# THE BUILDINGS OF ENGLAND

FOUNDING EDITOR: NIKOLAUS PEVSNER
ADVISORY EDITOR: JOHN NEWMAN
EDITOR: BRIDGET CHERRY

## LONDON 4: NORTH

BRIDGET CHERRY AND NIKOLAUS PEVSNER

THE BUILDINGS BOOKS TRUST

was established in 1994, registered charity number 1042101.
It promotes the appreciation and understanding
of architecture by supporting and financing
the research needed to sustain new and revised volumes of
The Buildings of England, Ireland, Scotland and Wales

The Trust gratefully acknowledges:

the generous contribution of
THE SAINSBURY FAMILY CHARITABLE TRUSTS
which makes possible the work of revision,
the extension of the series to all the countries of the British Isles,
and the effort to bring appreciation of our architectural heritage
to a wider public

grants toward the costs of research, writing and illustrations from
———      ENGLISH HERITAGE

JOHN AND RUTH HOWARD CHARITABLE TRUST

THE PAUL MELLON CENTRE FOR STUDIES
IN BRITISH ART

assistance with photographs from
THE ROYAL COMMISSION ON HISTORICAL
MONUMENTS OF ENGLAND

# London

# 4
## NORTH

BY
**BRIDGET CHERRY**
AND
**NIKOLAUS PEVSNER**

THE BUILDINGS OF ENGLAND

PENGUIN BOOKS

PENGUIN BOOKS
Published by the Penguin Group
27 Wrights Lane, London W8 5TZ, England
for
THE BUILDINGS BOOKS TRUST

Penguin Putnam Inc., 375 Hudson Street, New York, New York 10014, USA
Penguin Books Australia Ltd, Ringwood, Victoria, Australia
Penguin Books Canada Ltd, 10 Alcorn Avenue, Toronto, Ontario, Canada M4V 3B2
Penguin Books India (P) Ltd, 11, Community Centre, Panchsheel Park, New Delhi – 110 017, India
Penguin Books (NZ) Ltd, Private Bag 102902, NSMC, Auckland, New Zealand
Penguin Books (South Africa) (Pty) Ltd, 5 Watkins Street, Denver Ext 4, Johannesburg 2094, South Africa

Penguin Books Ltd, Registered Offices: Harmondsworth, Middlesex, England

First published 1998
Reprinted with corrections 1999, 2001

ISBN 0 14 071049 3

Typeset at Cambridge Photosetting Services, Cambridge
Made and printed in Great Britain
by Butler & Tanner Ltd, Frome and London
Set in 9/9.75pt Monotype Plantin

TO J, E AND T

# CONTENTS

# LIST OF TEXT FIGURES AND MAPS

# PHOTOGRAPHIC ACKNOWLEDGEMENTS

We are grateful to the following for permission to reproduce photographs:

Architectural Review: 113
Martin Charles: 7, 48, 49, 52, 58, 60, 79, 86, 102, 108, 110, 112, 118, 121, 123, 124, 125
Bridget Cherry: 96, 130
Country Life: 43
English Heritage Photographic Library: 1, 47, 105
A. F. Kersting: 3, 9, 15, 41, 61, 65
Warburg Institute: 59

All other photographs are reproduced by kind permission of the RCHME (Crown copyright).

The photographs are indexed in the indexes, and references to them are given by numbers in the margin of the text.

# ABBREVIATIONS
## AND LIST OF COUNTY COUNCIL ARCHITECTS

*Area Authorities*
MBW    Metropolitan Board of Works (1855–88)
LCC    London County Council (1888–1965)
GLC    Greater London Council (1965–86)
ILEA   Inner London Education Authority (1965–90,
       covering the area of the former LCC)
MCC    Middlesex County Council (1889–1986)

In order to avoid repetition, chief architects of public authorities are not mentioned on every occasion in the gazetteer. Borough architects are mentioned under individual boroughs. The chief County Council architects are as follows:

*Architects to the Metropolitan Board of Works, the London County Council and the Greater London Council*

*Superintending Architects*
Frederick Marrable 1856–61
George Vulliamy 1861–86
Thomas Blashill 1887–99
W. E. Riley 1899–1919
G. Topham Forrest 1919–35
E. P. Wheeler 1935–39
F. R. Hiorns 1939–41
J. H. Forshaw 1941–46
(Sir) Robert Matthew 1946–53
(Sir) Leslie Martin 1953–6
(Sir) Hubert Bennett 1956–71
(Sir) Roger Walters 1971–8
F. B. Pooley 1978–80
P. E. Jones 1980–86

*Fire Brigade Branch*
Edward Cresy 1866–70
Alfred Mott 1871–9
Robert Pearsall 1879–99
Owen Fleming 1900–

*Housing of the Working Classes Branch*
Owen Fleming 1893–1900
John Briggs 1900–2
Rob Robertson 1902–10

*Education Branch (until 1904 architects to the School Board for London)*
E. R. Robson 1871–84
T. J. Bailey 1884–1910
Rob Robertson 1910–

*The Constructional Division (absorbed the Fire Brigade Branch and the Housing of the Working Classes Branch from 1910, and the Education Branch from 1920. Housing was placed under the Valuers Department from 1946 until 1950, when the whole of the Architect's Department was reorganized under Sir Robert Matthew, with separate heads of department for housing and education.)*

*Housing*
H. J. Whitfield Lewis 1950–9
K. J. Campbell 1959–74
G. H. Wigglesworth 1974–80

*Education*
S. Howard 1950–5
M.C.L. Powell 1956–65
*Schools:* C.E. Hartland 1965–72
*Education:* M.C.L. Powell 1965–71
G.H. Wigglesworth 1972–4
P.E. Jones 1974–80

*Special Works (a separate department responsible for fire and ambulance stations, magistrates' courts, civic buildings, etc.)*
G. Horsfall 1960–76 (also senior architect Civic Design, 1965–70, and Thamesmead Manager from 1970)
R.A. Michelmore 1977–80 (from 1980, principal Construction Architect)

*Surveyors to the Metropolitan Police*

Charles Reeves 1842–66
Thomas Charles Sorby 1867–8
Frederick Caiger 1868–81
John Butler Sen. 1881–95
John Dixon Butler 1895–1920

G. Mackenzie Trench 1921–47
J. Innes Elliott 1947–74
M. Belchamber 1974–88
T. Lawrence 1988–

*Architects to the Middlesex County Council*

H.T. Wakelam (County Surveyor from 1898)
H.G. Crothall (Surveyor of Schools from 1903, then architect to the Education Committee; County Architect from 1908)

W.T. Curtis (County Architect 1930–46)
C.G. Stillman (County Architect 1946–59)
H.J. Whitfield Lewis (County Architect 1959–65)

# FOREWORD

*This book, the fourth in a six-volume series covering Greater London, includes the area of north London between Edgware Road and the Lea Valley. The gazetteer of places following the Introduction is arranged under the modern boroughs of Barnet, Camden, Enfield, Hackney, Haringey and Islington, each divided into areas which follow the boundaries of the older local authorities based on historic parishes. Each of these subdivisions has its own introduction and its own map or maps. The introductory essays preceding the gazetteer, and the sequence of photographs each provide a chronological overview of the whole area.*

*A few exceptions to the above principles have been made for ease of reference. The large area of Barnet is divided into a greater number of centres than the pre-1965 local authorities; and there has been some rationalization of the awkward boundaries of St Pancras. Highgate is treated as*

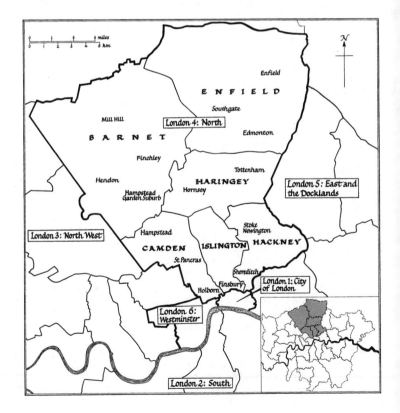

*an entity although it lies partly within Haringey; Euston Road is taken as the boundary between St Pancras and Holborn, whereas the historic division lay a little further* S; *and the* E *fringe of Regents Park, which lies within Camden, is omitted from this book as it is described with the rest of the park in* London 3: North West.

*The territory covered here previously formed part of two very early* Buildings of England *volumes: Nikolaus Pevsner's* Middlesex *(1951) and* London except the Cities of London and Westminster *(1952), both invaluable landmarks in their time, particularly in the appreciation of buildings of the* C19. *The original texts provided the skeleton, but the progress of research and the broadening of architectural appreciation, together with architectural developments since the 1950s, have necessitated extensive revision and expansion.*

*The arrangement of the gazetteer*

*The order of subject matter follows the principles established in earlier* Buildings of England *volumes. Main headings are indicated in a list at the beginning of each borough. The order followed within these is broadly as listed below, with a few exceptions to cope with areas of particular complexity, such as Holborn. Important individual buildings or groups requiring long accounts, such as the British Museum, British Library, and University of London have separate entries following the Public Buildings section. In general buildings are listed under their present use, cross referenced when necessary.*

RELIGIOUS BUILDINGS *and their furnishings, alphabetically by current name, are divided into:*
*Church of England*
*Roman Catholic*
*Other places of worship*
*Cemeteries*

PUBLIC BUILDINGS *are arranged in approximately the following order:*
*Civic and official buildings (town halls, municipal offices, law courts, police stations, fire and ambulance stations, post offices)*
*Local authority and other community buildings (libraries, baths, community and sports centres)*
*Hospitals and health centres*
*Prisons*
*Markets*
*Parks*
*Utilities and transport*
*Educational buildings (universities, colleges, secondary schools, (former) Board Schools, primary schools)*

MAJOR HOUSES *and other large buildings or groups follow Public Buildings.*

PERAMBULATIONS *are listed at the beginning of each borough. These cover domestic and commercial and industrial buildings and other building types not included under public buildings, such as lesser institutions, pubs, cinemas, theatres and smaller open spaces.*

*It should be stressed that mention of a building in no way indicates that it is open to the public. Where two dates are quoted, the first is generally for the final designs, the second for completion of work. For modern buildings names of job architects are given in addition to the name of the firm, when that information is available; County Council heads of departments are set out on p. xiii and to save space are not mentioned under every reference; likewise details of borough architects are mentioned in the individual introductions. As with previous volumes the aim is that information on buildings up to c. 1830 of more than local interest should be as complete as recent research and the space of the volume permit, for C19 and C20 buildings the bulk of the material and the space available has made greater selectivity necessary. Church furnishings omit bells, plate, and lesser items such as plain fonts and furniture. Movable furnishings in secular buildings also are excluded. Failure to mention a building or feature may not inevitably imply it is of no interest; while efforts have been made to keep abreast of information up to early 1998, there will always be new buildings, new discoveries and reassessments.* The Buildings of England, *as ever, will be grateful for information on errors and omissions and for suggestions for future editions.*

*BC April 1998*

# ACKNOWLEDGEMENTS

*As with* London 3: North West, *this book owes much to those who helped with the creation of its forbears of 1951 and 1952:* Middlesex, *for which the research was carried out by Dr Gertrude Bondi, and* London except the Cities of London and Westminster, *which was prepared by Mrs Katharine Michaelson. The books also benefited greatly from the help given by the librarians and staff of the London public libraries, from the photography collections of the National Buildings Record, from the then as yet unpublished statutory lists of historic buildings prepared by the Ministry of Local Government and Planning, and from much information collected by J. H. Farrar of the Historical Records Department of the LCC. Furthermore, access was kindly given to H. S. Goodhart-Rendel's notes on Victorian churches and to Sir Thomas Kendrick's index of Victorian glass. Others from those years whose help should be recorded are Miss Darlington at the Members' Library, County Hall, Mr Stonebridge at the St Marylebone Public Library, Mr Wesencroft at the University Library, Mr Rayne Smith at the Guildhall Library, the Jewish Historical Society of London, the Public Relations Department of the London Transport Executive, and the many rectors and vicars, local historians and occupiers of houses, who went to much trouble in providing answers to written questions.*

*Although* London 4: North *has expanded very considerably from its progenitors, it owes an incalculable debt to the vision and breadth of interests of Sir Nikolaus Pevsner who provided the core around which the present volume developed. Over forty years of correspondence testify to the mixture of enthusiasm, affection and irritation which the old volumes inspired among those eager to know more about London's architecture, and to understandable frustration over omissions, lack of indexes, and the long gestation of the new London editions. The quantity of information engendered by the growth of scholarly interest in the built fabric of London, the activities of both national and local amenity societies, the development of the conservation movement and the consequent expansion of statutory protection of historic buildings (in all of which Pevsner and the* Buildings of England *volumes played an active part), not only increased the complexity of the task of revision, but makes it difficult to thank adequately all those who have directly or indirectly contributed to this work.*

*The activities and interests of the Victorian Society, of which Pevsner was a founder member, demonstrated that there was much of value not mentioned in the old* London except, *and much that deserved fighting for; many buildings included in the present book owe their survival to such campaigns. More recently the Twentieth Century Society has similarly opened eyes to the interest of buildings of this century, encouraging a wider appreciation of the variety of styles than was current among Pevsner's generation. A collective acknowledgement is due to the work of both these societies, and to others who have battled to promote a better appreciation of* *the architecture of their localities. The growth of interest in local history over the last forty years has been fostered by numerous local societies; their publications and expertise have also made substantial contributions to a better understanding of the different areas of London (*see *Further Reading p. 708).*

*From the early years of the century the London County Council took a lively interest in preserving London's historic buildings, a tradition continued by the GLC's Historic Buildings Division, and after 1986 by the London Division of English Heritage. I gratefully acknowledge the considerable debt this book owes to the detailed research amassed over the years by these bodies, to which I have generously been given access, and to the friendship and encouragement of English Heritage's London historians both past and present. For sharing discoveries, answering countless queries, and pursuing individual problems I must thank in particular Susie Barson, Roger Bowdler, Elain Harwood, Frank Kelsall, Chris Miele, Andrew Saint and Robert Thorne. Other branches of the London Division have kept me up to date with current conservation issues, and I have benefited also from the expertise of my fellow members of English Heritage's London Advisory Committee and Post-War Steering Group. The staff of the Survey of London, before 1986 within the GLC, now part of the Royal Commission on the Historical Monuments of England, have also been most helpful, as have the RCHME's Threatened Buildings Section; I owe thanks especially to their respective heads, John Greenacombe and Peter Guillery, and among other RCHME staff, to Charlotte Bradbeer, Alan Brodie, Alan Cox, Stephen Porter and Chris Stell.*

*The local history collections and archives maintained by the boroughs have continued to be an essential resource for details on individual areas, as they were for the first editions. For this volume I have had much help from many often hard-pressed local librarians and archivists: I must thank particularly Pamela Taylor and Joanna Corden at Barnet and Graham Dalling at Enfield, who provided guidance and suggestions on how to deal with these large outer boroughs, and also checked text; I am also grateful to Malcolm Holmes and his colleagues at Camden, David Mander at Hackney and Rita Reid at Haringey, and the staff at Islington. The help of conservation officers of the various boroughs has also been invaluable: thanks are due especially to Robin Harper and David March (Camden), Kay Owen and Robert Harding (Hackney), Steve Gould (Haringey), and Alec Forshaw and Mike Bruce (Islington) for finding time both to discuss general issues and answer detailed queries. For information on recent developments I gratefully acknowledge the assistance of the many planning officers and architects who answered numerous enquiries from the Buildings of England office. I thank in particular Alan Weitzel, former borough architect of Haringey, who took me on a tour of 1970s architecture in Haringey, Birkin Haward, with whom I investigated recent houses in Camden, and Professor Sir Colin St J. Wilson, for an enlightening tour of the British Library.*

*The book has also benefited from the expert local knowledge of many people. Several groups helpfully assembled suggestions and information for the new edition: the Finchley Society and the Hendon and District Archaeological Society in Barnet, and the Enfield Preservation Society and Southgate Civic Trust in Enfield. I have learnt much also from discussions with members of the Camden History Society, the Edmonton Hundred Historical Society, the Hackney Society, the Hornsey Historical Society and Islington History Society. The chore of reading and commenting on parts of the gazetteer was kindly undertaken by Mervyn Miller (Hampstead Garden Suburb), Christopher Wade (Hampstead), Andrew Saint (Camden); Ken Gay, Joan Schwitzer, Steve Gould (Haringey); Elizabeth Robinson, Robert Thorne, Chris Miele (Hackney), Martin O'Rourke (Shoreditch); Mary Cosh, Tanis Hinchcliffe (Islington), Alan Cox (Clerkenwell). In addition many helped on individual topics: Victor Belcher contributed the account of Sutton House, Michael Shippobottom, with the late Edward Hubbard, researched and wrote the entry on The Hill, Hampstead. On churches I was helped by discussions with the late B.F.L. Clarke, the late Donald Findlay, and Michael Gillingham. Geoffrey Brandwood provided details on Victorian churches, Denis Evinson lists of Roman Catholic churches, Martin Harrison, Peter Cormack and Caroline Swash supplied information on C19 and C20 stained glass, Geoffrey Fisher commented on C17 and C18 monuments (abbreviated GF in the gazetteer).*

*The many people who gave me access to buildings and responded most helpfully to enquiries on particular topics are too numerous to mention individually, my debt to them is great. I must single out in particular John Allan (Lubetkin and Tecton); Peter Barber (Lauderdale House); Richard Bond (timber-framed buildings); Susie Barson (Metropolitan Police buildings); David Bieda (Seven Dials Monuments Trust); D.L. Collins (Mill Hill School); Miss B.J. Franks (University of London); Marjorie Caygill (British Museum); Geoffrey Gillam (Grovelands, and also, together with John Griffin and Andor Gomme, Forty Hall); Dr Negley Harte and John Byway (University College London); Guy Holborn (Lincoln's Inn); Tony Hunt (J.S. Alder); Roland Jeffrey (St Pancras Housing Association); Richard Kennedy (Highgate School); W.J. Mol (St Joseph's Convent, Mill Hill); Jack Morris (Building Design Centre); Alan Powers (C20 houses); Stephen Porter (the Charterhouse); Nicholas Redman (Whitbread's); Margaret Richardson and Helen Dorey (Sir John Soane's Museum); Dr Aylward Shorter (Holcombe House, Mill Hill); Chris Stell (Nonconformist churches); Rev. Gordon Taylor (St Giles-in-the-Fields); Theresa Thom (Gray's Inn); Barbara Wheeler-Early (Freeform Artworks). Among many others who have provided information and encouragement over a long period, I must especially mention John Brandon-Jones, Sir Howard Colvin, Michael Robbins and Alastair Service.*

*The book owes a special debt to Malcolm Tucker, who as in previous London volumes has contributed the entries to the gazetteer concerning industry and transport, as well as a separate introduction dealing with these subjects in north London. I am grateful also to Eric Robinson and to Joanna Bird who have updated their general introductions for this volume, respectively on Geology and Building Materials and on Prehistoric and Roman Archaeology.*

*The main Introduction has benefited considerably from the scrutiny of John Newman, Simon Bradley and Elain Harwood. Errors that remain are my own; despite so much help I am well aware that there are inadequacies and unsolved problems in a book that attempts to cover so much ground.*

*A large number of the photographs were specially taken for the book by Sid Carter and Steven Cole of the RCHME, an arrangement which is much appreciated, for others we are grateful to English Heritage and Martin Charles. For providing material for text figures we need to thank especially Richard Bond at English Heritage, the staff at the Guildhall Library and Michael Clements at the Survey of London. Other text figures were drawn by Alan Fagan, the maps were prepared by Reg and Marjorie Piggott.*

*Not least is my debt to former and present colleagues at* The Buildings of England, *without whose help this book could not have been completed. Initial preparation for the London volumes was undertaken by Susan Rose-Smith, and further research was most efficiently carried out by Helen Hills and Tye Blackshaw. Elizabeth Williamson prepared and wrote parts of Islington and Hampstead Garden Suburb, Stephany Ungless assisted on Barnet, Simon Bradley contributed useful additional information, Charles O'Brien and Sue Machin speedily solved last minute problems. Copy editing of the text was undertaken by Judith Wardman and Stephany Ungless and the design by Georgina Widdrington. Alison McKittrick has been most resourceful in gathering together the text figures and of great help in ensuring that the last stages of the book have gone smoothly. The debt to my family, who have lived with this book for longer than is reasonable, is acknowledged in the dedication.*

# INTRODUCTION

## BY BRIDGET CHERRY

The most prominent physical landmarks of north London are the twin hills of Hampstead and Highgate, which define the skyline of so many early views of the metropolis, and provide panoramic vantage points for views to the s. Looking across the open space of Hampstead Heath, between the two hilltop settlements, to the city spreading over the Thames basin and reaching to the Surrey hills beyond, one

Early C17 London, looking N to St Pancras church and Highgate Hill.
Detail of engraving by Wenceslas Hollar

still has an illusory impression of a built-up area confined to the river valley. But modern London stretches far further. To the N its outer boroughs reach to the Hertfordshire border, where C20 suburban expansion over the Middlesex countryside was curtailed only through the creation of the green belt just before the Second World War.

The area covered in this book is bounded on the w by the Edgware Road, the Roman Watling Street, and on the E by the River Lee in whose flat valley the Old North Road, another straight Roman route, makes its way. The range of hills, known as the Northern Heights, which forms the steep northern edge of the London basin stops abruptly on the edge of the Lea Valley. The waterways of the Lee attracted industry from an early date; elsewhere there were woodland, pastures and scattered settlement, increasingly focused on serving

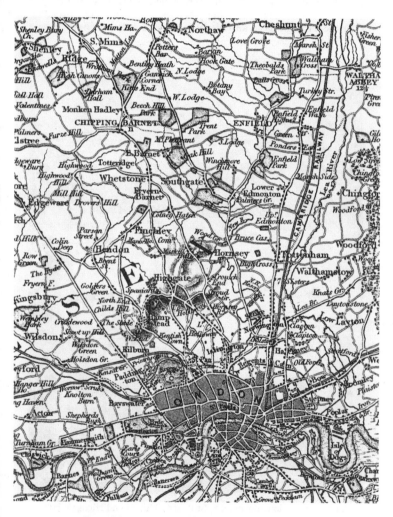

From 'New Map of the Environs of London', 1838

the needs of the metropolis. As the City of London and the separate court suburb of Westminster grew together in the C17, housing spread to their N, over the open land with its scatter of villages and hamlets. By 1800 the built-up area was approaching Euston Road, the mid-C18 bypass around London, with tentacles stretching beyond along the main roads. During the C19 it covered most of the slopes leading up to the Northern Heights, with the important exception of Hampstead Heath and its adjacent land preserved as open space. This built-up area was included within the bounds of the London County Council, created in 1888. The outer boroughs of Greater London (formed 1965) incorporated growth from the later C19 of commuter suburbia, which had been encouraged first by the expansion of the suburban railway lines; then in the C20 by the extension of the underground lines to Barnet and Cockfosters.

North London is well served by railways, but the rail traveller from the N, whose views are obscured by frequent cuttings and tunnels, sees less of London than those approaching from S or W. The exception is the fascinating cross-section of Victorian suburbs visible from the largely elevated North London line laid out in 1850 around the then built-up area. It runs from E to W past a medley of grey slate roofs and miscellaneous industrial backyards interspersed with bright new housing squeezed on to old railway land. For a broader picture one should survey the scene from Hampstead Heath and Parliament Hill Fields, or from the terraces of Alexandra Palace at the eastern end of the Northern Heights.

## THE MIDDLE AGES TO THE LATER C17

### Monasteries and churches

In the Middle Ages London extended only a little beyond the walls which had defined the bounds of the Roman city. The separate royal palace and abbey at Westminster lay upriver to the SW, linked to the City by the Strand, along which a string of riverside mansions developed, a large number of them the town establishments of bishops and other leading ecclesiastics. On the open land around the fringes of the walled city MONASTIC HOUSES were founded, especially in the C12, when enthusiasm for monasticism was at its height. The greatest concentration of these was to the NW: no doubt the good water supply from the springs in this area was an attraction. Here, more clearly than anywhere else in London, much of the present street layout is still conditioned by the legacy of these medieval precincts. Outside the walls (although within the present City of London, and described in that volume), St Bartholomew's priory and hospital were established in 1123; a little to their N, in the area which became known as Clerkenwell from one of the local springs, the first priory in England for the Knights Hospitallers was founded in the 1140s by Jordan Briset and his wife, who around the same time also built a nunnery nearby. From St Mary's Nunnery only a few traces of the cloister walk are now visible, but much more is known of the Hospitallers' Priory of St John. Their first church had a choir above a rib-vaulted crypt, attached to a circular nave, used in 8 deference to the church of the Holy Sepulchre at Jerusalem. The foundations of this mid-C12 nave, and the entire crypt, enlarged

in the later C12, are among London's most important Norman
survivals. The other military order, the Templars, also favoured the
circular nave; their transitional Gothic nave still stands in the area
which later became the legal precinct of the Temple (now in the City
of London). The Templars' first home (c. 1121) was near Holborn,
but of their buildings here we know nothing. The principal remnant
above ground of the Hospitallers' buildings at Clerkenwell is the
smart stone and brick priory gatehouse of 1504, which survived
various post-Dissolution uses to become part of the present headquarters of the modern Order of St John. In the same neighbour-
16, hood are the more coherent remains of the Charterhouse. This was
17 built for Carthusian monks in 1371, and preserved through conversion
first to a C16 mansion and then to Sir Thomas Sutton's early C17
foundation of school and almshouses. The buildings are still contained
within a distinct precinct, although the different periods are difficult
to disentangle. The present chapel occupies the Carthusians' chapter
house; its vestibule has a late medieval vault. To the w of the site of the
church is an attractive group of early Tudor brick domestic quarters,
and to the N the exceptionally large cloister green (now within St
Bartholomew's medical school) with traces of some of the twenty-
four individual monk's cells which lay around it. From the other
monastic foundations in the area of this book no buildings remain.
Off Shoreditch High Street, Holywell Lane and Row recall Haliwell
Priory, for Augustinian nuns, founded before 1127, rebuilt in the early
C16; and the church and neighbourhood of the evocatively named St
Giles-in-the-Fields, Holborn, trace their origins to the leper hospital
founded by Queen Matilda in 1101 on the main route w from the
City. Much further w, at Kilburn on the Edgware Road, there was a
Benedictine nunnery, founded by the Abbot of Westminster in 1139.

Much land around London was owned by the church. The
Bishop of London could escape from the city to his hunting park at
Highgate, where a moated site on Highgate golf course remains
from his palace. Other senior ecclesiastics needed bases within or
close to the capital. Nearly all evidence of their houses has long since
vanished; the principal survivors lie s of the river, Lambeth Palace
and the ruins of Winchester Palace (see London 2: South). In our area
there is one important relic in Holborn, the present R.C. church of
11 St Etheldreda, which originated as the private chapel of the Bishop
of Ely's mansion. The chapel dates from the later C13. The two-
storey building has lost much of its ornamental detail but must once
have made a proud show. Its large E and w windows demonstrate
the experimental forms of the period of transition between the
Geometric and Decorated tracery.

It is difficult now to visualize the countryside that once lay immediately N and w of the City. Up to the C17 the roads out of the city
began with a scatter of large suburban mansions with their own
gardens and orchards; in the country beyond were timber-framed
manor houses, farms and the occasional stone church. Among
MEDIEVAL PARISH CHURCHES the oldest evidence is to be found
at St Pancras. The tiny stone building tucked away behind the railway station, though much altered, is essentially C12, but contains an
altar stone dated to the C7. Together with the dedication to a Roman
saint this suggests an early origin for the church, perhaps indicating
a post-Roman settlement or cemetery in this area. Nothing remains

of pre-Conquest buildings, which, as in other regions poor in good building stone, would have been of timber. The transition to stone buildings for local churches, with walls of local rubble and dressed stone brought from elsewhere, took place in the C12; but to see details preserved better than at St Pancras one needs to travel some way from the pollution of inner London, to East Barnet and Friern Barnet, where there are small churches whose Norman origin is still evident. St James, Friern Barnet, a possession of the Hospitallers, has a simple chevron decorated doorway. At All Saints, Edmonton, which belonged to the abbey of Walden in Essex, fragments of arches are preserved from more elaborate Norman work, with carving including grotesque heads. St Mary, Hendon, has a very substantial Norman font, but that is the sum total of early survivals.

One reason why the church of St Pancras remained small was because the parish had two subsidiary medieval chapels (both long since rebuilt), serving growing settlements at Kentish Town and Highgate. Likewise, the area around the church at East Barnet also remained a backwater, in contrast to the expanding market centre of High Barnet on the main road, which had its own chapel. In other parishes, medieval churches followed the usual pattern of extension and piecemeal rebuilding from the C13 onwards, to cater for expanding populations and changing liturgical needs. By the end of the Middle Ages the usual result was an aisled nave, the aisles often continued by chapels flanking an extended chancel, with a tower at the W end. The North Middlesex examples are generally not spectacular, but substantial enough for something to remain from many of them, despite the pressures of later suburban growth. The exceptions are the churches of the parishes closest to London, mostly rebuilt in the C18.

Detail from the C13 to C15 is simple and not easy to date; nave arcades generally have octagonal piers and chamfered arches, the number of nave bays is modest: three at Hendon, four at Edmonton and Finchley. Tottenham appears to have had a four-bay nave arcade continued by three bays in the chancel. High Barnet has an arcade with quatrefoil piers, datable by a bequest to the mid C15. Enfield is the most ambitious: the church of a small town, with a five-bay nave, also with quatrefoil piers, the whole made light and lofty by a clerestory added in 1522. The finest early C16 rebuilding must have been that of Hackney, with a total of seven bays, paid for by the lord of the manor Sir John Heron, but demolished, apart from the W tower, in the C18.

Sculptural decoration is sparse; remains of a C13 foliage capital at Hendon, Perp capitals carved with angels at St Mary, Hornsey, and Monken Hadley. There are good late medieval roofs at Monken Hadley, Edmonton and Hendon. The most distinctive feature of the region's churches is the military-looking stumpy W tower, sturdily built to hold a peal of bells, with diagonal buttresses, battlemented top and corner stair-turret. The type was popular from the C15 to early C16 and appears all over the Thames Valley and beyond: North Middlesex examples are at Edgware, Edmonton, Finchley, Hackney, Hornsey, and Monken Hadley, the last dated 1494. Enfield has a W tower whose thick lower walls and absence of buttresses and turret make a C12 or C13 date likely; the tower at Tottenham, with a stair-turret within the thickness of the wall, may also be earlier than the rest. In the early C16 brick became acceptable as a building material for churches. The tower at Hornsey, of *c.* 1500, has a brick interior and is faced in rubble. But the handsome early C16 porch at Tottenham is all of brick, and when St Mary at Stoke Newington was rebuilt in 1563, brick was used for the entire structure.

Medieval church furnishings have not survived, apart from a few early C16 STAINED GLASS fragments at Enfield, and a few examples of brought in pieces: a C15 Flemish Virgin and Child at St Dominic, R.C., and an English C15 alabaster at St Mary Brookfield (both St Pancras, Camden). Nor do many MEDIEVAL MONUMENTS remain. In the Charterhouse a fragment of a C14 tomb canopy and in St John's Priory the excellent cadaver effigy of Prior William Weston (†1540), indicate the quality of what must have been lost from the major foundations. In the parish churches BRASSES were the more common form of memorial, but these too have mostly gone, although a handful of minor C15 and C16 examples with figures can be found at Edmonton, Enfield, Finchley, Hackney, Hendon, Hornsey and Islington, and the head of a nun, found on the site of Kilburn Priory, is preserved at St Mary Kilburn, Hampstead. The only outstanding brass is the large one to Joyce Lady Tiptoft (†1446) at Enfield, beneath an elaborate canopy in the style of the

Easter Sepulchre erected by Christopher Urswyck, 1519,
St John, Hackney

Royal Works which was probably added in an early C16 embellishment of the family chapel. There are two examples of the early C16 tomb design which occurs in a number of churches in the London area. The type consists of a small wall monument with four-centred Perp arch with splayed reveals, generally framing a brass and sometimes doubling as an Easter Sepulchre. The earliest is at St Mary Lambeth (1507). The monument at Hackney, dated 1519 and bearing the name of the eminent rector of Hackney, Christopher Urswyck, formerly Dean of Windsor (†1521), was made as an Easter Sepulchre, and was originally separate from Urswyck's own brass which is now on the tomb-chest. The design appears to have been favoured at first by ecclesiastics, and was then taken up more widely, as in the case of the version used for the tomb of a local landowner at Edmonton, John Kirton (†1529). Simpler small early C16 wall monuments used as a setting for a brass were once common; an undated example remains at St Pancras.

CHURCH MONUMENTS of the later C16 to mid C17 fall into several categories. One exceptional work from the late C16 should be mentioned first – the exquisite, sensitively carved Vergara monument at St John, Clerkenwell, attributed to the Spanish sculptor *Esteban Jordan*, brought from Spain in the early C20. Most English monuments look prosaic by comparison. A rustic looking contrast is the large slab to George Rey †1599 (now in St Mary with St George, Hornsey), boldly incised with three figures, a type found in the Midlands. It has been attributed to *Jasper Hollemans*, working at Burton-on-Trent, and its presence here is no doubt explained by the fact that Rey came from Staffordshire. In general the grand monument of these years is less frequent in north London than in the churches of west Middlesex (*see London 3: North West*). A noteworthy alabaster effigy, to Lady Latimer †1583, survives at St John Hackney. A late example of the recumbent effigy is the alabaster monument to Thomas Ravenscroft at High Barnet (†1630); unusually, it has a consciously Gothic canopy. A more progressive approach, which began to be adopted in the later C16, was to depict the deceased as reclining figures, but the only major example of this is the formal two-tier monument to Sir Nicholas Raynton at Enfield, †1646, which seems disappointingly old fashioned from the patron of Forty Hall (*see* p. 15). Far more common is the small wall monument with carved figures of the deceased kneeling before a prayer desk, a type that developed out of pre-Reformation representations of figures kneeling before religious images. A very simple example in low relief is that at Enfield to Robert Deicrowe †1586. A more elaborate Enfield monument is that of 1610 to the Middlemores, with two figures within a surround with armorial in strapwork above. Others of the early C17 can be found at Hackney, Finchley and the Charterhouse. At Tottenham, the Canteler monument of 1602 is unusual in having two pairs of figures within arches flanked by obelisks. The type continued into the 1640s; Tottenham has two contrasting examples. Sir John Melton †1640, and wife, are shown as the usual stiff little puppets, but they kneel within a bold classical surround with columns supporting a broken pediment; the monument nearby to Sir Robert Barkham †1644 and family, carved in black and white marble by *Edward Marshall*, shows the new interest in a more lively figure style.

Tomb of George Rey †1599 and wives,
St Mary with St George, Hornsey. Rubbing

Marshall was a pupil of NICHOLAS STONE (*c.* 1587–1647), and it was Stone, influenced by his training in Holland, who revolutionized English monumental sculpture in the early C17. After his return to England in 1613 one of his first works was the large and crowded tomb to Sir Thomas Sutton at the Charterhouse. It was carried out together with *Nicholas Johnson* and *Edmund Kinsman*, and indeed looks as if it was composed by a committee. It combines a traditional recumbent effigy and a pictorial scene of Sutton's pensioners with elegantly elongated allegorical figures in Stone's typical Mannerist style. Stone's other monuments are very varied in type but are always worth a special look: Martha Palmer at Enfield, 1617, has a cartouche flanked by swaying figures of Faith and Charity; two other Stone monuments in north London feature the portrait bust, that to John Law at the Charterhouse, †1614, and the Wilbraham monument (†1616) at Monken Hadley, which has a pair of busts in a more elaborate composition in different coloured marbles. The bust, as a revival of a classical tradition, became increasingly popular: another from the earlier C17 is at Hackney (D. Doulben, †1633), and many more were to follow in the later C17. Elaborate allegorical and pictorial themes had a briefer flowering. Examples in this spirit are the monument at St Pancras to Philadelphia Woolaston †1616, with reclining effigy in a curtained recess, and the delightful small armorial tablet at Edmonton to George Huxley †1627, crowned by an elegant figure of Father Time.

## Domestic building

Much of the countryside N of London was woodland in the early Middle Ages. Small settlements grew up in clearings, often developing subsidiary centres (the origin of many 'end' place names in Middlesex) rather than growing into single large nucleated villages. Larger farmsteads and manor houses were timber-framed buildings, often protected by moats. Some of these early MOATED SITES are still recognizable. Camlet Moat, a reputed seat of the C12 Geoffrey de Mandeville, lies in a romantically overgrown setting in the woodland of Trent Park, Southgate, Enfield; the moated sites of

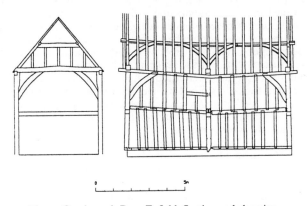

No. 17 Gentleman's Row, Enfield. Section and elevation

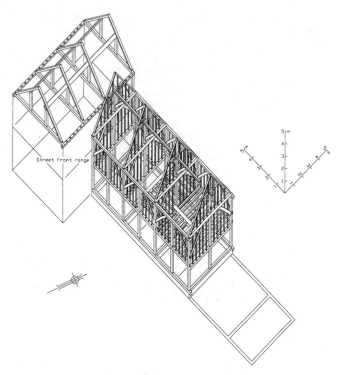

No. 1264 High Road, Whetstone. Axonometric

early manor houses at Barnsbury and Highbury are defined more prosaically by the C19 suburban street pattern that developed around them.

As so many of the larger houses were successively rebuilt in later centuries, little of their early history remains visible, even when buildings survive. An example of such multi-phase development is Broomfield, Southgate, Enfield, whose complex history was unravelled in investigations after a fire, but even here the oldest surviving part, a timber-framed wing, goes back only to the early C16. Although over 400 timber-framed buildings are known in the Greater London area, they are mostly to be found in the more rural areas to the NW, E and SE, rather than in north London.* In the London area by the later Middle Ages the aisled hall had been superseded by the open hall without intermediate supports, generally with a roof of crown-post construction, and studded walls. Houses of yeoman farmers were commonly on a two-cell plan, the open hall and screens passage with a storeyed part at one end, all under a continuous roof. A surviving example in north London is No. 17 Gentleman's Row, Enfield. A crown-post roof, partially smoke-blackened, also remains as the rear wing of Nos. 1264–1270

---

* For a full account of this subject see the Introduction by Malcolm Airs in *London 3: North West*, also Richard Bond, *Timber-framed buildings in the London region* (forthcoming).

Whetstone High Road, Barnet. From the early C16 onwards such halls were invariably divided by an inserted floor and chimneystacks. The stacks were often placed centrally, to provide heating for rooms on each side of the house, on two floors, thus creating the 'lobby-entrance' plan. A C17 example of such a plan, in brick, is Church 22, Farm House, Hendon. p. 163

Brick had begun to replace timber as the principal building material from the early C16, although timber-framing continued in use for lesser buildings into the C17. The largest surviving example of the timber-framed rural house in our area is Lauderdale House, p. Highgate. Its long jettied s range with first-floor long gallery probably 406 dates from the later C16 when the house was owned by Richard Bond, a wealthy London goldsmith. In the City and its immediate suburbs gabled timber fronts remained the rule, despite the risk of fire. The appearance of such buildings is demonstrated by a remarkable, if restored, survival, the long timber-framed group of Staple Inn Buildings in Holborn, built in 1586. An early example of the newly fashionable use of brick for major houses is Bruce Castle, 24 Tottenham, which encapsulates an early C16 brick building from the time of the court official, Sir William Compton. Bruce Castle also has a mysterious detached circular brick tower of around the same date, or perhaps earlier. Also originating from the earlier C16 is Sutton House, Hackney, whose significance as an early brick build- pp. ing of the 1530s has only recently been appreciated. This compact 492 brick house, built by another court official, Ralph Sadleir, made an $^{-3}$ exterior show with its row of brick gables; it had – and still has – comfortably panelled parlours, but its hall was single-storeyed and of moderate size, a departure from the medieval tradition of the open hall.

The common arrangement for grander medieval establishments, as is known from plenty of examples in other areas, was of ranges grouped around one or more courtyards, approached through a gate-house, with a great hall open to the roof as the principal focus. Such was Ely House, Holborn, already mentioned, destroyed in the C18, apart for its chapel, and such was Brooke House, Hackney, sadly demolished after major damage in the Second World War. Canonbury, Islington, is a tantalizingly partial survival (E range and NW corner) of a courtyard house which until the Dissolution was a country retreat of the Priors of St Bartholomew. The much altered and sub-divided E range may be early C16 in origin, as the rebus of Prior Bolton indicates; the commanding NW brick tower is perhaps a little later. The most indicative examples of this kind of plan in our area are the two surviving Inns of Court in Holborn, Gray's Inn and pp. Lincoln's Inn. These lawyers' colleges each took over a suburban 282, aristocratic mansion in the C14, and in both cases later rebuilding 285 continued the medieval tradition of ranges around a courtyard. At Lincoln's Inn both hall (1489–92) and gatehouse range (1518) 15 display the contemporary fashion for colourful diapered brick walls; the hall still has its original arch-braced roof. At Gray's Inn the hall dates from 1556–8, although much restored after gutting in World War II.

The influence of French and Italian RENAISSANCE TASTE began to make itself felt from the early C16 onwards in furnishings and fittings of Henry VIII's principal palaces. These lay along the

Thames and to its s; to the N the only important royal survival is the sumptuous mid-C16 heraldic fireplace at Enfield, which bears the royal arms with initials ER (which could stand for either Edward VI or Elizabeth). It is likely to have come from Elsyng, a courtyard house of the early C16 (demolished in the C17), built by Sir Thomas Lovell, chancellor to Henry VII and Henry VIII. The house was acquired by Henry VIII for use as a hunting lodge convenient for the royal forest of Enfield Chase and used as a residence for his children. Compared with Henry VIII's activities royal building in the later C16 was minimal, and it was the courtiers' houses which were built to impress. For such men new opportunities were provided by the major upheaval in the ownership of landed property following the Dissolution of the monasteries. Much monastic property in the London area passed to leading courtiers, either for conversion as their own homes, or to be sold for a profit. The hospital of St Giles-in-the-Fields became the property of Lord Dudley. The domestic buildings of the Charterhouse, owned first by Lord North and then from 1564–72 by Thomas Howard, Duke of Norfolk, were transformed into a grand courtyard mansion, whose main features still exist. Its core is a great hall, with oriel and open timber roof; unusually for this date, the hall backs on to a range with great

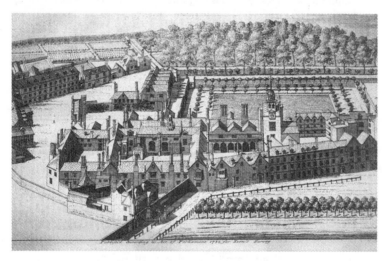

The Charterhouse, Finsbury. Engraving, 1755

chamber which retains an elaborate fireplace and a (restored) plaster ceiling. This range connects with a long raised garden terrace created above the old W cloister walk. This is Elizabethan courtier building on a grand scale, a rare survival within the London area. Canonbury House in Islington was acquired by one of the richest City merchants, Sir John Spencer; some elaborate plaster ceilings and panelling survive from his refurbishment of c. 1600, showing that City merchants could also put on a show. About other great

houses in the area frustratingly little is known. At Highgate by the
early C17 there were two aristocratic mansions in large grounds;
Arundel House and Dorchester House. They both gave way to
smaller houses in the later C17, and all that remains is a garden wall
with bastions from Dorchester House in the gardens of houses in
The Grove.

As these few examples show, by the C17 it was established practice
for both courtiers and merchants to acquire or build houses within
easy reach of London, but from the later C17 onwards those who
chose to live N and E of London tended to be City or professional
men. From the reigns of James I and Charles I, courtiers had
increasingly gravitated toward the court at Westminster and the
new West End suburbs. The change was gradual. By the early C18
aristocratic residents in Hackney were only a memory. Strype's
edition of Stow (1720) refers to the 'pleasant and healthful town of
Hackney where divers nobles in former times had their country
seats'. In C17 Clerkenwell the Duke of Newcastle lived in a house
made from the cloister ranges of St Mary's Nunnery, and the Earl of
Aylesbury in a house within the former precinct of St John's Priory.
But it is symptomatic that the greatest mansion here, the Charterhouse,
through Thomas Sutton's bequest of 1611, became a school for
boys and foundation for pensioners rather than a private house. The
joinery and stone doorcases and fireplaces, added as part of the
interior alterations carried out at this time by *Francis Carter* and 16,
*Edmund Kinsman*, demonstrate a lively mannered classicism of the 17
type developed through the influence of Netherlandish pattern
books, a little more disciplined than the coarsely flamboyant late
C16 woodcarving of the screen in the hall at Gray's Inn. Surviving
early C17 interior decoration in lesser houses some way from
London shows a continuing interest in all-over patterning, as at
The Priory, Tottenham, where elaborate plasterwork and panell- 18
ing of *c*. 1620 was installed by Joseph Fenton, a barber-surgeon.
More refined detail dependent on Netherlandish pattern books
could also be found, as on an overmantel at Salisbury House,
Edmonton.

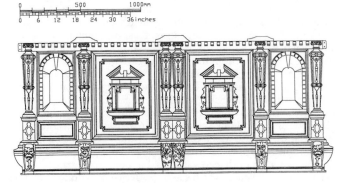

Overmantel, Salisbury House, Edmonton,
early seventeenth century

*Urban developments from the early C17*

During the second half of the C16 London's importance as a trading
port increased dramatically, and the population grew very rapidly,
reaching *c.* 200,000 by *c.* 1600. A city of this size required a more
effective water supply than that which had been supplied by the
springs and conduits immediately outside the walls, and in 1607 and
1608 two Acts were passed to enable the City to bring water from
further afield. The ambitious task was carried out by Sir Hugh
Myddelton, London goldsmith and entrepreneur, and completed in
1613. The NEW RIVER wound its way from the Hertfordshire
springs of Chadwell and Amwell along a 100 ft contour in a tortuous
route originally over 38 miles long, through the parishes of Enfield,
Tottenham, Hornsey and Islington, to end in a reservoir at the New
River Head at Sadlers Wells. From here water was conveyed by
wooden pipes into the City. Apart from its practical benefit, the existence of the New River was to have a significant effect on building
activity in its neighbourhood, providing a ready-made landscape
feature and a picturesque outlook for new houses and villas built N
of London. These were yet to come; in the C17 its route still ran
through open country. But S of the New River Head, and indeed all
around London, beyond the authority of the City Corporation,
undisciplined and insalubrious building activity was in progress.
Proclamations against such building began in 1580 and were repeated
during the reign of James I. By the 1630s the need to acquire licences
to build in the area immediately outside the City had not stopped
such activity, but operated as a useful source of revenue for the crown;
requirements to use brick rather than timber may have helped to
restrict shoddy work, at least in the more respectable western suburbs,
if not in the expanding E end hamlets along the riverside.

Overcrowding within the City was no doubt an additional reason
for the wealthy to prefer spacious suburban locations, or even more
remote villages further W, such as the Chelsea riverside or Kensington
(*see London 3: North West*). The well-established sites along the
Strand, convenient for the court at Westminster, remained popular
for aristocratic suburban houses, and others grew up along Holborn.
In the early C17 some major houses in both areas began to receive
additions and improvements which demonstrate the growing interest
in creating a show front, in contrast to the inward looking character of
the medieval courtyard house hidden behind a gatehouse. Although we
have only the scantiest evidence about these new buildings, it is clear
that they played a significant part in the spread of new architectural
fashions. Part of the site of the Bishop of Ely's mansion was taken over
by Sir Christopher Hatton in the late C16; his house passed to his
nephew Edward Coke's wife, Lady Hatton, and it was her new Holborn
frontage, with its fashionable broad shaped gable, pronounced cornice
and cross windows that was recorded in a sketch by the visiting
Midlands architect John Smythson in 1618–19. On the same visit he
drew a nearby house which the poet and courtier Sir Fulke Greville,
Lord Brooke, had just acquired from the Earl of Bath; part of this also
has the new type of shaped gable, and a 'pergola' or balcony in the
Italian manner, features which can be paralleled on a drawing by Inigo
Jones. Jones's influence began to make itself felt when he became
Surveyor of the Royal Works in 1615, but was at first restricted to court

Sir Fulke Greville's House, Holborn.
Drawn by John Smythson, 1619

circles. The evidence of the 'Holborn gables' indicates how Jones's Italian-influenced architectural ideas were at this time spreading beyond Westminster and were being sought out by cognoscenti. The Norfolk landowner Sir Roger Townshend was another visitor to Greville's house in 1618; his gabled Raynham Hall displays the influence of the new London buildings he saw.

These houses and many others of this time have long gone, so it is difficult to gauge how rapidly such new fashions became widespread in the countryside around London. Only a few key buildings of this period remain. Swakeleys, Hillingdon, and the house known as Kew Palace, both of the 1630s, each display varied forms of the shaped gable (*see London 3: North West* and *London 2: South*). Two rather different houses of similar date in our area are Forty Hall, Enfield, and Cromwell House, Highgate. Forty Hall was built by Sir Nicholas 25 Raynton, haberdasher and Lord Mayor. It now seems convincing that its building date of 1629 applies to the main features of the existing house, including the precocious hipped roof. It is thus an early example of a compact brick house with three regular show fronts and a double-pile plan. The hipped roof can be compared to p. some of Inigo Jones's designs of the 1630s, as can the pedimented 443 gateway to the service yard. Inside, nevertheless, there are still busy plaster ceilings in the Jacobean tradition. Cromwell House, Highgate, 26 of 1637–8, has a comparable mixture: the lavishly carved well stair-case rising from basement to top floor is in an older tradition, but p. belongs to a house with an up to date double-pile plan. The exterior 405

with elaborately detailed brickwork is in the spirit of City bricklayers dependent on Netherlandish sources; however, the symmetrical front and the use of a parapet in place of gables suggest the influence of Jones, as does the first-floor wreathed ceiling. An important lost example of another forward-looking building was the Earl of Southampton's new manor house at Bloomsbury, just outside built-up London, probably begun shortly before the Civil War, although the interior was not completed until the 1660s. The novelties here were not only the restrained hipped-roofed elevation, long and low, with a piano nobile above a basement storey, but the inclusion of a
p. cour d'honneur in the French manner: an open front courtyard
18 flanked by service wings, closed off by only a low wall, so that the house could make a show when seen from the street.

During the 1630s–40s the area between the City and Westminster began to be built up more densely, although development was erratic, dependent on the interests of individual property owners. The most ambitious undertaking lies outside this volume: the fourth Earl of Bedford's development of his land at Covent Garden, the former kitchen gardens of the monastery at Westminster, which lay N of the garden of Bedford House on the Strand. Building began in 1631 to designs by Inigo Jones. The formal layout of a square was prophetic. Although the houses above Italian-inspired arcaded walks (or 'piazzas' as they became known) filling two sides were not imitated elsewhere, the classical regularity of the whole stood as a standard of excellence. The houses provided a convenient urban alternative for those who wished to avoid the expense of maintaining a large London establishment and became fashionable with the aristocracy. Other speculators soon followed suit. In the later 1630s William Newton built a row of houses nearby in Great Queen Street, now demolished, which was given a unified appearance by the use of giant Corinthian pilasters. Newton was also responsible for the development of Lincoln's Inn Fields, which had been built up on three sides by 1658. Only one of the first buildings remains, Lindsey
27 House, dating from 1639–41, originally the centrepiece of the W side, and thus distinguished by a balustraded parapet instead of the more usual wooden eaves. The design of this accomplished classical façade with Ionic pilasters, heavy pedimented windows, and balustraded parapet, so clearly reminiscent of Jones's Whitehall Banqueting House, has been plausibly linked with the circle of Inigo Jones, and his colleague Nicholas Stone is indeed known to have been a friend of the patron, Sir David Cunningham.

The scattered development beyond the City's boundaries was recognized by the wide extent of the defences put up by Parliament in 1642–3. On the N side of London they ran from Kingsland Road in Hackney to near the N end of St John Street, Clerkenwell, then roughly SW, with an outwork at the New River and a pair of batteries behind Southampton House, to St Giles. A little way along Oxford Street the line turned more sharply S toward Hyde Park Corner and then skirted around Westminster. The defences were never tested, and London was spared siege or destruction, but the war and the unsettled years that followed cannot have been an encouraging time for building. Nevertheless expansion around London continued. A remarkable survival from the Commonwealth period is at Newington Green, a hamlet on the fringe of Islington: a terrace of four houses

dated 1658, whose elevation with giant pilasters displays the influence 28
of recent houses in Holborn. It is the oldest known existing brick
terrace in London. This urban outlier is also interesting for its plan,
which has an arrangement predating the one which became standard
in terrace houses from the end of the C17: the staircase rises between
front and back rooms and there is an internal lightwell between each
pair of houses. Other tantalizing evidence of lost buildings shows
that the elevation with pilasters emphasizing the upper floors
appears to have become an accepted formula in the London area by
the middle years of the C17. Pilasters appeared, for example, on
Thanet House, an aristocratic mansion in Aldersgate Street in the
City, on the rebuilt Holborn frontage of Furnival's Inn, one of the
Inns of Chancery, and on Balmes, Hackney, a country house whose
eccentric remodelling with paired pilasters and steep hipped roof
with two tiers of attics may date from the ownership of Sir George
Whitmore (†1654, Lord Mayor 1631–2).

The restoration of the monarchy in 1660 after the disruption of
the Civil War once again reinforced the importance of Westminster,
and encouraged the building of both individual houses and speculative terraces in the growing suburbs. N of the development fringing
the river between the City and Westminster there was still room for
PRIVATE MANSIONS with substantial grounds behind. For such
buildings a new type of designer began to be employed, the gentleman architect who had some knowledge of continental classical
architecture. The house which attracted most attention was the short-
lived Clarendon House on Piccadilly, designed for the Lord Chancellor
by Roger Pratt, under construction in 1664, but demolished in 1682.
During its brief life it was one of the acknowledged sights of London,
and its balanced frontage with projecting wings, hipped roof and
central pediment was influential all over England. Another flamboyantly ambitious mansion was built in 1675–9 in Great Russell Street,
close to Southampton House, for Ralph Montagu, the ambassador
to Paris, to designs by the architect and scientist *Robert Hooke*. It was
at least partly rebuilt after a fire in 1686, when it acquired an idiosyncratic French roofline, ascribed to a French architect called *Puget*.
It survived as the C18 home for the British Museum until replaced
by the museum's present buildings. One of the few survivors of
major late C17 houses in inner London (although altered inside) is
Newcastle House, in Lincoln's Inn Fields, begun in 1685–9 by
*William Winde* for William Herbert, first Marquess of Powis. It is on
a much larger scale than the first houses in the Fields. Its brick front
of three storeys with central pediment, over a high basement,
although reconstructed in the C20, gives a good impression of the
plainer type of post-Restoration house, influenced by the more
austere manner of later C17 Dutch architecture.

## NORTH LONDON:
## THE LATE C17 TO THE END OF THE C18

### *Domestic building from the late* C17

Large mansions remained the exception, and it was the terrace
house which was to dominate London's suburban development for
the next two centuries. Individual houses in their grounds continued

to be built on the urban fringes, but they were first surrounded, and
eventually almost invariably replaced by more profitable rows of
smaller houses, whose rents could line the pockets of aristocratic
landowners, property speculators and small builders, or provide
income for charitable bodies. Such houses were often rebuilt after
the initial lease ran out, or at least refronted and modernized. As a
result, and because of pressure on valuable sites in inner London for
other uses, there are only a relatively small number of survivals from
the later c17, although the street patterns that were then established
are still evident.

The urban SQUARE, already known in Italy and France, had been
introduced to London by the fourth Earl of Bedford's development
at Covent Garden. In 1661, immediately after the Restoration, the
fourth Earl of Southampton obtained a licence to develop his
Bloomsbury estate, and laid out Bloomsbury Square as a formal
prelude to his own manor house, a novelty. The houses were leasehold, so that the ground landlord retained control, but the builders
bore the cost of the work, a pattern that was to be repeated in the
development of later London estates. The early character of the
square is known only from old views: all the houses have been
rebuilt except for a few on the w side, hidden behind later fronts.
The houses on the three sides of the square (the new term appears
first in 1663) had a uniform general appearance, three storeyed, with
dormers in steep roofs, although they were not all identical in width
or plan. The square was at first successful in attracting aristocratic
residents; lesser streets to the w, and a market (long vanished)
provided for services. In these smaller streets a little late c17 fabric
remains here and there, sometimes recognizable by the low height of
the ground floor in comparison with houses rebuilt later (see for
example Little Russell Street). The next squares were in Westminster:

NW corner of Bloomsbury Square, Holborn, laid out 1661.
Detail of engraving, published 1754

St James's Square, conveniently close to the court, built from 1665, and Golden Square in Soho, 1673. Meanwhile the catastrophe of the Great Fire of 1666 had ensured that building in brick became the rule in the City. The Rebuilding Act of 1667 laid down regulations for materials, and specified the different categories of houses appropriate for different locations. Four storeys was regarded as suitable for the most important thoroughfares, three storeys for lesser streets. It is this latter type that most commonly survives.

Extensive development N and W of the City took off in the 1680s: Hoxton Square and neighbouring streets were laid out on the edge of built-up Shoreditch; Hatton Garden, a broad street with large houses, covered the gardens of the former mansion of the Bishop of Ely; and Red Lion Square and Queen Square were built on virgin ground N of High Holborn. The streets and squares remain, but none retains any of its first buildings. In the C19 Hatton Garden became commercial and the centre of the diamond trade; Hoxton was taken over by furniture making. The Holborn squares remained homes for professional families into the C19 but their houses were gradually taken over for offices or showrooms, or in the case of Queen Square for specialist medical purposes. However, building of the 1680s can still be appreciated in those havens of tradition, the lawyers' quarters at the Inns of Court: New Square at Lincoln's Inn, begun in 1682, and Gray's Inn Square, c. 1685–93. These plain brick ranges, enlivened only by sturdy stone portals, were planned as lawyers' chambers, with each set opening off communal stairs. They therefore have windows of equal height on each floor, unlike private houses where the lesser importance of the top floor was indicated by smaller openings. A surviving domestic example from the 1680s is a modest group on the S side of Great Ormond Street (most of Nos. 49–61), which belong to the developments of c. 1686 around Queen Square. For these the notorious Dr Nicholas Barbon was responsible. Barbon was among the most active entrepreneurs of this period; his undertakings outside the area of this volume included buildings in the City, and houses in the Temple and in Essex Street off the Strand. Within Holborn, in addition to Queen Square, he completed New Square, Lincoln's Inn, and laid out Red Lion Square for building, despite the protests of the lawyers of Gray's Inn, who valued the rural outlook of their famous Walks planted by *Francis Bacon*. Building spread outward from the areas begun by Barbon, and from the first twenty years of the C18 much more remains. Among them are the streets of the Rugby estate N of High Holborn, where particularly good houses can be found in and around the E part of Great <sub>31</sub> Ormond Street; there are others of similar date in the neighbouring Great James Street, and in Bedford Row, built 1717–19 as the last part of the Red Lion Square development. The old hamlet of St Giles-in-the-Fields also expanded: Seven Dials, with its novel layout of six streets radiating from a central pillar, was admired by Evelyn in 1694.

From these examples some generalizations can be made about the CHARACTER OF LONDON TERRACE HOUSES of the late C17 to the 1720s. The narrow-fronted single-family house arranged on several floors, inhabited by the aristocracy as well as the gentry and the middling classes, was a London phenomenon which intrigued visitors from abroad accustomed to a greater display from the wealthy.

The most common type has a three-window front of brownish-red
brick. In early examples the floors may be divided by brick bands.
Segment-headed windows (as in Great James Street) were smart in
the earlier C18. The straight-headed window, which required skilful
bricklaying with expensive soft red bricks 'rubbed' to shape, became
the norm from the second quarter of the century, although less carefully detailed segment-headed windows were often still used for
windows at the back or in the basement. Doorways were often
sheltered by flat canopies supported by lavishly carved brackets,
whose variety demonstrates how the craftsman was not yet constrained by the architectural conventions that gained currency from
the 1720s. From the end of the C17 it became common for windows
to be glazed with sashes instead of the older type of cross-window
with casements. Early sashes were set close to the outer wall; they
were heavy affairs with thick glazing bars, and have almost invariably
been replaced with lighter, late Georgian sashes with thin glazing
bars, or by Victorian plate glass. These replacement sashes were still
set close to the outer wall, although this was prohibited in the
Building Act of 1709, which sought to reduce the amount of exterior
timber to diminish the risk of fire. The change to deeper reveals for
the windows, which appears to have become widespread only from
around 1720 or later, is one of the most easily recognizable visual
differences which distinguishes later terraces from those of the first
decades of the C18. An earlier Building Act, of 1707, forbade timber
cornices; if the early Holborn houses ever had them, they have all
been replaced by brick parapets.

As should be clear from these comments, individual houses are
likely to have a complicated history of alterations, and the date of
building by no means will apply to all visible details. What remained
fairly constant was the PLAN of the smaller terrace house. The three-
bay front allowed for two rooms on each floor and a staircase rising
from front to back in a narrow hall at one side. In late C17 and early
C18 examples the back room commonly has a small projecting closet
for more private use, the two rooms being served by adjacent corner
fireplaces, an arrangement generally given up later in the C18.
Kitchen and service rooms were in the basement. In front this was lit
by a sunken area below the level of the road, railed off from the
street, at the back these rooms were at ground level, opening on to a
narrow back garden, which (to judge from C18 views) would have
been laid out with formal walks. Inside, partitions were often of
timber studding, and the main rooms of ground and first floor were
panelled from floor to ceiling. A surprising number of interiors of
this kind survive behind later refronting. Occasionally larger houses
diverged from this plan. An example is the four-bay No. 11 Bedford
Row, which was broad enough to have a large front stairhall with
37 mural painting (executed after *c.* 1720 by *John Vanderbank*). Another
example of a stairhall of this type, with painted ceiling, is No. 99
Great Russell Street. Outside Holborn more fragmentary remains of
domestic terraces of this kind can be found in Clerkenwell, where
Britton Street has houses of *c.* 1719, filling in gaps left among the
remains of St John's precincts. Another centre grew up N of the City
around the early C18 church of St Luke Old Street, but here very
little of the C18 is left. The best individual house in this area is the
large early C18 one in Chiswell Street, which later became the

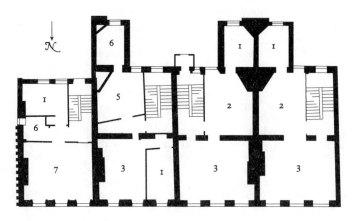

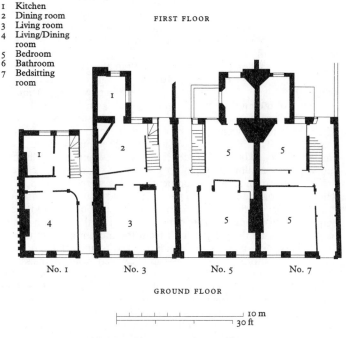

1  Kitchen
2  Dining room
3  Living room
4  Living/Dining
   room
5  Bedroom
6  Bathroom
7  Bedsitting
   room

**FIRST FLOOR**

No. 1        No. 3        No. 5        No. 7

**GROUND FLOOR**

10 m
30 ft

Nos. 1–7 Great Ormond Street, Holborn.
Plans showing room use after conversion in 1975

Partners' House for Whitbread's Brewery; further E there is another in Charles Square, Hoxton.

It would be misleading to think that all houses were of this standard. The older suburbs close to the City, old hamlets such as St Giles-in-the-Fields, and the eastern settlements close to the river, were filled with poorly built, overcrowded and insanitary dwellings crammed into back lanes and courts. In such places conditions deteriorated as the population multiplied. By the middle of the C18

London was the largest city in Europe, attracting a continual flow of immigrants both from the countryside and abroad. The population grew from *c.* 200,000 in 1600 to around 575,000 in 1700. During the first half of the C18 it remained relatively static, probably because of the disastrous effect of gin drinking (limited by the Gin Act of 1751), but by the time of the first census in 1801 the figure was 900,000. As the suburbs became increasingly significant, the numbers of people living in the City itself declined: *c.* 208,000 in 1700, 134,000 in 1801.

The expanding suburbs with their grand squares on the great estates in Mayfair and St Marylebone drew the aristocracy westward; the better Holborn houses (convenient for the legal Inns) remained popular with lawyers and professionals, but were no longer the leaders of fashion. Larger mansions were few. Apart from Southampton House and Montagu House there was Powis House, which stood N of Great Ormond Street. Rebuilt after a fire in 1714, it survived until 1784, but this was an exception. Engravings show a grand elevation with giant fluted pilasters and heavy attic storey.

North London lacks major domestic examples of the PALLADIAN STYLE, the stricter classical manner inspired by the C16 Italian architect Palladio and his disciple Inigo Jones, which developed in the 1720s in reaction to the Baroque of Wren and Hawksmoor. The best example is the restrained Nos. 57–58 Lincoln's Inn Fields, rebuilt by *Henry Joynes* in 1730, a deliberately reproportioned rendering of the ingredients of its older neighbour, Lindsey House. There are nevertheless some good examples of lesser terrace houses where Palladian influence can be seen in the form of more precise classical details, which were now increasingly popularized through pattern books. The timber doorcase with columns or pilasters supporting a pediment began to replace the canopy on carved brackets. In ambitious developments streets were designed as a whole, as a 'palace front' with centre and end houses emphasized. A more refined effect was achieved by the use of recessed sash windows with slimmer glazing bars, and often by the use of a stone band to mark off the ground floor from the more important upper floors. This could be used to suggest the base of an 'implied order', following the more precise proportions derived from the classical Orders, even when pilasters or columns were not present. Later in the C18 the contrast between the floors was accentuated by the application of render or stucco to the ground floor. Another change was in the colour of brick, brownish-red giving way to paler yellow brick, popular with the Palladians because its cooler tone (until discoloured by London's sooty atmosphere) appeared closer to stone. Some dignified houses in this manner remain to the S of Bloomsbury Square, designed by *Henry Flitcroft* (architect of the Palladian St Giles-in-the-Fields and master carpenter to the Office of Works from 1746). They were built in the 1740s–50s for the Bedford estate, which had inherited the Southampton lands through Rachel, the daughter of the fourth Earl, who had married Lord William Russell. A little speculative building was also carried out elsewhere in Holborn: spacious streets with good houses remaining from this time are John Street N of Theobalds Road of 1756–9, and Percy Street and Goodge Street, W of Tottenham Court Road, of the 1760s.

*Building in the countryside*

The new type of brick house, both the large detached building and the terrace, was adopted in places outside the immediate London suburbs. The compact house with double-pile plan and symmetrical front, often with a cupola crowning its hipped roof, was an accepted form in the London countryside by the end of the C17, especially in the villages N of London which were convenient for those with City connections. Most can now only be appreciated in old views. Belsize, built by a courtier, Daniel O'Neal, on the slopes of Hampstead in the 1660s seems to have been an early example. From the later C17 there were others: a grand house built for Sir William Ashurst, Lord Mayor, on the site of the Banqueting House of Arundel House, with grounds spreading over the slopes of Highgate Hill, and Clapton House, one of many fine houses which once existed in the then fashionable village of Hackney. Another was Abney House (named from residence in the early C18 of another Lord Mayor), in Stoke Newington, a village 'pleasantly situated and full of fine country houses for citizens' (Strype, 1720). The best surviving example is 30 Fenton House, Hampstead, built *c.* 1693, with its restrained brick front with central pediment, and an interior which still has its p. staircase and much of the original room layout. The grounds behind 216 surrounded by raised terraces give an impression of the formal garden of this time.

A good vista was a strong element in the choice of sites for C18 houses around London. Hampstead and Highgate maintained a perennial appeal. Further N, one can still appreciate (thanks to the green belt) the rural views from the ridges of Mill Hill and Totteridge which attracted both gentry and self-made city men to these more remote spots. A pattern which recurs through the C18 and the early C19 is the siting of both individual houses and terraces around commons, often some way from old village centres. Monken Hadley, Barnet, right on the fringe of our area, still preserves this effect of spacious Georgian houses loosely scattered around open common land, and other areas now suburbanized must once have given a similar impression. At Southgate, Enfield, once a secluded rural hamlet away from the main road village of Edmonton, a number of large mansions and fragments of their grounds still remain among C20 suburbia. Arnos Grove, Southgate, a surprising survival now enveloped in a C20 office building, was rebuilt *c.* 1720. Behind its standard pedimented seven-bay front is a grand entrance hall with staircase, decorated in the grand Baroque manner with mural painting by *Lanscroon*. Local example could have an effect: at Broomfield, Southgate, early C18 improvements included a staircase hall, much smaller than that at Arnos Grove, but also painted by *Lanscroon*. This stairhall and its paintings await reinstatement following a fire, but the grounds (now a public park) retain an avenue and a sequence of lakes which are relics of a formal layout of the type common in the late C17 and early C18. Forty Hall, Enfield, whose grounds were extended in the mid C17, also has remains of avenues and water features. A minor but interesting example of an early C18 garden layout is at Mill Hill, where an older house, Littleberries (now St Vincent's), was enlarged by a pedimented pavilion on axis with a long garden. This originally had a series of formal ponds, and

still ends in a small C18 banqueting house. A more complete early
C18 mansion is East Finchley Manor House (now the Sternberg
Centre), a plain building of 1723 which replaced an older moated
manor house.

The terrace house also made an appearance in places outside the
City. Nos. 79–85 Essex Road is a rare survival (much rebuilt) of a
late C17 terrace in Islington, by this time a prosperous little market
town N of the City, among the flat dairy pastures which supplied the
growing needs of the metropolis. Hampstead grew for a different
reason: mineral waters were discovered here in the late C17, and the
place became a spa, popular throughout the C18 both with day
trippers and as a healthy hilltop summer resort for Londoners, away
from the smoke of the city. The spa lay E of the High Street, near
Flask Walk (where the water was bottled). To its w a more select
area grew up with a mixture of detached houses, terraces and
cottages fitted intricately along narrow lanes or on banks above the
steep slopes. Much from the C18 remains, indeed too much to list
here, but mention must be made of the best of the early C18 terraces
in the London area, Church Row, Hampstead, built *c.* 1720. Its
uniformly three-bay houses have backs which enjoy a magnificent
southward view toward London. The other hilltop settlement,
Highgate, remained more exclusive, with a preponderance of detached
houses, and – a novelty – semi-detached ones. The pairs in The
29 Grove of *c.* 1688, replacing Dorchester House, were built as an
unsuccessful money-raising venture for a school. Their plans are of
the mid- to late C17 type with staircase between front and back
rooms. Other examples show that the pair of houses was a not
uncommon type outside London. At Southgate Green is a very
handsome early C18 example, three storeys with emphatic rusticated
quoins in a Baroque manner. Another from the same period is

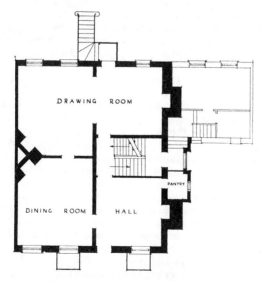

No. 4 The Grove, Highgate, *c.* 1688. Ground-floor plan

Nos. 808–810 Tottenham High Road. Such houses are generally set back further from the road than an urban terrace, sometimes with forecourt behind big gatepiers in a manner reminiscent of larger C17 houses such as Lindsey House, Lincoln's Inn Fields. The approaches to some of the larger individual houses of the earlier C18 are treated similarly, for example the two handsome examples of *c.* 1720 in Stoke Newington High Street, and Nos. 47–49 North Hill, Highgate, which appears to have begun as a single house with flanking lower wings. But no general pattern developed in the centres within easy reach of London during the first half of the C18; the result was a medley of brick houses of many different types and sizes, as can still be seen most attractively in the centres of Hampstead and Highgate, in a more fragmented fashion in Stoke Newington Church Street and along the High Road at North Tottenham, and further out, still in more rural surroundings, at Forty Hill, Enfield.

A particular type of housing that must be mentioned is ALMSHOUSES for the elderly, a medieval tradition of planned housing which continued as a recognized expression of personal charity throughout the C17 and C18. Many were built on the edge of the City of London by the City Livery Companies for their own members, but these have all been replaced later, either on their original sites, or more frequently on cheaper land further out. The earliest survivals resulted from private bequests. Lawrence Campe 23 Almshouses, Friern Barnet, *c.* 1612, are a row of two-storey brick cottages with mullioned windows. Sir Roger Wilbraham's group at Monken Hadley, of the same date, are one-storeyed. Bishop Wood's Almshouses at Lower Clapton Road, Hackney (1665, much rebuilt), are a little more ambitious, with projecting end wings with shaped gables. At High Barnet the Ravenscroft Almshouses of 1679 have been rebuilt apart from an archway but retain two excellent busts of the founders. The Nicoll Almshouses at Mill Hill of 1696 are still a row of one-storey cottages. By this time there were some architecturally more impressive exemplars, such as Hooke's group for the Haberdashers' Company at Shoreditch (1695, rebuilt 1825) and these may have had an effect on the group which has a claim to be the most attractive in our area, the Geffrye Almshouses (now 32 Museum) in Shoreditch, built 1712–14. This has two-storey ranges p. around three sides of a courtyard (four entered from a single door, 521 rather like lawyers' chambers), and a central chapel which retains its C18 furnishings, as well as a handsome wall monument to the founder, Sir Robert Geffrye (†1703) brought from a demolished City church. Among more modest later examples are the Wollaston Pauncefort row in Southwood Lane, Highgate (1722), single-storeyed, with taller centre block which was used as a school; and Garrett's Almshouses, High Barnet (1731), also simple one-storey cottages; the Daniel Almshouses at Hendon, (1727–9) are a more sophisticated composition with two-storey centre and gabled end pavilions. Almshouses continued into the C19; good examples are the Victorian Tudor group for the Metropolitan Benefit Society in Balls Pond Road, Islington (1829), the more elaborately detailed Leathersellers' Almshouses at High Barnet (1836–7, 1851), and the minimally Gothic Drapers' Company Almshouses at Bruce Grove, Tottenham, by *Herbert Williams* (1868–9).

*Churches: late C17 and C18*

In the inner suburbs all the older churches were rebuilt in the C18, with the exception of the isolated little building of St Pancras. Before this happened, private chapels for the residents of the new suburban streets had begun to supplement the medieval churches. St George the Martyr, Queen Square, originated in this way; the simple building erected in 1705 was embellished in 1718–20 so that it could be elevated to a parish church. The money came from the Fifty New Churches Act of 1711 which was responsible also for funding two entirely new churches in our area, St George Bloomsbury and St Luke Old Street, the first by *Nicholas Hawksmoor* alone, the second by *Hawksmoor* with *John James*. The Commissioners for the Act were ambitious in their aims, requiring stone buildings, properly oriented

33 and suitably monumental. St George, built 1716–31, has a six-column portico – the first C18 London church to have one – which because of the tight site is placed on the s side, and a w steeple inspired by the description of the mausoleum of Halicarnassus, a Hawksmoorean eccentricity only matched by the steeple of St Luke (built 1727–33) which is in the form of an obelisk. The rest of St Luke is more conventional, but sadly has been an unroofed shell since 1960. St George still has many of its original fittings, although C18 reordering has disguised the original arrangement with two grand family pews for the chief local magnates, the Duke of Bedford and Lord Montagu. Hawksmoor had prepared plans for rebuilding St Giles-in-the-Fields, but he lost the job to *Henry Flitcroft,* who in

35 1731–3 produced a handsome new preaching box in the tradition of Wren's St James Piccadilly, in an up to date Palladian style, with a steeple, but without portico or Baroque extravaganzas. Next came

34 St Leonard Shoreditch, rebuilt by the City Surveyor *George Dance Sen.* in 1736–40, a more monumental building with portico and fine steeple placed behind the portico in the manner of Gibbs's St Martin-in-the-Fields, and a grand interior with giant columns.

The villages around London followed suit: St John, Hampstead, in 1745–7, where *John Sanderson* was preferred to Flitcroft, and where the intended spire was never built; St Mary, Islington, in 1751–4 (*L. Dowbiggin*), where only the tower and steeple now date from the C18. At Kentish Town the chapel was rebuilt by *James Wyatt* in 1782–4, but has been drastically altered since. At Hackney a very large, original building based on a Greek Cross plan was built on a new site in 1791–4 by *James Spiller*. Such a plan had also been used for St Mary Paddington (1788–91), but the exceptional size of

36 the Hackney church creates a quite different effect, more akin to the interior of a theatre. A tower, also of novel type, was added in 1812–14. Minor work was carried out in the more distant villages: brick naves at Edgware and Totteridge; repairs to aisles at Enfield, Tottenham and Edmonton, but nothing spectacular. Tottenham had a curious mausoleum to Lord Coleraine attached to the e end of the church, but this disappeared in the C19. Many of the more rural churches have noteworthy churchyards with early headstones and good chest tombs. Those at East Barnet, Edmonton, Enfield, Hendon and Tottenham are particularly rewarding.

As for interior fittings and monuments, St Giles-in-the-Fields (Holborn), St Leonard (Shoreditch) and St James (Clerkenwell) are the places to visit to enjoy especially good collections of C17 and C18 work. All three have richly carved organ cases, and among much else the pulpit at St Giles and the excellent Rococo clock at St Leonard 39 are especially memorable. St Giles and St James also have well-preserved vestry rooms, an indicator of the significance of the vestry in C18 parochial administration. Elsewhere, Tottenham has a rare example of late C16 French stained glass, St Paul Mill Hill has a window with unusual painted glass of 1809 (by *Charles Muss* and *W. H. Hodgson*). Among monuments which should be singled out are the C17 shrouded figure by *Joshua Marshall* for the tomb of Lady Frances Kniveton at St Giles; and the striking wall monument to Elizabeth Benson †1710, with two skeletons, at St Leonard. A number of late C17 and C18 fittings from City churches were dispersed to new suburban churches in the late C19 and early C20: St Bartholomew, Tottenham, has a C17 pulpit and font with cover; St Olave, Stoke Newington, another C17 font and cover; St Peter le Poer, Friern Barnet, a late C18 pulpit; and St Benet Fink, Tottenham, a fine C18 organ and organ case.

Nonconformist survivals from this time are few, although the evocatively crowded Bunhill Fields Cemetery, Finsbury, in use by Dissenters from the late C17 to 1854, testifies to the strength of Nonconformity during this period. The oldest surviving building is the Unitarian Chapel at Newington Green, Stoke Newington, of 1708, now with a later front; the most significant is Wesley's Chapel in City Road, of 1777, considerably altered since but still with a recognizably C18 pedimented front, flanked by Wesley's own house on its right.

*Other secular buildings: C17 to C18*

The suburbs immediately N and NW of the City attracted only a few buildings representing communal endeavour. At the New River Head, Finsbury, reset within later buildings, the splendid interior of the late C17 Boardroom of the New River Company has been preserved, with plasterwork and woodcarving in the most sumptuous 38 City taste. From the C18 there is Armoury House, built for the Honourable Artillery Company in 1734–6 just outside the City boundary where there was space for training grounds. It is memorable for the exploding cannon balls on the parapet which enliven its otherwise routine Palladian front. On Clerkenwell Green the Middlesex Sessions House was built in 1779–82, by *Thomas Rogers* (though *John Carter* claimed responsibility for the design), a Palladian front in the lighter manner of the late C18, embellished with sculpture by *Nollekens*, but a good deal altered since.

The most ambitious undertaking was for a charity, Thomas Coram's Foundling Hospital, built 1745–53 to designs provided free of charge by the City merchant and architect *Theodore Jacobsen*. The buildings were plain, but generously laid out on three sides of a courtyard, on open land just to the N of the parish of Holborn. They survived until 1926. The Foundling Hospital was mid-C18 London's most fashionable charity, and its public rooms were decorated in style: some of this work is preserved in the C20 premises of the Thomas Coram Foundation at Brunswick Square, including a sensitively carved fireplace by *Rysbrack* and a ceiling by *William Wilton*. 40

Thomas Coram's Foundling Hospital, Holborn, *c.* 1750

The existence of the Foundling Hospital is a salutary reminder of the less appealing aspects of C18 London, where poverty, destitution and vice flourished in the back streets and alleys behind the elegant Georgian terraces, as Hogarth's paintings and engravings demonstrate. St Giles-in-the-Fields with 'a mixture of rich inhabitants to wit the Nobility, Gentry and commonalty, but withal filled with an abundance of poor' (1720) and the Seven Dials district immediately to its s were the most notorious, the setting for Hogarth's *Gin Lane.*

There were other HOSPITALS, the most visible results of the stirring of public conscience about such matters. They were established or enlarged throughout the C18, supported by voluntary subscriptions, and built on a scale far larger than any other public benefaction. Those with the best surviving C18 buildings lie outside our area: the rebuilding of St Bartholomew's in the City, Guy's Hospital, a new foundation in Southwark, and the London Hospital, Whitechapel. Other C18 foundations were rebuilt later (Westminster Hospital, St George's Hospital, Middlesex Hospital, all in existence by 1750). In north London there were two specialist hospitals, but both have disappeared: the City of London Lying in Hospital in City Road (1771) and St Luke's Hospital, which had been founded in 1751 to assist the older Bethlem Hospital for the insane at Moorfields and was rebuilt in Old Street by *George Dance* in 1782–9. It ended its life as the Bank of England's printing works and was demolished after the Second World War.

SCHOOLS were also established, but few survive from before the C19, and these are mostly in the towns on the fringes of London. The most important one was the Charterhouse, already mentioned, which remained on its site close to the City until 1872. Generally schools were unambitious; C16 schools often consisted simply of a large hall for teaching, as in the case of the brick building at High Barnet which is now part of Barnet College, although dormitories were soon added above the hall. The Grammar School at Enfield (*c.* 1577) which was built two-storeyed from the beginning, has been more altered but still has some of its brick mullioned windows. Highgate School was also founded in the C16; but its modest buildings were replaced when it was refounded as a C19 public school. During the C17 and C18 it became common practice to send London children to private schools in healthier spots outside the city; many of these were established in large, older houses, thereby assisting their survival when they were no longer fashionable as residences. The popularity of Hackney for this purpose is well known from the comments in Pepys's diary. Among the Charity schools which catered for poorer children are the unusually elegant former Welsh Charity School at Clerkenwell of 1738 (much restored; now Marx Memorial Library); a charming little example at Edmonton, dating from 1784; and a simple late example at High Barnet, the former Elizabeth Allen School of 1824. In Hatton Garden, Holborn, are two refixed figures of Charity children which came from a school of 1696.

*Developments from the later C18: country and town*

The stylistic revolution which overtook London in the later C18 owed much to *Robert Adam*. Inspired by his studies of antique Roman domestic building he introduced a lighter and more delicate version of the Neoclassical style, which was quickly taken up by other architects, builders and decorators. North London has a supremely successful example of his work, the transformation of Kenwood House, the country house of Lord Mansfield overlooking Hampstead Heath. Adam began work here in 1766, embellishing the exterior with an entrance portico and the garden side with decorative stucco pilasters, and adding to the main building a library or grand room with shallow curved vault, exquisitely decorated and furnished, making ingenious use of large mirrors. The other country house in our area with good work of this period is Arnos Grove, Southgate, where around 1765 *Sir Robert Taylor* added two excellent rooms in his characteristically elegant style. pp. 369 –70 47

A typical house of the London countryside of the later C18 was, however, not the mansion in large grounds but the VILLA. The prototype Palladian villas of the 1720s, such as Chiswick and Marble Hill, were built close to the Thames, w of London. The type became more widespread only in the later C18, when Sir Robert Taylor developed his own version of the villa, characterized by skilful planning in a tight compass, with rooms of different shapes cleverly fitted into a compact plan with projecting bays. A lost example in north London, plausibly suggested as a work by Taylor, was Beaver Hall, Southgate, of the 1760s, demolished 1870.* There is tantalizingly little information about other buildings of this type that once existed in the Middlesex countryside, and nearly all those that remain have been compromised by alterations. The earliest survivor appears to be the much altered Hendon Hall, whose core, with canted bay window, may date from the 1760s, although with embellishments of the early C19, probably by its then owner, *Samuel Ware* (they include the incongruous addition of a giant portico, with capitals possibly brought from Wanstead House).

Two well-preserved villas of the 1770s remain at Mill Hill, a popular retreat for rich merchants in the late C18: Belmont, and

* See Richard Garnier, Two Crystalline Villas of the 1760s, Georgian Group Journal VII, 1997.

Holcombe House. Belmont by *James Paine Jun.* is a quirky building, borrowing some ideas from his father, with some very elegantly detailed rooms of different shapes arranged around a great circular core containing a cantilevered staircase. Holcombe House by *John* 44 *Johnson* is more restrained, but has a good staircase and interior decoration and makes ingenious use of differing levels at front and back. Also from the 1770s is the former Southgate House (now within the Minchenden College campus), once a fine house, with central staircase fitted into a half circle. Neoclassical planning with curved rooms is also a feature of Millfield House, Edmonton, probably of the 1790s.

One of the most intriguing losses is the house at Trent Park, Southgate, built in 1777 when parts of Enfield Chase were enclosed. It was a small pavilion in a sophisticated French manner, designed by *Sir William Chambers,* for the royal physician Sir Richard Jebb. Its exterior is known only from a sketch, although the core survives within the much enlarged present mansion now used by Middlesex University. A second house built in Enfield Chase at the same time, Beech Hill, survives as a golf club, with a decent but less remarkable classical front possibly attached to an older building. Many other houses have gone; the Fitzroy villa at Highgate, for example, was built *c.* 1770 and lasted only until 1828, when it was replaced by a more rambling stuccoed house by *George Basevi*. Highbury Hill, a house by *D. A. Alexander* of *c.* 1790, survived within built-up Highbury until 1928.

From the 1790s two good buildings remain. Clissold House, Stoke Newington, built as Newington Park House, sited so that a view over the New River could be enjoyed from its raised Grecian p. colonnade. Its plan is unusual. The curved staircase descends to a 539 basement which is partly given over to neatly planned services, partly to a circular garden room projecting into a s bow. The second, very 45 different house is Grovelands, Southgate, designed by *John Nash* p. in 1797. It is by far the most accomplished of these late C18 463 Neoclassical villas, articulated by a giant Ionic order, with *Coade* stone trimmings, and with a well-planned interior with reception rooms around a grand staircase. The *pièce de résistance* is a breakfast room painted as a birdcage.

Fine LANDSCAPED GROUNDS with water were an important 1 aspect of late C18 estates. Those at Kenwood are the best preserved. Here, as was the general pattern in the C18, earlier formal planting was replaced in the mid C18 by lawns sloping down to a lake to the s of the house. The picturesque eyecatcher of a 'sham bridge' by the lake was added in the later C18; and in the 1790s, when *Repton* was consulted, there were further improvements, including a model farm, dairy and cottages. *Repton* was also involved at Grovelands, which likewise has a lawn sloping down to a lake, sheltered by woodland. Part of the grounds at Grovelands remain as a public park, as does a fragment of those of Arnos Grove. Here both the Pymmes Brook and the New River ran through the grounds. Until the New River was straightened in the mid C19, its tortuous route provided a ready-made landscape feature for numerous other houses. Many, such as Harringay House, Hornsey, have vanished without trace; elsewhere remains are fragmentary, as at Woodside Park, Wood Green, where an attractive early C19 octagonal lodge remains from

Chitts Hill House. A survivor is Myddelton House, Enfield, a classical villa built in 1818 by *Ferry & Wallen*, for H. C. Bowles, with shallow bow overlooking the grounds, where an iron bridge of 1832 remains above the New River's former course.

The New River Head, sited on high ground on the fringe of Clerkenwell, stood on the edge of the countryside until the later C18. For Londoners it was still only a short walk to the pleasure grounds of nearby Sadlers Wells, or to other places of rural amusement beyond the New Road which had been laid out around the City in 1756. But by the end of the century London was creeping northward.

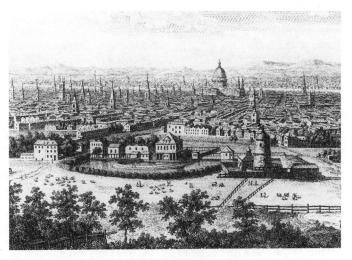

New River Head, view towards the City.
Engraving, published 1794

The finest URBAN DEVELOPMENT of this time is Bedford Square 3 of 1775–86, the start of the Bedford estate's late C18 development of Bloomsbury. Each side of the square is treated as a single unit, with stuccoed and pedimented centrepiece, the only London square of this type to survive complete. The broad doorways with *Coade* stone 42 rustication and handsome fanlights, and the use of stucco for the ground floor, echo Adam's developments around Portland Place, St Marylebone. The interiors differ, making use of a variety of combinations of rooms with curved ends, often with bows overlooking p. the gardens behind, the main rooms with refined plasterwork detail 324 in the Adam manner. The most unusual is No. 1, designed by *Thomas Leverton*, which has a centrally placed doorway, leading to an entrance hall filling the whole width of the three-bay front. 43 Leverton was involved in some other interior work in the square, although there is no evidence that he designed the exteriors. He also worked in Lincoln's Inn Fields at this time (No. 65, and perhaps some interiors in Newcastle House). More routine lesser streets followed, but most of Bloomsbury was built up only from the 1790s. Further afield, Islington also expanded in the 1770s: Cross Street, off Upper Street, has a sophisticated pair in Adam style of this time;

to the E of the High Street the picturesque banks of the New River attracted a steady growth of houses from the 1760s onwards (one of the best places to study houses of this period); and to the W, just N of the New Road, the streets of Pentonville were laid out in the 1770s, although here little is left. Some way further out a lone terrace, Highbury Place, was erected in Highbury Fields in 1774; a similarly isolated urban outlier is Grove Terrace at the N end of Kentish Town.

The developments of the 1770s were a prelude to the interest in NEOCLASSICAL URBAN PLANNING which was especially evident around 1790. Bath had provided an English precedent for the use of the geometric forms of squares, circuses and crescents to impose order on the city. The introduction of these principles to London was due to the younger *George Dance*, Clerk of the City works from 1768, and familiar with Neoclassical design from his study in Italy, but his work has not fared well. The first example, on a miniature scale, was the development from 1767 of the Minories estate in the City of London. Dance made more ambitious plans for the development of Moorfields N of the City; Finsbury Square was built up from the 1770s, but Finsbury Circus (within the City) not until 1815. Neither retains any original houses. Nor are any left in the small development of two linked crescents which he carried out on a City estate E of Tottenham Court Road (1796). Ambitious proposals by Dance which were not executed included a grand crescent at St George's Fields Southwark, and in north London, preliminary proposals for the development of Camden Town for the Earl of Camden, following an enabling Act of 1788. This was to have had linked crescent, circus and oval, but was abandoned in favour of a simpler grid of streets to the E of Camden High Street. An unusual scheme, long since demolished, was a polygon of houses at Somers Town, of 1793 by *Jacob Leroux*, who had earlier built a similar polygon at Southampton.

Most of the plans that came to fruition were less ambitious, relying on the tested earlier C18 ingredients of a square surrounded by service streets. Among the most successful compositions is Fitzroy Square, of 1789, the centre of a development on the Southampton estate W of Tottenham Court Road, a late work by *Robert Adam*. 
46 The two grand stone-fronted palace fronts (only E and S sides of the square were built at first) are closer to Adam's Edinburgh work than to his other London speculative developments. Around the same time *S. P. Cockerell* made plans for the Foundling estate property, which eventually resulted in the large expanses of Brunswick Square and Mecklenburgh Square flanking the hospital grounds. (Only the latter retains some of its original buildings, completed after 1808 by *Joseph Kay*.) At the same time the adjacent Bedford estate was being developed, with Russell Square, laid out in 1800, as a principal new focus, linked to the older Bloomsbury Square across the site of the demolished Southampton House. The very large square provided the opportunity for greenery; Russell Square was landscaped by *Repton*, as was Bloomsbury Square at the same time, marking a switch from the older custom of squares with plain gravelled walks to the romantic landscape tradition. But Russell Square was too big to read as coherent townscape; moreover it yielded less profit than a denser network of streets. In the later parts of Bloomsbury, developed by the builders *James Burton* and *Thomas Cubitt*, the 'squares' become long, narrow rectangles. The influence of the later C18

interest in formal planning is seen most clearly in the development of Finsbury and Islington, where squares were made central features of many of the small estates built up in the first half of the C19, starting c. 1805 with Northampton Square and Canonbury Square, both on Northampton estate land.

Some generalizations can be attempted about the character of TERRACE HOUSES of c. 1790–1830, of which numerous examples remain in the areas mentioned above. The London Building Act of 1774 had consolidated earlier legislation, making clearer distinctions between the different grades of houses, and ensuring better super-vision of standards through district surveyors. Thus established practice continued, and terrace houses differed only in detail from earlier examples. In plan, small and middle-sized houses usually followed the earlier C18 pattern, although especially in larger houses there may be rooms and stairhalls with curved end walls in the Neoclassical taste. Externally, a notable feature was the rising popularity of stucco. Adam and his contemporaries had experi-mented, not always successfully, with early patented types of hard plaster. A reliable version was patented in 1796 and its use became more general in the early C19. Stucco painted a stone colour, and often lined to give the impression of masonry, became popular as a brighter (although not maintenance free) alternative to the dinginess of smoke-blackened London brick. At first it was most often con-fined to ground floor and basement; from the 1820s it was more widely applied to the whole frontage. Large expanses of plain brick-work were also diminished by a greater proportion of window to wall; from the 1790s long first-floor windows down to floor level became fashionable, to provide maximum light to the main living room. These windows are often framed by arches, breaking up the wall surface still further. The legacy of Adam is seen in a liking for pretty, delicate detail, rather than formal classical features: ground-floor arched windows with thin glazing bars, sometimes with intersecting heads, elegant iron balconies with patterns that range from Grecian to Gothic. After timber doorcases and porch hoods were prohibited by the Building Acts, traceried fanlights received more emphasis, and *Coade* stone features, most often in the form of keystones with heads, could be an additional embellishment. The fashion for Neo-Grecian of the early C19 is expressed principally by the occasional appearance of Greek Doric doorcases. A light touch is also apparent inside; walls plastered rather than panelled (wallpaper was becoming fashionable); staircases have plain stick balusters rather than carved or turned ones. Grander houses might have ceilings with delicate plasterwork.

There were larger and more elaborate houses of this period, but these tend to be in fashionable Westminster rather than in the northern suburbs. However, the most extreme demonstration of what can be done behind a three-bay frontage is in Holborn, No. 13 Lincoln's Inn Fields, where *Sir John Soane* created from 1808 to 1813 an astonishing range of varied spaces within the house that became his museum, making ingenious use of skylights, coloured glass and mirrors to bring light into the building in different ways. The exterior, with its projecting stone centre, is also out of the ordinary. His dwelling house at No. 12, built in 1792–4, and No. 14, of 1823, are good examples of the standard type of terrace house given distinction by subtle details and ceilings of unusual shape.

48
p.
297
49

Among the terraces of the new estates, the late Georgian SHOP with elegant purpose-made shopwindow begins to make an appearance in the thoroughfares away from the more exclusive squares. There are good survivals in several streets around Fitzroy Square, and a whole stuccoed group in Woburn Walk on the edge of Bloomsbury.

## LONDON FROM AROUND 1800 TO 1914

The increase of shops – not just small shops in the new suburbs, but fashionable bazaars and markets in the West End – is just one indication of how London by 1800 had become above all a place of commerce, larger than all other known cities, inspiring awe and amazement in visitors from abroad. The first census, of 1801, counted a population of 900,000. The building of the first enclosed docks dates from this time, soon to be followed by the construction of a canal network linking them with the Midlands (see p. 95). Working-class housing expanded rapidly in the East End around the docks. Along the s bank of the Thames, linked to the City and Westminster by an increasing number of bridges, steam-powered manufacturing industry grew up, adding its smoke to the fog created by countless domestic fires. Immediately N of the City, where breweries and distilleries already existed in the c18, small specialized industries continued to expand, taking over domestic terraces and building over their backyards. Furniture making was concentrated in Shoreditch, metalworking and watchmaking in Clerkenwell. The open land beyond the built-up area was dominated by urban needs. A confused area of clay and gravel pits, brick kilns and rubbish dumps around the edge of town gave way to pasture land for the dairy cattle which provided London with milk. The flat countryside around Islington was the principal dairying area. The richer land of the Lea Valley further E had a scatter of market gardens, although they were less extensive than those along the Thames w of London. Further N, rising up toward the Northern Heights, were hay meadows, essential for the city's vast population of horses.

A desire to create better communications and to impose some appropriate civic dignity on this teeming hive of activity led to schemes for improving the main thoroughfares, a recurrent c19 endeavour, but one where achievement fell far short of original vision. The first and most ambitious of such improvements, albeit not completed as intended, was Regent Street and Regents Park, planned by *John Nash* for the Crown estates from 1811. This offered opportunities for a grander and more selfconscious type of scene-setting than London had seen hitherto, characterized by great sweeps of stucco-covered buildings with plenty of applied classical detail. In and around the park, laid out on the site of the farmland of the old Marylebone Park, Nash's final scheme provided for a ring of tall, palace-type terraces, a scatter of grand villas within the park, service squares further E, and the smaller individual houses of two Park Villages.* Soon after, travel to and from London to the N was eased by a rationalization of the main turnpikes and the creation of

*The squares (since rebuilt) and the two Park Villages E of the Park, are described in this volume; for the rest of Regents Park see *London 3: North West*.

new roads. Caledonian Road, Camden Road and Finchley Road, providing new links to the West End, were all begun in the 1820s. Improved transport also had an effect on the fabric of London. Welsh slate for roofs, brought by sea and canal, became ubiquitous, replacing local clay tile, and once the railways arrived – the London and Birmingham at Euston in 1837, the Great Northern at King's Cross in 1852 – a wide variety of building materials could easily be imported as alternatives to the yellow London stocks, the locally made bricks that hitherto had been the cheapest and most widely used building material.

*Suburban houses, 1800–1860*

Nash's Regents Park developments provided a fertile source of inspiration for the suburban house builders, to whose activities we must now turn. From *c.* 1800, new housing, principally for the middle classes, spread N from the increasingly industrial quarters of Clerkenwell and Shoreditch, and expanded around the core of late C18 developments at Bloomsbury, Somers Town and Camden Town. Between 1801 and 1841 the population of the parish of Islington grew from *c.* 10,000 to *c.* 56,000, and of St Pancras from *c.* 32,000 to *c.* 130,000. The line of the North London railway, laid out in 1850, enclosed an area which was already almost entirely built up. The history of individual areas is given in the borough introductions, but the general character of the new building may be summed up here.

In Holborn, an early manifestation of the new fashion promoted by Nash was the final part of the Foundling estate's development. The stuccoed E side of Mecklenburgh Square, a composition with giant Ionic columns, is by *Joseph Kay*, who was also responsible for town improvements in Greenwich. The later squares of Bloomsbury built by the great contractor *Thomas Cubitt* from the 1820s – Gordon Square, Tavistock Square – also have noticeably more stucco. Stucco terraces, with a little variety in their composition to add interest, were a speciality of Cubitt's, as can be seen not only in his major development of Pimlico in Westminster, but also in his more modest north London estates E of Gray's Inn Road and at Stoke Newington. The influence of the Nash style can also be traced in the increasingly elaborate terraces of the Islington estates, although these never aspired to the grandeur of their West End contemporaries, such as Tyburnia in Paddington. The most flamboyant demonstration of the Nash manner is in parts of the Thornhill estate, developed by *Joseph Kay*, where memorable sphinxes and obelisks guard the doorways of Richmond Avenue. Other Islington estates were less ostentatious; on the Scott estate, the 1820s houses with eccentric Ammonite capitals still have the delicate elegance of the Regency period.

The very tall, fully stuccoed, terrace houses with Italianate trimmings which became the standard type on smart west London Kensington estates in the mid C19, were imitated only occasionally in north London and not with great success: Arundel Square, Islington, begun 1852, was never completed, and the more ambitious development of the Belsize House estate in Hampstead, begun 1855, bankrupted the builder. The SQUARE with formal terraces nevertheless remained popular in Islington into the 1860s. In general, details are predictably Italianate, with the exception of *Roumieu &*

79 *Gough's* Milner Square (1839–44), where eccentric proportions transmuted traditional classical terraces into strange, powerful compositions of verticals and horizontals. In Hackney, further E, increasingly considered part of the industrial east end, squares were not built after the 1840s; the poorer streets have terraces of only two storeys above basements, but the builders of the smarter areas 80 developed their own style; the 1860s terraces of Dalston are a good hunting ground for lush and exuberant mixed ornament.

The suburban adoption of variants on the VILLA, previously associated with the country rather than the town, gathered pace during the C19. The detached or semi-detached house was a declaration of unease with the civilized urban ideal in a city made increasingly inhospitable through overcrowding and pollution. It could be in a 54 variety of styles, as Nash demonstrated in his Park Villages. Its romantic, rural affiliations were expressed most clearly by the *cottage orné*, with decorative bargeboarded gables and patterned window panes, or by battlements and Tudor detail. The best surviving north London example of such a building (now in a suburban setting, but once on its own) is Hunter's Lodge, Belsize Lane, Hampstead, of 1810 by *Joseph Parkinson*, a survival from the once numerous gentlemen's houses of the early C19 which maps show scattered over the countryside close to London. A late and very charming group in 56 the *cottage orné* style is Holly Village, designed in 1865 by *Henry Darbishire* as an eyecatcher on the edge of Baroness Burdett-Coutt's estate at Highgate.

Nash was not the only architect to introduce the villa into a more suburban context. The idea was current already in the 1790s. Detached villas had been proposed in 1794 for the Eyre estate in St Marylebone, although it was only from the 1820s that much of St John's Wood, further N, was developed in this way. South of the Thames around Blackheath (an area perhaps less affected by metropolitan aspirations than the northern suburbs) *Michael Searles* had also been experimenting with various forms of single, semi-detached and linked houses.

The simplest types of classical villas were modest hipped-roofed pairs built cheaply along the main roads: Camden Road, laid out in the 1820s, has an instructive sequence, becoming more ambitious by the mid C19 as the area developed. A well-preserved neighbourhood of small stuccoed villas is Downshire Hill and Keats Grove on the edge of Hampstead, and a distinguished little group remains 78 at Chalk Farm, Hampstead, as part of the development of the Eton estate from the 1840s, by the estate's surveyor *John Shaw Jun.* These exhibit a discreet use of Grecian detail, used more emphatically for the small idiosyncratic paired and pedimented villas on the Lloyd 55 Baker estate, Finsbury, where building began in 1825. The paired villa with shared pediment appears also in a more restrained form in the neighbourhood of London Fields, Hackney. Exceptions to regular terraces also begin to appear in the more prosaic formal squares of Islington laid out in imitation of Bloomsbury. Barnsbury, developed piecemeal from the 1820s–40s, mixes terraces and villas of various types; the gabled Tudor-Gothic houses of Lonsdale Square (1838–45 by *R. C. Carpenter*) are the most extreme departure 57 from classical tradition. The De Beauvoir estate in Hackney, mostly built up from the end of the 1830s, has as its centrepiece a square of very pretty Tudor villas with shaped gables and patterned glazing.

By the mid C19 the trim, small-scale aesthetic of Keats Grove was no longer felt to be appropriate for the wealthier middle-class Londoner, and substantial Italianate houses, either detached or in pairs, with plenty of room for servants, began to appear, often laid out along curving streets. Islington developers had some success with houses of this kind: Canonbury Park, begun 1837, Highbury Crescent, 1844–50, Alwyne Road, 1847. Gloucester Crescent, *c.* 1845–50, between Camden Town and the more fashionable Regents Park fringe, is also in this style, embellished with picturesque accents of Italianate towers. Much more unusual is the playful and eclectic mixture of Lombard or Venetian Gothic and classical found in *Charles Hambridge*'s houses in Highbury New Park, Islington, of 1851 onwards; *George Truefitt* planned a similar mixture at Tufnell Park from the late 1850s, although only a little remains.

*Domestic building from the 1860s*

A more eclectic choice of sources, no longer predominantly classical, becomes increasingly evident from the 1860s for houses, as for other types of buildings which will be mentioned later. Large mansions in their own grounds are now rarities in north London, although more once existed. The type is illustrated by Avenue House, East Finchley (mid C19, embellished in the 1870s), and even more eccentrically by The Logs, Well Road, Hampstead, by *J.S. Nightingale*, of 1867–8, which mixes Italianate, Gothic and French motifs in extravagant abandon. Caen Wood Towers (now Athlone House) Hampstead Lane, of 1870–2 by *Salomons & Jones*, adopted an elaborate Jacobean style, but has lost much of its detail. The inventive enthusiasm of church architects for developing Victorian versions of the GOTHIC STYLE had only a limited influence on domestic building. The most interesting efforts are by architects closely involved with church building and decoration. Outstanding among these is the terrace in Worship Street, Shoreditch, built by *Philip Webb* in 1862–3 for the 68 philanthropist Colonel Gillum, which included both workshops and housing. Although Gothic arches appear, the style, as in so much of Webb's work, defies classification. A more overtly Gothic example is the pair in Lyndhurst Terrace, Hampstead, of *c.* 1864–5, by and for the stained-glass designer *Alfred Bell* and his father-in-law *John Burlison Sen.* (assistant to Scott). The type of house that most commonly is given a Gothic flavour is the VICARAGE, intended to complement its church but also to appear domestic. Even where the church has disappeared the original function of the house is often unmistakable (for example the former vicarage in Oakley Square, St Pancras, by *John Johnson*). Especially good is St Chad's vicarage, Shoreditch (1873–4) by *James Brooks*, who was particularly skilled at composing the ancillary buildings around his churches. Such efforts were in a different league from the speculative development by conservative-minded builders dependent on pattern books. But the interest in polychromy and in Gothic detail which was fostered by Ruskin's writings had its effect. The standard type of terrace house continued, but from the 1870s stucco doorcases are commonly a hybrid type with segment-headed arches, Gothic capitals and naturalistic foliage. Flat frontages are broken by bay windows;

parapets give way to exposed eaves and sometimes to gables. More enthusiastically Gothic houses such as the large gabled detached ones of Crescent Road, Crouch End, of the 1870s, remain uncommon.

The 1870s brought a fresh approach to house design through the introduction of the style known as 'QUEEN ANNE', inspired by English domestic buildings of the C17 and by the tradition of tall, urban brick building in Holland and Flanders. Chelsea is well known as a home of the style, but Hampstead is the place to study it in north London. *Philip Webb* made an early, original contribution with Nos. 2–4 Redington Road, a deceptively simple tile-hung pair of 1876. *Norman Shaw*, one of the principal pioneers, built for himself the tall, red brick No. 6 Ellerdale Road (1874–6). It has a seemingly arbitrary arrangement of windows, explained by the siting of rooms inside, and a minimal use of exterior ornament. It was followed by other Shaw houses in Hampstead, less severe, and all inventive. Hampstead had long been celebrated as a home for artists; now from the later C19 it became fashionable to have an 'artistic' residence. Individual houses in the Shaw tradition include one in Redington Gardens by *Basil Champneys* for the artist Henry Holiday (1873), Champneys' own house in Frognal Lane (1880), and *Ewan Christian*'s own house in Well Walk (1881). Whole streets of informal, picturesquely grouped red brick houses, relieved variously by terracotta ornament, tile-hanging and painted timber balconies and porches, were built around Fitzjohn's Avenue, and elsewhere by the firm of *Batterbury & Huxley*, who were especially busy around Well Walk and England's Lane. Studios became a speciality, either within large houses, or as separate buildings tucked 81 into mews spaces. Among the many highly original architects working in a Free Style at this time, *C. A. Voysey* must be singled out; his masterpiece in north London is No. 8 Platt's Lane, Hampstead, of 1895, remarkable for its use of plain roughcast and skilful massing in place of ornament of any kind.

By the 1890s the new manner had matured into the relaxed Free Style of the Arts and Crafts movement which continued into the early C20, employing a skilful mixture of simple classical features and vernacular detail, often enlivened by original decorative work. It was adopted with enthusiasm for the larger houses built in the countryside which suburban trains had brought within easy reach of London, particularly Mill Hill and Totteridge, where the fine views were a special attraction. At Totteridge, where *Shaw* had already built a house in his Old English manner in 1876–7, the successful London architect *T. E. Collcutt* built his own house in 1895, and followed it by other work here and at Mill Hill which displays his own picturesque blend of Arts and Crafts and Old English detail. A further artistic strand was added by the Nicholson family, who owned the Totteridge manor house; *Charles Nicholson*'s first building was the vicarage of 1892 in a bold Queen Anne style.

Suburban versions of the Free Style are amply demonstrated in Hampstead by the West Hampstead estate, around Redington Road, developed from 1898, where *C. H. B. Quennell* was the principal architect, and by houses of similar date by *Amos F. Faulkner* in Elsworthy Road. By this time the style had been taken up by builders elsewhere. Muswell Hill, developed at the turn of the century, is a prime example, still very complete; with houses lavishly provided with pargetting and painted timberwork, in streets laid out around central shopping parades in a busy developers' Baroque. There is also more subtle work by the *Collins* family (responsible too for the Rookfield estate at the foot of Muswell Hill), who built not only houses, but some highly original Arts and Crafts mansion flats. Further out, the new railway suburb of Bush Hill Park, between Edmonton and Enfield, developed from 1880, had detached houses already in a minimal Queen Anne manner, and one exceptional house by *A. H. Mackmurdo* of 1883, defying current trends by its use of a stripped classical style. Bush Hill Park also had its working-class part, its humbler terraces sited in the classic position E of the railway line. They are a part of the general trend determined by the introduction in 1872 of workmen's trains with cheap fares on some of the Great Eastern lines, which resulted in the rapid development of working-class housing in both Tottenham and Edmonton.

### Urban rebuilding and planned housing

New working-class suburbs, with their plain but healthier two-storey terraces with gardens were one way of reducing the pressure on inner London, although the overcrowded London slums with a population of the very poorest remained problematic throughout the later C19 and beyond. The need to tackle the slums had been recognized from 1842, when the *Report on the Sanitary Conditions of the Labouring Classes* was published, and successive cholera epidemics reinforced the argument for action. In Holborn attention was focused on two problem areas, the notorious rookeries of St Giles and Seven Dials, and the slums on the edge of the Fleet valley. The initial approach was to flatten the worst areas for new roads. The first was New Oxford Street, cut through St Giles in 1841–7 to provide a more direct E–W link between High Holborn and Oxford Street. It was intended as part of a more elaborate scheme, but of the new N–S routes then proposed, only Endell Street was built; Charing Cross Road and Shaftesbury Avenue were not created until the 1880s. One experimental scheme of model dwellings resulted from the 1840s efforts and is still standing. Parnell House in Streatham Street, of 1849, was designed by *Henry Roberts* for the Society for Improving the Condition of the Labouring Classes, founded in 1844, one of several philanthropic bodies established at this time with the intention of providing model working-class housing. The five-storey block of flats, with balcony access, arranged around a courtyard, is on a comfortably humane scale, but hardly adequate to cope with the disruption caused by the clearances. The Fleet valley was the subject of more wide-reaching improvements, carried out by the City Corporation from 1863 to 1869, which included the culverting of the Fleet River, by then an offensive open sewer, the bridging of the valley by Holborn Viaduct and the creation of Farringdon Road and new access roads to Smithfield market. Here too some model dwellings resulted, provided by the Corporation, the first local authority to put up such buildings, but the only surviving ones are a small, later group of 1874 N of Charterhouse Street.

Still standing elsewhere are some of the flats built by Alderman Sydney Waterlow's Improved Industrial Dwellings Company,

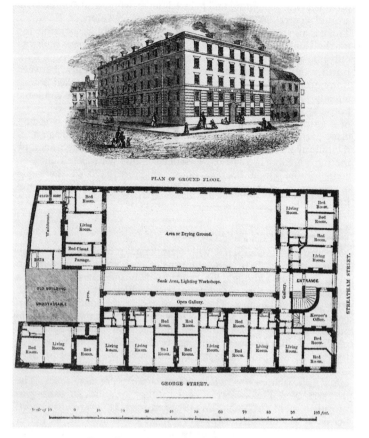

PLAN OF GROUND FLOOR.

Parnell House, Streatham Street, Holborn.
Ground-floor plan, 1849

founded in 1863. They adopted a standard design, based on *Henry Roberts*'s model dwellings shown at the Great Exhibition in 1851: flats reached by an open stair recessed in the centre of each block. The first, near Waterlow's printing works in Shoreditch, no longer stand; later, extant examples include one in Mark Street, Shoreditch (refurbished and not unattractive now), and the evocative Stanley Buildings of 1864–5, close to King's Cross Station. The Peabody Trust, founded in 1862 by the American banker George Peabody, had similar aims, but was able to acquire much larger sites. After an initial, not wholly satisfactory venture in Spitalfields, the Trust built its first major estate in Greenman Street off Essex Road, Islington, in 1865, establishing a pattern repeated elsewhere (e.g. Clerkenwell Close and Whitecross Street, Finsbury). The flats, designed by *Darbishire*, are in large four-storey blocks, around a courtyard, with access by internal stairs; the earlier estates had an additional top drying floor. The style is an austere but dignified Italianate, with distinctive striped grey brickwork. A different type of housing was produced by the Artisans, Labourers and General Dwellings Company, a self-help group founded in 1867, whose aim was to provide modest suburban housing for the skilled working class. Their first estate was in Battersea (1872); Noel Park, Wood Green, was built in 1883–1907, a simple layout with straight roads of neat terraces enlivened by some gables and a little terracotta ornament. Most of this philanthropic housing could only be afforded by the better-off artisan. Lodging houses for single men were provided in the 1890s by Lord Rowton's houses. One example (still in use) of these great red brick piles remains in Arlington Road, Camden Town. Industries in London were generally too small to build housing for their employees; exceptions are the long row of cottages at the Royal Small Arms Factory, Enfield; railway workers' terraces at Cricklewood, Barnet; and Aeroville, an attractive Neo-Georgian square for workers at Hendon aerodrome, built 1917.

As a result of the Housing Act of 1890, the local authorities were beginning to build too. The LCC, formed in 1888, established a Housing Branch in 1893, and full of the idealism of the 1890s, aimed to provide a more attractive type of housing than the philanthropic tenements. Boundary Road, Bethnal Green (*London 5: East*), was their first major effort, with blocks arranged around a *rond-point*, and given striped brick and gables to provide visual interest. The slums of Somers Town were another focus of attention: the LCC's first work here (1899), in Churchway, N of Euston Road, was flats in an attractive Arts and Crafts style. Later on pressure to accommodate as many as possible produced the more cramped blocks of the vast Bourne estate on Clerkenwell Road, Holborn, of 1901–7, housing 3,900 people. Other more recently established housing bodies such as the Samuel Lewis Trust and the Guinness Trust also endeavoured to make their flats look less utilitarian; the Samuel 98 Lewis Buildings in Liverpool Road, Islington (1909–10), have mansard roofs and a little ornament, and look rather like private mansion flats. Navarino Mansions (note the classier name), in Hackney, built by the Four Per Cent Industrial Dwellings Company (1903–4) is an equally striking group, with bold entrance archways.

By the early C20 it was clear that rebuilding within London would not on its own solve the housing problem, nor was the accommodation provided affordable by the very poor. An Act of 1900 allowed the LCC to provide housing outside its boundaries, and led to the development of cottage estates beyond the built-up area, the first in south London, begun 1903. But the most significant and influential suburban development of the early C20, nationally as well as locally, was Hampstead Garden Suburb, begun in 1907 through the efforts of Dame Henrietta Barnett. It differed both from the usual speculative development and from the paternalistic approach of the philanthropic trusts by being built through co-partnership companies, which enabled residents to remain involved in the management. Despite difficulties at various stages, this ensured that the suburb retained its architectural character, if not its original social aim of a model neighbourhood combining houses for a range of social levels. In contrast to the average speculative working-class terrace, the artisans' houses were practically planned, with wide 100 frontages that made it possible to eliminate light-swallowing back extensions. The simple cottage style, with much use of roughcast and gables, and the imaginative layouts with winding roads and plentiful open spaces were devised by the architects *Barry Parker & Raymond Unwin*, who had already tried out some of these ideas at Letchworth Garden City, Herts. The larger houses were by a variety of architects, and were more formal, those by *Lutyens* and some others making use of a late C17 or Neo-Wren style, but with many

99 variants. *Baillie Scott*'s Waterlow Court, with its simple arcaded cloister, built for single women, is particularly pleasing. The concept of the low-density garden suburb was to be immensely influential in the first half of the C20, given official recognition after Unwin became involved in government planning for new public housing after the First World War, and imitated also by private builders between the wars. The LCC began to adopt the principles of Unwin's picturesque layouts for their cottage estates on the fringe of London: the change of approach can be seen in the development of the White Hart Lane estate, Tottenham, begun 1903, and continued into the 1920s. A small but attractive example of the Suburb's influence is Finchley Garden Village of 1909–14, a co-partnership enterprise, with cottagey houses by *Frank E. Stratton*.

### C19 *industrial and commercial architecture*

Tracing the development of the suburbs poses the question of where the growing numbers of London residents found employment. The City, conveniently accessible by tram or train by the later C19, drew a stream of workers from the northern suburbs. Closer at hand were the many small labour-intensive manufacturing industries which occupied large areas of Camden Town, Finsbury, Shoreditch, Islington and Hackney, and an industrial strip along the Lea Valley, to an extent difficult to realize today when so many industrial sites have given way to housing or are merely used for warehousing (*see* Industrial Archaeology p. 101). There was also an increasing range of service industries within the suburbs themselves, indeed the most visible evidence now of Victorian small-scale enterprise is the vast number of undistinguished small shops that developed along the main roads, often built out in the later C19 over the front gardens of earlier houses; Holloway Road is a classic example.

Among commercial buildings which made an architectural show, BANKS were important already in the earlier C19. A surprising and attractive survival is the stuccoed Italianate Finsbury Savings Bank by *Alfred Bartholomew*, of 1840, a showpiece in the contemporary Sekforde estate in Finsbury. A sober classical style remained a respectable style for banks: a mid-century example is No. 212 High Holborn (*H. Baker*, 1854). Later in the C19 suburban banks tended to take on the more florid style of neighbouring shops and pubs, as in the case of the flamboyantly gabled example at Enfield Market Place by *W. Gilbee Scott*, of 1897, but settled down to more sober versions of Neo-Georgian from the early C20. Suburban banking halls do not have the grandeur of city-centre banks; their distinctive feature is their relatively small and high windows, ensuring privacy and security.

The large C19 OFFICE BUILDING only gradually made an appearance in the suburbs. Holborn became the home of several

INSURANCE HEADQUARTERS. The Prudential, requiring more space than could be found in the City, moved here in 1876. Its buildings by *Waterhouse* (first building 1876, but the present ones mostly 1895) are in an insistent red brick and terracotta Gothic, 63 which was adopted as the company house style, a rare case of Gothic used wholeheartedly for a financial institution. The principal interiors, lavishly decorated with glazed tiles, were also intended to impress. Further w in High Holborn is *Moncton and Newman*'s Pearl Assurance (1912 onwards) in an overblown Baroque, and (jumping to the 1920s) round the corner in Southampton Row are the grandly scaled but sober Neo-Grec premises of the Liverpool Victoria Friendly Society by *C. W. Long*, also with well-appointed interiors in matching style. Neo-Grec appears a little earlier with *Beresford Pite*'s accomplished London Edinburgh and Glasgow Assurance, Euston 108 Square, of 1907. The main display of early C20 commercial build-ings in Holborn was along the newly laid out Kingsway, opened 1905, soon lined by a palatial series of grandiosely decorated stone-faced offices, many of them by *Trehearne & Norman*. Among them is *Burnet*'s offices for Kodak (1911), unusually plain, and so qualifying as one of Pevsner's 'pioneers' of modern design.

In the suburbs some way from central London, developers provided purpose-designed SHOPPING PARADES, with flats above individual shops. They follow the styles of contemporary houses, though tend to be more showy; Italianate up to *c.* 1870, then more eclectic, with brick or stone trimmings and gabled rooflines. The most imposing date from the 1890s onwards. Crouch End and Muswell Hill have 5 busily detailed parades, by the builder and developers *Edmondsons*, the former given a sense of urban importance by a clock tower of 1895. Golders Green has some interesting groups of *c.* 1908 onwards, the later ones by *Welch & Hollis* echoing the vernacular and Neo-Georgian styles of Hampstead Garden Suburb just up the road (where shops were excluded). The inventive Free Style of the Arts and Crafts movement generally made little impact on commercial centres, but an exception is the rather Voyseyish parade in Palmers Green, Southgate, 1909 onwards, by *Arthur Sykes*. Sykes also built a good bank here, but in a more sedate C17 style. In Bloomsbury, early C20 Bedford estate rebuilding produced two distinctive Edwardian creations: a spiky Art Nouveau range (now Dillons) between Gower Street and Malet Street by the estate surveyor *Fitzroy Doll*, and the agreeable pedestrian street, Sicilian Avenue, terracotta Renaissance by *R. J. Worley*. A particular type of 105 small shop given special attention in the late C19 was the dairy, often a corner building with large arched windows for good ventilation, and with tiled interiors which could be decorative as well as hygienic (good examples are in Amwell Street and Great Sutton Street, Finsbury, and Coptic Street, Holborn).

The suburban DEPARTMENT STORE, a late C19 development, has largely disappeared or been rebuilt, though Holloway Road still has the former 1890s premises of Jones Brothers and some other quite showy buildings of this date. The shopping pattern in inner London has also drastically altered. There is little trace now of Holborn and High Holborn's former role as a major shopping artery, with Gamages near its E end as its principal store. Rebuilding after the Second World War replaced many shops and restaurants by offices;

Gamages was demolished in 1974. Tottenham Court Road remains a shopping street, although with only a little from the boom years of the early C20 when large showrooms were built to display the products of the local furniture trade: from this time there remain the rather fussily detailed former premises of Catesbys, a leading linoleum store, and in contrast to this, *Smith & Brewer*'s rational and reticent design for Heal's of 1912–17. Specialist WAREHOUSES AND SHOW-ROOMS were also built in other industrial areas. Shoreditch still has a rich and inventive variety untroubled by polite C19 architectural conventions. Nos. 125–130 Shoreditch High Street, built *c.* 1878 for an ironworks, displays this material with some panache, and iron is also used extensively on exteriors around the W end of Old Street.

INDUSTRIAL BUILDINGS, when they occupied a prominent position, responded with a façade in the style of the day. Few now remain from the earlier C19; notable survivals are the (altered) classical frontage of a floorcloth factory in Essex Road, Islington (1812), and the long sober front to St John Street, Clerkenwell, of a distillery building of 1828. Later C19 buildings adopted the Venetian Gothic palazzo, with rows of arched windows and coloured brickwork, as an appropriate industrial show front; there are some excellent examples in Farringdon Road, which was built up from the 1860s and attracted firms connected with the printing industry, and others in Cowcross Street. Gothic could be adapted too for the tall ware-house, with loading doors contained within twin arches under a gable as at Nos. 18–20 St John Street, Finsbury (William Burges built a much illustrated prototype in Upper Thames Street in 1866). An eclectic Italianate could also be employed, as at Farmiloe's lead and glass works in St John Street (1868 by *Isaacs*). Such display is excep-tional in comparison with the more numerous small, plain brick factories and workshops, ranging from piano factories in Camden Town to speculatively built ranges of small workshops for furniture makers in Shoreditch (*see* further p. 102). A more self-conscious architectural approach is increasingly evident from the 1890s, illus-trated by the sophisticated treatment given to industrial premises on the Sturt estate, Hoxton, for which *Ernest Newton* was responsible, and the Shannon furniture factory in Dalston of 1903 by *Edwin O. Sachs*.

Further out, almost nothing is left of the C19 and early C20 industrial buildings which developed along the Lea Valley, with the one important exception of the Small Arms Factory, the vast, isolated government establishment at the remote site of Enfield Lock. It opened in 1816, but the great period of expansion took place from the 1850s. The showpiece was the large steam-powered factory of 1854–6, built on American mass-production principles, single-storeyed and roof lit, its façade decorated in up to date fashion with polychrome brickwork.

An attractive trend from the later C19 was the embellishment of industrial and commercial buildings with sculpture or other orna-ment as a form of advertisement: a prominent example is the clock 66 manufacturer's premises overlooking the railway cutting at Farringdon (1875 by *Rowland Plumbe*). Friern Manor Dairy Company at Crouch Hill, Islington, advertised itself by large sgraffito panels of *c.* 1890 showing milk production and delivery. Booth's Gin Distillery (1903 by *Mountford*) has an excellent series of reliefs of gin making by

Royal Small Arms Factory, Enfield, 1861

*F. W. Pomeroy*, on its frontage re-erected in Britton Street. Another example is Treasure House, Hatton Garden (*Niven & Wigglesworth*, 1907), with reliefs of the diamond trade.

### Public buildings from 1800

Amidst the ever expanding streets of houses, specialized buildings sprang up to assist the functioning of a great city. Those in the north London boroughs covered by this book are a diverse collection. Some in inner London have a national or metropolitan function, others were built to serve the residents of the growing suburbs; there are those whose location was dictated by the availability of cheap land on the urban fringe, and others yet further out which were deliberately sited in what was then countryside. Many are no longer used for their original purposes, but enough survive to convey the complexity of the rapidly expanding capital during this period. It was administered by a confusing range of authorities: the Metropolitan Police Authority (from 1829), the workhouse unions (from 1834), the Metropolitan Board of Works and the Boards of Health (from 1855), and the vestries and district authorities which were the predecessors of the borough councils created at the end of the century. To these must be added the School Boards set up after the Education Act of 1870, and a whole host of private organizations and companies which provided utilities and transport, and (to a

limited extent) education, health care, welfare and housing. From
1888 an increasing number of these responsibilities were taken over
by the London County Council (LCC) which superseded the
MBW, and in the outer areas, by the Middlesex County Council
(MCC), both creations of that year.

Most of London's national public buildings are concentrated
around Westminster, but it was Holborn which became the home
of the British Museum. Its site was determined in the C18, when a
parsimonious government decided to acquire the late C17 Montagu
House for the collections given by Sir Hans Sloane and others,
rather than build a new museum. The need to accommodate major
collections of sculpture from Greece, Egypt and elsewhere, acquired
at the beginning of the C19, led to rebuilding on the same site by
58 *Sir Robert Smirke* from 1823 to 1852. It gave the residential suburb of
61 Bloomsbury London's most monumental Grecian building, setting a
precedent for the burgeoning of learned institutions which, by the
later C20, had eroded much of the original character of this area.
The austere Greek detail of Smirke's great colonnaded frontage was
a universal European taste at the time of its conception, although
out of fashion by the time the museum was finally opened. The
1820s was the high point for Grecian Neoclassicism, adopted as an
appropriately serious dress for a variety of institutions. It was favoured
particularly by Nonconformists. Mill Hill School, established in 1807
as the first Nonconformist public school, was provided in 1825–7
with imposing but very plain buildings by *William Tite*, a long
frontage with Grecian colonnade dominating a high ridge of North
Middlesex. At the northern end of Bloomsbury, not yet built up,
the non-denominational University College was founded as the
University of London and begun in 1827; here *William Wilkins* more
60 eclectically combined a Grecian portico with a central dome (the
charter enabling the university to grant degrees, which it eventually
received in 1836 after a long battle, marked the wider acceptance of

The entrance to Euston Station, St Pancras in 1870,
from Euston Square

Nonconformity in public life). Other Grecian buildings of these years included the Highbury College for Dissenters, 1825–7 by *John Davies* (demolished), the London Orphan Asylum at Hackney, 1823–5 by *W. S. Inman* (from which only a portico remains) and *D. R. Roper*'s Haberdashers' Almshouses at Shoreditch, 1825–7, which was later adapted as a Technical College and still exists.

By the mid C19, as has already been observed with houses, the Grecian taste had given way to more ornate styles, either Italianate or Gothic. The latter was used for certain secular buildings, although never as extensively as for churches. A notable example in our area is the New Hall and Library at Lincoln's Inn, begun by *Philip Hardwick* and completed by his son *P. C. Hardwick*, 1842–5, in an effective and scholarly version of Tudor Gothic. This style remained popular with institutions which wished to emphasize their long traditions, as in the case of the much later Chapter House of the Order of St John at Clerkenwell, of 1901–4 by *J. Oldrid Scott*.

The new building types of the industrial age created different problems, and selecting an appropriate manner for these was one of the great Victorian dilemmas. Nowhere is this better illustrated than in the treatment of the three great railway termini on Euston Road. At the first, Euston (no longer extant), the London and Birmingham Railway's station was prefaced by a severe Greek Doric entrance, completed in 1838 by *Philip Hardwick*; a monumental great hall in a more Italianate spirit was added by *P. C. Hardwick* in 1846–9. King's Cross, of 1851–2 for the Great Northern Railway, by *Lewis Cubitt*, adopted a functional solution, the brick frontage with its two large arches clearly expressing the two train sheds behind, with a detached station hotel of 1854 in an uneventful Italianate. For the much larger St Pancras hotel of 1868–74, forming the approach to the Midland Railway's vast train shed, *G. G. Scott* adopted a full-blown Gothic of the most elaborate and picturesque type, one of the most eloquent expressions anywhere of Victorian romanticism on a grand scale. 64
p.
363

King's Cross Station,
St Pancras, 1851

Land-hungry PUBLIC INSTITUTIONS seized upon the open areas on the fringes of town, their lowering presence often casting a blight on the suburbs which soon surrounded them. Pentonville Prison was laid out in 1840–2 by Col. *Joshua Jebb* as the second national
p. prison, its radial plan designed to achieve both constant supervision
671 and total isolation of prisoners. Within Clerkenwell was another radially planned prison, the Clerkenwell House of Detention by *William Moseley*, 1845–7 (the basement that remains is accessible to visitors). Holloway Prison, built as the City House of Correction on open land to the N of Pentonville, by the City architect *J. B. Bunning*, followed in 1849–51. While Pentonville is a utilitarian complex hidden behind high walls, Holloway (now entirely rebuilt) originally expressed its function to the outside world by a forbidding mock-medieval castle entrance. Bunning was responsible too for the Caledonian Market, a well-organized model cattle market laid out in 1850–5, also on the edge of expanding Islington, more easily accessible for drovers than the City's congested cattle market in Smithfield which it replaced. Its clock tower and some ancillary buildings remain. Another category of institution which catered for more than a local clientele was the EXHIBITION BUILDING. North London has two surviving examples which made use of great iron and glass roofs (in both cases considerably reconstructed), though, unlike the pioneering Crystal Palace, they have solid walls: the former Royal Agricultural Hall in the centre of Islington, 1861 by *Frederick Peck*, now Business Design Centre, and Alexandra Palace,
p. dominantly but impractically sited on the hill above Wood Green,
581 the Crystal Palace's equivalent for the northern suburbs, built 1865–73 by *John Johnson*.

The alarm over the epidemics which swept through the over-crowded and unhealthy slums in the 1840s–50s led not only to the reconstruction of London's sewage system, but to the building of new HOSPITALS away from the centre of London. The extensive sites of many of those in the suburbs had their origin either as isolation hospitals (St Ann's Tottenham, part of the site of the present Royal Free Hospital, Hampstead) or as workhouse infirmaries. An interesting example is the Whittington Hospital on Highgate Hill (Islington), which combines the two types: buildings survive from a Smallpox Hospital of 1848–50 by *S. W. Daukes*, and from three different workhouse infirmaries built from 1868 to 1900 by inner London Workhouse Unions who wanted to move their sick from insalubrious city surroundings. Of these, the infirmary built in 1868 by the St Pancras Union was one of the first to be built separately from its workhouse (whose dour later buildings survive as St Pancras Hospital near King's Cross). The central administration block of such complexes was often a dignified classical composition. Daukes's building at the Whittington is of this type, as is the centrepiece of the old London Fever Hospital of 1848–52 by *Fowler & Moccatta* in Liverpool Road, Islington, likewise the centre of the former Hampstead Workhouse at New End, 1849 by *H. E. Kendall* (both now converted to housing). A late example is Colindale Hospital, Hendon, originally the infirmary for Central London District, 1898–1900 by *Giles, Gough & Trollope*. The largest complex of all is
73 that of the former Friern Hospital, built in open countryside in 1849–51 by *Daukes*, as Colney Hatch Asylum, the second Middlesex

pauper lunatic asylum, a vast self-sufficient establishment in its own grounds, its overwhelmingly long front relieved by an Italianate centrepiece with tall dome.

As these large institutions continued to expand during the later C19, often to the detriment of their once orderly layouts, the alternative of the COTTAGE HOSPITAL provided non-specialist care and treatment on a smaller and friendlier scale. Their buildings were deliberately domestic with Arts and Crafts touches, as at Hornsey (1907–10 by *G. Lethbridge*) and Finchley (1908 by *I'Anson & Son*). The SPECIALIST HOSPITAL tended to remain in London. Holborn has several in and around Queen Square, where a number started in the C19 in private houses, and were rebuilt and expanded later. The National Hospital, 1883–5 by *Manning & Simpson*, and the Italian Hospital 1898–9 by *T. W. Cutler*, both have handsome frontages, which are, as one would expect, considerably more elaborate than the workhouse infirmaries. Most remarkable is the little Neo-Byzantine chapel of 1876, by *Edward Barry*, hidden within the much rebuilt 90 Great Ormond Street Hospital for Sick Children. Nearer the City is Moorfields Eye Hospital with buildings of 1897–9 onwards by *Young & Bedell*. Another medical area developed around University College, which had a teaching hospital attached to it from 1833. This was rebuilt from 1896 to an ingenious cruciform plan by *Alfred Waterhouse*, faced in his favourite hard red brick and terra- 74 cotta, and designed to provide maximum light and air for its wards projecting from a central core of services and operating theatres.

The London countryside attracted a variety of other institutions. There was a long tradition of sending children to be brought up out of London. The buildings of the severe C19 orphanages have mostly disappeared. The London Orphan Asylum in Hackney has already been mentioned, another was the Caledonian Asylum for Scottish children, built in 1827, on the newly laid out Caledonian Road. The most formidable survival is the High Victorian pile at Wood Green (converted to Crown Courts) built as the Royal Masonic Institute (1865 by *Pearce* and *Wilson & Son*). Its use of elaborate Gothic detail for a grandly scaled composition echoes the Royal Patriotic Asylum at Wandsworth of 1857–9. On a more humane scale was the progressive industrial school at East Barnet, for poor boys from St Pancras, established in 1860 by Colonel Gillum, who lived nearby and employed *Philip Webb* and others for its low-key buildings. The Barnet area also acquired a remarkable number of convents, sometimes with schools attached. Along the ridge of Mill Hill there is a whole string of R.C. religious establishments of the later C19; St Joseph's College (begun 1869) and St Mary's Abbey (1888–9), each with domestic buildings and chapel by *Goldie & Child*; and St Vincent's, with chapel of 1886–7 by *F. W. Tasker*. This last is in an airy Perp style, in contrast to the serious early Gothic of the other two institutions. An ambitious scheme was begun at Edgware for the Convent of St Mary at the Cross, a country offshoot of a convent in Shoreditch; *James Brooks* planned a large abbey church in 1873, but only one chapel was completed. At Hendon there is St Joseph's Convent, which moved from Whitechapel in 1882.

SCHOOLS were among the most distinctive Victorian contributions to the buildings required for the expanding population of the suburbs.

At the beginning of the C19 schools generally consisted of little more than a large schoolroom, with teacher's accommodation and perhaps an additional classroom. Among large boarding schools Mill Hill was exceptional in providing as many as four classrooms in addition to its main hall. The early C19 Church of England schools providing elementary education in their parishes were modest adjuncts to their parish churches, and adopted styles of the time: the Clerkenwell parochial schools in Amwell Street of 1828–30 are simple battlemented Tudor; Tottenham Green school of 1848 resembles a *cottage orné*; the former St James schools in Lower Holloway, of 1854, crammed onto a small site, are in a gaunt Italianate. By the mid C19 a more serious Gothic was the generally accepted style for church schools, usually built under the aegis of the National Schools organization, and designed by church architects. Good examples of this once common type are the former East Finchley school, 1847–8, and St Michael's Highgate, 1852, both by *Salvin*; Christ Church Hampstead by the *Habershons* (1854–5), and, especially lavish in its detail, Colvestone, Hackney, by *T. E. Knightley*, 1862. The usual type of modest church school, with single schoolroom and teacher's house, was hardly adequate for the crowded city slums. A novel solution was adopted in 1860 by *E. M. Barry*'s St Giles Schools Holborn, a tall polychrome Gothic building planned for 1,500 pupils and incorporating a soup kitchen in the basement. Not far off in Old Gloucester Street *S. S. Teulon* provided another tall Gothic school for St George's Queen Square in 1863–4.

The move in the 1860s to improve secondary education led to the refoundation of many older schools and extensive building activity. Highgate School, an old grammar school, was provided with new buildings in 1865 by *F. P. Cockerell*; the ambitious Gothic group of chapel and hall still dominate the centre of Highgate. Another Gothic survival of the 1860s is the odd, incomplete former Christ's College Finchley (1861, by *E. Roberts*). The Merchant Taylors' school moved into part of the Charterhouse site in 1872, but all that survive from their occupation are a fanciful Gothic Lodge by *I'Anson* and the former headmaster's house. Other City Livery Companies used their charitable funds to establish schools in the new suburbs. Near Tottenham Green a large, spikily Gothic building of 1860–2 survives from a group originally also including almshouses, built for the Drapers' Company by their surveyor *Herbert Williams*. Schools were built by the Grocers in Hackney, and the Stationers in Hornsey, but of these only a lodge from the former remains. Survivors are the former Haberdashers' school in Hampstead, and the Skinners' Company school at Stamford Hill, Hackney, of 1889 by *E.H. Burnell*; by this date the Queen Anne style of the Board schools had become the model (*see* below). More unusual is the City-type Italianate of *E. N. Clifton*'s former City and Guilds College, Finsbury, 1881–3 (now Shoreditch County Court). Among the private schools the outstanding buildings of the 1890s onwards are at Mill Hill: a chapel by *Basil Champneys* and library and other buildings by *T. E. Collcutt*, all in a spirited Free Classical manner. In similar vein, but rather more restrained, are the buildings for the former Westfield College, one of the first women's colleges, at Kidderpore Avenue, Hampstead, 1889 onwards by *R. Falconer Macdonald* (a pupil of J.J. Stevenson and Ernest George). Early C20 Baroque is best represented by

University College Boys' School, Hampstead, 1905–7 by *Arnold Mitchell*, which has a fine assembly hall.

After the 1870 Education Act local School Boards were set up to provide non-denominational elementary education. The School Board for London (covering the area of the future LCC) led the way, appointing *E. R. Robson* as its architect in 1871, under whom 289 schools were built by 1884. The outer areas were more variable in their achievements. Tottenham was prompt, with a Board set up in 1871, kept busy coping with the demand created by a rapidly expanding working-class population; the more rural Hendon, where strong opposition came from the Church, held back until 1897. The London School Board rapidly became celebrated for its new type of school: in place of austere classical or poky Church Gothic, the tall, brick schools, rising high on tight sites, contained airy rooms with large windows. They made use of the latest fashion among progressive architects led by J.J. Stevenson and Norman Shaw, an adaptable domestic Queen Anne style with a little terracotta embellishment. A good early example is the former school in Bowling Green Lane Clerkenwell (1873–5), but Robson's early schools have mostly been added to, for at first the inclusion of a hall and a large number of classrooms was regarded as too extravagant. Under his successor *T. J. Bailey*, who took over in 1884, a standard type evolved: the compact, symmetrical 'three decker', ingeniously planned with superimposed halls for the three separate departments of Infants, Boys and Girls. Classrooms were ranged along one side of the hall and in flanking wings. The separate departments each had their own entrance, staircase and cloakrooms. Small additional buildings, often attractively detailed, housed a caretaker and the manual instruction and housecraft centres, subjects forming part of the curriculum from the 1890s. The picturesquely grouped decorative gables, staircase turrets, and high hipped roofs with bell-turrets of these schools still tower high over many parts of London. The 1890s was the apogee of the type; impressive examples, among many, are Hungerford and Montem, both in Islington, and Gainsborough at Hackney Wick. From the same period are the robust buildings of the School Board's central stores at Clerkenwell, demonstrating the scale of the London schools enterprise. The most active School Boards further out were in those areas already densely built up by the 1890s: in this book Tottenham, Edmonton and Hornsey. Here private architects who specialized in schools were employed, and, though influenced by the LSB, put their own stamp on their buildings. Among the most prolific and accomplished was *G. E. T. Laurence*, active in both Tottenham and Edmonton (e.g. Bush Hill Park, Edmonton, 1896, Woodlands Park, Tottenham, and Alexandra, Wood Green, both 1897). Hornsey's most original architects were *Mitchell & Butler*, responsible for Stroud Green, 1894–7, an Arts and Crafts version of the LSB three-decker. Further out, where space was less constricted and the population less dense, lower buildings were possible, such as the modest rural Board School at Edgware, of 1895. 71

The local authorities which took over from the School Boards in 1901 continued the tradition of increasingly flamboyant buildings, often by the same architects that the Boards had employed. Among the LCC's buildings especially memorable are the proudly Wrenaissance Cassland Road School Hackney (1901–2), and New

End, a boldly Baroque, almost Hawksmoorean group squeezed onto a cramped site in a poor quarter of Hampstead (1905–6). The additional teaching facilities required for Higher Grade Schools (i.e. schools including classes for pupils over fourteen) could produce some impressive groups, as in the case of *Mitchell & Butler*'s Free Baroque complex at Mattison Road, Hornsey (1902–5). The innovation of the early C20 was the building of new secondary County Schools. Here Middlesex made an impressive show under its architect *H. G. Crothall*. His buildings are handsome compositions, variants on the traditional front range with the centrepiece of hall flanked by entrances and stair-turrets, dignified by classical detail and a greater use of stone. Notable examples are the former Southgate County School, Enfield County School for Girls, and
72 Wood Green County School, all built 1909–12. Less formal is the *LCC*'s Clapton School for Girls (1914–16), in a quieter but original version of Free Classical.

Among colleges of this time is the Central School of Arts and Crafts, Holborn (now London Institute), of 1905–8, a grandly urban building in an eccentric quasi-classical style, apparently reflecting the influence of *W. R. Lethaby*, the School's principal.

The School Boards were only one of a number of PUBLIC BODIES which during the period *c.* 1870–1914 stamped the London suburbs with a recognizable, repetitive building type that contributed to the collective identity of the capital and its satellite suburbs. Another was the POLICE. The Metropolitan Police Authority had been set up by an Act of 1829, covering an area extending over a four- to seven-mile radius of Charing Cross. Its stations built by the first surveyor, *Charles Reeves*, appointed 1842, were small and unostentatious, of brick with stone quoins. A more ambitious example (which survives as a Traffic Wardens' Centre), in firm and stately Italianate, is the former divisional headquarters in King's Cross Road (Finsbury), by *T. C. Sorby*, of 1869–70. An alternative, more domestic manner was adopted for *Norman Shaw*'s station at Kentish Town (1894), establishing a precedent for the most characteristic type which can be recognized all over London. These date from the surveyorship of *John Dixon Butler* (1895–1920), when an extensive building programme provided London with stations in a severe yet quite domestic style, red brick with spare classical trimmings, distinguished by Butler's trademark of elongated stone consoles to doors or windows. Hampstead and Highbury Vale are good examples among many. Butler was also responsible for several larger court houses where his originality in the bold use of Free Classical elements could be given more play. Notable examples (both 1906) are in Old Street, Shoreditch, and the Clerkenwell Courts in King's Cross Road.

The POST OFFICE also had a recognizable house style in these Edwardian years; the small, cheerfully Baroque frontages of the sorting offices built by the *Office of Works* still make their mark in suburban streets (e.g. Leighton Road, Kentish Town; Church Street, Edmonton; Station Road, Winchmore Hill); the Northern District Post Office in Upper Street Islington of 1906 is Baroque on a grander scale.

The FIRE BRIGADE BRANCH of the LCC was another London-wide organization. It had to provide accommodation for both

engines and firemen; solutions were lively and original. The example
at Tabernacle Street, Shoreditch (1895–6), resembles a French
château, but from 1900, led by *Owen Fleming* and *Charles Canning
Winmill*, the Branch drew freely on English vernacular sources,
creating romantic compositions of gables and chimneys above a
mixture of brick, stone or rendered walls. The prime north London
examples are in Camden: Euston Road, St Pancras (1901–2); West
End Lane (1901) and Lancaster Grove (1914–15), both in Hampstead.
UNDERGROUND STATIONS also developed a distinctive house style
during this period, the most familiar being the ox-blood-tiled
stations of *c.* 1906 by *Leslie W. Green* for the Northern and Piccadilly
lines.

As London-wide organizations made their mark on the capital,
the individual local authorities also developed ambitions to make
architectural statements. The Vestries, given new powers by the
Metropolitan Management Act of 1855, built vestry halls with council
chambers and offices, generally dignified Italianate efforts on a compact plan. Shoreditch Vestry Hall, built for the booming industrial
suburb in 1863–8 by *Caesar A. Long*, is an outstandingly lavish early
example, which included a large public hall on the first floor. The
Hampstead Vestry Hall, of 1877–8 by *Kendall & Mew*, also survives,
as does the Clerkenwell Vestry Hall, by *C. Evans Vaughan*, 1895: the
last no longer Italianate but in the livelier northern Renaissance style
popular at this date. Most authorities replaced their early buildings
after they became boroughs at the turn of the century. A weighty
Baroque style, often reinforced with sculpture, and with a stately
grand stair leading to the main rooms, was used to impress in the
early C20 (as used influentially by John Belcher at Colchester,
designed in 1898). North London representatives from this period
of burgeoning civic consciousness are Hendon Town Hall, 1900 by
*T. H. Watson* (with rather old-fashioned Free Renaissance detail);
Tottenham, by *Tayler & Jemmett*, 1905; and Holborn by *Hall
& Warwick*, 1906–8. At Shoreditch the older Vestry Hall was
incorporated as part of an enlarged complex by *W. G. Hunt* (1898–
1902). Considerable effort was also put into the other public buildings
for which the local authority was responsible. Here also Shoreditch
is again of especial interest, building an innovative combination in
1895–7: a refuse destructor which powered a generating station,
with steam to provide power, and waste heat used for the adjoining
swimming baths. The machinery and the baths have gone, but
turbine and generating halls survive, also the neighbouring Library
by *H. T. Hare*, a Free Classical composition of 1895–7 in the Scotland
Yard manner of Norman Shaw.

PUBLIC BATHS and LIBRARIES were buildings for which local
authorities were empowered to raise local rates, but it took some
time before this was generally practised. The period *c.* 1890–1914
was the great time for library building, assisted through the funds
provided by Passmore Edwards and Andrew Carnegie. Central
libraries were supplemented by numerous branch libraries from the
1900s. In the 1890s playful Free Renaissance, Tudor or Jacobean
details were used to entice the user: Holborn 1894; Tottenham 1896
(by *Edmeston & Gabriel*) and Edmonton 1897 (by *Maurice B. Adams*)
are good examples (all now in other uses). As with town halls, in the
early years of the C20 classical and Baroque styles dominated. Both

Islington and Hackney employed architects of repute for their buildings, with worthwhile results; in Islington there are two libraries
(1905–7) by *Hare* and one by *Mervyn Macartney* (1916), and a
102 particularly original one by *Beresford Pite* (1905–7); in Hackney *Edwin
Cooper* built three in 1912–14, of which two remain. The first branch
library of St Pancras was built at Highgate in 1906, Renaissance
style by *W. Nisbet-Blair*; Hornsey has two of 1901, unusually in a
domestic style to match neighbouring houses, while Enfield has two
mildly Baroque examples of 1909–12. While all these buildings
remain (though many do not have a secure future), C19 BATHS have
survived less well. They had a dual function, to provide swimming
pools for recreation but also baths and washhouses for those without
such facilities. The latter need diminished with rebuilding and
housing improvements after the Second World War. Some remain
with swimming pools, for example the magnificent example at
Haggerston built for the Borough of Shoreditch by the Baths expert
*A. W. S. Cross* (1903–4), and the Hornsey Road Baths in Islington
(1892–5) by another Baths specialist, *A. H. Tiltman*, while at Kentish
101 Town (St Pancras) there remains an especially festive Baths frontage
by *T. W. Aldwinckle*, 1898.

The new public libraries provided an alternative to the more
exclusive subscription-based organizations, such as Literary and
Scientific Institutions. Most of these have disappeared, although the
one at Highgate, established 1840, still flourishes in buildings of a
mixture of dates. More distinctive architecturally is the example in
Almeida Street, Islington, now a theatre, with severe front by
*Roumieu & Gough* of 1837–8, near the same architects' Milner
Square. A later C19 curiosity was a different kind of club, the drill
hall built for Volunteers. Two examples remain in Bloomsbury, for
the Bloomsbury Rifles (1882–3 by *Samuel Knight*) and the Artists'
Rifles (1888–9 by Colonel *R. W. Edis*); both have frontages with
appropriate ornament, and functional interiors now adapted for
other purposes (arts centre and dance theatre respectively).

Another type of institution which developed in the later C19 was
the socially purposeful 'settlement', usually staffed by university
graduates, designed to provide a centre of culture for the poor. Most
were concentrated in the East End, but the most architecturally enterprising of such buildings is to be found on the edge of Bloomsbury,
97 Mary Ward House in Tavistock Place, founded as the University
Hall Settlement and built 1895–7 by *Smith & Brewer*. It is a delightful
and highly original building, closely designed for its purpose in a
friendly Free Classical style, with touches of Lethaby-influenced
symbolism. Among other establishments providing adult education,
the Northampton Institute, built on the Northampton estate in
70 Clerkenwell, 1893–8 by *E. W. Mountford*, is an accomplished example
of the more usual style of the 1890s, a free French Renaissance.
*W. D. Caröe*'s Working Men's College, in Camden Town, of 1904–6,
is in a more restrained Board School manner. The movement to
provide buildings for community use also took the form of adapting
(and thereby saving) some important survivals from earlier periods:
Sutton House, Hackney, was preserved as St John's Institute; the
Geffrye Almshouses in Shoreditch were converted to a furniture and
craft museum by the LCC; Canonbury Tower became a community
centre.

THEATRES had for long provided an alternative, frequently more frivolous way of occupying leisure time. They had flourished on the northern fringe of the City and on the South Bank in the C16, but when theatres were revived again after the Commonwealth the theatrical focus shifted to Covent Garden and Westminster. From the C18 to early C19 more rustic attractions were the country inns, pleasure gardens and spas on the rural fringes, of which there were many on the healthier high ground to the N of London, at Kilburn, Hampstead, Kentish Town, Highbury Barn, Hornsey Wood, and elsewhere. The present Sadlers Wells theatre can trace its origins back to a theatre of 1765 which replaced an older music hall. This is an exception; other rural entertainments disappeared as the suburbs encroached. Alternatives were the numerous urban public houses, which were often provided with their own performance areas. Hoxton Hall, Shoreditch, is a rare survival of a purpose-built small music hall of 1863, with iron gallerys on three sides. Toward the end of the C19, larger purpose-built theatres were provided in many suburban centres, as lavish in their decoration as any in the West End. Most have gone. The splendid Hackney Empire of 1901 by *Frank Matcham*, with its ornate terracotta exterior and sumptuous 77 galleried auditorium, is the best example in use. Others now adapted for different purposes are the Royal Camden Theatre, Camden Town (1900–1 by *Sprague*), the Tottenham Palace, Tottenham High Road (1908 by *Wylson & Long*), and the Golders Green Hippodrome (1913 by *Crewe*).

C19 PUBLIC HOUSES appear frequently, punctuating terraces of housing, thickly scattered in industrial areas such as Shoreditch and Clerkenwell, and along the main roads, where they often replaced older buildings with a venerable history (as in the case of the Angel Islington, rebuilt 1899, which gave its name to the area at the southern end of the Islington High Street). Early C19 pubs are little different from neighbouring houses. In the mid C19 they stand out by the use of more florid debased Italianate ornament, but are not substantially larger in scale. The firm of *Finch Hill & Paraire* put up such buildings: the Museum Tavern in Great Russell Street *c.* 1855; the Hat & Feathers, Clerkenwell Road, 1860, and the still more elaborate and larger Horseshoe Hotel, Tottenham Court Road, 1875. But it was in the late 1890s that the great pub rebuilding took place, led by the major breweries. These grander buildings, which often functioned also as hotels, were prominent additions to the suburban centres. Their eclectic exteriors sported turrets and gables, and their bar space, divided into socially distinct sections by elaborate joinery, was enhanced by engraved glass and tiles. Among the specialist firms active in this field were *Shoebridge & Rising* (Great Northern, Hornsey, The Crown, Cricklewood) and *Thorpe & Furniss* (the Assembly House, Kentish Town, Boston Arms, Tufnell Park) to name only a few of the best examples of 1897–1900. The developer *J. C. Hill* was responsible for the Salisbury, Green Lanes, Wood Green, and the Queen's Hotel Crouch End, both distinguished by a 76 lively use of *Cakebread Robey*'s coloured glass. The Fox and Anchor at Smithfield and the Adam and Eve at Homerton should be visited for their flamboyant tiled frontages. The grander type of HOTEL of the same period is illustrated by *Fitzroy Doll*'s monumental terracotta-clad French château in Russell Square, Holborn (1898).          75

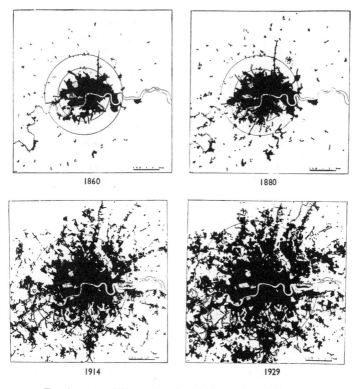

Development of Greater London's built-up area, 1860–1929

By the end of the century industry, housing, railways and services in the inner suburbs were closely packed together, and the built-up area already extended beyond the LCC's boundaries. As London expanded into a countryside already disfigured by brickfields and miscellaneous industrial activity, pressure grew for the retention of some OPEN SPACES. The Metropolitan Commons Act of 1866, achieved through the Commons Preservation Society, secured the public use of existing common land. Hampstead Heath was saved from building in 1871 after a long battle with the lord of the manor, Sir Thomas Maryon Wilson, and extended later by Parliament Hill Fields and other additions. Highgate Wood was acquired by the Corporation of London in 1885; Queen's Wood by Hornsey in 1898. But for areas already built up a different approach was needed. The first of the PARKS to be made N of the Thames was a creation of the government. Victoria Park was opened in 1845, on the boundary of Hackney and Bethnal Green, picturesquely laid out, by *James Pennethorne*, with lakes, a gravelled drive and varied planting. The suburbs overtook a planned Albert Park in Highbury; instead the smaller Finsbury Park further N was laid out by *Alexander McKenzie* for the Metropolitan Board of Works on the site of Hornsey Wood and opened in 1869. *McKenzie* was also responsible for the design of Alexandra Park, completed in 1863 to complement the Palace still under construction on the farmland of Wood Green. Islington remained without official open spaces until Highbury Fields was acquired by the MBW in 1885. A notable development of the later C19 was the acquisition of private grounds for public benefit.The philanthropist Sir Sydney Waterlow showed the way in 1889 by the gift to the newly formed LCC of his grounds in Highgate, now Waterlow Park. Clissold Park, Stoke Newington, with its house, was acquired by the LCC in the same year. Bruce Castle, Tottenham, became a public park in 1892, Pymmes Park, Edmonton, and Golders Hill Park, Golders Green, in 1898.

The CEMETERY was another type of open space achieved by the C19 reformers. The scandal of the overcrowded inner city church-yards led to the creation first of Kensal Green cemetery in 1833, then of others, the early ones run by private companies. In north London, Highgate, opened 1839, is an outstandingly atmospheric example, with its romantic paths winding past countless memorials to culminate in a solemn 'Egyptian Avenue' with catacombs. The 53 well-landscaped Abney Park Cemetery in Stoke Newington also 52 uses the Egyptian style for its entrance. The municipal cemeteries of the later C19 generally adopted the formula of paired chapels at the entrance for Anglicans and Dissenters, as at Highgate, but their landscaping is of a lesser order, although many have some good individual monuments, particular the two at Finchley which were laid out for St Pancras and Islington and for St Marylebone. The most impressive group of buildings is to be found at the crematorium at Golders Green, a fine Neo-Byzantine sequence of 1902 onwards, by *George & Yeates*.

## C19 *churches*

The lack of churches in the expanding suburbs became a matter of public concern after the end of the Napoleonic wars. To establish a completely new parish church an individual Act of Parliament was required, a complicated business rarely achieved. One London example was Islington's first new parish church, St Mary Magdalene Lower Holloway, a rather stodgy classical box of 1812–14 by the Middlesex County Surveyor *William Wickings* (his only known building). The needs of middle-class communities continued to be met erratically by private Anglican chapels, some of which later developed into full parish churches: St Thomas Upper Clapton began this way *c.* 1774 (much rebuilt since). St John, Downshire Hill, Hampstead, was also founded as a proprietary chapel, and still preserves its original character, a charmingly modest stuccoed build-ing of 1818–23 among the contemporary villas of the area.

Much more challenging architecturally was the new church for the 50 parish of St Pancras, built in 1819–22 on a site S of Euston Road convenient for the expanding suburb of Bloomsbury, the medieval building remaining in its burial ground further N. The architects, winners of a competition, were *William Inwood* (son of the bailiff of Lord Mansfield of Kenwood) and his son *H. W. Inwood*. The latter travelled to Greece to study appropriate classical sources, specifically the Erechtheum on which he published a monograph; the result was the scholarly application of Grecian detail to the well-tried C18 formula of pedimented portico with tower behind, with the quaint innovation of a pair of porches inspired by the Erechtheum, which formed grand entrances to the burial vaults below. The *Inwoods* built two less ostentatious Grecian chapels in St Pancras, the elegant All Saints, Camden Town, and St Peter Regent Square (demolished), but generally the Grecian style had only a short popularity with Anglicans. The impressive if stolid St John the Baptist, Hoxton, by *Francis Edwards* 1824–6, is the other contemporary north London example, a later one is *Pennethorne*'s heavy, eclectic, Christ Church Albany Street (1836), a late addition to the E fringes of Nash's Regents Park.*

The Hoxton church was built as a result of the 1818 Church Building Act, as was St Peter Regent Square. This provided public funding for part of the building costs of a new church, and thus encouraged a rapid church-building programme, felt to be desirable by a government which was concerned both with the dangers of popular unrest in the years following the Napoleonic wars and with the Nonconformist threat to the established church. A second Act of 1824 speeded the process and in the Diocese of London thirty-eight churches were completed before 1830, mostly within the new suburban areas. The emphasis was on speed and economy; the most common type was not classical, which required expensive stonework, but a brick box with galleried interiors to seat the maximum number of people, and pared down Gothic detail; the grander examples had a slim w tower. This type of 'Commissioners' Gothic' was the prevalent style from the 1820s to the early 1840s. Few examples now are in their original form, because it became standard practice in the later C19 to 'beautify' such buildings by removing the galleries, inserting tracery in the plain lancet windows, and adding a chancel in place of the shallow sanctuary. Even so, the earnest, austere evangelical mood of these early C19 buildings is often still apparent. An early example of the type is St Mary Somers Town of 1822 by the *Inwoods*. No less than three rather solider versions were built by
82 *Charles Barry* in 1826–8 for the new Islington suburbs. In the smarter villages outside London some handsome examples were provided: at Tottenham Green *James Savage*'s Holy Trinity (1828–30); at Highgate *Vulliamy*'s St Michael (1831–2). Lesser architects followed suit: *William Lochner* at De Beauvoir Town, Hackney (his home ground), and in the distant working-class hamlet of Enfield Highway. *Thomas Ashwell*, a Tottenham carpenter, built Jesus Church at Forty Hill, Enfield, at the expense of the lord of the manor, modelled on Holy Trinity, Tottenham. Other remote rural areas deficient in convenient churches also adopted the type: Mill Hill (through the patronage of William Wilberforce), Winchmore Hill, Whetstone and Arkley all received churches by 1840.

Few non-Anglican churches of this period remain in our area; Nonconformist buildings were almost invariably rebuilt more ambitiously later in the century. A plain brick front with pediment was the generally accepted form, as can be seen at the simple Friends Meeting House at Winchmore Hill of 1790; the former Claremont Chapel (now Crafts Council), Finsbury, 1818–19 by *W. Wallen*, and the former Maberley Chapel, Hackney, 1825–6.

From 1836 a new spur to Anglican church building was provided by the Metropolis Church Fund set up by Bishop Blomfield. Fifty

---

* Single dates given here are starting dates only. For more details *see* the gazetteer.

churches were planned in the diocese in eight years, and the fund finally assisted a total of seventy-eight.* Their character rapidly evolved in a very different direction from that of the Commissioners' churches, for the 1840s saw a radical change of approach to Anglican church building. From this time the Ecclesiological movement sought to introduce more elaborate liturgy, with emphasis on the chancel rather than the pulpit, in parallel with the campaigns of A.W.N. Pugin, who idealized the architecture and society of the Middle Ages in contrast to that of early C19 industrial Britain. Pugin's *Contrasts* of 1836 (second edition 1841) castigated the cheap detail of St Mary Somers Town, contrasting it with true medieval Gothic. The growing antiquarian understanding of medieval architecture which developed from the early C19 provided sources on which the new ecclesiologically minded church architects could draw. The change of approach becomes apparent by the mid 1840s: stone exteriors instead of brick, a deep, externally visible chancel; traceried windows with stained glass; and more solid and emphatic towers and spires. Modest early examples of this trend are St Barnabas, Homerton, by *Arthur Ashpitel*, 1843–52, with a tower of late medieval Middlesex type. Others are Christ Church High Barnet, stone and flint-faced, an early work by *G. G. Scott*, 1845, and Holy Trinity East Finchley by *Anthony Salvin*, 1845–6, both small, and built for still semi-rural settings. In the inner suburbs much larger buildings were needed: an early example was *E. C. Hakewill*'s grandly scaled St John of Jerusalem in South Hackney (1845–8), a somewhat clumsy rendering of early Gothic forms, with an ambitious crossing tower and spire.

In the 1850s the new churches made an increasing impact on London's skyline. The majority were Gothic buildings of ragstone, designed to act as a dignified focus for their middle-class suburbs, a romantic re-creation of the medieval stone-built village church in an age of faith. Inspired by the Puginian ideal, they were generally intended to have towers and spires. Not all spires were built and some have gone, but enough remain to make a substantial contribution to the suburban townscape. Enthusiasm and funds for building spires waned after the 1850s, although there are some fine later examples: from the 1860s *Scott*'s Christ Church, Southgate, and *Bury*'s St Ann, South Tottenham, and later still: *Scott*'s St Mary, Stoke Newington (completed in 1890), and *J. S. Alder*'s St James, Muswell Hill, a prominent site on its hill top. In the 1860s *Champneys*'s St Luke (Kentish Town) broke the pattern with its forceful gabled tower of brick.

For those concerned with church building along the lines advocated by the Ecclesiologists, one of the first significant achievements of the later 1840s in north London was St Mary Magdalene, built in a 83 poor area just N of Euston Road by *R. C. Carpenter*, a serious exercise in 'second pointed' Gothic, the early C14 style which the Ecclesiologists favoured above all others. Its lavish interior, with richly decorated chancel and plenty of furnishings and stained glass, was due largely to the generosity of its vicar, the Rev. Edward Stuart. Even though its intended tower and spire were never completed, this church set standards for those who wished to build in the medieval Gothic style. Meanwhile, contemporary work by *William Butterfield* pointed in a different direction. His St Matthias Stoke

* These figures are from B. F. L. Clarke's *Parish churches of London*, 1966.

Newington, of 1849–53, paid for by a local resident, Robert Brett, was built at the same time as his more famous All Saints Margaret Street, St Marylebone. Both are of brick, designed for an urban setting. The saddleback tower at St Matthias which soars above the chancel is inspired by northern European rather than English medieval precedent. *Butterfield*'s St Alban Brooke Street, built in 1856–62 in the slums of Holborn, was in the same spirit; but, apart from its powerful w tower and clergy house, was largely rebuilt after the Second World War. It was notable both for its forceful poly-chromatic brick decoration and for its rich fittings. A miniature echo of these new ideas can be seen in the little brick mission church of St John the Baptist, at Clay Hill, Enfield, of 1857, by *J. P. St Aubyn*. *Butterfield*'s own later work in the outer suburbs included additions to All Hallows Tottenham and St John High Barnet, the latter a bold and successful reworking of the medieval church, and the quieter St Mary Magdalene, Enfield. Another innovative architect was *William White*, responsible for St Saviour Aberdeen Park (1865–6), an isolated example of High Church fervour in evangelical Islington, and remarkable not only for its use of constructional polychromy, but for its interior covered later with insistent all-over stencilling.

The 1860s onwards saw a developing interest in a tough, robust Gothic, inspired by the boldly massed forms of Early Gothic on the continent rather than the prettier (and more expensive) carved details of home-grown Dec. Curved apses and high roofs to long, aisled naves are characteristic: *Christian*'s Holy Trinity New Barnet (1865), *Champneys*'s St Luke, Kentish Town (1867–9), and *Manning*'s St Mary Hampstead (1870–2) are variants on this type all worth a look. The most ambitious examples are the churches by *James Brooks*, built to make an impact in the poorest areas of Shoreditch. The impetus came from the Haggerston Church Scheme begun by the vicar of Shoreditch, and supported by, among others, Robert Brett of Stoke Newington. The first of Brooks's churches was the rather atypical St Michael, which makes use of coloured brick in the Butterfield manner. The two still in use are St Chad and the former 86 St Columba, both begun in 1867, partly vaulted inside, and with impressively lofty basilican naves. Brooks also built St Chad's vicarage, and a fine group of clergy buildings at St Columba. The tradition of the long brick basilica on a tight urban site was con-tinued in the 1880s by the prolific *Cutts*' firm; their big, rather dull, towerless buildings are easily recognizable. When enough money was available, they can be impressive inside; as in the case of St Mary the Virgin, Tottenham, funded by Marlborough College.

Not all churches followed the precepts of the Ecclesiologists, and it is interesting to look at some alternative trends, particularly appar-ent in evangelical Islington. Christ Church, Highbury, of 1847–8 by *Thomas Allom* (better known for his classical work for the Ladbroke estate in Kensington), is a successful and original use of Gothic for a building on a cruciform plan with broad octagonal crossing. The cross-plan with broad nave and crossing was popular for churches in the low church tradition where an effective auditorium for the spoken word was preferred to a plan designed for an elaborate liturgy. Another example is St Mark, Tollington Park, of 1853–4, by *A. D. Gough*, architect of several suburban Islington churches. Their

eclectic Gothic detail and galleried interiors did not meet with the
approval of the Ecclesiologists, so they were prone to later alterations
or demolition. St George Tufnell Park (1865–8, *G. Truefitt*) is an
interesting later example of an experimental polygonal plan. In the
same tradition, but departing still further from accepted norms, is
St Martin Gospel Oak by *E. B. Lamb*, 1864–5, where the broad
space is pulled together by a bizarre roof structure of wonderful
complexity. The more lavish treatment of St Martin no doubt owed
something to its rich patron, the glove manufacturer J. D. Allcroft.
Well-heeled parishioners also explain the sumptuousness of the most
magnificent example of this low church tradition, St Stephen, 85
Rosslyn Hill, Hampstead, by *S. S. Teulon*, built 1869–73, remarkable
both for its powerful exterior in Teulon's most aggressive Early
Gothic, and for its vast, stately interior, disused since 1977, but once
richly decorated. The influence of Teulon's building is surely to be
seen at two buildings in Hackney, *E. L. Blackburne*'s elaborate w
tower for St Mark, 1877–80, which does much to add presence to
its large but ungainly church of the 1860s, and *Ewan Christian*'s
Holy Trinity Dalston, 1878–9, which like St Stephen has a tough,
dominant crossing tower.

At this point it is appropriate to mention the NONCONFORMIST
CHURCHES, whose importance in the C19 suburbs is often overlooked, as so many buildings have disappeared or have changed
their purpose. Hackney, Islington and Haringey nevertheless remain
good hunting grounds.* The Nonconformists often employed their
own architects (generally ignored by the contemporary architectural
periodicals), and had different requirements from the High Anglicans,
although their emphasis on a broad, often galleried, preaching space
was comparable to the low church faction within the Church of
England. The classical preaching box continued to be built, the later
examples making a show on the street front with increasingly rich
Italianate detail, as seen for example at the Hampden Chapel,
Hackney (1847), the Swiss Protestant Church, Holborn, by *Vulliamy*,
(1853), and still more grandly, at the former New Court Congregational 94
Church (now St Mellitus R.C.), Islington, by *C. G. Searle* (1870),
which has an imposing temple front. Medieval styles, associated with
the Church of England, were at first avoided, although interestingly the
substantial Bloomsbury Central Baptist Church of 1845 by *John
Gibson* is an example of the brief Neo-Norman fashion of the 1840s,
the English archaeological equivalent to the *Rundbogenstil* of the continent. Gothic is used tentatively at Vernon Baptist Chapel, Finsbury
(1843), more confidently for the King's Cross Welsh Tabernacle,
Finsbury (*H. Hodge*, 1853), and for the wealthy and well fitted up
Unitarian Chapel Hampstead (1862 by *John Johnson*). Much more
ambitious than these is *Raphael Brandon*'s Catholic Apostolic
Church of 1853, in Bloomsbury (now the university church of Christ
the King), employing archaeologically correct Gothic on a cathedral
scale, with liturgical fittings of equal magnificence. By the later 1860s
use of Gothic became more widespread, particularly in the buildings
by *John Tarring*, one of the most accomplished of the Nonconformists'
architects. His Lady Margaret Methodist church at Kentish Town

*In Islington this has been demonstrated well by the RCHME's research: Philip
Temple, *Islington Chapels*, 1992.

(1864) has a stone Gothic exterior with tower and spire not dissimilar to an Anglican church, but its interior with gallery on iron columns is characteristically Nonconformist. Another Tarring church, complete with fine spire, is Christ Church Congregational at Enfield (1874). A particularly idiosyncratic example, also with a prominent
91 spire, is the church built for the Agapemone sect at Clapton, Hackney
92 (1892), memorable for its intense stained glass by *Walter Crane*.

Other varieties of expression range from the minimal Gothic of a temporary 'tin tabernacle' (Shrubland Road, Hackney), a rare survival of a type of building that often preceded permanent buildings, to brick buildings in a robust transitional or Early Gothic, such as the Baptist churches at Hackney Downs (1868 by *M. Glover*) and Seven Sisters Road, Tottenham (1882, *Paull & Bonella*), and East Finchley Methodist Church (1896 by *E. Hoole*). The former Islington Congregational church of 1887 by *Paull*, unusually, is in an appealingly domestic Norman Shaw style.

A type of particular interest is the galleried 'auditorium', which develops a plan form that had already been used by Nonconformists in the C18 and which was adopted in the C19 for some of the most
93 ambitious chapels. The Round Chapel in Hackney of 1869 by *Henry Fuller* (not in fact circular, but with a rounded end with continuous gallery with slender iron columns), is one of the most impressive examples. The adaptation of Gothic for a central plan is particularly
95 successful at the splendid Union Chapel, Islington, by *James Cubitt*, 1876, a specialist in chapel building: the only example of this group to retain its excellent fittings. A later example is the polygonal former Congregational Chapel at Hampstead by *Waterhouse*, 1883.

Several ROMAN CATHOLIC CHURCHES were founded by French émigrés in the early C19, and flourished through the C19 as the centres of Irish and other immigrant communities. At the modest end of the scale is the charming building in Holly Place, Hampstead (1816, with an Italianate front of 1850 by *Wardell*). Ambition grew after the establishment of the Catholic hierarchy in 1850. An interesting, very Italian example is St Peter, Holborn (1862, *J. M. Bryson*), built for the poor Italian community of Saffron Hill. Many of the principal buildings were the result of foreign missions and included school and convent as well as church, as for example the Gothic group of St Monica Hoxton (*E. W. Pugin*, 1864). A much larger Gothic church, formerly also with convent, is the richly furnished St Dominic, Kentish Town (*C. A. Buckler*, 1874), built for the Dominicans established here in 1861, which was intended to be one of the chief R.C. centres for north London. Even more imposing is the Passionists' St Joseph, Islington (*A. Vicars*, 1887, replacing an earlier building of 1859). Here the style adopted is Italian Renaissance (as at the Brompton Oratory, designed 1878). The vast Italian dome dominates the climb up Highgate Hill; there is a sumptuous Italian Renaissance interior as well. A later landmark is the twin towered front of the Jesuits' St Ignatius, Tottenham (*B. Williamson*, 1902), inspired by Spanish Transitional Gothic.

*Churches: the late C19 to 1914*

Serious medieval Gothic continued to inspire a number of the best church architects in the 1880s–90s, and although funds were no longer so plentiful, rarely allowing for towers, there are some out-standing Anglican churches of these years. *Bodley*'s refined yet powerful work can be seen at St Michael Camden Town, begun 1880, and St Mary of Eton, Hackney Wick, part of a mission group of the 1890s. St John, West Hendon (1895–6), by *Temple Moore*, is in a similar tradition. *Moore* also was responsible for a sensitive addition to St Mary, Hendon, in an original version of late Gothic. All Hallows, St Pancras, begun 1889, has a noble, though unfinished late Gothic interior by *Brooks*, quite different from his earlier work. St John, Friern Barnet, by *Pearson* 1890–1, also has a fine interior, in 84 this case making inventive use of early Gothic detail. These are the highlights, but there are plenty of late C19 churches of character by lesser architects, often with interiors which are more rewarding than the outside might lead one to expect; a short list might include Holy Cross, Holborn, spiky original Gothic by *Joseph Peacock*, 1887; St Mark, Noel Park, by *Rowland Plumbe*, a good focal point in the Artisans' estate at Wood Green (1889); and the spacious St Thomas Islington and St Olave Stoke Newington, both by *Ewan Christian* (1888, 1893).

There are also some notable departures from tradition. The powerful Italian Renaissance of Holy Redeemer, Finsbury, by *J. D.* 89 *Sedding* (1887), is the most unexpected, a radical contrast to his more customary free Gothic, which can be found at St Augustine, Archway Road, Haringey (1884). A more frivolous late Gothic is exhibited by *Champneys*'s St Luke Hampstead (1897).

In the early years of the C20 this variety continued in the churches built for the Edwardian suburbs. Gothic was still the most common style but it was employed in a number of idiosyncratic ways. St John the Evangelist, Southgate, by *J. O. Scott* (1903), is a mature building by an accomplished Gothic architect, satisfyingly rich and eclectic in its details and materials. *W. D. Caröe* developed a homely Arts and Crafts version of the basilican church, using free Perp detail; St Aldhelm Edmonton (1903) and St Bartholomew Tottenham 88 (1904) are good examples. In contrast, *C. H. B. Quennell*'s St John Edmonton has an unexpectedly monumental interior (1905), as has *J. S. Alder*'s St Benet Fink, Tottenham (1911), the one odd and quirky, the other lofty and serene. St Silas Kentish Town (St Pancras) is the first of *E. C. Shearman*'s intense and eccentric Gothic churches (1911). Alternatives to Gothic also appear. Holy Trinity Holborn by *Belcher & Joass* (1909) is inspired by Italian Baroque, while at Hampstead Garden Suburb, *Lutyens* provided the central square with an imposing and original pair, for Anglicans and Noncon- 87 formists (1909, 1911), successfully blending Baroque with Byzantine and medieval sources.

A number of Nonconformist churches of the Edwardian years drew attention by their cheerful street frontages, derived from the free Gothic of Sedding and his followers, generally with an asymmetrical turret and big Perp window. The *Baines* firm produced many good examples, making effective use of brick, flint and terracotta; among them the Baptist and Presbyterian churches at Muswell Hill (1900, 96 1903) and another Baptist Church at Bounds Green (1907). The two Baptist churches have pleasingly unaltered interiors with origi-nal joinery and patterned glass. The most individual and lavish Nonconformist interior of this time is that by *Beresford Pite* for the

Paget Memorial Mission Hall (1910), an unexpected gem in an unpromising area of Islington.

From the later C19 an increasing number of SYNAGOGUES were built for the Jewish communities of the new suburbs. Hackney examples have unostentatious brick exteriors, as at Brenthouse Road (1896 by *Delissa Joseph*), even when they were very large, as in the case of the former synagogue, now mosque, in Shacklewell Lane (1903 by *Lewis Solomon*). The Hampstead Synagogue (1892–1901 by *Joseph*) is exceptional among Victorian suburban synagogues both in its outward display – a towered Romanesque front – and in the sumptuousness of its galleried interior. Its Edwardian counterpart is the New Synagogue at Upper Clapton (1914–15 by *E. M. Joseph*), the sober classical style with galleried interior and coffered apse following the tradition of its early C19 City predecessor.

This introduction can only touch on the vast subject of CHURCH FURNISHINGS and STAINED GLASS of the Victorian and Edwardian years; the numerous excellent individual examples must be sought in the gazetteer. Most often furnishing and windows were accumulated gradually, often as memorials. The most lavish decoration generally dates from the later C19 and the early C20 when the fashion for the rich effects of mixed materials could lead to the clothing of sanctuaries and chancels in tile or mosaic, as well as stencilling or wall painting. The embellishment of St Mary Magdalene, Munster Square (St Pancras), is typical. Some of the best collections of fittings were lost in the Second World War, as at St Alban, Holborn (although the survivals here are still worth a visit). Elsewhere much was reduced in the C20, when plainer tastes prevailed. St Mary, Primrose Hill, Hampstead, provides a fascinating case study of contrasting approaches of the C19 and the early C20 (when the reforming Percy Dearmer was vicar). Complete sequences of stained glass by single firms tend to be exceptional – good examples are the excellent *Morris* windows of a variety of dates at Christ Church, Southgate, those by *Clayton & Bell* at St John, Friern Barnet, and the glass and wall painting at St Andrew, Stoke Newington, by *Heaton Butler & Bayne*. Another interior decorated from the 1880s onwards is All Saints, Oakleigh Park, Barnet, following a scheme devised by *S. Gambier-Parry* and carried out mostly by *Ward & Hughes*. C19 and early C20 efforts to bring the preaching boxes of an earlier age into line with current taste, such as Butterfield's redecoration of St Leonard, Shoreditch, have largely disappeared, but a remarkable surviving example, recently restored, is the elaborate and effective early C20 ceiling painting of St John Hoxton. *F. P. Cockerell*'s remodelling of St John Hampstead in the 1870s is an interesting example of the acceptance of a classical style, with Renaissance fittings by *T. G. Jackson*. Among sculptors in the Gothic style *Thomas Earp* was one of the most accomplished; good examples of his work can be seen at St Saviour, Hampstead, and the Union Chapel, Islington.

## NORTH LONDON BETWEEN THE WARS

During the two decades between the World Wars London expanded into Middlesex, until almost the whole county was transformed into continuous suburbia. Its growth depended on new public transport:

the Northern Line Extension from Golders Green to Edgware (1923–4) and the Piccadilly Line Extension from Finsbury Park to Cockfosters (1932–3). *Charles Holden*'s clean-cut, well-planned stations on the Piccadilly Line, inventive variations based on simple iii geometric forms in the spirit of the latest Scandinavian architecture, seemed to herald a new age. Yet they remained exceptional. It was the potent combination of romantic rural imagery and genteel Neo-Georgian, promoted so successfully at Hampstead Garden Suburb before the First World War, that inspired the repetitive winding roads of commuters' semi-detached houses put up by the large building firms. Public buildings and services provided by the fledgling boroughs and urban districts were at first similarly traditional. In the inner areas the architectural scene was confused. The classical style, shorn of its Edwardian exuberance, remained the safe solution for official architecture and institutions. Buildings for commerce and entertainment were more adventurous, looking to America both for new constructional techniques and for exotic ornament, while architectural ideas from the continent were beginning to influence those looking for radical solutions for the worst social conditions. Here émigré architects played an increasingly important role.

### Domestic building

The extreme example of traditionalism was the re-creation by Sir Philip Sassoon of a Georgian country house at Trent Park with materials salvaged from demolished buildings (1926–31). The parts of Hampstead Garden Suburb built between the wars also carried on with familar pre-war styles, often in a very accomplished manner. Lytton Close by *C. G. Winburne*, 1935, in a modernist style, is one of the few exceptions. A domestic Wrenaissance remained widely popular, not only for superior private houses, but for such buildings as *Lutyens*'s YWCA in Great Russell Street Holborn (1930–2); C17 detail is also a source for *Baker*'s grander and more eclectic London House in Holborn, for students from the Dominions (1933). For more modest accommodation in the suburbs, a simple cottage style in the Parker & Unwin tradition became the solution, and was used to great visual effect for the houses on the LCC's large Watling estate at Hendon, begun 1926. Inspired by Unwin's planning principles, this was the style generally adopted for the first 'homes for heroes' council housing put up immediately after the war by the Middlesex local authorities, where there was plenty of space for low-density housing. Good examples are Hyde estate, Edmonton; Woodhouse estate, Finchley; Durnsford Road, Wood Green. Attempts by Laings, one of the chief north London builders, to introduce a similarly pared-down style for private housing (Sunnyfield, Mill Hill, by *T. Alwyn Lloyd*) did not meet with success. Private owners wanted their houses to be more distinctive; this was often achieved by the addition of a little decorative timber work; the most 6 ubiquitous type, the semi-detached house, was usually given twin gables and canted or curved bay windows whose top lights might have some fancy glazing. Progressive modernism did not make much headway in the private market, although a few tentative experiments can be found in the Hendon suburbs.

There were still parts of inner London with acute problems of overcrowding and poverty, and the reconstruction of the worst of these inner areas was a major concern between the wars. Both the LCC and the London boroughs acted as housing authorities, and independent housing trusts also were active. Together they transformed large swathes of inner London. Low-rent housing in the inner areas most frequently took the form of walk-up flats of four or five storeys, usually with balcony access at the back. The sturdy brick blocks put up by the LCC can still be distinguished by their well-proportioned sash windows (when they have not been replaced), hipped roofs, and nicely lettered ceramic name plates. The type is

LCC Name plate, Whitmore Estate, Shoreditch

well illustrated by the Whitmore estate in Shoreditch (1924–37); many others are scattered through Islington and Hackney. The Ossulston estate at Somers Town, St Pancras (1927–37), was more novel: for this the LCC adopted a courtyard plan with seven-storey centrepiece, influenced by the ambitious mass housing of Vienna. Courtyard layouts were popular between the wars; they provided the opportunity for more formal architecture, as well as for tenants' amenities, although gardens rarely survived the later advent of car ownership. They range from the strikingly austere, rather Expressionist police flats in Merlin Street, Finsbury (1927–30 by *G. Mackenzie Trench*), to the LCC's grand, almost fortress like Stamford Hill estate in Hackney. The energetic St Pancras Home Improvement Society (founded 1924) also adopted a courtyard layout for its 'garden city', the Sidney Street estate in Somers Town by *Ian Hamilton*, begun 1929; its blocks are arranged around a large court, and the tenants could be diverted by the playful ceramic decorations by *Gilbert Bayes* which embellished both buildings and drying yards. Housing for the boroughs tended to be less inspired: *E. C. P. Monson* in Islington, and *A. J. Thomas* in St Pancras mostly built in a Neo-Georgian idiom; the work by Messrs *Joseph* in Hackney was more austere in appearance, although when space allowed, as on the fringes of Clapton, amenity space could be generous. The most original experiments were by housing associations. Lennox House, near Well Street, Hackney, by *J. E. M. McGregor*, 1937, has flats stepped back over a covered space intended for a market, a remarkable precursor of the type of A-frame construction developed for housing in the 1960s, although without immediate imitators. Kent House, by *Connell Ward & Lucas* (1935–6), built by a splinter group of the St Pancras Home Improvement Society at Kentish Town, was an early example in England of the application of progressive continental Modern Movement principles to working-class flats: built of concrete, with electric services, large windows and generous balconies, all features that would be taken up after the war.

Most progressive architects did not have such an opportunity to put their ideals to the test, and it was private patronage that made other Modernist buildings possible. The principal examples in north London are some of the most significant nationally: the Isokon Flats at Hampstead by *Wells Coates*, 1934, for the furniture maker Jack Pritchard, and Highpoint One and Two at Highgate, 1933–5 and 114 1938, superior flats built by the émigré architect *Berthold Lubetkin* and his firm *Tecton*, for Sigmund Gestetner. Both made visible use of concrete in the tradition of Le Corbusier. The earlier Highpoint flats are particularly ingenious in the planning of their communal areas, the later ones in the internal arrangement of their double-height apartments. Highpoint Two has rather less exposed concrete surfaces, a trend noticeable in other buildings of the later 30s. A similar tempering of the extremes of Modernism can be seen in the few private houses which espoused this cause: the plain white concrete of the early ones at Hampstead (*Maxwell Fry*, 1934–5, *Connell Ward* 113 *& Lucas*, 1937) contrast with *Goldfinger*'s group in Willow Road, a subtle, brick-faced trio including his own house (1937–9), and *Tayler & Green*'s tall, compact studio house in Duke's Head Yard, Highgate (1939).

A few other examples of private housing built in the 1930s were in a Modernist spirit to a varying degree: the White House, Albany Street, service flats by *R. A. Atkinson*; brick flats by *Ernst Freud* in Frognal Close and on the edge of Hampstead Garden Suburb, a hostel by *Maxwell Fry* in North Gower Street, and (the most Corbusian, but altered) a concrete group by *A. V. Pilichovski* at Golders Green. Other architects were more eclectic, none more so than *Oliver Hill* whose Glenamoy, Mill Hill, of 1936, has a steep thatched roof, although his work at Upper Terrace Hampstead makes use of more streamlined effects. Mill Hill also has the oddity of a house imitating Frank Lloyd Wright's textile houses of the 20s (The White House, Hyver Hill, by *D. E. Harrington*, 1934).

*Public Buildings*

Most of the boroughs which had not already rebuilt their old vestry halls adopted a formal, though not routine, classical style for their new TOWN HALLS. Common features are a stone-faced exterior, a traditional ceremonial stair leading to a council chamber, and a public hall with separate entrance. Islington (*E. C. P. Monson*) was the first, begun 1922, with quite a small frontage, given dignity by being set back from Upper Street. St Pancras (*A. J. Thomas*) and Hackney (*Lanchester & Lodge*) both begun 1934, are imposing blocks dominating their tight urban sites; Stoke Newington (*R. Truelove*, 1935) in the centre of the old village, has a gentler curved front. The stylistic exceptions are Hornsey, by *R. H. Uren*, begun 1933, a spare, asymmetrical brick composition, which daringly took its inspiration from Dudok's Hilversum Town Hall, with the modern spirit carried through to its internal fittings, and Friern 112

Barnet, 1939 by *Sir John Brown, Henson & Partners*, with a reticent brick concave front, which owes something to the c20 classical tradition of Sweden.

Other building types demonstrate a similar development. In the 1920s a friendly domestic Neo-Georgian was favoured for smaller buildings serving the community, for example *F. Danby Smith*'s attractive Health Centre, Kingsland Road, of 1920–2, built for the benefit of the poor of Shoreditch. The style was found equally suitable for small LIBRARIES built for the new middle-class suburbs; those at North and East Finchley by the Finchley borough architect *Percival T. Harrison* are elegant examples. The TECHNICAL COLLEGES built by the Middlesex County Council at Hendon and Tottenham, and the SENIOR SCHOOLS such as Edmonton County (1931) were in a similar tradition; under *W. T. Curtis*, county architect from 1930, restrained classical proportions, more simply detailed than the county's Free Baroque of pre 1914, were used to give these appropriate gravitas. More unusually, a powerful, quite mannered version of the Arts and Crafts tradition was used for the 1920s additions to Latymer school, Edmonton. Private schools could also be more enterprising: the best is Mill Hill Junior, with good Lutyensesque buildings by *J. C. S. Soutar* (who had worked at Hampstead Garden Suburb).

In the 1930s pressure on the Middlesex County Council's services as a result of the rapid expansion of population led to a different approach, developed by Curtis together with his education architect *H. W. Burchett*: plain brick surfaces, metal windows, and cubic massing in the manner of Dudok were found to be economical as well as architecturally progressive. The bulk of the schools built at this time were in the developing areas of north-west and west Middlesex (*see* further on this *London 3: North West*); in our area a good representative of the streamlined secondary schools of this era is Copthall North, Mill Hill, 1936. The new county style was maturing just as the war ended building activity. The further reaches of the Piccadilly Line are a good hunting ground: near Oakwood there is both the De Bohun Primary School, a skilfully massed composition of 1936, and a library of 1939. At New Southgate there is a well-composed group of swimming baths, library and clinic (1939). Meanwhile the combination of public baths and laundries was still required in the poor inner boroughs full of substandard housing; at Finsbury they are in a Neo-Roman style by Messrs *Cross*, the baths specialists (1931, extended 1938); in Hackney, the Borough Engineer *Percival Holt* gave the early 1930s frontages a slightly Art Deco flavour; in 1938 a more streamlined style was adopted for the borough clinic in Elsdale Road. A new, airy and hygienic approach to design, achieved through the use of light, bright materials, was eminently appropriate for the health centre, a new building type of this time, intended to encourage healthier living standards in the community. The prime exemplar was the Finsbury Health Centre of 110 1935–8 by *Lubetkin* and *Tecton*, their first public work, skilfully planned to be both functional and welcoming, with splayed wings extending on either side of its generous curved entrance. Hospitals also began to adopt a modern style at this time, for example the crisp steel and brick wing by *Burnet, Tait & Lorne* added in 1935–6 to the German Hospital at Hackney, and the streamlined extensions for the National Hospital in Queen Square, Holborn, by *Slater Moberly & Uren*, 1937–8.

As these examples show, a range of Modernist idioms for public service buildings was beginning to emerge by the end of the 1930s. The laboratory at the New River Head, Finsbury, by *Easton & Robertson*, 1938, with its handsome glass-brick staircase tower, also belongs in this category. But it was by no means a universal style. Public taste craved something more exotic, and nowhere was this better satisfied than in the SUPER-CINEMA of the 1930s, whose bulky mass now intruded in every suburban centre. The earlier ones used loose, showy classical detail both outside and in (King's Cross, 1920, Dominion, Tottenham Court Road, 1928–9). Then in the 1930s the American 'atmospheric' interior with clever lighting effects became fashionable. The best of these in north London is the Astoria, Finsbury Park (*E. Stone* 1930), plain outside, but with a fabulous escapist interior: a 'fountain court' as a foyer, and a vast auditorium with starry ceiling and rooftops of an 'Andalucian Village'. The Odeon High Barnet (1934) has Moorish decoration, while Egyptian was the novelty used for the exterior of the Carlton, 116 Islington, by *George Coles* (1930). *Coles* also could work in a minimalist streamlined style, well preserved at the Muswell Hill Odeon of 1935–6. The grand classical manner remained the answer for the former Gaumont (now Odeon), Holloway Road, by *C. Howard Crane* (1937–8). The Gaumont, Wood Green (now closed), is a good example of German inspiration, which took over from American in the mid 1930s. THEATRES adopted similar styles. The use of subtle overlapping planes, in a similar spirit to the Muswell Hill Odeon, is to be found earlier in the interior of the Cambridge Theatre at Seven Dials, Holborn, a distinguished design by *Chermayeff* of 1929–30, inspired by 1920s Berlin cinemas. The Phoenix in Charing Cross Road has a more traditional Renaissance interior by *Komisarjevsky* of 1930. The PUB was another opportunity for escapism – no longer offering the glitter of the Victorian gin palace, but now, especially in the outer suburbs, exhibiting nostalgia for a more genteel timbered Tudor. The Railway Hotel, Edgware, and the Goat, Forty Hill, are good examples.

Exotic styles were also used more occasionally for COMMERCIAL BUILDINGS which sought to give their products a smart image. Egyptian Art Deco enjoyed a certain vogue in the 1920s following the Paris exhibition of 1925 (Carreras cigarette factory, Mornington Crescent, by *M. E. & O. H. Collins*, 1926 (later stripped off, but to be restored); offices in Shaftesbury Avenue by *Hobden & Porri*, 1929). A sharp Expressionist use of faience was the choice for Austin Reed's offices in Red Lion Square, Holborn (*Westwood & Emberton*, 1925). A crisp modern façade drew attention to Crawford's Advertising Company in High Holborn (*Etchells & Welch*, 1930) which claimed to be the first Modern Movement building in central London, and a mature version of the continental brand of Modernism appeared at Gilbey's gin offices in Jamestown Road, Camden Town (*Chermayeff*, 1937). The more practical concerns of the suburban household were reflected in competing gas and electrical showrooms. In central Hackney they are classical (borough electrical offices, 1924; Gas Light & Coke Co. showrooms by *Tapper* and *Hall*, 1931); in Hornsey they are in tune with the brick Modernism of the neighbouring Town Hall (Gas by *Dawe & Carter*, 1936–7; Electricity 1938 by *Uren*). Some of these buildings provided an opportunity for imaginative artistic decoration, with good lettering, discreet low-relief sculpture and decorative metalwork used as a foil for plain exterior surfaces. The work by *Arthur Ayres* at Hornsey is especially notable, as is the low relief cast-stone frieze by *Gilbert Bayes* which adorns the Modernist exterior of the Saville Theatre in Shaftesbury Avenue (*T. P. Bennett*, 1931).

Large INSTITUTIONS played a safer game and were more likely to be in an established style. The extremes of theatrical display exhibited in the colossal headquarters of the Freemasons in Great Queen Street, Holborn (*Ashley & Newman*, 1927–33), are something of an exception: flamboyantly classical outside, and with a grandiosely Egyptian central hall. A more sober classical approach is that of the Wellcome Building, Euston Road (*Septimus Warwick*, 1931–2). For the buildings in Holborn connected with the University, classical also at first seemed an obvious choice: *Richardson*'s rather fussy 1920s additions to *Wilkins*'s buildings at University College; *Horder & Rees*'s more restrained stripped classicism for the London School of Hygiene and Tropical Medicine (1926–8). A new scale and a new aesthetic arrived with the appointment of *Charles Holden* in 1931 as architect for the University's central site. His colossal tower for
109 Senate House and Library was completed in 1937. The tower, with its powerful stepped massing of plain cubic forms, was London's tallest 'inhabited' building at the time, and its most prominent departure from tradition, although it seems to have made less of a stir than Holden's earlier London Transport offices at Westminster. It was intended as the centrepiece of a precinct surrounded by quieter brick buildings, but this only came to fruition gradually after the war.

Finally in this period between the wars, CHURCHES need to be considered. The main activity was in the outer boroughs, but the list of highlights is short; much had already been built before 1914. An original, spare version of Gothic was used by *C. G. Hare* for the 1920s nave of St Benet, Kentish Town. Arts and Crafts free Gothic was skilfully employed by *Giles G. Scott* at St Alban Golders Green (1932–3), its brick skin concealing reinforced-concrete construction. Concrete is used more overtly for the parabolic transverse arches of *Seely & Paget*'s St John Tottenham (1939), which has an oddly proportioned rather mannered exterior, but is impressive inside. *Cyril Farey*'s St Peter Southgate (1939–41) is modern without but Romanesque within. The most radical in both style and function is
115 *Martin-Smith*'s John Keble Memorial Church, Hendon (1935–7), rational and symmetrical in a French Modernist manner, with a grand, blocky brick tower and broad undivided space. Nonconformist building is surprisingly varied. Among the most impressive is Woodcroft Evangelical Church, a very sober Tuscan hall on the Watling estate, by *Sir John Burnet* (1927–8). Methodist churches are especially original: Trinity at Golders Green (*Withers*, 1922) has a central plan in a kind of Neo-Byzantine; Hendon, by *Welch & Lander*, has mild brick Expressionist detail; Grange Park, Southgate, is cheerful Art Deco (*Brightiff*, 1938). The Methodists were also active in more urban areas at this time: their Central Hall in Mare Street, Hackney, has an impressive classical exterior of 1926–7 by *Gunton & Gunton*. Friends House, the Quaker headquarters in

Euston Road (*H. Lidbetter*, 1925–7), is more austerely Grecian, echoing the entrance to Euston Station opposite. SYNAGOGUES were most frequent in Golders Green, Hackney and Stoke Newington; the most impressive is United Synagogue, Dunstan Road, Golders Green; a dignified classical building of 1921 by *D. Soloman*, enlarged 1921–7 by *E. Joseph*; the Synagogue at Lea Bridge Road, Hackney (*M. Glass*, 1931), is Romanesque with an Art Deco flavour.

Among church fittings of this time the most original are those by *Sir Charles Reilly* in St Barnabas Shacklewell Lane, Hackney. There is a surprising early painting by *Ivon Hitchens* in the Unitarian church at Golders Green (1925), and some remarkable wall paintings of the 1920s by *Walter Starmer* in St Jude, Hampstead Garden Suburb, the earlier ones forming a war memorial. FIRST WORLD WAR MEMORIALS of other types are numerous and varied, but few are spectacular. Tottenham Green has a sculpture by *L. F. Roslyn*, Spa Green Finsbury an angel and pictorial plaques by *Thomas Rudge*; Golders Green a Clock Tower. At Finchley there is an unusually dramatic French bronze sculpture: 'La Délivrance', a female figure by *L. Guillaume*, 1920. Mill Hill School has a rather good restrained Beaux Arts archway by *Stanley Hamp*, 1919–21

A note should be added on three manifestations of what might be termed alternatives to traditional religion. Conway Hall, Red Lion Square, built for the South Place Ethical Society by *F. H. Mansford*, 1929, has Baroque exterior trimmings to an austere toplit hall. Cecil Sharp House, in Gloucester Avenue, Camden Town, for the Folk Song Society, is in a demure Neo-Georgian, by *H. M. Fletcher*, also 1929 (inside, it has a post-war folksy mural by *Ivon Hitchens*). Most remarkable of all is the intense, revolutionary fresco of the 1930s by *Jack Hastings*, in the Marx Memorial Library, Clerkenwell Square, an C18 Welsh Charity School which became a radical meeting place from the late C19.

## NORTH LONDON 1945-c. 1970

PLANNING for post-war London began during the war. The challenge of adapting and expanding the pre-war plans for slum clearance and housing improvement, to cope with the consequences of wartime destruction, was addressed by the LCC's *County of London Plan* by J. H. Forshaw and Patrick Abercrombie, published in 1943, and Abercrombie's *Greater London Plan* of 1944. The latter recognized the need to look at a wider area than that within the LCC's boundary, although this co-ordination only became an administrative reality in 1965 with the creation of the Greater London Council. The plans were not concerned with housing alone, they had a wider vision, embracing transport networks, relocation of industry, and the need for open space, services and amenities. Optimistic post-war enthusiasm for better living conditions was coupled with impatience over the grimy, shattered legacy of a haphazard mixture of industry and poor housing. There was also a firm belief in the need to resist unplanned sprawl of the type that had preceded the establishment of the green belt in 1938.

In 1943 the population within Greater London (then defined as a slightly larger area than in 1965) was 8,379,948. It had dropped by around 300,000 since 1919, but more significantly, the balance was shifting; an increase in the new outer suburbs and a decline in the older inner areas, which by 1943 had only around $2\frac{1}{2}$ million of the total. The 1943 Plan defined a range of maximum residential densities, from 200 persons per acre in the centre (which assumed largely flat dwellers), to seventy in the outer suburban areas, a compromise between urban ideals and the garden suburb approach, both of which had their protagonists. The green belt of 1938 remained sacrosanct, but, it was hoped, would surround a city whose housing would be better organized, with six new towns beyond which would take the overflow population. The plan also proposed a concentric series of ringways to improve traffic circulation; only the outermost ring (the M25) was eventually completed as intended, although the threat of 'Ringway One' (through Islington and Camden) for long blighted large stretches of north London. A zoning system was devised to encourage the separation of residential areas from industry (the future decline of London industry and the docks was not foreseen), and much increased open-space provision was recommended through the creation of new parks.

## Public housing from 1945

In the austerity years housing was the priority. The LCC took responsibility for the most problematic war-damaged neighbourhoods, declaring comprehensive development areas in south London and in much of the East End. Although the LCC continued to build housing estates elsewhere, especially where they had already been active before the war, the reconstruction of north London was largely left to the individual boroughs. Finsbury had led the way before the war in producing a plan for rebuilding; the other London boroughs, particularly St Pancras, Holborn and Hackney, now developed their own schemes. In Middlesex, Edmonton was especially energetic. The first decade of building after the war also saw a considerable range of experimental new housing types. Many were built by private firms employed by the boroughs, which resulted in greater visual variety than in the East End, where so much was done by the LCC. The boroughs themselves generally did not have the resources for this quantity of activity, and the creation of borough architect's departments, independent from the borough engineers, was a gradual process.

The NEW HOUSING falls into a number of categories. What appears now as the most conservative type was strongly influenced by garden city principles, with streets mixing short terraces and culs-de-sac of houses, but including also a few blocks of three- or four-storey flats as visual counterpoints. Introducing this kind of varied layout in place of the usual walk-up flats was an innovation in inner London. The styles adopted reflected the influence of the brick Scandinavian-Dutch modernism which had become familiar from the late 30s for public service buildings. There were also echoes of the few modern private houses built before the war, especially Goldfinger's Willow Road. Occasionally delicate details were drawn from the English Regency style – a British version of Swedish modern. The best-known example is the Lansbury estate in the East End, the 'living architecture' section of the Festival of Britain of 1951 (which so irritated more radical architects seeking greater urban excitement). *Sir Frederick Gibberd*, who worked at Lansbury, had earlier used this type of housing very successfully for the Somerford and Shacklewell Road estates, 1946–7, the first of several which he designed for Hackney. Simpler versions of the type were used imaginatively for early humanely scaled estates elsewhere: as at Colney Hatch Lane, Friern Barnet, 1946–51, and Sebastopol Road, Edmonton, 1950.

A more formal tradition, developed on the continent before the war, especially in Germany, was the *zeilenbau* layout with blocks of flats well spaced out in rows, generally at r. angles to the street so that the buildings could enjoy better light and views. It was first adopted on a large scale for the LCC's Woodberry Down estate at Stoke Newington (planned by *J. H. Forshaw* from 1943), where the showpiece is two pairs of seven-storey slabs, some of the first English public housing to be provided with lifts. *Hening & Chitty*'s flats in the large cleared area around Cromer Street (Holborn), built for St Pancras (1949–51), was an early and rigorous example of this type of lay-out on a denser inner city site. An adaptation of the principle, but following the line of the road and given careful traditional detail, is *Farquarson & McMorran*'s housing in Parkhill Road, Hampstead, c. 1948–50.

An alternative was a looser grouping of flats, breaking away from what was considered to be the constricting monotony of the street front. St Pancras experimented with various small layouts of this kind: *Norman & Dawbarn*'s well-detailed six-storey group on Camden Road of 1946–8, the borough's first post-war flats to be completed, was widely admired; *Hening & Chitty* made similar efforts in Holborn in the more restricted bomb-damaged areas N of Theobalds Road. The 'point' block, a tower with flats grouped around a service and circulation core, was another solution used for tight sites; an imaginative early example of unusual shape is Medway Court, Judd Street (Holborn), for St Pancras (*Clarke-Hall*, 1949–55), intended as the first of three. A variant was the Y-shaped block with wings radiating from central stairs or lift. This type was popular in the mid 50s (Tottenham Hale; Gee Street, Finsbury; also Clem Attlee estate, Fulham, in west London), but the earliest and most remarkable example is Bevin Court, Finsbury, 1952–5 by *Skinner, Bailey & Lubetkin*, which has a spectacular central staircase demonstrating 117 both the Baroque potential of cantilevered concrete, and Lubetkin's fascination with abstract geometry. This firm was successor to Tecton, which, as has been mentioned, had already been involved with Finsbury before the war. Tecton produced two other housing schemes for the borough, both of marked originality. At the earliest, Spa Green (1946–50), a reduced version of a much more ambitious 118 pre-war rebuilding scheme for the area, the symmetrical arrangement of large slab blocks is given interest by a lower curved range and by unexpected curved entrance canopies and ramps, all enlivened by a variety of colour and textured surfaces. The later and larger Priory Green estate at Pentonville (1947–57), which suffered from economies in its building, has a more formal arrangement of four- and eight-storey blocks. The radical reconstruction of Finsbury was carried on into the 1960s, with some visually quite dramatic set pieces of slabs and towers by *Emberton, Franck & Tardrew*. Islington continued in a more old fashioned manner with *E.C.P Monson*'s firm, whose post-war flats were mostly updated versions of the pre-war walk-up blocks, although there were also a few quite impressive taller showpieces, such as the linked slabs of the Aubert Park estate (1946–53).

The architectural importance of the LCC as the largest housing authority in Britain was established when a new architect's department was set up in 1950 under (Sir) *Robert Matthew*, attracting a large young and forward-thinking staff. The LCC's new approach, developed from the early 50s, was the principle of mixed development: estates with both high and low buildings, and with flats and houses of different sizes, in contrast to the more uniform pre-war solutions. The inclusion of high-rise blocks provided an opportunity for introducing mighty slabs of Corbusian type, the ideal among the 'carnivores', the more extreme of the Modernists. Alton West, the second phase at Roehampton in south London, built 1954–8, provided the examples that became most famous. Slightly earlier prototypes were built at Loughborough Road, Brixton, and at Bentham Road Hackney (1952–4). At Hackney the monumental eleven-storey concrete slabs with open ground floors are individually impressive, but lack the ample setting that such buildings demand. The gentler approach of the Swedish-influenced Modernists (the 'herbivores') is well illustrated by the LCC's attractive Quadrant estate, Highbury (1954), with its open lawns scattered with neatly detailed five-storey flats in pale brick. The LCC principles of mixed development became standard practice for other local authorities, but over the next fifteen years the blocks of flats increased in height, and four- or six-storey maisonettes became more common, as can be seen at *Gibberd*'s later estates for Hackney, or, less appealingly, at Fellows Court, Shoreditch, where older housing was replaced by a clumsy composition of two bulky towers and lower ranges of flats.

St Pancras's two major development sites, Regents Park Estate and West Kentish Town, both illustrate the unfortunate results of protracted rebuilding programmes with many changes of plan. In both areas more was demolished than would now be thought necessary, and neither hangs together as a whole, although the zoos of housing types include some interesting specimens. At the Gospel Oak end of West Kentish Town, *Powell & Moya* were responsible for an early mixed development group combining the extremes of a trim ten-storey curtain-walled slab juxtaposed with a neat low terrace (1952–4). At Regents Park, a little later, a new type of precinct layout was introduced by *Armstrong & MacManus*, four-storey maisonettes grouped around a square, in a Modernist reinterpretation of traditional London planning (1957–9). Kiln Place, Gospel Oak (1959–62), by the same firm, is similar. There were other precincts or squares of this time elsewhere in London, for example the LCC's Brandon estate in Southwark, and a little later, the more complex and influential Lillington Gardens, Westminster, by *Darbourne and Darke*, planned in 1960. The type might have flourished further had it not been for the continuing pressure to house ever larger numbers, and also to cope with car-parking.

TOWERS seemed to the authorities to be the fastest and simplest way to pack in large numbers of people. From the early 60s the government encouraged the use of industrialized building techniques with factory-made parts, in the belief that this would both speed up and reduce the costs of major housing schemes. Both hopes proved to be illusory. The economics of industrialized building demanded increased scale and simpler details, at the expense of quality. The result was a scatter of indifferent tower blocks and slabs of maisonettes, crudely built of large panels, without the careful detailing or skilful siting that had characterized earlier post-war work. By the 1970s many such towers could be found in Hackney, Islington and Haringey, although by the late 90s they were less obvious, as some had been demolished (Holly Street and Trowbridge estates, Hackney) and others reclad (Harvist estate, Islington, and many others). The borough which embraced industrialized building most enthusiastically was Edmonton, carrying out the building work through its own Direct Works Department. The Edmonton towers of the later 60s have a certain panache, with their patterned surfaces and decorative tops, and form prominent landmarks along the Lea Valley. The tallest are of twenty-three storeys.

An alternative to towers was linked slabs, as used most famously at Park Hill Sheffield, a type only occasionally adopted in London, as at the relatively small Weston Rise estate, Finsbury, a dramatic cluster on a slope, by *Howell, Killick, Partridge & Amis* for the GLC, 1964–9, and at the system-built Packington Square, Islington (1967–9). More elaborate multi-level schemes were encouraged by the greater resources available to the larger London boroughs created in 1965: they include the forbidding Abbey Road, Hampstead, begun 1965, and Broadwater Farm, Haringey, 1966–71. Still more ambitious was the multi-level centre with housing above shopping. There were two major attempts at this type of brave new urban world with complete segregation of people and traffic. Edmonton Green, planned by Edmonton but carried out after 1965 by Enfield, has towers of flats rising from a deck above shopping mall and market. At Wood Green Shopping City, by *Sheppard Robson & Partners* for Haringey, planned from 1969, and intended as a central focus for the new borough, housing clusters are piled up over garages and two levels of shops. But neither was completed as intended; at Edmonton the public buildings which were to have made the green into a genuine civic centre remained unbuilt, and at Wood Green the road plans were drastically simplified. Visually there is a telling difference between the two schemes: a bold use of concrete at Edmonton and the employment of deep red brick and pitched roofs at Wood Green, demonstrating the shifting of taste toward 'friendlier' materials. The fascination of planners and architects with the complexities of multi-level urban restructuring in the 60s is seen too in internal planning. The extreme example is the 'scissor plan'; developed for some of the largest of the GLC's tower blocks (e.g. on the Banner estate and St Luke's estate, Finsbury), where individual maisonettes overlap each other across a central corridor so that each has rooms facing in different directions.

A prime object of multi-level structures was to provide for the car. Although the separation of pedestrian and vehicular circulation was received wisdom in road planning, early post-war planners had not anticipated that council tenants would become car owners. As numbers of cars increased, from the later 1950s much ingenuity was devoted to devising ways of incorporating car-parking tidily within housing schemes, generally by raising the flats on a podium or deck over garaging. The City of London led the way with plans for the Barbican (from 1956), following it with an astonishingly ambitious plan (adopted 1959) to create a network of raised pedestrian walk-ways throughout the City.*

7 In north London the most influential prototype was the Brunswick Centre on the edge of Bloomsbury, planned by *Sir Leslie Martin* and *Patrick Hodgkinson* from 1959 although not built until 1968–72. Unlike the Barbican, with its freely grouped towers and slabs, the Brunswick Centre was simpler to grasp, a linear plan of a raised

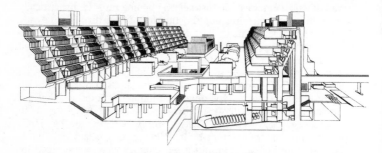

Brunswick Centre, built 1968–72. Axonometric

shopping street flanked by stepped-back flats within two vast A-frame structures. It was intended to be twice the length that was built and was at first to be for private owners, though it was eventually taken over as council housing. This grand ideal of the self-sufficient urban megastructure incorporating not only cars and housing but services and amenities (a new version of Le Corbusier's Unité d'Habitation), was not easy to implement, and most linear deck schemes built in the later 1960s–70s were for housing alone. The influence of the Brunswick Centre can be seen most clearly in the work of the Architect's Department created by the new borough of Camden in 1965. An inventive team, inspired by *Neave Brown*, imaginatively adapted stepped housing on decks over car-parking for a variety of

124 sites; the earliest is at Dunboyne Road Hampstead (designed 1966), another is at Highgate New Town. Others range from the sylvan heights of Branch Hill to the wastelands behind King's Cross, cul-

123 minating in the great sweep of Alexandra Road in West Hampstead (designed 1969, built 1972–8).‡

Housing of this type not only rejected the tower, whose diminish-ing reputation as satisfactory family housing had been further dented in 1968 by the dramatic collapse of Ronan Point, a tower in the Borough of Newham. It also provided individual entrances in place of access galleries or corridors, a return to the traditional pattern of the street. A shift away from towers also became the policy in Islington, where *Darbourne & Darke*'s large Marquess estate (1966–76) was intended to provide an alternative: dense, picturesquely grouped medium-rise housing with small gardens,

---

* See *London 1: the City of London*.
‡ See further the Introduction to St Pancras p. 342.

with decks over garaging and flats along intimate high-level streets. Although visually attractive, the size and intricacy turned out to be too complex to manage, and as with other decked housing schemes the podium garages proved to be a gift to vandals.

Not many PRIVATE FLATS of the 1960s need to be singled out here. The most memorable are a few forceful examples built at the height of the fashion for expressive concrete construction in the early 1960s, for example by *Douglas Stephen* at Swiss Cottage and Southwood Park, and by *Owen Luder* at Hendon. PRIVATE HOUSES of the 1950s–60s include a number of interesting buildings mostly designed by architects for themselves in Hampstead and Highgate. St Anne's Close Highgate has a simple, self-effacing group of 1950–2 by *Walter Segal*, an indicator of his later involvement with low-cost housing. Several experiment with the innovative planning that their designers were at the same time exploring in public housing, notably *Howell* and *Amis*'s narrow fronted row in South Hill Park, Hampstead (1953–6), and *Neave Brown*'s unusually planned terrace in Winscombe Street, Highgate (1963–4). The fringes of Highgate, then still quite rural, attracted a number of individual houses in the 1950s. Fitzroy Park has a rewarding collection, including a Scandinavian timber-clad house by *Erhard Lorenz* (1958), and there is another little cluster off Bacons Lane, among them several by *Leonard Manasseh* of 1961. The Hampstead fringe of Barnet has three good houses by *Patrick Gwynne*, one in Spaniards End (1959), and two of the 1960s in Golders Green. 1960s houses are fewer and bolder: the other outstanding examples are *James Gowan*'s austere, individualistic Schreiber House, in West Heath Road, Hampstead, of 1962–4, and *John Winter*'s own house with bold Cor-ten steel frame (1966–9), perched on the edge of Highgate cemetery. By this time permission for such *outré* designs was becoming harder to obtain in affluent areas; attention turned to Camden Town, where neglected mews lanes offered opportunities for small, ingeniously planned buildings. The trailblazer here was *Edward Cullinan*'s house in Camden Mews, built for and by himself from 1962, followed by others in Murray Mews on the other side of Camden Square; the most original are those by *Team 4*, *Richard Gibson* and *Tom Kay*. This interest in fitting small buildings into an existing setting was a foretaste of some of the concerns which became dominant in the 1970s (*see* below).

## Public Buildings

Before carrying the story of housing further, the record of PUBLIC BUILDINGS AND SERVICES in the post-war years should be examined. Next to housing PRIMARY SCHOOLS received early attention. This book includes schools built by three different authorities. The one that set the pattern for post-war schoolbuilding was Hertfordshire, two of whose schools of the early 1950s are in East Barnet (then in Herts). These low, light, curtain-walled buildings, made of prefabricated parts, are as different as possible from the tradition of the urban Board School. Post-war Middlesex primary schools, built rapidly to provide for the young families of the outer suburbs, generally continued to use brick, but are quite varied in plan, ranging from the rather barrack-like formal finger plan of

Cuckoo Hall, Edmonton, of 1948, to subtleties such as the circular assembly hall on two levels surrounded by a fan of classrooms (Rokesly, Hornsey, 1952–3).

The LCC's new primary schools in reconstructed areas followed the lead of Hertfordshire in using standardized components for their low buildings, set in more generous play spaces than their predecessors. They are usually too modest to make much contribution to the townscape. The more architecturally striking examples are by outside architects, such as Ashmount, Islington (1957–8 by *H. Cadbury Brown*), with its two-storey curtain wall of frosted green glass facing the street. After 1965 when the Inner London Education Authority took over, more varied planning developed, encouraged from 1966 by the Plowden Report's advocacy of open-plan classrooms. Vittoria, Islington, with split-level planning, was the ILEA's most experimental response. Hugh Myddelton, Finsbury, by *Julian Sofaer*, 1966–70, is a refreshingly individual group with a sturdy presence in a confused area.

SECONDARY SCHOOLS were a major preoccupation after the war. Middlesex County Council's efforts concentrated on SECONDARY MODERNS. Hornsey has two attractive examples with buildings from the 1950s: Fortismere by *Richard Sheppard & Partners* (1952–5) and Highgate Wood by *E. D. Mills & Partners* (1956–7). The LCC's School Plan of 1944–7 included the total reorganization of secondary schools on comprehensive lines, though the most significant early examples were in south London.\* Much of north London had to make do with the unsatisfactory expedient of split sites, often using adapted Board School buildings. The first completely new comprehensive was built by the LCC for the new housing estate at Woodberry Down, Stoke Newington (1950–5). Another early school is Hackney Free and Parochial, by *Howard Lobb & Partners*, 1951, notable for its careful interior detailing. The large 1960s comprehensives by a range of private architects make more of an impact; and are interestingly individual, the most impressive from these years making bold use of concrete. Among those in the area of this volume are Haggerston, Shoreditch, a mature and harmonious work by *Goldfinger*, 1962–7, and Acland Burghley, Kentish Town, by *Howell, Killick, Partridge & Amis*, 1963–6, where the forceful bulk, squeezed onto a small site, is deliberately broken up into recognizable parts. *James Cubitt* built Highbury Grove, Islington, *Stillman & Eastwick-Field* provided well-proportioned additions for Hampstead School, and a powerful composition of brick and concrete buildings at Stoke Newington.

Apart from the University of London (*see* below), few HIGHER and FURTHER EDUCATION buildings were built before the 1960s. Styles progressed predictably from reticent curtain walling in the early 60s, as for Southgate Technical College and the early part of Kingsway College Holborn, to more expressive use of concrete, as at the Polytechnic (later University) of North London, 1966, which has a tough landmark tower on Holloway Road. The most important higher education buildings were those of the UNIVERSITY OF LONDON. Building according to Holden's pre-war plan was resumed in the 1950s, and a series of uneventful brick buildings went up to the N of the Senate House. Various other university buildings were

---

\* See further the Introduction to *London 2: South*.

built, to no coherent plan. An early one was the quietly modern range on the N side of Gordon Square for the Institute of Archaeology (*Booth, Ledeboer & Pinckheard,* 1954–8); a more aggressive contribution was University College's Engineering tower, 1961 by *H. O. Corfiato,* the first UCL building to react against the classical tradition preserved by Sir Albert Richardson, Corfiato's predecessor as Professor of Architecture. Then in 1965 an extension to Holden's precinct was planned by *Denys Lasdun,* enlarging it to the NE. The general principle of extending the university precinct had already been advocated in the County of London plan and by a development plan by Sir Leslie Martin, but the Lasdun scheme was now resisted by those anxious to preserve older Bloomsbury, and not all was built. The buildings completed in 1976 nevertheless compose most effectively around the new pedestrian area N of Russell Square: 122 a library added for the School of Oriental and African Studies, and a long range running N between Russell and Gordon Squares, with a dramatic stepped wing running back from it (more wings were to have been built further N). Through this an upper raised walkway was planned, an idea which Lasdun had developed earlier at the University of East Anglia, another manifestation of the general 1960s enthusiasm for three-dimensional planning and upper pedestrian routes.

Of other major INSTITUTIONAL BUILDINGS only two need mention here. The first, Congress House, TUC Headquarters, a 120 transparent, cleverly lit design of as early as 1948 by *Aberdeen,* is a breath of fresh air when compared with the stodgy traditionalism of so many institutional headquarters, and notable too for its bold *Epstein* War Memorial. Another refreshing post-war design is the 119 Indian YMCA in Fitzroy Square, by *Ralph Tubbs,* 1952.

Post-war reconstruction also required new CHURCHES, many of which had disappeared as a result of war damage. A few were entirely remodelled inside: St Barnabas (now St Clement), Finsbury, by *Norman Haines,* became grandly classical; Butterfield's St Alban Holborn was given a much quieter Gothic interior by *Adrian Scott* (1959–61), with a grand mural on the E wall by *Hans Feibusch* (1966), the most dramatic of his work in post-war churches. The Stations of the Cross and a later exterior sculpture are also by *Feibusch.* St John Clerkenwell was repaired by *Seely & Paget,* who added a curious oval ceremonial stair at the W end leading down to the Priory crypt. *Seely & Paget* also rebuilt St Mary Islington; the plain, light interior has paintings by *Brian Thomas.* Three of the devastated churches of Hackney were rebuilt by *Cachemaille-Day;* the most innovative was St Michael (1959–60), with a shell concrete roof and cheerful paintings and sculpture by *John Hayward.* Outer suburban churches were supplemented by St Alphege, Edmonton, a simple but well-detailed building by *Sir Edward Maufe,* 1957–8. R.C. churches had a new burst of life in the 1960s and were more innovative, encouraged by the liturgical reforms inaugurated by Vatican II. St Joan of Arc, Islington, by *Walters & Kerr Bate,* is an angular modern version of Gothic with lively gabled front and slim tower (1960–4). St Aloysius, St Pancras (*Burles Newton & Partners,* 1966–8), and two later 1960s churches by *Gerard Goalen,* St Gabriel, Holloway, and St Thomas More, Hampstead, make little external show but have quiet, contemplative interiors of interesting curved shape. The Poor Clare Monastery at Arkley by *Owen Fogarty*, 1968–70, is in a similar spirit. An unusually flamboyant Nonconformist building is the United Reformed St John, New Barnet (*Finlayson* and *Langlands*, 1967–9), with dramatic sloping roof; a more noticeable trend after the formation of the United Reformed Church was the demolition of redundant buildings and a practical-minded rebuilding on old sites, with a smaller church combined with low-rent housing. *Peter F. Smith*'s United Reformed Church in Stoke Newington (1969–70) showed the way. In older buildings the most remarkable new furnishings are those in the Polish church in Devonia Road, Islington: stained glass by *Adam Bunsch* of 1939–45 and bronze Stations of the Cross by *J. Z. Henelt*. The outstanding stained glass of the 1950s is the E window of St Michael, Highgate, by *Evie Hone* (1954). Other notable windows can be found in St Mark, Hampstead, by *John Hayward* and *Brian Thomas*.

LIBRARIES received much attention after the war. The aim here was to produce light, friendly buildings, where all ages would be welcomed and a range of facilities provided, including exhibition and meeting spaces, and a children's library. Holborn Library in Theobalds Road, by *Sidney Cook*, the borough architect, was a trendsetter when opened in 1960, with its cheerful decoration, contemporary furnishing, and accommodation spread over four floors. The airy two-storey building by *Ley & Jarvis* at Hornsey, and the skilfully planned library in St John Street Finsbury by *C. L. Franck*, are in a similar spirit; both intended as borough libraries before the changes of 1965. Some smaller branch libraries in the outer boroughs are similarly appealing: Ridge Avenue Edmonton (1959–63), which is combined with a clinic, has an exciting timber roof; other good examples are at Friern Barnet and Edgware. On a different scale is the more monumental concrete group at Swiss Cottage by *Basil Spence*. The library and swimming pool were planned as a single composition, built 1962–4, which was to have formed part of a large civic complex for Hampstead; the rest of the plan was abandoned when the borough became part of Camden.

Plans for TOWN HALLS were disrupted by borough reorganization. Post-war ideals embraced the concept of the civic centre which would include cultural facilities as well as council premises, but this was rarely achieved. The abortive schemes for Edmonton and Hampstead have already been mentioned. At Wood Green *Sir John Brown, Henson & Partners* planned a complex with a spacious foyer leading to council chamber and meeting rooms, with public hall and library in a range behind, but only the front part was built (1955–8) before interest shifted elsewhere when the borough became part of Haringey. Enfield began a handsome town hall in 1957–61, by *Eric G. Broughton & Assocs.*, but this was overpowered by the tower of offices added in 1972–5 after it became the administrative centre of the new borough.

PUBLIC BUILDINGS of the 1960s by government agencies included a rebuilt Euston Station, 1962–8, a low, indifferent substitute for past glories, and a new addition to the skyline, the slim cylinder of the Post Office Tower (later British Telecom). It was joined by other TALL BUILDINGS. Up to this time tall offices had only occasionally been built outside the City, but developers now began to look westward. Several towers emerged as an outcome of road improvements: the first was the brash zigzag of *Seifert*'s controversial Centre Point at the junction of Tottenham Court Road and New Oxford Street (1959–66), followed a little later by the similarly detailed but lower Space House, off Kingsway (1964–8). At the N end of Tottenham Court Road a much larger group was the extensive but more neutrally curtain-walled Euston Centre (*Sidney Kaye, Eric Firmin & Partners* 1962–72). Official encouragement at this time for the relocation of offices outside central London also led to a scatter of blocks in the outer suburbs near good transport connections, as at Whetstone and New Barnet.

## NORTH LONDON FROM THE 1970S

In the 1970s–80s three strands came together to affect the appearance of north London. The first was the growing disillusion with very large redevelopment schemes and tall blocks of flats. The second was the increasing strength of the conservation movement, and the third was a rediscovery and reworking of older building forms and styles.

In the north London suburbs ALTERNATIVES TO HIGH RISE for family housing were already being explored in the 1960s, mostly on very large sites, as at Marquess Road, mentioned above. From the late 60s a new approach developed, which involved tackling smaller areas, and integrating them more carefully with existing buildings. Islington and Haringey were among the London boroughs which led the way, employing a large number of outside architects who produced an interesting range of solutions for small, awkward sites, bearing in mind the need for better security and more private space than had been provided in earlier, larger schemes. In Islington notable early schemes of this kind are the tiny row of houses with gardens, off Popham Street, by *Andrews, Sherlock & Partners* (designed 1968) and the housing behind Barnsbury Street by *Pring, White & Partners* in Barnsbury (1969–71). In Haringey there is a wide variety of small groups of low terraces and flats from *c.* 1971 onwards, especially in South Tottenham around Seven Sisters Station and along a disused railway line between Seven Sisters and Wood Green Common. An especially attractive group is the sheltered housing at St Michael's Terrace, Wood Green Common, by *D. Hayhow*, completed in the 1980s. A similar concern to fit in tactfully is seen in the sheltered housing by *Neylan & Ungless* at Danby Court, near Gentleman's Row, Enfield (1974–8), and in the houses and flats by *Colquhoun & Miller* deliberately keeping in scale, in Caversham

Housing, Brownlow Road, Hackney, by Colquhoun & Miller, completed 1984 (third and fourth from the left) within nineteenth-century context. Elevation

Road, Kentish Town (1976–9), and later on, at Brownlow Road, Hackney (1981–4) where they reinterpret the shared pediment motif used in the early C19. Regrettably few private developers were similarly sympathetic; the best examples are *Ted Levy, Benjamin & Partners*' small groups in Hampstead, Highgate and Camden Town.

Infill schemes were sometimes devised in conjunction with the rehabilitation of older houses, as in the case of Barnsbury, just mentioned, or, as at South Tottenham, they might be an expression of a more general concern to preserve the low-rise, intricate nature of the existing later C19 neighbourhood. In central London the Comyn Ching Triangle, Seven Dials, was a pioneering transformation of a dilapidated group of Georgian terraces and shops (from 1977) by *Farrell Grimshaw Partnership*, demonstrating that a tactful integration of old and new could also be achieved with commercial buildings. Sensitivity to context responded to the growing pressure to preserve not only individual 'listed' buildings, but the historic character of an area (an approach which was encouraged by the creation of Conservation Areas from the later 1960s). This was assisted from the later 1970s by the encouragement of low-rise building through a less stringent approach to housing densities and by a general winding down of local-authority housing programmes.

CONSERVATION of older buildings was a movement which gathered strength gradually. After the war there were some important repair jobs at major damaged sites, together with what might now be described as 'contextual infilling'. At Gray's Inn *Sir Edward Maufe* tactfully restored hall, chapel, and chambers, and rebuilt the early C20 library in his own Regency-Swedish manner. At the Charterhouse *Seely & Paget* were in charge, rather freely restoring the damaged Master's Court to emphasize its Tudor character. Historic groups of this kind fell within the accepted canon of buildings to be preserved; those of the later C19 were another matter. Nash's work was on the borderline. In the end his Regents Park terraces were repaired, but his humbler squares E of the park (damaged although not destroyed in the war, but already earmarked for clearance) were swept away. Not only were terraces unregarded, so too were major C19 architectural works. The famous conservation battles over these individual buildings took place in the 1960s. In north London they were about railway stations: lost at Euston, demolished in 1960–1, won at St Pancras, which was listed in 1967, although it took another ten years for British Rail to accept that it should be preserved (and despite many plans, the hotel building is still disused at the time of writing). Large parts of Holborn also became battlegrounds: in 1964 the streets S of Great Russell Street were designated for a huge extension for the British Museum; in 1965 other parts of Bloomsbury were threatened by Lasdun's proposals for the University of London. Several of the Bloomsbury terraces disappeared for the University, but with the eventual decision in 1974 to move the British Library site to St Pancras, the area S of the Museum was preserved. By the mid 70s a change of attitude was widespread. Government funding became available for rehabilitation work, while growing gentrification of run-down C19 housing in Islington and Camden led to repair by private owners. In Islington the borough began to tackle the much reviled Milner Square in

1973, with remarkable results. In 1975 repairs at last began on the scandalously neglected early c18 terraces of the Rugby estate in Holborn. Many smaller battles fought by local residents elsewhere overturned longstanding plans for comprehensive clearance which had blighted whole streets. Instead, constructive efforts were made to retrieve the character of areas eroded by unsympathetic alterations or neglect. In Holborn, Fitzrovia was one of the areas to benefit in this way in the 1980s, as did Seven Dials, where a replica of the late c17 central pillar was installed in 1989 by the Seven Dials Monuments Trust. In the 1990s public money was directed toward poorer, problematic areas further E. The effects of this are evident in Hackney, where parts of Dalston and Shoreditch began to be dramatically transformed through repair, new building and public art. The King's Cross area is likely to be the place to watch in the early c21. Elsewhere, lottery funding of the late 1990s is beginning to make a difference to parks and public spaces, for example along the line of the New River.

A new approach to industrial buildings also began to develop in the 1970s. In 1975 a compromise rescued the façade of Booths Gin Distillery in Clerkenwell for re-erection; the establishment of the Clerkenwell Workshops the same year in the former London School Board warehouses reversed a policy that replaced industrial building by housing and demonstrated that there could be a future for redundant buildings of this kind. But the general decline of London's manufacturing industries could not be halted. By the later 70s industrial buildings in Clerkenwell were beginning to be converted to offices (Alan Baxter's engineering firm was an early arrival in Cowcross Street in 1979). In Camden Town, also in the 1970s, *Sheppard Robson* adapted industrial buildings for their offices, and a piano factory in Fitzroy Road was converted to housing (an early example). In Endell Street (Holborn) on the edge of Covent Garden *Rock Townsend* converted Lavers & Barraud's c19 stained-glass works to offices (1983). Larger buildings posed more problems; ambitious and successful schemes were the eventual rescue of the Royal Agricultural Hall in Islington as the Business Design Centre (1983–5), partial refurbishment of the even bigger Alexandra Palace (1980–90), and the sensitive conversion and rebuilding of the old Royal Free Hospital, Islington, for housing (1987–92), a pattern followed on other hospital sites in the 90s.

CONVERSIONS and adaptations in the 1980s–90s became bolder and more radical, particularly during the boom in the 1980s. Older offices were hollowed out to provide a central toplit atrium in American fashion: an early example (1980–5) was *Sheppard Robson's* remodelling of *Belcher's* Edwardian Royal London House on Finsbury Square. This device was particularly used for City offices, but was applied elsewhere, as at the Crowndale Centre, community offices at Camden Town, created by *Rock Townsend* in 1987–9 in an old Post Office building. A burst of 1980s regeneration around the Battlebridge Basin near King's Cross produced some flagship office conversions of industrial buildings, notably Porters South by *Fitch Benoy*. Such efforts diminished in the more stringent 1990s, when throughout London conversion to housing became the most common solution for a wide miscellany of unused buildings, from churches and hospitals to warehouses and offices. Another type of adaptation which became

popular from the late 1980s was the roofing over of courtyards. This
was achieved most elegantly and economically with tensile fabric,
at Store Street, Holborn, for Imagination, by *Herron Associates*
(1988–9). On a much larger scale is *Foster & Partners'* grand scheme of
1994 for covering the central court of the British Museum with a
curved glazed roof, which will not be completed until after 2000.

The third strand of the 1970s is the change of approach to design.
A common theme was the rejection of the extremes of brutalism of
the previous decade and a general reaction against concrete, but
the alternatives offered in this AGE OF PLURALISM are various. At
one end of the spectrum is the thin stream of the scholarly classical
tradition, represented by *Raymond Erith's* common room at Gray's
Inn (1970–2), at the other the minimalist high-tech version of
modernism, as developed by *Norman Foster*, best represented in our
125 area in the 70s by the *Hopkins'* own house at Hampstead (1975–6),
and later by *Foster & Partners'* building for ITN in Gray's Inn Road
(Holborn, 1989–92) and their plans for the Channel Tunnel Rail
Link station at St Pancras. A similar reductionist approach is found
in a few other architects' houses such as the pair by *Spence & Webster*
in Belsize Park. Between these extremes are a large range of buildings
which draw eclectically on past traditions. The most monumental
121 example is *Sir Colin St John Wilson's* British Library, 1978–97, the
greatest national building of the later C20, an impressive, lovingly
crafted creation which is given resonance by its allusions to the
architect's favourite Modernist heroes, and to other sources as well.
Deliberate homage to early Modernism can also be found in a number of lesser buildings of the early 70s (some of Camden's public
housing in Kentish Town, *Georgie Wolton's* studios at Cliff Road).
Inspiration from older architects, particularly Soane's handling of
light and space, is also a theme that can be traced, for example at St
Alban's Church Centre, Holborn (1989–91, *Anthony Richardson
Partnership*). *John Melvin's* work in Islington makes effective use of
the traditions of older architecture, for example his Edwardian
inspired flats in Essex Road.

A more populist approach was the revival of vernacular imagery:
pitched roofs and friendly tile and brick surfaces; the classic expression of this taste in London was RMJM's Hillingdon Civic Centre
of 1973–8 (*see London 3: North West*). A similar concern can be seen
in the buildings for Middlesex Polytechnic (now University) at Cat
Hill, Southgate, by *HKPA*, 1972–9, at the library at High Barnet
(1985–9), and in a more jazzed-up form, at Islington's numerous
small neighbourhood centres of 1981 onwards, an extreme reaction
against town hall pomp and bureaucracy. A more localized approach
was the adaptation for new housing of motifs from the C19 vernacular
of debased Italianate used by C19 London house builders. *Hunt
Thompson* made a speciality of this, as at The Mothers' Square,
Hackney (1987–90). An alternative is the quaint folksy detail adopted
for some Islington borough housing of the 1980s (as in Hillrise
Road). Another approach was an industrial aesthetic allied to high-
tech traditions, as at *Nicholas Grimshaw's* Sainsbury's, Camden Town
128 (1985–8), where there are also flats fitted on to the back of the site
which are self-consciously dressed up as space-age capsules.

Dressing up is indeed the great characteristic of POSTMODERNISM,
whose influence, in its American-inspired form, began to be seen

during the 1980s, chiefly on commercial buildings in the City. Flamboyant expressions in north London are by *Chassay Wright* at Battlebridge near King's Cross, and by *Rock Townsend* at the Angel, Islington (1987–91). The liberating influence of Postmodernism's free use of colour, texture and shape can be seen in a number of ways from the later 1980s. The inventive creations of *CZWG* range from an eccentric private house in Britton Street, Clerkenwell, to subtly detailed mews houses N of King's Cross (both 1987). Witty 127 quotation is another game, played effectively by *Allies & Morrison*'s Grimaldi Park House, Pentonville Road (1988–90), offices with a frontage recalling the C18 church they replaced. On a more serious level is the church of St Paul, Harringay, by *Inskip & Jenkins* 129 (1988–93), which employs striped brickwork and simple geometric shapes to powerful effect. An alternative approach, relying resolutely on plain surfaces and good proportions in the tradition of the Modern Movement, was continued by some architects, such as *Bertram Dinnage* in Haringey; and there are many good small housing schemes, e.g. by *Avanti Architects*, *Jestico & Whiles*, *Levitt Bernstein Associates* and *Anthony Richardson Partnership*, which use a variety of materials in a straightforward but original manner. By the 1990s such building activity was almost always undertaken for housing associations. The GLC's housing role ceased with the abolition of the council in 1986 by the Conservative government, and the boroughs were given ever-diminishing funds for new building. Attention focused instead on refurbishment of older housing stock (which was further reduced by the introduction of tenants' 'right to buy'). A trendsetting example was *Hunt Thompson Associates*' transformation of Hackney's 1930s Lea View estate in Clapton (1980–2), given private gardens and jazzed up with colourful trimmings.

What can be added about BUILDING TYPES of this period? For many, and especially the two largest categories, offices and housing, any style was possible, as will already be clear. There was a fashion from the 1980s for some PUBLIC SERVICE BUILDINGS to adopt cheerful Postmodern trimmings, as in the somewhat brash and colourful exteriors for the Police (Stoke Newington Road, Hackney) and Fire Brigade (Upper Street, Islington). Health-care buildings are generally more restrained, adopting a deliberately friendly image; there is a striking shift from the impersonal 1960s tower of the Royal Free Hospital (1968–75) to the low, homely pitched-roofed buildings of Homerton Hospital, Hackney, arranged around small courtyards (*YRM* 1980–7). An interesting new type is DOCTORS' SURGERIES, which inspired a variety of carefully thought-out buildings, free from clichés, generally based on rooms around a central toplit waiting area. Good examples are by *Douglas Stephen & Partners* at Highgate and by *Pentarch* at Adelaide Road, Hampstead. *MacCormac Jamieson Prichard*'s Canning Crescent (1994), Wood Green, is an attractive, imaginatively designed Day Centre (another new health care category). Leisure and sports buildings are more numerous than in the 60s, but so far rarely of distinction. In the 90s one can discern a move away from flamboyant expression toward quieter brick exteriors and well-handled interior spaces, as in a number of EDUCATIONAL and CULTURAL BUILDINGS. *Rock Townsend*'s Southgate School (1990–2) uses pale brick but still makes quite a show; more restrained are *Nicholas Hare*'s sensitive Brunei Gallery and *Troughton McAslan*'s

Clore Management Centre, both at London University, likewise the ambitious Shoreditch Community College (*Perkins Ogden* and *Hampshire County Architects*), where elegant buildings are set off by a generous quantity of excellent artwork, including gates by *Matthew Fedden*, a sunken garden with pool, by *Susanna Heron*, and much else. In 1998 grander Lottery-funded cultural buildings are also beginning to take shape; Sadlers Wells Theatre (*RHWL* and *Nicholas Hare*) is among the first.

The sponsorship of ART in public places has been uneven. In the 1950s the LCC encouraged public sculpture on its new housing estates: a rare north London example is 'The Neighbours' by *Siegfried Charoux*, at Highbury Quadrant. Post-war schools also received works of art, but few remain (a good mural by *Fred Millett* at Danegrove, East Barnet, has been boarded over). The few civic buildings built by the boroughs in the 1960s were complemented by sculpture: the most progressive collection is at Swiss Cottage, Hampstead, where there is a sculpture of Freud by *Oscar Nemon*, a more abstract figure by *F. E. McWilliam*, and a patterned concrete wall by *William Mitchell*. Mitchell also contributed a similar type of decorative wall to the North London Polytechnic (now University) in Holloway Road. Elsewhere a Festival of Britain aesthetic continued: Enfield Civic Centre has a bronze 'Enfield Beast' by *R. Bentley Claughton* and an appliqué wall panel by *Gerald Holtom;* Hornsey Library a fountain with bronze figure by *T. E. Huxley-Jones*. From the 1970s commercial buildings were occasionally given some eye-catching sculpture, but there is not much of this in north London: a notable example is the steel-and-cable composition by *William Pye* at Kings Cross House, Pentonville Road (1974). The artist best represented in north London is *Sir Eduardo Paolozzi*. His works range from the transformation of Tottenham Court Road Station with intensely colourful tiles (planned 1980), to major sculptures. Piscator, 1980, outside Euston Station is the earliest, a large, semi-abstract form. 'The Artist as Hephaestos' at Bracton House, High Holborn, 1987, is an arresting self-portrait on a speculative office block; more apt for its position is the monumental figure of Newton outside the new British Library (1997). The Library forecourt is also to have a sculpture by *Antony Gormley*; in the foyer is a major tapestry designed by *R. B. Kitaj*, 'If Not, Not', on the theme of T. S. Eliot's *Waste Land*. Churches have been the traditional place for interior works of art, but there is not very much to single out from the 1970s onwards. There are interesting windows in St Paul R.C., Wood Green (*Moira Forsyth, Carmel Cauchi*), and at St Monica R.C., Southgate (*Carmel Cauchi*). St Edmund R.C., Edmonton, has two striking abstract designs by *Mark Angus*, 1982. The most original furnishings of the 1980s are the exceptional works in porphyry by *Steven Cox* in St Paul, Harringay (Hornsey).

The 1990s saw an energetic growth of interest in public art, allied to a deliberate policy of enhancing open spaces. Straightforward, recognizable themes with popular appeal were preferred to abstract compositions: especially successful are the decorative railings by *Jane Ackroyd* at Old Royal Free Square, Islington. Public art of this kind has proliferated in Hackney, where artists' studios began to multiply from the 1980s. The playful sculptures and railings provided by *Freeform Artworks* (Stonebridge Common, London Fields and 130 elsewhere) which brighten some long-neglected areas provide a cheerful note on which to end.

## GEOLOGY AND BUILDING MATERIALS

### BY ERIC ROBINSON

The geology of Middlesex and north London, like its topography, is uncharacteristically subdued and almost subtle. It consists of two simple elements, a foundation of *solid* rock, and a *superficial* cover of sands and gravels principally found in the valleys.

Beneath the entire area, the Chalk forms a solid basement which rises to a surface outcrop to the w of the Colne Valley, to the N of Watford, and the line of the Great North Road beyond Potters Bar. Within this curving arc, the Chalk dips below the surface to form a shallow basin below Greater London so that its top surface lies some 200 ft (61 metres) below Camden Town, overlain by a thickness of Tertiary sands and clays. In the past, the Chalk has provided building material in the form of hard chalk ('clunch'), but more especially the hard and irregularly shaped flints which occur as discontinuous seams throughout its thickness. At one time, flint was worked from shallow mine shafts around Pinner and Hatch End, but has always been more readily available from the weathered top surface of the Chalk ('clay-with-flints') or from the river gravels within the basin.

The Tertiary rocks which fill the basin consist of Thanet Sands (up to 20 ft, 6 metres, in thickness), Reading Beds (again up to 20 ft), London Clay (as much as 200 ft, 61 metres, in places), and finally Bagshot Sands of up to 30 ft (9 metres) in thickness capping the Middlesex heathlands. Before human activities took a hand, these Tertiary rocks must have given rise to well-wooded sandy heaths (the Reading Beds), or heavy-clay-floored valleys (the London Clay), while the isolated higher hill cappings of heathland correspond with the Bagshot Sands outcrop.

Of the Tertiary beds, the Reading Beds were ancient river deposits and so consist of sands and gravels, mainly flints derived from the Chalk below, with less frequent bands of clay. Locally, patches of flint gravel have been cemented by siliceous springs to produce the distinctive pebble rock known as Hertfordshire Puddingstone, used as a building material in the St Albans area. A speciality of south Hertfordshire, rocks of a similar kind and origin could occur in the Colne Valley and have provided the dark-brown pebbly sandstone seen in Pinner church, or the sarsen-type green sandstone seen in the tower of the church at Harlington (for both *see London 3: North West*). Such rocks can develop patchily in beds of unconsolidated sand as groundwaters rich in silica or iron salts permeate and bond together the sand grains and create an extremely hard rock.

The London Clay is a marine mud deposit which had a great influence upon topography and buildings in Middlesex, for as a rock type, this clay has both a high plasticity and a dynamic response to weathering. (Exposed to air, sulphide minerals within the fresh clay oxidize and expand, producing a visible upheaval of the ground.)

Hot summers produce drying out and deep cracking of the surface, allowing penetration of moisture in succeeding wetter periods. So is initiated a continuing cycle of ground movement which, even in the more modest hill slopes of north London, can produce worrying landslip and subsidence. In Middlesex, the London Clay was always a prime source of brick-making clay (Hampstead Heath, Copenhagen Fields, Edgware).

Within the London Clay, from time to time, nodules of hard, lime-rich clays occur in thin seams. Internally, they are calcite. When the clay weathers, these septarian nodules accumulate on the surfaces of the open country of north Barnet and Enfield Chase from where they were collected and used in churches in the northern part of the present study area. The tower of Monken Hadley church is a notable example.

The *superficial* rocks of Middlesex and north London are principally a legacy of the Ice Age. Roughly 150,000 years ago, glaciers from the north came to a halt in the Vale of St Albans, with a southernmost lobe pushing down the Dollis Brook into Finchley. The ice left behind a sticky, pebbly clay ('chalky boulder clay') which runs through Finchley to end beyond the North Circular Road in the cemeteries of East Finchley. Further N a well-marked ridge of pebbly gravel extending from Chipping Barnet through Arkley, which we can project westwards to Brockley Hill, Stanmore (*London 3: North West*), and Bushey (*Herts*), represents a water-washed moraine of the same pebbly clay and the same ice sheet.

The melt waters of these great ice sheets were responsible for the second category of superficial rocks, the sands and gravels of the Thames drainage in west and north-west Middlesex, spread out as broad, flat-surfaced terraces extending beneath Uxbridge, Heathrow, Hayes, Ealing, and Kensington. The deposits of ancient Thames watercourses, the principal materials of the gravels, are flints either washed from the Chalk outcrops of the Chilterns and the North Downs, or derived from the older gravels and sands of the Tertiary solid geology described above. Undoubtedly the terrace deposits have long been the source of the flints used in medieval churches and grander buildings, just as they are the continuing source of bulk material for foundation work, ballast, and ready-mix concrete in the present age.

It follows from what has been said of the geology of Middlesex and the London Basin that the area is lamentably short of good-quality building stone. For this reason, Norman masons naturally looked to the Caen Stone from Normandy which they had been accustomed to use for work of importance. In the Lea Valley the major example is the early Norman Waltham Abbey, just over the Middlesex boundary in Herts, for which a prodigious quantity of Caen stone was imported, still visible in its truncated abbey church. Later, they made do with the gritty limestone collectively known as 'Kentish Rag', limestones ranging from shelly ragstone from Kent through to stone of freestone quality, Reigate Stone from north Surrey. Easy to work and dress into all forms of mouldings, Reigate often proved too readily weathering for external use and has often been replaced by other stone. No such weakness characterizes the limestones from Lincolnshire, originally brought into London by the Romans and used also in the well-known C12 carved doorways of Harlington and Harmondsworth churches (Hillingdon, *London 3:*

*North West*). The shelly Jurassic oolite stone in both cases is thought to be Barnack Rag quarried from the area a few miles s of Stamford (*Lincs*).

Much later, Bath Stone and Cotswold and Oxfordshire oolite arrived by canal from the West Country for c18 and early c19 work, mainly the stone dressings to churches. Later still, when the Great Western Railway made the same stone still cheaper to procure, more and more of the deep orange freestone appeared in large houses, municipal halls, and offices as well as newer parish churches in London suburbs.

Ancient gravels of the Ice Age Thames underlie Hackney and Edmonton and provided occasional blocks of iron-cemented gravel and sand in older churches of those areas. The Lea Valley itself is a testimony to the Ice Age. Some two miles wide between Stoke Newington and Walthamstow, it was cut when melt-waters flooded southwards from the ice fronts of Ware and Hertford.

Sand and gravel aggregate and the new ubiquitous flint derived from the Chalk have always been the available material for London and Chiltern builders. The aggregate forms a brown puddingstone in south-west Middlesex and can occur in quite large lumps (see the base courses to the great barn at Harmondsworth). Further N it takes the form of a darker and denser carstone, hard enough to be used for quoins, as in Pinner church; iron-cemented sands from the Bagshot Sand outcrop in Highgate provided the striking brown sand rock in Hornsey Church tower. The local builders' handling of the materials produced fabric and styles just a shade different from those found a short distance away in Buckinghamshire, Hertfordshire, Suffolk and Essex where in all respects builders started with the same disadvantages.


# PREHISTORIC AND ROMAN ARCHAEOLOGY*

## BY JOANNA BIRD

The founding of London shortly after the Roman invasion of A.D. 43 established a focus for trade, government and general human activity which has been growing and changing almost continuously ever since. This growth has obscured much of the natural landscape of the area, and it is difficult now to see that Greater London actually incorporates parts of several distinct regions. Earlier patterns of settlement have been largely destroyed and much of our knowledge of London's archaeology is dependent on chance finds and imprecise records, and on comparison with more fortunate areas. Even those parts – mainly in the outer boroughs – where information does survive are under constant threat from building, and modern archaeological effort is almost completely devoted to 'rescue' work.

Despite the problems, however, it is still possible to draw some general conclusions about the occupation of the area during prehistoric

---

*This Introduction covers the whole of Greater London. For areas not included in this gazetteer, the relevant volume is indicated by: (*1*) for *London 1: The City of London*, (*2*) for *London 2: South*, (*3*) for *London 3: North West*, and (*5*) for *London 5: East and the Docklands*.

and Roman times from the distribution of finds and settlement sites. During the Palaeolithic and Mesolithic periods, light woodland and river banks were favoured for their game, fowl, fish and fresh water; the presence of flint for tools may also have had an influence. From the Neolithic onwards, the need was for soils that could be easily cleared and farmed using primitive implements, with good drainage and abundant water supply; the light soils over gravels (notably in west and north-east London) and along the springline of the North Downs were consistently chosen, while the intractable and densely forested London Clay was as consistently avoided.

Several features of London's archaeology are of particular importance, and are discussed in more detail below. Briefly, they include the wealth of Lower Palaeolithic material, the complex of Neolithic monuments in the Heathrow area, the presence of what must have been a major Late Bronze Age metalworking centre, and the evidence for some of the earliest Saxon settlements in England; while the Thames in west London has produced a range and quantity of Bronze and Iron Age metalwork that is without parallel.

Now for GEOLOGY. The basic shape of Greater London's landscape is formed by a fold in the Chalk, which has produced ridges to the N (the Chilterns) and S (the North Downs), and left a wide basin in the centre through which the Thames now flows. Much of the Chalk has been subsequently covered by later geological deposits, producing a variety of soils and surface cover. The first, consisting of a series of sand, clay and pebble beds, which provide relatively light soils of varying utility where they reach the surface, occur mainly in south-east London, and there is a springline at the junction with the Chalk. The London Clay, deposited subsequently by a warm sea, forms much of the land surface, notably in north Middlesex and across the centre of the southern portion. It is heavy and impermeable, and naturally carries dense forest. In places it is overlain by sands mixed with clay and pebbles which form a dry light soil with springs at the junction with the clay: Hampstead and Highgate in north London are instances of this. The most recent geological deposits consist of gravels, mainly laid down during the later Ice Ages. In particular, the wanderings of the Thames have deposited a complex series of gravel terraces, forming a broad band beside the modern course of the river. Springs occur at the junction with the Clay, and light, easily worked soils are produced; the upper levels of the gravels are often a clay-like loam ('brick-earth'), naturally wooded but not difficult to clear.

The area is roughly divided by the Thames, and a major feature is the number of smaller rivers draining into it from N and S; those in the central area, such as the Fleet, have now been led into the artificial drainage system. The presence of these rivers and the flatness of the river basin has meant that much of the area bordering the Thames is naturally marshy: places such as Southwark, Lambeth, and Westminster, and large tracts of east London, would not have been habitable until relatively recently. In these areas, the river gravels are overlain by silts. Southwark was first drained during the Roman period, and the problem of securing London from flooding continues to exercise the authorities today.

The earliest traces of human activity in Greater London belong to the PALAEOLITHIC (Old Stone Age), ranging from 450,000 to 12,000 B.C. This was also the period of the later Ice Ages, and it is unlikely that the area was continuously habitable. The wide variations of climate during and between the glaciations are reflected in the animal remains: those of cave bear, mammoth, and reindeer indicate arctic and sub-arctic conditions, those of the hippopotamus show hot conditions. The archaeology of this immense period is complicated by the contemporary geology. The course and depth of the Thames varied considerably, and a series of gravel terraces was laid down by the river: their number, sequence, and chronology are not yet fully understood, and it is from them that most of the Palaeolithic finds have come.

The Palaeolithic can be broadly divided into three phases, distinguished by the types of tools in use: they are the Lower (450,000–100,000 B.C.), with flint axes and crude flint flakes; the Middle (100,000–40,000 B.C.), with more advanced flake tools; and the Upper (40,000–12,000 B.C.), with fine flint blades (it is to this last phase that the painted caves of France and Spain belong). Almost all the material in Greater London comes from the Lower Palaeolithic; the few Middle and Upper Palaeolithic finds probably represent the debris of brief hunting sorties. The Upper Palaeolithic coincided with the last Ice Age, and it is probable that the area, lacking natural shelters such as caves, was largely uninhabitable.

Some of the most important Lower Palaeolithic sites in Europe lie along the Lower Thames Valley, and some of the richest are within Greater London: at Yiewsley-West Drayton (3), Ealing-Acton (3), Stoke Newington, and Crayford (2). Other concentrations occur in the West End, at Wandsworth, and along the springline of the North Downs. These sites would have been the camps of small hunting communities, and animal remains have been found with tools at Southall (3), King's Cross and Stoke Newington. Acton, Stoke Newington and Crayford have produced evidence, in the form of flint waste, for the manufacture of implements. Other evidence is fragmentary and tantalizing: a few birch stakes woven with clematis and fern, perhaps a shelter, from Stoke Newington, and burnt stones, possibly a hearth, at West Drayton.

The MESOLITHIC (Middle Stone Age), c. 12,000–4,000 B.C., followed the last glaciation, and for much of the period Britain was still joined to the continent. Initial sub-arctic or tundra conditions were succeeded by forest, and the climate became warmer and wetter; arctic fauna were replaced by forest animals such as boar and deer. The typical tools of the period are small neatly worked flint 'microliths', made to be mounted in bone or wooden shafts as hunting and fishing weapons, saws, and scrapers. Heavy flint axes ('Thames picks'), antler hammers, and tools of bone (e.g. harpoons) were also produced. There are a number of known settlements where hunters and fishers had their camps, including sites where flint waste indicates working, and one site, at Twickenham (2), where a midden of shells and tools was found. The main areas of occupation lie beside rivers, on the less heavily wooded soils, and along the springline of the North Downs, including Hampstead Heath, Harefield Moor (3), Ham Fields (3), Wimbledon Common (2), and Putney Heath (2).

The NEOLITHIC (New Stone Age), c. 4,000–1,800 B.C., saw the introduction of agriculture and pastoralism, which spread gradually from the Near East and the Balkans and reached Britain during the fourth millennium. The process must have been slow, with a considerable overlap between old hunter-gatherer and new farmer. Some at least of the Neolithic settlements would have been the permanent homes of farmers, who would for the first time have begun to change their environment by clearance and by sowing and stock-rearing. In the London area, most of the known Neolithic settlement is concentrated on easily drained and worked soils, the gravels of west London and the sands along the springline of the Downs, where water and flint were abundant. Settlements include Putney (2), Harlington and Harmondsworth (3), Twickenham (2), Brentford (3), Rainham (5), and Baston Manor (near Hayes, 2); some have also produced flint-working debris. Flint tools were modified to new needs (e.g. sickles) and a characteristic axe type, of polished stone or flint, was in use: some of these were traded considerable distances, and the London area has produced axes originating in the Lake District and the Alps. A further innovation at this period was pottery; despite its technical crudity – it was handmade, and probably fired in bonfires – distinct forms and decorative styles can be recognized. A quantity of Neolithic pottery indicates a further settlement at Kingston (2).

In addition to settlements, there are more substantial monuments of the Neolithic, of which there was clearly an important complex in the Heathrow area and westwards beyond the Greater London boundary in the areas of Staines, Runnymede, Stanwell and Shepperton. Henges, roughly circular ritual enclosures marked by a ditch within a bank (and sometimes containing rings of stone or wooden uprights), are the most famous Neolithic monuments, and there are remains of hengiform enclosures at Heathrow and East Bedfont. Earlier Neolithic causewayed camps (ditched enclosures with access causeways) probably served a social and religious purpose; none have so far been identified within Greater London, but there is at least one nearby, at Yeoveney (Middlesex). Another typical Neolithic monument was the cursus – a long, straight earthwork distinguished by two parallel banks and ditches – for which a ritual use is generally suggested. Part of a cursus has been identified running northwards across the western end of Heathrow (3); it was around 66 ft (20 metres) wide and at least $2\frac{1}{2}$ miles (4 km) long, and there is probably a second one crossing it. Another long earthwork traced at Heathrow was probably a mortuary enclosure. The characteristic burial rite was inhumation beneath a long, gently wedge-shaped 'long barrow': this might contain galleries, chambers, or simply burials, of considerable variety, and was normally flanked by a ditch from which the mound had been excavated. Only the Queen's Butt, on Wimbledon Common (2), is a serious candidate for a long barrow in London, and must, if genuine, have been altered in more recent times.

The main feature of the BRONZE AGE, c. 1800–800 B.C., was the introduction of metals, first copper and later bronze. The metals had to be imported, copper from Wales or Ireland and tin from Cornwall, and implements were made by casting in clay or stone moulds. Imports of metal objects bear witness to trade with the continent, probably carried along the Thames. Flint and stone continued to be of importance, particularly for heavy agricultural tools for which bronze was unsuitable. Several settlement sites are now known, often with associated field systems – e.g. Hayes Common (2), Upminster (5), Uxbridge, East Bedfont, Heathrow and Harmondsworth (3) – and indicate a similar pattern to that of the Neolithic. A group of stone hut circles once visible on Wimbledon Common may have been of this date. A number of log or brushwood trackways, probably all of Bronze Age date, have recently been discovered at marshy sites, including Barking (5), Beckton (5), Erith (2) and Bermondsey (2). Bronze Age burials were placed beneath a round barrow, one of which has been excavated at Teddington (2); there are a number of other possibilities, notably the mound on Parliament Hill and King Henry VIII Mount in Richmond Park. Later Bronze Age cremations, placed in a pottery urn, were sometimes buried in a stone chest beneath a barrow or inserted (like the secondary burial at Teddington) in an older barrow. The latest rite was to bury groups of urns together, and some evidence for such urnfields comes from Yiewsley (3), Acton (3), Kingsbury (3), Coombe (2), Upminster (5), Ilford (5), and Ham Common (2).

Two features of the Bronze Age in the London area are of outstanding interest. One is the high number of Late Bronze Age smiths' hoards (broken implements, copper ingots) found along the edge of the North Downs; these indicate a major metalworking industry in the area, probably trading its goods over considerable distances. The second is the enormous quantity of Middle and Late Bronze Age metalwork recovered from the Thames, mainly in west London. This cannot at present be accounted for as debris from riverside settlements: although there are very likely to be unknown sites – notably in the area of Old England, Brentford (3) – much of this metalwork is likely to represent ritual or funerary offerings to the river deity.

The IRON AGE, c. 800 B.C.–A.D. 43, saw the introduction of iron, a metal more easily obtainable (e.g. from the Weald) and worked than bronze, and with wider uses. Another innovation, later in the period, was currency, in the form both of metal bars and of coinage. Continuing trade with the continent is shown by imported goods, including fine wheel-made and kiln-fired pottery and Mediterranean luxury items such as wine and silverware. The most notable monuments of the period are its 'hill forts' (not necessarily on hills), some at least of which were first constructed in the Late Bronze Age. They were enclosed in single or multiple bank and ditch defences, and vary widely in complexity and sophistication. The best surviving examples in Greater London are the two 'Caesar's Camps', at Keston (2) and Wimbledon (2); more fragmentary ones are known at Edmonton (Bush Hill), Carshalton (2) (Queen Mary's Hospital), and Hadley Wood. Uphall Camp Ilford (5) contains a number of round houses, rectangular buildings, including granaries, and internal enclosures; massive ditches excavated at Woolwich Power Station (2) also enclosed round houses. Settlement sites follow the pattern of preceding periods, with concentrations along the North Downs (e.g. Beddington, Coulsdon and Keston 2) and in the w (notably at Harmondsworth and East Bedfont, both 3 and NE (notably at Upminster, Romford, Rainham and West Ham, all 5). The site of Heathrow Airport (3) included a temple, and there may also have

been a shrine at Hounslow (3). Many settlements formerly classed
as Iron Age can now be seen to have continued into the early Roman
period: the distinction is often difficult with small rural sites of the
first centuries B.C./A.D., in the absence of distinctive pottery. To this
group belong the sites at Charlton (2) and Old Malden (2), and a
number in the Cray valley, as well as the only surviving ancient field
system, on Farthing Down (2). As in the Bronze Age, there is a concentration of metalwork from the Thames in West London, and it
includes some of the finest from Britain: the Battersea shield and the
Waterloo helmet, both now in the British Museum, are among the
best known pieces.

The ROMAN invasion of A.D. 43 and the founding of Londinium
shortly afterwards affected the settlement pattern of the area considerably. A system of major roads radiating from the city to the military
and civil centres of the province attracted new villages, and there is
some evidence for activity in the areas of the London Clay, although
the main rural pattern continued to follow that of earlier periods.
Apart from Londinium, there was an important suburb at Southwark,
and there must have been a bridge across the Thames on the
approximate site of Old London Bridge. Southwark began as a
settlement of small clay and timber buildings laid beside the road to
the bridgehead, but was later occupied by more spacious stone
buildings, including one beneath the cathedral. Another, with finely
painted wall plaster and part of an inscription, lay on the site of
Winchester Palace, Southwark, and may have had some official
function. A well-preserved wooden warehouse has also been found
close to the Roman waterfront. There is evidence for at least two
stone buildings at Westminster, including the abbey site. Large
cemeteries lay outside these centres, notably in Bloomsbury and
Aldgate (1), and along the road to the SE. Settlements include
Brentford (3) on the Silchester road, Brockley Hill (possibly the
Sulloniacae named in the later Roman Antonine Itinerary) on the
Verulamium (St Albans) road, Enfield and Edmonton on the
Lincoln Road, Old Ford (5) where the Colchester road crossed the
Lee, and Crayford (2) (probably Noviomagus) on the Dover Road,
with further probable sites at Croydon on the Lewes road and Merton
on the Chichester road. Settlements at Putney (2) and Fulham (3)
must have served a river crossing, and many smaller roads with
farms and villages must have lain between the major routes; the
most densely occupied areas seem to have been the Cray valley,
the 'brick earths' and gravels to the w and NE, and the edge of the
Downs. There is not a great deal of evidence for villas, in the sense
of large country houses with estates, but there is some, notably at
Keston (2), Beddington (2), Orpington (2), Wanstead (5) and perhaps
Leyton (5). A large building in Greenwich Park has produced a
number of fragmentary inscriptions, and was probably a temple of
some importance. A square stone tower within a ditched enclosure
has been excavated at Shadwell (5) and provisionally identified as a
late Roman Signal Station; another late Roman military-style structure has been found at Uphall Camp Ilford (5). Industrial activity is
represented by two pottery sites, one at Brockley Hill on a large
scale, exporting its wares as far as the military sites in Scotland and
Wales, and a more local one in Highgate Wood, and a tileworks at
Canons Park (3).

The earliest SAXON settlers (early C5 onwards) were probably mercenary soldier-farmers, and their sites ring London to the S, combining a reasonable closeness to the city with good agricultural land. Few actual settlements are known, but cemeteries have been found at Mitcham, Beddington, Croydon and Orpington (all *2*). At the Battle of Crecganford (probably Crayford, *2*), of A.D. 454, described in the Anglo-Saxon Chronicle, the Britons, officially abandoned by the Roman authorities after A.D. 410, were defeated by the Saxons. Later (C6–C7) pagan barrows can still be seen in Greenwich Park and on Farthing Down (*2*), and pagan settlements are also indicated in Middlesex by place-name evidence. The linear earthwork known as Grim's Ditch, which runs across the borough of Harrow, is probably Saxon, and may be a defence against invaders from the north.

# INDUSTRIAL ARCHAEOLOGY

### BY MALCOLM TUCKER

For the industrial archaeologist, north London's interest lies in the transport routes which run north from the capital city, the utilities which have served it over the years and the numerous manufacturing enterprises which once supplied its considerable consumer market.

TRANSPORT BY WATER goes back to ancient times on the RIVER LEA or LEE. Despite Elizabethan aspirations for its improvement, the navigation depended on inefficient flash locks until artificial cuts with pound locks were made in 1767–9, upon the recommendations of *John Smeaton*. Further improvements in the 1850s and 60s allowed 100-ton barges to reach Enfield, encouraging industrial development. Corn and malt were carried from Hertfordshire, and materials such as softwood, hardwoods and metals from the Docks. The tradition of weirs composed entirely of lifting gates, which controlled the water levels through drought and flood, is represented at Newman's Weir, Enfield (rebuilt 1907).

The REGENT'S CANAL of 1812–20 had onward connections to the Midlands, via the Grand Junction Canal at Paddington, both becoming parts of the Grand Union Canal in 1929, but it was a major carrier of local necessities such as coal, building materials, fodder and refuse. With its connection to the Thames at Limehouse it had excellent access to the up-river docks and continued to carry cargoes until the docks closed in the 1960s. It features a reservoir near Hendon, double locks and good bridges best seen at Camden Town, the fine tunnel under Islington hill and several large basins as in Islington. Kingsland Basin in Hackney retains its industrial character in the face of modern housing developments elsewhere.

The first of the trunk RAILWAYS was the London and Birmingham (1833–7), out of Euston. It became the London and North Western Railway and is now part of the West Coast Main Line. The Northern and Eastern Railway (1836–40, later part of the Great Eastern) ran up the Lea Valley, bound for Cambridge. There followed the Great Northern Railway (1846–52) from King's Cross (now the East Coast Main Line) and the Midland Railway's London extension (1863–8)

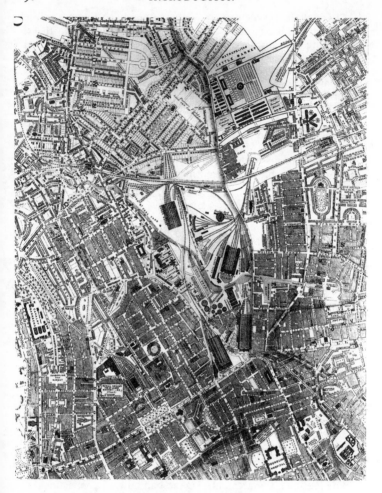

Railway lines around St Pancras and King's Cross, 1891

into St Pancras. An important circumferential line began life as the East and West India Docks and Birmingham Junction Railway (1846–51), mercifully renamed the North London. Various branches were built in the 1860s and 1870s. Cheap workmen's fares on the Great Eastern encouraged later C19 suburban development in the E. The line out of Euston had a long, 1-in-77 climb to pass over the Regent's Canal, requiring stationary winding engines until locomotives grew in power in the 1840s. From similar considerations, the line out of King's Cross has to dive beneath an aqueduct, while St Pancras Station is raised on a viaduct.

Tunnels were necessitated by the rising ground of north London, among them *Robert Stephenson*'s Primrose Hill Tunnel, Camden (1837) with elaborate E portal. The twin-bore elliptical tunnels at Highgate (Hornsey) on the former Finsbury Park to Edgware branch line (1867) and the Dollis Viaduct on the same line at Mill Hill East, are examples of the sophistication of *(Sir) John Fowler*'s work. The demolished Euston Station was the first with iron-roofed train sheds (1837), while its Doric entrance propylaeum (completed 1838) and Great Hall (1846–9) were of unmatched monumentality. King's Cross Station (1851–2) is among the earliest with overall arched roofs, which are functionally expressed in the main façade. Neighbouring St Pancras (1866–8) has the widest spanning train shed in Britain, fronted by *Scott*'s high-Gothic hotel. In the suburbs may be noted the round-arched Italian style of the North London Railway at Camden Road and Hackney (*c.* 1872), the scalloped valances of surviving canopies on the Great Eastern line to Enfield (1872) and late C19 and early C20 details particularly in the Great Northern Company's stations such as Enfield Chase (1910). Neo-Victorian of the 1990s has replaced 1950s functionalism at Hampstead Heath Station, but some post-war railway buildings at West Hampstead and Hackney Downs are now 'listed'. Cricklewood has Midland Railway housing of the 1870s.

The extensive GOODS STATIONS have been largely redeveloped. Camden, of the LNWR, retains its iron-roofed Round House (1847), a fine group of stables (1850s onwards) and the Interchange Warehouse (*c.* 1905) above a canal dock. King's Cross Goods Station of 1850 was then the world's largest, and its substantial buildings remain relatively intact, including goods sheds, granary, goods offices and distinctive coal drops. Bishopsgate Goods Station (Shoreditch) has impressive entrance gates.

A Royal Commission of 1846 decided that surface railways should not enter the central area, s of the New Road. In 1859–63 the world's first UNDERGROUND RAILWAY, the Metropolitan by *(Sir) John Fowler*, was built mainly in cut-and-cover tunnels to link the northern termini with the City at Farringdon Street. It is distinguished by tall buttressed retaining walls in cuttings and the wide vaulted stations beneath the New Road at Great Portland Street and Euston Square. With contortions of alignment, links could be made with the main lines to N and S, and the duplicate City Widened Lines (now Thameslink) were opened in 1866–8, when the neat iron roofs at Farringdon were built.

Electric traction and lifts and new means of tunnelling in the London clay allowed the building of deep underground lines from the end of the C19, the 'tube' network being effectively complete in the central area by 1914. The Great Northern and City reached Finsbury Park in 1904 and, alone of these lines, was sized for main-line rolling stock. The Piccadilly Line was opened to Finsbury Park in 1906 and the 'Hampstead Tube' (now part of the Northern Line) to Golders Green and Highgate Archway in 1907. Both lines have some distinctive red-glazed terracotta stations and coloured-tiled platforms, by *Leslie Green*. The extension above ground to Edgware (1922–4) has neo-Georgian buildings, while the Piccadilly Line Extension to Cockfosters (1930–3) has expressly modern architecture by *Charles Holden* (yet conservative, brick-arched viaducts). The Highgate branch (Hornsey) was extended in 1936–41 to intercept the 1860s–70s branch lines serving Mill Hill East and Barnet, part of a more ambitious scheme that was halted by the war and the Green Belt. Thus large parts of the northern suburbs were given direct rail access to central

London. The Victoria Line was added in 1963–9. During World War
Two, some deep air-raid shelters were built on the Northern Line in
the manner of tube tunnels, intended for future railway lines but
never used as such, as at Store Street (Holborn) and Belsize Park.

POSTAL SERVICES have the unique facility of the Post Office
Railway, a 6½-mile narrow-gauge 'tube' line of 1914–27 centred at
Mount Pleasant (Finsbury). The 1860s Pneumatic Despatch Railway
(St Pancras) was of similar concept, but spurned by the Post Office.

MAIN ROADS are especially prominent in north London. The
Romans built Watling Street, now the Edgware Road, on the
western edge of our area, and Ermine Street, later the 'Old North
Road' through Tottenham in the E. Other, medieval routes climbed
the Northern Heights and one, via Holloway and Highgate Hill,
became the Great North Road which was turnpiked in the early C18.
Modern road building commenced with the New Road (now Euston
Road etc.) from Paddington to Islington, spaciously laid out under
an Act of 1756 as London's first bypass. Highgate Hill was bypassed
in 1813 by the ambitious Archway Road (*see* Hornsey), with a 60 ft-
(18 metre-) deep cutting in lieu of an uncompleted tunnel. New
North Road (1822), Caledonian Road (1826), Junction Road
(*c.* 1813) and the 6 mile (10 km) Finchley Road (1825) were built as
connections to the Great North Road. These roads, together with
Camden Road-Seven Sisters Road (1824–34) were paid for by tolls,
which were mostly abolished in 1864.

NEW STREETS were driven through the older parts of north-
central London in the later C19, viz. New Oxford Street (1844–7),
Farringdon Road (1854–6), Theobalds Road-Clerkenwell Road
(1872–8), Great Eastern Street (1872–6) and Rosebery Avenue
(1885–92), while others were widened. Such opportunities did not
recur.

Horse-drawn cartage and public transport services have left many
remains of late C19 STABLES, often on two or more floors joined by
ramps for economy of land, e.g. the former Whitbread's Brewery
stables in Garrett Street, Finsbury. The first horse buses ran in 1829
along the New Road from Paddington to the Bank. More trams
ran in north London from 1871 and offered cheap fares for workmen, but they were banned in the central area. Highgate Hill had a
cable tramway (1884). ELECTRIC TRAMS ran from 1904 in north
Middlesex, while the LCC commenced services through the central
area in 1906, via the Kingsway Tram Tunnel. Their trams were fed
from conduits in the road surface rather than obtrusive overhead
wires. Power from the Greenwich generating station (*see London 2:
South*) was transformed at substations which provided unusual
104 architectural opportunities, notably at Rivington Street (Hackney)
and Upper Street. Tramways also occasioned an early reinforced-
concrete girder bridge at New North Road (Hackney) in 1912.
Trolleybuses mostly replaced the trams after 1935 and were phased
out in their turn by 1962.

For the MOTOR AGE, the North Circular Road, the Watford and
Barnet Bypasses, and Great Cambridge Road were built in the 1920s
and 30s through still rural parts of Middlesex. The viaduct across
the Lee at Edmonton (1927) by *Sir Owen Williams* had monumental
pylons, since cleared away for successive widenings. The M1 motorway reached Hendon in 1967 and Staples Corner in 1975. The

three-level junction at Brent Cross of 1962–5 was one of the first of the ever more complex works of later C20 trunk-road improvement. In the inner area, the County of London Plan of 1943 proposed sweeping changes, but the cost and futility of providing for limitless traffic growth was acknowledged by the mid 1970s and there have been very few changes to the C19 street network. An early multi-storey car park of 1931 in Herbrand Street (Holborn), by *Wallis, Gilbert and Partners*, is still in use by taxis.

AVIATION is represented by the RAF Museum at Hendon, in Belfast-trussed hangars of *c.* 1917 at the site of Claude Grahame White's London Aerodrome of 1911. Some features of his adjacent aircraft factory (1915–16) may shortly be relocated there.

London's early WATER SUPPLIES came by wells and conduits from the superficial gravels, or were carried from the Thames. The reservoir ponds at Hampstead (1589 onwards) and Highgate (later C18) supplied parts of St Pancras until the 1850s. In 1604, work started on the engineer *Edmund Colthurst*'s 40-mile (64-km) water channel along the contour from springs near Ware (Hertfordshire). He joined forces with the entrepreneur and financier *Sir Hugh Myddelton* and their NEW RIVER was completed in 1613 to the New River Head at Clerkenwell, above the City. Widened and consider-ably straightened with embankments and tunnels as in Enfield and Haringey, curtailed at Stoke Newington since 1946 and much modified in its water sources and treatment arrangements (the Lee itself being the principal source) the New River still makes a significant contribution to London's water supply and its scenery and ecology. Some sections have excellent cast-iron bridges as in the centre of Enfield. Former pumping stations include the wind-pump base (*c.* 1708) and beam-engine house (1768 and later) at New River Head, and the spectacular 'castle' (1854–6) at Stoke 62 Newington. Complementary to these are the hilltop service reser-voirs as at Claremont Square, Finsbury (1708, rebuilt 1852). Hampstead reservoir has a rare C19 cast-iron standpipe tower; Whitewebbs, near Enfield (1898), and Campsbourne Well at Hornsey (1887) represent two of the many C19 pumping stations which exploited the underlying chalk aquifer with deep wells.

The later C19 clay-embanked reservoirs of the East London Waterworks Co. and those of its successor the Metropolitan Water Board, dominate the Lea Valley from Tottenham to Enfield. Their engineer, *W. B. Bryan*, cast aside the obligatory Italianate of (now demolished) earlier pumping stations for shapely roofs and corbel tables, or half timbering as at Ponders End (Enfield), before turning to classical mannerism as at King George the Fifth, Enfield (1913). The latter has preserved gas-driven pumps on a novel oscillatory principle. 1850s filter beds at Lea Bridge (Hackney) are now a nature reserve.

From the early C20, supplementary water was piped to north London from the Thames, near Staines. The 19 mile (30 km) Thames-Lee Raw Water Tunnel (1955–61) pioneered the techniques used in the tunnelled Ring Main for treated water (1985–94). Also deep in tunnels are inner London's INTERCEPTOR SEWERS of the 1860s (by *(Sir) Joseph Bazalgette*) and the 1900s. Further N, Tottenham has a fine sewage pumping engine of 1886 and sludge settlement tanks preserved.

Two of the world's earliest gasworks were at Curtain Road, Shoreditch, and Central Street (Brick Lane), Finsbury, from 1814. Large plants were established in the 1820s by the Regent's Canal, at St Pancras and Shoreditch. Almost nothing remains of these or later establishments in north London, excepting GASHOLDERS. London led the world through much of the C19 in the size and number of its
2 gasholders. The holders at St Pancras are unequalled as a townscape feature and they have guide columns both of traditional cast iron (1880) and innovative latticework (1886). There are diagonally framed guide frames at Hornsey (1892) and New Barnet.

ELECTRICITY generating stations have come and gone, leaving the shell of the pioneering refuse-burning station at Shoreditch (1895–7) and the operational refuse destructor (32 megawatts) at Edmonton (1971–4). The first municipal electricity undertaking, at St Pancras, is commemorated by arc-lamp standards of 1891–2 in Tottenham Court Road (Holborn). In TELECOMMUNICATIONS, north London has the world's first television mast at Alexandra Palace (Wood Green), of 1934–6, and the 620 ft (190 metre) British Telecom Tower (Holborn), of 1961–4.

The scale of activity in London has caused other, less prominent services to be manifested in constructional form. Thus, until mechanical freezing plants became widespread in the 1900s, natural ice was imported in bulk from Norway and stored in huge commercial ICE WELLS, particularly along the Regent's Canal. These were brick-lined cylinders up to 100 ft (30 metres) deep and up to 40 ft (12 metres) across, carved out of the London clay. The first was built at Cumberland Market (St Pancras) in 1825 and examples survive in Jamestown Road (St Pancras) and New Wharf Road, Islington). Major EXCAVATIONS were also made for the tanks of gasholders, the deepest (55 ft or 16 metres) at St Pancras in 1860–1. Near these, the largest such excavation in the London Clay, of 1982–7, contains the five-basement book store of the British Library.

The King's Library of 1823–8 at the British Museum (Holborn) was innovative in its STRUCTURAL IRONWORK, with cast-iron open-webbed girders and wrought-iron arched plates for fireprotecting the timber upper floor, devised by *Sir Robert Smirke* and *John Raistrick*.* The British Museum Reading Room has *Sidney Smirke*'s cast-iron-ribbed dome of 1854–7. It should be noted that 'fireproof' floors in London were mostly the preserve of prestigious public and commercial buildings, rather than industrial ones, but iron and concrete composite slabs were used also in model tenements, as at Streatham Street, Holborn, of 1849–50. Ornamental cast-ironwork is used for mullions, piers or spandrels in the façades of some 1870s and 80s commercial buildings in Finsbury, particularly around
69 Clerkenwell Road, and a screen of gothic frames fronts Nos. 20–24 Old Street. Railway structures have already been mentioned, but a cast-iron-arched roof of train-shed proportions spans the Business Design Centre in Islington, formerly the (Royal) Agricultural Hall of 1861–2, while the former German Gymnasium (1864–5), Pancras Road, in St Pancras, has LAMINATED TIMBER arches, similar to those which originally roofed King's Cross Station.

---

*Thin wrought-iron fire plates, devised by *David Hartley* in 1773, had been used to protect domestic timber floors on the Bedford estate.

Clay and brickearth, admixed from the late C17 with domestic cinders, were the basis for extensive BRICKMAKING, often a peripatetic industry with the bricks fired in simple clamps on land destined for development. However, the railways enabled the characteristic pink or yellow London Stock bricks* to be supplemented with reds, Gaults, Flettons and engineering bricks from elsewhere. Fused wasters and fireclay kiln furniture were used extensively in garden walls around 1900, as in Hornsey and Southgate. Conical tile kilns, making drain pipes and chimney pots, were a feature of the King's Cross area through much of the C19.

The clay pasturelands of north Middlesex were a springboard for the FOOD INDUSTRIES. The Royal Agricultural Hall was built for livestock shows near to the Metropolitan Cattle Market which moved from Smithfield in 1855 and has some features remaining.‡ Slaughterhouses and gut scrapers followed the market to west Islington, but have now gone. Bacon curing and cold storage continued until the 1970s around the dead-meat market at Smithfield (*see London 1: The City of London*); some bacon stoves have been converted to studios behind Nos. 44–46 St John Street, Finsbury. Dairying, though often performed from urban cow lairs until the early C20, has left the model College Farm (1883) at Finchley, the remarkable sgraffito-decorated depot (*c.* 1890) at No. 1 Crouch Hill, Islington, and various preserved shopfronts of a slightly later period. Until mid-C19 development, there was market gardening on the gravels in Hackney, where Loddiges' famous plant nursery had the most spectacular series of iron-framed GLASSHOUSES of the 1810s and 20s.

GRAIN MILLING is represented by the active Wright's Flour Mill at Ponder's End (Enfield) on the River Lee and the preserved windmill at Arkley (Barnet). In the later C19, steam mills were clustered along the Regent's Canal near the railway granaries at King's Cross. BREWING was a staple metropolitan occupation until the 1960s and later. It first achieved an 'industrial' scale after 1750 at Whitbread's Brewery on the borders of Finsbury, where the converted buildings retain *John Smeaton*'s several beer-tight vaults made with pozzolanic mortar (1775–86) and the timber roof trusses of 66 ft (20 metre) clear span over the Porter Tun Room (1784). Late C19 brewery buildings remain at the former Cannon Brewery, Finsbury, and the former Tottenham Brewery, Tottenham. GIN DISTILLING was another essential trade, concentrated particularly in Finsbury, where Nicholson's in St John Street (1873–5 etc.) and Booth's façade re-erected in Britton Street (1903) are architecturally prominent, as is Gilbey's at Camden Town (1894 and 1937, of both periods in concrete). The one-time Carreras TOBACCO factory at Mornington Crescent, of 1926–8, was then inner London's largest reinforced concrete building; its flamboyant 'Egyptian' decoration to be restored in 1998.

London's MANUFACTURING INDUSTRIES were so numerous, but so diverse, that they created no single image. Relative immunity from the 'industrial revolution' and the generally small scale of individual enterprises disguised the fact that London was always

---

* The yellow colour is attributed to additions of chalk.

‡ The site was near to railways; before that, livestock converged on north London 'on the hoof'.

(until the mid C20) Britain's biggest manufacturing centre in terms of total numbers employed. The architectural impact was usually mute, with much tucked away in back streets or mixed with housing, and the later C20 exodus of industry from the capital has further reduced the prominence of industrial buildings, which survive mostly in other uses.

Within this diversity, some strong local characteristics are apparent. The LEA VALLEY was largely rural until the late C19, but water power and navigation attracted early, small-scale industries, such as gunpowder in the C17, and pigment grinding in the C18. The isolation probably suited the rubber works (now gone) at Tottenham and the Linoleum works at Edmonton, from the 1860s, and at that time Hackney Wick attracted chemical and related trades, notably early aniline dyes and cellulose-based plastics. Their architectural legacy is scanty. The Royal Small Arms Factory, established at Enfield Lock in 1812 and remodelled as a vast single-storeyed mass-production establishment in 1854–6, was in every respect remarkable (*see also* p. 452).

PRECISION CRAFTS were first concentrated under the control of guilds in the City of London but spread N, particularly to CLERKENWELL in the late C17 and C18 and remained there in strength until the C20. Gold and silversmithing, watch and clock making, instrument making of various sorts, engraving and typography required the good day-lighting of attic workshops (topshops) or wide-windowed rooms below. Most of such accommodation has been cleared away and the potentially best examples at Nos. 42–46 Clerkenwell Close are a crude rebuilding; some altered attics may be seen in Britton Street and scattered elsewhere. In the late C19, grand premises for clock makers, typographers, printers and others were erected around Farringdon Road and lesser ones in Clerkenwell Road, while clock-trade outworkers built back-garden extensions (now rebuilt) in the N parts of St John Street. In Cowcross Street and the S end of St John Street, on the City fringes, there are exuberant high-Victorian warehouses for miscellaneous trades (*see also* pp. 627 and 629). LIGHT MANUFACTURES, including printing, stationery, leatherwork, pharmaceuticals and light metal goods, were carried on in eastern Clerkenwell and western Shoreditch, often in densely packed late C19 or early C20 buildings characterized by large, metal-lintelled windows between brick piers. S Shoreditch became the centre of the FURNITURE trade in the C19, the many surviving buildings being large and later C19, either purpose built for particular firms as in Curtain Road or designed as rows of units. They usually have sash windows between the pilasters of giant arcades, but casements under very broad segmental heads may be found in older (mid-C19) premises.

High-class furniture was also made around Tottenham Court Road, while PIANO MAKING was centred on Camden Town, with several distinctive mid-C19 buildings: chapel-like, pedimented façades at Nos. 30–31 Lyme St and No. 44 Fitzroy Road, a polygon with radial jack-arched floors for streamlined production (1850–2) in Oval Road and a very large block in the Shoreditch workshop style in Belmont Street. Some later examples are arranged around yards, e.g. No. 7 Chalcot Road, and, with less distinction, they extend through Kentish Town and Islington.

Small C19 factories were also scattered in the suburbs of Islington and Hackney, with certain concentrations around York Way and Caledonian Road, Holloway, and Dalston. There was a band of IRONWORKS and other engineering activity along the Regent's Canal, notably the Regent's Canal Ironworks in Eagle Wharf Road, Hoxton, of which only a distinctive mid-C19 chimney survives. In the early C20, industry such as furniture and aircraft-component manufacture spread N through Tottenham and Edmonton, and also Cricklewood in the W, and then onwards along the arterial roads around Enfield. Here and on expanded sites in Islington and Hackney, LIGHT ELECTRICAL and ELECTRONIC INDUSTRIES became prominent. But there was little of the expressive interwar architecture found in west London and much has been cleared away or emasculated. The present day offers a severe anticlimax.

# BARNET

Barnet became a borough within Greater London in 1965. Its origins are diverse. Before 1965, High Barnet and the medieval parishes of Totteridge, East Barnet and, more briefly, Monken Hadley formed two urban districts within a s peninsula of Hertfordshire. Nearer London were four old parishes which had become three local authorities within the old county of Middlesex: tiny Friern Barnet to the E; Finchley, a long, thin area with a number of hamlets in the neighbourhood of the Great North Road; Hendon, a huge medieval parish bounded on its w side by the Roman route of Watling Street, including the areas of Cricklewood, Golders Green and Hampstead Garden Suburb, and Edgware, a separate parish to the N, joined to Hendon in 1931. Description of the modern borough under comprehensible headings is no easy matter; this gazetteer therefore subdivides some of the old administrative areas into districts with a recognizable identity.

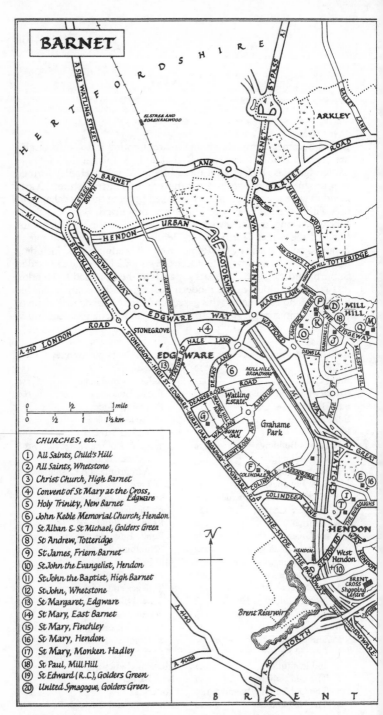

# BARNET

*HERTFORDSHIRE*

ELSTREE AND BOREHAMWOOD

ARKLEY

**CHURCHES, etc.**

① All Saints, Child's Hill
② All Saints, Whetstone
③ Christ Church, High Barnet
④ Convent of St Mary at the Cross, Edgware
⑤ Holy Trinity, New Barnet
⑥ John Keble Memorial Church, Hendon
⑦ St Alban & St Michael, Golders Green
⑧ St Andrew, Totteridge
⑨ St James, Friern Barnet
⑩ St John the Evangelist, Hendon
⑪ St John the Baptist, High Barnet
⑫ St John, Whetstone
⑬ St Margaret, Edgware
⑭ St Mary, East Barnet
⑮ St Mary, Finchley
⑯ St Mary, Hendon
⑰ St Mary, Monken Hadley
⑱ St Paul, Mill Hill
⑲ St Edward (R.C.), Golders Green
⑳ United Synagogue, Golders Green

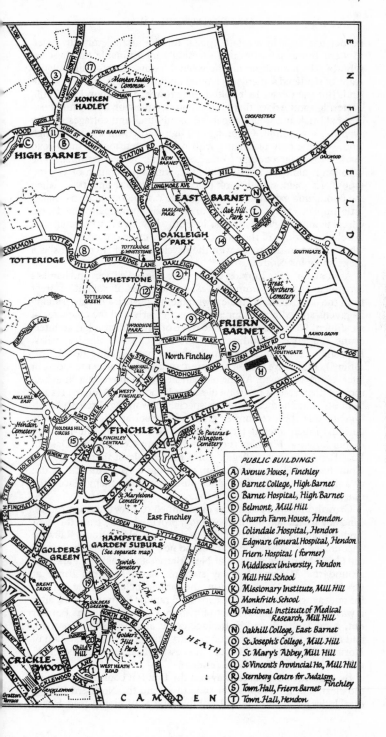

PUBLIC BUILDINGS
- (A) Avenue House, Finchley
- (B) Barnet College, High Barnet
- (C) Barnet Hospital, High Barnet
- (D) Belmont, Mill Hill
- (E) Church Farm House, Hendon
- (F) Colindale Hospital, Hendon
- (G) Edgware General Hospital, Hendon
- (H) Friern Hospital (former)
- (I) Middlesex University, Hendon
- (J) Mill Hill School
- (K) Missionary Institute, Mill Hill
- (L) Monkfrith School
- (M) National Institute of Medical Research, Mill Hill
- (N) Oakhill College, East Barnet
- (O) St Joseph's College, Mill Hill
- (P) St Mary's Abbey, Mill Hill
- (Q) St Vincent's Provincial Ho, Mill Hill
- (R) Sternberg Centre for Judaism, Finchley
- (S) Town Hall, Friern Barnet
- (T) Town Hall, Hendon

## INTRODUCTION

Barnet has little immediate appeal for the architectural traveller. Modern routes pass through seemingly interminable middle-class suburbs which mushroomed between the wars, transforming a landscape of scattered settlements among undulating farmland and woodland. But the Green Belt halted this growth, and around Mill Hill, Totteridge and Arkley there is still countryside with a handful of traditional brick and weatherboarded farmhouses and cottages. Arkley even has a windmill. Chipping or High Barnet, on a ridge of high land, was the only old centre with urban pretensions, a main-road market town far enough from London not to be swamped. The borough is almost entirely residential, with a population of 312,500 (1995). Its main growth took place between 1901 and 1939, when the population expanded from 76,208 to c. 296,000. Industry makes little impact except along the main roads, principally the North Circular and Edgware Roads; in both these areas vast retail and warehouse groups of the later C20 are now more dominant, a trend which began in the 1970s with the development of Brent Cross as a major shopping centre.

As in much of the London countryside, the old villages and hamlets expanded, especially from the C18, as the better-off sought a retreat from the city. Monken Hadley, with handsome brick houses fringing its greens and commons, preserves particularly well the character of an affluent Georgian village. The ridge of Mill Hill also has an interesting sequence, including two fine late C18 Neoclassical villas, Holcombe House and Belmont (both now parts of educational institutions). Elsewhere only a few pre-C19 buildings are embedded in later suburban growth. All the old parishes retain interesting churches, most of them at least partly medieval; at Hendon and Monken Hadley both buildings and contents are specially rewarding. Pre-C19 buildings include the C16 former grammar school at High Barnet, the curious, much altered Hendon Hall (now a hotel), the fine C18 manor house at Finchley (now the Sternberg Centre), and Oakhill, East Barnet (now a college). On a humbler level there is the C17 Church Farm House at Hendon, which has a sympathetic new use as a museum. Simple rural almshouses remain in many places: the oldest, at Friern Barnet, are of 1612.

Growth in the C19 and C20 owed much to new transport routes. Finchley Road, laid out in the 1820s, provided a link from the West End of London through Finchley to the Great North Road. Railways encouraged the development of brand new later C19 suburbs around the Great Northern stations at New Barnet and Oakleigh Park, and around the Midland Railway stations on the western fringe at Cricklewood and West Hendon, the former including long terraces for railway workers. Finchley expanded rapidly from the 1870s, after it was linked by a branch line to Finsbury Park and the City. Further out, rural Mill Hill and Totteridge could also be reached by train, and attracted large picturesque country mansions in the tradition of Norman Shaw, several by the successful London architect *T. E. Collcutt*, himself a Totteridge resident.

By 1900 the effect of railways on the London countryside was all too clear, and the proposal in 1902 to extend the Northern Line of the Underground to the still unbuilt land N of Hampstead Heath met with stiff resistance from Hampstead residents. This had wide-reaching results: the preservation of the Heath Extension, the rapid development of Golders Green, where the station was eventually built in 1907, and the creation of Hampstead Garden Suburb, a planned settlement established in 1907 by Henrietta Barnett as an alternative to indiscriminate growth, and idealistically intended to cater for a diverse social range of residents. Henrietta Barnett and *Raymond Unwin*'s planning of the Suburb, with winding roads, preserved open spaces and picturesque closes of cottages – and an absence of shops and pubs – was widely influential; in Barnet its effect can be seen immediately and charmingly in Village Way, Finchley, and on a much larger scale in the big Watling Estate, Hendon, built by the LCC from 1926. By then the extension of the Northern Line from Golders Green to Edgware (1923–4) and new roads (the North Circular, Falloden Way, Watford Way) were opening up the rest of Hendon to developers. The Arts and Crafts cottage tradition of Parker and Unwin and their numerous followers was transmuted, here as in other suburbs, into the semi-detached house designed for the mass market, the style which Osbert Lancaster dubbed 'bypass variegated'. More particular to the area, especially on the edges of Hampstead Garden Suburb, are accomplished, if repetitive, versions of Neo-Georgian which were favoured for superior houses between the wars. The Modern Movement made only tentative and occasional appearances, and remained the exception for private houses after the Second World War; for these the Hampstead fringe of Golders Green is the best hunting ground.

Public housing by the local authorities is of less interest and less extensive here than in the inner London boroughs. Characteristic examples of different decades are Finchley's 1920s Woodhouse Estate, in pleasant garden suburb mode, and its 1930s Grange Estate, East Finchley, with flats. Friern Barnet provided a good early post-war combination of flats and houses in Colney Hatch Lane. The most ambitious development is the GLC's Grahame Park, laid out on the site of Hendon Aerodrome in 1969, with a deliberately urban pedestrian walk as its central focus. Among public buildings Friern Barnet's Town Hall of 1939 is a dignified example of the cautious compromise between traditional and modern typical of the late 1930s.

The London countryside attracted many institutions serving more than a local catchment. College Farm, a delightful model dairy built for Express Dairies at Finchley in 1883, is a reminder of the importance of the pastures of the area for London's milk supply. The Victorians colonized the countryside for cemeteries; the two at East Finchley serving inner London parishes have the most notable monuments, the Crematorium group at Golders Green by *George & Yeates* of 1905 etc. has the finest buildings. The largest establishment of all was the formidable Colney Hatch Asylum at Friern Barnet, of 1849–51, by *Daukes*, built as Middlesex's second pauper lunatic asylum, now converted to housing. Still surviving are numerous religious foundations, a particular feature of Barnet, especially around Mill Hill, which has the massive R.C. St Joseph's College and St Mary's Abbey, both by *Goldie*. At Edgware *James Brooks* began a convent to highly ambitious plans, but only a fraction was carried out. In severe Grecian contrast to these Gothic buildings is the earlier Mill Hill School of 1825–7 by *Tite*, built for Dissenters. The school also has notable, less austere buildings by *Champneys* and *Collcutt*.

Among the civic and religious buildings built to serve the new suburbs are some outstanding churches. The old Anglican churches were supplemented in the earlier C19 by very modest buildings (*see* Arkley, Mill Hill and Whetstone, and *Scott*'s prettier Christ Church, High Barnet). The more ambitious Gothic of the later C19 is demonstrated by *Butterfield*'s grand extensions to St John, High Barnet, *Pearson*'s noble St John, Friern Barnet, and *Temple Moore*'s refined St John, West Hendon. *Lutyens*'s St Jude and Free Church provide a distinctive twin focus for Hampstead Garden Suburb, and *Young*'s St Edward R.C., 1915, and *Giles G. Scott*'s St Alban, 1925–33, are worthy landmarks in Golders Green. Nonconformity was also strong in the suburbs; its churches are still numerous throughout Barnet, with a particularly good late C19 to early C20 range in Finchley and Golders Green. Golders Green is also rich in synagogues. Finally, mention must be made of *Martin-Smith*'s innovative John Keble Church, Hendon, 1935–7, one of the most progressive churches of its time, not only in Hendon but nationally.

ARCHAEOLOGY. The few early prehistoric finds have been mainly from the northern part of the borough. An Iron Age hill fort at Hadley Wood is defended by a single bank and ditch. Mill Hill had an Iron Age or Romano-British settlement. The high ground at Brockley Hill at the NW tip of Barnet gives an impressive view southwards of Roman Watling Street which ran from London to Verulamium and the NW. The road forms the western boundary of the borough; Brockley Hill was probably the Sulloniacae named in the Antonine Itinerary; it was also the site of a major Roman pottery industry during the first and second centuries. Evidence of Roman occupation has been found at Hendon, including fragments of mosaic flooring.


# ARKLEY

Arkley, in Hertfordshire until 1965, is still almost countryside; only a scatter of C20 suburban houses fringes the road which runs along the ridge w of High Barnet.

ST PETER, Barnet Road. 1840 by *George Beckett*. Humble lancet-style chapel of rough brick (formerly rendered?) with aisleless nave and transepts. Two small octagonal pinnacles. The flint-faced chancel was added in 1898 by *J. C. Traylen*. Plain plastered nave interior; timber-vaulted chancel. STAINED GLASS. E window 1903 by *Kempe*. Chancel N and S attributed to *Heaton, Butler & Bayne*, 1898, 1903 (M. Coles). MONUMENT. Very simple wall tablet to Enoch Durant †1848, at whose expense the church was built; signed by the *Westminster Marble Company*.

POOR CLARE MONASTERY, Galley Lane. 1968–70 by *Owen Fogarty* for an enclosed order of nuns established at Notting Hill in 1857. Purple brick with aluminium roofs. From the entrance an apsed chapel is visible on the l.; visitors' building, two-storeyed with a pitched roof, on the r. Beyond is a three-storey range of cells, and single-storey workrooms around five tiny courtyards linked by well-lit corridors. Taller central refectory, given dignity by a boarded ceiling. L-shaped CHAPEL, one half for the public, the other divided off for the nuns, with free-standing altar facing each wing at 45 degrees. Spare, lofty interior with subdued lighting from narrow windows in the angles of the slightly broader apse, and asymmetrical sloping ceilings.

ELM FARMHOUSE, No. 2 GALLEY LANE. A picturesque rural oasis. Early C18 farmhouse with C19 front on partially timber-framed structure. Barn to r., weatherboarded with tiled roof.

In BARNET ROAD, BROCKET. Mid-C18; roughcast, two storeys, two bays, with central pedimented porch. Later additions to l. and r. LANE HOUSE. 1961 by *S. & M. Craig*. On a steep slope, with entrance at mezzanine level. Stock brick inside and out. Off Barnet Road, in ALYN CLOSE, a house by *John Voelcker*, 1960. Well set back behind trees; three ranges around a courtyard opening to the garden. An important early example of two trends which became popular later: the use of a vaguely vernacular idiom (sloping roofs, blind brick walls) and the achievement of maximum privacy by an inward-looking design.

WINDMILL, N of the church, off Brickfield Lane. A circular brick tower mill, built between 1822 and 1840. Worked until 1916; repaired in 1930 and 1974. Three sails and a fantail, and the drive to one pair of stones, remain. Nearby BARN of 1788 for storing grain. Timber-framed and weatherboarded.

WATER TOWER, Rowley Lane. A cluster of concrete tanks on many tapering legs, 1965 by *Scherrer & Hicks*. A striking design.


# BRENT CROSS

When built in 1970–6 this was for a short time the prime example in England of the American type of out-of-town centre designed for shoppers arriving by car. Architecturally it is undistinguished. The site lies close to the junction of the M1 and the North Circular Road. The SHOPPING CENTRE by *Bernard Engle Partnership* for Hammerson Properties is set in a sea of car parks: 3,500 parking places in 1976, much increased since, with no mitigating landscaping, despite public enquiry recommendations. Externally the buildings appear as a clumsy accidental agglomeration, a far cry from the minimalist elegance of the Milton Keynes shopping building of 1973–9. Different types of cladding are used for the main stores at each end: a plain concrete wall for Fenwicks, dour granite with vertical slits for John Lewis. Their height was intended to provide for rooftop servicing, but this was not carried out. Yet the plan is straightforward, based on a 200-metre-long galleried spine route (smaller than American prototypes but similar to earlier centres in France). Large stores on two levels. Extended N in 1995, with upper link to new car parks, part of a refurbishment by *Building Design Partnership*. This transformed the interiors with simpler detailing, natural lighting with new roof-lights in curved ceilings, and big glazed domes at the cross-axes. Major expansion to the S by the same firm: completion planned 1999.

## CRICKLEWOOD AND CHILD'S HILL

Cricklewood straddles the Barnet–Brent boundary along Edgware Road. After the railway arrived, the rural hamlet within the parish of Hendon developed into a late C19 suburb, which became the terminus of the trams from London, which ran along the Edgware Road. Superior late C19 residential parts lie to the w in Brent (*see London 3: North West*), industrial and working-class areas to the E. They grew around the extensive Midland Railway sidings and marshalling yards N of the station (now largely redeveloped), and by the 1930s Cricklewood was Hendon's main centre of industry. Child's Hill was an old settlement further E, connected to Cricklewood by Cricklewood Lane, but now has nothing older than the mid C19.

ALL SAINTS, Child's Hill. Hidden away between Finchley Road and Cricklewood Lane. The original ragstone church was of 1853–6, by *Thomas Talbot Bury*, the first new church for the southern part of the parish of Hendon. N aisle 1878 by *John Young*; s aisle 1884. Much rebuilt by *S. C. Ramsey*, 1952, after a fire in 1940. Plain columns and plastered walls inside; clerestory with timber windows and low-pitched C20 roof.

    VICARAGE, now CHURCH WALK HOUSE, also by *Bury*, tall and spiky, with red brick diapering.

ST PETER, Cricklewood Lane. Small, plain building with crude dormers of 1977 poking through a tiled roof. It replaced a late C19 church by *T. H. Watson*. It is attached to an attractive Arts and Crafts CHURCH HALL of 1910, from which some lessons might have been learned.

ST AGNES (R.C.), Cricklewood Lane. 1930 by *T. H. B. Scott*. Sober Early Christian style in plain brick, outside and in. Transverse arches between sanctuary and apse, N passage aisle and s chapel. Neo-Byzantine capitals to the entrance, by *Philip Lindsey Clark*. Sanctuary reordered 1975–6 by *Campling and Iliffe*.

CLAREMONT BAPTIST FREE CHURCH, Cheviot Gardens. 1931 by *C. W. B. Simmonds*. Brick with broad half-timbered gable in cosy domestic vernacular mode, in the contemporary estate by Laing, donor of the site.

CHILD'S HILL PRIMARY SCHOOL, Dersingham Road. One of four Board schools opened by Hendon in 1901. Two-storeyed; sparing terracotta trim.

WHITEFIELD SCHOOL, Claremont Road. Long three-storeyed ranges with shallow pitched roofs and blue and white trim, the result of the *Borough of Barnet*'s recladding and enlargement in 1993–5 of a secondary school opened in 1954 and extended in 1967 and 1991.

CRICKLEWOOD STATION. Opened to passengers in 1870 by the Midland Railway. Station offices rebuilt 1906; red brick and terracotta with a bold chimney and an Art Nouveau touch.

CRICKLEWOOD BROADWAY is part of the Edgware Road. Its most flamboyant building is THE CROWN, 1898–1900, a substantial pub set back from the road on the E side, one of Cannon Brewery's ambitious rebuildings by *Shoebridge & Rising*. Free Flemish Renaissance, with two stepped and voluted gables in front of a slate mansard roof, a battlemented turret at one end. Plentiful terracotta ornament; four handsome cast-iron lamp standards in front. To its N, a tall, quite elaborate terrace in pale brick, dated 1900. Nothing else of note in the Broadway apart from the TELEPHONE EXCHANGE further N of 1929–30, which shows how good proportions can do much to mitigate colossal bulk. Three storeys over a tall basement, eight by three bays, in the dignified classical manner adopted for such buildings by the *Office of Works* between the wars. Two show sides in grey brick with red dressings, with a little ornament provided by carved stone keystones to some of the first-floor windows.

Immediately to the N, tucked away between main road and railway, C19 railway workers' housing in parallel rows of simple two-storeyed brick terraces, with back yards to service roads, and front doors opening onto paths with gardens beyond. GRATTON and NEEDHAM TERRACES are the earliest, of the 1860s. Some of the gardens are arranged as communal spaces, others are individual tiny enclosures of delightful variety. Allotments beyond.

CRICKLEWOOD LANE starts on the S side with CROWN TERRACE; standard bay-windowed terrace houses of *c.* 1900, but, unusually, raised up so that the front doors are reached from a railed terrace over the roofs of the shops below. Opposite St Peter's, No. 134, a former COMMUNITY HALL of 1920–1 for the local railway workers and others (see foundation stones). On the N side a mid-C19 stuccoed row, very plain and humble; Nos. 41–53 with doors in recessed bays, Nos. 55–69 with flat fronts. At the end a contemporary pub, the former CRICKLEWOOD TAVERN, three storeys, the ground floor smartened up in the later C19 by elaborate green glazed tiles.

To the N, industry was concentrated along CLAREMONT ROAD, parallel to the railway. The W side is taken up by a straggle of cream painted buildings, former premises of the EXPRESS DAIRY CO. BOTTLING FACTORY, opened in the late C19 and much added to. Opposite, CRICKLEWOOD TRADING ESTATE, developed from 1914 with munition and aircraft component factories. No. 1, at the N corner of Somerton Road, was the former Handley Page aircraft works: a polite painted brick one-storey frontage to the road hiding a long row of roof-lit workshops behind. Handley Page's short-lived Cricklewood Airport lay to the N (1912–29); on its site is an intrusion of middle-class Hendon: one of Laing's earliest London housing developments, prim brick semis symmetrically laid out in concentric ovals around PENNINE DRIVE. To the W, on a narrow strip of land beside the railway, BRENT TERRACE, railway workers' cottages with backs to the road and front doors to the railway line, in a single long row, a less sociable layout than those W of the railway (*see* above).

From CLITTERHOUSE FARM a former C19 farmhouse remains in Claremont Road, three bays with a little polychrome brickwork; its fields, first taken for the airport, are now football pitches fringed by stolid brick council housing begun by Hendon after the First World War. Later additions of after 1945 in WALCOTE AVENUE and PRAYLE GROVE include two-storey prefabricated houses, whose shallow pitched roofs and painted ribbed cladding provide a touch of crisp 1950s modernism. To their N is the world of the North Circular Road and Brent Cross (q.v.), with its big retail sheds of the 1980s onwards. TESCO, off Tilling Road, deserves singling out. Pale brick and cream enamelled panels, elegantly detailed, with glazed entrance canopy on columns, and another glazed roof to lighten the area in front of the tills. Built in 1993 by *Lyons Sleeman & Hoare*, together with the neighbouring HENDON YOUTH SPORTS CENTRE, where the same materials are used. This houses gym, sports hall and other facilities under a big, shallow curved roof.


## EAST BARNET

A southern peninsula of Hertfordshire until 1965. East Barnet, a settlement of early origin in the Pymmes Brook valley, still preserves a rural air, due to the park in the valley between the church and Oakhill, the only major surviving large mansion in the area (*see* Enfield). Up to the late C19, when suburbs began to expand from the stations at Oakleigh Park and New Barnet (q.v.), there was little apart from the church and several large houses in their grounds.

ST MARY, Church Hill Road. A remarkable survival. This was the mother church of the later settlement of Chipping or High Barnet; despite C19 additions, it is still recognizable as a simple Norman church. The plain rendered N wall retains three tiny single-splayed windows and a blocked round-headed doorway belonging to a formerly aisleless nave. Inside, another slightly larger S doorway. Both are of Reigate stone, finely jointed, probably second quarter of the C12. The church belonged to St Alban's Abbey. Small uncouth yellow brick Neo-Norman tower of 1829 by *R. Kelsey*, originally free-standing. S aisle of Kentish rag with plate tracery and one gross red marble column, 1868 by *A. R. Barker*. Chancel enlarged 1880, vestries 1911. PULPIT and CHOIR STALLS, minor work by *Street*, 1850–1. STAINED GLASS. E window 1880, good, by *Clayton & Bell*, Crucifixion and other scenes. Minuscule ancient fragments reset in N windows. Only minor monuments inside, but a fine CHURCHYARD with an old cedar tree S of the tower and many memorials including a number of large chest tombs. N of the church, a delightful series of tombstones to the Grove family, all of the same design, decorated with putto heads and topped by obelisks, the earliest Francis White †1755. Another stone with putti to Joseph Answorth †1727. Their rustic flavour is a nice contrast with the elegant (but badly decayed) monument to John Sharpe †1766, a large urn of Carrara marble on a big base under a heavy arched baldacchino, perhaps by *J. Wilton* (cf. his monument to Sloane at Chelsea), and a tapered classical sarcophagus on lions' feet further E. General Prevost †1787, sarcophagus with Gothic detail, by *John Bacon*. Sir Simon Haughton Clarke of Oakhill †1832 and family: railed Gothic monument with octagonal lantern on octagonal plinth.

BROOKHILL METHODIST CHURCH. *See* below.

GREAT NORTHERN CEMETERY, Brunswick Park Road. An ambitious private cemetery established in 1861, originally connected by a special branch line to the main railway at New Southgate. Laid out by *Alexander Spurr* on a concentric plan, intended to cover

200 acres; attractively mature landscape in the s part. Gothic gatepiers; chapel in the centre, E.E. with a fine tall spire (interior converted to crematorium in 1950s). Among the MONUMENTS, tall late C19 obelisk erected by the Society of Friends. In a walled garden a very large marble column to Shogi Effendi, Baha'i leader, †1957.

OAKHILL COLLEGE see Enfield p. 464.

Near St Mary's Church, CHURCH FARM SCHOOL. This originated as an industrial school, established in this rural spot in 1860 as an offshoot of a school for destitute boys in Euston Road, St Pancras. The site was bought by Colonel William Gillum, philanthropist and early patron of the Morris circle, who employed *Philip Webb* to build workshops in Shoreditch (*see* Hackney) and his own house in East Barnet as well as the additions to the farm buildings here. These include the w wing of white-painted brick with a much altered schoolhouse of 1868, flanked by schoolroom (1878) and playroom (1880), both by Webb's friend *C. G. Vinall*. s and e wings were added in 1925–6, with mansard roofs and a copper-clad clock turret in the angle. Cottages Nos. 1 and 2, in Webb style, with segment-headed doors, drastically altered, are perhaps by *Vinall*, Nos. 2a and 2b by *Charles Nicholson*, 1912, pink brick, with ground-floor windows under Gothic arches. To the N a reinforced concrete water tower, clad in brick and tile with hipped roof; 1912, by *J. C. Mellis*, engineer, with *Nicholson* as consultant, and a swimming pool.

TREVOR LODGE, Church Hill Park. The lodge to the demolished Trevor Park, Colonel Gillum's house. By *Philip Webb*, 1868–70. Square, with a steep tile-hung gable on each side, but, alas, windows altered and central chimney lowered.

ST MARY'S CHURCH OF ENGLAND SCHOOL, Church Hill and Little Grove. 1871, the usual rural type with two end gables. Mullioned windows.

POST-WAR PRIMARY SCHOOLS. Two early examples in East Barnet of the type of schools that made Hertfordshire County Council famous after the Second World War. MONKFRITH, Knoll Drive, 1949–50 by the *Herts CC Architect's Department*, and DANEGROVE, Ridgeway Avenue, 1950–1 by *Architects Co-Partnership*. Both make use of a modified form of the Hills 8-ft 3-in. steel-framed system, and are similar, but Danegrove is the more pleasing composition. It has one-storey buildings nicely set on a green slope, the classrooms generously glazed, balanced by a taller assembly hall with flat projecting roof, facing the entrance. The hall had a particularly fine mural by *Fred Millett* (boarded over at the time of writing).

The suburban centre of East Barnet is at the junction of CAT HILL and BROOK HILL ROAD, where the prim Neo-Georgian CLOCKHOUSE PARADE of 1926 faces BROOKHILL METHODIST CHURCH, an ungainly complex, mostly of 1967. JACKSON ROAD to the sw was the first suburban development, laid out in 1889 with plain brick pairs of houses, leading towards Oakleigh Park Station.

BRUNSWICK PARK further s also began to be developed in the late C19. e of the Great Northern Cemetery (*see* above), there was still open land in the 1930s, when a sprinkling of daring speculators'-modern flat-roofed houses appeared, e.g. Nos. 11–12 in the appropriately named WHITEHOUSE WAY.

OSIDGE, No. 151 CHASE SIDE (Sir Thomas Lipton Memorial Hostel). In its own grounds. Newly built in 1808, when it was sold by John Kingston, the owner of Oakhill. Yellow brick with stucco trim. Three storeys, five bays, with later additions.

# EDGWARE

Edgware lies on the borders with Hertfordshire, its northern part still rural Green Belt, although sliced through by the M1. The suburban development further s resulted from the London Transport extension from Golders Green, completed in 1924. In 1931 the parish became a part of the urban district, later borough, of Hendon. The population grew from 1,516 in 1921, 5,352 in 1931, to c. 17,096 in 1946. The old village centre lay along the Edgware tract of Watling Street, where it is known as High Street, extending across the parish boundary into Little Stanmore (*see London 3: North West*, Harrow). The church lies near the crossing of Watling Street with the route to Mill Hill. This is now Station Road, with a shopping centre around the station.

ST MARGARET, Station Road. A sturdy late medieval w tower of the usual Middlesex type: of ragstone with Reigate dressings, much renewed. Diagonal buttresses, and a NE turret higher than the battlemented parapet. w doorway; arched belfry windows. The rest of the church was rebuilt in brick in 1763–4. The shallow sanctuary and transepts date from 1845, by the young *Charles Barry Jun.* The Perp N and s aisles were added in 1928. They have arcades with dying mouldings cut through the old walls. Small w gallery of 1791. Boarded ceilings and plastered walls. A little carved decoration flanks the sanctuary arch. The sanctuary retains its attractive mid-C19 FITTINGS, still simple and pre-ecclesiological: stone dado arcade on the E wall, wooden COMMUNION TABLE with Gothic tracery, similarly detailed STALLS extending into the transept; COMMUNION RAILS with curly ironwork; black and white marble PAVING. COMMANDMENT BOARDS, now in the s aisle, near the handsome C18 marble baluster FONT. STAINED GLASS. E and transept windows of three lights: E (Ascension), 1851, rather bleached, old-fashioned classically modelled figures, by *Wailes*. Probably also by him the s and N windows: †1858: St Timothy, in coloured quarries; †1868: Christ with Mary and Martha, with harder detail. Nave s (Good Shepherd and Sower), c. 1925, and N (Moses and Dorcas), c. 1928, both by *Jessie Jacobs*, good colours. sw (St Paul and Nehemiah), *A. K. Nicholson Studios*, c. 1948. BRASS. Anthonie Childe †1599, tiny babe in swaddling clothes. MONUMENT. Randolph Nicoll †1658, Baroque tablet with broken segmental pediment. In the crowded churchyard, behind railings, a large Neoclassical tapered sarcophagus to Francis Day †1826; also a headstone to Ivy Glen McSweeney †1943, good relief in the Gill tradition.

ST ANTHONY OF PADUA (R.C.), Garratt Road. Red brick with stone dressings, Perp. Nave, N aisle, N chapel and short chancel, 1910–13. Enlarged 1930–1. Aisles, baptistery and sanctuary extensions by *Burles and Newton*, 1956–8, when the brick piers were replaced by steel supports.

(BAPTIST CHURCH, Station Road. By *W. Allen Dixon*, *c.* 1872. Three-bay pilastered front with pedimented centre.)

EDGWARE DISTRICT REFORMED SYNAGOGUE, No. 118 Stonegrove. Good, boldly detailed three-storey group of red brick with aggregate-faced bands and brown boarding. 1960s, with many later extensions. By *Hildebrand & Glicker*.

LIBRARY, Hale Lane. 1960–1 by *Hendon Borough Council* (*B. Bancroft*, Chief Assistant Architect). Pleasant L-shaped building with shallow copper roofs and a dominant glazed gable end; light interiors with large windows in the welcoming manner favoured by post-war libraries. Reference library in a gallery above the main library.

EDGWARE JUNIOR SCHOOL, Garratt Road. 1895, built by the Edgware and Little Stanmore School Board. Somewhat altered (the domed clock turret over the entrance has been truncated), but an attractive example of a rural Board school; one-storeyed, with shaped gables and tall chimneys, rather in the tradition of Ernest George, who worked for the Harrow School Board.

ORANGE HILL SCHOOL, Hamonde Close. 1965 by the *MCC* (*D. R. Duncan* and *D. L. Pelham*). Straightforward one- to three-storey curtain-walled buildings on a concrete frame. Built as a girls' grammar school; the last by the MCC before secondary education passed to the new boroughs. Ample practical facilities demonstrated the county's post-war policy that grammar schools should not be purely academic.

CONVENT OF ST MARY AT THE CROSS (Benedictine Community of Sisters of the Poor), Prioryfield Drive, off Hale Lane. This began as an offshoot of a convent and hospital founded in Shoreditch in 1865. The Edgware site was bought in 1873; it became the main centre after the Shoreditch house closed in 1931. The early buildings, by *James Brooks*, make an impressive group, best viewed from the NW. They consist of a residential block of 1874, in picturesque brick Gothic with crested tiled roofs and bold chimneys, linked by a cloister of 1893 to an apsed chapel, completed *c.* 1891. This was intended merely as the Lady Chapel of a huge abbey church. On the N side one can still see the beginning of the stone wall arcading intended for the main apse. The exterior is of brick with stone traceried windows between hefty buttresses, and a very steep roof. (Elaborate capitals inside; STAINED GLASS in the E window.) Narthex for lay use added 1965–6 by *Norman Davey*. To the S: hospital blocks and isolation unit, 1937–41 by *Collcutt & Hamp*. (Mortuary chapel with stained glass and tiles from the Shoreditch convent.) W of the cloister, HENRY NIHILL HOUSE, for the elderly, 1990–2, by *Woods Hardwick* of Bedford. A long calm range, of brick with stone dressings, its upper floor linked by a glazed bridge to the chapel. The priory grounds were built up with private housing in the early 1990s; much decorative half-timbering in the tradition of between-the-wars suburbia.

EDGWARE STATION, Station Road, 1923–4. On the Edgware extension of the Northern Line; by *S. A. Heaps*, architect to London Underground Electric Railways. A unique variant of the classical style he used for the stations of the Edgware extension. The E wing was destroyed in 1938, the W wing in 1988–9. Entrance through a colonnade of paired columns; pantiled roofs.

In STATION ROAD, opposite the church, the RAILWAY HOTEL, 1931 by *A. E. Sewell* for Truman Hanbury & Buxton, the most exuberant of their neo-Tudor inns, complete with half-timbering, clustered brick stacks, carved bargeboards and decorative rain-waterheads. Further E, the predictable mix of a suburban centre: genteel, quite urban Neo-Georgian interwar shopping parades; an obtrusive dumpy curtain-walled slab and podium of out-of-town offices and shops (by *Morgan & Branch*, 1962), and a brash shopping arcade and superstore of 1990 on the site of the old GNR station. At the junction with HALE LANE, a dignified Neo-Georgian BANK, built for the National Provincial, 1928 by *Palmer and Holden*. Superior interwar houses in the streets off Hale Lane; PENSHURST GARDENS has a good selection.

The borough and parish boundary runs along Edgware Road (Watling Street), here named the HIGH STREET. The E side has little of note; on the W side, a group of more interesting buildings of C16 and earlier origin remains (*see London 3: North West*, Harrow). Further N the road becomes STONEGROVE. On the E side the DAY ALMSHOUSES of 1828: a row of eight; a symmetrical, gabled Gothic group, cement-rendered. Near the present borough boundary was the probable site of the Roman settlement of SULLONIACAE on Watling Street.

BURY FARM, Edgwarebury Lane, between Edgware Way and the M1. A rural survival: L-shaped, with a C17 double-gabled wing, partly jettied over a brick ground floor, and a brick C18 wing.

# FINCHLEY

The medieval parish stretched from the Spaniards Inn on the edge of Hampstead Heath and the present fringes of Hampstead Garden Suburb as far N as Whetstone (qq.v.). It is now a wholly urban area of the later C19 and earlier C20 but still with much green surrounding it and penetrating into it. The main ancient route is the High Road, the medieval Great North Road running N from Highgate through what was once Finchley Common. The road from the West End of London (Finchley Road and Regents Park Road, linking up with Ballards Lane) was made only in 1827. Small scattered settlements grew up around the edges of the common: Church End was connected by East End Lane to East End, the hamlet which became East Finchley, whose principal house was the manor house of Bibbesworth, now the Sternberg Centre. Another early centre was North End, on the W side of the present Whetstone; the present North Finchley developed along the Great North Road only after the enclosure of Finchley Common in 1816.

Suburban development was encouraged by the opening of a railway line from Finsbury Park to Edgware and High Barnet (1867–72). The parish had only 1,503 inhabitants in 1801 and still only 7,146 in 1871. Thereafter growth was rapid: 16,647 in 1891, 39,419 in 1911, 59,113 in 1931, 69,991 in 1951. Finchley became an Urban District Council in 1895, a Municipal Borough in 1933.

There are a few mid-C19 developments, but the predominant character is late Victorian and Edwardian, with housing ranging from simple cottages to ornate Edwardian villas and deliberately picturesque rural revival (Garden Village, Finchley Central).

## RELIGIOUS BUILDINGS

### 1. Church of England

ALL SAINTS, Durham Road, East Finchley. 1892 by *J. E. K. & J. P. Cutts*. Red brick with stone dressings, Perp, with a typical Cutts long clerestoried nave. Chancel 1912, with tall E apse. The intended NE tower was not built.

CHRIST CHURCH, High Road, North Finchley. 1867–9 by *J. Norton*. Coursed ragstone, with a big W rose window above a narthex; gabled aisles added 1874 (N), 1880 (S); E end 1891. A spire was intended. Impressive Victorian interior, with red brick walls and tall stone clustered piers and foliated capitals, made rich and dark by much STAINED GLASS (the windows are better collectively than individually). S aisle first from E, 1868 by *W. H. Constable*, rather harsh; a fine W rose of c. 1870, with abstract patterns by *Bell & Co.*; s chapel by *A. L. Moore*, c. 1891–2; six-light E window with Te Deum, c. 1911 by *James Powell*. Brass GAS BRACKETS in the chancel. WAR MEMORIAL on W wall.

HOLY TRINITY, Church Lane, East Finchley. 1845–6 by *A. Salvin*, who lived at East Finchley and was Vicar's Warden. Set in quite a large leafy churchyard. A modest effort for a humble neighbourhood, at that time still more of a village than a suburb. Ragstone with freestone dressings, with an octagonal bell-turret corbelled out between two W lancets. Aisles with plate tracery, added in 1860 (S) and 1866 (N). STAINED GLASS. Geometric E window and two W lancets by *Willement*, 1846. Aisle windows of the 1860s by *Gibbs* (S aisle, first from E) and *O'Connor*. CHURCH HALL to the E, now community centre, the main part dated 1913, brick with mullioned windows.

ST BARNABAS, Holden Road, Woodside Park. 1912–14 by *J. S. Alder*. Red brick with stone dressings. W front with tall Dec window above a baptistery, flanked by turrets. Surprisingly grand inside: stone arcades with clustered piers; clerestory; apsed and aisled choir. W end divided off 1970. STAINED GLASS. E window, 1947 by *A. E. Buss*. Lady Chapel, 1922 by *George Daniel*. Three windows by *Goddard & Gibbs*, 1973. HALL by *Patricia Brock*, 1985.

ST MARY, Hendon Lane. A low, broad C15 building of ragstone with a modest battlemented W tower with diagonal buttresses and a SE corner turret continuing only up to belfry level. Some fragments of Norman zigzag and foliage are reset in the W wall. The interior is oddly shapeless, with a N aisle, s aisle and outer s aisle. The N aisle is of medieval origin (described as new in 1496, although a N aisle and chantry chapel already existed in the C14), but its arcade, together with the clerestory, was rebuilt when *Newman & Billing* added the inner s aisle in 1872. Both arcades have octagonal piers. The outer aisle is by *Sir Charles Nicholson*, 1932. A remarkable feature of the old parts is a narrow skewed four-centred arch on each side of the chancel arch, to allow for the fact that the chancel is narrower than the nave. Flat-pitched C15 nave roof, with moulded tie-beams and curved braces, uncovered in the early C20. The chancel was extended and its w end repaired by *Caröe & Partners* in 1953 after severe war damage.

FONT. C13 Purbeck marble on modern shafts; small octagonal bowl with two pointed blank panels to each face. FURNISHINGS. Pale wood, in the Comper tradition, 1953, partly displaced by bald reordering of the chancel. STAINED GLASS. Fragments from a window by *H. Holiday*, 1880, s aisle E, above three mosaic panels with flowers, set in the lower part of the window. Other pieces in the s aisle w window. Chancel and NE chapel E, 1953–4 by *Harcourt Doyle*. BRASSES. One elegant C15 lady (w wall). In the N chapel a smaller lady (husband missing), Juliana, wife of Richard Prate, †1488. – Simon Skudemore †1609 and wife, two figures and shield; another wife of the same period on the same slab. Several other inscriptions. MONUMENTS. Alexander Kinge, Auditor to the Exchequer, †1618 and wife; of Finchley Manor House (q.v.). Kneeling figures in profile facing each other across a prayer desk, in a Corinthian aedicule with columns on cherub corbels and an arch with cherub heads in the coffering; a shield on the entablature. – Thomas Allen †1681 and wife †1663, 'erected by Edward Allen' and signed '*Allen* fecit'. Bold architectural wall monument with a curtain framing the inscription and a top-heavy broken pediment with flaming urn, on thin black marble columns. – John Searle †1682. A simpler version of the above; architectural wall monument with flaming urn, trophies of arms and a shield below. – Thomas Allen †1780, flat Adamish tablet of coloured marbles, very pretty. – Several minor tablets.

CHURCHYARD. Some handsome monuments and chest tombs. Major Cartwright, the radical, †1824, obelisk erected 1835 by public subscription. Richard Norris †1779, with reclining veiled woman and urn; some good tombstones, especially two of the 1730s near the s door, with cherubs' heads, skull, hourglass etc.

ST PAUL, Long Lane. 1886 by *J. Ladds*. Ragstone, Geometric tracery; the intended tower was not built.

### 2. Roman Catholic

ST PHILIP THE APOSTLE, Regents Park Road. 1933 by *T. H. B. Scott* and 1959–60 by *T. G. B. Scott*. Romanesque, on an elevated site. Figure of St Philip by *Philip Lindsey Clark*.

ST ALBAN, Nether Street. 1909 by *P. A. Lamb*. Plain red brick Perp. w tower porch with niche and statue.

### 3. Other places of worship

The new C19 suburbs of Finchley had plenty of Nonconformist supporters. There were sixteen congregations by 1903. Surviving buildings demonstrate the crescendo of building activity around the turn of the century, and the falling off since.

EAST FINCHLEY METHODIST CHURCH, High Road. 1896–7 by *Elijah Hoole*. A striking red brick landmark; lancet style, with nice moulded brick detail, a turret on the r. Lofty interior, plain apart from some moulded brick patterning on the E wall. Pulpit removed 1992. The gallery retains its decorative balustrade; the space behind is divided off. Former hall to the w by *G. E. Withers*, 1908–9.

EAST FINCHLEY BAPTIST CHURCH, Creighton Avenue. The original building (converted to housing) 1902 by *G. & R. P. Baines*, knapped flint and freestone dressings, one of their playful Free Gothic designs, typical of the turn of the century. Tapering octagonal buttresses flank the central bay. Art Nouveau iron work and cresting. The present church of 1930 is a tired echo by the same firm; now entered through a recent side extension.

FINCHLEY METHODIST CHURCH, Ballards Lane. 1904 by *H. E. Jones*, red brick, Dec Gothic detail, with tower and spire. Beside it the plain Gothic earlier church, yellow brick with stone dressings, 1879 by *Charles Bell*, now a hall. Porch of 1973.

ST MARGARET UNITED REFORMED CHURCH, Victoria Avenue. Built as a church hall for Presbyterians; 1907 by *W. D. Church & Son*, free Perp in red brick with stone dressings. The planned church was not built.

NORTH FINCHLEY UNITED REFORMED CHURCH. 1864–5, Dec Gothic, with tower and spire. E extensions, 1894. STAINED GLASS in transepts brought from New College, Swiss Cottage.

FRIENDS MEETING HOUSE, Alexandra Grove. 1966–7 by *H. V. Sprince*. Stock brick, with corner windows, and flat roofs stepping up from the hall to the warden's flat at the back.

FINCHLEY UNITED SYNAGOGUE, Kinloss Gardens. 1964–7 by *Dowton and Hurst*. Very large, to accommodate 2,000. Reinforced concrete with Portland stone cladding on the front elevation. Severe interior with panels of dark mosaic.

## 4. Cemeteries

ST PANCRAS AND ISLINGTON CEMETERY, High Road, East Finchley. Vast. Eighty-eight acres acquired by the St Pancras Vestry were opened in 1854; a further ninety-four acres for Islington were added to the NE in 1877. The winding routes and fine mature trees give the landscape of the older parts considerable appeal, despite unworthy C20 buildings cluttering the approach, tarmac surfaces and crude municipal road signs. Of the original ragstone Gothic buildings by *Barnett & Birch* there remain a northern pair of gatehouses with their railings (but not gates) and the Anglican chapel, cruciform, with Dec windows and central spire. Simple R.C. chapel further E, 1896, also Dec. More remarkable is the Islington chapel of 1896 by *Forsyth & Maule*, progressive Arts and Crafts Gothic in brick and stone, with a playful timber cupola and a canted apse with buttresses thrusting through the tiled eaves. Crematorium 1937 by *Albert Freeman*. The most splendid MONU-MENT is the Mond Mausoleum for Ludwig Mond, Lord Melchett, †1909, a fine grey granite and Portland stone Grecian temple by *T. A. Darcy Braddell*, based on the Temple of Nemesis, Rhamnus. Two fluted Ionic columns *in antis* below a pediment. Amidst countless tombs lost in rampant undergrowth, a scatter of smaller mausolea. The most prominent are S of the Islington chapel, a classical temple to Henry Carter †1876, and two in Mausoleum Road nearby: Penfold Family, classical, with rusticated walls; Davey family, 1882 etc., Gothic, with steep roof of stone slabs.

St Marylebone Cemetery (East Finchley Cemetery), East
End Road. Founded in 1854. Notoriously sold in 1987 after long
neglect by the City of Westminster; the ragstone buildings by
*Barnett & Birch* were at last restored in 1994–6. Elaborately railed
approach with Gothic Lodge and Dec Gothic Anglican chapel
with crocketed flèche over the entrance. Further w, the smaller
Dissenters' chapel, and the Crematorium by *Sir E. Cooper*, 1937.
Slightly Early Christian (cf. Golders Green Crematorium, which
set the fashion), with low-pitched pantiled roofs and careful tile
detail to the round-arched windows. The chimney, with receding
octagonal top, does not quite convince as a campanile. Dignified
brick interior with white plastered vaults.

The grounds have a formal central yew-lined avenue leading s,
and a square of straight paths to the w. The cemetery is particularly rich in ambitious Edwardian MONUMENTS. – E of the
Anglican chapel, Sir Peter Nicol Russell, engineer, †1905, by *Sir
Bertram Mackennal*, 1919. Against a tall pedestal a dramatic
bronze group: a workman to whom an angel gestures upward
towards a portrait bust of the deceased. – Further E a clutch of
quite grandiose tombs: among them John George Abraham †1912
and family, stone enclosure with very large standing angel. – Faith
Sparrow †1910, angel under a classical aedicule. – Glenesk
Mausoleum, by the circle on the central avenue, 1899 by *Arthur
Blomfield* for Lord Glenesk. A substantial Gothic chapel with
sculpture: N gable with Christ flanked by angels and soldiers.
Corner buttresses with evangelist finials. – Further s: Thomas
Skarratt Hall †1903, 'for forty years an Australian colonist'. Mighty
granite sarcophagus in Napoleonic taste, raised high. Intricate
artistic lettering. Based on the Roman sarcophagus of C. L. Scipio
Barbatus. – Thomas Tate †1909. A bronze youth rising from an
elaborate Roman sarcophagus. By *F. Lynn Jenkins*, 1910. – Harry
Ripley †1914, by *William Reid Dick*. Also bronze; a restrained
draped female mourner, set on a rough granite plinth. – William
Calvert †1927, female figure in low relief. – Duncan Monro
Macdonald †1949, fine art dealer. Abstract pierced form.

## PUBLIC BUILDINGS

Barnet Law Courts, Regents Park Road, Finchley Central.
1980s, with moderate Postmodern trimmings. Primrose House
adjoining is the former St Mary's Infants School, pretty Arts and
Crafts style of 1905.

North Finchley Library, Ravensdale Avenue. 1936 by
*Percival T. Harrison*, Borough Engineer and Surveyor. Pleasant
Neo-Georgian, the ground floor of rusticated brick with arched
windows. Reading room and children's library flanking the entrance,
separated by glazed screens.

East Finchley Library, Great North Road. 1938, also by
*Harrison*, and in a similar spirit, with assembly room on the upper
floor. Regular front, but with the surprise of a quadrant-shaped
adult library with saucer domes, approached through a circular
inner hall.

Church End Library, Hendon Lane. 1964 by *F. G. F. Nutter*

of the Borough Engineer's Department. Small and informal: a curtain wall with zigzagging windows to the ground floor; free-standing bookshelves.

LEISURE CENTRE, High Road. Uninspired but unmissable massive group in American style, developed in 1993–6 by *SBT Planning* for THI Leisure Parks on the site of the old municipal Lido. Around a large car park, Warner Bros' vast HOLLYWOOD BOWL (bowling alley and cinemas), SWIMMING POOL and a row of low restaurants. All of grey blockwork and red trim, overlaid by garish advertising. The swimming pool is pleasantly light and airy inside, with hinged laminated trusses and ridge lighting. The cinemas, by *Unick Architects*, have a huge upstairs space-age foyer where flashing disco lights provide the 1990s equivalent to the atmospheric interiors of the 1930s.

HEALTH CENTRE, Oak Lane, East Finchley. 1938, built by the Borough together with the Grange Estate (*see* Perambulation 1). Neat, two-storeyed and flat-roofed in the functional manner favoured for health buildings in the 1930s.

FINCHLEY MEMORIAL HOSPITAL, Bow Lane. The earliest part was built as a cottage hospital, 1908 by *E. I'Anson & Son*; a busy mixture of materials in Arts and Crafts fashion, with tile-hung gables and turreted porch. In the entrance hall, bronze busts to the principal donors, Mr and Mrs Ebenezer Homan of Friern Watch. War memorial wing 1921–2, many later additions.

NATIONAL HOSPITAL NEURO REHABILITATION UNIT, High Road, East Finchley. Or, in the more friendly terms of the foundation stone of this pretty building, a Country and Convalescent Home, for the Hospital in Queen Square Bloomsbury. 1896–7 by *R. Langton Cole*. Projecting wing with a tile-hung gable and a large window with patterned leaded lights. Half-timbered lodge by Bishop's Avenue.

AVENUE HOUSE, East End Road. A villa built in 1859 and largely reconstructed and extended after it was acquired in 1870 by H. C. Stephens, son of Dr Henry Stephens, the inventor of Stephens Ink. He left house and grounds to the borough in 1918. Confused Italianate stucco front to the road with gabled E wing. Eclectically picturesque garden front, L-shaped with NE turret. In the angle, a rustic Italianate tower with projecting eaves, enlivened by Anglo-Norman doors and windows. The addition to the E end is of 1884; of stone, with mullioned windows and a quirky corner bay looking out over the grounds from a large drawing room. Entrance hall with panelled staircase and remains of stencilled beams and elaborately crafted Victorian joinery. The bold beamed and stencilled ceilings of drawing room and anteroom were restored after a fire in 1989.

LODGE and STABLE BLOCK, with a little turret, *c.* 1880. Further E by the road, swathed in ivy, a WATER TOWER which once served a now demolished laundry. To its N a crenellated enclosure around gardener's house and garden, intended as a picturesque eyecatcher from the house; derelict at the time of writing. Excellent, well-cared-for GROUNDS, planted by Stephens with specimen trees; mounds to E and S shut out the surroundings and create the illusion of greater size.

STERNBERG CENTRE FOR JUDAISM, East End Road. Established here in 1981. It includes the Leo Baeck College and Library, a synagogue, primary school, museum and much else. The present C18 house is a successor to the medieval moated house of the Finchley submanor of Bibbesworth, owned by the Bishop of London and occupied by a succession of wealthy London merchants through the Middle Ages. In 1622 it was acquired from the family of Alexander Kinge by Edward Allen, whose descendant, Thomas Allen, rebuilt it on a new site (rainwater head 1723).

The house faces NE, large, plain and dignified Early Georgian, seven by three bays, with three storeys over a basement. An attic floor and N extension were added for the convent and school of St Marie Auxiliatrice, in occupation 1921–81. The centre bays of each side project slightly. Decoration is confined to a flat rusticated door surround, quoins, and urns on the parapet. Windows with straight heads of rubbed brick. Entrance and garden sides are identical, except that a staircase with original iron railings appears on the entrance side. A minor entrance on the short SE side leads to a central corridor. The entrance hall occupies the central bay and two bays to the r., and has on its r. side a lofty panelled stair-hall with a fine stair with twisted balusters and fluted Corinthian newels. The rest of the hall is single-storeyed. To its l. a three-bay reception room; the plaster decoration on walls and ceiling may be embellishment of the early C20 (the owner from 1905 to 1918 was A. W. Gamage, of the department store). Upstairs rooms with plain panelling, on either side of a central corridor with pilasters; secondary stairs at the SE end.

NW of the house, one-storey outbuildings, extended and converted to museum and offices, 1991. SCULPTURE: in the forecourt, Renew our days, by *Naomi Blake*, 1986, fibreglass; by the approach to the house, Jacob and the Angel, by *Fred Kormis*, resin. Biblical garden in the grounds to the W, where part of the MOAT survives. Until the late C19 there was a long formal canal around an island, across the road to the E, on axis with the house; there were fishponds here by 1692.

NORTH LONDON ISMAILI CENTRE, No. 273 East End Road. 1996. Discreet traditional materials and massing. A substantial building. Stock brick with slate roof, deep eaves, projecting centre in cream render framing entrance and window above with stepped top.

EAST FINCHLEY UNDERGROUND STATION. 1939 by *Charles Holden* and *L. H. Bucknell*, carefully refurbished by *Avanti Architects*, 1996. Built as the terminus of the Northern Line, incorporating staff offices. Red brick, with a long rather unbalanced wing of offices to the W. Cream-tiled foyer lit by a triple window with decorative glazing. The platforms have cantilevered concrete roofs and integrated signs and lights, and the tracks are crossed by a bridge of offices approached, in Bauhaus mode, by curved glazed staircases. On a parapet, a large stylized metal statue of an archer by *Eric Aumonier* (recast 1957), symbolizing the former hunting forest of North Middlesex.

WEST FINCHLEY STATION. 1933, though in a style similar to the earlier (1872) stations on the Finchley–High Barnet line. Fittings from old stations in Northern England were used. Footbridge from Wintersett and Ryhill, near Barnsley.

WOODSIDE PARK STATION. Built 1872. A modest brick building,

still with attached one-storey coal offices by the Woodside Park Road entrance. Two traditional weatherboarded signalboxes on the W side of the line.

RAILWAY VIADUCT, Dollis Road. 1863–7 by *Sir John Fowler* and *Walter Marr Brydone*. Thirteen red brick arches with parapet. It has an unusual pier construction: the piers being subdivided into two sub-pieces. Built for the branch line from Finsbury Park to Edgware.

## Educational buildings

BISHOP DOUGLASS R.C. HIGH SCHOOL, Hamilton Road, East Finchley. A striking composition to the road, unified by the use of a pinkish brick, crisply and unfussily detailed. From l. to r.: workshops with a zigzagging profile of N lights; a four-storey classroom block containing the recessed main entrance under a plain brick end wall, the hall with dramatic concave roof, and a lower flat-roofed wing. The hall is L-shaped; the back part is closed off by movable screens. These parts by *Gerard Goalen*, 1972–80. Behind are earlier buildings by *David Stokes & Partners*, 1967–9.

FINCHLEY CATHOLIC HIGH SCHOOL, Woodside Grange Road, North Finchley. On this site from 1928. C20 buildings are grouped around the WHITE HOUSE, an asymmetrical stucco-Gothic villa known as Woodside Grange, built between *c.* 1885 and 1894. Unpleasant surfaces deprive it of charm. Battlemented, with an irregular E entrance front of 3–2–2 bays, with stair-tower rising behind. S front with four very shallow bows. Entrance hall with marble paving, staircase behind with good iron balustrade. C19 Gothic LODGE on Woodside Grange Road, rendered and ashlar-lined.

PARDES HOUSE SCHOOL, Hendon Lane, Church End. Founded as Christ's College, 1858. The first buildings (by *Salvin*) do not survive. The existing tall two-storey gabled block in diapered red and blue brick, with its odd circular stair-turret, is by *Edward Roberts*, 1861, the start of an ambitious scheme which was not completed, towering over the more modest village church across the road. Former boarding school block, 1925–6 by the *MCC*, a long L-shaped group with mullioned windows; Dec tracery to the hall window facing the road.

WOODHOUSE SIXTH FORM CENTRE, Woodhouse Road. A long stuccoed house, extensively rebuilt for G.W. Wright Ingle in 1888. The NE service wing (with former billiard room) is all of this date, but the main range incorporates an earlier five-bay house with a bow to the rear, probably the house which belonged from 1788 to the plasterer Thomas Collins (†1830), friend and executor of the architect William Chambers. In the entrance hall, two classical roundels (a man reading and a man teaching a youth), possibly C18; other interiors all late C19.

ELEMENTARY SCHOOLS. Two attractive Edwardian examples. MANORSIDE SCHOOL, Squires Lane. *c.* 1900; long, one-storey frontage of brick and terracotta, with some eccentric free Wrenaissance motifs and boldly lettered entrances. Big segmental gables to the two main halls. MARTIN SCHOOL, High Road, East Finchley. 1912. A low S-facing group attractively composed behind handsome railings; central hipped-roofed hall flanked by lower ranges with gables; just a little restrained brick patterning over windows and doors.

Former SCHOOL, No. 451 High Road. 1903. Two-storey Neo-Georgian front of fourteen bays; Baroque doorcases to the end bays and bold curly keystones to the ground-floor windows.

## PERAMBULATIONS

### 1. East Finchley

As with North Finchley, the commercial centre lies along the GREAT NORTH ROAD and has the usual ingredients. On the E side the PHOENIX, an early cinema of 1910, remodelled by *Howes & Jackman*, 1938; austere black and white exterior, decorative frieze inside. A terracotta-trimmed Edwardian parade climbs smartly uphill to the junction with Fortis Green. N of the station MCDONALD'S, an obtrusive horseshoe of brown brick offices, five and six storeys, 1987–92 by *Ardin Brookes & Partners*, and the plain C19 BALD FACED STAG (with stag on parapet) at the corner of East End Road.

EAST END ROAD led from the old hamlet to Finchley village. Now unpleasantly busy, yet still with some green stretches along its winding route. A few older buildings and a few new ones worth noting amidst unexceptional suburbia. First on the S side, No. 250, adapted in 1993 as the BOBATH CENTRE for children with cerebral palsy. Built in 1847–8 as a National School by *A. Salvin*, the architect also of Holy Trinity East Finchley. An attractive low U-shaped composition, red brick with Tudor detail. Slightly projecting centre with high gable terminating in a bellcote, porches in the angles. On the N side, No. 273, the North London Ismaili Centre (*see* Public Buildings, above). Further w, the FIVE BELLS, a plain gabled brick pub of the 1860s pleasantly set back from the road, a rebuilding of an older inn. Some way on, a diversion down Trinity Avenue brings one to No. 1 ELMHURST AVENUE, by *Newton Clarke, c.* 1989. A layered front: a gable of concrete blocks, with inset entrance, in front of a larger roughcast gable echoing the neighbouring houses. Forceful jutting dormers at the sides. Back in East End Road, on the S side, FAIRACRES, three bays, three storeys, C19 stuccoed. Then NAZARETH HOUSE (home for the elderly), on the site of a mid-C19 house in its own grounds. A decent plain C19 brick two-storey wing of 1–5–1 bays remains, to the r. of 1970s buildings with a prominent slate-hung pyramidal steeple. Extensive rear parts by *Plaskett Marshall Architects Partnership*, completed 1980. Opposite St Marylebone Cemetery (*see* above), No. 61, CONVENT OF THE GOOD SHEPHERD. Its core is East End House, a nice early C19 five-bay villa with Greek Doric porch. The grounds now much filled up with C20 housing. Particularly attractive are the groups to the N, 1976–9 by Chalice Housing Ltd: houses and three-storey flats in closes, with angled paths running off from irregular parking areas.

The most appealing parts of East Finchley lie between East End Road and the High Road, where the intricate road pattern still reflects the haphazard growth of the area. The OS map of 1863 shows two main centres; the s one, all rebuilt, lay around the old

Market Place. N of this, earlier C19 small villas and terraces remain on the s side of CHURCH LANE near the High Road and later ones of *c.* 1865–7 on the w side of LONG LANE, parallel to the new railway line, and in TRINITY ROAD. The latter has an unusual and charming group: six pairs of cottages with fringed eaves of the type found on station buildings, over central recessed balconies; rendered fronts with quoins. ALBION VILLAS, plainer brick pairs opposite, have the date 1869.

Rebuilding began in the 1930s and continued after the Second World War. Around RED LION HILL and OAK LANE much was cleared for the three- and four-storey red brick flats of the Borough of Finchley's GRANGE ESTATE (first block completed 1938). The centrepiece is CHALLONER CLOSE, with a formal curved centre range, MOWBRAY HOUSE, three storeys with hipped roof. Contemporary Health Centre (q.v.) in Oak Lane. Other blocks were flat-roofed in a more modernist idiom, but most were given new top floors with slate roofs in *Barnet*'s refurbishment scheme of 1989.

WILMOT CLOSE and THACKRAH CLOSE, off Tarling Road. A group of parish almshouses. Cleeve House, 1895 by *Stephen Salter & Adams*, is a simple red brick two-storeyed range with gables and a continuous wooden balcony. Polygonal meeting room at the end, added 1900. Behind, pale brick groups of 1957 (Haynes House), 1963–7 (Norris House) and 1972–3. THACKRAH CLOSE is more decisively neo-vernacular, red brick with dark pantiled roofs, 1985 by *Manning & Clamp*.

In STRAWBERRY VALE, E of the High Road, HAWTHORNE DENE, now painfully close to the widened North Circular Road, is a remarkable pair of back-to-back cottages of *c.* 1825–6 by the builder *James Frost*. A yellow brick cube with hipped slate roof. The interior is probably unique: the shallow vaulted ceilings are plastered tiles on fluted iron ribs and the staircases are of stone with cast-iron balustrades. Apparently an early form of fire protection and perhaps influenced by Soane's Bank of England.

Further on, the long curving five-storey barrier block is part of a high-density mixed housing development by *Bickerdike Allen Bramble*, 1978–9. Sheltering behind, tightly packed clusters of low houses with abrupt monopitch roofs, all in the same monotonous brown brick.

## 2. North and West Finchley

The centre of North Finchley is marked by the TALLY HO, rebuilt at the wedge-shaped junction of Ballards Lane and Great North Road *c.* 1924–35, with gables all round and Shavian Ipswich windows. To its s, the dubiously named GRAND PARADE, an effort in a streamlined Dudok manner, with passage linking the two roads. Brick fronted; in the arcade, coloured tiles, and some period shopfronts. Further s the huge bulk of the GAUMONT (*W. E. Trent*, 1938) went in 1989, leaving an empty space at the time of writing.

Along the HIGH ROAD scattered efforts at Edwardian urbanity or 30s modernity catch the eye above the mediocre shopfronts. From s to N, on the E side: No. 704 (Argos); expressionist moulded stone verticals. After a quiet C19 pale brick stucco-trimmed terrace comes the most dynamic contribution, No. 776 at the N corner of Friern Park, dated 1906. Free style with Art Nouveau leanings, in brick with yellow terracotta. Two punchy towers with shallow bows and undulating parapets. No. 790, also clad in terracotta, is more traditionally gabled. Further on a 1980s SAINSBURYS provides some ground-level interest by a brick arcade masking the shop windows. On the W side, No. 759 (Harveys' Beds), of the 1930s, quite tall, with some fancy brickwork and attachments for flagpoles. At the corner of Hall Street, No. 765, a former bank dated 1905, brick with stone dressings, with a festively garlanded pediment on pilasters.

VICTORIAN HOUSING. TORRINGTON PARK to the E has the best of the earlier to mid-C19 classical stucco villas remaining in the area, Nos. 32–38; the centre of the first pair projects, that of the second is recessed. There are a few others left in the High Road S of the Tally Ho (Nos. 653–665; 659–661). The most coherent later C19 development is further S, W of Ballards Lane, where MOSS HALL CRESCENT, THYRA GROVE and ALEXANDRA GROVE were laid out between 1870 and 1890 on part of the Moss Hall Estate. The crescent has twelve Victorian villas in a gentle curve, pale brick with simple Italianate stucco detail. Semi-detached pairs in Thyra Grove and Alexandra Grove. Further N, LODGE LANE, a humbler artisan development of the 1820s onwards. Simple terraces remain on the N side; also TORRINGTON COTTAGE, a small early C19 three-bay villa by CHURCH PATH. This is an old right of way preserved amidst the suburban houses, which runs towards the church in Finchley village.

The area of WOODSIDE PARK, W of the High Road, developed around the station in the later C19, but only a few of the substantial original villas remain amongst an assortment of C20 replacements. The variety can be sampled along WOODSIDE PARK ROAD. In WOODSIDE AVENUE, No. 21, NANSEN VILLAGE, housing for overseas students. A cluster of flats, 1969–71, by *Lush & Lester*, brutally romantic in red brick with monopitch roofs and abrupt concrete chamfers. GREEN BANK, the turning marked by a big Corinthian capital, has attractively grouped two-storey terraces, reminiscent of Span, 1961 by *Ronald Salmon & Partners*. Weatherboarded upper floors, communal landscaping with tiny back gardens. In ST ANDREW'S CLOSE opposite, nicely detailed detached houses of *c.* 1930, still in an Arts and Crafts tradition, a demure contrast to No. 42, a pale brick mid–late-C19 villa with bold bracketed eaves and Doric porch. Opposite is the NORTH LONDON HOSPICE, one to three storeys tucked into a slope, brown brick and pantile roofs, 1990–2 by *Peabody Design Group (Kit Platten)*.

To the W of the railway line in WEST FINCHLEY was the Brent Lodge Estate. A stuccoed lodge remains as No. 361 NETHER STREET. The estate was acquired by the Brent Garden Village Society and building plots leased from 1911. The house, a handsome bow-fronted villa, was demolished after the Second World War. CEDARS COURT, The Drive, was part of the early development, 1912 by *Taylor & Huggins*; a block of flats with Baroque trim, an unusual scheme of cooperative flats with shared services, intended for middle-class families.

Between the Great North Road and Friern Barnet open land remained until the First World War. A large area of Finchley UDC council housing was begun on the Woodhouse Estate, s of WOODHOUSE ROAD, in 1915. The most attractive area is the second phase, laid out in garden suburb tradition in 1919–21. The broad-verged INGLEWAY leads to a large green; houses around it are grouped in pairs and short terraces, and cluster picturesquely on the northern slopes. Some houses are plain brick, others painted or plastered. Indiscriminate window renewal and the replacement of most of the small grey slates of the roofs by coarser tiles have, alas, diminished the appeal. To the s, around FALLOWFIELDS DRIVE, yellow brick housing of the 1990s, a denser but friendly streetscape mixing houses and low flats.

### 3. Finchley Central

The junction of the old route of HENDON LANE with Regents Park Road, made in the 1820s, is marked by the corner turret of KING EDWARD HALL, shops with hall above, 1911 by the local firm *Taylor & Huggins*, in a distinctive hard classical style. Stone mullioned windows to the first-floor hall. Only a little remains as evidence of the old village. The medieval church (*see* above) is tucked away in Hendon Lane; opposite are some c19 cottages in COLLEGE TERRACE. The best house is No. 56 Hendon Lane, PARK HOUSE, an excellent five-bay house of 1739. Two storeys on a basement. Rubbed brick segmental window heads and pedimented Doric doorcase. Roof parapet with recessed brick panels. No. 58, at the corner of Hendon Avenue, is a much modified and added to c19 LODGE of the former Grass Farm, built by *Edward Roberts*, red brick and tile-hanging.

Points of interest in the surrounding suburbs are described roughly anti-clockwise, starting from Hendon Lane.

HENDON AVENUE was laid out c. 1900 on the Grass Farm Estate. It winds w past affluent early c20 houses; the N side largely by the local firm *Bennett & Richardson*, those on the s side in more various Arts and Crafts styles, e.g. No. 19 by *Paxton Hood Watson*, 1903. Tucked away down a drive, No. 30a, 1956–8 by *Chamberlin, Powell & Bon*, a discreet modern house which sits on slim supports over a garage, with an external staircase giving access to wide first-floor balcony and main room. Dark weatherboarding and white painted timber walls; a brick core projects above with clerestory lighting.

VILLAGE ROAD at the bottom of Hendon Avenue leads to FINCHLEY GARDEN VILLAGE, built by Finchley Co-Partnership Society, formed in 1908. A charming garden suburb of 1909–14; small pairs of houses mostly roughcast and gabled, laid out very attractively around an informal green. Designed by *Frank E. Stratton* of the local firm *Bennett & Stratton*. He is commemorated by a memorial lamp on the green.

COLLEGE FARM, Fitzalan Road. A surprising interlude among the streets off Regents Park Road built up in the garden suburb tradition. Now a show farm with rare breeds grazing beside the poplar-lined drive, but built as the Express Dairy Company's pioneering model dairy, 1883 by *Frederick Chancellor*. Picturesque five-gabled front, the centre gable half-timbered, the end ones tile-hung. Foreman's house at the end in similar style. Behind is a double courtyard with brick buildings built to house cows and ancillary dairy functions. Attractive dairy (now teashop) with timber lanterns crowning a double pyramid roof and decorative tilework inside. Silo with a pair of full height convex bays, each with an integral loading bay. The dairy was the first to practise tuberculin testing (1921).

At the s end of Regents Park Road, near the North Circular Road, bronze SCULPTURE of 'La Délivrance' by *L. Guillaume*, 1920. Woman with raised arms and sword, on a hemisphere.

Near the N end of EAST END ROAD, AVENUE HOUSE and its grounds and the STERNBERG CENTRE further s are the chief points of interest (for both, *see* Public Buildings, above). Immediately N of Avenue House, HERTFORD HOUSE (council offices), a hefty Italianate villa with a tower with tall crested mansard roof, *c.*1860. Near the station, Victorian roads for early commuters: LICHFIELD GROVE, starting with close-set pairs of stucco-trimmed houses and turning Edwardian further s; GLENHILL CLOSE, off to its s, a select period piece of the 1930s. BALLARDS LANE, the long dull main route between Finchley Central and North Finchley, has Edwardian and later parades of shops and flats, with adjacent streets of similar date. In CORNWALL AVENUE one older house remains: CORNWALL HOUSE, a three-bay stucco-fronted villa, probably late C18; at the back a bow and a long wing, of painted brick. To the s, in BOW LANE, opposite Finchley Memorial Hospital (q.v.), some good decorative Edwardian villas.

# FRIERN BARNET

A small, thin parish E of Finchley, stretching N to Whetstone. It became an Urban District in 1895, a borough in 1933. Its population grew from under 1,000 in 1851 to 11,566 in 1901 and 23,101 in 1931. The name Friern derives from the brothers of the Order of St John Hospitallers, who held an estate here. Older buildings are strung along Friern Barnet Lane, whose winding course and many old trees still reflect a rural past.

ST JAMES, Friern Barnet Lane. A small medieval church swamped by *W.G. & E. Habershon*'s Gothic enlargement of 1852–3. An attractive mixture of local materials, grey flint and brown pebbly iron conglomerate, used both for the walls of the old church (now the s aisle), and for the C19 N aisle, chancel and small sw tower. Polygonal N extension of the 1970s in disappointing drab brick. C12 s door of one order, very much renewed, with zigzag ornament to the columns, voussoirs and border of the tympanum; segment-arched lintel; tympanum with diapering. C19 chancel arch with coarse foliage corbels. STAINED GLASS. E window by *Alan Younger*, 1974, abstract, red and pink shapes against clear glass. In the nave, late work by *Clayton & Bell*, 1910 etc. Enjoyable minor MONUMENTS. John Cleeve †1725, fine architectural surround, veined marble, broken pediment with two urns. John Cleeve †1748, cartouche with putto and drapery. Four sons and four daughters

of Richard Down, by *J. Bacon Jun.*, 1804, fine and sensitive in its
very shallow relief, with a composition of urns, and on top, under
a pointed arch, a group of ascending figures clearly inspired by
Flaxman.

St John, Friern Barnet Road. A late work by *J. L. Pearson*, begun
1890–1. Completed by *Frank Pearson*: nave 1899–1901, w end to a
modified design, 1911. An ambitious stone building, though not
with an impressive exterior; the intended NE tower was not built.
Tall clerestory windows between prominent flying buttresses,
which tell at once that the church is vaulted throughout. The style
is Gothic of *c.* 1300, continental rather than English, cool but
satisfying. The apsed E end was inspired by the German Cistercian    84
church of Heisterbach, at the request of the vicar, Frederick Hall
(a former curate at Pearson's St Augustine Kilburn). Subtle
spatial effects; the narrow ambulatory around the apse and the s
chapel allow for cross vistas between a variety of pier forms; tall
transept at the w end (the N side is now screened off). FONT.
Handsome polished grey marble multifoil bowl on shafted base. –
COVER in Perp style, from Exeter Cathedral. – PULPIT, *c.* 1920.
A fine eclectic Arts and Crafts piece, octagonal, combining
marquetry in C17 style with carved Gothic foliage brackets and
back panel with angels and shield. – STAINED GLASS. A complete scheme by *Clayton & Bell*. E windows, Adoration of the
Lamb; s chapel, angels (†1892); s transept, St Paul preaching
(†1911); s aisle, bishops; N aisle, Protestant worthies.

   PARISH ROOM to the N, pale brick with canted bay, by *Triforum
Architects*, 1992.

St Peter le Poer, Albion Avenue. 1909–10 by *Caröe & Passmore*,
funded by the sale of the City church of the same name in Old Broad
Street. Red brick, with free Perp tracery, rather plain, but with some
characteristic Caröe detail, especially the bushy eyebrow effect of
the tiled arches between the buttresses framing the aisle windows.
The E end has three irregular gables, the w end rises surprisingly
as a low saddleback tower with belfry dormers. Vaulted chancel;
broad nave with barrel ceiling and five-bay stone arcades (the w two
divided off *c.* 1990) with crenellated capitals. The chief FITTINGS
from the City church are an ample alabaster FONT, *c.* 1873, and an
elegant curved PULPIT with a little restrained carving and (shortened) stairs with twisted balusters, probably dating from the rebuilding of the City church in 1788–92. STATIONS OF THE CROSS,
engraved and coloured wood, by *Wilfred Lawson*. Also by him the
good STAINED GLASS of the seven-light E window (1923): Christ
in Glory and the angels of the seven churches, effectively crowded.
Lady Chapel E: Annunciation, by *J. H. Lawson*, 1969.

Christ Church (Baptist and United Reformed), Friern Barnet
Road. 1909–10. Cheerful Free Perp in the manner of the Baines
firm; red brick with stone stripes, large transepts, on the l. a tower
with battered buttresses and spirelet. Plain lancet CHURCH HALL
behind, 1883.

Methodist Church, Manor Drive. 1931 by *Farrow, Turner &
Cooper*. Plain and substantial, cruciform with polygonal apse.

Town Hall, Friern Barnet Road and Friern Barnet Lane. By *Sir
John Brown, Henson & Partners*, 1939–41. A pleasant accommodating piece of design. Swedish-Modern, with such traditional

features as a porch on attenuated piers below a continuous balcony and a slim cupola rising from a roof of green Westmorland slate. Concave façade, embracing the side of the circus at the crossing of two main roads. The council chamber projects at the back. Staircase lined with marble; two green octagonal columns on the landing.

LIBRARY, Friern Barnet Road. By *W. T. Curtis* of the *MCC*, 1933. Simple brick and stone. Tudor, with three gables and central entrance.

LIBRARY and CLINIC, Colney Hatch Lane. 1963 by *Friern Borough Council*. Pleasant L-shaped group with pantiled roofs, set on a slope; the library entered at first-floor level. Large window in the gable end.

HOLLY PARK SCHOOL, Bellevue Road. Pretty Edwardian elementary school. Chequerwork centre between two big gables.

FRIERN BARNET LANE. The s end starts with an indifferent crossroads shopping centre opposite the Town Hall (pubs dated 1909 and 1910), followed by genteel suburbia. Pleasantly extensive open spaces remain on the w side. First FRIARY PARK, with Statue of Peace on a pile of rocks, splendidly sited on a ridge, 1910. Then the medieval church in its spacious churchyard (q.v.), and North Middlesex Golf Course. The clubhouse is the former MANOR FARM HOUSE, quite a grand stuccoed house with a pediment to its taller central bay, earlier C19, but much altered.

23    On the e side a delightful gem, LAWRENCE CAMPE ALMSHOUSES, *c.* 1612. Some of the oldest surviving almshouses in London. Entirely in the vernacular tradition: a long straight range of brick, with stone stringcourse between its two floors. Seven tenements, with four-centred arched doors, and low windows of three lights on the ground floor, two lights above. Renovated 1843, 1899, and by *John Phillips* in 1982. Next door, a pretty former Victorian SCHOOL (now All Saints and St John Nursery), paid for by John Miles (*see* All Saints, Whetstone), flint-faced with two gables. Off the n end, near the High Road, a few nice early–mid-C19 cottages in SHERWOOD STREET and GREEN ROAD.

COLNEY HATCH LANE runs s from the Town Hall. At the s end its character merges into Edwardian Muswell Hill (*see* Haringey). Between this part and the North Circular Road, a good early postwar council estate by *Friern Borough Council* (*J. Marshall* Engineer and Surveyor), 1946–51. Trim brick flats of three and four storeys, with flat roofs, surrounded by low terraces spaciously laid out around GEORGE CRESCENT. These have concrete porches with portholes, a motif used also on the balconies of the flats. The landscaping took note of Ministry recommendations of 1948 that there should be plenty of trees and open grass areas.

PRINCESS PARK MANOR, Friern Barnet Road. Built as Colney Hatch Asylum, the second Middlesex pauper lunatic asylum (the first was at Hanwell), planned for 1000 patients. Designed by *S. W. Daukes*, built 1849–51. Closed 1994; converted to private

73    housing from 1998. The front range faces n, set well back in spacious grounds, approached down a main avenue past an Italianate LODGE dated 1893. The formal central block is in mixed Italianate style; its centrepiece is an awkwardly tall octagonal domed tower, an echo of Sydney Smirke's dome at Bethlem

Hospital, Lambeth, of a few years earlier. The E-shaped plan adopts the principles of Alderson's Hanwell Asylum of 1829–31: a central block with chapel, assembly hall and kitchens, and on each side seven wards with bedrooms opening onto long day rooms with canted central bays looking s. They are connected by a bleakly disorientating corridor – reputedly the longest in Europe – running the whole extent of the N front. Extended 1857–9 with one- and three-storey blocks. By 1896 the population was over 2,500, partly housed in temporary timber buildings which burnt down in 1903. Seven brick villas for special categories of patients were built around the perimeter in 1908–13. The establishment was originally self-supporting, although almost all traces of its service building to the s – gasworks, water supply, sewage farm, brewery etc. – have disappeared. In the grounds, octagonal arcaded SUMMERHOUSE and water tower.

# GOLDERS GREEN

Golders Green, between Hampstead and Hendon, was part of the parish, later borough, of Hendon. The southern fringe merges with the affluent borders of Hampstead, where large houses (now mostly replaced) began to appear from the late C19 among the cottages let out for summer visitors. Most of the rest was farmland with a few scattered villas until rapid development followed the opening of the station on the Northern Line in 1907, the extension of the line to Edgware (1924) and the construction of the North Circular Road and Hendon Way in the 1920s. The distinctive Jewish character of Golders Green, which began as a result of migration from inner London, was strengthened by émigrés from Eastern Europe and, after the Second World War, by the depopulation of the East End.

In contrast with the disciplined planning of Hampstead Garden Suburb, Golders Green is haphazard in its development. Idealistic planners in the 1960s devised a destructive scheme to divert the traffic of Golders Green Road around a rebuilt multi-storey shopping area* (cf. Wood Green, Haringey), but this was abandoned when Brent Cross was developed as a major centre, and the shops of the Green remain Edwardian. The earlier streets have attractively various small middle-class houses reminiscent of the Suburb's Arts and Crafts cottage style, but, alas, they lack comparable protection and have too often been spoilt by window replacements and car parking.   ·

## RELIGIOUS BUILDINGS

*1. Church of England, R.C. etc.*

ST ALBAN AND ST MICHAEL, North End Road. Planned 1925, built 1932–3, by *Sir Giles G. Scott*. A compact cruciform brick church, the broad crossing tower with battlements and a low tiled roof. Pleasant exterior, carefully detailed in Scott's free Gothic. The tower has subtly tapering canted corners. Hipped tiled roofs

* Report and proposals by *W. S. Atkins & Partners, Minoprio Spenceley & Macfarlane,* and *Nathaniel Lichfield & Associates,* 1965.

to nave and chancel, homely porches with timber lintels, straight-headed windows with ogee-headed lights, of Clipsham stone. The narrow facing bricks disguise a construction of reinforced concrete. The interior is effectively lit by the lantern tower, above a crossing with plain pointed arches. Plastered walls above a dado of Blue Hornton stone. Fittings designed by *Scott*: delicately wrought stone REREDOS with Crucifixion below canopywork; chunky alabaster FONT with tall canopy.

CHURCH HALL to the s, 1909 by *Herbert Wills*, with timber windows and dormers, built as the first church.

ST BARNABAS, Cranbourne Gardens, Temple Fortune. This began as a church of 1915 by *J. S. Alder*. Apsed chancel and Lady Chapel 1932–4 by *E. C. Shearman*; the apse with thin lancets, the chapel with one of Shearman's typical vigorous oversize rose windows with patterned leading, set in a tilted octagon. Nave rebuilt 1962 after bomb damage, by *Romilly B. Craze*, in an etiolated Gothic; very tall, thin, mannered nave windows, w rose in weak imitation of the Lady Chapel. Future uncertain.

ST EDWARD THE CONFESSOR (R.C.), Finchley Road, near Hoop Lane. 1915 by *Arthur Young*. Brick with lively stone dressings. Cruciform; low crossing tower with corner turrets and chequered parapet; w end with corner turrets, also chequered. Nave arcades on quatrefoil piers; clerestory. Timber barrel roof with bosses. Wood carving by *Alfred Robinson*; stone carving by *Joseph Armitage*. STAINED GLASS. Five-light e window by *R. L. Hendra & G. F. Harpes*, 1947. Three windows by *Goddard & Gibbs*, 1968–73.

CARMELITE MONASTERY (nuns), Bridge Lane. Plain brick Gothic buildings of 1908; later additions.

HOLY CROSS AND ST MICHAEL'S CATHEDRAL (Greek Orthodox), Golders Green Road and The Riding. Built as St Michael C. of E., 1913 by *J. T. Lee*; very simple lancet style. w additions in cuspy Gothic by *Caröe & Passmore*, 1924–5. Plain NW tower-porch with spindly classical cupola of 1960 by *James Barrington-Baker*. He also designed a reredos *c.*1938. (STAINED GLASS. E window by *Heaton, Butler & Bayne*, *c.* 1914. – N chapel N wall and N aisle windows by *George J. Hunt* 1914–41.) To the s a huge CHURCH HALL by *Stellios Constantinou*, 1993. Sharp Postmodern detail: red brick with blue brick buttresses, dark mirror glazing.

TRINITY CHURCH (Methodist and United Reformed), Hodford Road. 1922 by *George E. Withers*, for the Methodists. An original building: square church with corner turrets, lit by big clerestory lunettes above lower surrounding rooms and offices. A mixture of Byzantine and Neo-Grec detail; brown and red brick with stone dressings. Low porch with Byzantine capitals, flanked by two squat towers. The windows have patterns of herringbone brickwork below stone architraves. To the w, HODFORD HALL, 1936.

UNITARIAN CHURCH, Hoop Lane. 1925 by *Reginald Farrow*. Small pedimented building with plaster groin vault and apse with semi-dome, designed for a mural PAINTING on canvas by *Ivon Hitchens*, an early work made in 1920–1. The subject is a symbolic forest scene: deer and other animals among trees, in the tradition of Morris & Co. Sturdy Arts and Crafts PULPIT, originally made by Belgian refugees for Cardinal Mercier.

SHREE SWAMINARAYAN TEMPLE, Finchley Road. Built as a Presbyterian church, 1910–11 by *T. Phillips Figgis*. Broad front of brick with conventional stone Perp tracery.

## 2. Synagogues

UNITED SYNAGOGUE, Dunstan Road. The first and grandest of the many synagogues of the area, by *Digby Soloman*, begun 1921 for a congregation which first met in 1915. Main hall completed 1925 by *Ernest Joseph*, who also added entrance portico, E vestibule and classrooms, completed 1927. Plain Neo-Georgian exterior, brick with stone dressings. Dignified, well-detailed classical interior: oak panelled galleries on three sides on Doric columns, with Ionic ones above (now painted white, originally black); top lighting from a central lantern and E roof-lights. Contemporary FITTINGS: ARK at the E end; marble PULPIT; much STAINED GLASS. Central BIMAH added 1878. Joseph Freedman Hall, 1939; Nursery 1958 by *Ivor Warner*.

NORTH WESTERN REFORM SYNAGOGUE, Alyth Gardens. By *Fritz Landauer*, 1936. Built for a congregation of émigrés. Plain two-storey brick front, slightly splayed ends. To the S, Leo Baeck Centre, 1959 by *Ervin Katona*. Extensions of 1971 by *G. Rottenberg Associates*.

BETH HAMADRASH SYNAGOGUE, The Riding. 1959 by *Shaw & Lloyd*. Large group of hall and synagogue with porch link. Synagogue with brick aisles on a slight zigzag plan; E wall of the centre clad in grey mosaic; inscription panel framed by a big angular-headed window.

MACHZIKE HADATH SYNAGOGUE, Highfield Road. 1983. Grey and red brick with small arched windows; two angled pitched roofs with clerestory roof-lights.

## 3. Crematorium and Cemetery

CREMATORIUM, Hoop Lane. Opened 1902. The first crematorium within easy distance of London; it rapidly became the most important in England. A large, very impressive group spread along the S side of Hoop Lane, best appreciated from the fine grounds which lie behind. The buildings date from 1905 to 1939; they are in a consistent Early Christian or Lombard Romanesque, red brick with round arches and pantiled roofs, but picturesquely irregular in their grouping, linked by a long cloister walk which looks out onto the grounds. The main cloister was built in 1912–16. The buildings behind, from W to E, start with the WEST COLUMBARIUM, a low tower, 1902–3, and the WEST CHAPEL and campanile, 1905 by *Sir Ernest George & Yeates*. In the chapel, original fittings and bust of Sir Henry Thompson, pioneer of cremation, by *Frith*, 1904. EAST CHAPEL by *Mitchell & Bridgwater*, 1938; EAST COLUMBARIUM, 1910–11, with a tall tower, the main focus of the group; behind it the small BEDFORD CHAPEL built in 1911 for the Duke of Bedford. ERNEST GEORGE COLUMBARIUM, by *Alfred B. Yeates*, 1926–8, set back behind an arcade. Galleries on three sides, with a small tower at either end, and a small copper-roofed apse to the N. CHAPEL AND HALL OF

MEMORY, 1939 by *Mitchell & Bridgwater*. At the w end of the
walk in front of the cloister, WAR MEMORIAL, 1919–20, a stone
Ionic temple with segmental pediment, in front of a lily pool.
Opposite, at the E end, MARTIN SMITH MAUSOLEUM, 1904–5
by *Paul Phipps*; of brick and stone, small but quite ornate. To its N
a garden with exedra, formerly with a pergola laid out by *William
Robinson*, 1907. Off the E walk, PHILIPSON MAUSOLEUM, by *Sir
Edwin Lutyens*, 1938: severely classical: circular, of stone with
bronze doors, open shallow dome, surrounded by a stone lattice
screen. Inside, two small urns on a plinth. The grounds start as an
open field in front of the cloister, then become an informal woodland garden with pools, a very English conception. SCULPTURE:
'Into the Silent Land' by *Henry Pegram* R.A., 1924. An impressive
bronze, shrouded figure raising a girl above a sea of souls.
Chanshyam da Birla †1983, standing bronze figure.

GOLDERS GREEN CEMETERY FOR SEPHARDI JEWS, Hoop
Lane. Founded 1895. Two halls linked by an archway, in red and
blue brick, with some patterned tiles. Domestic-looking LODGE
with roughcast and half-timbering. The burial ground is in two
areas, flat slabs in the NE part for Sephardi Jews, more elaborate
upright memorials in the SW part, for members of the West
London Synagogue.


## PUBLIC BUILDINGS

METROPOLITAN POLICE STATION, No. 1069 Finchley Road.
1916 by *J.D. Butler*.

LIBRARY, Golders Green Road. 1935–6. Decent Neo-Georgian.
The Borough of Hendon's first purpose-built branch library.

IVY HOUSE (MIDDLESEX UNIVERSITY), North End Road. An
early C19 villa, much altered; irregular with castellated parts. Home
from 1840 to 1851 of *C.R. Cockerell*, who created a library with
casts of the Bassae frieze, and from 1934 of Anna Pavlova, who
converted the library to a dining room. Later the New College of
Speech and Drama from 1962, then part of Middlesex Polytechnic.

KING ALFRED SCHOOL, Manor Wood, North End Road.
Established 1898 in Ellerdale Road Hampstead as a 'rational',
progressive, co-educational day school; moved to this site on the
Manor House Estate in 1919. Between 1919 and 1934 new buildings in Garden Suburb tradition by *Barry Parker* gradually replaced
old army huts. On the NW corner of the site *E.C. Kaufmann*
added in 1934–6 a one-storey Junior School, in reinforced concrete, in the international style of the 30s, with classrooms which
could be opened up on one side for open-air teaching. They were
replaced from 1991 by new Lower School buildings by *Van
Heyningen & Haward*, built on a rapid programme during school
holidays. As in the older scheme, classrooms are arranged in pairs
on an L-plan, with hall in the angle, looking out over the central
playing field, and continuing the principle of outdoor teaching.
The buildings are timber-framed with gently pitched roofs with
substantial overhangs, and toplighting to the indoor spaces.

LA SAGESSE CONVENT SCHOOL, Golders Green Road. *See*
Perambulation 1.

MANOR HOUSE HOSPITAL, North End Road. Founded 1917 in the Manor House (*c.* 1792 and possibly earlier), which was demolished *c.* 1962. Additions of the 1930s and later; demure four-storey Neo-Georgian wing of 1969 in place of the original building.

GOLDERS HILL PARK. Acquired by the LCC as a public park in 1898. The house (C18, with additions of 1875 by *E. F. Clarke*) was close to North End Road; it was demolished after damage in the Second World War. The grounds were improved in the 1870s for Thomas Spencer Wells, a royal surgeon, by *Robert Marnock*, an advocate of the English landscape tradition. His aim was to create a 'natural gardening' effect, with an enlarged lake to the park. Walled kitchen garden, laid out by the LCC as an 'Old English' garden with pergola and sundial. BANDSTAND in the same spirit. SCULPTURE. Water Baby FOUNTAIN by *Bainbridge Copnall*, *c.* 1950, originally in Victoria Park. Diogenist by *Mark Batten*. Golders Hill Girl by *Patricia Finch*, 1991.

GOLDERS GREEN STATION. 1907; originally the terminus of the Charing Cross, Euston and Hampstead Railway (now the Northern Line). Five curved platforms with a fine array of cantilevered steel canopies.

## PERAMBULATIONS

*1. The Green and the area to its north*

The heart of Golders Green is the crossing of Finchley Road with the old route of North End Road and Golders Green Road. Restrained stone WAR MEMORIAL CLOCK TOWER at the junction, 1923, possibly by *Frank T. Dear*. The Green has become an irregular square, quite urban on its S side, with tall gabled shopping parades of 1908 flanking the approach to Finchley Road, contemporary with the station opposite. The centre is all buses. On the NE side the grand GOLDERS GREEN HIPPODROME by *Bertie Crewe*, opened as a music hall in 1913 (BBC recording studio from 1968). Stuccoed, with Ionic pilasters and rather French-looking channelled rustication. The auditorium has giant Doric columns flanking the boxes; above them, free-standing figures of charioteers drawn by lions.

GOLDERS GREEN ROAD continues NW with shopping parades on each side which demonstrate the stylistic shifts of the Edwardian period. The terraces on the S side, of 1909, start with emphatic upper windows with arched stone transoms. Opposite, CHEAPSIDE, 1911–13, by *H. A. Welch* with *A. Clifford Hollis*, attractive domestic vernacular, with tile-hung gables, in the spirit of Hampstead Garden Suburb. The terrace further along the S side, also by *Welch & Hollis*, is in a quieter Georgian style, with timber cornices and dormers.

Further N the road becomes low and residential with only a few larger punctuations. The first is LA SAGESSE CONVENT SCHOOL, mostly of the 1920s, which began as Woodstock House, an early C19 stuccoed villa. No. 208, YEHOSHUA FRESHWATER CENTRE, a Jewish home and centre for old people of 1990–2 by *Rosenfelder Associates*, rises to three and four storeys in cheerful Postmodern style, L-shaped with a bow across the angle. EAGLE LODGE, mansion flats of 1935–7 by *M. V. Braikevitch*, has classical detail awkwardly applied to tall gaunt blocks. In contrast, HIGHFIELD COURT, in Highfield Road to the E, 1935 by *A. V. Pilichovski* is a Modern Movement composition: flats in an L-shaped group of three storeys of reinforced concrete, painted, framing a half-sunken garden. On the main road, another small shopping centre is marked on the w by two pubs: THE SWAN, an old inn rebuilt in the C19 and early C20, and the PRINCE ALBERT, decoratively neo-Tudor. Further N, off Princes Park Avenue, HARMONY CLOSE, sheltered accommodation and hostel by *David Stern & Partners*, 1977–9, an informal group designed around a mature oak tree, making use of different levels. Two four-storey blocks of pale brick with slate hanging, linked by a bridge; lower buildings around a courtyard behind. Abstract SCULPTURE: Fidelity, by *Naomi Blake*, fibreglass.

FINCHLEY ROAD, created after an Act of Parliament of 1826, and built up only in the C20, has little to note to the N of Golders Green apart from the shopping centre at TEMPLE FORTUNE on the edge of Hampstead Garden Suburb (q.v., below).


## 2. North End and West Heath

NORTH END ROAD and its hinterland belong in character to the fringe of Hampstead. NORTH END itself, once an isolated hamlet among woodland on the Hampstead border, is described under Hampstead (*see* p. 235). Its major houses within the old parish of Hendon were the Manor House, rebuilt as Manor House Hospital, and Golders Hill House opposite, from which the park remains (for both, *see* Public Buildings, above).

Edwardian houses SW of North End, around Golders Hill Park, are interspersed with a scatter of individual modernist buildings of the 1960s. Starting by St Alban's Church (q.v.), WEST HEATH DRIVE has a complete row of *c.* 1910 on the w side with nice Arts and Crafts detail. WEST HEATH AVENUE has superior detached examples of the same date. Here also is a clutch of post-war houses in a variety of styles. No. 17 by *Jellicoe, Ballantyne & Coleridge, c.* 1961, rather Scandinavian: L-shaped, of small buff bricks, shallow copper roof to the main range; simple timber windows, split level plan. Round the corner in GOLDERS PARK CLOSE, No. 6 by *David Stern*, completed 1966, in the more austere style of the 60s; dark blue brick vertical panels at the sides contrasting with horizontal window panels in front and full-height glazing at the back; two storeys over a basement. No. 5 has a curtain-walled upper storey floating over a brick base. Back in West Heath Avenue, No. 21, with a long transparent upper floor overlooking the park, is by *Anthony Levy*, 1961. In WEST HEATH ROAD, which starts on the w side of the park, No. 191, WESTFIELD, also of the 1960s, a large site with a long low house. Overhanging first floor above a ground floor faced in rough yellow stone; the same material used for panels along the boundary wall, effectively alternating with fencing and trees. Opposite, Nos. 114–116, one of the few surviving late Victorian mansions; gable with half-timbering, Tudor porch. Another is No. 84, St Margaret's, tall, with tile-hanging. No. 88 by *David Stern*, completed 1962; simple horizontal lines.

Off West Heath Road, CENACLE CLOSE by *Ted Levy Benjamin & Partners*, 1969–72, one of this firm's attractive developments of small two- and three-storey houses, crisply grouped, with a picturesque broken skyline of monopitch roofs; dark weatherboarding above white brickwork. Opposite, BEECHWORTH CLOSE, built up with individual houses from the 1960s. Two by *Patrick Gwynne*: at the end, No. 4, 1961; two storeys with set-back upper floor, crisp and rectangular. Rooms are arranged around a central top-lit staircase to allow maximum views of the older garden. No. 3, 1963, also with central staircase, has curved corners and canted front and back, and curving garden walls. WESTOVER HILL has larger and sleeker houses in brown brick, mostly by *Gerd Kaufmann*, 1976–9, extended 1986–9. Back downhill to WEST HEATH CLOSE, a 1930s development; mostly commonplace apart from No. 2, Art Deco with green tiles, and No. 7, a carefully composed modernist house, 1932–4 by *R. A. Duncan* of *Percy Tubbs, Son and Duncan*. Roughcast with ribbon windows and sun terraces, and a full-height curved glazed corner. A path at the end leads to HERMITAGE LANE. On the s side, near the borough boundary, medium-rise council housing built for Hendon in 1964 by *GMW*: arranged around a lawn, four-storey flats and maisonettes with inset concrete balconies, also some low old-people's housing and a two-storey shopping terrace.

## HAMPSTEAD GARDEN SUBURB

Pevsner's introduction of 1951 should be quoted in full: 'The aesthetically most satisfactory and socially most successful of all C20 garden suburbs. The conception of the garden suburb is not the same as that of the garden city. The garden city, industrially and commercially an independent unit, was first proposed by Ebenezer Howard in his book of 1898, and first realized at Letchworth, Herts, founded in 1903. The garden suburb goes back to Bedford Park, Acton, begun in 1875, and to Port Sunlight and Bournville. In its social character the Hampstead Garden Suburb comes nearest to what Bedford Park was in its beginnings. The population is on the whole comfortably off and ranges from true sensibility to amateur arty-craftiness. While the garden suburb is not meant to have its own factories, warehouses, etc., it yet needs a social centre to be more than a dormitory. This the Hampstead Garden Suburb has, and it is something to be proud of, as it should be.'

The paragraph above was written when the Suburb was not yet fifty years old. It was famous among planners, but its detailed architectural history had yet to be written. The following expanded account owes much to the Suburb's archive and to recent research, and especially to Mervyn Miller and A. Stuart Gray's *Hampstead Garden Suburb*, 1992.

### History

The Hampstead Garden Suburb was founded in 1907 at the inspiration of Dame Henrietta Barnett (1851–1936), whose experience first as a friend of Octavia Hill and then as the wife of Samuel Barnett,

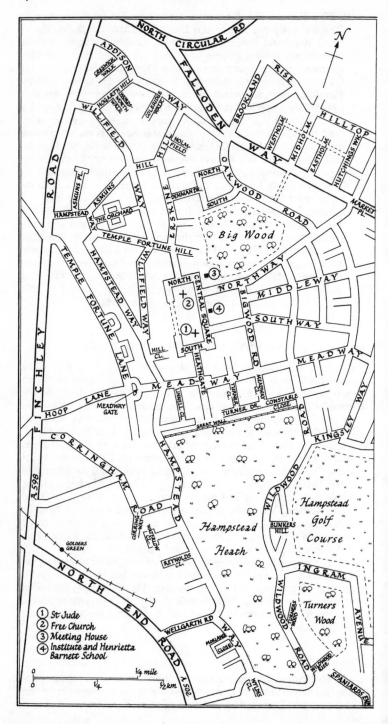

① St Jude
② Free Church
③ Meeting House
④ Institute and Henrietta
   Barnett School

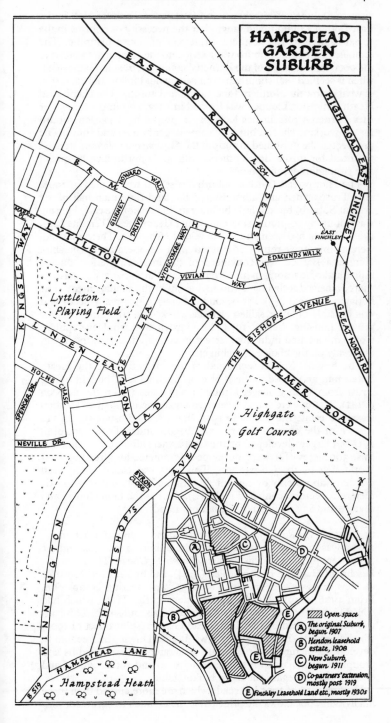

HAMPSTEAD
GARDEN
SUBURB

EAST END ROAD A.504

HIGH ROAD EAST FINCHLEY

BRIM

HOWARD WALK

GURNEY

DRIVE

MARKET PL.

KINGSLEY WAY

LYTTLETON

WIDECOMBE WAY

HILL

DEANS WAY

EAST FINCHLEY

EDMUNDS WALK

VIVIAN WAY

Lyttleton
Playing Field

LEA

ROAD

RICE

THE BISHOP'S AVENUE

GREAT NORTH RD.

LINDEN LEA

HOLNE CHASE

SPENCER DR.

NEVILLE DR.

NORRICE

ROAD

AYLMER ROAD

Highgate
Golf Course

AVENUE

BYRON CLOSE

N

WINNINGTON

THE BISHOP'S

HAMPSTEAD LANE

B 519

Hampstead Heath

Ⓐ

Ⓒ

Ⓓ

Ⓑ

Ⓔ

Ⓔ

⧄ Open space

Ⓐ The original Suburb,
begun 1907

Ⓑ Hendon leasehold
estate, 1908

Ⓒ New Suburb,
begun 1911

Ⓓ Co-partners' extension,
mostly post 1919

Ⓔ Finchley Leasehold Land etc., mostly 1930s

vicar of St Jude's Whitechapel and founder of Toynbee Hall in the East End of London, had taught her the necessity of reforms in the social as well as the aesthetic principles of house planning. The establishment of the Suburb was a sequel to the campaign to preserve the open land to the N of the Barnetts' country retreat at Hampstead, when it seemed that suburban expansion would follow the extension of what is now the Northern Line, sanctioned in 1902. The Hampstead Heath Extension Council was formed in 1903, and in the same year Mrs Barnett wrote in her local paper proposing a garden suburb for the working classes, but with some larger houses and shops. The prospectus she published in 1905 in the *Contemporary Review* stressed the need for mixed development, with its opportunities to spread 'the contagion of refinement'.

The Hampstead Garden Suburb Trust Ltd was floated in 1906. The Trust owned and administered the land (less than half of the present Suburb) but did little building itself; most of the early housing was put up by co-partnership companies (Hampstead Tenants Ltd), like those that had been set up to develop Letchworth. Their principles were commercial return combined with co-operative ownership. Henrietta Barnett was convinced of the improving effect on the individual of investing in his own property. Participants purchased a share, received a dividend and had a say in the management. The initial investment (£5) was beyond the grasp of the really needy and was possible only for skilled artisans, clerks and tradesmen. As for private housing, before 1914 the Garden Suburb Development Company advised individual lessees in conjunction with the Trust, especially on the choice of architect.

The original Suburb consisted of the roads fringing the Heath Extension, and those to the N of it on freehold land bought by the Trust from Eton College, a total of 243 acres (A on the map on p. 141). To these were added several leasehold parcels. A small Hendon leasehold estate was added in 1908 (B); a second estate (C) of 112 acres E of the original Suburb, was begun under Trust control in 1911 but largely developed by the Co-partners after 1919. N and E of this, 300 acres (D) were developed commercially after the First World War by the Co-partners. This tract was called Hampstead Garden Suburb only by agreement with the Trust, and was outside their architectural control. Finally (E), there is the Golf Course and roads E and S of it (Finchley Leasehold Land).

PLANNING. *Sir Raymond Unwin*, who had met Canon Barnett in the 1880s, was involved in the lay-out of the Suburb from 1904 and the plans were prepared by his practice, *Parker & Unwin*. Their plan for Letchworth had just been revealed (1904), and housing for Rowntree at New Earswick, near York (1902–3), was nearing completion. From 1906 to 1914 Unwin was architect to the Trust, which had control over aesthetic matters such as materials and siting. This control was reinforced by the Hampstead Garden Suburb Act of 1906, which overrode the Hendon by-laws. It gave Unwin the freedom to develop his picturesque plan, with a hierarchy of road widths and groupings of houses – in staggered terraces and round greens and closes – that disregard the usual building line.

His first plan of 1905 has roads which are more curved than those finally built, but shows the principal features much as executed, with the northern parts given up to working-class cottages, the s to larger houses, and the public buildings concentrated in Central Square. As at Letchworth, the pattern of streets and squares takes the contours carefully into consideration: Hampstead Garden Suburb is quite hilly. The Central Square is placed on the highest eminence and dominates the Suburb on all sides. Patches of wood are preserved in two places as well as smaller groups of old trees, and the streets are shown planted with new trees. The main streets are neither all straight nor all winding, but rectangular crossings are almost universally avoided for the sake of more interesting compositions and *points-de-vue*. Occasionally footpaths allow short cuts – a pedestrian network in embryo.

Building began in 1907 to a plan that shows the first part of the Suburb, the 'Artisans' Quarter', much as we know it today. By then residential closes had been introduced. The idea was also tried out at Letchworth (Bird's Hill, 1906), but it was at Hampstead Garden Suburb that planners learnt the benefits of such closes. Density is very low (no more than eight houses per acre) and all houses have private gardens, divided from the street only by hedges, never by walls (an innovation for England, though the accepted practice of the United States). Only towards the Heath Extension in the s was a retaining wall with a series of gazebos (*see* p. 151) introduced as a more formal boundary.

Central Square, with its two churches, was intended from the start to be more formal than the rest of the Suburb and has a monumental approach from the s up Heathgate. Unwin's first plans had included shops along the approaches, but as built by *Sir Edwin Lutyens*, appointed consultant architect in 1906, the shops were omitted and the square became a high-minded enclave of churches and public buildings with a fringe of smart houses. Lutyens was known to the Chairman of the Trust, Alfred Lyttleton (for whom he had designed Greywalls, Gullane, Lothian, in 1900) but he did not get on with Henrietta Barnett and was dismissed. The omission of shops from Central Square has proved a disadvantage; the square has never become a real social centre. Not only shops, but also cinemas, pubs and cafés have been refused admission. Institute education and divine worship have not proved to be as much of a lively attraction as the social reformers hoped for. In the end shops were provided only at Temple Fortune, the main point of entry from the w, although others had been planned, e.g. at the junction of Willifield Way and Temple Fortune Hill. Another unexecuted scheme was a sw entry from the Heath at Wellgarth Road with a 'gateway' crescent of startlingly modern houses by *Edgar Wood*, shown in the plan published in 1909.

The Suburb Extension or 'New Suburb', laid out by Unwin in 1911–12, followed the formal planning of Central Square, with three avenues radiating NE from it and with a formal Market Square on the projected continuation of Addison Way. It was necessary to depart radically from these plans when in 1926–7 the government drove a link from the Great North Road to the Barnet bypass (Falloden Way–Lyttleton Road) along the line of Addison Road through the centre of the extended Suburb. Northway, Middleway and Southway reflect the original scheme, but the Market Square, which would have provided a central focus for the area, had to be abandoned; the differently sited Market Place on Falloden Way is a poor substitute.

Social development has not turned out as it was projected by the originators. The mixed character gradually disappeared, especially as the Suburb extensions made very little provision for working-class housing, and none at all for local employment. Inevitably, the pretty artisan houses have proved attractive acquisitions for the middle classes, so the population is now very much of one kind. Visual variety remains in the Old Suburb, but much less in the New Suburb's streets of more uniform, relatively wealthy houses laid out in the 1930s by Unwin's successor *Soutar*. Despite these drawbacks, Hampstead Garden Suburb has been of the greatest importance in the history of town planning in England and influential also in Germany and the United States. The Hampstead Garden Suburb Act of 1906 can indeed be described as the starting-point of C20 town-planning legislation. Moreover, strict planning regulations and local vigilance have ensured that on the whole the character of the Suburb has been well preserved.

The STYLE of the buildings is of no less interest than the planning of the Suburb. The architects who designed most of the older artisan houses, headed by *Unwin*, believed in a free and comfortable neo-vernacular architecture which has stood the test of time splendidly. The walls are either roughcast or brick, with occasional tile-hanging and half-timbering. The detailing is sensitive throughout, with brick-work of uneven surface and ranging in colour from grey to dark purple-reds. The roofs are of dusky brown tiles, usually steep-pitched, with many gables and judiciously placed chimneys. The charm of the roofscape owes much to the Act of 1906, which permitted the waiving of the regulation which required party walls to project above the roof-line. Windows are homely casements; porches are often tucked beneath low eaves. Even the wooden garden gates are designed with care. Unwin determined house type and plan as well as street lay-out. The prototype (*see* Foundation Cottages, Hampstead Way, Perambulation 2), was not exactly repeated but subsequent semi-detached and terraced houses had similar accommodation, based on that used earlier by Unwin at Starbeck, Yorks, 1902–3: parlour with inglenook, scullery, bath, w.c., and a dog-leg staircase to bed-rooms with fireplaces.

The informal, picturesque vernacular idiom was established by *Parker & Unwin* in the Artisans' Quarter, where they designed the greater number of the houses, and was continued by other architects in the rest of the Suburb. Greater unity was achieved where one architect designed a whole close or square. Where that is not the case, each design has its own individuality, but control by the Trust secured a general harmony of character. Among the other architects who made important contributions were *M. H. Baillie Scott, Courtenay Crickmer* and *Geoffrey Lucas* (all also involved at Letchworth); *Michael Bunney* (*Bunney & Makins*), *E. Guy Dawber, W. Curtis Green, Edwin Palser, Herbert A. Welch*, and *T. M. Wilson*. Most of them also made use of the formal late C17–early C18 style which *Lutyens* had introduced in 1910–11 for the houses in Central Square and its approaches. The characteristic type is a five-bay house, usually sym-metrical with a hipped roof. Its most faithful exponents were *C. H.*

*James, C. H. B. Quennell, J. C. S. Soutar* and *G. L. Sutcliffe*, especially
round the fringes of the Heath Extension. The first individual distinctly Neo-Georgian house seems to have been *C. Cowles-Voysey*'s
No. 19 Wellgarth Road of 1910. After that, and especially after 1918,
Neo-Georgian predominated for wealthier houses in the Suburb.
The most lavish but least accomplished examples are in the fringes
of the Suburb beyond the Trust's control. Apart from the architects
mentioned, over sixty others were involved in the original Suburb,
though most of them built no more than one or two houses. There is
room in this account only for the highlights.

## PERAMBULATIONS

### *1. Central Square, churches and institution*

Lutyens's formal design of *c.* 1906–8 for the centre of the Suburb
was never completely realized, but the bones are there. The composition is unified by style, chiefly English late C17, and by materials,
silver-grey and red brick. The Institute makes an imposing but
unintimidating backdrop to the broad, grassed Central Square. It is
flanked to N and S by the equally balanced churches and houses of
North and South Square, but Central Square was left open to the W
to catch the view towards Harrow church, one of the inspirations for
the Suburb; alas, trees have since grown up too high and destroyed
the effect. In Lutyens's original scheme the E side was closed off by
wings that extended the Institute's pavilions and the churches were
linked by church halls to three-storey flats. They would have had a
more positive role in the scheme than the present houses, and the
flavour would have been closer to Inigo Jones's Covent Garden.

St Jude, mainly 1909–11, is one of *Lutyens*'s most successful buildings. It exhibits all his best qualities and even turns that 'naughtiness'
or wilful originality which often mars his late buildings into a decided
advantage. The church has a Gothic silhouette (in deference to 87
Mrs Barnett's conventional belief in Gothic as the true religious
style), but otherwise is defiantly eclectic. Lutyens called it 'Romantic
Byzantine-cum-Nedi' (Nedi was his nickname); however, English
Baroque and, inside, Quattrocento influences are equally strong.
Nave and aisles are covered by a huge roof starting uncommonly
close to the ground – expressly required by Mrs Barnett to prevent
the church overwhelming surrounding houses. The roof is broken
by very tall dormer windows of aedicule form; the E chapels have
separate hipped roofs. This discord between medieval and Baroque
features is what Lutyens must have enjoyed as much as, say,
Norman Shaw before him in the church of Bedford Park. The
façade (added in 1935 but to the original designs) also shows it.
The tall crossing tower (built 1915) has layers of open arches,
reminiscent of Byzantine brickwork, and a Gothic spire with
chevron leading. It looks magnificent from whatever the distance
it is viewed.

Inside the discord perhaps goes too far. The church is tunnel-
vaulted, with a dome over the crossing, which leads to a painful
conflict with the open timber roofs of the aisles; their Wealden
crown-post trusses are threaded through the brick arches. The E

chapels, with domes and apses, are more harmonious. Spacious sanctuary with herringbone brick and stone floor. Byzantine-style ALTAR of coloured marbles. Good iron SCREENS to the chapels. Vaults were intended to be pure white and Brunelleschian, but proposals for painting the Lady Chapel N of the chancel were made already in 1912. WALL and CEILING PAINTINGS are by *Walter Starmer*, 1919–30.* The present scheme originated in 1919 as a result of a meeting at Arras in 1918 between the war artist Starmer and the Vicar of St Jude, the Rev. Bourchier. Starmer's spirit fresco WAR MEMORIAL PAINTINGS in the Lady Chapel – highly unusual in both style and subject-matter – were completed in 1922. They show women of the Bible and Victorian women engaged in charitable works, strongly drawn ochre-coloured figures, against misty impressionistic backgrounds. The paintings elsewhere date from 1922–30; in the main apse, the Risen Christ and angels, in the S chapel the Revelation of St John. ORGAN. C19 by *Father Willis*, brought from St Jude's Whitechapel (Canon Barnett's previous church) when it was demolished in 1923.

The FOUNDATION STONE of 1910 is by *Eric Gill*.

FREE CHURCH. Begun 1911 by *Lutyens*, W end completed in the 1960s, adopting a diluted version of *Lutyens*'s design, but one bay shorter. A variation on St Jude, with the same roof and dormers and façade, but a low concrete dome instead of the spire. Interior with large, bold forms; nave with raked floor and barrel vault, divided from flat-ceilinged aisles by large Tuscan columns on high brick plinths. The interior, intended to be white, was later decorated in pastel colours.

FRIENDS MEETING HOUSE, North Square. By *Fred Rowntree*, 1913. A low retiring building set back from the road, modelled on the famous Meeting House of 1688 in Jordans (Bucks).

INSTITUTE AND HENRIETTA BARNETT SCHOOL. Exterior with dominating roof-line and tall cupola. A complicated building history. The N wing with the 'old hall' was begun as the Suburb's cultural centre in 1908, to designs by *Lutyens*, and by 1912 had been enlarged with a new brick skin, under *J. C. S. Soutar*, as part of a larger institute. Matching S wing (Queen Mary Hall) begun in 1918, completed 1924. The centre block, based on a *Lutyens* scheme of 1916, was not built until 1925–6; interior planning by *C. E. Hanscombe*, working with *H. G. Crothall*, Middlesex County Architect. The N and S pavilions are used by the Institute, the rest by Henrietta Barnett School, established in the Institute *c.* 1920. Behind it, facing Bigwood Road, an independent part designed as the Junior School in 1938 by *J. C. S. Soutar*. Feeble Neo-Georgian.

HENRIETTA BARNETT MEMORIAL, W side of Central Square. By *Lutyens*, *c.* 1938. Airy bronze arches raised on stone pylons intersect over a plinth with a stone laurel wreath. Intended to frame Henrietta Barnett's beloved view towards Harrow church.

Lutyens was right about the height of the HOUSES. As executed, they are a little too low and too much like a mere fringe to the public buildings. They are nevertheless fairly grand (the Co-partners' first venture in middle-class housing), arranged in terraces and, in the SE corner, detached. *Lutyens* designed Nos. 1–8 NORTH

---

*I am grateful to Dr Chris Miele for details on the paintings.

SQUARE and the well-disguised pairs (Nos. 1–7, odd) round the corner in ERSKINE HILL (*see also* below), which leads up to the Square. The façades of the houses in Erskine Hill, and *Lutyens*'s two parsonages facing the Institute, are of a fine restrained late C17 formality. Those round North Square have façades varied with less formal incident (bay windows, balustraded parapets etc.). The interiors were planned by the Co-partners' architect *G. L. Sutcliffe*, who did the houses at the NE corner of North Square. SOUTH SQUARE (mostly flats) was designed by *C. G. Butler*, with greater restraint. Henrietta Barnett lived at No. 1. The even more formal approach from the S, up HEATHGATE (with a fine view of the Heath from Central Square), has houses by *Sutcliffe* and other architects, also handling late C17 and early C18 forms (Nos. 1 and 4: *J. C. S. Soutar*; No. 6: *Quennell*). Several were not finished until the 1920s.

## 2. The Old Suburb north of Central Square, starting from Temple Fortune, Finchley Road

The N part of the Suburb, where building began in 1907, was planned with artisan and working-class housing. Most of it was built by 1912. The junction of Hampstead Way and Finchley Road at TEMPLE FORTUNE was intended by *Unwin* to be the main 'gateway' to the Suburb. It is made important by tall shopping parades, with arcades facing FINCHLEY ROAD, detailed by Unwin's assistant *A. J. Penty* (1909–11). Their Germanic silhouettes are inspired by the medieval towns, like Rothenburg, that inspired Unwin (cf. the S end of Hampstead Way, below). Identical hipped gable ends with faintly Regency vertical iron balconies, but otherwise the buildings are subtly different: Arcade House (originally a tea room) partly timber-framed, Temple Fortune House (flats) with lattice timber balconies. Close to the shops No. 166 HAMPSTEAD WAY, the area manager's office, Neo-Georgian. QUEEN'S COURT opposite, with long low ranges round the curve of Hampstead Way, is a late addition of 1927, built by the United Women's Homes Association, over the garden behind the tea room. *Parker & Unwin*'s groups along HAMPSTEAD WAY and Farm Walk were carefully orchestrated around this former open space. They have less impact now, although Nos. 136–138 Hampstead Way is an especially good example of the careful handling of a focal point: the pair has Voyseyesque hipped projections facing the entrance from Temple Fortune. Nos. 140–142, FOUNDATION COTTAGES, were the first houses to be completed (1907). Their design is unique, but they set the mood for the streets which radiate from here, all with houses by *Parker & Unwin*, 1907–9.

The houses, mostly in twos and fours, vary between roughcast in Hampstead Way and Asmuns Hill, and brick in ASMUNS PLACE, which opens delightfully into a green originally laid out as a skittle alley. The terraces, detailed by *Charles Wade*, include carefully composed 'twittens' or passages, a characteristic of the Suburb. ASMUNS HILL is also by *Parker & Unwin*, apart from the plainer 100 stretches, Nos. 44–56, by *Hubbard & Moore* for the Improved Industrial Dwellings Company, 1909–10. At the top of Asmuns

Hill, WILLIFIELD GREEN, a deliberate piece of village revival, with red brick groups at the junction of Willifield Way by *Crickmer* (No. 113 rebuilt), the rest by *Parker & Unwin*. Those next to No. 113 on the SW side were also rebuilt after war damage, Neo-Georgian rather than to the original designs. The lynch-pin of the group, the Club House, with a tall Germanic tower (echoed in Birnbeck Court, Finchley Road, *see* below), stood opposite. It was, alas, badly damaged in the Second World War and replaced by a detached 1950s house and by FELLOWSHIP HOUSE, an unobtrusive old people's centre of 1958 by *M. Darke* and *K. Williams*. Behind the Green (W), BROOKLANDS SCHOOL, conforming in cottage style to its surroundings, 1956, replacing a school by *W. G. Wilson*.

To the NW of the Green, in WILLIFIELD WAY, brick once more gives way to roughcast. This part too is by *Parker & Unwin*, as are HOGARTH HILL and ADDISON WAY (1911), the latter with low groups of flats, mostly with staircase access to the upper pairs, though the block facing Hogarth Hill is more flamboyant, with a flourish of symmetrical outer staircases leading to a long upper balcony. The charming retired closes of 1909–10 should not be missed: WORDSWORTH WALK off Hogarth Hill (*Herbert A. Welch*), CRESWICK WALK (*G. L. Sutcliffe*) and COLERIDGE WALK (*Welch*) off Addison Way. They have long cottage fronts, half-timbered parts and linking twittens. Addison Way originally continued with flats and cottages, but in 1927 it was brutally transformed into part of Falloden Way.

ERSKINE HILL leads back to the centre. The lower slopes are all by *Crickmer*; his traits here are brick with roughcast upper floors, and a liking for symmetry (paired hips or end gables). More interesting are *Parker & Unwin*'s special groups of 1911–14, off to the E in HOLMEFIELD. Three Lutyensish blocks, used for children in care, for the elderly (now Abbeyfield House, raised in height) and for 'tired servants'. A little further N, the BARNETT HOMESTEAD (1916–17) was designed by *Soutar* as flatlets for war widows; cottage-style. The junction with Asmuns Hill is also by *Parker and Unwin*. After this, plain cottages by the Improved Industrial Dwellings Company on the W. Opposite (Nos. 20–68), *Bunney & Makins*'s work, mostly in pairs with prominent overhanging mansard roofs, and in the short closes off it houses by *T. M. Wilson* (CHATHAM CLOSE), *Bunney* and *Welch* (DENMAN DRIVE, which leads into the New Suburb, *see* below) and *W. H. Ward* (WOODSIDE). *Bunney*'s No. 20 ERSKINE HILL is a more individual design, with a shell porch and low, Voyseyesque windows beneath the eaves. It is set close to the road, as are *Lucas*'s Nos. 16–18, preparing one for the heightened architectural experience of *Lutyens*'s more formal Neo-Georgian groups along the approach to Central Square. Nos. 1–13 are by *Lutyens* himself, Nos. 2–4 by *Sutcliffe* after his design. In contrast, round the corner, the diagonally set chimneys and irregular gables of *Sutcliffe*'s Nos. 55–61 and 52 TEMPLE FORTUNE HILL (1912) form a delightfully picturesque setting, rather in an early Lutyens manner, to the entrance to the Big Wood. Temple Fortune Hill returns W past Willifield Way, another carefully managed junction with three different symmetrical groups of 1909–10 by *Crickmer*. From No. 36 down to Hampstead

Way, and N along the W side of Willifield Way it is all *Parker &
Unwin* again. In the angle between is THE ORCHARD, originally
enclosed by *Parker & Unwin*'s old people's flats, replaced in
1970–4 by *M. Darke* with a group that, though well-intentioned,
does not live up to the high aesthetic pitch of its surroundings.
In FINCHLEY ROAD, s of the junction with Willifield Way, at Nos.
860–864, the HAMPSTEAD GARDEN SUBURB TRUST OFFICES
by *J. C. S. Soutar*'s office (1935). It continues the style and materials
of Central Square. PANTILES, Mediterranean-Moderne flats of
1934–5 by *J. B. F. Cowper*, are much more eye-catching. BIRNBECK
COURT, 1985 by *Architech*, has a hipped-roofed tower which pays
homage to the vanished Willifield Green club house (*see* above). It
replaced the Finchley Odeon (1930 by *Yates, Cook & Darbishire*).

*3. The Old Suburb west and south of Central Square, starting at the
south end of Temple Fortune Lane by Meadway Gate*

This part of the Suburb, built in 1908–10 with a mixture of housing
designed by a wide variety of architects, is not as easy to characterize
briefly as the more homogeneous first part. Many of the most
successful groups were designed for private developers with advice
from the Garden Suburb's Suburb Development Company, for
example the *Baillie Scott* houses in Meadway, *Lucas*'s Lucas Square,
and *Bunney*'s Linnell Close.

The streets W of Central Square belong in character to the earlier
streets just to their N (*see* above). Cottage groups set back round
greens create satisfying unified stretches in both Temple Fortune
Lane and Hampstead Way. TEMPLE FORTUNE LANE was on
the edge of the original Suburb and so only its E side was built up,
with open-ended squares and crescents overlooking the countryside. The following can be singled out (S to N): Nos. 12–32
(PALSER SQUARE) by *James & Edwin Palser*, consciously old-
world (leaded windows); Nos. 34–36 by *Arnold Mitchell*, with brick
and tile-hanging, a mixture more characteristic of Mitchell than of
the Suburb; Nos. 38–48 (DAWBER CRESCENT) by *Guy Dawber*,
asymmetrical elements arranged with symmetrical precision; Nos.
50–54 by *Parker & Unwin*, with the pretty device of an archway in
the link connecting the house on the l., which is set at an angle;
Nos. 56–78 by *Albert Lakeman*, the diverse treatment of porches
worth noticing, from No. 84 to the end by *Parker & Unwin*.
HAMPSTEAD WAY (N to S) is one of the Suburb's most varied roads.
The simple Nos. 110–114 and, set back, LITCHFIELD SQUARE
(Nos. 84 on) are by *Parker & Unwin* (the former actually designed
by *C. M. Shiner*); the fussier LUCAS SQUARE (Nos. 60–82, round
a tennis lawn) by *Geoffrey Lucas*. Larger, individual houses begin
to appear after that; they resemble those in the predominantly
middle-class area S of Meadway. Those which catch the eye are
No. 48 by *Parker & Unwin* (1908), with a recessed porch and big
chimney; No. 46, by *T. M. Wilson* for himself (1908), with pargetting by *Bankart*; and No. 40 by *T. Laurence Dale* (1909), prominently sited at the corner with Willifield Way with an eye-catching
bow, and an oriel (pargetted by *Bankart*) over the doorway in the
angle. No. 38 is by *Bunney & Makins*, No. 36 by *Dawber*. In HILL

CLOSE (1910–12), the roofs of the cottage-style houses (No. 2 by *Watson Hart*; Nos. 3–5 by *Howard Goodchild*; No. 7 by *Rowntree*; Nos. 4–6 by *Bunney & Makins*) step up towards the accent of St Jude's spire. On the other side of Hampstead Way further down, an unusual inward-looking group of cottages (Nos. 135–141) by *Curtis Green*, with entrances between closely set pairs of projecting wings. It contrasts with *Parker & Unwin*'s more open grouping of Nos. 143–149. WILLIFIELD WAY, designed in *Parker*'s Letchworth Office, returns N, starting with low buildings so as not to obscure the view up the path to Central Square. Further N, Nos. 9–47 are all by *Geoffrey Lucas*, yellow and red brick, partly set back in a curve; Nos. 46 and 48–54 are by *Bunney & Makins*.

Meadway runs across Hampstead Way. At the W end around MEADWAY GATE, at the junction with Temple Fortune Lane, cottage groups by *Palser*. At the meeting with Hampstead Way, Nos. 6–10 and No. 22 Hampstead Way (1909) are by *Baillie Scott*, the most picturesque group in the Suburb, a rambling but finely balanced design, with the architect's typical bold chimneys, swept eaves and a wide variety of motifs and materials. The other groups here, by *Sutcliffe*, use similar elements but without the same finesse. Further E in MEADWAY, houses by *Bunney & Makins* (Nos. 12, 14–16, 22, 7–13), *Curtis Green* (No. 20) and *M. J. Dawson* (Nos. 1, 36–42; No. 38 was for himself). After Heathgate, most of the houses are set back and play less part in the composition. MEADWAY COURT is a formal close, in brick with stone dressings, by *Sutcliffe*. E of Wildwood Road the houses are all later.

It is the more intimate CLOSES AND DRIVES OFF MEADWAY that make the most enjoyable compositions. They would have been more effective if the N–S ones on the S side had been left open at their end to frame views of the Heath, as Unwin had intended. To the N there is the small RUSKIN CLOSE, with pairs by *Crickmer* (Nos. 1–3, 2–4) and *Dawber* (Nos. 5–6). The closes to the S start with LINNELL CLOSE, 1909–11, especially satisfying, with No. 1 by *Parker & Unwin*, the shell-hooded Nos. 2–7 by *Bunney & Makins* (among the first classical designs in the Suburb) and No. 8 by *Crickmer*. It turns the corner into LINNELL DRIVE, with No. 6 by *Dawber* and No. 10, a fine, slightly later *Welch & Hollis* house. W of Heathgate, TURNER CLOSE leads to TURNER DRIVE, with large detached houses in a more formal late C17 style, Nos. 1–15 by *Soutar*, No. 12 by *Quennell*, and No. 14 by *T. M. Wilson*, all of 1914, and No. 8 by *Braxton Sinclair* as late as 1920–3. At the end of MEADWAY CLOSE, two intriguing houses, No. 1 for H. L. Coffin by *Arnold Mitchell* (1910), convincing late C17 style with tall, heavily moulded, rubbed brick panels under a square hipped roof, and the cottagey No. 3 for Coffin's son by *E. P. Powell* (1920), with its upper parts tile-hung right to the chimneytops. More large Wrenish houses in CONSTABLE CLOSE by *T. Laurence Dale*; No. 11 by *Soutar*.

## South of the Great Wall

Around the Heath Extension the S part of Hampstead Way and Wildwood Road was mostly built up between 1908 and 1914. Their houses demonstrate the growing taste for symmetrical fronts with Neo-Georgian elements, the type which Lutyens introduced in his designs for Central Square *c.* 1906 and which became dominant for larger houses in the extensions to the Suburb built after the First World War (*see* below). Brick becomes the favoured material. Georgian elements such as pedimented or bracketed doorcases, occasional sash windows and discreet brick pilasters begin to appear. The late C17 style, with cross-casement windows and hipped roofs, is used as often as sash-windowed Neo-Georgian. The cottage-style does not entirely disappear but cottagey roughcast is given up in favour of often gloomy brownish brick and leaded panes.

The GREAT WALL picturesquely divides the Heath from the gardens of the houses to its N. It was detailed for *Parker & Unwin* by *Charles Wade*. In inspiration it is like a medieval town wall but punctuated with Lutyensish pavilions rather than conventional bastions. Only the w half had been built by 1914; the rest was never completed. At the end of Heathgate, a raised viewing terrace, with pavilions framing the vista to St Jude.

In HAMPSTEAD WAY S of the junction with Meadway, the best houses are (E side) Nos. 16 and 18, 1912 by *Bunney & Makins*, identical and exceptionally charming, with carved keystones, and Nos. 10–14 by *Quennell*, austere in late C17 style. Opposite (W), Nos. 99–101, a good Neo-Tudor composition by *H. A. Welch*; Nos. 87–89 by *M. J. Dawson*, 1910, with pretty details; and Nos. 79–81, a Lutyensish pair by *Ernest Willmott*, 1910–11. At the top of the rise, No. 27 by *Welch & Hollis*, *c.* 1913, an early example in the suburb of a convincingly C18 treatment, except for its boldly placed chimneystacks.

Beyond Wild Hatch in CORRINGHAM ROAD, CORRINGWAY, *c.* 1909, had flats for chauffeurs over the block of garages, replaced in 1996 by a pastiche in Parker & Unwin style (*David Baker* of *Lawrence & Wrightson*). *Parker & Unwin* also built the closes of Neo-Georgian houses at Nos. 16–90, 101–117. Alongside the Heath, blocks of flats predominate. REYNOLDS CLOSE and HEATH CLOSE by *Parker & Unwin* (1911–12) cleverly exploit this narrow swathe of land with deep cul-de-sacs. Their houses are in overblown cottage style, of brownish brick with unpainted leaded casements (Reynolds Close), and latticed timber balconies (Heath Close).

WATERLOW COURT at the end of Heath Close, approached through a lychgate, is by *Baillie Scott*, 1907–9 for the Improved Industrial Dwellings Company. It provided 51 self-contained flats for working ladies. A masterly job – a quadrangle with low arcades 99 on four sides of a lawn and a gabled and bellcoted feature opposite the entrance. Roughcast walls, an exception in this middle-class area.

The most obtrusive flats in Hampstead Way are the huge group of Neo-Georgian 'labour-saving' ones called HEATHCROFT, 1923 by *J. B. F. Cowper*. Beyond these at the s end of Hampstead Way and in the roads off it, an eclectic mixture. On the corner of WELLGARTH ROAD (where *Edgar Wood*'s shocking Wellgarth Gateway to the Suburb was meant to stand: *see* Introduction to Hampstead Garden Suburb) is a spreading butterfly-plan house by *Barry Parker* (No. 16 Wellgarth Road, 1914), paired with No. 19 by *C. Cowles-Voysey* (1910), the first straightforward Neo-Georgian

houses in the Suburb. Further down, Nos. 12–14 by *Bunney &
Makins* have a row of four boldly hipped gables. Then the former
Nursery Training College (now YHA) by *A. J. Penty* for *Lovegrove
& Papworth*, 1915; unwieldy Neo-Tudor.

MORELAND CLOSE has a characteristic range of houses: No. 3,
steeply roofed, is by *Bunney & Makins*, Nos. 4–7 by *Quennell*, on a
different scale. On Hampstead Way, Nos. 7–11 are also by
*Quennell*, typically eclectic, followed by Nos. 3–5 by *A. J. Penty*
of *Unwin*'s office and No. 1 by *C. H. James*, thorough-going
Neo-Georgian. Just in WYLDES CLOSE, GATES HOUSE, by *T.
Laurence Dale* (1915), decorated with a putto cast from
Frampton's sculpture for Selfridge's entrance. At the back, flanking a canted bay, flat-roofed extensions by *Thomas Tait*, 1930, for
himself. For Wyldes, *see* Camden: Hampstead, Perambulation 3.
In WYLDES CLOSE, FAR END, 1911 by *Evelyn Simmons* for himself, and WYLDES CLOSE CORNER, by *Parker & Unwin*, 1912.

WILDWOOD ROAD, between Heath Extension and golf course, was
built up largely from *c.* 1912. Some of the best houses are in closes
off the E side. In WILDWOOD RISE, furthest S, No. 5 is an unusual
type for the Suburb, with a stone frontispiece and Jacobean details;
1913 by *Field & Summers*. In contrast, No. 2 by *Cyril Farey* looks
extremely modern for 1912–13, and slightly American, with a
spreading hipped roof and a rigorously pared-down façade. It won
a *Country Life* small-house competition. In TURNERS WOOD,
eight vernacular-style houses of 1915 by *G. L. Sutcliffe* for the
Hampstead Heath Extension Company, his best work in the
Suburb. At No. 16 INGRAM AVENUE, a replica of the Hampstead
Garden Suburb Trust Offices in Finchley Road, by *J. C. S. Soutar*'s
office, 1935. Earlier restrained Neo-Georgian work by *C. H. James*
(1929) in FAIRWAY CLOSE; No. 3 was his own house. In
BUNKERS HILL, an especially good pair by *C. Cowles-Voysey* for
himself, Nos. 1–2, of 1928–9. Symmetrical, with end wings, chimney
over the central 'twitten' entrance. Finally, in Wildwood Road
itself, Nos. 56–60 by *Hennell & James*; No. 48 by *Robert Atkinson*;
No. 44 by *James & Bywater*; and Nos. 34–42 by *C. Cowles-Voysey*.
Just S of Kingsley Way, a handsome group, Nos. 1–15 (Frank Pick
lived at No. 15), with hipped gables, sash windows and incidental
timber-framing, not unlike rectories by Street.

### 4. *The New Suburb: east of Central Square*

#### *Central Square to Market Place*

The 412-acre area developed after 1911 E of Central Square and E of
the Heath Extension was brutally bisected in 1927 by the trunk road
(Falloden Way–Lyttleton Road). Artisan housing (1907–30) was
continued E and N of Central Square by the Co-partners; it is
divided in two by Falloden Way. To the E lies middle-class housing
of post-1927, modest N of Falloden Way and more affluent S of it,
reaching extremes of opulence and injudicious design in Winnington
Road and (just outside the Suburb) in The Bishop's Avenue. A few
more styles were introduced into the late Arts and Crafts and Neo-
Wren or Neo-Georgian repertoire of the Old Suburb: between the
wars a very cautious International Modernism, Art Deco, Cape-

Dutch and Spanish. Watered-down Neo-Georgian persisted after 1945, joined in the 1980s by bland Postmodernism.

NORTHWAY, MIDDLEWAY and SOUTHWAY, three avenues radiating from Central Square, were laid out across the first tract of 112 acres in 1911–12 following plans by *Unwin*. But within this formal lay-out the only formal housing consists of SOUTHWOOD and BIGWOOD COURTS between the avenues, simplified late C17-style flats for ex-servicemen round three sides of a grassed court; by *Soutar*, 1925. Otherwise the cottage style predominates, with a few houses in the late C17 and Neo-Georgian manner described above. Some pre-1914 houses in SOUTHWAY include an ingeniously planned, square studio house at No. 10 by *Lucas*, 1910; No. 16 by *S. B. K. Caulfield*; and No. 18 by *Bunney & Makins*. Among several of the 1920s, the best is the symmetrical group, Nos. 28–34, by *C. H. James*, with Neo-Georgian end houses flanking neo-vernacular ones. BIGWOOD ROAD has white-rendered cottagey groups behind high privet hedges: *Bunney & Makins* did the satisfactory Nos. 5–7 and 6–12, widely spaced pairs with big gables, and the groups at the corner of Meadway: Nos. 45–7 Meadway, Nos. 1–3 Bigwood Road.

### Market Place to East Finchley Underground Station

The MARKET PLACE which Unwin envisaged as a commercial focus for the area is marked only by discordant quadrants and parades of 1930s shops and flats on Falloden Way. To its SW, OAKWOOD ROAD and DENMAN DRIVE NORTH and SOUTH have plain artisan housing laid out by the Co-partners (1912–13): roughcast, brick-quoined houses by *G. L. Sutcliffe*, not as refined as the Co-partners' earlier work. The rest of this phase lies N of Falloden Way in the 'Holms' and in Brooklands Rise, Brooklands Hill and Hill Top. *Sutcliffe* began the work with WESTHOLM (1914–15); EASTHOLM by *E. A. Aston* dates from 1920, the rest is post-1927 by *C. G. Butler*, Sutcliffe's successor as Co-partnership Tenants' architect.

The planning of the 'Holms' has great charm. Each one is linked to the next by twittens, footpaths with arched entrances (cf. Coleridge and Wordsworth Walks in the Artisan Quarter, Perambulation 2) and opens out into a green or shrubbery. MIDHOLM has good set-back terraces with pretty angle bay windows as emphasis; WESTHOLM is closed by a linked timber-framed pair. The other houses are plain and those in red and yellow brick have a neo-Victorian flavour different from the villagey character of the early Suburb. The latest ones have slight Art Deco touches, especially in MIDHOLM CLOSE, HILLTOP and NEALE CLOSE, 1928–9. BROOKLANDS RISE etc. to the w, of 1929, continue Sutcliffe's plain roughcast style.

Modest middle-class private houses, many hardly more elaborate than the Co-partners' work, begin to the E. Off Hilltop in HUTCHINGS WALK, and further E off Brim Hill (the continuation of Hilltop) in HOWARD WALK, classic 1930s semi-detached houses with sun-trap windows and hipped roofs by *Crickmer*, 1935–6, remarkably unspoilt (the same designs appear in Brunner Close s of Falloden Way); some good brick houses of the same

type round the corner in BRIM HILL. S of Brim Hill, the E part of
GURNEY DRIVE has larger, gracious houses by *P. D. Hepworth*
(1930), with some charming Neo-Georgian detail. Further E,
turning the corner of Brim Hill into WIDECOMBE WAY, Nos.
76–78 by *G. B. Drury & R. F. Reekie*, 1936, are a messy compromise between International Modernism and traditional forms.
Butterfly-plan, with main and service doors towards the road. At
the S end of Widecombe Way, in VIVIAN WAY, a small, spoilt
group, Nos. 22–30, of flat-roofed houses by *Brian Herbert*, 1937.
On the main LYTTLETON ROAD, BELVEDERE COURT of 1938
by *Ernst Freud*. Clear International Modern influences, with strong
horizontals and Mendelsohnian wings with curved ends, but combined with sections of pantiled mansard roof. Most of the houses
on the N slope are in reduced versions of the older Suburb's styles,
but the less common half-timbered Tudor appears as well, most
elaborately in the extensive group of 1936 by *R. H. Williams* and
*Burgess Holden & Watson* round EDMUNDS WALK and into
DEANSWAY, the route to East Finchley Station.

*Market Place to Hampstead Golf Course*

From the S side of Market Place, Kingsley Way starts with good
1930s houses with sun-trap windows in KINGSLEY CLOSE.
KINGSLEY WAY is more monotonous but has one interesting
transitional house of the 1930s at the corner of LINDEN LEA,
No. 2. At the E end of Linden Lea is the more adventurous
LYTTON CLOSE, 1935 by *C. G. Winburne*, small houses with
bold, completely glazed staircase towers appearing above roof
terraces. Opposite the end of Linden Lea, in NORRICE LEA, six
traditional small houses of the 1930s, Nos. 33–43, by *Robert Atkinson*,
more precisely early C18 than their vaguely Neo-Georgian neighbours. At the N end of Norrice Lea, KEREM SYNAGOGUE and
SCHOOL, 1937; Doric portico with balustrade.

The roads near the Golf Course boast very showy houses.
WINNINGTON ROAD is almost universally genteel Neo-Georgian
on an ample scale, apart from BRAEWOOD, opposite the S end of
Norrice Lea, which resembles a miniature Jacobean mansion with
shaped gables, and, further S, No. 61, SPANIARDS MOUNT, by
*Adrian Scott* for himself, 1936, which quite harmoniously combines
brick-facing and sash windows with a more Modernist central
balcony. To the W, NEVILLE DRIVE has a more entertaining
medley: most eye-catching is the weatherboarded No. 16 by
*Gerald Warren*, *c.* 1935, with its massive stepped gable and weathervane. No. 18 is more reticent but also Cape Dutch. No. 21 opposite
is International Modern (partly re-roofed) by *Ernst Freud*, 1935,
originally planned to be one of a group of four, and at the corner
of SPENCER DRIVE No. 17 is a 1930s Hispanic fantasy with a
Richardsonian porch by *Katona*. No. 23 Spencer Drive is a small
symmetrical semi-modern house by *Welch, Cachemaille-Day &
Lander*, with pantile-fringed parapet, similar to their houses in
Hendon. Further W, at the junction of Neville Drive and Kingsley
Way, BUNKER'S DIP, 1930 by *P. D. Hepworth*, in mellow brick
and pantiles, with arched windows and a stair-tower. Opposite, in
EMMOTT CLOSE, cottage flats round a secluded green; 1928 by
*Hendry & Schooling* for the United Women's Homes Association.

*5. The Bishop's Avenue from north to south*

THE BISHOP'S AVENUE, otherwise known as Millionaires' Row, and a by-word for opulence and vulgarity, has some of the most ambitious suburban houses in London. It is not strictly part of the Suburb. It was laid out in the 1890s through woodland as a link between Hampstead and East Finchley and was not fully developed until between the wars. Much rebuilding has taken place since. The name comes from the medieval hunting lodge on the Hornsey estate of the Bishops of London, whose moated site lies in the grounds of Highgate Golf Course just to the E.

Starting from Lyttleton Road, the w side has some of the earlier houses: GABLE LODGE, 1927 by *P. D. Hepworth*, and STRATHEDEN, both Cape Dutch with big stepped gables, the latter a bigger, brick version of No. 18 Neville Drive (*see* above). ELIOT HOUSE (formerly White Walls), 1924, and TURQUOISE, No. 42, are Lutyensish, the former also by *Hepworth*, an imposing composition of whitewashed brick and swept roofs with sea-green Swedish pantiles. Then a clutch of 1980s replacements in a hotch-potch of classical and Postmodern styles, e.g., on the E side, THE FOUNTAINS, an older house aggrandized by an inept portico with four huge Corinthian columns, Nos. 43–45, which could easily be mistaken for a branch library or similar small public building, and SUMMER PALACE. Most pretentious of all, set back in grounds like a country house, is the Neo-Wren No. 53. A favourite motif of many of the pseudo-classical fronts is a grandiose portico with fully glazed wall behind, exposing an overwhelming entrance hall. Next to No. 53, ARDEN COURT GARDENS, a well-landscaped group of smaller houses of the 1980s; steep, wide-eaved roofs over squarish houses with cut-away corners. A few big but mostly unexceptional early houses remain at the S end, where wooded grounds still convey something of the original character of the road. EAST WEALD by *Ashley & Winton Newman*, illustrated in *The Studio*, 1915, is a symmetrical dark red brick pile with a huge roof and a round-arched doorway with tilework and carving. On the w side, KENSTEAD HALL is a Neo-Tudor mini-stately home of the 1920s; beyond is BARON'S COURT, 1980s pseudo-Palladian. Tucked away at the end of BYRON CLOSE to the w, No. 5 by *Michael Manser*, 1962, a rare case in this area of a thoroughgoing Modernist house; white walls with flat roof.

In SPANIARDS END, a secluded cul-de-sac N of Spaniards Road just within Barnet: No. 24, THE FIRS, 1959 by *Patrick Gwynne*. Brick with timber boarding, large windows to the garden, the colourful variety of materials characteristic of the 1950s. Good interior with fitted furniture; HEATHBROW, 1959–61 is by *H. C. Higgins* of *Higgins & Ney*.

# HENDON

Hendon is now a continuous suburban area with only a handful of buildings older than the later C19. After Harrow, Hendon was the most extensive medieval parish in Middlesex, with small settlements scattered over an area bounded by Edgware Road on the w and stretching s–n from Cricklewood to Mill Hill. The large medieval church and its monuments surviving at Church End are the chief reminders of this early history. Growth accelerated rapidly in the early C20, especially following the extension of the Northern Line, opened in 1926. The population figures tell the story: 1871: 6,972; 1891: 15,843; 1911: 40,039; 1921: 57,529; 1946: c. 158,000. The parish became an Urban District in 1895 and (together with Edgware, q.v.) a borough in 1931. By then several of the old hamlets had become flourishing suburbs with their own distinctive characters (they are described separately here – see Cricklewood and Child's Hill, Golders Green, and Hampstead Garden Suburb, above, and Mill Hill, below). The burst of building activity between the wars encouraged development around the stations: at Hendon Central on the new Hendon Way bypass, and at Colindale and Burnt Oak further n. The open land between Colindale and Edgware was filled by the LCC's Watling Estate and, after the Second World War, by the GLC's Grahame Park, which covered most of the site of Hendon Aerodrome, now recalled only by a few early relics and the aircraft museums.

The overwhelmingly sedate domestic character of suburban Hendon is interrupted by the bypasses which sliced through the area in the 1920s: the A1 (Hendon Way and Watford Way) as an alternative to the old Great North Road, and the North Circular Road (dualled 1935). The M1 was extended s in 1966–75 to meet the North Circular in a maze of slipways and roundabouts. Industry, now largely replaced by warehouses and large retail sheds, sprang up along these routes as well as along Edgware Road; the largest single development was the massive out-of-town shopping centre at Brent Cross (see above) of the 1970s.

## RELIGIOUS BUILDINGS

CHRIST CHURCH, Brent Street and Heriot Road. 1881 by *Stephen Salter*. Small plain ragstone building; early Dec style. (Rood screen by *Temple Moore*, 1896.)

JOHN KEBLE MEMORIAL CHURCH, Deans Lane. Built for the Rev. O. H. Gibbs-Smith, 1935–7, by *D. F. Martin-Smith*, winner of a competition in 1934. The assessor was Edward Maufe. One of the most interesting of the few pre-war London churches in the modern idiom. Reinforced concrete frame clad in stock brick. The
115 w front has much presence, the sides stepping up to a flat roof with strongly projecting eaves, then to a square tower and concrete lantern, rather in a French taste. Inside, a plain square main room, very light and spacious, with a w gallery and a coloured 'diagrid' ceiling with diagonal coffering (the first use of such a ceiling in an English church).

The dedication of the church was inspired by Keble's concern to bring the church to the people. Gibbs-Smith introduced novel forms of service (family communion followed by parish breakfast), and the liturgical arrangements also broke new ground: the choir is placed not in the shallow sanctuary but in low stalls within the main body of the building, with the congregation arranged around it. FONT. A mortar, set in oak. A curiosity, said to come from Devonshire House, Piccadilly. FURNISHINGS. Original, designed by the architect; two plain PULPITS and SEDILIA built into the wall. LIGHT FITTINGS. Designed specially to throw light sideways. BALDACCHINO over the altar by *A. F. Erridge*. MOSAIC panel in blue and gold with central dove.

VICARAGE, Deans Lane. 1952 by *Braddock and Martin-Smith*. Open-plan ground floor.

ST ALPHAGE, Montrose Avenue, Watling Estate. Brick basilica with an apse, in Early Christian style; 1927 by *Charles Nicholas & J. E. Dixon-Spain*. W end, completed later, with open narthex between porches. A SE campanile was planned but not built. Restored in 1952 after war damage. Festive interior; all white, with low arcades on piers, and a lofty ceiling with heavy tie-beams on gilded modillions. Small Perp FONT and octagonal timber PULPIT, from St Mark, Goodmans Fields, Stepney (1838–9 by *Wyatt & Brandon*, demolished 1927).

ST AUGUSTINE, Grahame Park. By *Biscoe & Stanton*, 1971–5. Brick, polygonal, with lower offices attached.

ST JOHN THE EVANGELIST, Algernon Road, West Hendon. An early work by *Temple Moore*, 1895–6. Plain stock brick contrasts with stone dressings and elaborate Dec tracery. Interior modelled on the C14 Austin Friars Church in the City, with tall, austere stone arcades without capitals or clerestory; the N arcade provided for an aisle which was never built. Chapel, vestries, parish room 1911. FITTINGS from City churches. Noble mahogany PULPIT of *c.* 1760, from St Michael Bassishaw. Elegant FONT in the style of *Wren*, small cup on a bulbous baluster, with ogee-shaped FONT COVER. These and the wooden REREDOS are from St George, Botolph Lane, installed there in 1673, moved here 1909. The reredos has lost its side panels and pediment. Vestry panelling also from City churches. STAINED GLASS. Memorial window over Lady Chapel altar, 1935 by *F. C. Eden*. BRASS. Rev. W. H. Ogle-Skan, the first vicar, †1912, erected 1928. Large portrait brass of priest in vestments, designed by *Leslie Moore* (who designed another of the same subject for his later church of Holy Cross, Greenford, Ealing).

The roughcast VICARAGE of 1900 is also by *Moore* (alas, reglazed in front). The three gables mirror what was intended for the church.

ST MARY, Church End. Both size and contents indicate that this was the church of a large medieval parish. A rewarding building, much more so than the exterior, with its little C15 W tower of ragstone and its cemented walls, would make one expect. The interior is two churches in one, a C13 nave, chancel, N aisle and S arcade, with early C16 N chapel, and a second, larger nave replacing the old S aisle, but with its own spacious S aisle. This addition, obviously the work of a sensitive as well as bold architect, is by *Temple Moore*, designed 1911 and built 1914–15, one of the rare cases in which a Gothic revival architect, by respecting old work and adding frankly new work to it, has considerably enriched the original effect.

The C13 remains indicate that a church of some ambition replaced a Norman building, from which fragments are set into the W stub of the S wall. The E end of the old chancel has the remains

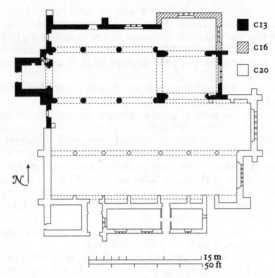

St Mary Hendon. Plan

of wall arcading on foliated C13 capitals. Low nave arcades on octagonal piers, with double-chamfered arches on moulded capitals. Late medieval N aisle ceiling, one boss with a green man. The chancel arch was renewed in 1827; the N chapel arch is perhaps of the same time.

Temple Moore's arcade is higher than the C13 ones, allowing the S aisle the same height as the new nave and keeping the old clerestory openings as windows from one nave into the other. The C20 extension is by no means conventional in its use of Gothic. It has an understated entrance in a plain projecting S wing which also houses the organ chamber; tall, slim clustered piers with a thin band instead of capitals separating shafts from arch mouldings, and aisle windows with a wall passage in front.

FURNISHINGS and MONUMENTS are of unusual variety and good quality. – FONT. Heavy square bowl on short shafts; each side has eight intersected arcades on short columns with block capitals. Of the Norman fonts of Middlesex this is the most successful. – WALL PAINTING. Monochrome fragment of royal arms, with unicorn (i.e. after 1603). – CHARITY BOARDS in the tower. – STAINED GLASS. N chapel N: 1887, Faith, Hope, Charity, semi-Pre-Raphaelite figures. N chapel E: 1897, forming a reredos, framed by elaborate painted wooden panelling by *Bodley*. Chancel E: Christ in Glory, with angels, in the style of Kempe. Chancel N: Christ Preaching. Pictorial, 1913. Nave W: 1917, a war memorial; archangels and knightly scenes. – MONUMENTS. In the N chapel: tiny brass to John Downer, 1515. – Magnificent large black marble slab on a low tomb-chest to Sir Jeremy Whichcot †1677, with nothing but bold lettering, a large coat of arms, and a border. – Sir William Rawlinson †1703, standing wall monument with rather bad semi-reclining life-size figure. Attributed to *Francis Bird* (GF). – Bishop Fowler of Gloucester †1714, with a long inscription between Corinthian pilasters and weepy cherubs perched left and right (cf. Smythe Monument, Cranford, Middx). Attributed to *Edward Stanton* (GF). In the N aisle: William Nicoll of Hendon Place †1644. Tablet with carved strapwork surround. Sir William Herbert Lord Powis (Lord of the Manor of Hendon) †1655. Inscription in Mannerist pedimented frame. Judith Bell †1722. Cartouche with putto head. Nave w wall: Charles Mordaunt †1681. Good curly cartouche. Attributed to the partnership of *Grinling Gibbons* and *Arnold Quellin* (GF). Nave: John Nicoll †17?31 and wife †1735. Tablet on coloured marbles. Against the chancel arch: Sir Charles Colmore and family, erected 1800 by a surviving son, by *Flaxman*. Small, with standing figures of Faith and Hope. – Giles Earle †1811, by *J. Smith*, with seated figures of Faith and Hope. Many other minor tablets and ledgers.

Large and attractive CHURCHYARD with green views over the valley to the N, and a good range of tombstones; some large sarcophagi, including a Neoclassical one with urn to Theodore Brinckman of Hanover †1741, and a dour Egyptian temple to Philip Rundell †1827. Near the E end of the chancel, *Henry Joynes* †1754, the architect. Square pedestal with moulded cornice.

ST MATTHIAS, Rushgrove Avenue, Colindale. The original church of 1934 is now the hall: red brick with arched windows and pan-tiled roof. Behind is the church of 1971–3 by *R. W. Hurst*: an ungainly exterior profile in brick and slate, but an impressive space within, lit obliquely by narrow slits in a folded E wall, and by big western clerestory windows. w gallery on tapering concrete piers. Roof-lit baptistery behind.

CHURCH OF THE ANNUNCIATION (R.C.), Thirleby Road, Watling Estate. Consecrated 1928. Modest Neo-Byzantine, with pantiled roofs. Plastered interior with arcades on short stone columns with abaci but no capitals. Further columns to an outer N aisle with chapels E and W. Octagonal dome over the crossing.

ST MARGARET CLITHEROW (R.C.), Grahame Park, *c.* 1970. Polygonal, with a tiled roof split to provide clerestory windows.

OUR LADY OF DOLOURS (R.C.), Egerton Gardens. 1863, com-pleted 1927 by *T. H. B. Scott*. Cruciform, of ragstone; E.E. detail.

HENDON BAPTIST CHURCH, Finchley Lane. 1886 by *J. E. Sears*. Tall stone front with a pair of big Dec windows, above a basement hall.

HENDON METHODIST CHURCH, The Burroughs and Egerton Gardens. By *Welch & Lander*, 1937. Dark brick, rectangular, with a clerestory, with some of the Expressionist feeling of their some-time partner Cachemaille-Day's St Saviour, Eltham. Curved buttresses flow organically out of the walls to accentuate the w end and divide the aisle windows. Canted w porch with jambs with angled brickwork. Interior subdivided and refurnished 1982. (STAINED GLASS. E window by *Christopher Webb*; the work of women: St Agnes to Josephine Butler.) Methodist Institute behind, 1910, now YAKAR (Jewish Adult Education).

WOODCROFT EVANGELICAL CHURCH, Watling Avenue. 1927–8 by *Sir John Burnet*. A focal point at the main crossroads of the Watling Estate. Built as a Christian Brethren church and paid for by the builder Sir John Laing, who had just established his London office at Mill Hill (q.v.). Laing came from a Brethren background at Carlisle. A severe, well-proportioned Tuscan barn, with main hall raised over a basement. Red brick, pedimental gable with strongly overhanging eaves; sturdy porch with Tuscan columns.

SYNAGOGUE, Raleigh Close. Opened 1935. (Streamlined fittings.)

HENDON CEMETERY, Holders Hill Road. Founded in 1899 by the Abney Park Cemetery Company (*see* Hackney: Stoke Newington). Crematorium added 1922. Gatehouse by *A.A. Bonella* in quaint Old English style, with half-timbered entrance arch and roughcast walls with Gothic lettering in stone. Neat flint-faced CHAPEL with Perp detail, flanked by an archway beneath a tower with corner turret and spike. (In the chapel, a terracotta REREDOS by *Cantagalli*, a copy of della Robbia's Resurrection in Florence Cathedral.) MONUMENTS. C.H. King †1919, standing bronze figure. – Edwin Roscoe Mullins, sculptor, †1907, with tondo of kneeling woman signed by *Mullins*.

### PUBLIC BUILDINGS AND INSTITUTIONS

The chief public buildings of Hendon make quite an impressive show along the N side of The Burroughs, typical examples of official architecture in brick with stone dressings, the earlier still quite jolly, the two later ones more genteel.

TOWN HALL, The Burroughs. By *T.H. Watson*, 1900. A broad Free Renaissance front in red brick and stone, with a hipped roof with timber lantern rising behind a lively balustraded parapet. Arches with blocked voussoirs to the ground floor. A pair of stone corbelled-out mullioned-and-transomed oriels light the Council Chamber on the first floor. This has a coved ceiling and original seating. SCULPTURE: Family of Man, by *Itzhak Ofer*, 1981, bronze.

PUBLIC LIBRARY, The Burroughs. By *T.M. Wilson*, 1929. Eclectic Neo-Baroque. A recessed centre with two attenuated fluted columns *in antis*, and projecting pedimented wings, whose main windows have swan-necked pediments with brick niches above.

FIRE STATION, The Burroughs. *Herbert A. Welch* won the competition in 1911, with a design intended to relate to the Town Hall. He was clearly influenced by the LCC's admirable fire stations in a free Arts and Crafts spirit. Red brick over a stone ground floor with three arched openings; two canted stone oriels with mullioned windows; the stone surfaces very smooth and the mouldings minimal.

CHURCH FARM HOUSE MUSEUM, Church End, *see* Perambulation 1.

CENTRAL PUBLIC HEALTH LABORATORY, Colindale Avenue. Founded in 1907 as the Government Lymph Establishment for making vaccines. A forceful pyramid of laboratories by *Robert Matthew, Johnson-Marshall & Partners*, 1981–5. The earlier buildings were by *Maxwell Ayrton & Partners*, 1950–3, reinforced concrete construction, brick-faced but with concrete cornice and other details.

BRITISH LIBRARY NEWSPAPER LIBRARY, Colindale Avenue. First built 1900–3; enlarged 1930–2 by *J.H. Markham* of the Office of Works, with storage on six floors. An extension of 1956–7 replaced the 1903 building (destroyed in 1940). The superintendent's house of 1903 survives. The 1930s building is of brick, very austere, yet with a few simplified classical trimmings. Later additions 1969–71 (microfilm building) and 1972 (reading room extension and restaurant).

LIBRARY, Watling Avenue, Burnt Oak. 1966–8 by the *Borough Architect's Department*. Concrete-framed, two-storeyed, with a rhythm of narrow windows.

PILLAR OF FIRE SOCIETY. *See* Perambulation 3.

ST JOSEPH'S R.C. CONVENT AND SCHOOL, Watford Way. The Sisters came to Hendon in 1882 from Whitechapel. They belonged to an order known as Poor Handmaids of Jesus Christ, founded at Dernbach in the Rhineland in the mid C19, invited to England by Cardinal Manning in 1875. They moved to Norden Court, now Westminster House, *c.* 1887. This has an eclectic later C19 brick front, in a Franco-Flemish style, small but elaborate. Above the porch a colonnaded balcony with steep pointed roof; on the r. a far-projecting gable with heavy bargeboards. The once fine grounds were built over to the N *c.* 1995 (an ICE HOUSE remains). To the S, plain school buildings, the block of 1900 by *A. J. C. Scoles* with an apsed chapel.

ST ROSE'S CONVENT, Orange Hill Road. Formerly Orange Hill House; a Dominican convent from 1930. Built *c.* 1877 by Sir Blundell Maple (of the furniture store); from 1912 to 1915 the home of Claude Grahame-White (*see* Hendon Aerodrome, Perambulation 4). A bold outline of tiled gables, hipped roofs and tall chimneystacks in the manner of Shaw. N entrance front with stone mullioned windows and a four-storeyed tower rising to a belvedere. Other parts very busy and undisciplined: red brick with plentiful terracotta and brickwork embellishment. LODGE and STABLES by *J. G. Buckle*, with even more fanciful coloured and moulded brickwork; illustrated in *The Builder*, 1881.

COLINDALE HOSPITAL, Colindale Avenue. Built as the Sick Asylum for the Central London District, 1898–1900 by *John Giles, Gough & Trollope*. Dignified three-storey central block in a festive free Italianate, brick and stone, with cupola and tripartite centrepiece; entrance flanked by blocked columns. Lower wings, tall ward blocks behind. Later additions and rebuilding (operating theatre 1923, new wing 1934, physiotherapy department 1966, etc.) added quite tactfully. Big, brash BLOOD TRANSFUSION CENTRE to the NW, 1990 by *Design Team Partnership*. T-shaped, with a series of stepped-back storeys with white enamel cladding, backed by taller wings with yellow-trimmed glazing. Echoes of Stirling in the oddly angled windows.

EDGWARE GENERAL HOSPITAL, Edgware Road, Burnt Oak. Opened 1927. Demure central administration building, standing out among a mess of additions.

BRENT RESERVOIR. Created by damming the River Brent in 1832–4, and used to maintain the level of the Regent's Canal. The dam was raised in 1852–4. Also known as the Welsh Harp reservoir, after an inn on Edgware Road which became a popular centre for C19 day excursions.

STATIONS. The Northern Line stations at BRENT CROSS, HENDON CENTRAL and BURNT OAK are all of 1923–4 and by *S. A. Heaps*, in a Neo-Georgian style. COLINDALE was rebuilt after destruction in World War II. Hendon Central forms the NE quadrant of the grandiose composition of Central Circus (*see* Perambulation 3).

RAILWAYS. The nineteen-arch VIADUCT across the Brent at Staples Corner was built in 1867 and widened *c.* 1895. No longer impressive, as the valley has been partly filled in and the whole area vastly altered for the junction of the North Circular Road and the M1.

ROAD BRIDGES. BRENT CROSS FLYOVER, carrying Hendon Way over the North Circular Road, has a compact three-level interchange, the first of its type in Britain. 1962–5, by *Sir Bruce White, Wolfe Barry and Partners* (consulting architects *Robert Atkinson & Partners*). New high-intensity lighting was used, on 100-ft-high tubular masts. Further w on the North Circular, STAPLES CORNER FLYOVER, completed *c.* 1976, a half-mile-long elevated ribbon of prestressed concrete with transverse beams in the thickness of the deck. A network of long span footbridges at a lower level, of steel box girder construction.

HENDON AERODROME. *See* Perambulation 4.

*Educational Buildings*

MIDDLESEX UNIVERSITY, The Burroughs. This campus of the University started as Hendon Technical College; built by the *MCC* (*H. W. Burchett*), 1937. Serious classical building of brown brick with hipped roof on stone eaves. A forceful archway, with ascending voussoirs in stone, leads into a restrained courtyard with Neo-Georgian ranges in three colours of brick. Extensions of 1955 and 1969 (refectory and engineering blocks). Lighter and brighter 1990s additions for the University.

METROPOLITAN POLICE COLLEGE, Aerodrome Road. An enormous complex of buildings, developed from 1935 on part of the aerodrome site, and much rebuilt and extended in the 1970s. Bronze STATUE of Sir Robert Peel, by *William Behnes*, formerly in Cheapside near St Paul's, moved here 1974. (QUEENS BUILDING contains a very large chimneypiece in Renaissance style, possibly brought from Grahame-White's Aerodrome Club House, the College's original location.)

HENDON COLLEGE, Abbots Road (built as a boys' school). 1932; quite a grand two-storey front range dignified by stone surrounds to some of the windows.

BOARD SCHOOLS. Four were opened in 1901 (the Hendon School Board was formed only in 1897, delayed by Anglican opposition). MONTAGU ROAD, West Hendon, is a pretty design with central shaped gable, and pargetted dormers. BELL LANE, plainer, was built as Hendon Central Board School. The others were at Cricklewood (q.v.) and Burnt Oak (closed).

SCHOOLS BETWEEN THE WARS. New housing demanded an energetic building programme of elementary schools by Hendon, which acted as its own education authority (the MCC being responsible for secondary schools until 1965). The Watling Estate provides characteristic examples of 1928–32, when traditional styles were still current and before generous school grounds were the rule. Main ranges are tightly sited, close to the road, with lower wings behind. WOODCROFT JUNIOR and INFANTS SCHOOL (originally junior and senior girls), Goldbeaters Grove, 1928–30 by *H. A. Welch*, is still in an Arts and Crafts tradition, with big sweeping tiled roofs. BARNFIELD SCHOOL, Silkstream Road, 1928, and GOLDBEATERS SCHOOL, Thirleby Road, 1931, are Neo-Georgian. In contrast, COLINDALE PRIMARY SCHOOL, Woodfield Avenue, for the new suburb, 1933, is traditional in form, but with slightly Art Deco buttresses between the windows.

POST-WAR SCHOOL BUILDING, which provided secondary schools for the maturing suburbs, adopted modernist principles of light and informal buildings. ST MARY'S CHURCH OF ENGLAND HIGH SCHOOL, Downage, 1957–60, has a gently elegant front of three storeys; curtain walling with timber bands. ORANGE HILL JUNIOR HIGH SCHOOL, Hamonde Close, 1963–5 by *D.R. Duncan* of *MCC*, is also curtain-walled. By the 1970s a different, tougher tradition was established: the Senior School of ST MARY'S CHURCH OF ENGLAND HIGH SCHOOL, Summerfields Road and Church Path, 1976–7 by *K.C. White & Partners*, is a rigorously plain two-storey cube with internal courtyard; of russet bricks with pebbly floor bands.

## PERAMBULATIONS

### *1. Hendon village*

W of the church is the GREYHOUND INN, rebuilt in 1896, and St Mary's Church Hall, opposite, of 1894, plain Neo-Georgian. Next to it was CHURCH END FARM, given model farm buildings in 1889 by *Wimperis & Arber* for C.F. Hancock of Hendon Hall. The chief survival is the long MILKING PARLOUR, a low brick range with crested ridge, at r. angles to the road. The hay loft at the N end is quaintly apse-shaped, with a finial. The adjoining house, also part of the farm, is in a picturesque Norman Shaw style, tile-hung and half-timbered.

CHURCH FARM HOUSE, on the N side of Church End, now a 22 museum, is a delightful survival from rural Hendon, acquired by

CI7

CI8–EARLY CI9

LATER CI9–EARLY C20

Parlour    Hall    Kitchen

10 m
30 ft

Church Farm House. Ground-floor plan

Hendon Council in 1944 and restored in 1954. Chiefly C17, with red brick three-bay front of two storeys divided by a platband; three widely spaced gables with original dormer windows. Other windows with later sashes; early C19 brick porch. Fine grouped chimneystack with four flues, between parlour (l.) and hall (r.). Kitchen to the r. of the hall, with large rear fireplace. Behind is an C18 service wing, later heightened to two storeys. The lobby entrance in front of the main stack now leads to a passage cut through the stack in the late C19, with early C19 staircase beyond. Some reused C16 panelling in the hall, formerly upstairs. Upstairs the main chamber lies over the hall, with closet over the entrance lobby.

To the s of the church little remains from before the C20. The later C19 streets that grew up between Church Road and Church End were replaced by plain low- and medium-rise housing by the Borough Architect's Office (*B. Bancroft*), 1975–9, in loose cul-de-sacs behind a range along Church Road. W of Church End, one older house with irregular cross-wings, much altered. The most notable survival is the DANIEL ALMSHOUSES, Nos. 1–10 Church Road. Built 1727–9. Two-storeyed centre with pedimented gable, little gabled corner pavilions with newly fashionable Diocletian windows, one-storeyed tenements between. The school in the E wing has an inscription dating it 1766, but it was much restored in the C19.

THE BURROUGHS started as a separate older centre, now linked to Church End by the civic buildings and a row of later C19 cottages with rustic porches. By Watford Way, on the N side an irregular group of C18–early C19 frontages in stucco and brick, concealing an early C18 red brick house of six bays, visible from the N. On the s side one dignified C18 house, BURROUGHS HOUSE, four bays with a parapet. (Good staircase; rebuilt behind.) To the s, suburban streets were laid out from the late C19. BRAMPTON GROVE existed by 1896; a few generously spaced tile-hung houses had appeared on the N side by 1913; elsewhere and in adjoining streets are superior brick villas of between the wars.

### 2. *Parson Street*

The rising land NE of the village centre attracted large mansions, now mostly replaced by flats. On the E side of PARSON STREET, once in fine grounds, the VICARAGE, a simply detailed house of *c.* 1800 with three-bay s front and projecting bracketed eaves, but unfortunate modern roughcast. In the late C19 C.F. Hancock of Hendon Hall developed the area with big detached houses by *Wimperis & Arber*. From these remain the COTTAGE on the N side, prettily turreted and diapered, formerly a lodge to the demolished Langton Lodge; No. 35, IVY TOWER, a substantial 1870s house with a corner turret, and No. 39, IVY COTTAGE, dated 1879, built as a lodge to a house called Downage. On the s side, No. 54, formerly ST SWITHIN'S, with crenellated and turreted roof-line, extended *c.* 1900 to designs of *George Hornblower*.

HENDON HALL, Ashley Lane, a hotel since 1912, is now very hemmed in, but once had much more extensive grounds. The house is a puzzle. It is dominated on its E entrance side by a colossal but ill-fitting four-column Corinthian portico with pediment, patently out of scale, and clearly an addition to the six-bay front. Capitals and entablature are of stone, finely carved, but the columns are simply banded brick. C.F. Hancock, a London jeweller, who bought the house in 1869, added the straggling N wings, much remodelled in the C20. The core of the house is a three-storey red brick Palladian villa of the mid-to-later C18, as can be seen from the neat rounded full-height bow in the centre of the S side, and the canted bay at the S end of the W side. The latter has recessed angles of the type favoured by James Paine. The bays and the brickwork between them include black headers, not found in the SE and E parts, which were perhaps remodelled when the portico was added. There is a balustraded parapet with urns, perhaps also a later addition.

The house has attracted numerous myths, principally that its interior decoration was due to David Garrick, and that the portico came from the Duke of Chandos's mansion at Canons. There is a reference to a 'newly built house' on a map of 1754, but Garrick, although Lord of the Manor of Hendon from 1765 to 1778, never appears to have lived here. By 1828 the house was owned by the architect Samuel Ware. Keane's *Beauties of Middlesex* (1850) describes Ware's property with carriage front 'adorned with pillars and enriched capitals, brought from Wanstead House'. Colen Campbell's Wanstead was demolished in 1824, so was it *Ware* who embellished his house with relics of Campbell's mansion? He may also have been responsible for the balustrade and urns (Wanstead had similar features), the statues in pedimented niches in the S front, which are mentioned by Keane, and the moulded timber frames to the windows. Ware's work on major houses would have given him plenty of opportunities to gather material of this kind.

The interior has been much altered. A passage from the portico of the E side leads to a central stairwell with an awkwardly placed stair of earlier C18 type (fluted balusters, carved tread ends), perhaps also architectural loot. The low cornice to the passage to the W garden door looks C18. The rooms to the S are taller; they include the SW dining room, which has a rectangular C18 ceiling painting with classical figures. A smaller ceiling painting identified as a study by Tiepolo was sold in 1954. Its origin is unclear.

The GROUNDS in Ware's time celebrated the association with Garrick by two obelisks with inscriptions to Garrick and Shakespeare, which survive in the forecourt. A temple with statues of the muses has disappeared, as has a more distant monument to Shakespeare which survived in Manor Hall Avenue until *c.* 1957.

HENDON HALL COURT, Great North Way, backs onto the hotel car park. A forceful range of flats in shuttered concrete, now painted, with a rhythm of inset balconies. By *Owen Luder*, 1961–6.

In the surrounding streets developed by Haymills Ltd, among unexceptional suburban houses, a few of 1932–5 by *Welch, Cachemaille-Day & Lander* are in more daring modern dress: in ASHLEY LANE, Nos. 29–37, with flat roofs with a frill of pantiled parapets, and Nos. 42–46. More convincing and better preserved is the white cubic composition of No. 72 DOWNAGE, by *Evelyn Simmons* of *Simmons & Grellier*, 1936, with tall stair-tower on the l., a curved wing on the r., and a sunroof.

### 3. South and east of the village centre

BRENT STREET was an early hamlet, but is now an indifferent shopping street. To the E, in VICTORIA ROAD, SPALDING HALL, 1901 by *F. W. Troup*, built as Sunday Schools for Hendon Congregational Church (demolished). Chequered brickwork with nicely detailed Arts and Crafts entrance under a big splayed arch.

Further S in Brent Street, PILLAR OF FIRE SOCIETY and ALMA WHITE BIBLE COLLEGE, with a picturesque entrance archway flanked by two cottages. Built as St Saviour's Homes, for women in need of care, by *H. A. Prothero & G. H. Phillott*, 1897. A brick Tudor group planned as self-contained homes arranged around a quadrangle. Dining hall on the N side, with a projecting bow and mullioned windows; chapel to the E with Perp gable to the road. At the corner of Shirehall Lane, PENFOLD HOUSE: stuccoed front to Brent Street, with pretty Regency-style door canopy dating from 1924 but with an L-shaped timber-framed core said to have originated as a drovers' hostel. A few modest houses remain in SHIREHALL LANE, Nos. 2, 4, 8 and 10 (late C17–early C18 but all much altered).

CENTRAL HENDON grew around Watford Way and the Northern Line station. There were plans for the area already in 1912, but building only took off after work on the railway began in 1922. The pivot is the enormous CENTRAL CIRCUS, loose compositions of meagre, thinly stretched Georgian motifs to NW and SW, facing the Underground station (q.v.) and a cinema of 1932.

WEST HENDON, close to the Edgware Road and the Midland Railway line, had become a suburb by the late C19, as its Board school and church indicate (qq.v.).

### 4. Colindale, Hendon Aerodrome and Grahame Park

COLINDALE dates mostly from between the wars, but scrappy earlier development of soon after 1900 remains along COLINDALE AVENUE. This was the site of 'Leatherville', thirty dwellings for workers at Garston's trunk factory, established here in 1901. The British Museum Newspaper Library opened in 1905, the Central Public Health Laboratory in 1907 (qq.v.). The suburban area further S is worth visiting for the COLIN PARK ESTATE, with houses put up in 1927 for F. H. Stucke & Co., 'artistic' house builders, by the eccentric *E. G. Trobridge* (who did similar work in Brent, *see London 3: North West*). Four groups in COLINDEEP LANE (Nos. 89–97), flanking Court Way, with tile-hanging alternating with half-timbering, and Trobridge's typically emphatic star-shaped chimneystack.

### Hendon Aerodrome

The aerodrome was developed from 1910 as a private venture by the pilot, aircraft designer and manufacturer Claude Grahame-White (†1959), and became well known as a centre for training pilots, test flights and flying displays. Rapid growth took place during the First World War, when the aerodrome was used also by the Royal Air Force and other companies, with expansion S of Aerodrome Road onto the present site of the Police Training College. The government bought out Grahame-White in 1925; the aerodrome was closed after 1945.

The EARLY BUILDINGS lie along the N side of Aerodrome Road. In 1915–16 Grahame-White's architect *Herbert Matthews* built a FACTORY with Neo-Georgian show front along Aerodrome Road, workshops behind, and at the N end Grahame-White's offices, with a belvedere or 'control tower'. The GRAHAME-WHITE HANGAR (S of the RAF Museum) is in two parts. The earlier and lower W part, *c*. 1917 (originally one of a pair), is constructed with Belfast trusses, an inexpensive type of wide-span roof with bow-string trusses of timber, invented in Northern Ireland in the C19 and widely used during the First World War. Its N front, now of brick, originally had sliding doors. The E part, of 1918, has four cross-braced steel roof trusses. There are plans to re-erect the hangar in the museum. The former ENTRANCE GATES to the Grahame-White Aviation Co. Ltd are now at the entrance to the Museum. The Neo-Tudor building dated 1917, later the OFFICERS MESS, was formerly the 'London Aerodrome Hotel'.

RAF MUSEUM. Concrete and glass galleries of 1969–72 by *Industrial Development Group Ltd*. BATTLE OF BRITAIN MUSEUM, next to the RAF Museum, 1977–8. BOMBER COMMAND MUSEUM, 1983, by *Anne Machin* of *Wimpey Architects*.

AEROVILLE, off Booth Road. A delightful formal square of terraced Neo-Georgian cottages for 300 employees of Hendon Aerodrome; 1917 by *Herbert Matthews*. Mansard roofs with pedimented dormers. Doric colonnades to the sides flanking the approach and to the centre opposite.

*Grahame Park*

A miniature new town, planned with a mixture of public and private housing for 10,000 people, on the site of the aerodrome runways. The housing is by the *GLC*, with private and Ministry of Defence housing around the fringe; the community buildings are by *Barnet Architect's Department*. Designed 1968, begun 1969, two-thirds completed by 1975. By then the somewhat simplistic and rigid urban ideals which had inspired the design already seemed out of date.

The long N–S central spine is a landmark from afar, with tall buildings of six to seven storeys concentrated along a winding pedestrian central route, in an effort to give the flat featureless area some urban identity. Early plans proposed a megastructure, but this was reduced to a series of linked blocks, from which lower housing reaches out into surrounding parkland. The plan, influenced by the GLC's unbuilt new town at Hook, and by the early plans for Thamesmead, aimed at an alternative both to Corbusian 'towers in a park' and to amorphous low-rise suburban estates. With similar good intentions, the central spine was from the beginning planned with shops, pub and amenity buildings, complemented by careful hard landscaping; but more diverse commercial activity was not permitted, so the centre could not develop a truly urban character. The original design with its relentless use of dark brick made both the tall blocks and most of the lower terraces disappointingly dour. Remodelling by the *Borough of Barnet* from 1989 to 1995 created a new, more picturesque image: the original rugged Louis

Kahn-inspired profile of the ranges along the spine route was crowned by roofs of orange tiles, and the cliff-like elevations, with large bleak expanses of obscured glazing to the circulation areas, were transformed by recladding, new staircases and coloured trimmings.

Low COMMUNITY BUILDINGS, built together with the flats, ring the changes by the use of angular forms, echoing the cranked line and materials of the brick-paved spine route. Near the centre the route widens into an irregular square. On its N side is the LIBRARY, with shallow sloping roof and small projecting windows. It faces the COMMUNITY CENTRE, polygonal, with irregular projections and pyramid roof, set in a planted 'moat'. Opposite, projecting from one of the tall blocks, a DAY CENTRE looks out through bay windows, with a HEALTH CENTRE nearby. Two churches (*see* above) lie just off the main route; schools are sited around the edge, with ample open space. The ingredients are fine, but architecturally the results are disappointing.

### 5. *Watling Estate*

Laid out in 1926 by the *LCC* under *G. Topham Forrest* on open land between Hendon Aerodrome and Edgware. The first houses were occupied in 1927; 4,000 were completed by 1931. Like the LCC's earlier estates at Old Oak, Hammersmith, and White Hart Lane, Tottenham, the Watling Estate adopted the principles developed in the garden cities and garden suburbs and applied them successfully to low-cost houses.

The main route is WATLING AVENUE, running NE from Burnt Oak Station. The clever grouping and the play of contrasting textures also recall Frank Baines's Office of Works Estate at Well Hall, Eltham. The vistas in the undulating streets, with the many old trees preserved, are excellent, and there are many open spaces: WATLING PARK in the centre, SILKSTREAM PARK further S, and THE MEADS along the northern fringe. Along The Meads the houses are simple rows of brick cottages. Elsewhere they vary pleasantly between brick, roughcast, and stained timber weatherboarding, sometimes with orange pantile roofs, interspersed with an occasional three-storey block of flats. In DEANSBROOK ROAD, N of Watling Park, housing of the late 1970s by *Mayorcas Guest & Partners*.

The amenities provided over such a large area were few. Shops were developed only at the W end of Watling Avenue: the streamlined (but now shabby) pair of shopping parades, SILKSTREAM PARADE, close to Burnt Oak Station, dates from 1929–31, by *Burnet Tait & Lorne*. Daring for its time, with grey rendered brickwork and horizontal window bands, an interesting contrast to the classical character of the neighbouring Woodcroft Evangelical Church (q.v.) by *Sir John Burnet*. Other early buildings also have Roman echoes: the churches of St Alphage and The Annunciation (qq.v.) and the WATLING CENTRE in Orange Hill Road, built for the Watling Community Association in 1931 by *Granville Streatfield*, with pantiled roofs and pedimental end gables. SCHOOLS were provided by Hendon (*see* Public Buildings, above).

Savoy Cinema, Edgware Road, Burnt Oak. Now a bingo hall. By
  *George Coles*, 1936. Classical stone dressings, pleasant interior with
  stepped ceiling, to seat 2,000.


# HIGH BARNET

High or Chipping Barnet was formerly part of a peninsula of
Hertfordshire extending into Middlesex. The town developed on a
main route to the N, to the W of the older settlement of East Barnet;
St Alban's Abbey established a market here in 1199. Numerous inns,
encouraged by this favourable position, are still a feature of the
town. The distinctive urban character of the centre owes much to
the position and personality of the parish church standing at the
crest of the hill.


## RELIGIOUS BUILDINGS

Christ Church, St Albans Road. An attractive group. Two big
  gables to the road, flint with stone dressings, with a little wooden
  bell-turret. The original building 1845 by *G. G. Scott* of *Scott and
  Moffatt*. Aisle and porch 1855 by *W. G. & E. Habershon*. The
  pretty Church Hall of brick, flint and stone in a fancy Tudor
  style, 1907 by *L. W. Ridge & Waymouth*. To the s, the former
  School, flint and brick.
St John the Baptist, Wood Street. The architecture of the
  church, which is largely Victorian, makes the most of its position,
  more than the medieval church had done. It started as a chapel-
  of-ease to East Barnet, and was rebuilt at the expense of John
  Beauchamp, as is recorded in an inscription in the spandrel of
  one of the arcade arches. He died in 1453. When *William Butterfield*
  was commissioned to enlarge the old building, he decided to keep
  the medieval nave and N aisle and to add to it a new higher nave
  with its own aisle to the s. His work dates from 1871–5. He also
  removed the old W tower, leaving only parts of its N and s walls,
  and replaced the old chancel with an organ chamber. So the present
  church seems to have two naves and two aisles. From the N you see
  the low medieval aisle, rubble with some flint, with sparing stone
  dressings, much renewed, and with three-light clerestory windows
  above. The medieval s clerestory windows look into Butterfield's
  nave. Butterfield's own, much taller church, has somewhat perverse
  alternating three-light and circular cinquefoil windows. His walls
  have plenty of low stone bands and chequerwork to enrich the
  rhythm of the flint work. His W tower is most impressive, big and
  broad, a beacon when you come up from London, and a dominant
  accent for the town. The timber and metal flèche over the nave
  roof was added by *J. C. Traylen* in 1893.
    The C15 church has an arcade with piers with four attached
  shafts, four hollows in the diagonals, and complex mouldings to
  the two-centred arches. The inside face of the N wall (stripped
  1985) displays evidence for much rebuilding: a confused mixture
  of chalk blocks and Reigate stone and changes to window openings in old brickwork in English bond. In the E wall of the organ

chamber, a C15 embattled doorway with original traceried door, formerly in the S wall of the old chancel. Butterfield's loftier church has more robust detail: tall octagonal red sandstone piers; chancel arch striped pink and white. The chancel has a prettily decorated roof, and – a typically Butterfieldian piling on of effects – a mosaic REREDOS set against bright STAINED GLASS: the Ascension by *Heaton, Butler & Bayne* (1880–2). – FONT also by *Butterfield*, splendid polished red Devonshire and grey Derbyshire marble. – Framed oak CHEST. – The noble canopied FONT COVER, the elaborate PULPIT and no fewer than 159 historiated BENCH ENDS, designed by *J. C. Traylen* and made by *H. Hems*, were added in the 1890s. – STAINED GLASS. N and s windows of the aisles, good Arts and Crafts style, 1887–9, by *Henry Holiday*. W window of St John the Baptist, 1974, designed by *Alfred Fisher* and painted by *Peter Archer*. – MONUMENTS. Thomas Ravenscroft †1630, excellent recumbent alabaster effigy under canopy. The details of the canopy are an interesting example of Gothic survival: cusped arches, rib-vault, quatrefoil frieze to the top cornice. – James Ravenscroft †1680 and his wife †1689, two small marble busts made in 1913 (copies of those made for his foundation, the Ravenscroft Almshouses: *see* Perambulation, below), set in a Neo-Gothic surround incorporating four ledger stones, with cusping inspired by the earlier tomb. – Thomas Leverton †1824 by *J. Kendrick*.

ST STEPHEN, Bells Hill. Built as a Mission Church, 1896. (FONT. Octagonal; C15?)

ST MARY IMMACULATE AND ST GREGORY (R.C.), Union Street. 1974, built by *Lanner Buildings* after a design by *Steel, Bretman & Partners* (also used for St Margaret Clitherow, Grahame Park: *see* Hendon, above). Polygonal, with steep split-pitched roof; the taller part over the E end lit by clerestory windows. Presbytery by *Scott & Jakes*.

UNITED REFORMED CHURCH, Wood Street. 1884, extended 1892. Capacious building in mixed late Gothic with broad stone gable flanked by asymmetrical turrets, a projecting entrance lobby, and a wooden flèche over the crossing. To its W, EWEN HALL, brick, with pretty bay window with leaded glazing, 1906 by *W. Charles Waymouth*.


## PUBLIC BUILDINGS

REGISTRY OFFICE, No. 29 Wood Street. The competition for new Urban District Offices was won in 1913 by *H. A. Cheers*. Brick, in the English Baroque tradition, the entrance emphasized by a big segmental pediment on Ionic columns, matched by a central curved gable above.

COURT HOUSE, Barnet Hill. 1913, Neo-Georgian.

LIBRARY, Stapylton Road. By *Barnet Borough Architect's Department*, 1985–9. Red brick with big sweeping tiled roofs, a deliberately vernacular image in the tradition of Hillingdon Civic Centre. Ingenious plan based on interlocking octagons. Octagonal public hall; main library with reference section on mezzanine floor above, leaving the ground-floor spaces around the edge open to the boarded roof, with well-lit corner sitting areas.

BARNET COLLEGE, Wood Street, s of the church. The former Queen Elizabeth Grammar School is now the TUDOR HALL of the college. It was built *c.* 1577 and altered C19. Tudor brickwork, with diapers of vitrified headers, three-window front, the windows with modern mullions, at the angles two hexagonal turrets. The E turret led to dormitories, added a little later. The hall was originally open to the roof. The interior was remodelled in 1968. Behind the hall, three phases of local authority architecture. The buildings are grouped informally around a quadrangle. Modest library of 1957; competent curtain-walled blocks of 1965 (*Hertfordshire County Council Architect's Department* (*G. C. Fardell*), linked by a glass bridge with red brick towers at either end. They demonstrate the confidence with which the Herts CC could mix new with old buildings. Heavier puce brick additions to the SE (*Barnet Borough Architect's Department: B. Bancroft*), 1974–6.

HYDE INSTITUTE, Church Passage. Now part of Barnet College. Built from a bequest of 1887; 1903–4, a late work by *T. G. Jackson.* Large stone mullioned windows and brick pilasters in his favourite English Renaissance style. Galleried reading room with open timber roof, now with inserted floor.

QUEEN ELIZABETH'S BOYS' SCHOOL, Queen's Road. Long Neo-Tudor range by *C. F. Skipper*, planned 1929, built 1931–2. Central bay window to first-floor library. Quadrangular plan behind.

QUEEN ELIZABETH'S GIRLS' SCHOOL, Barnet Hill. Established in Russell House on Barnet Hill in 1890. Successive extensions and rebuilding by *J. Ladds* from 1890, and by *J. W. Fisher* 1924–7 (classrooms, dining room, library), Neo-Georgian. Large plain extensions of the 1960s.

RAVENSCROFT SCHOOL, Barnet Lane. 1955. The one-hundredth school built by the *Herts County Council Architect's Department* since the war.

BARNET GENERAL HOSPITAL, Wellhouse Lane. Originated as the Barnet Union workhouse infirmary. Neat plain brick extensions (psychiatric unit and boiler house), 1975–6 by *Gollins, Melvin, Ward & Partners*. Phase 1a of major rebuilding programme, 1996 by *Percy Thomas Partnership*. Many cheerful colourful brick gables.

ODEON CINEMA, Great North Road, at the bottom of Barnet Hill. 1934 by *Edgar Simmons*. Prominent double-height windows in Moorish style, flanked by brick towers with diapering. Obelisks at the sides. Well-preserved interior, the two-level foyer with Moorish payboxes and green marble columns. Now subdivided, but in the upper cinema much of the balconied Art Deco auditorium is visible; it continues the Moorish theme with stepped mouldings around ogee lancets. Cubist light fittings; ceiling with octagonal centrepiece with jazzy lozenge pattern.

## PERAMBULATION

The raised causeway up BARNET HILL was made in the 1820s to lessen the steep slope. The town is heralded at the start of the HIGH STREET by a tall former London and Counties Bank dated 1892, of the type found in late C19 suburban commercial centres; corner oriel with pretty Jacobean detail. But building on this scale failed to take over the rest of the High Street, and a number of small low buildings, some timber-framed in origin, still reflect the town's older history, although old fabric is well hidden and the scene fails to add up to anything consistently picturesque. On the E side, Nos. 52–58, low stucco fronts with a passage through No. 56, and the MITRE, at No. 58, with good C19 etched glass. Nos. 60–64 is a four-bay Georgian house with later shopfront. On the w side, the CROWN AND ANCHOR has one of Truman Hanbury & Buxton's elaborately half-timbered frontages (like the Railway Hotel, Edgware, by *A. E. Sewell*?).

Past the church the following can be singled out among the High Street shops: E side: Nos. 114–118, a four-bay, three-storey C18 house with a good C19 shopfront on its l. side. Fluted Greek Doric columns to the entrance. On the w side, near the little green by the church, an exuberant Edwardian POST OFFICE of *c*. 1903–4, with tall shaped gable in striped brick and stone. LLOYDS BANK, low but grand Baroque revival, by *T. M. Wilson*, *c*. 1931; central arch and pilasters, all in rusticated brick, window with swan-neck pediment (cf. Hendon Library). Nos. 105–107, a former interwar BURTON'S, has the store's typical flashy interwar detail to the upper floor. Beyond St Albans Road, Nos. 151–153, in origin a timber-framed house (see the steep roofs), well hidden behind later alterations and additions.

THE SPIRES shopping centre, 1986–9 by *Essex Goodman & Suggitt*, starts on the w side of the High Street between the twin turrets preserved from a Methodist church of 1891, and stretches back over a long narrow site to Stapylton Road. Banal detail but pleasant planning: first a toplit arcade with shops on two levels, then shops around two planted open courtyards, ending with supermarket and car park fronting Stapylton Road, where the histrionic pyramid roof of the entrance hall is shown up by the more subtle contemporary library opposite (q.v.).

STREETS OFF THE HIGH STREET. MOXON STREET to the E has a series of earlier C19 villas, No. 9 the best preserved; elegant curved sashes to the ground-floor windows and a little fanlight. UNION STREET to the w was laid out in 1837; at first a very modest mid-C19 stuccoed terrace, then simple paired cottages, Nos. 52–66.

WOOD STREET, running w from the church, has the best of the older houses, on the s side mostly stuccoed, on the N side a pleasant mixture of brick, stucco and old tile roofs. The s side, after Barnet College, starts with No. 15, right on the road, now pebbledashed and drab, but possibly early C17 in origin: see the four pilasters to the low ground floor, and the platband, broken by the two later two-storeyed bay windows. No. 17 is timber-framed behind the stucco. Then, set back, the MUSEUM, in four bays of a two-storeyed stuccoed terrace. No. 35, BOW HOUSE, has a very large shallow bow, and a doorcase with channelled pilasters, early C19. Further on, some early C19 villas, No. 53 with Ionic porch. No. 55 is a more substantial C18 house with C19 seven-bay stucco front, later a maternity hospital, converted in 1996 to flats, with extensions to l. and r. Next to this the MARIE FOSTER HOME, single-storey, dark brick, by *Peter Barefoot & Partners*, 1974. Further on, the small former ELIZABETH ALLEN SCHOOL; centre block with pedimented gable, dated 1824.

On the N side the pretty group of Nos. 14–18 is timber-framed in origin, Nos. 14–16 now rendered with canted bays, No. 18 with red brick front. No. 20, also red brick, early C18, is of seven bays with cornice and parapet and a doorcase with carved brackets. Like its neighbour, much repaired after bomb damage. Nos. 30–32 again have timber frames behind their render, and were possibly built as part of a range of C16 tenements.

ALMSHOUSES are a special feature of Wood Street. On the N side, first the RAVENSCROFT ALMSHOUSES, the Jesus Hospital Charity founded by James Ravenscroft, 1679, although of that date now only the central archway and gable, and the gatepiers with carved stones 'JR' and '1679'. Single row of one-storeyed dwellings, largely rebuilt in the C19. In RAVENSCROFT LODGE, Union Street, an annexe of 1976–8 by *R. E. Barnes*, are displayed the fine alabaster busts of James Ravenscroft, dated 1670, and his wife Mary, dated 1672, attributed to *Thomas Burman* (GF). GARRETT'S ALMSHOUSES, 1731, a very simple one-storey row of six cottages, much restored *c.* 1902 and modernized 1981. LEATHERSELLERS' ALMSHOUSES, at the N end of Union Street (the entrance just off Wood Street), were a foundation of 1544, moved from Bishopsgate in the City of London. Three ranges round a courtyard. Centre range in a timid Tudor, with stone-fronted Dec chapel, 1866, rebuilt 1926. The wings of pale brick, originally single-storeyed, 1836–7 (W) and 1851 (E), were tactfully rebuilt in 1964–6 by *Kenneth Peacock* of the *Louis de Soissons Partnership*. Lodge of 1861. Excellent iron gates (brought from St Helen's Place, Bishopsgate, in 1926). Beyond Ravenscroft Park, PALMER'S ALMSHOUSES, founded in 1585 on land given by Mrs Eleanor Palmer †1558; rebuilt 1930.

THOMAS WATSON COTTAGE HOMES, Leecroft Road, S of Wood Street. 1914. One-storey cottages for 'old and loyal employees of Mssrs Sutton & Co. carriers', spaciously arranged on three sides of a large court. Central community building in a free C17 style, with tall oriel windows and steep hipped roof.

RAVENSCROFT PARK, beside Wood Street, originated as part of Barnet Common, laid out as a public recreation ground in 1883. On its N side, two mid-C19 three-bay stuccoed villas, then substantial brick and tile-hung houses of the 1890s. Near the junction of Wood Street and Galley Lane, THE WHALEBONES. Early C19 two-storey three-bay stuccoed house, with whalebone gate.

PHYSIC WELL, WELL APPROACH, off Wellhouse Lane. A mineral spring was discovered here *c.* 1650 and visited by Pepys in 1664 and 1667. C17 brick well chamber, reached by a flight of stone steps, with brick floor and two shallow pools. Arched over and given a pump in 1808. Sheltered by a picturesque cruciform timber-framed structure put up by *Barnet Surveyor's Department* in 1937, when the area was surrounded by council housing.

## MILL HILL

Mill Hill was part of the parish, later borough, of Hendon. The suburban part lies around The Broadway, near Mill Hill Broadway Station (opened 1868). The old farming hamlet, three quarters of a mile to the NE, is an oddly diverse but rewarding scatter of buildings, strung out for a mile along the high ground of the Ridgeway, looking out in both directions over Green Belt countryside. Brick and weather-boarded cottages of rural Middlesex are interspersed with a large number of rambling institutions, successors to the earlier private mansions of wealthy Londoners attracted by the fine views. A surprising number of these older buildings remain embedded in the later complexes. Highwood Hill further N, like Totteridge imme-diately to its E, remains a favourite spot for substantial houses in secluded grounds (*see* Perambulation 2).

## RELIGIOUS BUILDINGS

ST PAUL, The Ridgeway. 1829, by *Samuel Hord Page*, built as a chapel by William Wilberforce, who had a house on Highwood Hill. A typical cheap church of its date in the Commissioners' style, cement-rendered, with the plainest of turrets on the W and E angles. Pointed windows with Y-tracery, the W front with a more fanciful Gothic window, and originally with two doors. Simple interior, little altered. Plain ashlar-lined walls, original pews (moved later), shallow chancel with ribbed plaster vault and panelling. Later SCREEN. ALTAR and ALTAR RAILS. In the E window, within an inappropriate surround of 1887 by *E. R. Frampton*, an exquisite panel of PAINTED GLASS, signed and dated 1809 by *Charles Muss* and *W. H. Hodgson*. Muss trained as a china painter and became enamel painter to George IV. The painting is a copy of Annibale Caracci's *Dead Christ and the Three Marys*.

ST MICHAEL AND ALL ANGELS, Flower Lane, off The Broadway. Built for the new suburb near the station. Begun 1920 by *Herbert Passmore*. Quiet traditional Gothic (based on *W. D. Caröe*'s designs of *c.* 1911 for another unexecuted church), coherent, despite a long building period. E part completed 1922, extended W 1932, 1938; W end, vestries and Lady Chapel completed by *Alban Caröe* in 1956. Exterior of uncoursed ashlar; dignified interior with clerestory above stone arcades on piers without capitals. STAINED GLASS. E window 1959 by *A. E. Buss*: five biblical appearances of angels. To the N, HARTLEY HALL, brick church hall of 1909.

SACRED HEART AND ST MARY IMMACULATE (R.C.), The Broadway. Polygonal church by *PRC Partnership* (*S. G. Crawford*), 1994–5 (replacing a building of 1922–3 by *Williamson & Foss*). Parish Centre of 1968.

ST VINCENT (R.C.), The Ridgeway. 1887 by *F. W. Tasker*. *See* St Vincent's Provincial House, below.

MILL HILL EAST FREE CHURCH, Salcombe Gardens. By *R. R. Wilkins* of *Beard, Bennett, Wilkins & Partners*, 1963. A big glazed W gable lights the broad meeting hall. Laminated timber roof; movable furnishings. Attached to HALL and CLASSROOMS of 1951.

UNITED REFORMED CHURCH, The Broadway. Low, domestic-looking hall with tiled roof and mullioned windows, 1927. Church of 1936, designed by *Arnold Harwood* and *Martin S. Briggs*, mem-bers of the congregation. Red brick, plain Gothic, with an open timber roof and a low rather bald W tower.

UNIVERSAL SPIRITUAL SCHOOL OF PRACTICAL CHRISTIANITY, The Ridgeway. Built for the Methodists. Humble red brick Gothic of 1893 by *I. Sitt & J. Adkin* of Bradford.

PADDINGTON CEMETERY, Milespit Hill. Opened 1936. Blocky brick chapel with polygonal apse and flat coffered ceiling, by *E.E. Lofting*. (Dutch cemetery with war-time graves. Opened 1965, with bronze figure by *van Kraligen*.)

## COLLEGES AND INSTITUTIONS

MILL HILL SCHOOL, The Ridgeway. Founded in 1807 as a 'Protestant Dissenters Grammar School' to provide for 120 boys; the most important establishment of its kind in the early C19. It began in a house called The Ridgeway, which had belonged to the C18 botanist Peter Collinson. New buildings were provided in 1825–7 by *Sir William Tite*, his first major work, a long, austere Neo-Grecian composition facing SW over the older grounds. A giant Greek Ionic six-column portico and pediment fronts a double-height dining hall with three tall windows, the walls between them treated as a lesser order of Doric pilasters. Plain two-storey wings of pale brick are relieved only by a stone band and arched recesses to the windows. On the entrance side the simpler centre has flat paired giant pilasters. Rooms are ranged along a central spine corridor lit by two elongated octagonal light-wells, the approach to the dining hall marked out by eight pairs of Ionic columns. The dining hall is dignified by a coffered ceiling, latticed windows above the side doors, and a latticed mirror over the taller central door. The room is flanked by a plain stair to the dormitories and by a room planned as library and common room. The NW wing had four schoolrooms, unusually many for the early C19, when a single schoolroom was still common. The SE wing had masters' and service rooms on the ground floor. Tite's plan proposed end pavilions linked by colonnades, for headmaster's house and chapel, but these were not carried out.

Later buildings, in contrast to the Grecian severity of Old School, display the more playful and homely free style popular around the turn of the century for educational buildings. From S to N: BIG SCHOOL, linked to Old School by a pretty three-arched open passage. 1905 by *T. E. Collcutt*, absorbing a C19 chapel which became a school hall. Asymmetrical free classical front to the road, rendered with stone dressings, the hall expressed by a blank wall with decorative foundation stone. Beyond is a low LAUNDRY, and SWIMMING BATHS of 1874. Then the CHAPEL, 1896–8 by *Basil Champneys*. Pretty brick and sandstone exterior with S turret, Baroque detail, Venetian window to the W front. Good interior in a free C17 spirit, dignified yet lively: opposed stalls, college fashion, in dark wood, marble floor, apse with Ionic columns on a high plinth, and a barrel vault with festive plasterwork. W gallery and NE gallery. Large, thickly mullioned round-headed windows, each with a central panel of STAINED GLASS in paler surround, attributed to *Powell* of Whitefriars. W window †1903.

The charming U-shaped group of TUCK SHOP, WINTERSTOKE LIBRARY and MURRAY SCRIPTORIUM, 1907 by *Collcutt*, faces the playground at r. angles to the chapel. Low and picturesque, with half-timbering, brick and tile-hanging; the steep roofs and a turret over the arched entrance are reminiscent of the American H. H. Richardson. The library has a decorated plaster barrel vault. The McCLURE MUSIC SCHOOL beyond, 1912 by *Martin S. Briggs*, is similar but plainer. Sweeping tiled roof over a barrel-vaulted music room; practice rooms in the wings. The SCIENCE SCHOOL across the playground, 1924 by *Stanley Hamp*, Collcutt's partner, returns to a rather severe classicism; 2–3–2 bays, the ends recessed. Stone centrepiece with little balcony over the entrance. The Regency feel is continued inside by a vaulted corridor and octagonal lobby. Also by *Hamp* is the GATE OF HONOUR, the war memorial in front of the main entrance, 1919–21, an accomplished Beaux Arts classical archway incorporating a screen with names.

More recent buildings lie further N: ART SCHOOL, plain brick, minimally classical detail. SIXTH FORM CENTRE, 1970–1 by *Alex Gordon & Partners*. Two blocks linked by a bridge, with some brick and dark weatherboarded projections to give character. Down a slope, brick-faced SPORTS HALL of the 1980s. Further off to the N, SANATORIUM, by *T. Roger Smith*, c. 1877.

BOARDING HOUSES and other buildings began to be built from the later C19 along the lines of other public schools. S of the main buildings, along WILLS GROVE, from E to W, first THE LODGE, c. 1900, a steep rendered gable on each side and a corner entrance. Opposite, WINTERSTOKE HOUSE (Pre-prep School). Formerly a vicarage. The front is a formal five-bay red brick composition in Queen Anne style with projecting porch, big egg-and-dart eaves cornice, and hipped roof. Boys' quarters extend in a large wing behind. Two further boarding houses on the W side, COLLINSON HOUSE, render above red brick, by *Collcutt*, and ST BEES, late C19. Further S, RIDGEWAY HOUSE, also by *Collcutt*, c. 1905, in a eclectic style similar to his Big School. Large, on a dog-leg plan; mostly white render, with window surrounds, bay and porch of stone. *Hamp*'s BURTON BANK of 1938 is of buff brick in plain Neo-Georgian; a slightly more elaborate master's end faces downhill. Nearby, CRICKET PAVILION and PARK LODGE, both with trim white weatherboarding.

The GROUNDS with their fine trees still reflect something of the planting established by the botanist Peter Collinson (†1768); the C18 wall of his botanic garden remains between Old School and Wills Grove.

BELMONT (MILL HILL JUNIOR SCHOOL), The Ridgeway. The present Headmaster's House was built in 1771–3 for Peter Hammond, a London brewer, by *James Paine Jun.*, his only significant architectural work. A substantial three-storey Palladian villa, somewhat in his father's manner, but full of unusual quirks. Five by three bays, of stock brick, with stone bands hinting at classical proportions. The corners have recessed chamfers (a device much used for Paine Senior's bay windows); the projecting three-bay centre to the SW front breaks out into a two-storey shallow bow housing an elliptical porch with balcony above (both now glazed). Paine's first proposal included unfluted Greek Doric columns to the porch, but this precocious idea was abandoned for more conventional Tuscan. The SE front has a curious segmental recessed centre bay, also of two storeys, flanked by superimposed orders and crowned by a Diocletian window and open pediment. Some of these eccentricities are explained by the plan, a tour-de-force of ingenious Neoclassical planning in the manner of Paine Senior or Sir Robert Taylor. The elliptical entrance hall opens into a toplit circular stairhall. Large niches containing curved doors lead into the main rooms on the SE side: the dining room is an elongated octagon, the drawing room is elliptical, with a delicate Neoclassical ceiling and fireplace. Elegant saucer-domed corridor to the back entrance. On the first floor the iron balustrade of the cantilevered stair is continued as a gallery around the drum of the hall, with more doors in niches, and an elliptical room over the entrance, possibly originally an open balcony. The basement has cellars within the central drum and service rooms on the SE side. In the grounds to the E a pretty early C19 Gothic GARDEN BUILDING with battlemented corner turrets and a small stuccoed LODGE.

SCHOOL BUILDINGS to the W of 1919 onwards, the earliest block later converted to an assembly hall. The other buildings are by J. C.S. Soutar. W of the old house, a tactful Neo-Georgian wing with canted central bay, 1923. Further N the CHAPEL of 1924–5. An attractive Lutyensesque exterior; pedimented entrance in front of a steep sweeping roof crowned by a pretty bell-turret. Sober classical interior with apse, barrel-vaulted nave, and passage aisles. The chapel faces a classroom wing of 1928, which forms a quadrangle with two Quattrocento-style arcades which have a view through to the grounds.

ST VINCENT'S PROVINCIAL HOUSE (Sisters of Charity of St Vincent de Paul), The Ridgeway. Set back from the road, with two C19 stuccoed lodges. The nucleus is Littleberries, a property acquired in 1691 by George Littleberry, a London bookseller who married Mary Snow of Hendon Place. The entrance side is a much altered refronting of the C18 or early C19. Red brick, seven bays, the recessed centre with pretty early C19 balcony on timber columns. Convent extensions to the NW of the 1920s, to the SE of the late C19. Projecting from the back, not on axis with the entrance, is the most interesting survival, probably added c. 1712, when Littleberry paid Lord Powis, Lord of the Manor, for improvements made to his house and grounds. It consists of a three-bay pedimented pavilion of chequer brickwork with stone dressings, housing a single room over a vaulted basement. Fine coved ceiling, its plasterwork probably of c. 1740, as is indicated by the quilted patterns and the medallions portraying William III, George I, George II and Caroline of Ansbach. The walls, now plain, were once also lavishly decorated. The room faces down a long terraced avenue towards a BANQUETING HOUSE in the form of a pedimented Ionic temple, shown on an estate map of 1754, and probably part of Littleberry's improvements. J. F. Pawson, the owner from 1847, glazed the front and added the plasterwork inside. Traces of the early C18 long narrow garden remain, a rare survival. A round and a square pond (now filled) lay along the avenue; beyond the banqueting house was a walled garden and pleasure ground.

Many additions for the convent. CHAPEL, attached to the SE wing, by F. W. Tasker, 1886–7. Perp, of stone; spacious interior with aisles as high as the nave and an E transept of two bays planned for lay use. Furnishings stripped out in 1973, when two SCULPTURES by *Sean Crampton* were added: Our Lady of the Assumption, and a seated Risen Christ in open metalwork. STAINED GLASS. Seven-light E window with archangels and saints under canopies. DAMASCUS HOUSE, NE of the chapel, built as an orphanage in 1887, converted to a retreat centre in 1972–3. E-shaped, with a tower, in a distinctive austere Italianate, white brick with deep eaves, with upper windows in recessed panels. A less forbidding two-storey balconied range behind, built as a nursery. Former PRESBYTERY across the lane, *c.* 1886, handsome red brick, with hipped roof and big chimneys. ST VINCENT'S R.C. SCHOOL (JMI), 1896; stock brick with some half-timbered gables.

MISSIONARY INSTITUTE LONDON, Holcombe Hill. The core is HOLCOMBE HOUSE, a handsome two-storeyed three-bay stucco villa, built in 1775–8 by *John Johnson* of Leicester for John William Anderson, a glove merchant who was Lord Mayor of London in 1797. Set back behind rusticated stucco gatepiers with fluted vases. An elaborately detailed front on an apparently modest scale: three bays, rusticated ground floor of unpainted stucco, semi-circular porch flanked by windows recessed in arches, first floor with fluted pilasters; balustraded parapet. A delightful interior. In the elliptical entrance hall a cantilevered staircase with wrought-iron S-shaped balustrades sweeps elegantly up to the first floor. A small groin-vaulted lobby behind leads to the two rear rooms, which overlook the sloping grounds at first-floor level. Both have excellent Neoclassical plasterwork: the sober dining room has a ceiling with simple radiating pattern, urn-and-thyrsus frieze and large figures on three walls: Eros, Muse of Tragedy, Priestess at an altar. The former drawing room is more light-hearted, with three windows, and an elaborate ceiling with decorative plaster lunettes and pointed ovals which have painted figures of the Muses, after designs attributed to *Angelica Kauffman*. The house was attached to an older range to the E, now much remodelled and extended. In 1866 it was acquired by Herbert Vaughan (later Cardinal) as the first premises for St Joseph's College; it passed to Franciscan nuns in 1881, who remain in the adjoining buildings to the NW (qq.v.). The SE wing was built as a school; gaunt institutional Tudor, 1892–4 by *F. W. Tasker*. Rear wing to the E, 1978 by *A. F. Peel* of the *City Design Group* for the Missionary Institute London, which took over the buildings in 1977. In the grounds, NUNS' CEMETERY, not far from the site of a now vanished C18 Grecian temple.

ST MARY'S ABBEY, Holcombe Hill. Built for the Franciscan nuns who occupied Holcombe House from 1871. Large brick cruciform CHAPEL; 1888–9 by *Goldie, Child & Goldie*. Chunky plain geometric shapes, the crossing tower with pyramid roof and a folded star ceiling inside; other roofs with timber barrel vaults. Good STAINED GLASS in the five W lancets: the Evangelists and the Foundress, Mother Mary Francis (†1886), by *Heaton, Butler & Bayne*, *c.* 1910; some clerestory windows probably also by them. Sacristies and low barrel-vaulted passages with robust joinery around the E end of the church. Convent wing 1883, red brick Gothic, with rounded stair-turret to the front and the apse of an upper chapel projecting at the back.

St Joseph's College, Lawrence Street. By *Goldie & Child*, begun in 1869. On a commanding site. The tower, with its saddle-back roof and gilt statue of St Joseph, by *J. Baumeister* of Munich, is the chief landmark of Mill Hill. The buildings are the culmination of Herbert Vaughan's endeavours to build a foreign mission-ary college (*see* Missionary Institute London, above). Ambitiously planned; spacious cloister with two tall ranges of convent build-ings (1869–71) beside the large apsed chapel with its SE tower (1871–4). W wing added 1898, N wing 1922, E wing 1929–30. Carved tympanum over the main entrance by *James Forsyth*. The CHAPEL has a grandly conceived interior, reflecting Vaughan's own detailed instructions. Ambulatory arcade with carved angel capitals on granite columns, and a five-bay nave in the rich but sombre spirit of Mediterranean Early Gothic. Pointed arches, timber barrel vault; aisles forming six transversely vaulted side chapels (from which only three altars remain) lit by circular windows. The enrichments were much reduced *c.* 1973. Bands of gilded WALL PAINTINGS and roundels survive from the nave decoration begun in 1886 by Father *Joseph Rettori*. They are on the theme of missions. The HIGH ALTAR now in the N aisle was given by Lady Herbert, a major benefactor. Of Roman marble, by *Leonardi*. Delicate Early Renaissance detail with much colourful inlaid work. Three sumptuous SIDE ALTARS. St Mary, 1873: frontal with Italian relief of the Flight into Egypt, large alabaster reredos with naturalistic flowers, and a painting by *Soldadich*, flanked by carved angels. St Peter (formerly in the N aisle). Fine marble standing statue flanked by good low-relief scenes from his life, dramatically rendered. St Joseph, 1874, by *Earp*. Dark red-brown Spanish marble; with a statue by *Coyers* of Louvain (copied from the one on the tower), under a rich Gothic canopy. Decoration and glass in the chapel by *Lavers, Barraud & Westlake*. STAINED GLASS. Older figural glass in six roundels to N and S. E windows of *c.* 1973 by *Goddard & Gibbs*; bright abstract wiggly shapes, increasing in intensity towards the centre of the apse. Effective, but hardly appropriate in this setting. In the cemetery, large recumbent granite cross to Cardinal Vaughan †1903.

National Institute for Medical Research, The Ridgeway. By *Maxwell Ayrton*. A bulky brown brick colossus; the land was bought in 1922, the shell of the building put up 1938–42, completed 1946–50. In a pared-down country-house style, an odd choice, reminiscent of Vincent Harris. Seven storeys with steep roofs, tapering chimneys and splayed wings. The butterfly plan was chosen in order to provide maximum light and air. Very austerely detailed. Arched central doorway in a canted porch, some green tile patterning to accentuate the upper floors. Lodge with canted corners and hipped roof. Older buildings to the E: two long ranges of red brick with pantiled roofs, one with a hoist.

## OTHER PUBLIC BUILDINGS

Branch Library, Hartley Avenue, off The Broadway. Decent Neo-Georgian, single-storeyed. 1937 by *A. O. Knight & Arthur Smith*.

FIRE STATION, Hartley Avenue. Opposite the library, and just a little less traditional. Tower with a stepped top.

COPTHALL SPORTS CENTRE, Page's Lane and Great North Way. In the extensive former grounds of Copthall, a mansion of C17 origin demolished in 1959. Stadium and swimming pool of the 1970s.

ST PAUL'S CHURCH OF ENGLAND PRIMARY SCHOOL, The Ridgeway, beside St Paul's Church (q.v.). Founded as a charity school. Simple Gothic of 1835, gabled and stuccoed; extended 1874 and 1969.

COPTHALL NORTH SCHOOL, Page Street. The best example in the area from the great burst of school building between the wars. Built in 1936 as the County School for Girls, one of *W. T. Curtis* and *H. W. Burchett*'s distinctive secondary schools for the MCC. The front is a two-storeyed L-shaped composition of multi-coloured brick, with entrance tower in the angle, and some polygonal-headed windows to individualize the streamlined modern image. Classrooms round a quadrangle behind.

THE MOUNT SCHOOL. *See* Perambulation 1.

## PERAMBULATIONS

### 1. The Village: Milespit Hill, The Ridgeway, Holcombe Hill

Mill Hill is one of the few parts of outer London where there is still plenty of evidence of the timber, weatherboarded or brick vernacular of rural Middlesex. This tour starts at the top of MILESPIT HILL by the former Methodist church. Facing the pond are the NICOLL ALMSHOUSES, 1696, charmingly minimal. A row of six brick cottages, single-storeyed with simple wooden mullioned casements and a steep tiled roof. Next door, ANGEL COTTAGES, 1964–6 by *R. Seifert & Partners*, which try to be sympathetic by using red brick, timber boarding and tiled roof, but spoil the effect by obtrusive mansards. Further down the hill on the E side, PARKFIELD COTTAGES, a pretty group with plaster coving and half-timbering above a carriageway, probably built together with THE MOUNT (now a school), which is of *c.* 1875 by *T. E. Collcutt*, a substantial brick house with timbered gables and tall chimneys in the picturesque Old English manner of Norman Shaw. Collcutt later lived at Totteridge and did much work in this area (*see also* Mill Hill School, above). Back now to The Ridgeway, where a little to the E Collcutt enthusiasts can find another house by him in similar style, THE PRIORY, also of 1875, now a good deal altered, but with an attractive LODGE by the road.

The chief buildings at the E end of THE RIDGEWAY are institutions (*see* above: National Institute of Medical Research and St Vincent's). At the pond one can turn off along the HIGH STREET, an attractive short parallel stretch with brick C19 cottages, two dated 1911, by *M. S. Briggs* (St Augustine and Ridgeway Cottage), roughcast with tile-hung gables, which seem to have strayed from Hampstead Garden Suburb. BLENHEIM STEPS has an C18 front of six bays with an older wing behind. Formerly stuccoed (as the crude brickwork indicates); the bows flanking the entrance were added after 1948, when the house was used as the school shop. Back in The Ridgeway, on the N side, ROSEBANK, a long weather-

boarded timber-framed building, a good deal altered; six windows
irregularly spaced. It was used as a Quaker meeting house from
1678 to 1719. Then KINGSLAND, *c.* 1970, with monopitch roofs
building up to a taller part at the back. Opposite Mill Hill School
(q.v.), THE GROVE, now the headmaster's house, an appealing
white weatherboarded house end on to the road. Timber-framed,
possibly C16 in origin. Lobby entrance main range with large brick
stack; cross wings. Remodelled as masters' hostel by *Stanley Hamp*,
*c.* 1912. Then CLEVELAND, three bays, neat Regency stucco, and
THE BUNGALOW, built in 1903, but converted into a quaint 30s
*cottage orné*, a three-storeyed confection of timbers and tiled roofs.
After the group of church and school, CHURCH COTTAGES, an
irregular group, mostly C18 and C19, in red and yellow brick.
Opposite Belmont (*see* above), POST OFFICE COTTAGE, C18
red brick, three bays, with weatherboarded extension to the l.

At the W corner with HAMMERS LANE, a picturesquely irregular
group of late C18 weatherboarded cottages is centred on HILLTOP,
which has a butcher's shop built out in front, and two nicely
proportioned Georgian sashes above. Further down Hammers
Lane, MURRAY HOUSE, at r. angles to the road, rendered, and
WEST GROVE, with an early C19 stuccoed front of five bays, with
Doric porch.

LINEN AND WOOLLEN DRAPERS COTTAGE HOMES, Hammers
Lane. Two attractive garden-villagey groups of cottages. To the w,
the MARSHALL ESTATE, by *George Hornblower*, established in
1897 by James C. Marshall, son of the founder of Marshall &
Snelgrove, on part of his father's estate of Goldbeaters. The first
phase consists of sixty-one one- and two-storey cottages, red brick
with half-timbering or roughcast, arranged around a garden.
Central Institute and Clubhouse with decorative terracotta gabled
front and cupola. Smoking and Reading Room extension behind,
1901. On the E side of Hammers Lane, the CHALET ESTATE,
1927 onwards; seventy-one cottages informally disposed around a
central group of one-storey flats. To the N, BEDFORD HOUSE,
1961, five blocks and rest homes for the aged, and a nursing centre,
with extensions of 1994.

On HOLCOMBE HILL, the NW continuation of The Ridgeway,
another picturesque group: houses called St Mary and St Francis,
part of St Mary's Abbey (*see* above), clad in unpainted weatherboarding. A steep path (formerly the main road) leads downhill
past THE OLD FORGE, white render with hipped roof, to
LAWRENCE STREET. SUNNYFIELD, off Lawrence Street, was an
experimental development of 1932–4 by *Laings*. Its simple brick
and pantiled houses with metal windows were intended as an
alternative to the usual suburban clichés. Estate plan by *T. Alwyn
Lloyd*, who designed most of the houses; others were open to competition. They did not sell well and have been much altered.

## 2. *Highwood Hill*

At the junction of HIGHWOOD HILL and Marsh Lane, the RISING
SUN INN, licensed 1751; in origin a late C17 brick two-bay cottage.
Opposite, HIGHWOOD ASH has an C18 painted brick front with
parapet and a full-height canted bay on the garden side; the core is

older, with some timber-framed parts, and was enlarged in the 1660s. Celia Fiennes lived here 1713–37. Stables to the s. Further E, HIGHWOOD HOUSE. A neat stuccoed front; three-bay recessed centre with semicircular Ionic porch. Wings with shallow pediments and ground-floor windows recessed in arches. Built shortly before 1817 by William Anderson; acquired by Sir Stamford Raffles after 1825. Interior much altered c. 1950. The house was a rebuilding of an older one (minor parts of which remain at the back), on an estate which had belonged to Lord William Russell (executed 1683). Along Highwood Hill a fringe of outbuildings and estate cottages remains; the most elaborate are OAK COTTAGE and HILL COTTAGE, c. 1900, with half-timbering and tile-hanging. More cottages tucked away up NAN CLARK'S LANE, then more affluent houses of the 1930s. THE BARN, in part of the former grounds of Highwood House, is a polygonal half-timbered studio house of c. 1937, with tiled roof and tall chimney. In its garden, LADY RUSSELL'S WELL, a late C17 chalybeate well. Circular enclosure of brick with steps down, restored 1937; inside is an original cartouche inscribed 'MRS RACHEL RUSSELL'S GIFT JUNE YE 10 1681'. At the end of the lane, GLENAMOY, built 1936–8 for Donald Sessions by *Oliver Hill*, a late example of his romantic Arts and Crafts style; limewashed brick with a dramatic thatched roof. Splendidly sited. A curved plan, with main rooms and central open loggia on the outer curve, looking s over the valley.

Returning w, on the s side of Highwood Hill, EDGEHILL, a large mansion in Free Classical of c. 1910, four dentilled gables, Georgian sashes. Then HIGHWOOD LODGE, an exceptionally pretty early C19 cottage with barge-boarded gables, the lower parts heavily castellated.

Further w, in MARSH LANE, large suburban houses of the turn of the century onwards. The best is GREYSTANES, c. 1907 by *G. & A. Gilbert Scott*. L-shaped plan. Roughcast with high prominent gables and chimneys, now painted white. Stark unmoulded mullioned windows, but in the main gable a mannered elongated central window with segmental pediment, recalling the Arts and Crafts manner of Edgar Wood. On the N side, POWERSCOURT, c. 1900, roughcast with three tile-hung gables and a quaintly inappropriate late C20 French-château extension. Off Marsh Lane, in HANKINS LANE by the golf course, COVENTRY FARMHOUSE, C17, timber-framed, with later stucco front.

HYVER HILL. Select houses in a secluded woodland setting E of Barnet Way. Near the end of the lane, HIGH ACRE by *Jane Drew*, 1960. A two-storeyed flat-roofed house with brick ends and upstairs living rooms with floor-to-ceiling windows to exploit the view. A large upper terrace projects in an irregular curve at each end. Further on, THE WHITE HOUSE. A curiosity. 1934 by *D. E. Harrington* for Fred Daniels, a film cameraman who worked at the Elstree Studios. He demanded a house in the style of Frank Lloyd Wright's houses of the 1920s, which he had seen when visiting Hollywood. The result appears to be unique in England. L-shaped, with large ground-floor studio, veranda with piers emphasized by banding. The angular effects which Wright achieved in his 'textile houses' in cast concrete are here done mostly in white brick (painted later).

*3. East, south and west of The Ridgeway*

SE of The Ridgeway the Green Belt has preserved the rural character of a long loop of lanes. In BURTONHOLE LANE, THE FARM-HOUSE, an attractive C18 three-bay two-storey house, cedar-shingled with tiled hipped roof and a simple dentilled cornice. OAKFIELD, *c.* 1898. Large red brick house with elaborate painted stone facings, balustraded porch and windows and a corner turret. PARTINGDALE MANOR in PARTINGDALE LANE is a picturesque stuccoed agglomeration, its exterior chiefly early C19; a variety of windows, including Gothick traceried ones. Doric porch with radiating fanlight. NETHER COURT, Frith Lane. A large Victorian house by *Percy Stone*, Neo-Jacobean, now Finchley Golf Club.

Among the C20 suburbia to the W, only a few buildings of interest. FEATHERSTONE HOUSE, Wise Lane, *c.* 1700 but given a new front and windows in the C18. Rusticated doorcase with flat hood on brackets. PAGE STREET was a hamlet by the early C19; one good survival in Bunn's Lane: CHASE LODGE. Early C19, yellow brick with two-storey centre and front and rear porches, one Tuscan, one Doric. It faces the extensive headquarters of the builders *John Laing & Son*, the firm responsible for much of the area's suburban development, established here in 1926; offices much enlarged from 1956 onwards. Between Page Street and the A1, the former grounds of Copthall, now a sports centre (*see* above). The much altered mansion of 1624 was demolished in 1959. Near the junction of Watford Way and THE BROADWAY, LAWRENCE FARM HOUSE, now offices, a solid red brick house probably built in 1729. The Broadway itself consists of quite varied shopping parades on a homely scale, in late Arts and Crafts taste. They expanded E from the station from *c.* 1910 to 1925. W of the railway in HALE LANE, by Lillie Lane, ST ANTHONY'S SCHOOL, incorporating a house of possibly early C17 origin. L-shaped timber-framed building behind a three-bay C18 brick front, with large central chimneystack. To the NE, a later, taller brick addition.

# MONKEN HADLEY

A pleasantly semi-rural spot between High Barnet and Cockfosters. The parish, originally in Middlesex, formed part of East Barnet Urban District in Hertfordshire between 1895 and 1965. 'Monken' refers to the abbey of Walden, Essex: a hermitage at Hadley, together with the church at Edmonton, was given to the abbey in the C12. The church lies amid a little cluster of houses between the informal open spaces of Hadley Green and Hadley Common, 'one of the most felicitous pictures of Georgian visual planning which the neighbourhood of London has to offer', Pevsner wrote in 1953, and, happily, the scene is little altered.

ST MARY, Hadley Green Road. The date 1494 appears in arabic numerals – an unusual feature for this date – on a stone on the W tower, convincing not only for the tower but for much of the present

church. Tower and w walls of the aisles have an attractive irregular
chequer of flint and ironstone. w tower in three stages, with three-
light arched belfry windows, diagonal buttresses, battlements, and
higher sw turret. On top is a copper BEACON, renewed in 1779, a
great rarity. The *Beauties of England* suggested it could be 'nearly
a unique vestige of the manners of the Middle Ages'. The other
walls of flint with white Ancaster stone dressings are largely C19,
replacing brick. *G.E. Street*'s restoration of 1848–9 included
widening the aisles and removing plaster ceilings and a miscellany
of galleries added in the C17 and C18. s porch rebuilt 1855. Aisled
nave of two bays, with a further bay embracing the tower; chancel
chapels of one bay, perhaps older than the rest, as their arches have
the simplest mouldings (concave double chamfers). The nave
arcades have moulded four-centred arches on piers with capitals
towards the arches, more elaborate than average for a rural
Middlesex church. Tower arch similar. On the nave E responds,
capitals with angels, and hoodmould stops with a probably recut
carving of a bird with wheatear, a rebus of the Goodyeres (*see*
brasses, below). Medieval nave roof with a tie-beam with struts to
arch braces; tracery in the spandrels. Raised chancel and seating
of Street's time.

FONT. Simple octagonal type, with quatrefoils; tall attenuated
Gothic COVER of 1952. – ORGAN, *c*. 1860, brought from Hull in
1991. – STAINED GLASS. Chancel s and s chapel E by *Wailes*,
*c*. 1850, small scenes still in an engraving style. N chapel N (dated
1857) and s chapel s by *Powell & Sons*, heraldic. Chancel E 1952,
designed by *Francis Stephens*, painted by *John Hayward*, small
figures on clear glass, in C20 style but sympathetic to the Wailes
windows. Memorial windows by *Clayton & Bell*, in the s aisle,
one with sentimental Victorian deer in a landscape, 1877. – An
unusual number of small BRASSES, reset on the walls. The oldest
to Philip and Margaret Green, and Margeret Somercotes, all
†1442 (two effigies of ladies). W. Turnour †1500, wife and four
daughters; Joan Goodyere (1504, according to a lost inscription):
woman in demi-profile. T. Goodyere †1518 and wife (inscription
lost); William Gale †1615 and family (now concealed by carpet).
Anne Walkedon †1572, inscription. Many MONUMENTS. The
best of the larger ones is to Sir Roger Wilbraham †1616 by *Nicholas
Stone*. Two busts of outstanding quality, in oval niches, the attitudes
of exquisite Mannerism. Alabaster and black and pink Belgian
marble, less austere in colour than some of Stone's works. – Alice
Stamford and her son Henry Carew †1626, an entirely wooden
wall monument with painted portrait of the son and painted surround. – Elizabeth Davies †1678, wall monument with curved
tablet framed by garlands and achievement, signed by *William
Stanton*. – Richmond Moore †1796, with mourning woman by
broken column. – Frederick Cass (of Little Grove, East Barnet,
patron of the church) †1861, brass, with one large and four small
quatrefoils. Rev. Charles Cass †1896, plain tablet. Charles Tempest-
Hicks †1918, marble, with portrait medallion. Many minor classical
tablets with urns of every shape.

CHURCHYARD with many chest tombs, also some wooden
'bedheads'.

s of the church, two pretty Gothic cottages of 1822, built as almshouses, flint-faced, with quatrefoil windows and on the N side a tall blind arch. Part of a group united as Paggits's Ecclesiastical Charity in 1958. It includes the little stuccoed GATEHOUSE to the s, built for the parish clerk, early C19 with later Gothic windows. Behind is the RECTORY, the E-facing front with Tudor dripstones built 1824, the additions in a more solid domestic Gothic of 1846 by *Street*, his first secular work.

## Perambulation

The houses along the sides of Hadley Green and Hadley Common include only a few of high individual merit. It is their universally satisfying standard and their variety of scale, texture, and juxtaposition that make them so enjoyable. This was Pevsner's verdict of the 1950s and it still holds good forty years later. There is indeed very little to remind one of the later C20 apart from a discreet increase of security. The highlights are described roughly from NW to SE.

On the w side of HADLEY GREEN, OLD FOLD MANOR HOUSE, Old Fold Lane, five-bay, two-storey Georgian, *c.* 1750, stuccoed. Remains of a moat to the w. To the N, OLD FOLD MANOR GOLF CLUB HOUSE, two houses of *c.* 1820, two-storeyed, with rounded full-height bays, the N one with doorway with good fanlight and sidelights. Adapted in the early C20 by *W. Charles Waymouth* as club house, with an added central link with four columns and broad parapet with Soanian incised line ornament. Along the Great North Road, here called HADLEY HIGHSTONE, small cottages, including the KING WILLIAM IV, a picturesque timber-framed pub, C17 and later. Two gables to the road with decorative C19 bargeboards, the r. one rendered, the l. one weatherboarded. The Highstone is the OBELISK on the Great North Road, erected in 1740 by Sir Jeremy Sambrooke to commemorate the Battle of Barnet of 1471. Of Portland stone. Originally 200 yds further S; moved to present site *c.* 1840.

HADLEY GREEN ROAD runs along the SE edge of the Green. It starts on the fringes of High Barnet with OSSULSTON HOUSE, built soon after 1764 by John Horton, three bays, red brick, with Gibbs surround to the arched door and brick stringcourses. On the r. a three-storey house at r. angles. Then two cottages with early C19 fronts, the OLD COTTAGE clearly with an older core. Four detached Neo-Georgian houses follow, replacements for bomb damage. Then HADLEY HOUSE, the most ambitious property along the Green, of *c.* 1760. Stately mid Georgian, 1–3–1 bays with a bow and three further bays to the l. Central pediment, ground-floor windows in arches, big Roman Doric porch with fluted columns. The doorway with continuous fanlight and side lights looks a little later. Contemporary STABLES to the r., half H-shaped, with central archway with clock turret. Then FAIRHOLT, *c.* 1750, five bays, three-storeys, stuccoed. MONKENHOLT, also stuccoed and of five bays, with a bow front built soon after 1767. HOLLYBUSH, *c.* 1790 of yellow brick, with good fanlight, earlier section to l., now heightened and reroofed, of red brick with blue headers. After some new or renewed cottages, the WILBRAHAM ALMSHOUSES, founded in 1612 by Sir Roger Wilbraham, six one-storey red brick cottages with two-light brick windows with arched tops to the two lights, and paired diagonal stocks. Extended at the back in 1815. The almshouses mark the beginning of the funnel-like access from the Green towards the church and the common.

DURY ROAD runs from Hadley Highstone towards the church. A varied sequence on the E side: No. 1, early C18 plum brick; Nos. 3–11, 15 and 17, all timber-framed, Nos. 5–9 with Victorian Gothic front with three bargeboarded gables and pretty timber Gothick veranda. No. 29, THORNDON HOUSE, good early Georgian, two storeys and basement, five bays with narrow end bay, an extension at each end. Nos. 27 and 31, of similar date, with segment-headed windows. No. 39, STOBERRY LODGE, *c.* 1830, a three-bay stucco villa. No. 43, HADLEY BOURNE, red brick, mid–late C18, Tuscan doorcase with fanlight. Round the corner towards the church, a group of mid-C20 Neo-Georgian houses, set back, on the site of THE PRIORY (C16 and early C19 Gothic Revival). GROVE HOUSE follows, late C18, very thoroughly Neo-Georgianized by *H.A. Welch*, and BEACON HOUSE, directly N of the church, timber-framed with brick front, C17 and early C18. Opposite, SW of the church, WHITE LODGE, all stuccoed, three Early Georgian bays with ornate Gibbs-surround doorcase, three-bay late C18 addition to the E.

The group of church, almshouses and rectory (*see* above) closes the vista completely, and only after one has passed it does the view open onto the common, with Hadley Wood as the background. Along HADLEY COMMON, quite a chain of pleasant houses on the s side. GLADSMUIR HOUSE, a five-bay villa of *c.* 1830 with Victorianized front. Red brick with stucco trim, Doric porch with fluted columns. C18 timber-framed weatherboarded BARN in the grounds; queenpost trusses; weathervane dated 1775.* HURST COTTAGE, five-bay, two-storeyed, early C18, with an attached gabled Tudor cottage on the l. THE CHASE, stuccoed, seven bays, early C18; C19 alterations to the façade, windows with very broad moulded frames. HADLEY HURST, a good large house of *c.* 1700. Red brick, three storeys and five bays, with a three-bay addition. Curly broken pediment above the (former) central door with Roman bust. (Original internal features include a panelled stairhall with three turned balusters to each step.) HADLEY HURST COTTAGES (Nos. 1–3), C18, built as stables for Hadley Hurst. Three bays on either side of a tall archway; three large full-height semicircular niches. Further on, MONKENHURST, No. 15, tall romantic Gothic of 1880, with tower over the entrance, big Gothic staircase window to the l., and half-hipped roof. Enlarged 1915 (stained glass brought from Northumberland House, Charing Cross). A little further on, by THE CRESCENT, one of the many access gates to Hadley Common, a fine C18 five-bar gate with octagonal piers with caps and decorative ironwork.

ST MARTHA'S CONVENT SCHOOL, Camlet Way, Hadley Common. Formerly Mount House. A handsome C18 house in its own grounds. Five-bay red brick s front with stone dressings, quoins and stringcourse, the central three bays set forward under a pediment with bullseye window. Doorway with elaborately

---

* Another good C18 timber-framed BARN in the grounds of MONKENMEAD, Hadley Wood Road.

decorated Ionic surround and pediment. E side with two rounded bows of *c.* 1800. Cantilevered stair. To the w an C18 stable range, with arched ground-floor openings and Baroque domed clock turret. School additions behind of 1960 and 1968.

# NEW BARNET

Like the older settlement of East Barnet (q.v.), part of Hertfordshire until 1965. Thorne in 1876 observed that New Barnet had 'one of those new half-finished railway villages that we have come to look on as almost a necessary adjunct of every station within a moderate distance of London'. The Great Northern Railway arrived in 1850, and the area began to develop while there was still open land further s.

The approach to the station now has indifferent tall offices of the 1960s, characteristic of the vogue at that time for out-of-town offices close to transport centres. At the junction with STATION ROAD, the usual Edwardian BANK, a slim WAR MEMORIAL, and No. 32, the former COUNCIL OFFICES, now a restaurant; modest Italianate with a clock tower. Built for East Barnet Valley Local Board, 1891–2 by *F. W. Shenton* of Whetstone, winner of a competition. The more affluent of the late Victorian houses are spread over the higher slopes to the sw, built on the Lyonsdown Estate by the British Land Company.

HOLY TRINITY, Lyonsdown Road. 1865, an early work by *Ewan Christian*. Stock brick with red brick banding. Well sited on a corner, with its strong rounded apse to the fore, flanked by curved chapels. Transepts and big sweeping slate roof with small E flèche.

ST JAMES, Station Road. 1911 by *W. Charles Waymouth*. Nave with passage aisles, apse.

ST MARK, Potter's Road, Barnet Vale. 1896–9 by *J. L. Pearson*, but not a spectacular example of that excellent architect's work. Executed by *Frank Pearson*. Four-bay nave only, the E end a temporary structure. Lively surfaces of rough flint and rubble with stone dressings; chequerwork in the w gable; two-storeyed porch with carved figures over the entrance. Large Perp aisle windows with four-centred heads. The aisle arcades with tall piers; no clerestory.

ST JOHN (United Reformed), Somerset Road and Mowbray Road. By *Jon Finlayson* and *Iain Langlands*, planned 1964, built 1967–9. An arrestingly angular design. Polygonal, with steep zigzagging slate roof whose eaves almost touch the ground. Long narrow roof-lights along the folds of the roof, and other windows in all kinds of odd positions. Church hall beneath, taking advantage of the slope.

GREAT NORTHERN CEMETERY. *See* East Barnet, above.

LIVINGSTONE PRIMARY SCHOOL, Baring Road. On the fringe of the Green Belt. 1952–3 by *James Cubitt & Partners* for *Hertfordshire County Council*, using their 8-ft 3-in. module. Curtain walling with blue spandrels and pebble-coated cladding. Light and airy, with split-level hall between ranges of classrooms opening onto play areas. The glazed library annexe to the hall is later, as are the large brick-faced pitched-roof classroom extensions to the rear (1996).

In Park Road, No. 89, a large stuccoed house, used as a folk
museum before the Second World War. In the grounds, a small
medieval timber-framed BARN, brought from Birchington, Kent,
now a private house.

# TOTTERIDGE

Totteridge is on the outermost perimeter of London, chiefly a
scatter of buildings around the Green, and a ribbon of affluent
houses along the old route named Totteridge Lane, Totteridge
Village and Totteridge Common. This runs E–W along a gravel
ridge, with panoramic views towards London over open land. The
district was once a medieval estate of the Bishop of Ely, and the
dedication of the church was originally to Ely's patron saint, St
Audrey or Etheldreda. In the C18 Totteridge was still only a tiny
hamlet with a few major houses in large grounds. These have largely
disappeared, but village church and green remain, and some modest
C17–C18 buildings.

Survival of the rural setting is due to the Green Belt and to the
efforts of the Totteridge Preservation Society before the Second
World War and the Totteridge Manor Association, formed in 1955,
which took over management of surrounding common and woodland. Wealthy late Victorian and Edwardian mansions and their
smaller successors hide behind curved signposts and bold white timber
gates which are a signature of the village. Architectural standards
were high in the Edwardian period, when local residents included
the architects T. E. Collcutt and Charles Nicholson. The sprinkling
of secretive security-conscious houses of the later C20 makes less
impact.

St Andrew, Totteridge Village. Rebuilt in 1790 by *William
Ketteridge*, an aisleless nave of brick with arched windows in Gibbs
surrounds and heavy W pediment. Pretty weatherboarded bell-
turret, battlemented, with weathervane dated 1706. W porch 1845.
*James Brooks* added the modest apsed chancel, nave roof and plate
tracery in 1869. Plentiful STAINED GLASS transformed the interior
into a dark, cosy Victorian space. – Chancel: three lancets by
*Clayton & Bell*. – Nave S and N: one window each, by *Kempe*,
1896 and 1897; another in the NE chapel, 1907. N side, W end: an
Arts and Crafts window in glowing, uneven glass, to Sir Charles
Nicholson †1903 (of The Grange, *see* below) by his son, *Archibald
K. Nicholson*. The wife of another son, the architect *Charles
Nicholson*, decorated the chancel roof in 1899. It has bold vine-
scrolls. – ALTAR FRONTAL, 1936. Beaten metal panels between
wooden pilasters. – PULPIT. Jacobean, with arcading and strap-
work, said to come from St Etheldreda, Hatfield. – MONUMENTS.
Fine ledger stone to Sarah Long †1718, with coat of arms. John
Puget †1805, by *John Bacon Jun.*, garlanded urn in low relief
above a long inscription; matching tablet below to Catherine
Puget †1842.

CHURCHYARD with remarkably large ancient yew tree and many
enjoyable tombs. Several C18 chests with curly Baroque decoration: Peter Meyer †1727; Elizabeth Gildart (by *J. Hockley*); also

some early shaped headstones: Samuel Sureties †1739, with
cherubs' heads; Richard Burdett †1747, with skull. Scrimgeour
family, 1863 etc., draped urn on tall plinth. Slender Gothic Cross
to Sir Charles Allom and family, *c.* 1918.

VICARAGE, E of the church. By *Charles Nicholson*, probably his
first building, 1892. Simple but not standard Queen Anne style;
orange brick with hipped roof and big hood to an asymmetrically
positioned door. (Stained glass roundel over the door by *A. K.
Nicholson*; good interior features.)

Close to the church a weatherboarded C17 BARN and POUND
ENCLOSURE. Next to it, POUND HOUSE by *J. Leonard Williams*,
1911, a trim villa in the Old English tradition with roughcast, half-
timbering and shaped bargeboards; the neighbouring PRIOR'S
CORNER is in a similar spirit. THE PRIORY, No. 54, at the corner
of Barnet Lane, is a timber-framed C17 building; its name is early
C19, its appearance mostly *c.* 1900: pebbledashed with an old tile
roof. On the S side of Totteridge Lane a Georgian group: GARDEN
HILL HOUSE, No. 43, with irregular front in red brick with tall
parapet, and a wing to the S with Venetian window. (Good C18
staircase.) SOUTHERNHAY, No. 49, is a late Georgian stuccoed
villa. Close to them was one of Totteridge's major houses,
Copped Hall, demolished in 1928. It had extensive grounds to the
S, shown formally laid out on a print of *c.* 1700. Relandscaping in
the late C18 is attributed to *Repton*; a lake survives, now part of
Darlands Nature Reserve.

From the church TOTTERIDGE VILLAGE runs E towards the
GREEN, a large informal triangle of land to the S, with some good
houses along its W side. Near the lane, ST ANDREW'S SCHOOL,
rebuilt in 1938 in a demure domestic style with dormered hipped
roof and green-shuttered windows. Surprisingly, by *Wallis, Gilbert
& Partners* (better known for their factories). It includes Kemp
Hall, built for shared use with the parish. Extensions 1954, 1959.
The W side of the Green starts with THE ORANGE TREE, a rural
pub, much rebuilt. Further on, GREEN LODGE, a former lodge
to Copped Hall, picturesque late C19 Gothic with angular windows
and patterned tiled roof. Then THE CROFT, very picturesque, by
the successful late Victorian architect *T. E. Collcutt* for himself,
1895 and later. His rural style is a simplified and more relaxed
version of Norman Shaw's early 'Old English' work, very different
from his London buildings. Three ranges in a U-plan around a
court. Brick with roughcast upper floor, Tudor windows, and a
little half-timbering. (Interior with some pretty plasterwork and
*De Morgan* tiles. Remains of formal gardens behind, with sculpture
of a triton by *Henry Pegram*.) Towards the tapering S end of the
Green, FAIRSPEIR, in a similar idiom, a small roughcast house
with jettied gable, dated 1899, also by *Collcutt*. STRATHEARN
COTTAGES are an early C19 pair, brick with shallow hipped roof.
Also by *Collcutt*, another large but altered house of 1898–9, from
1968 CONSOLATA COLLEGE. Roughcast with half-timbered
gabled wings, an angled wing to the r.; bold tall chimneys. The
Green ends with a group around a pond: HOME FARM, a C17
timber-framed house with brick end stack and irregular rendered
front; LAUREL FARM, of similar date and construction but much
restored. Converted C18 barn in between.

At the NE corner of the Green, OLD HOUSE, plain tall Georgian, rendered; porch with two thin columns. Further E in Totteridge Lane, TREVANION, Nos. 131 and 133, by *Norman Shaw*, 1883–4, tile-hung, not Shaw at his best. Repaired after a fire in 1975.

Now to the W of the church. TOTTERIDGE VILLAGE has an attractive group of rural houses demonstrating the change from timber to brick buildings in the C16–C18. No. 56, TOTTERIDGE HOUSE, and No. 58, C18 brick, much extended. OLD TOTTERIDGE FARM, a three-bay brick early C19 farmhouse divided in two and extended to l. and r. No. 74, ROSE COTTAGE; much altered early C18 brick front to an earlier timber-framed house. Lobby entrance with central chimneystack. Nos. 76–84 are a complicated cluster, with an early C18 brick front to probably early timber framing. Opposite, on the S side, No. 51, RIDGEWAY COTTAGE, timber-framed and weatherboarded, and Nos. 53–55, a simple painted brick pair.

THE GRANGE, Totteridge Common and Grange Avenue. This was one of Totteridge's major C18 houses, with grounds covering the area of Grange Avenue. Rebuilt as flats after a fire in 1899, by *Charles Nicholson*, son of the owner. Brick Neo-Georgian, two storeys, following the lines of the former building, and using old materials. S front with a two-storey bow. GRANGE HOUSE was formerly the coach house and stables. Then on the N side of TOTTERIDGE COMMON, MANOR HOUSE, a good five-bay, two-storey mid-Georgian house, red brick with hipped tile roof; very neglected in 1996. Built within the grounds of Totteridge Park (*see* below). No. 4 was a LODGE to Totteridge Park; minimal early C19 Gothick, with a veranda on slender Doric columns.

Among later houses in this area on the S side: LONGBOURNE, *c.* 1973 by *L. R. Harbinson*, tucked into the slope, with long slate roofs of uneven pitch, and a staircase drum as a feature of the entrance courtyard. REDINGS, 1961–2 by *Boissevain & Osmond*, a low brick house with fully glazed main rooms facing S.

TOTTERIDGE PARK is the one surviving older mansion, now subdivided. Basically C18 but substantially altered in the early C20. Until then it was a plain mid-Georgian composition of three ranges around a courtyard facing W; the central one with a projecting three-bay centre with pediment and cupola. Rainwater heads and an Ionic doorway with keystone give the date 1750. The alterations of *c.* 1900 turned it into a picturesque, asymmetrical, gabled composition; roughcast was added on the S side, the N wing was demolished, and a new main entrance was made on the N side of the S range, with broad round-arched porch. All this is in the style of *Collcutt*, who added the very pretty stable courtyard (now THE PADDOCKS) to the N, with cupola (reused from the house?) and timber arcade. C18 WALLED GARDEN.

Also on the N side: No. 38, WILLOW HOUSE (formerly Denham Farm House); Late Georgian painted brick front to an earlier timber-framed house, and No. 56, WEST END HOUSE, early C19 stucco front with timber framing behind. On the S side several large houses. ELLERN MEDE, 1876–7 by *Norman Shaw* for William Austin; one of Shaw's asymmetrical Old English L-plan compositions, with lower service wing to the l., big, bold half-timbered gable over the entrance, and broad tile-hung flank with half-hipped gable, all anchored by tall chimneys. By the road LODGE and stable block; early C20 garage between, kitchen garden beyond. Further W, FAIRLAWN, No. 51, early C18, with large roughcast and half-timbered Edwardian extensions, and THE LYNCH HOUSE, Nos. 55 and 57 by *T. E. Collcutt*, 1905–7, rendered, three-gabled and symmetrical, with windows of every shape and a segmental hood to the door.

ST EDWARDS COLLEGE, N side of Totteridge Lane (from 1958 White Fathers Missionary College). Present college buildings by *A. F. Peel*, 1977–80. They occupy part of the larger site of Totteridge Lodge, where a R.C. orphanage was founded in 1875 by Cardinal Manning (born at Copped Hall). A gaunt brick CHAPEL with round-arched windows remains further E, converted to housing.

# WHETSTONE AND OAKLEIGH PARK

Whetstone, on the borders of the old parishes of Friern Barnet and Finchley, developed along the Great North Road, probably soon after this stretch was made in the C14. But apart from St John's Church and a group of old buildings on the E side, nearly all the High Road is now of the C20, and of little note. To the E is OAKLEIGH PARK, a superior suburb served by the station on the Great Northern line. Thorne noted in 1876 'recent collections of genteel villas'; a handful of large houses remains behind shrubberies and conifers along the undulating roads.

ALL SAINTS, Oakleigh Road North and Myddleton Park. Founded by John Miles of The Manor, Friern Barnet; 1881–3 by *Joseph Clarke*. Flint-faced with stone dressings, in an already old-fashioned C13 lancet style. Canted apse, N tower with fine stone spire. Similar to All Saints, Reading, where the founder's son, Henry Miles, was curate, before becoming the first vicar here. Very tall interior with plastered walls, circular piers with foliage capitals. Iron SCREEN incorporating the pulpit. The special feature is the elaborate decoration, still complete, carried out from the 1880s to the 1920s. Devised by *S. Gambier-Parry* and the Rev. Miles, with spiky gabled REREDOS, STAINED GLASS by *Ward & Hughes* (Life of Christ in the chancel, pictorial scenes showing Works of Mercy in the aisles), and chancel WALL PAINTING: a frieze with angels and other figures above bold stencilling. The last part, Christ in Glory over the chancel arch, was completed 1923 after a design by *Heaton, Butler & Bayne*. SE Chapel of the Holy Spirit added 1905, with good glass of *c.* 1909–11 by *T. F. Curtis* of *Ward & Hughes*.

ST JOHN, High Road, 1832. The first additional church to be built in the old parish of Finchley. Small and plain, with the polygonal turrets typical of the date. White painted turret, Gothic, with battlements and an ogee dome. Square-headed windows. In 1879 *James Brooks* supplied C13 tracery to the windows, provided a new scissor roof and seating and built a chancel and vestry (cf. Totteridge). STAINED GLASS. E window by *William Morris & Co.*, Crucifixion, with leafy background. W window by *Lavers & Westlake*.

CONGREGATIONAL CHURCH, Oakleigh Road. 1900, by *E. F. Knight.* An odd specimen of its date and of the fanciful leanings of the Congregationalists about 1900. Red brick with slim flèche and two w turrets with a curved parapet between. Perp w window in a deep recess with eleven chamfers; the bottom part disappears behind the curved top of a lower chapel.

ST MARY MAGDALENE (R.C.), Athenaeum Road. 1958 by *Wilfred C. Mangan.* Dull red brick, with angular window lights. w tower; steeply pitched steel-framed roof.

Along the HIGH ROAD indifferent interwar shopping parades are punctuated by a tall office block at each end, the s one BARNET HOUSE (borough offices), 1966 by *R. Seifert & Partners,* twelve and three storeys on a T-plan, with mosaic cladding and tapered stilts in Seifert's 1960s manner. On the E side, N of Oakleigh Road North, some older remnants: Nos. 1264–1270, an irregular two-storey group with tiled roofs of differing heights. Ground floors altered for shops. Behind the brick front range of No. 1264 a late medieval timber-framed rear wing, a rare survival in this area. Close studded walls with arched braces, and a crown-post roof, smoke-blackened at the ends, suggest that at least part of the range was an open hall. Further N, BANK BUILDINGS of *c.* 1900, ending with a green corner dome.

On the w side, Nos. 1331–1339, a brick group, mostly early C19 and C20 in Georgian style, but incorporating No. 1339, early C18, two bays, red brick, with two-bay extension to the l.

# CAMDEN

Camden was created in 1965 from the three LCC Metropolitan Boroughs based on medieval parishes: Holborn, St Pancras and Hampstead. Holborn was already expanding as a north-western suburb of the City of London in the C16, and it was entirely built up by the early C19. St Pancras, to its N, owes its name to its ancient church near the southern end of the parish, but until the whole area was built over in the C19, its main settlements were further N at Kentish Town and Highgate. The southern part is now dominated by the great C19 railway termini on Euston Road: Euston, King's Cross and St Pancras. Camden Town was a new settlement which developed in the early C19; by 1900 a continuous suburb stretched from here through Kentish Town to Highgate, at the top of the hill. Across Hampstead Heath, north London's most important open space, is Hampstead, still a distinctive hill-top settlement, with C19 development on its lower slopes. The population of the whole of Camden was 184,900 in 1995. The architectural achievements of the modern borough, particularly in housing, are more notable than

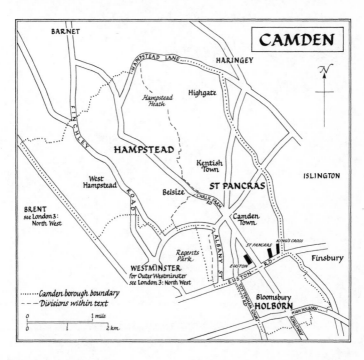

those in many other parts of London; they are discussed in the Introduction to St Pancras.

The following account divides the modern borough into its three historic components, with a few exceptions in the interest of coherence. The centre of Highgate is all described under St Pancras, including the part E of Highgate High Street within the Borough of Haringey. Likewise the southern tip of St Pancras, which lies s of Euston Road, is described, with the rest of Bloomsbury and adjoining areas, under Holborn. Regents Park and its buildings w of Albany Street are described in *London 3: North West*. Buildings s of the road named Holborn (including the old parish church of St Andrew Holborn), now within the City of London, are included in *London 1: The City of London*. To the sw the boundary cuts through the fringes of Covent Garden. Covent Garden itself is covered in *London 6: The City of Westminster*.

## INTRODUCTION

The character of Hampstead is conditioned by the 'Northern
Heights' of London, the sand and pebble-capped hills rising up from
the London clay which run from West Hampstead to beyond
Highgate. Early settlement is indicated by Palaeolithic finds in the s
part of the area, and West Heath was an important Mesolithic site. A
mound on Parliament Hill may be a Bronze Age barrow.* In the
Middle Ages there was a village with a parish church near the top of
Hampstead hill and, downhill to the w, a nunnery at Kilburn, by the
Roman road that became known as Edgware Road and formed the
w boundary of the parish. The main manor houses were Hampstead,
belonging to the Hicks family of Chipping Campden, later the Earls
of Gainsborough; Frognal to the w; Belsize to the s. The great time
for Hampstead was the c18, and of all the former villages of north
London it has most visibly preserved its character of a favourite
*villeggiatura* near the town, for the summer months or for retirement. This is due to two causes: the open spaces of Regents Park,
Primrose Hill and Hampstead Heath preserved between London
and Hampstead, and the steepness of the hill on which the village
lies. A hill, as at Harrow, if steep enough to rule out trams and

---

*The mound lies *c.* 300 yards NE of the N end of Hampstead ponds and is now *c.* 115 ft
in diameter and *c.* 10 ft high. Excavation has shown the external ditch to be relatively
modern, but there is a burial ditch inside, and additions to the mound were visible; no
human remains were found, but a pocket of charcoal near the centre.

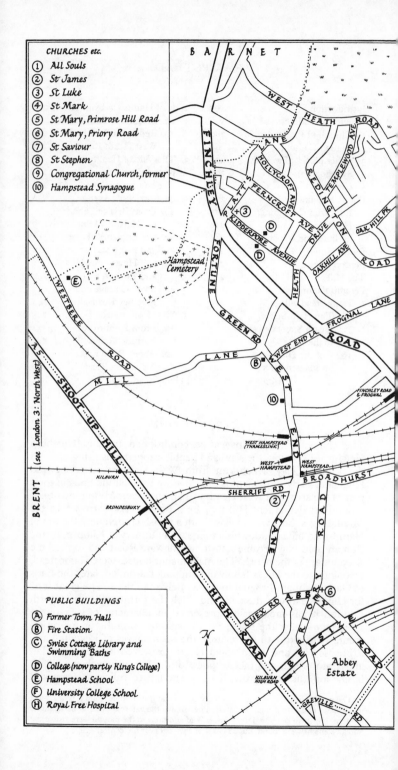

CHURCHES etc.

1. All Souls
2. St James
3. St Luke
4. St Mark
5. St Mary, Primrose Hill Road
6. St Mary, Priory Road
7. St Saviour
8. St Stephen
9. Congregational Church, former
10. Hampstead Synagogue

PUBLIC BUILDINGS

A. Former Town Hall
B. Fire Station
C. Swiss Cottage Library and Swimming Baths
D. College (now partly King's College)
E. Hampstead School
F. University College School
H. Royal Free Hospital

BARNET

WEST HEATH ROAD

PLATT'S LANE

HOLLYCROFT AVE
FERNCROFT AVE
REDINGTON DRIVE
TEMPLEWOOD AVE
OAK HILL PK
OAK HILL AVE
OAK HILL ROAD

KIDDERPORE AVENUE

FINCHLEY ROAD

FORTUNE GREEN RD

HEATH DRIVE

FROGNAL LANE

FROGNAL ROAD

Hampstead Cemetery

WESTBERE ROAD

MILL LANE

SHOOT UP HILL

A5 (see London 3: North West)

WEST END LANE

WEST END

FINCHLEY ROAD & FROGNAL

WEST HAMPSTEAD (THAMESLINK)

WEST HAMPSTEAD

WEST HAMPSTEAD

KILBURN

BRONDESBURY

BRENT

SHERRIFF RD

BROADHURST

QUEX RD

ABBEY ROAD

PRIORY ROAD

BELSIZE ROAD

KILBURN HIGH ROAD

Abbey Estate

GREVILLE RD

N

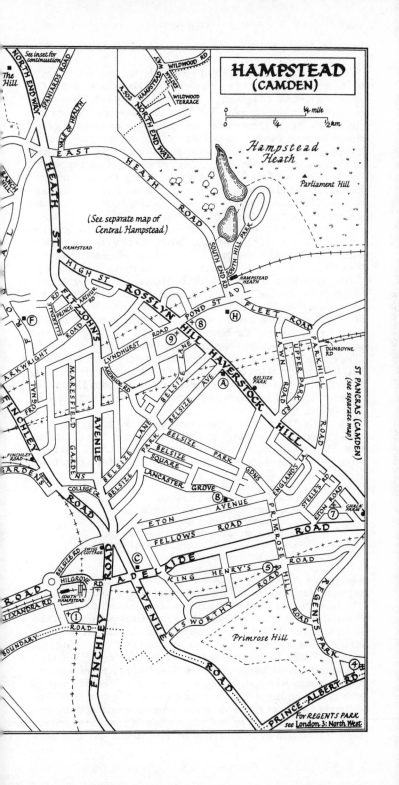

# HAMPSTEAD
## (CAMDEN)

See inset for continuation

The Hill

WILDWOOD RD
WILDWOOD WAY
NORTH END WAY
HAMPSTEAD WAY
A502
WILDWOOD TERRACE
HAMPSTEAD WAY

0 — ¼ mile
0 — ¼ — ½ km

SPANIARDS ROAD

NORTH END WAY

VALE OF HEALTH

EAST

HEATH

Hampstead Heath

Parliament Hill

BRANCH HILL

HEATH ST

HEATH ROAD

(See separate map of Central Hampstead)

SOUTH HILL PARK

HAMPSTEAD

HIGH ST

ROSSLYN HILL

POND ST

FLEET ROAD

SOUTH END RD

HAMPSTEAD HEATH

RD
FITZJOHN'S
PRINCE ARTHUR RD
ELSWORTHY
LYNDHURST ROAD

(F)

(8)
(9)

HAVERSTOCK HILL

(H)

AKENSIDE RD

BELSIZE LANE

BELSIZE AVE

(A)

BELSIZE PARK

LAWN RD

UPPER PARK RD

PARKHILL ROAD

DUNBOYNE RD

ST PANCRAS (CAMDEN) (see separate map)

ARKWRIGHT

FROGNAL

FINCHLEY

MARESFIELD GARDENS

BELSIZE

AVENUE

BELSIZE PARK

BELSIZE SQUARE

LANCASTER GROVE

BELSIZE PARK GDNS

ENGLANDS LANE

FINCHLEY ROAD

GARDENS

COLLEGE CR

ROAD

(8)
AVENUE

ETON

FELLOWS ROAD

PRIMROSE HILL ROAD

STEELE'S RD

ETON ROAD

CHALK FARM

(7)

ROAD

BELSIZE RD
SWISS COTTAGE

ADELAIDE ROAD

KING HENRY'S ROAD

(5)

HILGROVE RD

(C)

SOUTH HAMPSTEAD

ROAD

ALEXANDRA RD

FINCHLEY ROAD

(1)

AVENUE

ELSWORTHY ROAD

REGENTS PARK ROAD

REGENTS PARK

BOUNDARY

ROAD

Primrose Hill

(4)

PRINCE ALBERT RD

For REGENTS PARK see London 3: North West

buses, is bound to help in keeping the character of a place from adulteration.

The popularity of Hampstead grew with the discovery of chalybeate springs in the late C17, known as the Hampstead Wells. The site lay between the High Street and East Heath Road. Waters were not only taken on the spot (Well Walk) but were also bottled and sold (Flask Walk). There was a lesser spa at Kilburn, and in the early C18 Belsize was also opened as a place of entertainment and became a kind of Vauxhall. Hampstead village now grew prodigiously. The first completely urban-looking terraces of wealthy houses appeared, Church Row and Elm Row. Defoe in 1725 said 'the concours' was incredible, and Hampstead was growing 'from a little village almost to a city'. Yet there were still only 691 inhabited houses in 1801, and the population was only 4,300.

By the early C19, in addition to a dense tangle of terraces and cottages on both sides of the High Street, there were a number of commodious larger houses in the centre of the village and close to it. Remarkably many of these survive: among those W of the High Street are Fenton House; Old Grove House; Frognal Grove; The Old Mansion, Frognal. E of the High Street are Burgh House, Squire's Mount and Foley House, and on top of the hill, by Jack Straw's Castle, Heath House, which was the start of big houses along the ridge to the E on the fringe of the Heath, ending with Kenwood, the most ambitious, over the parish border with St Pancras (q.v.). Around the village were hamlets, of which North End and the Vale of Health (a late development of the early C19) are still recognizable. Frognal and New End, once distinct settlements, now merge into Hampstead village; West End has been swallowed up by the suburbs of West Hampstead.

The early C19 spread of Hampstead down the hill in neat stuccoed cottages and terraces is best preserved at and near Downshire Hill. That was the time when Keats lived in Keats Grove and Leigh Hunt in the Vale of Health. This is what Hampstead was to Leigh Hunt:

> A steeple issuing from a leafy rise,
> With balmy fields in front and sloping green,
> Dear Hampstead, is thy southern face serene,
> Green hills and dells, trees overhead now seen,
> Now down below, with smoking roofs between,
> A village revelling in varieties.

The spread of London northward began to affect the area in the 1830s, as Regents Park and the land around began to be developed. The first building leases on the Eton College Estate, around Chalk Farm, date from 1827; Adelaide Road was developed from c. 1840. In the 1850s, on the Belsize Estate, which had been divided up already c. 1808, villas in their own grounds began to give way to stuccoed terraces. Similar large and heavy stuccoed houses with big porches, emulating the respectability of the new West End suburbs of Belgravia, Tyburnia and Kensington, began to appear in West Hampstead around the Finchley Road, a new turnpike road begun in 1826. High Victorian Gothic of the 1860s makes only occasional appearances, for example in the pair by *Bell* and *Burlison* in Lyndhurst Terrace. Some extravagant detached mansions were built at this time, especially on sites commanding views over the Heath, but they have mostly disappeared. The best survivor is The Logs, East Heath Road.

The next phase, in conscious reaction, reclaimed Hampstead as a favourite district for artists and for the artistically minded (Romney, Constable and Ford Madox Brown had all lived and painted at Hampstead). From the 1870s, wealthy red brick houses, mostly in elaborate versions of the new Queen Anne style, sprang up in and around the newly laid out Fitzjohn's Avenue and elsewhere. The most original were by *Norman Shaw*; others, by *Philip Webb* in Redington Road, by *Champneys* in Redington Gardens and off Frognal Lane, established Frognal as an area for the avant-garde, a trend that was to continue in the C20. The new fashions were rapidly taken up for superior developments by speculative builders, often with picturesque results, as in the groups of the 1870s–80s off Haverstock Hill, around Well Walk and on the Eton Estate. A little later, the more relaxed Free Style of the 1890s onwards is competently demonstrated by *Quennell* around Redington Road, by *Faulkner* in Elsworthy Road, by *Horace Field* around Lyndhurst Road. The most remarkable individual house of those years is *Voysey*'s in Platt's Lane of 1895, remarkably precocious in its absence of ornament.

Churches multiplied to serve the expanding suburbs. The old village church of St John in Church Row, which had been rebuilt in 1745–7, was supplemented at first by private chapels; St John Downshire Hill is a rare and well-preserved survival of the type. The first Victorian church was Christ Church (1851–2) at New End, at the time a poor corner of the village. As the suburbs spread between the village and expanding London, others followed: St Saviour on the Eton Estate (1856), St Mary Kilburn (1857–62), St Peter in Belsize Park (1858–9). But the comfortable Hampstead suburbs did not inspire fervent High Church building activity, and among later churches the only Anglican building of real grandeur is *Teulon*'s St Stephen Rosslyn Hill (1869–73), which adopts the broad nave and short chancel of Low Church tradition. St Mary Primrose Hill is the best example of a church with rich later C19 furnishings; St Luke, by *Champneys* (1898), is a lively representative of turn-of-the-century originality. The wealth and confidence of other congregations of the 1880s is expressed by *Waterhouse*'s former Congregational church in Lyndhurst Road, while the Hampstead Synagogue of 1892 is one of the most lavish in London.

Suburban expansion of the later C19 is reflected in the population figures which rose only slowly up to the mid C19 (1801: 4,300; 1821: 8,600; 1851: 12,000) and then speeded up considerably (1861: 19,000; 1881: 47,000; c. 1900: 80,000). In the C20 there was only a gradual increase to 95,000 in 1951. Although West and South Hampstead were by the end of the C19 almost entirely covered with buildings, development of the Heath was resisted. It was expanded by 240 acres in 1866; Parliament Hill Fields (267 acres) was added in 1890, Golders Hill Park in 1897, the 'Heath Extension' N of Spaniards Road (80 acres) in 1905, and the grounds of Kenwood (121 acres) in 1924.

The growing desire to preserve both Hampstead's existing open spaces and old buildings, as well as local opposition to anything unconventional, provided relatively little scope for novel C20

architecture in the centre of the village. The important early landmarks of the Modern Movement remained the exception, and so are
all the more striking: *Wells Coates*'s Isokon flats in Lawn Road
(1934), houses by *Connell, Ward & Lucas* and by *Maxwell Fry* in
Frognal and by *Goldfinger* in Willow Road (1937–9). After the
Second World War there were plans for a grand civic centre at Swiss
Cottage, but all that was built were *Spence*'s Library and Swimming
Baths. Early post-war public housing by the Borough of Hampstead
was tactfully in keeping with its surroundings, while private developments such as Oak Hill Park were fitted in sensitively. Individual
houses only occasionally impinge on the street scene, as in the case
of *Howell* and *Amis*'s terrace of 1953–6 in South Hill Park, and
*Gowan*'s Schreiber house in West Heath Road of 1962–4.

A change came in the 1960s. The dynamic programme of housing
by the Borough of Camden from 1965 (*see* Introduction to St Pancras)
nevertheless had little effect on the tightly knit village centre, although
it made its mark on the periphery, most notably at Dunboyne Road,
at Alexandra Road and stepping up Branch Hill near West Heath
(*see* pp. 243, 247 and 230). In the 1970s the southern slopes became
a favoured area for radical architects' houses (the *Hopkins* house
in Downshire Hill, *Spence & Webster*'s in Belsize Park Gardens
and others in the Belsize Lane area), while space was found for a
number of ingenious small-scale developments in and around the
village, the best by *Ted Levy, Benjamin & Partners*. Less appealing
are the exclusive precincts of private housing which greedily filled
the gardens of big houses in the 1980s–90s, especially around West
Heath.

## RELIGIOUS BUILDINGS

### 1. Church of England

ALL SOULS, Loudoun Road, Swiss Cottage. Redundant in 1985,
now Grace Chapel (Celestial Church of God). Humble polychrome
brick Gothic of 1864–5 by *J. F. Wadmore* (brother of the vicar);
apsed chancel, no clerestory, a little flèche (originally shingled)
over the E end of the nave. Eclectic additions of 1904–5 by
*Nicholson & Corlette* give the building more presence: a severe S
aisle, vestry, and miniature westwork composed of turret porches
and saddlebacked W tower above a W baptistery. Sumptuous High
Church fittings were also added in the early C20, but few remain.
Surviving at the time of writing: grand REREDOS, a carved triptych
by *C. G. Hare*, 1909, in the style of his partner Bodley. Alabaster
PULPIT, 1884. Much STAINED GLASS. The best of the 1870s
windows in the S aisle, by *Clayton & Bell* (s5 and S aisle W), scenes
in small panels. Two unusual windows in the N aisle: N4,
Adoration of the Kings, in bright colours, by *Dunstan Skilbeck*; N5,
SS James and John, boldly outlined, by *W. J. Nelson*, 1913.

CHRIST CHURCH, Hampstead Square, New End. 1851–2 by *S. W.
Daukes*; built to replace a proprietary chapel in Well Walk. Correct
but dull ecclesiological Middle Pointed instead of the Perp which
Daukes had used a few years earlier for St Andrew Wells Street
(now at Kingsbury, Brent: *see London 3: North West*). Ragstone
exterior; the NE tower with slim spire is the best feature. W porch

1876 by *G. G. Scott Jun.* (who succeeded his father as architectural consultant); gabled outer N aisle and extension to N porch 1881 by *Ewan Christian*. Plain five-bay arcades, nave and aisles, all with lofty open roofs, the outer N aisle now divided off. Reordered with nave altar 1972–4, leaving the chancel empty apart from the mosaic REREDOS of 1912 by *Powell*'s and the ORGAN with pipe front by *Gilbert Scott* (a member of the congregation). *Scott*'s w gallery of 1860 was removed; it had been praised for its 'lightness and beauty' by the *Illustrated London News*. STAINED GLASS. e window, with lively Old and New Testament scenes around the Sacrifice of Isaac, 1881; w window with vine scroll and shields.

EMMANUEL, Lyncroft Gardens, West Hampstead. Chancel and four nave bays 1897–8 by *J. A. Thomas* of *Whitfield & Thomas*, the rest 1903. Typical late C19 lancet-style basilica in red brick; apsed, with w baptistery and a N porch intended as a base for a tower. Plain but spacious interior, stock brick banded with red, a timber barrel vault over nave and chancel. REREDOS, with carved oak panel of the Last Supper, by *A. Robinson*, 1908. PULPIT, 1901, with flamboyant tracery. s chapel furnished 1952, with PAINTING by *Frank Salisbury*. In the w baptistery, FONT of 1898, with openwork cover of 1902, and STAINED GLASS of 1904 with pretty landscape backgrounds. e apse windows by *Kempe*, 1903.

HOLY TRINITY, Finchley Road. Rebuilt in 1978 by *Biscoe & Stanton*; an unassuming red brick exterior, with corner entrance approached up steps, and large foyer windows to the street. It replaced a traditional High Victorian Kentish-rag-faced church by *Henry S. Legg* (aisled nave 1871–2, brick-vaulted chancel 1875).

ST CUTHBERT, Fordwych Road, West Hampstead. 1987–8 by *Jeremy A. Allen*. Another replacement, but more satisfactory than Holy Trinity: a low, polygonal brick building set back from the road in a pleasant garden. Slate roof with broad eaves, centrally planned main room with a boarded ceiling. STAINED GLASS: two panels from a two-light window in the old church: the Raising of Lazarus, by *Henry Holiday*, 1904. In front of the church, a bell of 1906 from its predecessor (a lancet-style brick basilica of 1886–7 and 1903, by *W. C. Street*), whose site is occupied by a block of sheltered flats, DAVINA HOUSE.

ST JAMES, West End Lane and Sherriff Road, West Hampstead. 1885–8 by *A. W. Blomfield*. Large, of red brick inside and out, sound and dignified. Lancet windows, no tower. Square carved FONT, 1888. STAINED GLASS. Lancets in the N chapel apse, also of the 1880s, by *Lavers, Barraud & Westlake* (prophets and life of the Virgin). Excellent, crisply drawn figures with jewelled backgrounds and intricate leading. Other windows by *Kempe*: grouped lancets at e and w ends (1890, 1892), in sober colours, figures under white canopy work; N chapel N windows also by *Kempe*, 1893. SCULPTURE. Life-size figure of St James, C18, Spanish (?), uncoloured wood.

ST JOHN, Church Row. 1745–7. The old parish church was in need of repair by the C18. *Henry Flitcroft*, a local resident, offered to rebuild it in 1744, but the parish rejected his designs and turned instead to another parishioner, the minor Palladian architect *John Sanderson*. His building has a plain brown brick exterior; the tower was placed at the e end (to save expense, as the ground fell towards the w), with an entrance on either side. The tower breaks through a pediment; Sanderson intended it to be completed by a spire, but this remained unbuilt owing to lack of funds. The upper part of the tower was reconstructed more modestly by *Samuel Steemson* in 1759, with battlements and urn finials at the corners; a slim spike was added in 1782–3. After long disputes about the need for enlargements, repairs were carried out in 1834, and eventually a w extension consisting of transepts and a w gallery was added in 1843 by *R. Hesketh*. This soon proved inadequate; a competition was held in 1874 for an entirely new building, which led to a successful public campaign to save the c18 tower. *F. P. Cockerell*, the winning competititor, was employed to repair and improve the existing building in 1877–8, reversing the orientation. A choir vestry was added at the w end by *Temple Moore* in 1911–12; the crypt room beneath was created by *J. Brandon-Jones* in 1964–5.

The c18 interior was in the tradition established by Gibbs' St Martin-in-the-Fields, with tall unfluted Ionic columns supporting arches which cut into the tunnel vault, and galleries appearing between the columns. *Cockerell* moved the altar from the e to a new sanctuary at the w end and added new fronts to the galleries. Furnishings in Renaissance style were added: ALTAR, REREDOS with paired Ionic columns, fine inlaid STALLS, and a turreted ORGAN CASE, all by *Sir T. G. Jackson*, who redecorated the chancel in 1883. There was also elaborate Renaissance ceiling decoration by *Alfred Bell* (painted out in 1958). *Ellis Wooldridge*'s large wall painting, Baptism of Christ, has also gone, although his STAINED GLASS of 1884 in the w window remains. The other windows have glass by *Clayton & Bell*. – PAINTING. Wooden panel after Filippo Lippi, by *Clement Burlison*, 1869. – PULPIT, hexagonal on a single stem, 1746 by *Launcelot Dowbiggin*. – Carved Hanoverian ROYAL ARMS. – COMMANDMENT BOARDS (in the gallery); fine surround with putti and drapery. – In the NW chapel, reused mid-c17 balustrades and a pillar from the former stone FONT. The Chapel of St Mary and St John, N of the sanctuary, was arranged by *Temple Moore* in 1913. In its s window STAINED GLASS (the Queen of Heaven) by *Joan Fulleylove*, 1918–19. s vestries also by *Temple Moore*.

MONUMENTS. Many, all minor; the best in the galleries. – Large oval epitaph with two allegorical figures in relief by the *Younger Bacon*; to the Hon. Frances Erskine †1805 (erected 1809). – Among the smaller tablets in the nave, Dorothy Harrison †1802 and George Todd †1809, both by *Westmacott Sen.* – Charles Duncan †1806 by *John Bacon Jun.*, with an urn. – Charlotte Wortham †1810, also with urn. Louisa Lowndes †1811, Marianne Beresford †1818, two small memorials to children, each with a broken flower, by *John Bacon Jun.* – William Bleamire †1803 by *Kendrick*, with a mourning figure. – Rev. Thomas Ainger †1863 by *G. G. Scott*; marble and mosaic, with portrait medallion. – In the gallery, T. N. Longman †1842, bust by *Christopher Moore*.

In the crowded CHURCHYARD many big c18 memorials. Buried here, for example, were Constable †1837, and Norman Shaw †1912, with a table tomb by *Ernest Newton*. The fine iron GATES and RAILINGS at the Church Row entrance were bought in 1747 from the sale of the Duke of Chandos's house at Canons, Little Stanmore (*see London 3: North West*). In the extension churchyard across the road, *Coade* stone monument to George Todd †1829, and the tomb of George du Maurier by *T. Armstrong*, 1896. Notable C20 monuments include those to A.R. Orage by *Eric Gill*, Temple Moore by *L.T. Moore*, and Kay Kendall by *Reynolds Stone*.

ST JOHN, Downshire Hill and Keats Grove. 1818–23; probably by *William Woods*, a Kennington builder. Built as a proprietary chapel. An attractive stuccoed exterior, with w cupola and porch with oddly detailed Doric columns (old views show that the exterior formerly had more ornament). An exceedingly charming, neat and light interior. Three galleries between two orders of slim columns, the upper order carrying the shallow tunnel vault of the nave. No separate chancel. Restored by *Horace Field* in 1896 and by *Edward Cullinan* in 1964–71, when the glass screens at the w end were added. – Box pews, large pulpit, classical reredos. – STAINED GLASS. Good E window of 1882.

ST LUKE, Kidderpore Avenue. An appropriate church for this turn-of-the-century area of affluent artistic houses at the NW end of Hampstead. 1897–9 by *Basil Champneys*. A most picturesque w front, with two porches and a gallery stair projection, raised up above a basement. Completely asymmetrical. Orange brick and stone, the main w window Perp with Flamboyant touches. No tower, but a pretty SE turret. Tall and impressive interior, light and open, with no chancel arch. The brick walls of the long five-bay nave (whitened later) are crisply articulated by angular wall-shafts rising from slender hexagonal stone piers without capitals. Tall clerestory with paired three-light windows; low aisles, w gallery with baptistery below. The early C20 S annexe, at first open to the S aisle, was walled off in 1949 by *Harold Dicksee*. The restrained Gothic furnishings by *Champneys* include a plain REREDOS with texts, canopied STALLS, and a fine large ORGAN CASE above a more whimsical sedilia and priest's door. STAINED GLASS in the chancel by *Powell & Sons*. Neat First World War memorial SCREENS at the back of the pews.

The gabled red brick VICARAGE to the S, 1902–3 by *Champneys*, echoes the massing of the w front of the church. The garden side is tile-hung and more domestic.

ST MARK, Prince Albert Road, Regents Park. 1851–2 by *Thomas Little*. Ragstone exterior, NW tower with pinnacles and broached spire. Dec detail; the aisle windows in two parts indicate the former existence of galleries. These were removed in 1890 as part of a reordering by *A.W. Blomfield*. Tall, wide, somewhat bleak nave with circular columns; the clustered pair at the E end originally marked off the chancel ('a tendency in the right direction' was the *Ecclesiologist*'s very qualified praise for the liturgical arrangements). A C19 drawing suggests there were plans for a more ambitious E end; a new chancel was eventually added by Blomfield in 1890. The E wall and all the roofs date from repairs by *A.B. Knapp-Fisher*, 1957, after gutting in the Second World War. Grand REREDOS by *Comper* (replacing one destroyed in 1940). Figures against a gold background. REREDOS, N chapel. Similar in type, but more appealing, with larger figures. STAINED GLASS. An interesting collection. Oldest survivals are three pretty quatrefoils with infants in Blomfield's W baptistery, presumably c. 1890. Five grisaille lancets above by *Goddard & Gibbs*, 1956. C20 window in the N aisle: two by *John Hayward*, first from W, Life of St Mark, bright stylized figures, 1966; and N aisle E, with the vicar's cat and a sputnik. N fourth from W, by *Brian Thomas*, 1957: SS Peter and Mark; an effective design with figures in oval roundels, good colours, heavily leaded. E rose: Benedicite, somewhat harsh. – MONUMENT. Rev. W.B. Galloway †1903. Mosaic panel with Adoration of the Kings.

ST MARY, Primrose Hill Road and King Henry's Road. 1870–2 by *M. P. Manning*, on a site given by the Eton College Estate. A red brick French Gothic basilica in the manner of Brooks's East End churches. Apsed, with a transept; lancet windows. The interior has broad arches on low cylindrical piers with lively stiff-leaf capitals, and a clerestory, bound together by a big timber barrel vault in the nave, and by a vault over the raised sanctuary. Choir vestry added 1890, S aisle with vaulted chapel 1891–2. Such churches were intended to provide a simple but noble background for rich FURNISHINGS, which began to appear in the 1890s. The effect here was modified by the 'Old English' liturgical reforms of Percy Dearmer (vicar 1901–15), which included the whitening of the walls, the simplification of the sanctuary, and a low curtained altar, ideas which were much copied elsewhere. The dominant ROOD of 1914 by *Gilbert Bayes* now eclipses *Bodley & Garner*'s REREDOS of 1895, a carved and gilded triptych, which was remodelled and reduced in height by *Bayes* in 1915. Painted angels on the wings added by *F. C. Cleverly*, centre repainted 1983. The PULPIT by *Bodley & Garner* of 1893 remains; their stalls of the same date have been simplified (return stalls now in the S chapel). SANCTUARY LAMP by *Frank Knight*, 1954. At the W end, by the FONT of 1872, large enamelwork Crucifixion panel in low relief, by *Henry Holiday*, formerly on the artist's house. OAK SEATING (W wall) by *Temple Moore*, 1910. In the S chapel, later C20 Resurrection figure, bronze, by *Francis Stephens*. Beaten copper MEMORIAL TABLET, 1907 by *Harold Stabler*. STAINED GLASS. Original windows by *Clayton & Bell* (apse centre, S chapel, N aisle †1887, †1890). Small window by the font, 1893 by *Comper*. Fine W window, 1895 by *Kempe*. S aisle windows by *H. V. Milner* (†1894). – WAR MEMORIAL, at the corner of Elsworthy Road. 1921, with Virgin and Child by *Philip Turner*, 1988.

ST MARY, Priory Road, Kilburn. 1857–62 by *F. & H. Francis*, typical of church building of its date in a new fairly well-to-do suburb. Large ragstone Dec church, with a commanding SW tower and spire, transepts and clerestory. Lofty four-bay nave with alternating piers, and capitals with the rather gross naturalistic carving favoured by Francis. Standard later Victorian fittings, little altered. Alabaster REREDOS 1885, with seven mosaic panels of 1902. Carved stone and marble PULPIT; carved PEWS. STAINED GLASS by *Clayton & Bell* and *Westlake* (BFLC). The best is the E window, c. 1883 (Resurrection and Miracles). BRASS. A C15 fragment, the head of a nun (height of face c. 2½ ins), discovered in 1877 on the site of the medieval nunnery at Kilburn, near Edgware Road. Later CHURCH HALL behind, with Gothic windows under gables.

St Peter, Belsize Park. 1858–9 by *W. Mumford*; chancel and sw
tower-porch by *J.P. St Aubyn, c.* 1875. Earnest ragstone Dec
Gothic (cf. St Mary, Priory Road). Spiky gables over the nave
windows. Lofty interior with alternating columns with naturalistic
capitals; open timber roofs. Sanctuary reordered 1927 and 1965.
STAINED GLASS. E and W windows by *O'Connor*, the E one with
figures under canopies, the W one (†1873) a pictorial Ascension.
MONUMENT. Rev. F.W. Tremlett, the first vicar, †1913. Portrait
bust by *Kathleen Shaw*, 1915.

St Saviour, Eton Road. The body of the church is of 1855–6 by
*E.M. Barry*, his first independent work. Cruciform, of random
Kentish rag with lancet windows, plain and old-fashioned for its
date. The sw tower and spire were part of the original scheme but
were built only in 1864. They have the richer detail of the 60s:
belfry level adorned with thick foliate capitals, coloured shafts, a
busy band of paterae below the eaves. Choir vestry 1882 by *E.
Christian*. Chancel lengthened 1902 by *Caröe*. Simple interior with
widely spaced circular columns; whitewashed later. The original
fittings (praised by the *Ecclesiologist*) include the octagonal FONT,
decorated with tiles, and the PULPIT, by *Thomas Earp*, with delicately carved angels in niches with naturalistic foliage. – Carved
stone REREDOS, 1885 by *Earp*. Figures in niches under gables with
tall pinnacles. – SCREEN, 1890. STAINED GLASS. N transept N,
Transfiguration (†1858), attributed to *Ward & Hughes*; theatrical
groups of large figures, very weak in comparison with the richer
colours and more assured medievalizing style of the windows by
*Clayton & Bell*: E window (†1872), small scenes with the Life of
Christ; SE chapel S, nave S2, N2 and N3 of the 1880s. MONUMENT.
Basil Miller †1925. Quattrocento-style relief in painted frame. Of
metal, simulating wood.

HALL to the W, 1967–8, and VICARAGE to the SE, 1972–3, by
*D.S. Martin*; both octagonal and of brown brick.

St Stephen, Rosslyn Hill. 1869–73 by *S.S. Teulon*, one of his most
mature and powerful works. The site was given by Sir T. Maryon
Wilson; principal donors were R.H. Prance and Charles Woodd, a

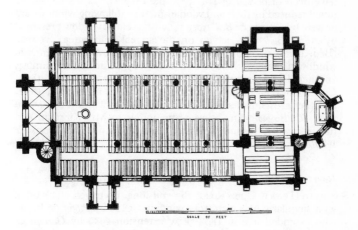

St Stephen. Plan

friend of Ruskin. Hampstead's chief Victorian church was made redundant in 1977, and its brutally vandalized interior was still awaiting a new use twenty years later. Exterior of dark red
85    Dunstable brick with stone and granite dressings; over the crossing a big bulky tower with steep capped pyramid roof rises above gabled transepts and short polygonal apse. The E end is raised up above a crypt because of the slope of the hill. The rounded corner turret to the tower is a typical Teulon touch, as is the use of robust plate tracery for the nave windows and for the rose in the W gable above the tripartite vaulted porch. These early French Gothic features are waywardly combined with domestic-looking straight-headed and transomed aisle windows. 'Exceedingly insensitive' and 'unmistakable Teulonesque hamfistedness' were Pevsner's 1952 comments on the detail, but since then appreciation has grown, both of this forceful and original architect and of buildings outside the ecclesiological canon. St Stephen, an offshoot of St John Downshire Hill, is ostentatiously Low Church, with a short sanctuary, emphasized by a brick vault rather than by greater height, a broad, well-proportioned and well-lit nave, and a W gallery (which rests most perversely on segment-headed arches, in contrast to the pointed arches of the nave arcade).

The wealthy congregation ensured that the INTERIOR was as richly dressed as any High Victorian lady. The circular piers carry lushly carved foliage capitals by *Thomas Earp* and elaborately notched and chamfered arches (particularly ornate at the crossing and transepts); the walls are striped in grey, yellow and white brick; the sturdy arch braces of the roof rest on carved stone corbels. There is even a little exterior sculpture, also by *Earp*. All this survives, although the fittings and decoration in a variety of materials have suffered badly since 1977. They included a FONT given in 1869 by *Ewan Christian*, mosaic roundels by *Salviati* in the chancel, gilt mosaic on the W gallery and in the nave arcade spandrels. In 1881–3 alabaster roundels were added, probably by *Clayton & Bell*, with incised portraits of martyrs (including 'Wickcliffe' and the Protestant Latimer, given by Ewan Christian). Other furnishings have been dispersed or smashed, the excellent STAINED GLASS much reduced by theft and vandalism. The following windows are or were by *Clayton & Bell*. Apse 1869 (the central window presented by *Alfred Bell*, who served on the appeal committee). W rose (Benedicite) after 1873. The S transept E window was a memorial window to Teulon, 1874; S transept S, 1893. S aisle: easternmost, another Teulon memorial, 1873; Whitehouse memorial, 1892; Coe memorial, 1905–6. Baptistery (Jennings memorial), 1892. By other artists: tower base, N side, St Cecilia window by *Heaton Butler & Bayne*, 1870; N aisle, memorials to Mrs Kirkman and the first vicar, Joshua Kirkman, 1892 and 1902 by *Lavers & Westlake*.

## 2. *Roman Catholic*

SACRED HEART, Quex Road. Big and long, no tower, stock brick with singularly ugly clerestory windows. 1879 by *Pugin & Pugin*, who extended it E in 1898–9. W extension 1959 by *Gordon & Gordon*; further E extension and new sanctuary, 1964–5, by *F. G.*

*Broadbent & Partners*. Incoherent interior. Behind, the PRIORY of Oblates of St Mary Immaculate, in buildings of 1965.

ST MARY, Holly Place. A charming composition, the tiny church in the centre of a recessed terrace of cottages. One of the earliest R.C. churches of London. It was built in 1816, under the French émigré Abbé J.J. Morel, at the expense of the congregation. The stuccoed front was added by *W. Wardell* in 1850: it has a Tuscan doorway, a statue of the Virgin in a niche above, and a picturesque open bellcote with segmental pediment on top. Interior altered 1878, sanctuary and two E chapels added 1907 by *G. F. Collinson & A. M. Cock*; baldacchino by *Adrian Scott*, 1935. Reordered in 1976 by *Williams & Winkley*. MONUMENT. Perp-style tomb-chest to the founder, Abbé Morel, †1852 by *Wardell*, with recumbent effigy.

ST THOMAS MORE, Maresfield Gardens. 1968–9 by *Gerard Goalen*. An elliptical plan, broadside on to the road. Undramatic externally, impressive inside, the concrete elements elegantly handled, as at Goalen's earlier St Gabriel, Islington, and St Gregory the Great, South Ruislip (Hillingdon). A ring of slender columns pierces a shallow gallery and continues up to support massive concrete beams set on edge. These run (liturgically) W–E, and so counteract the lateral emphasis of the elliptical form. The forcefulness of the concrete is relieved by the brick relief surfaces of the lower walls, and by the pattern of circular gallery roof-lights supplementing the even lighting from the clerestory. STAINED GLASS above the altar by *Alfred R. Fisher* of *Whitefriars Studios*.

### 3. Other places of worship

BRONDESBURY CHRISTIAN CENTRE, Iverson Road. 1989. Replaces an ornate Neo-Norman Baptist church and hall of 1878 by *W. A. Dixon*.

Former CONGREGATIONAL CHURCH, Lyndhurst Road. 1883–4 by *Waterhouse*, one of his most satisfactory works. Centrally planned, like several progressive Nonconformist churches of this time (cf. Union Chapel, Islington, 1876). Purple brick and coloured terracotta decoration, with lancet windows and round-arched entrance. Clear, hard and rigid. The interior was altered when subdivided for concert hall and recording studios in 1991–2 by *Bernard Parker* of *Heber-Percy & Parker*. Originally the irregular hexagon had deep galleries on three sides. Pulpit and organ faced the entrance. The HALL behind is in similar style.

Former EBENEZER STRICT BAPTIST CHAPEL (now WOMEN'S MISSIONARY FELLOWSHIP), Belsize Road, Kilburn Vale. 1870.

FRIENDS MEETING HOUSE, Heath Street. 1907 by *Fred Rowntree*. Small, with a pretty curved timber porch, copper-roofed. Restored 1990–1. Garden in front with nice gateway.

HEATH STREET BAPTIST CHURCH, Heath Street. 1860–1 by *C. G. Searle*. Stone front with Dec detail and two towers, hall below, adjoining wing of 1871 built for a British School. Well-preserved interior with cast-iron columns, traceried gallery fronts and pew ends, and a steep roof with traceried spandrels. Large PULPIT, 1880; ORGAN and organ chamber, 1901. Patterned Art

Nouveau STAINED GLASS of 1887. Entrance vestibule 1964; lecture hall wing 1871. In the wing, memorials to ministers of the church, and a Second World War memorial by *Walter Godfrey*.

ST ANDREW UNITED REFORMED (former Presbyterian) CHURCH, Finchley Road. 1904 by *Pite & Balfour*. Good composition on a sloping site with (ritual) NE steeple. Kentish rag. Interior with piers without capitals. Detail Dec. Striking STAINED GLASS by *Douglas Strachan*.

SEVENTH DAY ADVENTIST, Haverstock Hill. Formerly Oxendon Presbyterian, 1877 by *Thomas Arnold*.

UNITARIAN CHAPEL, Rosslyn Hill. 1862 by *John Johnson*. Kentish rag. W end and gallery 1867. N aisle and chancel 1885 by *Thomas Worthington*, the Manchester architect, in the same style. The main entrance was moved to Rosslyn Hill in 1898. Broad, spacious nave with ceiled roof, four-bay N arcade. Furnishings and monuments of high quality indicate the strength of Hampstead Unitarianism. – WOODWORK. Stalls beneath W gallery, 1904; FRONT, 1908, both by *Ronald P. Jones*, incorporating wood with brass panels, brought from the demolished Essex Street Chapel. – SCULPTURE. Four excellent Neoclassical reliefs. The two in the chancel (formerly flanking a third relief, now destroyed) are calm and noble compositions of women with children, attributed to *Flaxman*. Very different in spirit are two reliefs beside the chancel arch (copies after Flaxman models), which show the sculptor at his most vigorous. The subjects, a woman and children borne aloft by angels, and demons wrestling over a man, were used also for the Baring monuments at Micheldever, Hampshire, of 1801–13. – STAINED GLASS. Chancel E: 1886 by *Wilson & Hammond* – Nave S. Three windows of 1867–71, in the style of *Hardman*. N aisle E, another similar one moved from the S aisle, adapted by *Clayton & Bell*, 1887. – N aisle N. First from E: a fine work by *Henry Holiday*, 1887. Allegorical figures of Purity and Simplicity, deep colours. Second from E: 1886 by *Wilson & Hammond*. Third from E: 1888 by *William Morris* and *Burne-Jones*. Fourth from E: 1889 by *Lavers & Westlake*. – N aisle W. 1889, after cartoons by *Burne-Jones*. Three figures on white glass. Nave N. 1887 by *Mayer* of Munich, typically colourful. – MONUMENTS. – Thomas Sadler †1891. Bronze table with lettering by *William Morris*. – Dr James Martineau †1900. Marble relief portrait by *H. R. Hope-Pinker*. – Dr Brooke Hereford †1905, by *Wragge*; Isaac Solly Lister †1913 by *Kathleen Shaw*: two bronze panels with Art Nouveau detail. – Rev. Stopford Brooke †1916. Marble and mosaic.

Former WEST HAMPSTEAD CONGREGATIONAL CHAPEL. *See* Public Buildings, below: Parsifal College.

### 4. Synagogues

BELSIZE SQUARE SYNAGOGUE. 1958 by *H. W. Reifenberg*, incorporating the 1915 vicarage of the neighbouring St Peter's Church; hall added 1973.

HAMPSTEAD SYNAGOGUE, Dennington Park Road. 1892–1901 by *Delissa Joseph*. One of the largest synagogues in London, built for Hampstead's prosperous Jewish community. Impressive red brick exterior; a tall tower with corner turrets over the entrance, elaborately detailed in a mixture of French Gothic and Romanesque. Generous entrance hall. Interior on a grand scale; a polygonal plan with a central dome on octagonal marble piers, galleries on three sides. Lavish, eclectic decoration. Classical marble surrounds to the ark, with choir gallery above. The *bimah* (reading desk) is placed on a platform directly in front (not in the centre of the building, as was the older practice). The E end is lit addition-ally by two lesser domes with playful coloured glass. STAINED GLASS throughout: mostly foliage and bird designs of 1902–13, with clear borders which let in plenty of light. Four gallery windows with lily and flower designs are by *Morris & Co.*, *c.* 1907–13. Bright post-war glass in the four lunettes of the main dome (creation themes) and in the large W window (the New Jerusalem).

SOUTH HAMPSTEAD UNITED SYNAGOGUE, Eton Road. 1962 by *H. J. Georghiou.*

## 5. Cemetery

HAMPSTEAD CEMETERY, Fortune Green Road. Lodges and a pair of chapels linked by an arch, by *Charles Bell*, 1874–6, Kentish rag. (STAINED GLASS by *J. Dudley Forsyth*.) Grounds laid out to a formal plan by *J. F. Meston*. The MONUMENTS include a large number of Celtic crosses of the type made popular from the 1890s by the sculptor *G. C. Maile* (†1929), who is buried here. James Wilson †1906; massive Egyptian sarcophagus by *Cramb*, the monu-mental mason whose Egyptianizing premises remain opposite in Fortune Green Road (*see* Perambulation 5a). Fine standing bronze figure by *William Goscombe John* to his wife Marthe †1923. The most unusual monuments are in the NE corner. Charles Barritt †1929 is commemorated by a stone organ, the Bianchi family by a colossal gateway with Art Deco angel. Artistically, the most notable was to H. R. Fischer †1977: a plain stone block incorporating a small but powerful bronze relief by *Ernst Barlach* showing three anguished figures (sinced removed).

## PUBLIC BUILDINGS

Former TOWN HALL, Haverstock Hill. An Arts Centre by *Burrell, Foley, Fisher* with a new dance and concert hall, created 1998–2000 from the Vestry Hall of 1877–8 by *Kendall & Mew*. Red brick and stone, Italianate with a pediment on two of its sides and a corner tower. Toplit hall, imperial stair with cast-iron balustrades. Public hall on the first floor. When Pevsner damned it in 1952 as 'crush-ingly mean' and 'a disgrace to so prosperous and artistic a borough', plans for new civic buildings were under discussion (*see* Swiss Cottage Library below), although nothing transpired; the building lost its function in 1965 when Camden chose St Pancras Town Hall as its main headquarters.

POLICE STATION, Rosslyn Hill. By *J. D. Butler*, 1910–13, with that architect's typical long corbels supporting the door hood, and a steep pediment with windows.

FIRE STATIONS. Two admirable examples by the *LCC's Fire*

*Brigade Branch.* WEST END LANE, 1901, by *W.A. Scott,* was one of the first fire stations to adopt a domestic vernacular style: a trim, rather Voyseyish building with deep eaves, roughcast walls, and a projecting stone-mullioned ground-floor bay on one side. Firemen's cottages behind. LANCASTER GROVE, 1914–15, by *C.C. Winmill,* is one of the most accomplished of the Branch's early C20 achievements. An L-shaped composition; one wing with firemen's quarters, the other with garages, a powerful brick hose and water tower marking the junction. Well-handled detail in the free vernacular in which Winmill excelled: steep wide-eaved roofs, irregularly grouped mullioned and bay windows. For the former Fire Station in the High Street, *see* Perambulation 1a.

SWISS COTTAGE LIBRARY and SWIMMING BATHS, Avenue Road. Built 1963–4 by *Basil Spence, Bonnington & Collins.*\* Intended as the first phase of an ambitious CIVIC CENTRE on the seven-acre island site E of Swiss Cottage. The original scheme for the Civic Centre, under discussion from 1943, was to have included a new town hall and offices, but by the time Basil Spence was appointed architect in 1958, Hampstead's future as a borough was uncertain, and only the first phase went ahead, becoming the dominant group in an unsatisfactorily disparate development. Both library and baths delight in their use of concrete, as was fashionable at the time, and are distinguished externally by powerful geometric contrasts (Spence created a similar effect at his contemporary science buildings at Exeter University). The baths are a cube with horizontal slatting to keep out the sun; the library has rounded N and S ends, with vertical slatting. Inside, both are concisely planned, and have good-quality finishes. Lending and reference libraries are airy spaces at each end of the first floor, approached by a recessed entrance under the N end, and then by a stair rising through a broad central toplit exhibition space. The cube was designed with pools and sports halls at the corners, and with central café, private baths and circulation space slotted through at mezzanine level. To the S the symmetry is disturbed by a projecting angled sun terrace, screened by a sculptured concrete wall with forceful blocky motifs by *William Mitchell.* W of the pools, seated figure of Sigmund Freud by *Oscar Nemon*; N of the library, abstract sculpture: the Hampstead Figure by *F.E. McWilliam,* 1964.

The rest of the site is an unhappy story of indecision during the time when the borough's chief efforts were focused on its major housing schemes. Successive proposals variously incorporating hotel, theatre, sports centre and housing were explored without result. The compromise of 1980 provided sheltered housing at the NE corner, and some low-key community buildings financed by bright and brash offices along Avenue Road. The advice centre, a hipped-roofed pavilion, and the gabled community centre to its E, both in dark brick, are, like the Avenue Road offices (*see* Perambulation 4e), by *Ted Levy, Benjamin & Partners.* Between library and offices, the Hampstead Theatre Club continued in temporary buildings. The remaining open space was half-heartedly landscaped, broken up by walls pierced by arches overlooking

\* The library alone was listed in 1998, the future of the baths is uncertain.

a sunken games area. The sheltered housing, a tall, somewhat gaunt terrace along Winchester Road, is by *Clive Alexander & Partners*, 1982. The whole area deserves a coherent plan, respecting the Spence buildings and providing the Theatre Club with worthy premises.

CAMDEN ARTS CENTRE, Arkwright Road. Built as Hampstead Central Library in 1897 by *Arnold S. Tayler*. Arts and Crafts Tudor on a substantial scale; extended 1909 and 1926, gutted in the Second World War, and adapted for its present purpose after the main library moved to Swiss Cottage in 1964.

LIBRARIES. COTLEIGH ROAD, Kilburn, 1902 by the Borough Surveyor *Charles H. Lowe*; a modest building with two shaped gables. DENNINGTON PARK ROAD, West Hampstead, 1954; ANTRIM ROAD, Belsize; rebuilt 1934–7 by *H.A. Gould* and *R. de W. Aldridge*. Progressively simple, with apsidal reading room, and pantiled roof. KEATS GROVE, a discreet addition to Keats House (*see* Perambulation 1b), 1931 by *Sydney Trent*.

Former PUBLIC BATHS, Flask Walk. *See* Perambulation 1b.

*Educational Buildings*

*Colleges*

Former WESTFIELD COLLEGE (now partly King's College), Kidderpore Avenue. Built as Westfield College, which was founded as a women's college in 1882 in Maresfield Gardens, off Finchley Road, and moved to this site in 1889. The core is the villa of 1840–3 (now SPIRO INSTITUTE OF JEWISH HISTORY AND CULTURE), built on the crest of the hill by *T. Howard* for John Teil, a retired merchant who traded in leather from Kidderpore near Calcutta. His house originally stood quite on its own in its gardens. It has a bold Grecian stucco front with slightly projecting colonnade of six Ionic columns, but with pediments on the sides, projecting on bracketed eaves, that is, on the point of changing from pediments into gables. On the garden side to the E, four columns *in antis*, to the N a bow, also with columns. Several original handsome interiors.

To the S are the first additions for Westfield, by *R. Falconer Macdonald*, a pupil of J.J. Stevenson and Ernest George. The Maynard Wing with students' rooms, 1889–91, with its main front facing S across a terrace, is in an economical but agreeable Queen Anne style, continued by later additions around the informal courtyard: red brick, steep pedimental gables, curly brick aprons to the windows. The library of 1903–4 has a bolder Baroque front to Kidderpore Avenue, sporting a stone first-floor bay with Ionic columns as its main features. Only the meanly detailed S range of the 1960s breaks the mood. The CHAPEL is hidden away in the garden NE of the villa. An impressive, spare design of 1928–9 by *Horder & Rees*. Rendered, with deep eaves, and small rectangular windows high up lighting an austere but well-proportioned interior. The interior comes as a surprise, for the Doric porch leads into a foyer at gallery level from which two flights of stairs descend. The later buildings by *Verner Rees* are of less interest: dining hall interior (1935), Orchard Wing (1936).

Post-war college buildings are on the w side of Kidderpore Avenue.
First comes the QUEEN'S BUILDING, *Verner Rees's* awkward
science block of 1957–62, a red brick monster with an unhappy
double-height classical entrance, later extended w in brutalist
purple brick. Further N, the indifferent REFECTORY of 1962–3.
From the mid 1960s *Casson & Conder* were in charge (as at so
many universities). Their main contributions date from 1968 to
1972: the large and forceful SKEEL LIBRARY, and KIDDERPORE
HALL, bleakly detailed linked students' residences in red brick,
opening onto a paved terrace walk parallel to Kidderpore Avenue.
The reaction against the blocky gigantism of 1960s university
buildings is demonstrated by the QUEEN MOTHER'S HALL, also
by *Casson & Conder* (1981–2), with its friendlier pitched roofs and
oriel windows. SUMMERHOUSE in the grounds, probably coeval
with the C19 villa. SCULPTURE, on Kidderpore Avenue. Crouching
Arab woman by *Enrico Astori*, 1900, erected here 1971.

PARSIFAL COLLEGE (London Regional Centre, Open University,
since 1977), Finchley Road and Parsifal Road. 1887 by *M. P.
Manning*. A long asymmetrical brick building with buff terracotta
dressings. Tudor windows of several lights in irregular surrounds.
Built for Hackney College, a training college for Nonconformist
ministers; later amalgamated with New College, College Crescent,
Finchley Road, when the rear parts, of 1934, were added by
*G. E. T. Laurence & Partners*. To the N, THE OCTAGON is the
former West Hampstead Congregational Chapel, founded by the
college, of 1894 by *Spalding & Cross*, tall, centrally planned, with
a terracotta gable on each side flanked by little turrets. Converted
to flats in 1991.

*Secondary schools*

HAMPSTEAD SCHOOL, Westbere Road. Along the road, buildings
originally for Haberdashers Aske's Boys' School (which moved to
Aldenham, Herts, in 1961). Main block of 1902–3, brick with
stone dressings, a turret at one end, by *Henry Stock* of *Stock, Page
& Stock*; technical block to the N, 1910, with bold upper lunettes,
science block to the s, by *Noel D. Sheffield*, in the dry institutional
classical of 1930. Behind, in a very different spirit, a square block
by *Stillman & Eastwick-Field*, 1966, for the newly formed ILEA
comprehensive (1,135 pupils). A tough, compact concrete building of two and three storeys, with widely spaced uprights, plain
but well proportioned, the varying fenestration reflecting a mixture of functions (classrooms, houserooms with dining areas, staff
rooms). Ranged around a central courtyard, which is on several
levels, with a tree.

UNIVERSITY COLLEGE SCHOOL, Frognal. A boys' day school
founded in 1830 in Gower Street as part of University College;
moved to Hampstead in 1907. Handsome buildings of 1905–7 by
*Arnold Mitchell*, one of his major works. Planned for 500 pupils. In
an early C18 manner, of brick with floridly decorated stone frontispiece and cupola. Splendid great hall, panelled, with curvaceous
barrel-vaulted ceiling pierced by large lunette windows, well
restored by *Michael Foster* after a fire in 1978. Additions of *c.* 1957
onwards (laboratory, music room, library); sixth form centre,
1974, by *Michael Foster* of *TFP Architects*.

*Special schools*

JOHN KEATS and FRANKLIN D. ROOSEVELT SCHOOLS, Avenue Road and Adelaide Road. 1959 and 1955–7 by the *LCC* (job architects *A. J. Lyne* and *W. Kretchmer*). Two reticent single-storey schools for handicapped and delicate children, on well-landscaped linked sites, arranged around internal courtyards.

FRANK BARNES SCHOOL FOR DEAF CHILDREN, Harley Road. 1976–7 for the ILEA by *Ivor Plummer* of the *GLC Architect's Department*. Adjacent to the above schools, but more prominent. A technologically progressive design for its time: defensive walls to the N to protect it from vibration, large glazed areas to the S; the octagonal module was dictated by the horseshoe shape of fixed hearing-aid equipment.

*Primary schools*

VOLUNTARY SCHOOLS originating from before the Education Act of 1870, mostly with C19 buildings in picturesque Gothic, close to their associated churches, are unusually numerous in Hampstead. A mid-C19 example is CHRIST CHURCH, Christ Church Hill, 1854–5 by *W. & E. Habershon*, with porch of 1879 and a former teacher's house. EMMANUEL, Mill Lane, West End, has a pretty tile-hung and gabled teacher's house of 1874 on the r., brick schoolroom on the l. with Gothic plate-tracery windows (end wall rebuilt), originally of 1845, by *Charles Miles* of West End Hall, but enlarged and extended 1874 and 1892. In between is the former teacher's house of 1845, of stone, with mullioned windows, converted to a classroom in 1874. HAMPSTEAD PAROCHIAL, Holly Bush Vale, has boys', girls' and infants' schools of 1856, *c.* 1862 and 1887; MORELAND HALL is by *Shaw*, much altered by *Ashley & Newman*, 1938.

Of a different origin is ROYAL SCHOOL, No. 86a Fitzjohn's Avenue, which incorporates school and headmaster's house of the Royal Soldiers' Daughters' Home, all that survive of the buildings of 1856–8 by *William Munt*. The home occupied Vane House, one of Hampstead's large mansions, remodelled by Munt in 1858 and demolished in 1972. *LCC* additions of 1954.

LONDON SCHOOL BOARD buildings of after 1870 and their LCC successors are squeezed onto cramped sites. The first in Hampstead were in FLEET ROAD (now Education Centre), 1879, extended 1881 and 1890. KINGSGATE SCHOOL, Messina Avenue, Kilburn, 1903 by *T. J. Bailey* has a circular lantern and the emphatic stone details typical of Bailey's late work. NEW END SCHOOL, New End, 1905–6, is one of *Bailey*'s most remarkable buildings; dramatically tall, planned for 612 children, squeezed onto a tiny hillside site, and handled in an exceptionally confident free Baroque manner; the pilastered centre flanked by stair-towers is a standard Bailey composition, the back is more unusual, with fifth-floor classrooms in corner pavilions with broad arched windows emphasized by mannered stone voussoirs.

POST-WAR PRIMARY SCHOOLS, reacting against the tall, formal Board school (and in response to a declining child population), are low and unassuming. Examples from different decades are FLEET ROAD, LCC work of the 1950s; ST PAUL CHURCH OF

ENGLAND, Elsworthy Road, Primrose Hill, 1972–6, in land-scaped grounds; ST MARY KILBURN CHURCH OF ENGLAND, Quex Road, low with pantiled roofs, around a courtyard, by *Hans Haenlein Associates*, 1990–1.

SARUM HALL SCHOOL, Eton Avenue. Elegant buildings by *Allies & Morrison*, 1996, with traditional pitched roof to blend with the neighbourhood.

*Hospitals*

ROYAL FREE HOSPITAL, Pond Street. The Royal Free, in Hatton Gardens from 1828 and in Gray's Inn Road from 1840, like several other centrally located hospitals, determined on a move out of central London after the Second World War. The decision was taken in 1954; the first phase, by *Watkins Gray Woodgate International*, was built 1968–75. As at the new Charing Cross Hospital, Fulham, the dominant feature is a cruciform tower of wards. It is of eighteen storeys, with a forceful pattern of concrete balconies. Outside, a decorative iron tympanum of 1894, from Gray's Inn Road. The fifteen-acre site was inherited from two earlier establishments which had become part of the Royal Free group in 1948: the North Western Fever Hospital, which had begun in temporary buildings in 1870, and the Hampstead General Hospital of 1905 by *Young & Hall*, both now demolished. SCULPTURE by *Jesse Watkins*, two interlocking curved forms, 1974.

Former NEW END HOSPITAL, New End. *See* Perambulation 1b.

QUEEN MARY'S HOUSE, Heath Street and East Heath Road. Neo-Georgian of 1921–2 by *B. Kitchin* and *T. Danby-Smith*. Built as a military maternity home; converted 1990–1 by *Stillman & Eastwick-Field* as a home for the elderly.

*Utilities and transport*

PUBLIC CLEANSING DEPOT, Cressy Road. 1981, by *John Winter*. Functional metal box with exposed steel frame and corrugated cladding.

HAMPSTEAD PONDS. Three (formerly four) very early reservoirs for the Hampstead Waterworks, 1589 and later, with earthen dams across the Fleet valley. The VALE OF HEALTH POND is C18.

HAMPSTEAD RESERVOIR, s of Whitestone Pond. 1859 for the New River Co., with iron roof pillars and a rare, 40ft high cast-iron standpipe.

PRIMROSE HILL TUNNEL, Primrose Hill Road. For the line from Euston *see* p. 365. By *Robert Stephenson*. A magnificent stone E portal by *W. H. Budden*, 1837, with sunburst rustication flanked by massive Italianate towers. Curved wing walls with rusticated piers. The tunnel and its portals were duplicated in 1879, while the electric suburban lines of *c*. 1920 burrow beneath.

BELSIZE TUNNEL, under Belsize Park. For the Midland Railway by *W. H. Barlow*, 1865–7, duplicated in the 1880s. 1m long, with massive strainer arches and heavily buttressed cuttings in the E arch.

UNDERGROUND STATIONS. CHALK FARM, BELSIZE PARK and HAMPSTEAD. Like the Northern Line's stations in St Pancras (q.v.), all of 1906–7 by *Leslie W. Green*, with rows of arches and characteristic ox-blood glazed tiles. Hampstead is the deepest underground station in London. (Near Belsize Park Station, shafts near Downside Crescent belong to the Belsize Park Deep Shelter (Ministry of Defence); a quarter of a mile of twin tunnels below the station, constructed 1944.)

KILBURN HIGH ROAD (LNWR). A stuccoed Italianate station house, *c.* 1852.

WEST HAMPSTEAD THAMESLINK STATION. Originally erected at Queens Park, Kilburn, in 1945 by *J. L. Martin* and *R. Llewelyn-Davies* under *W. H. Hamlyn* of the LMS Railway, as a prototype for prefabricated stations. The first of its kind. Wall panels clipped to a framework on a 3-ft 4-in. module. Cantilevered platform roof.

WEST HAMPSTEAD POWER SIGNAL BOX. An early example of a new type. 1977 by *J. S. Wyatt, British Rail Regional Architect*. Very large; red brick and steel cladding.

## BURGH HOUSE
### New End Square

A handsome mansion acquired by the Borough of Hampstead in 1947, run by the Burgh House Trust as a community arts centre and local museum. The house was built in 1703, probably for a Quaker family called Sewell, and from 1720 it belonged to William Gibbons, physician to Hampstead Wells, whose initials appear on the iron gates. The name comes from a C19 owner, the Rev. Allatson Burgh. Five-bay brick front facing Well Walk, three storeys above a basement, with dentilled cornice, segment-headed windows and plain doorway. It was originally only one room deep. The back part, probably added by Gibbons, can be distinguished by the bright red brick used for quoins and window heads. It extends a little to l. and r. of the original house, and has rear closets projecting on either side of the central staircase. The Music Room extending to the l. at the front dates from the 1920s; a tactful rebuilding of an earlier addition built as a drill hall. Inside, the front range of the house has been altered, with entrance hall and room to the r. thrown into one. In the Music Room C18 brought-in panelling (probably from the demolished Weatherall House in Well Walk). Excellent staircase of *c.* 1720, with twisted balusters and carved tread ends; original panelling in the back rooms, and on the first floor. The front terrace was laid out by *Gertrude Jekyll* in 1908, the only part of the large garden which has survived.

## FENTON HOUSE
### Hampstead Grove

One of Hampstead's most attractive houses, given to the National Trust in 1952. Built probably in 1693, the date on a chimneystack brick. Both the original owner and the architect or builder are unknown. In 1707 it was bought by Joshua Gee, a silk merchant, in 1793 by Philip Fenton, a Baltic merchant.

The original approach is through a fine iron gate with Gee's initials.
30    Handsome s front of five bays, of brown brick with red brick dressings. Two storeys and basement, with a pediment over the three
central, slightly projecting bays. High hipped roof with attics, its steep
pitch still in an earlier C17 tradition. Otherwise the simple details
reflect the straightforward domestic classicism of the William and
Mary period: doorcase with pediment on Doric pilasters; plain
platband, prominent modillion cornice of timber. The narrower
windows in the end bays are a typical late C17 device, lighting
closets off the main rooms. All the windows now have Georgian
sashes. The E front, also of five bays, has projecting end bays with
flat balustraded roofs, the chimneystacks rising behind, an eccentricity which makes the main hipped roof irregular. In front of the
centre three recessed bays is a one-storey Doric entrance loggia,
added when this was made the principal entrance, probably after
James Fenton inherited the house in 1807. On the garden side to
the N the service basement is exposed, and the considerable height
of the building, with its tall attic storey, is more evident.

The plan is a compact square, with chimneystacks on the E and
W walls and thin internal partitions. Originally with four rooms on
each floor, divided by stairs and corridors. Between the N rooms,
a robust staircase to the first floor, with twisted balusters on a closed
string; on the W side, the service stair from basement to attics. The
rooms on the E side have their corner closets (now without doors)
in the projecting end bays, ingeniously tucked around the chimneystacks. On the ground floor the two s rooms were united by double
doors (satisfying a characteristic later Georgian desire for a large
dining room) when the main entrance was changed to the E side.
The doors were replaced by the present arch c. 1965. Original
panelling in the SE room and simpler panelling in the first-floor
NW room give an idea of the original fittings. The building now
houses the fine porcelain collection of the last owner, Lady
Binning, and the Benton Fletcher Collection of musical instruments given to the National Trust in 1937.

The delightful walled GARDEN to the N has a high raised terrace
walk on its E and N sides, probably original to the house and
designed to overlook a formal parterre.

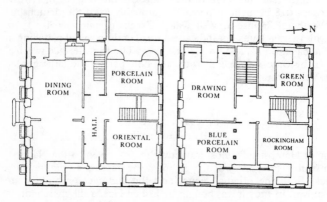

Fenton House. Plans of ground and first floors

## THE HILL*
North End Road

The London home of the first Viscount Leverhulme (†1925), founder of the soap firm Lever Brothers and creator of Port Sunlight, near Birkenhead. Later known as Inverforth House, when it was part of the Manor House Hospital. A large brick Neo-Georgian house in its own grounds, in 1996–8 converted to flats with some new houses to the N. Most of the grounds and great PERGOLA adjoining the Heath were acquired by the LCC for public use in 1960, passing to the Corporation of London in 1989.

The house had been rebuilt *c.* 1895, and was bought by W. H. Lever (as he then was) in 1904. His passion for building resulted in successive remodellings and enlargements, right up until the time of his death in 1925, with some of the architects who were active at Port Sunlight being employed. Equally characteristic was the development of spectacular gardens, which, like those at his Cheshire seat and on the stupendous hillside site at Rivington in Lancashire, were entrusted to *Thomas H. Mawson*. Of all his many houses, however, only at the Hill was accommodation provided specifically for parts of his constantly growing art collection. The interior, which reflected his eclectic tastes, has been much altered. *Grayson & Ould's* Adam drawing room and Jacobean dining room survive, as does the richly 'Wrenaissance' entrance hall.

The W front to the garden has Queen Anne wings, with Ionic brick pilasters, originally single-storeyed and balustraded, which were added by *Grayson & Ould* of Liverpool, *c.* 1905. The upper parts are post-Leverhulme, in connection with hospital use. Some plasterwork only remains of a barrel-vaulted Carolean music room which occupied the N wing. *James Lomax-Simpson*, later company architect of Lever Brothers, worked on this while articled to Edward Ould. In the S wing were small rooms for showing ceramics; the Stuart Room, incorporating C17 woodwork, was fitted up *c.* 1917. By *Grayson & Ould*, possibly *c.* 1905, is a terrace extending along the garden front. *Mawson* built an Ionic veranda onto it *c.* 1910, and the whole was reconstructed and widened when a ballroom by *Leslie Mansfield* was formed underneath in 1923. The ballroom ceiling was originally painted to show the night sky with constellations in position for Leverhulme's birthday. In 1924–5 *Mansfield* (who was not one of those who worked at Port Sunlight), in conjunction with *T. H. Mawson & Sons*, extended and internally remodelled the S wing in a simple and refinedly detailed classical style. The Stuart Room was retained, with its floor lowered, and sculpture and picture galleries (no longer intact) were formed. They communicated with a marble vestibule from which leads the staircase (remaining but altered) to the ballroom. Other work included the addition of a library wing on the l. of the E (entrance) front, by *William & Segar Owen* of Warrington, 1913–14.

The GARDENS involved collaboration between *Mawson* and *Lord Leverhulme* himself. Most of the formal grounds are now a public garden, and have been little altered. They are among the most impressive of their date in London. The original sloping site

---

* This entry was largely written by Edward Hubbard and Michael Shippobottom.

became a terraced lay-out, raised above Hampstead Heath. Curving steps by *Lomax-Simpson*, and a pool with a boy-and-dolphin STATUE by *Derwent Wood*. The main garden structures are by *Mawson* and his firm. Raised Doric pergolas give a disciplined architectural unity, though initially their continuity was broken by a conservatory on the w and on the s by a loggia. Hungry for expansion, Leverhulme bought and demolished two neighbouring houses, so as to include their gardens with his own. An ingenious link was formed to one of these *c.* 1912, extending the main axis w from where the conservatory had stood earlier. Flanked by further colonnaded pergolas, the route bridges a public footpath, changes direction at a circular domed TEMPLE, and ends at a BELVEDERE, with a view towards Harrow on the w horizon. The belvedere

107

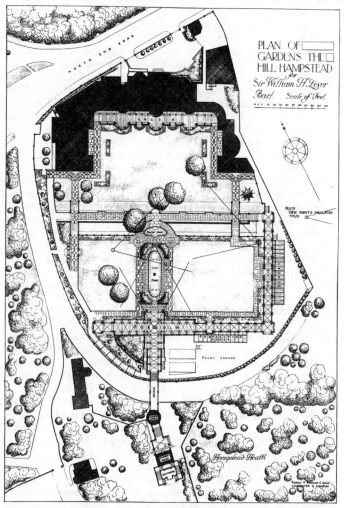

The Hill, garden lay-out by T. H. Mawson

is two-storeyed, complicated, and very Mannerist and freely detailed. A flight of steps descends from here to the garden. The second extension was southwards; after long neglect it was repaired by the Corporation of London and given a new garden at the foot of the pergola in 1995.

KEATS HOUSE, Keats Grove. *See* Perambulation 1b, p. 227.


## PERAMBULATIONS

### 1. Hampstead village

Perhaps the most remarkable thing about Hampstead village is that it has kept nearly all of its pre-Victorian street pattern, very close and intricate, so much so that London street atlases substitute an odd pattern without names for the dozens of narrow passages, stepped lanes and tiny squares. The scale is also uncommonly well preserved. With the exception of the late C19 rebuilding around the central crossroads and some Victorian flats and similar structures, the houses in the centre of Hampstead have pretty well kept the character which they had in the early C19. Most of the views painted by Constable are still easily recognizable.

The perambulation is divided into two circular tours: 1a, the High Street, Heath Street and streets to the w; 1b, the area E of the High Street and Heath Street, between the Heath and Downshire Hill.

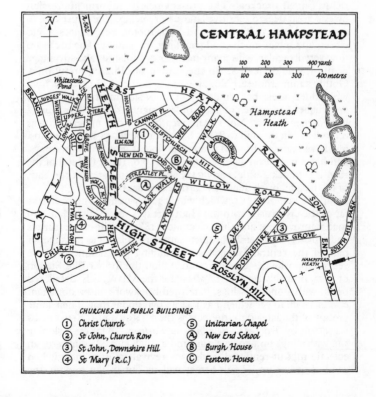

*1a. The High Street, Heath Street and streets to the west*

Starting at the Underground station at the crossing of the High Street, Heath Street and Holly Hill, first impressions are Victorian; the HIGH STREET starts with tall late C19 shopping terraces of no great merit. Further s the early C18 character is better preserved, apart from the intrusive shop windows. The best group is on the w side: Nos. 70–76 and 82–84 (with an insensitive 1970s Post Office in between) and, set back a little, STANFIELD HOUSE of *c.* 1730 (formerly two houses). At No. 83, ZENW3, an elegantly minimalist restaurant by *Rick Mather*, 1986. PERRINS LANE leads w past C18 and C19 cottages and some C20 infilling on a tactful scale to the s end of Heath Street.

CHURCH ROW, leading w from Heath Street to the parish church, is the best street in Hampstead, and was better still before *Sherrin*'s overpowering Gardnor Mansions were built in 1898. The terrace houses, used in the C18 as summer retreats by Londoners and by spa visitors, demonstrate how urban forms were beginning to invade the villages around London. The s side, Nos. 28–17, gradually descends in stages towards the church. The houses, built between 1713 and 1730 as a speculative development by Richard Hughes, a gentleman of Hampstead, are handsome examples of a common early C18 type. Each is of three bays, three storeys over basements, of brown brick with red dressings, with slender segment-headed windows and doorways with straight hoods on richly carved brackets. The present nearly uniform impression owes a great deal to sensitive later C19 refacing. The houses are to a standard plan, with front and back rooms, rear staircase and closet, and retain much good panelling and joinery. The backs are now very irregular, with many later bows added to take advantage of the splendid views s. (In the garden of No.24 a pretty brick Gothic summerhouse.) No. 26 was the home of *G. G. Scott Jun.*, who added a rear bay window. On the N side most of the houses are smaller and more cottagey, of less regular design. Some are a little earlier in date. No. 5, with weatherboarded upper bay, was remodelled in the mid C18, but has a fine early C18 staircase. Nos. 6–7 have segment-headed windows; No.9 is grander, of five bays, and has a good iron gate, as has No. 8. No. 12, at the end of the row, is set back a little, early C18, with brick pilasters at the ends of the façade, brick dentilled cornice and later doorway

Now up HEATH STREET, which winds gently uphill. The stretch as far as the crossroads with the High Street is the result of late C19 road improvement and slum clearance (1883–7), the corner turrets and pink terracotta embellishments marking this out as the superior part of the central Hampstead rebuilding programme of those years. Opposite the Underground station the former Fire Station of 1873, probably by *Robert Pearsall* for the MBW; E.E. detail, red brick, with stone dressings, patterned brickwork and a dominant corner clock tower which has lost its pyramidal roof. Then some groups of the later C20: the best is the KINGSWELL SHOPPING CENTRE, by *Ted Levy, Benjamin & Partners*, 1972, on a sloping site with shops on two levels around a small curved courtyard; an eclectic mix of rendered walls, 30s revival railings and pitched roofs. Further up, Heath Street widens out in the middle, the

higher w part being called THE MOUNT. It is separated from the
E by a strip of greenery (Madox Brown's painting *Work* portrays
this spot). On the E side is an irregular group of low cottages and
the Baptist Church (q.v.), then a group of terrace houses: Nos.
92–94, *c.* 1700 (perhaps built as one house); No. 96 early Victorian,
tall and stuccoed with pilasters; No. 98 early C19, with the late
Georgian motif of windows framed by tall blind arches. In The
Mount, first a group of early C19 stuccoed houses, then No. 6,
CLOTH HILL, behind a good iron gateway: a fine mansion of
1694, four bays with a lower projecting N wing (staircase with
twisted balusters). After the plain early C19 Nos. 8–9, a little higher
up, at r. angles, CAROLINE HOUSE and HOLLY COTTAGE are
mid-Georgian, each of two bays. Close to the top of Heath Street
Nos. 113–125 are a pretty group of two- and three-storeyed
Georgian cottages, each of only one or two bays. At the top of the
hill (420 ft above sea level) is WHITESTONE POND, the old horse
pond (to refresh horses which had pulled carts up the steep
streets). This once attractive meeting point of West Heath and
the main Heath is now overwhelmed by traffic. West Heath Road
is described in Perambulation 2c; this route now returns s into the
intricate network of small streets w of Heath Street.

## West of Heath Street

HAMPSTEAD GROVE runs parallel with Heath Street. Here, as is
frequent in the C18 development of villages, are bigger individual
houses, behind the terraces of the main street. They were
colonized in the C19 and C20 by eminent artists and writers, as the
blue and red plaques show. First a detour w down ADMIRAL'S
WALK to the white ADMIRAL'S HOUSE (formerly The Grove),
familiar from Constable's painting. Built in 1700, with mid-C18
doorway and later alterations. The curious quarterdeck on the
roof was added by an eccentric late C18 owner, Fountain North,
who lived here 1775–1811. Back in Hampstead Grove the first
major houses are NEW GROVE HOUSE, C18 brick, stuccoed and
Tudorized *c.* 1840, and the adjacent OLD GROVE HOUSE, a
complex early C18 house with a 1730 wing to the w, a stuccoed
projection with Regency ironwork to the E, and a yard with a
cottage. *Parker & Unwin* renovated the main house *c.* 1912; the
s front was refaced *c.* 1959. Three by four bays, brown brick
with red dressings. Towards the street a Tuscan pedimented doorway. The stables were rebuilt by *Parker & Unwin* in Georgian
style as No. 8 MOUNT SQUARE. This minute and picturesque
square belongs to the maze of alleys and squares tucked between
Hampstead Grove and Heath Street (another is GOLDEN
SQUARE, at the foot of HOLLYBUSH STEPS).

Further s on the E side of Hampstead Grove are cottages, then
Victorian flats; on the w is the best individual house in Hampstead,
FENTON HOUSE, of 1693 (*see* above). Its contemporary iron
gates to the s face a triangle with other remarkable buildings. It
must have been a perfect spot before MOUNT VERNON cruelly
broke the spell and dwarfed all the rest by its pretentious mass.
It was built as a Consumption Hospital in 1880 by *T. Roger Smith*;
with wings added 1893 and 1903. The style is early C17 French.
The hospital moved to its Northwood (Hillingdon) branch in

1913 and the buildings became the National Institute for Medical Research. Converted to flats in 1997 by *IKA Architects*.

At the top of HOLLY BUSH HILL, s of Fenton House, ROMNEY'S HOUSE, picturesque and weatherboarded. This began as a picture and statue gallery built by *Samuel Bunce* in 1797–8 for the painter George Romney, on the site of stables of No. 6 The Mount (q.v. above). Enlarged in 1807 as the Hampstead Assembly Rooms, with tea room, upper ballroom, and new card room. Much altered 1929–30 by *Clough Williams Ellis* as his own house. Now divided up. (Inside, a geometrical staircase and pilastered upper room.) Holly Bush Hill and HOLLY HILL continue downhill towards the station, past some pretty Georgian houses. HOLLY MOUNT, off to the E, has a rural Victorian pub, a disused chapel with three arched windows, and a few Georgian cottages.

w of Fenton House is a good group of tall houses, of the type that is more frequent in Highgate village. First ENFIELD HOUSE, with late Georgian canted front, then an early C18 terrace consisting of WINDMILL HOUSE, BOLTON HOUSE and VOLTA HOUSE, each of three bays, brown brick with red brick dressings; straight doorhoods on carved brackets, nice moulded brick stringcourse. Now a detour N from the corner of Volta House up WINDMILL HILL, leading up to West Heath. At the corner with Admiral's Walk, BROADSIDE, by *P. Boissevain & B. Osmond*, a crisply designed, well-detailed house of 1960; brick end walls, shallow-pitched roof with broad eaves embracing a chimneystack. The N front has a double-height glazed central entrance hall, with an elegant spiral stair to the first-floor living room. N of Admiral's Walk, TERRACE LODGE, stuccoed early C19, with *cottage orné* fancy glazing, then, set back, No. 10 LOWER TERRACE (NETLEY COTTAGE), a late C18 former farmhouse. Nos. 1–4 Lower Terrace are a pretty late Georgian terrace facing s. Constable lived at No. 2 from 1821 to 1822. Further w on the s side, No. 14, an Arts and Crafts house with chequered chimneystack, and FROGNAL RISE, at the corner, early C19, with carved stone porch of *c.* 1907–8 (attributed to *Parker & Unwin*), and bold garden walls and gate of the same period. Higher up is the grander UPPER TERRACE, with Nos. 1–4, an irregular row of tall Georgian houses and No. 5, by *Rick Mather Architects*, 1998. UPPER TERRACE HOUSE with gardens to Judges' Walk has a restrained classical front of nine bays: three C18 houses remodelled as one in 1931–3 by *Oliver Hill* for Colonel Reginald Cooper. Additions by *Forbes & Tate*, 1937–8 (Hill's interiors survive: oval dining room, stairs with Ionic screen). In between, a lane to JUDGES' WALK on the brow of the hill, with CAPO DI MONTE, a tiny stuccoed *cottage orné*.

Back now to Fenton House and to the s, up the raised bank called MOUNT VERNON. MOUNT VERNON HOUSE, C18, hides behind high garden walls. Nos. 1–6 is an early C19 brick terrace with tall blind arches (cf. No. 98 Heath Street); the lower No. 7, ABERNETHY HOUSE, dates from *c.* 1819. No. 9 HOLLY WALK, at the corner, is the watch house built for the Hampstead Police *c.* 1830, four storeys, with broad segment-headed windows. Then s along Holly Walk, where there is a delicious little early C19 composition, HOLLY PLACE, 1816, with the R.C. church (q.v.) in the centre. Tiny lanes of houses lead off to the E: HOLLYBERRY

LANE, BENHAM'S PLACE (1813) and PROSPECT PLACE. On
the W side is MORETON HOUSE, 1896, with a rendered front by
*Garner*, in the style of a Jacobean manor house. Most of its terraced
garden has disappeared beneath mediocre late C20 houses. Holly
Walk continues towards the parish church beside the churchyard
extension, across which one has an excellent view of the complex
backs of the northern terrace of Church Row (*see* above).

*1b. East of the High Street and Heath Street*

This part of the village developed around Hampstead Wells. This
was a fashionable place to visit from the late C17, with Flask Walk
and Well Walk as the main thoroughfares. Grander houses are more
thinly scattered than to the W of the High Street. A dignified early
C18 group developed at Hampstead Square, and the neighbourhood
of the Heath attracted larger houses in their own gardens. But by
the C19 the hamlet of New End on the slopes immediately above the
wells was crowded with the cottages of the poor; the towering
Edwardian school and the remains of the former workhouse and
public baths are reminders of the once lowly status of the area.

FLASK WALK leads E from the High Street, especially picturesque:
early C19 cottages with only a few intrusions. Early in the C18 the
Upper Flask Inn at the top of Heath Street was the meeting place
of the Kit-Kat Club (whose members' portraits are in the
National Portrait Gallery). The name of the inn comes from the
bottles in which the waters of the Hampstead Wells were sold.
The present pub (THE FLASK) is solid Victorian, with good
patterned tiles. On the N side, neatly fitted in, No. 29 and LAKIS
CLOSE, an alley of well-detailed houses, grey brick and exposed
concrete, 1973 by *Gerson Rottenberg*. At the bottom of the street
GARDNOR HOUSE, a detached house of 1736 (with original staircase); three-bay E front refaced later, large bowed W projection.
On the N side the street steps back to a row of low Georgian
houses and the former PUBLIC BATHS, 1888 (closed 1978 and
converted to housing). Built by the Wells and Campden Charity.
Low front of red brick, boldly lettered. Then No. 75, with rendered
front and some mid-C19 detail, and, set back, the handsome BURGH
HOUSE, 1703 and later, now a local arts centre (*see* p. 215). It
is surrounded to the N and E by tactfully Georgianizing council
flats, also only of three and four storeys, by *C. H. James*, 1948,
built after the house had been acquired by the borough. A
detour S into GAYTON ROAD can take in Nos. 36–38, a group
of houses and flats whose bulk is broken by staggered frontages
and oversailing top floors, by *Ted Levy, Benjamin & Partners*,
1969.

WELL WALK continues E; the WELLS TAVERN, dignified early
C19, with arched first-floor windows, is followed by several late
Georgian houses (Nos. 32–34, 36–40). No. 40 was Constable's
main home. The one of special note, and indeed of exceeding
charm, is No. 46, which originally adjoined the spa's Pump Room
and Long Room. It has a pretty Gothick oriel, tripartite window
above, and porch with clustered columns. The towering late
Victorian Nos. 11–13, directly opposite, exemplify the picturesque

of a century later. They date from 1879, part of the development of the area by the landowner, the Wells and Campden Charity (of which more below). In front, the FOUNTAIN of 1882 by the Charity's surveyor, *H. S. Legg*, commemorates the chalybeate spring.

## New End and Hampstead Square

Now back to Burgh House and NEW END SQUARE, an irregular space to its w; Nos. 16–20, Georgian but much rebuilt. To the w, off New End, STREATLEY PLACE, a tiny passage between the workhouse site (*see* below) and New End School (q.v.). Next to the tall workhouse chimney, of 1897–8 by *Young & Hall*, a cottage-style terrace of 1996 (part of the workhouse conversion by Berkeley Homes), then MANSFIELD PLACE, a little cul-de-sac of genuine mid-C19 cottages behind long front gardens. In telling contrast, NEW COURT opposite consists of two bleak five-storey blocks of artisan tenements, one of 1854–5, and a slightly more decorative one of 1871, the latter perhaps by *T. G. Jackson*, whose father, Hugh Jackson, a local solicitor, paid for the earlier one. Back in NEW END the tall, plain former dispensary and soup kitchen, erected in 1853 after the area escaped the cholera epidemic, providing a further reminder of the social level here at this time. Here also Nos. 10–14, a terrace of the early C18 with typical segment-headed windows and doors with straight hoods on simple carved brackets. The former workhouse, later New End Hospital, extended up to Heath Street. The conversion of the site to housing by Berkeley Homes, 1996–7, preserved the main frontage to New End, an emphatically detailed classical composition by the younger *H. E. Kendall*, 1849. Three storeys with lower wings, 2–3–4–3–2 bays with a strongly projecting pedimented centre and a heavy scrolled pediment over the entrance. Of the ward blocks, there remain, converted to housing in 1996, GILES BUILDING, 1869 by *John Giles*, and the ROTUNDA, 1884–5 by *Charles Bell*, an early example of a circular ward, with central chimney and square tower to one side.

N of New End, CHRISTCHURCH PASSAGE leads to Christ Church (q.v.), past Christchurch Cottage, with a nicely detailed Arts and Crafts extension facing the passage, and Christ Church Lodge, a semi-detached Gothic pair overlooking the church school to the E (q.v.). Christ Church replaced an earlier chapel in Well Walk serving this part of C18 Hampstead. W of the church is an C18 enclave around HAMPSTEAD SQUARE, a loose group of separate five-bay houses of the early C18 (like Church Row, with much tactful C19 refacing); Nos. 1 and 2 facing E, and No. 6, VINE HOUSE, facing S, a fine three-storey house with doorway on carved brackets. To the S, abutting No. 1, an ambitious C18 terrace on the N side of ELM ROW, No. 1 with straight-headed, Nos. 3–5 with segment-headed windows. On the s side No. 2, Elm Lodge of *c.* 1732, five bays with projecting centre, main entrance at first-floor level. From Hampstead Square a glimpse N can take in HIGH CLOSE, in HOLFORD ROAD, a lofty pile of 1884 by *W. H. Murray*, in the manner of Ernest George, generously tile-hung and half-timbered. (Its former garage, BOADE'S MEWS, is off Flask Walk.) To the E, CANNON PLACE, built up with stucco-trimmed mid-

Victorian villas on the s side, with later terraces opposite. No. 10 (built as the Christ Church Vicarage) is a substantial house of c. 1900 in a plain Arts and Crafts manner in the style of Horace Field. Then CANNON LODGE, early C18, originally twice its size, the front fancy-tiled around 1900. CANNON HALL is also early C18, more irregular, of two plus four bays, with segment-headed windows. Low stable block projecting to the l. At the end, the most substantial mansion, SQUIRE'S MOUNT (and CHESTNUT LODGE, formerly part of it) of 1714 with an extension by *Horace Field* in matching style, giving the three-storey s front a total of eleven bays; straight-headed windows and parapet. To the N a row of cottages, one with a (reused) name plate with the date 1704. CANNON LANE leads downhill, skirting the tall garden wall of Cannon Hall. Within it a parish lock-up of c. 1730.

### Around East Heath Road

Between CANNON LANE and WELL ROAD are the grounds of THE LOGS (now subdivided and partly called LION HOUSE), a formidable atrocity of 1867–8 by *J. S. Nightingale*, for and perhaps partly designed by *Edward Gotto*, a civil engineer and developer. Elaborate gateway with lion-crested gable in WELL ROAD. The house exhibits yellow, red and black brick and excrescences in all directions, arches pointed and round, motifs Gothic and Frenchified, and a remarkably wilful tower with château roof (its iron cresting has gone). The conversion to six maisonettes (preserving the grand central staircase) was carried out in 1952 by *Alexander Gibson*, an early case of appreciation of the Victorian. Gibson also added in 1955 a neat two-storey house in the former kitchen garden; brick-faced, with a large upper sun terrace, one of the first post-war houses in the modern idiom. At the s corner of Well Road and East Heath Road, FOLEY HOUSE, built in 1698 for J. Duffield, the first spa manager (see the back), but with a mid-C18 three-bay front with bay window in the centre incorporating a Tuscan doorway. Venetian windows l. and r. Early C18 stables, weatherboarded. Round the corner in WELL WALK, Nos. 21–29 (inscribed Foley Avenue), built in the former gardens of Foley House, then owned by Edward Gotto of The Logs (*see* above); two showy piles by *H. S. Legg*, 1881–2, with corner dome on one fat granite column. Contemporary building opposite on the Wells and Campden Charity land was more consciously artistic, as a result of a campaign by local residents. No. 50, KLIPPAN HOUSE, formerly Thwaitehead, was built by *Ewan Christian* for himself, 1881. Set at an angle to provide views of the Heath (since blocked by flats of 1904 by *Hart & Waterhouse*). Boldly scaled, with mighty chimneys and complex roofs in the manner of Shaw, brick with some tile-hanging, large stone-mullioned windows, and the curiously eclectic feature of some delicate ironwork on the garden side. No. 8 East Heath Road is also by *Christian*. Further w, off Well Walk, GAINSBOROUGH GARDENS, an exclusive development begun 1884, a private road with its own LODGE, by *Legg*, dated 1886. Houses are arranged around a well-planted oval circus (its shape dictated by a former lake). They are tall and red with tile-hanging and timber porches, but of considerable variety. The architects include *E. J. May* (Nos. 3 and 4, 1884, with attractive slate-hanging), *Legg* (No. 6) and *Field* (Nos. 11–13, slightly Neo-Georgian). No. 14, also by *Field*, 1895, has Jacobean gables. No. 9a has a Gothic entrance and sgraffito frieze. By the s gate one can return towards the Heath, past HEATH LODGE and HEATH SIDE, a charming pair of cottages of 1805, symmetrical, with bow windows. EAST HEATH LODGE is a pair of the later C18, very plain, with a big s pediment. The canted bay with balcony may be an addition of 1775 by *James Wyatt*.

*Willow Road to Downshire Hill*

WILLOW ROAD runs w from East Heath Road, overlooking open grass at its e end. Apart from WILLOW COTTAGES near the n end, a pretty terrace with round-arched windows of *c.* 1840, most of the road is indifferent late C19. It now seems strange that the quiet brick terrace at the s end, Nos. 1–3, by *Ernö Goldfinger*, aroused so much hostility from local conservationists when first built in 1937–9. Pevsner, writing in 1952, still felt the need to justify the design: 'Here is the contemporary style in an uncompromising form, yet by the use of brick and by sheer scale the terrace goes infinitely better with the Georgian past of Hampstead than any-

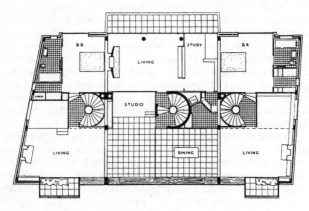

Nos. 1–3 Willow Road. First-floor plan

thing Victorian'. But by the 1990s views had changed. No. 2, Goldfinger's own house, was acquired by the National Trust in 1994, its first modernist house, and opened to the public in 1996 after restoration by *Avanti Architects*. The terrace was a deliberate effort to combine variety of plan (each house is different) within an overall design capable of extension as a continuous street frontage. The structure is of reinforced concrete, with columns exposed on the ground floor, and with concrete used also for framing the openings in the brick-faced walls (a detail much imitated in the 1950s). Three storeys in front, four storeys at the back. The basement and ground floor have garages and services. In each house an elegant toplit spiral stair leads to the first-floor living area, which is emphasized externally by the larger windows. In Goldfinger's own house the front and back rooms can be thrown together, but are made distinct by a change of level and by different textures. The staircase walls are grey and blue. Tall well-lit front dining room and studio (the glazing on different planes should be noted). Living room at the back, up steps, with warm-coloured oak panelling, floor-to-ceiling glazing to the balcony, and a formal fireplace at one end set in a curved projection. Much ingenious experimental furniture by the architect, both built in and freestanding, making original use of artificial materials such as Bakelite. It is complemented by a notable collection of modern art.

The s end of Willow Road runs into SOUTH END ROAD, which has a pleasant irregular sequence of early C19 houses. At the end, No. 71, RUSSELL HOUSE, one of a C19 pair, with clearly visible alterations by *Voysey* of 1890, his earliest surviving work in London.

For those who wish to pursue C20 themes a diversion E can take in SOUTH HILL PARK, a C19 encroachment into the corner of the Heath, which became a favourite spot for experimental designs by the first generation of post-war architects. Nos. 80–90 is a terrace of six houses (built on a bomb site) by *S. Amis* and *W. Howell* (later of *HKPA*), the centre two for themselves. They date from 1953–6, when the architects were working for the LCC at Roehampton, and reflect their concern there with compact low-cost housing. A reticent, well-proportioned three-storey street frontage with exposed concrete floors and white panels between dark brick cross-walls. Ingenious planning (each house is slightly different) makes the best of the very narrow width of 12 ft, with central staircase and services, and a spacious double-height living room at the back, overlooking the Hampstead Ponds. An open grid of generous balconies creates a more forceful rear elevation. No. 78 is by *Brian Housden*, a strange brutalist composition of concrete and glass bricks. Nos. 29–31 are a pair clad in yellow brick, with first-floor entrances and contrasting elevations: No. 31 is by *Michael Brawne*, 1959, with strong vertical mullions to the windows; No. 29 is by *T. Ingersoll*, 1962, with a playful polygonal bay. No. 7, Oliver Court, five storeys of flats with a syncopated pattern of recessed balconies, is another neat demonstration of cross-wall construction.

DOWNSHIRE HILL and KEATS GROVE, running back from the Heath towards Rosslyn Hill, are two of the most attractive streets in Hampstead, with early C19 houses in a setting of generous foliage. In Keats Grove, No. 10, KEATS HOUSE, 1815–16, built as a semi-detached pair; a museum since 1925. Formerly WENTWORTH PLACE, a simple three-bay stucco house with ground-floor windows in blind arches. Keats lodged in the eastern house with his friend Charles Brown in 1818–19. The two houses were united in 1838–9, when one of the staircases was removed and a one-storey E extension of drawing room and conservatory was added. Immediately to the w, a discreetly designed branch LIBRARY of 1931 by *Sydney Trent*. St John's Church (q.v.), a former proprietary chapel, sits happily at the junction of the two roads. No. 14a DOWNSHIRE HILL was its former school, demonstrably Grecian, one-storeyed like a lodge. Downshire Hill is especially characteristic of the stuccoed architecture of *c.* 1820, and the delightful thing is the preservation of so much, yet no uniformity. Apart from Nos. 16–17 (Portland Place), a brick group dated 1823, most of the rest are stuccoed. Nos. 7 and 8 have a joint crenellated pediment. Everywhere much nice ironwork. The few later additions are very discreet. The tiny No. 13 is *M. J. H. and Charlotte Bunney*'s own house, 1936, on an ingenious deep plan; rendered exterior with just a few modernist details (curved sun roof). No. 49a is by and for *Michael and Patty Hopkins*, 1975–6, so skilfully sited that the building is scarcely noticeable from the road. A radically modern design in the minimalist High Tech manner pioneered by Foster. The transparent steel and glass house became an established type in the American countryside from the 1940s (cf. the Wichita house by Charles and Ray Eames), but is rare in England. A structure of great elegance, six bays wide and five deep. Two storeys high, but set well below the road, to which it is linked by a bridge to the upper floor. Ceilings and walls are of silvered ribbed metal cladding; back and front are entirely glazed, with some blue cross-bracing. A calm, free-flowing interior, barely disturbed by an open circular stair linking the two floors. Adaptable partitions and blinds and two free-standing service cores allow for maximum flexibility.

Finally back towards the High Street. In ROSSLYN HILL at the corner of Pilgrim's Lane, LLOYD'S BANK, 1891 by *Horace Field*, in an accomplished Wrenaissance style with corner entrance and boldly rusticated arched windows to the ground floor. In ROSSLYN MEWS, BLACKBURN HOUSE, 1989 by *Chassay Wright & Wilson*. In the HIGH STREET, through an archway on the E side dated 1869, OLD BREWERY MEWS. A former brewery building of the same date, converted to offices in 1971–3 by *Dinerman Davison Dyke-Wells Associates*, with terrace houses fitted into the lane behind, yellow brick with slate hanging. TRINITY CLOSE nearby, off Willoughby Road, incorporates the converted Trinity Hall of 1862, with Gothic windows preserved in the end walls.

### 2. West of Hampstead village

#### 2a. Frognal to Branch Hill

Frognal was a community of its own in the C17 and C18, with its own manor farm and a number of larger houses and cottages scattered picturesquely along FROGNAL, the road which winds uphill to the w of the village centre. Something of this character still remains, despite the additions made when this became a favourite area for artists' and architects' houses in the late C19 and early C20, and then for wealthy private houses. On the higher slopes the former grounds of the larger mansions, although built up later, still give this part of Hampstead a romantically rural atmosphere.

Starting at the s end of Frognal, opposite University College School (*see* Public Buildings), the corner house (No. 28 Arkwright Road), with Flemish moulded brickwork and a large turret, is by *R. A. Briggs*, 1891. No. 39, 1884–5, is by *Norman Shaw*, for Kate Greenaway, and therefore just a little pretty-pretty with its lavish use of tile-hanging in a ruralist mode. The Victorian street pattern is broken by No. 41, low, with horizontal brick bands, set back in its own grounds; by *Alexander Flinder*, 1966–8. FROGNAL CLOSE is a well-planned and well-designed group of small houses by *E. L. Freud*, 1937, in the International Modern style, but (like Goldfinger's houses in Willow Road) discreetly brick-faced, with windows emphasized by slightly raised panels. Nos. 49–51 Frognal are by *Reginald Blomfield*, No. 51 for himself, No. 49 for Cobden Sanderson, in an uneventful Free Classical, 1886. On the E side, at the corner of Frognal Way, No. 66, by *Connell, Ward & Lucas*, 1937, in the extreme idiom of the day, now something of a classic. The design was perhaps originally a little too concerned to *épater le bourgeois*. The effect has been diluted by alterations which disrupt the original balance of solids and voids. Concrete construction with plastered walls, entrance at first-floor level. The ground floor is partly on stilts. The top floor was planned as an open sun deck, but was later filled in for bedrooms (by *Trevor Dannatt*, with the approval of the original architects). Immediately to the E in FROGNAL WAY, and better preserved, the excellent SUN HOUSE 113 by *Maxwell Fry*, 1934–5, an object lesson in façade composition. White rendered walls, three-storeyed window bands of different heights, large first-floor balcony on thin steel supports and then a broad projection at the r. end on the first floor, and a narrow one on the l. on second-floor level. The effect is surprising and shows what a design of quality can make of relatively elementary material. The window frames are not original. (*Hans Feibusch* made a mural for the interior: Apollo and Dionysius, a leopard and Helios.) Otherwise Frognal Way has an assortment of interwar villas from Neo-Georgian to Hollywood Spanish-Colonial and South-African Dutch (with pantiles). No. 5, SHEPHERD'S WELL, was by and for *Adrian Scott*, mannered Neo-Georgian of 1930 (the front doorcase has been removed). No. 13 is by *C. H. B. Quennell* (of whom more later), late 1930s. A more recent addition is No. 22, a low brick house with a circular entrance hall and two big wings to the garden, by *Pank Goss Associates*, 1975–7.

Now back to Frognal and w down FROGNAL LANE, the old route between the hamlets of Frognal and West End. On the r., behind their own drive, Nos. 19–23 are late C18, altered. No. 21 has a nice iron gate. On the l., down a path, No. 40, a villa of 1813 built for the manor bailiff near the site of the Manor Farm, and No. 42, HALL OAK, *Basil Champneys'* own house, red brick, very snug and solid, 1880. Symmetrical exterior with shaped gables and a big hipped roof with four central chimneys, a viewing platform between them, originally with balustrades. Converted to flats 1958; interior reunited 1984.

FROGNAL N of Church Row has some relics of the early C18; FROGNAL LODGE, No. 88, is a long white two-storey house with early C18 door canopy on carved brackets and later s wing with bows to the garden. No. 94, THE OLD MANSION, is a nine-bay brick house of two storeys; the even-bay centre is of *c.* 1700, but considerably changed; the wing of *c.* 1900 was added by *James Neale*. No. 100, of 1891, with heavy corner dome and tile-hung gables, is also probably by Neale, who designed the tall houses on the E side of FROGNAL GARDENS, laid out in the 1880s in the grounds of the Old Mansion. They have a variety of playful gables. The stuccoed houses of the 1920s on the other side are by

*E. B. Musman.* No. 1, the large free-style house at the sw corner, is of *c.* 1900 by *Thomas Worthington* for *Henry Herford*, an amateur wood-carver, who was responsible for the interior carved decoration. On the w side of Frognal, No. 81 (THE OAKS, now flats) started as a Georgian house but was extravagantly embellished in 1902 with balconies and roof pavilion by *George Hornblower* for E. P. Musman. The Regency-style No. 85, set back behind, is of 1920, perhaps by the latter's son, *E. B. Musman.* Further on, No. 95, a small early c19 former lodge with octagonal corner, and No. 97, soaring mansion flats of the 1890s (by *Palgrave & Co.*). On the e side, No. 102, FROGNAL COTTAGE, 1906 by *Amyan Champneys* (son of Basil), a very pretty free Edwardian design with oriel windows flanking a pilastered centre crowned by twin tile-hung gables. Then Nos. 104–106, an early c18 pair; No. 108, larger and more irregular, also c18; and No. 110 (formerly an inn), c17 in origin, with tall hipped roof.

On the w side of Frognal, No. 99 is mid-c18 and later, three bays and three storeys with full-height canted bay on the s side. Next to it a much altered group, UPPER FROGNAL LODGE, No. 103, and FROGNAL GROVE (Nos. 105–111). A muddle, but with an interesting history. The core is of *c.* 1745 and is by *Henry Flitcroft*; No. 107 was his own house, a villa of four bays and three storeys, with a central cupola. Nos. 105 and 109 are later wings. The house was altered by *G. E. Street* and re-Georgianized in 1926, with a painted brick front. No. 111, with two pedimental gables, is the former stables, adapted by *A. & P. Smithson* in 1960. From the drive raised above the road one looks across Frognal Rise to a bold c20 house in WINDMILL HILL by *Ted Levy, Benjamin & Partners*, 1968–70 (almost invisible from elsewhere); steel-framed, of two storeys, set into the side of the hill, with the first floor on brick piers and a deep upper balcony behind sturdy uprights supporting the projecting roof beams.

The area w of the upper part of Frognal had few houses until Redington Road was developed from 1875 (*see* Perambulation 2b). A little earlier, OAK HILL PARK was laid out *c.* 1851. Only two of its tall stucco mansions remain; the rest were replaced after the Second World War by a mixture of houses and flats carefully disposed in the mature landscape, a Roehampton for the rich. In OAK HILL WAY No. 3 is by *Trevor Dannatt*, 1958, built into the hill, originally with a terrace above a garage, extended since. A still rural path leads to OAK HILL HOUSE, one of the original survivors, and to the three seven-storey point blocks and well-sited lower flats, by *Michael Lyell Associates*, 1962. Further up the hill the major estate was BRANCH HILL. The former lodge (THE GARDENS), an attractively quirky little building dated 1868, may be by *Teulon*. The main house, BRANCH HILL LODGE, now an old people's home, is an Edwardian monster in red brick and terracotta chiefly of 1901. It is on the site of an c18 mansion which was altered by *Flitcroft c.* 1745, by *George Gibson c.* 1800, and by *Teulon* in the 1860s. Unsympathetic c20 additions. The garden front looks w over the ingenious but alien interlocking houses of the BRANCH HILL ESTATE, stepping down the slope in the hill-village fashion made popular in the 1960s by the work of the Swiss firm Atelier 5. Designed by *Gordon Benson* and *Alan Forsyth* of

*Camden Architect's Department*, one of the last large-scale enterprises from an adventurous decade of Camden housing. The form
is similar to Maiden Lane (*see* St Pancras, Perambulation 3b), but
works better here, because of the smaller site and steeper slope.
Built in 1974–6, after long delay, and at notorious expense. Pale
render and shuttered concrete throughout, with roof gardens;
narrow passages in between, the rigorously mathematical lay-out a
startling contrast to the unkempt surrounding landscape.

Back in BRANCH HILL, a surprising C19 Gothic terrace with crowstepped gables. Beyond it, steps lead up to Judges' Walk on the
brow of the hill (*see* end of Perambulation 1a), with West Heath
Road beyond (Perambulation 2c).

## 2b. The Redington Road area

The area between Frognal and Finchley Road is the ideal place to
study the transition from late Victorian to Edwardian architecture.
The following account is much indebted to Alistair Service, *Victorian
and Edwardian Hampstead*, 1989.

REDINGTON ROAD was laid out in 1875 and built up slowly, starting from the Frognal end. Nos. 2–4 are by *Philip Webb*, 1876,
attractively self-effacing, with tile-hung upper floor and crisp
dormers. The controlled simplicity contrasts with the more self-
conscious Gothic of No. 6, now flats, but built as the vicarage for
the parish church, 1875–6 by *T. K. Green* (cf. Ellerdale Road etc.,
Perambulation 4a). No. 12, Wellesley House, 1877–8, is in an old-
fashioned Italianate. More interesting is ONE OAK, No. 16, of
1889 by *A. Mackmurdo*, with plain six-bay front with tall sash
windows below a mansard roof, its simplicity forward-looking for
its date, as with his earlier house at Bush Hill, Enfield (q.v.). The
wings and separate studio were added in 1927 by *Maxwell Ayrton*
for Sir Owen Williams. On the other side of the road, little of note
until one comes to REDINGTON LODGE (Nos. 35–37), 1887 by
*Horace Field*, with big strong gables and tile-hanging. No. 39, at
the corner of Oak Hill Avenue, is an extravagant Free Style design
of 1903, probably by *W. W. Bull*, a pupil of James MacLaren. On
the N side again No. 20, the Red Cottage, 1909, for the developer
G. W. Hart, probably by his partner *C. H. B. Quennell* (*see* below).
Nos. 14 and 16 are also Edwardian; No. 28 is of *c.* 1907 in the
Free Classical style of Arnold Mitchell. No. 30 with big bargeboarded gables looks earlier, perhaps by *T. K. Green*. No. 50 is by
*Ted Levy, Benjamin & Partners*, 1966, discreetly filling a narrow
site, with sloping roofs stepping up from a one-storey garage and
entrance to taller parts at the back.

The developments of the 'West Hampstead Estate' undertaken by
Hart, with Quennell as his architect 1898–1914, are scattered
around the area between Redington Road and Finchley Road.
Nos. 41–49 Redington Road, 1907–8, are typical examples of
those years, mixing orange and red brickwork with gables, oriels,
and occasional classical features to create a relaxed style loosely
reminiscent of English architecture of the mid C17 to early C18.
Nos. 51–67 of 1904–5 are equally varied. No. 69, with Voyseyish
roughcast, is by an unknown architect; Nos. 71–77, again by

*Quennell*, 1907–8. Then a patch not built up until after 1918:
No. 81 by *Maufe*, 1921, in stripped classical style; No. 87, the
HILL HOUSE, by *Oliver Hill*, 1936–7 for G.L. Schlesinger, but
sadly altered when converted to flats. A long, asymmetrical brick
villa in strictly modern forms, well placed on a sloping site.
Originally with a flat roof. Curved ends, one with an upper terrace,
the other a loggia with sleeping porch above (now filled in).
Ground floor with single long living room with high-quality plain
panelling. The gardens were laid out by *Christopher Tunnard*. On
the other side Nos. 54–64 are *Quennell* of 1908–9, the last house
surprisingly Baroque. No. 66, THE WABE, is a maverick design of
1902 by *William Garnett*, educational adviser to the LCC, for himself:
big canted bays and a crenellated parapet. No. 70, 1912–14, is one
of *Quennell*'s last designs, a large house in the more staid Neo-
Georgian characteristic of the years just before the First World War.
Quennell-land extends over several other streets in this area. Off
Redington Road to the N is TEMPLEWOOD AVENUE, with comfortable large detached houses, No. 15, along with much else, by
*Quennell*, *c.* 1905. No. 5a is a small interloper by *Trevor Dannatt*,
1960, originally a single-storey brick house with three wings
around a courtyard. TEMPLEWOOD GARDENS dates from
*c.* 1912, REDINGTON GARDENS from 1915–17. At the far end the
older OAK TREE HOUSE, 1873 by *Basil Champneys* for the artist
Henry Holiday, a tall compact brick house (now flats) with coved
eaves, high segment-headed dormers and tall chimneys, one of
Champneys' first houses in a Queen Anne style, precociously
similar to its Edwardian neighbours. The first-floor studio has a
big Venetian window at gallery level.
s of Redington Road, HEATH DRIVE, a pleasantly leafy road of
1890 onwards, has some of *Quennell*'s best work: Nos. 22–33 date
from 1905–7, well-composed pairs with canted bays, steep gables
and massive tiled roofs. The detached corner house, No. 33, with
open arched corner porch, was given three illustrations in his
*Modern Suburban Houses*. More Edwardian Arts and Crafts houses
to the s in OAKHILL AVENUE, 1909. To the w in KIDDERPORE
AVENUE, No. 9 by *Quennell* and No. 1, with Dutch gables, probably by *Arthur Keen* (for his brother E.H. Keen). Smaller *Quennell*
houses in KIDDERPORE GARDENS, in a cosy vernacular, *c.* 1906.
Further on in Kidderpore Avenue, past the college buildings (*see*
Public Buildings), No. 12, the vicarage of 1899, like St Luke's
Church (q.v.), is by *Champneys*, with recessed porches, and
No. 14 is by *Arthur Keen*, 1901, a studio for G.H. Swinstead,
extravagantly decorated, with dome and sculpture.
In PLATT'S LANE the most interesting house is No. 8, ANNESLEY
LODGE, the best *Voysey* house in London, built for his father in
1895. L-shaped plan with front door in the inner angle. Typical
Voysey sloping buttresses and roughcast, with stone dressings to a
remarkable long band of low first-floor windows just below the
eaves. The mullions have no mouldings at all, and the whole
house is astonishingly ahead of its date. The main entrance is in
the angle of the two wings, leading to a large corner entrance hall.
The interior has been subdivided.
Part of Platt's Lane (Nos. 29–39, *c.* 1898; Nos. 41–47, 1903; and
Nos. 18–24) and the streets off it were also developed by Hart,

with a mixture of detached and semi-detached houses, many of them by *Quennell*. BRIARDALE and CLORANE GARDENS of 1896–7 were followed by FERNCROFT AVENUE, with more mature designs of *c.* 1900–4. HOLLYCROFT AVENUE dates mostly from *c.* 1905–6, with Nos. 33–49 by *Quennell*, and No. 46 by *Guy Dawber*, 1907, a satisfying informal composition with asymmetrical chimneys, reminiscent of Lutyens's early work. ROSECROFT AVENUE, built up slowly from 1898, has some good early Quennell houses, Nos. 17 and 18 with plaster panels by *Benjamin Lloyd*, 1898, and the larger PHYLLIS COURT, 1900.

## 2c. West Heath Road

WEST HEATH ROAD winds its way from Finchley Road to Whitestone Pond at the top of the hill. The rural appearance of this area in the early C19 is known from Constable's sketches; even in 1895 there was only a handful of wealthy houses standing in large grounds, looking out over the mature landscape of the West Heath. The W part of the road gradually filled up in the early C20 with a variety of sedate villas in well-treed grounds. There was little change until the 1980s, when the large houses disappeared and one site after another sprouted self-consciously designed flats and exclusive precincts of small houses. For West Heath Road W of Platt's Lane, *see* Barnet: Golders Green.

E of Platt's Lane is the most flamboyant contribution of between the wars, No. 23, SARUM CHASE, unashamed Hollywood Tudor, 1932 by *Vyvyan Salisbury* for his uncle, the artist Frank Salisbury. Still in the tradition of fashionable late Victorian artists' houses. Stone and brick, with a showy half-timbered part, and a projecting l. wing with big oriel window. An early C20 group follows, of which the most lavish is BURLEIGH HOUSE, No. 19, Neo-Tudor, with stone oriel window to a double-height great hall. No. 15 was replaced by fussy flats by *Hough & August*, 1986. No. 13, ASHMOUNT, at the corner of Redington Road, is late C19, red brick with much rubbed brick enrichment, Dutch gable and picturesque angle turret enriched with pargetting. At the opposite corner, No. 11, MIDDLEHEATH, substantial gabled Tudor of *c.* 1900; fine garden walls and gatepiers.

No. 9 is a rare London example of a lavish private house from the brief period when the austerity of the Brutalist aesthetic was in the ascendant. Built in 1962–4 by *James Gowan* for the furniture manufacturer C.S. Schreiber. A precisely geometric exterior with no domestic allusions, planned on a 3-ft module, and immaculately faced with dark blue-grey engineering brick. The house is of four storeys, although this is hard to guess from the anonymous ladder windows, which give no indication of scale. Inside, the restraint is tempered by the use of high-quality materials, with *Schreiber*'s own built-in furniture used as room dividers to achieve an uncluttered plan. Rooms extend N–S through the whole house to minimize the N-facing aspect. Domed swimming pool to the W, 1968, also by *Gowan*.

Across Templewood Avenue, HEATH PARK GARDENS, by *Igal Yawetz & Associates*, 1985–8, a pile of flats with aggressively flamboyant cantilevered balconies, replacing *Quennell*'s Neo-Georgian Templewood House of 1913. To the E and S, MANSION GARDENS and GRANGE GARDENS, tight cul-de-sacs of select town houses, 1981–3 by *Ted Levy, Benjamin & Partners* for Barratts. They cover the site and grounds of The Grange (a C19 house remodelled in Edwardian times, which replaced the 'Salt Box' painted by Constable). Simply detailed, well-composed groups – this time in brown brick, as in Levy's earlier development at Millfield Lane, Highgate. Sympathetic landscaping by *Derek Lovejoy*. In sharp contrast, BIRCHWOOD DRIVE, which opens off Grange Gardens, has wilful Postmodern trimmings. This is on the site of another large C19 house, Spedan Tower, the home of the store-owner John Lewis and his son, John Spedan Lewis. The land, like that of neighbouring Branch Hill (*see* above, pp. 230–1), was earmarked for Camden housing in the 1970s but was eventually filled in 1982–7 by dense clusters of eighteen private houses by *Bickerdike Allen Simovic*. At the corner of Branch Hill, in FIRECREST DRIVE, the thirty flats in ST REGIS HEIGHTS and SAVOY COURT are part of the same development, two domineering piles, eclectically detailed with Stirlingesque sloping glazed porches. At the E end of Judges' Walk, SUMMIT COURT, quieter in its details, but far too prominent on its hilltop site near Whitestone Pond; a group of thirteen flats, 1987–8 by *Architectural Design Associates* (successors to Ted Levy, Benjamin & Partners). It replaced Hawthorne House, a big Neo-Tudor composition of 1883 by *George & Peto*, built for the china merchant W.J. Goode.

### 3. The Vale of Health and the northern fringes of the Heath

The VALE OF HEALTH is a curiously isolated pocket of houses in a hollow to the E of Whitestone Pond. Its name, recorded in 1801, may have been ironic, for in addition to a handful of cottages, the remote area attracted anti-social activities such as tan pits and a varnish factory. From the early C19 its picturesque quality appealed to impecunious writers, notably Leigh Hunt, who lived there 1815–19. In the 1860s some suburban villas appeared, as well as two hotels, neither of which survives. After 1872, when further encroachment on the Heath was forbidden, expansion was limited to the existing built-up area. Hence the most attractive feature of the Vale: the passages no more than four feet wide between some of the streets. Among older houses: VALE LODGE, late Georgian, beautified in the C20; MANOR LODGE, white-washed brick; WOODBINE COTTAGE, weatherboarded. VILLAS ON THE HEATH date from the 1860s; Nos. 3–6 are attractive stuccoed Tudor of 1862.

Elsewhere around the top of the hill are more isolated buildings. N of the Whitestone Pond at the crossroads, JACK STRAW'S CASTLE. The famous pub was destroyed in the Second World War and rebuilt in 1963–4 by *Raymond Erith* in Georgian Gothick: a timber-framed building with white boarding, crenellations, and pretty intersecting Gothic glazing bars, but on a scale that is unmistakably C20. Nearby, OLD COURT HOUSE is C18, much altered. Opposite, at the beginning of Spaniards Road, HEATH HOUSE faces S, a very plain early C18 five-bay mansion of brown brick with red brick dressings and an Ionic porch, with a more elaborate balustraded E extension with canted bay. SE of Whitestone Pond a group of older houses, with GANGMOOR, C18, and BELLMOOR, a block of C20 Neo-Tudor flats, not obtrusive (yet a sad addition). A detour down SPANIARDS ROAD between the Heath and the Heath Extension takes one past an attractive group of C18 houses on the N side: THE CHANTRY and WHITE HOUSE (formerly one house called The Firs), c. 1734 with early C19 alterations (Greek Doric porches). HEATH END HOUSE has a SW weather-boarded part. EVERGREEN HILL (formerly called Erskine House) is C18, but mostly rebuilt c. 1923. In the late C19 this was a rural retreat from the East End of London for Canon Samuel Barnett and his wife, Dame Henrietta Barnett, founder of Hampstead Garden Suburb (see Barnet). Then THE SPANIARDS at the borough boundary, a picturesque corner which has happily defied road widening: a whitewashed C18 pub, and an C18 TOLL HOUSE on the opposite side. For Spaniards End to the N of Spaniards Road, see p. 155. On the S side of Spaniards Road, beyond high walls, the picturesque neo-Jacobean outline of gables, turret and chimneys belongs to THE ELMS, later ST COLUMBA'S HOSPITAL, altered and extended for residential use, 1998. It began as an older house transformed before 1870 and then embellished for Lord Duveen in 1888–95, possibly by *T. E. Collcutt* (with grand double-height reception room with lavish French Renaissance style woodwork).

The remains of the hamlet of NORTH END can be approached through the woodland N of Spaniards Road, or along NORTH END WAY from Jack Straw's Castle, past INVERFORTH HOUSE (The Hill) on the W side, converted to flats in 1996 (for the house and grounds, see The Hill, p. 217). The road then runs downhill through the Heath Extension between steep banks to NORTH END, once an isolated hamlet on the boundary between the parishes of Hampstead and Hendon (see also Barnet: Golders Green). The Hampstead Heath Extension to its N and E still gives it a rural feeling. In NORTH END ROAD is THE OLD BULL AND BUSH, a pub made famous by a music-hall song, much rebuilt 1923–4, although the two bay windows and Venetian window are older features. Behind the pub, a cul-de-sac, NORTH END, with Nos. 1 and 3, C18, on the N side. On the S side was Pitt House (originally North End House), demolished 1952, a big, gloomy, featureless C18 mansion, the largest in Hampstead, where the elder Pitt retired to nurse his melancholy in 1766. (A brick pedimented archway in woodland to the S may belong to improvements of 1766–7 by *James Paine*.) Further E, beyond a tiny green, BYRON COTTAGE, a pretty, irregular C18 house, and WILDWOOD, also C18, but tile-hung in the later C19. WILDWOOD LODGE is a mid-C19 *cottage orné*. No. 19, with low gabled roof, is by *Michael Ventris*, 1953. A little further N, overlooking the unkempt woodland of the sandy wood, is the surprisingly urban Gothic WILDWOOD TERRACE, built, with WILDWOOD GROVE to its W, by a local builder in 1866–7.

WYLDES, just to the N (strictly speaking in Barnet). Wyldes and Old Wyldes are remarkable survivals with an interesting history, tucked away between Hampstead Way and the Heath Extension.

OLD WYLDES is the former farmhouse, probably early C17, a timber-framed, two-storey lobby-entry house with weatherboarded exterior and C18 SW extension. Another extension, of *c.* 1820, links it to WYLDES, built as a large brick and weatherboarded barn. The farmer occupied the partly converted barn, and the farmhouse was let out as a holiday house. John Linnell and other artists came in the 1820s; Dickens stayed for five weeks in 1837. From 1884 it was occupied by Mrs Charlotte Wilson, an early Fabian, and became the meeting place of the Hampstead Historic Club, a radical political discussion group. She remodelled the house in 1885, giving it an oriel window and veranda, and completed the conversion of the barn. In 1905 the house was directly threatened by the proposed Underground extension; its site was to be a car park, and Hampstead Way was laid out as an approach road. Instead, when the plans for the Heath Extension and Hampstead Garden Suburb were adopted, it became the home of *Raymond Unwin*, the designer of the Suburb (*see* Barnet). He reconstructed the barn as drawing and estate offices.

## 4. The southern slopes of Hampstead

### 4a. Around Fitzjohn's Avenue

The upper slopes below the village were developed with large houses in the later C19 and enjoyed a good, if passing, popularity with prosperous artists. This tour starts at the top of Fitzjohn's Avenue.

ELLERDALE ROAD belonged to the Greenhill Estate, and was built up in the early 1870s with grand Gothic villas, many of them by *T.K. Green*, whose own house, No. 2, makes a bold show with oriel-bedecked tower and tile-hung upper floor. More daringly progressive is No. 6, by *Norman Shaw*, built in 1874–6 by W.H. Lascelles for Shaw himself, who lived there 1876–1912. It belongs to the years of Shaw's most inventive compositions in Kensington and Chelsea, where he explored the potential of tall urban frontages. Here height is used to exploit the views S. The house is so tall that, especially from the back, it appears craggy. It has a completely asymmetrical four-storeyed front with a three-storeyed pargetted oriel on the r., balanced by a tall canted bay and gable on the l. Windows of the very attenuated 'Queen Anne' type, with rubbed brick heads and aprons, are set apparently without any order, yet forming themselves into nice playful compositions, between large expanses of red brick. The entrance on the r. (formerly in front, now at the side) leads into a low panelled hall from which stairs rise to the dining room, taller than the other rooms, hence the asymmetry of the front. It has a heavy beamed ceiling, panelled walls with tapestry above, and a huge inglenook lined with Spanish-style tiles and embossed leather. Above it is Shaw's 'den', or workroom, with a window looking down above the fireplace, approached by a tiny corner stair lit by a porthole. The SE drawing room (now chapel) was enlarged by a big back wing in 1884–5. This retains a delicate inlaid screen with attenuated urn balusters, marking a change of level.

Further tall Gothic villas to the s, with dates of the 1870s, in PRINCE ARTHUR ROAD, and in ARKWRIGHT ROAD, where there are some especially ornate houses by *Green*: the multi-gabled No. 13 (1878); No. 4, with much carved detail, for the artist F.W. Topham, and No. 1. No. 13b, the NEW HOUSE, is a modern house of 1939 by *Val Harding*, a member of Tecton. Brick-faced, with exposed concrete floors, somewhat like Goldfinger's houses in Willow Road (*see* Perambulation 1b). The front is given interest by a large recess with glass bricks. On the NE corner of Arkwright Road, FIELD COURT, No. 77 FITZJOHN'S AVENUE, housing for Camden by *Pollard Thomas & Edwards*, 1977–8, a compact, neatly detailed bricky cluster: nine houses and twelve flats in a tall, rather gaunt gabled block with pitched roofs intended to echo the massing of its Victorian neighbours. No. 75, UPLANDS, is another house by *Green*, for P.F. Poole, R.A., in elephantine Gothic with bargeboarded gables.

The development of the southern part of FITZJOHN'S AVENUE, laid out through the lands of the Maryon Wilsons, lords of the manor, was proposed from the mid C19, but delayed by long disputes. The broad and now busy avenue leading downhill to Swiss Cottage eventually took shape from 1876, lined by substantial but only occasionally distinguished houses. No. 73 has alterations of 1901–3 by *Voysey* for P.A. Barendt (see the front bay). No. 69, 1877 for C. Kemp Wild, is in a polychrome *Rundbogenstil*. The best is No. 61, with No. 50 NETHERHALL GARDENS, built in 1878 as a single house for the artist Edwin Long by *Shaw*, and thanks to the architect's inexhaustible fantasy completely different in motifs and composition from his own house in Ellerdale Road (*see* above). It is low, comfortable, broadly composed, with two Dutch gables, and below, in the middle of them, a projecting studio with large bow at the end. No. 55, THE TOWER, 1880 for H.F. Baxter by *J.T. Wimperis*, is a massive Baronial creation, with stone balconies and tourelles; grand gatepiers and gates to match. No. 47 (ST MARY'S CONVENT) is by *George Lethbridge* for L.M. Casella, *c.*1880; much terracotta detail. The outstanding houses further s have been demolished (No. 6, Three Gables, 1881 by *Shaw* for Frank Holl, and *Flockhart*'s studio house for John Pettie). A detour to the w can take in the best house in the 1880s hinterland, No. 6 NETHERHALL GARDENS, 1882–3 for the artist Thomas Davidson, by *Batterbury & Huxley*, with a large studio wing with big leaded-light window. Among more of the 1880s in MARESFIELD GARDENS, several later additions: No. 16a, 1930 for the Danish glass designer Arild Rosenkrantz, plain brick; No. 20, a broad symmetrical Queen Anne house, home of Sigmund Freud, now the FREUD MUSEUM, with interior alterations by his son, *Ernst Freud*; No. 58, 1938–9 by *H. Herry-Zwiegenthal* for Paul Jolowitz, a modernist house of brick, with an angled projecting room on the l., carrying a bold pierced metal balcony.

The area E of Fitzjohn's Avenue around LYNDHURST ROAD formed the freehold Rosslyn Park Estate, which belonged to the Dean and Chapter of Westminster. Streets were developed slowly from 1853, covering the former grounds of Rosslyn House (which survived until the 1890s on the s side of Lyndhurst Road). Nos. 1 and 3 LYNDHURST TERRACE, a flamboyantly Gothic pair, were

designed *c*. 1864–5 by and for *Alfred Bell*, the stained-glass designer,
and his father-in-law *John Burlison Sen.*, assistant to Gilbert Scott;
united (as Bayford House) in 1870 by *Bell* and *Charles Buckeridge*;
subdivided since. No. 1 exhibits the bold geometric forms of the
masculine Gothic of the 1860s, packing in a rounded stair-turret,
a square corner turret, and a triangular oriel. Lively polychrome
window heads. (Inside, remains of elaborate interiors with stained
glass and stencilled decoration.) The free composition of the pair
has been somewhat marred by the heightening of the centre, but
can still be contrasted with No. 5, where angular Gothic detail is
constrained within the form of a symmetrical villa. To the N,
THURLOW ROAD has solid pairs of a more conventional type
(No. 30 by and for *Horace Field Sen.*). The houses of the earlier
1860s are still stuccoed Italianate. Urbane stucco-trimmed pairs
continue along ELDON GROVE, back to LYNDHURST ROAD. At
the NW corner, TOWER CLOSE, a group of 1982 by *Pollard
Thomas & Edwards*, with a gabled corner tower with a half-
skeletal top, looking like a deconstructionist version of the type of
Germanic fortification that was an inspiration in Hampstead
Garden Suburb. Opposite to the S, beyond a disturbingly prominent parking area, OLAVE CENTRE (Headquarters of the Girl
Guides Association) has as its core ROSSLYN LODGE, a small
stuccoed villa built *c*. 1800, with ogee-topped turret and shallow
bow. Extensions, tactfully white-rendered but dwarfing the original house, by *John Dangerfield*, 1980–91. Slotted in behind is
WATERHOUSE CLOSE, housing for the elderly, in a neat L-shaped
two-storey group, with distinctive deep timber eaves. By *Camden
Architect's Department*, 1980–2. From here a glimpse of another
pre-suburban survival, the C18 garden front of ROSSLYN GROVE
hidden behind the former Congregational Church (q.v.).

Back W along LYNDHURST ROAD. Among a mixed bag of
large villas, the most interesting group is on the S side, built on the
site of Rosslyn House (demolished 1896). At No. 19 part of an
1860s outbuilding by *Teulon* remains. Nos. 19–21 of 1897–8 are by
*Horace Field*, in the quiet Neo-Georgian which he had adopted by
this date. In the streets immediately to the S one can study Field's
earlier style: No. 17 LYNDHURST GARDENS, 1890, has a shaped
gable to the road, and a demure tile-hung S front with a big
hooded porch. In contrast, Nos. 22, 24 and 26 belong to one of
*William Willett*'s developments, designed by *H. B. Measures*: three
very tall detached gabled houses with plenty of spirited Queen
Anne detail. Along the leafy WEDDERBURN ROAD, further ample
gabled houses on the N side; on the S side, first WEDDERBURN
HOUSE, a nicely proportioned small mansion block of 1884–5,
then some early experimental work by *Horace Field & Moore*. Nos.
3 and 5 are set back, detached houses of *c*. 1886 with mullioned
windows in Tudor manor house fashion; Nos. 7–9, *c*. 1891, is a
long frontage with Georgian sashes. The more showy Nos. 11 and
13 have Dutch gables.

A little to the S a housing scheme for Camden fits in discreetly; 1979
by *Neylan & Ungless*. Dug into the slope above DALEHAM
GARDENS is a trim red brick block of old people's housing, with a
lower more intimate garden side, and across the gardens, at Nos.
48–52 FITZJOHN'S AVENUE, a five-storey block of maisonettes,

ingeniously planned with garden access at two levels, and long sloping roofs above. The street side is more formal, with entrances within a ground-floor arcade.

### 4b. The southern slopes from Belsize Lane south to England's Lane

This area is now largely of the second half of the C19, with the occasional older building, although the street pattern still reflects its pre-suburban history. BELSIZE takes its name from Belsize House, which faced E down a drive that has become Belsize Avenue. The house was expensively rebuilt in 1663 by a courtier, Daniel O'Neill, and gained notoriety in the early C18 as a place of entertainment. It was rebuilt or remodelled *c.* 1744–6, and survived, together with its elaborate gardens and grounds, until 1853. By then other houses had begun to appear, but until the mid C19 much of the area, like the Rosslyn Park Estate to the N (*see* Perambulation 4a), consisted of houses in parkland. The earlier houses then began to be replaced, and suburban terraces and villas developed in distinct patches as different areas were released for building.

BELSIZE LANE, as its winding character indicates, predates the late Victorian development at its E end (probably of *c.* 1883 by *Henry Spalding*). No. 5, HUNTER'S LODGE, is one of the few early C19 houses remaining in the area; a stuccoed and castellated Gothic *cottage orné*, a rare survival for London. Ogee windows and a varied composition of two turrets and a tall gable towards the garden, exceedingly pretty in a toy way. It was built for William Tate by *Joseph Parkinson*, who exhibited the design at the Royal Academy in 1810, on the site of an earlier cottage of 1808. Further on the lane winds S, past an assortment of C20 infilling. No. 17a, and No. 40 ORNAN ROAD nearby, are by *John Winter*, 1970, two austere but well-proportioned three-bay houses with pale grey mosaic cladding. They are based on a 10-ft module, but differ from each other in both height and plan. No. 34 Belsize Lane, by *Georgie Wolton*, 1975–6, is almost entirely hidden behind a tall garden wall. A spacious, self-effacing one-storeyed house with the main living area with glazed walls to enclosed gardens on both sides. Bedroom wing and studios at either end, the S studio added 1983, linked by a conservatory, with a further garden court beyond.

The triangular meeting point of the lane with Belsize Crescent and Terrace is a small shopping centre of stucco-trimmed terraces, known as Belsize Village, which developed on the site of Belsize farm. In the later C19 this part of Belsize Lane developed into a service road for the grander neighbouring streets, with a series of mews, mostly much rebuilt. One of the most elaborate is the BELSIZE COURT GARAGES off Belsize Place, a long range with half-timbering above red brick, built by *Willett* as livery stables in 1880. Further on, BAYNES MEWS, 1871, also by Willett, with an unusually grand street front of three storeys with arched windows, coloured brickwork, and a still genuine cobbled area and garage doors behind.

N of Belsize Lane building began in 1868: the rather cramped Italian-ate houses in BELSIZE CRESCENT are the builder *William Willett*

*Sen.*'s first Hampstead undertaking, on the fringe of the main development to the s. This began in 1855: by BELSIZE TERRACE one reaches BELSIZE PARK, BELSIZE PARK GARDENS and BELSIZE SQUARE, which form the core of the large Belsize House Estate, whose long streets were laid out in a fashionable Kensington stucco style, designed to attract prosperous professional commuters to southern Hampstead instead of west London. The main activity took place from 1855 to 1870, when the builder, Daniel Tidey, went bankrupt. BELSIZE AVENUE and the N side of BELSIZE PARK have slightly busier houses of the 1870s by *Willett*. Stucco terraces extend w from here to Swiss Cottage (see Perambulation 4e), where College Crescent was developed already in 1849, and where there is a little more in similar manner in BUCKLAND CRESCENT and at the w end of Belsize Lane (Nos. 79–93).

BELSIZE PARK GARDENS is the most impressive stretch, a grandiose and relentless march s of massive paired palazzi with Ionic porches and robust vermiculated quoins. The only diversions are at the ends. Nos. 2c and 2d, at the back of a N corner site, almost hidden behind a high wall, is an elegantly minimal one-storeyed pair of houses by *Spence & Webster*, 1978–81, built for themselves. A bold demonstration of a radically different form of housing, associated with China or Chicago rather than with London's urban traditions. The houses look inward to a shared central courtyard. Each has a compact plan, without corridors, with a central service area and spacious rooms at either end, the living area on the garden side divisible by screens. At the far s end of Belsize Park Gardens, Nos. 83–89, a well-composed group of homely brick Willett houses of 1896, display the late Victorian reaction against stuccoed pomp.

To the E, BELSIZE GROVE runs towards Haverstock Hill. The earlier terrace near its E end, Nos. 26–38, is typical of the attractively modest scale of the 1820s: stuccoed with central pediment, reticently detailed, set back behind generous front gardens. In HAVERSTOCK HILL, Nos. 129–133, a taller group, brick above stucco, with projecting pedimented centre, is part of the same development. No. 148 opposite, CROWN LODGE, is a small Grecian villa of the earlier C19, with stuccoed front, paterae and pilasters, an isolated survival among the usual main road mixture of late Victorian houses and C20 flats. The best landmark further downhill is the LOAD OF HAY, a handsome Italianate pub dated 1863.

*4c. South of England's Lane and Eton Avenue*

The lower slopes of the hill are described roughly from E to W, starting from Chalk Farm Underground Station at the foot of Haverstock Hill. CHALK FARM derives its name from Chalcots, an estate owned by Eton College, which began to make plans for the area already in the 1820s, although nothing was built until *c.* 1840. The long straight streets lined with respectable but plain mid-Victorian villas and terraces were never very exciting, and much was rebuilt in the C20. More appealing patches are a picturesque triangle of early development (Eton Villas), and some artistically inspired groups built after 1870.

In ADELAIDE ROAD there has been much rebuilding; only seven pairs of substantial but plain stuccoed houses of c. 1845, by the developer *Samuel Cuming*, survive on the s side. To the N, reached by ETON COLLEGE ROAD, is an attractive triangle of more complete streets – PROVOST ROAD, ETON ROAD, and ETON VILLAS, with St Saviour's Church (q.v.) as their focus. These smaller middle-class villas built in the 1840s–50s, reminiscent of 78 Nash's earlier Park Villages and the contemporary St John's Wood, reflect the more refined taste of the Eton Estate surveyor *John Shaw Jun.* They are mostly semi-detached, with rendered fronts and shallow shared gables in a rustic Italian manner, but with restrained Grecian detail for the window surrounds. In a different spirit, but also of an appealing intimacy, is BEAUMONT WALK, at the corner of Eton Road and Adelaide Road, a homely brown brick cluster of three-storey buildings, with a mixture of 44 houses and flats. 1976 by the *GLC Architect's Department* (*J. Bancroft, D. Parris, N. Hamdi*). Appearance and lay-out, with private spaces and a network of little paths set with poetic quotations, illustrate the new efforts at this time to provide imaginative and flexible public housing on a friendly scale. Interiors were constructed to permit easy internal alterations, based on the theories of the Dutch architect J. N. Habraken.

The area immediately N of Eton Road, where Richard Steele's cottage retreat stood in the C18, was not built up until the 1870s, and then attracted artists' houses similar in spirit to those built elsewhere in Hampstead at this time. The detached, highly individual examples in STEELE'S ROAD are mostly by *Batterbury & Huxley*, and are very much in the vanguard of the new taste: of red brick, with brick decoration, floral tiles and Dutch and Queen Anne motifs just beginning to appear. As the N-facing studios are at the back, the houses have a fairly conventional villa appearance from the street. From w to E: No. 39, 1872, still Gothic and gabled; No. 38, with rubbed red bricks, and No. 37, Gothic again, both of 1873; No. 36, with Dutch gables, 1875; No. 35, 1875, with very deep cove and emphatic dormers. Nos. 32 (1876) and 31 (1874) are by *J. M. Brydon*, but altered. At the SE end, STEELE'S MEWS, with arches to N and S, but much rebuilt behind. Nearby, but approached from England's Lane, WYCHCOMBE STUDIOS, 81 a curious oasis by *Batterbury*, 1879–80, with three studio blocks around a little garden. No. 6 is a substantial house by *Paskin Kyriades Sands*, completed 1989, brimming with fashionable details of its time; double gable with circular window, curved balcony, glass bricks. Backing onto Steele's Road, CHALCOT GARDENS, off England's Lane, has more studios: No. 15 is by *Batterbury & Huxley* for Hal Ludlow, 1883, with half-timbered garden studio. No. 16 is of 1881, but with front and back additions of 1898 by *Voysey* for Adolphus Whalley. Arthur Rackham had a studio here from 1903.

ENGLAND'S LANE was an old lane which (like part of Belsize Lane) became a small shopping street in the later C19, with stucco-trimmed terraces on the N side. To its N, hemmed in close to the Library (*see* Public Buildings), No. 15 ANTRIM GROVE, a small stuccoed house of c. 1820, a survivor from the rural villas once scattered over this area. Further w, opening off Primrose Hill

Road, is the sequence of long parallel roads which carved up the hillside and formed the main C19 development of the Eton Estate. ETON AVENUE, continuing England's Lane, is the latest and most characterful part, a *Willett* development begun *c.* 1886, with houses designed by *H. B. Measures*, their terracotta trimmings and shaped gables acknowledging the artistic trends of the 1870s (see especially Nos. 43–45, 57–65). Later houses by *Amos Faulkner* (e.g. No. 13, 1904). The plainer nature of the earlier FELLOWS ROAD to the s (1860 onwards) is still evident from the pale brick houses with tall basements along the N side.

The s side and all of the w part of ADELAIDE ROAD was for long under threat from the inner ring road, first proposed in the 1940s. After this had been abandoned it was eventually rebuilt in 1965–70. The rehousing scheme for 3,680 people was a joint public and private venture, designed by *Dennis Lennon & Partners*. An array of twenty-three-storey concrete tower blocks of Camden council flats is starkly juxtaposed with closes of plain low-rise private housing. On the s side, GROUP MEDICAL PRACTICE by *Pentarch*, a later addition of 1992, quite dramatically sited over a car park and approached like a ship by a gangway from the street. Timber-clad, with toplit central waiting room, and a shallow curved roof with deep projecting eaves. Further w, the REGENTS PARK MARRIOTT HOTEL (formerly the HOLIDAY INN). Part of the original scheme by *Dennis Lennon & Partners*; in a diffidently frivolous Mediterranean manner, with round-headed arches and a light grid of balconies.

HARLEY ROAD to the s has a few houses remaining from the 1870s; beyond lies the leafy enclave of WADHAM GARDENS and the w part of ELSWORTHY ROAD, built up after 1895 on the site of the Eton and Middlesex Cricket Ground. The substantial houses, detached but tightly packed, are grouped picturesquely along the curved roads. This is another *Willett* development, mostly by *Amos F. Faulkner*, here employing the comfortably relaxed eclecticism of the Arts and Crafts movement in almost indigestible profusion. The area abounds in judicious alternation of patterned tile-hanging and roughcast, domed corner bays, asymmetrical gables and mullioned windows, and pretty porches with shell hoods or roofs suspended from iron ties. Nos. 45–51 Elsworthy Road are especially good examples.

AVENUE ROAD, running s, has a little more from the 1890s in a similar spirit, e.g., on the w side (in the City of Westminster), Nos. 45, 43, and 31, and a few others further s. No. 29, an early C19 Neo-Grecian villa, recalls the earlier phase of development here, related to the growth of St John's Wood to the w (see *London 3: North West*, St Marylebone). On the E side No. 16 is a handsomely proportioned formal design of *c.* 1900, with dentilled cornice and brick quoins; but the rest is now largely flaccid between-the-wars Neo-Georgian, mixed with even less appealing later flats.

### 4d. East of Haverstock Hill and Rosslyn Hill

The eastern strip of Hampstead, which merges into Kentish Town in the old borough of St Pancras (q.v.), consists of a disparate mixture of public and private housing.

Off Haverstock Hill near Belsize Park Station, the RUSSELL NURSERIES ESTATE, Camden housing of 1987–90 (*Bill Forrest* and *Oscar Palacio*), was the borough's last new-build housing; plain pale brick terraces, a fancy baldacchino at the entrance. Further s, PARKHILL ROAD and UPPER PARK ROAD were laid out with substantial villas from 1862, mostly by the builder *Richard Batterbury*. Squeezed among them is No. 30a Parkhill Road, a minute house by *Hugh Cullum* and *Richard Nightingale*, 1983–8. An irregular front with an angled bay; white render above a dark-banded ground floor. Cleverly planned, with a formal double-height toplit centre, a staircase tucked behind the hearth, and an asymmetrical bow to catch the sun on the garden side. On the w side, BARNFIELD and WOODFIELD, two long blocks of decent post-war council flats in a Neo-Georgian spirit, *c.* 1948–50 by *Farquarson & McMorran*. In TASKER ROAD, the MALL STUDIOS of 1872 by *Thomas Batterbury*; residents between the wars included Herbert Read, Ben Nicolson, Barbara Hepworth and Henry Moore. At the e end, three compact brick houses by *Walter Segal*, 1963, projecting garage wings, glazed garden fronts.

GARNETT ROAD has some of Hampstead's earliest borough housing, very plain five-storey blocks by the Borough Engineer *O. E. Winter*, 1905–6. Near the n end of LAWN ROAD, the ISOKON FLATS, built in 1934 by *Wells Coates*, a milestone in the introduction of the modern idiom to London. The flats 'put a forbidding face towards the street, with large unmitigated concrete surfaces, especially the long horizontals of heavy balcony parapets and the diagonals of staircase parapets. It is all in a spirit of revolution, unaccommodating and direct to the verge of brutality.' Thus Pevsner described the flats in 1952. The building was commissioned by the furniture designer Jack Pritchard and his wife, in place of the private house they had originally intended. The name comes from Isometric Unit Construction, the building company Pritchard set up in 1932; the object was to provide inexpensive accommodation for young professional people. The four-storey block was planned with 22 'minimum flats' for single people, each provided with much built-in furniture, larger flats at the s end, and a rooftop penthouse for the Pritchards. The reinforced concrete structure was based on a 10-ft 8-in. module related to the width of the main rooms, so that no internal columns were necessary; the narrow shape of the flats is defined externally by the balcony brackets. The progressive spirit was enhanced by a residents' club known as the Isobar, created on the ground floor in 1937 by *F. R. S. Yorke* and *Marcel Breuer* (who was one of several eminent artistic refugee residents in the 1930s). The flats passed to Camden in 1972. In 1983–4 the concrete was repainted off-white (the original colour was a pale greyish pink).

Further N, past the curious contrast of Nos. 21–25 Lawn Road, a well-detailed traditional Arts and Crafts group of *c.* 1934, to FLEET ROAD. On the s side is the DUNBOYNE ROAD ESTATE, precise white-rendered ranges with distinctive slit-eyed windows, a Camden housing scheme designed by *Neave Brown* in 1966, although not carried out until 1969. It had much influence on later borough housing as an early alternative to high-rise. Three paired blocks, with nothing over four storeys. Tightly planned, with ingenious provision of carefully delineated (but somewhat overlooked) private and public spaces on different levels, including generous communal roof gardens. The concentration on upper levels developed from the introduction of garages (this was the first Camden scheme to provide a garage space for each dwelling). The 1960s interest in elaborate traffic segregation is reflected in the unhappily hefty ramps, planned as part of an unexecuted scheme for upper-level walkways over Southampton Road to connect with the big new housing areas of Gospel Oak (*see* St Pancras, Perambulation 4b). The two big point blocks of the Borough of Hampstead's FLEET ROAD ESTATE, 1960–3 (*E. F. Jacob*), show what Camden was rejecting. Further N, Nos. 4–32 FLEET ROAD demonstrate a more contextual approach: housing for Abeona Cooperative, 1988–91 by *Anthony Richardson Partnership*, conversions with discreet new parts behind.

Back w past the little centre of SOUTH END GREEN with granite Gothic DRINKING FOUNTAIN of 1880 by *J. H. Evin*. Up POND STREET dominated by the Royal Free Hospital (q.v.), to the main road, here called ROSSLYN HILL. Just to the N, HAMPSTEAD HILL GARDENS has an enclave of red brick artists' villas of 1875–83, largely by *Batterbury & Huxley*. Their steep tiled roofs and dormers group picturesquely around the curve of the road. They start with No. 12 Rosslyn Hill, 1876–7; and, opposite, No. 1 (Sunnycote) Hampstead Hill Gardens, dated 1876, enlarged by *Batterbury & Huxley* in 1883. No. 3 was enlarged by the same in 1881; Nos. 5 and 7, probably also by them, are of 1879; No. 5 has a surprisingly formal five-bay front, with curly lintels to Neo-Georgian sashes. No.9, 1879, was built for the watercolour painter Thomas Collier; No. 2 is of 1881.

## 4e. Swiss Cottage and Finchley Road

SWISS COTTAGE is a busy junction overlooked by an ill-assorted medley of different dates. The SWISS COTTAGE appeared in the 1840s as an inn on the new Finchley Road. Rebuilt and enlarged since, but still a low chalet, whose backdrop from 1937 has been the ODEON CINEMA, a good tall straightforward brick block by *H. Weedon*, and REGENCY LODGE, one of *R. Atkinson*'s blocks of flats, good, though a trifle stodgy in the English manner, and with some mannerisms in the mouldings. To the w, in AVENUE ROAD, in place of the public building previously intended here, No. 100, by *Architectural Design Associates* (formerly *Ted Levy, Benjamin & Partners*), 1981–4, is a cream travertine-faced slab of offices with crisp red trimmings in the fashion of the day, tactfully stepping down from six to three storeys as it approaches the community buildings and open space to the s. Its back faces onto THE SQUARE, intended in the 1960s to be the setting for a grand civic complex (*see* Public Buildings).

FINCHLEY ROAD was laid out as a turnpike road from 1826 by Colonel Eyre, owner of the Eyre Estate, on which St John's Wood developed (see *London 3: North West*, St Marylebone). The w side near the Swiss Cottage is largely C20: No. 137, CENTRE HEIGHTS, is an early example of the concrete idiom of the 1960s (1961 by

*Douglas Stephen* and *Parios Koulermos).* A low interlude of a boldly detailed gabled Edwardian shopping parade (Nos.167–173), with stone pilasters carrying large balls, is followed by ST JOHN'S COURT, No. 191 by *T.P. Bennett,* 1936–8, which shows that modern clichés such as window bands and long balconies sweeping round corners do not prevent the unconvinced user of such forms from indulging in polygonal bay windows as well. Opposite, COLLEGE CRESCENT, named after the Nonconformist college which used to be here, with a few battered stuccoed houses, and an octagonal granite Gothic DRINKING FOUNTAIN of 1904 (a memorial to Samuel Palmer, biscuit manufacturer). The crescent is a prelude to the mid-Victorian development of Belsize to the E (*see* Perambulation 4b). N of Finchley Road Station, on former railway land, shops and leisure centre by *Hellmuth Obata & Kassabaum,* planned 1996. S of Finchley and Frognal Station, in LITHOS ROAD, housing by *Pollard Thomas & Edwards* for the Notting Hill Housing Group, 1992; a long range with striped brickwork and steel balconies squeezed onto a tight site by the railway line.

## 5. West Hampstead

### 5a. From Kilburn to Fortune Green

The development of the northern part of West Hampstead dates entirely from the late C19 onwards. It is divided from Hampstead proper by the C19 creation of Finchley Road; a land of minor late Victorian terraces and mansion flats which in 1952 Pevsner considered worth visiting only by those in search of Victorian churches: 'The houses and streets require no notice'. Few of the patches of council housing and private flats that have arrived since are of much merit, although they have broken the monotony and given the older survivals some rarity value. The neighbourhood grew after the arrival of the three railway lines, the Hampstead Junction (1860), the Midland (1868) and the Metropolitan Line (1879), which later opened stations on West End Lane. Before this there was only the retired hamlet of West End, down the hill from Frognal: its former centre is still marked by a small green at the junction of West End Lane and Mill Lane, where the Fire Station (*see* Public Buildings) is the best building. Round about was a scatter of gentlemen's houses, which disappeared as piecemeal development extended over the land E and W of the main thoroughfare. This consists of Fortune Green Road climbing N from the green towards Cricklewood, and West End Lane winding S from it towards Kilburn on the parish boundary with Paddington.

The OLD BELL by Kilburn High Road Station on Edgware Road is an average main-road pub of 1863, oblivious of its history. It marks the site of a little C18 resort, although there is nothing now to recall the medicinal springs and pleasure gardens that once attracted Londoners on their excursions from the city. Earlier still this was the site of Kilburn Priory, a nunnery founded in 1139, now recalled only by a few street names. Further S, GREVILLE ROAD and GREVILLE PLACE were built up in 1819–25 by *George Pocock* on the Abbey Farm Estate, and share something of the character of St John's Wood to the s. Other early suburban development in this area was replaced by post-war council housing, chiefly the KILBURN PRIORY ESTATE, the earliest parts with decent brick blocks, not too crowded, of 1948–57, by *J. B. K. Cowper*. Around PRIORY ROAD an enclave of trim mid-C19 stuccoed streets remains around St Mary's Church. Further N along West End Lane one can sample the variety of suburban forms developed over the last hundred years. KING'S GARDENS are superior mansion flats of 1897; WOODCHURCH ROAD has an attractive assortment of detached houses of 1878. At the w corner with West End Lane, SIDNEY BOYD COURT, a Hampstead Borough showpiece of 1953: six- and seven-storeyed centre with curved front and modish balconies; four-storey staircase-access blocks behind. At the e end, OLIVE WAITE HOUSE, old people's flats on a beehive plan of flat-roofed hexagons by *Noel Moffet & Associates*, 1967. Ingeniously angled views, but disappointingly detailed. Based on their similar scheme at White City, Hammersmith. N of the railway lines, in LYMINGTON ROAD, low-rise housing for Camden by *Sheppard Robson & Partners*, completed 1980, tightly packed pantiled-roofed terraces at r. angles to the road. Apart from the taller pair on a deck above garages, a decided departure from the style of Camden's own grand schemes of the 1970s.

Between West End Lane and Kilburn High Road the meaner late C19 terraces began to be replaced by council housing in the 1970s, but by the 1980s a mixture of rehabilitation and rebuilding had become the pattern. Further N, FORTUNE GREEN, surrounded by small, more haphazard C19 houses, is still somewhat rural in feeling. It was saved from development in 1897. In FORTUNE GREEN ROAD, opposite the entrance to the Hampstead Cemetery (q.v.), No. 128, an oddity, with the most flamboyant stucco Graeco-Egyptian detail, of the kind that was favoured in cemeteries in the earlier C19, built for the monumental mason Cramb, *c.* 1886.

### 5b. Abbey Road and Alexandra Road

Two prominent council schemes close to the railway line epitomize the ambitions of borough housing in the period which reached its apogee in the late 1960s. Comprehensive rebuilding of this northern fringe of the Eyre Estate was discussed from 1959. The first stage was the ABBEY ESTATE, planned in the early 1960s by *Austin-Smith, Salmon, Lord Partnership* for Hampstead Borough Council, but not built until 1965. It consists of an ungainly group of three coarsely detailed twenty-storey towers, a grossly ugly multi-storey car park and a pair of eight-storey slabs. They are awkwardly linked by bridges across Abbey Road and Belsize Road, a half-hearted demonstration of the 1960s concern with pedestrian segregation, for the convenience of the traffic clearly comes first. Slabs and car park have unrelenting horizontal aggregate-faced concrete bands to their upper floors. Shops, a health centre and a community centre (refurbished 1991 by *Neil Thomson Associates*) provide a little relief at ground level.

The long curving swathe of concrete terraces to the s of the railway line between Abbey Road and Loudoun Road, on the site of ALEXANDRA ROAD, is in many ways a reaction to the type of housing provided by the Abbey Estate. The building dates are 1972–8, but the detailed design by Camden's project architect *Neave Brown* goes back to 1969, when the Borough Architect's Department was at its most innovative and energetic. Other

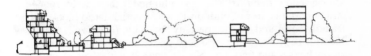

Alexandra Road Estate. Section, looking east

members of the team included *Lynn Cohen, Graham Frost, Geoffrey Griffiths*, and *Gordon Benson* and *Alan Forsyth* (cf. Branch Hill, Perambulation 2a). The early 1960s proposals for a mixture of private and public housing in low terraces and towers (cf. Adelaide Road, Perambulation 4c) were rejected in favour of council housing only, arranged in three long ranges, for 1,664 people, at the highest permissible density (210 p.p.a.), with all vehicles banished to the level beneath, and generous open space at ground level. The design is closely related to contemporary Camden schemes exploring alternatives to high-rise, such as Fleet Road (Perambulation 4d) and Highgate New Town (*see* St Pancras), a quest influenced by earlier studies by Sir Leslie Martin, and given urgency by the Ronan Point disaster of 1968. The scheme reflects the 1960s interest in the concept of the megastructure, but unlike the earlier Brunswick Centre in Bloomsbury the flats here are approached directly from the main pedestrian route, giving it the feeling of a traditional street.

Alongside the railway a six-storey barrier block is cantilevered out over the tracks like the underside of a vast grandstand. The stepped-back fronts of these flats overlook a gently curving pedestrian walk, ROWLEY WAY, with a lower terrace of maisonettes on the other side. The array of concrete cells, with their forceful repetitive pattern of sloping dividing walls, seems to stretch to infinity, a breathtakingly grand conception. The open flights of steps to the upper flats seem uncomfortably steep and narrow, but the flats themselves have generous balconies, and the stepped-back profile gives them plenty of light. The lower terrace has a friendlier and smoother face to the s side, where it looks onto a large green. Beyond this are three low blocks of houses. The open space is heavily landscaped and divided up by play areas, approached rather unhappily by tall concrete walled alleys. At either end are community buildings. The play centre at the w end is a low concrete bunker hidden among trees, a late arrival of 1981; near the e end a mixture of buildings on different levels and by different architects creates greater variety: in addition to a community centre, there are two buildings by *Evans & Shalev*, both discreetly sited and so difficult to appreciate. Their well-detailed exteriors combine dark-stained timber windows with fairfaced concrete blockwork. The northern building, in LANGTRY WALK, was built as a children's reception centre but functioned as such only briefly (conversion to housing under discussion, 1998). The southern one, No. 48 BOUNDARY ROAD, was planned as a home for young disabled people, innovative at the time for its combination of private rooms with their own s-facing outdoor terraces. The spatially ingenious toplit communal areas incorporated wheelchair ramps as a deliberately forceful element of the design. Converted by *Evans & Shalev* as a home for the elderly, 1996–7. At the entrance from Loudoun Road two brick-faced blocks on a friendly scale add to the diversity, both by *Tom Kay Associates*: No. 49, 1975–80, with workshops under a stepped range of two-storey houses and flats, and No. 61, 1974–9, with n-facing studios above shops. Further w, between Boundary Road and BOUNDARY MEWS, housing of the 90s is represented by a group of flats by *Avanti Architects*, 1995–6, for Notting Hill Home Ownership. Attached to an older terrace and discreetly contextual to the road, with more innovative pavilion blocks behind.

# HOLBORN

## INTRODUCTION

Holborn derives its name from the Holbourne, the name given to the part of the River Fleet running down to the Thames along the valley W of the City. Farringdon Street follows its line. The Roman road leading from the City, which crossed the river where Holborn Viaduct now stands and climbed the steep hill to its W, became known as Holborn and High Holborn. From the Middle Ages grand suburban houses were built along Holborn. A number of them became lawyers' colleges; by the C17 these precincts stretched from N to S down to the Thames; the two surviving ones in Holborn are Gray's Inn and Lincoln's Inn. Still further W the manor house of Bloomsbury stood in open country to the N, while the main road passed through the small settlement of St Giles-in the-Fields, which originated as a medieval leper hospital.

The big individual establishments close to the City included the Bishop of Ely's London mansion, a courtyard house which stood in what is now Ely Place; its late C13 chapel survives as the Church of St Etheldreda. From the later C16 the Elizabethan courtier Sir Christopher Hatton occupied part of the site, and in the early C17 the poet Fulke Greville, Lord Brooke, had a house nearby. Holborn could not rival the sequence of palaces along the Strand to the S, but the fashionable new gabled frontages built for Lord Greville and for the formidable Lady Hatton, wife of Edward Coke, were possibly p. 15

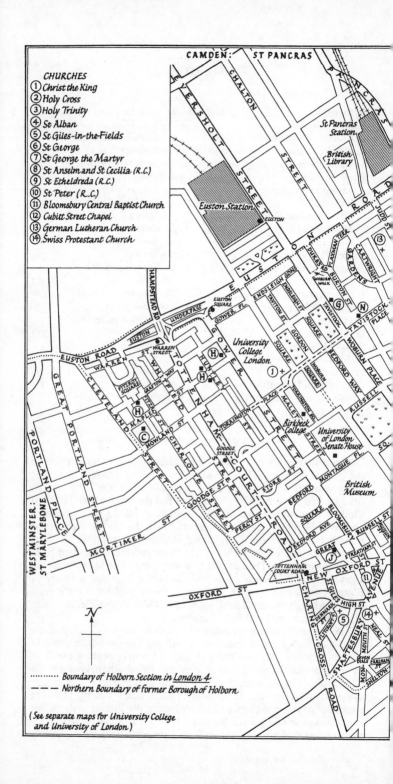

CAMDEN: ST PANCRAS

CHURCHES
① Christ the King
② Holy Cross
③ Holy Trinity
④ St Alban
⑤ St Giles-in-the-Fields
⑥ St George
⑦ St George the Martyr
⑧ St Anselm and St Cecilia (R.C.)
⑨ St Etheldreda (R.C.)
⑩ St Peter (R.C.)
⑪ Bloomsbury Central Baptist Church
⑫ Cubitt Street Chapel
⑬ German Lutheran Church
⑭ Swiss Protestant Church

St Pancras Station

British Library

Euston Station

EUSTON

WESTMINSTER: ST MARYLEBONE

EUSTON ROAD

University College London

University of London Senate House

British Museum

N

·········· Boundary of Holborn Section in London 4
— — — Northern Boundary of former Borough of Holborn

( See separate maps for University College
  and University of London )

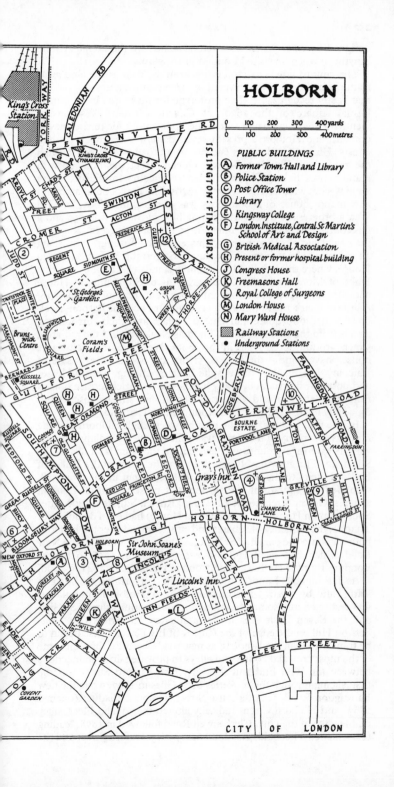

# HOLBORN

| 0 | 100 | 200 | 300 | 400 yards |
| 0 | 100 | 200 | 300 | 400 metres |

**PUBLIC BUILDINGS**

Ⓐ Former Town Hall and Library
Ⓑ Police Station
Ⓒ Post Office Tower
Ⓓ Library
Ⓔ Kingsway College
Ⓕ London Institute, Central St Martin's
    School of Art and Design
Ⓖ British Medical Association
Ⓗ Present or former hospital building
Ⓙ Congress House
Ⓚ Freemasons Hall
Ⓛ Royal College of Surgeons
Ⓜ London House
Ⓝ Mary Ward House

▨ Railway Stations
● Underground Stations

King's Cross Station

KING'S CROSS (THAMESLINK)

PENTONVILLE RD

YORK WAY

CALEDONIAN RD

KING'S CROSS RD

ISLINGTON : FINSBURY

SWINTON ST

ACTON ST

FREDERICK ST

CROMER ST

ARGYLE ST

CHADS ST

REGENT SQUARE

SIDMOUTH ST

JUDD ST

St George's Gardens

GOUGH ST

WREN ST

CALTHORPE ST

PAKENHAM ST

GRAY'S INN ROAD

GUILFORD STREET

MECKLENBURGH SQUARE

DOUGHTY STREET

Coram's Fields

Brunswick Centre

TAVISTOCK PLACE

HUNTER ST

MARCHMONT ST

BRUNSWICK SQUARE

BERNARD ST

RUSSELL SQUARE

GUILFORD STREET

MILLMAN STREET

JOHN STREET

SOUTHAMPTON ROW

QUEEN SQUARE

GREAT ORMOND STREET

CONDUIT ST

ORMOND ST

HORTHINGTON STREET

BEDFORD PL

BEDFORD SQUARE

BURY PLACE

BLOOMSBURY WAY

NEW OXFORD ST

HIGH HOLBORN

MUSEUM ST

PROCTER ST

RED LION SQUARE

PRINCETON ST

RED LION STREET

THEOBALDS ROAD

JOCKEY'S FIELDS

Grays Inn

BOURNE ESTATE

PORTPOOL LANE

LEATHER LANE

CLERKENWELL ROAD

HATTON GARDEN

SAFFRON HILL

FARRINGDON ROAD

ROSEBERY AVE

FARRINGDON

GREVILLE ST

ELY PLACE

CHARTERHOUSE ST

HOLBORN

HIGH HOLBORN

CHANCERY LANE

BROOKES MARKET

Sir John Soane's Museum

Lincoln's Inn

LINCOLN'S INN FIELDS

KINGSWAY

STUKELEY ST

PARKER ST

MACKLIN ST

QUEEN ST

WILD ST

GREAT QUEEN ST

SARDINIA ST

LONG ACRE

ENDELL ST

COVENT GARDEN

ALDWYCH

STRAND

FLEET STREET

FETTER LANE

CITY OF LONDON

Cromer St
Frederick St
Old Gloucester St
Dombey St
Lamb's Conduit St

① ② ③ ④ ⑥ ⑦ ⑧ ⑨ ⑩ ⑫

designed by *Inigo Jones*, and were sketched by the architect John Smythson when he visited London in 1618–19.

The countryside began to disappear in the C17, as the land away from the main roads was covered by streets and squares in a pattern that is still recognizable. The prototype for these was Inigo Jones's formal square of the 1630s at Covent Garden, Westminster. Gentlemen entrepreneurs seized the opportunity for further development, and Holborn's present street pattern owes much to their efforts. Hatton Garden was laid out as a broad new street through the grounds of Ely House. Great Queen Street was built up with grand houses, linking Covent Garden to Lincoln's Inn Fields, whose s and w sides were developed by the 1640s. The Earl of Southampton's new manor house of Bloomsbury was also begun before the Civil War, a progressive design with a long hipped-roofed frontage and a forecourt in the French manner. After 1661 it formed the N side of the newly laid out Bloomsbury Square. More houses grew up along an old lane to its w, now Great Russell Street; the largest, Montagu House, where the British Museum now stands was built by the first Duke of Montagu in 1676. The grounds of Southampton House and Montagu House stretched into open country until the mid C18. A little to their E the notorious speculator Dr Nicholas Barbon developed Red Lion Square and Queen Square and their surrounding streets from the 1670s; to the s, Thomas Neale laid out the radiating streets around Seven Dials in the 1690s. Nearly all the really large houses have gone – the best survivors are two on the w side of Lincoln's Inn Fields – but despite later rebuilding, wartime losses and post-war destruction, many handsome red brick terrace houses from this late C17 and early C18 period can still be discovered, especially in Bedford Row and around Great Ormond Street.

By the mid C18 most of the area between High Holborn and the northern boundary of the parish was built up; the Foundling Hospital with its extensive grounds was laid out on the open land just to the N in 1742. The growth of Bloomsbury, on the estate of the Dukes of Bedford, heirs to the Southampton Estate, began in the later C18, with Bedford Square of *c.* 1775, the best preserved of all London squares. Gower Street followed *c.* 1790; Russell Square *c.* 1800, after Southampton House (by then Bedford House) had been demolished. To the N the sequence of squares and streets spread over the Holborn boundary into the parish of St Pancras, up to Euston Road, the New Road which had been laid out across fields in 1756 to bypass London. By 1801 Holborn had 67,000 inhabitants, by 1841, 93,000.

As fashionable London moved w, the City fringe declined in status, and by the C19 a large proportion of Holborn's population was crammed into some of London's most notorious slums: St Giles and the Seven Dials area made famous by Hogarth's *Gin Lane*; Saffron Hill on the edge of the City, N of Ely Place. These began to be transformed in the later C19 as new roads were cut through some of the most crowded courts and alleys to provide better connections between the West End and the City. New Oxford Street was the first, slicing through the rookeries of St Giles in 1847, while the new Farringdon Road, Charterhouse Street, Holborn Viaduct (opened 1869) and Holborn Circus radically altered the squalid Fleet valley on the edge of the City. Clerkenwell Road followed in 1878, leading to a widened Theobalds Road, thence to New Oxford Street and the

new Shaftesbury Avenue of 1886 and Charing Cross Road, opened
1887, while Rosebery Avenue, completed in 1892, provided a new
route to Islington. Along New Oxford Street dignified but hardly
grand buildings were erected; the later streets were meaner, lined with
tall and generally grim mansion blocks to rehouse some of those
displaced by the new roads, a requirement of the Metropolitan
Street Improvements Act of 1877. The most extensive area of new
working-class flats was in the area s of Clerkenwell Road near St
Alban's Church, mostly now rebuilt, although the LCC's Bourne
Estate of 1901–7 still remains as a reminder of the pressure to provide
housing in this area. Another area of public and philanthropic housing developed around Judd Street, s of Euston Road (originally within
the old borough of St Pancras). The only effort at Edwardian
grandeur was Kingsway, the new N–S route leading to the Strand,
achieved after many decades of unsuccessful plans to provide an
improved route leading N from the Strand. It still retains much of its
Beaux Arts panache, lined with commercial buildings on a colossal
scale. Others appeared in Holborn and High Holborn, where the
principal survivors range in style from the monumental Gothic of the
Prudential to the overblown Baroque of the former Pearl Assurance
Building.

Elsewhere institutions were taking over. Some started in the private
houses of professional men when Holborn was still a respectable
residential area. The collections which formed the nucleus of the
British Museum were at first in Sir Hans Sloane's house in Bloomsbury
Place. From 1759 they were in Montagu House, until this was replaced
from 1823 by the Museum's own monumental Grecian premises. Sir
John Soane's Museum was established in his own house in Lincoln's
Inn Fields, and still remains there, preserved according to his bequest
of 1837 as a highly individual combination of museum and dwelling
house. Specialized hospitals, of which Holborn has a large quota,
also often started in private houses. Queen Square became, and
remains, a centre for these, ending up much rebuilt as a result. London
University similarly took over much of Bloomsbury, although it
started on an open site with William Wilkins's grand Neoclassical
buildings for University College, begun in 1827 at the still unbuilt N
end of Gower Street.

The combined result of slum clearance, commercial expansion and
the growth of institutions was a decline in the residential population:
1861: 93,000; 1881: 78,000; 1901: 59,000; 1931: 39,000. These
trends were accentuated by the Second World War, in which Holborn
suffered badly, with one seventh of its buildings destroyed. Among
the worst affected areas were those around New Oxford Street, the
w end of Theobalds Road, Brunswick Square, Gray's Inn and
Portpool Lane. Although post-war building included some flats, it
was the growth of offices and institutions (especially the University
and hospitals) at the expense of residential areas that was most
marked. The main routes of Theobalds Road and High Holborn,
the latter once full of inns and theatres, developed into sterile tracts
of vast offices; N of St Giles High Street the tower of Centre Point,
completed in 1966, appeared to herald the expansion of skyscrapers
w from the City. Even new residential development, such as the
radical Brunswick Centre, could be disturbingly disruptive of familiar
patterns, although grand schemes of this type were few, for most of

the new Borough of Camden's major housing schemes of the late 1960s–70s lay outside Holborn. By the early 1970s opposition grew as the erosion of character resulting from piecemeal large-scale rebuilding began to be recognized. The plan for redeveloping much of Covent Garden was abandoned after a public enquiry in 1971, encouraging the preservation of the small streets around Seven Dials. In 1973 the area s of the British Museum was reprieved when the site for the new British Library was moved to St Pancras. The following year Camden initiated repairs to the long neglected terrace houses on the Rugby Estate in the neighbourhood of Great Ormond Street. A similar change of attitude prevented the completion of the expanded university precinct as originally planned by Sir Denys Lasdun, and produced university buildings more deferential to Bloomsbury's past, although whether this invariably produced architectural benefits is debatable. In the 1980s–90s a policy of repair and tactful infilling became more widespread, rejuvenating also the shabbier parts of C18 Fitzrovia, w of Tottenham Court Road. Exploring the streets off the main routes can now be rewarding for new as well as older buildings.

Holborn's surviving churches are not numerous but rank high in quality and variety. The oldest is the former private chapel of the Bishop of Ely, a progressive design of the late C13 (now the R.C. Church of St Etheldreda). The medieval parish church, St Andrew Holborn, rebuilt by *Wren*, lies within the City of London (*see London 1: The City of London*). It was supplemented as the City expanded westward by one of the most majestic of London's C18 churches, *Hawksmoor*'s St George Bloomsbury. Not far from it St George Queen Square originated as a modest proprietary chapel for the new suburb (its interior modified by an individual C19 recasting by *Teulon*). Further s the church of the separate parish of St Giles-in-the-Fields was handsomely rebuilt in the C18 by *Flitcroft*. Later Anglican efforts have been much diminished by demolition* or, in the case of *Butterfield*'s St Alban, by extensive rebuilding, but two rewarding C19 churches remain which were built for other denominations: *Brandon*'s former Catholic Apostolic Church, with an exceptionally sumptuous Gothic interior (now the University Church of Christ the King) and *Bryson*'s R.C. St Peter Clerkenwell Road, which surprises with Early Christian. As for the C20, Edwardian classicism is demonstrated with aplomb by *Belcher & Joass*'s Holy Trinity Kingsway, Gothic eclecticism by *Walters*'s St Anselm and St Cecilia, latest Gothic Revival more quietly by *Adrian Scott*'s post-war rebuilding of St Alban.

## RELIGIOUS BUILDINGS

### 1. Church of England

CHRIST THE KING (University of London Chaplaincy), Gordon Square. Built for the Catholic Apostolic Church in 1853 by *Raphael Brandon* (author of *An Analysis of Gothic Architecture*). Studiously E.E., on a cathedral scale and in cathedral style, the

---

* Demolished: Christ Church, Woburn Square, by *L. Vulliamy*, 1831–2; St John, Red Lion Square, by *J. L. Pearson*, 1874–8; St Peter, Saffron Hill, by *Barry*, 1830–2; also Scottish Presbyterian Church, Regent Square, by *Tite*, 1824–7. *See also* p. 340n.

first large building for this sect which had developed from the Irvingites *c*. 1837. Eastlake described it enthusiastically in 1872 as 'one of the largest and most imposing churches in England ... Its internal length is 212 ft; width from north to south of transepts 77 ft ... Built of Bath stone, with groined chancel and presbytery ... the central tower and spire to be carried up 300 ft.' The spire was never built and the exterior, with its mechanical Bath stone surfaces, is less impressive than the lofty interior, which has a full-dress gallery above the arcades and a tall lancet clerestory. The nave (intended to be two bays longer) has a richly ornamented hammerbeam roof; the choir is on three levels, and has a multi-ribbed stone vault, diapered spandrels, and other scholarly Gothic detail of the 1230s–40s, i.e. the period of Lincoln Cathedral nave and Westminster Abbey choir. Many of the original choir furnishings remain, reflecting the elaborate ritual practised by the Apostolic Church: special reading desks, 'Angel's throne', stalls for the 'Apostles' or elders. Oil lamps were used instead of candles. The church was planned to be served by a staff of sixty-four.* The most original feature is the thin tripartite Dec screen behind the altar, opening into an E chapel, originally the assembly place of the Apostles. It has blank arcading round the walls, large roof bosses and much other decorative carving. STAINED GLASS by *Lilian Pocock*. The S transept rose is by *Archibald Nicholson*.

The church is entered from an arcaded cloister walk on the N side. Next to this, THE CLOISTERS, built as flats for the clergy; the asymmetrical four-bay Gothic façade has a big bay window with bold tracery and a long stone balcony.

HOLY CROSS, Cromer Street. 1887 by *Joseph Peacock*. Plain tower-less exterior of stock brick with lancets and W bellcote. Dignified, lofty interior: stone arcades, polychrome brick walls, more restrained than some of Peacock's work, although with some odd features, especially the low-starting flying buttresses in the narrow aisles and the demi-strainer arch separating nave from W bay. E end more elaborate, with trefoil-headed arcading and a little carving. FONT in Norman style by *J. L. Pearson*. Many Anglo-Catholic fittings of the early C20; ROOD by *Sir Charles Nicholson*, 1913, tile and mosaic STATIONS OF THE CROSS. Other fittings from Peacock's St Jude, Gray's Inn Road, demolished 1936. STAINED GLASS. Good Shepherd window, S aisle (†1920) by *Martin Travers*; deep colours, heavily leaded.

Former HOLY TRINITY, Kingsway. 1909–11 by *Belcher & Joass*. Built to replace a church in Little Queen Street, demolished for Kingsway in 1909. Redundant in 1992. Plans in 1998 propose retention of the frontage with new commercial building behind, by *Sheppard Robson*. The impressive stone façade is a little like that of Santa Maria della Pace in Rome by Pietro da Cortona. Concave, the curved walls with niches and with urns at the ends. In the centre a semicircular projecting portico crowned by a shallow dome. Behind the porch a tower was meant to rise. It was never built; instead there is only a funny little bellcote. The ornamental detail has the wilful angular classical motifs characteristic of Belcher and even more of Joass. (The plan was a square nave,

---

* See *The Ecclesiologist*, April 1854, pp. 83–8.

with apse. The nave was given a concrete tunnel-vault penetrated by the central windows, instead of the intended dome.)

ST ALBAN, Brooke Street. 1856–62 by *Butterfield*. Built on a congested site in what were at the time some of Holborn's worst slums. The land was given by Lord Leigh and the church paid for by J. G. Hubbard. This was one of Butterfield's most powerful buildings, but only the w tower and clergy house survive to convey the original character. The rest was seriously damaged in 1941 and was rebuilt on the remains of the old walls in 1959–61 to a new design by *Adrian Scott*. *Butterfield*'s big w tower is of red brick with stone bands, and has a saddleback roof (inspired by St Cunibert, Cologne) and a staircase turret climbing to the middle of the w front of the tower. Adjoining to the s, Butterfield's tall CLERGY HOUSE (1859–63) with bachelor flats and communal dining room. Its polychrome brickwork contrasts well with the trees of the small adjacent courtyard. The clever use of the cramped space is clearly modelled on All Saints Margaret Street. *Scott*'s rebuilding of the rest retains something of Butterfield's exterior proportions: very tall nave and tall aisles (a general impression of uprightness whose contrast with the surroundings is maintained by the low new housing to the s and w). But the new work is in plain buff brick, and the window tracery is Scott's. On the s wall, facing the entrance way to the church, a SCULPTURE by *Hans Feibusch*, 1985: a half-figure of Jesus being raised from the dead.

The original interior was one of Butterfield's most lively works, with much abstract polychrome patterning in white stone, brown and red brick, and brown terracotta (used for wall-shafts). The blind E gable wall had a grid of frescoes designed by *Henry Styleman le Strange* and completed by *Frederick Preedy*. Scott's interior is quite different; calm and restrained Gothic in pale stone, tall arcades without capitals, no clerestory, transversely vaulted aisles. The main adornment is a staggeringly large and dramatic MURAL on the E gable wall, by *Hans Feibusch*, 1966, in predominantly pastel shades of blue and mauve: The Trinity in Glory, surrounded by a large number of muscular figures including the clergy of St Alban's. STATIONS OF THE CROSS, painted panels, also by *Feibusch*.

From the beginning the church was famous as a controversial centre of Anglo-Catholic ritual, but most of the elaborate FURNISHINGS were lost in the war.\* Something of their character is conveyed by the survivals, mostly at the w end. MACKONOCHIE CHAPEL to the SW, used as a weekday chapel, 1890 by *C. H. M. Mileham*. An effective re-creation of a richly decorated late medieval chantry chapel: highly ornamented walls with much carving, stone vault, carved REREDOS, and STAINED GLASS by *Kempe*, 1892. It contains the MONUMENT to the first vicar, Rev. A. Mackonochie †1887; recumbent marble effigy in a Perp wall niche with painted background. In the w vestry (former mortuary chapel), WALL PAINTING on the w wall; Christ in the Sepulchre, 1890 by *Christopher Whall*, and three windows by *Kempe*. – MONUMENT in the nave: Rev. A. Stanton †1913; fine recumbent bronze effigy by *Hamo Thornycroft* on a Neo-Perp tomb-chest with alabaster angels

---

\*They included a huge REREDOS by *Bodley & Garner*; ROOD by *C. H. M. Mileham*, 1893; elaborate FONT COVER, 1908, and STATIONS OF THE CROSS, 1912 (one of which is preserved), all by *Comper*.

on pinnacles: traditional forms, but the mixture of materials very much of its time. It originally stood in an elaborate chantry chapel by *Ninian Comper*, one of his most important works. – SCULPTURE. Virgin and Child, C17 Italian. Coloured and gilded statue of St Alban, by *Comper*, post-war. S chapel: REREDOS (Pietà and two angels); STAINED GLASS by *Comper*, repainted after 1945. N aisle, E end: STAINED GLASS: three *Kempe* figures reset in clear glass.

CHURCH CENTRE, 1989–91 by *Gordon Fleming* of *Anthony Richardson & Partners*. A visual as well as a functional asset, in pale brick with generous glazing and touches of colour. Adjoining the church to the E, approached from the N choir aisle by a heightened Gothic doorway. The interior spaces interlock most ingeniously. A tall airy foyer alongside the main hall ends in an exhibition tower used to display some of the church's notable VESTMENTS and FABRICS. An upper floor with meeting rooms floats above the main hall, suspended from the shallow segmental girders of the roof, allowing top lighting to reach the sides of the ground floor, a Soanian device. At the E end of the main hall a gallery is thrown across a shallow apse. The w end consists of *Butterfield*'s E gable, its brick textures giving warmth to the white interior. Caretaker's flat on the S side.

ST ANDREW, Holborn. The ancient parish church of Holborn lies just beyond the modern borough boundary: *see London 1: The City of London.*

ST GEORGE, Bloomsbury Way. By *Nicholas Hawksmoor*. One of the churches built under the Fifty New Churches Act of 1711. Begun in 1716, completed 1731, after the Commission had rejected schemes by Gibbs and Vanbrugh, and an earlier scheme by Hawksmoor for a church with an oval plan. Perhaps the most grandiose of all London's C18 churches, with all Hawksmoor's vigour, and less odd in its proportions than e.g. Christ Church Spitalfields. When built it was already hemmed in by houses; the splendid six-column Corinthian portico (the first example of this feature at a London church) is therefore placed on the S side. It has an extra row of columns along the back wall and a coffered ceiling. The idea goes back to Hawksmoor's scheme of 1708–9 for Queen's College, Oxford, and appears again in London churches of the 1720s (St George, Hanover Square; St Martin-in-the-Fields). Here the portico is intended only as a show front, for the main entrances were originally up stairs on the N and S sides of the tower. The tower (built 1729–31) is not in conflict with the portico, but placed to the w, so as to be visible unimpeded from solid base to fanciful spire. The spire is stepped on the example of Pliny's description of the mausoleum of Halicarnassus, and is crowned by a figure of George I. It was formerly made even odder by lion and unicorn supporters at its base (see the miniature reproduction on the lamp-post). The N front of the church, towards Barter Street, is interesting too: stone-faced, like the whole church, very secular and palatial. Five bays in two storeys, two orders and a big pediment, the ground floor with blank arches between windows, the upper-floor windows arched. C19 NW vestry by *J. Peacock*.

The awkward site, longer N–S than E–W, was cleverly handled by Hawksmoor so that the altar could be to the E, as required by the Commissioners. One does not appreciate this now, as the entrance is through the portico, and the altar, moved in 1781, faces one on the N side. Its theatrical frame of two sets of columns was not Hawksmoor's intention. The plan is a square, with different additions on all four sides: a small projection to the W for the former entrance vestibule beneath the tower, an apse to the E with fine plaster vault by *Isaac Mansfield*. N and S sides have coupled columns projecting from the side walls, with bits of architrave, joined by a segmental arch. Behind were N and S galleries, for the Dukes of Bedford and Montagu respectively. To the N the column motif is repeated further back, with two pairs of columns and piers instead of double columns; the space beyond, later occupied by the altar, may have been for a baptistery. In the reordering of 1781 the N gallery was replaced by an E gallery; a W gallery had already been added in 1731. In *Street*'s restoration of 1870–1, E and W galleries were taken out; in 1930 Street's tiles were removed; in 1972–4, under *Laurence King*, the church was redecorated and a glass screen added below the S gallery.

FONT. Small, of 1726. – Excellent mahogany fittings: original REREDOS: niche with big open pediment on Corinthian columns, gilding added 1974. – PULPIT also original; hexagonal with inlaid panels. – ORGAN CASE by *Gray & Davison*, *c.* 1850, from Emmanuel, St John's Wood. – MONUMENT. Beneath the tower. Charles Grant †1823 by *J. Bacon* and *S. Manning*. He is seated, obviously exhausted; a figure of Faith bends over him. His clothes are in the fashion of the day.

ST GEORGE THE MARTYR, Queen Square. Founded in 1705 by a group of gentlemen as a chapel of ease to St Andrew Holborn; the builder was *Arthur Tooley*. It was repaired and beautified by *Hawksmoor* in 1718–20 for the Fifty New Churches Commissioners, adopted as a parish church, and consecrated in 1723. The basic C18 plan survives, a rectangle with domed centre on four columns (probably additions by Hawksmoor), with cruciform arms and four corner rooms. Transformed in 1867–8 by *S. S. Teulon*, who removed two Grecian porches of 1813, stuccoed the exterior and provided a thin Gothic flèche (clock added 1880), larger windows with tracery and some carved decoration. Inside Teulon remodelled the N gallery, removed the other galleries, and formed an elaborately fitted chancel within the S arm, an odd but distinctive imposition. It has a mosaic REREDOS with canopied arches, patterned tiled floor and much distinctive WOODWORK: STALLS and PULPIT are in a minimal punched-out Gothic. Gallery front in the same style. Low marble SCREEN inset with coloured tiles and knobs. C18 baluster FONT with oval gadrooned bowl. The C18 REREDOS remains on the E wall, mahogany, with texts in well-carved surrounds.

ST GILES-IN-THE-FIELDS, St Giles High Street. A leper hospital of St Giles was founded by Queen Matilda in 1101; its chapel, also used as a parish church, survived the Reformation, was rebuilt in 1624–30, and again in 1731–3 by *Henry Flitcroft*. Entirely in the Wren–Gibbs tradition. Flitcroft's design can be seen as a restrained Palladian riposte to the Baroque eccentricities of Hawksmoor, whose plans of 1730 for rebuilding the church were rejected. Stone-faced, with rusticated ground floor. Two tiers of windows, the upper ones round-headed, NW porch. E window of the Venetian variety. W front without portico, its doorway with Gibbs surround and Flitcroft's name prominently displayed above. The steeple rises straight out of the façade. The bell-stage has coupled pilasters just like Gibbs' St Martin which must have been the inspiration for the whole spire. Pretty decoration at the clock stage above. Tall octagonal lantern with attached columns, little balustrade, and obelisk with a number of raised bands around, resulting in a curiously bossy outline. In front of the W façade a GATEWAY of 1800 by *Leverton*. In it, a tympanum with wooden RELIEF of the Resurrection of the Dead, crowded with figures, a copy of the original carved in 1687, which is now in the S porch. The original is signed by *Love*. A very similar one is at St Mary-at-Hill in the City.

The interior is modelled on the pattern of Gibbs' St Martin, i.e. with a wide tunnel vault without clerestory. The aisles are groin-vaulted. Square pillars with Ionic columns above at gallery level. The arches penetrate into the tunnel vault. Reordered by *Blomfield* in 1875; restored by *Butterfield* in 1896. W end with circular lobby flanked by staircases. REREDOS. An eared frame in the manner of Kent, with scrolly pediment on top on which perches a pelican. Separate frames to l. and r. hold paintings of Moses and Aaron by *Francesco Vieira the Younger*, a Portuguese court painter who was in England in 1798–1800. – PULPIT. Hexagonal, fine crisp carving and delicate marquetry. Supposed to have been given by John Sharp, Rector of St Giles and later Archbishop of York, probably in 1676, although it looks later; reduced in height. – 'Wesley's PULPIT', N aisle, part of a plain painted three-decker pulpit of *c.* 1700 from West Street Chapel. – FONT. Tapering octagonal shaft and circular bowl; very classical decoration with Greek key, honeysuckle, etc. made in 1810 and attributed to *Soane*. – ORGAN CASE. 1734, richly decorated. – CHEST in the S porch; of iron, dated 1630 (presented 1924). – Four CHANDELIERS of brass, the largest C17 Flemish, the others probably C18. – The original MODEL for the church is under the tower. Note how it shows the N doorway approached up steps, and an upper gallery in place of the organ. – MONUMENTS. Many famous residents of the parish were buried here. – George Chapman, the poet †1634. His monument is in the unusual form of an upright Roman tombstone (very badly preserved). It is said by Vertue and in the inscription (recut 1827) to be *Inigo Jones*'s own design. Chapman in a letter called Jones 'my exceeding good friend'. – Lady Frances Kniveton † before 1645, recumbent figure in a shroud, by *Joshua Marshall*, 1669. – Richard Pendrell †1671, 'preserver and conductor' of the future Charles II in 1651; Purbeck slab, from a tomb in the churchyard. – Sir Roger L'Estrange †1704, ascribed to the *Stanton* workshop (GF). Good tablet, curly cartouche. – John Hawford and wife †1712 and 1714, cartouche on drapery with cherubs' heads. – The poet Andrew Marvell †1678 has a plain tablet erected 1764. – John Barnfather †1793, oval with female by an urn, signed by *Taunton & Brown*. – M.W. Poore †1828 by *W. Pitts*, relief of mourning father and children. – Memorial to Flaxman, put up in 1930 by the Royal Academy. It is a bronze cast of the Baring Monument at Micheldever (Hants) with two angels bearing a soul. – MOSAIC PANEL (in S porch), 1884, after Watts's 'Time and Death followed by Judgement', presented to Canon and Mrs Barnett in Whitechapel; from 1925 to 1970 on the exterior of St Giles's National Schools at the corner of Endell Street.

Large VESTRY ROOM, adjoining the S porch, by *Flitcroft*, 1731; panelled inside with names of churchwardens and incumbents, gilt on black.

## 2. Roman Catholic

ST ANSELM AND ST CECILIA, Kingsway. 1909 by *F. A. Walters*. A stone façade inspired by Belgian churches of the C18. Eclectic interior with Renaissance details, especially the REREDOS, which is in the style of François I. Nave with clerestory and timber tunnel vault; balcony across the chancel arch; stone arcades (blind on the N side) with classical columns. S aisle added by *S. C. Kerr-Bate*, 1951–4, when the façade was also rebuilt. PAINTING. Large Deposition of Christ, probably from the old Sardinian Chapel, to which St Anselm is the successor; late C18, strongly influenced by Correggio.

ST ETHELDREDA, Ely Place. An important survival of the later C13, built as the chapel of the town house of the Bishop of Ely. It was referred to as the 'new chapel' of John de Kirkby (Bishop 1286–90) in an enquiry after his death. After the rest of the house was demolished (*see* Perambulation 1a) it became a Welsh chapel, until acquired in 1873 by the Order of Charity (Rosinians) for R.C. use. Restored by *J. Young* in 1874–9,* and again in 1935 by *Giles Gilbert Scott*. Originally with four octagonal corner turrets (as at St Stephen, Palace of Westminster, a little later). Two-storeyed, an arrangement typical of private chapels (cf. the royal examples of the Sainte Chapelle in Paris and St Stephen Westminster). The upper chapel has an entrance bay with elaborately moulded N and S doorways and blind tracery. Five main bays with two-light windows with pointed trefoil tracery (restored from the example of a single window remaining at the E end). Interesting E and W windows (unblocked after 1874), similar but not identical, showing the evenness of the Geometrical just on the point of disintegrating into the illogicalities of the coming Dec style. The combination of intersecting arches and a top circle can be compared to the choir aisles of Old St Paul's; similar motifs occur in Exeter Cathedral Lady Chapel, also of the late C13. Between N and S windows and l. and r. of the E and W windows, tall narrow blank arcades with crocketed gables. Traces of triple SEDILIA on both sides of E bay. – Purbeck marble FONT. – ROYAL ARMS, nicely carved, of oak, late C17. – ORGAN CASES, a pair, and W SCREEN by *J. F. Bentley*. On the walls, medieval corbels carry painted STATUES of English martyrs, of resin and fibreglass, 1962–4 by *Mary Blakeman*. STAINED GLASS. E window by *Joseph Nuttgens*, 1952, Christ Enthroned, deep colours in a brilliant mosaic style. Side windows with Old and New Testament themes, 1952–8, and W window, with English Martyrs, 1964, all by *Charles Blakeman*.

* See *St Paul's Ecclesiological Soc. Trans. I*, 1880–1.

The plain CRYPT has C19 columns. Repaired and reordered by *Charles Blakeman*, 1968–70, who also designed its STAINED GLASS and STATIONS OF THE CROSS.

ST PETER, Clerkenwell Road. A mission church for the poor Italian community then living around Saffron Hill. 1862–3 by *John Miller Bryson*, probably influenced by more ambitious unexecuted plans of 1853 by *Francesco Gualandi*. Tall narrow two-bay front. Entrance loggia of two arches; upper parts 1891 by *F. W. Tasker*, brick and stone with pediment. Before Clerkenwell Road was made, a grander E façade to Herbal Hill was intended. Surprisingly large and impressive interior, an Italian basilica with straight entablature on marble Ionic columns and T-plan transept. Upper galleries were closed off in 1885–6, when walls and ceiling were painted by *Arnaud* and *Gauthier*, artists from Piedmont. Pevsner found this work sufficiently Baroque to have 'an un-English, nicely Mediterranean effect'. Its impact was lightened when the architectural surrounds were painted out in 1953. Baldacchino with black marble columns, partly obscuring a PAINTING of the Annunciation, signed by *Bon Einler*, Wien, 1861. Four Italian Baroque terracotta STATUES of evangelists, apparently brought from the Manchester exhibition of 1857. PRESBYTERY and offices at No. 4 Back Hill, 1865–6, Italianate.

## 3. Other places of worship

AMERICAN CHURCH (Whitefield Memorial Church), Tottenham Court Road, 1957, brick, plain but stately. Reticent classical detail, steeply pitched roof. On the site of the chapel of the C18 preacher George Whitefield.

BLOOMSBURY CENTRAL BAPTIST CHURCH, Shaftesbury Avenue. 1845–8 by *John Gibson* for Sir Samuel Morton Peto. Prominently sited on the road, unlike earlier Dissenters' chapels. Broad front of white brick, with two Romanesque towers flanking a big rose window. The spiky roof-line was destroyed by the removal of spires in 1951 and the addition in 1914 of a top floor in place of the central gable. Interior with steeply raked galleries on iron columns, the centre gallery slightly curved. Sanctuary blandly refitted 1963–4 and upper gallery removed.

GERMAN LUTHERAN CHURCH, Thanet Street and Sandwich Street. 1974–9 by *Maguire & Murray* (job architect *Ekkehard Weisner*). In the basement of the INTERNATIONAL LUTHERAN STUDENT CENTRE, a lively and ingenious urban design on a tight site. Six storeys, with tall oriel windows, and circular stair windows at the side. At ground-floor level large multi-paned lunettes act as clerestory windows to the church, with a larger one incorporating the door. The church is a square within a square, the centre defined by columns and higher ceiling (cf. the same architects' St Paul, Bow Common). FITTINGS by the architects.

SWISS PROTESTANT CHURCH, Endell Street. Narrow façade between taller houses; 1853 by *George Vulliamy*. Two-storeyed with two outer giant pilasters and two inner giant columns. The details one might call incorrect Palladian. Interior (stripped of old fittings) with unusual barrel vault pierced with windows, and small apse. MONUMENT, small bronze tablet by *Sir W. Goscombe John* to his wife Marthe †1923.

## PUBLIC BUILDINGS

Public buildings and institutions in Holborn are numerous and diverse. University buildings, the Inns of Court, the British Museum and Sir John Soane's Museum are described in separate entries following this section. Others are arranged here as follows:

1. Civic and municipal buildings
2. Educational buildings (non university)
3. Medical buildings
4. Other institutions

### 1. Civic and municipal buildings

Former TOWN HALL and LIBRARY, High Holborn. E wing, formerly St Giles's Library, by *W. Rushworth*, 1894, with a double-height oriel and pretty French Renaissance ornament. The W wing, the former Holborn Town Hall, 1906–8 by *Hall & Warwick*, has the bolder Baroque detail and generous finishes typical of Edwardian public buildings. Circular stairhall; panelled court room, domed council chamber. Ironwork by the *Bromsgrove Guild*. Conversion by *Scott, Brownrigg & Turner* under discussion, 1998.

POLICE STATION, Theobalds Road. 1962–3 by *J. Innes Elliott*. Subdivisional station with low Portland-stone-faced block to the street with a pattern of slit windows on the top floor, and a tower behind.

BRITISH TELECOM TOWER, Cleveland Street. 1964 by the *Ministry of Public Building and Works* (chief engineer *L. R. Creasy*, project engineer *H. C. Adams*). The (former) Post Office tower is a notable 1960s landmark. Reinforced concrete shaft, 620 ft high above street level, with prestressed concrete foundations on London clay. A distinctive top profile: circular bands of differing diameter carrying aerials, above them a broader part intended as observation areas and restaurant with revolving floor.

LIBRARY, Theobalds Road. By *Sidney Cook*, Holborn Borough Architect; completed 1960. A lively street front with a pattern of hexagonal concrete panels below two main floors with continuous glazing and a brick-faced top storey. Imaginatively planned on four floors; the light, purpose-made fittings and deliberately informal furnishings reflect the post-war desire to be friendly and accessible. Double-height entrance hall with glazed wall to main library and mezzanine; basement children's room, lecture hall on the top floor. Staircase hall faced with an unusual combination of timber and patterned panels.

PUBLIC BATHS. For the Oasis Leisure Centre, *see* Perambulation 1b, High Holborn p. 305.

TOTTENHAM COURT ROAD UNDERGROUND STATION. Opened 1900 (Central Line); 1907 (Northern Line). The forceful, brilliantly coloured tile decoration in the underground areas by *Eduardo Paolozzi* is the most ambitious example of the cosmetic treatment for Central Line stations planned in 1980. Plans for rebuilding and extensions above ground were made by *Michael Hopkins* in 1991.

KINGSWAY TRAM TUNNEL, by the *LCC*. Constructed 1902–4 as part of the building of Kingsway (see p. 314), opened 1906. Deepened for double-decker trams in 1930–1. The N entrance ramp in Southampton Row remains as abandoned in 1952.

Distinctive conduits for electrical pickup built into the road surface.

ST GEORGE'S GARDENS. A delightful retreat between Handel Street and Gray's Inn Road. Acquired in 1713 as the burial ground for St George's Bloomsbury and St George the Martyr; made into a garden with the help of the Kyrle Society in 1882. Repairs and landscape improvements planned 1998. Winding paths between C18 sarcophagi with bulgy pilasters, an obelisk, and a big altar tomb with urn, to Robert Nelson †1715. Terracotta figure of Euterpe from a series in *Fitzroy Doll*'s Apollo Inn, Tottenham Court Road (demolished 1961). By the Handel Street entrance, a plain early C19 pedimented LODGE. Attached to it a pretty engraved tablet with rustic architectural ornament to Clare Taylor †1763 and other members of her family; 'life how short, eternity how long'; signed *W. Wooton Kegworth*.

## 2. *Educational buildings (non-university)*

ARCHITECTURAL ASSOCIATION, Bedford Square. *See* p. 325.

BOARD SCHOOLS. All squeezed onto cramped sites. TOWER STREET: irregular four-storey pile of 1874, with lively turrets and gables; converted to offices 1990. PRINCETON STREET, 1877, now studios. ARGYLE SCHOOL, Tonbridge Street: 1881 and 1902, with a tower to the earlier part.

CITY LITERARY INSTITUTE, Stukeley Street. 1939 by *E. P. Wheeler*. An adult education institute; functional 30s-style brick frontage on a narrow street.

KINGSWAY COLLEGE, Gray's Inn Road. Two parts: the front is an aggressive composition of ribbed concrete surfaces, blocky projections and angled windows, containing teaching areas, dining room and common room; 1974 by the *GLC* for ILEA, a clumsy relation of Pimlico School. Along Sidmouth Street, behind trees, the *LCC*'s restrained earlier classroom block of *c.* 1960: neat white cladding above a set-back ground floor, unfortunately reglazed in the 1990s.

LONDON INSTITUTE: Central St Martin's School of Art and Design, Southampton Row. Built 1905–8 as the Central School of Arts and Crafts. By the *LCC Architect's Department*, then under *W. E. Riley*, but with considerable input from *W. R. Lethaby*, who was head of the school. He examined the design in 1903; he wanted it 'plain, reasonable and well-built' with little ornament. According to Lethaby's biographer, Godfrey Rubens, the plan is probably by *Nelson Dawson*, and the design by a former student, *A. H. Verstage*. Portland stone above granite, an original elevation with an odd restless rhythm of round-arched and segmental windows, and, for its date, a remarkable absence of decoration. The most prominent features are the heavy top cornice and lead ogee corner dome. This crowns a dramatic staircase. Low entrance hall and, between the two wings, a toplit exhibition space. Sturdy granite columns and round-headed arches.

## 3. *Medical buildings*

Medical buildings are a special feature of Holborn. The largest cluster is in and around Queen Square, where most started as

specialist institutions in private houses (*see also* Perambulation 2b).
The other main centre, around Gower Street and Huntley Street,
had a more deliberate origin, growing around the hospital founded
by University College in conjunction with its medical school.

QUEEN SQUARE clockwise from NE corner. NATIONAL HOSPITAL
FOR NEUROLOGY AND NEURO-SURGERY. Richly ornamented
terracotta frontage (Albany Memorial Wing), designed 1880 by
*J. W. Simpson* (of *Manning & Simpson*), built 1883–5, the third
phase of expansion of a hospital founded in 1860 at No. 24 for the
treatment of the paralysed and epileptic. Good staircase with
stained glass in a Venetian window, CHAPEL with pair of marble
columns. Extension to the S, 1937–8 by *Slater, Moberly & Uren*;
streamlined brick bands, sculptural panels by *A. J. Ayres*. Later
top storey. To the N, towards Guilford Street, INSTITUTE OF
NEUROLOGY, an ugly ten-storey concrete pile, by *Llewelyn-Davies
& Weeks*, 1970–8.

    ROYAL LONDON HOMEOPATHIC HOSPITAL, at the corner
with Great Ormond Street. On this site from 1859. Earlier part
1893–5 by *W. A. Pite*, the stone-faced wing in the square by *E. T.
Hall*, 1909–11.

    Former ITALIAN HOSPITAL, S side of the square, founded
1884; 1898–9 by *T. W. Cutler*. Four storeys, of brick and stone,
with giant Corinthian pilasters in a quite dignified, plain Baroque.
Tower and dome to the former chapel behind. Extended to
Boswell Street by *J. D. Slater*, 1911.

HOSPITAL FOR SICK CHILDREN, Great Ormond Street, round
the corner from Queen Square. Founded in 1851. The oldest surviving part until the 1990s was of 1872–7 by *E. Barry*, with a S
wing of 1890–3 by *Charles Barry Jun*. Major rebuilding by *Hall,
Easton & Robertson*, planned in the 1930s, started with the Nurses'
Home (facing Guilford Street), 1933–7, and continued with the
eight-storeyed Southwood Building between Guilford Street and
Powis Place. Along Great Ormond Street, low, pale brick wing for
Outpatients, completed after the war. At the corner of Outpatients,
sculpture of St Nicholas and three children by *Gilbert Ledward*,
1950–1. Adjoining the Southwood Building, and replacing the
parts by Barry, are additions by *Powell & Moya*, 1991–3. Towards
Lamb's Conduit Street (*see* Perambulation 2b, pp. 312–13), the
Camelia Botnar Laboratories, 1993–5 by *DEGW*. CHAPEL, 1876
by *Edward Barry*, formerly within the older buildings, transported
to a new site adjoining the Powell & Moya buildings in 1992.
90  A moving and remarkable interior: a little Neo-Byzantine gem
glowing with richly coloured materials; apse, nave with four marble
columns and a dome. Child-sized PEWS; WALL PAINTING,
Cosmati work, REREDOS of alabaster, marble and brass, contemporary light fittings, much STAINED GLASS by *Clayton & Bell*.

UNIVERSITY COLLEGE HOSPITAL AND MEDICAL BUILDINGS,
Gower Street. The first hospital was founded by University
College in association with its medical schools and built opposite
the main college buildings in Gower Street in 1833. It was replaced
74  in 1896–1906 by a spectacular cruciform building by *Alfred* and
*Paul Waterhouse*. Closed as a hospital and reacquired by the
college in 1996 for teaching purposes; refurbishment by *HLM*

*Architects* from 1997. Red brick and terracotta, a functional Gothic riposte to the college's classical tradition. A basement fills the whole site, with cross-shaped plan above, set diagonally to Gower Street, planned with operating theatres in the centre and wards in the wings, a scheme devised by Dr G. V. Poore to promote maximum ventilation and isolation of the wards. The plan breaks the harmony of the street as much as do the jagged elevations, very tall with turrets at the ends of the cross-arms.

MEDICAL SCHOOL, Gower Street and University Street. 1905 by *Paul Waterhouse*, Baroque and ridiculously grand, a busy brick and stone frontage with giant Ionic order to centre and end pavilions. In contrast, the NURSES' HOME and PRIVATE PATIENTS BLOCK, Grafton Way, 1936 by *Michael Waterhouse* and *Cedric Ripley*, is dour and reticent, dark brick above stone, in interwar stripped classical. In Huntley Street, OBSTETRIC HOSPITAL, 1923 by *George Hornblower*, and ROYAL EAR HOSPITAL, 1926–8 by *Wimperis, Simpson & Guthrie*, and the colossal ROCKEFELLER NURSES' HOME, very large and heavy, the earlier part of orange brick with stone quoins.

NEW BUILDINGS for University College Hospital, on the large site to the N fronting Euston Road, the first government private finance initiative for a hospital. Plans by *Llewelyn-Davies & Weeks* approved 1998.

EASTMAN DENTAL HOSPITAL, Gray's Inn Road. Formerly part of the Royal Free Hospital. The N building is *Sir John Burnet*'s last work, 1926, still firmly in the Beaux Arts tradition; festive pilastered and pedimented centre and wings (the r. wing truncated), with central entrance to an inner courtyard. To the S, a C19 part, a nice plain classical composition of 3–7–3 bays, brick with stone bands and keystones, horribly insulted by modern glazing. Recessed centre with tripartite entrance. This began life as the Light Horse Volunteer Barracks: centre 1842; wings 1855, 1876.

HEALTH CENTRE, No. 8 Hunter Street. Built as the London School of Medicine for Women, established by Dr Elizabeth Garrett Anderson. 1897–8 and 1900 by *J. M. Brydon*; Queen Anne domestic with some Baroque dormers.

ST LUKE'S HOSPITAL, Fitzroy Square. *See* p. 336.


## 4. *Other institutions*

BRITISH MEDICAL ASSOCIATION, Tavistock Square. On the site of James Burton's villa (*see* p. 329). Designs were begun in 1911 by *Sir Edwin Lutyens* for the Headquarters of the British Theosophical Society, with which his wife was closely involved. His plans of 1912 were for an ambitious English Baroque composition: two courtyards, the range between them with a tall domed centrepiece, flanked by wings with steep hipped roofs and central chimneys. Only the main range and flanking wings at the back of the site were begun; Lutyens's revised plans of 1915 omitted the rest. The building was requisitioned by the War Office, and completed by the British Medical Association in 1923–5; ranges to Tavistock Square by *C. Wontner Smith* 1925–9, extended by *Douglas Wood*, 1938–50.

The courtyard is entered through iron memorial gates, designed by Lutyens for the BMA after his grand dome had been abandoned.

Central range with six pairs of Corinthian columns in brick, and a pediment; the back to Burton Street is a finely detailed brick palazzo with windows with alternating pediments (intended to have two attic storeys above). The main windows light the great hall, completed by Lutyens to a revised design in 1925, with Corinthian columns and an open roof to the centre (original colouring gold, blue and green); a barrel vault at each end. Converted to library in the mid 1980s, with committee rooms inserted in the roof space. In the Council Room in the half-basement, panelling from the BMA's former premises by *Holden* in the Strand. In the courtyard, WAR MEMORIAL, with four large statues round a pool, by *James Woodford* and *S. Rowland Pierce* (Sacrifice, Cure, Prevention and Aspiration), 1954. Smith's wings extending to Tavistock Place carry on Lutyens's brick and stone, but are simpler; their special feature is giant columns of brick.

CONGRESS HOUSE (Trades Union Congress Memorial Building), Great Russell Street. By *David du R. Aberdeen*. One of the first important post-war buildings in London. Built 1953–7, but the design won a competition in 1948 and so is earlier than even the Festival Hall. A far cry from the stodgy tradition of so many 1930s institutions. The inspiration was Le Corbusier's early work of the 1920s. The ingeniously planned, airy building, designed without

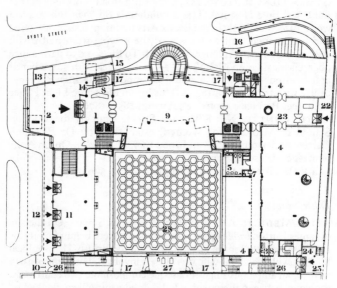

Congress House. Ground-floor plan

120 corridors, is particularly effective when viewed from Dyott Street. From here one can see through the transparent ground-floor foyer, with its curving stair down to the lecture hall, right across
119 the inner courtyard to where *Epstein*'s powerful War Memorial of 1955–6, in the form of a vast stone Pietà, is placed against the far wall – originally of green marble, replaced later in rather dis-

appointing grey-green mosaic. The floor of the courtyard consists
of hexagonal glass roof-lights to the lecture hall. The projecting
parts which give interest to the Dyott Street frontage also serve to
bring extra light into the basement. More formal seven-storey
front to Great Russell Street, clad in granite and blue tiles, with
large figural sculpture over the projecting porch, The Spirit of
Brotherhood, by *Bernard Meadows*. Minor alterations (enlargement of entrance lobby, reusing original doors) and upgrading
and renewal of services by *Huckle Tweddle Partnership*, completed
1990, following an appraisal by *Cedric Price*, a notable example of
tactful treatment of an early post-war listed building.

FREEMASONS HALL, Great Queen Street. The third masonic hall
to be built in Great Queen Street. Its predecessors, by *Sandby*
(1776) and *Soane* (1828), lay to the E (*see* Perambulation 3c, p.
320). 1927–33 by *Ashley & Newman*. Bewilderingly self-possessed,
in gleaming Portland stone, with a corner frontage like the Port of
London Authority and all the detail in an embellished Classical
Revival. Five storeys on an irregular pentagon surround the
principal rooms, which are sumptuously detailed in marble and
mahogany, and approached by a grand marble stair starting in
two flights. Domed corridors lead to the galleried library and
museum. A series of three lavish vestibules, the first with War
Memorial shrine and lamps by *Walter Gilbert*, leads to a theatrically
awesome great hall 62 ft high. Allegorical mosaics on the cove of
the ceiling, with 'celestial canopy' in the centre. Massive bronze
doors by *Gilbert*; pictorial subjects on the outside (Solomon's
temple); symbolic themes inside. SCULPTURE. Standing figure of
the Duke of Sussex, by *E. H. Baily*, 1846. Busts of sons of George
III: George IV and Duke of Sussex by *Chantrey*; William IV by
*J. Francis*; Dukes of York and Kent by *Baily*.

LIBRARY ASSOCIATION, Ridgmount Street and Store Street.
1963–5 by *Sir Giles Scott & Partners*. Straightforward, unfussy
concrete-framed four-storey blocks around a courtyard, decently
proportioned. Ground floor with tapering piers.

LONDON HOUSE, Guilford Street and Mecklenburgh Square. Built
as a college-type hostel around a large quadrangle, for students
from the Dominions. Planned from 1933 by *Sir Herbert Baker*.
Brick on a flint and stone base, as at Baker's Church House,
Westminster, intended to symbolize different ages of building.
S and E wings 1936–7; W wing on the same plan by *A. T. Scott*,
1949–50 (Baker died in 1944); N wing, to a simpler design, 1961–3.
Symmetrical S front 'in which Baker's motifs and foibles are only
too noticeable' (Pevsner). The quadrangle face is quieter, with an
arcaded cloister and balcony above. Characteristically pompous
public rooms in this pre-war part: dining hall with canted bay,
coved ceiling and gilded imperial emblems; library with ceiling in
late C17 style; between them a grand stone staircase. The plasterwork is by *Lawrence Turner*. Chapel by *Vernon Helbing*, 1963.

MARY WARD HOUSE (from 1961 the National Institute for Social
Work Training), Tavistock Place. Built in 1895–7 for the University
Hall Settlement founded by Mary Ward (the novelist Mrs Humphry
Ward), with funds provided by Passmore Edwards. The young
architects who won the competition were *A. Dunbar Smith* and
*Cecil Brewer* (the partnership later responsible for Heal's in

Tottenham Court Road). One of the most charming pieces of
architecture designed at that time in England. The detail is
remarkably original; connections with Voysey (cornice and roof),
Townsend and Lethaby (entrance) and the Shaw tradition (tripartite
windows) are evident, but the grace of handling and the combination of formal symmetry with intimate scale are the architects'
personal contribution. The building provided the neighbourhood
with hall, library, gymnasium and common rooms; on the second
floor are small, rather monastic rooms for the residential students
97  running the settlement. This is clearly expressed on the outside.
Barrel-vaulted first-floor hall in the centre, of brick with roughcast
below the eaves, lit by dormers and a big Venetian window to the
w; small rising windows to the staircases up to the hall. To the
road a big stone porch, dignified by two eggs symbolizing creation
(a Lethaby influence), providing the entrance to the common
rooms. On the w side, approached through spirited iron gates, a
separate entrance for the residents, their rooms indicated by the
small windows above. Inside as well as out, the details repay
study. Rooms are tightly planned around a plain courtyard with
glass-roofed gymnasium. Low doors, excellent door furniture
(with monograms indicating donors), and a series of delightful
tiled fireplaces designed by the architects' friends (*Lethaby, Troup,
Voysey, Dawber, Newton*); individual attributions are uncertain, but
the spirit of Voysey is evident. Common room at the back, with
cupboards for storing away the tables designed by the architects.
On the E side, drawing room and library, each with a big bow
window. Library with stone fireplace (a memorial to T.H. Green)
and original fittings. In the hall, busts to notable C19 thinkers,
given by Passmore Edwards, and a memorial to Mary Ward.
The second-floor corridors were boldly decorated, with red walls
and green paintwork. Alterations to improve circulation with lift
and new roof to the courtyard, by *Karen Butti* of *Patricia Brock
Associates*, under discussion 1998.

No. 9 Tavistock Place, by the same firm, 1903, more simply
detailed. Built as a school for invalid children.

ROYAL ACADEMY OF DRAMATIC ART, No. 62 Gower Street.
Founded 1904 by Sir Herbert Beerbohm Tree, on this site from
1905. The present premises rebuilt 1927 by *Geoffrey Norman*. Very
tall, brick-faced with some arched windows. Masks of Comedy
and Tragedy by *Alan Durst* guard the door. At the back, with
entrance to Malet Street, a theatre, planned 1913, built 1921, also
by *Norman*. Reconstructed after war damage 1954; rebuilding
planned 1996.

ROYAL COLLEGE OF SURGEONS, Lincoln's Inn Fields. 1835–6 by
*Sir Charles Barry*. But the principal motif, the noble giant Ionic
portico with straight entablature, comes from the predecessor to
Barry's building, designed by *George Dance* and built in 1806–13.
Barry reused it, though he had to shift it slightly, and he added
fluting to Dance's plain columns. Barry's front was of two more
bays l. and r. of the portico than Dance's, and higher by one half-
storey. Then in 1888 *Stephen Salter* added two more bays l. and
two r., the giant pilasters, and alas the two top storeys, one with
wreathed circular windows. Barry's façade thus lost most of its
sense. The yet heavier and higher angle erections are of 1937.

Barry's vestibule with Greek Doric columns and his delightfully reposeful library survive, the latter with bookcases only against the wall and not projecting into the room. The cases are divided by pilasters and there is a gallery with a cast-iron railing above with another tier of bookcases. The attractive light green colour is said to be original. In the inner hall, statue of John Hunter by *Weekes*, 1864. The College's busts include Dr John Belchier by *Roubiliac*, John Hunter by *Flaxman*, 1805, and W.H. Baillie by *Chantrey*, 1823.

THOMAS CORAM FOUNDATION, No. 40 Brunswick Square, and CORAM'S FIELDS. The successors to the FOUNDLING HOSPITAL established by Captain Thomas Coram, demolished in 1926. Plain but ample buildings were laid out in 1745–53 by *Theodore Jacobsen* on an open site N of the present Guilford Street. Attempts to save them after the children were moved to Hertfordshire came to nothing, but important contents were preserved in the Foundation's offices on the N side of Brunswick Square, a quiet neo-Georgian house of 1937 by *J. M. Shepherd*.*

The original FITTINGS include a heavy oak staircase with closed string and symmetrical balustrades, from the Boys' Wing. The reconstructed COURT ROOM demonstrates the artistic significance of the Hospital in the mid-C18. Fine Rococo ceiling by *William Wilton*; fireplace with charming relief over the mantel by *Rysbrack* of charity children engaged in husbandry and navigation, in a frame by *John Deval Sen.* On the walls large biblical pictures of appropriate subjects (The Finding of Moses, Suffer little children, etc.), between plaster embellishments, and painted medallions showing London hospitals. Many of the artists (who included *Hogarth*, *Hayman*, *Highmore*, and *Wilson*) and Rysbrack were governors, giving their services free, and in the 1750s the Hospital was a notable showplace for contemporary painting. In the picture gallery, another original fireplace of coloured marbles with small relief of putti. Among the sculpture: terracotta bust of Handel, another governor (the Hospital was also famous for its music), by *Roubiliac*, *c.* 1739; reclining baby by *E. H. Baily*; terracotta group of girl and foundling by *George Halse*, 1874. Portable *Coade* stone FONT with reliefs of doves, supported by lambs' heads. The picture collection includes *Hogarth*'s splendid portrait of Coram. (See further: B. Nicholson, *Treasures of the Foundling Hospital*, 1972.)

After the buildings were demolished, an infant welfare centre was built at the N end of the site, and the rest of the GROUNDS were laid out in 1936 as a children's park by the *LCC Parks Department*, with buildings of stuccoed concrete by *L. H. Bucknell*. Central pavilion with circular conical roof and clock, quite original, with a white terracotta frieze with reliefs of children playing by *Marjorie Meggitt*. Flanking the entrance, two discreet low halls (for Scouts and Guides). The Doric colonnades along the E and W walls are part of the original scheme, but were much rebuilt in 1964–8.

YMCA and YWCA, Great Russell Street. *See* p. 322.

YMCA INDIAN STUDENT HOSTEL, Fitzroy Square. *See* Perambulation 6b, p. 336.

---

* Font, pulpit and organ case from the hospital chapel are now in St Andrew Holborn, where Coram is buried (*see London 1: The City of London*).

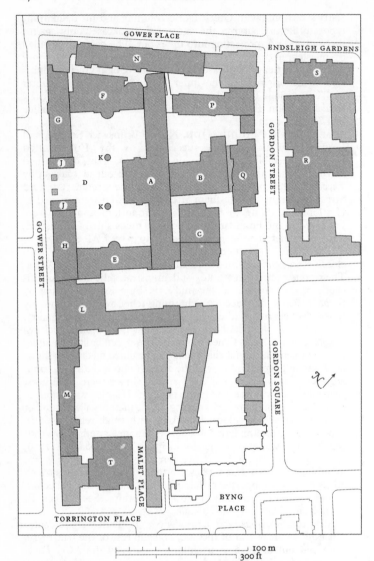

A   Wilkins Building, 1827–9
B   Library, 1849 (additions by Richardson)
C   Bernard Katz Building, 1993
D   Front Quadrangle
E   South Wing, 1869–76
F   North Wing,
      Slade School of Art, 1870–81
G   NW Wing, 1913–14
H   SW Wing, 1891, completed 1923
J   NW and SW Wing extensions, 1984–5
K   Observatories, 1905–7
L   Anatomy, 1922–3
M   Biological Sciences, 1959–64
N   Kathleen Lonsdale Building, 1912–13
P   Physics, rebuilt 1954
Q   Bloomsbury Theatre, 1964–9
R   Chemistry, (Christopher Ingold
      Building), 1969
S   Wates House, 1975
T   Engineering, 1961

University College. Plan

## UNIVERSITY COLLEGE
Gower Street

University College owes its existence to the desire for university education without an exclusively Anglican bias. In 1825 two Scots, the poet Thomas Campbell and Henry Brougham, later Lord Chancellor, inspired by the universities of Scotland and Germany, proposed a London University for 'the youth of our middling-rich people'. According to Campbell's letter in *The Times*, 'all that would be necessary would be to have some porticoes and large halls independent of the lecture rooms to which they might resort for relaxation'. Land intended for a Bloomsbury square was acquired, and *William Wilkins*, one of the leading enthusiasts for the Greek Revival, won the architectural competition in 1826 with a grand scheme for an E-shaped building with a Corinthian portico and three domes, around a large quadrangle which was to have been closed off to Gower Street by a screen of Doric columns. Tite's exactly contemporary Mill Hill School for Nonconformists is also Grecian. This was the style then associated with Nonconformity, as was noted by Pugin, who detested both. He pointedly described the architecture of University College as 'in character with the intention and principles of the institution'.

The institution opened as the University of London in 1828 and obtained its first charter (becoming University College London) in 1836, when the present University of London was formed as a separate degree-giving body (*see* below). At first there were only funds to build the central range, the WILKINS BUILDING of 1827–9, intended to house great hall, library, museums and lecture rooms. It is an impressively monumental composition, more concentrated and intense than Wilkins's later National Gallery, and more ornate than his earlier Downing College Cambridge. It had to be built to a much simplified design, worked up by Wilkins together with his fellow competitor *J. P. Gandy*. After several changes of plan the central great hall behind the portico was abandoned in favour of a hall to be built at the rear. The dome over the vestibule thus appears more prominently than Wilkins had at first intended, Renaissance competing with Grecian. The massive ten-column portico, set above a steep flight of steps, was without precedent in England, modelled on the Temple of Jupiter Olympus at Athens. It was roofed with cast-iron tiles, replaced by slate in 1858. Iron was also used in the construction of the building, but outside all is concealed by Portland stone. The portico is flanked by plain two-storey ranges, sparingly decorated with a band of wreaths, and with pilasters over channelled rustication.

The INTERIORS of the Wilkins Building were remodelled in 1848–9 by *T. L. Donaldson*, the first of a series of college Professors of Architecture to make additions, and restored by *A. E. Richardson* after major damage in the Second World War. Donaldson built the main staircase and, with *C. R. Cockerell* and *Sir Charles Eastlake*, from 1849 to 1851 adapted the space below the dome to house the Flaxman collection of over 200 casts donated to the college. These were fixed under the dome and in the vestibule.

They were restored in 1986, reverting to Donaldson's original rich mid-C19 arrangement, with the reliefs set against deep terracotta-coloured walls. Below the dome, the model for the large group of St Michael conquering Satan, brought back from the Victoria and Albert Museum in 1994. The design commissioned by Lord Egremont for Petworth in 1821. The balustrade around it survives from Richardson's post-war restoration, when an oculus, now filled, was made to bring light to the lower floor. The dome is enriched with bands of coffering with rosettes; the walls below have lunettes above two orders of columns. The LIBRARY was created by Donaldson in 1849 on the site of Wilkins's incomplete great hall, damaged by fire in 1836. Sober, heavily modelled interior, with coffered barrel vault, columns at each end, and deep side bays flanked by pilasters, restored by *A. E. Richardson* after being gutted in the Second World War. The library has expanded along the corridors to N and S; at the N end, an addition by Richardson in the Regency manner in which he felt most at home; two floors, each with galleries, the upper one with an elegant, shallow Soanian dome with central lantern, the lower one with a northern bow. On the lower floor of the main building, an arcaded ground floor known as the cloisters, glazed later. Two sculptures: Flaxman, seated figure by *M. L. Watson*, 1851; Locke by *Westmacott Sen.*, 1834. In the S cloister, Marmor Homericum, a large picture in coloured marbles of scenes from Homer, by Baron *H. de Trinqueti*, 1865 (designer of the Albert Memorial Chapel at Windsor). S of the S cloister, the college's most eccentric posses-sion, the remains of Jeremy Bentham †1832, in an upright wooden case like a cupboard, his clothed and seated figure with wax head displayed 'in the attitude in which I am sitting when engaged in thought'.

The back of the main building is of brick and very plain, ori-ginally with semicircular lecture theatres projecting at each end (destroyed in the war). Attached to the S end and respecting its height is the BERNARD KATZ BUILDING, plain yellow brick, decently proportioned, 1993 by *Casson & Conder*, a medical research building shared with a pharmaceutical company, which has its own foyer at the E end. The building ingeniously extends N with two sunken storeys below a lawn on a level with the S cloister. On the lawn a black marble slab commemorates twenty-four Japanese students who studied here in 1863–5 'and returned to lay the foundations of modern Japan'.

The FRONT QUADRANGLE is now almost entirely surrounded by later wings, apart from a narrow entrance from Gower Street with Wilkins's little one-storey brick LODGES, which he intended to be temporary. Although departing from Wilkins's original lay-out, the result is both successful and sympathetic, sheltering the college from the busy Gower Street, while tactfully continuing the pattern of the main range. The S WING, occupied by University College School until 1907, was built in 1869–76, the N WING, with the SLADE SCHOOL OF ART, in 1870–81; both are by *T. Hayter Lewis*. The centre of each is marked by a half-rotunda with Corinthian columns, developed from Wilkins's early proposals. Large studios at the back, with some inserted mezzanines. As new departments and students grew in numbers (the intake at first was only *c.* 600 a year), further additions followed along Gower Street: NW wing (Pearson) by *F. M. Simpson*, 1913–14, for the new Bartlett School of Architecture; SW wing (Chadwick), with ground floor of 1891, completed in 1923 by *A. E. Richardson*. In 1984–5, after many abortive plans, these wings were extended towards each other by additions by *Sir Hugh Casson*, ingeniously conforming with the Wilkins elevation on the quadrangle side while fitting in an extra floor. Each ends with a pilastered attic carried up to form twin towers facing the entrance, a neat solution; only the recesses between the towers are recognizably of the 1980s. The quadrangle is now a calm grassed area with two little former OBSERVATORIES of 1905–7, greatly benefiting from the reduction of parked cars.

The college extensions fill nearly the whole rectangle bounded by Gower Street, Gower Place, Gordon Street and Gordon Square, and Byng Place, with some outliers to the E. The classical legacy of Wilkins remained a strong influence, rejected only occasionally. Buildings are described clockwise, starting in Gower Street.

GOWER STREET. S of the main quadrangle buildings, ANATOMY by *A. E. Richardson*, 1922–3. A fussier classical front than those in the Wilkins tradition; recessed centre with tripartite windows and busy ornament. Further S, BIOLOGICAL SCIENCES (Darwin), also by *Richardson*'s firm, 1959–64. The opposite extreme, a long stone-faced range, ultra-plain, but keeping to classical proportions, with rustication to basement and ground floor. It replaced houses along Gower Street (from one of these, occupied by Lady Diana Cooper, murals by *Rex Whistler* of the goddess Diana, painted for Lady Diana Cooper, now in a dining room in the college). Behind Anatomy, PHYSIOLOGY, 1909 and PHARMACOLOGY, 1912, forming the S range of a small S quadrangle created on the site of University College School's playground.

GOWER PLACE. The attractive rounded corner with Gower Street, now the university language centre, was rebuilt in 1931–2 for Lewis's bookshop. It bears a bust of its founder, H. K. Lewis. Then KATHLEEN LONSDALE BUILDING, built for the Chemistry Department; 1912–13 by *Simpson*, memorably coarse, the centre with a pair of mighty Corinthian columns *in antis*, the rest with giant pilasters and gross paterae. Converted with new top floor by *Stillman & Eastwick-Field*, 1985. HEALTH CENTRE, No. 3 Gower Place, by *Farrell Grimshaw Partnership*, 1972, spanning a road with a sprightly curtain-walled block; planned vertically, with doctors' rooms above waiting area.

GORDON STREET. The end wall of PHYSICS, by *Richardson*, rebuilt 1954 after bomb damage. Five storeys, very plain reduced classical. Then, filling part of the gap left by bombing, and breaking with the classical tradition, the BLOOMSBURY THEATRE, built as the Collegiate Theatre, by *Fello Atkinson* of *James Cubitt & Partners*, 1964–9. An elegant façade with giant arcade of slender concrete piers supporting a coved overhanging top storey which hides the fly tower behind. Adaptable auditorium seating 500. Students' social and sports rooms packed in behind. Renamed in 1982; porch of 1988 with spidery graphics by *Gerald Scarfe*. (On the bombed site was the college's Memorial Hall, a post-First-World-War conversion by *Richardson* of *Donaldson*'s All Saints Church of

1846.) On the E side of Gordon Street, CHEMISTRY (Christopher Ingold Building), 1969 by *Architects' Co-Partnership*, with an inset curtain-walled entrance relieving the heavy concrete walls, and WATES HOUSE, by the same firm, completed 1975, unappealing, with vertical piers in dark brick. The W side of GORDON SQUARE has C19 terraces now used by the college. Behind is the Bernard Katz Building (*see* above) and to its S, fortunately not easily visible from the road, a disappointingly crude building for the Medical Research Council, 1990s by *Ansell & Bailey*; yellow brick with weak Postmodern detail. Towards the S end of Gordon Square, Dr Williams Library (*see* below), a mammoth Neo-Jacobean frontage of 1849 by *T. L. Donaldson*, which needs to be mentioned here because it was built as the college's first hall of residence. Behind it is a rusticated GATEWAY dated 1668, a trophy brought from Pewterers Hall in the City by Professor Richardson in 1932.

Facing BYNG PLACE to the S, FRIENDS INTERNATIONAL CENTRE, a tall plain stuccoed house of nine bays with central pediment, built in 1834 as the Unitarian Coward College. It became UCL's College Hall, opened for women in 1882. (Women were admitted to degrees from 1878.) Adjacent is the eleven-storey steel-framed tower of ENGINEERING, opened 1961, by *H. O. Corfiato*, who succeeded Richardson as Professor in 1946. The college's first resolutely modern building, concealing the clutter behind and looking boldly S towards Senate House and the more timid post-war university buildings. Stone-faced uprights, narrow facing bricks harking back to Dudok and the 30s, and a long projecting glazed bay on the third floor, which helps to give the tower a human scale. Extra floor added 1991. Behind, MALET PLACE leads to FOSTER COURT, with utilitarian ranges adapted by Richardson from Shoolbred's warehouse and mattress factory in 1931. Pretty classical clock turret added by *Richardson*, dated 1937. W of this, two-storey former STABLES, still with a horse ramp, now Museum of Egyptian Archaeology.

BENTHAM HOUSE, Endsleigh Gardens. Acquired for the Law Department in 1965; built for the General and Municipal Workers Union, 1954–8, by *H. and H. Martin Lidbetter*. The design looks pre-war. An eccentric mixture: a tall corner, Grecian columns carrying an angular first-floor balcony, windows with fluted mullions, and some applied relief sculpture. Stonecarving and bronze mouldings by *Esmond Burton*.

## UNIVERSITY OF LONDON
### Bloomsbury

The University of London began in 1828 with University College (*see* above), known as the University of London until 1836, when the University as a degree-giving organization was set up for students from University College and its Anglican rival, King's College in The Strand, founded in 1824. Over the next hundred years other new colleges and institutions were established both in Bloomsbury and elsewhere in London, and in 1900 the University became a teaching as well as an examining body. Eventually the pressing need for central buildings for administration, library and some of the schools was met in 1927 by the acquisition of land between the British Museum and University College. Development was interrupted by the Second World War and has been intermittent since, owing to shortage of funds, changes of plan, the rival claims of different establishments, and to bitter divergence of opinion over the destruction of Bloomsbury's civilized late Georgian squares and terraces and the exclusion of traffic. The precinct planned in 1932 and enlarged after 1957 for long remained incoherent, and only a few buildings have had the confidence to challenge the established urban pattern. Meanwhile individual institutions have sprung up in an uncoordinated way on other scattered sites, and the traffic continues.

## 1. Central site

*Charles Holden* was appointed architect for the central site in 1931, and produced a preliminary plan in the same year. On the site there was already one brick institute, *Burnet*'s Chemistry building (No. 30 Russell Square); nearby was the classical stone-faced Institute of Hygiene and Tropical Medicine (*see* below). Holden's first scheme was for a battleship of a building, a huge tower near the s end, a long central spine running N from it to a lesser tower at Byng Place, and branching off it a regular grid of lower buildings for the different schools and departments, swallowing up Torrington Square and filling the whole area between Malet Street and Woburn Square. The single unified scheme recalls Holden's early experience as a hospital architect dealing with complex institutions. His revised plan of 1932 omitted the central spine and the N tower, replacing them by separate buildings ranged around the perimeter of the site. Building began in 1933. Senate House and its tower were completed in 1937, then progress was interrupted by the war. In the 1940s–50s fragments of the scheme were built to the N: ranges along Malet Street for Birkbeck College, and the Students' Union; and on the E side the School of Oriental and African Studies (SOAS) and the Warburg Institute.

Forshaw and Abercrombie's London plan of 1943 proposed a larger traffic-free university precinct. The outline development plan of 1959 by *Sir Leslie Martin* endorsed the principle on a more limited scale, but had to accept two main traffic routes through the area, across Byng Place and down Malet Street. His plan proposed the completion of Holden's precinct and the creation of a further one on the sites of Woburn and Gordon Squares, with new buildings conforming to the heights of the older terraces, but preserving only the w side of Tavistock Square. Growing resistance to the destruction of Bloomsbury failed to halt the demolition of the E side of Woburn Square, with its central feature of Christ Church, but ensured that only the first phase of the replacement was built, *Denys Lasdun*'s library for SOAS and his powerful range for the Institutes of Education and Advanced Legal Studies, completed in 1976. A change of approach in the 1980s produced a fake Georgian range of university offices along Russell Square in place of Holden's proposed university hall; in the 90s this was followed by the discreet SOAS Extension and Brunei Gallery by *Nicholas Hare* and a restrained extension for Birkbeck by *Stanton Williams*. The central precinct is now beginning to make sense as a pedestrian area, as clutter is replaced by landscaping.

109 SENATE HOUSE AND LIBRARY, Malet Street. *Charles Holden's*
building of 1932–7, of smooth Portland stone above a base of
Cornish granite, has its main fronts facing E and W. A broad
entrance lobby below the library tower leads s to library, halls and
council rooms, N to the School of Slavonic Studies and Institute
of Historical Research (the latter completed after the war).
Holden's ability at massing on a grand scale had been demonstrated a little earlier by his headquarters building for London
Transport, No. 55 Broadway, Westminster. Pevsner, preferring the
'vigour and directness' of Holden's later and simpler Scandinavian-
inspired London Transport stations, found the style puzzling: 'a
strangely traditional, undecided modernism; the general block
shapes are clearly of the C20, and ornament and mouldings
reduced to a minimum. But the window shapes remain Georgian,
and steel window frames in such windows always look unpleasantly
mean. What there is of mouldings is heavy, especially the odd
broad buttresses leading with set offs up the centres of the E and W
sides of the tower. Equally baffling are the small balconies representing the only emphasis on the centre of the Senate House front
and the balconies and arches squeezed into the corners between
the tower block and the lower projecting wings of the tower before
the upper parts step back.'

Inside, spacious public areas, finished with dignified restraint:
Travertine marble floors; handsome doors, light fittings and railings in bronze (London plane leaves are the chief motif). Holden's
Arts and Crafts background shows through here, as with the decorative dated rainwater heads outside. Two large halls (Macmillan
and Beveridge) occupy the ground floors of the internal courtyards, on each side of a generous processional stairhall with
balconies along the sides. On the upstairs landing, models of the
early scheme, and a bust of Holden †1960, by *L. Tarling*. Beyond,
over the entrance, the plain Chancellor's Hall, completed later. To
the E administrative dignity is expressed by the lavish panelling of
the suite ending in Senate Room and Court Room, with heraldic
glass in the lobbies by *Erwin Bossanyi*. Refectories and common
rooms on second and third floors were given some tentative ceiling decoration by students from London art schools. The LIBRARY
has its main reading rooms on the fourth floor, the two Middlesex
reading rooms (given by the MCC) furnished in oak, the

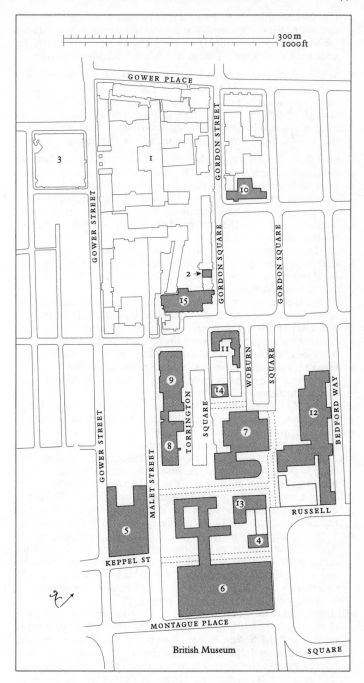

University of London. Plan

Goldsmiths' Library in English walnut with a ceiling of cypress, and with glass by *Bossanyi*. The 209-ft tower contains book stacks, planned for 950,000 books, supported by an internal steel frame, unlike the rest of the building, which is of traditional masonry.

The rest of the central site is described clockwise, starting in Malet Street, followed by the buildings of the extended site to the E. Holden's buildings of the 40s–50s are well mannered but disappointingly dull, four and five storeys, of red brick with stone bands hinting at classical proportions; their main fault is that they face outwards and fail to present an interesting face to the central garden.

BIRKBECK COLLEGE, Malet Street. Founded as the London Mechanics' Institute, 1824. The steel frame was put up in 1939, the building completed in 1951. N extension 1962–6 by *K. Urquart* of *Adams, Holden & Pearson*; the same height but squeezing in seven storeys over the basement, and so more crowded with windows, but with the benefit of an open ground-floor passage leading to the garden behind.

STUDENTS' UNION, Malet Street. 1947–55. Similar proportions to Birkbeck, with sports facilities in the basement. Three big hall windows to the N; to the E two wings project, with later glass barrel roof between.

WARBURG INSTITUTE, Woburn Square. 1955–8. The tall top floor at the back was built for the Courtauld Institute Gallery (now in Somerset House). The front to the square is elaborated by stone frames to some of the windows, to cluttered effect. In the entrance
59    hall *Coade* stone panel of the nine muses, from Charles Fowler's architectural office at No. 1 Gordon Square, demolished 1955.

To the S, five of the original houses of Woburn Square survive, despite numerous rebuilding schemes.

CLORE MANAGEMENT CENTRE for Birkbeck College, facing Torrington Square. By *Stanton Williams*, 1996–7. Pale brick, with big upper windows to the garden; top floor set back behind a thin projecting stone band. The height respects the older terraces.

SOAS BUILDINGS (School of Oriental and African Studies). The earliest part, dated 1940, the first and best of Holden's lesser buildings on the site, N of the E–W pedestrian way from Russell Street created in the 1990s. Pleasantly proportioned, the central entrance with three doors, a rounded end to the E as a special feature. Attached behind is the library extension by *Denys Lasdun*, 1968–73, which forms part of Lasdun's development towards Bedford Way (*see* below). Tough, seven-storey exterior in concrete, with windows set back between strong horizontals. An interesting library space within: stepped-back balconies and toplit centre with diagrid ceiling. Outside, SCULPTURE: seated figure of Tiruvalluver, Tamil philosopher, given 1996.

BRUNEI GALLERY and SOAS EXTENSION. By *Nicholas Hare Architects*, completed 1995. Between the NW corner of Russell Square and the Senate House. Two parts; a five-storey teaching block and a lower gallery wing to the W. The taller part has a layered exterior: modernity behind a brown brick skin. The brick wall lines up neatly with the W terrace of Russell Square, but sings its own tune. The top floor has a busy rhythm of small openings; the square glazing pattern of the deeply inset windows below is continued by a recessed all-glass stair-tower and set-back attic floor. Ingenious spaces inside: basement lecture theatre; toplit upper corridors. The gallery entrance hall is a tour-de-force in fair-faced concrete: a toplit drum with punched-out openings and upper balcony. Exhibition space on two floors, with shallow brick vaulting, and a delightful oriental roof garden with water feature and pergolas.

No. 30 RUSSELL SQUARE. 1913–14 by *Sir John Burnet*, pre-dating the Senate House. Built for the Royal Institute of Chemistry, now used by Birkbeck College. The counterpart to the SOAS Extension at the opposite end of the Russell Square terrace. A thoughtful free classical composition which can hold its own. Brown brick; the same height as the older terrace but of different proportions, with pronounced cornice. Three bays to the square, a longer asymmetrical s front in two parts with differing floor levels, divided by a big doorway. In its broken segmental pediment a seated figure of Sir Joseph Priestley by *Gilbert Bayes*.

STEWART HOUSE (Schools Examination Board), Russell Square and Montague Place. 1985, designed by *Gabriel Epstein* of *Shepheard, Epstein & Hunter*, executive architect *Charles Tarling* of *Adams Holden & Pearson*. On the site of Holden's proposed assembly hall next to Senate House. A concession to the conservation movement. The long Neo-Georgian frontage to Russell Square looks fine from a distance, copying the proportions of the genuine terrace to the N. Closer up, the broader windows pretending to be doorways just look silly. Facing Montague Place an (unused) Grecian porch inspired by the one opposite, then after a glazed link the building turns modern; above first-floor balconies big projecting oriels with bronze glazing run up above the roof-line.

INSTITUTE OF ADVANCED LEGAL STUDIES and INSTITUTE OF EDUCATION, Bedford Way. On the extension to the central site. By *Denys Lasdun*, planned 1965, completed 1976. Only part of the original scheme was built. The best approach is from the NW corner of Russell Square, where an agreeably landscaped pedestrian route starts between Lasdun's SOAS extension on the l. (*see* above) and a terrace dramatically stepping down on the r. The original conception belongs to the era of urban megastructures (cf. Brunswick Centre, Holborn; Alexandra Road, Hampstead). There were to have been five stepped spurs, linked by a long range defining the perimeter of the site along Bedford Way, with an upper pedestrian route threaded through on the precinct side. The layering and stepping, the pedestrian routes at different heights, and the use of a long single range tying all together can be traced back to Lasdun's earlier buildings, especially the University of East Anglia designed in 1962, but in this urban context they appear in a more rigidly diagrammatic form. The single spur that was built is highly effective visually, with a strikingly sculptural 122 silhouette of angular concrete escape stairs rising above the floor levels and curtain walling with bronzed aluminium spandrels. Similar contrasts of texture and shape appear along Bedford Way, where the strong horizontals of the curtain-walled main range are punctuated by projecting concrete lecture rooms and service towers. Here the effect, unrelieved by landscaping, is starker and forbiddingly monolithic, although tempered by the cut-away corners on

slim concrete piers and by the transparency of the set-back
entrance floors of the Institute of Education. This has a foyer on
two levels running through to the back of the building, arranged
around an impressively monumental stair descending around a
well to Logan Hall, a fan-shaped auditorium in the basement.

## 2. Other university buildings in Bloomsbury

Converted terraces (*see* Perambulation 4) rub shoulders with buildings put up on whatever sites became available. The main effort was
in the 1950s, when styles compromised uneasily between Georgian
traditions and a timid modernism.

DR WILLIAMS LIBRARY, No. 14 Gordon Square. 1849 by *T. L.
Donaldson,* the first Professor of Architecture at University College
(*see* above). Used as a library from 1890, but built as the college's
first hall of residence. In contrast to Wilkins's Neo-Grecian,
Donaldson chose a more domestic battlemented Neo-Jacobean.
On a ridiculous scale, though with a certain ungainly charm. The
seven storeys are disguised by running two sets of tall mullion-
and-transom windows through two floors. Big central entrance
with oriel above, flanked by turrets.

INSTITUTES OF ARCHAEOLOGY AND CLASSICAL STUDIES and
EXAMINATION HALLS, Gordon Square. 1954–8 by *Booth,
Ledeboer & Pinckheard.* In 1958 hailed by the *Architects' Journal* as
a 'genuine C20 building'. The Institutes have a nice recessed
ground floor, but the brick wall above with six rows of small windows is painfully dull. The Examination Halls are distinguished
by larger windows.

INSTITUTE OF CHILD HEALTH, No. 30 Guilford Street. 1953–5
by *S. E. T. Cusdin* of *Easton & Robertson,* built as a maternity and
child welfare centre at the corner of Guilford Place; enlarged
1962–6. A varied and successful design; curtain-walled front with
ground and top floors treated differently; a brick flank steps back
to Guilford Place with a projecting window strip at third-floor
level. Two storeys of lightweight attic floors with lively monopitch
roofs, 1994 by *ORMS*. No. 20 Guilford Street, 1968–9, also by
*Easton & Robertson* and curtain-walled, but routine.

LONDON SCHOOL OF HYGIENE AND TROPICAL MEDICINE,
Keppel Street and Gower Street. 1926–8 by *P. Morley Horder and
Verner O. Rees.* Stripped classical fronts in meticulously cut
Portland stone; in a comparable spirit to Holden's slightly later
Senate House, but more old-fashioned. Four storeys rising to five
and six behind. Austerely detailed, with large wreaths and names
of medical scientists in relief, the sculpture by *Alan Howe*. The
chunky carving contrasts oddly with the delicate gilded flora and
fauna decorating the balconies.

SCHOOL OF PHARMACY and EXAMINATION LABORATORIES,
Brunswick Square. By *Herbert J. Rowse*, begun 1939, completed
1960. The site, with the shell of the building, was acquired in
1949 from the Pharmaceutical Society. Grimly symmetrical with
raised ends and centre, overpowering the N side of the square. Tall
ground-floor windows, a long strip high up for the laboratories.
Nicely detailed bronze doors.

HALLS OF RESIDENCE in Bloomsbury are uninspiring. COLLEGE HALL (for University College), Malet Street, 1931 by *W.J. Walford*. Seven storeys, crudely detailed in brick and stone. After the Second World War some halls were created behind existing frontages, e.g. CONNAUGHT HALL, Nos. 36–45 Tavistock Square, 1958–61 by *Booth, Ledeboer & Pinckheard*; others replaced derelict or bomb-damaged terraces. One of the largest is the INTERNATIONAL HALL OF RESIDENCE, Brunswick Square, s side, 1958–62 and 1964–7 by *S. E. T. Cusdin* of *Easton & Robertson*. Long, dull brick frontage, with the concrete box-frame exposed on the end walls. In Cartwright Gardens, COMMONWEALTH HALL, planned 1949, built 1960–3, by *K. Urquart* of *Adams, Holden & Pearson*, and HUGHES PARRY HALL, 1967–9 by *Booth, Ledeboer & Pinckheard*.

## GRAY'S INN
### Gray's Inn Road

The Society of Gray's Inn was on this site from the C14, occupying the manor house of Purpoole, which belonged to the de Grey family. The Inns of Court, or colleges of lawyers, similar in architectural character to a certain extent to the colleges of Oxford and Cambridge, form a belt of legal precincts w of the City of London, starting by the river with the Temple. Gray's Inn is the least known and the most northerly. The historic core is the C16 range with Hall and Chapel to the s of the entrance from Gray's Inn Road, now standing between two courtyards created in their present form in the late C17 and C18. A third more informal court lies to the w looking out over the famous Walks, laid out by Sir Francis Bacon in the early C17. 'The many contrasts between heights and sizes of open spaces should be specially studied: narrow paved spaces, wide turfed spaces, and finally the long expanse of the gardens. It is English visual planning at its best.' So Pevsner wrote in 1952, when the buildings were still being extensively reconstructed after substantial war damage. The restrained and sensitive post-war repair and rebuilding was by *Sir Edward Maufe*; more recent schemes have been more variable in quality.

HALL. Rebuilt in 1556–8; of brick with stone dressings, revealed in the 1890s when stucco of 1826 was removed. Typical unadventurous mid-C16 Tudor detail, much restored. The hall is raised above an undercroft and has straight-headed windows of three uncusped lights with transom, set high up between buttresses. To the N a canted bay with cusped lights; the s bay is a post-war addition. The battlements date from 1826, but the crowstepped gables are an original feature, as are the N and s doors with four-centred arches, now concealed within later porches. At the w end, buttery in C18 Gothic style, an addition of 1970–2 by *Raymond Erith* (*see also* below). INTERIOR. The hall was gutted in 1941, but faithfully restored by *Maufe* from 1948. The hammerbeam roof follows the original design, archbraces with a little tracery below the hammerbeam, simple mullions above; diagonally set pendants. In the N bay window a good display of ARMORIAL STAINED

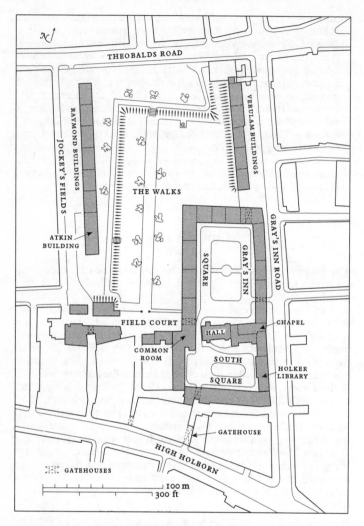

Gray's Inn. Plan

GLASS of the C16 onwards; *William Peckitt* supplied armorial glass in 1763–4. SCREEN, rescued in pieces in 1941 and reassembled. Late C16, with much strapwork decoration in shallow relief. Five bays with Ionic columns between shallow arches; reclining female figures in the spandrels. Above the columns an ornate entablature. The gallery above has a lively profile: modillions carrying terms punctuate individual scrolled and pierced frontages.

CHAPEL. Much rebuilt by *Maufe* after major war damage. The medieval chapel had been remodelled in the C16, with chambers above; it was rebuilt in 1619–24 and again, without chambers, in 1689, and stuccoed in 1826. Restorations took place in 1893 and in 1930–1, when the stucco was removed. Maufe's exterior has a peeled appearance: plain brick, parapet, small Perp doorway with lozenge stops and four-centred arched windows with minimal mouldings. Inside, blocked C16 mullioned windows visible in the formerly external S wall. The five-light E window breaks into the Gray's Inn Road front. Post-war fittings of Canadian maple. ORGAN by *N. P. Mander*, 1993. STAINED GLASS. E window with archbishops, 1895. N side, Bishop Lancelot Andrews by *Selwyn Image*, c. 1910; War Memorial window by *Christopher Whall*, c. 1920.

GRAY'S INN SQUARE. The large square N of Hall and Chapel was formed from two smaller spaces in the later C17; rebuilding was hastened by three fires in the 1680s, and the range between the two older courts was demolished in 1685. The work appears to have been complete by 1693, when it was ordered that a ball was to be set over every door 'with figures for distinction'. The arrangement is similar to New Square, Lincoln's Inn, of the same date; plain, regular brick ranges of four storeys over basements, doorways with broken segmental pediments leading to the staircases to individual chambers. Original joinery in No. 1; staircase with heavy balusters. The rest repaired and rebuilt after war damage. GATEWAY to Gray's Inn Road, 1688, two bays wide, marked by a pediment; rusticated stone surround to the entrance facing the road. The work was supervised by the Society's surveyor Mr *Rider*.

SOUTH SQUARE. Only No. 1 on the S side is pre-war: of 1759, with three widely spaced bays, remaining from the C18 rebuilding of C16 chambers. The rest of the S side rebuilt by *Maufe*. On the E side, Maufe's HOLKER LIBRARY, in an attenuated late classical style. It replaced *Edwin Cooper*'s lusher building of 1929, destroyed in the war. Shallow pediment over the centre five bays, with first-floor library windows opening onto tapering metal balconies, in a Swedish 30s spirit. Inside, a good semicircular staircase; library with galleries framed by tall unmoulded round-headed arches. On the N side, pedimented projecting entrance dated 1952 to offices and treasury, backing up against the chapel, in place of C19 buildings. W of the hall, No. 10, COMMON ROOM, 1970–2 by *Raymond Erith*, his last major work. Dignified four-storey front with central pediment. Dentilled cornice in deference to the older buildings. The mixture of different styles is deliberate; continued by Erith's Georgian Gothic buttery opposite, attached to the Hall but linked underground to No. 10. In South Square, bronze statue of Bacon by *Pomeroy*, 1912.

GATEHOUSE to Holborn. Land to provide access to Holborn was acquired in 1593. The gatehouse was a timber structure, encased in stucco in 1867. The present building, a reconstruction with facsimile exterior, was put up in 1965–6 after the original collapsed during rebuilding of the premises to the E. Square bay window above an elliptical arch, with niches to l. and r.

FIELD COURT, reached by a passage from Gray's Inn Square. An attractive, irregular area with old paving, open to the Walks on the N side. SE corner much rebuilt. On the S side, No. 2, only one room deep, with an authentic early C18 frontage preserved during refurbishment in 1990–1. More elaborate than the earlier chambers; segment-headed windows with triple brick keystones and aprons below. Alleys lead from here to Holborn: gateway to Fulwood Place with stone griffins; entry to Warwick Court bridged by indifferent buildings for the School of Law, 1964. Opposite, No. 4, grand Edwardian chambers, with an exuberantly Baroque doorway with Doric columns and pediment. Further w, No. 5, C18, two-storeyed and domestic-looking, with stucco above rustication, good railings, and tented balconies to the N front.

VERULAM BUILDINGS, 1803 and 1811, by *Joseph Wigg*, and RAYMOND BUILDINGS, 1825, by *George Wigg*, flank the Walks to E and w. Both are exceedingly plain; four storeys over basements, with entrances on the sides away from the Walks. Stock brick with parapets and minimal stone banding, in contrast to the red brick and dentilled cornices of Gray's Inn Square. Raymond Buildings is continued s by ATKIN BUILDING, a pastiche in similar style, 1987 by *Vigers*, surveyors to the Inn. Proposals in 1990 to build over the N end of the Walks were fortunately rejected.

WALKS. First laid out in the late C16: walls were built in 1597 around the field to the w of the area which later became Gray's Inn Square, and trees and hedges were planted under the direction of *Francis Bacon*, a bencher of the Inn. Further improvements were made after 1606 when Bacon became treasurer, including a banqueting house built on the upper Walks to the w in 1608–9. Bacon's basic lay-out remains, although none of his planting. The Walks became a fashionable place of resort; early C18 views show them with gravelled paths running s–N between rows of trees (at first elms and sycamores, replaced in the C18 by limes and later by planes), raised terraces to w and N, and an open aspect to Highgate Hill. The fine IRON GATES at the s end were added in 1723. The lay-out was simplified in 1755, probably by *Capability Brown*; the mount was removed and walls to the upper Walks were replaced by slopes. Raymond Buildings now occupies part of the w terrace; the N terrace has some mighty plane trees, with early C19 railings to Theobalds Road. On the lower ground, a single broad walk with an avenue of red oak planted after the hurricane of 1989.

## LINCOLN'S INN

Lincoln's Inn preserves exceptionally well the collegiate character of the colleges of lawyers on the edge of the City. It should be wandered through, just as one wanders through Oxford and Cambridge colleges. There are entrances in Carey Street and in Chancery Lane, but the start should be at the Gatehouse in Chancery Lane (where the main door is open on weekdays).

The Inn was founded some time in the C14 on land which had been the Dominicans' before they moved to Blackfriars in 1276. It then became the mansion of the Earl of Lincoln, and he left it as a residence to lawyers. Yet there are no certain records of before 1422. Old Buildings, that is the E court with the Gatehouse, was built *c.* 1490–1520.

GATEHOUSE. Built in 1518, but reconstructed in 1966–9 by *K.A. Williams*, together with the adjoining range to the s, Nos. 25–26 Old Buildings. It has square angle towers to the outside as well as

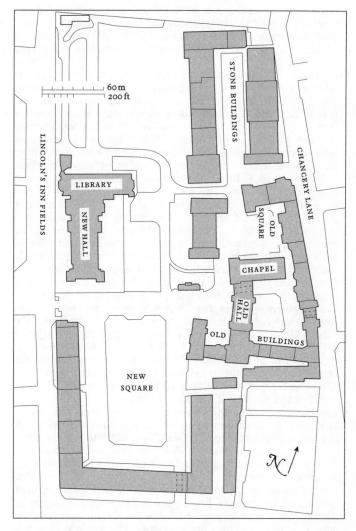

Lincoln's Inn. Plan

the inside and a gateway with a four-centred arch and a pedestrian
entrance to its N. Over the archway are the arms of Henry VIII,
the Earl of Lincoln, and Sir Thomas Lovell. The heavy oak doors
date from 1564. The gabled buildings to the S, before their reconstruction in 1969, were partly of *c.* 1520 and partly a remodelling
of 1609, with later windows.

OLD BUILDINGS, entered through the Gatehouse, is a quadrangle
of irregular shape closed entirely by buildings except for a gap E of
the Chapel. Chambers to the E and S, the Old Hall to the W,
Chapel to the NW, all of red brick except for the rendered Chapel.
On the S side, Nos. 24–21 are Tudor redone in 1609, with two

polygonal stair-turrets and windows, and plain rusticated doorways of the late C17. (Interiors altered, but some original timberwork was retained in Nos. 21, 22 and 23.) The old work continues
to the W, as will be seen later. Between it and the Hall is a passage
made in 1583.

OLD HALL. Built in 1489–92 (although it owes its present appearance to a thoroughgoing restoration and part-rebuilding by *Sir
John Simpson* in 1924–8). It is unusual in having four oriel windows,
two at each end. The matching S ones at the screens end date
from 1583; they are part of a S extension by *John Symons*. The wall
between the oriels is of diapered brick (rebuilt after removal of
later stucco), buttressed, with three three-light windows under
four-centred arches. Attached on the N is an archway. This dates
only from 1926–8. Inside, the hall has an elaborate arch-braced
roof with collar-beams, two sets of moulded purlins and cusped
wind-braces. It was exposed and restored in 1924–8, when a simple
plaster barrel vault of 1720, probably by *James Gibbs*, was
removed. The walls have linenfold panelling. Re-erected against
the S wall is a SCREEN, with elaborately studded termini pilasters
carrying busts, and an upper gallery also with termini pilasters. It
was made in 1624 by *Robert Lynton*, and is a descendant of the C16
ones at Gray's Inn and the Middle Temple. The strapwork
surround to the clock above may be an addition of 1627. In the
former gallery openings, heraldic paintings of 1819, added when
the screen was placed against the wall. Of the same date the
plaster Gothick ceiling in the passage behind, added by *James
Wigg* during the alterations. Against the N wall, *Hogarth*'s big
PAINTING of St Paul before Felix, installed in 1750. Inside the
covered passage between hall and Chapel, a reset C13 arch on
shafts, with dogtooth ornament. It probably comes from the wall
arcading of the N wall of the original Chapel.

CHAPEL, rebuilt 1619–23. The benchers opted for a building in
traditional style 'answerable' to the other buildings of the Inn. It
was carried out by the mason *John Clark*, who was asked to draw
the 'platforme' of the model in 1618. The traditional attribution to
*Inigo Jones* is derived from a brief reference which suggests that his
advice was sought earlier in 1618, but, it seems, not followed. The
Chapel stands on an open undercroft with Gothic four-centred
arches and lierne vaults. Its only up-to-date feature is the use of
Tuscan demi-columns attached to the piers. Buttresses with five
set-offs separate the bays of the Chapel. The windows have still
completely Perp tracery of a familiar pattern. The E window was
renewed in 1795–6 by *James Wyatt*, who also renewed the roof.
The latter was reconstructed again in 1882 by *Samuel Salter*, also
responsible for the pinnacles on the buttresses and the W bay and
forebuilding. – PULPIT with tester. Charming early C18 work. –
COMMUNION TABLE of *c.*1700, given in 1938. – COMMUNION
RAIL. Late C17, with twisted balusters. – PEWS. The ends are contemporary with the Chapel. – STAINED GLASS. Much-restored
figures of apostles in the S windows, by the *van Linge* brothers,
early C17. The figures opposite are largely reconstruction after an
air raid in 1915.

The N end of the E range carries on E of the Chapel, then continues
W with an uninspired gabled Neo-Elizabethan range of brick: Nos.

8–10 is by *Sir George Gilbert Scott*, 1874; Nos. 11–13, 1878–80 by *J. Oldrid Scott*, Nos. 14–15 of 1886. Just N of the Chapel it forms a small and pretty court, OLD SQUARE, with a centrally placed tree, a nice contrast to the previous quadrangle. From the SW corner one can reach another Tudor court, formed by the continuation of Old Buildings W of Old Hall, with ranges of 1524 and 1534 on S and W sides, again with polygonal stair-turrets. The N side is open towards spacious lawns with old trees, and the large buildings of the later C18 and early C19.

NEW SQUARE lies to the SW, a complete late C17 square of remarkable size. This was begun by Henry Serle in 1680 as a private venture, largely on his own land. Members of the Inn objected and by an agreement of 1682 the square was laid out for the benefit of the Inn, completed after Serle's death in 1690 by Nicholas Barbon.* The gardens, with a large central lawn and trees, were laid out in 1843. The buildings are of identical design, designed as chambers (cf. Gray's Inn), with four storeys of even height and with open segmental pediments over the doorways to the staircases. On the E side, Nos. 1–2 are the backs of the C16 buildings. On the S side is a broad gateway of 1697 to Carey Street. It has a four-centred arch and a wide segmental pediment with big volutes on the N, a wide open pediment with double-curved scrolly sides on the S – designs evidently not in the court taste of Wren and his masons. On the W side, No. 10 was rebuilt in 1862, and No. 11 was rebuilt after war damage by *A. F. R. Anderson*.

The N half of Lincoln's Inn, consisting of Stone Buildings, the New Hall and the Library, forms a contrasting picture, visually highly successful, the Palladian chastity of the one set against the picturesque large-scale Neo-Tudor of the other.

STONE BUILDINGS was designed by *Sir Robert Taylor* and built in 1774–80. The main front is to the W, stone-faced (hence the name) and with angle pavilions emphasized by attached giant columns with pediments. The long middle part is entirely plain. The S end of this range has pilasters. The oblong back court is completely regular. The S end of the W range again has attached columns, to make a *point-de-vue* for those coming from Chancery Lane through the gate facing this pavilion. The shorter E range has a stone-faced centre with arched principal windows, but the ends and sides are brick. The narrow N end of this court or close is a part of the composition of the W range; at its E end, one bay flanked by pilasters. Obviously some change of plan was made here. The S end of the W range was added by *Philip Hardwick* in 1842–5 to Taylor's original design.

The NEW HALL and LIBRARY were designed by *Philip Hardwick* in 1842, and completed under the supervision of his son, *P. C. Hardwick*, in 1845. *J. L. Pearson* was chief assistant and worked on the details. It is an eminently successful piece of romantic design. In spite of the size, which by that time had become necessary for the population and reputation of the Inn, it keeps up a vivacious variety. The buildings are of red diapered brick, lighter than the old ones. The Hall has two big bay windows at the high-table end

*I owe these details to Frank Kelsall.

and two square tower-like erections at the other. A louvre in the
middle adds to the picturesque appeal. From the street connecting Lincoln's Inn Fields with the older buildings the hall is reached
by a nicely and freely arranged staircase. The Library follows,
connected with the Hall by a room with an octagonal lantern, and
smaller, less formal rooms to l. and r. The Library, which was
enlarged to the E in 1871–3 by *Scott* (with much interference from
E. B. Denison, *Lord Grimthorpe*), now comes forward into the
garden, giving the whole group an L-shape. Hardwick's E window
was reused, and at the SE angle a spire of moderate height was
added. Towards Lincoln's Inn Fields the façades of Hall and
Library are in line, but here the variety is maintained by a low
house attached to the Library to the N, and the archway (by *P. C.
Hardwick*) to the S of the Hall. The Hardwicks' work at Lincoln's
Inn is no longer as naive as Tudor work of 1830, nor is it yet as
pedantic as Tudor imitation was to become soon. HALL INTERIOR.
The roof, redesigned by *P. C. Hardwick*, has the appearance of a
hammerbeam, as was originally intended, although it is suspended
from iron rods. It has a lantern in the centre. The lively colours
are a restoration of 1987, based on the original scheme. At the S
end there is a screen, and on the N wall *George Frederick Watts*'s huge
early fresco of The Lawgivers (1852–9), with Minos and Mahomet,
Moses and Solon, Charlemagne and Edward I and many others.
The style is decidedly Raphaelesque, derived from the Stanze, but
filtered, as it were, through the German Romantics such as Schnorr
von Carolsfeld or Führich. Watts described it as the only true
fresco in England. It did not survive well; it needed treatment in
1870, 1890 and 1927, and was damaged in the Second World War,
but has since been successfully restored. The LIBRARY INTERIOR
is also very tall. It has big canted bay windows at E and W ends.
Shelves on three levels, with iron galleries. The interior work was
done by *Scott*. STATUE of Lord Erskine by *Westmacott*, 1830.

## BRITISH MUSEUM
### Great Russell Street

*Sir Robert Smirke*'s monumental Grecian building of 1823–52, set
back behind an ample forecourt, comes as a surprise in the narrow
Bloomsbury street. It houses the first public museum in Europe
with a collection that was accepted as a national responsibility, a
development from the princely and private collections that had
begun during the Italian Renaissance. The most important additions are the famous Round Reading Room, added in the central
courtyard by *Sydney Smirke* in 1854–7, and the fine classical N wing
facing Montague Place, by *Sir John Burnet*, 1907–14. *Sir Norman
Foster & Partners'* bold plan for transforming the space around the
Reading Room was adopted in 1994.

### History

Sir Hans Sloane's collections were acquired for the nation, after his
death in 1753, by means of an Act of Parliament which established
the British Museum for their display, together with the Cotton Library,

given to the nation in 1700, and the Harley Manuscripts, acquired with funds provided through the Act. For reasons of economy, the government did not provide a new building for the collections, but acquired Montagu House, the grand mansion in Great Russell Street built for the first Duke of Montagu in 1675–9 by *Hooke* and rebuilt after a fire in 1686. It was opened to the public in 1759. Early gifts included the old Royal Library given by George II in 1757, exotica from Captain Cook's voyages, and Sir William Hamilton's collection of Greek vases (1772). The museum's famous larger items arrived later: Egyptian antiquities, including the Rosetta Stone, obtained in 1802 from the French after the defeat of Napoleon's forces in Egypt, and then the great classical collections – all purchased by the government – the antique sculptures collected by Charles Townley in 1805, the Bassae Friezes in 1815, the Parthenon sculptures (Elgin Marbles) in 1816. A Department of Antiquities was established in 1807. The Townley Marbles and Egyptian sculpture were housed in a new NW wing built by *George Saunders* in 1804–8, the Parthenon sculptures in a temporary building to its W. As the collections grew – a major collection of colossal Egyptian sculpture was acquired in 1819 – so did pressure for an entirely new building. In 1820 *Sir Robert Smirke*, architect to the Office of Works, was invited to review the requirements of the museum, and the matter became yet more urgent with the acquisition of George III's library in 1823. Parliament voted £40,000 to provide this with a suitable home. Smirke's task was thus to create both a library and space for a very substantial quantity of bulky pieces of sculpture, as well as the smaller collections.

Smirke's scheme of 1823, conditioned by the existing building and by limited funds, proposed a phased rebuilding to a courtyard plan, starting with two parallel wings to the N of the existing Montagu House. The E wing was to house the King's Library, with an upper floor at first intended for a picture gallery (the latter was abandoned after the decision to create the National Gallery in 1824). This E range was to be linked to a N range, and eventually to a S entrance range replacing the old house. The building dates are: E wing 1823–8, W wing N section 1825–34 (Egyptian collections), N wing 1833–8 (library and reading rooms), S wing 1842–6. The residences for the officers, extending E and W from the S wing, were added in 1844–9. The western galleries, which required the demolition of the Townley Gallery of 1804–8, were begun in 1846, providing accommodation for, among other things, the Assyrian relics from Layard's excavations, an indication of the broadening of academic interests by the mid C19. Gates and forecourt were completed in 1852, when the building was at last opened to the public. It did not meet with universal enthusiasm, for by then taste had shifted away from Smirke's pure, monumental Neo-Grecian. Nor was the building adequate for the continually expanding collections. The library alone was growing by *c*. 30,000 books a year, faster than any other library in the world. In 1852 Antonio Panizzi, the celebrated Keeper of Printed Books, proposed a circular reading room to fill Smirke's central courtyard. It was designed by *Sydney Smirke*, who had succeeded his older brother as architect in 1845, when the latter retired owing to ill health. The Reading Room was built in 1854–7, with book storage in the surrounding quadrants.

In the later C19 parts of the original collections moved elsewhere: portraits to the National Portrait Gallery in 1879, the natural history collections to Waterhouse's new museum in South Kensington in 1880–3. Other sections grew as scholarly interest and archaeological activity expanded to include British, medieval and oriental antiquities. The Trustees acquired the freehold of the surrounding buildings from the Bedford Estate in 1894–5. New galleries were added to Smirke's core; the most ambitious, the King Edward VII Wing to the N, 1907–14 by *Sir John Burnet*, was all that was executed of a much more extensive scheme, including new outer wings to E and W. The failure to provide links to the rest of the museum left a difficult legacy. Later additions and changes were piecemeal, heavily dependent on private donations. The Duveen Gallery to the W, providing a new setting for the Parthenon sculptures, was completed in 1938 by the American Beaux Arts architect *John Russell Pope* but, because of disruption by the war, was not opened until 1962. Some radical remodelling of older galleries took place from the 1960s, notably the classical sculpture galleries by *Robin Wade*, 1969, followed by the Assyrian galleries, 1970, and Egyptian sculpture gallery, 1981. A new wing, W of the S wing, with restaurants, exhibition gallery and offices by *Colin St John Wilson*, was opened in 1980; new Japanese galleries were created in the roof space of the Edward VII Wing by *Gordon Bowyer & Partners*, 1985–90.

After the Second World War the museum abandoned Burnet's ambitions plans for expanding E and W at the expense of Montague Street, Bedford Square and Bloomsbury Street (the area to the N was by then occupied by London University). Instead, a site to the S of the museum was designated for a new library, around a grand forecourt opening up a long vista to the museum. Plans for this, by *Sir Leslie Martin* and *Colin St John Wilson*, were published in 1964, but in 1967 the scheme was rejected by the Labour government after local objections to the destruction of the character of Bloomsbury. A smaller site was agreed on in 1970, excluding the W side of Bloomsbury Square. In 1972 the British Library Act decreed that the library was to become a separate institution. Although plans for building the library S of the museum were confirmed by the Conservatives in 1973, the new Labour government of 1974 dropped the scheme in favour of a site at St Pancras, where building eventually began in 1982.

In 1994, with the imminent departure of library and manuscripts (including the books from the King's Library), the firm of *Sir Norman Foster & Partners* was selected in a competition whose brief involved making use of the reading rooms and the surrounding vacant spaces, and providing improved circulation inside the museum – a desperate need for a building with six million visitors a year. Enabling work began in 1997.

*The original building: exterior*

*Sir Robert Smirke* did not publish his total design until 1844, but there is sufficient evidence to prove that his splendid entrance front, with its noble array of Greek Ionic columns forming portico and colonnade, was conceived by 1823.* The design of the

58

* See J. M. Crook, *The British Museum*, 1972, and *The King's Works*, Vol. VI, 1973, for a discussion of Smirke's sources.

museum thus belongs to the same era as the vast Glyptothek at Munich by Klenze (1815–30) and Schinkel's Altes Museum in Berlin (1823–30), the first with eight-column Ionic portico, the second with long Ionic colonnade. Like other museums and libraries of this time they reflect the period's new faith in humanism, its great respect for *Bildung* and its new democracy of learning. Their inspiration can be traced back to the gargantuan designs for museums and libraries done by the young French architects of the late C18 for their *Grands Prix*, and hence such spectacular and at the same time nobly Grecian work as the reconstructions inside the Louvre for Napoleon's collections and inside the Vatican for the Papal collections. The British Museum's unusual combination of portico and colonnade (forty-four columns in all), applied to the Palladian formula of a main block with projecting wings, possibly looks back to the C18 Dublin Parliament House, but the treatment is rigorously Grecian in form, the fruit of Smirke's visits to Sicily and Greece, and his deep admiration for the severe logic of Greek architecture. Thus the portico is an entrance, the colonnade is deep enough to be functional, there is no meaningless rustication or balustrading, the walls are of plain, smoothly jointed ashlar. The Grecian detail is not slavish copying but is adapted from a number of sources, the Ionic order based principally on the Temple of Athena Polias at Priene, Asia Minor.

The CONSTRUCTION of the building, though not visible, was innovative. The massive Portland stone slabs are fixed by iron cramps to a brick core. Concrete was used for foundations from 1833, slate for fire-proof flooring, and cast-iron beams, disguised by timber and plaster, were used from the beginning for all roofs and ceilings. Those for the King's Library, spanning 41 ft, with a flanged section to support a ceiling of thin arched iron plates, were designed by the engineer *John Raistrick*.

SCULPTURE: the result of enrichment of the design in the 1840s, a concession to changing taste. Sculpture was planned for the apex and corners of the pediment, for friezes behind the columns, and free-standing groups flanking the steps (drawings show the Wrestlers and Laocoön). But all that was executed was the group in the pediment by *Sir Richard Westmacott* (†1856), his last major work. 61 Solemn clusters of figures illustrate the progress of civilization, from primitive savage on the l., through paganism to the study of astronomy in the centre, to the sciences and arts on the r., terminating in natural history, and encompassing thus the scope of the museum's collections at this time. A blue background (soon obscured) and gilding, renewed after cleaning in 1978, were part of Westmacott's original scheme.

FORECOURT. Completed by *Sydney Smirke* after 1845. On either side KEEPERS' RESIDENCES project forward with pedimented end over sober Doric pilastered front. Each has a link to the museum, originally one-storeyed, heightened on the E side by the similarly detailed White Wing of 1884 by *Sir John Taylor*, and on the W by the discreetly modern glazed upper part of *C. St J. Wilson*'s restaurant extension of 1980. *Sydney Smirke* designed the small GATE LODGES in 1850 and the admirable cast-iron RAILINGS AND GATES, lushly mid-Victorian in their elaboration of

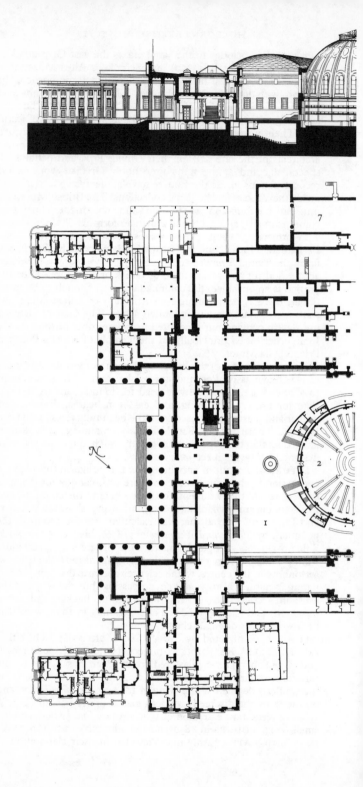

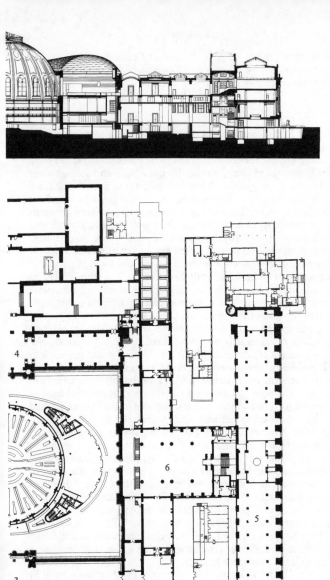

1  Central Court          5  King Edward VII Wing
2  Round Reading Room     6  North Library
3  King's Library         7  Duveen Gallery
4  Egyptian Gallery       8  Keepers' Residences

British Museum. Section and plan, showing *Foster & Partners'*
Great Court scheme

classical detail, made by *John Walker & Co.* of York (models by
*Lovati*, completed by *Thomas* and *Collman & Davis*). The granite
gatepiers were intended to have sculpture.

*Interior*

The PLAN of *Robert Smirke*'s building was simple, a front range two
rooms deep, with grand staircase to the l. of an entrance hall leading through to the central courtyard. The other three ranges were
originally one room deep, but additional offices and storage were
added to the E wing in the 1840s and galleries to the W wing from
the 1840s to the 1880s. Both crowds and collections now make it
difficult to appreciate Smirke's architecture. Greek Doric columns
are used sparingly, to articulate the approach to the staircase, and
to mark the centre of the Egyptian Gallery in the W wing. Doors
are placed on axis, emphasizing the symmetry of formal vistas lit
by high clerestory windows above the cases, and by top lighting on
the upper floor. The great stair breaks into a double flight; its
stone balustrades have a pierced guilloche pattern, but otherwise
ornament is confined to discreetly enriched coffered ceilings. At
the top of the stairs there was originally a wall with two doors and
a niche (destroyed in the Second World War). Robert Smirke had
intended the interiors to be stone-coloured. In 1846 *Sydney Smirke*,
aware of recent discoveries about the use of paint on ancient
Greek buildings, persuaded the Trustees to agree to a colourful
decorative scheme for entrance hall and stairhall. It was carried out
by *Leonard Collman* of *Collman & Davis*, and applauded by *The
Builder* in 1849. The coffered ceilings (restored in 2000) were painted
blue with yellow stars; red and white were used for other enrichments. The galleries in the S and W wings were given deep red
walls, so as to make the London dirt on the sculptures less apparent.
    Little now remains of the original displays; but Smirke's early
case design can still be seen in Room 73. In contrast, the western
sculpture rooms of 1969 (W wing extension, first floor), designed
by *Robin Wade* with *R. D. Russell* and *R. Y. Goodden*, were the first
in the museum to depart radically from the C19 tradition of even-
handed, symmetrical presentation in tune with Smirke's architecture. They adopt a selective, chronological presentation and make
use of dramatic lighting, emphatic display cases, and ingenious
viewing points at different heights.
The KING'S LIBRARY in the E wing, begun in 1823, completed in
1827–8, is one of the great rooms of London, restrained but
festive. Fluted Corinthian pilasters flank the doorcases at either
end, the 300-ft length is broken by four granite columns defining
the broader centre area (reduced from eight, because of expense),
flanked by yellow scagliola pilasters. The ceiling patterns also
break up the space, alternating between coffering and circles.
Brown scagliola panels provide a warmer touch, and so too did
the fine C18 bindings of the books before their removal to the new
British Library. Bookcases on two levels, the upper ones behind a
narrow gallery with brass handrail; the glazing of the cases is later.
The rooms to the S were devoted to manuscripts; the N wing, now
much altered, originally had library and reading rooms. The
ARCHED ROOM at the W end of the N range, built in 1840–1 and

used as a library for incunabula, has three floors of projecting
shelving dramatically linked by a series of arches.

## Courtyard and Round Reading Room

The central COURTYARD, impeccably faced in Portland stone,
remained clear for only a few years. It was planned with porticoes
to both S and N ranges, but simplified in execution; each side has
a central pediment, but with engaged Ionic columns *in antis*
instead of the free-standing N and S colonnades first envisaged by
Smirke. The S entrance was replaced in 1879 by an extension to
the front hall; the N entrance was almost entirely destroyed by
later additions. *Sydney Smirke*'s ROUND READING ROOM of
1854–7, built with bald brick exterior wall, was only intended to be
seen from within. It has a diameter of 140 ft, with a dome of
exposed cast-iron ribs pierced by tall arched windows of two lights,
a pragmatic mid-Victorian approach vastly different from the
Grecian dress of the museum. Neither plan nor construction were
novel (the Radcliffe Camera, George III's library at Buckingham
House, and unexecuted schemes in Paris all provided precedents
for circular libraries, the Coal Exchange for an iron dome). There
were various proposals for decoration of the dome with statuary
and for an elaborate allegorical scheme of painting and sculpture
by *Alfred Stevens*, but this was never executed, so the interior lacked
the panache of its later imitators, such as Washington's Library of
Congress. But the size is spectacular and the accommodation for
the books was ample, in four quadrants of densely packed iron
shelving around the domed space. Users appreciated the heating
(hot-water pipes) and ventilation (a complicated arrangement
with air chambers between ceiling and roof). Sydney Smirke
designed the original chairs, *Panizzi* the black padded reading
desks (now blue) and iron bookshelves.

*Foster*'s GREAT COURT, planned from 1994, swept away the book
store quandrants and later clutter to reveal Smirke's courtyard walls
as the setting for a new covered circulation and exhibition space,
with a semi-elliptical building enclosing the dome. The same firm's
ingenious transformation of the (albeit smaller) forgotten inner
spaces of the Royal Academy provided a London precedent for a
bold interior mix of classical and high tech. Educational facilities
and lecture theatres were added below ground, Smirke's courtyard façades restored, and spacious stone-clad stairs wrapped
around the Reading Room, providing access to exhibition space
and restaurant, with a high level bridge to Smirke's N wing. Work
began in 1997 and was completed in 2000. The triumph is the
vast glazed roof, a network of glazed panels rising effortlessly in a
shallow curve to unite Museum and Reading Room.

## King Edward VII Wing

*Sir John Burnet*'s massive N wing, 1906–14, needs to be approached
from the N, and to be appreciated it has to be understood as an
incomplete fragment. The site for the museum extensions was
bought from the Bedford Estate in 1894, the Scottish architect
appointed in 1904; this was his first London building and made

his reputation in England. The long range is a successfully eclectic mixture in the chastest Beaux Arts style: a dominating parade of giant fluted Ionic engaged columns which echo Smirke, large plain openings which are clearly C20, the whole given dignity and repose by a high basement and tall, plain attic. The weakest element is the central entrance at basement level, with surround butting up awkwardly against the columns above. It is flanked by seated lions by *Sir George Frampton*. The tall, plain tapering pylons at the ends were also to have had sculpture by Frampton. They were to have formed junctions with wings returning s around the older museum (the wing replacing the w side of Bedford Square with a grand entrance portico leading to a domed lecture theatre). Within, the space is handled with originality: an oculus between entrance hall and the long gallery above, and an impressive but rather cramped staircase, with marble-faced balustrade and mighty black columns, rising around a gilded lift shaft made by the *Bromsgrove Guild*. On the top floor Ionic columns flank the entrance to the galleries. The construction is steel-framed; columns and staircase are of reinforced concrete. Connecting the N wing and the Round Reading Room is Burnet's NORTH LIBRARY, once a noble interior, with central space defined by Ionic columns standing forward from bookcase bays, but drastically altered by the insertion of mezzanines in 1934–6 by *J. H. Markham* of the Office of Works, and due to be transformed at the end of the C20 for the Department of Ethnography.

106

### SIR JOHN SOANE'S MUSEUM
Nos. 12–14 Lincoln's Inn Fields*

If anybody still believes that Sir John Soane was a Neoclassical architect, let him go to Lincoln's Inn Fields and see what Soane did in the exterior and interior of his own house. The building history is not simple. It starts with No. 12, which Soane rebuilt for his own occupation in 1792–4. Then when he sold his country seat at Pitzhanger, Ealing, he acquired No. 13 and rebuilt it in two stages, in 1808–9 and 1812–13 to house his collections. In 1823 he bought and rebuilt No. 14 as well, incorporating the rear of the site into No. 13, and letting the front as a separate house. He rebuilt the façade of No. 14 to match the plain Georgian front of No. 12.

On his death in 1837 Soane left his house to the nation as a museum 'for the study of Architecture and the Allied Arts'. Although the museum expanded into the rear of No. 12 in the later C19, and into its front in the C20, the impression is still of two private houses, albeit one of them highly eccentric. A scholarly restoration programme begun in 1990 restored the interiors of No. 13 and the ground floor of No. 12 to their appearance in Soane's time. In 1997, with the help of the Heritage Lottery Fund, the Museum acquired No. 14 for use in the future.

EXTERIOR. The façade is not neo-antique in the sense of, say, Smirke. No. 13 is of yellow brick, with arched windows on the

---

*I am grateful to Margaret Richardson and Helen Dorey for assistance in expanding and updating the original account of the museum by Sir Nikolaus Pevsner.

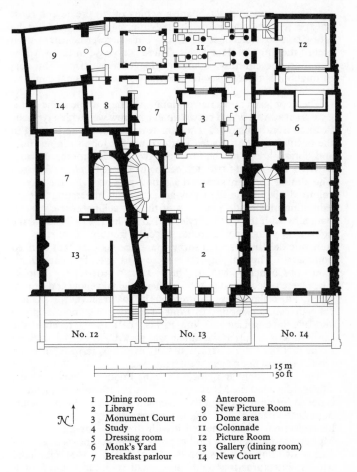

|  |  |  |  |
|---|---|---|---|
| 1 | Dining room | 8 | Anteroom |
| 2 | Library | 9 | New Picture Room |
| 3 | Monument Court | 10 | Dome area |
| 4 | Study | 11 | Colonnade |
| 5 | Dressing room | 12 | Picture Room |
| 6 | Monk's Yard | 13 | Gallery (dining room) |
| 7 | Breakfast parlour | 14 | New Court |

Sir John Soane's Museum. Ground-floor plan

ground floor. The centre of three bays projects and is stone-faced 48 throughout ground, first and second floors. On the second floor the middle bay continues the projection. At the angles above the outer bays are caryatids (of *Coade* stone). The third floor, extended at the front in 1825, is all recessed, and has typically Soanian pilasters and a typically Soanian balustrade with acroteria. The first floor is arched and was originally an open loggia. The ground floor of the loggia was glazed by Soane in 1829, the first and second floors in 1834. Between the arches the most surprising feature of the façade – two Gothic brackets, from the C14 N front of Westminster Hall. Two more between the windows of the ground floor. But even without this demonstrative solecism no one could call the front Greek or Roman. There is in fact hardly a single motif of direct antique derivation.

INTERIOR. No. 13 is a combination of living quarters, office and museum, and as such decidedly congested. However, it was just that congestion that set Soane's genius off to create the most unexpected and capricious spatial interplay. Not only did he refuse compositions of straight axes, but wherever he can he even breaks the unity of floor levels. There is no ease in the way it is done, on the contrary, a kind of dogged fanaticism. The goal throughout is to confuse and to mystify, and what goal could be less classical?

The door leads into a narrow lobby and then to the stone canti-lever STAIRCASE, which curves up in a narrow well with a typically Soanian iron balustrade. It widens towards the far end owing to the peculiarities of the site. To the r. are Sir John's dining room and library, above on the first floor two drawing rooms. In both DINING ROOM and LIBRARY, ceiling paintings by *Henry Howard*. The dining room has muted lighting produced by the use of coloured glass. The library is an extremely interesting design, exhibiting in the odd pendants of the flat ceiling Soane's secret sympathy with the Gothic style, and in the mirror walls above the bookcases, with hanging arches placed in front of the mirrors, his romantic delight in spatial surprise and the concealment of fixed boundaries. The hanging arches were used again by Soane in his Court of Chancery of 1824. The DRAWING ROOMS are simpler. They were redecorated in 1986 in their original yellow and bronze green. The ceilings have two versions of Soane's favourite shallow yet taut vaulting motifs. In front of the drawing room window and overlooking Lincoln's Inn Fields, the LOGGIA received the most curious details at the time it was glazed. On the half-landing to the first floor is the SHAKESPEARE RECESS, restored in 1990. On the second floor there were bedrooms.

The dining room and North Drawing Room overlook a narrow courtyard, called the MONUMENT COURT. Remarkably, its level is not the ground floor but the basement level of the house. Soane built at the back of Nos. 13–14 a lower range of rooms to house his collections and connected it with the house by a room W of Monument Court and a kind of passage E of it. The passage con-sists of two tiny rooms, STUDY and DRESSING ROOM, crammed with architectural fragments and small sculpture, much of it collected in Rome in the 1790s by C. H. Tatham on behalf of Henry Holland. Both rooms were restored in 1990–1: the pump and washbasin were re-created and the dressing room passage narrowed to its original width. The dressing room has an E as well as a W window. The E window opens towards the MONK'S YARD, which contains medieval rather than antique fragments, and also goes down to the basement. The medieval pieces, mostly from the Palace of Westminster, are assembled to form the tomb and cloister of a legendary Padre Giovanni.

N of the dining room and W of Monument Court is the
49    BREAKFAST PARLOUR with a shallow canopy dome on the centre of which rises a little lantern. The dome is supported at the corners only. Light comes in from skylights to N and S, and from the central lantern, but the spandrels have convex mirrors giving a reduced perspective of the room. The effect is eerie, and presents, in Soane's words, 'a succession of those fanciful effects which constitute the poetry of Architecture'. To the l., the ANTE-ROOM, in Moorish style, and the NEW PICTURE ROOM to the N, behind

No. 12, were both built in 1889–90 to the designs of *James Wild*, curator from 1878 to 1892. The semicircular glass dome and Pompeian-style painted decoration of the New Picture Room were re-created in 1992. Soane's part of this back range consists of three rooms, if rooms they can be called. The first is the DOME, an oblong room with a glass dome, again full of bits and pieces. This was built at the back of No. 13, on the site of former stables, in 1808–9, and annexed to the back of No. 12. The central space of the dome area is a two-storey tribune connecting with the crypt below – as in the Dôme des Invalides in Paris – to allow the visitor to look down on the sarcophagus of Seti I, which Soane had bought for a high price.

To the E follows the COLONNADE, an extremely crowded and confusing area with columns arranged in a pattern not at once comprehensible. The columns carry the UPPER DRAWING OFFICE, installed in 1821, and then altered by Soane in 1824. The room is curiously constructed, independently of the main walls, so that the two long skylights light the ground-floor area on the S, and the crypt below on the N. E of the Colonnade the PICTURE ROOM was added in 1824, again with an extraordinary ceiling construction with pendants and a curved skylight along the middle axis. Equally original and perverse is the fireplace. The great peculiarity is the 'moveable planes' on three sides of the room, which open to display further pictures. The original paint scheme was restored in 1988.

From here a staircase leads down into the basement, where smaller rooms of the museum connect with the yards. The most remarkable room is the MONK'S PARLOUR, small, absurdly high, and in a tricky way in its upper part connected with the Picture Room. The adjoining MONK'S CELL was restored in 1992.

No. 12, now part of the museum, is one of Soane's few surviving town houses. The two rooms on the ground floor were dining room and breakfast parlour. The latter has a vaulted 'star-fish' ceiling decorated with a painted trellis, honeysuckle and columbine, as if the room were open to the sky like a pergola. It was painted by *John Crace Sen.* in 1794 (restored 1993–4). The dining room was opened as an exhibition gallery in 1995, with free-standing cases by *Eva Jiricna*, arranged in an offset cross formation. On the first floor are two drawing rooms (now the museum's research library), the front one with a domical ceiling and finely carved white marble fireplace.

No. 14 (not yet open to the public) is perfectly preserved, with many variations of Soanian themes, including a star-fish ceiling in the first-floor front room.

It is not for this volume to describe the collection brought together by Sir John Soane and exhibited to the public. But his collection of models ought at least to be mentioned, also the many Soane drawings, the more than 8,000 Robert Adam drawings, the famous book of drawings by John Thorpe of Elizabethan and Jacobean houses, and the large number of models by Flaxman. In addition there are paintings and drawings by Soane's contemporaries, such as Piranesi, Clérisseau, James Barry, Mortimer, William Hamilton, Fuseli and Turner.

PERAMBULATIONS

*1. South-east Holborn*

*1a: A circular tour starting from Holborn Circus*

The old heart of Holborn forms a dense NW fringe to the City of London. The parish church of St Andrew indeed lies within the City (*see London 1: The City of London*). It is an area of contrasts: relics of Victorian commercial pride along the main roads and of over-crowded housing behind; reminders of grand medieval houses, remnants of suburban respectability of the C17 and C18.

ELY PLACE, off Charterhouse Street to the NE, contains a fragment of one of the great medieval houses of London: the chapel which once formed part of the Bishop of Ely's establishment and is now the R.C. Church of St Etheldreda (q.v.). The great hall and cloister survived until the C18, as did the gatehouse, built by Bishop Arundel in the C14. The bishops retained possession until 1772, when they moved to Dover Street in the West End. The street called Ely Place was laid out by *Charles Cole* in 1773, retaining only the chapel, whose front appears amidst a select development of neat, regular, four-storeyed terrace houses, with identical door-ways framed by columns and entablatures. On the E side they are nearly complete, on the w only Nos. 8 and 9 remain. Beside them ELY COURT, a narrow passage, with the OLD MITRE, two bays, C18, tucked in behind. This emerges in HATTON GARDEN, a broad street which was laid out in the grounds of Ely House as the centre of a smart new suburban development, with spacious brick houses of *c.* 1680. It was developed by Sir Christopher Hatton, descendant of the C16 courtier of the same name, who had acquired the lease of the Bishop's gatehouse. Hatton Garden became com-mercial in the C19, and the centre of the diamond trade; only scattered evidence now remains from its domestic past. On the E side, No. 5, mid-C18; on the w, Nos. 86–87 (London Diamond Club, disguised by later stucco). Some excellent carved panelling of *c.* 1730 from a room in No. 26 is in the Victoria and Albert Museum. The oldest survivals are at No. 43, two lively figures of Charity children from the parochial school established on this site in 1696 in a former chapel. The building was gutted in the Second World War and restored as offices. Three-bay front, doorway with segmental pediment, large arched upper window with keystones. Among the commercial buildings the best is TREASURE HOUSE, Nos. 19–21 on the E side, by *Niven & Wigglesworth*, 1907, stone-faced, remarkably sensitively detailed, with six fine relief carvings of appropriate subjects. On the w side, much less appealing, Nos. 73–83, a long range of 1930s offices, refurbished in 1979 with new back and a landscaped courtyard behind, by *Halpern & Partners*.

By GREVILLE STREET or ST CROSS STREET, both with a few battered C18 houses, one reaches the narrower LEATHER LANE with its street market overlooked by a mix of lesser domestic and commercial buildings, e.g. No. 23, late C19 with jolly gable and chequered tympana. The s end of Leather Lane, now pedestrian, has been taken over by buildings on a different scale: the Prudential on the w side (*see* Perambulation 1b) and on the E VESAGE COURT, an 80s tower of flats built behind big British Telecom offices fronting Holborn. To the N, GREVILLE STREET leads to BROOKE'S MARKET, with an open square overlooked by the redeveloped back of the Prudential, all sleek purple granite (*see* below, Perambulation 1b). Squeezed into the NW corner, St Alban's Church (q.v.), and close to it No. 16, by *Halsey Ricardo c.* 1900–10, five storeys, whitewashed, with coloured shutters, rather Austrian or south German-looking. The narrow passages around the church lead to BROOKE'S COURT and BALDWIN'S GARDENS, a once overcrowded area badly damaged in the Second World War, transformed in the 1970s by a mixture of friendly, compact, low-rise housing, a surprising oasis. Further N much miscellaneous post-war rebuilding and clearance, which destroyed some of the very earliest planned working-class flats, the Thanksgiving Model Buildings in Portpool Lane of 1850–1 (with open staircases of the type much copied by other model housing). Back now to Leather Lane, where at the N end a few good houses remain, Nos. 83–89, early C18, with brick cornice and segmental window heads. They stand near the SE corner of the BOURNE ESTATE between Portpool Lane and Clerkenwell Road. 1901–7 by the *LCC* (*W. E. Riley*). Tightly packed five- and six-storey blocks of balcony-access flats, for 3,900 people, the third largest of the County Council's early schemes, but architecturally less adventurous than Boundary Street (Tower Hamlets: *see London 5: East*) and Millbank (Westminster). Livened up by red and yellow brickwork and by classical trimmings (pediments and pilasters). Large archways through the perimeter blocks lead to the central area, where the ranges run N to S, alternately with narrow gardens in between.

The slums that had developed on the slopes of the insalubrious Fleet valley were tackled by C19 road improvements (*see also* Islington: Finsbury Perambulation 3). CLERKENWELL ROAD was completed in 1878. On the N side, the DUKE OF YORK, an elaborate debased classical pub elevation. ROSEBERY AVENUE running N towards Islington dates from 1889–92. At its S end CAVENDISH MANSIONS, rather grim six-storey blocks, then a widening with identical terraces called ROSEBERY SQUARE (*see* below, Perambulation 5, p. 332, and for the area further N, *see* Finsbury, p. 632). To the W the older route of MOUNT PLEASANT with a surprising survival, a modest early Georgian terrace (Nos. 47–53); Nos. 47–49 is the least altered, with brick bands and cornice and segmental window heads. The plaque 'Dorrington Street 1720' seems appropriate but is not *in situ*; it comes from a street near Brooke's Market. E of Rosebery Avenue, on the borders with Clerkenwell (*see* Islington: Finsbury Perambulation 3), is a confused area of small lanes with evocative names such as Vine Hill and Saffron Hill. These slopes above the Fleet River were slums in the early C19 (the setting for Fagin's den in *Oliver Twist*). They were cleared when the river was covered over by FARRINGDON ROAD, this part completed in 1856. The C19 commercial and industrial buildings that followed are now in their turn disappearing: the best survival within Holborn is Nos. 25–27 at the corner of Greville Street. The proud six-storey Venetian Gothic frontage of 1873 by *Harding & Bond* was built for Bradbury, Wilkinson

& Co., engravers. Polychrome brick and terracotta detail; iron-mullioned windows with stone tracery. Interior reconstructed 1988–93. Off Greville Street, SAFFRON HILL turns s past a glimpse of ST ANDREW'S HOUSE, landlocked flats with iron balconies, 1874 by the Corporation of London (*Sir Horace Jones*), built for those displaced by Holborn Viaduct. The passage then climbs a flight of stairs beneath No. 17 Charterhouse Street (DIAMOND TRADING COMPANY), 1976–9 by *Chapman Taylor*. This has a fortress-like ground floor to the street, made interesting by narrow, deeply chamfered windows and attractively pitted stone facing; curtain walling steps out above.

## 1b. Holborn and High Holborn, starting from Holborn Circus

The ancient route leading from the City, Holborn starts w of the Fleet valley (spanned from 1869 by Holborn Viaduct) and is continued by High Holborn w of Gray's Inn Road. Once with numerous inns, and up to the mid C17 a favourite site for grand suburban houses (*see* Introduction to Holborn), but now lined by commercial buildings of the later C19 and C20, too many of them unappealingly large and dull. Only here and there do a few narrow frontages echo a more distant past.

PRUDENTIAL ASSURANCE, Holborn, N side. One of London's Victorian Gothic showpieces, and one of the first major financial enterprises to be established beyond the City boundary. The company had been founded in 1848 and was formerly on Ludgate Hill. An overwhelming mass of bright red terracotta and brick with tall ranges around internal courtyards. Built piecemeal by *Alfred Waterhouse* on the site of C19 buildings which had replaced Brooke House (demolished for Brooke Street *c.* 1676) and Furnival's Inn (one of the minor Inns of Chancery, which disappeared in the early C19). The dates are various but the character remained consistent, establishing a house style for Prudential offices which was copied all over the country. The first portion was built at the corner of Brooke Street in 1876–9, with extensions to Brooke Street and Greville Street in 1885–8; the N range of the main courtyard was begun in 1895; most of the rest followed in 1897–1901. The 1879 parts were then rebuilt in 1932 by *Messrs Joseph*.

Pevsner's description of 1952 displayed respect rather than enthusiasm: 'The Prudential is an earnest thoughtful design even if without warmth. Long symmetrical façade of fiery red brick and red terracotta, amply gabled, and with a big central tower crowned by a pyramid roof with spike. The windows all lancets except that on the second floor simple plate tracery is introduced. It seems in the details all done from the best models. Yet the sheer multiplication of the motifs deprives them of their efficacy.' The street front is only part of the story. The approach to the heart of the complex is contrived with drama: first comes a deep rib-vaulted archway beneath the turreted tower, then a small courtyard which opens on the N side by a very wide arch into the generous main court, now a semi-public space called Waterhouse Square. This is dominated by a symmetrical N block whose broad end gables rise to five storeys. On the ground floor both N and E ranges have

63

arched windows, some of them opened up to form a kind of cloister walk when the building was refurbished in 1990 (design by *Prudential Architects' Dept*, executed by *EPR Architects*). Bronze WAR MEMORIAL by *F. V. Blundestone*, 1922: two angels support a dying soldier; below are standing women with wreaths.

The front range of 1897–1901 has the best INTERIORS, lavishly faced in *Burmantoft*'s glazed terracotta. Waterhouse had used terracotta to good effect in the Natural History Museum, but here it is more brightly coloured. On the r. the former public office, and on the l. hall and vaulted director's staircase, with terrazzo floor. The interiors were restored in the 1990 campaign, when later partitions were removed. Columns faced in terracotta conceal steel supports, used by Waterhouse from the 1880s. Parts of the building also incorporate Lindsay's patent steel decking, used with concrete for fireproof flooring.

The new work of the 1990s by *EPR Architects* replaced the parts to Greville Street and Brooke Street by a deep back range, with a large atrium entrance from Greville Street. Along Brooke Street sleek purple granite cladding and elementary mouldings butt up against the older parts.

The s side of Holborn is in the City (*see London 1: The City of London*)

### High Holborn: from Gray's Inn Road to Kingsway

N SIDE from the E. The street begins beyond the site of Holborn Bar, marking the City boundary. Except at the w end, almost all the buildings are of after 1945. At the corner of Gray's Inn Road, offices by *Gordon Collis* for the Prudential, 1986; seven storeys, plain brown brick. BISHOP'S HOUSE by *Trehearne & Norman, Preston & Partners*, 1955–7, an up-to-date façade (thin verticals, green spandrel panels) but with a two-storeyed entrance feature conventionally placed in the centre. Roof originally with opentrellis canopy. No. 20, blue brick with marble-faced floorbands, 1964–5 by *Fitzroy Robinson & Partners*, next door to the gatehouse to Gray's Inn (q.v.), which had to be rebuilt as a result. The SAMUEL SMITH CITTIE OF YORKE (formerly Henekeys Tavern) is a narrow stone-faced pub, rebuilt in 1923–4 (possibly by *Ernest R. Barrow*), still with the pretty Tudor detail of the type favoured by Treadwell & Martin in the late C19; two shallow bay windows and two little gables. Atmospheric interior, partly older than the frontage, a long narrow space with open timber roof and cubicles off. BRACTON HOUSE, one of the few late C20 intrusions, a brash front designed by *D. Y. Davies*, 1987, with flat Postmodern patterning in brown, white and pink, and a forbidding bronze SCULPTURE in a niche at street level: The Artist as Hephaestos, a self-portrait by *Eduardo Paolozzi* (commissioned by the developers, London & Bristol). An odd, dislocated combination. A dull post-war stretch follows: Nos. 29–30, ALLIANCE HOUSE, another narrow frontage, 1964–5 by *Jackson & Greenen*; Nos. 40–49, FIRST AVENUE HOUSE, 1949–51 by *Gordon Jeeves*; Nos. 55–57, by *George, Davies & Webb*, 1956–7, curtain walling in a stone frame. The most interesting 1950s building on the N side was demolished in 1993: STATE HOUSE by *Trehearne & Norman, Preston & Partners*, 1956–60. It was one of the first post-war London offices to break the conventional mould, a group of three blocks of different height placed in landscaped courtyards, the tallest with projecting uprights carried above and over its roof. In 2000 replaced by a vast pile by *Kohn Pederson Fox*.

W of Red Lion Street, uninspired mammoth frontages which are partly war-damage replacements: Nos. 81–87, TEMPLAR HOUSE, stone-faced, with little Neo-Georgian motifs, by *Richardson & McLaughlin*, completed 1959; No. 88 (ICL) treated as a centre-piece to this and the adjacent Nos. 90–93 (SUNLEY HOUSE), by the same firm, 1969; Nos. 94–99, TURNSTILE HOUSE, stone, classical, with columnar reliefs on top, by *Wimperis, Simpson & Guthrie, c.* 1937. Then PROCTER HOUSE, with the sleek horizontals of the 1960s, by *Dynley Luker & Moore*, built together with the blocks behind in 1960–2, when Procter Street was created on the bomb-damaged W side of Red Lion Square to take traffic coming from Theobalds Road. Originally there was a big canopy over the road beneath. Nearer Southampton Row, Nos. 114–115, and a group of gabled houses of *c.* 1900 by *Arthur Keen*, who also built the adjacent Baptist headquarters in Southampton Row (*see* Perambulation 4, p. 327).

S SIDE from the E. At the site of Holborn Bar, the old boundary with the City, Nos. 337–338, STAPLE INN BUILDINGS, a long and high group of C16 timber-framed houses, the most impressive survival of such buildings in central London. However, survival here means the preservation of the frontages only, when the rest was extensively reconstructed in 1937. There was a previous restoration in 1886 (by *Waterhouse*), when the front windows were copied from surviving first-floor casements of No. 337. The back of the range was faced in brick already in 1826. No. 338, on the l., is of 1586: symmetrical with five gables, central arched doorway into Staple Inn behind (*see London 1: The City of London*). Two jetties, oriel window to each upper floor below the gables. Larger oriels in the centre. No. 337 may be a little later. It is a slightly taller two-gabled house, also double-jettied, also symmetrical, except for coving below the r. first-floor oriel. Close-studded walls without any deco-ration. Shopfronts on the ground floor. No. 336, STAPLE INN BUILDINGS NORTH, 1903, is as red and gabled as the Prudential, though Tudor rather than Gothic. Indeed also by *Waterhouse*.

After Staple Inn, the S side of High Holborn is all of the C20. No. 30, SOUTHAMPTON BUILDINGS (British Gas), built as offices for the National Westminster Bank by *Gordon Charratou* of the *J. Seymour Harris Partnership*, 1965–8. Soberer and less memorable than its predecessor, *Knightley*'s Doulton-tiled Birkbeck Bank of 1895–6. A long façade to High Holborn, several times slightly broken. Eight storeys, the ground floor partly recessed. The upper floors have long window bands; the floor levels are marked by concrete projections. Main entrance at the SW corner. In the reception area, three splendid gryphon brackets in Doulton ware, which once supported the gallery of the Birkbeck Bank. HERON HOUSE, adjoining in High Holborn, 1967–9 by *E. S. Boyer & Partners*, has been designed on the same pattern, except that three times on each floor from the second to the top are what might be described as the semblance of balconies. Some lively Victorian buildings flank Chancery Lane; on the E side the corner building is of 1851, revamped in 1921 for a bank, with pilasters added, by

*Bourchier, Tatchell & Galsworthy*. Further on, deadening blocks of the 50s, some stone-faced (LINCOLN HOUSE by *Ley, Colbeck & Partners*, 1955–6), some curtain-walled (Nos. 283–287 and 277–282, by *Morrison, Rose & Partners*). Then Nos. 266–267, a modest Palladian front, and Nos. 262–265, plain, seven storeys, by *T. P. Bennett & Son*, 1956. In GREAT TURNSTILE, DOLPHYN COURT, 1986 by *Michael Aukett Associates*, reticently stone-clad, with neat recessed entrance.

The former PEARL ASSURANCE buildings are the only effort in High Holborn to achieve Edwardian grandeur. By *Moncton & Newman*, 1912–19. Conversion to a hotel under way, 1998, by *T. P. Bennett & Son*. Channelled grey granite ground floor, a giant Ionic order to three upper floors, two attic floors above a big cornice. Baroque dome over the central entrance, which leads into a court-yard which had a WAR MEMORIAL (St George) by *Frampton*. Other ranges completed later; E 1929–30 by *Moncton*; SE 1954–6 and W 1959–60 by *Bates & Sinning*; W extension 1960–3 by *T. P. Bennett & Son*.

Between LITTLE TURNSTILE and KINGSWAY, No. 233, by *Frederick Etchells & Herbert A. Welch*, 1930, a pioneer work in the history of modern architecture in England. Etchells was the trans-lator of Le Corbusier into English. A remodelling and extension of an existing building for Crawford's Advertising Company. The façade uses a minimum of motifs, but uses them sensitively. Corner block with chamfered corner, ground floor of black marble. The rest white cement-rendered, with long uninterrupted bands of windows subdivided by stainless steel mullions. Prismatic glass, also used for internal corridors, allowed the deeper than average offices to be well lit. Steel staircase. Nos. 229–231 uses the same style later, without personality.

*High Holborn west of Kingsway*

S SIDE. Nos. 215–222, featureless offices by *Fitzroy Robinson & Bull*, 1957–8, with canted corner. No. 212 (NATIONAL WESTMINSTER BANK) by *H. Baker*, 1854, but except for the segmental arches on the ground floor, surprisingly pure Palladian. Nos. 208–9, PRINCESS LOUISE, with an excellent late C19 pub interior: engraved mirrors by *Richard Morris & Son*; stained glass, tiles etc. Nos. 199–206, 1978 by *Sidney Kaye, Eric Firmin & Partners*, incorporating the frontage of Nos. 199–201. This was built in 1869–70 by *W. J. Trehearne* for George Kent, inventor of a patent knife-cleaning machine and other gadgets. A typical functional Victorian front; bands of windows all over; only shapes and sizes differ: top two storeys with eighteen windows, twelve windows below. Ground floor all glass and columns.

After the former Library and Town Hall (*see* Public Buildings) the street curves SW, away from New Oxford Street towards St Giles. Behind a frontage heightened and reclad in 1990 by *DEGW*, OASIS LEISURE CENTRE, 1960 by *S. A. G. Cook*, Holborn Borough Architect, and *J. Seymour Harris & Partners*, incorporating an older outdoor swimming pool and a new covered pool, separated by a sliding glass wall. Play area and two rooftop sunbathing terraces. On the site of baths and washhouses built in 1853 as part of the improvements to the slums of St Giles.

N SIDE. At the corner of Southampton Row No. 125, a Franco-Flemish composition in brick and stone by *Ford Son & Burrows*, 1899–1902. Nos. 127–129 is an early work by *Charles Holden*, 1904, worth studying. Characteristic angular detail and principal windows. They have columns, and the entablature above curves back and outward into the frames. Nos. 139–144, in line with New Oxford Street, NATIONWIDE BUILDING SOCIETY, 1959–62 by *L. Blease* and *J. A. Rawlinson*, a straightforward tower block. Nearby, in front of an office block refurbished for BUPA, a sculpture by *Peter Randall-Page*: Chain of Events, 1996, Portland stone and African granite. High Holborn then branches SW, past the circular end of COMMONWEALTH HOUSE, 1939 by *H. P. Cart de Lafontaine*, its smart modernism expressed by mechanical horizontal bands of windows. The former Post Office building (converted in 1997 for a British Museum store) is by *E. T. Serjent* of the *Ministry of Public Building & Works*, 1961–9. Long bands of Portland stone and glass, weakly angled at the corner of Museum Street. Finally the SHAFTESBURY THEATRE (formerly Princes Theatre), 1911 by *Bertie Crewe*, with a jolly rotunda as the top feature of the rounded corner.

## 2. Southern Holborn east of Kingsway

### 2a. South of High Holborn: Lincoln's Inn Fields

At the beginning of the C17 Lincoln's Inn Fields was some leftover fields surrounded by small property of no quality. William Newton, the developer of houses in Great Queen Street just to the w, bought the Fields in 1629 and 1638 and, against the wish of the gentlemen of Lincoln's Inn, who wanted them to be a public open space like Moorfields, obtained a licence to build thirty-two houses. By 1658 there were houses on the w, N and s sides. Piecemeal C19 rebuilding ignored both original height and style; late C20 replacements have sought to restore a Georgian appearance to the square. The earliest survivors are on the w side, but this account follows the numbering and starts at the NW end with the N side, the most varied of all.

### North side

Nos. 1–2, early C18, joined together in 1820; good staircase with finely twisted balusters and carved tread ends. Also good fireplace, carved doorcase and ceiling. Nos. 3–4, reticent Neo-Georgian of 1972 by *T. Saunders & Associates*, five storeys and dormers, replacing a tall Victorian monstrosity. No. 5, late Georgian. Nos. 6–8, mid-C18, with brick floorbands and simple doorcases (No. 8 with original features inside). No. 9 late Georgian. Nos. 10–11, 1980s, by *Westwood, Piet, Poole & Smart*, replacing a big red brick building of *c.* 1900; dark brick, a restrained, decently proportioned front, with metal first-floor bay windows as its main feature.

Nos. 12, 13 and 14, in triptych symmetry, include SIR JOHN SOANE'S HOUSE and MUSEUM, created from 1792 to 1824. The story is complicated and is discussed above (p. 296). No. 15 is of *c.* 1742; rusticated doorcase with Ionic columns, bulgy frieze and pediment. Excellent fireplace with termini caryatids and fine plaster ceilings. No. 16 is similar. Nos. 17–18 is by *Waterhouse*, 1871–2, for

Equity and Law Assurance. Gothic, of stone, with typical stilted window-heads. Not fussy in the details, but one of the first to break the skyline of Lincoln's Inn Fields. No. 19 is by *Philip Webb*, 1868–9, also tall, three bays, brick with stone-faced bay and polygonal buttresses. The side windows have Webb's characteristic mixture of Gothic and Queen Anne. Heavy door-hood of forms not of any period of the past. Nos. 20–23, by *Wimperis, Simpson & Guthrie* and *W. Curtis Green*, 1936–7. Large; of smooth stone with pilasters at the top. Not an ornament to the square. No. 24, 1787, with blind balustrade below first-floor window. Nos. 25–27 have brick C18 fronts; good carved doorcase to No. 26. No. 28, offices of *c.* 1870 with a good Renaissance carved frieze. No. 29 (former Royal Institute of Chartered Surveyors), by *F. H. Greenaway & J. E. Newberry*, 1924, originally of three storeys only, which was a handsome gesture to the square; altogether a well-mannered building in the Palladian tradition.

The E SIDE is all Lincoln's Inn (*see* above, p. 284).

*South side*

Strictly speaking beyond the Holborn boundary, but mentioned here for completeness. Tall C19 and C20 institutions have entirely replaced the original houses. LAND REGISTRY by *The Office of Works*, 1901–7 and 1911–14, big, symmetrical Neo-Jacobean, with four towers on the four corners. NUFFIELD COLLEGE OF SURGICAL SCIENCES, red brick and stone, tamely Neo-Georgian, 1956–8 by *A. W. Hall* (consultant *Sir E. Maufe*). ROYAL COLLEGE OF SURGEONS, by *Sir Charles Barry*, 1835–6, incorporating the Ionic portico from its predecessor of 1806–13 by *George Dance* (*see* above, p. 268). IMPERIAL CANCER RESEARCH FUND building, by *Young & Hall* (consultant *John Musgrove*), 1959–62, with an extension of *c.* 1972 which replaced some good C18 houses. Six storeys with a tall attic (originally windowless), neatly detailed, with dark metal window frames and brick spandrel panels.

*West side*

The SW corner was closed by an archway until 1909, when much was disturbed by the building of Kingsway immediately to the W. What remains is of high value. Near the centre the C18 Nos. 57–58 and the mid-C17 Lindsey House, Nos. 59–60, are interesting to compare.

LINDSEY HOUSE must be considered first. The name comes from the Earl of Lindsey's occupation in the early C18. This is the only surviving original house in the Fields, built in 1639–41 as a speculation by Sir David Cunningham. Colen Campbell illustrated it in *Vitruvius Britannicus* and attributed the design to Inigo Jones, but the only further evidence known which might point to this is that Cunningham was a friend of Nicholas Stone. The house is well set back, in a forecourt defined by rusticated brick piers. When built it formed a tall centrepiece on the W side, with a balustraded parapet instead of the eaves cornices of its neighbours. A broad front of five bays, with rusticated ground floor and six Ionic pilasters 27 above. Built of red brick, with pilasters stuccoed to look like stone (the walls have later stucco, now painted red). Summerson found in it 'pioneering roughness and coarse craftsmanship'; Pevsner argued that the broad proportions and emphatic detail – the wreathed capitals, and the boldly pedimented first-floor windows, the central pediment open and segmental – added character. Whether or not by Jones, this design with *piano nobile* and pilasters is a rare early survival of the type of regular, classically detailed street elevation that Jones had promoted at Covent Garden, and which was beginning to appear elsewhere in the 1630s. The *Vitruvius Britannicus* plan shows a double-pile plan with further rooms to the rear of a small light-well. The house was altered inside when subdivided in 1751–2, possibly by *Isaac Ware*. The lowered first-floor windows may date from this time. (Inside, some C17 joinery remains, and an alcove attributed to Ware.)

Nos. 57–58 by *Henry Joynes*, of 1730, rebuilt for Charles, Lord Talbot, solicitor general, deliberately takes its motifs from its neighbour, but is all stone-faced, and the Palladian composition is perhaps just a little too smooth and well behaved in comparison: see the small trim pediments to the first-floor windows, all identically triangular, and the undiminished pilasters. Semicircular porch with fluted Roman Doric columns, added when the house was subdivided by *Soane* in 1795. He added a central party-wall, removed when the houses were reunited in 1909, but his toplit staircase and other details survive in No. 57.

No. 63 is an odd intruder, plain, honest commercial Victorian of 1888 by *William Simmons*, seven storeys, with rows of slightly arched windows, in concrete, an early use of the material. No. 64, early C19, with Ionic pilasters and an attic floor. No. 65 is by *Leverton*, 1772 for Sir Henry Kendal; three bays wide and three and a half storeys high, with rusticated ground floor and pediment over the central first-floor window. (Stone staircase; delicate ceilings.)

Finally NEWCASTLE HOUSE on the NW corner, a tall seven-bay house of brick with stone dressings. Built in 1685–9, after a fire, by *William Winde* for William Herbert, first Marquess of Powis, completed by *Wren* in 1694, and sold to the Duke of Newcastle in 1705. A rare survival of a late C17 aristocratic London house on a grand scale, although much altered. It was subdivided in 1771 by Henry Kendal, but reunited by Sir William James Farrer in 1906, when the back parts were demolished for Kingsway. The present late C17 appearance is the result of restoration by *Lutyens* and *Dendy Watney* in 1930–1 for the Farrer brothers (for whom Lutyens had worked at The Salutation, Kent). The E and N outside walls, which had become unstable, were rebuilt and the late C17 detail was re-created, including the central pediment and steep roof with dormers, following an engraving of 1754. The rebuilding was tactfully and tastefully done. The grand curved double stair leading up to the entrance is a later addition, possibly from 1771. The covered passage along the N flank wall facing Remnant Street is an original feature. Inside, the S side retains much from the later C18, including part of the main stairs, an elegant cantilevered stone back stairs and two rooms with fine plaster ceilings, the SE ground-floor room with peacocks in the spandrels of an oval centre. This work may be by *Leverton* (who built No. 65 for Henry Kendal, *see* above). The bolder plasterwork of the SW room looks mid C18. There is no obvious trace of *Vanbrugh*'s internal alterations made in 1714–17.

In the gardens in the square, open octagonal SUMMERHOUSE, 1880
by *James Wild* (curator of the Soane Museum), originally with
two-tiered roof, simplified in 1934. Two MEMORIAL SEATS: one
to Margaret MacDonald, with bronze figures by *Richard Goulden*,
1914, another to W.F.D. Smith, Viscount Hambleden (†1928)
formerly with bust. At the NE corner, SCULPTURE: Camdonian, a
large flat metal cutout, 1980 by *Barry Flanagan*.

*2b. Around Red Lion Square and Queen Square, between High Holborn
and Guilford Street: a circular tour starting from Holborn Underground
Station*

The development of this part of Holborn began in the 1680s, when
the notorious builder and speculator Nicholas Barbon made plans
for residential districts around two new squares, Red Lion Square
and Queen Square. Red Lion Square was in progress in 1684, when
the lawyers of Gray's Inn attempted to disrupt building activity
which was encroaching on their rural setting. The squares themselves retain nothing as early as this, but much of interest remains in
the surrounding streets, where development continued after Barbon's
death in 1698.

RED LION SQUARE lies N of High Holborn, connected to it since
1961 by PROCTER STREET, which sliced off its W end. Much
here had been destroyed in the war, including *Pearson*'s St John's
Church (1874–8) at the SW corner. The gardens were relandscaped in 1991 by *Charles Funke Associates* with two circular lawns.
Bronze bust of Bertrand Russell by *Marcelle Quinton*, 1980. The
oldest houses are near the SE corner: Nos. 16–17 has a Victorian
front but is older behind. Rossetti lived here, and it was later the
first offices of William Morris's firm. Nos. 14–15 are mid-c18,
refronted in the early c19, with good fanlights and first-floor
windows in arched recesses. E of these, SUMMIT HOUSE by
*Westwood & Emberton*, 1925, built for Austin Reed. An Art Deco
period piece; faced with glazed yellow tiles, with vertical bands
emphasizing the steel frame. Bold lotus-leaf railings; two carved
panels by *Percy Metcalfe* reset in the doors (formerly over the
entrance). On the N side at the W end, No. 35, by *Lander, Bedells
& Crompton*, 1956, the former offices of Cassells, a neat frontage
with unbonded tiles. No. 34, a plain narrow front of *c.* 1960 with
hammered concrete band decorated with dividers and T-square;
formerly architects' offices for Seiferts. Then, on a forbiddingly
large scale, NEW MERCURY HOUSE, a cliff of polished granite
with bland square openings by *Austin-Smith: Lord*, completed
1980. At the NE corner, CONWAY HALL, built for the South
Place Ethical Society in 1929 by *F.H. Mansford* (Waterhouse's
chief draughtsman). Grey brick with a rather jolly two-storeyed
Baroque entrance topped by urns. Urns also crown the flank of
the hall along RED LION PASSAGE. Large foyer with shallow
arches on a polished granite column; hall with curved glazed roof.
On the E side of Red Lion Square and on the S side of PRINCETON
STREET, flats of the 1950s, brick-faced, the taller ones raised on
stilts, the lower buildings scaled to fit into RED LION STREET to
the E. This is a nicely varied service street with shops, still with

some older houses, among them No. 46, with brick band and moulded cornice, and No. 50, with rubbed brick window heads. In the E part of Princeton Street, an early Board school of 1877, very plain apart from some decorative plaques.

BEDFORD ROW at the end of Princeton Street is an uncommonly wide street, which also started as a Barbon development, begun c. 1690. Brick terraces on both sides, with good iron railings. The W side is much rebuilt, although still superficially Georgian; the E side, built 1717–19, although also partly reconstructed, gives a good impression of street architecture of the early C18. Houses are of four storeys, the tallest type of Georgian terrace, mostly of three bays, though a few are of four. Slender straight-headed windows, brown brick with red dressings, doorcases and fanlights of different patterns and dates. Inside, the staircases have graceful groups of three twisted balusters to the tread. No. 11, of four bays, is especially grand, one of the few surviving examples of an C18 London town house with a painted stairhall occupying the front of the house. It was decorated by *John Vanderbank* (probably after 1720, for Dame Rebecca Moyer). On the walls an equestrian George I between painted columns, allegorical figures of the Arts, and Britannia. Ceiling with Mercury, History and Justice in an oval. The staircase (which rises against the front wall in complete disregard of the window pattern), is appropriately sumptuous, with Corinthian column newels and pilastered dado. Towards the S end of Bedford Row, the early C18 houses are interspersed with some later rebuilding. A few more C18 houses (Nos. 46–48) and a nice C18 cast-iron pump in the part of the street which turns E towards Gray's Inn (q.v.). In HAND COURT, a passage running towards Holborn, No. 23, 1897–8 by *Horace M. Wakley*; built as the City of New York pub. Four-storey brown terracotta front with lavish Renaissance detail; ornate plasterwork inside. The tour continues from the N end of Bedford Row into Theobalds Road.

THEOBALDS ROAD, a main thoroughfare running W–E, began as a royal route to James I's mansion of Theobalds in Hertfordshire and was widened in 1877–8. The W end is of little interest, rebuilt in 1948–50 after extensive war damage with deplorable, crushingly utilitarian government offices (architect *Arthur S. Ash*), under the Lessor scheme. W of New North Street, MERCURY HOUSE, a 1950s building by *Gordon Jeeves*, remodelled by *Austin-Smith: Lord* for Cable and Wireless Co. in 1993, has a tight central atrium with a surprising vertical water cascade between the lifts by *William Pye* and carpet by *Susan Pye*. Around Bedford Row the street scene improves. No. 24, at the E corner of Bedford Row, is a handsome former BANK of 1902, Queen-Anne-style going Baroque, with brick and stone quoins, aedicules high up, and a weighty cornice. Round the corner in JOCKEY'S FIELDS, beside Gray's Inn gardens, No. 18, MEGHRAJ BANK, 1989–91 by *Jestico & Whiles*, an ingenious transformation of a mews building, all white render with bands of narrow-paned windows, sloping back at the top, with passage through to a similarly handled courtyard. On the N side of Theobalds Road, first Holborn Library (q.v.), then Nos. 14–22, c. 1770, with pedimented doorcases and nice iron railings; No. 18 especially good, with cornice and stone bands marking an implied Order in the Palladian manner. At the corner of Gray's Inn Road a heavily modelled block of 1877 by *J. W. Brooker* with the YORKSHIRE GREY pub; sculptured horseman in the gable.

### North of Theobalds Road

The return W is through the grid of streets running N from Theobalds Road.

GRAY'S INN ROAD starts on the E side with a series of tall red brick mansion flats of *c.* 1900: TIVERTON, DULVERTON and CHURSTON MANSIONS, enlivened by curved parapets and curly gables. Then No. 200, ITN, *Foster & Partners'* first major commercial building in London, 1989–92 for Stanhope Properties, taken over for Independent Television News and media offices. A deep-plan atrium building with glass and aluminium curtain-walling, not innovative, but with the firm's usual good proportions and immaculate detail. A sleek pale front, its eight-storey bulk reduced by setting back the top two floors, and recessing the two lowest ones behind slim, widely spaced structural columns. The columns are visible above through elegantly sheer glazing. Double-height entrance hall; long central toplit atrium descending to the basement, with secondary atrium opening off to the E. Across the S end are dramatically silhouetted bridges, against a big window with opaque glazing. All white and silver, apart from a coloured MOBILE by *Ben Johnson*. No. 236, with a heavy-handed rhythm of concrete arches, was built as New Printing House Square, for *The Times*, 1972–6 by *R. Seifert & Partners*, after the 1967 merger of the paper with the *Sunday Times*, which had its presses here. Four ranges of seven to eleven storeys, kept low to Gray's Inn Road. On the W side No. 85, with a dark, glossy exterior by *Comprehensive Design Group*, completed 1992; tower with a convex bite and a grid of thin blue brises-soleil. On this side, fragments of early domesticity remain: some typical early C19 terraces with first-floor windows under arches (Nos. 61–71, 75–81).

NORTHINGTON STREET leads W; No. 8 has a modest C18 front with pair of doors and bowed shopfront neatly set below a single lintel.

JOHN STREET is the next street running S–N. Built up 1756–9 by *John Blagrove*, carpenter. Wide and well preserved, a good demonstration of the mid C18 in contrast to the earlier streets to the W. Yellow stock brick is used instead of red brick. Many pattern-book Ionic doorcases and other good details. No. 2 has a later doorcase, Greek Doric, and an iron overthrow. Good interiors also: stone staircases to Nos. 2 and 3, and an unusual Chinese fretwork staircase in No.5. Opposite, No. 33, larger than most, with four bays and a pediment (good first-floor ceiling). Further N the houses have wider doorways with some good fanlights. For the later continuation N, Doughty Street, *see* Perambulation 5e. This route continues W along NORTHINGTON STREET, past mews lanes and No. 13, a cheerful coachhouse of 1903, with flamboyant segmental gables and tapering chimneys (erected by Henry Finch, J.P.), to Great James Street.

GREAT JAMES STREET is dated 1721 on a cartouche on No. 16. A gem, very complete on both sides, with segment-headed windows, doors in pairs with door-hoods on carved brackets, staircases with twisted balusters. Only the original sashes with glazing bars are missing. The terraces are unusually uniform for their date. A few exceptions: Nos. 21–22 were refronted in 1779; Nos. 23–24 were rebuilt in the 1960s, reusing rather ineptly a very grand pedimented early C18 doorcase from Great Ormond Street. This area makes an interesting study in changing approaches to historic streetscape. MILLMAN STREET, which continues N from here, had on the E side another terrace of 1721, which collapsed in 1971. It was replaced in 1974 by terraced housing for Camden by *Farrell & Grimshaw*, firmly C20, a little dour with its facing of hard uncoursed red brick. The minimal Georgian echoes in the form of simple round-arched doorways and stuccoed ground floors, unusual for public housing at the time, reflected the shift towards sympathetic infilling in historic settings. At the N end Nos. 52–58, sheltered housing for Camden, by *Hunt Thompson Associates*, 1991–2. A pleasantly proportioned block of yellow brick, with entrance under an oriel sparkling with glass bricks. Nos. 1–25 on the W side were rebuilt in 1888 by the Rugby Estate, in pale brick with bands of coloured tiles, and restored by *Donald Insall & Partners* for Camden after 1975, when the borough bought some of the Rugby Estate property in order to set the pattern for much needed repairs.

GREAT ORMOND STREET is the main artery of the estate belonging to Rugby School, running E–W from Millman Street to Queen Square. Development was begun at the W end by *Barbon* in 1686, and was continued after his death in 1698 by *Millman*. The stretch E of Lamb's Conduit Street was built up *c.* 1721. At the E end each side has tall, handsome four-storey-and-basement houses in
31     brown and red brick (the grander ones on the S-facing N side). The sites were leased to separate builders, so the frontages have an appealing individuality. Several doorways with fluted pilasters and flat hoods with carved brackets. The condition of many of the houses became a scandal in the 1960s, and in 1974 Nos. 9–15 were partly demolished as dangerous structures. Camden acquired Nos. 1–17 in 1975, and major repair began by *Donald Insall & Partners*. The first conversions to flats, Nos. 1–7 on the S side, succeeded in retaining original panelling and staircases, as well as
p.     much of the original plan (stairs behind the entrance hall, two
21     main rooms on each floor with the characteristic late C17 back closet off the rear room). Nos. 9–15 are entirely new, with replica façades of 1980. Progress elsewhere was slower: Nos. 19 (C19), 21–25 (with C19 fronts to older houses) and 27 (C18 altered) were still under repair in 1993, by *Lander Associates* for the Rugby Estate.

LAMB'S CONDUIT STREET runs N–S across Great Ormond Street. Its name is derived from a conduit, provided by William Lamb (†1577), from which water was piped to the City. It was taken down in 1755. A lively local shopping street, a rarity now in inner London, with enjoyable C19 shopfronts and pubs behind the clutter of C20 pedestrian impedimenta. New buildings at either end. Those at the N end of the W side are the CAMELIA BOTNAR

LABORATORIES for Great Ormond Street Hospital, 1993–5 by *DEGW*, a neat brick range, four storeys to the street, adjoining an C18 house which has been adapted for hospital use. Taller behind, with a row of silver chimneys which act as air-conditioning vents. To the S are older stretches: the street was begun by Barbon in 1690 and built up by *c.* 1710; plenty of panelling and staircases of this date remain behind some of the later refronting (e.g. Nos. 28–38, 59, 83–85). On the W side, Nos. 29–37, of *c.* 1765–7. A detour to the E can take in RUGBY STREET, where the eyecatcher is Nos. 10–16, a fine group of *c.* 1721 (tactfully restored by Rugby School in 1981), including No. 12, with excellent carved doorcase and railings. No. 13 opposite incorporates below its back closet a medieval conduit chamber built for the Greyfriars in the City.

Now W along DOMBEY STREET, with minor C18 houses on both sides, converted to flats by *Levitt Bernstein Associates* in 1988. Extensive early C18 panelling preserved in Nos. 18–22. The W end of Dombey Street and NEW NORTH STREET were badly damaged in the war. The C18 terraces were replaced by blocks of flats by *Hening & Chitty*, begun 1948–9. They were among the first post-war flats, and earned high praise from Pevsner in 1952: 'eight-storeyed and one eleven-storeyed range, not lavish, but of delicate precision and agreeably devoid of mannerisms. Red brick, the short sides of the individual slabs roughcast, a little colour in the prettily detailed balconies' (cf. also Cromer Street, Perambulation 5c). The taller, plainer towers are later additions. Back by ORDE HALL STREET, with a C19 terrace on the E side, to Great Ormond Street.

The W part of GREAT ORMOND STREET is all hospital buildings on the N side (*see* Public Buildings), but on the S side Nos. 41–61, incorporating the entrance to ORMOND CLOSE, include some of Barbon's first houses in this area. A regular group with straight-headed windows, brick floorbands and some original doorways with square top lights. Freely carved original doorcase, especially good, to No. 41; a more precise C18 classical one to No. 49. Nos. 45 and 51 have attractive modest C19 shopfronts. No. 61 has a C19 front. On the N side, squeezed in among the hospital buildings, are Nos. 2–4 POWIS PLACE, late C18. Powis Place is on the site of Powis House, a very grand late C17 house rebuilt after a fire in 1714 and demolished soon after 1784.

QUEEN SQUARE. Planned in 1686, and built up by *c.* 1729, but, like the adjoining N side of Great Ormond Street, now over-whelmed by hospitals and medical buildings (q.v.). The square was originally open to the N, and in a letter of 1770 Fanny Burney could still praise 'the delightful prospect of Hampstead and Highgate'. On the W side there remain a few older houses of the C18 or early C19: Nos. 1, 2, 6, and 7; Nos. 13–15 have rebuilt fronts to match. No. 6, the most interesting, has an C18 staircase with twisted balusters and carved tread ends and, behind, an atmospheric toplit hall by *F. W. Troup*, added in 1914 for the ART WORKERS GUILD (founded in 1884). Panelled walls with portraits and the names of members; above are four reliefs and twelve oval niches with busts of former Masters (all by distinguished sculptors). A bust of William Morris by *Conrad Dressler* is in an arched niche in the place of honour above the Master's

chair. (Morris's firm was at No. 26 from 1865.) Most of the later
buildings on the w side of Queen Square have medical associations.
Nos. 8–11, Sir Charles Symonds House, grand Neo-Wren, was
built as a medical examination hall, 1909 by *A. N. Prentice*.
No. 12, St John's House, was a Church of England training
institute for nurses, 1907 by *Eustace Frere*. No. 17, Alexandra
House, tall Neo-Georgian, replaced a children's hospital on the
site from 1867 to 1920.

On the N and E sides the National Hospital, established in 1860,
on the E side and in Great Ormond Street the Royal London
Homeopathic Hospital, which moved here in 1859; on the s side
the former Italian Hospital, founded here in 1884 (*see* Public
Buildings). Of domestic buildings, No. 33 alone remains on the E
side and Nos. 42–43 on the s side, with good later C18 doorcases
(and a staircase in No. 43). There were trees in the square from
the end of the C18; the lead STATUE of Queen Charlotte dates
from 1775. At the s end an C18 cast-iron pump, and paving of
1975.

OLD GLOUCESTER STREET leads s from Queen Square. Near the
corner the former St George's Schools, tall gloomy Gothic,
1863–4 by *S. S. Teulon* (who also reordered St George the Martyr
q.v.); on the N side the Boys' school in similar style, 1877–8 by
*J. & S. Flint Clarkson*. s of this a few early C18 houses, refaced
later. w of the square, by St George the Martyr (q.v.) COSMO
PLACE, a pleasant paved passage leading to Southampton Row.
No. 9 has a good early C19 double shopfront.

### 3. South-west Holborn

### 3a. Kingsway

The need for a street to connect Holborn with the Strand was discussed frequently during the C19. Destruction of the slum area
around the s end of Drury Lane was begun by the new LCC as early
as 1889, but the plans for the new road were published only in 1898.
The formal opening took place in 1905. It was the most prestigious
of the LCC's Edwardian street improvements: a broad tree-lined
avenue 100 ft wide, with a tunnel beneath for electric trams (from
1961 used for cars), laid out on a scale to rival the boulevards of continental capitals. The buildings came slowly, from 1903 to 1922.
Architectural attention focused on the new Aldwych crescent linking
Kingsway to the Strand (*see London 6: The City of Westminster*). Most
of the other tall stonefaced buildings are not individually outstanding, although impressive in the aggregate; the lion's share went to
*Trehearne & Norman*. This account covers those at the N end, within
Camden.

E SIDE, N–S. Nos. 64–78, AFRICA HOUSE, *Trehearne & Norman*,
1921–2; a pompous, rather busy front with two orders of giant
columns and lots of sculpture above the cornice (by *Benjamin
Clemens*: Britannia with African workers and animals). Double-
height entrance hall with imperial stairs and much good ironwork
by *Singer & Sons*. No. 48–58, IMPERIAL BUILDINGS, with
carved figures over the doorway signed by *L. F. Roslyn*, 1914.

Light relief is provided at Nos. 44–46, 1914–15 by *Metcalfe & Grieg*, Art Nouveau Gothic with plentiful curves, two strong stone mullions flanking a shallow bow, carried up to intersect the curved gable. No. 40–42 is a *Lutyens* building of 1906, originally for William Robinson's magazine *The Garden*. Doric ground floor derived from Sanmichele (cf. Heathcote, Ilkley, Yorks). VICTORY HOUSE, another rather confused front by *Trehearne & Norman*, 1919–20; giant fluted columns to the upper part. QUEEN'S HOUSE by *M. E. Collins*, 1913–1914, PUBLIC TRUSTEE OFFICES, by the *Office of Works*, soothingly restrained 1912–15.

w SIDE, S–N. SPACE HOUSE. An intruder, by *R. Seifert & Partners*, 1964–8, later than Centre Point, and developed from it. The front to Kingsway is perfectly harmless except for the heavyweight antics of the Kemble Street corner. Behind, connected by a two-storey bridge, is a high circular block (circular in response to the angular street pattern behind), supported on splayed stilts like the Mercedes trademark. The tower is constructed of cruciform precast concrete members similar to those of Centre Point, though a little less crudely shaped. The windows do not join in the resulting zigzag game. Nos. 61–63, built as KODAK HOUSE, 1911 by *Sir John Burnet*. Pevsner singled this out in 1957 as 'the only building of architectural importance in Kingsway. For here is an early example in London of that straightforward treatment of a commercial building to which the future belonged.' Ground floor and mezzanine, except for the doorway, almost unrelieved by mouldings. Above, uprights reaching up through four floors. They have bases but no capitals at all, and lead flush into the top frieze. Between them four tiers of horizontal windows, and between the windows metal panels. The top cornice is coved. Nos. 77–97, WINDSOR HOUSE and REGENT HOUSE, 1913 by *Trehearne & Norman*; Nos. 97–107 by *Sykes*, 1906–7, with plenty of motifs attached without any discrimination.

## *3b. St Giles: west of Kingsway and south of New Oxford Street, from north to south*

In the Middle Ages a hamlet grew up around the hospital of St Giles-in-the-Fields, to which the present c18 church traces its origin. St Giles High Street, a continuation of High Holborn, still exists just N of the church. Its surroundings were hopelessly fragmented by the new c19 roads, which were deliberately driven through to eliminate some of the most notorious London slums. The first of these was New Oxford Street, bypassing the curve of St Giles High Street, planned by *James Pennethorne* from 1841 and opened in 1847 as part of a grand scheme of major thoroughfares through London, which was never fully realized. The hope was that the street would become a fashionable shopping area, but developers were deterred by the rookeries remaining behind; the only effort at new housing for the poor was the block of flats built to the N in Streatham Street (*see* Perambulation 4, p. 323). Pennethorne also created Endell Street, providing a N–S link to Covent Garden, but major links with Westminster were formed only with the creation of the E part of Shaftesbury Avenue through a widening of 1877–86 and Charing Cross Road, laid out 1887.

NEW OXFORD STREET. In the central part of the street a little still stands of the original 1840s houses: stuccoed, with loose bits of enrichment which appear debased when compared with e.g. Nash's West Strand of c.1830. Remaining examples are Nos. 36–60 (N); 33–37, 43–45, 47–53 (S). The most striking is No. 53, because it contains James Smith's magnificent umbrella shop with its original brass and mahogany shopfront and counters of c.1870.

Later buildings at either end. To the E, extending to Bloomsbury Way and towering over St George, ST GEORGE'S COURT, 1948–50, by *Lewis Solomon*; giant screens of columns to Bloomsbury Way with set-back upper parts behind; plenty of sudden aedicules of the type derived from Lutyens and Baker. For Pevsner the worst and most mechanical of the Lessor buildings (cf. Theobalds Road).

To the W, on the S side, CASTLEWOOD HOUSE and ST GILES COURT to its S, begun 1950, by the same firm (*Lewis Solomon, Son & Joseph*) and much more neutral. Plain, and not over-glazed, the two buildings making something of a composition. On the N side, No. 80, 1929 by *Gunton & Gunton*, a very long frontage, the centre with fluted Corinthian columns, four bays on each side with giant arches. For BURTON'S at the corner *see* Tottenham Court Road (Perambulation 6a, p. 333).

CENTRE POINT, at the junction with Charing Cross Road, 1959–66 by *R. Seifert & Partners* (designer *George Marsh*), a thirty-four-storey tower 398 ft high, with a lower block linked by a bridge on tapered piers over a road. The group aroused violent feelings when built, partly because of its size and style but also because it became a symbol of opportunistic exploitation during the 1960s office boom. It was built as a result of a deal between the developer Harry Hyams and the LCC, which thereby gained the land for a traffic route around the building (proposed already in 1956); but the tower stood unoccupied until 1975, and the traffic route never functioned as intended. The tower was designed for offices but later converted for housing. Pevsner's view in 1973 was that 'Centre Point has the merit among London skyscrapers of looking slim, at least from N and S. But that is its only visual merit. The drooping arms of the cruciform precast concrete members which result in a remorseless horizontal zigzag across the sill zone of every floor is coarse in the extreme ... Who would want such a building as its image?' Several decades later, the tower, so much smaller than what has been built since, can be seen as a classic expression of bright and brash 'pop architecture' of the 60s, inspired distantly by Le Corbusier and the Pirelli tower in Milan, its angular profiling (intended to reduce wind currents) curiously reminiscent of Czech cubism of the early C20. The frame of precast concrete sections is claimed as the first in London which eliminated the need for scaffolding.

ST GILES HIGH STREET and streets to its S. For the N side *see* New Oxford Street, above. On the S side just a few older buildings remain at the time of writing: W of the church No. 59, early C19, and a few more, including some late C17 houses in DENMARK STREET, laid out c.1687: No. 27 with passage through to the back. Fragments remain from the once dense network of streets and alleys. In FLITCROFT STREET, a narrow lane S of the church,

the ELMS LESTER PAINTING WORKS, 1903–4, the only working example of a scene-painting workshop in the West End.
Pedimented gable above tall doors: toplit painting room on the
first floor, with four paint frames. Flitcroft Street continues past a
Gothic warehouse of 1878 and emerges in Charing Cross Road,
between Nos. 114–116, 1888 by *Roumieu & Aitchison*, with heads
in roundels, and the PHOENIX THEATRE, 1930 by *Giles Gilbert
Scott*, who did the elevation, and *Bertie Crewe*. Italianate exterior,
circular entrance lobby with tiles, leading to a Renaissance interior
by *Komisarjevsky*, with painted panels by *V. Polunin*.

SHAFTESBURY AVENUE, linking the West End to New Oxford
Street, was created 1877–86. N of High Holborn it runs through
two awkward interlocking triangular spaces. Facing these on the W
side, the Neo-Romanesque Bloomsbury Central Baptist Church
(q.v.) and No. 233, Britannia House, offices by *Hobden & Porri*,
1929, with bold Egyptianizing columns and pilasters; side by side
the two look like an Osbert Lancaster drawing. Opposite, Nos.
228–234 and 210–224, King Edward Mansions; *c.* 1902–8, with a
series of jolly terracotta tourelles, probably by *C. Fitzroy Doll* (surveyor to the Bedford Estate; *see* Perambulation 5, Bloomsbury);
he built the Black Lion at No. 226 in 1904. On the W side, the
SAVILLE THEATRE by *T. P. Bennett*, 1931 with *Bertie Crewe*, quite
an original façade. A long low-relief frieze in cast stone by *Gilbert
Bayes*, Drama through the Ages, above the stonefaced ground
floor, and then a windowless red brick wall along High Holborn,
punctuated by raised red brick bands. Interior reconstructed in
1970 as two cinemas, by *William Ryder & Associates*.

*3c. From Seven Dials to Drury Lane, from west to east*

SEVEN DIALS. The district S of St Giles and N of Covent Garden
was developed in the 1690s by Thomas Neale, M.P. and entrepreneur. He was given the land by the Crown in return for establishing the first lottery, and let it to individual builders. The narrow
streets allowed for a large number of profitable frontages. The
unusual plan, with seven streets radiating from a central pillar, was
seen and admired by John Evelyn in 1694. The PILLAR, a column
bearing six sundials, and forming the seventh itself, was designed by
*Edward Pierce*. It was removed in 1773 (in a vain attempt to stop the
mob from congregating), but a facsimile by *Whitfield Partners* was
installed in 1989 as a result of a campaign begun in 1984. Its reinstatement is a great improvement to the area. For long Seven Dials
was remembered only as the centre of the closely packed district of
vice and crime into which it had deteriorated, recorded in Hogarth's
*Gin Lane* and other pictures and chillingly described by Dickens in
*Bleak House* as 'Tom all alone's'. Clearance began in the 1840s and
continued into the 1880s. The residential character was largely
replaced by commercial and industrial building, although a surprising number of houses survived, some still with panelling inside.
Redevelopment of the area began after Covent Garden Market
departed in 1974 and threatened redevelopment was halted. Much
ingenuity was devoted to finding new uses for existing buildings.*

* On Seven Dials *see* further *The Environment Handbook* by the Seven Dials Monuments Trust, 1997. On Covent Garden *see* further *London 6: the City of Westminster*.

STREETS RADIATING FROM SEVEN DIALS, clockwise. MONMOUTH STREET (N): a scatter of c18 houses on both sides; facing the pillar, the CROWN, 1865, by *Finch Hill & Paraire*. Houses on the E side together with commercial buildings facing SHORT'S GARDENS (NE) were neatly converted by *Levitt Bernstein, c.* 1980; flats open onto a raised court at the back, a shopping arcade below connects with Neal's Yard, of wholefood fame, now very consciously picturesque. Between Short's Gardens and EARLHAM STREET (E), a stretch of c19 warehouses, including Nos. 29–43 Short's Gardens, a former brewery warehouse of 1882, converted to a shopping mall in 1992 with central galleried atrium. Brick vaulting and iron columns remain, but swamped by fussy detail. Nos. 29–39 are former brewery stables, Nos. 36–40 are an early c19 terrace. On the S side of EARLHAM STREET, warehouses. The CAMBRIDGE THEATRE at the Seven Dials corner is by *Wimperis, Simpson & Guthrie*, 1929–30, plain, stonefaced and classical on the outside, but with one of the best-preserved London theatres of its date. *Serge Chermayeff*, then working for Waring & Gillow, was involved in the design (shortly before he worked with Mendelsohn on the Bexhill Pavilion theatre). Auditorium with curved overlapping planes with concealed lighting, an early example of progressive German ideas, adopted later in English cinemas. In the foyer two reliefs of dancers by *Anthony Gibbons Grinling*.

Between MERCER STREET (SE), MONMOUTH STREET (S) and SHELTON STREET is the block known as the COMYN CHING TRIANGLE after the ironmonger's shop of that name, with some of the most complete domestic terraces. Modest houses from the late c17–c19, with small c19 shops. They were rescued from long-standing dereliction with an ingenious and tactful scheme by *Farrell Grimshaw Partnership*, a model of its kind, begun in 1977. From the street, little change is apparent, apart from careful repair and new buildings at the corners. The N corner facing Seven Dials has a small tower (the c19 and c20 handling of the seven sharply angled corners deserves comparative study). Within the triangle, in place of a confused muddle of buildings, an attractive courtyard was created; inventive Neo-Baroque porches provide access to a mixture of residential and commercial accommodation, with warehousing below. To the court, the new corner buildings have curved projections in each of the angles; on the outside they are of striped brick, of the c20, but not aggressively so. On the W side of Monmouth Street (S) more c18 houses, backing onto a small early c19 group in TOWER COURT, and a few more in EARLHAM STREET (W).

The following streets have only their northern parts in Camden. For the rest, *see London 6: The City of Westminster.*

NEAL STREET, now pedestrian, has tactfully restored small shopfronts. On the W side Nos. 27–37, a good late Georgian group; opposite, some early c18 houses, especially No. 64, with rubbed brick window heads and original staircase, and No. 78, with workshop dormers.

ENDELL STREET. Planned 1839, laid out in 1843–6 as part of the street improvements of the 1840s (*see* New Oxford Street, above), in an effort to simplify the tortuous street pattern around Drury Lane. A nicely varied collection of buildings on the W side. At the

NW corner, first the former ST GILES NATIONAL SCHOOLS, 1860 by *E.M. Barry*. Lively polychrome brick front with Gothic windows and asymmetrical gable; N front more restrained, with a high roof. Designed for a total of 1,500 children, with soup kitchen and industrial school in the basement. Next to the Swiss church (q.v.), No. 81, stuccoed and, like the church, by *Vulliamy*. No. 71, C19 commercial, with fine carved stone frieze, and entrance to a cobbled yard. Part of the W side of Endell Street belonged to an earlier street and so has some late C18 houses, Nos. 51–59 and 63–69. Then the CROSS KEYS, a lavish mid-C19 pub front. On the E side DUDLEY COURT, six-storey housing by *Powell & Moya*, completed 1983, which replaced the tall and grim Dudley House, the former Workhouse (by *Lee & Smith*, 1879, with infirmary of 1886 by *Beresford Pite*). No. 22 is of 1859 by *Withers* for Lavers & Barraud, the makers of stained glass. Gothic, quiet and even. A flat front of red brick made decorative by blue and yellow diapers and bands. Stepped S gable. Five symmetrically arranged corbelled-out dormers on the W front are the only light relief. A remarkably early example of its style. In the S gable, stained-glass window by *Brian Clarke*, added when the building was converted to offices in 1983 by *Rock Townsend*. BETTERTON STREET, with a few C18 houses, leads E to Drury Lane.

DRURY LANE has been much rebuilt, on an inappropriate scale. The dominating WINTER GARDENS by *Paul Tvrtkovic* dates from 1967–72, when rebuilding of the whole of this area was being considered. It incorporates a 900-seat theatre, adaptable for theatre-in-the-round, by *Chew & Percival* and *Sean Kenny*, as well as banqueting rooms, shops, sixty-two flats and a car park. These are grouped in a large chunky pile, the tallest part faced with brown brick, the lower parts mostly curtain-walled below thick white roof bands. Further N on the W side a large ugly hotel on a raised podium replaced a hospital; the NW corner has large offices by *Geoffrey Spyer & Partners*, 1972. Opposite, a few narrow C18 and C19 frontages remain.

STREETS BETWEEN DRURY LANE AND KINGSWAY, from N to S. A poignant contrast to Kingsway close by. A network of small streets still with the crowded diversity of a poor C19 quarter, although now with less of its squalor. In MACKLIN STREET on the N side, behind a tall wall, No. 17a, ST GILES'S ALMSHOUSES, rebuilt 1885 by *E.H. Burnell*, Neo-Tudor, facing a tiny courtyard, and No. 23, built as a scene-painting workshop in 1851–2 by the leading Victorian scene-painter Thomas Grieve (see the tall doors). On the S side, the low ST JOSEPH'S R.C. PRIMARY SCHOOL; quite cheerful red and yellow brick of *c*. 1870. At the corner of STUKELEY STREET, a former mortuary, later C19; Dec windows and pretty Gothic detail. Nos. 20–22 Stukeley Street, a plain warehouse transformed inside by *Jestico & Whiles*, 1990–2, into passive solar offices, with a steel and glass atrium. DRAGON COURT, 1980s infilling on a humane scale. On the E side of NEWTON STREET, HOLLAND and THURSTAN DWELLINGS, tall late C19 working-class flats, colourfully reconditioned for the Islington and Shoreditch Housing Association in 1986 with new balconies, gates etc., by *CGHP Architects*. Further S, offices encroach from Kingsway: MANAGEMENT HOUSE, 1964–6; a hexagonal tower on columns straddles a low rectangular block. Designed by *James A. Crabtree*, reclad in the 1980s. s of this, ELIZABETHAN HOUSE, a large group by *Sir John Burnet, Tait & Partners*, 1959–61. Twelve-storey tower with four- and nine-storey attachments, the kind of varied grouping for which some English architects showed a fondness in the 50s. An opening through it leads to Great Queen Street. But first a diversion r. down PARKER STREET, which has on the N side an LCC Lodging House of 1892 by *Gibson & Russell*; over the fireplace in the reading room was placed in large letters the inscription: Labour!

GREAT QUEEN STREET was an important route between Covent Garden and Lincoln's Inn Fields, and had some major C17 houses. It is a great shame that nothing remains of *William Newton's* terrace of *c.* 1635–40 with giant pilasters, which made the C18 call this 'the first regular street in London'. On the N side some of the remaining houses are early and mid-C18: Nos. 6, 27–29 (with two nice doorcases), 33–35 (with brick bands) and 36–37. In between, Nos. 30–31, by *E. R. Barrow, c.* 1923–4, quite grand with Corinthian columns, built as the Royal Masonic Institute for Girls. Nos. 24–26, *c.* 1913 by *Bird & Walters*, built with offices of the Royal Masonic Institution for Boys above. Dark stone front with some Masonic ornament. Opposite is the colossal Freemasons Hall of 1927–33 (*see* Public Buildings, p. 267). Adjoining it to the E, the CONNAUGHT ROOMS occupy the site of earlier Freemasons' premises. No. 61 preserves part of the front added in 1869 to the Freemasons Hall built by *T. Sandby* in 1775–6 (demolished 1932). No. 63 also has a frontage of 1869, built as a pub. At the back a banqueting hall by *F. P. Cockerell* remains, added behind a later Freemasons Hall (1828 by *Soane*, extended 1838 by *P. Hardwick*, demolished 1863). To its E, with its main entrance in the narrow WILD COURT to the s, WESLEY HOUSE by *Gordon & Gunton*, 1910–12. Built as a Wesleyan Mission Centre. Quite jolly red brick with stone dressings, a Palladian window on the first floor. KINGSWAY HALL added to it in 1912–13 by the same firm has been demolished.

### 4. Bloomsbury: a circular tour starting in Bloomsbury Square

The development of Bloomsbury started in 1661 with the laying out of a residential square by the Earl of Southampton, to the s of his house begun before the Restoration. This became Bloomsbury Square. It is mentioned by Evelyn as early as 1665, and Pope in a letter refers to it as a fashionable address. To its w, Montagu House was erected by the Duke of Montagu in 1675–9, on the site N of Great Russell Street later to be occupied by the British Museum (q.v.). In 1720 Great Russell Street was called by Strype 'very handsome and well-built'. Streets grew up to its s, but to the N the grounds of the two great houses stretched into open country until the later C18. The Southampton Estate passed by marriage to the Russells, Earls of Bedford, who did a little building around the square in the mid C18. Then in 1775–80 Bedford Square (still admirably complete) was developed further N, and Gower Street followed. More far-reaching development of the extensive Bedford property began in 1800 when Southampton House was demolished, and the fifth Duke's builder, *James Burton*, laid out Russell Square, connected to Bloomsbury Square by Bedford Place, on the site of Southampton House. Other squares and streets followed, continued under *Thomas Cubitt*, until they filled the whole area up to Euston Road. Bloomsbury remained a select residential area throughout the C19, gated at its N end. In the early C20 it fell into gentle decline, and the name became the term for the set of intellectuals and artists who lived cheaply here in those short years around the First World War.

The present character of Bloomsbury appears in two strata. The first is the world of the squares and terraces, pleasant leafiness in alternation with equally pleasant architectural restraint, an ideal example of the right mixture of formal and informal. There are later C19 intrusions, for example in Great Russell Street and Russell Square, but they are not too damaging to the whole. The second stratum is the *Cité Universitaire*. This began with University College (q.v.) as early as 1828, but became a menace to the old Bloomsbury only from the 1930s onwards. The scale of the buildings grew; they overpowered and occasionally entirely destroyed the squares. Around the new intellectual centres a welter of university institutions, students' clubs and small hotels took possession of what were once private houses. After 1950 yet more was destroyed. Still more was threatened, but the decision to build the new British Library at St Pancras reprieved the area s of Great Russell Street, which benefited from rehabilitation in the 1980s.

The following account proceeds from s to N, omitting purpose-built university buildings, which are described in their own section above, *see* p. 275.

## Bloomsbury Square and Great Russell Street

The licence to build the square was granted to the Earl of Southampton in 1661; the early views show E, W and S ranges of p. 18 regular terraces with steep roofs with dormers, forming a kind of forecourt to the Earl's own mansion, Southampton House, on the N side of the square. E and S sides have been rebuilt: to the E there is now the back of the former Liverpool Victoria Friendly Society (*see* Southampton Row, below); on the s side the COLLEGE OF PRECEPTORS makes a handsome show with a tall front in debased Northern Renaissance style, 1887 by *F. Pinches*. In the middle of the s side, SOUTHAMPTON PLACE runs s, with an ensemble of neat Palladian houses on both sides, 1757–63 by *Henry Flitcroft*; doorcases with attached columns and pediments, some Doric, some Ionic.

The sw corner of Bloomsbury Square (Nos. 5 and 5a) is slightly earlier, 1744, also by *Flitcroft*, a good example of a carefully proportioned Palladian astylar elevation with the emphasis on the first floor. No. 5a, facing Bloomsbury Way, has two wings flanking a pedimented centre with tripartite window arrangement and lunette above. (Good staircase.) Along the w side of the square, C19 frontages conceal older building. Behind quite elegant stucco of *c.* 1862, Nos. 9–14 retain the proportions and some fabric of the 1660s. No. 12 has a back closet, and a staircase between back and front rooms, a type of plan preceding the standard Georgian terrace-house plan. In No. 14, the upper part of the stairs is original. No. 15 was rebuilt in 1889 by the Pharmaceutical Society, which also added the top floor and porch of *c.* 1860 to No. 17. No. 17, with Nos. 72–73 Great Russell Street, is a group of C17 origin remodelled in 1777 by *John Nash*, a very early example of his grand stuccoed style. A dignified front to the square with a tall first floor with Corinthian pilasters and pedimented windows. Good interiors, restored 1981: toplit stairs rising against a curved wall; decorative ceilings to first-floor rooms.

The regular terraces on the N side of the square, with the street running N from it (*see* below), replaced Southampton House *c.* 1800.

In the SQUARE, *Westmacott*'s STATUE of Charles James Fox, a seated figure of 1816, looks towards the Duke of Bedford in Russell Square. The square was originally laid out in quarters divided by paths. It was landscaped by *Repton, c.* 1806; around the perimeter he planned a compact hedge and broad gravel walk with grass margins, with an irregular walk in the centre. Trees remain around the edges, but the centre was replanted after the insertion of an underground car park in 1972–3, an ingenious double-helix construction seven storeys deep.

GREAT RUSSELL STREET, an old lane, was built up from *c.* 1661–2. Nos. 74–77 on the N side, although with later stucco, are the remains of a longer terrace built in the 1660s, partly destroyed *c.* 1802 for Montague Place, when the side of No. 77 was given its pretty iron balcony and veranda. Opposite the British Museum (q.v.) a former hotel (now part of the YWCA), 1895 by *Hayward*, breaks the mood with its craggy busy, many-gabled front ('A cat may look at a king' was Sir John Summerson's reaction). Also on the S side, much rebuilding by the Bedford Estate took place in the mid C19. Nos. 43–48, and the MUSEUM TAVERN at the corner, are by *William Finch Hill, c.* 1855–64, a distinctive, slightly French, stucco elevation with moulded round-headed and oval windows. Good interior of 1889 by *Wylson & Long*.

W of Bloomsbury Street, first the KENILWORTH HOTEL on the N side, busy brick and stone of 1903 by *G. Waymouth*, then Nos. 98–99, late C17, although externally altered. No. 99 is wider than average, five bays; to the l. of the central entrance is a grand staircase hall: stairs with twisted balusters, and the rarity of a painted ceiling. No. 105 is neatly fitted up as an artists' colourman's shop (established 1855). Further W the Central London YMCA at the corner of Tottenham Court Road, rebuilt 1972–7 by *Michael Mulchinet* of the *Elsworth Sykes Partnership*. A bulky complex clad in horizontal ribbed concrete. A cluster of four staggered towers with accommodation for 764, above a seven-storey podium (five floors underground) with many sports facilities. (Its predecessor was of 1911 by *Rowland Plumbe*, with reinforced concrete structure concealed behind a Neo-Greenwich Baroque exterior.) Less disruptive is the tall but chaste composition of the YWCA on the S side, by *Lutyens*, 1930–2. Brick with stone dressings, with a big Neo-Early Georgian portal. Four storeys with basements and attics. The tall windows in front light an entrance hall with concert room above. Large hall in the back wing. On the first floor near the centre a library, and a chapel lit by two Diocletian windows at the sides. To its E, Congress House, the TUC Headquarters, strikes a different note (*see* Public Buildings, p. 266).

STREETS S OF GREAT RUSSELL STREET. An area of much character: small service streets with varied shops, in origin late C17, but much rebuilt after New Oxford Street was cut through the slums of St Giles in the 1840s (*see* Perambulation 3b). From the 1980s the neighbourhood benefited from sensitive infilling and repair, after the threat to the area had been removed with the decision to move the British Library site from Bloomsbury to St Pancras.

MUSEUM STREET, partly of *c.* 1855–64, carries on the spirit of the Museum Tavern (*see* above). Nos. 42–47 are a refronting of a terrace of *c.* 1700. At Nos. 40–41 a decorative iron hanging sign for Allen & Unwin, possibly by *Walter Crane*. In LITTLE RUSSELL STREET, Nos. 18–21 is another early C18 group concealed by a mid-C19 façade (see the proportions). E of BURY PLACE, two pleasant new pedestrian courts, GALEN COURT and PIED BULL YARD, form a link to Bloomsbury Square. By *Chapman Taylor Partners*, *c.* 1980. At the w end of Little Russell Street, between COPTIC STREET and BLOOMSBURY STREET, crisp new housing by *Avanti Architects*, 1988–91, trim yellow brick, with angled windows and metal balconies at the corner. Opposite, PIZZA EXPRESS occupies No. 30 Coptic Street, 1888 by *R. P. Whellock*, for the Dairy Supply Company, with the large round-headed arches on the ground floor that became a hallmark of the company's dairy buildings. The area further w, which bordered on the C18 rookeries of St Giles-in-the-Fields, began to be rebuilt by the Bedford Estate in 1763 and was much rebuilt again *c.* 1844, when New Oxford Street was laid out. On the w side of Bloomsbury Street, Nos. 1–5, now stucco-fronted, date from the 1760s. No. 5 was leased by a tapestry maker and had until the 1980s an C18 tapestry weaving workshop behind in STREATHAM STREET, disguised to look domestic. On the N side of Streatham Street, PARNELL HOUSE, inscribed Model Dwellings for Families, p. 40 erected by *Henry Roberts*, 1849, for the Society for Improving the Condition of the Labouring Classes (founded 1844). The only effort to provide housing for the poor in this area after the demolition for New Oxford Street. One of the earliest blocks of flats of its kind, and (at least from outside) surprisingly dignified. Open-access galleries in the courtyard; again one of the earliest examples of that device. Five storeys including basement.

## Bedford Square

Bedford Square, reached by Bloomsbury Street, was the first extension of Bloomsbury northward, 1775–86. It remains without any 3 doubt the most handsome of London squares, preserved completely on all sides. The first occupants included many lawyers, attracted by its nearness to the Inns of Court. In the C19 it was popular with doctors and architects. Now it is almost all offices. The planting of the oval garden of the square is particularly abundant. The meaningless extra pavement space is a creation of the 1970s.

Each side of the square is treated as a whole, with stuccoed, pedi- 42 mented and pilastered five-bay centre. The houses have entrances with window slits flanking the doors so as to make a tripartite pattern, and surrounds of *Coade* stone with intermittent vermiculated rustication and bearded faces on the keystones. Similar detail appears on the adjoining houses in Bloomsbury Street. *Thomas Leverton* was involved in finishing some of the houses, as is known from his correspondence, but there is no firm evidence to attribute the elevations to him; the perverse treatment of N and s centrepieces, where a pilaster appears beneath the centre of the pediment, argues against the involvement of a designer familiar with classical principles. The builders *Robert Grews* and *William Scott*, responsible for many of the houses, are possible candidates.

No. 1 on the E side is an exception. Its exterior at once marks it out from the others, and its interior does not disappoint. Built for Sir Lionel Lyde (patron of Revett's Grecian church at Ayot St Lawrence, Herts) and completed by 1782, it has been ascribed to *Leverton* on the basis of his other known work in the square. It is relatively narrow (27 ft), and its arched doorway is centrally placed, flanked by niches with crossed spears, all set in an exquisitely detailed stuccoed projection. The plan is also unusual. The door is centrally placed and leads to an entrance hall opening on the r. to an oval space with corner niches, and on the l. to the staircase, also set in an oval. Stone stairs with elegant iron balusters; rear rooms on both ground and first floor are the full width of the house, and have rounded corners. In the upper room an excellent ceiling with painted medallions after designs by *Angelica Kauffman*. Other interiors have more traditional, but not identical plans. Many of them still display the refined and elegant taste of the late C18: curved walls and delicate patterning, pretty plaster ceilings to the tall first-floor reception rooms, fine stone staircases with slender iron balustrades. (For fuller details see Andrew Byrne, *Bedford*

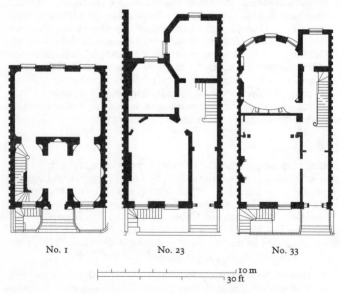

No. 1          No. 23          No. 33

10 m
30 ft

Bedford Square. Ground-floor plans

*Square*, 1990). Specially noteworthy: No. 6 in the centre of the E side, of five bays (restored as a single house in 1985), completed by *Leverton* for Lord Loughborough, the Lord Chancellor, with handsome toplit staircase. No. 9 has good ceilings and staircase. No. 10, completed by Leverton for Lionel Lyde's brother Samuel, with many details similar to No. 1, and a front room with barrel-vaulted ceiling with painted panels. No. 13, leased and completed by Leverton in 1781–2, was his home from 1795 until his death in 1824. Good ceiling to the main front room. No. 14, good plaster-work and staircase. Nos. 18 and 19, the two centre houses of the N side, each with stairs against a curved wall. Behind Nos. 19 and 21 contemporary outbuildings. No. 25, at the end of the N side, has fine interiors: an inner hall with fanlight, staircase with curved wall, good plasterwork. No. 31, good ceilings. No. 32, centre of the W side, with screens between entrance and stairhall, one of the them with columns, in a rather old-fashioned style; very pretty iron stair balustrades. Nos. 34 and 35 were taken over by the ARCHITECTURAL ASSOCIATION in 1917. Interiors were remod-elled by *Robert Atkinson* (head of the school since 1913); the ground-floor front rooms were combined as common room (now lecture room), with reproduction decoration to match the original; the library on the first floor was created in 1919–21. No. 36 was acquired in 1927, and further extensions were made at the back. Alterations by *John Winter*, 1961–75, included a new members' room on the roof. Further remodelling by *Rick Mather Architects*, 1978–82, created a basement bookshop, bar and restaurant and new exhibition gallery.

On the S side Nos. 40–53 were repaired and adapted as offices by *Ellis, Clarke & Gallannaugh* for Abbey Life Assurance, 1970–92, linked to extensions provided in the rebuilt mews behind. Original decoration was meticulously restored; much good plasterwork, e.g. in Nos. 44, 47, 48, 50 and 51. The mews to the S were replaced in the 1890s by BEDFORD AVENUE, with BEDFORD COURT MANSIONS on the S side, seven-storey brick and Portland stone flats by *Purchase & Martin* and *Allan F. Vigars*.

N OF BEDFORD SQUARE, development began at the end of the C18. GOWER STREET was built from the 1780s on with long, almost wholly unadorned brick terraces, even, soothing, dignified, and with a sense of overall planning, although certainly without much imagination. To Ruskin the street was 'the nec plus ultra of ugliness in street architecture', and G. G. Scott agreed. The Bedford Estate made concessions to C19 taste by adding some stuccoed entrances (Nos. 51–85). (At the S end, No. 2 (later the residence of the Master of Birkbeck College) has interior decoration by *Rhoda* and *Agnes Garrett* of *c.* 1875.) Another square was intended near the N end, but before it was built the land was sold for the new London University (*see* University College), thus beginning the academic encroachment that has overtaken so much of the area.

*Russell Square*

Reached from Bedford Square by MONTAGUE PLACE, leading E between the back of the British Museum and Senate House. It was begun in 1800 and is larger than any earlier London square, including even Grosvenor Square. It was laid out by *Repton* with a horseshoe of paths, in the new landscape style, and is still Bloomsbury's leafiest spot. The centre formerly had a garden building; its three flat fountain bases date from 1959. On the s side a bronze statue of Francis Duke of Bedford by *Westmacott* (1809) faces Fox's statue in Bloomsbury Square. Tall pedestal with reliefs of rural scenes; playful putti at the foot of the statue. The square is connected to the earlier developments of Bloomsbury Square and Great Russell Street by BEDFORD PLACE and MONTAGUE STREET. These should be studied first, for they are characteristic and perfectly preserved examples of the style of the Duke of Bedford's new developments of this time by his builder *James Burton*; absolutely plain, decently proportioned, with stuccoed ground floors. Bedford Place is complete on both sides. Montague Street dates mostly from 1802–11. No. 29a, a detached villa set back between the two streets, was built as the Bedford Estate Office in 1841–3 by *Thomas Stead*.

Russell Square had similar terrace houses, but only a stretch at the N end of the W side remains in its original state. To its s is a pastiche creation by the University (q.v.). The houses remaining on the s and N sides are original, but were beautified with terra-cotta bits *c.* 1896 by *Philip P. Pilditch*. RUSSELL SQUARE HOUSE on the N side, Regency classical stretched thinly over eight storeys, is by *Richardson & Gill*, 1941, extended later. The E side was replaced by two colossal late C19 hotels. Only the northern of these survives, the RUSSELL, by *C. Fitzroy Doll*, 1898, a super-François-Premier château with decided borrowings from the Château de Madrid, but magnificently inflated to a height of eight storeys. The materials, red brick and terracotta, and the details of the centre and top gables have no parallel in the C16. Sumptuous entrance hall. Its companion, the Imperial Hotel, also by *Fitzroy Doll* (in a vicious mixture of Art Nouveau Gothic and Art Nouveau Tudor), was replaced in the 1960s by two tawdry affairs with sawtooth fronts, entirely unworthy of their position.

*North and east of Russell Square*

The original character of this area has been heavily eroded by C20 university buildings (q.v.). Walking between these one reaches the remains of WOBURN SQUARE (*c.* 1829), with converted terraces to E and W. Of TORRINGTON SQUARE to the W (*c.* 1821–4) only a few houses are left on the E side, framing the vista towards Senate House. In BYNG PLACE to the N, squeezed by the taller University Church of Christ the King (q.v.) beside it, a large detached house of 1834 (FRIENDS INTERNATIONAL CENTRE), built as Coward Unitarian College: stuccoed, of nine bays, its projecting centre to the E emphasized by pilasters. To the W, between Malet Street and Gower Street, another terracotta creation by *Fitzroy Doll*, of 1907, now occupied by DILLONS, a wild block very elaborately detailed in a restless, flamboyant, Franco-Flemish Gothic style. Art Nouveau railings on Gower Street. In Malet Street DILKE HOUSE (Union of Shop, and Distributive and Allied Workers), a well-proportioned classical front skilfully coping with seven storeys; 1916 by *Lander, Bedells & Crompton*.

N OF TORRINGTON PLACE the pattern of elongated squares continues, built up by *Thomas Cubitt*. Surviving from the original lay-

out: GORDON SQUARE, E side, Nos. 36–46 and 55–59, c. 1824–5.
The rest of Gordon Square was completed only c. 1850, as can be
seen from the heavier Italianate of Nos. 47–53 and Nos. 16–25 on
the w side. In TAVISTOCK SQUARE, Nos. 29–45 on the w side
retain a façade of c. 1824, designed by *Lewis Vulliamy*. In the
gardens, bronze STATUE of Gandhi, c. 1968 by *Fredda Brilliant*,
and a MEMORIAL to Louisa Aldrich Blake †1925: seat and base
by *Lutyens*, bronze busts by *A. G. Walker*. On the s side the
TAVISTOCK HOTEL by *C. Lovett Gill & Partners*, 1951. N of
Gordon Square a complete block remains, bounded by ENDSLEIGH
PLACE, Nos. 1–7 (where houses were built by *Lewis Vulliamy* for
James Humphries, builder, in 1827), the E side of TAVITON
STREET, and the w side of ENDSLEIGH STREET, begun in 1824.
To the N, ENDSLEIGH GARDENS; on the N side a neat six-storey
block by *Avanti Architects*, 1992–4; ground-floor maisonettes; flats
for the elderly above, with curved glass-walled entrance.

In UPPER WOBURN PLACE, only one original group, much altered
(now the CORA HOTEL), 1821–4, formerly part of a symmetrical
terrace. Also ENDSLEIGH COURT, by *Richardson & Gill*, 1935,
and the COUNTY HOTEL by *C. Lovett Gill* alone, 1940. Recessed
centre with angled bays. For developments by Burton and Cubitt
further E *see* Perambulation 5.

*Southampton Row*

SOUTHAMPTON ROW continues s from the E side of Russell Square
(*see* above) towards Holborn. The s end is grandiose Edwardian,
widened as a continuation of the new Kingsway to its s. On the w
side, Nos. 8–10, CARLISLE HOUSE, 1905–6 by *Bradshaw, Gass &
Hope*, built as hotel and offices, with an exuberant roof with double
mansard, copper-domed corner turrets and gabled flank walls.
Nos. 2–6, KINGSGATE HOUSE, 1901–3 by *Arthur Keen*, was built
as headquarters for the Baptist Union, then at the height of its
influence. Free Baroque, Ionic columns to the upper floors, and a
lively skyline of gables and tall stacks, recalling that Keen was a
pupil of Shaw. Statue of Bunyan by *Richard Garbe*. Handsome
interiors to the main rooms: good panelling, fireplace reliefs by
*Tinworth*, ceilings by *L. Turner*. The front hall had a bronze standing figure of C.H. Spurgeon by *Derwent Wood*, 1905. At the back
an octagonal chapel (later inserted floor), with pretty plaster reliefs
by *Richard Garbe* (trees from the Bible). Future uncertain. Partial
demolition, with new back parts by *Craig Hall & Rutley*, proposed
at the time of writing. Opposite, VICTORIA HOUSE, built for
the LIVERPOOL VICTORIA FRIENDLY SOCIETY, 1921–34 by
*Charles W. Long*, an island block with grand frontage also to
Bloomsbury Square and lesser ones to N and s. A very large Beaux
Arts Grecian composition, with the conventional combination of
glass and metal upright bays and giant Ionic columns, quite
dignified and acceptable. Steel-framed, with the top two storeys in
a tall mansard rising behind the central pediment with sculpture
by *H. W. Palliser*. The ground floor to Southampton Row has
shops, originally set behind an arcade. Sumptuous, well-preserved
interiors with much marble and bronzework, arranged around two
light-wells. Basement meeting hall, octagonal public office on the
ground floor, mahogany-panelled third-floor board room. The

company occupied the N end of the building; the rest was let. Conversion to a hotel by *Anthony Blee* proposed in 1997, involving the transposition of the N staircase to the S end to improve circulation.

Further S, SICILIAN AVENUE by *R. J. Worley*, 1905–10 for the Bedford Estate, a most attractive and unusual pedestrian shopping street; upper storeys with turrets and tourelles of brick, terracotta and marble. Pretty colonnaded screens separate the diagonal avenue from Southampton Row and Bloomsbury Way. Two lamp-posts in the centre, with blue faience pedestals.

*5. East of Bloomsbury: Brunswick Square to Gray's Inn Road: a circular tour starting from Russell Square Underground Station*

The story begins with Thomas Coram's Foundling Hospital, laid out in 1746–52 on open land in the parish of St Pancras, just over the Holborn border. The main buildings were demolished in 1926, but the grounds in front survive as Coram's Fields, and some important relics are preserved in No. 40 Brunswick Square (*see* Public Buildings). In 1790 a grand scheme for developing the Hospital's estate was made by *S. P. Cockerell*, although his plans were not followed exactly. Brunswick Square to the W and Mecklenburgh Square to the E were laid out, with lesser streets around them. Building was carried out from 1792 by *James Burton*, who was also involved in contemporary development of other estates to the N. The whole area up to Euston Road was built up by the mid C19. It was badly affected by bomb damage and subsequent clearance after the Second World War, but the early C19 pattern can still be traced, although much interspersed with later rebuilding.

*Between Brunswick Square and Russell Square*

BERNARD STREET, completed by 1802, connects Russell Square with Brunswick Square. We start with a head-on confrontation between C20 and Georgian design: to the N the elevated Brunswick Centre, to the S a plain, decently proportioned brick terrace (Nos. 12–28), with arched doorways and neat rubbed brick window heads. BRUNSWICK SQUARE itself was almost totally rebuilt after major damage in the Second World War. Thomas Coram is commemorated by a STATUE in the square, a seated bronze figure, 1963 by *William Macmillan*. N and S sides of the square have university buildings (q.v.).

The BRUNSWICK CENTRE, replacing the W side of the square and the parallel street beyond, has its main entrance facing Brunswick Square. This was London's first influential megastructure, designed as a prototype for a new approach to urban living. It was originally intended to extend N as far as Tavistock Place; a linear scheme, unlike the Barbican. The single mammoth concrete structure provides housing, shops and other facilities in a pair of A-frames linked by raised decks, allowing for complete separation of vehicles and pedestrians, as was all the rage in the 1960s. The initial design by *Patrick Hodgkinson*, with *Sir Leslie Martin*, was begun in 1959; Hodgkinson was sole architect from 1963. Building took place only in 1968–72 and was not completed as first planned. The five storeys of flats and maisonettes, with two storeys of car parking below, were originally intended for private owners, but the whole was taken over by Camden as local authority housing.

The excitement of the design lies in the contrast between the grandeur of the framework and the intimacy of the flats facing each other above a busy concourse, a mixture not achieved in most of the imitations which followed. The main entrance, cutting through the long horizontal lines of stepped-back flats, is marked by mighty tapering concrete piers, curiously reminiscent of the early C20 visionary schemes of Sant'Elia, the Italian Futurist. The humanizing touch is a low box-like entrance to a cinema, tucked in between. Steps lead up to the pedestrian deck between the two A-frames, with shops on either side. A disappointingly bleak upper deck for the use of the residents covers part of the central space; this was originally intended to be glazed over. (Alterations to the shops, as part of general refurbishment by *RHWL*, planned 1998.) Cheerful stepping zigzags of greenhouse roofs above the balconies of the flats – a late addition to the original design – temper the severity of the concrete. The Piranesian effects of which concrete structures are capable can be seen in the lofty cavernous spaces within the A-frames, where the front doors to the flats are ingeniously, but not ideally, sited.

MARCHMONT STREET, a service street for Brunswick Square, preserves on its W side a long terrace of *c.* 1801–6 with a flourishing mixture of small shops and pubs. The contrast with the neighbouring Brunswick shopping centre should be pondered on. Facing Bernard Street another part of the *Martin* and *Hodgkinson* scheme: a large, restrained office block with hotel behind, with long bands of windows. To its W, HERBRAND STREET with the lovable landmark of the LONDON TAXI CENTRE, built as a DAIMLER GARAGE, 1931 by *Wallis, Gilbert & Partners*. Stuccoed concrete, with a bold spiral ramp continuing to the roof, as if more floors were intended; abstract Art Deco ornament around windows and staircase entrance. Daimler-owned cars were kept on the upper floor, private cars below, with waiting rooms at the side. This fringe service area between the Bedford and Foundling estates became slummy in the C19 and was rebuilt from 1898. Near the N end of Herbrand Street a Peabody Estate in the usual grey brick contrasts with three red brick gabled ranges of flats by the *LCC*. In KENTON STREET working-class housing provided by the Foundling Estate: five-storey blocks with decent Neo-Georgian detail, refurbished in 1978.

*North of Tavistock Place*

TAVISTOCK PLACE, built up *c.* 1800, divides the Foundling Hospital development from the area to the N, which was an eastward extension of *James Burton*'s development of northern Bloomsbury for the Bedford Estate (Perambulation 4). On the S side, Nos. 18–46 are original, Nos. 2–14 a facsimile frontage of *c.* 1975, an early, earnest example of the move towards contextual infilling. Much of the land to the N belonged to the Skinners' Company; Burton developed the area from 1809 to the 1820s, around his own villa, which stood between Tavistock Square and Burton Street on the site now occupied by the buildings of the British Medical Association (q.v.). The best survival of his time, reached from the N end of Marchmont Street, is the generous crescent of CARTWRIGHT GARDENS (now largely university halls of residence). Two quadrants of houses; stuccoed ground floors with arched windows. In the gardens a STATUE to Major John Cartwright, a resident of the crescent, 1831 by *George Clarke*. In the centre of the crescent BURTON PLACE leads W, between Greek Doric porches on the flanks of each quadrant. Nos. 4–7 were built as four houses disguised as a single one (converted to flats, 1986 by *Anthony Richardson & Partners*). BURTON STREET has some minor terraces. Just to the N, and not to be missed, are WOBURN WALK and DUKE'S ROAD, with three-storey Grecian frontages and shop windows belonging to the original *Cubitt* design of *c.* 1822. The shops have curved bay windows; the upper windows are tripartite, smartly decorated with paterae. Built for the Bedford Estate, on its border, so that the shops would not disturb the prime residential areas. Also in Duke's Road, No. 17, THE PLACE THEATRE. Built as the drill hall of the Middlesex (Artists') Rifle volunteers, 1888–9 by their colonel *R. W. Edis*. Attractive terracotta front with free Renaissance detail, and a medallion of Mars and Minerva by *Thomas Brock*. To the NE, FLAXMAN TERRACE, early St Pancras Borough housing, 1907–8 by *Joseph & Smithem*. Six storeys, with much consciously pretty detail: roughcast top floor, domed corner towers and Art Nouveau railings. Similar features on the engaging little caretaker's lodge at the corner of Burton Street. In MABLEDON PLACE, HAMILTON HOUSE, the stately premises of the National Union of Teachers, Edwardian classical by *W. H. Woodroffe*, 1913–14 (assembly hall added in the central courtyard 1961–2 by *Hulme Chadwick*).

E of Cartwright Gardens the early C19 street pattern of the Skinners' Estate remains but with only scattered survivals from the original buildings. Minor terraces survive in SANDWICH STREET and in THANET STREET (only two-storeyed); in LEIGH STREET is a complete terrace on the S side, with shops, and there is a taller stretch along JUDD STREET (Nos. 87–103), No. 95 with a Corinthian-columned shopfront. Scattered late Georgian houses also in HUNTER STREET (Nos. 3–4) and HANDEL STREET (Nos. 4–7) among miscellaneous medical institutions and mansion flats.

*Between Judd Street and Gray's Inn Road*

In this area planned working-class housing began to replace the older terraces from the end of the C19, continued by a variety of new housing types after the Second World War. MEDWAY COURT on the W side of Judd Street, by *Denis Clarke-Hall*, was an experimental point block built for St Pancras, 1949–55 (two others were intended); nine storeys, made interesting by lively massing and detail. Above a ground floor with shops the plan has three wings, with only two flats to each access balcony. Concave and convex sides, and much use of patterning and colour. E of Judd Street REGENT SQUARE, badly damaged in World War II; now with post-war flats on all except the S side (Nos. 1–17). This is of *c.* 1829, a quiet palace front with slightly projecting centre distinguished by arched first-floor windows. A few more houses in SIDMOUTH

STREET to the E. The N side of Regent Square is of *c.* 1958 by *Davies & Arnold*, with blocks of flats of different heights, the type of mixed development advocated by the LCC; one twelve-storey point block, others of four to seven storeys. E side rebuilt later. CROMER STREET further N offers an earlier, more formal alternative to the traditional street: a striking sequence of nine six-storey slabs of flats of 1949–51 by *Hening & Chitty* (cf. Dombey Street, Perambulation 2b), placed at r. angles to the street, with lawns alternating with service courts, to provide plenty of light and air. They were singled out by Pevsner in 1952 as some the first good post-war flats. Projecting staircase towers; decorative front balconies. Two blocks elaborately refurbished *c.* 1996. Four others by the same architects between Argyle Street and St Chad's Street. The small early C19 streets further N, run-down and overcrowded by the end of the century, were replaced by flats put up by the East End Dwellings Company. Their depressingly grim early blocks, arranged around cramped internal courts, can be seen N of Cromer Street, around TONBRIDGE STREET (WHIDBORNE STREET, TANKERTON STREET, 1893). TONBRIDGE HOUSE of 1904 is more cheerful, its open front courtyard and use of red and yellow brick marking the change of spirit initiated by the LCC's early housing.

Towards King's Cross is ARGYLE SQUARE (approached from Cromer Street by Whidborne Street), one of the last areas to be built up, laid out on the site of the unsuccessful Royal Panharmonium Gardens opened in 1830. Four-storey terraces on three sides. The mouldings around the upper windows betray the date: *c.* 1840–9. The surrounding streets are earlier, CRESTFIELD STREET and BIRKENHEAD STREET built up from 1825, ARGYLE STREET from 1826, ST CHAD'S STREET from 1827. Argyle Street, the most complete, leads to GRAY'S INN ROAD where the W side has a little more of the same period.

The N end of GRAY'S INN ROAD offers a miscellany of commercial and public buildings (*see also* pp. 263, 265). On the E side, Nos. 356–364, WILLING HOUSE, 1910 by *Hart & Waterhouse*, very fanciful three-bay front of freely mixed Tudor and Baroque elements. Carving by *Aumonier*; a figure of Mercury on the roof by *A. Stanley Young*. Good S annexe. BATTLE BRIDGE HOUSE; seven storeys, red brick bands, with yellow brick at the side. By *Sidney Kaye, Firmin & Partners, c.* 1975. ACORN HOUSE (NUJ Headquarters) is by *Robert Sharpe & Son,* 1966.

*East of Gray's Inn Road*

Streets developed E of Gray's Inn Road as early as 1773: in SWINTON STREET Nos. 51–59 are late C18, although the rest of the S side, with stuccoed ground floor, like ACTON STREET to the S, is of *c.* 1835 onwards. S again is FREDERICK STREET, part of a quite ambitious lay-out of *c.* 1827–32 by *Thomas Cubitt* (whose building yard lay just to the S off Cubitt Street). Minor grandeur in the Nash manner is achieved by the exploitation of vistas and by the use of groups with giant pilasters, or with stuccoed pediments to first-floor windows. Nos. 48–52 have elegant covered balconies facing down AMPTON PLACE to a group with pedimented porches in AMPTON STREET. Low-key neo-vernacular housing of the 1980s (WELLS SQUARE, FLEET SQUARE) fills the area further s. Nearby in CUBITT STREET the FIELD LANE COMMUNITY CENTRE, built as a Baptist Chapel in 1861. Two-storey three-bay front, all windows arched. Further s, PAKENHAM STREET, with a modest early C19 terrace, leading to WREN STREET and CALTHORPE STREET, another Cubitt development, planned from 1816, but built up slowly, as the different designs of the houses indicate. The streets are linked by GOUGH STREET, where No. 50 and GREEN YARD are worth a special look: sympathetically scaled infilling by *Pollard Thomas & Edwards*, completed 1990: stock brick corner house with mews houses behind. Perky but not over obtrusive late C20 details of early Modernist derivation (ground-floor portholes and mesh balconies). E from here, ROSEBERY SQUARE, near the borough boundary. The square forms a slight widening in ROSEBERY AVENUE, a new road laid out in 1889–92 and built up with plain working-class flats. Cheered up in the 1990s to designs by *Peter Mishcon*. For the N part of Rosebery Avenue *see* Finsbury, p. 632.

Back to Gray's Inn Road, where some formerly domestic stretches survive, which belong with Calthorpe Street on the E side and Guilford Street on the w. The CALTHORPE PROJECT, Nos. 258–274 Gray's Inn Road, is a community garden, a series of intimate spaces created by local effort in 1981–4, the outcome of a campaign to thwart an office development. Post-and-beam timber community building, 1991 by *Architype*, following Walter Segal's self-build construction principles. Deep overhanging eaves; flat roof planted with herbs.

*Doughty Street and Mecklenburgh Square*

Returning w, Guilford Street is crossed by DOUGHTY STREET, built up by the Doughty Estate from 1792 to 1820 as a link between the Foundling Estate and the older area to the s in the parish of Holborn (the parish boundary ran along Roger Street). Still impressively complete. Long ranges of terraces on both sides, with plenty of assorted balconies, fanlights and doorcases, including surprisingly sturdy Greek Doric entrances to Nos. 57–59. DICKENS HOUSE, No. 48, built *c.* 1807–9, where Charles Dickens lived 1837–9, was restored as a museum in 1925. It demonstrates the lay-out typical of these houses: basement service rooms (back washroom and wine cellar reconstructed); front ground-floor dining room with curved end, opening into a back parlour; first-floor drawing room (decorated and furnished in the style of *c.* 1837, with lilac cornice and woodwork). In the garden a *Coade* keystone with head of Jupiter from No. 1 Devonshire Terrace, where Dickens lived later.

MECKLENBURGH SQUARE, at the N end of Doughty Street, is in a different mode. Built from *c.* 1808 by *Joseph Kay*, Cockerell's successor as Surveyor to the Foundling Estate. Damaged in the Second World War but restored since. The E frontage is in the new grand manner of street architecture adopted also for Tyburnia and for Nash's Regent's Park. Stuccoed eleven-bay centre with giant Ionic columns and angle accents with recessed giant columns. The garden laid out in 1808–9 retains much of its original lay-out, with four serpentine paths from the corners to the centre. Some plainer original houses in MECKLENBURGH STREET to the N, also Nos. 43–47 on the N side of the square. On the N side is London House, *see* p. 268. From the N side a path leads W across the N end of Coram's Fields past the Coram Foundation (*see* p. 268) to the N side of Brunswick Square.

S of Coram's Fields in GUILFORD STREET *Burton's* original terraces of 1791–4 survive in patches, mostly rather altered. The best group is on the SE corner of GUILFORD PLACE, a wider area with DRINKING FOUNTAIN of 1870 opposite the entrance to Coram's Fields. Nos. 3–6 at the SE corner were sensitively restored in 1985 when converted to sheltered flats; two delicate fanlights, blue-painted railings. Some more in LANSDOWNE TERRACE (Nos. 1–4, 1794), and further W, where Nos. 70–72 GUILFORD STREET, 1793 onwards, fill what was once the vista N from Queen Square, hence their unusually grand elevations with giant Doric half-columns and pilastered attic floor.

## 6. North-west Holborn

### 6a. Tottenham Court Road

TOTTENHAM COURT ROAD, the main route from Holborn to Hampstead, derives its name from Tottenham Court, the Tottenhall manor house which stood N of Euston Road (*see* St Pancras, Perambulation 1a). Now entirely commercial, Victorian and post-Victorian, and indeed post-1950: of the six buildings singled out by Pevsner in 1952 only three remain. In the C19 this was a centre of furniture making, hence the grand department stores and warehouses that appeared in the early C20 among remnants of domestic terraces. This character has largely gone; only Heals survives in its original buildings. The speciality at the S end is now computers and electrical equipment. On islands down the centre of the street are lighting columns for electric arc lamps of 1892, refurbished 1990, celebrating Britain's first municipal electric light undertaking.

E SIDE. The S end is between-the-wars commercial classical: head-quarters and shop for the tailors MONTAGUE BURTON, *c.* 1929–30 by *Harry Wilson*; Neo-Grec, metal windows between Corinthian pilasters. DOMINION THEATRE, 1928–9 by *W. & T. Milburn*, with quite narrow concave stone-faced front hiding a very large Neoclassical auditorium (seating for 3,000); cinema conversion 1930, 1933 and 1953. Then the HORSESHOE HOTEL, 1875 by *Paraire*. A 'gruesome Victorian abomination' (Pevsner), but very typical of the freedom with which pubs, gin palaces and music halls treated period material at that date. After the YMCA (*see* Great Russell Street, Perambulation 4), a stretch with little of note apart from the BEDFORD CORNER HOTEL (Nos. 234–236) with a sturdily detailed elevation of *c.* 1870.

Now a small diversion E along STORE STREET, where the City Surveyor *George Dance* was responsible for some ambitious planning in 1796 on a small estate belonging to the City of London. ALFRED PLACE was laid out with a crescent of houses at either end, completed in 1810. The domestic character disappeared as the area became service roads for the Tottenham Court Road shops, and then began to be redeveloped for offices. Nos. 8–10, with nice wavy roof-line, are the industrial back of the more formal Jacobean Nos. 216–219 Tottenham Court Road, all of 1908 by *Read & Macdonald*. Opposite, Nos. 19–29, glossy black granite-faced offices, *c.* 1972, in the severe, angular, slightly Egyptian mode favoured by *R. Seifert & Partners* at this time. In the centre of SOUTH CRESCENT, hidden behind a tall, demure red brick Edwardian front, the spectacular premises of IMAGINATION, a design consultancy, by *Herron Associates*, 1988–9. The space between the front building and a second one behind has been transformed into a tall atrium with walls painted white, roofed by tensile fabric supported by slender steel supports, and crossed by light metallic bridges. Next to it, on the curve, the BUILDING CENTRE, built *c.* 1920 as Daimler showrooms. In front of NORTH CRESCENT, the lumpish top of lift shafts to concrete-lined UNDERGROUND TUNNELS, 1941–2 by the engineers *Halcrow & Partners*, one set of eight built in London as deep shelters for government personnel. (Intended for later use by the underground railway, but only used for storage.) Further E on the S side of CHENIES STREET, former Drill Hall, now Arts Centre, built for Bloomsbury Rifles, a volunteer corps: a romantic Tudor front with battle-mented entrance tower, 1882–3 by *Samuel Knight*.

HEAL'S, Tottenham Court Road E side, Nos. 191–199. The centre, of 1912–17 by *Smith & Brewer*, is the best commercial front of its date in London, with fine reticent stone uprights in a rhythm which avoids uniformity. Decorative cast-iron panels by *Joseph Armitage*. S extension and additions by *E. Maufe*, 1936–8, continuing with the same proportions. N addition (the part now occupied by Habitat) by *Fitzroy Robinson & Partners*, 1968, similar, but with simplified detail. The ground floor of the original building had shop windows discreetly set back, so that the uprights were emphasized. This effect was lost, alas, when new windows of 1986 eliminated the covered walk (they replaced non-reflecting curved windows installed in 1937 to display deep room settings). N of Grafton Way an austere granite and mosaic-faced complex of 1976 by *R. Seifert & Partners*, for MAPLES (replacing their showy furniture store of 1928–30); shop below offices and flats, E wing with laboratory for University College Hospital.

TOTTENHAM COURT ROAD W SIDE. The S end was for long a curious mess of small properties on the Gort Estate, partly replaced by a greedy granite-clad hulk, six storeys rising to ten at the back, intended but never used as headquarters for the music company EMI; by *Sidney Kaye Firmin Partnership*, completed 1980. Behind, in GRESSE STREET, Nos. 32–34, a lively refurbishment of a 1915 warehouse by *CZWG*, 1983. At the corner of Tottenham Court Road and Windmill Street, No. 46, RISING SUN, 1896, in *Treadwell & Martin*'s typically fanciful Art Nouveau Gothic. N of Goodge Street, Nos. 64–67, formerly Catesbys, a department store specializing in linoleum; 1903–5 by *Henry A. Whitburn*; a froth of eclectic detail to the upper floors. No. 85, completed 1992 by *EPR Architects*, six storeys, offices above shops, sleekly clad with triple glazing, the front given interest by the partial recessing of ground, first and top floors behind the structural columns (cf. Heal's opposite).

## 6b. Fitzrovia

The narrow grid of streets w of Tottenham Court Road, centred on Fitzroy Square, is the heart of the area dubbed Fitzrovia, an appealing small-scale mixture of domestic and commercial Georgiana with a Bohemian aura, which was popular with artists and writers in the C19 and early C20. Threatened by redevelopment in the 1960s, but since redeemed by some careful conservation attention. Most of the land belonged to Tottenhall manor. The s part was developed piecemeal during the C18, then more consistently in the 1760s; the N part took shape after the freehold was acquired in 1768 by Charles Fitzroy, later Lord Southampton. Fitzroy Square, the single grand setpiece, was laid out in 1789.

CHARLOTTE STREET, the main s–N artery, is still Georgian in scale, with a scatter of C18 houses of the 1760s onwards, mostly with inserted shops and restaurants. Nos. 18–36 on the E side, c. 1766, is the best group. (No. 26 has a rococo ceiling and a good later shopfront.) The N end is more disrupted: on the site of the old Scala Theatre (1904 by *Verity*), an undistinguished podium and slab development with cinema, offices and flats (by *Sidney L. Belser*, 1974) provides an indication of what could have happened to the whole area.

Many Georgian survivals, mostly of the 1760s, are to be found if one zigzags along the streets which run E–W across Charlotte Street. From s to N: PERCY STREET, developed 1764–7. Houses of varying size on both sides, planned as two balanced compositions centred on No. 11 and No. 29. Shops inserted later, but some original interior features (e.g. in No. 29, also staircases in No. 4 and No. 36). CHARLOTTE PLACE, with small shops, links up with Rathbone Place to the s (*see London 3: North West*, St Marylebone). Further N, WINDMILL STREET (once a track leading to a windmill in Charlotte Street), developed from c. 1723 but with existing houses of the 1760s. COLVILLE PLACE, pleasantly domestic, with smaller houses of the same date, complete on the N side, leads to WHITFIELD STREET. This is the back lane to Tottenham Court Road and has suffered accordingly. Original houses at the N end. Further s, among the later buildings, Nos. 54–60, 1914–19 by *Ernest H. Abbott*, with giant pilasters and two segmental pediments; built as premises for a goldbeater, hence the decoration on one of the capitals. GOODGE STREET, one of the wider E–W streets, is mostly of the 1760s, built by the speculator-architect *Jacob Leroux*. Nos. 33–41 are a good group of 1767, with dentilled cornice. No. 35 has a first-floor ceiling roundel with musical instruments, and a good (restored) early C19 shopfront with curved corners. N of Goodge Street GOODGE PLACE, specially attractive, with minor Georgian terraces still in domestic use, and Nos. 17–18 by *Parry Frame Associates*, c. 1989, for a housing association, C20 detail in traditional materials. A few more C18 houses in TOTTENHAM STREET and SCALA STREET.

FITZROY SQUARE is the centre of a planned development of the 1790s by the first Baron Southampton, which included Fitzroy Market (now Whitfield Place) and surrounding streets. E and s sides of the square were designed by *Robert Adam*, one of his last

major works before his death in 1792. E side (built 1793–8) of fine
Portland stone; a unified composition in subdued relief, reminiscent of his Edinburgh work rather than his earlier London terraces.
Rusticated ground floor with arched windows; broad doorways with
sidelights and fanlights. Centre with recessed, attached unfluted
Ionic columns, the angle pavilions with shorter recessed columns
forming a tripartite window with tripartite lunette window above.
The S side of 1794 etc. made the latter its centre motif, with still
smaller angle motifs of recessed columns and pairs of relief medallions. This side was damaged in the Second World War; the exterior was restored in facsimile and refurbished as offices by *Rolfe
Judd Group Practice c.* 1980. The LONDON FOOT HOSPITAL
occupies the end houses. The interiors of both E and S sides have
stone stairs with iron balusters. N and W sides were built only in
1827–35 and have stuccoed fronts, the centre of the W side with
Ionic columns *in antis*, the N side with Ionic pilasters. The plain
classical stone fronts of Nos. 13–14 on the N side are an intrusion
of the 1920s, built for ST LUKE'S HOSPITAL FOR CLERGY,
established here in 1907. In the square, SCULPTURE by *Naomi
Blake*, 1977, View II.

    Some plain late C18 houses remain S of the square in FITZROY
STREET and MAPLE STREET (the Fitzroy Chapel of 1788 stood
here until destroyed in the Second World War). Others in GRAFTON
WAY, especially the N side, Nos. 56–60 with good fanlights. To the
N good groups of the 1790s in CONWAY STREET with pairs of
delicate iron balconies. No. 35 has a nice dairy shopfront of
*c.* 1916. Lesser streets in this area have a good scatter of Georgian
survivals, including some elegant early shops with characteristic
bowed fronts: see WARREN STREET (Nos. 21–22), CLEVELAND
STREET (No. 106) and WHITFIELD STREET (No. 135).

YMCA INDIAN STUDENT HOSTEL, corner of Fitzroy Street and
Grafton Way. 1952 by *Ralph Tubbs*, with an extension by Tubbs of
1962–4 along Grafton Way. Well-composed, L-shaped building
faced in brick; a stone flank wall with honeycomb pattern of
windows marks the corner of Fitzroy Square, with a transparent
glazed staircase set back beside it. A glazed link connects it to the
later extension. Inside, a broad, airy staircase leads down to
Mahatma Gandhi Memorial Hall in the basement, a tall galleried
space with raking windows to the courtyard to let in the light.
Library and common room on the first floor; prayer room with
curved roof on the top floor. New wing at the back with bedrooms
and conference room, planned 1997, by *Tubbs Davis*.

## INTRODUCTION

St Pancras forms the centre of the Borough of Camden. Its name is derived from its oldest building, the ancient parish church, tucked away in its churchyard in an incongruous setting just N of St Pancras Station; the dedication to a Roman saint and the survival of a Saxon altar suggest that the church was a very early foundation. The medieval parish which later became the metropolitan borough extended in a narrow strip for 4 miles, from the borders of Bloomsbury uphill to Highgate on the Northern Heights.\* By the later Middle Ages there was a chapel on the main road N at Kentish Town, and another at Highgate, on the edge of the Bishop of London's large N Middlesex estates. Highgate grew into a little hilltop town by the C18; its remote position kept it distinct, and its story is told separately (*see* Perambulation 5). Apart from Highgate, it was Kentish Town which developed into the principal settlement, and the old church of St Pancras stood alone among fields until the end of the C18.

Just to the s of the old church, the New Road, of which Euston Road is a part, was made in 1756 to bypass central London. Built-up Bloomsbury crept N during the C18 but did not reach Euston Road

---

\*The irregular southern boundary is shown on the Holborn map on pp. 250–1. For the sake of convenience the area between this and Euston Road is described above under Holborn. The NE boundary with Hornsey (now part of the Borough of Haringey) passes through the centre of Highgate, which is all described under St Pancras.

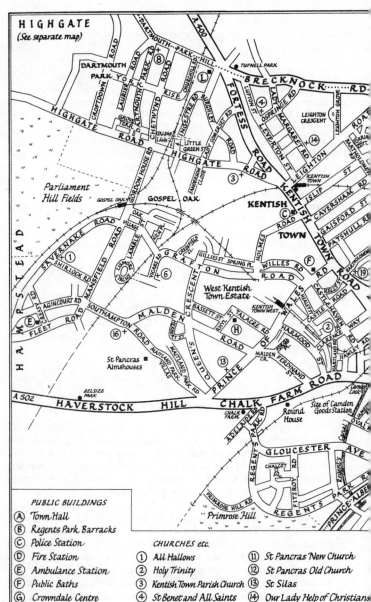

# HIGHGATE
(See separate map)

PUBLIC BUILDINGS

Ⓐ Town Hall
Ⓑ Regents Park Barracks
Ⓒ Police Station
Ⓓ Fire Station
Ⓔ Ambulance Station
Ⓕ Public Baths
Ⓖ Crowndale Centre
Ⓗ Interaction Centre
Ⓙ Royal Veterinary College
Ⓚ Working Men's College
Ⓛ Acland Burghley School
Ⓜ Camden School for Girls
Ⓝ Jewish Free School

CHURCHES etc.

① All Hallows
② Holy Trinity
③ Kentish Town Parish Church
④ St Benet and All Saints
⑤ St Luke
⑥ St Martin
⑦ St Mary
⑧ St Mary Brookfield
⑨ St Mary Magdalene
⑩ St Michael

⑪ St Pancras New Church
⑫ St Pancras Old Church
⑬ St Silas
⑭ Our Lady Help of Christians
⑮ St Aloysius (R.C.) (R.C.)
⑯ St Dominic (R.C.)
⑰ All Saints
⑱ Friends House
⑲ St Andrew (Greek Orthodox)
⑳ St George (Greek Orthodox)

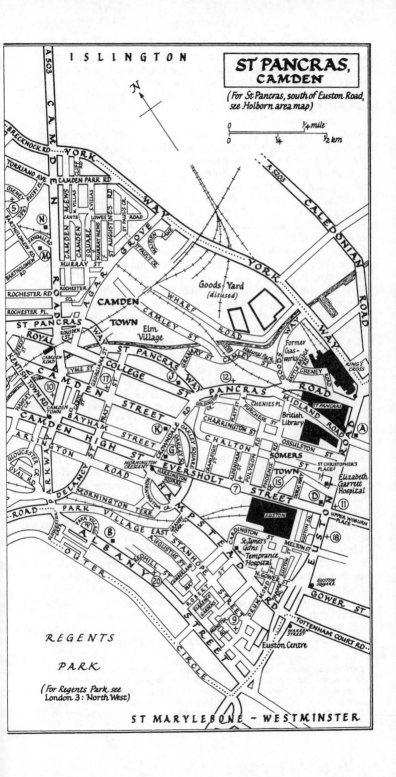

50 until c. 1820, the date when a new, Grecian St Pancras Church was provided for the neighbourhood. N of Euston Road development had begun in the 1790s, both at Somers Town, where a polygon of houses (now demolished) was built as an unusual setpiece by Lord Somers, and on the Earl of Camden's land to the E of what became Camden High Street. When Dickens lived there as a boy, in Bayham Street, there were still fields all round. Further w the fringes of the Crown's Regents Park development were built up in the 1820s, and building also started on the Southampton Estate w of Camden High Street. By the 1860s houses covered the whole area between Camden High Street, Regents Park and Primrose Hill. Camden Road, a new route cutting NE to Tottenham from Camden Town, was laid out in the 1820s, and streets off it followed, although the area to its N, between Kentish Town, Highgate and Hampstead, was not fully built up until the second half of the C19. Close to Gospel Oak the traditional fair was still held in 1857. The population of the borough grew from 46,000 in 1811 to 130,000 in 1841 and 199,000 in 1861, reaching a peak of 236,000 in 1881, after which it declined. In 1931 it was 198,000, in 1951 138,000.

The new suburbs of St Pancras were not a match for the smarter areas of West London. Squares were built in the neighbourhood of Euston Road in the early C19, continuing the pattern of Bloomsbury, in Bedford New Town further N and on Nash's Regents Park estate, but were less successful in the later suburbs. The largest, Camden Square, took twenty-five years to complete. Nash's delightfully varied
54 miniature villas in the two Regents Park Villages remained exceptional, although larger detached or paired villas were popular along the main roads – Camden Road had the grandest examples. Formal circuses and crescents in the Neoclassical manner also appear only occasionally (e.g. Mornington Crescent from 1821, and the later Oseney Crescent of the 1860s). Nothing came of more ambitious schemes such as the sequence of circuses for Camden Town proposed c. 1790 by *George Dance jun.*; the railway to Euston disrupted a later grand plan for the Southampton Estate centred on Oval Road and Gloucester Avenue. For the most part the C19 suburbs consist of simple grids of streets lined with the usual London brick terraces with stucco dressings. They became more ornate as the century progressed, and in the northern parts of Kentish Town are given a certain irregular picturesqueness by the hilly terrain.

Until the later C19, churches were the principal social amenity for the new suburbs. By 1851 the old parish had twenty-six Anglican churches and chapels, although only a few of these now remain in the southern part of the parish.* Those of the earlier C19, erected with the encouragement of Dr James Moore, vicar of St Pancras from 1814 to 1846, started with the enlargement of Kentish Town Chapel and the building of the new church of St Pancras on Euston Road. They aimed to meet the needs of a respectable expanding

---

*Demolitions include: two older chapels (St James, Hampstead Road, 1788; St Bartholomew, Gray's Inn Road, 1811). Also St Peter, Regent Square, by the *Inwoods*, 1822–6; Holy Trinity, Gray's Inn Road, by *Pennethorne*, 1838; All Saints, Gordon Square, by *T. L. Donaldson*, 1841; St John Evangelist, Fitzroy Square, by *H. Smith*, 1846; St Paul, Camden Square, by *Ordish & Johnson*, 1847–9; St Luke, King's Cross, by *J. Johnson*, 1856–61; St Jude, Gray's Inn Road, by *Peacock*, 1862–3; St Matthew, Oakley Square, by *J. Johnson*, 1851–6; St Andrew, Haverstock Hill, by *C. F. Hayward*, 1864–6.

population with large preaching spaces filled by profitable rented
pews, built over capacious burial vaults. The novelty of St Pancras
and its followers, All Saints, Camden Town, St Peter, Regent Square
(demolished), and Christ Church on the edge of the Regents Park
Estate, was the adoption of a demonstrably Grecian style. Still more
exotic was Highgate Cemetery, with its atmospheric Egyptian cata- 53
combs, which provided burial space for North Londoners from
1839. But it was Gothic which was to become the accepted style
for churches, used minimally for St Mary, Somers Town, more
ambitiously at St Michael, Highgate. Tractarian ideals of the 1840s
were expressed first by new fittings (Christ Church), then architecturally by St Mary Magdalene, *R. C. Carpenter*'s early and notable 83
exercise in Dec Revival. Later c19 survivors further N have fared
better; those of national distinction include *Lamb*'s strikingly eccentric
St Martin, *Bodley & Garner*'s St Michael, *Brooks*'s cathedral-like
fragment of All Hallows. Even more ambitious is St Dominic,
planned as a major R.C. centre for North London.

The arrival of the railways had drastic effects on the southern part
of St Pancras. Euston Road was transformed by the great termini, all
major architectural monuments: Euston (1836, demolished), King's
Cross (1851) and St Pancras (1868). N of the stations stretched a
noisy industrial landscape of marshalling yards, goods yards, gas- p.
holders and canal wharves. There were railway works also at Chalk 96
Farm (including the famous Round House) and at Kentish Town.
The vast constructions gave rise to a temporary population of navvies;
the results of their work destroyed large areas for living purposes
(including nearly the whole of Agar Town N of King's Cross) and
reduced the value of others. These areas with their streets going
grimy attracted the new poorer class of workers for the railways and
their goods and passenger stations. The result is vividly clear on
Booth's poverty map of 1889, showing the houses of the poor densely
concentrated N of Euston Road, but extending also into large areas
of Camden Town and Kentish Town. The drive to tackle overcrowding and bad housing – notoriously, before the 1890s the railways
were not obliged to rehouse the people they displaced – gathered
momentum in the later c19, fuelled at first by private philanthropy.
The first LCC housing in Somers Town was begun in 1899, the first
borough housing in 1904. By 1939 over 3,000 flats had been built by
the local authorities and by private organizations, among which the
most active was the St Pancras Home Improvement Society (later St
Pancras Housing Association). Somers Town was largely transformed
by these various endeavours, although traces of its early c19 character
can still be recognized. Schools and other amenities, which began to
be provided by the local authorities from the later c19, have also left
their mark: architectural highlights range from the public baths in 101
Kentish Town to one of the LCC's most inventive Edwardian fire 103
stations in Euston Road.

Post-war St Pancras, ruled by a Labour council from 1945 to 1949,
was one of the most energetic housing authorities in the country,
executing and expanding a programme already being planned during
the war. A thousand flats were complete by 1951. The council's
traditional watered-down Neo-Georgian blocks by *A. J. Thomas*
were soon supplemented by new styles and lay-outs by other architects;
early post-war examples were a tower and crisp low terraces by

*Powell & Moya* at Gospel Oak, and Modernist rows of flats by *Hening & Chitty* in Cromer Street (*see* Holborn, Perambulation 5, p. 331), and by *Norman & Dawbarn* in St Pancras Way, Camden Town. Major redevelopment was also put in hand (initially by *Gibberd*) on the Regents Park Estate, acquired by the borough from the Crown Commissioners. An idealistic borough plan in 1949 concluded that 50 per cent of the housing stock would need to be rebuilt within the next 20 years. From the 1950s grand schemes were discussed for the almost total reconstruction of West Kentish Town; there was much destruction and rebuilding here, continuing into the 1970s, but unhappily neither a coherent plan nor many buildings of distinction resulted.

When the Borough of Camden was created in 1965, a Borough Architect's Department was set up under *Sidney Cook* (1965–78), who had been Borough Architect of Holborn from 1945. The planning department was under *Dr Bruno Schlaffenberg*, who came from the LCC. Camden embraced the St Pancras housing programme and developed it energetically in new directions; for the next ten years its new buildings were among the most innovative and ambitious of all the London boroughs. The borough was among the first local authorities to reject the principle of high-rise blocks and to experiment with various forms of low- and medium-rise housing with integrated but segregated accommodation for people and cars. There were already some trailblazers, most influentially *Patrick Hodgkinson*'s experimental
7 prototype, the Brunswick Centre in Bloomsbury (*see* p. 328), with its stepped-back flats overlooking a central deck above garages. Exploration of this type for different sites was a distinctive theme in the work of Camden Architect's Department inspired by *Neave Brown*, and results can be found in Hampstead as well as St Pancras. Stepped
124 housing appeared first on an intimate scale at Dunboyne Road Estate (South Hampstead, *see* p. 243). Another group was fitted comfortably onto a hillside at Highgate New Town. The type was adopted in its most monumental form as a concrete barrier block bordering the
123 railway at Alexandra Road, and in romantic hill-village style at Branch Hill (Hampstead, pp. 247, 230). Within the St Pancras area variants include a spreading red brick group in Somers Town and the vast, white, rigorously austere Maiden Lane Estate N of King's Cross. But by the later 1970s disillusion with awkwardly large and expensive schemes had set in, and the fashion for concrete megastructures gave way to more homely compositions in brick and timber; the change is tellingly illustrated by the later phases of Highgate New Town.

It was not only the public-sector housing which drew attention to Camden, but also the private houses, often designed by architects for themselves. In the 1950s it was the still inexpensive semi-rural fringes of Highgate that attracted such buildings; from the 60s onwards tighter urban sites were found for new houses discreetly
126 disposed among the Victorian terraces and mews of Camden Town and Kentish Town. No other part of London can boast such a range of individual modern buildings of the later C20. The architectural self-consciousness generated by such activity may have helped to ensure that work of high quality continued in the 1980s–90s as local-authority housing gave way to more modest housing-association
127 developments and flamboyant modernism to more contextual approaches.

The preference for rehabilitating older housing has meant that since the 1970s it is derelict industrial and railway land that has offered most scope for new architecture. So far this has only occasionally produced non-domestic buildings of note, as in the case of *Grimshaw*'s Sainsbury's in Camden Town. By far the most significant development is *Sir Colin St John Wilson*'s British Library, on the site of St Pancras goods station, at last revealed as one of the most distin- 121 guished contributions to the area, and Britain's only major public building of the later C20. The full potential of the vast railway lands N of King's Cross has yet to be realized.

## RELIGIOUS BUILDINGS

### 1. *Church of England*

ALL HALLOWS, Shirlock Road, Gospel Oak. 1889–1901 by *James Brooks*, the chancel 1913–15 by *Giles Gilbert Scott*. One of the noblest churches of its date in England, and no doubt (in spite of the Ascension, Lavender Hill, Battersea) Brooks's masterpiece. Tall, long, without a tower, all of Ancaster stone with ashlar dressings. Meant to be vaulted throughout. A hall church, i.e. with aisles of the same height as the nave. High slender circular piers into which the springers of the vaulting ribs and arches die without capitals. Scott's vaulted chancel has chapels opening into it; the N one has an organ gallery above. The exterior most impressive on the N side. Tall slim windows, and between them bold buttresses, their whole upper part running up to the projected vault at a steep diagonal instead of the usual set-offs connecting vertical planes. These two slopes of N and S buttresses also characterize Scott's addition. The chancel E end has three lancets and two short polygonal stair-turrets. Brooks's W front is less impressive. – CREDENCE TABLE and base of pillar, Jacobean, from All Hallows the Great, Thames Street. STATIONS OF THE CROSS from St Alban, Holborn. VICARAGE, Savernake Road, 1889–91, by *Brooks*.

ALL SAINTS, Camden Street. Now Greek Orthodox; *see* below.

CHRIST CHURCH, Albany Street. *See* St George, Greek Orthodox, below.

HOLY TRINITY, Clarence Way, Kentish Town. 1849–50 by *T. H. Wyatt & Brandon*. Kentish rag battlemented W tower (the spire destroyed in the Second World War). Clerestory, narrow aisles, and an odd tripartite chancel arch. The N aisle was replaced by a church hall and the big W gallery removed *c.* 1950.

KENTISH TOWN PARISH CHURCH, Highgate Road. Redundant. A small medieval chapel on a different site was replaced in 1782–4 by *James Wyatt*'s first church, a trim Palladian chapel inspired by Jones's St Paul Covent Garden. It had a Tuscan portico and cupola, removed in 1843–5 when the building was deplorably remodelled in Neo-Norman style by *J. H. Hakewill*. The *Ecclesiologist*, outspoken as usual, called it 'the very meanest and most contemptible' of churches. Hakewill extended the E end with an E front replacing the portico. Two stunted towers flank a flat chancel. Side porches lead into odd transeptal extensions. Riding-school interior, on a large scale, created by removing the ceiling. The three eastern bays open out into galleried aisles on octagonal columns (N aisle closed off *c.* 1960). All detail round-headed, but early C13. The w end remains from the older building, with a curved w extension for an enlarged w gallery (removed 1889). This was added in 1817 by *James Spiller* as part of a reordering which provided extra seating in large curved E and w galleries (*see* the model now at the RIBA Drawings Collection; cf. St John Hackney). – FONTS. The present one C19, alabaster, with openwork wooden cover, from Chelmsford, Essex. Two older octagonal fonts. STAINED GLASS. E window and nave windows, brightly coloured small scenes, by *Wailes*, 1845. (A window by *Burne-Jones*, 1863, is now in St Benet.) MONUMENTS. Among many minor tablets: – John Finch †1797, festooned sarcophagus, by *Charles Regnant.* – Alexander Bureau †1808. Mourning woman by an urn. James Redfern †1826. Draped urn. – Mary Huggins †1835. Woman and child in low relief. – William Minshull †1836, with portrait profile, by *Chantrey*.

ST ANNE BROOKFIELD, Highgate West Hill. The ambitious type of spired church as they were erected in the mid C19 in so many well-to-do suburbs. 1852–3 by *George Plucknett*, a partner of Messrs Cubitt. E.E., dull apart from the sw tower and spire, a pleasant landmark at the foot of the hill. Clerestoried nave with plain five-bay arcades on circular columns. Stiff-leaf roundel commemorating the foundress, Anne Barnett of Brookfield, †1858. Reordered 1978, when the chancel was levelled; w end glazed off in 1984. The chief interest is the STAINED GLASS by a wide range of artists.* Chronological study of the work of *Lavers & Barraud* is instructive. By *F. P. Barraud*: N and s aisle w windows, 1859: good colours with rather Italian modelling of the figures; N 3rd from E, Good Samaritan etc., 1860. Also by *Lavers & Barraud*, s 2nd from E, Finding of Moses, 1862, in a harder clearcut drawing style, and s aisle 3rd from E, designed by *R. R. Holmes*, in a more Pre-Raphaelite manner, six medallions with the Acts of Mercy, *c.* 1865. Good w window, 1874 by *W. G. Saunders* s aisle E, a later six-medallion window, well-drawn scenes of the Life of the Virgin, 1879 by *N. H. J. Westlake* (who became a partner in the firm in 1868). *Heaton, Butler & Bayne* were responsible for the fine N aisle 1st from E, a Coronation, *c.* 1870, and N chancel N, Preaching at the Temple, *c.* 1874. *Ralph B. Edmundson*'s old-fashioned N aisle E, and N aisle 4th from E, 1863, are a comedown after these. Later windows are by *Burlison & Grylls*: chancel N, St John, 1881; and chancel E, Crucifixion, *c.* 1903, in the style of Kempe. MONUMENT. Tile mosaic to Elizabeth Hannah Bartlett †1911; two angels holding an inscription below a canopy.

ST BARNABAS, Kentish Town Road and Rochester Road. *See* below, St Andrew (Greek Orthodox).

ST BENET AND ALL SAINTS, Lupton Street, Kentish Town. By *C. G. Hare*; chancel 1908, nave 1928, replacing the first nave of 1884–5 by *Peacock*. Hare was successor to Bodley, and chancel and s chapel are still in a Bodley tradition, Dec, with elaborate tracery and gabled buttresses. E wall with a Crucifixion high up on the exterior. The nave is more restrained; tall and aisleless, with concrete barrel vault, and bays alternately wide and narrow, as in G.G.

* Identified by Michael Coles.

Scott Jun.'s design for Liverpool Cathedral. The broader bays have three-light windows with gables above, cutting into the roof. Inside, the nave walls have low blind arcading; the vault is banded by transverse arches. The calm, lofty, white-plastered interior originally formed a foil for rich furnishings, now mostly gone. – ROOD, 1912 by *Hare*, who also gave the lively continental Baroque painted STATUE of Virgin and Child and provided its bracket. From *Peacock*'s church the elaborate alabaster FONT and the STAINED GLASS in the Lady Chapel w window, attributed to *Clayton & Bell*. – Nave STAINED GLASS, pairs of archbishops (*c.* 1928), and Lady Chapel N, attributed to *Burlison & Grylls*. – Two lights by *Burne-Jones*, the Building of the Temple, 1863, brought from Kentish Town Parish Church. – PAINTING (in vestry). Entombment. Italian (?).

ST LUKE, Caversham Road and Oseney Crescent, Kentish Town. Redundant. Built to replace St Luke, King's Cross, demolished for the Midland Railway. *Basil Champneys*' first work of importance; 1867–9. (His father was the Vicar of St Pancras.) A big, bold, rather coarse, red brick building with a polygonal apse, narrow lean-to aisles, clerestory, and a high E tower (cf. Butterfield's St Matthias, Stoke Newington, Hackney). The tower top has four steep gables, a North German, not an English motif, and large, forceful belfry openings. The details E.E., simple lancet windows, except for the apse, which has plate tracery. Nave with low circular piers; brick-vaulted chancel under the tower, sanctuary six steps higher, with decorative TILES and SEDILIA. Three E windows with fine STAINED GLASS designed by *Holiday* and made by *Heaton, Butler & Bayne*, 1868; large standing figures; in the central circular window the Six Days of Creation, derived from Burne-Jones's design for Waltham Abbey. Also by *Heaton, Butler & Bayne* the w windows with archangels and musical angels. Two s clerestory windows by *Morris & Co.*, 1910 and 1914 (in store). – Brass eagle LECTERN, 1882, from St Paul, Camden Square.

ST MARTIN, Vicars Road, Gospel Oak. 1864–5 by *E. B. Lamb*, one of Goodhart-Rendel's 'rogues', and indeed the craziest of London's Victorian churches, inconfutable proof that the Victorians were not mere imitators in their ecclesiastical architecture. For here, although individual elements can easily be traced back to period precedent, their mixture with completely original ones results in an unprecedented whole which is both striking and harrowing. The attitude has rightly been compared with that of the innovators of Art Nouveau about 1900.* The exterior is comparatively harmless, of Kentish rag, low, but with an uncommonly tall N tower close to the w end, which forms the apex of the picturesque view from the SE, the composition building up into an agglomeration of roofs and turrets reminiscent of a northern French medieval town. The tower originally had a yet taller stair-turret with a spirelet (total height 130 ft). The church itself has tall transomed windows, many gables, and a polygonal apse, narrower than the shallow, also slightly polygonal s transept. The N transept is straight-ended. The tower at first had lofty open arches to N, E and w; the w arch now leads to a large later C19 extension with details matching the church,

---

* The above is all Pevsner's description of 1952.

converted to hall and church offices in 1985 by *Pickard & Palmer*, when the other arches were glazed.

The interior plan is a mixture of the longitudinal and the central, designed to suit a low-church emphasis on preaching and visibility. The W three bays of the nave are broad and aisleless; then come three aisled bays of central character, cut into by the transepts, equal in height. The other bays of the aisles are treated as angle chapels (the NW one, near the entrance, was originally the baptistery). Then the chancel arch and apse. Hammerbeam roof running right through, with the fussiest, busiest details, and resting on shafts which do not go down to the ground, but start from Cistercian-looking brackets. The square piers between nave and aisles have four such bracketed shafts attached to their four sides (a sight never before seen).

The patron who paid for all this was the wealthy J. D. Allcroft, glove manufacturer, of Stokesay Court, Shropshire. His monogram appears on the exterior of the nave S wall; on its reverse inside is the date 1867; opposite is Lamb's monogram. On the S wall large carved ROYAL ARMS, an old-fashioned touch. Lamb's low church FURNISHINGS match his building: STALLS with curved brackets hinting at Art Nouveau, READING DESKS and PEWS also are stamped with his individual style. – PULPIT with sounding-board. – FONT with curious overhanging tracery. – FONT COVER with pinnacle. MOSAICS with evangelists' symbols in tracery in the E angles of the crossing. They appear to be an early replacement of Creed and Commandment Boards. Low alabaster SCREEN and LECTERN, 1898. E apse STAINED GLASS of *c*. 1867 by *Clayton & Bell*.

ST MARY, Eversholt Street, Somers Town. 1822–6 by the *Inwoods*, as thin and papery as their St Pancras Parish Church is solid and substantial, 'perhaps the completest specimen of Carpenter's Gothic ever witnessed' (*Gent. Mag.*, 1827). Derided by Pugin in his *Contrasts* of 1836. The Commissioners paid the whole cost. Front of stock brick, with starved W tower with pinnacles, interior with thin cast-iron piers and plaster vaults, broad, low and aisled. Chancel enlarged and side galleries removed 1888 by *E. Christian*. W gallery removed and interior embellished by *R. C. Reade*, *c*. 1890, when the marble FONT and PULPIT were added.

ST MARY BROOKFIELD, Dartmouth Park Hill. 1869–75 by *Butterfield*; Dec chancel 1881 by *W. C. Street*. Not of special merit, though the lofty interior makes a show of Butterfield's beloved pattern of yellow, red, and blue bricks, and stone dressings. Tall clerestory. – FONT and PULPIT by *Butterfield*. ROOD 1913, on a pair of filigree ogee arches and other fittings, by *Comper*. – SCULPTURE. C15 Nottingham alabaster panel.

Plain rendered VICARAGE by *Temple Moore*, 1911–12.

ST MARY MAGDALENE, Munster Square. 1849–52 by *R. C. Carpenter*. Paid for by a Tractarian, the Rev. Edward Stuart, and intended as a deliberate contrast to his previous church, Christ Church, Albany Street (now St George, Greek Orthodox, *see* below). A hall church with broad aisles and no clerestory, in the tradition of the Austin Friars; reminiscent of Carpenter's contemporary St Peter the Great, Chichester. Exterior of irregularly coursed ragstone; details studiously in Second Pointed style. The intended sw tower and spire were never built. N aisle and N chapel, with a small bell-turret, were added 1883–4 by *R. H. Carpenter* according to his father's plans. A fine interior, restful, not fussy in effect, with five-bay arcades on tall quatrefoil piers with moulded capitals, and a lofty arch-braced roof with two tiers of wind-braces. The raised chancel has crocketed and gabled blind arcading incorporating sedilia; very large E window of seven lights.

The High Church embellishment begun under Stuart (†1877) continued into the 1930s. CHANCEL DECORATION: Paintings in N and E arcades begun 1867 by *Daniel Bell* and *Richard Almond*; s side later. – REREDOS by *Sir Charles Nicholson*, 1933. ROOD, BEAM and low PARCLOSE SCREENS by *J. T. Micklethwaite*, 1903–5. – REREDOS, S CHAPEL. Made up in 1935, with a large wooden Crucifixion of 1903. – PAINTING. Over the S door which led to the school: Christ among the Doctors; by *Clayton & Bell*, *c.* 1890. Also in the S aisle the FONT, correctly Second Pointed with canopies and ballflower, on marble columns, with tall COVER enlarged 1931, and SPONSORS' SEAT in the form of an oak settle, 1929. – STATIONS OF THE CROSS. 1905 by *Charles Beyart* of Bruges, after Fürich. STAINED GLASS. E window, Crucifixion flanked by saints under canopies in C14 style, by *Hardman*, to designs by *Pugin* of *c.* 1850 (one of his last works). Much restored, in 1905 by *A. K. Nicholson* and in 1952 by *Goddard & Gibbs*. The S windows were badly damaged in World War II; a Virgin and Child attributed to *Lavers & Barraud* remains. There was also early work by *Clayton & Bell*. Also by *Clayton & Bell* the surviving N and S aisle w windows (1884, 1891), and N aisle E. The four N windows with pictorial scenes with agitated figures are by *Heaton, Butler & Bayne* (1884–92); fifth N window by *A. A. Orr*. S chapel E 1935 by *A. K. Nicholson*, replacing a window by *Hardman*.

CRYPT. Remodelled *c.* 1975 as a social centre. STAINED GLASS set in panels, 1931–3 by *Margaret Rope*, from St Augustine, Haggerston (*see* Hackney: Shoreditch); Life of the Virgin and six saints, vignettes of local festivities below.

ST MICHAEL, Camden Road, Camden Town. A fine church by *Bodley & Garner*, the nave 1880–81, the chancel 1893–4. A tall w front rises from the street; the intended tower was never built. The external character, deliberately urban, is that of a C14 Friars' church, with big flying buttresses. An impressive interior, very tall, with much stone wall surface left bare and windows high up. Dec arcade of seven bays, with stone transverse arches over nave and aisles; tall clerestory. No structural division between nave and chancel. Low rib-vaulted NE chapel. The chancel was also intended to have a stone vault. Stone screen s of the chancel 1898. – STAINED GLASS in chancel, chapel and N aisle by *Burlison & Grylls*, *c.* 1881–1907. BRASS to the first vicar, Rev. E. B. Penfold, †1907.

ST MICHAEL, South Grove, Highgate. Set back from the road, on the site of Ashurst House (*see* Highgate, Perambulation 5a). 1831–2, replacing the chapel of ease which had been attached to the grammar school. The architect was *Lewis Vulliamy*, the builders William and Lewis Cubitt. Chancel 1878 by *C. H. M. Mileham*. Thin stock-brick front with spired steeple very similar to Vulliamy's now demolished Christ Church, Woburn Square. The sloping aisle roofs (originally with pinnacles) are visible in the front. The aisle w fronts oddly canted at the angles. Interior with octagonal piers, three poor wooden galleries (on iron beams) and clerestory. Roof with cast-iron trusses. – Some furnishings, including the Gothic REREDOS and reordering of the sanctuary, by *Temple Moore*, 1903. – STAINED GLASS. E window by *Evie Hone*, 1954, her last work. The Last Supper. Brilliant colours. Part of the former E window by *Kempe* (damaged in the Second World War) was re-erected in the chancel aisle. N clerestory by *Powell & Sons*, 1873. – MONUMENTS. Several from the old chapel (others went to St Pancras Old Church and St Mary, Hornsey). John Schoppens †1720 (W gallery); Sir Edward Gould †1728 (with putti heads); Samuel and Mary Forster †1752 and 1744 (mourning putti). Samuel Taylor Coleridge †1834, by *George Martin* of Highgate.

ST PANCRAS OLD CHURCH, Pancras Road. Both the dedication to a Roman saint (cf. Canterbury) and the discovery of a C7 altar stone suggest that this was one of the earliest churches to be established in the London area. However, by the Middle Ages the main settlement in the parish had shifted northwards to Kentish Town, and the little building stood alone in its large churchyard until surrounded by expanding London in the early C19. The medieval church consisted of chancel, nave and W tower. Surviving details, much restored, indicate a C12 rebuilding: in the chancel a Norman s doorway with two-way chevron, in the nave traces of a Norman N door (visible inside). Remains of a C13 lancet in the chancel N wall. The church was crudely Normanized in 1848 by *Roumieu & Gough*, who removed the medieval tower and replaced it with a W extension with W gallery, and a s porch with tower and spire above, truncated later, when the incongruous half-timbering was introduced. The interior was restored in 1888 by *A. W. Blomfield*, the side galleries removed in 1925. Restoration 1979–80 by *Erith & Terry*. – ALTAR STONE. Discovered in 1847. Dated from the cross types to the early C7. Carved ALTAR PANELS made up from the C17 pulpit. REREDOS by *Blomfield*. PISCINA and SEDILIA. C13 but wholly retooled. – FONT COVER. Pretty carving of *c*. 1700. – STAINED GLASS. Three apse windows of 1866, possibly by *W. M. Teulon*, who was on the committee for redecoration. Other windows 1881. – MONUMENTS. Early C16 recess with tomb-chest and indents for kneeling brass figures against the back. – Philadelphia Woolaston †1616, wall monument with semi-reclining effigy, l. and r. standing allegorical figures in the style of Nicholas Stone. – William and Mary Platt †1637 and 1687, wall monument with frontal busts in two oval recesses (from Highgate School Chapel). – John Offley and family, big, ornamental architectural tablet of after 1678 with inscription on feigned drapery, signed by *W. Linton*, but based on a drawing by *William Stanton* now in the Victoria and Albert Museum. – Samuel Cowper, the miniature painter 'Angliae Apelles', †1672 and his wife †1693, pretty cartouche with cherubs, attributed to *Edward Pierce* (GF). LEDGER to Frances Wintour †1720, with arms. – Isabella Jackson Hernon by *Coade & Sealy*, 1813.

The GARDENS around the church, opened in 1877, are made up of part of the old churchyard, enlarged in 1800, and a separate burial ground for St Giles-in-the-Fields, added in 1803. Near the church many C17 and C18 sarcophagi and tombs, some moved when the E part of the churchyard was destroyed for the Midland Railway in the 1860s–70s. In the 1803 extension the outstandingly interesting MONUMENT by *Sir John Soane* to his wife, who died in 1815, extremely Soanesque, with all his originality and all his foibles. A delicate marble monument beneath a heavy Portland stone canopy. Four piers with incised Ionic capitals; a pendentive vault carries a shallow drum encircled by a tail-biting snake (symbol of eternity), with a pineapple-shaped finial. The tomb is surrounded by a low balustrade with distinctive acroteria, which also encloses the steps down to the burial vault. Sir John Summerson suggested that the tomb can be interpreted as civilization (the monument) within eternity (the surrounding canopy). Also in this area, replacement slabs to Flaxman (†1826) and his wife, within dwarf cast-iron railings, and a renewed plain monument to William Godwin (†1836) and his wife, Mary Wollstonecraft (†1797). Near the entrance to the garden, large Gothic marble SUNDIAL erected by Baroness Burdett-Coutts, 1877, designed by *G. Highton*, with bas reliefs by *Facigna*, commemorating the graves disturbed for the Midland Railway. Fine iron GATES and RAILINGS, 1891.

ST PANCRAS NEW CHURCH, Euston Road and Woburn Place. Built to serve the suburbs expanding N from Bloomsbury to Euston Road. The site was bought from Lord Southampton in 1818. Built 1819–22 by *H. W. & W. Inwood*. William Inwood was a local architect; it was his son Henry who was responsible for the detail which makes this the earliest church in London in a pure Neo-Grecian style. He visited Greece in 1819. The six-column portico has fluted Ionic columns on the model of the Erechtheum in Athens. The three doors behind it go back to the same building (Inwood took moulds at Athens). At the E end, the otherwise box-shaped church has two lower additions, duplicated versions of the portico of the caryatids of the Erechtheum. Their fine bronze doors provide entrances to the burial vaults. The caryatids above, holding ewers and reversed torches as symbols of mortality, were modelled by *J. F. C. Rossi* and are made of terracotta over an iron core. The pagan looks of these (it is true, decently attired) maidens seem not to have worried parishioners; Pugin of course resented the whole church ferociously. The tower stands in the uncomfortable position sanctioned by Gibbs's St Martin-in-the-Fields. It consists of three octagonal stages of decreasing size, the lower two with fluted columns. The model is the Tower of the Winds. Interior with three galleries on lotus columns. Flat ceiling. Big unfluted Ionic columns of scagliola in the curve of the apse. The interior was originally in pale colours, redecorated in dark tones in the 1880s, lightened again in the post-war restoration by *R. N. Vanes*, c. 1948. – ALTARS. The original High Altar of 1822 now in the Lady Chapel; moved 1914 when the sanctuary was remodelled by *Adams & Holden*, with new altar and marble facing to the apse. – PULPIT. Splendid square structure on four Ionic columns; octagonal body above. – STAINED GLASS. By *Clayton & Bell*: E window 1866, others of 1881–2.

ST SILAS, St Silas Place, Prince of Wales Road, Kentish Town. 1911–12, by *E. C. Shearman*, the first example of the odd, expressionist Gothic style which he developed for later churches in the N and w suburbs. Approached from the s, close to the e end. Of the exterior otherwise only the upper parts visible, tall, no tower. Remarkably original, if somewhat mannered interior, perhaps a little of the character of Berlage's work. Exposed brick with narrow pointed arcade without capitals. Narrow aisles and narrow gallery above them. Extremely narrow ambulatory.

## 2. Roman Catholic

OUR LADY HELP OF CHRISTIANS (R.C. from 1969), Lady Margaret Road, Kentish Town. Built as LADY MARGARET METHODIST CHURCH, 1864–7, by *John Tarring*, who built so many large Nonconformist churches. The prominent spire forms a landmark half-way up the road. Pevsner found Tarring's churches 'ugly and uninspired'. The *Illustrated London News* in 1867 said that 'the whole of the external appearance ... makes it an ornament to the neighbourhood'. Kentish rag to the top of the sw spire. Gabled aisle walls. The usual Nonconformist plan with a galleried interior; iron piers with twisted shafts and iron spandrels with ivy-leaf decoration.

ST ALOYSIUS, Phoenix Road, Somers Town. 1966–8 by *John Newton* of *Burles, Newton & Partners*, interesting in itself, but alas replacing a church of great historic importance, which was built *c.* 1806 for the numerous French émigrés in the area. It had a chapel-like Tuscan exterior, and the interior, with recessed altar room with Tuscan reredos, and three galleries on thin supports, preserved 'like no other Catholic Church in London the atmosphere of the age before emancipation' (Summerson). The present building has an inconspicuous exterior apart from the broad flight of steps up to the western foyer. Elliptical plan, well lit, with a clerestory of coloured glass in the brick drum over the centre, and large plain windows (one-way glazing) to the street. Suspended wooden ceiling; seating on three sides around the altar. Curving s ambulatory with chapels. – SCULPTURE. Risen Christ by *D. Purness*. – Virgin and Saints by *G. Beningfield*. – CERAMIC TILES in Blessed Sacrament Chapel by *A. Kossowski*. STAINED GLASS. Clerestory and baptistery windows by *Whitefriars Studios*, 1967.

ST DOMINIC (Our Lady of the Rosary and St Dominic), Southampton Road. The Dominicans were invited to London by Cardinal Wiseman in 1861, and bought the site the following year, intended as one of the major Roman Catholic centres planned for the London suburbs. *Gilbert Blount* was the first architect, but he only prepared the foundations for the e end of the church. Owing to shortage of funds, it was not built until 1874–83, to a new design by *Charles Alban Buckler*, son of the antiquarian artist. One of the largest Roman Catholic churches in London, 299 ft long. Unbroken roof-line and no tower, as the Dominican tradition prescribed. Tall rather narrow, E.E. front with lean-to aisles. The interior long, high, simple, and impressive. All of yellow brick with stone dressings. Nave of eight bays, polygonal apse. Tall slender circular piers with stiff-leaf capitals, steep pointed arches, tall clerestory (the mean iron balcony running inside the building as a passage in front of it is a later addition). Quadripartite timber vault. Aisles with pointed transverse arches to support the lean-to roofs, with an outer ring of gabled chapels (a total of fourteen). To the r. a transept of two bays depth and three bays width, with altar chapels. Highly elaborate contemporary FURNISHINGS. – HIGH ALTAR, with canopied tabernacle, by *Buckler*; mosaics by *Salviati* . – LADY CHAPEL ALTAR (N transept) also with *Salviati* mosaics. – ALTAR PAINTING (Chapel of St Dominic, N transept) by *Philip Westlake*. – CHAPEL ALTARS each with a sculptural altar-piece with scenes from the life of Christ (Mysteries of the Rosary), the first, with the Annunciation, given by Buckler. SCULPTURE. Black Madonna shrine, a piece made up in 1913 of wood-carving of different dates, incorporating a C15 Flemish Virgin and Child, a C13 standing angel, and four later evangelist figures, all much restored. The canopy comes from *Blore*'s choir stalls for Peterborough Cathedral. – FRAGMENT. Purbeck column and oddly detailed moulded capital, C13, from the old Blackfriars site on the edge of the City. – STAINED GLASS. Much, but mostly not outstanding. By *Gibbs & Howard* (S aisle W; N transept E rose window); *Hardman* (apse windows); *Westlake* (N transept N chapel). Other work by *Saunders*, 1878. – MONUMENT. War memorial with lettering by *Eric Gill* and *Joseph Cribb*, 1921.

S of the church are the plain former CONVENT BUILDINGS, now converted to housing. W range with common room and library of 1863–7 by *Gilbert Blount*; brick with some stone Gothic detail. S range with cloister and clock tower with pyramid roof, 1867–8 by *W. K. Broder*.

## 3. Other places of worship

ALL SAINTS, Camden Street, Camden Town. Greek Orthodox since 1948. Built as Camden Chapel by *W. and H. W. Inwood*, 1822–4, in a simpler version of Grecian than their earlier New St Pancras. A rectangle, 'neat and substantial' (*Gent. Mag.* 1824), with semicircular portico of fluted giant Ionic columns. The circular tower placed behind it, not concentric with the portico (as Archer had done at Deptford and Smirke was to do at St Marylebone). The façade is of stone, the sides brick. Curved apse. Interior with flat ceiling and three galleries on Ionic columns, 'very neat approaching to elegance' (*ib.*). Now filled with Neo-Byzantine fittings.

FRIENDS HOUSE, Euston Road. 1925–7 by *H. Lidbetter*. Built over most of the S half of Euston Square (known as Endsleigh Gardens); the principal frontage faces N along a newly widened Euston Road. Brick with stone trimmings. A well-mannered classical building, in scale with the late Georgian terraces which once surrounded it, with a Grecian portico *in antis* on the N side to keep to the flatness of those terraces. Lesser entrances to E and W. A rational interior: the main portico leads to a broad corridor around a square meeting room seating 1,500, with small meeting room to its S. E part with library and committee rooms around a courtyard; W side (Drayton House) built as offices to let.

HIGHGATE ROAD BAPTIST CHAPEL. Large Kentish rag, Second Pointed church of 1877 by *F. C. Satchell & R. C. Edwards*. Gables over the aisle windows, no tower. Spacious galleried interior with carved pulpit at the E end (stairs added in the 1930s). Sunday schools behind, 1879 by *Dixon*.

LADY MARGARET METHODIST CHURCH, Lady Margaret Road.
*See* Our Lady Help of Christians (R.C.), above.

NEW CAMDEN CHAPEL (Methodist), Plender Street, Camden
Town. 1889 by *T. & W. Stone*. Decent debased classical. Stock
brick with stucco dressings; recessed entrance between columns,
rather squashed central pediment.

Former PRESBYTERIAN CHURCH, Camden Park Road. 1867–9,
for Scottish Presbyterians formerly in Caledonian Road. By *Finch
Hill & Paraire*, better known for their music-halls. Ragstone
Gothic, with a spire truncated later, and given disturbing high-
tech excrescences when the building was rescued from use as a
warehouse and converted to offices in 1990. Some quite sensitive
new details, for example the new w windows discreetly recessed
behind the original stone tracery.

ST ANARGYRIE (SS Cosmas and Damian; Greek Orthodox),
Gordon House Road. Humble red brick Gothic exterior with
trefoil-headed lancets, late C19. Resplendent inside with traditional
Greek Orthodox fittings.

ST ANDREW (Greek Orthodox), Kentish Town Road and Rochester
Road. Built for the C. of E. as St Barnabas. 1884–5 by *Ewan
Christian*. Brick, E.E., with an asymmetrical w end with apse and
turret. Apsed E end. Neo-Byzantine carved fittings, 1976.

ST GEORGE (Greek Orthodox), Albany Street. Formerly Christ
Church; 1836–7 by *James Pennethorne*, built to serve Nash's development E of Regents Park. Blocky grey brick building in a heavy
Grecian style. No portico. Main entrance on the s side, which has
a single bay with two giant pilasters and pediment. The only light
touch provided by the tower, whose upper stage is embellished
with columns with lotus-leaf capitals below a short spire. On the
longer sides two big pedimented doorcases flank tall arched
windows. At the angles small square pavilions. The austere classical
building with spare galleried interior was far from the ideals of the
Tractarians of the 1840s, and the interior was much embellished
by the Rev. William Dodsworth. (His curate, Edward Stuart,
moved on to become the builder of St Mary Magdalene, Munster
Square, q.v. above.) Chancel added and organ gallery removed
1843, by *Salvin*. LECTERN, 1849, *Butterfield*'s first work in the
church, a brass eagle and dragon, based on a lectern in Malta.
Carved STALLS, 1853, and PEWS, 1866, also by *Butterfield*, responsible for general restoration and redecoration 1866–85, with lavish
use of marble and tiles. His fittings included the FONT, recased in
marble 1868; PULPIT, 1884, carved by *Earp*, tiled dado and marble
floor, and ALTAR FRONTAL with Agnus Dei. A SCREEN was
added in 1904. STAINED GLASS. One window on the (ritual) s
side by *Morris & Co.*, designed by *Rossetti*, 1864 (Sermon on the
Mount), with quarries by *Morris*. The other windows mostly by
*Clayton & Bell*.

SPIRITUALIST TEMPLE, Rochester Square. 1926 by *T. Yorke*. With
large lunette window, in an Arts and Crafts tradition.

UNION CHURCH, South Grove, Highgate. 1859 by *T. Roger Smith*,
for Congregationalists. E.E. stone front without tower, lying
back from the street, but disturbing the C18 character of South
Grove.

## 4. Cemetery

HIGHGATE CEMETERY, Swain's Lane, Highgate. The most atmospheric of London's great Victorian cemeteries. The cemetery of thirty-seven acres covering the southern slope of Highgate Hill was established by the London Cemetery Company, founded in 1836. The older part, opened in 1839, is w of Swain's Lane; the extension of 1855 lies to the E. Both rapidly became popular, as is clear from the proliferation of tombs to the Victorian establishment. By 1888 *c.* 100,000 burials had taken place. The Friends of Highgate Cemetery took over the administration in 1975, and adopted a most successful policy of preserving the romantic character by maintaining both buildings and monuments and the rampant vegetation in a state of 'managed neglect'. The Friends' landscape plan of 1975 was by *Jenny Cox*; their architects *Caröe & Martin*.

Highgate was the third private cemetery created on the fringe of built-up London, after Kensal Green of 1833 and Norwood of 1838, and has by far the most remarkable buildings. The original ones are by *Stephen Geary*, the founder of the Company; later additions are probably by the Company's Surveyor, *J. B. Bunning*, appointed in 1839. The steeply sloping site was formerly the park and orchard to the s of the late C17 Ashurst House; St Michael's Church (q.v.) was built on the site of the house. The highly successful landscaping by *David Ramsay*, with 'circuitous roads winding about the acclivity' (*Islington Athenaeum*, 1853), was designed to take account of existing trees.

GATEHOUSE in thin brick Gothic, a plaster rib vault over the entrance. The Anglican and Nonconformist CHAPELS are in attached wings, an early example of an arrangement which became common in later cemeteries. They have little oriel windows. The Nonconformist chapel to the N, a gutted shell by 1975, was in 1985 tactfully converted to offices, with an inserted mezzanine. The Anglican chapel to the s, now used as an exhibition area, starts with an octagonal space with triple responds perhaps intended to take a plaster vault. The two E bays are in a more serious Gothic, with naturalistic carving on the corbels and Dec windows, and were probably added when the land for the E cemetery was acquired in 1854. Coffins reached the East Cemetery from the chapel by means of a hydraulic bier and a tunnel beneath the road. NE of the chapels the one-storeyed cemetery office and South Lodge match the style of the gatehouse; across the courtyard the retaining wall of the cemetery is hidden by a curving Gothic loggia, built to accommodate mourners.

MONUMENTS. As one ascends the hill, draped urns, obelisks and broken columns emerge romantically from the undergrowth among the low slabs and chest tombs. These restrained classical motifs are supplemented by the angels and tall crosses which became acceptable a little later. The most remarkable effect is at the top of the site, where a sunken ring of tombs, the Circle of Lebanon, was planned around an existing cedar tree. It is approached through a monumental stuccoed portal, flanked by tall obelisks and adorned 53 with pairs of bulbous columns of highly Egyptian detail, one of the most extreme expressions of this style to be found in England. A sequence of tombs with heavily tapering doorways lines the atmospheric 'Egyptian Avenue' which leads to the Circle. Here too the mausolea have Egyptianizing detail. The N half of the Circle has an outer ring of tombs added in the 1870s. These have tapering doorways, but also heavy classical pediments, and are in a variety of materials. Massive iron doors decorated with reversed torches. Above them towers the most strikingly spectacular indi-vidual monument, erected in 1876 by Julius Beer, proprietor of *The Observer* (†1880). It has a stepped pyramid of Halicarnassus type as its top. The interior is in the Quattrocento style. The architecture is by *J. Oldrid Scott*. Inside, behind the fine bronze doors, three sarcophagi, and a relief sculpture of a child being raised by an angel, by *Armstead*. Higher up, immediately below St Michael's Church, are the Catacombs, passages for tombs made below the terrace surviving from Ashurst House: the exterior with some Gothic detail, *c.* 1840 by *Bunning*. The broad railed terrace walk above them, with its fine views s, provided a place for promenades for the congregation of St Michael's.

In the neighbourhood of the Beer Mausoleum are some of the other more exceptional monuments: a tall statue of Religion by *Joseph Edwards*; George Wombwell, menagerist, †1850, is commemo-rated by a lion asleep (cf. Brompton and Woolwich cemeteries) and, further E, Tom Sayers the pugilist †1865 by a bust and figure of his dog. Remarkable also is the tall Gothic monument to George Peckett †1866, with much cast-iron tracery. There are fewer out-standing individual tombs than at Kensal Green or Norwood, but plenty of engaging oddities, such as the large tomb for the family of General Sir Loftus Otway †1854, with railings of reversed cannons. The Dissenters' section (s of the entrance) is generally more restrained, with a dignified sequence of catacombs along the eastern walk.

The EASTERN CEMETERY starts with three grand classical family mausolea in red granite: Strathcona and Mountroyal (1914), Pocklington, and Dalziel of Wooler. The rest is less eventful, apart from the most visited monument, the tomb of Karl Marx †1883, with colossal bronze portrait head on a granite plinth, 1956 by *Laurence Bradshaw*. Not far off are the tombs of George Eliot †1880 and of George Holyoake, social reformer, †1906, with a bust. Near Swain's Lane a Gothic monument by *Lutyens* to William Frieze-Green †1921; near the s entrance an obelisk to Ann Jewson Crisp †1884 with portrait head of a dog, 'her faithful friend'.

## PUBLIC BUILDINGS

*Civic and Municipal*

TOWN HALL, Judd Street and Euston Road. 1934–7 by *A. J. Thomas*, Lutyens's office manager until 1935. Portland stone, with columned centrepiece above channelled ground floor. A cautious Neo-Palladian design, with some Lutyens mannerisms (vanishing rustication around the windows). Decent finishes inside, marble for the entrance hall and grand stair, good panelling to the com-mittee rooms. Symmetrical plan, with first-floor council chamber approached by long corridors with domed and groined vaulting.

At the E end a public hall, entered from Bidborough Street. Beyond this, a coarse extension by *Camden Architect's Department*, 1973-7. Eight storeys of precast panels with curved window corners, with curved bays projecting to Euston Road.

ST PANCRAS CORONERS COURT, Camley Street. 1886 by *Frederick Eggar*. A small Gothic building at the back of the churchyard; *see* St Pancras Old Church, above.

REGENTS PARK BARRACKS, Albany Street. Part of *Nash*'s plan for Regents Park. Designed for 450 men and 400 horses. Much rebuilt, although the lay-out still reflects the original arrangement of 1820-1, with buildings grouped around a parade ground. To the E the only original survival, the Officers' Mess, a plain brick two-storey block, extended in 1866-7. The simple Gothic Chapel School to its N was added in 1857. At the N end, the former hospital, rebuilt in 1877, its decorative red brick dressings now concealed by render. The three parallel blocks to the S, with soldiers' quarters and stables, replaced earlier ones in 1891, when there was much utilitarian rebuilding under Col. *R. Athorpe*, including the service buildings around the perimeter, and the riding school (now garage) on the Albany Road frontage, with steel trussed roof spanning 60 ft.

POLICE STATION, Holmes Road. By *C. Reeves*, remodelled 1894 by *Norman Shaw*. Low-key domestic detail matching the neighbouring houses (the sash windows with echoes of Philip Webb); authority is conveyed by a stern rusticated archway.

FIRE STATION, Euston Road. 1901-2. An outstanding example of the Free or Arts and Crafts style characteristic of the *LCC*'s *Fire Brigade Branch* (cf. the two examples in Hampstead). Lively asymmetrical façade of five and six storeys with dormers. Stone ground floor, brick above, with a stone band at third-floor level. Prettily irregular domestic fenestration. [103]

AMBULANCE STATION, Cressy Road. By the *GLC*'s *Architect's Department* (*Henry White* and *Derek Wells*), 1975. Crisply detailed red brick and glass in the manner of Stirling's buildings of the 1960s. Polygonal offices stepping back, with plenty of curves and chamfers to the big garage behind. The back (in Agincourt Road) is worth a look too.

BERNARD SHAW THEATRE, Euston Road. By *Elidir L. W. Davies & Partners*, 1964-71. Built as public library and theatre with twelve storeys of offices above. Theatre and library had a large shared entrance hall, leading through the library arranged around a courtyard, and down on the r. to the theatre. This had an apron stage and a single tier of seats. Remodelled as hotel and theatre, 1998. Outside, SCULPTURE by *Keith Grant*, 1970, an abstract based on a polyhedron, entitled St Joan. At the back a small pub, the ELIZA DOOLITTLE.

HIGHGATE BRANCH LIBRARY, Chester Road. A cheerful little Renaissance composition with a central pedimented loggia. 1906 by *William Nisbet-Blair*, St Pancras Borough Engineer. The borough's first branch library, built with a Carnegie grant; earlier proposals were stalled by reluctant ratepayers. Interior remodelled by *John Winter* in the 1970s.

PUBLIC BATHS, Prince of Wales Road, Kentish Town. 1898 by *T. W. Aldwinckle*. An especially exuberant example of its type. [101]

Free-Tudor-François-Premier style in yellow brick with glazed terracotta bands, Dutch gables, sculpture over the door, bold lettering and other fun and games. Interiors much altered.

LIDO, Mansfield Road, Parliament Hill. One of the few open-air swimming baths built by the LCC still in use. By *Rowbotham & Smithson*, c. 1938.

CROWNDALE CENTRE, Eversholt Street and Crowndale Road. Large Edwardian *Office of Works* Post Office converted for community services in 1987–9 by *Charles Thomson* of *Rock Townsend*. Fussy new trimmings to an already busy stone and brick exterior, but impressive remodelled spaces inside. An atrium is carved out of the centre with a cleverly cantilevered roof. Prominent central escalator and exposed services in the high-tech tradition (cf. the same firm's buildings for Middlesex University at Bounds Green, Haringey). LIBRARY on the ground floor. HEALTH CENTRE and SURGERY behind, in a new building with an elegantly simple rendered exterior, ingeniously planned around a toplit space, by *Rivington Street Studio*, 1987–9.

CAMDEN UNITED THEATRE, Greenland Street and Greenland Place, just behind Camden High Street. Perhaps by *Bodley & Garner*, as it began life as a church hall for St Michael. Pretty late C19 vernacular detailing, with tiled tops to the buttresses between the windows. First-floor hall, segment-headed ground-floor windows.

INTERACTION CENTRE, Talacre Road, Kentish Town. By *Cedric Price*, for the radical community organization founded in 1968 by Ed Berman. Planned 1974, built 1976–7. A rare demonstration of the *Archigram* vision of the high-tech plug-in city that fired younger architects in the late 1960s. A flexible no-frills construction, intended to be easily altered. Steel frame with plastic-coated steel sheet cladding. Offices, hall, social club etc. in the main structure, with prefabricated cabins attached to provide for special facilities. Future uncertain.

*Educational buildings*

ROYAL VETERINARY COLLEGE, Royal College Street. Founded 1791; the original low pedimented buildings were replaced by reticent red brick ranges by *H. P. G. Maule*. College block 1936–7, around two courtyards, with central lecture hall; pathology department (s end) 1924–5; Beaumont Animal Hospital (N end) 1932.

WORKING MEN'S COLLEGE, Crowndale Road, Camden Town. Founded 1854. 1904–6 by *W. D. Caröe*, very subdued for this often fanciful architect; perhaps influenced by the C18 houses in Great Ormond Street which the College occupied as its first home. A free, varied Neo-Georgian; the hall at the end with a curved wall with segmental pedimental top, the classroom block symmetrical, with a central steep pediment and cupola, and finely lettered name. Extra floor added by *Alban Caröe* in the 1930s.

ACLAND BURGHLEY SCHOOL, Burghley Road and Dartmouth Park Hill. By *Howell, Killick, Partridge & Amis*, 1963–6. A comprehensive planned for c. 1,300 pupils, from the years when the LCC was a keen patron of Brutalism. An arresting urban composition on a tight site, unlike the LCC's earlier secondaries in the outer South London suburbs. It consists of a forceful cluster of bulky concrete buildings with emphatic profiles of chamfered floor bands. The three five-storey classroom towers were intended for lower, middle and upper schools, expressing the desire at the time to break up the formidable size of such schools into visually distinct units. The towers are linked by angular corridors, and radiate from a low hexagonal roof-lit hall. This has a boarded interior; elsewhere there is bleaker exposed concrete or brick. Workshops and gymnasium beyond, the latter ingeniously straddling the railway.

CAMDEN SCHOOL FOR GIRLS, Sandall Road and Camden Road. Founded in 1877 in Prince of Wales Road; established here in the buildings of its sister school, the North London Collegiate, which had moved to Canons, Little Stanmore (see *London 3: North West*, Harrow). *Stillman & Eastwick-Field*'s plain well-proportioned four-storey wing with hall and classrooms, of 1965–7, is sandwiched between the remains of a furniture store converted and extended by *E. C. Robins* in 1879 (mostly destroyed in the Second World War) and a large addition of 1908 by *J. T. Lee*. SCULPTURE. Youth, a bust by *Epstein*, 1955; Orpheus, a seated figure from the Festival of Britain, 1951. STAINED GLASS (from Prince of Wales Road), displayed in a corridor. By *Henry Holiday*. St Catherine, St Ursula and the Queen of Sheba, 1909–10; female figures representing Truth, Righteousness, Faith and Hope, 1921–3. In the library, memorial window to the foundress, Frances Mary Buss, 1927 by *A. K. Nicholson*.

HIGHGATE SCHOOL, North Road, at the top of Highgate Hill.* Founded as a grammar school in 1565 by Sir Roger Cholmeley; refounded in 1832. New buildings of 1865–7 by *F. P. Cockerell* were put up for the expanding public school under the headmastership of the Rev. John Dyne (†1874). Red brick Gothic, the French C13 variety. The main block, 'Big School', set back from the road, is a first-floor hall with mullion and transom windows and decorative band of shields. The traditional composition with oriel and porch at either end is disturbed by a formal central stair, added as a war memorial in 1949. Interior with open timber roof; stage and panelling added 1933–4. The undercroft below was filled in tactfully by *James Cubitt & Partners*, 1992. On the l. a classroom block with cloister walk below; on the r. the CHAPEL, of five bays with a small w clock turret, slim timber flèche and apse. Richly polychrome interior, embellished in the 1880s: apse ceiling painted by *Heaton, Butler & Bayne*, 1889, possibly to a design by *A. W. Blomfield*. Much STAINED GLASS, the earliest in the apse, 1867 by *R. R. Holmes*, and w rose. Smith and Tatham memorial windows 1882, 1889, designed by *Holmes*, made by *Lavers & Barraud*; Fayrer and McDowell windows 1893, 1895, by *Clayton & Bell*. Two s windows by *Francis Stephens*, 1953. To the w is the small GRAVEYARD of the chapel's predecessor, which was used by Highgate Anglicans until St Michael's Church was built. MEMORIAL GATES on to North Road, 1947. The school expanded N from 1877: Central Hall by *C. P. Leach*, 1898–9; science buildings 1928, extended 1983. On the e side of Southwood Lane, DYNE HOUSE, music

---

and arts centre, by *Ansell & Bailey*, 1967, brick and concrete and rather overpowering, and the former HIGHGATE TABERNACLE, a Baptist chapel rebuilt in 1836, converted to school library 1985. A long side to the street with two tapered Egyptian doorcases, and five windows, the three central ones emphasized by arched heads and a pediment. Further buildings in BISHOPSWOOD ROAD, adjoining playing fields: JUNIOR SCHOOL, 1938, and C19 boarding houses, of which No. 7 was converted to a pre-preparatory school in 1993, with new canopy and entrance hall by *James Cubitt & Partners*.

JAPANESE SCHOOL, No. 1 Gloucester Avenue. A former convent, Holy Rood House, 1908–10 by *W. H. Romaine-Walker*. Stark Italianate. T-shaped plan; apsed and barrel-vaulted basilican chapel; the domestic quarters at r. angles.

JEWISH FREE SCHOOL COMPREHENSIVE, Camden Road. The successor to the Jewish Free School which was in Bell Lane, Spitalfields, from 1817. Extensive buildings by *Sidney Kaye, Firmin & Partners*, 1956–72, for 1,400 pupils. The unifying motifs are blue ceramic spandrel panels and some white stone-faced walls.

ST RICHARD OF CHICHESTER SCHOOL. On two sites. Partly in the *LCC*'s former ROYAL COLLEGE STREET SCHOOL of 1910–13. Grander than their average buildings, and considered the finest school in London when it was built. Stone porch and other stone dressings. Another part in Prince of Wales Road in the former HOME FOR AGED GOVERNESSES built by the Governesses' Benevolent Institution in 1847–9 by *Wyatt & Brandon*. An irregular stone front with gables and some Gothic details, altered and extended in 1877–8 for the Camden School for Girls (q.v.). Good wrought-iron gates of early C18 type (brought in 1849).

SOUTH CAMDEN COMMUNITY SCHOOL, Charrington Street. A former Board school, with post-war LCC additions, to which is attached a community building by *van Heyningen & Haward*, 1991–2. This has a restrained exterior in yellow and black brick, with glazed bricks between square windows.

WILLIAM ELLIS SCHOOL, Highgate Road. Original buildings 1938 by *H. P. G. Maule*; many additions.

BOARD SCHOOLS. Good examples of every period. In addition to the buildings mentioned above: HOLMES ROAD, Kentish Town (now Camden Institute); an early example by *E. R. Robson*, 1873–4, asymmetrical with gables and some Gothic detail. PRINCESS ROAD, Camden Town, 1884–5. With nice curly gables. RHYL STREET, 1898, handsome example of the symmetrical classical type. TORRIANO AVENUE, 1910. Roughcast gables in an Arts and Crafts spirit. For Highgate, *see* Hornsey Board Schools p. 556.

ST MICHAEL'S C. OF E. PRIMARY SCHOOL, North Road, Highgate. Founded in 1833; relaunched on this site in 1852 as a model National and Industrial School, for 420 children, through the influence of Harry Chester, local resident and Assistant Secretary of the Privy Council Education Committee. Buildings of 1852 by *A. Salvin*, a picturesque low brick and stone composition of gables of different sizes, with Dec Gothic windows. The generous grounds originally included agricultural land for practical training in farming and gardening.

*Hospitals and health centres*

ELIZABETH GARRETT ANDERSON HOSPITAL, Euston Road and Churchway. A pioneer women's hospital, which originated with a dispensary founded by Dr Elizabeth Garrett in St Marylebone in 1872. Pleasant unexceptional red and yellow brick exterior of 1889 by *J. M. Brydon*, deprived of some of its tall chimneys. The original circular ward block at the N end was replaced by later additions.

ST PANCRAS HOSPITAL, York Way. Built as replacements for older St Pancras Workhouse buildings; 1885–9 by *H. H. Bridgman*, tall and gaunt, with central clock tower. Later parts to the N by *A. & C. Harston*, 1890–5, including chapel and hall.

TEMPERANCE HOSPITAL, Hampstead Road. Opened 1873. W wing 1885; outpatients department 1903.

HOSPITALS, Highgate Hill and Dartmouth Park Hill. *See* Whittington Hospital, Islington, p. 669.

CAVERSHAM HEALTH CENTRE, Bartholomew Villas, Kentish Town. By *Camden Architect's Department (P. J. Watson)*; completed 1973. Low L-shaped building for two doctors' practices, incorporating a teaching unit.

GROUP PRACTICE, North Hill, Highgate *see* Perambulation 5b, p. 411.

*Transport and utilities*

GASHOLDERS, Goods Way. The most impressive array of gasholder 2 frames anywhere. Of the present seven frames, three of 1880 are in a unique triplet formation, around tanks of 1861, which, 52 ft in the ground, are probably the deepest ever constructed. These have cast-iron columns with classical capitals in three tiers, connected by wrought-iron lattice girders. Another, similar, is of 1883. Three others have very early lattice columns, of wrought iron or steel, *c.* 1887. Site constrictions made all these holders tall and narrow. They have an uncertain future at the time of writing, as their site lies on the confirmed line of the Channel Tunnel rail link. The adjoining gasworks of the Imperial Gas Light and Coke Company, long ago cleared away (*c.* 1911), had two monumental Doric chimneys by *Francis Edwards*, 1822–4.

CANALS AND CANAL STRUCTURES. The REGENT'S CANAL, designed by *James Morgan*, was begun in 1812 and opened from Paddington as far as Camden Town in 1816. From there, it starts its descent to the Thames and was completed in 1820. In the W, it passes the leafy suburbs of Primrose Hill, with two good brick bridges of the 1820s. At the end of Oval Road, PIRATE CASTLE, a children's centre in the form of a brick toy fort, by *R. Seifert & Partners*, 1977. The climax is at 'Camden Lock', properly called HAMPSTEAD ROAD LOCKS (1820). Alone now of the locks on the Regent's Canal, these retain intact the twin lock chambers, side by side, which were adopted throughout as much to save water as to accommodate heavy traffic; one lock could be partly emptied into the other.* (The duplicate chambers lower down the

---

* This was the site of *Sir William Congreve's* hydro-pneumatic caisson locks of 1815, an unsuccessful attempt to avoid the discharge of water from the upper to the lower level in working a lock.

canal were converted to overflow weirs in 1975.) The LOCK-
KEEPER'S COTTAGE is castellated and stuccoed, its extension
remodelled in the same style in 1975.

The view W is a fine industrial landscape, framed by the LNW
Railway warehouse and Gilbey's (*see* below) and culminating in a
distant accumulator tower. The cast-iron ROVING BRIDGE of
*c*. 1854 has an unusual and striking tied-arch design of 80-ft span.
Under the later railway warehouse, a railway INTERCHANGE BASIN,
enlarged *c*. 1856, with a neat cast- and wrought-iron arched BRIDGE.
Massive gritstone parapets on the approach ramps to these bridges.
Re-erected here, a WINCH of 1865 which was originally used to
open and close the gates of the Lee Navigation entrance lock at
Limehouse. Below Chalk Farm Road, a twisting section of the
canal as it negotiates what was the edge of the town, with three
brick BRIDGES of *c*. 1820 in close succession.

ST PANCRAS BASIN, *c*. 1867, was for coal from the Midland
Railway. Almost opposite, a cast-iron bridge marks the former
arm into the Great Northern Coal Depot. (Other canal features
are described below, under *Railways*.)

HIGHGATE PONDS, Millfield Lane. Six earth-embanked reservoirs
for the Hampstead Waterworks Co., after 1777, now ornamental
and bathing ponds.

HIGHGATE SERVICE RESERVOIR, the Grove; *c*. 1850 for the New
River Co., with a daintly stuccoed valvehouse.

*Railway lines*

Euston Road and the area to its N are dominated by the termini of
the main lines. The first was the London and Birmingham Railway
(later London and North Western), which arrived at Euston Square
in 1837. A decision of 1846 forbade the erection of main-line
stations in central London. So the Great Northern Railway also
ended at Euston Road, at King's Cross Station, built in 1851–2.
Between these routes the Midland Railway extended its own main
line from Derby into London in 1863–8, clearing before it most of
the shanty town of Agar Town and much of the old St Pancras
burial ground. Around and to the N of the stations, vast expanses of
land were taken up by goods yards, warehouses, engine sheds, repair
sheds and sidings. The London and Birmingham's goods yard lay at
Chalk Farm, the Midland Railway's in Somers Town, Agar Town
and Kentish Town. The network of lines was further increased by
the North London Railway (until 1853 called the East and West
India Docks and Birmingham Junction Railway), built in 1846–51 by
*Robert Stephenson* to connect the Birmingham main line at Chalk
Farm with the docks at Poplar. It was extended (as the Hampstead
Junction Railway) via Gospel Oak to Willesden Junction, en route
to Richmond, in 1853–60. The rail traveller still glimpses evidence
of these huge enterprises, although much of the land has been
disposed of for other purposes or stands derelict at the time of
writing awaiting the construction both of the Channel Tunnel rail
link into St Pancras and new connections for the Thameslink line.
Only King's Cross and St Pancras retain their original passenger
stations. The three main termini on Euston Road are described first,
followed by other surviving railway structures and the suburban
stations.

*The main-line stations*

EUSTON STATION, Euston Square. The London and Birmingham p.
Railway, 1833–7 by *Robert Stephenson*, was the first trunk line into 46
London. It became the London and North Western in 1846.
Originally it was to stop on the banks of the Regent's Canal at
Camden Town (where the goods station was sited in due course).
The 1-in-77 descent to Euston Station was considered too steep
for locomotives and was worked until 1844 by stationary engines
with two monumental chimneys beside the track at Camden
Town. The station at Euston was planned by *Stephenson* in
1836–7, with two platforms 200 ft long, and sheds by *Charles Fox*,
the first to be built with iron roofs.

Applied architecture on the grandest scale was commissioned
from *Philip Hardwick*. His buildings were swept away in 1960–1 in
the interests of modernity, despite widespread protest. The battle
was lost, but the case became a landmark in the developing appreciation of Victorian architecture. Hardwick's buildings, completed
in 1838, consisted of a Greek Doric propylaeum (i.e. a gateway,
not an arch as it was commonly called), with iron gates (designed
by Hardwick and made by *Bramah*), and a pair of lodges on each
side. The propylaeum was 72 ft high, with 44-ft columns. The
early station buildings were modest and not at all demonstrative
architecturally. After the entrance arch and its lodges they must
have come as a remarkable anticlimax to passengers. What then
made Hardwick go all out for the sublime in his Doric display?
The answer is no doubt pride in the achievement of the railway
line. Here was something as grandiose of its kind as anything the
Greeks had ever accomplished. So it deserved the highest rhetoric
available, and that was in the 1830s without doubt Doric. In 1838–9
Hardwick added two modest buildings SW and SE of the propylaeum, the one on the r. planned as a hotel, the one on the l. as long-
term lodgings. Then in 1846–9, to celebrate the creation of the
LNWR, *P. C. Hardwick* added a monumental Great Hall with an
iron gallery and flat coffered ceiling, and a board room and shareholders' meeting room to the N, approached by a grand staircase.

Now for what one sees today. The only buildings not wiped out
in 1961 are two outer LODGES on Euston Road by *J. B. Stansby* of
1869–70, with the names of stations in gold lettering on the quoins
and sculpture by *Joseph Pitts*. Between them a WAR MEMORIAL
by *Reginald Wynn Owen*, 1921, a stone obelisk on a granite base
guarded by four bronze figures. Beyond lies an approach road for
buses, then the forecourt above a car park (where there would
have been plenty of space to retain the Arch). The forecourt is
dominated by *R. Seifert & Partners'* office development added in
1974–8. Three sleek squat black towers (Camden forbade taller
buildings), linked by a lower range with emphatic projecting fins.
They are a substitute for British Rail's plans of 1965 for four towers,
rejected because of the government's ban on central London office
building at the time. Also here is a statue of Stephenson by *Marochetti*
preserved from the old station, and a striking SCULPTURE by
*Paolozzi*: Piscator, 1980, a silvered block with curved hollows, and
rectangular shapes above. The new STATION was begun in 1962.
The Passenger Hall, 1966–8 by *R. L. Moorcroft* (London Midland

Regional Architect), is a low neutral building clad in black polished granite and white mosaic, with a glazed s wall to the spacious entrance hall (now cluttered with shops). Within, there is access to the Underground, ticket offices to the l. and waiting rooms and refreshments to the r., all under one roof. In the entrance to the cafeteria, the pediment by *Thomas* of 1859, from the old shareholders' meeting room. Ramps lead down to the low utilitarian train shed (only steam trains needed lofty roofs). The shed exteriors are long and monotonous, with steel cladding on black brick, no asset to the neighbouring streets.

p.  KING'S CROSS STATION, Euston Road, was built in 1851–2 by
47  *Lewis Cubitt* as the terminus of the former Great Northern Railway, the line to Lincolnshire and Yorkshire constructed in 1846–50 by *Sir William Cubitt* and his son *Joseph Cubitt*. Like Euston, this station was also designed with a façade to the road, but the design is conceived in a spirit completely opposed to that of Hardwick's Euston front, where the connexion with the purpose of the building was wholly associational. Cubitt looked at his job with equal pride but no romanticism. The façade reflects the plan of the station. Departure and arrival sheds are spanned by two round-arched roofs (originally with laminated timber arch ribs, replaced by ribs of wrought-iron plate in 1869 and 1887), each with a span of 105 ft. They rise from dignified brick arcades, with wider arches where carriages were traversed between the two sides. The arches of the roofs are frankly displayed as the predominant motif of the main (s) façade, separated by a clock tower 120 ft high. At the foot of the arches there were originally two plain three-bay arcades with segment-headed arches. A third large arch (though much lower than those of the platforms) marks the former covered cab drive on the arrivals side on the r. On the l. is the office and waiting rooms building. The former main entrance, in the w front, is marked by taller storeys and a wrought-iron-trussed porte-cochère. This has the thin, somewhat debased, Venetian windows of the classical revival on its last legs. The roof of the clock tower marks the heyday in the 1840s of the contemporary Italian villa fashion, already indicated at Cubitt's Bricklayers' Arms Station in South London (Southwark). The geometric simplicity and functionalism of the rest may owe something to the influential theories of the French architect J. N. L. Durand, a pupil of Boullée. The architect was satisfied to depend, as *The Builder* put it in 1851, 'on the largeness of some of the features, the fitness of the structure for its purpose, and a characteristic expression of that purpose'. The E front on York Way is forbidding, but also strictly honest. The two upper floors were added in 1869.

w of the station *Cubitt* added the Italianate GREAT NORTHERN HOTEL in 1854, built on a curved plan to follow the former line of Pancras Road. The space left in front of the station after Pancras Road had been diverted to the w was filled by a clutter of sheds, replaced by a low travel concourse in 1974 (*J. Green* of British Rail's Regional Architect's Department).

ST PANCRAS STATION and the MIDLAND GRAND HOTEL, Euston Road. No one would use for St Pancras any of the terms applied by *The Builder* to King's Cross, or at least not to the archi-tecture of the HOTEL which fronts onto Euston Road, designed by

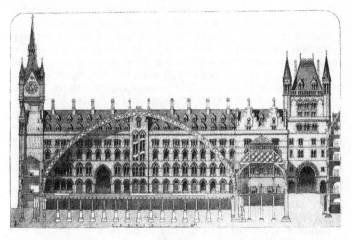

St Pancras Station. Section of train shed and north elevation of
Midland Grand Hotel, 1867

*G. G. Scott* in 1865–7 and built in 1868–74. Admirers would not
speak of plainness and firmness but exclaim with Walford (1897):
'It stands without rival ... for palatial beauty, comfort and convenience. The style of architecture', Walford goes on, 'is a combination of various medieval features the inspection of which calls to
mind the Lombardic and Venetian brick Gothic ... while the
critical eye of the student will observe touches of Milan and other
terracotta buildings, interlaced with good reproductions of details
from Winchester and Salisbury cathedrals, Westminster Abbey,
etc.' The 'ornaments of Amiens, Caen, and other French edifices'
are also mentioned. Building materials come from diverse sources:
the exterior faced with *Gripper*'s patent Nottingham bricks, with
dressings in Ancaster, Mansfield and Ketton stone and shafts of
grey and red granite. The story that Scott used for his St Pancras
the rejected design for the Government Offices in Whitehall is a
legend. All that is true is that he had made a thorough study of
French and Italian details for that building, and put them to good
purpose now. No London hotel at that time (or ever) was quite so
splendid and varied in appearance. The front is huge, although
not as huge as Scott's winning competition design with 300 bedrooms (twice the number asked for). In the final design one storey
was omitted and the clock tower reduced in height. The building
has 'fireproof' floors of concrete jack arches on corrugated-iron
soffits and wrought-iron beams, also early hydraulic lifts.

Contemporary appreciation did not guarantee continuing
admiration in the C20, and it was uphill work to rekindle public
enthusiasm for the building. In 1952 Pevsner sought to enlist
sympathy by giving its virtues a topical relevance: 'The composition
can perhaps be appreciated more justly now than it was immediately
after the Victorian age. It is decidedly done on the principle of free
grouping, so dear to present-day architects. Besides, the façade is,
with the exception of the five bays of the entrance on the extreme

left, set at an angle to the street, and the connexion between the five l. bays and the rest is a curve. The skyline also has great variety, starting from a stepped gable and two turrets on the l., going on to the big, broad main tower over the l. drive-in to the station, with its steep pavilion roof, and ending (after plenty of dormers and another small stepped gable) with a tall, but slimmer, clock tower in the manner of Big Ben. The carriage ramp up to the drive-in should also delight the eye of the modern designer.' After a long campaign by the Victorian Society the building was finally listed Grade I in 1967, but only in 1977 did British Rail accept that demolition was out of the question. Plans made in the 1980s to convert the building back to a hotel were shelved, pending a decision on the future of the station and the railway land behind, but in preparation for this the exterior was meticulously repaired and cleaned in 1991–5 by *Margaret and Richard Davies & Associates*, revealing once again the variety and colour of the materials and the quality of the detail. Inside, removal of later partitions recovered the character of the main rooms, still with many of their original features, although obscured by cream paint. In 1998 *RHWL* were selected as architects for converting the building to hotel and loft apartments.

HOTEL INTERIOR. The main entrance is in the w wing, completed 1873. In the lobby (restored 1994–5) a splendid Venetian Gothic doorway and window, and a floor with Minton tiles and mosaic. Gilding and stencilling were added for the opening of the whole building in 1877. The most important room, the dining and coffee room, stretches for 100 ft along the curved front. Its former splendour is indicated by grand marble fireplaces and attached columns of red Devonshire and green Connemara marble, carrying supports for the iron tie-beams decorated with ornate pierced mouldings. Scott designed furniture for the coffee room, and employed *Frederick Sang* to carry out interior decoration until 1873, when the directors, alarmed by rising costs, ceased to involve Scott in the interior and turned instead to *Waring & Gillow*. The walls of the coffee room were given panels with textured wallpaper instead of the tapestries which Scott had intended. At the junction of the curved w wing and the main range is the magnificent double staircase lit by three enormous two-light windows in the gable facing Midland Road. It extends through three storeys, supported on frankly exposed iron girders, and has excellent iron balustrading. At the top is a vaulted ceiling, painted with stars. On the vault spandrels, wall paintings of 1876–7 by *A. B. Donaldson* of Waring & Gillow: eight panels with Virtues, and the arms of the Midland Railway, restored 1994–5. The corridor walls have stencilled decoration, probably dating from a later redecoration scheme. Electric lighting was installed in 1885–9.

On the first-floor landing a later addition, a niche painted by *T. W. Hay* with a garden from the Romance de la Rose. On the first floor was a restaurant and writing room. Here too, good fireplaces and ceilings remain. The reading room above the porch is subdivided by a Gothic arcade. Walford (1897) reported that its ceiling 'glows in an atmosphere of gold and colour, yet free and graceful in its figures and ornaments designed by Mr Sang'. Other accommodation was in similarly rich and sumptuous High Victorian taste, a little old fashioned by the 1870s. Moncure Conway (*Travels in South Kensington*, 1882), complained that 'one does not desire to sleep amid purple and gold'. The luxurious appointments included passenger lifts, and pianos and clocks in some sitting rooms of the three hundred bedrooms on the upper floors.

TRAIN SHED. The iron shed of 1866–8 behind the hotel has the unprecedented clear span of 240 ft and a length of 690 ft. It is one of the outstanding surviving examples of Victorian functionalism and daring, designed by *W. H. Barlow*, assisted by *R. M. Ordish*. The ironwork was made by the *Butterley Company* and was originally painted sky-blue. Wrought-iron lattice arch ribs rise 100 ft to meet in a slightly pointed apex. They spring from platform level, without supporting columns. The floor supporting the platforms and tracks acts as the tie to the arch. The upper part of the roof was entirely glazed (the glass was reduced to two narrow strips when repaired after damage in the Second World War). The iron-pillared 'vaults' beneath, of dimensions precisely calculated (on a grid of 14 ft 6 in.) for storing Burton beer barrels, raise the tracks nearly 20 ft above Euston Road, so that trains could run on the level from Camden Town, over the Regent's Canal and Fleet River. There was a wagon hoist to the vaults on the central axis outside the shed. On the W side of the station, the BOOKING HALL, with linenfold panelling and originally with an open timber roof, 1869. The tie-beams are supported on columns with delightful carved capitals with railwaymen. Through an elaborate archway, a CAB ROAD with glazed, lattice-trussed roof. 65

Plans for the use of the station as a terminal for the Channel Tunnel Rail Link were developed by *Foster & Partners* in 1997–8. These include a low additional train shed to the N, as long as the existing station, the refurbishment of the original shed, and adaptation of the space beneath as arrival and departure areas, with new links to the Underground.

*Other railway structures*

LONDON AND BIRMINGHAM RAILWAY (later London & North Western Railway). Substantial survivals at Chalk Farm, Camden Town, just N of the Regent's Canal. Nothing remains of the chimneys for the short-lived early stationary engines which powered the stretch into Euston (*see* above), but the ENGINE HOUSE VAULTS of 1837 remain. The boiler houses were served by coal stores in vaults running towards the canal, with parallel vaults for the rope-tensioning mechanisms. Adjoining, an Italianate HYDRAULIC ACCUMULATOR TOWER which may be as early as 1853. There are portions of retaining walls and cast-iron railings of the period, and the sandstone abutments of the bridge across the canal, in Egyptian style.

GOODS STATION. On an embankment; the buildings stood on brick vaults used for stabling and later for wine and spirit stores. None of the early buildings remains above ground. The four-storey WAREHOUSE by the canal is of *c.* 1905, in splendid red engineering brick trimmed with blue brick, with water tower for fire fighting. Wooden upper floors, on steel beams and columns. At ground level there were road and rail loading platforms, and a hydraulic platform crane is preserved. In the basement there is a canal dock. Partly converted to offices in the 1980s.

W of this, by Oval Road, OFFICES, probably of the 1850s, with a toplit drawing office under a lantern roof.

RAILWAY STABLES, Chalk Farm Road. c. 1855 and later. Part of one range original, one and half storeys with hay lofts. Handsome semicircular wooden windows and round arches. Three other ranges raised to two and three storeys in 1881. On the roadside range a second storey of stables, added c. 1905, with red and blue brickwork and cantilevered walkway. To the W a two-storey range of stables over cartsheds, 1883, by *H. Woodhouse*. Horses reached the goods station by a subway through the vaults (*c.* 1855). Adjoining, a fragment of a four-storey BONDED WAREHOUSE of the 1880s for Gilbey's behind. Along the street, a retaining wall with pilasters and crisp sandstone cornices and, parallel to this, a kerb made of old SLEEPER BLOCKS from the original London and Birmingham Railway.

ROUND HOUSE, Chalk Farm Road. Built as an engine house for the LNW Railway in 1847 by *R. B. Dockwray*. 160 ft in diameter, with a shallow conical slated roof on 24 slender cast-iron columns. The engine entrance was on the W side, and a central turntable (36-ft diameter) distributed the engines to 23 berths, with repair pits beneath. From 1869, after engines had become too large, the building was used as a wine store by Messrs Gilbey, who added the wooden gallery. In 1965 it was acquired by Arnold Wesker's Centre 42; low-key conversion into theatre and arts centre by *Bickerdike, Allen, Rich & Partners* began in 1967, with an adaptable 900-seat theatre with gallery. A studio theatre below was opened in 1975. The enterprise struggled on until 1983, when its Arts Council grant ceased and the building was acquired by Camden Council. Structural repairs were carried out, but numerous plans to convert the building to other uses came to nothing, until 1997, when work began on tactful transformation to an Arts Centre for the Norman Trust by *John MacAslan*.

PRIMROSE HILL TUNNEL, *see* Hampstead, p. 214.

GREAT NORTHERN RAILWAY. The line to Lincolnshire and Yorkshire was constructed in 1846–50 by *Sir William Cubitt*. The section between the Regent's Canal and King's Cross passenger station dates from 1851–2. The passage under the canal through the MAIDEN LANE or GASWORKS TUNNEL presented problems of limiting gradients and clearances; the requisite cast-iron aqueducts are concealed from view. The original two-track tunnel was supplemented on the E in 1878 and on the W in 1892. (The Copenhagen Tunnel in Islington was triplicated similarly.) The earlier tunnels have simple circular portals with stone voussoirs and cornice.

GREAT NORTHERN GOODS YARD. A remarkable complex of C19 buildings to the N of King's Cross Station. In 1987 British Rail announced its intention to develop the site (59 acres: 24 ha). *Sir Norman Foster*'s scheme won a competition in 1988 but was thwarted by the recession. At the time of writing the southern part of the GOODS YARD retains many of its facilities of the 1850s, designed by *Lewis Cubitt* as the largest goods station of the period. Most prominent is the six-storey GRANARY of 1852, simple stock brickwork with stone cornice. Cast-iron columns and beams. Hydraulic power was used for operating the hoists. The granary is flanked by large TRANSIT SHEDS of 1850, each 580 ft long. Between the transit sheds, an area originally used for marshalling trains under cover with, raised above a mezzanine office floor of 1897, one bay of the original wrought-iron roof of 1850. The rest reroofed in the C20. There was formerly a canal basin in front, with large docks beneath the granary and transit sheds. Stables were provided under the transit sheds, reached by ramps, but they were soon inadequate (800 horses were employed by 1859). To the E is the substantial GOODS OFFICE (Regeneration House). To the E also is the MIDLAND GOODS SHED, built 1850 as the carriage shed for the Great Northern's temporary Maiden Lane terminus, then adapted for Midland Railway before it had its own facilities. Two lines of track at ground-floor level; iron columns and girders inserted in the late C19 support a timber upper floor with later roof. The adjoining roof of 1888 to the E for an extension of the potato market held here in the later C19 incorporates some spandrel beams from the temporary passenger station of 1850. At the N end of the Midland shed is a HYDRAULIC ACCUMULATOR TOWER, possibly built to serve the potato market sidings of 1861–4. Hydraulic power had been employed at the goods yard from 1851, an early use of the method. To the SW the COAL and FISH OFFICES, a curving block between Wharf Road and the canal, of 1852 with later additions. To the W is the former COAL DEPOT. The handling of coal was one of the goods yard's chief functions, and the COAL DROPS, despite later alterations, are still eloquent testimony to the size of the trade. They consist of long covered viaducts with impressive rows of arches on two levels. The rail tracks entered on the upper floor, beneath a wide-span wooden roof. The eastern coal drops (damaged by fire in 1985) date from 1866. From the four lines of railway track coal from the wagons was discharged into hoppers on a mezzanine floor carried on cast-iron columns and beams, and thence into carts in loading bays below. The S part was converted to warehouses in the late C19. The western coal drops date from 1856 have cast-iron beams used also to carry the tracks, and a more elaborate roof spanning 48 ft.*

MIDLAND RAILWAY. The first St Pancras Goods Station of the 1860s, at Agar Town, was demolished in the 1970s. An additional Goods Station was approved in 1877 in Somers Town W of St Pancras Passenger Station, displacing 10,000 people. This two-level station was built in 1883–7 (engineer *John Underwood*) and extended in 1896. It was partly damaged in the Second World War and largely demolished for the British Library in the 1970s. Only fragments of its extensive and excellently detailed boundary walls remain at the time of writing. They have (or had) buttresses alternating with Gothic arches containing hammered open iron grilles by *John Potter* of South Molton Street. A pair of wrought-iron

* For a detailed survey made in advance of proposed redevelopment, see S. Duckworth and B. Jones, *King's Cross development site, an inventory of architectural and industrial features*, Report for English Heritage, 1988; also R. Thorne with S. Duckworth and B. Jones, 'King's Cross Goods Yard', in *Change at King's Cross*, ed. M. Hunter and R. Thorne, 1990.

gates is re-erected at Camley Street Natural Park. N of St Pancras
Station the tracks are carried by heavy plate girder BRIDGES by the
*Butterley* company, 1867. By Goods Way is a WATER POINT of
2    1867, i.e. a water tank to serve steam engines, its iron tank encased
in Gothic arcaded brickwork (its relocation under discussion in
1998). On Pancras Road a row of COAL DROP ARCHES, now
garages, with remains of timber chutes. Opposite, Gothic COAL
OFFICES of 1896, from a two-level coal depot demolished in the
1970s for housing. On the N bank of the canal in the former
Goods Yard a red brick hydraulic PUMPING STATION with
remains of a stylish accumulator tower, converted to a boat club.
Near the N end of St Pancras Way the garden centre is converted
from three-storey STABLES.

Former RAILWAY CLEARING HOUSE, Eversholt Street (Nos.
163–203). A long anonymous range stretching N of Euston Station.
The clearing house was set up in 1842 to transmit business between
the railway companies. By 1914 2,500 clerks were employed. The
earliest section, of 1849 by *Philip Hardwick*, was demolished for
the new station; surviving parts, in a similar late Georgian style,
added from S to N, date from 1874–5 (*James B. Stansby*), 1882, and
1896, with a taller addition at the N end of 1901–2. Refurbished,
with new back extensions, in the 1980s.

PNEUMATIC DESPATCH RAILWAY of 1863–5 and 1869. This ran
from Euston Station to Eversholt Street and from Euston Station
to the Head Post Office at St Martin-le-Grand via Tottenham
Court Road and High Holborn. *T. W. Rammell* and *J. L. Clark*
were the designers. Wheeled containers were propelled by air
pressure through a horseshoe-shaped tunnel only 4 ft 6 in. high,
built under the streets. A speculative venture, it did not win the
favour of the Post Office and closed in 1874. Sections remain as
telephone and electrical ducts, e.g. under Tottenham Court Road.

*Suburban stations*

CAMDEN ROAD STATION (North London Railway). 1870, the only
survivor of several fine stations by *E. H. Horne* in a restrained
Italo-Romanesque style, which replaced the original wooden
stations on the line. To the W three-storey goods department
offices, also with round-headed windows.

Former KENTISH TOWN STATION (Midland Railway). At the
entrance, a platform canopy (*c.* 1890), re-erected from another station
on the line. Fragments of the engine shed of the 1860s to the N.

UNDERGROUND STATIONS. CAMDEN TOWN, KENTISH TOWN
and MORNINGTON CRESCENT (also the disused South Kentish
Town) were built in 1907 in the distinctive house style which
*Leslie W. Green* used for stations in Charles Yerkes's Underground
Group. They have characteristic ox-blood glazed tiles and bold
arches incorporating a mezzanine office floor.

KENWOOD

1    Kenwood, set in a landscaped park bordering Hampstead Heath, is
the finest C18 country house in North London. Most of the estate
was acquired for public benefit when it was threatened by building

in 1922. The contents of the house had been sold, but the building itself was acquired by the Earl of Iveagh in 1924, and bequeathed to the public in 1927, together with his fine collection of paintings. From 1949 house and grounds were run by the LCC, passing from the GLC to English Heritage in 1985.

The estate was bought by the Lord Chief Justice, William Murray, first Earl of Mansfield, from the third Earl of Bute in 1754. It contained a house close to the N boundary, with an admirable view over the S slopes towards London. The early C17 house appears to have been remodelled *c.* 1700, when an early C18 orangery was added to the W of the S front. In 1764 Lord Mansfield engaged *James and Robert Adam* to carry out improvements. The work took place between 1766 and 1774, and is described in the Adams' *Works*, published in 1774. The main external changes were the addition of an anteroom and library to the E, to balance the orangery, and an entrance portico on the N side. In 1793–6 *George Saunders* added two wings for the second Earl. These project to the N, and contain music room and dining room, with anterooms. The E offices, kitchen and other buildings in the grounds also belong to this date.

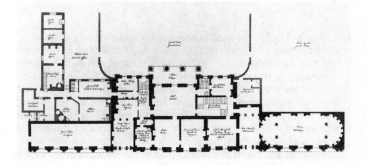

Kenwood. Ground-floor plan, 1774

The HOUSE is approached from the N: *Adam*'s Ionic portico, with four fluted columns and Grecian capitals, entablature with delicate swags, and pediment, stands in front of a stuccoed three-storey block of nine bays. On either side *Saunders*'s plain projecting wings, of white brick, with Venetian windows in the end walls. The S side is reached past a pretty veranda of the 1790s and then through a dramatic ivy tunnel leading out onto a terrace. This front makes a greater display. The nine-bay centre is of two storeys with an attic (a late addition to Adam's scheme). Giant pilasters above a rusticated ground floor, with centre and end bays emphasized by slight projections. Two closely set pilasters for each end bay, and paired pilasters below the ends of the central pediment. The delicate enrichment of pilasters and panels with Grecian honeysuckle and arabesques was removed after 1793, because Adam's patent stucco had begun to decay, but in 1975 it was restored very successfully in fibreglass, following a drawing in the *Works*. The one-storey orangery and library have windows within arches framed by Ionic columns, originally fluted.

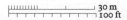

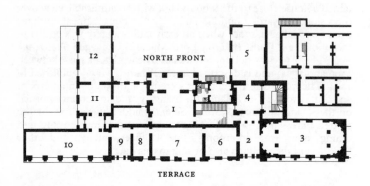

NORTH FRONT

TERRACE

INTERIOR. The rooms in the centre of the older house, adapted by *Robert Adam,* are comparatively modest. The rather low entrance hall has a modest stucco ceiling with painted panels by *Antonio Zucchi,* 1773, the central one with Bacchus and Ceres indicating that the room was also used as a dining room. Formerly doors led from the hall into the drawing room and parlour on the s side. The route proceeds E into Adam's staircase hall. The roof-light was added after the landing window was blocked by the later N wing. Staircase with iron balustrade and cast brass honeysuckle decoration. Beyond the stairhall Adam's extension; first comes the restrained anteroom, designed by *James Adam* in 1764. Venetian window looking s to the view, and facing it a screen with two Ionic columns. Wall niches for statues. Beyond is the library or Great Room, created in 1767–9, infinitely the most important of the interiors, a large apartment with a segmental tunnel vault and apses at both ends, screened off in the typical Adam manner by giant columns supporting a beam-like entablature. The tympanum above is left open. The bookcases are recessed between pilasters in the apses. In the first design of 1764 they continued in the recesses in the main walls, but instead Robert Adam lightened the effect by filling the recesses with exceptionally large mirrors, brought from France, set below decorated tympana. Mirrors also between the windows. All the decoration is of exquisite delicacy, with panels by *Zucchi* set in. Redecoration in 1969 in blue and pink followed the original colours found from paint scrapes.

N of the anteroom, in the wing added in 1793 by *Saunders,* the dining room lobby is small but ambitious, in the manner of Henry Holland, with a coffered ceiling and balustraded lantern resting on four thin segmental arches. The dining room beyond (now picture gallery) is now very plain. In Adam's time the rooms along the s front, in sequence from the anteroom, were Lord Mansfield's

| 1  | Entrance hall |
|----|---------------|
| 2  | Anteroom |
| 3  | Library or Great Room |
| 4  | Dining room lobby |
| 5  | Dining room |
| 6  | Lord Mansfield's dressing room |
| 7  | Breakfast room |
| 8  | Lady Mansfield's dressing room |
| 9  | Housekeeper's room |
| 10 | Orangery |
| 11 | Green Room |
| 12 | Music Room |
| 13 | Cold bath |
| 14 | Kitchen |

Kenwood. Ground-floor plan

dressing room, then drawing room and parlour (these two were united in 1815 and later became the breakfast room). Beyond Lady Mansfield's dressing room, a small chamber at the end of the old house, is the housekeeper's room, which has a Venetian window to balance the one in the anteroom. It forms a link to the formerly free-standing orangery, originally entered through the garden from the w. Behind this was the original service wing, replaced by the new w wing of 1793–6: green room with screen of Ionic columns, music room beyond, originally elaborately furnished, with organ and painted decoration. On the first floor the most notable survival is a colourful chinoiserie chimneypiece in the room above the entrance hall, all that remains from Adam's 'Chinese' room of 1773.

The two-storey SERVICE WING E of the house, added by *Saunders*, 1793–6, is of dark brick behind a Doric colonnade of white painted columns. Kitchen with octagonal roof and domed cupola (now a restaurant), flanked by splayed wings. The cafeteria occupies the laundry and brewery. S of the colonnade an C18 COLD BATH, restored with reconstructed marble lining after C19 use as a store. Originally with niches and shell decoration.

GROUNDS. Landscaping was begun by the first Earl, who enlarged the estate in 1789 to prevent development around Millfield Farm and Highgate Ponds. Further work was done from 1793 under the second Earl, who took advice from *Humphry Repton*, and was continued by the third Earl from 1796.

In the early C18 there were formal gardens s of the terrace (shown on Rocque's map of 1745), with fishponds and woodland beyond. The gardens were remodelled by the 1750s, to provide lawns, enclosed on each side by trees, sweeping down to the lake, where there is a SHAM BRIDGE with a pretty false front of timber, designed purely as an eye-catcher. The bridge is first recorded in

1786 and was rebuilt in 1791. W of the house, the looped ivy passage framing the view S and the flower garden, with its winding paths between rhododendrons, can be attributed to *Repton*, who is known to have made a Red Book for Kenwood for the second Earl. The drives from Hampstead Lane, which was moved N away from the house, also date from the 1790s, as do several buildings in the grounds by *Saunders*. W of the house, the DAIRY and DAIRY COTTAGE, *c.* 1795, three buildings around a forecourt, brick with hipped slate roofs with wide eaves. To the E, a MODEL FARM of the same date (partly demolished), and a walled garden. One-storey pedimented LODGES of white brick on Hampstead Lane. The gatepiers by the W lodge were brought from *James Stuart*'s Montagu House in Portman Square. The C20 SCULPTURE was added when the house was in the hands of the LCC. Near the W lodge, Bird Cage, 1951 by *Reg Butler*; forged and welded iron, made for the Festival of Britain. On the W lawn, Monolith (Empyrean), 1953 by *Barbara Hepworth*; further W a large bronze by *Henry Moore*, Two Piece reclining figure, 1963–4.


### BRITISH LIBRARY
Euston Road

1978–97 by *Sir Colin St John Wilson*. Britain's only major public building of the later C20, achieved after much agonizing over the site, and after drastic economies as a result of government parsimony. The assemblage of orange brick walls and grey roofs, rising behind a spacious courtyard opening off Euston Road, occupies the site of Somers Town Goods Station of the Midland Railway, constructed 1883–7 and closed 1967. When chosen, the location was criticized as too remote, a quarter of an hour's walk from the old library in the British Museum. Perceptions are changing; if the Channel Tunnel rail link terminus at St Pancras is built, this area could become as important a centre as any in London.

The British Library was originally part of the British Museum (p. 288). Its collections included the King's Library, given to the nation by George III, and housed in the splendid room in the E wing of Smirke's museum (q.v.). To cope with expansion, the famous Round Reading Room was added in the central courtyard in 1854–7. By the mid C20 these premises were totally inadequate, and many books were housed elsewhere. With the object of bringing the dispersed collections together and providing more space for readers and staff, plans were made to expand the Bloomsbury site. In 1962 Wilson, a Cambridge lecturer, who, in association with *Sir Leslie Martin*, had just made his name with Harvey Court, a powerfully monumental set of Cambridge students' lodgings, was appointed architect, jointly with Martin. The plan of 1964 involved ruthlessly sweeping away existing buildings S of the Museum (apart from Hawksmoor's St George's Church) to provide space for a new library and for the grand setting that Smirke's museum had always lacked. The extent of proposed demolition fired opposition from the growing conservation movement; the proposed site was reduced in 1966, then, after long delay, rejected in 1973 in favour of the present one next to St Pancras Station. At the same time the British Library was made formally independent of the Museum (involving a wrench-ing apart of the collections: manuscripts and maps, as well as the book collection, were assigned to the new building, while prints and drawings remained with the Museum). In 1978 Wilson's plans for the St Pancras site were approved; building of the first of three planned phases began in 1982, to provide seven reading rooms accommodating 3,440 readers, and storage for 25 million books. Reduced funding led to the abandonment of the later phases and a revision of the plans in 1988: a new N frontage was designed to com-plete the N side of the first phase, overlooking the empty spaces which had been designated for the later additions. The result in 1998 is eleven reading areas for 1,176 readers and storage for 12 million books.

The scale and complexity of the building invite comparison with the new universities of the 1960s, begun at a time of optimism and expansion for higher education. But universities serve a multitude of purposes; the Library is a single organism conceived with one chief aim, the storage and consultation of written matter, though with the addition of ancillary functions – exhibition spaces, refresh-ment areas and lecture and meeting rooms. Despite all the changes to the plans during an agonizingly protracted birth, the result has an impressive coherence, a building which despite its complicated func-tions is easy to understand, grand, yet friendly in its details. In some ways it is out of its time, designed before the impact of the new technology of the late C20 was fully appreciated, and only time will reveal whether it is flexible enough to adapt to changing needs. But it is built to last, with superb craftsmanship intended for a 300-year life, now a rare approach, and that deserves appreciation.

The building consists of two wings of unequal length, set back on a wedge-shaped site behind a generous courtyard which distances the entrance from the busy Euston Road. The COURTYARD, designed as a public space, is an important prelude to the Library itself, entered near the SW corner through a great red sandstone gateway which borrows its proportions from the doors of the old King's Library. Splendid openwork bronze gate composed entirely of the words British Library, by *David Kindersley* and *Lida Lopez Cardozo Kindersley*. Beyond is *Eduardo Paolozzi*'s powerful sculpture of Newton, 1997, based on the image by Blake: science and the arts brought together. The courtyard has a strong paving pattern of red brick squares in a white stone grid. The visitor's route crosses diagonally, down and up shallow steps, between enclosures for planting and seating, and a small open amphitheatre (to have a SCULPTURE by *Antony Gormley*, of incised granite blocks). Entrance and bookshop are in the W wing, which houses the humanities; the E wing has the science and Asian libraries, and an auditorium at the S end, which can be approached by a lesser SE entrance. The irregular space between the wings has areas for the use of both readers and the general public: entrance hall, exhibition areas and restaurants.

The wings are built up by sweeping horizontal layers of orange brick, enlivened by occasional round windows, deep red paintwork and emphatic horizontal lines of green sunblinds. Tiers of grey slate roofs, without eaves to disturb their geometric precision, step back to a slim brick clock tower marking the junction of the two parts. The brick and slate deliberately echo Scott's St Pancras Hotel, whose decorative gables tower over the lower roofs of the E wing. Wilson's view of St Pancras is significant. He sees it as a link in a chain – a representative of the 'English free style' – a flexible approach adaptable for the new building types of the C19, which led, via Richardson and Frank Lloyd Wright in America, to the Modern Movement on the Continent and so to his own building. The Library is full of allusions to the great heroes of modernism, but not so much to the rationalist stream, epitomized by Le Corbusier, as to the more organic and romantic tradition of Aalto and Scharoun. Aalto, Wilson's particular hero, is evoked not only by the brick, the sloping roofs and the stepped approaches, but inside by the curved partitions, tactile surfaces and ingenious natural lighting, used with the aim of creating a humane environment within the colossal scale of the whole. There are more exotic resonances as well; the layered roofs and the use of red are a conscious echo of another form of public architecture on the grandest scale, the Chinese temple.

The ENTRANCE HALL is a cool, airy monumental space, four storeys high, lit from a clerestory. Plain brick surfaces and stone bands continue themes from the exterior. The floor is paved with Portland and Purbeck stone; the three big square piers are faced with white Travertine marble, which is used lavishly throughout the building. Detail is minimal; all depends on space and light. A leisurely ceremonial staircase fills the centre (cf. Wilson & Martin's Law Library stairs at Oxford). More stairs and escalators beyond provide access to the white balconies which link the upper levels and provide magnificent, varied cross-vistas. The grand scale is tempered by details which reward examination: brass and leather handrails, differently patterned wooden doors. The good signage throughout the building was designed with *Pentagram*. Low marble screens define ticket desks and information areas, reminiscent of Early Christian furnishings, a hint that this is indeed a sacred building, a temple to the book. Art work provides a diversion: on the W wall a vast, colourful tapestry woven to a design by *R. B. Kitaj*: titled If Not, Not, inspired by T. S. Eliot's *Waste Land*. Also on this side, a row of roundels with busts of the Library's founders. Excellent hanging lamps by the Finnish architect *Juha Leiviska*.

The principal focus of the entrance hall is the TOWER OF BOOKS, gleaming behind the balconies at the far end, rising mysteriously from the depths of the basement storage areas. Ironically, this symbolic heart of the building was not part of the original scheme, but was devised to fill the space originally allocated for the catalogues but redundant after the introduction of electronic technology. The Tower's practical function is to house the C18 collection of books from the King's Library in the British Museum, which were originally to have been placed around the walls of the catalogue hall. The concept of the treasure chest of books can be compared to the plan of the Beinecke Rare Books Library at Yale (SOM, 1960–3), but the difference is that here the books are not hidden, but placed so that the spines of their fine bindings are displayed, as if forming part of the structure.

The PUBLIC AREAS cluster around the tower. To the l. the spacious EXHIBITION AREAS: Rare Books below, Manuscripts in the gallery. In contrast, the upper RESTAURANT AREAS, on two levels, have windows to the N front designed after 1988. Their pleasantly curved outdoor balconies are in a more relaxed mood than the rigidly angular front courtyard.

The READING ROOMS each have a distinctive character, dictated by the character of research: science subjects require open shelf access for rapid brief enquiry, humanities more prolonged study of books brought from the stacks. On the E side are the RARE BOOKS AND MUSIC READING ROOM (replacing the old North Library) and the GENERAL HUMANITIES ROOM. Rare Books is entered through a lobby which has busts and portraits. The main area is a calm clerestory-lit space, with much emphasis on wood, chosen as a friendly material: white columns panelled at the base, a slatted ceiling, and excellently crafted furniture in American white oak, with chairs designed by *Ron Carter*. Manuscripts are displayed in the gallery. The larger Humanities Room, also clerestory-lit, has two upper galleries projecting from one corner, providing an interesting variety of views and seating areas. The long E wing has at the back the ASIAN READING ROOM, for the Oriental and India Office collections, double-height, with high windows above a wall area intended for pictures. To its S the SCIENCE AND PATENT READING ROOMS, a very long and impressive galleried space with coffered ceiling; it opens to deep plan bookshelves to its E which form a buffer to the road beyond. On this frontage a staircase in a glazed angular projection breaks the long horizontals of the exterior and provides a view to the outside world. S of this is the CONFERENCE CENTRE, again with much wood apparent, and with a porthole to the courtyard. The LECTURE THEATRE is approached by gentle steps from a skilfully handled informal FOYER.

The BASEMENT, 75 ft deep, has four storeys of air-conditioned storage. Books are brought to the reading rooms by motorized rollers and paternosters.

## PERAMBULATIONS

*1. Euston Road and Somers Town*

*1a. Euston Road, from west to east*

Until around 1800 EUSTON ROAD marked the edge of built-up London. It was laid out as part of the New Road of 1756, intended as a bypass 'to avoid the stones', as Horace Walpole put it, the first example of such a road on record. Houses began to appear only at the end of the C18. The chief development was Euston Square, a widening of the road to N and S, built up *c.* 1811 as part of the northern expansion of Bloomsbury. The residential character has long gone, and the mile-long road, widened in the 1960s and with an underpass at Tottenham Court Road, now has a sequence of C20 offices punctuated by three main line termini and a few public buildings.

Starting at the W end, at the junction with Marylebone Road, the most prominent C20 contribution is the EUSTON CENTRE, 1962–72 by *Sidney Kaye, Eric Firmin & Partners*, occupying most of the N side up to Hampstead Road. The tall cross-shaped curtain-walled tower and the lower blocks stretching bleakly beside the widened road and underpass were early intrusions of large-scale offices into the West End, the result of a notorious post-war property speculation by the Levy brothers created at the same time as the underpass in front. The heavy modelling and bowed end of No. 338, the lower tower at the W end, is part of an ingenious refurbishment of 1991 by *Sheppard Robson* for British Land. The original plain curtain walling was replaced by ducting, and extra lifts were built out from the floor slabs. Piecemeal redevelopment of other parts of the site followed in an effort to regenerate the area; the most prominent addition to date is No. 50 TRITON SQUARE, large, elegant offices by *Arup Associates*, completed 1997.

To the E of Hampstead Road there stood until the C18 the manor house of Tottenhall or Tottenham Court, in its latter days a place of resort of dubious reputation. The corner site is now filled by a disturbing faceted cliff of glossy mirror glazing, 1975–82 by *Renton Howard Wood*, the commercial part of the compromise reached after the lengthy planning battle over Tolmers Square (*see* below). Further on, No. 222 on the N side, the former NATIONAL UNION OF MINEWORKERS, was one of the many trade union headquarters put up in this area within convenient reach of the railway stations. 1954–8 by *Moiret & Wood*; a framed front of marble and granite, spoilt after the Union left in 1982, when curtain walling was inserted in place of an opaque glass mural in the double-height board room.* No. 200, BENTLEY HOUSE (formerly CAMBRIDGE UNIVERSITY PRESS), 1937 by *Curtis Green & Partners*, not happy, with its two stunted angle turrets crowned by obelisks and the many small motifs of the slightly projected stone-faced front between.

The S side of Euston Road between Tottenham Court Road and Gower Street was rebuilt in the 1960s with an indifferent 1960s office scheme of mixed heights by *Stone, Toms & Partners*. To be replaced by buildings for University College Hospital (*see* p. 265). Then Nos. 195–205, sleek bronze granite with tinted windows, 1979–83 by *Carl Fisher & Partners*, built as speculative offices, and UNITY HOUSE, headquarters for the National Union of Railwaymen. Stained-glass mural of railway workers, 1983 by *Goddard & Gibbs*, and some other glass upstairs from the previous Unity House of 1910. The WELLCOME BUILDING, 1931–2 by *Septimus Warwick*, has a four-storeyed conventional Classical Revival front with giant Ionic columns and pediment. Built as a research institute and museum for the Wellcome Foundation, established in 1924 by the pharmaceutical magnate Sir Henry Wellcome. Interior remodelled 1989–92 by *Mlinaric, Henry & Zervudachi*, as headquarters, library and conference centre for the Wellcome Trust, with an exhibition gallery on the fourth floor. FRIENDS HOUSE (*see* p. 351), built over part of the gardens of Euston Square, is also classical, in deference to the spirit of the first Euston Station.

On the N side, No. 194, 1932 by *W. H. Gunton*, borrows its neighbour's giant Ionic columns but has none of the freedom, not to say naughtiness, of *Beresford Pite*'s former LONDON EDINBURGH

---

* The mural, and a sculpture of miners by *Moiret*, were removed to Sheffield.

AND GLASGOW ASSURANCE building, 1907. The main front, in MELTON STREET, faces E to Euston Square. Heavy, picturesque 108 Neo-Grec detail. Ionic giant order with bulgy volutes, some of the columns with projecting bits of entablature above, others squeezed back painfully. The centre of the top floor, with its extremely odd skyline with three gables, was added in 1913, the two N bays in 1924. Handsome inventive railings. Pite's decoration survives in the entrance hall: green and cream tiled walls, floor with zodiac mosaic. WALKDEN HOUSE, No. 10 Melton Street, by *W. W. & S. H. Fisk*, opened in 1958 as headquarters of the Railway Clerks Association.

EUSTON SQUARE, now a prelude to Euston Station (q.v.), was origi- nally just a broadening of the New Road to S and N, built up from 1811 as an extension of Bloomsbury. A pair of bow-fronted houses remains on the E side, Nos. 70–71. On the N side were stuccoed and pilastered terraces of *c*. 1811, of quite a distinguished design (demolished in 1937), and the famous 'Euston Arch' which dis- appeared in the 1960s with the rebuilding of the station. In their place are sheer black towers of offices around a piazza in front of the station (q.v.), built in 1974–8 by *Seifert & Partners*, after the rejection of British Rail's own office scheme.

The rest of Euston Road E of the station consists largely of public buildings (qq.v.) – Fire Station, Shaw Theatre, the new British Library and St Pancras and King's Cross Stations on the N side; St Pancras Church and Camden Town Hall and borough offices on the S. At the corner of Chalton Street, the RISING SUN, a typi- cally elaborate 1890s pub by *Shoebridge & Rising*, turreted and gabled. On the S side, CLIFTON HOUSE, 1935 by *Richardson & Gill*, stone-faced, in a straightforward modern vernacular, and NALGO HEADQUARTERS, *c*. 1970 by *Godfrey-Gilbert & Partners*, ribbed concrete.

*1b. North of Euston Road: between Hampstead Road and Euston Station*

The rebuilt TOLMERS SQUARE is more humane than the glassy front to Euston Road leads one to expect. Sheltered from the main roads by the tall offices are three- and four-storey brown brick terraces, partly residential, partly commercial, tightly arranged around a polygonal open space. The commercial blocks and the offices on Euston Road are separated by a glazed arcade (not visible from the square). The fate of the original stuccoed houses of the 1860s, blighted by intended office development, became a *cause célèbre* in the early 1970s when local squatters led community opposition to commercial redevelopment. The rebuilding of 1975–82 by *Renton Howard Wood* with a mixture of offices, housing and amenities was a compromise achieved by Camden working together with more sympathetic developers. The barrier-block housing along Hampstead Road is by the same firm.

In NORTH GOWER STREET, No. 195, the CECIL RESIDENTIAL CLUB, a hostel for girls, by *Maxwell Fry*, 1939–40, a straight- forward building in the style of the mid C20, diversified by a corner in glass bricks (now altered), and patches of tiles in a strong blue in other places, an early example in England of colour used in this way. The building is happily in scale with its older neighbours in North Gower Street, EUSTON STREET and DRUMMOND STREET. These form a surprisingly complete residential area, built up by the Southampton Estate *c.* 1820, with modest terraces and small shops. Its character has been respected by discreet 1970s infilling with small-scale housing by *Renton Howard Wood* (STARCROSS STREET, COBOURG STREET), which followed on from the Tolmers Square redevelopment. Larger hotels along CARDINGTON STREET buffer the area from the unprepossessing flank of Euston Station. Further S, in STEPHENSON WAY, a bleak back lane behind Euston Road, No. 14, *Jestico & Whiles*'s own offices, 1987–9; an elegant interior with double-height upper studio created within the shell of an older building.

To the N a lone survivor of once extensive railway service buildings lies just S of ST JAMES'S GARDENS. The gardens were made in 1887 out of St James's Churchyard, established as a burial ground for St James Piccadilly in 1791, with a church by *T. Hardwick* (now demolished). A few tombstones remain. Next to the site of the church, No. 108 HAMPSTEAD ROAD, the former ST PANCRAS CHARITY SCHOOL for poor girls (founded 1776); rebuilt in 1904 by *E. W. Hudson & S. G. Goss*; quite a colourful Edwardian Baroque front with pilasters, bold keystones and chequerwork tympana. It replaced a building of 1790.

## 1c. North of Euston Road: Somers Town, between Euston Station and King's Cross

An intricate neighbourhood around the railways; low rental housing, the result of over one hundred years of piecemeal slum clearance, intermixed with a few older terraces and the occasional trendy small late C20 office. N of King's Cross at the time of writing is an evocative decaying industrial landscape of canal, gasworks and goods yard awaiting a decision on the Channel Tunnel rail link. The area was built up by *c.* 1850, but much had gone slummy before the coming of the railways hastened the decline. Nothing remains now of the earliest development, Somers Town, an ambitious undertaking by Lord Somers, begun in the 1790s. It lay between Eversholt Street and Pancras Road, and had as its chief feature a polygon of outward-facing houses, designed by *Leroux* in 1793. E of this lay the poor working-class area of Agar Town, built up from 1840 on the estate of the Agar family, demolished from 1868 for the Midland Railway and St Pancras Station. Further N a little remains of a more respectable development by the Brewers Company around Charrington Street. The first initiatives to provide better housing in the King's Cross area (all now demolished) were made as early as the 1840s: they included some cottage housing in Pakenham Street, off King's Cross Road, designed by *Henry Roberts* in 1845, and a block of flats: Metropolitan Buildings, Pancras Square, built in 1847 by Dr Southwood Smith's Metropolitan Association for Improving the Dwellings of the Industrious Classes. More followed in the 1860s (two blocks remain behind King's Cross Station), but the main rebuilding effort began only at the turn of the century. The most extensive work was carried out from the 1920s, when both the LCC and the energetic St Pancras Home Improvement Society (later St Pancras Housing

Association), founded in 1924 by the Anglo-Catholic priest Basil
Jellicoe, looked to the example of the workers' flats of Vienna, and
created some courtyard lay-outs on the grandest scale.

EVERSHOLT STREET, on the E side of Euston Station, has on its E
side the pompous EUSTON HOUSE, No. 24 (British Railways
Board), 1934 by *A. V. Heal* and *W. Hamlyn*, modernistic and quite
uncommonly bad. Further N a long even stretch of early C19
houses remains (Nos. 140–182), with first-floor windows within
brick arches. Opposite, N of the station are the long plain ranges of
the former Railway Clearing House (*see* Public Buildings: Other
railway structures).

DORIC WAY to the E has the earliest new buildings put up by the St
Pancras Home Improvement Society. Their architect was *Ian B.
Hamilton*. The site was acquired in 1926. Three big five-storey
blocks with prominent mansarded roofs fill the triangular plot
bounded by Drummond Crescent: ST MARY'S, completed 1930,
ST ANN'S, 1935, and ST JOSEPH'S, 1936. Sculpture and ceramic
decoration, as on the other flats by the society, by *Gilbert Bayes*,
part of a campaign started in 1930 to provide 'things of beauty' for
brightening the lives of residents. St Mary's, with splayed wings,
faces across a pedestrian route to two-storey cottages of 1954 by
*Hamilton & Chalmers*.

CHURCHWAY, leading N from Euston Road, is shown on Booth's
map of 1889 as a narrow lane crowded with poor housing; rebuilding here was begun in 1899–1900 by the *LCC Housing Branch*
(*E. H. Parkes*). Brick blocks of flats, very pretty for their date,
varied by broken frontages, and by informal top floors, rendered,
with casement windows, in an Arts and Crafts spirit. On the E
side, further N, quite an elaborate Gothic terrace of 1882 with
coloured tile decoration.

CHALTON STREET, reached by a passage from Churchway. On
the E side the back of the LCC's Ossulston Estate of 1927–37
(*see* also Ossulston Street, p. 380). Built together with it, the
SOMERS TOWN COFFEE HOUSE, homely and domestic, with
big chimneys. On the W side, tucked away near the S end in ST
CHRISTOPHER'S PLACE, SPEECH, LANGUAGE AND HEARING
CENTRE by *Troughton McAslan*, 1995, a neat concrete grid with
ingenious steel windows. The rest of the W side is a haphazard
mixture: No. 57, tall polychrome Gothic, No. 71, boldly Postmodern, in two colours of brick, with very perverse railings, 1987
by *Philip Wharmby Architects* for St Pancras Housing Association.
Further N, No. 42 PHOENIX ROAD, opened in 1931 as the
Margaret Club and Day Nursery for mothers and children: nicely
detailed in a free Regency style; canted oriels with swept roofs;
arched ground-floor windows. Opposite was *Leroux*'s Somers
Town Polygon (*see* above), replaced in 1894 by flats for people
displaced by the Somers Town Goods Yard, which were demolished for OAKSHOTT COURT, 1972–6, one of Camden's grand
schemes (job architect *P. Tabori*). Lower and less monumental
than Alexandra Road (Hampstead) or Highgate New Town.
Instead of parallel terraces, an L-shaped arrangement of long red
brick tiers stepping up above garages. A friendly front, with
minute private forecourts and balconies overlooking an open

space, but forbiddingly overbearing rear parts. No. 101 Chalton
Street, MARY WOLLSTONECRAFT HOUSE, for the elderly,
1990–2 by *Gordon Fleming* of *Anthony Richardson Partnership*. Nos.
103–117, flats and houses for Covent Garden Housing Project, by
*Jim Monahan*, 1989–90. An urban composition with two bow-
fronted parts, intended to have a matching N section.

The SIDNEY STREET ESTATE, W of Chalton Street, was the final
phase of the St Pancras Housing Association's second major
scheme in Somers Town, planned in 1929, when it was described
optimistically as 'a miniature garden city'. An ambitious lay-out,
with *Hamilton*'s flats arranged around a generous central court. A
central assembly hall was intended, also shops along the street
front. Unusually grand forecourt with iron gates to Chalton Street
in front of ST ANTHONY'S, 1938–9. Clock and coloured ceramic
roundels on the flats, by *Bayes*, but his delightful decorative finials
to the drying-yard posts have gone. They included dolphins,
galleons and 'four and twenty blackbirds'. The top floor of ST
NICHOLAS, 1933–4, had a NURSERY SCHOOL with roof garden
planned by *Lady Allen*, with Hans Andersen reliefs, and fountain
by *Bayes*.

CHARRINGTON STREET, further E, has mid-C19 terraces of the
Brewers' Company Estate, complete on the E side, stucco-
trimmed, with pediments to the tall first-floor windows of the end
houses. More of the same date in the streets to the E. Opposite
GOLDINGTON CRESCENT, *K. D. Young*'s GOLDINGTON BUILD-
INGS, Royal College Street, 1902–3, the earliest housing put up
by the Borough of St Pancras, five storeys in cheerful orange and
yellow brick.

PANCRAS ROAD leads S past the LODGE and entrance to Old St
Pancras Churchyard (p. 349). Opposite are two proud cliffs of high-
density post-war flats by the Borough of St Pancras, *c.* 1948–50, by
*Thomas Sibthorpe* of St Pancras Borough Architect's Department,
eight and ten storeys, with the big windows of lift shafts and stairs
made into streamlined vertical features. In total contrast is the
low-rise area behind, demonstrating Camden's rejection of monumental schemes in the later 1970s. Around COOPERS LANE and
PURCHESE STREET, on the site of the St Pancras Coal Depot,
informal brown brick maisonettes and houses ending in a small
park.

Now back S to OSSULSTON STREET. On the E side, facing the flank
of the British Library, is the LCC's showpiece of between the
wars, the experimental OSSULSTON ESTATE, (principal assistants
*R. Minton Taylor* and *E. H. Parkes* under *G. Topham Forrest*). It
was planned to cater for housing needs not met by the cottage
estates on the edge of London, and was also intended to be a
visual improvement on the standard four- or five-storey walk-up
block of flats. CHAMBERLAIN HOUSE (1927–9) was the first part
to be built. Three blocks around a courtyard, with roughcast walls
above a granite-faced ground floor with arched windows. LEVITA
HOUSE, to the S, of 1930–1, is more boldly massed, with a formal
approach to a seven-storey centrepiece, flanked by splayed wings
with balconies enclosed within tall arches. Both the courtyard lay-
out and the drama of solid and void unrelieved by any ornament
pay tribute to the grand housing schemes of Vienna, which Topham

ST PANCRAS 2: ALBANY STREET 381

Forrest visited at this time. Earlier proposals had been even more novel, for American-influenced plans of 1925 had proposed nine-storey blocks served by lifts, with central heating, and with a small number of flats for private tenants on the upper floors. This proved unrealistically expensive; revised plans of 1927 reduced the height and cut down on the lifts. Top-floor studios and the idea of sub-sidizing public housing by private flats proved unacceptable, but a remnant of the concept remains in the formal courtyard to Ossulston Street, which was to have provided a segregated entrance to the superior apartments. All flats had the novelty of electric servicing (although heating was provided by coal fires). Behind the main frontage are three large internal courtyards; community facilities included the coffee house in Chalton Street (*see* above) and, N of Phoenix Road, THE COCK. Here also the first phase of WALKER HOUSE (1929–30), in the same spirit, but the large court behind is surrounded by plain brick six-storey ranges of 1936–7, typical of more routine 1930s LCC flatted estates.

### East of Pancras Road

Beyond the railway bridges, the area known as BATTLEBRIDGE (from an old bridge over the now culverted River Fleet) remained in limbo through the 1990s. Surviving to the N of King's Cross Station, STANLEY BUILDINGS, an atmospheric group, much beloved by film-makers. Some of the oldest surviving working-class flats in London. Five-storey blocks of 1864–5 by Waterlow's Improved Industrial Dwellings Company, on the usual plan (derived by *Waterlow* and his builder, *Matthew Allen*, from Henry Roberts's model dwellings of 1851), with cast-iron access balconies served by an open central staircase. No. 26 Pancras Road ('Turnhalle') is the entrance to the former GERMAN GYMNA-SIUM, built for the German Gymnastic Society in 1864–5 by *E. A. Gruning*, in imitation of such institutions in Germany. Laminated timber arches supporting iron spandrels span the breadth of the hall, a construction used also for the original roofs of King's Cross Station. In Battlebridge Road, CULROSS BUILDINGS, 1891–2 for the GNR, a rare survival of the tenement style of flats applied to railway housing. Mission Hall to railway workers alongside.

N of GOODS WAY, CAMLEY STREET, formerly Cambridge Street, which ran through Agar Town, whose houses were demolished for the Midland Railway. On the E side, adjoining the Regent's Canal, CAMLEY STREET NATURAL PARK, an enterprising creation of 1983, on the site of the GNR's coal drops. For the area to the N *see* Camden Town (p. 392).

### 2. Albany Street and the Regents Park Estate

The boundary between the parishes of St Marylebone (Westminster) and St Pancras (Camden) runs through Regents Park. The park and its buildings are described in *London 3: North West*. This account is concerned with the service area to the E, divided off from the grander houses by Albany Street. The close relationship between the two areas has largely been lost in the post-war rebuilding, apart from the important exception of the two Park Villages, with their select small villas. In addition to these *John Nash* built a working-class quarter around three squares, which were originally intended for markets. Rebuilding in this area began already in the 1930s; after extensive war damage most of the land was handed over to the borough, and the humble terraces around the squares were swept away and replaced by the Regents Park Estate.

At the s end of ALBANY STREET, the WHITE HOUSE, a large star-shaped nine-storeyed block, now a hotel, built as service flats; by *R. A. Atkinson*, 1936, quite modern for its date. Further N most of the Nash frontages were rebuilt after the war: on the W side by the *Louis de Soissons Partnership* for the Crown Commissioners, on the E by St Pancras Borough Council (*see* below). The original character of the street is shown by Nos. 34 (1812) and 36–48 (*c.* 1830); plain four-storey stuccoed houses. Around REDHILL STREET on the E is the beginning of a heavy Neo-Georgian pre-war rebuilding scheme by the Crown Commissioners (Windsor House etc.) by *C. E. Varndell*, 1933–7. On the site was *Nash*'s Ophthalmic Hospital of 1818. The former Christ Church follows (*see* Churches, above: St George, Greek Orthodox) and then the extensive utilitarian REGENTS PARK BARRACKS (*see* Public Buildings, above), also part of Nash's plan. At the N end of Albany Street, GLOUCESTER GATE, an iron-girder BRIDGE across the abandoned arm of the Regent's Canal which led to the markets, with elaborate quatrefoils and leafy candelabra lamp standards, 1877 by *W. Booth Scott*, engineer to St Pancras vestry.

PARK VILLAGE EAST and PARK VILLAGE WEST lie on either side of the canal site. They are one of the most interesting of *Nash*'s Regents Park extensions, laid out and begun by Nash in 1824 when most of the terraces around the park were finished, and completed by *Pennethorne*. In the two Park Villages Nash established the tradition of the small suburban villa (an idea already current a little earlier, as is shown by a plan of 1794 for the Eyre Estate at St John's Wood). In this way he rounded off the Regents Park planning scheme, a scheme unparalleled anywhere in its comprehensive character, ranging from the rich villas inside the park to the small villas of the two Villages, and the terraces, squares and markets E of Albany Street. Picturesque model villages had existed before (Nash himself had built the one belonging to Blaise Castle near Bristol in 1809), but the application of the village idea to the suburb was new and had a universal future. The villas are too closely set, therein also anticipating Victorian suburbs. Also they exhibit a certain variety of styles, which again was repeated by the Victorians: classical, emerging Italianate (with projecting eaves), and gabled Tudor.

Park Village West is grouped around a little winding street. The showpiece is No. 12, with octagonal tower porch and curved parts behind. No. 17 is gabled Gothic; the others vary the Italianate theme with round-headed or straight-headed windows. All stuccoed, with gatepiers to match. Park Village East is simply a row of substantial villas, differently detailed, strung along a straight line between street and canal. At the end, SILSOE HOUSE, Crown Commissioners' flats of 1972 by *Elsom, Pack & Roberts*, red brick, a lush variant on the Brunswick Centre type of plan; stepped-back profile; front doors on two levels opening onto a generous roof-lit

54

central corridor above garages. To the s, RICHMOND HOUSE, 1961 by *Fitzroy Robinson & Partners*; plain, four storeys.

REGENTS PARK ESTATE, by the Borough of St Pancras, fills the rest of the area. *Nash*'s plan had provided for a canal basin with landing docks leading s from the Regent's Canal, and three market squares: for hay and straw, meat, and vegetables, linked by the N–S axis of Osnaburgh Street. Cumberland Market was the northernmost, opened as a haymarket in 1830, to replace the market off Piccadilly. The two southern markets were not built as planned, but as modest residential squares: Munster Square and Clarence Gardens (1823–4). They were badly damaged in the Second World War. The various phases of rebuilding reflect changing post-war fashions in both planning and architectural detail. It is a muddled story; no overall plan was followed, although several were prepared. The first, by St Pancras in 1946, proposed a uniform lay-out of five- and ten-storey flats, which was rejected by the LCC; a later master plan was by *Sir Frederick Gibberd*, who also built some of the first flats, and there was another by the LCC in 1952.

The first phase, NE of Cumberland Market and adjoining the Crown Commissioners' pre-war rebuilding (*see* above), was begun in 1951. Eight-storey L-shaped blocks E of AUGUSTUS ROAD, with chequerboard fronts in the manner of Tecton, by *Gibberd*; six-storey blocks to the w, with blue tiles in Festival of Britain style, by the Borough Architect *T. Sibthorpe*, 1953. (These were originally planned with nine storeys, typical of the borough's eagerness for maximum density.) Phase 2, s of Cumberland Market, by *Davies & Arnold*, 1952–3, reflects the new principles of mixed development developed by the LCC at this time; there are both low houses and a row of eleven-storey blocks of flats, the highest in London when built. Their lift-tops are neatly concealed, a new achievement at the time. Plainly detailed apart from playful windows in the end walls. By the same firm the E part of ROBERT STREET and the VICTORY pub in Albany Street (1959). s of Robert Street is a quite different lay-out, precincts of low buildings proposed by *Armstrong & MacManus* in 1955 and accepted by the LCC in preference to their own plan. Built in 1957–9. Past a little shopping precinct with branch library one enters CLARENCE GARDENS, surrounded by four-storey maisonettes of light purple brick with white-painted window frames. For practical reasons access balconies appear on some sides but not on others, a marriage of modern planning with the tradition of the London square (cf. other contemporary London schemes such as the later parts of the Brandon Estate, Southwark). However, two eighteen- and nineteen-storey towers had to be added in order to bring the density up to the required 200 p.p.a. The estate ends with MUNSTER SQUARE and St Mary Magdalene (q.v.). In LONGFORD STREET, the former ST MARY MAGDALENE SCHOOL, an Arts and Crafts building of 1901, facing the back of the Euston Centre (*see* Perambulation 1, above). Rebuilding here destroyed *Butterfield*'s St Saviour's Hospital of 1850–2, an Anglican religious house established by Dr Pusey in what was then an area of slum housing.*

---

* The late C17 woodwork from Buxheim, South Germany, was moved to the hospital's new chapel at Seabrook Road, Hythe, Kent.

## 3. Camden Town

The development of Camden Town dates from the Act of 1788 which
allowed Charles Pratt, Earl of Camden, to lay out streets on his
property, to the E of what is now Camden High Street. *George Dance
Jun.* prepared an ambitious Neoclassical plan *c.* 1790, composed of a
linked crescent and oval, with a still larger circus to the NE. The
diagonal line of the new Camden Road leading to Tottenham
appears on this plan, but around it a simpler grid plan of streets was
laid out instead. The area W of Camden High Street, part of Lord
Southampton's estate, began to be developed in the early C19, but
its progress was disrupted by the cutting of the railway line to
Euston in the 1830s. The unassuming early C19 terraces of Camden
Town were not fashionable, and by the later C19 the district had an
aura of impoverished gentility (*see* George Gissing's *New Grub Street*),
with pockets of industry and services near the canal and railway
lines. Piano making was a speciality.

Further social decline followed, as expanding industry decreased
the appeal of the residential parts. Some areas were entirely rebuilt
after the Second World War, but, especially in the parts towards
Regents Park, older terraces returned to respectability as gentrification took over. From the 1960s Camden Town became particularly
popular for architects' offices and homes. They are thicker on the
ground here than anywhere else in England, squeezed, often with
great ingenuity, into inexpensive plots along mews and back lanes
behind the larger houses. Some of the earliest are around Camden
Square, but they are now ubiquitous and have spread to Kentish
Town as well. The high standard which they set for sensitive small-
scale infilling was followed by a variety of low-rent housing developments in the 1980s, making this a rewarding area for architecture of
the last thirty years of the C20.

The fabric of the centre of Camden Town is still essentially C19,
lively and scruffy, a mixture of shabby terraces and robust industrial,
canal and railway survivals, with the Camden Lock markets, over-
flowing with C20 youth, dominating the N end.

### 3a. Camden High Street and the area to its west

CAMDEN HIGH STREET starts with the statue of Cobden by *W. &
T. Wills*, 1863, and the CAMDEN PALACE (built as the ROYAL
CAMDEN THEATRE), 1900–1 by *W. G. R. Sprague.* A perky frontage with paired Ionic columns, sharply curved broken pediments
and odd observatory-like copper dome (its lantern has gone).
Interior altered but still impressive. Elaborate plasterwork by
*Waring & Gillow*; two cantilevered galleries, the boxes at the side
divided by giant columns. Originally it seated 3,000. The rest of
the High Street has been overtaken by the usual suburban shopping miscellany, with some early terraces visible at the S end
above shops, and a few more emphatic pubs, e.g., on the W side,
the former SOUTHAMPTON ARMS, with two tiers of pilasters.
The busy crossroads with Camden Road is marked by the former
MOTHER REDCAP (now WORLD'S END), 1875 by *H. H.
Bridgman.*

*West of Camden High Street, from south to north*

MORNINGTON CRESCENT, on Southampton Estate land at the N end of Hampstead Road, dates from 1821–32, a curved terrace with pretty balconies and doorcases with inset fluted columns, unhappily overshadowed by the bulk of the 550-ft-long former tobacco factory filling the garden in front sold off by the borough council. The factory was built for the tobacco giant CARRERAS in 1926 by *M. E. & O. H. Collins* with *A. G. Porri*. It was equipped with progressive machinery and air-conditioning and given one of the most extravagant Art Deco exteriors in London, said to be inspired by the Egyptian temple to the cat-goddess at Bubastis: a giant order with showy Egyptian detail along the long frontage, a solar disc to the sun-god Ra, and two gigantic bronze cats flanking the entrance. The detail was stripped off in 1961 when the building was unimaginatively converted to offices, but restored in colourful spendour in 1998–9. To the W, MORNINGTON TERRACE and MORNINGTON PLACE are cut short by the widened Euston railway line. ARLINGTON ROAD leads N, with complete stucco-trimmed terraces on its W side. On the E side, indifferent council flats, then No. 88, tactfully scaled rebuilding by *Phippen Randall & Parkes*, 1996. Beyond Delancey Street, No. 104, a former tramways electricity substation, 1908 by the *LCC*; perhaps by *Vincent Harris* (cf. his tramway generating station at Islington: Perambulation 1a). A serious classical front, with channelled brick ground floor and pediment. In DELANCEY STREET, more early C19 terraces and DELANCEY STUDIOS, a tiny balconied group around a court-yard, by *Camden Architect's Department*, 1981. Parallel to Arlington Road, ALBERT STREET, broad and handsome, with brick and stucco terraces on both sides, 1844–8, built by the surveyor *George Bassett*. Nos. 124–126 are restrained 1970s offices by *Richard Sheppard Robson & Partners*, the windows lined up with its C19 neighbours; recessed entrance and top floor.

PARKWAY, a shopping street leading uphill towards Regents Park, starts with late Victorian terraces, interrupted on the N side by a former Gaumont CINEMA of 1935 by *W. E. Trent*. Most of the interior detail was removed in the 1960s. Reopened in 1997 as a multiscreen cinema. The notable feature is the dramatic pantiled roofslope to the ARLINGTON ROAD flank, in place of the more usual blank bulk of most cinema rear quarters. Opposite this, Nos. 201–209, neat brick terraces for two housing associations, by *Jestico & Whiles*, 1993–5, with a rhythm of paired doors and window each divided by a column. Opposite is ROWTON HOUSE, 1905 by *H. B. Measures*, one of the men's lodging houses built by Lord Rowton, still functioning. The tall red brick bulk is given character by turreted corners. Refurbished by *Levitt Bernstein Associates* (*Nicholas Wood* and *David Bernstein*), 1983–8, and cheered up by bold art work inside.

Back in Parkway, through an archway on the S side, No. 77, *Sheppard Robson*'s own offices, C19 industrial buildings grouped around a small irregular courtyard, ingeniously transformed 1973–6, an early example of this type of rehabilitation. A glass bridge was added over the entrance to the courtyard, a large glazed porch opposite; the smooth expanses of glass are echoed by the single panes inserted in the big industrial windows, in discreetly recessed teak frames. Next door the offices of *Hunt Thompson Associates*, a conversion of 1987–8, handled in a different way: a warehouse with original windows retained, and a low addition with a show of colourful ironwork. At the top of Parkway, the flamboyant mood of the 1980s is demonstrated by DESIGN HOUSE; the sleek offices curving round the corner are a former Henly's garage of the 1930s, transformed with blue trimmed glazing by *Troughton McAslan* in 1983.

N AND NW OF PARKWAY. This district was developed only after part of the Southampton Estate was sold off in 1840, and suffered from the intrusion of the Euston line, which prevented completion of the intended grand lay-out with two crescents. The optimistically named OVAL ROAD runs beside the railway line and starts with a distinctive insertion: Nos. 1a–e by *Ted Levy, Benjamin & Partners*, 1963, a staggered group with large partly segment-headed first-floor windows. Beyond this, paired stucco-trimmed villas, facing the long even stretch of REGENTS PARK TERRACE of 1845–6. To the r., GLOUCESTER CRESCENT, the most ambitious part, *c.* 1845–50; big Italianate terraces in the form of linked villas with rather disorganized elevations and a variety of embellishments: towers, massive eaves brackets (No. 5), shared pediment (Nos. 13–14). Further N, towards the canal, the area goes industrial. At the N corner, a striking polygonal building of five storeys, built in 1852 as Collard & Collard's piano factory, one of Camden Town's prime C19 industries. The pianos were hoisted down a central well (now divided off, although the ring of iron columns remains), so that different parts of the manufacture could be carried out on each floor. The windows of the two top floors were replaced after a fire in the 1970s. At the corner of JAMESTOWN ROAD, offices built for Gilbeys, the wine merchants, by *Serge Chermayeff*; remarkably good modern of 1937. Well preserved apart from the loss of its lively lettering at the corner. One front slightly broken so as to appear curved, the other provided with an angular bay window projecting above the main entrance. The building is of reinforced concrete, and was remarkable at the time for its careful insulation, with cork foundations, double glazing and air-conditioning. Ground floor faced with grey tiles, plain rendered walls above, all windows teak-framed. Adjoining in Oval Road is a less distinctive extension of 1960, also by *Chermayeff*. To the N, the Regent's Canal and buildings of the former Camden Goods Yard (*see* p. 365). Round the corner in JAMESTOWN ROAD, the big C19 warehouse with channelled stucco was built as Gilbey's bottling works, 1894 by *William Hucks*, a very early example of a reinforced concrete structure.\* Further E, JS PATHOLOGY LABORATORY, 1989–91 by *Hutchinson & Partners*; ground floor recessed behind columns, a dramatic staircase through the centre of the building. Radical rebuilding for the stretch down to the High Street planned in 1998: hotels and offices by *CZWG* at SUFFOLK WHARF. This opens onto the towpath s of the canal with its BRIDGE and attractive battlemented early C19 LOCK-KEEPER'S COTTAGE.

Back to CAMDEN HIGH STREET, lined with scruffy early C19

---

\* At No. 34 Jamestown Road, by the canal, an underground ICE HOUSE of *c.* 1839. 100 ft deep and 34 ft in diameter, one of the largest ever built.

terraces above the crowded shops which have become an overspill from the market at Camden Lock. N of the canal a large area of former railway land with the ROUND HOUSE (*see* p. 366), and some forcefully profiled recording studios by *R. Seifert & Partners*, 1975.

### Between the railway and Regents Park

To the SW of the Euston railway line a smart and sedate residential area can be approached by a bridge over the railway at Chalk Farm. It is ringed by REGENTS PARK ROAD, and has uneventful stuccoed terraces lining the streets between GLOUCESTER AVENUE and Primrose Hill. CHALCOT SQUARE is the centre, built in the late 1850s, three sides with crowded stucco façades. Off its W corner, CHALCOT CRESCENT, with houses of varied sizes round a tiny double bend; a quite complicated rhythm of window pediments to the façades at the W end. E of Chalcot Square, FITZROY ROAD, a broad thoroughfare whose terraces are interrupted by a bold brick former piano factory of Messrs HOPKINSON (No. 44), 1867 by *J. T. Christopher*, five storeys with a big gable.* A radical conversion to flats took place in 1975–80 (*Peter Clapp* and *Adrian Pettit* of Camden Architect's Department), after demolition for a new housing scheme had been refused. The flank wall was opened up, with balconies set behind some of the original window openings, overlooking careful hard landscaping and hopeful pergolas and a Community Centre in HOPKINSON PLACE. In the mews on the other side of Fitzroy Road, the PRIMROSE HILL STUDIOS, developed before 1882 by the builder *Alfred Healey*, quite progressive, with red brick trim, and half-hipped roofs with studio lights. Just to the S in KINGSTOWN STREET, a small house by *Stout & Lichfield* at the back of a garden to Regents Park Road: a neat group of monopitch roofs over four rectangular spaces of varied sizes and levels.

On the fringe of this area, on the Crown Land adjoining Regents Park, PRINCE ALBERT ROAD has a row of grand stuccoed villas of *c.* 1842, elegantly varied in their design. No. 15, by the canal, has a corner tower, Nos. 8 and 9 and 12–13 have pilasters; Nos. 10–11 columns *in antis*. In REGAL LANE, the service lane behind, a house by *John Winter* for himself, 1959–61, top floor rebuilt 1979, refurbished and extended by *Winter*, 1995–7. Nos. 7 and 9 also by *Winter*, 1962–3.

CECIL SHARP HOUSE, at the junction of Regents Park Road and Gloucester Avenue, 1929 by *H. M. Fletcher* for the English Folk Song Society (repaired and rebuilt in 1951 by *Stillman & Eastwick-Field* after war damage). Quiet well-detailed Neo-Georgian. In the main hall, big MURAL by *Ivon Hitchens*, 1951–4; abstract swirls with folksy motifs. Nearby two pieces of infilling worth study. In REGENTS PARK ROAD No. 10 is by *Ernö Goldfinger*, 1953: a well-handled, rational five-storey elevation with exposed concrete frame and red brick panels, shuttered concrete columns on the ground floor; projecting balconies above. In GLOUCESTER AVENUE the stucco sequence is broken by Nos. 37–41, four storeys of flats above open garages, by *James Stirling*, 1963–4; bands of harsh red

---

* Off Chalcot Road, in Utopia Village another former piano factory (Messrs Spencer) around a yard. Big windows with rubbed brick heads of *c.* 1900.

Accrington brick, the material Stirling used for his contemporary
Engineering buildings at Leicester.

### 3b. East of Camden High Street

Starting at the s end, one terrace of HARRINGTON SQUARE and the
N side of OAKLEY SQUARE remain from what was first known as
Bedford New Town, stucco-trimmed terraces developed from
1834 on the Duke of Bedford's small Figs Mead Estate. Arched
first-floor windows in stucco panels with paterae are the distinctive feature. The s side of Oakley Square and the whole of Ampthill
Square were replaced by St Pancras's indifferent AMPTHILL
SQUARE ESTATE, by *Eric Lyons & Partners*, mixed development
with three clumsy tower blocks of *c.* 1960, reclad in 1988 with
trimmings in primary colours, and E of EVERSHOLT STREET, a
dense cluster of brown brick maisonettes, *c.* 1965, mostly of four
storeys, with a pedestrian spine leading through grassed courtyards
and car parking tucked away beneath. On the N side of Oakley
Square, a former vicarage, boldly Gothic in polychrome brick,
*c.* 1861 by *John Johnson*, built for St Matthew's Church, which
stood next door. At the corner with CROWNDALE ROAD a low
stucco LODGE to the square remains, opposite the Working Men's
College (*see* p. 356). Further E in Crowndale Road, No. 26 is the
former Old St Pancras Church House, a mission house and hall of
1896–7 by *C. R. Baker King*. Baroque doorway with figure of St
Pancras by *Hems*.

Off Camden High Street some humble terraces remain from Lord
Camden's development of the 1790s onwards, amid later industry
and council rebuilding. In PRATT STREET, some battered survivals
near the High Street (No. 6 with eccentric Gothick doorway) and
Nos. 82–86, with nice Gothick glazing. Others on the w side of
BAYHAM STREET. The E side has two large council schemes,
each characteristic of their era. WESTERHAM of 1955–61 is a tall
range with canted wings, the old-fashioned symmetry of its
frontage relieved by lightweight balconies and Festival-of-Britain
coloured tiles. Camden's CURNOCK STREET ESTATE, *c.* 1967–70
by *Boissevain & Osmond*, offers an alternative to high-rise in the form
of trim three- and four-storey blocks in yellow brick, approached
along pavements raised above a podium of well-concealed garages.
Behind this urban face are hidden surprisingly generous planted
enclosed squares and playgrounds.

Further N in Bayham Street, modest stock brick ALMSHOUSES of St
Martin-in-the-Fields, 1818 by *H. H. Seward*, with additions of 1881
and more houses of the 1820s. GREENLAND STREET HALL, carefully detailed late C19 Gothic, with tile-hanging, is probably by
*Bodley & Garner*, architects of St Michael's Church (q.v.). More
coherent terraces of the early to mid C19 in the streets to the E:
GREENLAND ROAD, CAMDEN STREET and in CAROL STREET,
where the southern terrace has been ingeniously rehabilitated with
substantial C20 back extensions, visible from the public gardens
behind. The gardens were laid out in 1889 in the former ST
PANCRAS BURIAL GROUND, for long a sad and neglected space
with tombstones lining the walls and a few battered MONUMENTS.
A two-tier Gothic sarcophagus to the Woodburn family, a lesser

one to the Moore family, and a large Celtic cross to Charles
Dibdin, erected 1880, are the chief survivals. Refurbishment with
lottery money planned 1998.

To the N, by way of GEORGIANA STREET, past more of the mid
C19, one reaches LYME STREET, where there is a curiosity: on the
W side a formal composition consisting of a piano factory (built
*c.* 1852–5), with four-storey pedimented centre and lower wings,
flanked by slightly earlier houses (built by 1849). These are three-
storeyed grey brick pairs with arched windows, a conscious contrast to the small semi-detached stuccoed villas opposite.

## *Around Camden Road and the canal*

CAMDEN ROAD, a new route running NE towards Tottenham, was
laid out in the 1820s and soon flanked by the usual progression of
terraces and villas, now much interrupted by later rebuilding. W of
Camden Street, Nos. 18–60, a long terrace from the first phase,
with pretty balconies and some original doors and railings. The
road is crossed by the canal which runs E from Camden Lock
towards Camden Road, before it turns S towards King's Cross,
attracting industry along its banks. Derelict sites have provided
the opportunity for several late C20 developments.

SAINSBURY'S, between Camden Road and Kentish Town Road,
occupies the site of the Aerated Bread Company factory of 1915–38.
1985–8 by *Nicholas Grimshaw*. Not a cosy building, all grey like an
aircraft hangar, and revelling in its dour engineering image.
Grimshaw's first supermarket, and one of the first to demonstrate
that such a building can have not only architectural quality but an
urban form. Camden demanded maximum use of the site, with
new housing and industry as well as the shop. A wasteful sea of
car parking was avoided by the invention of ingenious shopping
trolleys which slot into moving ramps leading to an underground
car park. The entrance to this is from Kentish Town Road, beneath
a long utilitarian range of workshops. Camden Road has a tall
frontage with a forbidding upper expanse of plant and staff rooms
behind ribbed cladding. The recessed vertical members form part
of the tensile structure supporting the big curved roof of the deep-
plan column-free shopping floor. The roof profile is visible on the
flank elevation to the N, although, disappointingly, it is masked
inside by a standard Sainsbury's interior. At the back of the site,
overlooking the canal, some futuristic space-capsule flats have 128
been fitted in; convex aluminium walls, with tall windows recessed
in between.

At the junction of Kentish Town Road and HAWLEY CRESCENT,
the ELEPHANT HOUSE, a decent red brick former brewery backing into the canal, dated 1900; centrepiece with some terracotta
decoration. Further on, the former TVAM STUDIOS, by *Terry
Farrell*, 1981–2, a brash and jokey piece of advertising for breakfast
television created from a disused Henly's garage. Along the curving
street a windowless curving wall clad in ribbed aluminium enlivened
by coloured stripes and bold lettering in relief (now covered up).
The forecourt is entered by an openwork archway with skeletal
keystone. On the canal side the jagged skyline of the industrial
wall remains, topped with giant eggcups.

For the area N of here, *see* Kentish Town Perambulation 4b, p. 396.

*South of Camden Road*

By the canal, LYME TERRACE, a little stuccoed group, curves attractively along a raised walk above the towpath. It leads into Royal College Street. Opposite is BRUGES PLACE, overlooking the canal, workshops with flats above, in a lively Postmodern combination of materials; concrete columns, striped brick, coloured window frames, with a gabled roof-line; 1987–9 by *Jestico & Whiles*. Back towards Camden Road, ROUSDEN STREET, with the GREENWOOD ALMSHOUSES, 1840, built as twelve dwellings in a terrace of four three-storey stucco houses, windows with Tudor dripmoulds. Refurbished after long neglect as six sheltered flats by *Peter Mishcon & Partners*, 1984–6, with lift and stair-tower added behind. On the w side of ST PANCRAS WAY, another nice curving terrace, with balconies and railings.

ST PANCRAS WAY ESTATE, at the corner of Camden Road, crisply designed council flats by *Norman & Dawbarn* for the Borough of St Pancras, 1946–8, were the borough's first post-war flats to be opened, amid much publicity. Both the lay-out, in rows instead of around courtyards, and the straightforward modern design were innovations of more than local interest. Six-storeyed and steel-framed, faced in yellow brick. The patterned balcony walls replaced plain glass in a refurbishment of the 1980s. Further on, the houses lining Camden Road are detached or semi-detached villas: at first the lowly early C19 type. The most coherent group are Nos. 142–170. No. 152 is a replacement by *Andrews Sherlock & Partners*, 1991, extending with tactfully lower buildings to the mews behind. Further on (No. 208 onward) villas of the 1850s–60s, taller, less practical, and less well preserved.

*Around Camden Square*

Mid-C19 streets to the SE start with ROCHESTER SQUARE. Its centre has been built over; stucco-trimmed terraces and villas to N and S. CAMDEN SQUARE to its N is much larger: too large to be coherent. It was developed slowly; a map of 1849 shows the square with St Paul's Church in the centre, three houses on the N side, three on the S. In 1860 there were still no houses E of the church, but all was built up by 1871. The SW corner house is grandest, with Corinthian pilasters. The later E end of the square and its continuations, NORTH and SOUTH VILLAS, reject urbane Italianate detail in favour of plainer, rather gaunt brickwork with arched windows and projecting eaves. The pattern continues N beyond Camden Park Road, into CLIFF ROAD, where industry intrudes in the form of a huge red brick repository. Opposite are the CLIFF ROAD STUDIOS, a piece of early modern revivalism, with rendered walls and glass brick windows, 1968 and 1972 by *Georgie Wolton*. The earlier N block has double-height studios facing the garden, the S studios are single-storeyed, with living accommodation behind.

Two long service lanes lie behind Camden Square, CAMDEN MEWS to the NW, the shorter MURRAY MEWS to the SE, curtailed after the success of the Camden Square development had been compromised by smoke from the Midland Railway tunnel vents. Only a few mews buildings were built to serve the grand houses of the square; other plots remained empty until recommended planning densities were raised after the Second World War. The small innovative houses which began to appear in the 1960s, mostly by architects for themselves, now have to be picked out among the less interesting gentrification that followed.

In CAMDEN MEWS an icon of its time was No. 62, by *Edward Cullinan*, built by and for himself from 1962 to 1965, a low-key, inexpensive family house squeezed onto a tiny site. Homespun use of simple materials: concrete piers, reused stock brick, and tough dark timbers, layered to interesting effect on the long s side. The living area on the first floor opens onto a raised garden on the adjoining garage roof, a courtyard in the air (although too overlooked to be ideal). The sideways lay-out with frontage onto the street (in defiance of planning recommendations then in force) was devised to take advantage of the view over an adjacent plot. For later houses, the principle of street frontages was accepted. No. 66 Camden Square, at the corner of Camden Mews, is a larger house, with delicate timberwork rising from behind a brick base formed from the former garden wall. By *Peter Bell & Partners*, designed 1980, built 1984–5. The main house is square, with toplit centre staircase; L-shaped service ranges around a small garden. Just to the N, No. 16 MURRAY STREET, a tiny one-storey house built for a disabled person, by *Edward Cullinan*, 1983. Further s, No. 2 CAMDEN MEWS, another house for the disabled, created from the ground floor of the corner house, with large living room in a one-storey brick extension behind, by *Tom Kay*, 1988–9.

In MURRAY MEWS the trendsetter was No. 20, of 1965–9, by and for *Richard Gibson*. Reticent L-shaped front in rough stock brick behind tall matching garden walls, a clever concession to the planning requirement for a set-back, while maintaining the urban character of the mews. Part of the courtyard glazed later. An impressive interior, with light penetrating to all parts from a toplit full-height central living area. Large open-plan galleried living room at first-floor level. Next door, No. 22 by *Tom Kay*, planned in 1967, built after a planning appeal in 1970–1. The stock brick matches the Gibson house so that the two read as one composition, with a strong pattern of layered planes created by the diagonal of the external stair up to a recessed first floor. Excellently planned inside, with a spacious L-shaped first-floor living area beneath a sloping roof with clerestory lighting, and a roof terrace. No. 30 is by and for *Jeff Kahane*, 1992, brick with a projecting circular concrete porch roof, and a central toplit staircase. At the NE end of the mews, among a clutch of tasteful stock brick or rendered walls, No. 43 by *John Townsend*, 1974–5, set back behind a tall garden wall. On the garden side a galleried living area with dramatic sloping glazed roof reaching nearly to the ground. At the other end of the mews, after No. 21, an original mews house, two storeys with gables, Nos. 15–19, of 1964–5 by *Team 4* (i.e. the early partnership including *Foster* and *Rogers*); a stark windowless red brick wall to the mews, the two floors behind toplit by a sloping glazed roof. Each house has a different plan. Opposite, a later arrival, No. 12, 1988 by *Sean Madigan* and *Stephen Donald*, displays the return to formality, a busy symmetrical front with square openings.

*Around the King's Cross railway lands*

AGAR GROVE, running E–W, marks the divide between the neighbourhood of Camden Square and the area to the S, where C20
council housing eats into the fringes of the vast railway lands
stretching towards the main termini. Among the Victorian villas of
Agar Grove, Nos. 9–11, housing association flats by *Levitt Bernstein*,
of the 1980s, a neat composition of six brick-faced flats on three
receding storeys, contained by rendered and channelled flank
walls which echo their older neighbours. To the N, in COBHAM
MEWS, an ingenious development by *David Chipperfield Architects*,
1990. A pair of two-storey studio offices with a forceful shared
formal entrance, each with an extension expanding into the limited
space available. Inside, a sophisticated late-modern-movement
mixture of austere low-cost concrete surfaces, white walls and
well-detailed joinery, reminiscent of the Japanese architect Tadao
Ando. Clever lighting: a hidden rear clerestory, circular roof-
lights, glass bricks in the long wedge-shaped studio.

Off ST PAUL'S CRESCENT to the S, two strikingly different develop-
127   ments. First ST PAUL'S MEWS by *CZWG*, 1987–91, select town
houses in a long double-curving sweep, with the panache typical
of this firm. Behind entrance gates, a single gatehouse-like block
echoes the terrace's shallow curved end gable. Dark green timber
ground floors with garage doors, brick above, at the ends whimsically intermixed with render.

MAIDEN LANE further S was one of the last of *Camden*'s grand
schemes, planned from 1973. Phase one, the W part, by *Gordon
Benson* and *Alan Forsyth*, was begun in 1976; phase two, running
up to York Way, was added in 1978–83. Like their housing at
Branch Hill, Hampstead (*see* Hampstead, p. 230), it owes much
to the influence of the crisp white stepped terraces by Atelier 5 at
Halen, Switzerland; there are reminiscences also of the Benson
and Forsyth terraces in Gospel Oak (*see* Perambulation 4b, p. 398).
But this is a much larger estate, and demonstrates only too clearly
that a predominantly low-rise form was not enough to guarantee
success. The ruthlessly diagrammatic grid of W-facing terraces
steps up above garages, with living rooms on the upper floors to
take advantage of the views towards central London. The height
varies from two to six storeys, with nine different types of dwelling;
but the general effect is of a chilly uniformity. The materials are
austere, white walls and stained timber. But there is not enough of
a hill to provide drama, and the narrow passages and pedestrian
open spaces which weave through the terraces are claustrophobic
rather than intimate.

ELM VILLAGE, between Camley Street and St Pancras Way,
provides an antidote: a deliberate return to traditional forms. The
name comes from a house built by William Agar *c.* 1810; on his
estate Agar Town rose in the 1840s, to be swept away in the 1860s
for the GNR marshalling yard. Instead of the council housing
proposed by Camden in the 1970s, a mixture of low-rental and
low-cost housing for sale was built, 1984–5 by *Peter Mishcon &
Associates*. Mostly of only two storeys. Short terraces and a crescent,
attractively grouped around ROSSENDALE ROAD, with plenty of
private space and variety of detail aimed to appeal to the owner-

occupier. The homely charm recalls the Duchy of Cornwall's Edwardian housing in Kennington, although the planning here is less formal. The brick and rendered surfaces are deceptive; the houses are timber-framed, to allow for speedy construction.

For the area further s, *see* Perambulation I.

## 4. Kentish Town

Kentish Town has a much older origin than Camden Town. The settlement which developed along the road towards Highgate had a medieval chapel, rebuilt in 1449. In the c18 it was a village 'where people take furnished lodgings for the summer, especially those afflicted with consumption' (Thornton, 1780). By 1800, as Milne's map shows, long ribbons of houses stretched N and S from the centre at the junction of Kentish Town Road and what is now Fortess Road. Traces of this early history can still be seen in parts of Kentish Town Road and in the back lanes of cottages behind the E side of Highgate Road. Development of the fields beyond took place from the 1840s; fifty years later the area was entirely built up. The c20 fate of the eastern and western areas has been very different. W of Kentish Town Road the arrival of the Midland Railway undermined the aspirations of the developers. Much of the area became working-class, was overcrowded by the early c20, and was extensively rebuilt in a long-drawn-out process from the 1930s to the 1980s. The occasional ragstone church, some stucco-trimmed terraces and a clutch of pretty cottages at Gospel Oak survive among a succession of ill-related public housing schemes, begun by the Borough of St Pancras and continued by Camden with many changes of plan. To the E the principal landowners – St Bartholomew's Hospital, Christ Church, Oxford, and St John's College, Cambridge – all developed their property from *c.* 1850, and the solid middle-class streets here are still stamped with the character imposed by their Victorian builders, leavened here and there by individual architects' houses, which began to appear from the 1960s.

### 4a. Kentish Town Road and its surroundings, starting at the south end

KENTISH TOWN ROAD branches N from the main crossroads at Camden Town. Industrial and commercial buildings cluster near the transport links of canal and railway (*see* Perambulation 3: Camden Town); further N, among the straggle of small shops stretching all the way to Kentish Town Station, one can still spot relics of the older domestic ribbon development depicted in J.F. King's earlier c19 'Kentish Town panorama'.*

By Hawley Road, a few battered early c19 stuccoed villas, the first pair gabled with Gothic and Tudor detail. On the E side the corner of JEFFREY'S STREET has a demure stuccoed group with pediment (partly rebuilt 1971–2), and a brick and stucco terrace (Nos. 57–63). Tall late c19 tenements follow at the corner with Royal College Street where road widening took place in 1877–86. Also, on the E side, a large factory (DUNN'S: the ground floor has nicely detailed 1930s windows with stained glass). On the W

---

* See *The Kentish Town Panorama*, London Topographical Society, 1986.

side post-war rebuilding has destroyed all coherence; one could hardly guess that until the C19 all this area was occupied by the pleasure grounds of the Castle Inn, alongside the Fleet River running S from Parliament Hill. KELLY STREET is the only Victorian street which was allowed to remain. Terraces of *c.* 1850, only two-storeyed, but surprisingly elaborate, with arched first-floor windows in uncommonly debased Italianate. To the W, in ANGLERS LANE, the former false-teeth factory of Claudius Ash, 1864, polychromatic. In HOLMES ROAD, Nos. 41–45, a former workhouse, *c.* 1900 in functional municipal style.

The centre of the E side of Kentish Town Road was rebuilt in the later C19 as shopping parades serving the new streets behind. The striped brick in reducing widths of the 1860s ABBEY TAVERN at the corner of Bartholomew Road provides some jollity; CAVERSHAM ROAD, the central road of the Christ Church Estate, is distinguished by elegantly canted corners with vermiculated quoins. Further on, miscellaneous early properties were replaced by post-war rebuilding of shops, library and flats, but the W side to the N of Prince of Wales Road still has a medley of narrow frontages with little alleys in between, reflecting the early date when this part of the street was built up. Nos. 325–347 are a long, even C18 terrace of some grandeur, visible above later shops.

At the junction of Kentish Town Road and Fortess Road, the centre of the old village, small-scale relics jostle against late C19 suburban rebuilding. In a prominent position facing S, No. 1a LEVERTON PLACE, a modest three-bay C18 front visible above a transparent shopfront of 1988–9 by *Jestico & Whiles*. To its S, Nos. 298–302 Kentish Town Road was the former Victorian Police Station (bold brick quoins and window surrounds). Next door is the ASSEMBLY HOUSE, in the C18 a rural place of resort for Londoners, but in its present form a lavish effort of 1898 by *Thorpe & Furniss*, with robust corner turret, elaborate ironwork, and well-preserved interiors full of etched glass and mahogany. The iron and glass ridge-and-furrow canopy erected in 1983 on the railway bridge opposite came from Elstree Station.

LEIGHTON ROAD, an old thoroughfare running E, starts with haphazard early C19 development: Nos. 20–22 with shared gable, No. 26 with Greek Doric porch, and more humble cottages from No. 36. No. 30 is a lively Edwardian former SORTING OFFICE of 1903. N of Leighton Road modest streets of stuccoed houses began to be laid out at the same time: LEVERTON STREET (somewhat over-gentrified) has terrace houses only one window wide; FALKLAND PLACE is a back lane whose cottages now enjoy a late C20 landscaped setting.

FORTESS ROAD, widened at the S end in 1891–5, has a late C19 POST OFFICE with shaped gable and pretty mosaic panels. Behind is FORTESS GROVE, an appealing small close of two-storey stuccoed houses, occupying the site of a reputed manor house. Taller respectable terraces of *c.* 1825 climb uphill: Nos. 44–94, three groups with channelled-stucco ground floors and unusual lyre-patterned balconies. Nos. 96 and 98 are a larger stuccoed pair with side entrances. Back now by FORTESS WALK to where Kentish Town Road branches E to become HIGHGATE ROAD. First the BULL AND GATE, rebuilt in 1871, with marble

1. Camden, St Pancras, Kenwood, remodelled by James and Robert Adam, 1766–74, from the south
2. Camden, St Pancras, gasholders, Goods Way, 1880s, and left, Midland Railway water point, 1867

3. Camden, Holborn, Bedford Square, 1775–86, from the south
4. Enfield, Gentleman's Row, eighteenth century and earlier, from the south
5. Haringey, Hornsey, Crouch End, Topsfield Parade, and Clock Tower by F.G. Knight, 1895
6. Enfield, Southgate, Meadway and Bourne Avenue, 1930s
7. Camden, Holborn, Brunswick Centre, designed from 1959 by Patrick Hodgkinson with Sir Leslie Martin, built 1968–72

| 3 | 5 |
| 4 | 6 |
|   | 7 |

8. Islington, Finsbury, St John's Priory, crypt, twelfth century
9. Barnet, Hendon, St Mary, font, twelfth century
10. Enfield, Edmonton, All Saints, twelfth-century fragments
11. Camden, Holborn, St Etheldreda (R.C.), former chapel of the Bishop of Ely, *c.* 1290
12. Barnet, Monken Hadley, St Mary, west tower, 1494

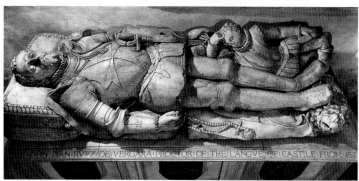

13. Enfield, fireplace, with sixteenth-century royal arms, now in No. 5 Gentleman's Row
14. Islington, Finsbury, St John's Priory, crypt, monument, probably to Juan Ruiz de Vergara of Castile, attributed to Esteban Jordan, late sixteenth century
15. Camden, Holborn, Lincoln's Inn, Old Hall, 1489–92, extended south, by John Symons, 1583. Screen by Robert Lynton, 1624
16. Islington, Finsbury, The Charterhouse, Great Hall, fireplace by Edmund Kinsman, 1614
17. Islington, Finsbury, The Charterhouse, Great Hall, gallery, early seventeenth century

<table>
<tr><td>13</td><td></td><td>15</td><td></td></tr>
<tr><td>14</td><td></td><td>16</td><td>17</td></tr>
</table>

18. Haringey, Tottenham, The Priory, ceiling, 1620
19. Enfield, Forty Hall, *c.*1629, hall screen and ceiling
20. Enfield, St Andrew, monument to Sir Nicholas Raynton of Forty
    Hall †1646

21. Enfield, Edmonton, Salisbury House, sixteenth century, from the north
22. Barnet, Hendon, Church Farm House, seventeenth century
23. Barnet, Friern Barnet, Lawrence Campe Almshouses, c. 1612
24. Haringey, Tottenham, Bruce Castle, south front, sixteenth century, remodelled 1684, with eighteenth-century east wing

25. Enfield, Forty Hall, *c.* 1629, from the south-east
26. Camden, St Pancras, Cromwell House, Highgate, 1637–8
27. Camden, Holborn, Lindsey House, Lincoln's Inn Fields, west side, 1639–41
28. Islington, Newington Green, west side, 1658

25 | 27
26 | 28

29. Camden, St Pancras, Nos. 1 and 2 The Grove, Highgate, *c.* 1688
30. Camden, Hampstead, Fenton House, *c.* 1693, from the south
31. Camden, Holborn, Great Ormond Street, north side, late
    seventeenth to early eighteenth century
32. Hackney, Shoreditch, Geffrye Almshouses (now museum), chapel,
    probably by Robert Burford, 1712–14

29 | 31
30 | 32

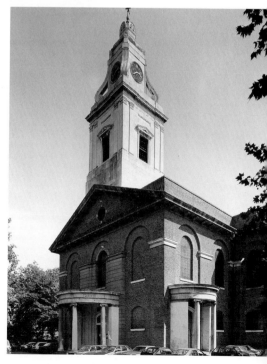

33. Camden, Holborn,
    St George, by
    Nicholas Hawksmoor,
    1716–31, from the
    south
34. Hackney, Shoreditch,
    St Leonard, by
    George Dance Sen.,
    1736–40, from the
    north-west
35. Camden, Holborn,
    St Giles-in-the-
    Fields, by Henry
    Flitcroft, 1731–3,
    from the south-east
36. Hackney, St John,
    by James Spiller,
    1791–4, tower
    1810–14

37. Camden, Holborn, No. 11 Bedford Row, stairhall with painting by
    John Vanderbank, *c.* 1720
38. Islington, Finsbury, New River Head, Oak Room, *c.* 1696–7, detail of
    panelling
39. Hackney, Shoreditch, St Leonard, clock, mid eighteenth century
40. Camden, Holborn, Thomas Coram Foundation, overmantel by
    J.M. Rysbrack, relief with charity children, mid eighteenth century
41. Camden, Holborn, Russell Square, statue of Francis Duke of Bedford,
    by Sir Richard Westmacott, 1809, plinth with rural scene

46. Camden, Holborn,
    Fitzroy Square, south
    side, by Robert
    Adam, 1793–8
47. Camden, St Pancras,
    Kenwood, Library,
    by Robert Adam,
    1767–9
48. Camden, Holborn,
    Sir John Soane's
    Museum, by Sir John
    Soane, 1812–23
49. Camden, Holborn,
    Sir John Soane's
    Museum, Breakfast
    Parlour, by Sir John
    Soane, 1812–13

| 46 | 48 |
| 47 | 49 |

50. Camden, St Pancras, St Pancras New Church, by
    H.W. & W. Inwood, 1819–22, caryatids modelled by J.F.C. Rossi
51. Camden, St Pancras, St Pancras Old Church, monument to
    Mrs Elizabeth Soane †1815, by Sir John Soane
52. Hackney, Stoke Newington, Abney Park Cemetery, by William
    Hosking, 1840, main entrance
53. Camden, St Pancras, Highgate Cemetery, by Stephen Geary, 1839,
    Egyptian Avenue

54. Camden, St Pancras, Park Village West, by John Nash, begun 1824, No. 12
55. Islington, Finsbury, Lloyd Baker Estate, designed by W.J. Booth, begun 1825, Lloyd Baker Street, 1833
56. Camden, St Pancras, Holly Village, Highgate, by Henry Darbishire, 1865
57. Hackney, De Beauvoir Square, north side, begun 1839

58. Camden, Holborn, British Museum, by Sir Robert Smirke, 1823–52, entrance front built 1842–6

59. Camden, Holborn, Coade stone panel of the Nine Muses, early nineteenth century, Warburg Institute, University of London

60. Camden, Holborn, University College, Wilkins Building, by William Wilkins, 1827–9

61. Camden, Holborn, British Museum, entrance front, pediment sculpture, by Sir Richard Westmacott, The Progress of Civilization, early 1850s

62. Hackney, Stoke Newington, pumping station, designed by Robert Billings, 1854–6

63. Camden, Holborn, Prudential Assurance, by Alfred Waterhouse, inner courtyard from the south, 1895–1901

64. Camden, St Pancras, Midland Grand Hotel, by Sir George Gilbert Scott, 1868–74, from the south-east

65. Camden, St Pancras, St Pancras Station, booking hall, 1869, capital

| 62 | 64 |
| 63 | 65 |

66. Islington, Finsbury, No. 34 Farringdon Lane, by Rowland Plumbe for John Greenwood, clock manufacturer, 1875

67. Hackney, Shoreditch, Nos. 65–83 Leonard Street, 1870s, furniture workshops

68. Hackney, Shoreditch, Nos. 91–101 Worship Street, by Philip Webb, 1862–3, houses and workshops

69. Islington, Finsbury, Nos. 20–24 Old Street, by Ford & Hesketh, 1880

75. Camden, Holborn, Russell Hotel, Russell Square, by C. Fitzroy Doll, 1898
76. Haringey, Hornsey, Queen's Hotel, Crouch End, by John Cathles Hill, 1898–1902, glass by Cakebread Robey
77. Hackney, Hackney Empire, Mare Street, by Frank Matcham, 1901

78. Camden, Hampstead, Eton Villas, by John Shaw Jun., 1840–50s
79. Islington, Milner Square, by Roumieu & Gough, 1839–44
80. Hackney, Nos. 90–92 Colvestone Crescent, by Edmund Hammond, 1860s
81. Camden, Hampstead, Wychcombe Studios, by T. Batterbury, 1879–80

82. Islington, Holy Trinity (now Celestial Church of Christ),
   Cloudesley Square, by Charles Barry, 1826–9
83. Camden, St Pancras, St Mary Magdalene, by R.C. Carpenter,
   1849–52
84. Barnet, Friern Barnet, St John, by J.L. Pearson, east end, 1890–1

82
83 | 84

85. Camden,
    Hampstead,
    St Stephen, by
    S.S. Teulon,
    1869–73
86. Hackney,
    Shoreditch, St
    Columba (now
    Christ Apostolic),
    by James Brooks,
    1867–71
87. Barnet,
    Hampstead
    Garden Suburb,
    St Jude, by Sir
    Edwin Lutyens,
    1909–11, crossing
    tower 1915
88. Enfield,
    Edmonton,
    St Aldhelm, by
    W.D. Caröe, 1903

89. Islington, Finsbury, Holy Redeemer, by J.D. Sedding, 1887–8, completed by H. Wilson, 1892–5

90. Camden, Holborn, Hospital for Sick Children, Great Ormond Street, chapel, by Edward Barry, 1876

91. Hackney, Church of the Agapemone (now Church of the Good Shepherd), by Joseph Morris & Sons, 1892–5, evangelist symbols by A.G. Walters

92. Hackney, Church of the Agapemone, west window, designed by Walter Crane, executed by J. Sylvester Sparrow, 1896, the Sun of Righteousness

93. Hackney, Round Chapel (formerly Clapton Park United
Reformed Church), by Henry Fuller, 1869–71
94. Islington, New Court Congregational Church (now St Mellitus),
by C.G. Searle, 1870–1
95. Islington, Union Chapel, by James Cubitt, 1876–7
96. Haringey, Hornsey, former Presbyterian Church, by
G. & R.P. Baines, 1903

| 101 | 103 |
| 102 | 104 |

105. Camden, Holborn,
Sicilian Avenue, by
R.J. Worley, 1905–10
106. Camden, Holborn,
British Museum, King
Edward VII wing, by
Sir John Burnet,
1906–14, detail of lion
by Sir George
Frampton
107. Camden, Hampstead,
The Hill, west pergola,
by T.H. Mawson,
c. 1912
108. Camden, St Pancras,
former London,
Edinburgh and
Glasgow Assurance,
Euston Square, by
A. Beresford Pite, 1907

113. Camden, Hampstead,
Frognal Way, Sun
House, by Maxwell
Fry, 1934–5
114. Camden, St Pancras,
Highgate, Highpoint
Two, east entrance,
by Berthold Lubetkin
and Tecton, 1938;
Highpoint One,
1933–5 beyond
115. Barnet, Hendon, John
Keble Memorial
Church, by D.F.
Martin-Smith, 1935–7
116. Islington, former
Carlton Cinema,
Essex Road, by
George Coles, 1930

117. Islington, Finsbury, Bevin Court, by Skinner, Bailey & Lubetkin, 1952–5, central staircase
118. Islington, Finsbury, Spa Green Estate, Spa Fields, by Tecton (executive architects Lubetkin and Skinner), 1946–50
119. Camden, Holborn, Congress House, War Memorial, by Sir Jacob Epstein, 1955–6
120. Camden, Holborn, Congress House, by David du R. Aberdeen, 1948–57, from Dyott Street

121. Camden, St Pancras, British Library, by Sir Colin St John Wilson, 1978–97, from the south-west
122. Camden, Holborn, Institute of Advanced Legal Studies and Institute of Education, by Denys Lasdun, 1965–76, from the south-west
123. Camden, Hampstead, Alexandra Road, by Camden Architect's Department, project architect Neave Brown, 1969–78, from the west
124. Camden, Hampstead, Dunboyne Road Estate, by Camden Architect's Department, project architect Neave Brown, 1966–9

125. Camden, Hampstead, Hopkins House, Downshire Hill, by Sir Michael and Patty Hopkins, 1975–6

126. Camden, St Pancras, Rochester Place, No. 44, 1977–85, No. 42, 1986–9, by David Wild

127. Camden, St Pancras, St Paul's Mews, by CZWG, 1987–91, from the west

128. Camden, St Pancras, flats behind Sainsbury's, Regent's Canal, Camden Town, by Nicholas Grimshaw, 1985–8, from the north-west

129. Haringey, Hornsey, St Paul, by Peter Jenkins, Inskip & Jenkins, 1988–93, from the south-west

130. Hackney, London Fields, flower sellers sculpture, by Freeform Artworks, 1988–9

pilastered ground floor, and Nos. 1–7, a tall urban group of altered late Georgian houses (built *c.* 1786). Then the former FORUM CINEMA, 1934 by *Beard & Bennett*; sumptuously detailed both outside and in: cream faience, with black columns with lotus capitals and Art Deco glazing; interior with elaborate use of Roman motifs, the auditorium with a coffered dome. Further N on the E side, ELSFIELD, stepped-back flats of 1972 by *Bill Forrest* of Camden Architect's Department; trim and cheerful and (unlike so much borough housing of this time) not too large. Smooth rendered walls and nautical-looking railings in the Modern Movement revival manner popular in the early 1970s. The dense industrial patch on the W side, with tall factories right on the street, comes as a surprise; it developed after 1870 in response to the vast expanse of Midland Railway land which lies immediately behind. Part of this area is filled by SANDERSON CLOSE: bleak brown brick Camden housing of the 1970s by *YRM*, in the form of a barrier block with lower terraces behind. Prominent from afar, approached from the S by Regis Road, is a vast blue hangar for WHITBREADS, 1984.

Older houses remain on the E side: Nos. 98–108, the late Georgian FITZROY TERRACE, with Gothic glazing to first-floor windows, and modest front doors curiously below street level. Then a Victorian terrace and No. 120, plain Georgian, altered. A rewarding late C18 patch follows: LITTLE GREEN STREET climbs uphill with an irregular group of pretty terraced cottages with bowed shop-fronts and a varied skyline; COLLEGE LANE, a back lane parallel to Highgate Road, winds N with haphazard cottages here and there. On its E side No. 30, by *Martin Goalen*, with triangular windows echoing a large sloping roof (double-height living area inside).

Back in HIGHGATE ROAD, on the W side, close to the railway bridge, No. 137, SOUTHAMPTON HOUSE, a handsome early C19 house, formerly a school; three broad bays, three storeys, with ground-floor windows recessed in brick arches and a good late Georgian doorway with incised pilasters and fanlight. Behind is a pleasant pocket of early C19 terraces: WESLEYAN PLACE, MORTIMER TERRACE. The S end was sliced off by the railway. Under the railway arches, M & A COACHWORKS, the space neatly adapted (note the good lettering beneath the railway bridge). N of Gordon House Road the HIGHGATE ROAD ESTATE, with HADDO HOUSE, six-storey flats with two glazed staircase towers and a well-detailed, pleasantly intimate group of lower houses behind, 1963–5 by *Robert Bailie* for St Pancras. The clumsy block with ugly sloping profile was added in 1971. Further N there is still No. 175, a solid stock brick three-bay villa of the early C19.

On the E side of Highgate Road, raised above it and separated from it by trees, first Nos. 150–152, large early C19 houses, and then the best group in this area, GROVE TERRACE. Nos. 1–5 are early C19, Nos. 6–27 late C18, a characteristic example of the Georgian urban terrace built in the countryside. Many of the doorcases have a shallow segmental arch between fat Tuscan columns, but there is much attractive variety of detail, especially in the ironwork, partly belonging to minor early C19 modifications – see the dropped window sills. Nice staircases, plasterwork and fireplaces inside. Between Nos. 21 and 22 a cobbled way to a mews lane behind. Soon after, the road begins the climb up to Highgate (*see* below), its once rural setting still preserved to some extent on the E side by the school playing fields on the edge of Parliament Hill Fields.

## 4b. West Kentish Town and Gospel Oak

Patchy remains of C19 suburbs largely replaced by fifty years of diverse council housing.

The S end of this area was built up in the earlier C19 with modest villas and artisan terraces. In HAWLEY ROAD a few early C19 villas remain on the S side. The grid of Victorian streets to the N was replaced by massive post-war council housing around CLARENCE WAY, 1947 etc. by *Hamilton & Chalmers*, one of the borough's three major new housing sites. More, on a less forbidding scale, in CASTLEHAVEN ROAD and CASTLE ROAD, 1970, 1958 etc. by *Max Lock & Partners*. Between Castle Road and HEALEY STREET, lower, more contextual terraces of 1979–84 by *Camden Architect's Department (David Webb)*. W of the railway line a mixture of rehabilitated modest terraces and tactful infilling also began to be adopted in the 1970s after disillusion had set in over grander schemes; see HAWLEY STREET and HARTLAND ROAD and *Camden*'s NEW HARMOOD ESTATE of 1978–81, arranged around landscaped courts. Among the older survivors the W end of CLARENCE WAY is especially appealing: little mid-C19 terraces with a curious rhythm of rising parapets. Other simple houses remain in HARMOOD STREET and POWLETT PLACE. Further W the area around FERDINAND STREET, shown as one of the poorest parts of Kentish Town on Booth's map of 1889, attracted borough enterprise on a grand scale in the 1930s. The FERDINAND PLACE ESTATE of 1936–7 is in the borough's usual pre-war style under *A.J. Thomas*; four-storey-and-attic walk-up blocks in grey and red brick, with Georgian sashes. Along FERDINAND STREET more monumental post-war council blocks of 1946 onwards, eight storeys, with classical doorcases and shaped brick balconies. Among them, KENT HOUSE, a daringly modern interloper. 1935–6, by *Connell, Ward & Lucas*, commissioned by a progressively minded group led by Lady Stewart, within the Northern Group of the St Pancras Home Improvement Society. A rare case of pre-war low-rent housing by Modern Movement architects, and the only such work by this firm. Two blocks on a humane scale: five storeys, reinforced concrete with pale rendered walls, far-projecting balconies with wire mesh. Two flats on each floor, built with all-electric services. Big concrete staircase (glazed 1980) approached through a partly open ground floor. Gates and landscaping 1980–2 by *Jeffrey Fairweather*. Off Chalk Farm Road in BELMONT STREET, Messrs CHAPPELL'S former piano works, 1860s, five storeys by eleven bays, on the scale of a textile mill.

Along MALDEN CRESCENT, the traditional grid lay-out of council flats is broken by DENTON (*Camden Architect's Department*, completed 1972), with a tower marking the corner of Prince of Wales Road, and four-storey maisonettes of brown brick with exposed concrete arranged in two whole and two half polygons. Grim hole-in-the-corner junctions between the blocks, but imaginative landscaping behind (*Gordon Cullen* and *Kenneth Browne* were advisers). Opposite, *Camden*'s FORGE PLACE and MUTTON PLACE have distanced themselves from such planning: lower, friendlier brick clusters of separate three- and four-storey houses and flats; 1980–1, with good landscaping by *Michael Brown Partnership*.

PRINCE OF WALES ROAD, the main W–E route, retains some of its C19 character. A development plan of 1840 for this part of the Southampton Estate proposed spacious villas, but apart from a group by Malden Crescent, from which one gabled pair remains at the E corner, the street was built up with terraces. Further w on the s side Nos. 131–149 are an especially handsome group, with excellent cast-iron balconies on two levels. The tone is maintained by the DRAMA CENTRE opposite, a former Methodist Church of 1871 with a grand stone front of five bays; pedimented centre with giant Corinthian columns *in antis*. Around St Silas' Church (q.v.), housing for Camden by *G. B. Drewitt*, 1966; intimate two- and three-storey pale brick terraces in closes tucked behind the larger blocks along the main roads.

QUEEN'S CRESCENT runs NE in a gentle curve from near the w end of Prince of Wales Road; the w side is still Victorian, with appealing little culs-de-sac of stuccoed houses opening off (Modbury Gardens, St Ann's Gardens, St Thomas's Gardens). HERBERT STREET has a sheltered hostel, three and one storeys, with courtyard between; by *Avanti Architects*, 1991–3. The other side of Queen's Crescent was replaced by council housing, at first a prewar symmetrical composition (on the site of the Journeymen Taylors' Almshouses), then a forbiddingly dense craggy group with long jutting balconies in brown brick (St Silas North, *Camden Architect's Department*, 1969–75), climbing up to a seven-storey range along MALDEN ROAD. The E side of Malden Road and the eastern part of Queens Crescent survived proposed clearance; the latter continues as a shopping street with a lively market between intermittently rebuilt stuccoed terraces. They form a human face between the big council schemes to N and w. To the s, in BASSETT STREET, an individualistic little terrace of pale yellow brick, with a long projecting glazed balcony providing access to top-floor flats. By *Castle, Park, Hook*, 1977. Nearby, at the corner of Rhyl Street, No. 47 TALACRE ROAD, 1989–90 by *David Baker*, for a housing association, a tall, elegantly Postmodern cornerpiece in red and yellow brick, with pedimental gable echoing the Italianate sources of the C19 housing. Around ATHLONE STREET, traditional St Pancras Housing Association flats of 1933–4.

The WEST KENTISH TOWN ESTATE replaced the Victorian streets w of the s end of Grafton Road. This was the area for which *Sir Leslie Martin* proposed in 1958 a revolutionary low-rise high-density scheme based on different-sized cross-over flats with internal corridors. It was rejected in favour of a more conventional mix of three- and four-storey blocks with one fifteen-storey tower, all built of prefabricated units (Reema storey-height panels), 1961–4. Unlike many other system-built estates, this had the benefit of architectural supervision (by *William Crabtree*); the spiral stairs at the end of the blocks, together with careful lay-out and landscaping, were intended to temper the impact of the clumsy concrete cladding panels. But more was demanded; the concrete is now completely concealed by awkward tile-hanging.

GOSPEL OAK was a tree marking the boundary between St Pancras and Hampstead parishes. The name became attached to the large area of C19 housing, mostly of the 1860s onwards, stretching N from Queen's Crescent to Mansfield Road, which was earmarked from 1959 for almost total redevelopment. A great range of housing types resulted, to no coherent plan. W of GRAFTON ROAD, long sleek parallel ranges by *Frederick MacManus & Partners* for Camden, 1971–9; mostly of three to five storeys, separated by well-landscaped open spaces. This is low-rise on the grand, overwhelming scale characteristic of the borough in the early 1970s, but with conscious use of delicate early modern motifs – pale rendered walls and wire-mesh private balconies – in contrast to some of Camden's own more brutalist creations. The flats are approached by stairs and not by long impersonal access balconies. A detour E of Grafton Road takes one to some smaller, more self-effacing sites developed in the 1980s. Among industry in GILLIES STREET, CARLTON CHAPEL HOUSE, 1983–4 by *Christopher Dean*, a compact block of flats for a cooperative tenants' association, given character by a lively gable end with open staircase rising within a trellised veranda. Nearby, WOODYARD CLOSE and CRESSFIELD CLOSE curl around the fringe of the railway lands, happily relaxed enclaves laid out in a homely suburban manner with low houses and flats with front gardens. 1977–81 by *Camden Architect's Department* (*Sheila Tribe, Diana Baker*). Back past the CITY FARM (the prototype for many) established in 1972 in old railway buildings, to GRAFTON ROAD.

N of the main Midland line are the earlier parts of the Gospel Oak redevelopment. To the E, KILN PLACE, by *Armstrong & MacManus*, 1959–62, four-storey brown brick blocks around courts and grassed areas, with details close to their buildings on the Regents Park Estate (*see* Perambulation 2). To the W, at the end of LAMBLE STREET, is an early trail-blazing group of mixed heights, by *Powell & Moya*, 1952–4; BARRINGTON COURT, a ten-storey slab of small flats with glazed balconies (cf. the details of the same firm's Churchill Gardens, Westminster), set on a low mound, with three small rows of neat two-storey terrace houses at its foot. Further W in Lamble Street a crisp and compact all-white terrace on a split-level plan, with car ports squeezed in (*G. Benson* and *A. Forsyth* of Camden, 1978–80). The cue for small-scale houses was no doubt provided by the attractive pairs of earlier C19 stuccoed cottages that were allowed to remain along OAK VILLAGE and ELAINE GROVE, narrow roads between Lamble Street and Mansfield Road, built up after a road (now Gordon House Road and Mansfield Road) was created in 1806 along the line of a footpath to Hampstead. *Benson* and *Forsyth*'s taller terrace, Nos. 17–79 MANSFIELD ROAD is less happy; the long white range has an ingenious mixture of public and private spaces, including large roof gardens (cf. Dunboyne Road Estate, Hampstead, p. 243), but neither the raised internal access gallery nor the cramped and overlooked sunken patios on the street side seem convincing assets.

The confused area further W was redeveloped in the 1970s after several changes of plan. At the W end of Lamble Street is LISMORE CIRCUS, a circular garden. It is hard to grasp that this was a focus of the Victorian suburb planned in the 1870s, with streets radiating in six directions. The houses have gone; all that survives from the C19 is the long walls of the Midland Railway's cutting, which early on disturbed the original plan, covered in peeling paintwork of 1970s murals. A bold scheme of 1962 by *Armstrong & MacManus* proposed a shopping crescent around the circus and courts of housing behind, but the crescent remained unbuilt, because it was decided to retain the Victorian shopping parades in Queen's Crescent. The result was an unhappy compromise of a few one-storey shops, a twenty-storey tower, and a low clinic with an incongruous glimpse of the Victorian tower of St Martin further s in Vicars Road (q.v.). To the N two long parallel grey brick blocks of WAXHAM and LUDHAM, 1969–72 by *F. G. MacManus & Partners*, shoot away to Southampton Road, entirely failing to relate to the space around the circus. To the busy MANSFIELD ROAD the taller five-storey block presents a deadening, streamlined face with glazed-in balconies. s of the Circus and E of MALDEN ROAD are a bewildering maze of courts, by *Armstrong & MacManus*, 1963 onwards, with maisonettes uncomfortably raised up above the garages suddenly demanded in such quantity at this time, and built to a higher density (over 136 p.p.a.) than the rest of Gospel Oak.

w of Malden Road the atmosphere changes. The tiny QUADRANT GROVE, with its intimate stuccoed terraces, is a welcome C19 survival. s of St Dominic's Priory (q.v.) in Southampton Road is the pretty group of the ST PANCRAS ALMSHOUSES, three humble Tudor ranges around a well-kept garden, 1851 and 1862 by *H. Baker*. Projecting, not identical houses at either end, the matron's house of the l. with turret, dated 1859.

MAITLAND PARK, further s, was once a neighbourhood of much character which had generously laid-out 1850s villas along its two curving roads, and plenty of open space around several charitable institutions. The villas were all replaced after the Second World War by flats by the *LCC*, its only work in this area. Those on the w side are the usual stodgy brick blocks of the 1930s, those to the E (1959–64) form a more sensitively scaled four-storey terrace of maisonettes, their plain modern detail now obscured by pitched roofs and other embellishments of 1991–2. Three six-storey point blocks in the gardens in the centre. At the s end, in the optimistic spirit of the post-war LCC, a SCULPTURE: Family Group, *c.* 1960. The flats on the w side occupy the grounds of ALEXANDRA HOUSE, founded as an orphanage and working school in 1847. Original battered gatepiers remain at the s end, and two buildings in a hard domestic Georgian by *Young & Hall*, 1906, brick with Bath stone trim. From the s end of Maitland Park one can return by Prince of Wales Road to Kentish Town, or take Haverstock Hill to Chalk Farm.

### 4c. East of Kentish Town Road

Mostly superior Victorian housing with some modernist interjections.

From Camden Road Station, first N up ROYAL COLLEGE STREET, which has plain early C19 Southampton Estate terraces with some well-preserved small shopfronts on the w side, and small alleys of

stucco-fronted terraces opening off: IVOR STREET to the W, REEDS PLACE to the E, still the characteristic late Georgian mix of large houses and service streets. The new focus of Reeds Place is No. 44 ROCHESTER PLACE by *David Wild*, planned 1977,
126   built 1980–5. A happy termination: height and pale render match the neighbours, but the frontage is in the Modern Movement tradition, worth study for its skilful handling of different planes. Recessed entrance below a large first-floor living room; top-floor studio hidden behind a large balcony. Inside, the structure is revealed by the concrete columns defining the three-bay depth, and the space is handled in a free Corbusian manner, with three low storeys at the back containing bedrooms and kitchen, and a living room of one and a half storeys, wrapped around a central hearth and glass-walled staircase. No. 42, 1986–9, also by *David Wild*, simpler, but in the same spirit. Near the canal, CAMDEN GARDENS by *Jestico & Whiles*, 1993; two crisply detailed closes in yellow brick for Community Housing Association.

Now into the St Bartholomew's Hospital Estate, built up by 1870. The area extending between BARTHOLOMEW ROAD and PATSHULL ROAD consists of straight leafy streets with solid pairs of brick villas and smaller stucco-trimmed terraces with iron balconies. No. 12 BARTHOLOMEW VILLAS is an intruder, a Japanese-inspired essay of 1963–4 by *Edward Cullinan*. First-floor galleried living room facing the garden, with only small windows under big eaves on the street side. Via Kentish Town Road into GAISFORD STREET, the southernmost of the roads laid out *c*. 1863–5 on the estate of Christ Church, Oxford; broader and showier than the preceding streets. Houses with Doric porches, taller centrepieces to the main terraces on each side. Between Gaisford Street and CAVERSHAM ROAD some ingenious infilling for Camden by *Colquhoun & Miller* (project architect *Richard Brearley*), 1976–9; progressive at the time for its combination of Modern Movement principles with a contextual approach. Nos. 6–10 Gaisford Street are a compactly planned block of five maisonettes, the whole in proportion to the street, but with neat horizontal lines and austere surfaces in deliberate contrast to the Victorian neighbours. A large opening was intended to lead to a tenants' hall behind, which remained unbuilt. Backing onto the site, No. 5 Caversham Road, two more deferential maisonettes, with floor levels which respect the proportions of the older houses.

The large paired villas of Caversham Road are disrupted by the Midland Railway line, which cuts brutally through the estate, but the vista E is satisfyingly terminated by St Luke (q.v.), sited on the curve of OSENEY CRESCENT. The S part of the crescent remains: quite stylish heavy Victorian houses with large porches and prominently bracketed eaves. The N part is all post-war flats. These follow the street line, but to the N, ISLIP ROAD is less happily lined by uninspiring ranks of pre-war blocks. Round the corner, TORRIANO COTTAGES, off Leighton Road, an unexpectedly rural cul-de-sac of Victorian cottages. At the end, No. 15, by *Philip Pank* of *Pank Goss Associates* for himself, 1965–7, an unassuming family house on a tiny site, one-storeyed, delicately detailed and landscaped, with a roof garden and a tree rising from an internal courtyard.

N OF LEIGHTON ROAD, less ambitious later Victorian developments. LEIGHTON CRESCENT off LEIGHTON GROVE is the
only formal lay-out, awkwardly laid out on a slope. A gap in the
late C19 villas is filled by a block of maisonettes and flats for
Camden by *E. Cullinan, P. Tabor, M. Beedle & M. Chassay*, 1974–9.
Like the contemporary infilling in Caversham Road (*see* above),
the massing respects the neighbours, but the detail here is quite
different: square windows and recessed attics, a sloping metal
roof, and cheerfully coloured grids of drainpipes and balconies.
An unusually airy central stairhall leads through to the garden.
Sixteen wide-fronted flats, placed back to back; an urban version
of Cullinan's housing at Highgrove, Hillingdon (*see London 3:
North West*). Just to the N, with access from Brecknock Road, is
one of the few pre-suburban buildings in this area: MONTPELIER
HOUSE, a villa of *c.* 1840 with broad projecting eaves; its grounds
are now a public garden.

LEIGHTON ROAD (for the w end, *see* Perambulation 4a) has stretches
of small terraces of *c.* 1830–40, with good varied ironwork and a
few pediments (Nos. 69–71). A grid of late C19 streets to the N fills
the triangle between Fortess Road and Brecknock Road. In LADY
MARGARET ROAD, No. 2a, by and for *Richard Burton* (of *ABK*),
provides an individualistic interlude, with a slightly Chinese circular
doorway next to a tree, and a steeply angled studio roof. Double-
height studio 1989; the rest of the house 1986–7, hiding behind
the boundary wall. Only the centre has two storeys. Kitchen,
living room and study are linked by a s-facing conservatory opening onto a garden. Spacious, experimental interiors, the rooms
crammed full of ingenious joinery and differentiated by much visible
variety of timber and steel construction.

Finally, N of the junction of Highgate Road and Fortess Road. The
streets around BURGHLEY ROAD were developed in the 1860s by
St John's College, Cambridge. No. 16, set back from the road, is
the vicarage to Kentish Town Parish Church, ample Gothic of
1863 by the estate surveyor, *Henry Baker*. In LADY SOMERSET
ROAD, No. 25a, a studio house by *Rick Mather*, 1977–9, of brick,
with curved turret-like end, and a neatly recessed entrance to the
lower wing. Further N, by the railway line, Camden's INGESTRE
ROAD ESTATE (1967–71, *J. Green*). It begins discreetly by College
Lane (*see* Perambulation 4a) with two-storey houses with informal
conservatory porches stepping up the slope, but ends with
maisonettes skied above gaping carports and aggressively large
concrete ramps. Across the railway by a pedestrian bridge one
reaches the friendlier brick blocks of the YORK RISE ESTATE of
the St Pancras Housing Association, 1937 by *Ian Hamilton*, five
four-storey blocks with large balconies, arranged round courtyards
which had ceramic-headed drying posts by *Gilbert Bayes* (now
removed) as in the Association's Somers Town estates (*see* pp.
379–80).

To the N of the railway is the area known as DARTMOUTH PARK, a
network of small streets laid out haphazardly in the last quarter of
the C19 over the undulating foothills of Highgate. YORK RISE,
the service street which binds the residential roads together,
has an informal mix of small Victorian shops and later infilling.
The best of the latter is No. 24, a compact studio house on a tiny

site, by and for *van Heyningen & Haward*, 1975, trimly and reticently detailed, of stock brick with a pitched roof. In LAURIER ROAD, No. IC is the same firm's later house and studio, 1986, a tall brick town house matching the scale of its neighbours, but in a discreetly modern idiom, the windows square or in multiples of squares. Ingeniously planned to combine family house with top-floor studio. Central stairs divide the double-height living room on the first floor, facing the garden, from the lower rooms at the front.

In the neighbouring streets, attractively diverse stucco-trimmed Victorian houses, e.g. in BOSCASTLE ROAD, and DARTMOUTH PARK ROAD. Here FIRST HOUSE is by and for *J. de Syllas* of *Avanti Architects*, 1990–3; unassuming brick exterior, spatially ingenious inside, with double-height roof-lit dining area. From the N end of Boscastle Road CROFTDOWN ROAD leads E into the BROOKFIELD ESTATE, St Pancras Borough housing of 1922–30 by *A. J. Thomas*; the lay-out is less routine than in the large 1930s estates, and the detail well preserved. Winding roads with homely groups of red brick houses. Compact four-storey blocks of flats (only eight in each) cluster further up the hill close to Highgate Branch Library (q.v.) and Highgate New Town. For this and the area at the foot of Highgate Hill, *see* Highgate, below.

## 5. Highgate

Highgate began as a hilltop hamlet on the edge of the Bishop of London's large Middlesex estates, on the boundary between the parishes of St Pancras and Hornsey. Until the early C19 there was no parish church, only a chapel at the top of the High Street incorporated within Highgate School. Along the approach from London up Highgate Hill from Holloway something of the C16 and C17 can still be found among the usual later ribbon development: on the W, Lauderdale House, a much-altered remnant of a partly timber-framed C16 house, and on the E side, Cromwell House, harbinger of the new type of compact brick building which began to appear in the London countryside from the C17 onwards. The main settlement at the top of the hill lay around a green with a series of ponds, the last of which disappeared in 1865. In the early C17 there were two aristocratic mansions, Dorchester House and Arundel House, standing in their own grounds. They disappeared in the later C17, giving way to handsome brick houses for City men, of which a considerable number still remain. By the end of the C18 Highgate was a small town, and the whole area still has the character of a favourite C18 residential settlement near London. The division between the parishes is perpetuated by the modern borough boundaries, but is ignored here so that the centre of Highgate can be described in one place. For churches and public buildings in Highgate, *see* pp. 343 ff.

## 5a. The Centre

The steep climb up Highgate High Street is rewarding. On the E side the houses are raised upon a bank above the road, still looking much as in C19 views. The principal one is Cromwell House. Opposite, set back on the edge of Waterlow Park, is Lauderdale House.

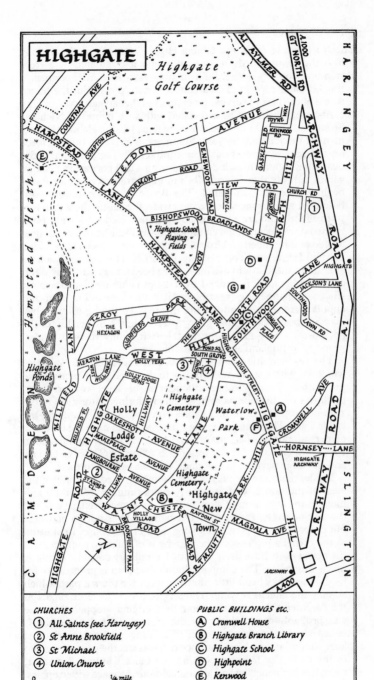

# HIGHGATE

*Highgate Golf Course*

*Hampstead Heath*

*Highgate Ponds*

HARINGEY

HARINGEY

ISLINGTON

CHURCHES
① All Saints (see Haringey)
② St Anne Brookfield
③ St Michael
④ Union Church

PUBLIC BUILDINGS etc.
Ⓐ Cromwell House
Ⓑ Highgate Branch Library
Ⓒ Highgate School
Ⓓ Highpoint
Ⓔ Kenwood
Ⓕ Lauderdale House
Ⓖ St Michael's C. of E. Primary School

0       ¼ mile
0    ¼    ½ km
(For the east part of Highgate see Haringey)

*Cromwell House*

The brick house (now the Ghana High Commission) fits happily into the group on the E side, although it originated as a free-standing country house, built in 1637–8 by Richard Sprignell, a trained band captain. The architect is not known, but the house is one of the best of surviving examples of the 'artisan style' of City craftsmen, which can be associated with such names as Nicholas Stone and Peter Mills, and whose hallmark is the elaborate treatment of brick detail. Sir John Summerson calls it 'a tour de force on the part of some bricklayer contractor'. The symmetry, the nearly flat treatment, window proportions and cornice in place of gables indicate that Inigo Jones's more restrained court style was beginning to be assimilated. The house is of two storeys with basement and dormers, seven bays wide; the centre three step forward slightly and are emphasized by quoins. Red brick with much rubbed brick decoration: central window embellished with a double lugged and moulded architrave. The other windows have moulded surrounds; the busy cornice is also of brick. The sashes are a later alteration: there would originally have been casements. The door, of ample breadth, is flanked by Tuscan columns placed against stuccoed channelling (possibly a later alteration). The roof and cupola were restored after a fire in 1865. To the l., an extra bay over a carriageway, added in 1678–9 during the ownership of the da Costas (1675–1749), the first Jewish family to own landed property in England since the Middle Ages.

The rear elevation is less formal, interrupted by the staircase windows, with a small oval window to the s and some pilaster-like projections. Possibly other ornament at this level was lost when the attics on this side were heightened (during restoration in the 1980s the outline of former gables on this side was visible on the inside wall). The wing projecting E dates in origin from the da Costa ownership but was heightened later, and was much remodelled in 1987–9, when the house was restored as offices by *Carden & Godfrey* and the large pavilion in matching style was added to the E.

Inside, the best room is the main stairhall, sited centrally at the back of the house, with its sturdy stairs running from the basement to the attic around a relatively narrow open well, as was still the fashion in the earlier C17. The handrail rests not on balusters but on panels with pierced carving, as at Ham House. In allusion to the owner's profession, the carving is of military trophies, and the newel posts have lively statuettes in military costume (replicas of the originals). The compact double-pile plan is progressive for its date and has been little altered except for the NE part, which adjoins the later rear wing. The service rooms were originally in the basement; the large NW room with original stopped doorcase was probably the kitchen. On the ground floor the stairhall is approached by a narrow panelled entrance passage, perhaps a later alteration, as a large entrance hall was still the general custom in the C17. The l. front room has no older features, but the r. room has C17 panelling and an original stone fireplace with trophies; behind it a smaller panelled parlour with corner chimneypiece (a curious irregularity in the plan is that the s wall of this room is not in line with that of the front room). On the first-floor landing are

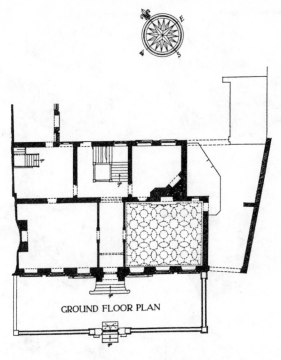

GROUND FLOOR PLAN

Cromwell House. Plan

four splendidly elaborate pedimented doorcases, the largest leading to the principal (sw) room. This has a ceiling reconstructed
after the fire of 1865, apparently authentically. Its broad ribs and
central oval are in the manner introduced by Inigo Jones, as at the
contemporary Swakeleys, Hillingdon (*see London 3: North West*).
In the room added to the s, a chimneypiece with the da Costa
monogram on the keystone. The NW room has a replica C18 fireplace; in two other rooms attractive tiled fireplaces of the 1980s,
designed by *Ian Angus* of *Carden & Godfrey*, one of them alluding
to the history of the house.

*Lauderdale House*

Community and arts centre since 1978. A low, unassuming five-bay
rendered front, lying back from the w side of Highgate Hill. Sash
windows, central pediment and lunette give a misleadingly C18
impression, for the house is older, one of the few survivals in the
London area of a large house still partly built in the timber-framed
tradition, although much altered. In the later C16 its occupant was
a City goldsmith, Richard Bond; in the 1660s it belonged briefly
to the Duke of Lauderdale, from 1686 to Sir William Pritchard, a
Lord Mayor. After 1705 it was occupied by a succession of tenants
until 1871. Various Victorian additions were removed after 1889,
when the house and grounds were given to the LCC by Sir Sydney
Waterlow. Repaired after damage by fires in 1963 and 1968.

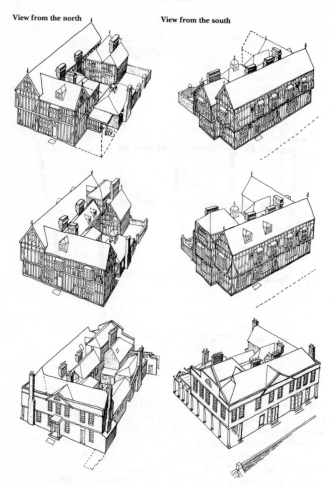

View from the north          View from the south

Lauderdale House in 1582, 1640, 1760 (top to bottom). Axonometric

The C16 house may have been on a courtyard plan, although
details are unclear. Behind the present entrance range was a NE
range, of which little is left, although the staircase tower that stood
in the angle between the two ranges remains. Long SE wing, its
timber frame rendered but still recognizable from the jettied upper
floor. This upper floor contained a long gallery. At the back of the
house a veranda with Doric columns, probably of the earlier C19,
opens onto the terraces overlooking the fine grounds that now
form Waterlow Park (see below).

Inside there is disappointingly little to see. The entrance hall
has an early C18 panelled closet (not *in situ?*). The staircase,
repaired after extensive fire damage, has an early C18 lantern with
restored plasterwork. On the staircase walls until the fire of 1968
was a trompe l'œil balustrade of the type found e.g. at Boston
Manor, Brentford, Hounslow (see *London 3: North West*), suggest-

ing alterations in the early C17. The roof over the long gallery was entirely rebuilt after the fire of 1963.

WATERLOW PARK and FAIRSEAT. In 1889 twenty-six acres of grounds belonging to Lauderdale House and a neighbouring house (since demolished) were given to the LCC as a 'garden for the gardenless' by Sir Sydney Waterlow (1822–1906), Lord Mayor of London in 1872 and chairman of the Improved Industrial Dwellings Company, who had added these estates to the grounds of Fairseat, his own house just to the N. W and S of Lauderdale House are terraces, with red brick walls perhaps of late C17 or C18 date, improved by the mid-C19 tenant, James Yates. A pair of gadrooned piers with statues to the S. Below the terraces lawns sweep down to two lakes. To the N, amid late C19 planting, a bronze statue of Waterlow, 1900 by *F. M. Taubman*.

FAIRSEAT (Channing Junior School) was Waterlow's own house from 1856, altered by him, 1867. It lies close to the road, reduced in size and refronted in red brick after road widening in 1909. The back is possibly a recasing of an earlier house. The steep French mansards and patterned slates date from Waterlow's time, as does the matching service block to the N with tall end pavilions.

On the E side of Highgate Hill, Cromwell House is followed closely by several excellent C18 terrace houses. IRETON HOUSE and LYNDALE HOUSE, Nos. 106–108, were originally a single building, early C18, with segment-headed windows. Then No. 110, with straight-headed windows. The doorways of the three houses, with Tuscan pilasters, are identical. Higher up, CHOLMELEY LODGE, an excellently composed block of modern flats by *Guy Morgan*, 1934; the front springs back twice in curves. IVY HOUSE and NORTHGATE HOUSE are another brick pair of *c.* 1700, of three bays each, with straight-headed windows and heavy modillioned cornice.

Along HIGHGATE HIGH STREET towards the top of the hill, the shops and terrace houses still convey the feeling of the separate little town that Highgate had become by the C18. Only a few houses are worth noting individually, but the late C17-to-C19 ensemble is pleasantly unspoilt, given character by C19 shopfronts and canopies extending over the pavement. Nos. 17–21 are a handsome terrace of 1733, with raised ground floors and segment-headed windows (No. 21 with original staircase). No. 23 is lower and broader, with a modillion frieze and straight-headed windows with fine rubbed brick lintels. It can hardly be later than *c.* 1710. Oddly irregular fenestration, with a double window to the l. of a central entrance, and the blank slit end windows that were fashionable at the beginning of the C18 (cf. Queen Anne's Gate, Westminster). Original staircase with closed string, chimneypiece and panelling. No. 42 opposite, of *c.* 1830, has a pretty carved straight hood to the door with the Ashurst arms, brought from Ashurst House, the large mansion of *c.* 1700 demolished for St Michael's Church in South Grove (q.v.). Also on the E side, No. 46 with C18 doorcase, No. 60, weatherboarded, with a hoist, and No. 64, built as a pharmacy in 1832, with four of the original six pilasters to the shopfront.

Off the High Street many lanes and alleys. Hidden in DUKE'S HEAD YARD to the E, STUDIO HOUSE built in 1939 for the artist Roger

Pettiward, an early work by *Tayler & Green*. Tower-like, because of the confined site, of brick with rendered walls, coloured, as originally, three sides red, one side grey, with a drum staircase to the garden side and a rooftop sun terrace. An unshowy, excellently thought-out modern house. The airy top floor is a single studio and living room with fitted furniture and two walls with continuous windows. These are of timber (imported from Switzerland) chosen in preference to metal; the choice of materials looks forward to the architects' post-war rural housing in Norfolk.

At the top of the High Street, on the w side, the GATEHOUSE, 1905, a half-timbered rebuilding of an inn at the boundary of the Bishop's estate. Almost opposite, SOUTHWOOD LANE runs N. On the w side, opposite Highgate School (q.v.), some good urban brick houses: Nos. 2–10, C18; No. 12, early C19; No. 18, probably of C17 origin. Further on, the stuccoed front of the former Highgate Tabernacle (*see* Highgate School). On the N side, the WOLLASTON PAUNCEFORT ALMSHOUSES, founded in the C17, rebuilt in 1722, a modest one-storey row with taller centre for a girls' charity school.

Off to the s, KINGSLEY PLACE, with a variety of yellow brick houses of one, two or three storeys, stepping down a dramatically steep slope, by the *Architects' Co-Partnership*, c. 1967. SOMERSET GARDENS is a little later, with pitched roofs and timber cladding.

For the rest of Southwood Lane, *see* Haringey (Hornsey: Perambulation 3).

### Highgate village west of the High Street

Among the jumble of shops at the E end of SOUTH GROVE are two substantial C18 houses: No. 9, RUSSELL HOUSE, the doorway with the curved-up entablature of the early C18 and later elaborate window frames and stucco, and No. 10, CHURCH HOUSE, plain red brick, five bays, three storeys, with segment-headed windows. Then follows the low stuccoed front of the HIGHGATE LITERARY AND SCIENTIFIC INSTITUTION. This was established in 1840 in a building previously used as a school; the front and porch date from 1882. Behind is the lecture hall with high timber roof and central lantern, added by *Rawlinson Parkinson* in 1879; the original hall at the back became the library. At the corner of Swain's Lane, a prettily detailed red brick terrace with roughcast gables, windows under segmental arches; built as the HIGHGATE DAIRY in 1891 by *Ernest H. Abbott*.

After the Union Church (q.v.), No. 14, MORETON HOUSE, 1715. Brick, of five bays, with Ionic doorcase, decorated central window and a fine staircase. Extensively and immaculately reconstructed by *Julian Harrap* after a fire in 1983. Originally one of a pair, and only one room deep until the C19. It was subdivided by floors soon after it was built. No. 16 is by *Leonard Manasseh*, c. 1961, on older foundations, and with a later roof. Then, behind extensive brick walls, No. 17, OLD HALL, dated 1691 on a rain-water head, a tall brown and red brick front of five bays, the parapet concealing the roof perhaps later, as is the slightly lower l. wing. Excellent iron gate. The house occupies part of the site of Arundel House, the large mansion which belonged to the Earl of Arundel in the early C17, and where Sir Francis Bacon died in 1626. The grounds were divided up in the late C17; on the site of the banqueting house, Sir William Ashurst, Lord Mayor in 1693, built a grand seven-bay house with pediment and cupola. This was demolished for St Michael's Church; its grounds to the s became Highgate Cemetery (qq.v.). Further w, VOEL HOUSE, No. 18, also late C17, though with front and top storey of the C18. At the w apex of the built-up area w of Pond Square, THE FLASK, with a modest late C18 exterior, but earlier inside. Discreet Neo-Georgian addition to the N of 1975 by *E. W. Edwards*.

In POND SQUARE itself, where houses have encroached onto the former green, Nos. 1–5 on the w side are a low C18 group; No. 6, ROCK HOUSE, is larger, with two upper projecting bays facing South Grove. To the N in WEST HILL, close to the High Street, No. 47, with an elegant five-bay, two-storey C18 front; open pediment over the central three bays (good staircase inside). Set back to its NW, Nos. 45–46, a taller, more forbidding pair, three plus five and a half bays, with rainwater head dated 1729. Some lintels with a little decoration. At the side of No. 45, a doorway (not *in situ*) with the curving-up mouldings typical of *c.* 1710.

THE GROVE lies a little further w, set back from the N side of the green. Here too there was a large mansion, Dorchester House. It disappeared at the end of the C17; parts of the garden walls with bastion and niches survive in the gardens of No. 6. Nos. 1–6 are the finest group in Highgate, built *c.* 1688 by a City merchant, William Blake, as part of a speculation intended to fund a charity school. Originally there were three pairs of semi-detached houses, an example of how at this date the urban terrace was not yet the universal form for speculative building in the villages outside London. Two storeys with dormers. The interiors have the pre-Georgian arrangement of staircases between front and back rooms and corner fireplaces. No. 1 has a specially handsome gate. Nos. 4 and 6 are the best-preserved, the stairs with twisted balusters and closed string of late C17 type. No. 5 was rebuilt in keeping by *C. H. James* in the 1920s. Nos. 7–9, of *c.* 1832, are taller. No. 12 is of the 1970s by *Lush & Lester*, with neo-Edwardian corbelled-out polygonal bays and turrets.

29

p. 24

## 5b. The surrounding area

A rural atmosphere survived around Highgate village into the C20, especially in the parts near the Heath, because of the large grounds which still surrounded a number of C18 and C19 houses. C20 sub-urbanization has surfaced the once muddy lanes and built over the gardens, but has also provided the bonus of some new buildings worth seeking out. The following tours radiate from the centre of the village, starting from the N and working anti-clockwise.

### North: North Road, North Hill and streets off*

From the top of Highgate High Street, NORTH ROAD, continued by North Hill, starts as a wide plane-tree-lined avenue flanked by Highgate School on the E and by houses set back from the road on the w. A good group, largely C18, starts with BYRON HOUSE,

* Partly within the Borough of Haringey.

No. 13, and HAMPTON LODGE with iron gate. Then BYRON COTTAGE, six bays and two gables and a plat band, perhaps C17. THE SYCAMORES, No. 19 (probably a pub in the C18), has segment-headed windows, a big doorway with curved pediment and a weatherboarded back. An attractive later miscellany follows, with Nos. 37–43, early C19 with giant pilasters. Then St Michael's School (q.v.), and a jolly half-timbered building built as a fire station by the Borough of Hornsey in 1906; converted to flats, 1981 (*Chris Palmer* of *Timothy Bruce Dick Associates*).

HIGHPOINT ONE and TWO. By *Berthold Lubetkin* and *Tecton*, 1933–5 and 1938, the first examples in London of the right siting of such super-blocks of flats. The client was Sigmund Gestetner, who had at first intended to provide housing for his employees (his factory was at Tottenham Hale) but ended up building private flats. No one here could object on the grounds of grimness or austerity. The gardens and views to the w and the old trees close to the E fronts create a scene from which the sheer rectangularity of the buildings receives the necessary relief. Le Corbusier called HIGHPOINT ONE the vertical garden city, a brilliant name, and of course quite wrong. In spite of its predominant rectangularity the building is by no means completely regular. At ground level it has a brick bulge, containing a winter garden, and a tearoom coming out to the w in a typical shape of the 1930s. Otherwise Highpoint One is a symmetrical double cruciform shape, with eight flats on each floor and small rooms for maids on the ground floor, as was required for luxury flats at this time. The construction is of reinforced concrete, following a system, specially devised by *Ove Arup*, which reused the shuttering as the building grew upwards. The upper floors rest partly on pilotis; the plain walls are relieved by curved balconies connected to the walls by iron bars, a favourite modern motif of between the wars. The flats (two living rooms and three bedrooms) are simply a series of rectangular rooms with no corridors; the spatial interest inside is concentrated on the circulation area, where there are curves and freely flowing spaces reminiscent of Le Corbusier. From the entrance foyer at the side of the build-

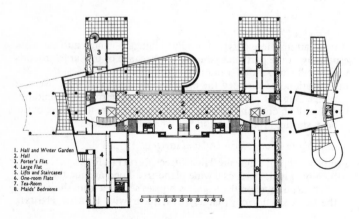

1. Hall and Winter Garden
2. Hall
3. Porter's Flat
4. Large Flat
5. Lifts and Staircases
6. One-room Flats
7. Tea-Room
8. Maids' Bedrooms

Highpoint One. Ground-floor plan

ing there are steps up to a raised landing below the main spine, from which one descends again to the tearoom overlooking the garden. This sequence comes as a surprise, for the façade is symmetrical, with the entrance beneath a projecting porte-cochère. Apart from some brick on the ground floor, Highpoint One is cement-rendered.

By the time HIGHPOINT TWO was built the architect had learned that for the London climate cement-rendering is not an advisable finish, so he used brick and tile as infillings. As the land for Highpoint Two was more expensive, the flats are larger (three living rooms and four bedrooms) and arranged in Corbusian fashion on two floors in an interlocking pattern so that the living rooms are double-height. Highpoint Two also has an entrance hall of interesting shape, and a porch which is unmistakably *Lubetkin*. The idea of using reproductions of two of the Erechtheum caryatids is significant. It is a case of surrealism in architecture, that is of the familiar made fantastic by a surprise setting. It is a most sophisticated effect, particularly since even spatially the figures are deprived of their original meaning. Instead of both turning one way, one of them seems to have decided on an independent right turn. Lubetkin himself occupied the penthouse of Highpoint Two; it has a large living room with shallow barrel vault, walls with rough timber panelling, and a fireplace whimsically provided with a window for the display of a *Calder* mobile. Photos show correspondingly eclectic furnishings.

HILLCREST, the group of flats opposite Highpoint, of 1946–9 by *T. P. Bennett* for the Borough of Hornsey, shows the Modern style handled in a routine way, not badly but without personality. For cost-conscious council housing the four- and seven-storey blocks are generously laid out, preserving trees from the grounds of Park House, with the lower buildings at the front in deference to village scale.

After Highpoint, NORTH HILL continues with intermittent C18 and C19 ribbon development on both sides. Nos. 3–7, modest Georgian of 1829, are followed by No. 9, discreetly tucked away behind a small entrance courtyard. This was built by *Walter Segal* for himself in 1962–8 (cf. St Anne's Close, S of the village, *see* below). Typically modest, a two-storey house of cross-wall construction, with much exposed timber inside. In the garden is the temporary building used while the house was under construction, a prototype for Segal's lightweight self-build houses developed later for the Borough of Lewisham. THE BULL is a low roadside inn, basically C18; the weatherboarded N bay and the upper E bay pre-date modernization *c.* 1900. On the E side, No. 6, grand early C19 stucco, with curved Tuscan porch, then small late Georgian villas, No. 10 with Gothic windows. Opposite, Nos. 47–49, which appear to have started as a single grand early C18 house, five bays and three storeys above basements, two-storey one-bay projecting wings. Urns on the parapet. At the corner of Rowlands Close, VERANDAH COTTAGES, plain three-storey workers' flats with minimal iron access balconies on two sides, built in 1863 by a Highgate society for working-class housing led by the Rev. Joseph Viney. At the corner of Church Road and North Hill, No. 44, a doctors' group practice. By *Douglas Stephen & Partners*, 1986.

Neat and airy. Doctors' common room in a glazed gable facing the road. Behind is a double-height toplit waiting area with surgeries on two levels.

PROSPECT PLACE, a pleasant group raised up on a bank on the W side (Nos. 109–117), dated 1811. Three storeys, with elegant honeysuckle balconettes. Further on, the early C19 development tails off with a very humble stuccoed terrace on the E side, Nos. 98–108, each house only one bay wide. Opposite, Nos. 193–215 and the enclave of two-storey red brick terraces around KENWOOD ROAD are early council housing of 1902 by the Hornsey Borough Engineer, *E. J. Lovegrove*, similar to Hornsey's other early estate off Nightingale Lane, Hornsey (Haringey), but also including some cottage flats. Later groups in GASKELL ROAD 1913, more simply detailed, with broad segment-headed windows. In TOYNE WAY, to the N, 1970s terraces with pantiled roofs and tile-hung upper walls; a self-conscious revival of vernacular imagery fifty years later, by *Robert Harrison* of Haringey Architect's Department.

Finally an excursion into the streets to the W, which have a mixed bag of affluent suburban building of the last hundred years. VIEW ROAD was built up on the N side from the 1890s with large Free Style detached houses: No. 1, with half-hipped gables; Nos. 3 and 7, 1897 by *A. Mitchell*, both of orange brick with lively white-dentilled gables. No. 9, 1899 by *M. Bunney*, with low mansard roof. No. 15, by *George Sherrin*, 1905, set back behind its tile-hung lodge, with half-timbered gable and a large porch with bold pargetting by *Daymond*: figures illustrate the motto 'The North Wind and the Sun. Persuasion is better than Force'. On the S side, No. 10, cautious Early Modern; at an angle to the road. A shallow monopitch roof with deep eaves; Deco lamps along the garden wall. VIEW CLOSE to the W is a crisp group of small houses of 1962 by *Dinerman Davies & Hillman*, somewhat in the Span spirit, pale bricks with dark tile-hanging, monopitch roofs. At the end, DENEWOOD ROAD leads NW to Highgate Golf Course, where the site of the moated medieval palace of the Bishop of London is marked by a few bumps. At the corner of BROADLANDS ROAD a mannered group strives for attention, full of jerky angled bays and porches. By *Assael Rowe-Parr Partnership*, 1984. Further W, BISHOPSWOOD ROAD skirts Highgate School Playing Fields, with school buildings interspersed with stately Victorian houses in pale brick, elaborately detailed. No. 20a is a compact modern house by *Stout & Lichfield*, *c.* 1973; double-height upper living room under an ingeniously syncopated roof. Finally back E along BROADLANDS ROAD, mostly Edwardian. No. 16 is the *pièce de résistance*, a spiky Gothic mansion in random stone, with steeply roofed porch turret and gables with decorated bargeboards, excellently preserved.

*North west: Hampstead Lane and Fitzroy Park**

HAMPSTEAD LANE runs W towards Hampstead from the S end of North Road. No. 3a is by *S. & M. Craig*, for themselves, 1967–8, a small, austere house of concrete blocks, with garden wall to match. After a C19 mixture of stuccoed terraces and large brick villas, the long garden walls of BEECHWOOD, one of the few

* Partly in the Borough of Haringey.

surviving mansions still in its own grounds. Built *c.* 1834 in the grounds of the former Fitzroy House (*see* below) by *George Basevi* for his brother. An uneventful two-storeyed stucco house, with two canted bays on the garden side, altered and added to. Yet further on, ATHLONE HOUSE (formerly Caen Wood Towers), now a nursing home, an ambitious Victorian red brick villa with superb views to the s. 1870–2 by *E. Salomons & J.P. Jones* for Edward Brooke. Much simplified. Originally with elaborate shaped gables, an oriel, and carved supporters instead of pinnacles on the tower above the porch. The sculpture was by *J.P. Philip*; the chimneys of Cosseyware. After this come the grounds and house of Kenwood and the start of Hampstead Heath (*see* above, p. 368).

On the N side there was woodland until suburban streets were laid out from *c.* 1910. Much of the development was by Walter Quennell, with many houses designed by his brother *C.H.B. Quennell* in a free English domestic style, paler versions of his work around Redington Gardens, Hampstead (*see* Hampstead, Perambulation 2b). Much diluted since; early examples remain in STORMONT ROAD, later ones in SHELDON AVENUE (Nos. 31 and 33, 1925; 16–24, 1923–4). For The Bishop's Avenue further w *see* Barnet, Hampstead Garden Suburb, p. 155.

FITZROY PARK can be reached from Hampstead Lane via The Grove. Its name comes from Fitzroy House, a Palladian villa built *c.* 1770 by Colonel Charles Fitzroy, later Lord Southampton. It was demolished in 1828. The grounds, reputedly landscaped by *Brown*, covered the whole of this area. Fitzroy Park, the former carriage drive, remained a secluded country lane until the later C20, and became a favourite place for select houses by architects for themselves. No. 6 was built for Ove Arup in 1958 by the Danish architect *Erhard Lorenz*; two storeys above garages, on a sloping site, end-on to the road. Elegantly detailed in the Scandinavian-modern tradition. Dark pine boarding, sloping back roofs, the corner entrance and the balcony on the garden side both inset behind thin columns. *Eva Jiricna* refurbished the interior in 1992 and added a refined, minimalist glass wing with dining room and gym overlooking a swimming pool. Nos. 7 and 7a are of 1957 by *June Park*, the larger house for herself and her husband (Cyril Mardall of YRM), the smaller one for her mother. Concrete framed with brick infill. The simple lines of both have been some-what altered: the ground floor of No. 7a was filled in, and No. 7 has an extension to the w by *Mardall* of 1967, with big brick piers in the more monumental style of that decade. The E porch is later. On the s side, No. 8, an early post-war house by *C.G. Stillman*, two storeys, stepping down the slope, 1953. No. 8a is by *H. Higgins* of *Higgins Ney & Partners*, 1964. An ostentatious luxury house, exploiting the slope of the hill, with a jagged profile of soaring brick staircase towers linking the different parts. On the N side, THE ELMS is set back behind its own lodge and drive. Much altered and added to, but its core is still the modest country villa built in 1838–40 by *George Basevi* for himself, together with the adjoining Beechwood (*see* above), after Fitzroy House was demolished. Stuccoed, with canted bays with iron canopies on the garden side; extended in 1863. On the s side No. 10, *Vincent*

*Harris*'s own house, 1932–4, Neo-Georgian in the Lutyens tradition, with careful use of small bricks (the recent pointing is an insult). A curved wall and a one-storeyed part to the road; terraced garden. Bequeathed by Harris to the Borough of Camden; now used for a horticultural training scheme. On the same side, THE HEXAGON, a cul-de-sac with six restrained brick and timber-clad houses of the 1960s by *Leonard Michaels*, and HIGHFIELDS GROVE, showier groups of the 1980s, built in the grounds of Witanhurst (*see* below). Round the corner, overlooking the fields of Kenwood, No. 53, with white boarding, by *Stephen Gardiner*, 1952, opposite a few engaging Art Deco period pieces with green tiles (Sunbury, Kenview). The road joins Millfield Lane at the entrance to the Heath by Highgate Ponds.

*South west and south: West Hill and Swain's Lane, a circular tour*

WITANHURST, the landmark at the top of HIGHGATE WEST HILL, is a palatial neo-Georgian mansion of 1913 by *George Hubbard* for the soap magnate Sir Arthur Crosfield, M.P., looking out over large grounds towards Hampstead Heath. The interior was designed in a variety of styles by *Percy McQuoid*, an authority on English furniture. Neo-Georgian LODGES of reused material, by *Seely & Paget*, 1929. Opposite, the houses on the s side of West Hill look over London. BROMWICH HOUSE, the grandest and most recent, is invisible from West Hill, tucked discreetly into the s-facing slope. Planned 1986 by *Elena Keats*, completed (after a planning enquiry) in 1996; interiors by *Conoley & Webb*. Living rooms at the top level, stepping down to wings flanking a diamond-shaped swimming pool. Then Nos. 81–84, C18 and perhaps partly older, with backs to the road, and HOLLY TERRACE, eleven houses, mostly built in 1807 on the site of a larger house, with some delightful verandas, balconies and gates facing s towards London over the former grounds of the Holly Lodge Estate (*see* below).

Further down Highgate West Hill, MERTON LANE, leading w towards the Heath, was a rural lane until the 1970s when, on the s side, WEST HILL PARK appeared, a luxury estate by *Ted Levy, Benjamin & Partners*, 1972–8, similar to those built by the same firm in Hampstead. Eleven types of houses and flats, clustered around little parks and courts; brick with pantiled roofs. Good landscaping by *Derek Lovejoy & Partners*. Merton Lane leads to MILLFIELD LANE, overlooking Highgate Ponds, a favoured spot for affluent C20 houses hidden behind garden walls. No. 23 is by *Robert Howard*, 1969–71; two wings linked by a circular staircase. From here also a view of the SOVIET TRADE DELEGATION flats overlooking the Heath, by *Eric Lyons*, 1957, the concrete and brick structure starkly exposed. Set back on the same site, hidden among trees is their four-storey office block (Nos. 32–33 Highgate West Hill), in the sleeker mode of the 70s; by *Dinerman Davies Associates*, 1973, the horizontals emphasized by white mosaic bands.

Further s in Millfield Lane, at the back of a spacious garden, No. 38 by *Pank, Goss Associates*, 1968–9. Stepped-back brick walls, with a large terrace to the first-floor living room. (Main rooms articulated by powerful ceiling beams with exposed joists.) By the bend in the road, MILLFIELD COTTAGE, C17 or earlier in origin (*see* the steeply pitched roof), once the farmhouse of Millfield Farm on the Fitzroy Estate. No. 16, a plain brick house of *c.* 1960, has attached to it a small house of 1985 by *Doug Clelland*. Discreet exterior with unpainted timber cladding and large oriel window. Ingeniously planned on a tight wedge-shaped site, with small rooms and clever built-in storage flanking a long theatrical roof-lit living space on two levels, with curved windows at either end. Hidden up MILLFIELD PLACE, a few handsome stuccoed houses of the earlier C19.

HIGHGATE WEST HILL still keeps in part its genteel C19 flavour; John Betjeman grew up in No. 31, one of a group of 1860 stucco and brick terrace houses uphill from Millfield Lane. Further S are more spacious stuccoed villas of 1839 (Nos. 6–7, 9, 10 and 11). On the E side the former vicarage near St Anne's Church is also early C19, grey brick with modillioned eaves. Tucked away in its former garden is ST ANNE'S CLOSE, a notable development of 1950–2. Planned as a co-operative scheme by *Walter Segal* for himself and his friends. Well-proportioned, economically planned two-storey houses with traditional brick walls, pantiled roofs with deep eaves, and minimal metal windows, the inexpensive details handled with exceptional care. Long frontages, with unfenced front gardens, carefully grouped around a communal green with trees.

A detour to the S to ST ALBANS ROAD can take in a mixed C20 bag: post-war St Pancras Borough flats, pale brick in slightly Swedish style; then HYLDA COURT, an Art Deco period piece. After some very lavish Victorian stucco, a formal group of flats and houses by *Chassay Last, c.* 1990. A three-storey terrace flanked by taller end pavilions with shallow barrel roofs. Striped brick enlivened by some mannered Postmodern window shapes, but all kept within control. (For more of the C20, a diversion can be made here to Highgate New Town, *see* Perambulation, South east, below.)

Back by Brookfield Park to SWAIN'S LANE. Immediately on the E, HOLLY VILLAGE, built by the fabulously wealthy philanthropist Baroness Burdett-Coutts in 1865; a picturesque eyecatcher from her estate further N. The group of eight buildings by her favourite architect, *Henry Darbishire*, is placed round a green. The material is stock brick; the fussy Gothic ornamental detail is in timber, with some stone carving. The gatehouse is symmetrical; the other houses, although balancing each other, are deliberately but only slightly asymmetrical, even the one forming the vista from the gateway. All immaculately kept, down to the rustic lattice fencing and thick holly hedges. Holly Village is a conception unusual for its date in London, comparable with rural rather than urban compositions, although its distant ancestors are Nash's Park Villages on the fringe of Regents Park. 56

HOLLY LODGE ESTATE, between Highgate West Hill and Swain's Lane, was built up after 1923 as a select garden suburb in the grounds of the early C19 villa which had been the home of the Baroness Burdett-Coutts (†1906). The grounds were landscaped by *J. B. Papworth* in 1825. The villa has gone; it stood close to Robin Grove, off Highgate West Hill, where select houses hide among the rhododendrons. Part of the gardens remains as a private park between Robin Grove and Holly Lodge Gardens. The stables were in St Albans Road. HILLWAY was the long carriage way through the grounds from the s. It now climbs uphill between manicured verges and trim half-timbered villas. The most prominent buildings on the estate are the weird half-timbered mansion blocks between Hillway and Swain's Lane, built in 1924 for 'Lady workers'. They had a restaurant and social centre in Makepeace Avenue. This, and some of the flats, were replaced with flats by Camden in 1975–7.

The steep slope of SWAIN'S LANE benefits on the E side from the greenery of Highgate Cemetery Extension and Waterlow Park. On the w side are the high walls of the older cemetery laid out over the former grounds of Ashurst House in South Grove (*see* Perambulation 5a). Ingeniously tucked into the boundary are two interesting modern houses by *John Winter*. No. 82, his own house, of 1966–9, is a tough but elegant box of glass and steel, three storeys high. An emphatic frame of Cor-ten steel, which weathers to a rusty brown (its first application in this country). Living rooms on top and ground floor, bedrooms in between; a central service core and chimney leave the broad bays of floor-to-ceiling glazing undisturbed, with splendid views from the spacious top floor. No. 85, 1978–82, has a steel upper floor cantilevered out from a concrete central spine, with an entirely glazed wall on the private side overlooking the cemetery. The street side is more self-conscious, with circular windows, diagonal bracing and dark blue steel cladding. On the E side of the lane, handsome gates to Waterlow Park, and a pretty castellated Tudor lodge of *c.* 1840. Near the top, Nos. 91–103, a neat terrace of pale yellow brick, facing s, by *Haxworth & Kasabov*, 1970–2; living rooms on the top floor.

Further w off South Grove, in BACONS LANE, a select group of architects' houses exploits the views over the cemetery. The earliest were built in the kitchen gardens and orchard of Old Hall (*see* South Grove, Perambulation 5b) and were designed to fit around existing trees. No. 4 is by and for *W. L. Youille* (of Design Research Unit), *c.* 1955, low and self-effacing, with pantiled roofs; a living and a bedroom range on a staggered plan, with entrance in the link between, making the best of its leafy setting. No. 5 is by and for *Anthony Cox* (of the Architects' Co-Partnership), 1955–7, a simple two-storey brick cube with a one-storey wing and a spacious open-plan ground floor on two levels. Nos. 1–2 is by *Peter Cocke* (from the same firm). Further E, on another garden, Nos. 6, 7 and 8, by *Leonard Manasseh*. No. 8 for himself, 1961. A square plan, two and a half storeys high, with sloping roofs. Impressive interior: clever use of a mezzanine level for the entrance hall combined with landing; a study gallery overlooks the large double-height living area. Interesting combinations of materials: brick, marble paving and timber ceilings.

*South east of the village; Highgate New Town*

This diversion can be included in the previous tour, reached by CHESTER ROAD from Swain's Lane, or the area can be approached from Kentish Town by Dartmouth Park Road.

HIGHGATE NEW TOWN, modest terrace houses of *c.* 1865–80, were earmarked for redevelopment in the 1960s when Camden was in its most ambitious mood. The first phase, the bold concrete

terraces stepping uphill from RAYDON STREET, was planned
c. 1967 by *Richard Gibson*, redesigned in 1972 by *P. Tabori* and *K. Adie*, and completed in 1977–8. The insistent rhythm of vertical
cross-walls and horizontal bands, with upper floors set back, is
similar to Camden's Alexandra Road (*see* Hampstead, p. 247),
but here the terraces are shorter, and only three storeys high. All
in unadorned pale concrete blockwork with concrete bands, and
when pristine undeniably impressive as street sculpture, although
at the expense of the identity of the individual unit. Painted later.
Between the terraces are play courts and pedestrian walks, with
car parks tucked beneath. Separate steep stairs to each upper
maisonette. At the corner of Chester Road a group of shops with
flats above (1972–6) in a different idiom; brightly coloured bolted
panels and railings. At the s tip of the area, a hostel (1972–4) of
the same fair-faced blockwork as the terraces. Enthusiasm for
concrete surfaces had evaporated by the time of the later phase
along Dartmouth Park Road (1978–81, *Bill Forrest, Oscar Palacio*);
here the more homely brick terraces of houses and flats have wide
overhanging eaves and are prettily ornamented with timber trellises
and colourful balconies. The final phase remained unbuilt, the
surviving Victorian terraces nearby bearing witness to doubts
whether so much reconstruction had ever been necessary.

Not far off, in WINSCOMBE STREET, is a small experimental group
of five houses and studio for a housing association, including
*Neave Brown*'s own house, 1963–4. Simple materials and details –
concrete blocks, brick and timber, as used later by Neave Brown
for Camden's schemes in Dunboyne Road and Alexandra Road.
Three storeys, in traditional terrace form, but with deliberately
untraditional planning designed for c20 family life. A circular stair
leads up to a first-floor front door. On this level are kitchen and
dining room with a large terrace overlooking the garden, children's and utility rooms are below, living room and main bedroom on the top floor. A circular stair inside as well. Communal
front and back gardens.

# ENFIELD

The borough of Enfield, composed of the older local authorities of
Edmonton, Southgate and Enfield, stretches N from Tottenham and
Wood Green to the borders of Hertfordshire, where the remains of
Enfield Chase and the Green Belt give the area some rural character.
The E boundary is the River Lee, the old eastern limit of Middlesex.
The population (1996) is 257,417.

# EDMONTON

## INTRODUCTION

Edmonton is the next settlement N on the Great North Road after Tottenham, with whose development it has much in common. It was famous for its fairs from the C17 to the C19. When Lamb and Keats lived here in the early C19 the parish had two main centres, linked by ribbon development along the main road: Upper Edmonton around Fore Street, Silver Street and Angel Road (now sliced through by the North Circular Road), and Lower Edmonton further N, which still retains some village character between the large medieval church in Church Street and the green at the junction with the Great North Road. Further N there was a hamlet along Bury Street. Other settlements to the w – Palmers Green and Winchmore Hill – were absorbed within the separate district of Southgate (q.v.), created in 1881. Railway stations arrived in 1840 (Angel Road on the Cambridge line) and 1849 (Lower Edmonton on the branch to Enfield); as at Tottenham, the transformation to suburb came after 1872, when workmen's trains on the Great Eastern encouraged the growth of working-class housing. The population jumped from 9,708 in 1851 to 23,463 in 1881. In 1911 (without Southgate) it was 64,797, in 1951 104,270.

During the C19 textile works and linoleum factories developed along the bank of the Lee Navigation. They were replaced in the C20 by other industries moving out of congested central London, and Edmonton became one of London's principal centres for furniture manufacture. To the w further building and industry was encouraged by the creation of the Great Cambridge Road (1923–4); the area was almost all built up by 1939.

A few pre-Victorian buildings remain. The brick and timber-framed Salisbury House is the sole relic of the hamlet of Bury Street; the late 21 C18 Millfield House is a similar reminder of scattered pre-Victorian settlement along Silver Street. Both are now arts centres (*see* Public Buildings). Some good Edwardian churches (including two by *Caröe*) mark the development of the suburbs. Of these suburbs the 88 most interesting are the 1880s 'Queen Anne' development at Bush Hill Park, on the Enfield borders, where a station opened in 1880, and the council's large Hyde Estate of between the wars, E of Haselbury Road.

In the post-war period, a much more radical building programme was initiated under the Edmonton Borough Architect *T. A. Wilkinson* (after 1965 architect to the new Borough of Enfield, largely carried out by the borough's long established direct labour force). Much of the neighbourhood of Fore Street was rebuilt, and through the 1960s Edmonton acquired the rash of high-rise system-built towers which dominate the skyline of this part of the Lea Valley. The grand plans for the total redevelopment of Edmonton Green were only partially executed; the shopping centre was completed but the proposed Civic Centre was abandoned when Edmonton became part of Enfield. The high-rise programme ended in 1968, after the Conservatives won the local election.

ARCHAEOLOGY. There is a small Iron Age hill fort at Bush Hill,

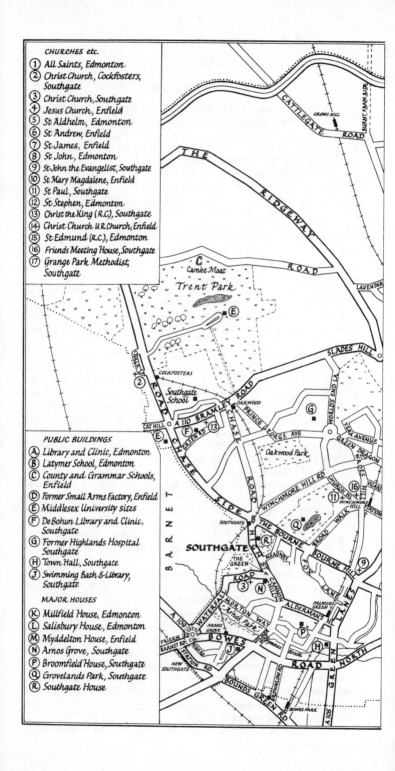

CHURCHES etc.
1. All Saints, Edmonton
2. Christ Church, Cockfosters, Southgate
3. Christ Church, Southgate
4. Jesus Church, Enfield
5. St Aldhelm, Edmonton
6. St Andrew, Enfield
7. St James, Enfield
8. St John, Edmonton
9. St John the Evangelist, Southgate
10. St Mary Magdalene, Enfield
11. St Paul, Southgate
12. St Stephen, Edmonton
13. Christ the King (R.C.), Southgate
14. Christ Church U.R.Church, Enfield
15. St Edmund (R.C.), Edmonton
16. Friends Meeting House, Southgate
17. Grange Park Methodist, Southgate

PUBLIC BUILDINGS
A. Library and Clinic, Edmonton
B. Latymer School, Edmonton
C. County and Grammar Schools, Enfield
D. Former Small Arms Factory, Enfield
E. Middlesex University sites
F. De Bohun Library and Clinic, Southgate
G. Former Highlands Hospital Southgate
H. Town Hall, Southgate
J. Swimming Bath & Library, Southgate

MAJOR HOUSES
K. Millfield House, Edmonton
L. Salisbury House, Edmonton
M. Myddelton House, Enfield
N. Arnos Grove, Southgate
P. Broomfield House, Southgate
Q. Grovelands Park, Southgate
R. Southgate House

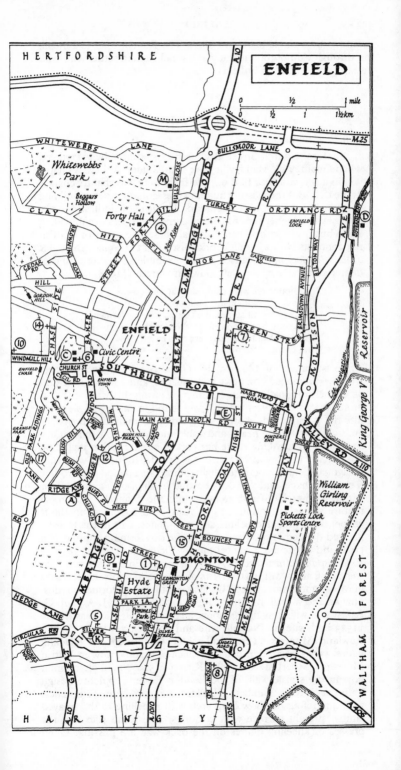

ENFIELD

HERTFORDSHIRE

WHITEWEBBS LANE

Whitewebbs Park

Beggars Hollow

CLAY HILL

Forty Hall

BULLSMOOR LANE

TURKEY ST

ORDNANCE RD.

ENFIELD LOCK

HOE LANE

EASTFIELD RD

ENFIELD

GREEN STREET

CAMBRIDGE ROAD

HERTFORD ROAD

MOLLISON AVENUE

BRIMSDOWN AVENUE

LITTON WAY

KING GEORGE V Reservoir

Lee Navigation

CEDAR RD

HILL

GORDON HILL

WINDMILL HILL

ENFIELD CHASE

Civic Centre

CHURCH ST

CECIL RD

ENFIELD TOWN

SOUTHBURY ROAD

NAGS HEAD ROAD

New River

GRANGE PARK

MAIN AVE

LINCOLN RD.

SOUTH ST

PONDERS END

BUSH HILL PARK

RIDGE AVE

CHURCH

WEST

BURY

STREET

Lee Navigation

VALLEY RD

WHARF RD

William Girling Reservoir

Picketts Lock Sports Centre

BOUNCES RD

HIGH ST

NIGHTINGALE ROAD

HERTFORD ROAD

MERIDIAN WAY

WALTHAM FOREST

EDMONTON

Hyde Estate

PARK LA.

Pymmes Park

SILVER STREET

MONTAGU ROAD

ANGELL ROAD

SILVER ST

FORE ST

EDMONTON GREEN

TOWN RD

HEDGE LANE

CIRCULAR RD

ANGEL ROAD

HARINGEY

M25

A10

scale: 0 ½ 1 mile / 0 ½ 1 1½ km

defended by a single bank and ditch. The Roman road to Lincoln ran through Edmonton; near it was a small Roman settlement, with burials nearby (*see also* Enfield).

## RELIGIOUS BUILDINGS

*1. Church of England*

ALL SAINTS, Church Street. A church existed here by *c.* 1136–43, when Geoffrey de Mandeville gave it to Walden Abbey. A chapel within it was endowed in 1292, and there were two chantry chapels in the C14. But the existing building is essentially a C15 rebuilding with a good deal of later alteration. The usual Middlesex C15 W tower, with a higher turret at the SE corner, and (less usual) with W angle buttresses rather than diagonal ones. The tower of Kentish rag contrasts with the yellow brick used in 1772 to face the tall N aisle, N chapel and chancel, a 'sad example of perverted taste' deplored in verse by the Rev. Dawson Warren (†1838):

> The buttresses were chipped away and cased
> The ancient battlements built up and coped
> With square cut stones, the Gothic window frames
> The costly work of our forefathers' zeal
> With sacrilegious hands were torn away
> And changed for timber ...

The restoration of 1889 by *W. Gilbee Scott* put back Gothic windows, removed box pews and galleries, and added S aisle and SE chapel (originally organ chamber). During this work CARVED FRAGMENTS of a Norman archway found in the S wall were set into the W wall inside. Larger voussoirs with small diaper, smaller arch with grotesque heads and cable moulding, voussoirs and a shaft with zigzag. One stone has part of an inscription including the letters IT DE WALTHAM. C15 N arcade: four bays with slim octagonal piers of moderate height; of the same period the two-bay N chancel chapel and NE vestry beyond (with piscina and old door within a low chamfered archway into the chancel). The roofs require special attention: C15 in vestry and nave, C16 in the N chapel, with moulded beams and wall-plates, C17 in the N aisle, flat and divided into sixteen panels, the ribs forming alternately a cross and a lozenge. Chancel mostly Victorian: restored 1855 by *E. Christian*, refurnished 1871 and decorated in the late C19 with stencilling and WALL PAINTINGS of angels and saints. PAINTINGS of Moses and Aaron, signed *W. Turner*, C18, from a former reredos, now on the W wall. BRASSES. Reset on the W wall: J. Asplyn, G. Askew and wife, tiny figures above an inset tablet; Nicholas Boone †1523 and wife, E. Nowell, wife and children †1616. N chapel: Rowland Monoux †1574, wall tablet with indent for kneeling figure, verse inscription below (replica of original now in British Museum). MONUMENTS. John Kirton †1529. Small altar tomb, now in the S aisle wall, of the London Easter Sepulchre design found at St Mary Lambeth, Hackney, and elsewhere. Tomb-chest with quatrefoils, shallow Perp arch with panelling to the splayed jambs; straight cornice with crestings. The tomb slab and the brasses of kneeling figures on the back wall are missing. Good late C17 LEDGER STONES, and many minor C17 and C18 monuments. George Huxley of Wyre Hall †1627, small armorial tablet of alabaster with black touch from Belgium and red marble, with skulls and a fine figure of Time above. Attributed to *Maximilian Colt* (GF). Others to the Huxleys in the S aisle: Anne Huxley †1653, wreathed oval. John Huxley †1661, architectural, with swags. Elizabeth Huxley †1730, Doric tablet. Edward Rogers and family, 1660s, architectural. Thomas Maule †1714/15, with fluted pilasters, feigned drapery at base. By *James Hardy* (GF). Galliard †1716, by *Edward Stanton* (GF). Elizabeth Chaplin †1720, erected 1726, with delicate marble Ionic columns. Rev. Dawson Warren †1838 (of the poem, *see* above). Chaste Neoclassical urn, signed *H. King*. Twin Gothic tablets to Charles Lamb †1834 and William Cowper †1800, erected to commemorate a visit by the London and Middlesex Archaeological Society in 1888.

Large CHURCHYARD with many good memorials. An enjoyable range of headstones. The earliest of 1667; some fine decorative ones of the C18, e.g. Sarah Silverthorne †1735, with figure of Time (SE of chancel). Several C18 chest tombs, also the tombs of Charles Lamb †1834 and his sister.

CHURCH HALL to the E, 1982 by *John Phillips*. The stone-faced former church hall opposite, now the Charles Lamb Institute, is by *J. S. Alder*, 1907–8.

ST ALDHELM, Silver Street. 1903 by *W. D. Caröe*. Brick, with low aisles, clerestory, steep-pitched roof and an idiosyncratic westwork building up to a W turret. Playful shingled flèche on the crossing. Free Perp detail enlivened by typical Caröe features: plentiful use of tiles, windows set in deeply splayed arches. Interior with W gallery and slim octagonal stone piers without capitals, the lower parts panelled in wood (originally dark green). Sturdy oak PULPIT with open arcading, from St Mary Spital Square, late C19, by *W. R. Dale*. REREDOS with large, effective painting of the Ascension, 1947–8, and STAINED GLASS, both by *Walter Starmer*, as Second World War Memorials. 88

VICARAGE N of the church also by *Caröe*, 1907; group of HALLS of 1883 and 1907–9.

ST ALPHEGE, Hertford Road. 1957–8 by *Edward Maufe*. Quiet, pale brick, a tall portal-framed centre with overhanging eaves and a slim SW bell-turret with sculpture of St Alphege. E wall with S Crucifixion against a circular window; aisle windows with 30s-looking stepped heads. Traditional long nave, originally made more interesting by a sunken choir area. N chapel with folding screen; to the S a hall enlarged from the original one in the S aisle. Simple FONT with wavy line decoration. PULPIT, neatly built out from the wall. PAINTINGS: Crucifixion and two smaller paintings by *C. Pearson*, given in the 1970s. The VICARAGE to the SE, also by *Maufe*, groups nicely with the church, with a pedimented gable at each end.

Former ST JAMES, Fore Street. Converted to flats; *see* Perambulation 2.

ST JOHN, Dyson Road. 1905–6 by *C. H. B. Quennell*. Lean, eccentric brick Gothic by an architect better known for his domestic work (*see* Hampstead). Powerful W front with layered brick planes and three tall lancets; niche with statue above, tiny baptistery windows below. Transepts and aisled nave of six bays, the piers panelled and with angular stone springers to the brick arches. Tall clerestory. The most striking feature is the way the narrower chancel with slim passage aisles allows for windows on either side of the chancel arch (cf. the medieval Spanish Cathedral of Gerona). ORGAN from Christ's Hospital, Newgate Street. SEAT made up from C17 woodwork. GLAZING with clear glass in leaded patterns, by *Paul Woodroffe*, who is named with other craftsmen on the foundation stone, a nice Arts and Crafts touch.

ST MARK, St Mark's Road, Bush Hill Park. *See* Enfield Churches, p. 437.

Former ST MARTIN, Town Road. *See* St Demetrios, p. 425.

ST MARY'S CENTRE, Lawrence Road, Lower Edmonton. 1970, replacing St Mary Fore Street, 1883 by *Butterfield*, demolished in 1957.

ST MICHAEL BASSISHAW, Bury Street. 1901 by *W. D. Caröe*, funded by the sale of the City church of the same name. Made redundant in 1982 and converted into flats, sensitively: the chief external alteration is a tactful lowering of the aisle windows. A substantial building of red brick with tall sweeping roofs and details characteristic of Caröe's Gothic. Big nine-light W window above W porch and baptistery. Deeply inset doors, flanked by a playful NW turret. A larger tower further E has windows to light the shallow chancel. The wide nave had passage aisles and a roof of hammer-beam type. The W bay remains undivided. Foundation stone by *Eric Gill*. Caröe's Rood of 1912 is now at St Alban, Ilford. Former VICARAGE in C17 style, 1901, also by *Caröe*.

ST PETER, Bounces Road. 1896 by *Newman & Newman*; impressively tall, brick with steep slate roof. Dec apsed chancel, narthex and porches of 1902, by *D. Newman*. (Chapel Reredos of old carved panelling.) VICARAGE, 1901, with heavy stone portal; hall 1908 by *Alder*.

ST STEPHEN, Park Avenue, Bush Hill Park. By *J. S. Alder*: E part 1906–7, W bays of nave 1915, SW tower not built. Stone, with Perp tracery, quite large and impressive. Tall nave of five bays with quatrefoil piers, wooden barrel roof, apsidal W baptistery. STAINED GLASS. E window 1938. Chapel E window 1936 by *Webb*. N aisle, Youth Fellowship window by *Francis Skeat*, 1969.

Baptistery windows by *Powell*. War memorial LYCHGATE, by *Alder*, 1919–20.

## 2. Roman Catholic

ST EDMUND, Hertford Road. Founded in 1903 by Redemptorist priests. 1905–7 by *E. Doran Webb*. Eclectic Gothic, coursed stone, with low lean-to aisles and squat crossing tower. A dark clerestory-less interior. ALTAR by *David Stokes*, carved by *Bernard Davies*, 1957. Worth a special visit for the two abstract STAINED GLASS windows of 1982 by *Mark Angus*: S transept, on the theme of light, with a strong vertical red band and blue-green around the edge; the chancel S window, symbolizing water and baptism, is mostly blue and green. PRESBYTERY (former monastery) to the W, 1907, gabled, with tall chimneys, and SCHOOL to the E, 1912 with additions, both in the same white stone as the church.

### 3. Other places of worship

BAPTIST CHURCH, Edmonton Green. 1974. Octagonal with a spike, a friendly contrast to the neighbouring shopping complex.

BUSH HILL UNITED REFORMED CHURCH, Main Avenue, Bush Hill Park. 1910. Lombard Romanesque front, round-headed windows within a larger arch under a gable; the gabled clerestory windows and hall of 1932, both roughcast, have an Arts and Crafts flavour.

EDMONTON TEMPLE (Universal Prayer Group Ministries), Grove Road. c. 1975. Polygonal, with angular clerestory windows below a shallow pitched roof.

ST DEMETRIOS (Greek Orthodox), Town Road. Formerly St Martin. 1909 by E. L. Warre, paid for by Mrs Elizabeth Mason. A large, plain church for a poor area. Red brick with stone dressings; lancet clerestory windows. The flying buttresses crowned by stumpy cupolas are the most distinctive feature. (Plastered interior; wide nave with braced tie-beams; timber w gallery. E window: Te Deum First World War Memorial.)

TANNERS END FREE CHURCH, Statham Grove, Bull Lane. 1886. Hall 1911 by F. Bethel.

### 4. Cemeteries

CEMETERY, Church Street and Great Cambridge Road. Chapels and mortuary, 1886–7. Apsed stone chapels with simple Perp tracery, linked by a carriage arch with spirelet above.

CEMETERIES, Montagu Road. Jewish Cemetery founded 1884; Tottenham Park Cemetery founded 1912.

## PUBLIC BUILDINGS

EDMONTON COUNTY COURT, Grove Street. 1940. In a formal stripped classical tradition; brick above a stone ground floor.

METROPOLITAN POLICE H.Q., Fore Street. Large red brick block of the 1980s with some fancy glazing at the entrance.

FIRE STATION, Church Street. Plain and symmetrical, with stone surrounds and bowed ends, but in 1930s modern dress, 1941 by Edmonton Architect's Department.

LEISURE CENTRE, Edmonton Green. 1970 by the Borough Architect T. A. Wilkinson. An unappealing box amidst car parking E of the Broadway, unintegrated with the rest of the new buildings of the shopping centre. This has a LIBRARY and careers office in South Mall, an adaptation of 1990–2 (see Perambulation 1).*

BRANCH LIBRARY and CLINIC, Ridge Avenue and Church Street. A fresh and airy group in the post-war Scandinavian style which succeeded the MCC's brick Dudok tradition. LIBRARY of 1959–63 by Brian van Breda of Edmonton Borough Architect's Department, an eyecatching L-shaped building on a corner site. Gabled, with monopitch roofs consisting of four segments of timber hyperbolic

---

*The old civic buildings in Knights Lane and Fore Street were demolished in 1989. The crenellated Perp Town Hall was of 1884 by G. Eedes Eachus, enlarged 1902–3 by W. Gilbee Scott, who also added swimming baths, likewise demolished.

parabolas, neatly boarded inside (consultants: Timber Development Association and *R. Hobin,* engineer). Asymmetrically arranged floor-to-eaves windows; red and yellow brick facing above a flint plinth. The adjoining CLINIC behind uses the same materials and has an entrance canopy with circular roof-lights.

HOUNDSFIELD ROAD CENTRE. Built as library and school 'feeding centre', 1937, by *T. A. Wilkinson* of the Borough Architect's Department, two storeys, plain but dignified, of dark brick with stone portal.

NORTH MIDDLESEX HOSPITAL, Sterling Way. A large complex, of C19 origin. The w part began as the Edmonton Union Workhouse, 1842; the E part was a separate Infirmary, opened 1910. Pymms Building 1986; Stirling House, a catering block with restaurant next to a pool, 1985–9 by *Llewelyn-Davies Weeks.*

PICKETTS LOCK SPORTS CENTRE. Built on an old refuse tip. One of the recreational centres developed for the Lee Valley Regional Park from 1973. Three large, functional white boxes arranged around a central swimming pool, linked by generous circulation areas. By *Williamson Partnership* with *J. V. M. Bishop* of the LVRP. Made a little less bleak by additions of 1993–4: restaurant, café and cinema, and an entrance block by *Fitzroy Robinson & Partners.*

REFUSE INCINERATION PLANT, N of Angel Road, on the edge of the marshes, in a setting which enhances its impressive scale. Built to generate electricity, 1971–4 by the *G. L. C.* Vast box-like forms clad in corrugated metal sheeting, pale grey and dark grey, approached by two big ramps on tapering piers. Huge cylindrical concrete chimney containing two flues.

NEW RIVER (*see also* Islington). A small SLUICE HOUSE spans the river as it passes under Bush Hill Road. It crosses Salmon's Brook on a high embankment which replaced the 'Bush Hill Frame', the original lead-lined trough, 666 ft long, removed in 1784–6. The arch over the brook has the arms of Sir Hugh Myddelton and the date 1682.

LEE NAVIGATION (*see also* Enfield). The locks date from the 1850s and 60s, rebuilt to take 100-ton barges. Except for Picketts Lock they were duplicated and mechanized *c.* 1960.

RAILWAYS. EDMONTON GREEN STATION (formerly Lower Edmonton), 1872, on a new suburban line of the Great Eastern Railway. Valanced saw-toothed platform canopies and good cast-iron work. Likewise the station at SILVER STREET.

ROADS. North Circular Road BRIDGE over the Lee Navigation at Angel Road, 1927 by *Sir Owen Williams* and *Maxwell Ayrton,* reinforced concrete, originally with two pairs of pylon-shaped towers with vertical ribs, and massive parapets. In contrast the weight of the carriageway is carried by shallow beams integral with the deck slab. VIADUCT to the E by the same engineer and architect, 1,700 ft long, of many short spans. The pylons E of the viaduct were demolished in the 1970s for road improvements.

*Educational buildings*

CHARITY SCHOOL, Church Street. *See* Perambulation 1.

BOARD SCHOOLS. Edmonton had an active School Board. Many of the early buildings are still in use. BRETTENHAM, Brettenham

Road, was their first building, opened 1882, enlarged 1885–9, 1892. The oldest parts two-storeyed, still with Gothic arched windows. In the centre of the rambling group, the prim villa-like SCHOOL BOARD OFFICES of 1900, by *Henry W. Dobb*. RAYNHAM, Raynham Road, dates from 1896, with infants' school of 1901. ELDON, Eldon Road, 1899.

BUSH HILL PARK SCHOOL, Main Avenue. 1896 (extended 1899, 1908), by *G. E. T. Laurence* for Enfield School Board, a handsome composition with a highly decorative skyline of gables and turrets, and much use of red terracotta.

LATYMER SCHOOL, Haselbury Road. A grammar school which traces its origins to bequests of 1606 and 1624. In Church Street until 1910. A long, striking Arts and Crafts frontage with sweeping tiled roofs. The original building of 1910 by *H. G. Crothall*, Middlesex County Architect, is at the N end, with hall sandwiched between two ranges of classrooms. This hall became a dining hall when the S extension of 1924–8 was added, with tall white-rendered and gabled entrance. Behind is a quadrangular lay-out with galleried hall to accommodate 1,000, and classrooms on two storeys. PERFORMING ARTS CENTRE by *Nicholas Hare Architects* planned 1996.

EDMONTON COUNTY SCHOOLS, Great Cambridge Road. Upper School built as Edmonton Grammar School, by *W. T. Curtis* of the MCC, 1931, altered 1962. A long dignified front in the Swedish classical tradition; big hipped roof with small cupola. Extended 1968 after it became comprehensive. LOWER SCHOOL, Little Bury Street, in secondary-modern buildings of 1960.

INTERWAR PRIMARY SCHOOLS. The expanding suburbs of between the wars demanded a stream of schools from the *MCC*. RAGLAN, Raglan Road, Bush Hill, 1928, infants 1934, has an earlier part still quite Baroque, a formal composition of one-storey pavilions. Centre with hipped roof and cupola. HAZELBURY, Hazelbury Road (juniors and infants, formerly secondary), 1930–1, is similar. Later examples: GALLIARD, Galliard Road, 1937; OAKTHORPE, Tile Kiln Lane, 1937, 1939.

WEST LEA SPECIAL SCHOOL, Haselbury Road. 1938, built by the *MCC* as an open-air school for TB sufferers; a special school from *c.* 1970. Low, formal composition facing S to playing fields. Hipped-roofed hall with generously windowed classrooms in projecting wings, formerly opening on to gardens. The E wing originally had unglazed openings to provide maximum fresh air.

POST-WAR PRIMARY SCHOOLS. The experimental 1950s produced schools of some variety. CUCKOO HALL, Cuckoo Lane, 1948. A formal finger plan, impressive but barrack-like, with one-storey rendered classroom ranges in long rows linked by corridors, very similar to Carterhatch Lane, Enfield. Taller adjoining buildings of 1952, now Salisbury Upper School. In contrast, WILBURY, Wilbury Way, 1951–3, by the *MCC*, is a compact group in a spacious setting. Upper floor timber-clad; two storeys, with a hall on each floor and classrooms used as circulation space. CHURCHFIELD, Latymer Way, 1974–8 by the *Borough of Enfield*, is in the style of the 70s. Built as linked junior and infants' schools. A spreading single-storey group with concrete-block walls and monopitch roofs. Free-flowing spaces with open-plan classrooms (partly altered) looking out to the surrounding greenery. Extra classrooms added 1984.

## MILLFIELD HOUSE
### Silver Street

Now part of MILLFIELD ARTS COMPLEX. The late C18 Millfield House was used from 1849 as a school for Strand Union Workhouse children, from 1915 as a hospital, and converted to an arts centre in 1971–9. Built by 1796, when it was let to the Imperial ambassador. Reticent w front of nine bays and two storeys, the centre three bays slightly recessed and with a shallow curved porch, the outer ones with pretty tented verandas, probably of the early C19. A surprisingly grandiose but loosely conceived Neoclassical plan, no doubt suitable for showy receptions. The porch forms part of a circular entrance hall (cf. Belmont, Mill Hill, Barnet). To the l. is an oval toplit stairwell, with elegant cantilevered stairs and curved doors on the upper landing. On the ground floor to the N are two reception rooms, the NW one with later bay window; to the s is a very large room with Neoclassical frieze of urns and husk garlands and a tripartite s window, the mullions with consoles and carved heads. SE service wing with later additions.

LODGE and outbuilding from the C19 workhouse period; another lodge of the early C20. Other institutional buildings were replaced by WEIR HALL LIBRARY and THEATRE, 1988 by *Enfield Borough Architect's Department*, w of Millfield House. The theatre, a brick box with green-painted windows, shares a foyer with the one-storeyed library projecting out towards the road.

## SALISBURY HOUSE
### Bury Street West

The one relic of the old hamlet of Bury Street, is incongruously surrounded by suburbia; a C16 gabled brick and timber house with clustered chimneystacks, part roughcast, part weatherboarded. Bought by the borough in 1936 and now an Arts Centre. Picturesque, despite the harsh rendered surfaces of the 1950s restoration. Repaired again in 1991–2. The house may once have been larger. It consists now of a range running N–S, with a C19 NW entrance hall attached to a w stair-turret. The earlier entrance was on the E side below the centre gable of three projecting from the N–S ridge. On each side are prominent external stacks. The door now opens into a single room, probably originally a N parlour, s hall and unheated central entrance space. The parlour has C18 panelling. Hall and entrance area each had access to the polygonal stair-turret on the w side. This is of brick on the ground floor, timber-framed above. It is now flanked by later additions blocking the lower windows in the main range. First-floor s room with early C17 fittings (sold in 1907 and taken to Edinburgh but returned in 1991–2). Small-paned panelling and a good overmantel with crisp classical motifs of the type copied from engravings: perspective

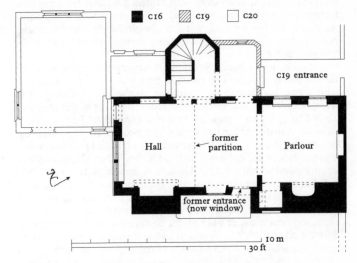

C16    C19    C20

C19 entrance

Hall    former partition    Parlour

former entrance
(now window)

10 m
30 ft

Salisbury House. Ground-floor plan

arches and aedicules with broken pediments. Fireplace with two
phases of PAINTING discovered on the reveals: fragments of strapwork, and over this, two later C17 cartouches with figures and
boldly drawn fruit and flowers. N room also with panelling,
painted over, an overmantel with geometric patterns and frieze,
and a pretty oriel overlooking the road with early C19 Gothic glazing. Basement with C16 moulded and stopped doorcase, possibly
moved from elsewhere. The S room with fireplace may have been
a kitchen.

## PERAMBULATIONS

*1. Church Street, Edmonton Green, Lower Edmonton*

CHURCH STREET preserves some relics of the old village and its C19
expansion. Starting at the church, to its W, on the S side, are two
low brick ranges of ALMSHOUSES, built 1679, rebuilt 1754 and
1903 (by *Henry W. Dobb*), modernized 1960. Nearby, No. 90,
JOHN ADAMS COURT, pleasant sheltered housing, yellow brick
with pebbly lintels and tiled roofs, *c.* 1979. Then Nos. 94–112, a
mid-C19 stucco-trimmed terrace, ruthlessly converted to flats. On
the N side the main focus is the CHARLES LAMB INSTITUTE,
1907–8 by *J.S. Alder*, a long stone range with Tudor detail, the
hall alongside the road ending in a turret. It is flanked by Nos.
71–77, two refurbished early C19 pairs of three-storey villas, and
Nos. 43–45, two mid-C19 stuccoed three-bay houses, each with a
projecting centre. Nearby is the early C18 cottage where Charles
and Mary Lamb lived from 1833.

Church Street continues E, with a little P.O. SORTING OFFICE
in jolly Edwardian Baroque on the S side, some low cottagey
terraces, and one small gem, the former CHARITY SCHOOL,

founded 1778, a narrow front with central door, two tall windows, inscription with the date 1784 and a niche above with charity girl. Adjoining red brick cottage for the schoolmistress. On the N side, No. 21, C18, a former three-bay three-storey pair with nice early C19 iron porch.

The transition from Church Street to EDMONTON GREEN at Lower Edmonton is abrupt. The green is now a series of roundabouts, with a C20 concrete conglomeration on the E side, facing away from Fore Street. Comprehensive redevelopment of the area was agreed in 1960, to a plan by *Frederick Gibberd & Partners*, for a radically transformed urban centre with pedestrian shopping area, car parking for 3,000, 750 flats, and new civic and amenity buildings in place of the old town hall and baths. When Edmonton was incorporated within the new Borough of Enfield plans for the civic buildings were abandoned, so this brave new world tails away to the S, with only a leisure centre set in a car park as an inadequate focus. Building began in 1965 and was completed in 1974. The shopping area is better than might be expected from the exterior. SOUTH MALL leads N, sheltered by a translucent roof (pleasantly airy compared with covered malls of the 1970s). Opening off is a LIBRARY and offices on three floors, converted from a former department store by *Rivington Street Studio*, 1990–2; a deep plan opened up by a handsome new toplit staircase (cf. Crowndale Centre, Camden). In the library, MEMORIAL BOARDS to local people, from the old Town Hall. The big, bustling no-frills MARKET SQUARE is a covered area lit by clerestory windows. NORTH MALL is treated differently, in the harder spirit of the later 1960s: a concrete coffered roof alternates with open light-wells, and ends in an open square, optimistically with two levels of shops and two storeys of flats above; brutalist dark brick and shuttered concrete. The backdrop rising from the deck above North Mall is composed of the huge slabs of system-built flats which the borough built so keenly at this time (*see also* below); their unimaginative bulk is only slightly mitigated by later two-tone painting. Further E, in TOWN ROAD, the shift to low-rise housing during the 1970s is demonstrated by two large two-storey groups in yellow brick by *Neylan & Ungless*.

HERTFORD ROAD to the N has a surprising contrast: THE CRESCENT, Nos. 84–132, reprieved from the town centre redevelopment scheme and repaired in the 1970s after long neglect. A leisurely early C19 urban sweep of three-storey houses comfortably set back from the main road: channelled stucco ground floor, first-floor windows below brick arches. S end and centre (the N end was not completed) accentuated by giant Corinthian pilasters; a pediment over the centre three houses. It was an unsuccessful speculation by a London solicitor, built 1826–51.

Little to single out among the later housing which fills the uneventful area between Edmonton and Enfield. THE COCK, at the corner of Houndsfield Road, *c.* 1900, is exuberantly gross Jacobean, with corbelled-out shaped pediment and a little dome. To the E, around CUCKOO HALL LANE, pleasantly laid out low-rise council housing, Edmonton's first post-war development, 1947–50, on the last greenfield site available in the borough.

## 2. Upper Edmonton

FORE STREET and the areas to its E and W have an instructive sequence of Edmonton's post-war housing, the result of the borough's enthusiasm for comprehensive development areas and innovative building types. The largest, at Edmonton Green, has already been described. S of it were Edmonton's C19 civic buildings, which were to have been rebuilt as part of the scheme, but which were demolished after the borough became part of Enfield.

In FORE STREET S of the shopping centre the best group is the housing of 1950 around SEBASTOPOL ROAD; exemplary 'mixed development' of the type introduced in Hackney by Gibberd and adopted by the LCC in the 50s, still in the gentle Scandinavian fashion of the post-war era. By the Borough of Edmonton (Job Architect *R. D. Kain*), after an outline plan by *F. Gibberd & Partners*. Two six-storey point blocks with canted sides; maisonettes with sawtooth fronts, decorative curved garden walls. On the W side, No. 337 is a former PASSMORE EDWARDS LIBRARY by *Maurice B. Adams*, 1897. Picturesque brick and stone three-storey symmetrical elevation, with projecting entrance bay and a roofline of shaped gables. (Inside were two fine portrait plaques by *George Frampton*, 1908, to John Keats and Charles Lamb, now in store.) One-storey rear lending library extension, 1931, by *Cuthbert Brown*, Borough Engineer, with coffered ceiling on Tuscan columns. Tucked away behind at the S end of SHRUBBERY ROAD, a 1950s industrial building with a carefully composed frontage: centre with glass bricks and a gridded projection above, wings with patterned tiles. Further S, No. 320, STATION HOUSE is a former police station, now flats; 1905 by *J. D. Butler*. Stone, with shallow ground-floor bay window and a big central gable. Near the North Circular Road a few remnants of C18 ribbon development remain, on a more modest scale than in Tottenham just down the road. Nos. 258–260, mid-C18 with Ionic doorcases; Nos. 236–238, an early C18 pair (No. 238 with Doric doorcase and iron railings), and Nos. 183–195 (Angel Place), a mid-C18 group of three linked blocks, two storeys, mostly with Doric doorcases.

This area, named the Angel after an old inn, was for fifty years disrupted by the busy North Circular Road (sunk in an underpass in 1997). To its S, among the shopping parades, Fore Street has a few more early houses, heavily disguised. The best are Nos. 186–192, an early C18 terrace behind later shops, and Nos. 60–64, three individual houses, No. 62 of three bays with central pediment. S of these, the PHOENIX, an attractive *c.* 1900 composition with ornamental plaster panels and half-timbered gables. Opposite is the former church of St James (now flats), 1850 by *Edward Ellis*; plain ragstone Gothic; vicarage to the N, 1868, also stone. Then a forceful range of shops with flats above, on the edge of another large area of post-war redevelopment by the *Borough of Edmonton*. This dates from 1956–61: big slabs of maisonettes faced in pale brick, arranged *en échelon*, mostly of nine storeys with a single taller block of fourteen storeys. They make a striking composition around COLLEGE GARDENS, despite deficient landscaping. Pleasant contemporary low PRIMARY SCHOOL of St John and St

James (1962) to the s in Grove Road. The four-storey blocks of flats at r. angles to LANGHEDGE ROAD, of similar date, are quite decoratively detailed in red and yellow brick. Further E, a later stage of borough housing can be seen at WOOLMER ROAD, just s of Angel Road. By the mid 60s the borough's priorities were speed and prefabricated construction; sensitive townscape was not an issue. ANGEL HOUSE, completed 1965, was built by the Edmonton Direct Labour Organisation as a prototype 18-storey block with precast units produced by a novel vertical battery casting system, developed by the borough with the Buildings Research Station and the Reinforced Concrete Steel Co. The technique was used for the borough's later towers.

PYMMES PARK, w of Fore Street, was opened as a public park in 1898. Agreeable lay-out of the usual C19 municipal type, with lakes and an island. At the s end, a walled garden with old walls and a mid-C19 WALL FOUNTAIN with dolphin decoration. Nearby was the site of Pymmes House, a brick and timber-framed mansion which belonged to the Cecils from the C16; it was burnt down in 1898. The name comes from Pymmes Brook, which can be followed from here upstream to Hadley Common.

The HYDE ESTATE, N of the park and E of HASELBURY ROAD, was the Borough of Edmonton's first major housing development, begun 1920. The architects were *Niven & Wigglesworth*. Roughcast semi-detached houses in garden suburb spirit, some with tile-hung twin gables to create variety. They are grouped round a series of little greens. E of Victoria Road, close to the railway, the extreme contrast of the borough's BARBOT ESTATE, by *Enfield Borough Architect's Department*, 1966–8 onwards. Four twenty-three-storey towers of concrete precast units made on site. Top fringe of tapering uprights above chequerboard cladding, a coarse descendant of Tecton's abstract patterning.

The E fringe of Edmonton along the Lee Navigation changed rapidly in the later C20 as industry was replaced by retail warehouses. The latter and their car parks dominate the junction of ANGEL ROAD and the new MERIDIAN WAY; to their N the ELEY INDUSTRIAL ESTATE still has some unassumingly functional brick factories of the 1950s.

### 3. Bush Hill

The suburb on the NW border of Edmonton was developed by the Northern Estates Company, established in 1875 with the intention of developing Bush Hill Park as a high-class building estate. Bush Hill Park Station was opened in 1880. The social divide is easy to see. E of the tracks a big pub and working-class terraces, beginning with First Avenue, laid out in 1880. MAIN AVENUE is the chief street, with a proud Board school and churches (St Mark's, United Reformed, qq.v.). In ST MARK'S ROAD, a former chapel of 1906–7, badly mauled by its conversion to flats, in a flamboyant debased Italianate; elaborate side porch with bellcote. To the w of the station is the indicatively named QUEEN ANNE'S PLACE, with some tile-hung shops of the 1880s in the tradition of Bedford Park, and a handsome former bank of *c.* 1900, with domed corner turret at the corner of Dryden Road, setting the tone for the middle-class development. The rest is a disappointment, for only a scatter of original houses remain. The contrast with 'aesthetic' Bedford Park (begun 1875) is interesting: there was little picturesque street architecture; the emphasis was on the detached house. The earliest were mostly by *R. Tayler Smith*; some remain along the main axis of WELLINGTON ROAD. A brochure praised them as 'rustic bijou villas', 'well built and detached with the four fronts equally well finished in the same style of architecture'. They are very plain, in a minimal Queen Anne style. The curving VILLAGE ROAD and PRIVATE ROAD (formerly gated) had larger plots with superior houses in a variety of styles, which have nearly all gone. The important exception is No. 8 (Brooklyn) PRIVATE ROAD, 1883 by the Arts and Crafts architect *A. H. Mackmurdo* for his brother. No. 6 (demolished), which Mackmurdo had built for his mother in 1874–6, was picturesquely half-timbered, but No. 8 is in a severe stripped classical style, reflecting Mackmurdo's growing interest in the Italian Renaissance. Unlike anything else of its date. Two storeys, six bays, with a flat roof. Roughcast walls, originally painted yellow, and articulated by strong horizontal bands and cornice, and by a tight rhythm of thick and thin pilasters between the ground-floor windows. These have terracotta panels and carry small terracotta figures.

BUSH HILL further W attracted several country houses but is now nearly all superior suburbia of between the wars and later. The mansion of Bush Hill Park stood until 1927 between Bush Hill and Park Avenue, close to the New River. Further S, HALLIWICK GATE, 1990s housing S of Bush Hill Road. This replaced a plain late C18 wing of Bush Hill House, or Halliwick, latterly used as a school. In the C17 Halliwick was the home of Sir Hugh Myddelton; his New River curved around the grounds and a sluice remains by Bush Hill Road (*see* Public Buildings). The one mansion surviving is OLD PARK, now BUSH HILL GOLF CLUB. The entrance front, facing E, consists of a S part of *c.* 1705, two storeys with parapet, of red brick, extended in 1838. In 1873 it was given a large but neat addition in Queen Anne style, and in the C20 ruined by horrible picture windows. C18 stables with clock turret. The house belonged to the C19 local antiquarian Edward Ford, who assembled various medieval fragments (there used to be two C15 corbel heads on the stables; three small carved C15 figures of angel, male and female saints on a cottage).

# ENFIELD

## INTRODUCTION

Enfield was the second largest medieval parish in Middlesex, with the principal town in the north of the county. The town developed midway between the forest of Enfield Chase on the higher land to the W and the Lea Valley to the E. The church was already sizeable by the C13. A market and fairs were granted in 1304; there is still a market place in front of the church, and the town centre has an urban rather than a suburban feel.

From the C15 the chief manor belonged to the Duchy of Lancaster and thus passed to the Crown, together with Enfield Chase. The royal connection and the appeal of the hunting forest gave Enfield a special cachet in the C16. In 1539 Henry VIII acquired the house known as ELSYNG, or Enfield House, which lay in the present grounds of Forty Hall and survived in part until the later C17. The royal accounts show that extensive repairs were carried out under Edward VI, who gave the house to his sister Elizabeth. Elsyng may be the provenance of some of the fittings which were in a house S of the market place known as ENFIELD PALACE. When this was demolished in 1927 the remains were preserved by the Leggatt brothers in an extension added to No. 5 Gentleman's Row. The chief feature
13 is a splendid stone fireplace in an accomplished mid-C16 Renaissance style, a rare survival of court work of this period. The overmantel is carved with royal arms and emblems set between Corinthian columns. Below are the initials E and R on panels with embryonic strapwork. There is also some enriched panelling with pilasters, and a geometric plaster ceiling with thin ribs and royal badges in the compartments. If also mid-C16 the ceiling would be a very early example of the type but is more likely to be later C16 and made for Enfield Palace.
25 Enfield's major surviving mansion is Forty Hall, built *c*. 1630 in an architecturally progressive style by Sir Nicholas Raynton, a wealthy Lord Mayor, and still standing in its own grounds. Around the fringes of the estate on Forty Hill the gentry built houses in the C18 and C19; the Green Belt has preserved this area at least partially as countryside. Enfield Town too became fashionable, with a series of
4 appealing houses along Gentleman's Row close to the New River, whose winding course also attracted picturesquely sited houses at Bulls Cross and elsewhere.

The eastern part of Enfield is a different story. Until the C19 the flat, swampy land of the Lea Valley harboured only a string of hamlets: Ponders End, Enfield Highway and Enfield Wash along Hertford Road, the line of the Roman Ermine Street, and Turkey Street straggling beside the Turkey Brook. The early industry of the Lea Valley is represented by the C18 flour mills at Ponders End. Lysons in 1795 mentions a tanyard and marbled paperworks as the only significant industries in the parish, but during the C19 good river and rail transport encouraged rapid development. The most remarkable was the government's Ordnance Factory, established at a remote site at Enfield Lock in 1816, which developed into a major industrial concern from the 1850s. Other factories grew up along the Lee Navigation, and more arrived in the C20, as industries moved out of

London to Ponders End and Brimsdown. The old hamlets became a continuous suburb, and the character of the riverside was transformed by a series of massive reservoirs along the Middlesex–Essex boundary. Further w, brickfields gave way to the Great Cambridge Road, which was built in 1921 to bypass the congested Hertford Road and was soon flanked by new factories, so that much of the area was built over. Much of the industrial activity vanished in the 1980s–90s, replaced by a more loosely knit mixture of sheds and supermarkets. Near the river, derelict industrial sites are now interspersed with efforts at reclamation by the Lee Valley Regional Park.

A station was opened at Ponders End in 1840, another at Ordnance Road in 1855. A branch line from Angel Road to Enfield Town opened in 1849, but extensive suburban building did not take off in the w part of Enfield until the c20.

ARCHAEOLOGY. There have been Paleolithic finds near the River Lee, and later prehistoric finds across Enfield Chase. There was a Roman settlement of some size beside the road to Lincoln, with burials nearby (*see also* Edmonton).

## RELIGIOUS BUILDINGS

### *1. Church of England*

JESUS CHURCH, Forty Hill. 1835, by *Thomas Ashwell* of Tottenham. According to the wishes of the patron, C. P. Meyer of Forty Hall, designed in imitation of Savage's Holy Trinity, Tottenham. It is the Commissioners' type all over, grey brick with paired lancets to aisles and clerestory and a narrow front showing aisles and nave in tight section. Originally with corner finials (E ones removed 1913, w ones simplified). The WAR MEMORIAL is made up from the old turrets. Interior with tall quatrefoil piers and w gallery. Perp chancel, 1926 by *A. E. Henderson* with carved stone angel corbels; given by H.C.B. Bowles. PULPIT by *R. H. Carpenter*, 1872. SCREEN (formerly around choir stalls), 1898 by *G. F. Bodley*. REREDOS, c. 1933, with three painted figures by *Wallace Wood*. WALL PAINTING, E wall, by *Lawrence Lee*, 1954, Benedicite, in memory of E.A. Bowles of Myddelton House. STAINED GLASS: four windows of 1869–81 and others of 1881–1914, all by *Ward & Hughes*; E window 1926 by *Percy Bacon*.

ST ANDREW, Market Place. The medieval church is a town, not a village, church, situated on the N side of the market place and visible from it in its full length. Overall length about 120 ft, w tower projecting, the rest, nave and chancel and N and s aisles, forming a complete rectangle, all battlemented. From the market place the tower with its colourful mixture of rubble stone and flint (cement render was stripped off in 1910) appears in contrast to a s porch and a s aisle rebuilt in brick in the early c19. The brick wall forms a fine background to several stately late c18 and early c19 sarcophagi and monuments in the churchyard. On the N side the aisle wall is medieval, of rubble, with projecting polygonal rood stair. The thick walls of the lower part of the tower may be c12 or c13; no buttresses or stair-turret. A c13 trefoiled lancet in the chancel s wall (visible inside) shows the substantial length of the church by this time. Nave and chancel arcades, chancel arch (widened 1779) and

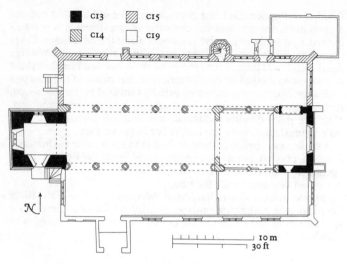

C13   C15
C14   C19

N↑

10 m
30 ft

St Andrew. Plan

possibly the upper part of the tower belong to an extensive rebuilding of the late C14. Five-bay nave with quatrefoil piers, and arches both moulded and chamfered. In the s aisle remains of three angel corbels. The nave upper walls are rubble, whitewashed. The clerestory is early C16. On the N wall are badges of Sir Thomas Lovell, Steward of the Royal Household and owner of the Elsyng estate, who paid for the clerestory windows in 1522. There were bequests for a s chapel in 1500.

Numerous repairs and restorations are recorded: by *Leverton* (1789); *Lapidge* (1810); *W. C. Lochner* (brick s aisle and gallery, 1824); *J. P. St Aubyn* (choir reordered in chancel, 1853); 1866–7 (new roofs); *J. O. & C. M. O. Scott* (1908–9, chancel and chapels refitted, galleries shortened).

WALL PAINTING above chancel arch: Crucifixion, 1923, by *Powell's.* BREAD SHELF in N chapel, *c.* 1630, with three columns supporting an entablature. ORGAN CASE of 1753 by *Richard Bridge*, exceedingly good of its period, with Baroque curves and excellent carving. CHARITY BOARD, 1772, with open pediment. STAINED GLASS. Two early C16 fragments in a s aisle window: arms of Thomas Roos, with garter collar, 1531; small piece with mourning nuns, from a window to Sir Thomas Lovell †1524, who was buried at Haliwell Priory, Shoreditch.

MONUMENTS. A fine collection. Joyce Lady Tiptoft †1446, large figure in heraldic mantle, under three crocketed and pinnacled gables with concave sides, on supports carrying shields. The elaborate late Perp setting of the brass dates from *c.* 1530, a canopy with a four-centred arch and a straight top cornice; a design deriving from the Royal Works. The tomb-chest with shields in diagonal cusped panels may be of this date too. – William Smith †1592 and wife, brass, two standing figures. – Robert Deicrowe †1586, Henry Middlemore †1610, Francis Evington †1614, all wall monuments with kneeling figures. – Martha Palmer, 1617, by *Nicholas Stone*, upright cartouche flanked by the graceful, very swaying, and very Mannerist figures of Faith and Charity, with attributes of books and children. – Sir Nicholas Raynton, builder of Forty Hall, Lord Mayor of London, †1646, with wife and family; standing wall monument of marble and alabaster in three stages; on the plinth, the kneeling minor figures facing each other, above, the reclining wife turned over towards us, holding a book, and immediately above her, on a higher shelf, Sir Nicholas also reclining, his cheek on his hand; top with arms in a broken segmental pediment. Attributed to *Thomas Burman* (GF). – John Watt †1701. Flowery cartouche. Attributed to *William Woodman Sen.* (GF). – Thomas Stringer †1706, by *G. B. Guelfi*, standing wall monument of marble, with bust in armour under a large tent-canopy with heavy opened draperies, the whole against a backpiece with entablature and broken pediment. CHURCHYARD with many good monuments both N and S of the church.

ST GEORGE, Hertford Road, Enfield Wash. 1899–6 by *J. E. K. & J. P. Cutts*. Tower planned but not built. Long aisled nave and chancel, baptistery.

ST JAMES, Hertford Road, Enfield Highway. 1831 by *W. C. Lochner*. A characteristic yellow brick Commissioners' church, thin and cheap with a narrow towered front, shallow buttresses, and battlemented throughout. Large barn-like interior. E.E. aisled chancel of 1864. Galleries removed 1952. Much rebuilt by *J. Barrington-Baker & Partners* after a fire in 1969 (chancel arch removed).

ST JOHN THE BAPTIST, Clay Hill. 1857 by *J. P. St Aubyn*. Still with the air of a rural mission building; a small aisleless church with shingled flèche set diagonally on a slate roof. Lively polychrome brick decoration both inside and out, E.E. detail. STAINED GLASS. Excellent set of windows by *Heaton Butler & Bayne*. VICARAGE to the N (now Glenwood House) also by *St Aubyn*, and even more colourful, with patterned tiles in the window heads and shaped bargeboards to the gables.

ST LUKE, Browning Road. 1899–1900, nave 1908, by *James Brooks*. In a commanding position, the long ridge of nave and chancel rising above the late C19 suburban terraces downhill to the S. Conventional E.E., chiefly red brick. Tall E end with two tiers of lancets, double transept showing outside in two half-timbered gables. A shingled turret over the crossing. A tower was planned. Chancel and N chapel STAINED GLASS by *Lavers & Westlake*, 1899. Parish room to the S. Across the road to the E, the substantial former VICARAGE (now Nursery School), also by *Brooks*. Brick and tile-hung, with playfully treated Gothic detail: hoodmoulds forming pointed arches, bow windows with trefoiled heads.

ST MARK, St Mark's Road, Bush Hill Park (*see* Edmonton). 1893 by *J. E. K. & J. P. Cutts*. Completed 1915 apart from the unfinished NW tower. One of the firm's typical long red brick basilicas; stone plate tracery windows.

ST MARY MAGDALENE, Windmill Hill. 1883, by *William Butterfield*. The patron was Georgiana Twells of Chase Side House, who built the church in memory of her husband Philip (†1880). Cruciform with W tower and spire, the absence of parapet between the two accentuating the solid geometry in a very Butterfieldian manner. The exterior otherwise unremarkable: Kentish rag with Bath stone;

Geometric tracery. Lofty nave with circular columns and clerestory. Lady Chapel added 1907. SCREEN (now at W end), 1898, the date also of the rich polychrome CHANCEL DECORATION designed by *Edward Turner* of Leicester: marble and alabaster panelling; ceiling painted with angels by *Buckeridge*, 1897–8, N and S walls with paintings by *N. H. J. Westlake*, 1899. Stone REREDOS by *Butterfield*, 1883, very architectural, its central roof silhouetted against the E window with STAINED GLASS by *Heaton Butler & Bayne*. This and other windows by the same firm (chancel N and S, S transept) were designed by *Butterfield*, and use the clear bright colours he preferred. War memorial window N aisle: striking design of a dead soldier at the foot of a Crucifixion, 1919, by *James Clark*, after his earlier painting.

Former VICARAGE (Ridge End House) by *Butterfield*, 1883, stone, matching the church, with a polygonal bay and oriel.

ST MATTHEW, South Street, Ponders End. Kentish rag with Geometric tracery. Nave and N aisle, 1877–8 by *H. J. Paull*, with chancel and chapel of 1900 by *J. E. K. & J. P. Cutts*. Plain former National Infants School to the W, dated 1840.

ST MICHAEL, Gordon Hill and Chase Side. 1874, by *Carpenter & Ingelow*. Exterior of irregularly coursed stone with Dec detail. Polygonal apse. W wall and narthex completed 1963, in stone, but feebly detailed. Handsome interior, with E and W parts carefully differentiated. Apse with brick vault, chancel with brick walls and stone shafts supporting stone transverse arches. The nave has three bays of stone columns, plastered walls, circular clerestory windows and a fine timber roof. Stone REREDOS; PULPIT, 1904, with marble shafts.

SS PETER AND PAUL, Ordnance Road. 1969 by *Romilly Craze*, pale brick with W apse, replacing a church destroyed in the war.

ST STEPHEN, Park Avenue, Bush Hill Park. *See* Edmonton, p. 424.

## 2. Roman Catholic

OUR LADY OF MOUNT CARMEL AND ST GEORGE, London Road. 1958 by *J. E. Sterrett & B. D. Kaye*. Pale brick with a large square W tower rising from the narthex. An Early Christian basilica: five bays with simple round-headed arches on columns; E end with barrel vaults. On the E side of London Road CONVENT OF THE HOLY FAMILY OF NAZARETH, occupying a Neo-Georgian range and lavish Victorian villa.

ST MARY, Nag's Head Road, Ponders End. 1921–4 by *Joseph Goldie*. Free Perp in yellow stone, SW octagonal turret with spire.

## 3. Other places of worship

BAPTIST CHURCH, Cecil Road. 1925, a late work by *W. Gilbee Scott*. Good, demure classical front in red brick, with shallow gable on big corner buttresses. Intended as a hall; the church was to have occupied the adjacent car park.

BAPTIST CHURCH, Totteridge Road. A capacious gabled building of 1871 amidst the small workers' terraces off Enfield Highway. Faintly Lombard Romanesque, with pilasters and coloured brickwork.

Bush Hill United Reformed Church, Main Avenue. *See* Edmonton (Religious Buildings), above.

Christ Church United Reformed Church, Chase Side. Built for Congregationalists to replace two earlier chapels. 1874–7, by the leading Nonconformist architect *John Tarring*, a Gothic building to vie with those of the Anglicans. Kentish rag with Bath stone dressings, cruciform with polygonal apse and a fine sw tower-porch with crocketed spire and diagonal buttresses topped by pinnacles. Delicately carved angel busts flank the doorway. The interior has arcades on slim quatrefoil piers with lavish carved capitals; transepts with elaborate Dec tracery. Fittings – marble pulpit, carved reredos and stained glass – also in the Anglican tradition. CHURCH HALL, 1939.

St Paul's Centre (formerly Presbyterian), Old Park Avenue. Large ragstone building on a prominent corner site, E. E. detail. E end added 1901 by *W. Wallace*. Subdivided 1987.

Trinity Methodist Church, Little Park Gardens and Church Street. 1889 by *F. Boreham*. Loose Gothic, of ragstone, with sw porch tower with spire and pinnacles. Raised over a basement. Interior rebuilt after a fire, 1919–20. HALL behind, 1913–14 by *F. Bethel*.

United Reformed Church, Lancaster Road.1885. Small, of polychrome brick, with circular w window.

*4. Cemetery*

Cemetery, Cedar Road. Finely sited at the top of Lavender Hill with views to the N. Buildings of 1870–1 by *T. J. Hill*: stone lodge and gatepiers with good iron gates, mirror-image chapels, each with canted apse and tower porch with broached spire. The Nonconformist chapel is now a store. Funereal landscape of mature conifers, with some varied early MONUMENTS picturesquely placed at the junctions of paths: William Buszard †1877, urn on tall plinth in red granite; Benjamin Godfrey †1872, Celtic cross; James Whatman Bosanquet †1877, big chest tomb.

PUBLIC BUILDINGS

Civic Centre, Silver Street. Dominant twelve-storey tower at the N end of the site, clad in stainless steel, of 1972–5 by *Eric G. Broughton & Assocs*. It was built for the post-1965 enlarged borough and so became double the original intended height, with further offices behind. The first phase, 1957–61 by the same firm, is a satisfying composition, consisting of the long brick administration range with upper floor projecting over a blue brick base, and the Council Chamber to the rear reached by a bridge from the main stairs. In front, a pool created from a loop of the New River; bronze sculpture of the Enfield Beast by *R. Bentley Claughton*. Inside, in the stairhall, an appliqué wall panel by *Gerald Holtom*.

Magistrates Court, Windmill Hill. 1900. By *H. T. Wakelam*. One-storeyed, of red brick with quite ornate stone dressings and a central shaped gable.

Post Office. *See* Perambulation 1.

LIBRARIES. The first is a CARNEGIE LIBRARY in Hertford Road, Enfield Highway, 1909 by *R. Collins*, District Surveyor. Classical detail treated with some licence; central gable, small segmental pediments over the windows. The CENTRAL LIBRARY, Cecil Road, of 1912, probably also by *Collins*, is more pompous, in a pedestrian English Baroque. Two storeys and seven bays, of red brick with stone quoins, the central bay with big segmental pediment, festooned circular window and an Ionic doorway with heavy curly broken pediment. Ponders End has a library of 1962 in the High Street, a neat L-shaped building in pale brick, with entrance recessed behind two columns. At Enfield Wash the building in Ordnance Road of 1976 by the Borough Architect *N. C. Dowell* is quite a dynamic concrete composition. Busy rhythm of paired uprights clasping pairs of beams. Between them, roof-lights to the one-storeyed parts of the open-plan ground floor, which wraps round a taller part with upper floor treated in similar manner.

ALBANY POOL, Hertford Road. *c.* 1990. Much glazing with red trim.

QUEEN ELIZABETH STADIUM, Donkey Lane, W of Great Cambridge Road. A period piece in a streamlined 30s-modern idiom. Under construction in 1939, interrupted by the war; completed *c.* 1952, and renamed after refurbishment in 1977. Sports pavilion with curved ends, projecting flat roofs, and a café at the E end with curved drum staircase.

CHASE FARM HOSPITAL (Enfield District Hospital), The Ridgeway. The oldest buildings, a single large building and a few detached cottage homes, were built as CHASE FARM SCHOOLS, an orphanage for workhouse children, by *T. E. Knightley*, 1882–6. The school closed in 1939.

HIGHLANDS HOSPITAL. *See* Southgate, p. 470.

NEW RIVER (*see also* Islington). Originally this wound through Enfield following the 100-ft contour line; parts were straightened in 1859 and *c.* 1890. On the line of the loop around the valley of the Cuffley Brook, a cast-iron aqueduct of 1820 (*see* Perambulation 2). Part of this loop was revived when WHITEWEBBS PUMPING STATION was built in 1898 (*see* Perambulation 2). The loop around Enfield Town, between Silver Street and Town Park, was retained as an ornamental water; it is still the original width, with several attractive early C19 iron bridges (*see* Perambulation 1).

LEE NAVIGATION. From the Thames to Hertford, an ancient navigation. Modest improvements to the natural river course began in the late C12 under the Abbot of Waltham; in 1424 an Act of Parliament – the first for this purpose – appointed commissioners to improve the navigable waterway. Following a report in 1766 by John Smeaton, *Thomas Yeoman* created a series of artificial channels and pound locks of modern type in place of previous flash locks. Yeoman's improvements included the broad and straight EDMONTON CUT, five miles long from Tottenham Hale to Ponders End, begun 1770, and the less regular ENFIELD CUT above Ponders End, following the earlier Enfield millstream. At ENFIELD LOCK, red brick cottages and toll office of 1889, with fanciful upper storey to the central projecting bay. Below the lock, a waterway maintenance depot, with a clock turret on the cruciform-planned office building of 1907. At the N end of the Small Arms Factory site (*see* Perambulation 3), NEWMAN'S WEIR: wooden sluice gates within cast-iron guide frames, as reconstructed in 1907 in succession to a series of timber weirs. Further N, RAMMEY MARSH LOCK and the adjoining cut are of 1864. Across the lock tail, a reused cast-iron beam footbridge dated 1835.

KING GEORGE THE FIFTH RESERVOIR, close to the Lee. A mighty earth-fill embankment by the Metropolitan Water Board, opened in 1913, covering 420 acres, the largest in London. At the NW corner, PUMPING STATION by *W. B. Bryan*, in an individual Classical Mannerist style in red brick and Portland stone. Still *in situ*, though last used in 1968, are some of the five pumps of novel design by *H. A. Humphrey*, which lifted water into the reservoir. There were no pistons and the water oscillated in giant U-tubes driven by explosions of gas on a four-stroke cycle. The combustion chambers are 7 ft diameter. Surrounding the surge towers is an elegant brick screen wall with coupled Doric columns in Portland stone.

Former ROYAL SMALL ARMS FACTORY *see* Perambulation 3.

RAILWAYS. ENFIELD CHASE STATION. Simple building of 1910, with an Art Nouveau entrance porch, and chaste, classical platform canopy pillars. On the line extended to Hertford, replacing an earlier terminus further W of 1868–71. On the Hertford line, RENDLESHAM VIADUCT, fourteen arches 1907–10, concrete with brick facing. SOUTHBURY STATION. 1891; one-storeyed with Jacobean gable, on a bridge.

## Educational buildings

MIDDLESEX UNIVERSITY, Queensway, Ponders End. Built for Enfield Technical College by the Middlesex County Council, 1939; completed after the war. Formal curtain-walled range with central tower over the entrance. Conversion of engineering workshop to teaching building, 1992 by *Rivington Street Studio*.

ENFIELD GRAMMAR SCHOOL, Enfield Town, immediately W of the church. The school originated as a pre-Reformation chantry foundation, but the earliest surviving building is late C16, tall and plain, of brick, two storeys and an attic. Lower windows altered but the three dormers in front and one in the N gable are original, each of three lights with brick mullions. The ground floor was one large schoolroom. Stair-turret on the W side. The school was refounded in 1876; S extension dated 1883. Edwardian wing with central stone oriel, 1904. Additions of 1938 behind (hall, library and classrooms). The LOWER SCHOOL occupies Enfield Court, Silver Street, which has a late C17 core with a long Georgian front, much altered and extended. Recent buildings to the N in a harmonizing style.

ENFIELD COUNTY SCHOOL, Holly Walk, Enfield Town. Built as a Girls' Grammar School; 1909 by *H. G. Crothall* of the MCC. An attractive formal composition in brick and stone, on an H-plan, similar to his other schools (cf. Edmonton and Tottenham) but personalized here by perky Art Nouveau copper domes on the corner turrets.

BOARD SCHOOLS. Enfield School Board put up several proud buildings on tight sites for a rapidly growing population. All by the schools specialist *G. E. T Laurence*: CHESTERFIELD ROAD, for the expanding hamlet of Enfield Lock, 1895–6; two-storeyed, with two central gables and cupola; pretty date plaques. CHASE SIDE, Trinity Street, 1899–1901; similar ingredients, with very red terracotta trim (cf. Laurence's schools for Tottenham School Board). Edwardian elementary schools continue the tradition of decorative terracotta and good detailing: SOUTHBURY, Swansea Road, 1905, EASTFIELD ROAD, 1909, LAVENDER ROAD, 1910, GEORGE SPICER, Southbury Road, 1912, gabled, with curly cartouches. *See* also Bush Hill Park School under Edmonton, above.

INTERWAR SCHOOLS. The *MCC*'s work is less interesting than in NW Middlesex: BISHOP STOPFORD, Brick Lane, has a core of 1934 on a splayed plan; ALBANY, Bell Lane, 1939, is a traditional two-storey group (both built as senior elementary schools and much added to). BRIMSDOWN, Green Street, is also of 1939.

POST-WAR PRIMARY SCHOOLS by the *MCC* are numerous, reflecting the needs of a still young outer suburb. CARTERHATCH, Carterhatch Lane, 1949, has a spread-out formal finger-plan, with low buildings on a grand scale (similar to Cuckoo Hall School, Edmonton); long rendered one-storey ranges of classrooms, linked by corridors; a clerestory-lit hall on each side. PRINCE OF WALES, Salisbury Road, Enfield Lock, 1950, has the special feature of a circular hall with low domed roof (cf. Grange Park, Southgate).

BULLSMOOR SCHOOL, Bullsmoor Lane. Purpose-built comprehensive of 1977.

CHACE SCHOOL, Churchbury Lane. Built as a secondary modern in 1956 by *C. G. Stillman* and *C. Hartland* of the MCC. Comprehensive from 1967. Assembly hall with brick gable ends, three-storey curtain-walled classroom block at r. angles.

# FORTY HALL

Forty Hall was built by Sir Nicholas Raynton, a wealthy haberdasher who was Lord Mayor of London in 1632. The date 1629 is on a brick near the E corner of the N side and on a ceiling inside. Forty Hall belongs with a number of progressive, compact brick houses built at this time by City men in the London countryside – among them Kew Palace, Cromwell House, Highgate, and Swakeleys, Ickenham – but its significance long remained in doubt because it was unclear to what extent it had been altered. Recent appraisals have reaffirmed the original date for the main features of the house. Here, therefore, is a combination of old-fashioned interior decoration and a precocious, trim, hipped-roofed exterior profile which seems to anticipate Inigo Jones's designs of the 1630s. In the late C18 the house was indeed attributed to Jones, though without any proof. But the story is complicated by later changes. Alterations were carried out by the Wolstenholme family (Sir John Wolstenholme married the Raynton heiress); Robinson's *Enfield* mentions rainwater heads dated 1708. There were further phases of modernization in the C18; Robinson states that after a sale in 1787 £4,000 was spent on repairs and alterations, including the rendering of the exterior. In 1799 the house was bought by James Meyer, whose initials appear on the present rainwater heads, with the date 1800. More radical changes,

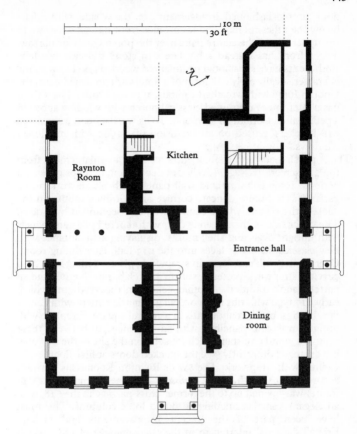

Forty Hall. Ground-floor plan

including a new main staircase, date from after 1895, when the house was sold following the death of a later James Meyer and bought by H. C. Bowles for his son, owner also of Myddelton House (*see* Perambulation 2). It was acquired by Enfield in 1951.

The main house is almost square, red brick with stone quoins; three-25 storeyed, with show fronts on three sides and service court and lower wings to the w. The sash windows and the hipped roof above modillioned cornice give an c18 impression, but both roof structure and plasterwork on the attic floor prove that the roof is original. It is the earliest known datable hipped roof of its kind – but only just the earliest: cf. West Woodhay, Berks, of 1635, and the grander Chevening, Kent, begun before 1630 but not finished until later. The sashes are of course later, as must be the present cement rendering of the broad-shouldered window surrounds. (The whole house was rendered in the late c18; the brickwork was exposed again only *c.* 1900.) Ground- and first-floor windows are of equal height, i.e. two floors of similar status, top floor lower. No visible basement; the kitchen (or serving room) was on the ground floor (an old-fashioned arrangement), on the w side, with cellars below the other rooms. The N entrance front has six windows to the upper floors, the centre pairs over the porch curiously narrow. The E front has instead a big late c19 stone staircase window. Both fronts have substantial pedimented wooden porches with the characteristically early c18 form of a lintel with upturned ogee; the E porch Ionic with wreathed capitals, N porch Doric. The s front has a later, more restrained classical porch with window above in a pedimented Corinthian surround. To its w a flat hood with carved c18 brackets, reused on an extension of *c.* 1900 with mullioned windows.*

The N porch leads into a small entrance hall, an enlargement from the c17 screens passage. Lively c18 decoration, perhaps of several periods: Ionic columns and wall panels with plasterwork busts, garlands, etc.; more delicate cornice and Gothick motifs on the back of the screen, whose central arch has been filled by a door.

19 The other side of the screen is c17, with tapered pilasters, panels with upright ovals and shell motifs, displaying acquaintance with new classical ideals. It faces into the c17 hall, later dining room. Overmantel with cartouche in strapwork; plaster ceiling with bold curving strapwork patterns still in the elaborate Netherlandish pattern-book tradition. Another ceiling in the SE room, typical early c17 type with ribs in an overall geometric pattern with corner floral sprigs; blank coat of arms in a central square. Fireplace with upright ovals and panelling with small panels. In between these rooms, a grand c19 stair which must be on the site of the c17 one, but arranged differently (see the blocked doors at first-floor level). Ceiling with strapwork. The sw or Raynton Room (his portrait, according to Gough, by *C. Jansson,* over the fireplace in a c18 frame) was opened up to the former cross-passage in the c18, with an elegant Venetian opening on fluted Ionic columns. This must have been part of the 'recent Improvements and tasteful Embellishments' referred to in the sale catalogue of 1787, which also observed how 'the singularity and boldness of the original ornament are ingeniously opposed to the *petite* neatness of the present'. Also of the c18 is the present arrangement of the back-stairs w of the hall, cut through a former ceiling. On the first floor the NE and SE rooms also have c17 ceilings, the SE room with a pattern of single ribs with floral sprays, and the date 1629. The room was formerly larger; the fireplace has been moved to a corner position. Early c18 bolection panelling in the NE room, also in the N room, whose present shape with corridor behind must go with the inserted backstairs. Over the kitchen a room with reused early c17 panelling. On the attic floor original coves to the NE and SE rooms, the latter with plaster heads at the corners.

The two lower wings which project w may both be very early additions; the s one was enlarged later. The service court has lower brick buildings (c17, but much remodelled as restaurant, exhibition gallery etc. in 1962–9) and is entered from the N by a flamboyantly c17 Mannerist gateway, all in brick, with rusticated piers

---

*G. Gillam, *Forty Hall,* 1997, refers to a marginal note in Gough's MSS notes for a history of Enfield which states that the house 'first had two bay windows on each side which were taken away by Nicholas Wolstenholme'. How should this be interpreted? Do the changes in the E front brickwork indicate alterations of this kind?

carrying obelisks and balls, flanking an arch topped by a shaped and pedimented gable. The details recall some of Jones's designs for Old St Paul's. It is flanked by battlemented walls, which look C18. WALLED KITCHEN GARDEN to the S. Further W an outer court, with remains of farm buildings, including two barns.

GROUNDS. The house stands in fine landscaped grounds, with a cedar on the lawn to the E. Immediately N of the house is a lake, now irregular but which may have originated as part of a formal layout of the later C17. A pair of lime avenues leads N, framing a view of the house, to a stream where there may have been another lake. W of the avenue is the site of ELSYNG, the house which belonged to Sir Thomas Lovell from 1492 (*see also* St Andrew Enfield) and which was used as a royal residence from *c.* 1540 (*see* Introduction to Enfield). It was demolished after 1656, when the grounds of Forty Hall were extended. No buildings are now visible, but excavations in 1963–6 revealed some brick foundations and drains. To the NE are substantial water features, a small and large lake above the level of the stream.

## PERAMBULATIONS

### *1. Enfield Town*

THE TOWN is the name of the Market Place, with St Andrew's Church on the N side and the Grammar School W of the church (qq.v.). In the centre a timber MARKET CROSS, octagonal with classical columns, rebuilt in its pre-C19 form for Edward VII's coronation (1902). Its predecessor was removed to Myddelton House, Bulls Cross (*see* below, p. 450). It is framed on the W by the KING'S HEAD, domestic Old English in character, with tile-hanging and half-timbered gables; by *Shoebridge & Rising*, 1899. On the E, a tall bank, dated 1897, by *W. Gilbee Scott*; exuberant Flemish Renaissance gables. To S and W, weaker stone-faced Beaux Arts frontages demonstrate the shift in urban ideals by the 1920s.

PEARSONS on the S side occupies the site of the house known as Enfield Palace, demolished in 1927 (*see* Introduction, p. 434). From the pre-suburban era there is now just one weatherboarded house on the S side, and the funny little OLD VESTRY OFFICES on the N, late Georgian with a tiny polygonal façade as if it were a toll house. Hidden away further S is a big pedestrian shopping precinct of *c.* 1980, trying to disguise its bulk by steep slated roofs. S of this an area known as Enfield New Town, with small roads laid out in 1852 by the National Freehold Land Association. Some typical simple cottages, single or in pairs (Frugal Cottages 1866), remain in RALEIGH ROAD.

Now to the E and N. The junction of The Town with SILVER STREET is marked by a DRINKING FOUNTAIN with two bronze cherubs, erected 1884, restored 1994. Silver Street runs N. On the W side, the old brick garden wall of the VICARAGE, No. 36. The oldest parts of the house are two wings, originally timber-framed, which belonged to a C16 hall house. There were alterations in 1801; Robinson (1823) illustrates the stuccoed and parapetted garden front. Part of the house was cased in brick in 1848 and kitchens and offices were added; further alterations in 1950, when the front was let as offices. Opposite, on the E side of Silver Street, No. 45, the CHURCH SCHOOL OF INDUSTRY, Tudor of 1876, red brick with stone dressings.

The Civic Centre (q.v.), with its overweening tower, faces a Georgian cluster, now mostly council offices. First a pair of tall three-bay houses with one-storey entrance links. Then WHITE LODGE, with a polygonal projecting bay, which is weatherboarded, but has unusually sophisticated decoration: classical friezes and dentilled eaves. No. 90 is of three bays, with pedimented doorway and a pediment over the central bay. Further on the former Enfield Court, with a five-bay Georgian front, much extended; now part of the Grammar School (q.v.). One can return by Church Lane and a path to the church; from here HOLLY WALK, a pleasant back lane, continues w between the Grammar and County schools (qq.v.) to emerge in Gentleman's Row (*see* below).

CHURCH STREET, w of The Town, is indifferent, apart from the POST OFFICE of 1906, with nice Free Classical stone ground floor and a pediment with royal arms. The scene improves near the crossing over the New River: an open space with the Library (q.v.) and TOWN PARK to its s, and No. 90, RIVER HOUSE, a three-storey, three-bay C18 house with C19 bay windows and lower extension. On the w side of the New River, offices of the 1980s, neat but rather large for this sensitive position, dark brick with stone-faced floorbands and tinted glazing.

GENTLEMAN'S ROW, the best street of Enfield, runs alongside the New River to the N. The name occurs from the C18. The houses face Chase Green, a remnant of the Chase preserved after the enclosure of 1803 (*see also* below). They start with the REGISTRY OFFICE, a formal five-bay mid-C18 house with three-bay wings. w entrance front with pedimented centre breaking forward, and a stone centrepiece: a pedimented window with false balcony above an Ionic doorway. At the back (E) the wings have lower windows under arches. Staircase within the entrance hall and to the r. In No. 5, well hidden from the road, fittings brought from Enfield Palace (*see* Introduction, p. 434). Gentleman's Row continues along a narrow path separating the houses from their front gardens.

4     The charm of the houses is their variety of detail and texture, with Georgian features often applied to older buildings, but showing the prevailing fashion for a five-bay symmetrical front. No. 9 has such a front, in brick, with parapet hiding an end gable. Good C18 iron gate. No. 11, FORTESCUE LODGE, five bays, two storeys, is stuccoed, with three gables to the flank wall and a link on the l. to THE COACH HOUSE, a weatherboarded projecting gabled range, formerly an outbuilding. Nos. 13–15 are a tall Victorian pair, Georgianized (C20 gentility has affected a good many houses round here). No. 17, where Charles Lamb stayed in 1827, has a charmingly crooked stuccoed front with parapet, obviously concealing something older. Investigations have indeed revealed that
p. 9     it began as a late medieval timber-framed hall house. Four-window front, with door in second bay from l. Upswept early C18 doorcase and an old tiled roof. Projecting rear wings are visible behind, and a chimneystack. No. 21, right on the path, is of five

bays again, with a big C18 central doorcase with fluted pilasters. The pale brick, late C18 No. 23 has a carriageway within the r. wing, a dentilled pediment over the central three bays with Tuscan doorcase, and a balancing blind arch to the l. The sequence tails off with Nos. 27–33, a plain small early C19 terrace, and Nos. 35–45, later C19.

RIVULET HOUSE on the w is an early C19 villa of three bays, the upper floor with just one window over the central door. The path turns w here to cross the New River (*see* Public Buildings) by a pretty iron bridge. On the e side of the river BRECON HOUSE, a large detached C18 house in its own grounds, five bays and three storeys with parapet. Then a small rather altered stuccoed house, and the CROWN AND HORSESHOES, a plain stuccoed C19 pub at a picturesque bend in the river. To the w, in HORSESHOE LANE, DANBY COURT, by *Neylan & Ungless*, 1974–8, tactful and appropriately unassuming sheltered housing of red brick, around courtyards with covered walks.

CHASE SIDE PLACE continues N along another path with small early C19 cottages, Nos. 7–8 the least altered, a bald pair with side entrances. Nos. 29–31 is another one, with front entrances. The path emerges on the busy CHASE SIDE, which continues with small brick, weatherboarded and stuccoed cottages and villas as far as Christ Church. No.77, VIONE HOUSE, early C19, has three broad C19 bays and an iron porch with palmette decoration.

Now back s along the w side of Chase Side. GLOUCESTER TERRACE, dated 1823, is a nice regular two-storey range of cottages with plain arched doors. On the e side, another small-scale mixture, mostly of the early C19: Nos. 43–45 and 39–41 are two pairs with central chimneys and hipped roofs. One can continue more pleasantly by a path to RIVER VIEW alongside the river. Near the s end a picturesque group backs on to the river: Nos. 2–14 GENTLEMAN'S ROW, part brick, part weatherboarded.

CHASE GREEN between Church Street and Windmill Hill has an unusual WAR MEMORIAL with a Grecian sarcophagus. To the s, in OLD PARK AVENUE, THE DRILL HALL SPORTS CLUB: quite jolly Free Tudor, with a very broad gable with little quirks and volutes broken by two polygonal turrets. On WINDMILL HILL, a routine Edwardian shopping parade near Enfield Chase Station of 1910, which replaced the earlier station further up the hill (*see* Public Buildings). Further on, the BYCULLAH ESTATE, developed from 1879 (the railway line to Hertford had to bypass it). Winding roads and trees remain but hardly any of the original large houses which once accompanied Butterfield's church at the top of the hill.

## 2. Outer areas to north and north-west

The NW parts of Enfield are some of the more attractive outermost fringes of London, despite the roar of the M25 just beyond. The patchwork of cottages and country houses, woodland and scrubby fields, golf courses and garden centres can still be called rural. Suburban spread was stopped by the Green Belt on the eve of the Second World War.

FORTY HILL. There was a hamlet already in the C16; by the C18 the elevated position was attracting the gentry. The worthwhile houses are dense enough to make a perambulation. At the top of the hill, the entrance to Forty Hall (*see* above), on the w, has C18 rusticated stone gatepiers with swags, and a half-timbered LODGE of *c.* 1900. Opposite, CLOCK HOUSE, a tall C19 stuccoed house right on the road, has a three-storey centre with vermiculated quoins; two full-height bows to the E. First to the N: WALTHAM COTTAGE, a three-bay C18 villa in dark brick, and SPARROW HALL, of similar size, also C18 but altered and reroofed in the C19. Further N, Jesus Church, built by James Meyer of Forty Hall, still stands in open country.

From the top of the hill the sequence to the s starts on the E side with ELSYNGE HOUSE, a long frontage with a flamboyant array of windows. Compact centre with a delicately detailed mid-C18 Venetian window (small Doric pilasters) on each side of a pedimented doorcase. Diocletian windows above. The pattern is repeated by two extensions to the l. and by a narrow C20 one to the r. LONGBOURN, stuccoed but basically C18, has a five-bay centre with Ionic porch and segment-headed windows; additions at each end. FORTY HILL HOUSE is on the big scale of the early C19, three bays, stock brick, with Doric porch and ground-floor windows within depressed arches. No. 37, the former Goat Inn, low and much altered, is perhaps C17 or earlier; projecting gabled wing on the r. It flanks GOAT LANE, where a few altered cottages remain. Then WORCESTER LODGE, s of Goat Lane, the classic five-bay, two-storey type of the early C18; straight-headed windows, dentilled eaves cornice below a steep tiled roof of double depth. The pedimented doorcase has a restrained mid-C18 elegance. On the w side, up a drive, the DOWER HOUSE (a C20 name; now two houses). Part of the Forty Hall estate until 1787. An attractive L-shaped house, probably early C17, but much refaced in the C18. Gables with casements, but later sash windows elsewhere. E front with two gables, with three plus two straight-headed windows and an Ionic doorcase. Brick platbands. The N front has three more widely spaced gables. (A panelled room on the ground floor; behind the panelling a painting of *c.* 1600 was found on the brick chimney breast: festooned urns in an arcade with stylized fluted columns.) Old garden walls.

Further downhill, on the E side, CANISTER HOUSE, No. 29, an odd thin building with four giant arches; two storeys of windows. A conversion from an outbuilding? On the w side, No. 78, THE HERMITAGE. a delightful house with the date 1704. Steep hipped roof with dormers, above a dentilled cornice, in the late C17 manner. But the irregular chimneys and six bays with off-centre entrance suggest an older house remodelled. Handsome early C18 doorcase with rusticated pilasters and Doric entablature. (Front rooms with panelling; closed string stairs; back rooms with square C17 panelling.) Weatherboarded timber-framed outbuilding attached on the l. Facing a little green, 'Cottage PLACE 1833', a terrace of four made stylish by ground-floor windows within arches. THE GOAT opposite is one of Truman Hanbury's elaborate interwar Tudor pubs, 1932 by *A. E. Sewell*; picturesque chimneystacks and intricately carved bargeboards (cf. the Railway

Hotel, Edgware). By the corner with Clay Hill the old brick wall and fine early C18 railings and gate belonged to Pattensware, the house of the antiquary Richard Gough †1809, demolished in the 1890s.

CLAY HILL runs W from the foot of Forty Hill. An alternative to the suburban start is the path beside the old course of the New River, which ran through the grounds of Pattensware. It leads to BEGGARS HOLLOW, off Clay Hill, and to the SOUTH LODGE to Whitewebbs (*see* below), a delicious pink confection: a little C19 *cottage orné* with elaborate bargeboards, patterned tiled roof and battlemented chimneys. CLAYSMORE LODGE, just to the N, one-storeyed and stuccoed with a central chimney, is a lodge of the more reticent C18 type. On CLAY HILL, the ROSE AND CROWN, very rural-looking; a long range with steep tiled roof, its timber frame concealed by a brick-faced front painted white. Extended to the E. On the S side, THE LODGE, probably built *c.* 1822, a simple square *cottage orné*, with Gothic windows. Up a drive, CLAY HILL HOUSE (residential home), in its own grounds with fine Victorian planting. Built for Joseph Toms, of Derry & Toms. Formal Italianate of *c.* 1860 in pale brick; two storeys and eight bays articulated by channelled quoins, all windows arched; a canted bay to the S and a projecting W wing.

Returning E along Clay Hill, one passes an older cluster on the S side. BRAMLEY HOUSE, now flats, has a three-storey five-window C18 centre, swamped by full-height former hospital extensions, the l. one dated 1881. Old garden walls. LITTLE PIPERS, behind a high wall, is a picturesque C19 recasing of an older house; stuccoed, with bargeboarding and hoodmoulds. THE FIRS, early C19 stucco, has seven widely spaced bays; the elaborate Gibbs surrounds to the ground-floor windows are probably a later alteration.

Scattered individual buildings in this area can be covered in a roughly circular tour; the pubs are the main interest. BAKER STREET is punctuated by suburban examples. No. 168, THE JOLLY BUTCHERS, 1906 by *William Stewart*, still has the florid exuberance of the turn of the century: roughcast gables, plaster frieze and twin domed turrets formerly flanking a central carriageway. THE BELL is demure and tile-hung; THE HOP POLES, 1909, expansive and half-timbered. Baker Street also has a few older houses: a group near the Jolly Butchers, including the C18 Nos. 172–174. CLAY HILL has two rural inns, the Rose and Crown (*see* above) and THE FALLOW BUCK, at the W end, C16 to C17; main range with four-centred doorway, short gabled wings, weatherboarded. THE KING AND TINKER, Whitewebbs Road, has early C19 sashes under big hoodmoulds, but an early C17 form: main range with projecting N wings, porch in the angle. Opposite to the N, WHITEWEBBS FARM: C17 brick farmhouse with hipped roof; timber-framed BARN with queenpost trusses.

WHITEWEBBS, Whitewebbs Road. Hidden within Whitewebbs Park (part wood, part golf course). The core is a house of 1791 built by Dr Abraham Wilkinson, which replaced an older building. But the dominant impression is of the late C19, when *Charles Stuart Robinson* dressed up the house as a French château, adding wings in 1881, and a large curved pediment to the W front. The E front has canted bays and balustraded balconies. LAKE with rustic

brick FOOTBRIDGE at W end. Pretty NORTH LODGE, similar to
South Lodge off Clay Hill (*see* above).

PUMPING STATION (now Transport Museum), Whitewebbs Road,
1898. Built to feed a loop of the NEW RIVER, which ran through
the grounds of Whitewebbs. Sturdy red brick building with large
arched windows and big pedimented porch. The end of the loop
was bypassed by a cast-iron AQUEDUCT of 1820 carrying the New
River over Cuffley Brook; an iron trough on brick columns. The
part of the loop thereby made redundant was made into an ornamental lake in the adjacent grounds of WILDWOOD, further W.

BULLS CROSS is another hamlet, with a group of old cottages around
the C17 PIED BULL, a small rendered house near the junction
with Bullsmoor Lane. Several larger houses on its fringes.

CAPEL MANOR, Bullsmoor Lane. Now a horticultural college, with
extensive model gardens. Red brick seven-bay C18 house with
one- and three-bay extensions, remodelled in 1908 in late C17
style for James Warren, a wealthy tea planter. Timber S porch with
excellent Corinthian columns, brought from Rotherhithe. Another
porch to the N. Lavish panelled interiors of 1908, with plaster ceilings to the SE and NW rooms, and an inlaid floor to the central
N room. Behind the house, handsome orange brick group of late
C19 STABLES and COACHHOUSE, U-shaped, with clock tower;
stables with high-quality original fittings. LODGE of 1876.

Off Bulls Cross at the W end of Turkey Street, GATE HOUSE, a five-
window two-storey C18 house with additions, and Nos. 120–122,
an C18 pair with Gothick casements. In Bulls Cross by Maiden's
Bridge, MAIDENS BRIDGE COTTAGES, C18 and C19, including
a tiny former Infants' School with Gothic porch, built in 1848 by
James Meyer of Forty Hall. Further S, GARNAULT, Italianate of
*c.* 1860, which had the old loop of the New River running through
its grounds. Humped BRIDGE over the Turkey (or Maiden's)
Brook, perhaps early C19, with circular flood arches on each side.

MYDDELTON HOUSE (Lee Valley Regional Park Headquarters),
Bulls Cross. An 'elegant villa' (Robinson), built for H. C. Bowles,
on the site of an older house, by *George Ferry & John Wallen*, 1818.
Of stock brick. E front of five bays, two storeys and an attic, with
an Ionic porch *in antis*. Later three-storey wing to the r., its bow
window decorated with Ionic pilasters. S front with a shallow bow
with tripartite ground-floor windows. Attached to it a conservatory, with two lead ostriches from Gough's house, Pattensware,
which stood at the foot of Forty Hill. STABLES, also early C19,
three bays with one-storey pedimented wings and a clock turret.

Robinson commented that 'the New River is a great ornament
to the grounds, which are laid out with taste'. The river, alas, was
diverted in the C19. A single-span iron BRIDGE, dated 1832,
remains. The plantsman E. A. Bowles (1865–1954) created a
famous garden from *c.* 1900, which partly survives, with lake,
terraces with older balustrades and urns, and other features,
including the 1826 Market Cross from Enfield. This is a square
Gothic structure, with flying buttresses to its second stage. It
stands in the centre of a formal garden with pergola and summerhouse in a brick wall. The wall incorporates at one end a curious
older brick pier of diamond shape, perhaps C18.

RURAL OUTLIERS. In Burnt Farm Ride, GLASGOW STUD

FARMHOUSE, mid-C17, twin gables. Red brick, the front rendered. (Staircase with strapwork balusters; first-floor stone fireplace with carved artisan Mannerist detail.) HOLLYHILL FARMHOUSE, Cattlegate Road. Mid-C19 villa, low hipped roof. OWLES HALL, Cattlegate Road. An early C19 stuccoed villa; rounded bow on the r.

## 3. East Enfield

As industry developed on the flat land beside river and railway, the rural hamlets along the main road to Hertford expanded into a string of artisan settlements, continuous by the end of the C19. Low terraces predominate, broken by the occasional tower block. The older centres are still recognizable. They are described from s to n.

PONDERS END has little to show from its early industrial history except for one remarkable survival near the river: WRIGHT'S FLOUR MILL in Wharf Road. There was a mill on the site already in the C16. Much added to, but the core is still the brick Georgian miller's house and offices flanking a three-and-a-half-storey water-mill of brick and white weatherboarding, c. 1789. They overlook fragments of water meadows by the Lee. An attractive ensemble, despite the large unloading bays built out in the 1970s in front of the mill. Dark weatherboarded sheds of different heights, taller steel-clad silos and milling plant behind. Small early C19 lodge with Gothic windows. Nearby, close to the Lee Navigation (*see* Public Buildings), NAVIGATION INN, created in 1995 partly within the shell of the Ponders End Pumping Station, 1899 by *W. B. Bryan* of the East London Waterworks Co. Half-timbering and roughcast below big tiled roofs, extended N in matching style in 1995.

Along NAGS HEAD ROAD, much late C19 workers' housing. SCOTLAND GREEN, formerly a small settlement on its own, has a characteristically disparate mix: some mid-C19 houses in Scotland Green Road, four dour 23-storey tower blocks of 1966–7, and 1990s low-rise housing on a former factory site. Neither is there much of note in the HIGH STREET apart from No. 221, decent municipal Neo-Georgian, built as a Technical Institute by *Middlesex County Council*, 1911. To the w, a set-back space with modest post-war library (q.v.). Along QUEENSWAY, industrial buildings of the 1920s onwards and a Middlesex University site (q.v.).

ENFIELD HIGHWAY. The next settlement to the N of Ponders End along the old line of Ermine Street. Its early C19 phase is marked by a Commissioners' church (St James, q.v.). Further N, WRIGHTS ALMSHOUSES, Hertford Road. Red and yellow brick; the heavy classical hoods over the doorways typical of the date, 1843. THE BELL, opposite Eastfield Road, is a big stuccoed house, early C19, with later one-storey portico. Edwardian library (q.v.) and indifferent long 1920s shopping parades.

ENFIELD WASH. A few old cottages in Hertford Road by the PRINCE OF WALES, much altered. Main landmarks are the bold C20 library (q.v.) and, opposite, a big 1920s-Classical CO-OP store (the Cooperative movement had a strong following in the area; the Enfield Highway Cooperative Society was established in

1873). TURKEY STREET, the site of another old hamlet, runs w beside Turkey Brook. A few early c19 houses, and four pairs of cottages, one dated 1838. Further w, in ALMSHOUSE LANE, ANN CROWE'S ALMSHOUSES, a group of four, with big central chimney and half-timbered gables. Built by H.C.B. Bowles of Myddelton House, 1893.

ENFIELD LOCK.\* On this remote spot E of Enfield Wash, an island between the river and the Lee Navigation, are the remains of the ROYAL SMALL ARMS FACTORY, the principal source of rifles for the British army throughout the c19. Land was bought by the Ordnance Board in 1812; the factory opened in 1816, and the finishing branch was transferred from Lewisham in 1818. Ambitious plans had been prepared by Captain *John By* in 1812 for a factory with three mills using existing waterpower; *John Rennie* advised the construction of a navigable leat with its own millhead and tailrace between the two waterways, to provide both improved waterpower and more convenient transport. The leat was made, although Ordnance Board economies provided for only one mill with two waterwheels. In 1822, in addition to the mill, there were workshops, forges, proof houses, coalhouses and storehouse. Workers' cottages were along the river, at first one-storeyed with two rooms, later with upper floors. There were sixty by 1841. A school was opened in 1846, an institute the following year, a church (since demolished) in 1857.

The factory remained quite modest until the 1850s, when the Crimean War called for vastly increased production. American rifles had attracted attention at the Great Exhibition, and a commission of engineers visited American factories (the chief prototypes were at Springfield, Massachusetts, and Harpers Ferry, Virginia). In 1854–6 a machine shop on American mass-production lines was built by the *Royal Engineers*, based on designs by *John Anderson* for a factory at Woolwich Arsenal. American machinery, run by steam engines, was installed, the workforce was increased to over 1,000, and by 1860 an average of 1,744 rifles per week was being produced. The factory became famous and, like Woolwich Arsenal, a spectacle for visitors. The work carried out in this model building was still piecework, not assembly-line production, but organized for maximum efficiency and on an unprecedented scale.

p. 45

Another major expansion began in 1886, when the original watermill gave way to steampower, and workshops were built over the site of the tailrace. The total number of steam engines grew to 16, with 23 boilers. By 1887 there were 2,400 employees. Production of the new model rifle by James Lee began in 1889; the famous Lee Enfield Rifle was designed in 1895. The factory expanded again during the First World War, but subsequently its character changed, and the specialized mass-production functions were replaced by machine shops and assembly lines. Decline set in after the Second World War; half of the site was closed in 1963, the rest in 1987.

The FACTORY of 1854–6 faces s across the great quadrangle, a long, low 23-window frontage of yellow brick with arched windows enlivened by red brick voussoirs, with a band of brick diapering above. Tall Italianate central clock turret in two stages. Interior of

---

\* This account is indebted to T. Putnam and D. Weinbren, *A Short History of the Royal Arms Factory, Enfield*, Centre for Applied Historical Studies, Middlesex University, 1992.

12 by 14 bays with slender cast-iron columns at 20-ft intervals supporting wrought-iron trusses with roof-lights, an impressive space. The line of the canal can be traced along the E side of the factory, turning W, with its head in the great quadrangle. To the W the quadrangle is closed by a two-storey range of stores and offices; to the S is an evocative cluster of buildings on the site of the first water-powered factory buildings, which stood next to the canal basin, now filled in. The existing buildings on the site of the former mill were used as an assembly shop. They are partly of 1910–16, partly earlier; behind, at r. angles, two-storey polishing shop (1863) and assembly and packing room, with central pediment (1889), and one-storey grindery (1887–8), with polychrome brickwork similar to the large factory. Further buildings to S and E.

Some way to the N, beyond the sites of gasholders, and in an eerily overgrown setting at the time of writing, the serried ranks of STORES near the canal wharves, of the 1850s onwards, used to house the wooden gun stocks; large two-storey ranges of 10 by 3 bays.

At the entrance is the former Factory School, opened 1846, later a police station. Fringing the factory to the W, GOVERNMENT ROW, a long line of plain C19 workers' cottages, overlooking a branch of the Lee. At the northern end, Nos. 71–76, a small group probably dating from 1857, still in a rural setting by a weir on the Lee Navigation (*see* pp. 440–1).

BRIMSDOWN. E of the railway line, S of Enfield Lock. An industrial area in transition in the 1990s. At the S end, by Lea Valley Road, big retail sheds of the 1990s; further N an older group with a tall brick chimney, and a 1950s lodge by the site of RUBEROID; in MILLMARSH LANE, smart new customized units with some jazzy details.

GREAT CAMBRIDGE ROAD. Begun 1921. This never became an industrial showpiece to compare with the 'Golden Mile' of the Great West Road. Factories grew up only gradually along the E side; by the 1950s, when many were built, ostentation was out of fashion. A characteristic plain brick group remains between Carterhatch Lane and Southbury Road, although the best has gone (Ferguson's colour TV factory by *Jellicoe*, 1956). Among the replacements, SAFEWAYS makes an effort to be elegant in a Postmodern manner, with moulded cornices and pitched roofs of the 1990s. In SOUTHBURY ROAD, near the station, RIPAULTS FACTORY, 1936 by *A. H. Durnford*. The only remaining interwar factory with some panache. The long, streamlined Art Deco frontage remains (derelict at the time of writing), white with black trim, original metal glazing. Taller centre with oriel and black vertical banding.

# SOUTHGATE

## INTRODUCTION

Southgate originated as a settlement at the south gate of Enfield Chase, at the NW corner of the parish of Edmonton. It became a separate district in 1881 and a borough in 1933, distancing itself from the working-class development to the E, just as Wood Green did from Tottenham. It remains a sedately respectable suburb whose monotony is broken by its gentle undulations and by a pleasantly large amount of parkland remaining from the large estates, which were not broken up for building until the late C19 and early C20. Several noteworthy mansions remain: Arnos Grove, Grovelands and Trent Park.

On Rocque's mid-C18 map the built-up area consisted chiefly of South Street, the present High Street stretching S from the south gate of Enfield Chase to the green at the junction with Cannon Hill, between the estates of Grovelands to the N and Arnolds (later Arnos Grove) and Broomfield to the W and S. In 1870 Thorne could still describe Southgate as one of the least changed villages around London, its large mansions inhabited by 'opulent citizens and the occasional nabob'. Development came with public transport. To the SW, New Southgate or Colney Hatch grew after the Great Northern Railway opened a station in 1851. The separate centres of Bowes Farm, Palmers Green and Winchmore Hill expanded after the railway came to Palmers Green in 1871 and trams were extended from Wood Green up Green Lanes to Enfield in 1907–8. The population of Southgate jumped from 10,970 in 1891 to 33,612 in 1911. The village itself and the area to its N filled up between the wars, with the opening of the Piccadilly Line Extension to Cockfosters. The population was 72,359 in 1961.

## RELIGIOUS BUILDINGS

### 1. Church of England

CHRIST CHURCH, Chalk Lane, Cockfosters. 1839 by *H. E. Kendall*. Paid for by R. C. L. Bevan of Trent Park. Still the London stock brick and lancet windows of the Commissioners' churches, but no longer symmetrical. The tower stands of the S side just E of the W gable. Chancel, N aisle, transepts and chapels added by *Sir Arthur Blomfield*, 1898, when the orientation was reversed.

CHURCH HALL, 1931, with triple-arched entrance.

CHRIST CHURCH, Waterfall Road and The Green. 1861–3 by *Sir George G. Scott*. Still in a seemingly rural spot. It replaced the chapel built by Sir John Weld of Arnolds in 1615. Stone, E.E. with cross-gabled aisles and NW tower with fine broached spire. Spacious interior, five-bay nave with quatrefoil piers and clerestory. Chancel with original REREDOS, 1868–9, with *Salviati* mosaic, and later marble embellishments: sedilia (1906), wall panelling, chancel arch columns (1913). (In the tower, MONUMENT to Sir John Weld †1622, black marble tablet.) STAINED GLASS. Decent work by *Clayton & Bell*: medallions in lancets (chancel E, nave W). But the remarkable windows are those by *Morris & Co.*, dating from the start of the firm to the early C20. Lady Chapel: four lancets of 1862, with evangelists, below canopies by *Philip Webb*. Three figures designed by *Morris* himself; St Matthew looks like a self-portrait. St Mark is by *Ford Madox Brown*. S aisle w, SS James and Jude, 1862–3, designed by *Rossetti* with canopies by *Webb*: fine and delicate; S aisle S, W end, SS Peter and Paul, *c.* 1866–71. Chancel N, Dorcas and Good Samaritan by *Burne-Jones*, 1876. N aisle: Christian virtues by *Burne-Jones*, riper and more luxurious than the earlier windows. The first two pairs, 1876 (Hope and Faith, Temperance and Charity); Prudence and Justice, 1885, Liberality and Humility, 1899. The draperies of Temperance and Charity especially lively. Two S windows, 1903, 1913, less good.

The site of the old chapel lies W of the church. Some good early HEADSTONES, e.g. Rebecca Shrawley †1683, with skulls and hourglass.

HOLY TRINITY, Green Lanes, Winchmore Hill. 1906–7 by *J. S. Alder*, but little of his building remains apart from the red brick saddleback tower-porch. After a fire in 1978 the E end of 1933 by *F. D. Danvers* was demolished, the nave arcades were removed, and the interior was remodelled by *Stanley Gidlowe*.

ST ANDREW, Chase Side. 1903 by *A. R. Barker*. Extensions by *Barker & Kirk*, 1916 (sanctuary, N chapel). Dull red brick and stone exterior. Flying buttresses to clerestory. W baptistery. Three-bay nave with passage aisles and stone piers, interior walls of yellow and red brick. Ambulatory behind the altar.

ST JOHN THE EVANGELIST, Green Lanes and Bourne Hill. 1903–9 by *John Oldrid Scott*. A rich, colourful exterior with a big crossing tower and two round E turrets with leaded spirelets. Plenty of flint rubble and flint panelling is used. Inside also the detail is original and eclectic. Stone columns, moulded capitals with some foliage; brick arches, thin brick shafts rising to tie-beams. Crossing arches on fat octagonal columns. The aisles have segmental-arched windows with intricate tracery lights in a free Perp. Flamboyant Dec E window with STAINED GLASS of 1924 by *J. H. Dearle* of *Morris & Co.*: Christ in Glory above eastern and western cities. It commemorates the church's chief benefactors, V. E. Walker and Mrs A. M. Baird. Chancel arch WALL PAINTING and quattro-cento-style REREDOS by *E. W. Tristram*, 1924. Much other late *Morris & Co.* glass (1911–47). N aisle (Patmos) window †1918, by *Frank Salisbury*, dark and dramatic. Also by *Salisbury* the WAR MEMORIAL E of the church, carved by *John Angel*, 1920.

W of the church the VICARAGE, 1909, by *J. S. Alder*, with porch at an angle and details echoing Philip Webb. ST JOHN'S HALL is also by *J. S. Alder*, 1908, of materials matching the church, with a small turret.

ST MICHAEL-AT-BOWES, Palmerston Road. The church of 1874 by *Sir George G. Scott* was replaced by a new church in the 1970s.

ST PAUL, Camlet Way, Hadley Wood. 1911 by *A. E. Kingswell*. Small, with lancets and a flèche. Hall at E end of 1977 by *L. P. Worby*.

ST PAUL, Church Hill, Winchmore Hill. 1826–7 by *John Davies*, on a site given by Walker Gray of Grovelands. A cheap church of the Commissioners type, aisleless, of yellow brick, originally without a chancel. W front with thin ogee niches flanking a central stone panel with ogee window, rising to a small bellcote. Barn-like interior with w gallery and flat ceiling. Refurbished after a fire in 1844, with oak PULPIT with Gothic canopies and STAINED GLASS with small scenes in medallions, formerly in the E window, now in the N and S windows of the chancel added in 1888–9. E window 1892. Low S chapel (also 1889) with good E and S windows by *Hardman*, figures effectively set against a red background.

ST PAUL, Woodland Road, New Southgate. Hidden in evergreens. 1873 by *G. G. Scott*, ragstone, routine E.E. Aisled, with thin SE bell-turret. Repaired 1950 by *R. S. Morris* after war damage. Parish hall to N of 1908, repaired 1952.

ST PETER, Vera Avenue, Grange Park. 1939–41 by *Cyril Farey*. Brick, with a low crossing tower and long chancel with canted apse. The exterior, with its rectangular windows, parapets and pantiles, looks Scandinavian-Classical, but the white plastered interior displays Farey's interest in Romanesque, with cushion capitals to the transept arches and low round-headed arcades to passage aisles. Building materials and furnishings came from war-damaged churches: most notable are the late C17 baluster FONT and COVER from the City church of St Katharine Coleman via St Katharine Hammersmith. STAINED GLASS in colourful panels, designed as a consistent scheme by *M. Aldrich Rope* for J.O. De Vile (vicar 1945–60): in the chancel the life of St Peter, in the nave Creation and Redemption.

ST THOMAS, Prince George Avenue, Oakwood. 1938–41 by *Romilly Craze*. Of brick, with a covered approach on the N side. w end and sw tower 1965 by *William Mulvey*. (STAINED GLASS. Three-light Lady Chapel window by *Alfred Fisher*, 1965.)

### 2. Roman Catholic

CHRIST THE KING, Bramley Road. 1940 by Dom *Constantine Bosschaerts*. The first stage of an ambitiously planned priory. Reinforced concrete faced in white brick. Modernistic cubic composition with a low window band to the aisle and a blank wall above. Tower with a recessed cross. Two-storey monastic buildings adjoining.

OUR LADY OF LOURDES, Bowes Road, New Southgate. 1935 by *J. A. Crush*. Simple Early Christian basilica in red brick; plain apse and round-arched arcades. Narthex 1986 by *Boris Kaye*.

PRIORY OF OUR LADY QUEEN OF HEAVEN, Priory Close. 1941, for Benedictine nuns.

ST MONICA, Stonard Road, Green Lanes, Palmers Green. 1913–14 by *Edward Goldie*. Rock-faced, Perp, two-stage SE tower. N vestibule, baptistery and sacristy 1963–4. Five-bay nave with low Perp arches and barrel vault. ALTAR in Sacred Heart Chapel with intricate mosaic work. STAINED GLASS. Aisle windows by *Mayer*, typically fussy; in dramatic contrast the E window, with pictorial Resurrection across five lights, 1984 by *Carmel Cauchi*.

### 3. Other places of worship

BAPTIST CHAPEL, Compton Road. 1907 by *W. Hayne*, a spreading late Gothic front in brick and stone, rather crude details.

FRIENDS MEETING HOUSE, Church Hill, Winchmore Hill. 1790, replacing a very early meeting house of 1682. Plain front of door and two windows with a pediment. Single rectangular room with simple old benches. Schoolroom and lobby added 1796, kitchen 1809, services and lobbies remodelled 1986–7. Burial ground to the w.

GRANGE PARK METHODIST, Old Park Ridings. 1938 by *C. H. Brightiff*. A striking Art Deco building on a corner site; brick, with square buttresses, a square w tower and rectangular windows in emphatic surrounds. The plain cubic forms relieved by stone carving of a Tree of Life over N and s doorways. Attractive and consistent interior; gently ramped nave, ceiling with an undulating profile, pretty pierced timber screens above the transepts and lower e end. Windows all with geometric patterns of yellow glass. Halls of 1970–3.

METHODIST CHAPEL, Green Lanes, Winchmore Hill. 1912 by *Albert Edward Lambert* of Nottingham. A broad front in free late Gothic; small domed turrets in striped brick and stone. Interior altered.

TRINITY-AT-BOWES METHODIST, Bowes Road, Palmerston Road. 1971–3 by *Edward D. Mills & Partners*. Square, with ambulatory on all four sides. Lower walls of brick, upper walls faced with aluminium cladding. STAINED GLASS window by *Gillian Rees Thomas*, in two layers.

UNITED REFORMED CHURCH (formerly Congregational), Compton Road, 1874, polychrome brick front with plate tracery and a tower with short slated steeple.

UNITED REFORMED CHURCH, (formerly Congregational), Fox Lane and Burford Gardens. 1914 by *George Baines & Son*, in their typical Late Gothic. Brick and stone with pretty flamboyant tracery. Broad nave with stone arcades on arches without capitals; transepts with pairs of taller arches. Hall to w in the same style, 1909.

WESLEYAN CHAPEL, The Bourne and Queen Elizabeth's Drive. 1929 by *A. Brocklehurst* of Manchester. Angular Gothic with sw tower.

*4. Crematorium*

ENFIELD CREMATORIUM, Great Cambridge Road. 1938 by *Sir Guy Dawber & A. R. Fox*. Two gabled and pantiled chapels connected by a triple-arched arcade. Central clock tower.

PUBLIC BUILDINGS

SOUTHGATE TOWN HALL, Green Lanes. Unassuming. The NW corner is the earliest part, 1893–4 by *Rowland Barker*; domestic-looking, with a half-timbered gable. Extended 1914–16 by *Barker*, with a red brick frontage in sober late C17 style. LIBRARY wing facing Broomfield Lane, 1938–40 by *J. T. W. Peat*, Borough Engineer; a bleak symmetrical front, slightly moderne, with fluted jambs to the central doorway.

POLICE STATION, No. 687 Green Lanes, Winchmore Hill. 1915 by *Butler*. Given character by shaped gables and a ground-floor bow window.

DE BOHUN LIBRARY and CLINIC, Green Road, Oakwood. By *W. T. Curtis & H. W. Burchett* of the MCC, 1939, in a similar

Dudok-modern style to their nearby school (*see* below). The MCC
were involved because Southgate had not adopted the Libraries
Act. A neat cubic composition faced in red brick, with a tall stair-
tower; generous glazing to the library on the first floor.

SWIMMING BATH and LIBRARY, Bowes Road, New Southgate.
Another MCC job by *Curtis & Burchett* of 1939. A stylish brick
group complementing Arnos Grove Station just down the road. A
novel combination of functions at the time; originally also housing
a juvenile employment bureau. The pool juts out on the l. with
an oval foyer with circular roof-lights. The first-floor library is
approached by a handsome curved concrete stair, lit by a slender
bowed oriel window. CLINIC to the w in similar style but with
less finesse.

BRANCH LIBRARIES. Two late works by the *MCC*: Green Lanes,
Winchmore Hill, 1961, with multi-angular children's library; High
Street, Southgate, 1964–6, simple one-storey steel box.

SOUTHGATE LEISURE CENTRE, Winchmore Hill Road. 1966 by
*J. T. W. Peat*, Southgate Borough Architect. Pool with a steel frame
clad in aggregate panels; ponderous zigzagging roof.

HIGHLANDS HOSPITAL. *See* Perambulation 4.

STATIONS. Southgate's first station was at New Southgate (1851).
The Great Northern Railway's line to Enfield opened in 1871. The
Piccadilly Line extension was built in 1932–3. Among the group of
1871, PALMERS GREEN is nicely preserved, with twin-gabled stock
brick booking office straddling the tracks, and fringed canopy over
the entrance. BOWES PARK (1880) has original platform canopies.

The PICCADILLY LINE extension has some of *Charles Holden*'s
best Underground stations. The skill in varying a fairly fixed number
of elements is wholly admirable. ARNOS GROVE has a circular
ticket hall of great repose and dignity. The canopy on the ground
floor is square in contrast to the curve above. The simple geometric forms recall Asplund's Stockholm City Library of 1928–31,
one of the most potent of the Scandinavian sources which inspired
Holden and his colleagues. SOUTHGATE also has a free-standing
circular ticket hall, but is given a playful little lantern (particularly
effective at night, as indeed are all the clerestory-lit stations).
Southgate is also carefully integrated with a curved shopping parade
and bus stops. The booking hall, as at Arnos Grove, has a roof
supported by a central column; around the edge, shops, ticket
office and staff quarters are tucked in neatly. The escalators have
their original elegant bronze uplighters. OAKWOOD (by *C. H. James*
and *Charles Holden*) is rectangular and yet essentially different
from, for example, Sudbury Town. COCKFOSTERS, at the end of
the line (by now above ground), has a long, low station building
with cantilevered canopy. The most striking part is the bold concrete-framed platform canopy, complete with its integrated fittings,
which slopes inward and has a clerestory above the central track.

Between Arnos Grove and Oakwood, brick VIADUCTS (engineer:
*Sir Harley H. Dalrymple-Hay*).

*Educational buildings*

MIDDLESEX UNIVERSITY, Chase Side and Cat Hill. Faculty of
Art and Design, built for the Middlesex Polytechnic. Tucked into

a wooded slope. The earliest part by the *MCC*, a neat factory-like block of workshops of the 1960s, with north roof-lights. Phase 2 is of 1972–9 by *HKPA*, and reflects the 1970s desire to give large buildings a friendly face. Unassuming outside, of one to three storeys. Red brick walls, timber windows and pantiled roofs hide a group of large steel-framed, wide-span teaching spaces, hall and library, surrounded by informally grouped smaller rooms and meeting spaces. Cheerful functional interiors with white-painted brick walls and exposed trusses.

SOUTHGATE COLLEGE, Southgate High Street. 1962–3 by the *MCC*. A large curtain-walled block tactfully set back from the road so that it does not dominate the older houses. Extended 1969–71. For the Minchenden Campus in former school buildings across the road, *see* p. 465, Southgate House.

PRE-1918 SCHOOLS. BOWES Junior and Infants, Bowes Road. Built by the Edmonton School Board, 1901. Tall three-decker on a tight site. Centre range with canted bay and a pretty cupola. TOTTENHALL INFANTS, Tottenhall Road. 1914 by the *MCC*. Much enlarged; the original part with nicely detailed symmetrical front to the road: hall with Venetian window between two-storeyed wings. Schools by the *MCC* in the developing outer suburbs had more space; HAZELWOOD, Hazelwood Lane, is one-storeyed, 1908 and 1911.

INTERWAR SCHOOLS. DE BOHUN PRIMARY, Green Road. A compact, well-composed example of an MCC school in the progressive cost-cutting modern manner adopted in the mid-1930s, by *W. T. Curtis & H. W. Burchett* of the MCC, 1936. BROOMFIELD, Wilmer Way. The core was built as a senior elementary school by the MCC (*Curtis & Burchett*), 1938, for 800 pupils. The MCC late 30s style at its most austere: a long range relieved only by a corner entrance forming part of an irregular cubic composition at one end.

POST-WAR SCHOOLS. The MCC introduced some new designs among its post-war primary schools. An interesting early one is GRANGE PARK, World's End Lane, 1951–2 (by *Anderson* of the MCC). Built on a slope, with the Infants' School at the front, with classrooms off a long ramped corridor, and an attractive circular hall with shallow dome pierced by a ring of circular central roof-lights (a design used also at Prince of Wales, Enfield Lock, q.v.). Other schools: WALKER, Waterfall Road, 1953; EVERSLEY, Chaseville Park Road, 1954 and 1957.

OAKTREE SCHOOL, Chase Side, Southgate. Special school of 1965, a low building in woodland, with a striking zigzagging hall roof.

GARFIELD PRIMARY SCHOOL, Springfield Road. Part of the 1970s rebuilding of New Southgate by the *Borough of Enfield*; a cluster of low concrete-block pavilions with monopitch roofs in generous open space (cf. Churchfield School, Edmonton), in place of an early Board school.

SOUTHGATE SCHOOL, Sussex Way, Cockfosters, replacing the County Grammar School, Fox Lane (now flats, *see* p. 469). The borough's only interesting late c20 secondary school. A large complex developed from 1960 to 1992. E wing 1959–61 by *Raglan Squires & Partners*, with minor S additions of 1972; sixth-form block 1980; W, N and S wings 1990–2 by *Rock Townsend (Andrew*

*Shorten, Chris Grasby*). The early part is a rectangular block in buff brick with grey curtain walling to the upper floors. Central courtyard, now roofed over, with clumsy red brick sixth-form block to the SW. The less formal additions of 1990–2 by *Rock Townsend* adopt the materials of the older building, pale yellow brick and glass brick, but use them with greater panache. The new parts are grouped to form three sides of a loose quadrangle with the E wing. The S end of the E wing was given a curved common room to balance the curved library at the end of the W wing. The curved motif was more marked in the early plans; the N wing was also to have had a circular projection. The courtyard has slightly cosmic overtones, with a N sign marked out, and a paved circular area with seats and planting. This interest in curved forms is displayed also in the roofs; most striking is the asymmetrical sweep of the sports hall, whose roof projects on one side over paired free-standing columns, and on the other is met by a lower reverse curve over the changing rooms. The interiors escape from rectangularity in a different way, by the use of wedge-shaped double-height spaces for the entrance foyer and between the classrooms.

## MAJOR HOUSES AND THEIR GROUNDS

Southgate retains a surprising number of large C18 mansions and grounds, which remained in private ownership until the C20, several of them owned by the related families of the Taylors and Walkers. They are arranged here alphabetically by their old names.

### ARNOS GROVE
No. 15 Cannon Hill

The Arnolds estate, owned by the Welds in the C17, was acquired in 1719 by James Colebrook. His house is enveloped in a vast red brick Neo-Georgian pile created for the North Metropolitan Electricity Supply Company from 1929, converted for residential care in 1997–8. This has absorbed a N wing of *c.* 1765, added for Sir George Colebrook by *Sir Robert Taylor*, and a S wing completed for Lord Newhaven in the later C18. From 1777 to 1918 the house belonged to the Walker family.*

The house of *c.* 1720 remains in the centre of the E entrance front: a dignified, well-proportioned three-storey front of seven bays, typical of its date, of dark red brick with brighter rubbed brick window heads. Dentilled cornice and slightly projecting three-bay pedimented centre; small cupola behind on the roof. Sashes all renewed. The W front also has a pediment. The C20 office additions consist of a broad stone porch and large brick wings in matching style and height (S wing 1929, 1932, N wing 1935), with lower balustraded links projecting on either side of the entrance. The wings extend the house in a U-plan to the W.

A remarkable double-height entrance hall remains, taking up five bays of the E front and containing the staircase, as was popular in grander houses of the earlier C18 around London (though the

* *See* further: R. Garnier, 'Arno's Grove', *Georgian Group Jnl* 8, 1998.

arrangement of the staircase may have been altered). The special feature here is the survival of the bold Baroque scheme of painting, dated 1723 and signed by the Flemish artist *Gerard Lanscroon*, an assistant of Verrio at Windsor and Hampton Court. On the staircase walls, Apollo and the Muses, and the Triumph of Julius Caesar; on the ceiling, the Apotheosis of Caesar. The hall opens to the long saloon on the w side with a shallow bow window to the garden, screened from the room by two columns. The bow is a later c18 addition, the Adam style decoration dates from the 1920s. Two rooms by *Taylor* remain to the n of the saloon: an elegant groin-vaulted anteroom with fluted pilasters and apsed ends (pretty floral plasterwork along the groins) and a taller square Dining Room in more severe Palladian taste, with a grid of ceiling beams, and walls with Venetian arches (a favourite Taylor motif) framing doorcases and a fireplace with a sunburst.

The GROUNDS were once extensive. A fragment remains further s as ARNOS PARK, opened to the public in 1928, with formal brick gatepiers at its n entrance in Morton Circus (*R. Phillips*, Borough Surveyor). Near the w end the long brick viaduct of the Piccadilly Line (q.v.) makes a handsome feature in the attractive informal landscape along the Pymmes Brook valley. Half-way up the slope, traces of a loop of the New River, which ran through the grounds until the c19.

BROOMFIELD

The public park between Alderman's Hill, Powys Lane and Broomfield Lane, opened in 1903, is the remains of the Broomfield estate. There was a substantial house here by 1624, when a house with 14 hearths is recorded, belonging to Joseph Jackson, a City merchant. The Jacksons enlarged and improved house and grounds in the early c18. In 1816 the property passed to the Powys family, who let the house to a series of tenants, and finally sold most of the land for development in 1901.

The HOUSE is a tragic story. It was latterly used by Southgate and Enfield Boroughs for a health clinic, museum and café, but was gutted by fires in 1984, 1993 and 1994. Before the fires the house was a large rectangular building with a misleadingly indifferent suburban appearance due to the fake timberwork added by the council in 1928–32. Subsequent examination of the pathetic remains revealed a complicated and interesting history. Rebuilding has yet to take place.* The house expanded gradually from the oldest part, a timber-framed two-storey farmhouse. Remains of framing for a jettied cross-wing, near the centre of the w front of the present building, may date from the earlier c16. A brick chimney-stack was added on its s side *c.* 1570, and was later altered to provide fireplaces for the rooms created when the adjoining hall to the s was given an upper floor (its timbers survive). In the c16 to early c17 additional ranges were added around the original house: a view of *c.* 1800 shows the w front with five gables, and a two-gabled

---

*This account is indebted to research by Richard Lea and Steven Brindle, see S. Brindle, *Broomfield, an illustrated history of the house and garden*, 1994, and Richard Lea, *Broomfield House, Enfield, the structural development of the house*, 1994.

wing facing s beyond the service end. The most important alteration was the insertion in the early C18 of a fine staircase in the
range N of the cross-wing, which probably became the principal
entrance at this time, with doorway on the w side, as shown in the
drawing mentioned above. The staircase (in store) is of oak, with
three different balusters to each tread, and carved tread ends. The
stairhall was decorated with paintings by *Lanscroon*, dated 1726,
three years after his work at Arnos Grove (q.v.). They were
removed after being damaged by the fire, and await restoration
and reinstatement. The ceiling had a figure of Victory and another
with carpenter's plane; on the walls classical gods and muses, and
figures representing the seasons, flanked by Corinthian pilasters.

Around 1820 a new brick range of reception rooms was built
along the N front, and the irregular gabled and rendered older
parts were given a classical appearance by sash windows. The w
front was regularized, with inset porch with Doric columns, and
the gables replaced by new roofs behind parapets.

The GROUNDS have much of interest. SE of the house old brick walls
of the C16–C18 and a fine brick ARCHWAY, on the outside with
four-centred arch, probably C16, and with C18 piers and wooden
pediment on the inner side. Brick piers also to the STABLE YARD
nearby. E of the house, against a garden wall, an early C18
SUMMERHOUSE with wooden Ionic columns. The formal grounds
lay to the w; they appear on Rocque's map of 1754, and are likely
to be contemporary with the early C18 improvements to the
house. There still remain a long avenue leading to the w front,
originally of elms, replanted with limes, and a sequence of three
formal ponds in front of the house. A fourth, oval pond was added
in the C20. Rocque shows another feature, possibly a canal, N of
the house. Half-timbered bandstand of 1926 by one of the ponds,
and a pretty conservatory. GARDEN OF REMEMBRANCE to the s,
by Powys Lane. Designed by the Borough Architect and
Surveyor, *R. Phillips*, opened 1929: a walled garden with pergola
flanking an arcaded temple; a memorial cairn in front.

### GROVELANDS
The Bourne

Built as Southgate Grove in 1797 by *John Nash* for Walker Gray
(†1834), a brandy merchant related to the Walkers of Arnos Grove.
The estate was extended by his nephew, John Donnithorne Taylor,
of the Taylor Walker brewery (who, it is said, disliked seeing other
men's chimneys). The family owned the house until 1921. From
1916 to 1977 it was used as a hospital. Rescued after long neglect
and restored in 1985 for use as a private psychiatric hospital, with
new buildings added discreetly at the back (architects *Bodnitz Allan
& Partners*, consultants *Donald Insall & Associates*).

The house is one of Nash's first mature buildings after he had returned
to London in 1796 from his bankrupt retirement to Wales, and is
the finest surviving example in the London area of a Neoclassical
villa of the end of the C18. Nash exhibited the design at the
Royal Academy in 1797; plans and elevations were published in
*New Vitruvius Britannicus* in 1802. The house is small but most

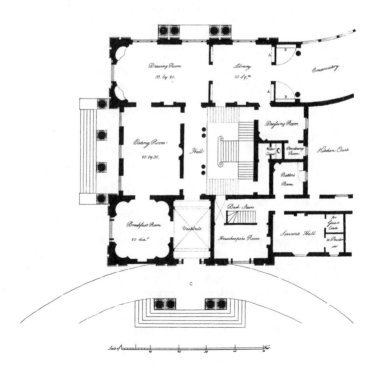

Grovelands. Plan and elevation, 1802

impressive, its rendered exterior given sophisticated grandeur by a giant order raised above a low basement; the spirit is slightly French, in contrast to the chaste English Palladian villas of the previous generation. The principal front to the E has a three-bay central loggia with four giant Ionic columns with *Coade* stone capitals, recessed between broader end bays with giant pilasters. Each end bay has a tripartite window under an arch filled with a shell, surrounded by the fanwise fluting so popular with Adam and his followers. The windows, which extend to floor level inside, have elegantly slim glazing bars; the sashes are of wrought iron with brass and copper mouldings. Interest in such an innovatory mixture (patented in the 1770s) was typical of Nash. Above the end bays an Ionic entablature and weighty attic with horizontal oval windows, originally surmounted by *Coade* stone sphinxes. The shorter entrance side of three bays uses a different arrangement of the same motifs, with paired columns flanking the doorway.

*The Beauties of England* (1816) especially commended the interior, 'with its strict attention to modern refinements': the reception rooms arranged en suite, and linked by central doors providing end vistas of windows or mirrors. The entrance leads to a low groin-vaulted vestibule with three grisaille panels of classical sacrificial scenes. Ahead is a generous toplit central stairhall, the stairs starting with a single central flight and dividing in two to reach the first-floor landing. Along the garden front the gem is the delightful Birdcage Room, an octagonal breakfast room conceived as a bamboo cage covered with greenery, with corner niches painted with views out to gardens. The centre room was the dining room, with drawing room beyond, a long room with windows on two sides; a broad niche at the E end (the original plan shows two corner ones instead); double doors to the square library to the w. Beyond this was a curved conservatory hiding the service side of the house from the garden. The show is all on the ground floor; the upper floor is low, with bedrooms and dressing rooms of modest size. The basement store rooms included an ice house.

45

GROUNDS. The house is finely positioned on rising ground; its site is said to have been selected by *Repton*, who refers to it in his *Enquiry* of 1806. The polygonal walled kitchen gardens sw of the house remain, also a small octagonal granary on staddle stones. Repton screened them and other service buildings from the pleasure gardens s of the house by planting. To the E he created a serpentine lake (now within the public park opened in 1913), leaving existing woodland beyond. J. T. Taylor carried out improvements after 1834, enlarging the lake and adding a second island. He also built a ha-ha (to contain his deer), a lodge and carriageway, and a second, grander approach to the house from Alderman's Hill, after he had enlarged the grounds and demolished the neighbouring house of Cullands Grove. *T. H. Mawson* advised the borough on the lay-out of paths in the new public park.

OAKHILL COLLEGE
Chase Side

An evangelical theological college from 1932. A long white mansion overlooking ample grounds with some fine trees, sloping down to

Pymmes Brook. The centre is a neat C18 villa which replaced an older house on the Monkfryth estate (so called from its early ownership by St Alban's Abbey). The house was called 'newly erected' in 1790, when bought by John Kingston, M.P. It then looked different: a drawing of *c*. 1800 by Oldfield (Herts Record Office) shows an E entrance with two-storey centre, recessed between lower three-bay wings, all raised above a basement. The present E front, flush with the wings and with a Diocletian window over a central pedimented Ionic porch, is probably part of a substantial remodelling by Sir Simon Haughton Clarke (†1832), a wealthy man who had married the heiress of a Jamaican planter and bought the house in 1810. He also probably added the conservatory to the N, and the large plain S extension (now library), perhaps for his picture collection; this has a dentilled cornice like that on the E front. Both extensions appear on the Tithe map of 1840. Further additions for the college: plain stone-faced chapel to the NE, 1957, dining hall and new wing to the S, 1964, octagonal dining room projecting W, 1982.

Inside, the two-bay entrance hall dates from the early C19: ceiling with Greek key decoration and garlands, three open arches to the spine corridor behind. A door to the SE opens to a delightful small spiral cantilevered stone stair with iron balusters, which must also belong to the C19 remodelling, a late example of its kind. The original stairs may have been behind, over the present stairs to the basement. An original service stair, behind a doorway with fanlight, remains in the adjacent wing. Plain reception rooms (the two central ones now united) along the W front. The rest much altered. The S extension had a central roof-lit space, now floored for the upper library. The conservatory has a pitched glazed roof on iron brackets.

To the S, remains of late C19 farm buildings. Behind the farmhouse, THE BYRE, with colourful ceramic tiles set between prominent timber struts. To the NW, small domed TEMPLE, early C19.

## SOUTHGATE HOUSE
### High Street

Now Minchenden Campus, Southgate College. As with Oakhill, the core is a late C18 Neo-classical villa. Probably built by Samuel Pole, who inherited the estate in 1776. From 1840 to 1922 owned by the Walker family; then sold to Middlesex Council and used as a secondary school.

The original house has a W front of three bays and two storeys and must have looked elegant before the later additions. Steps lead up to a curved segmental projecting porch with four Tuscan columns, flanked by cast-iron lampstands. The top-floor windows to l. and r. have been widened. On the E side the basement is exposed and the centre has a more pronounced curved central bow with three windows. A Venetian window to each side, and another in a bay to the N which appears to be an early extension. Parapet with intermittent balustrading. The curved projections hint at the Neo-classical plan, which employs a series of ovals through the centre of the house: an oval entrance hall with niches leads to a tightly planned semicircular toplit stairhall, the stair with iron balustrade rising elegantly against the curve. Cantilevered upper landings; the first is a half circle, but the top landing a complete oval, the cornice below decorated with garlands. Dining room in the centre of the E front with curved ends which have niches flanking the door from the stairhall. To the SE the large drawing room (now Principal's room) with handsome doorcases, each with a little carved scene below a broken pediment. Smaller rooms and service stair on the N side, with successive C19 additions beyond, the latest one a billiard room projecting forward on the W front. Some late C19 embellishment in an Arts and Crafts manner in the entrance hall. The grounds have been much diminished and built up. To the N, FARBEY BUILDING, by the *Middlesex County Council*, 1925, Neo-Georgian.

TRENT PARK. *See* Perambulation 5.

## PERAMBULATIONS

The major houses are described above. The character of the rest of Southgate is sampled in a series of tours, each starting at a station.

### 1. *Southgate Village: Southgate Station to Palmers Green Station*

The low station (*see* Public Buildings, above) forms the hub of five roads. First impressions are of the C20: 1930s shopping parades mixed with brusque offices of the 1960s. Only the low WHITE HART in Chase Road (near the site of the old South Gate to Enfield Chase) and the tall garden walls along THE BOURNE, now with flats behind, hint at the older village. W of the elegant curved brick parade built together with the station, BURLEIGH GARDENS may be examined as an example of 1930s suburban housing. Quite classy pairs on the S side, alternating between bow windows and Baillie Scott-derived jettied gables. Good details (tiled arches, stained glass, leaded casements) to those houses yet unaltered; *see* e.g. No. 86.

Along HIGH STREET the village can still be traced: between the suburban developments a straggle of cottages and smarter Georgian houses stretches S towards Southgate Green. The big curtain-walled range of Southgate College (*see* p. 459) is set back tactfully, and in front an older scale asserts itself: No. 117, weatherboarded, and Nos. 111–115, a group of *c.* 1800, with three-storey centre and lower side parts. Nos. 107–109 are an early C19 pair, a three-storey five-bay block with blind central window; mid-C19 stucco additions. On the E side is Southgate House (*see* Major Houses, above) within the Minchenden Campus of Southgate College. Much interwar housing follows, and a few Victorian cottages near the

6    entrance to MEADWAY, which has a formal prelude of terracotta-trimmed shops. Meadway and BOURNE AVENUE were laid out by Edmondson's on the Southgate House estate with superior suburban housing of between the wars, spaciously planned, with a picturesque medley of half-timbered, roughcast and tile-hung gables overlooking a little green. On the W side, in a different mood, ELLINGTON COURT, progressive flats of 1937 by *Frederick*

*Gibberd.* An informal three-storey frontage stepping back twice, with cantilevered porches and projecting concrete balconies in the style of Tecton's Highpoint One, Highgate, but with the brick facing that modernist architects were beginning to adopt in the later 1930s. Further on, a simple early C19 pair, Nos. 15–17.

THE GREEN starts with a picturesque sequence on the E side. No. 40 with a Georgian fanlight, Nos. 38–39, a tall pair built 1775–6 for Richard Goad, a local landowner; doorcases with reeded capitals and broken pediments; the canted bays are later alterations. Extension to the l. with two Venetian windows over a coachway. Nos. 23–31 are a lower group of three-bay rendered houses built in 1777 for Goad on charity land, apparently as almshouses. The south London architect *Michael Searles* made survey plans but whether he designed the houses is uncertain. Heavily reconstructed in 1981. The group ends with the OLDE CHERRY TREE, not all old, but an attractive mixture of brick, timber and stucco; on its l. a painted brick extension with simple assembly room over a coach entrance.

On the N side of The Green, a pair of very handsome Early Georgian houses, ESSEX HOUSE and ARNOSIDE, six bays, with rusticated brick quoins and doorways side by side in the middle. A detached low service wing projects forward on each side. Fine pair of Baroque gatepiers with urns, and original iron railings and gates. On the r., No. 2, OLD HOUSE, with a late Georgian doorcase; beyond this, the VICARAGE, set back.

In WATERFALL ROAD w of The Green, past Christ Church and the site of the older chapel (*see* Churches, above), MINCHENDEN OAK GARDEN, a pretty secluded evergreen garden created in 1934 by the borough around an ancient pollarded oak, in the C19 reputed to be the largest in England. More to see in CANNON HILL to the S. On the w side the vast Neo-Georgian offices screened by trees incorporate the principal mansion in the area, Arnos Grove (*see* above). Opposite, No. 6, CANNON HOUSE, is early C19, a two-storey three-window stock brick villa, with low weatherboarded former coach house. No. 2, the HERMITAGE, is late C18 in origin, a thatched *cottage orné*, quite large, of three bays, with bargeboarded gables and dormers and a Gothic doorway.

ALDERMAN'S HILL continues E, along the N boundary of Broomfield Park (*see* Major Houses, above), with a fine view across it to London and Alexandra Palace. No. 128, OLD PARK, dating from 1892, was built for himself by *J. B. Franklin.* Tall striped chimneys and a big Baroque window surround in the Shaw tradition; converted to flats 1995. Closer to Palmers Green, suburban streets of 1902–12 developed on the Old Park Estate. For Palmers Green, *see* Perambulation 3.

*2. New Southgate Station to Arnos Grove Station*

Building began after the railway came in 1850, but the Victorian reputation of the area was blighted by the proximity of the asylum just over the railway line in Friern Barnet (*see* Barnet); hence the change of name from Colney Hatch to New Southgate. The Victorian centre, much run down, can just be recognized.

FRIERN BARNET ROAD starts with THE TURRETS, a playful 1880s pub looking down Station Road, and continues with a few large C19 houses to BETSTYLE CIRCUS, which has a good inter-war parade in the Arts and Crafts tradition on the N side but is otherwise amorphous. To its S, HIGH ROAD, now a sad back-water among new housing, was once more important, as is shown by its cluster of churches. They range from the Anglican St Paul (q.v.), shrouded in evergreens, to a Sikh temple in a former Wesleyan chapel, its brick and stone spire rising incongruously above later pebbledash. Further E, in GROVE ROAD, a Baptist chapel of 1901 has become flats, quite a tactful conversion which maintains the character of the broad red brick Gothic front, with tower on one side ending in an octagonal turret. The green space nearby ought to be a focal point in this largely rebuilt area, but it all fails to cohere. Ranks of post-war four-storey flats to the N; cosier slate-hung low-rise cul-de-sacs of the 1970s further S.

Early efforts were bolder: the first phase of the borough's twenty-year redevelopment scheme was in HIGHVIEW GARDENS further E. Between dense Edwardian terraces and the railway line, an open landscape with four-storey maisonettes, and two thirteen-storey point blocks by *David du R. Aberdeen*, 1958–60. Transparent lift excrescences and balconies and bay windows to the corner living rooms make these towers livelier than later examples.

In BOWES ROAD, the styles of the 30s confront each other, the flabby half-timbered frontage of the ARNOS ARMS angled across a corner, and the taut brick groups of Underground station and library (qq.v.).

## 3. Palmers Green

Palmers Green is essentially Edwardian, a poor man's Muswell Hill, and indeed the same developer, Edmondson's, was active in both places. It expanded rapidly after parts of the Grovelands estate were sold for building in 1901. The station lies on ALDERMAN'S HILL, just W of the remnant of a triangular green overlooked by a tall free Jacobean BANK of 1904. The best bank is on a corner site further N up GREEN LANES: No. 288, the NATIONAL WESTMINSTER, a triumphant essay in rusticated brick, with purple and red brick dressings, and dramatically composed chimneys, 1913 by *Arthur Sykes*. Sykes specialized in shops and commercial premises; No. 286, of 1924–5, in a more sober Neo-Georgian, is also by him and so is the long parade on the W side, continuing to Devonshire Road, built in seven stages 1909–13. This has artistic leanings of the kind predating the vogue for commercial Neo-Georgian: free Tudor with plain Voyseyish details, an unusual choice (and also different from Sykes's earlier artistic shopping parade at Acton, Ealing). Roughcast walls enlivened by bay windows, and an effective skyline of gables, steep roofs and chimney-stacks. Further on, THE FOX, 1904, with exuberant corner turret and pargetting.

SKINNERS ALMSHOUSES, Pellipar Close, off FOX LANE, is a sensitive rebuilding of 1967–9 by *Alec Shickle* of almshouses formerly in Green Lanes. The older almshouses (1895 by *W. Campbell Jones*) had replaced others in inner London. From these are two small figures of *c.* 1700 standing in alcoves in the garden, a man from Great St Helen's, a woman from Mile End Road. The new buildings loosely follow a traditional almshouse lay-out, informal two-storey blocks with black-boarded upper floors, stepping back; with one-storey links to a taller polygonal community room.

CORIB COURT, further up Fox Lane, is the former Southgate County School by the MCC architect *H. G. Crothall*, 1909–10, now flats. In the free Baroque tradition which Crothall used so effectively for his secondary schools; seven-bay centre; stone surrounds to arched ground-floor windows, stone-faced projecting end pavilions, steep roof with decorative lantern. MENLOW LODGE, the former caretaker's house and manual instruction centre, uses similar details, including the perverse inset brick quoins at the corners, and has inspired a pale echo of the style in CROTHALL CLOSE.

Back to GREEN LANES for a few isolated items. S of Alderman's Hill on the E side, good examples of Edmondson's showy Edwardian terraces with quirky detail. Further S, opposite the Town Hall (q.v.), TRURO HOUSE, No. 176, a pleasant early C19 villa; Corinthian porch and projecting eaves, and an Ionic bow to the garden front overlooking the New River.

The METAL BOX FACTORY in Chequers Way, just S of the North Circular Road, is a quite stylish three-storey composition of between the wars; red brick with stone banding to accentuate centre and corners, staircase windows with crisp frames, angled brickwork. Three-storey centre of 1929 flanked by slightly taller wings of 1934 and 1938 by *S. N. Cooke*; outer additions of the 1950s.


## 4. *Winchmore Hill*

The top of Winchmore Hill still appears comparatively rural and nicely wooded, with Grovelands Park adjoining to the W. As at Southgate, C20 suburbia is leavened by a sprinkling of cottages and Georgian houses. The STATION opened in 1871, but there was little new building until around 1900.

The centre of the old hamlet is the irregular GREEN near the top of the hill. At the SE corner the former village bakery has an early C19 shopfront with fluted columns. In BROAD WALK, ROWANTREE HOUSE, now two houses, with an irregular early C18 front of nine bays; two storeys and parapet. To the W the bold and jolly KINGS HEAD of 1899. Beside it CHURCH HILL continues uphill with the Quaker meeting house on the r. and St Paul's on the l. (qq.v.). Further on, near an entrance to Grovelands Park (*see* Major Houses, above), the pretty group of WOODSIDE COTTAGES, three early C19 weatherboarded houses with low-pitched slate roofs. The central single-storeyed building was the village school house. Back to the Green and N up WADE'S HILL, which has some more weatherboarded cottages, and opposite, GLENWOOD HOUSE, one of a three-storey C18 pair. Other C19 cottages in VICARS MOOR LANE; also a polite mid-C19 terrace with Doric porches.

In STATION ROAD, downhill from the station, a prim sequence of small detached late Victorian villas with arched doorways and a little half-timbering below the eaves. Opposite, the delightful former POSTMEN'S OFFICE of 1904; spirited Edwardian Baroque on a miniature scale; canted frontispiece with blocked window surrounds. More average Edwardian development around the junction with Green Lanes and further s.

N of Winchmore Hill, WADE'S HILL leads to GREEN DRAGON LANE, where there are a few C19 cottages among the between-the-wars suburbia of GRANGE PARK. To the NW, WORLD'S END LANE. On its w side, incorporated in a dull Barratts housing development of 1995–7, a few buildings remain from the once remote HIGHLANDS HOSPITAL, 1884–7 by *Pennington & Bridgen*, built by the Metropolitan Asylum Board for those convalescing from infectious diseases. It had an unusual and distinctive lay-out: a winding street of pavilions in Queen Anne style around a central administration block. The original pavilions are in a friendly red and yellow brick with coved eaves and tall chimneys; the central block (extended after 1890, demolished 1997) was more formal, with engaged pilasters. At the NE end of the site was the original small ambulance station for the carriage which conveyed the infectious patients to the hospital.

### 5. Oakwood, Cockfosters, Hadley Wood and Trent Park

This area at the N tip of Southgate lay within ENFIELD CHASE, part of the old forest of Middlesex, which in the C18 belonged to the Duchy of Lancaster. Parts were enclosed in 1777 and two mansions were built, Trent Park and Beech Hill Park. Cockfosters developed as a hamlet between the two, with a church by 1839, but substantial development occurred only a century later, after the Piccadilly Line arrived in 1933. The earlier growth of Hadley Wood as a select Victorian suburb further N was due to the owner of Beech Hill Park, Charles Jack, who from 1882 laid out streets near the Great Northern Railway station, opened in 1885.

The 1930s suburbs of Cockfosters and Oakwood are notable princi-pally for their Underground stations, a few schools, and a library (qq.v.). CHASE ROAD, s of Oakwood Station, has suburban hous-ing with a few modernistic touches (curved corner windows). Cockfosters has some incongruously urban offices near the station; the church lies tucked away in CHALK LANE, but any village character has been swamped by late C20 houses in traditional sub-urban mode. Those surrounding WEST FARM PLACE,* a long, low rendered building of the early C19, date from the 1990s.

At the N end of Chalk Lane, THE COCK, a characteristic 1930s roadhouse by *J. C. F. James* for Benskins. Further N, built-up London stops abruptly at the Green Belt, with Trent Park on the E and Beech Hill Park Golf Course on the w.

BEECH HILL PARK, Beech Hill (Hadley Wood Golf Club since 1922), was built for Francis Russell, secretary to the Duchy of Lancaster (†1795), after the Chase enclosure of 1777. In a fine position looking s. Restrained exterior: seven-bay brick front with giant Doric pilasters to the centre. C19 one-storeyed pavilion wings, stuccoed, for billiard room (E) and conservatory (w). These are

---

* West Farm Place is within Barnet.

now integrated within the club's suite of reception rooms, with entrance from the w. In the original s entrance hall, two plaster medallions with classical scenes; another over the fireplace in the NE dining room. Behind the entrance hall, a plain but very elegant staircase with stick balusters and sinuous handrail, rising around a well. To its w a narrow room with elaborate Neoclassical decoration: two Corinthian columns at the E end, on the walls matching pilasters, honeysuckle frieze, and a row of moulded frames on each side (some blind). A staircase rises behind the columns to a mezzanine at the back: is this the remains of an older house enveloped in the new building? STABLES to the N, three ranges around a courtyard, with arched openings, somewhat altered.

CAMLET WAY continues from Beech Hill towards Monken Hadley (*see* Barnet), lined with affluent C20 houses in every style except modern. Among them a few earlier buildings: Nos. 83–89, dated 1878, are a picturesque group of 'Old English' estate cottages which served a mansion called Broadgates; steep gables and decorative tile-hanging. In CRESCENT ROAD near Hadley Wood Station, a sudden fragment of a Victorian suburb: substantial tile-hung houses of the 1880s, a development by Charles Jack, which failed to expand further.

WEST LODGE PARK HOTEL, Ferny Hill, is on the site of one of the ancient lodges for the underkeepers of Enfield Chase, which were in existence by the C16. The earliest part now is the two-storeyed s range, probably C18 but altered. Centre rebuilt in the later C19, N end 1923, N and W extensions 1972. Unified by white stucco, and set in nicely planted grounds. Large entrance hall with C18 staircase; above the half landing, a reset Jacobean overmantel.

Further W, FERNY HILL FARM; an attractive group of three-bay farmhouse and timber-framed, weatherboarded barn. In HADLEY ROAD, a tall PUMPING STATION for a well, 1903.

*Trent Park*

The buildings, from 1947 a teacher training college, became part of Middlesex Polytechnic in 1974 and of Middlesex University in 1992; the grounds were bought by the County Council in 1951 and are now a country park. The estate formed after the enclosure of part of Enfield Chase in 1777 was acquired by Sir Richard Jebb, a royal physician (†1787), knighted after he had saved the life of the Duke of Gloucester at Trent in the Tyrol. He built a small villa, described by the *Gentleman's Magazine* as 'a singular loggia in the Italian style', only *c.*30 by 40 ft, apparently an older building adapted by *Sir William Chambers*. This intriguing miniature, known from a sketch by Chambers's pupil Reveley, had a domed centre and paired giant columns. Jebb supplemented the house by outbuildings with library, billiard room etc., but after his death the original building was soon made unrecognizable by additions to E, W and S, and was much altered and extended by F. A. Bevan in 1894. Apart from the w service wing, the Victorian additions were demolished or disguised in 1926–31, when the house was again transformed, by Sir Philip Sassoon, M.P. and wealthy connoisseur (†1939), as a setting for his theatrical hospitality. The result was a large Georgian mansion 'in the pure English tradition' (as it was described by Christopher Hussey in

*Country Life*, 1931). Sassoon's architect was *Philip Tilden*, who had worked for him in a much more flamboyant and luxurious manner at his house at Lympne, Kent. Exactly what he was responsible for here is unknown.

The house now appears as a nearly symmetrical composition of 2–2–3–3–2 bays to the N of a paved forecourt. Sassoon added balancing projecting wings to the entrance front in place of irregular Victorian bay windows, and cased the house in red brick with stone dressings and a balustraded parapet. The materials came from the demolished Devonshire House, Piccadilly (1734–5 by *Kent*); the inspiration was said to be Wimpole Hall, Cambs. Doorcase with swan-neck pediment, from Chesterfield House, South Audley Street (demolished 1937). Inside, the sequence of reception rooms along the N front incorporates those of the older house. The saloon is entered from the entrance hall by a heavy arched door-way flanked by pilasters and niches, apparently adapted from Jebb's front. Sassoon's interiors, now devoid of their furnishings, appear bare and sad and convey little of the elusive 'country house' spirit – described by Hussey as 'an essence of cool flowery chintzy elegant unobtrusive rooms'. In the saloon, murals copied from Chinese wallpaper partly survive. The drawing room (NW), has C18 Kentian fireplaces with large consoles. The W end of the room, beyond a pair of fluted Ionic columns, is Sassoon's addition; Venetian window at the end, with *Rex Whistler* mural of dolphins. Panelled library (NE) with corresponding Whistler murals of mermaids; Blue Room (SE), with murals of Mars and Minerva. The blue colour scheme was originally contrasted with red lacquered furniture. SW dining room, also panelled. Brought-in C18 staircase, E of the entrance hall, a fine example with three types of balusters.

The SWIMMING POOL E of the house is framed by the splayed wings of Sassoon's red brick ORANGERY, designed by *Reginald Cooper*; balustraded parapet with urn and putti. Around the house some fine GARDEN STATUARY of *c.* 1700, added by Sassoon. On the entrance side, lead figures of Actaeon and Venus, from Wrest Park, Beds. At the E end of the terrace, a pair of charming lead sphinxes, by *Nost*, from Stowe, Bucks. Below the terrace, two more lead groups, also from Stowe, by *Nost* after Giovanni da Bologna, the detail excellent: Hercules wrestling with Antaeus, and Samson defeating a Philistine. At the W end of the terrace, a group of two female figures and a winged male figure, of marble, early C18. Also from Sassoon's time is the WISTERIA WALK to the SE, a pergola with Italian columns of pink marble; C18 GATE nearby.

Jebb's outbuildings were replaced in the C19. To the SE of the house, the STABLE COURTYARD, quite pretty, with Gothic gabled buildings on three sides and polychrome brick arches, and several estate COTTAGES, built by R. C. L. Bevan between 1837 and 1890. In this area, a scatter of indifferent buildings for the College of Education of the 1950s onwards by the *MCC*, others to the NE of the house by the Borough of Enfield (*N. C. Dowell*), 1972–4.

In contrast to the cluttered surroundings of the house are the splendid GROUNDS, carved out of the ancient woodland of Enfield Chase. The house overlooks a string of lakes to the N. The W approach is down a long lime avenue from the Cockfosters entrance, with gates in a semicircular brick and stone exedra masking a half-timbered Victorian LODGE. COLUMN and two OBELISKS brought by Sassoon from Wrest Park, Bedfordshire; early C18, the taller obelisk creating a fine *point de vue* near Ferny Hill. Not far from this is CAMLET MOAT, an impressively substantial moated site with traces of buildings, much overgrown, said to be the site of a manor house of the Mandevilles, Earls of Essex, and latterly a haunt of Dick Turpin.

# HACKNEY

Hackney was formed in 1965 from the three Metropolitan Boroughs
of Shoreditch, Hackney and Stoke Newington, the new borough
taking its name from the central and largest older local authority. All
three began as medieval parishes, and their story is one of gradual
absorption in the London suburbs: this happened to Shoreditch
already in the C16, to Hackney and Stoke Newington in the C18 and
C19. As fashionable London moved w, Shoreditch and southern
Hackney became part of the industrial East End, with a consequent
decline in social status in the C19 as the population increased. The
combination of bomb damage, slum clearance and decline in industrial activity, especially marked in the later C20, has led to a marked
drop in numbers: in 1951 *c.* 265,000; in 1995 *c.* 194,220.

# HACKNEY

## INTRODUCTION

The early history of Hackney is recalled by the tower remaining from the medieval parish church close to Mare Street. It was preserved as a bell tower after the large new church was built to its NE in 1792. The C16 is represented now only by Sutton House, sole surviving domestic reminder of Hackney's distinguished past. The area possessed a marked and acknowledged character in its own right to the middle of the C19, when its incorporation into the East End of London took place. From its wealthier and more leisurely days it has kept a general leafiness still pleasantly noticeable, especially in the common land preserved as open spaces, of which there are more than in most other inner London suburbs. Pepys records more than once that he goes out to Hackney 'to take the ayre', although an additional attraction to him was the boarding schools, or, to be more precise, 'the young ladies of the schools whereof there is great store'. Hackney schools also appear in Restoration comedy, and in *The Spectator* (No. 134), *The Tatler* (No. 82) etc. In 1720 Strype praises its 'healthful air' and refers to the 'divers nobles' who 'in former times had their country seats' at Hackney; Defoe also calls it 'remarkable for the retreat of wealthy citizens', with 'near a hundred coaches kept in it'.

Defoe (who lived in Stoke Newington) mentions twelve hamlets or separate villages, 'tho some of them now join'. Their existence explains the tortuous and confusing road pattern that still exists in much of Hackney. The old centres are nearly all still recognizable. The main settlement grew up around the long line of Mare Street stretching S from the parish church. To the N was Clapton with its pond and green; to the E lay Homerton, 'a retired village' as late as 1851, and, near Hackney Marsh, the more remote Wyck House, which gave its name to Hackney Wick. To the SE were Well Street, where the Knights of St John had a mansion, Grove Street, a very small hamlet, and Cambridge Heath on the edge of Bethnal Green. The W part of the parish is still bisected by the Roman route of Ermine Street, running straight N from Shoreditch towards Stoke Newington and Stamford Hill; its southern stretch is known as Kingsland Road from the hamlet of that name, where Pepys as a boy 'used to shoot with bows and arrows'. Defoe also mentions Dalston (still 'a small hamlet' in 1806), Shacklewell and Newington.

Rocque's map of 1745 already shows in addition to Mare Street the usual ribbons of houses along Lower Clapton Road N and S of Clapton pond, and along Homerton High Street. A hundred years later half the area of the parish was still grasslands, but urban grids of streets were beginning to appear to the E and W of Kingsland Road. Loddige's famous market gardens with their huge Palm and Camelia Houses of 1819–22, which lay E of Mare Street, disappeared in the 1850s. The population was *c.* 13,000 in 1801, 25,000 in 1821, 38,000 in 1861, 125,000 in 1871 (1840–70 are the decisive years of suburbanization) and 199,000 in 1891. The new churches marked the expansion. St Thomas, Clapton Common, was a former proprietary chapel, still with a tower of 1829; then came St James in Stoke Newington Road, by Smirke, 1821–4, a vast Commissioners'

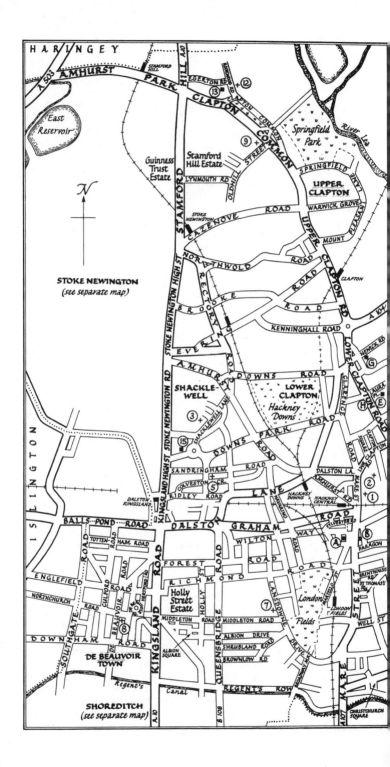

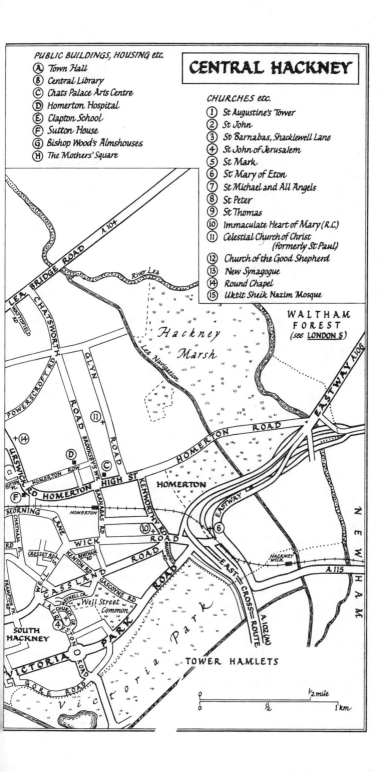

PUBLIC BUILDINGS, HOUSING etc.

- (A) Town Hall
- (B) Central Library
- (C) Chats Palace Arts Centre
- (D) Homerton Hospital
- (E) Clapton School
- (F) Sutton House
- (G) Bishop Wood's Almshouses
- (H) The Mothers' Square

# CENTRAL HACKNEY

CHURCHES etc.

- (1) St Augustine's Tower
- (2) St John
- (3) St Barnabas, Shacklewell Lane
- (4) St John of Jerusalem
- (5) St Mark
- (6) St Mary of Eton
- (7) St Michael and All Angels
- (8) St Peter
- (9) St Thomas
- (10) Immaculate Heart of Mary (R.C.)
- (11) Celestial Church of Christ (formerly St Paul)
- (12) Church of the Good Shepherd
- (13) New Synagogue
- (14) Round Chapel
- (15) Uktit Sheik Nazim Mosque

church in Doric style, destroyed in the Second World War. A burst of
activity from the 1840s produced St John South Hackney (an ambitious High Church rebuilding of a chapel of ease at Well Street), St
Barnabas Homerton, St Peter De Beauvoir Town, and St James
Lower Clapton. St Mark Dalston, another huge building, followed
in the 1860s. Around the churches respectable Victorian middle-class
housing burgeoned; in the 1840s it was classical, or occasionally
57 *cottage-orné* Tudor as in De Beauvoir Square; twenty years later it had
80 become more eclectic, with copious and inventive stucco trimmings.

By the later C19 the character of Hackney was changing; industries
(especially furniture and clothing) spread N from Shoreditch and
Bethnal Green, and colonized the Lea Valley to the E. Factories and
warehouses filled the backland of the older buildings remaining in
the old hamlets and often took over the larger houses as well. With
new jobs came overcrowding and pressure for more housing. The years
after the First World War saw a remarkable growth of estates of flats.
In the aggregate they altered the appearance of Hackney decisively.
The LCC contributed its usual solid walk-up five-storey blocks all
over Hackney. The borough began its main efforts in 1929, taking over
the more open areas remaining to the N. Its flats by *Messrs Joseph*
were increasingly ambitious in conception, grand formal lay-outs in a
minimal Neo-Georgian, but incorporating amenities for the tenants.
By 1940 the borough owned thirteen major estates. In addition
extensive building was carried out by the Guinness Trust, the Samuel
Lewis Housing Trust and other housing organizations. The pattern
continued immediately after the Second World War, for although
by 1951 the population had shrunk to 171,000, pressure for new
housing was unabated. Building was shared between the borough,
under the Borough Engineer *George Downing*, Director of Housing
from 1946, and outside architects.

By 1965, when the new borough incorporating Shoreditch and
Stoke Newington was formed, one-fifth of its population lived in
properties owned by the council. *J. L. Sharratt*, the former Borough
Architect of Shoreditch, became architect for the new borough, and
yet more schemes of radical reconstruction were planned. But the
mammoth estates of the later 1960s, especially their system-built
towers, proved increasingly unpopular, and during the 1970s plain,
less intrusive low-rise new housing became the norm, much of it
provided by the borough.* At the same time a more sympathetic
interest in Hackney's fast disappearing older buildings began to
develop, coinciding with government funding becoming available
for renovation and encouraged by a certain amount of gentrification.

Hackney's vigorous cultural variety, created by successive waves of
immigration (in 1995 black and ethnic minorities constituted around
91 half of the borough's population), is strikingly reflected by the
93 continuing diversity of its places of worship, from C19 chapels and
synagogues to C20 mosques. It is also an interesting place to explore
a whole gamut of approaches to conservation and reuse of other
types of buildings and to appropriate or less appropriate infilling in
sensitive areas. Improvement is an uphill struggle. In the 1990s, with
the decline of local industries, the borough was one of the poorest in

---

*In 1991, 36,242 households lived in borough-owned housing, 47.9 per cent of the
total (compared with 11.3 per cent in housing association property, 13.8 per cent in
other rented property, and 26 per cent owner occupied).

Britain. The effects of government-funded improvements are beginning to be apparent, as at Dalston, although they remain small oases among a traffic-ridden medley of shabby shopping streets, dingy empty factories, and run-down flats.* But there is plenty of interesting architectural activity to discover: factories converted to artists' studios (the borough has exceptionally many) or replaced by new housing; council flats transformed by radical rehabilitation; decaying c19 terraces repaired, and open spaces enlivened by sculpture.  130

ARCHAEOLOGY. The few Roman finds in this area include a handsome marble sarcophagus from Lower Clapton.

## RELIGIOUS BUILDINGS

### 1. Church of England

ST AUGUSTINE'S TOWER, Mare Street. Only the w tower remains from the medieval parish church of Hackney. It was retained initially as bell and clock tower for the new church (see St John, below). A tall elegant version of the usual Middlesex Perp tower, probably a little earlier than the early c16 rebuilding of the church at the expense of Sir John Heron, Lord of the Manor, and the rector, Christopher Urswyck. Kentish rag, of four stages, with four-centred belfry windows. SE corner staircase; its turret has been truncated. At the third level, an early c17 TURRET CLOCK. The iron frame and some of the mechanism are original, the two clock faces later. The rest of the church was demolished in 1798, apart from the Rowe Chapel, built s of the chancel in 1614, which survived until 1896.

ST JOHN, Mare Street. The new church of 1791–4 by *James Spiller*, adjoining the medieval churchyard, has a show front to the N facing Lower Clapton Road, emphasized by the N tower and semicircular porch added (to Spiller's designs) in 1810–14. It is in  36 many ways a remarkable building. First of all it is of vast size; secondly its plan is a Greek cross, that is, symmetrical all round; and thirdly its detail is distinctly original, not to say odd: Soanian perhaps, though parallel to rather than a derivation from Soane. The tower faces N, yet the High Altar faces E, an irregularity easily overcome by the Greek cross shape inside. The tower rides white on a big brick pediment. This pediment was originally repeated on s, w, and E sides; two were removed when the church was damaged by fire in 1955 and repaired by *N. F. Cachemaille-Day* and *William C. Lock*. Smaller semicircular porches on E and w sides, also added in 1810–14, originally gave access to the lobbies at the end of N and s arms. The external view is thus of an oblong with short w and E arms. The tower is of the most unconventional shape, first a massive square substructure, then the bell storey, also square with coupled pilasters and severely pedimented windows, and then an equally square and weighty, fantastically detailed top stage with broad volutes and a crowning motif that defeats description. Only St Anne Soho is comparable in oddity. The tower 'beautifully weathered and gleaming white seems to float in sublime independence of the

---

* An ambitious initiative, planned in 1997, involves the creation of a cultural quarter centred on the Town Hall in Mare Street, with improved facilities in the former Methodist Central Hall, Public Library and the Hackney Empire.

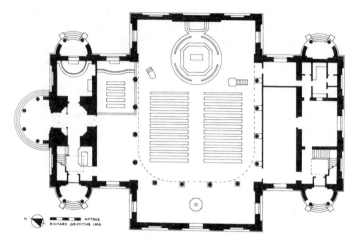

St John, Hackney. Plan

sturdy brown temple which really supports it' (J. Summerson). The rest is of plain stock brick, with arched windows in two storeys, very broad Tuscan pilasters and (originally) very deep eaves, effective by sheer mass, and more in the spirit of Hawksmoor than of the architects of 1800.

The interior also impresses first by size. It is wide not high, with a large open centre covered by a shallow vault (the roof ingeniously secured above with the help of steel by *Beresford Pite* in 1929). The short arms of the Greek cross have shallow tunnel vaults cut into by the windows. A gallery of Roman Doric columns fills the arms and curves round NW and SW corners. The E window is distinguished by width, by coupled pilasters and some little decoration.

Original REREDOS, CHOIR STALLS, ALTAR RAILS and semicircular BAPTISTERY RAILS. Gallery parapet also partly of metal. Excellent mahogany PULPIT, tall and free-standing on four Corinthian piers. The staircase has slim twisted balusters; the body is polygonal, with competent carving. STAINED GLASS. E window 1955–8 by *Christopher Webb*.

p. 6

MONUMENTS from the old church are in the lobbies. Christopher Urswyck †1522, Dean of Windsor and rector of Hackney. Canopied wall monument made as an Easter Sepulchre, formerly on the chancel N wall of the old church. Small chest with cusped quatrefoils, Perp canopy with canted panelled jambs and canted panelled four-centred arch, vine-scroll frieze and horizontal cresting. The design is that used for other early C16 London sepulchre-tombs (cf. St Mary Lambeth, St Helen Bishopsgate). On the back panel only the name and date 1519, probably inspired by the similarly simple inscription on the tomb in St Paul's Cathedral of Urswyck's friend John Colet. The BRASS to Urswyck now on the tomb-chest was originally on the chancel floor. – John Lymsey †1545, brass in armour; of his wife only the indent left. 4½-ft figures, surrounded by thin rectangular frames with corner roundels. Two shields are palimpsests, made from an early C16 Flemish brass. – Arthur Dericote †1562 and four wives, small tablet with kneeling brass figures. – Sir Thomas Rowe †1570, with wife and children, one of the usual monuments with kneeling figures facing each other, but now only the figures preserved (floor of NE lobby). – Lucye, wife of Lord Latimer, †1583, reconstructed free-standing tomb-chest with recumbent alabaster effigy of a quality good enough for Westminster Abbey (cf. the effigy of Lady Burghley there). Attributions to *Cornelius Cure* (GF) or *Garrett Johnson* (Adam White) have been suggested. – Hugh Johnson †1618, vicar of Hackney, brass of man on pulpit. – Henry Banister †1628 and his wife and children, kneeling figures (NE lobby). Attributed to *Humphrey Moyer* (GF). – David Doulben, Bishop of Bangor, †1633. Frontal bust in recess with open segmental pediment and small figures of angels seated to l. and r. Also attributed to *Moyer* (GF). – Thomas Wood, father of Bishop Wood, †1649 and wife and children. Perhaps made *c.* 1660, by *Thomas Burman* (GF). An interesting modification of the older type of monument with kneelers. Here the two main figures stand and look at each other across the prayer desk. The others still kneel, but style and expression are quite freed from Jacobean stiffness. – Richard de Beauvoir †1708, attributed to *William Woodman Sen.* (GF). – James Sotheby †1750, wall monument with crest by *Roubiliac*. – Captain Newcome †1797, by *Regnart*. Sarcophagus with large, vividly carved trophy on top. – Lieutenant Sedgwick †1811, also by *Regnart*, and the pendant to the other, though enriched by a battle relief on the sarcophagus.

CHURCHYARD. Large and leafy. Walled in 1707 and planted with avenues of trees in 1797 under the supervision of *Harry Sedgwick*. Burials ceased in 1859, and the tombs were rearranged in 1893 when a formal public garden was created. The large number of substantial tomb-chests are mostly now arrayed in line along the N side. The S part was relandscaped as a walled quiet garden in 1964 by the Borough Engineer.

HOLY TRINITY, Beechwood Road, Dalston. 1878–9 by *Ewan Christian*. A tall, spare, urban church in red brick, lancet style, cruciform. Most dramatic when seen from the E. A huge Teulonesque central tower with steep roof and circular turret broods over the sanctuary. Interior with broad brick arcades (now whitened). S transept lowered after a fire. E window by *A. F. Erridge* (BFLC). SCREEN at W end from the demolished St Philip Dalston (1841).

ST BARNABAS, Homerton High Street. 1843–52 by *Arthur Ashpitel*. Kentish rag tower of the Perp London type: interesting as an effort to copy local character. Interior with alternating circular and octagonal piers and thick foliage capitals and corbels. Repaired by *W. C. Lock* after war damage; chancel divided off for vestries. (FURNISHINGS include a large triptych, brought from St Andrew Bethnal Green.)

ST BARNABAS (Merchant Taylors' School Mission), Shacklewell Lane. 1909–11, an early work by *Sir Charles Reilly*, decorated by him 1935–6. Not visible from the street and therefore with a plain exterior, though the general shape and windows hint at the Byzantine character of the interior, which looks surprisingly spacious. Nave with concrete tunnel vaults and broad transverse brick arches. Low passage aisles with segmental-arched arcades, shallow dome over the chancel, apse and no transepts. The chancel screen in the Adam taste, with figures by *Tyson Smith* added in 1935, is a piquant addition which comes off much more happily than one might expect. Chancel fittings by *Reilly*. C19 Gothic PULPIT from Christ Church, Rendlesham Road.

MISSION ROOMS facing the road, 1890, minimal Gothic.

ST BARTHOLOMEW, Dalston Lane. On a prominent corner site. Built as church and vicarage in one building, 1884 by *John Johnson*. For long a ruin, converted to housing in 1995.

ST JAMES, Lower Clapton Road. 1840–1 by *E. C. Hakewill*. Lancet style, stock brick and stone, a curious design, with nave and transepts ending in lower polygonal chapels. Polygonal turret and passage to the main porch in the SE angle. Red brick E bay, chancel and N vestries added 1902 by *W. D. Caröe*. Also by Caröe the ORGAN CASE, CROSS and CANDLESTICKS. Nave divided off in 1978 as a centre for handicapped children.

ST JOHN OF JERUSALEM (South Hackney Parish Church), Church Crescent. By *E. C. Hakewill*, 1845–8. A large church on a prominent island site, an ambitious High Church replacement of the Well Street chapel of ease of 1806–10. Kentish rag walls with stone dressings. Cruciform, with a big w tower, its E.E. arcading reminiscent of St Mary Stamford. The original broach spire lost in World War II was replaced by a slender one by *Cachemaille-Day*. Interior on the grandest scale; the detail mostly E.E., quite progressive for the 1840s, but in places curious rather than good (see the odd clerestory tracery). Broad aisled nave with tightly placed columns, some circular, some octagonal, but not rationally ordered. Some competent stiff-leaf carving. Deep transepts (now subdivided) flank a vast crossing with intersecting timber roof. The chancel is apsed, with a stone vault. A black and white mosaic floor of 1893 dominates nave and aisles, exceptionally wide in the centre to allow for free seats, since removed. The sturdy poppy-head PEWS to N and S were probably originally closer together. The STALLS have in addition musical angels. STAINED GLASS. All post-war, attributed to *M. C. Farrer Bell*; apse with the theme of healing, N transept with prophets, S transept with St Augustine, Cranmer, Wesley and William Temple. MONUMENT. Rev. H. H. Norris †1850, the first rector. Brass in a quatrefoil recording that 'the church erected mainly through him is a monument to his zeal for the beauty of holiness'. His portrait is in the S transept.

ST LUKE, Chatham Place. 1871–2 by *Newman & Billing*; routine Dec, random ragstone. E.E. tower and spire 1882; the corner turret has its own bulky spirelet. (STAINED GLASS. E window 1950 by *H. Vernon Spreadbury*.)

ST MARK, St Mark's Rise, Dalston. 1862–6 by *Chester Cheston Jun.*, architect to the Amhurst estate (for which his father was the solicitor). E.E., with grouped lancets, enormous. The exterior dull except for the striking w tower, completed by *E. L. Blackburne* in 1877–80. Boldly striped upper part, the octagonal top with circular turrets clustered around a stumpy gabled spire, a Teulonesque piling on of effects. Large gargoyles. Very broad low-church interior, odd but impressive: slim iron quatrefoil piers; w gallery; polychrome brick walls, a big pointed wagon roof. The chancel was heightened in 1880, and the church much embellished during the time of the Rev. Joseph Green Pilkington, vicar from 1870. Sanctuary with arcaded panelling below painted diapering. Mosaic REREDOS.

Curious stained-glass panels in blue and gold, with angels, set into the roof above the arches to the transepts. STAINED GLASS of 1865–6 by *Lavers & Barraud* was replaced by richly coloured windows, a coherent set of Old and New Testament themes, with Virtues and Vices in the W rose. FONT with four large standing figures. PULPIT of coloured marbles. Prettily painted ORGAN. On the tower a turret BAROMETER.

CHURCH HALL to the SE, Gothic, with large dormers.

ST MARY OF ETON, Eastway, Hackney Wick. 1890–2 by *Bodley & Garner* for the mission founded in 1880. A church well worth a special visit. Red brick with Bath stone dressings. The E side faces the street with a sensitively grouped display of steep E gable, E ends of aisles, gabled SE chapel, taller than the aisles but lower than the nave, and big NE gate-tower giving access to the picturesque courtyard with the Eton Mission buildings. The two W bays were added by *Cecil Hare* in 1911–12.

The interior is equally impressive, in the tradition of Bodley's Pendlebury, Lancs (1870–4) and reminiscent of his church at Epping of 1889. Tall and wide nave with a gracefully painted boarded wagon roof. Tall square piers without capitals, tall narrow aisles, no clerestory. No structural division between nave and chancel. The fragile wooden SCREEN formerly in between is now near the W end. REREDOS 1930 by *W. Ellery Anderson*. On the W piers, memorial INSCRIPTION by *Eric Gill*, 1936.

ST MATTHEW, Mount Pleasant Lane, Upper Clapton. A converted church hall. *F. T. Dollman*'s much larger church of 1867–9 was burnt down in 1976 and replaced by sheltered housing (*see* Perambulation 2b).

ST MICHAEL AND ALL ANGELS, Lansdowne Drive, London Fields. A replacement for a C19 church on the opposite side of the Fields (by *J. H. Hakewill*), destroyed in World War II. By *N. F. Cachemaille-Day*, 1959–60. Unassuming compact brick-faced exterior, spacious inside. Square shallow-domed church between foyer and church hall (formerly opening to the latter by a screen). The dome is a light and elegant concrete shell. Between its curves and the walls, clerestory windows filled with mosaic STAINED GLASS designed by the architect, made by *Goddard & Gibbs*, blue and yellow at the sides, with red at the (liturgical) E end, where St Michael is shown. Large WALL PAINTINGS by *John Hayward*, sensitively drawn, of Old and New Testament scenes on the side walls, and of the Baptism of Christ on the W wall behind the font. On either side, a glazed wall opening to foyer and Lady Chapel, with stained-glass figures of the apostles, also by *Hayward*, 1961. W gallery above, with circular roof-lights. On the W front, metalwork SCULPTURE of St Michael by *John Hayward*.

ST PAUL, Glyn Road. *See* Celestial Church of Christ, below.

ST PAUL, Stoke Newington Road and Evering Road, West Hackney. By *N. F. Cachemaille-Day*, 1958–60, replacing *Smirke*'s bombed St James of 1821–4. An austere concrete-framed, brick-faced rectangle, set back from the street, with hall adjoining at r. angles at the back. Plain aisleless interior, with altar set forward within circular communion rails. Windows only to (liturgical) W and S. The low square S windows have effective STAINED GLASS of the four evangelist symbols; deep colours set in concrete, by *Goddard & Gibbs*. Other decoration more traditional: w window with conversion of St Paul weakly set against clear glass, by *John Hayward*, 1963; WALL PAINTINGS by *Christopher Webb*: Christ in Glory; St Christopher.

ST PETER, De Beauvoir Road. 1840–1 by *W. C. Lochner*. A stock-brick pre-ecclesiological preaching box raised up on a tall crypt, with minimal Dec Gothic detail. The w tower with corner pinnacles forms an entrance lobby. Interior with galleries on three sides on slim iron columns. Romanesque chancel of 1884 by *H. R. Gough*. E wall with three lancets, each with a STAINED GLASS panel with small figures; Crucifixion, St Peter and St Paul.

ST THOMAS, Clapton Common. This began as a proprietary chapel built *c.* 1774 by *John Devall*, contemporary with the neighbouring terrace. Sturdy channelled-stuccoed E tower facing the road, of 1829 by *Joseph Gwilt*. The top storey has aedicules with Ionic half columns to E and W, and Doric pilasters to N and S. The plain brick-faced body of the church, rebuilt after war damage, is of 1960 by *N. F. Cachemaille-Day*. Dignified basilican interior with tall, slender square piers, straight lintels, and square clerestory windows. E apse within the tower, gilded. Glazed w screen with Lady Chapel beyond. HIGH ALTAR and ROOD by *Martin Travers*, 1921. Painted panelled REREDOS to N altar, probably of similar date, from Lambeth Palace. CHAMBER ORGAN, *c.* 1800, handsome. Post-war heraldic STAINED GLASS by *Goddard & Gibbs*.

## 2. *Roman Catholic*

IMMACULATE HEART OF MARY, Kenworthy Road. 1875–7 by *C. A. Buckler*. Completed 1883. Apsed basilica with SE campanile, inspired by the Roman churches of SS Nereo e Achilleo and Sta Maria in Dominica. Gutted in 1941; rebuilt by *John E. Sterret*, 1955–7.

OUR LADY AND ST JOSEPH, Balls Pond Road, Kingsland. 1962–4 by *W. C. Mangan*. Yellow brick and stone, plain. Westwork with central tower, church with shallow arched roof.

ST JOHN THE BAPTIST, Triangle, Mare Street. 1956 by *Archard & Partners*; sanctuary and chapels remodelled 1972. It replaced *Wardell*'s church of 1847, damaged in the war.

ST SCHOLASTICA, Kenninghall Road. 1963 by *J. E. Sterret & B. D. Kaye*. Brick with white mullioned windows, plainly detailed. Front with gabled centre flanked by circular chapels. The gable motif used also for the porch and inside for the arcades.

## 3. *Other places of worship*

ASSEMBLIES OF GOD (formerly HAMPDEN CHAPEL), Lauriston Road. 1847. Dignified Italianate stuccoed front; projecting centre with Venetian window and pediment.

AZIZIYE MOSQUE, Stoke Newington Road. A stucco-fronted former cinema, altered in 1992 to create a domed prayer hall, with enlarged windows and small domes to corner towers.

CELESTIAL CHURCH OF CHRIST (formerly St Paul C. of E.), Glyn Road, Lower Homerton. 1890–1 by *Henry Cowell Boyes*, architect to the Grocers' Company. Cruciform, red brick with lancet windows, but with Arts and Crafts touches; a nice shingled central tower and slated spirelet. Aisled chancel. Interior cleared and altered with suspended ceilings in chancel and N aisle. Some older fittings remain: low SCREEN and COMMUNION RAILS with good ironwork: PAINTING above reredos, Christ in Majesty, by *Eva Allen Andrews*, 1898–1900; STAINED GLASS, s and w windows 1902 etc., by the local firm *Cakebread Robey*.

CENTRAL HALL, Nos. 276–280 Mare Street. Built for the Methodist Central Mission, 1926–7 by *Gunton & Gunton*. Hard, mannered classical front in yellow stone; giant pilasters, two copper-clad domes confronting the Hackney Empire opposite. Impressive galleried barrel-vaulted hall. To be converted to a music centre with Arts lottery money, 1997.

CHURCH OF GOD, Ritson Road, Dalston. 1875–6 by *E. P. Loftus Brock*; built as the Hamburg Lutheran Church, close to the former German Hospital. Cruciform, with sw tower and spire. Rose window in the gable. The excellent fittings, originally made *c.* 1680 for the German Church in Little Trinity Lane in the City, are now in the Victoria and Albert Museum. (They include an outstanding REREDOS richly carved in the style of Gibbons, possibly by *Robert Leighton*, contemporary ALTAR TABLE, and PULPIT.)

CHURCH OF THE GOOD SHEPHERD, Rookwood Road, Upper Clapton. 1892–5 by *Joseph Morris & Sons* of Reading. The spire forms a notable landmark to the N of Clapton Common. Built as the 'Ark of the Covenant', for the Agapemone sect, followers of Henry James Prince (†1899), who founded his 'Agapemone' (abode of love) at Spaxton, Somerset. Expensively faced with dark stone contrasted with Portland dressings. Big w tower and spire, displaying low down large stone sculptures by *A. G. Walters* of the 91 four symbols of the evangelists, and higher up on the buttresses bronze ones of the same subjects. Heavy Dec detail. Apsed, aisleless interior, with much symbolic decoration signifying the new creation. Carved corbels by *Walters*, and a complete set of stunning STAINED GLASS windows of 1896, designed by *Walter Crane* and executed by *J. Sylvester Sparrow* in antique glass. Intense colours with no white glass. In the apse windows the Dove of Peace and Lion of Judah, with the translation of Enoch and Elijah. Eight nave windows with symbolic flowers. w windows with the Sun of 92 Righteousness flanked by Sin and Shame and Disease and Death, elongated writhing figures tortured by flames and snakes.

THE DOWNS BAPTIST CHURCH, Queensdown Road. 1868 by *Morton M. Glover*. Robustly eclectic. w front with Romanesque wheel window flanked by stumpy towers ending in very Victorian steep mansards with decorative iron cresting. The flank to Downs Road is enlivened by two levels of round-arched windows with striped voussoirs and patterned iron glazing, carried on for the adjoining two-storey SUNDAY SCHOOL to the E. Galleried interior with iron balustrades and columns, aisles now partitioned off.

DOWNS ROAD METHODIST CHURCH, Downs Road. 1870 by *Charles Bell*. Flat gabled ragstone street front with coarse Dec tracery.

ELIM PENTECOSTAL CHURCH, Homerton High Street. *See* Perambulation 3, below.

EVANGELICAL CHURCH, Shrubland Road. An early 'tin tabernacle': a remarkable survival. A prefabricated iron structure of 1858, erected in ten weeks by *Turner & Co.* for Presbyterians who had seceded from St Thomas's Square Chapel when their minister became a Unitarian. Gothic detail.

HACKNEY SYNAGOGUE, Brenthouse Road. 1896 by *Delissa Joseph*, enlarged 1936. Red brick with stone bands, triple-arched side entrance with pediment above. (Stately galleried interior lit by clerestory lunette windows.)

Former MABERLEY CHAPEL, No. 47a Balls Pond Road. Built 1825–6. Simple pedimented front of brick, revealed in 1993 when stucco was removed during restoration work. Three windows, two wooden porches. S end with hipped roof. (Galleries on three sides, on iron columns.)

MEDINA MOSQUE, No. 2a Lea Bridge Road. An adaptation of 1987 by *Hackney Environmental Action Resource*. Red brick and stucco front with standard Islamic features: paired ogee-headed windows, domes and minaret.

NEW SYNAGOGUE, Egerton Road, Upper Clapton. Built in 1914–15 by *E. M. Joseph* for the prosperous Jewish community of Stamford Hill as a replacement for their City synagogue at Great St Helens (1837–8 by *John Davies*), on which this is modelled. Substantial, with Doric porch and gabled centre between two stone stair-turrets crowned by small domes. An impressive interior; gallery on Doric columns, with Corinthian columns above, continuing around a coffered apse. Fittings brought from the City synagogue.

NEW TESTAMENT CHURCH OF GOD, Downs Park Road. Built in 1876 for the Presbyterians, who moved here from the iron chapel in Shrubland Road (*see* Evangelical Church, above). Picturesquely composed, in a good corner position. Rough random ragstone, Dec tracery. Projecting SW tower-porch with angled pinnacles.

NORTH LONDON PROGRESSIVE SYNAGOGUE, Amhurst Park. Built as a Methodist church; after war damage, reconstructed as a synagogue by *Derek Sharpe*, in 1961. Gabled front with plate tracery.

ROUND CHAPEL, built as CLAPTON PARK UNITED REFORMED CHURCH, Lower Clapton Road. 1869–71 by *Henry Fuller* for Congregationalists. Original and impressive, one of the finest Nonconformist buildings in London, setting a pattern for some bold innovations in Nonconformist church building in the later C19. A large classical auditorium, stonefaced and balustraded, with round-headed windows, but with capitals and other details which are Transitional Gothic of *c.* 1200, a mixture that blends most success-
93 fully. The broad main hall has a rounded end facing the road, flanked by two octagonal stair-turrets. Magnificent interior, both festive and functional. A continuous gallery with lattice balustrade, on iron columns, with tall, slender columns above carrying an arcade with lattice spandrels. Contemporary PULPIT and ORGAN CASE. The original pews, alas, destroyed in 1990. Repaired and refurbished 1995–6 as a performing arts centre, by *Casanove Architects*. To the N the SCHOOLS, now converted as a chapel. T-shaped, of two storeys, with round-headed windows and W apse echoing the main building, but more overtly medieval; see the roofs and picturesque clustered chimneystack. 1873, by Fuller's partner *James Cubitt*, architect of the slightly later Union Chapel, Islington.

ST JOHN THE THEOLOGIAN (Greek Orthodox), Mare Street. 1873 by *John Drake* of Rochester, built for the Catholic Apostolic Church.

Polychrome brick exterior, aisleless interior with shallow transepts and E apse.

SHILOH PENTECOSTAL CHAPEL, Ashwin Street. A hefty former Baptist chapel of 1871 by *C. G. Searle & Son*, enlarged 1880. Coarse Lombard Romanesque front with circular windows, two porches with large foliage capitals.

SYNAGOGUE, Lea Bridge Road. 1931 by *M. Glass*. Cheerful Art Deco-Romanesque front; a large brick arch with recessed orders flanked by chamfered stair-towers; tiled zigzag and chequerwork decoration.

TRINITY CONGREGATIONAL CHAPEL, Lauriston Road. 1901 by *P. Morley Horder*. Red brick and sandstone, in a late Gothic style.

UKTIT SHEIK NAZIM MOSQUE AND CULTURAL CENTRE, Shacklewell Lane. Built as a synagogue, 1903 by *Lewis Solomon*. Central dome added in 1983 when it became a mosque (the earliest of Hackney's large mosques). Massive building faced with red brick, simple Italianate detail. Spacious galleried interior.

UNITED REFORMED CHURCH, Rectory Road. 1992–3 by *Martin Heine* of *Craig, Hall & Rutley*. Cheerful, compact corner building in yellow brick, with toplit church on the first floor. Staircase tower lit by a cross in glass bricks. The same material also used for a series of curved staircase walls to the flats at the back of the site.

## PUBLIC BUILDINGS

TOWN HALL, Mare Street. 1934–7 by *Lanchester & Lodge*. Set back behind formal gardens, which were laid out on the site of the previous vestry hall of 1866. A square building faced in Portland stone with a long symmetrical front, conventional but not showy. Pedimented centre with arched windows and stone balcony. Traditional courtyard plan with first-floor council chamber projecting in the centre, committee rooms in front, assembly room at the back. A generous central stairhall; original furnishings and fine Art Deco light fittings throughout, the half-column lights on the stairs especially handsome.

Former MAGISTRATES COURT, Stoke Newington Road. Built as Dalston Police Court, 1889 by *John Taylor* of the Office of Works. Dignified Italianate, 1–3–1 bays, with channelled stone ground floor and vermiculated quoins to the entrances.

POLICE STATIONS. Two by *J. D. Butler*. HACKNEY, at Nos. 2–4 Lower Clapton Road, 1903, in his characteristic free classical; brick with stone dressings, with a central pediment and tall chimneys. DALSTON, Dalston Lane, 1914 (converted to flats).

CENTRAL LIBRARY, Mare Street. Built on land acquired from the LCC after the widening of Mare Street. 1907–8 by *H. A. Crouch*. Partly stone-faced, with a nicely handled corner; semicircular Ionic porch, rusticated walls. Interior altered 1965.

LIBRARIES. Two bursts of activity: 1913 and the 1960s. CLAPTON, Northwold Road, 1913–14, is the most domestic of three Hackney libraries designed by the distinguished Edwardian architect *Edwin Cooper*. An attractive, carefully detailed brick front with two big arched entrances and a hipped roof with Cumberland slates. An intended tower was not built. Cooper's other libraries were at Dalston (1913, destroyed 1945; it had a tower and domed central hall) and at Nos. 42–44 Brooksby's Walk, Homerton, 1912–13, now CHATS PALACE ARTS CENTRE. This is small but monumental; a sober stone-faced portico with Doric columns *in antis*, pediment and tall plain attic. Two halls, their barrel vaults concealed by later ceilings. POST-WAR LIBRARIES are more austerely functional: DALSTON, Dalston Lane, 1957–9 by *Burley & Moore*, exposed concrete and glass. PARKSIDE, Victoria Park Road, within a housing development by *Gibberd*, 1964. ROSE LIPMAN, De Beauvoir Road, contemporary with the De Beauvoir Estate behind, *c.* 1967, a well-composed low block with community centre. STAMFORD HILL, Portland Avenue, an arresting two-storey front with glazing and stone-faced floor bands crisply contrasted, 1968 by the *Borough Architect's Department* (Borough Architect *J. L. Sharratt*). HOMERTON, Homerton High Street, 1968–70, is similarly bold, with a well-proportioned two-storey brick-faced frame.

HACKNEY EMPIRE. *See* Perambulation 1, p. 496.

BATHS. LOWER CLAPTON ROAD (N side), 1896–7 by *Harnor & Pinches*; tall, urban and stone-faced. Interior remodelled 1990–1. Smaller baths in SHACKLEWELL LANE, 1931, and in ENGLEFIELD ROAD, 1932 (not in use, but still with its bold lettering), both by the Borough Engineer *Percival Holt*; brick fronts with artificial stone dressings in a slightly Art Deco classical. The former baths at EASTWAY, Hackney Wick, of 1934–5, with a neat symmetrical front in artificial stone, included slipper baths and the novelty of a 'mechanical laundry'; the intended swimming baths were not built. Converted to studios by *Hook Whitehead Stanway*, 1994.

CLINIC, Elsdale Road. Built as a maternity and welfare clinic. Streamlined, brown brick. A neat period piece by the Borough Engineer, *Percival Holt*, 1938–9.

Former GERMAN HOSPITAL, Ritson Road, off Dalston Lane. Converted to housing 1995–8. Unexciting original buildings of 1865 by *T. L. Donaldson* and *E. A. Gruning*, enlarged 1876. More interesting is the progressive E WING facing Clifton Grove, by *Thomas Tait* of *Burnet, Tait & Lorne*, 1935–6, airy and hygienic, with a smart streamlined exterior. Steel frame clad in yellow brick; five storeys, L-shaped, with a projecting curved corner balcony to each floor, and a roof terrace for the children's ward on the top floor.

HOMERTON HOSPITAL, Homerton Row. By *YRM*, 1980–7, replacing two older hospitals on the site. Large, well-ordered complex, with four main groups of buildings on a friendly scale, with car parks in front but with pleasantly landscaped footpaths at the back. All two-storeyed, with plain, handsome brickwork and pitched roofs with deep eaves, each group with a small central courtyard, some with sculpture. SCULPTURE by *Kevin Harrison*, on the theme of adults and children. Near the entrance a small educational centre; to the E a separate day centre, by *Archimed*, 1996; more elaborately treated, in stone, brick and timber, with a large glazed entrance.

ST JOSEPH'S HOSPICE, Mare Street. *See* Perambulation 1, below.

MILLFIELDS ROAD DISINFECTING STATION. An unusual purpose-built group of 1900–1 by *Gunton & Gunton* for the Borough's Public Health Committee; unexpected Arts and Crafts detail. CARETAKER'S LODGE; SHELTER with recessed corner entrances, to accommodate those whose property was steam cleaned in the adjacent CLEANSING BUILDING: one-storeyed with twin gables, arched windows, and porches with pretty ironwork.

NORTH LONDON RAILWAY. Extended from Dalston Junction to Broad Street, 1861–5 by *William Baker*. Only fragments of the C19 DALSTON JUNCTION STATION remain (the station was moved to a new site at Dalston Kingsland), but to the W is a fine SIGNAL BOX, weatherboarded with arch-headed windows and hipped roof. In Amhurst Road, a former station of the late 1860s by *E. H. Horne*, round-headed arches.

GREAT EASTERN RAILWAY. On the 1872 line RECTORY ROAD STATION was rebuilt in 1984–5 in neo-vernacular style. HACKNEY DOWNS STATION was rebuilt in 1980 in crisp red brick. To its N, an early example of a power SIGNAL BOX, 1960 (*H. H. Powell*, Regional Architect, Eastern Region), with forceful far-projecting top fascia above a fully glazed control area.

BRIDGES. Across the East Cross Route and its slip-roads in the Hackney Wick area, several long-span steel box-girder rail bridges, including the Victoria Park Bridge of seven spans on a considerable skew. By *Rendel, Palmer & Tritton*, 1970–7.

VICTORIA PARK. *see* Perambulation 4c, p. 504.

*Educational buildings*

HACKNEY INSTITUTION, now COMMUNITY COLLEGE, Dalston Lane, Amhurst Road. Founded as the North East London Institute in the late C19; enlarged by the *LCC* in 1925. From this time, the front building, quietly dignified, with restrained detail of an Arts and Crafts kind; tiled quoins, large arched windows to the main floor.

HACKNEY COLLEGE, Kenninghall Road. On the site of Brooke House, an inadequate substitute for Hackney's most interesting house (*see* p. 499). Built as a secondary school, 1958–60 by *Armstrong & MacManus*. Two curtain-walled slabs, the taller one with curved staircase drums; reclad in the 1980s.

CARDINAL POLE SCHOOL. An annex occupies the former FRENCH HOSPITAL in Victoria Park Road, by *R. L. Roumieu*, 1865. Built to house forty men and twenty women over sixty, replacing an earlier building in Old Street. Brick, with dark brick diapering. Broadly symmetrical composition, with picturesque Franco-Flemish central tower and Franco-Flemish dormer windows. Very beefy. The main school building is in Kenworthy Road.

CLAPTON SCHOOL. The part facing Laura Place began as Clapton Secondary School for Girls. Attractive Free Classical stone-faced entrance with arched doorway and bowed oriel, 1914–16 by the *LCC*. Panelled entrance hall. To the rear, the galleried assembly hall (now library) with open timber roof. Plain steep-tiled roofed parts to the E, *c.* 1920–5; two-storey extension of 1959–60 to the r. by *J. M. Austin Smith & Partners*, with trim brickwork and coloured tiles. Behind are large *GLC* extensions of *c.* 1979 in dour dark brick, added when the school became a comprehensive, transformed as a technology centre in 1995 by *Hackney Design Services*. These form an incoherent backdrop (what a missed opportunity) to the impressive ruin at the end of Linscott Road. The tall Greek Doric portico and long flanking colonnade are all that survive from the LONDON ORPHAN ASYLUM founded by the Rev. Andrew Reid in 1813, and built in 1823–5 by *W. S. Inman*. The columns are of stucco, unfluted; the walls behind the colonnade of brick with stucco pilasters. The Salvation Army took over the buildings in 1881 and roofed the inner courtyard to create a congress hall seating 4,700.

CORDWAINERS COLLEGE, Mare Street. Built in 1877 for Lady Hollis's School for Girls (founded in 1711), which moved to Hampton in 1936. Front with shaped gables, the centre one added, with the rear wing, in 1905 by *F. S. Hammond*.

Former HACKNEY DOWNS SCHOOL, Downs Park Road. A Gothic lodge and diapered brick boundary wall remain from the school built by the Grocers' Company in 1875–6 by *Theophilus Allen*. Routine *LCC* exposed concrete and brick ranges, 1965–70, around the site of the main building, burnt down in 1963.

HACKNEY FREE AND PAROCHIAL CHURCH OF ENGLAND SCHOOL, Paragon Road. By *Howard V. Lobb & Partners*, 1951, a very early post-war secondary school, replacing a building of 1811. A compact spine range with two projecting arms, one with the hall, planned so that it could be used separately. One to three storeys, brick, decently detailed in the quiet modern of the 50s; library fittings by *Gordon Russell*. Extended 1995 by *Barron & Smith*: science block, English department and gymnasium.

KINGSLAND SCHOOL, Shacklewell Lane. The older parts built as Dalston County Secondary, 1938 by the *LCC* (*E. P. Wheeler*). Yellow brick, nicely grouped, if indifferent in the details. Rewindowed. Extensions to the s of the 1980s, a long range with the concrete frame crisply expressed; windows set back behind paired verticals.

LUBAVITCH FOUNDATION AND SCHOOL, Stamford Hill. 1967 by *David Stern & Partners*. Large, neat, abrasively modern block of dark brick and curtain walling.

SKINNERS' COMPANY SCHOOL FOR GIRLS, No. 117 Stamford Hill. 1889 by *E. H. Burnell*. Quite grand; Queen Anne detail, given presence by a tower-porch with cupola.

VICTORIAN CHURCH SCHOOLS. COLVESTONE, Colvestone Crescent, Shacklewell. 1862 by *Knightley*. Unusually florid Gothic. A low building, its picturesque porch with columns and thickly foliated capitals. ST PAUL'S, Brougham Road (now community centre), is simpler; pretty red and yellow brick trim, trefoil-headed windows.

BOARD SCHOOLS. A large variety of lively skylines still tower above Hackney's streets of Victorian terraces and their c20 replacements. As elsewhere in London, the type developed from the 1870s, with *E. R. Robson*'s picturesque asymmetrical buildings in the tradition of Philip Webb, to the full-blown formal three-decker compositions of *T. J. Bailey* of the 1890s and beyond.

A selection in chronological order: DE BEAUVOIR, Tottenham Road, 1873, with 1885–7 additions. Two buildings on a cramped site; the earlier one with three big gables to the E, and tall chimneys. CHELMER ROAD, Lower Clapton. Now part of the Community College. Romantically grouped shaped gables and dormers; blind tracery above some of the windows. MORNINGSIDE, Chatham Place. 1884, tall, with turrets. DAUBENY, Colne Road. 1884–6, simple one- and two-storeyed. GAYHURST, London Fields. 1893–4, with gabled bellcote and shaped dormers. WILTON ROAD, Lansdowne Drive. 1885, along frontage with arched windows, decorative shell niches and corbelled-out dormers; and typical caretaker's house and manual instruction centre, treated as separate pavilions. A former Central School to the s, tall and plain with pedimented centre, 1913. QUEENSBRIDGE ROAD and ALBION DRIVE (now teachers' centre). 1897; monumental composition with four-storey centre: giant arches to the w, Ionic pilasters to the e; stair-towers with spirited finials. GAINSBOROUGH, Berkshire Road. 1897–9, a grand turreted three-decker with shaped gables, overlooking the bleak wastes of Hackney Wick. PRINCESS MAY ROAD. 1900, with dignified gabled frontage to Stoke Newington Road. MANDEVILLE, Oswald Street. 1901–2, with terracotta. CASSLAND ROAD (now sixth-form centre). 1901–2 etc. by *T.J. Bailey*, magnificent Wrenaissance front with rusticated arches and pilasters and lavish use of cream terracotta. Handsome contemporary walls and railings.

POST-WAR PRIMARY SCHOOLS. Several of the post-1965 ILEA schools by the *GLC* demonstrate the reaction against standardized types. SHACKLEWELL, Shacklewell Row, has a split-level plan around a courtyard. BENTHAL INFANTS, Benthal Road, *c.* 1970, is a low cluster with classrooms of deliberately varied shapes, and a playground on different levels. BERGER, Flanders Way, Homerton, has low clustered polygonal pavilions with little pyramid roofs.

SPECIAL SCHOOLS. These also attracted varied approaches. DOWNSVIEW, Downs Road. 1969 by *ILEA*: concrete blockwork with awkward red brick trim and some curved windows. ICKBURGH, Brooke Road, 1971 by *Foster Associates*: a calm well-proportioned one-storey range set back behind trees and grass. Flexible open plan around a service core.

OUR LADY AND ST JOSEPH PRIMARY SCHOOL, Buckingham Road. The infants' school is a demure single-storey pale brick group of 1971–2. Junior school and nursery of 1989, with a colourful hipped roofed pavilion with clock turret. The carved Crucifixion facing De Beauvoir Road came from a church on the site; the school was established in its basement in 1856.

## SUTTON HOUSE*

A rare survival of a courtier house in the London countryside, built in 1535 for (Sir) Ralph Sadleir, who was rising rapidly in the king's service as right-hand man to Thomas Cromwell. It is a relatively modest-sized house, for a man who had yet to establish himself in the inner circles of power and influence, but remarkably it is built of brick, following the fashion of greater houses of its time. No building accounts or records of architect or builder are known. Sadleir continued to prosper and amassed a considerable fortune. In 1546 he built himself a much larger brick house at Standon in Hertfordshire (of which only a fragment remains), and he sold his house in Hackney in 1550. It was subsequently occupied by merchant families,

* This account is by Victor Belcher.

and in the later C17 housed a girls' school.* In the mid C18 the house was modernized; and, at the same time or slightly later, it was divided into two.

At the end of the C19 the two houses were purchased by the Rector of Hackney and converted into St John's Institute, a recreational centre for young men. In 1904 a substantial programme of restoration and adaptation was undertaken in the Arts and Crafts style by the architects *Crane and Jeffree* (principally *Lionel Crane*, son of Walter Crane) including the addition of the 'Barn' at the back for a meeting room. In 1914 the E cellar was converted into a chapel, an early work of *Edward Maufe*.

In 1936 the Institute decided to vacate the premises, and after concerted lobbying by amenity societies the National Trust purchased the house. It was leased to a variety of institutions but in the 1980s became vacant and was vandalized and squatted. A proposal to let the house to developers for conversion into flats met with vigorous local opposition, and the Trust agreed to adopt an alternative scheme for its restoration for community use. The full-scale restoration was undertaken in 1990–5 by the architect *Richard Griffiths*, initially with *Julian Harrap Architects*. Among Griffiths's additions were a café-bar in the form of a conservatory at the W end of the Wenlock Barn, a cupola above the Barn (dated 1991), and chimneys in a modern version of the Tudor style.

The house faces N. It has a basically conventional plan, essentially a development of the medieval hall house with cross wings, but carried up to three storeys and with brick cellars under the front of each wing. The wings were originally gabled. Their irregular shape may be the result of building on a constricted site, right up to the western property boundary; earlier buildings on the site (known

Sutton House. North elevation,
conjectural reconstruction as built in the sixteenth century

---

* It was never the home of Thomas Sutton, after whom it was mistakenly named. Sutton lived in an adjacent house to the W, which was demolished for the building of Sutton Place.

from documentary evidence) could also have affected the plan form. The lower part of the house, with the kitchen and a buttery or steward's parlour, was in the E wing, the hall with a great chamber above in the centre, and the private chambers in the W wing.

The brickwork of the centre of the ENTRANCE FRONT is of the mid C18, as are the parapets and window openings, although the sashes are replacements. The two entrances, reflecting the earlier division of the house, have tiled wooden porches dating from the alterations

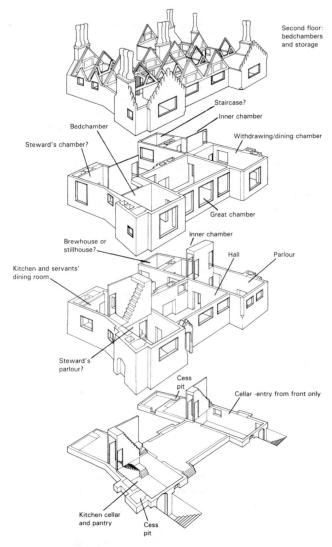

Sutton House. Exploded axonometric,
conjectural reconstruction as built in sixteenth century

of 1904. The oak door in the W entrance may be original but has been moved from the E, where the C16 entrance would have been. The E wing was rendered in the C19, with typical mouldings to the replacement large-paned C19 windows. The W wing has retained its warm red Tudor brickwork with remains of diapering, although reworked around the C18 window openings. The E FRONT is dominated by a huge projecting chimneystack with an odd niche at ground level and has retained its C16 brickwork, much repaired. The W front is also from the original build, with good survival of diaper patterning. The mullion-and-transom window at first-floor level on this front dates from the restoration of 1990–5 and was inserted in a previously blocked-up opening. A remarkable survival in the rear COURTYARD is a twelve-light window with oak mullions and transom at ground-floor level in the W wing, the only original window remaining in the house. Above it, at first-floor level, is an C18 Gothick window. The covered walkway is of 1904.

In the interior, the GEORGIAN PARLOUR in the E wing has early C18 panelling with a wooden dentil box cornice. Behind the C18 fireplace, and visible underneath a hinged panel, is the upper part of a C16 stone fireplace, with carving of vines and decorative shields in the spandrels. In the NE corner of the room is the lower stage of a GARDEROBE tower which served all three storeys. To the S, the E STAIRCASE, open-string with twisted balusters, carved tread ends and a broad, moulded handrail, was inserted in the mid C18, probably from another house. Beyond the staircase is the former Tudor KITCHEN, much altered, but surviving in the end wall is most of the large timber bressumer which spanned the original range.

In the centre of the ground floor, a leap of imagination is necessary to re-create the Tudor HALL, now divided into two passageways with a room between. Panelling and fireplace are of the mid C18, but the wide relieving arch of the hall fireplace is extant behind the later panelling. A change in floor level suggests a raised dais in the position now occupied by the W passage.

The LINENFOLD PARLOUR at the front of the W wing is one of the finest rooms in the house. The oak linenfold panelling itself, of very high quality, has been shown to be contemporary with the building of the house, but appears to have been adapted to fit the room and may have been brought from elsewhere by a later, but early, owner. There has been much subsequent rearrangement of the panelling. The lower panels on the E wall were formerly plain, but painted in a trompe-l'oeil linenfold pattern. These are now covered by actual linenfold panels which have been hinged in the recent restoration to show the decorated panels beneath. High on the E wall are the remains of a window opening, apparently inserted in the later C16, with reveals painted to match the panelling. These decorative features show that at this time the panels were highly colourful, in combinations of green, yellow-cream and red-brown. The stone fireplace in the room, though partially restored, is original. The remainder of the W wing has been much altered. The W staircase has undergone many changes and is now mainly Edwardian, but retains the remnants of an elaborate scheme of early C17 wall paintings, containing strapwork and cartouches. To the S is a room which now serves as an annex to the café-bar. Here a mid-C18 fire surround with an elaborate wooden frame for hanging rails or spits above suggests that the room may have become a kitchen when the house was divided.

On the first floor in the E wing the VICTORIAN STUDY dates mainly from the C19 but has a plaster modillion cornice, probably of the mid C18. The form of the GARDEROBE is more clearly visible off this room. In the centre the GREAT CHAMBER has retained its original proportions. The room is panelled throughout with high-quality oak panels of various dates (some dated by dendrochronology to the late C16), much rearranged, especially on the N wall, where the fenestration has been changed. The panels above the fireplace carved with a rose and fleurs-de-lys are modern copies of originals stolen when the house was empty. The fireplace itself, though of Tudor form, is a later copy. The LITTLE CHAMBER at the front of the W wing also has oak panelling of the mid to late C16 and an original stone fireplace decorated *inter alia* with the coat of arms of the Milward family, East India merchants who lived in the house in the second quarter of the C17. The room to the rear in this wing, now used for exhibitions, has been left with its C16 brick-work exposed. It contains another early C16 stone fireplace (partly hidden by a later flight of stairs), similarly decorated but in better condition because it was blocked up at an early date.

The CELLARS have much exposed original brickwork, that in the E cellar painted over when it was converted into a chapel. Both, but more particularly the W cellar, have unusual arched niches in one wall, perhaps to support the ends of barrels, the front resting on trestles.

The WENLOCK BARN, added in 1904 at the rear of the courtyard, is a large room in church-hall style with a good Arts and Crafts open timber roof. The gallery at the W end was added in 1991.

## PERAMBULATIONS

### *1. Central Hackney: a circular tour*

This tour starts in Clapton Square, the focus of the smart suburban village of the late C18 and early C19, and ends with the older centre, which lay around the narrow N end of Mare Street.

CLAPTON SQUARE was laid out piecemeal on Clapton Field from *c.* 1811 to 1818, and looks S towards the late C18 church in the northern part of the leafy old churchyard. Tall restrained houses remain on W and N sides, mostly terraced, with a few linked pairs. Round-headed ground-floor windows. No. 20 at the NW corner is grander than the others, with stuccoed pilasters. Next to it, in CLARENCE PLACE, No. 8, a former coachhouse, and Nos. 1–7, another terrace. E of the churchyard some tall pairs of *c.* 1800 with Doric porches remain on the S side of LOWER CLAPTON ROAD, interrupted by the grandiose classical front of the ELECTRICITY SHOWROOM, built by the borough in 1924.

CHURCHWELL PATH can be followed along the E side of the church-yard, past a glimpse of Sutton Square (*see* below) S to SUTTON PLACE, laid out in 1808, where paired houses on the N side face a continuous terrace of *c.* 1820, the latter with unusually well-preserved detail: marginal glazing and original doors with circular

mouldings flanked by fluted half columns. To the s is Sutton
House (*see* Public Buildings, above), Hackney's one remaining
older house. SUTTON SQUARE to the N is pop classical by *CZWG*
for Kentish Homes, 1984, timber-framed houses dressed up by
eclectic brick and plaster trimmings, pleasantly arranged around a
garden.

s of the railway and s of Morning Lane the mood changes; CHATHAM
PLACE continues s past dour C20 flats and factories on the sites of
C19 villas. The factory toward Morning Lane incorporates the
Old Gravel Meeting House (former home of the Round Chapel
Congregation). But to the w, in PARAGON ROAD, an attractive
group remains, Nos. 71–83, built 1809–13; half-stuccoed pairs of
three storeys, with low entrance links with broad doorways behind
four Doric columns (the inspiration must be Michael Searles's
similarly arranged Paragon, Blackheath). Surprising ogee-arched
fanlights. The development was on land of St Thomas's Hospital,
Southwark, the design possibly by the hospital surveyor *Samuel
Robinson*, or by the builder *Robert Collins*. Further w the tall
stretched-out Neo-Georgian former POST OFFICE of 1928–9,
and behind it, in Valette Street, VALETTE HOUSE, tall very plain
LCC flats of 1906–7, built on the site of Jerusalem Square for
those displaced by the widening of Mare Street. Also in Valette
Street the HACKNEY TRADES HALL, 1912, built as headquarters
of a Friendly Society.

MARE STREET, like so many old commercial thoroughfares, is a late
C19 and Edwardian jumble with neglected late Georgian frontages
visible intermittently above shopfronts. On the E side, just s of
Paragon Road, a late C18 group: Nos. 224–228, dating from 1780–1,
built by *Joseph Sparkman*. Further s only a few buildings worth
noting. No. 195 (LANSDOWNE CLUB) is the best remaining C18
town house in Hackney. Set back from the street, of five bays, two
and a half storeys with parapet. Brown brick with brick floor bands,
rubbed brick window heads. The flush window frames suggest an
early C18 date. Later Doric doorcase. (Good interiors.) Also on
the w side, THE DOLPHIN, No. 165, smart mid-C19 Italianate,
balustraded parapet with urns, possibly with an older core. Opposite,
ST JOSEPH'S HOSPICE: ranges around the front court with big
glazed windows and gently bowed floor bands; 1955 by *Stewart &
Hendry*, an enterprising design. Near the s end of Mare Street, a
few battered fragments of terraces of *c.* 1800.

There is more to see at the N part of Mare Street. No. 277 was
built for the Gas Light and Coke Company in 1931 by *Walter
Tapper* and *H. Austen Hall* (cf. their work for the same company
in Kensington), the showrooms to the street by Tapper, in well-
managed Neo-Georgian, the offices behind by Hall. Near the N
end, the Central Library, the 'cultural quarter' planned 1997,
composed of the Methodists' Central Hall, and the Town Hall
(*see* above), and the splendidly confident HACKNEY EMPIRE.
This is of 1901 by *Frank Matcham*, and is among the best-surviving
Edwardian suburban variety theatres. Exterior with Baroque
detail in buff terracotta, used especially lavishly on the elaborate
77      twin domes (1988 replicas of the originals). Sumptuous interior;
foyer with marbled walls and coffered ceiling; festive Rococo auditorium with much plasterwork: curved circle and two tiers of

cantilevered balconies. Behind the Empire, and on either side of the Town Hall, remains of an old back lane. At the end of the s part, HACKNEY GROVE GARDENS, a community garden with some lively railings, made on the site of a burnt-out factory, by *Freeform Artworks*, 1982. A few pre-Victorian houses survive here: in HACKNEY GROVE, Nos. 25–27 and No. 33 with Doric porch; in the n part, SYLVESTER PATH, No. 4, with late c18 front, older behind, and No. 13, early c18 but much altered. Nearby, SYLVESTER HOUSE, flats of 1910 with attractive Arts and Crafts detail. In WILTON WAY, CHRISTOPHER ADDISON HOUSE, flats and a housing office, by the *Borough Architect's Department*, 1993, four storeys, brick-faced, with trendy corner staircase drum of glass bricks and a curved stainless-steel roof.

Further N, AMHURST ROAD to the E is worth a glance for Messrs E. Gibbons's matching Art Deco shopfronts (Nos. 1–17). Back to Mare Street by KENMURE ROAD. At the corner of Brett Road, BRETT MANOR, a small block of maisonettes by *E. D. Mills*, 1946–8, built for a charitable trust. Brick-faced: four storeys and a penthouse, with inset balconies on alternate floors. Well-handled motifs, but very run-down at time of writing. It had the first reinforced-concrete box frame completed in London, designed by the engineer *Ove Arup*.

In NARROWAY, the narrow part of Mare Street, No. 354 (MIDLAND BANK), prominently sited close to the church tower; the stone facing with rusticated ground floor and the large Baroque entrance were added in 1900 to a house built in 1803 on the site of the medieval vicarage. The house was used for parish meetings until the mid c19. On the w side, No. 387, known as the MANOR HOUSE; built in 1845 for the manor steward, J. R. W. Tyssen. Latest Georgian in style, of plain yellow brick, seven bays with slightly recessed centre. Shops added on the ground floor. Further N, at the start of LOWER CLAPTON ROAD, THE CROWN, with relief and formerly with good pub detail of *c.* 1900.

## 2. Clapton and Stamford Hill

Clapton more than any other part of Hackney keeps memories of its former prosperity, despite the fact that its relatively open areas attracted some of Hackney Council's major housing efforts of the 1930s onwards. There is still plenty of green relief in and around the gently curving main artery, called at the N end Clapton Common, then Upper and then Lower Clapton Road, although the old spaciousness with low houses and tall trees has largely gone.

### 2a. Lower Clapton

LOWER CLAPTON ROAD can be reached from Clapton Square by CLAPTON PASSAGE, a footpath flanked by a busily Italianate terrace of *c.* 1880; triplet windows to the upper floor. The same design continues along POWERSCROFT ROAD to the E, opposite the Round Chapel (q.v.). The main road, Lower Clapton Road, once had older and grander houses (they included the late c17 Clapton House on the E side, N of the ponds, and a fine early c18 house, No. 179 on the w side). An appealing pre-Victorian group remains on the E side, overlooking CLAPTON POND. At the corner of Newick Road, BISHOP WOOD'S ALMSHOUSES, founded 1665. Wood (†1692) was Bishop of Lichfield but of Hackney descent. The six almshouses are very modest, one-storeyed, on three sides of a shallow courtyard. C19 Gothic chapel added at the NE corner; the tall chimneys also date from this time. Restored in 1888, and by *H. R. Ross* in 1930. POND HOUSE, No. 162, is a restrained stuccoed villa of *c.* 1800, on a generous scale, with semi-circular Doric porch, a basement with lunettes, and tripartite ground-floor windows. Flanking quadrant walls with former stables · to the N. (Interior with elegant curved staircase.) Then Nos. 158–160, a tall early C19 pair of four storeys above basements. Further S on the E side, Nos. 126–128, mid-C19, stucco trimmed; round the corner in LAURA PLACE, opposite Clapton School (q.v.), Nos. 8–12, an early C19 group, and No. 13, a good large five-bay house with Ionic porch.

On the w side, No. 143 has an C18 three-bay brick front with pretty open-pedimented doorcase on a house of older origin (surviving timbers suggest a mid-C16 to C17 date). Extended N and remodelled probably *c.* 1814. Nos. 145–153, set back, are three stately pairs of *c.* 1824, with ground-floor windows in arched recesses. These were formerly used by the Salvation Army's MOTHERS' HOSPITAL, and refurbished for housing by *Hunt Thompson*, 1992–3. Behind, by the same firm, THE MOTHERS' SQUARE, 1987–90, replacing the hospital. The new and adapted buildings provide housing, sheltered flats, day hospital and nursing home. The square is friendly but formal, a bevelled rectangle of continuous terraced houses, given character by coloured brickwork and cheerfully coarse classical detail in deliberate imitation of Victorian Hackney builders' vernacular. Busy rhythm of paired stumpy columns on the ground floor. A central pergola distracts from the parked cars.

ST ANDREW'S MANSIONS, at the entrance to ROWHILL ROAD, tall half-timbered and tile-hung mansion flats, introduce a whole street of the same, a late C19 development by *A. Bedborough* for W. Andrews of Wood Green. Further N, No. 167 onwards, two- and three-storey brick terrace houses of the 1980s with some minimal coloured brick trim. A path leads to more behind, and to ROBERT OWEN LODGE, homely sheltered housing in linked groups backing on to a communal garden. They replace Powell House, the dour council flats of 1937 by *Joseph*.*

A large area of council housing further W is prefaced at the corner with KENNINGHALL ROAD by GOOCH HOUSE, a seventeen-storey tower block for Hackney by *Harry Moncrieff*, 1959–63, the herald of many more. Concrete-framed, with projecting balconies and inset parts to break up the mass. Further W, HEALTH CENTRE by *Cassidy Taggart Partnership*, 1993. Circular, with central toplit waiting room ringed by lower consulting rooms. It provides some variety at the NW corner of *Hackney*'s vast NIGHTINGALE ESTATE, a bleak concrete expanse of the late 1960s, with an L-plan of linked slabs framing a forceful cluster of six stark point blocks overlooking Hackney Downs.

*Powell House replaced No. 179, later a Home for the Deaf and Dumb, built in 1710 for Markham Eeles, a City manufacturer. Its fine staircase and some panelling were given to the Geffrye Museum.

To the E of Lower Clapton Road a large area of minor Victorian streets remains, extending towards Hackney Marsh, developed on the Alderson estate from the 1860s by the London Suburban Land and Building Company. Off Lea Bridge Road in WATTISFIELD ROAD, ALMSHOUSES for Disabled Soldiers and Sailors, 1922–3 by *Gunton & Gunton*, a row of six cottages with a semi-detached house at each end. Recessed sitting areas beside the front doors, and other nice Arts and Crafts touches.

### 2b. Upper Clapton and Stamford Hill

UPPER CLAPTON ROAD starts N of the roundabout at the junction of Lea Bridge Road. On the W side, only a street name recalls Hackney's most important mansion, Brooke House, demolished in 1954–5, after partial war damage. Hackney College stands on the site.* To the N of the C20 widening the road becomes a bottle-neck with some older, much altered houses behind shops; then council flats take over. In ROSSENDALE STREET to the W, a rectangular semi-basement AIR RAID BUNKER of 1938, of concrete over 6 ft thick. (Original equipment inside includes an electric generator powered by a twin bicycle frame.) N of this, the decent proportions of the LCC's NORTHWOLD ESTATE (1934) are still recognizable, despite new windows. A detour along CAZENOVE ROAD to the W can take in samples of other types. On the S side Hackney's MORLEY HOUSE on the S, a long five-storey range, 1937–8 by *Joseph*, a meanly detailed exterior, although the planning of the individual flats was generous at the time. In contrast, HADLEY COURT, the block of private flats opposite of the same date, makes a stylish show of 'moderne' features.

Among the plain council flats in UPPER CLAPTON ROAD No. 26 comes as a relief, a tall Wrenaissance front with Baroque brick features and shaped dormers, built as a Home for Deaf and Dumb Women in 1933 by *A. Rubens Cole*, to replace the demolished No. 179 Lower Clapton Road (*see* above). E of Upper Clapton Road, some of the borough's most ambitious 1930s estates. WARWICK GROVE, by *Joseph*, of 1937–40, was planned with 280 flats in two groups, WIGAN HOUSE and WREN'S PARK HOUSE, designed on a grand axial lay-out with amenity buildings in the central courts. The planning reflected the progressive ideas of the time: a balcony for each flat and access to the five-storey blocks by stair-cases instead of by the more traditional and cheaper long balconies. Refurbished 1996–7. In MOUNT PLEASANT LANE, off Warwick Grove, No. 86, sheltered housing by *Anthony Richardson & Partners*, 1985, for Newlon Housing Trust, built on part of a church site. A startling composition in concrete blockwork and grey aluminium, broken up so that the whole is not too overpowering. Cleverly planned; on the entrance side a monopitch roof above overhanging floors, which step up sideways to five storeys; at the back they step down, with large windows overlooking the garden. Further N, LEA VIEW, along SPRINGFIELD, another model development of

---

* Brooke House was a courtyard house of medieval origin, whose owners included Henry Percy, Earl of Northumberland, Thomas Cromwell and William Herbert in the C16 and, from 1608, the Grevilles, Barons Brooke. A C15 wall painting from the chapel is in the Museum of London; panelling is in Harrow School.

1939–40 by *Joseph*; a similar lay-out of plain five-storey blocks around a large central area which housed unusually generous amenities: community hall, laundry, tennis courts etc. This estate was refurbished by *Hunt Thompson Associates* in 1980–2, the first of this firm's schemes to demonstrate how apparently no-hope housing could be transformed in consultation with the residents. Family dwellings were placed at ground level; entrances face outward to the street instead of to the courtyard, which was closed off as a private space. The most visible changes are the new lift towers in striped brick which brighten the N side, and the colourful wooden fences to the separate front gardens.

SPRINGFIELD PARK, opened in 1905, incorporating the spacious grounds of three houses, is in a delightful position on the slopes overlooking the Lea Valley. Charming pond, bowling green etc. One house was kept as a refreshment house: a stuccoed five-bay early C19 villa with Greek Doric porch, and two shallow bows to the N.

CLAPTON COMMON is the continuation of Upper Clapton Road. The E side makes a pretty picture from across the open green, with the ponds in front and a distant church (the Church of the Good Shepherd, q.v.), although the only older houses are No. 98, a half-stuccoed villa, doorway with Greek Doric columns *in antis*, and Nos. 94–96, with an C18 core but much altered. On the W side one especially good stretch remains: Nos. 49–69, a late C18 terrace, part three-storeyed, part four-, with nice pedimented doorways, and an early C19 Greek Doric porch to No. 57. Nos. 43–47 are also Georgian, but simpler (No. 47 is a replica). A good fanlight to No. 45. The group ends with No. 41, taller, C19, and the square classical tower of St Thomas's Church (q.v.) at the corner of OLDHILL STREET, a modest shopping street still with some feel of an old settlement. Off the N side, STAMFORD GROVE EAST and WEST, the remains of an elegant little early C19 enclave, with pairs of houses, and a single house, GROVE HOUSE.

STAMFORD HILL, the stretch of Ermine Street continuing N from Stoke Newington High Street (*see* Stoke Newington, below), is dominated by interwar flats which replaced large older houses. On the W side, the GUINNESS TRUST ESTATE of 1932 by *Joseph*, flat-roofed five-storey blocks in serried ranks nine deep, with minimal Georgian detail. On the E side, STAMFORD HILL ESTATE, one of the *LCC*'s larger estates (516 flats planned, 353 completed by 1936). A more interesting composition, influenced by Viennese mass housing: steep roofs with dormers, a formal central courtyard flanked by lower arcaded pavilions. Concrete balconies add a touch of modernity. Now full of drab car parks and in need of landscaping, but highly regarded at the time (according to Clunn's *Face of London* (1951), 'many quite wealthy people tried unsuccessfully to obtain accommodation here').

One older survival: Nos. 266–268, behind later shops, a five-bay house of *c.* 1730 (good original features inside No. 266).

### 3. Homerton and Hackney Wick

Homerton was once a small hamlet E of Hackney village, on the high ground above the Lea Valley. In the C18 it had a few large houses, and developed a strong Nonconformist tradition. A secluded mansion built c. 1727 by *Colen Campbell* for a Nonconformist merchant, Stamp Brooksbank, became a Dissenters' Academy in 1786. It was demolished c. 1799. Another Dissenters' establishment on Homerton High Street, Homerton College, was rebuilt in 1823 by *Samuel Robinson*. It became a teacher training college, which moved to Cambridge in 1893; the building survived, used as a school for the deaf, until demolished after war damage in 1940. Industries developed in the neighbourhood early. Berger's Paints was one of the largest, established on land off Shepherd's Lane in 1780, and surviving here until c. 1960. By the C19, much of the High Street was industrial, as was Hackney Wick, further E on the edge of Hackney Marshes.

HOMERTON HIGH STREET. At the w end, really belonging more to the centre of Hackney, is Sutton House (*see* above, p. 491). The rest of the s side is a haphazard assortment of factories, council flats and dingy hospital buildings, where only a very little survives to tell of the Georgian past. The best is Nos. 140–142 on the s side, with doorways with pediments on attached Tuscan columns. Nos. 168–170 are a later C18 pair, No. 168 also with nice doorcase, the l. house much altered. On the N side, first THE PLOUGH, 1898, with stucco decorated corner turret. The flats around COLLEGE ROW are on the site of Homerton College (*see* above). Further on, the High Street is cheered by a picturesque C19 ragstone group: church schools (now Elim Pentecostal Church), 1855–6 by *J. Edmeston*, a battlemented Tudor vicarage by *A. Ashpitel* of c. 1850, and St Barnabas (q.v.). E of the Library (q.v.) the only building of note is the ADAM AND EVE pub, a daring front of 1915; purple glazed tiles below cream terracotta with a large relief. From here the land slopes down to playing fields and the KINGSMEAD ESTATE, built on the Hackney Marshes in 1936–8 to provide 1,000 flats for people from a clearance scheme in Bethnal Green. The pre-war *LCC* at its least inspiring, with long rows of four- and five-storey blocks flanking a central axis leading to a school, built only after the war and too humble to serve as a focus. Along the Lee, much housing of the 1990s, replacing industry.

To the N of the church, BROOKSBY'S WALK has the surprisingly grand former library (q.v.), followed by a little modest early C19 development. It leads to CHATSWORTH ROAD, a bustling late Victorian shopping artery. s of the church, in BARNABAS ROAD, a few respectable mid-C19 paired villas (Nos. 2–8). Further s beyond the railway, near the R.C. church in Kenworthy Road (q.v.), the CONVENT OF THE SACRED HEART. This began as a country house, and still has a five-bay wing of c. 1800; arched first-floor windows on the E side, a shallow bow to the w, much hemmed in.

*Hackney Wick*

Once a hamlet on the fringe of Hackney Marshes. The C20 housing is now surrounded by desolate industrial areas, and isolated from the rest of Hackney by road and railway.

In EASTWAY, one group of architectural significance: ETON HOUSE, 1897, a MISSION HALL, close to St Mary of Eton, and, nearby, former Baths (qq.v.). To their E is the *GLC*'s unhappy TROWBRIDGE ESTATE, built 1967–70, which became famous in 1985 for the bungled demolition of the first of its seven system-built twenty-one-storey towers. Remodelled as 'Wick Village' by *Levitt Bernstein Associates*. The estate's traditionally built brick low-rise housing remains.

## 4. South Hackney

In the early C19 there were still fields between the hamlets of Well Street and Grove Street and the ribbon development along the southern part of Mare Street. A few pre-Victorian survivals can be spotted along the main streets, but elsewhere what has not been replaced in the C20 is mostly of the 1850s–60s. Victoria Park attracted some superior housing along the spacious streets to its N, although not the high-class villas for which its planners had hoped.

### 4a. St Thomas's Square to Well Street

On the E side of MARE STREET, St Thomas's Hospital, Southwark, was one of the major landowners: hence ST THOMAS'S SQUARE, developed already in 1772, but, alas, replaced by flats from the 1950s. At the W end, handsome circular granite DRINKING FOUNTAIN of 1912. On the S side, the REGAL CINEMA, 1935–6 by *W. R. Glen*, on the site of St Thomas's Chapel, founded in 1771. Behind, ST THOMAS'S BURIAL GROUND remains; gravestones tidied up around the walls. Between this and a strip of green to the E, ST THOMAS'S PLACE, a typical stucco-trimmed terrace dated 1859 (with earlier reset stone of 1807). On the N side, the overweening ten-storey PITCAIRN HOUSE of 1960 overlooks the formal garden made in the square. Beside this, LYME GROVE leads NE past THE PILGRIM LODGE, an almshouse of 1865 by *A. R. Pite*, red and yellow brick, with a canted bay to the path. To the E, a straggle of slabs of various ages and heights forms the FRAMPTON PARK ESTATE (earlier parts of 1953 by the LCC; continued in the 1960s by the GLC). More appealing is BRENT HOUSE, in BRENTHOUSE ROAD; 1931–2 by *Ian Hamilton*. Behind nice railings. A compact, decently detailed four- and five-storey block in a Neo-Georgian spirit; three ranges around a small garden, built for Bethnal Green and East London Housing Association (cf. Hamilton's work for the St Pancras Housing Association, Camden).

WELL STREET to the N of Cassland Road was the centre of the old hamlet, marked by a jumble of low shops and street market near the junction of WICK ROAD, with the typical C19 development of small industrial concerns behind. Among these, a handsome warehouse (James Taylor) in COLLENT ROAD, dated 1893. Blue facing bricks. Its back faces CRESSET ROAD. W of this is the remarkable LENNOX HOUSE of 1937 by *J. E. M. McGregor*, like Brent House built for the Bethnal Green and East London Housing Association. A friendly brick ziggurat of pantile-roofed flats with stepped-out private balconies, cantilevered out over a covered central space which was intended for a market. The traditional materials conceal an innovative reinforced concrete structure, precursor of the type of plan and mixed uses developed in more monumental fashion for the Brunswick Centre, Camden, and its 1960s successors.

*4b. East of Well Street to Well Street Common*

KENTON ROAD was built up with regular terraces in the 1860s, with the KENTON ARMS at the junction with Bentham Road cheerfully flourishing a decorative corner gable with swags and pretty cornice. On the s side of BENTHAM ROAD Nos. 4–28, of 1860–2, mark the shift from classical to tentative Gothic detail, with coloured brickwork and pointed hoodmoulds. They face part of the GASCOYNE ESTATE, another large and protracted LCC/ GLC post-war enterprise (1947 onwards). The most impressive elements are near the E end of Bentham Road: the two earliest of the tall slab blocks, built 1952–4, when the *LCC Architect's Department* was at its most adventurous. The engineer was *F. J. Samuely*. Eleven storeys. The airy open ground floors and shaped roof tanks proclaim their Corbusian allegiance; the projecting balconies with pattern of supporting beams give some life to the huge white façades. As at contemporary Roehampton, the slabs have the innovation of economic narrow-fronted maisonettes (12 ft 3 in. wide), much copied in later blocks.

Back w along CASSLAND ROAD. On the s side, opposite a semi-circle of 1860s villas, HACKNEY TERRACE, Nos. 20–54, comes as a surprise. It is the earliest survival in this area, a symmetrical composition of 1792–1801 of plain three-storey houses with simple fanlights. Central pediment with *Coade* stone garlands and the arms of the three developers, which included their architect, *William Fellowes*. The enterprise was organized as a building society with subscribers (a very early example), and the houses had originally not only private gardens but a communal pleasure ground behind (cf. Tyburnia, Paddington), opening on to Well Street Common.

WELL STREET COMMON is one of the few green areas in East London where there are no adjacent towers of flats to diminish the sense of space. The LCC flats on the NE side, along GASCOYNE ROAD, completed 1947, are five-storeyed, with a series of projecting balconies, a little more imaginative in design than the average at that time. On the N side, MEYNELL CRESCENT of the 1890s, and, opening off it at the w end, MEYNELL GARDENS, by *A. Savill*, a nice oasis of garden-suburb-type cottages, built in 1932–3 on the site of a house of 1787 (some remnants remain in garden walls). To the w, CHURCH CRESCENT skirts St John's Church (q.v.), with buildings of the 1840s by *George Wales*, surveyor to the Cass estate. The MONGER ALMSHOUSES, rebuilt in 1847–8, have Tudor doorways, shaped central gable, and an oriel with remains of lozenge glazing. The villas are of the same date, Nos. 1 and 2 also Tudor, with gables. s of the church the villa form is cleverly echoed by a semi-detached white-rendered group by *Colquhoun & Miller*, 1981–4, with dramatic deep eaves overhanging inset balconies and Mackintosh-inspired detail (see the side windows).

*4c. Around the north fringe of Victoria Park*

LAURISTON ROAD (a C19 realignment of Grove Street, an old hamlet) runs s to Victoria Park through a well-preserved enclave developed from the 1860s by the Norris estate, with spaciously laid out streets of stuccoed villas. See for example PENSHURST ROAD, with the contemporary PENSHURST ARMS at the corner, dated 1864.

The roads around the perimeter of the park were laid out by the Crown Commissioners at the same time as the park, but development was slow. At the E end of VICTORIA PARK ROAD, near the park gates, No. 220, the BEDFORD HOTEL, c. 1870, given character by its paired arched windows to the upper floors. Further w the stuccoed ROYAL HOTEL marks the junction with GROVE ROAD, which runs through the centre of the park. GORE ROAD, along the NW fringe, has a nice uniform stucco-trimmed crescent of the 1870s and some infilling by *John Spence & Partners* of c. 1966, planned as low-rental housing for local professionals. In a modern idiom, but an early example of low-rise housing making a deliberate effort to keep in scale with existing buildings, CHRISTCHURCH SQUARE and neighbouring closes, 1969–76, is by the same firm; friendly brown brick low-rise housing on the site of a demolished church. N of this, back in Victoria Park Road, an array of plain mid-Victorian detached villas, and near Mare Street, a tight enclave of stuccoed terraces in FREMONT STREET and WARNEFORD STREET, begun in the 1850s but mostly dating from the 1860s.

VICTORIA PARK straddles the border between Hackney and Tower Hamlets (*see London 5: East*). It was created after a petition was presented to the government in 1840, and belongs to the general movement to bring amenities to the labouring classes of East London; it was the first and largest of the new London parks of the C19. It was designed by *James Pennethorne* of the Office of Works, and opened in 1845. The S side is bounded by the Regent's Canal, the SE side by a canal of 1826 linking the Regent's Canal with the Lee Navigation. The landscape of the w part was embellished in 1849 by a large lake, with waterfall and islands, made in former gravel workings. Smaller lakes further E (originally four, now two). The park was much appreciated in the C19; planting by *John Gibson* introduced sub-tropical vegetation, there were celebrated bedding displays, and several ornamental buildings, including a pagoda on an island and a Gothic loggia, both destroyed in the Second World War, as was Pennethorne's elaborate Tudor lodge at Bonner Gate, the main S entrance. The Lido of 1936, which replaced earlier swimming pools, has also gone. The chief survivals are BONNER GATE itself, with Pennethorne's chunky Jacobethan gatepiers in brick and stone, and the oddly palatial DRINKING FOUNTAIN given by Baroness Burdett-Coutts in 1861, an elephantine polygonal structure with oversized putti and dolphin in niches, the whole in a Gothic-cum-Moorish style. It was designed by *Henry Darbishire*, also the architect of Baroness Burdett-Coutts's even more impractical and ambitious (and now demolished) Columbia Market in Bethnal Green and the Gothic cottages on the fringe of her Holly Lodge estate, Highgate (*see* St Pancras, p. 415). Near the E end are two SHELTERS, stone alcoves which came from *Taylor* and *Dance*'s London Bridge of 1758–62. In the 1980s the park was one of the first to benefit from the government funding which encouraged revival of interest in open spaces. New railings, lamp standards and entrance gates were provided, also a new café by the lake, and other improvements.

5. *Between London Fields and Kingsland Road; a circular tour*

Between the two N–S axes of Mare Street and Kingsland Road patchy survivals of the 1840s are interspersed with C20 rebuilding. Traces of an older settlement remain around Broadway Market, S of the common land of London Fields.

RICHMOND ROAD skirts the N side of London Fields and continues W with quite large *c.* 1840 villas. On the S side, Nos. 176–178 with pedimental gable; others linked by paired porches. Good cast-iron sill-guards. The E side of the Fields is more varied, with a typical Hackney mixture of small-scale industry and battered C19 houses. Along MARTELLO STREET, industrial premises (now studios) lie close to the railway line, alternating with once attractive individual villas overlooking the Fields. At the N corner of LAMB LANE, a picturesque gabled house of ragstone, built in 1873 as the vicarage for St Michael and All Angels (*see* Churches, above), which stood opposite. Near the SE corner of the Fields, an endearing pebbly SCULPTURE of flower sellers and sheep by *Freeform Artworks*, 130 1988–9, commemorating the use of the Fields by drovers on their way to Smithfield Market. On the W side, the S end of LANSDOWNE DRIVE, where Nos. 126–148 form a handsome early C19 terrace, three storeys with arched ground-floor windows and paired door-ways with Doric pilasters. Refurbishment of Nos. 140–148 dates from 1985, when this group was converted by *Hunt Thompson Associates* as housing for special needs, with new rear extensions. Further S, No. 172, a nice three-bay stuccoed villa with Ionic pilasters to the upper floor, then Nos. 174–186, a more irregular C18 group close to Broadway Market.

BROADWAY MARKET still has a pleasant early C19 feel, with a mis-cellany of low terrace houses and shops screening the C20 flats behind. No. 77 retains a shopfront of *c.* 1830 but may be older behind. Off to the W, DERICOTE STREET and CROSTON STREET, an appealingly modest development of *c.* 1830–40: small paired villas with shared gables, arched ground-floor windows and patterned fanlights. To the E, in ADA STREET, the C19 scale is shattered by eight-storey flatted factories, an expression of the post-war planning ideal of separating industry and housing. By *YRM*, completed 1966. Austere but well proportioned; long window bands articulated by three groups of inset balconies.

W of the Fields, uneventful streets of low stucco-trimmed villas and terraces were laid out from the 1840s. Redevelopment of the southern parts was begun by the *GLC* with piecemeal medium-rise maisonettes and terraces. They exhibit the variety of neo-vernacular styles that became popular in the 1970s as tall flats were abandoned. Along REGENTS ROW the U-shaped blocks make some effort to respond to their setting, with courtyards opening towards the canal. MARLBOROUGH AVENUE experi-ments with a long spine block with large upper balconies. Then in 1981, after Hackney took over from the GLC, *Colquhoun & Miller* were brought in to try a new approach. Their solution,

completed 1984, was a return to the villa form, slotted into the
p. existing street pattern among older houses. The group extends
81 from BROWNLOW ROAD (Nos. 37–39, 41–43) through to
SHRUBLAND ROAD and ALBION DRIVE. A mixture of flats and
houses, but all contained within the semblance of paired villas
with shared gables; entrances are within a rather grand inset centre
with single column. In similar vein though less original is the group
at the N corner of Albion Drive and QUEENSBRIDGE ROAD,
Nos. 214–226. No. 214 is a converted C19 villa, the rest replace a
terrace allowed to decay. Tall, but well proportioned, of brown
brick above rendered basements, with a pediment to the three-bay
centrepiece in each group.

The streets W of Queensbridge Road were laid out on the land of Sir
William Middleton in the 1840s. The part which deserves to be
explored centres on ALBION SQUARE, where a nicely railed square
is surrounded by a satisfyingly complete picturesque Italianate
composition of 1846–9. The builder was *Islip Odell*, who may have
been Middleton's surveyor. Villas on the N and S sides, terraces at
the W end. The villas are in groups of two or four, some windows
arched, others in squared stuccoed surrounds. The centre of the S
side is taller, with a shared gable. The W side, originally occupied
by a Literary and Scientific Institute of 1849–50, now has two
tactful pairs of bow-fronted villas of 1994–5. ALBION TERRACE
continues W with a simpler artisan row to STONEBRIDGE
COMMON, an informal triangular area with a green, embellished
by a colourful concrete and mosaic SNAKE play sculpture by
*Freeform Artworks*, 1981, and bounded by a railway line, pub, and
a small stone obelisk. To the N, MIDDLETON ROAD; paired villas
with pedimented doorcases on the S side.

KINGSLAND ROAD consists of the usual main-road mixture of
decaying fragments of early ribbon development overtaken by
shops and industry. The most impressive survival, rescued from
decline in 1995, is KINGSLAND CRESCENT on the E side (Nos.
318–346), fifteen houses remaining from a shallow crescent, a
once handsome late C18 group which had been much altered by
industrial use. Further N a few large C18–C19 pairs remain behind
Kingsland Road shops.

To the E of Kingsland Road are large areas which were intended for
comprehensive redevelopment by the borough after the Second
World War. Terrace housing along HOLLY STREET (1948 by the
Borough Engineer *George Downing*) is quite friendly and modest;
much less so the later parts of the HOLLY STREET ESTATE,
completed *c.* 1968. Its centrepiece is a bleak U-shaped group of
maisonettes. E of these, four twenty-storey system-built towers
were added, strengthened after the Ronan Point disaster in 1968.
Radical remodelling began in 1993, when two of the towers were
demolished, and a seven-year programme was begun of low-rise
rebuilding and rehabilitation by *Levitt Bernstein*. On the N fringe of
this area, some delicately detailed small earlier C19 villas remain in
FOREST ROAD (Nos. 62–70); others in PARKHOLME ROAD
(Nos. 1–13, partly rebuilt). The WILTON ESTATE, further E, has
early terraces of 1947 by *Norman & Dawbarn* s of Wilton Way,
trim three-storey blocks of yellow brick with projecting flat roofs
and jaunty angled balconies, and staircase access on the sides away

from the streets. But by 1949 this humane scale was abandoned, and large blocks by *Joseph*, similar to their pre-war ones, were planned, replaced since by lower terraces.

## 6. w *of Kingsland Road; De Beauvoir Town*

Plans for the development of DE BEAUVOIR TOWN go back to *c.* 1818, when a building lease was acquired by William Rhodes, a member of a family of London brickmakers and speculators. The land formerly belonged to Balmes House, a C17 mansion on a medieval site, which lay just N of the Regent's Canal. *James Burton* drew up plans for four squares and a central octagon. The diagonal routes of Enfield Road, Stamford Road and Ardleigh Road, and the position of De Beauvoir Square go back to this plan. But little was built, and the main development of paired villas and short terraces took place only from the late 1830s–40s, after the ground landlord, Benyon de Beauvoir, had regained possession. The fringes of the area were eroded by new housing in the 1960s–70s; later insertions have been more tactful in scale and detail.

In DE BEAUVOIR SQUARE the E side was complete by 1823 but has been rebuilt; the other three sides have pairs of very pretty Tudor 57 villas, begun on the N side in 1839. They have shaped gables and some still have their original lozenge glazing; on the w side the centre pair has steep gables with finials, and castellated bay windows.

The attraction of the surrounding streets lies in the combination of a spacious lay-out with a disarmingly haphazard variety of villa types, mostly two-storeys-and-basement, with the reticent classical stucco detailing that was still the norm up to the 1840s. The following highlights are described anti-clockwise from the Square. N of the Square, in HERTFORD ROAD, Nos. 97–107, three pairs with channelled stucco door surrounds, the centre pair with shared gables and a tablet 'BENYON COTTAGES A.D. 1839'. Further N, simpler hipped-roof pairs with recessed side entrances. The N side of STAMFORD ROAD has larger pairs with basements. Others in MORTIMER ROAD, which also has the TALBOT pub, three broad bays, and No. 82, a nice detached three-bay house with arched windows and bracketed eaves. S of the Square, by the church, No. 85, the former vicarage, with Tudor porch and hoodmoulds. No. 10 NORTHCHURCH TERRACE is also Tudor. St Peter's Church faces DE BEAUVOIR ROAD, which runs N–S. Its best groups are at the S end; on the W side the porches have fluted Ionic columns. Further W, NORTHCHURCH ROAD, an ample lay-out of paired villas, some with channelled stucco ground floors, some all stuccoed, with the odd feature of Ionic pilasters to the top floors. Grand balustraded approaches to side entrances. In UFTON ROAD short terraces, in SOUTHGATE GROVE groups of four, each couple with a shared pediment. Hidden to the S of this, a whimsical cul-de-sac, ORCHARD MEWS, by *CZWG*, 1984, for Kentish Homes. Quirky Arts and Crafts motifs, with corner towers and irregular windows. SOUTHGATE ROAD on the borough boundary has some earlier C19 terraces, as has BALLS POND ROAD (*see* Islington).

On the N and S fringes the C20 intrudes in contrasting fashion. At the N end around TOTTENHAM ROAD, the KINGSGATE ESTATE, designed for Hackney by *Frederick Gibberd*, 1958–61. An informal grid of four-storey terraces on a friendly scale, given interest by their rhythm of gables linking projecting party-walls, which are opened up by small arches on two levels. One eleven-storey tower. Hackney's DE BEAUVOIR ESTATE of *c.* 1962–1972, S of Downham Road, is more overbearing. Built for the population displaced by the Holly Street redevelopment. Tower blocks and a slab of six-storey maisonettes in dark brick, bleak spaces in between, tempered only by a group of low shops behind community hall and library (q.v.) at the corner of De Beauvoir Road. The estate stretches S towards the now semi-derelict industrial area that grew up around the Regent's Canal. Adjoining the Kingsland Basin, approached through an archway from Kingsland Road (No. 315), a former GRANARY, built in 1878 to provide for the *c.* 1,200 horses employed by the North Metropolitan Tramways Company. Of brick, with original timber and iron roofs.

### 7. Dalston, Kingsland and Shacklewell: a circular tour

The three old settlements can barely be distinguished. Along the main routes sparse remnants of the early C19 are swamped by a mixture of later commerce and industry (the latter increasingly replaced by C20 housing). In between are patches of more consistent Victorian domesticity.

At the junction of Balls Pond Road and Dalston Lane, the route of Ermine Street changes from Kingsland Road to KINGSLAND HIGH STREET, a crowded down-at-heel thoroughfare with plenty of character, if not much architecture, considerably smartened up from 1995 as a result of City Challenge money. It starts quite well: at the SE corner of the crossroads, the CROWN AND CASTLE, heavy Italianate of *c.* 1870; at the NE corner, a former BANK, also stucco-trimmed, restored in 1995. Behind, in KINGSLAND PASSAGE, a warehouse converted to *Levitt Bernstein Associates*' offices, 1992, an elegant trail-blazer for the rehabilitation of the area. Open-plan offices on two floors, with a glazed barrel vault and big end windows. Just to the N in BRADBURY STREET, a YOUTH ENTERPRISE CENTRE, 1997 by *Hawkins Brown*, a training centre in a white rotunda at the end of a rehabilitated terrace. E of the High Street, a trite entrance to DALSTON CROSS, a hygienic covered shopping centre of *c.* 1992, which contrasts with the lively and chaotic street market stretching down RIDLEY ROAD on the other side of the railway line. (Entrance to the market by *Freeform Artworks* planned 1997.) Back in the High Street, the Cockney spirit continues opposite with No. 41, a former Eel Pie and Mash shop, fitted up in 1910 with additions of the 1930s. Tiled interior with fishing scenes and much eely ornament; rear dining room of 1936 with coloured glass domes. Further N the Victorian mood is broken by THE RIO cinema, a building of 1913–15 by *Adams & Coles*, transformed in streamlined style by *F. E. Bromige* in 1937, when a lower auditorium was inserted below the still-surviving early C20 roof structure. The exterior simplified later. Curved corner entrance. A former cinema further N, cream-faience-fronted, at the corner of Trumans Road. On the E side, by Shacklewell Lane, quite dignified and coherent later C19 terraces with round-arched windows to the first floor.

SHACKLEWELL LANE leads NE, its old origin indicated by an attractive irregular early C19 group on the N side, converted to flats *c.* 1990, with new housing tactfully fitted in behind in GATEWAY MEWS. This was a slum area in the early C20. Hence the austere brick Hackney Borough flats in ARCOLA STREET, of 1939 by *Joseph.* The low amenity building in the centre, HINDLE HOUSE, was modernized and given a sparkly mosaic by *Hunt Thompson c.* 1987. Behind St Barnabas (q.v.), APRIL, PERCH and SEAL STREETS, laid out on the Tyssen estate with neat two-storey terraces by a Hoxton builder, *John Grover.* They have the dates 1881–4, and are reminiscent of progressive low-rise philanthropic housing of this time. s of Shacklewell Lane smart middle-class housing grew up in the 1860s around the colossal Church of St Mark (q.v.) in ST MARK'S RISE. Appropriately Gothic terraces of 1867 opposite and in SANDRINGHAM ROAD, the heart of the area developed by the local builders *Jordan & Paine.* On the s side of Sandringham Road, the vicarage by *Chester Cheston,* 1872–3. In COLVESTONE CRESCENT, an elaborately dormered Gothic church hall, 1874 by *E. L. Blackburne.* Nos. 90–104 Colvestone Crescent, built in the 1860s by a carpenter, *Edmund Hammond,* are among the most fancily dressed of Hackney's rich variety of  80 Victorian housing, with giant Ionic pilasters and especially eccentric doorcases. Its continuation, MONTAGUE ROAD, has a terrace of 1861–6: doorcases with mermen.

DALSTON LANE immediately to the s is a busy route connecting Dalston to central Hackney, with scattered remnants of C18 and earlier C19 terraces and villas: No. 113 is a large three-storey house of *c.* 1800; No. 127 has bows. No. 160 is part of a much altered C18 group ending with No. 164; No. 166, an early C19 villa. A few more villas in WAYLAND AVENUE off to the N, and in GREENWOOD ROAD and NAVARINO ROAD to the s. Here also is the flamboyant group of NAVARINO MANSIONS, 1903–4. Built by *Nathan S. Joseph* for Jewish artisans by the Four Per Cent Industrial Dwellings Society. An imposing series of tall five-storey blocks linked by a screen of triple arches along the road. Formerly with tall chimneystacks. These were lowered as part of a bold refurbishment by *Hunt Thompson Associates* (from 1986), when the mansions were given lifts, new private balconies and gardens, and community facilities in a new link block behind the screen.

Returning w along Dalston Lane, the SAMUEL LEWIS TRUST flats on the N side, 1990s, replacing an older Trust estate of the 1920s. s of the railway, the junction of Dalston Lane and Queensbridge Road is marked by the former Gothic church and vicarage of St Bartholomew (q.v.), long derelict, but converted to housing in 1995. To its w, No. 57, a good house of *c.* 1800, three bays, with Tuscan porch and fanlight, and some decaying early C19 pairs opposite, hidden behind later shops.

Off the N side of Dalston Lane nearer Kingsland an industrial area developed in the C19. The most impressive building is off TYSSEN STREET, the former Shannon Furniture factory of 1903–5 by

*Edwin O. Sachs.* Steelwork encased in concrete, brick-faced, with heavy eaves modelling. In ASHWIN STREET, the former premises of REEVES & SON, artists' colour manufacturer, on this site from 1866. The w part is a late C19 factory, with fourth floor added 1913; the E part, the 'Print House', is an extension of 1913 by *John Hamilton & Son.* Nicely decorated with mosaic in bands and in the tympana of three ground-floor arches.

## 8. Hackney Downs

An amorphous area between Shacklewell and Lower Clapton, largely rebuilt with housing estates between the 1930s and the 1960s. This route follows a roughly chronological tour of styles from the 1930s to the 1960s, starting at Hackney Downs station and ending with the chief asset, HACKNEY DOWNS, common land, preserved from the 1860s as open space, an early success of the Commons Preservation Society.

Starting from Hackney Downs Station, AMHURST ROAD leads NW. On the w side, a SAMUEL LEWIS TRUST ESTATE by *Joseph* of 1931–2, extended 1934 and 1937–8. The last part, with curved balconies (glazed 1969) was built as an 'all-electric' block of 40 flats. The traditional brick detail of these blocks and of the *LCC*'s DOWNS ESTATE opposite has an abrupt contrast further N, in EVELYN COURT. This is by *Burnet, Tait & Lorne,* 1934–5 for the Four Per Cent Industrial Dwellings Company, and was innovative for its date. Ten austere five-storey blocks with staircase access, laid out in rows, built of standardized reinforced concrete to save money, and said to be the first box-framed structures to use reinforced concrete in Britain. The walls, now pastel-coloured, were originally painted white, with green stair-towers.

To the w, off SHACKLEWELL LANE, are the SHACKLEWELL ROAD and SOMERFORD ESTATES, a long strip extending to Stoke Newington Road. Planned by *Frederick Gibberd* for Hackney in 1945, built 1946–7. An influential pioneer example of 'mixed development', including both houses and flats, in reaction to the standard pre-war solution of flats for the city, cottages for the suburbs. The flats are only three- and four-storeyed, not yet taller landmarks, as became the pattern a few years later. Informal but carefully considered grouping allows for attractive vistas. Pairs and terraces of low pitched-roof houses, set back or with small gardens, along an E–W spine route which is part street, part footpath. The taller flats, flat-roofed, are mostly in a series of L-shaped groups divided by grass courts. They end with a long, plain four-storey range with passage through to Stoke Newington Road. Although the detail has been coarsened by new windows, the ingredients of the Festival of Britain style are still recognizable: coloured ceramic tiles and delicate porches and little curved balconies of Regency inspiration (cf. Gibberd's contributions to the Festival site at Lansbury, Poplar). Amenities were provided too: a small community centre and a HEALTH CENTRE in Somerford Grove.

Back to the junction of Amhurst Road and RECTORY ROAD, where there is a little group of early C19 survivors: the AMHURST ARMS, mid-C19, stuccoed with pilasters, and Nos. 6–14, earlier C19.

No. 6 is of three bays with ground-floor windows in arched recesses, Nos. 8–10 have trellis porches. Further N on the E side, at the corner of DOWNS ROAD, THE BECKERS, another Hackney estate by *Frederick Gibberd*, planned in 1956. This has buildings of contrasting heights in the manner of the LCC, but different from them in style. Plain lower ranges with blue spandrel panels and shallow pitched roofs, simpler than Gibberd's work elsewhere. Two eleven-storey point blocks with livelier elevations: glass balconies, curved tops to the lift towers. They show the move away from the prettiness of ten years earlier towards a tougher urban image.

# SHOREDITCH

## INTRODUCTION

Shoreditch lies immediately N of the City of London. The High Street begins not far outside Bishopsgate. It was one of the first outer districts of London to merge with the City. What houses there were in the Middle Ages lay close to Haliwell (or Holywell) Priory, a house of Augustinian nuns founded before 1127, which lay W of the High Street. Its position just outside the boundaries of the City of London may be compared to that of the religious houses in Clerkenwell or St Mary Overies in Southwark. But nothing at all of Haliwell Priory exists today, so that there is no visual link with the medieval past. Even Elizabethan evidence is confined to street names and the like. Stow, in 1598, describes the ribbon of houses along the High Street, and another thinner ribbon down Old Street as far as Golden Lane. Manor houses or country houses also existed; Hoxton to the N was 'a large street with houses on both sides', Haggerston to the NE was still a village on its own. Immediately W of the High Street the first London theatres were built: The Theatre *c.* 1576 and, a little later, The Curtain (the name was that of the neighbourhood, derived from the walled close of Haliwell Priory, and had nothing to do with a theatrical curtain). Both were erected for James Burbage, and Shakespeare must have acted in them. The Fortune Theatre in Golden Lane, Clerkenwell, came later still.

More evidence remains of the late C17 and early C18. Hoxton Square and the adjoining areas to the N of Old Street were laid out then, in an attempt at introducing the new West End pattern to the N of the City. The ribbons along the main roads extended, with almshouses at their ends, as usual half-way between town and country. There were fifteen in the parish established earlier than 1750. The parish church was rebuilt in a decidedly urban style by *George Dance Sen.* in 1736–40. By the mid C18 the parish is supposed to have had 2,500 houses, that is, a population of *c.* 10,000. Shoreditch had become a part of London. By 1801 the population had grown to 35,000; in 1831 it was 69,000, in 1851, 109,000. This rapid rise indicates the decline of gentility. Trade began to dominate, notably the furniture and timber trades. These were at first centred round the part later occupied by Broad Street and Liverpool Street Stations, then around the 1860s moved N to the area around Curtain Road; by the end of the C19 they had invaded Hoxton Square.

The furniture industry has gone, and new occupants fill the Victorian and Edwardian offices, workshops and warehouses whose robust bulk and handsome detail still dominate the streets of southern Shoreditch; this is one of the most consistent and distinctive areas of its kind in London, despite encroachment by glossy City outliers of the 1980s. Shoreditch also still has several of the idealistic groups of Victorian churches, schools and clergy houses which reflect the C19 concern to minister to the urban poor. The most ambitious of these were built by *James Brooks* in the 1860s as a result of the Haggerston Church Scheme, promoted by two wealthy High Church laymen, Richard Foster, and Robert Brett of

Stoke Newington. Three Brooks churches survive (*see* below), but only one is in Anglican use at the time of writing.*

The cramped dwellings which housed the poor have been almost entirely replaced. Rehousing began as early as the 1860s with private philanthropy, by Sydney Waterlow, whose printing works were in Shoreditch, and with Colonel Gillum's workshops by *Philip Webb* in Worship Street. Between the wars both the LCC and the borough built flats, of which the largest group was the *LCC*'s Whitmore Estate, but the borough was still badly overcrowded right down to the Second World War. In 1938 Dr Mallon of Toynbee Hall spoke of the 'widespread squalour ... ill health and poverty' of Shoreditch. By 1951, the population had dropped to 45,000. The replacement of old terraces by blocks of flats continued ruthlessly after the war until the 1970s, with the loss of much that would now be cherished. The best new buildings are educational ones: *Goldfinger*'s Haggerston School of the 1960s and the more recent Shoreditch Community College by *Hampshire County Architects* and *Perkins Ogden Architects*.

The College is part of the vigorous 1990s regeneration whose effects are also apparent in Hoxton Square and Hoxton Market.

## RELIGIOUS BUILDINGS

### 1. Church of England

ALL SAINTS, Haggerston Road. 1855–6 by *P. C. Hardwick*. Ragstone exterior with Dec E and W windows. Soon after, the aisles were rebuilt and extended W by *T. E. Knightley*, with galleries on iron columns, set back behind broad, spare arcades, which are relieved only by carved foliage capitals.

HOLY TRINITY, Shepherdess Walk. 1848 by *W. Railton*. Simple lancet style church flanked by parish SCHOOL and VICARAGE (1868). SW tower with broach spire; within it a baptistery made in 1896 by *Spencer W. Grant*. Tall thin arcades on octagonal piers, whitened walls; many Anglo-Catholic fittings of the 1930s onwards. REREDOS with gilded relief of Crucifixion by *W. E. A. Lockett*. CONFESSIONAL with tall Corinthian pilasters, by *M. Travers*, possibly made up from old woodwork. Also by Travers, painting above reredos (1942) and roundel above chancel arch. Two older pieces: PULPIT, 1686, from the City church St Mary Somerset, carved with cherubs' heads and flowers. Part of a font cover from the same source, reused as a corbel for a statue.

ST ANNE, Hoxton Street. 1868–9 by *Francis Chambers*. Ragstone Gothic. W end with three gables; unfinished NE tower. E apse with tall two-light windows. Beneath it a curved stone and marble REREDOS, 1882. Wooden PULPIT with details in French C13 style. STAINED GLASS. E window by *A. L. Wilkinson*, 1956.

ST AUGUSTINE, Yorkton Street, Hackney Road. 1866–7 by *H. Woodyer*, his only London church. Converted to hologram and arts centre, 1997. Built under the Haggerston Church Scheme. W end hidden behind tall, minimally Gothic clergy house and hall of

---

* The many churches demolished include Christ Church, New North Road, by *Blore*, 1840; St Andrew Hoxton, by *C. A. Long*, 1865; St Mary Haggerston, by *Nash*, 1825–7, altered 1860 by *Brooks*; St Paul, Broke Road, by *A. W. Blomfield*, 1859–60; St Augustine's Convent, Ash Grove, with chapel by *Harold Gibbons*, 1925.

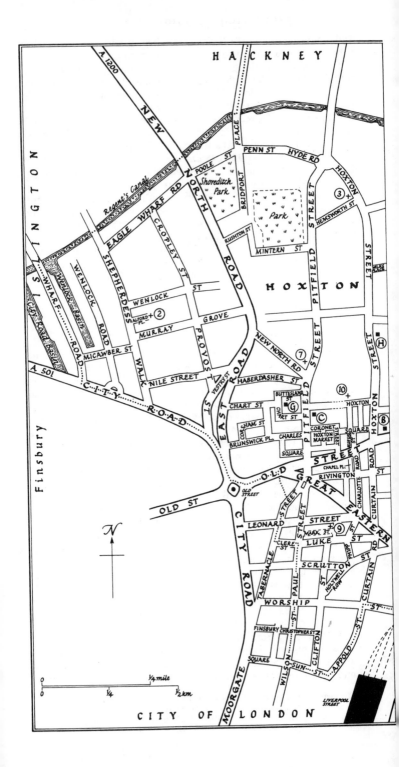

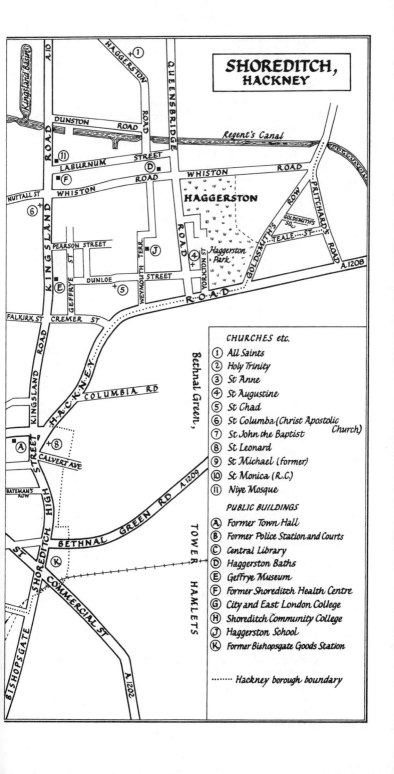

SHOREDITCH,
HACKNEY

Kingsland Basin
HAGGERSTON
Regent's Canal
DUNSTON ROAD
QUEENSBRIDGE
HAGGERSTON ROAD
A.10
ROAD
LABURNUM STREET
ⓕ
ⓓ
WHISTON ROAD
WHISTON ROAD
NUTTALL ST
KINGSLAND
ⓖ
PRITCHARD'S ROW
GOLDSMITH'S SQ.
PEARSON STREET
GEFFRYE ST
WEYMOUTH TERR.
ⓙ
HAGGERSTON ROAD
ⓔ
DUNLOE STREET
ⓢ
Haggerston Park
YORK'S
GOLDSMITH'S ROW
TEALE ST
A.1208
FALKIRK ST
CREMER ST
ROAD
ROAD
HACKNEY
Bethnal Green,
COLUMBIA RD
KINGSLAND
ⓐ
STREET
ⓗ
CALVERT AVE
BATEMAN'S ROW
ⓚ
BETHNAL GREEN RD A.1209
SHOREDITCH HIGH ST
COMMERCIAL ST
TOWER HAMLETS
BISHOPSGATE ST
A.1202

CHURCHES etc.
① All Saints
② Holy Trinity
③ St Anne
④ St Augustine
⑤ St Chad
⑥ St Columba (Christ Apostolic
        Church)
⑦ St John the Baptist
⑧ St Leonard
⑨ St Michael (former)
⑩ St Monica (R.C.)
⑪ Niye Mosque
PUBLIC BUILDINGS
Ⓐ Former Town Hall
Ⓑ Former Police Station and Courts
Ⓒ Central Library
Ⓓ Haggerston Baths
Ⓔ Geffrye Museum
Ⓕ Former Shoreditch Health Centre
Ⓖ City and East London College
Ⓗ Shoreditch Community College
Ⓙ Haggerston School
Ⓚ Former Bishopsgate Goods Station

········ Hackney borough boundary

1926–7 by *J. Harold Gibbons*. Tall simple church, under a single roof. w gable with circular window and bellcote, paired clerestory windows, e window with quite elaborate tracery. Well-proportioned interior with broad arcades on slim octagonal columns. Aisles now divided off. Furnishings included a spiky tall stone REREDOS probably by *Woodyer*, and hanging ROOD. STAINED GLASS by *Margaret Rope* now in St Mary Magdalene, St Pancras (*see* p. 347) and St Peter, Wapping.

ST CHAD, Dunloe Street. 1867–9 by *James Brooks*, the architect of several forceful churches built for the Haggerston Church Scheme. Now the only one of the group remaining in use by the Church of England. The tall, compact, cruciform building of red brick, in an austere Early Gothic, once towered above a square of modest early Victorian Tudor cottages. Plain and purposeful, the first of Brooks's East End churches to abandon polychromy, with only a timber bell-turret above the crossing, and no tower. The w front has three powerful plate tracery windows, the top one a rose, above a low narthex. Roses also to the transepts. The interior has short circular stone piers, the rest is again brick (whitened later). Lean-to, windowless aisles, non-projecting transepts, but plenty of light from the tall clerestory: lancets in the chancel; grouped lancets and a rose in the nave. The steep and lofty nave roof has a boarded seven-sided ceiling between arch braces. The chancel is brick-vaulted with a semicircular apse. The s chancel chapel is also vaulted. The vaulting shafts and ribs are of stone, and the capitals are the only ones in the church that have received the intended foliage carving. w bay of the nave divided off. Stone REREDOS by *Brooks*, carved by *Earp*. Wooden octagonal PULPIT by *Brooks*. Apse STAINED GLASS by *Clayton & Bell*. To the N of the church, the VICARAGE, also by *Brooks*, of 1873–4. Red brick, slate half-hipped roof and a circular turret, essential to the whole picturesque composition. Arched brick hood-moulds give it a slightly churchy feel.

ST COLUMBA, Kingsland Road. *See* Christ Apostolic Church, below.

ST JOHN THE BAPTIST, New North Road, Hoxton. 1824–6 by *F. Edwards*, a pupil of Soane. Unusually monumental for a Commissioners' church. Severe classical w front of three bays with two giant Ionic columns *in antis* and no pediment. The w tower appears above the broad parapet; it has a low square base, two circular, rather emaciated upper stages, and a stone cupola. The long sides of seven bays all stock brick, with bays one and seven emphasized by giant Tuscan pilasters. Impressively wide interior; galleries on three sides, with curved corners, on Tuscan columns. REREDOS, plain classical, 1937 by *J.E. Yerbury*, with painted panel by *L.A. Pownall*, 1911. PULPIT, 1902, mahogany, on runners. ORGAN CASE, acquired 1834, possibly from a City church, the design with three towers on leafy consoles reminiscent of *G.P. England*. STAINED GLASS. E window, 1958 by *F. Stephens*. MONUMENT. Rev. A.P. Kelly †1864, with ivy leaves and relief portrait bust.

The surprise is the ambitious CEILING DECORATION of 1902–14 by *J.A. Reeve*, returned to its original vigour after cleaning in 1993–4: angels of the Apocalypse in square panels, on a blue background. The decoration originally included the walls as well. The cleaning was the first phase of an inspiring programme of regeneration. The w end was screened off for a variety of uses by elegant oak and glass partitions, 1995, by *Tom Hornsby* of *Keith Harrison Associates*. In the crypt a café and gymnasium, with new s entrance, 1997.

Good CHURCHYARD RAILINGS on granite plinth.

ST LEONARD, Shoreditch High Street. The medieval parish church of Shoreditch was rebuilt in 1736–40 by *George Dance Sen.*, after the tower of the old church had partly collapsed in 1716. A church as stately as Hawksmoor's East End churches, if not as grandiose. The steeple is original in design, with its elongated stone cupola

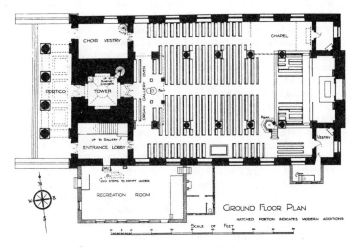

St Leonard, Shoreditch. Plan

crowned by a slim lantern with a square obelisk top. The cupola is 34 the covering of a square stage with attached columns at the angles (cf. St Mary-le-Bow), and the whole tower rises behind the portico in the awkward position for which Gibbs' St Martin-in-the-Fields is responsible. The steeple is 192 ft tall and seems even taller owing to the slenderness and elongation of its various members. The front of the church is of five bays and has a robust four-column giant Tuscan portico, originally with more steps than at present. The N and S sides are of seven bays, with two tiers of round-headed windows, above lunettes to the vaulted brick crypt. The front is of Portland stone, the rest red brick.

The interior gives the impression of bigness and solidity, but has not been helped by later alterations. The elevation is reminiscent of Hawksmoor's Christ Church Spitalfields: giant Doric columns each carrying a section of entablature with metope friezes and arches high up, with a clerestory above. The N and S galleries were removed in 1870 by *Butterfield*, when the aisle windows were blocked and the upper windows lengthened. The W gallery remains. It is stretched out between the NW and SW bays of the aisles, which are different from the others, with arched openings, and a circular window above the entablature towards the nave.

The same motifs are repeated for the last bay in the E opening towards the slightly projecting chancel, giving the interior a faintly centralizing tendency. The original staircase to the w gallery remains, with a bold balustrade. *Butterfield* redecorated the church in 1870–1, but his work was painted out in the C20 and the Victorian fittings reduced. Plans for comprehensive restoration by *Richard Griffiths*, 1997.

Some original furnishings of the highest quality remain. FONT. 1740. Stone, bulgy polygonal shaft and shallow fluted bowl. FONT COVER in keeping, 1914. – PULPIT. Also 1740, although lowered, with sounding board on two magnificent fluted Ionic columns, and an elegant staircase. – COMMUNION TABLE. 1740, mahogany, the front legs with claw-and-ball feet; enlarged in the C19. – Two large C18 voluted PANELS, perhaps stall ends. – CLOCK. Against the w gallery, with exquisitely carved rococo surround, of the best quality then available anywhere in England. Who may have made it? – Fine mahogany ORGAN CASE, w gallery, 1756 by *Richard Bridge*, with original console. – Two elegant C18 BREAD CUPBOARDS with pierced fronts. – Four BENEFACTORS' and two COMMANDMENT BOARDS in the chancel. Small carved ROYAL ARMS of George II. BELL BOARDS in fine frames, 1777, 1784 (eight bells were cast in 1739; there are now twelve). – STAINED GLASS. E window by *A. K. Nicholson Studios*, 1955. – MONUMENTS. Elizabeth Benson †1710, by *Francis Bird*. Wall monument of striking quality and design, an oak tree carrying an inscription on feigned drapery is riven by two skeletons pulling hard at the branches, a frighteningly convincing vision. It is derived from a 1640s design by *Stefano della Bella* (information from Roger Bowdler). A good range of minor tablets: Thomas and John Austen †1658, 1659, inscription under a broken pediment with arms. – Rev. Francis Clerke †1690 and wife †1709, inscription of feigned drapery. – Elizabeth Crossley †1760 and family, and Rev. Edward Kimpton and family, erected *c.* 1817, both of the same elegant design in coloured marbles. John Marshall †1840, with classical frame, by *Samuel Nixon*. – Large classical memorial erected by the London Shakespeare League in 1913 to Shakespeare's theatre associates, including James Burbage, who built the theatre in Shoreditch in 1576. – WHIPPING POST and STOCKS in the churchyard, under a tiled roof, as if it were a lychgate.

ST MICHAEL, Mark Street. 1863–5 by *James Brooks*, his first church in this area. Closed 1964; used since as a store for architectural salvage. Stock brick with bands of red brick and stone for windows, still in the Butterfield mould. The E and W windows have plate tracery, with lancets and groups of foiled circles set in patterned brickwork. Plain interior with tall clerestory and steep timber roof. Square chancel. A NW tower was planned but not built. STAINED GLASS. Excellent E window by *Clayton & Bell*. The church formed part of an eminently picturesque group to the w of the church, of which only the CLERGY HOUSE of 1870 and part of the adjacent school remain. The nicely landscaped garden, now open to the s, is on the site of the cloister and the Hospital of St Mary at the Cross, begun by Brooks, and completed in Franco-Flemish style by the young *J. D. Sedding*. (Furnishings from the convent chapel were moved to the convent at Edgware, q.v.)

## 2. Roman Catholic

St Mary Moorfields, Eldon Street. *See London 1: The City of London.*

St Monica, Hoxton Square. 1864–6 by *E. W. Pugin*. Narrow W front of brick, with Perp window and slender bell-turret. Chancel, eight-bay aisled nave with timber columns, tracery arches and vault. Lady Chapel 1880 by *John Young*. STAINED GLASS. Four windows by *M. E. Aldrich Rope*, 1924. Adjacent Augustinian PRIORY, 1862–4, also by *E. W. Pugin*, and former SCHOOL, *c.* 1870, plain Gothic.

## 3. Other places of worship

Christ Apostolic Church, Kingsland Road. 1867–71. Built as St Columba, an Anglican church by *James Brooks*, one of his finest buildings. The largest church built for the Haggerston Church Scheme, designed to seat 800. Like St Chad (*see* above) it is in a tall and severe Early Gothic, of red brick, with a decidedly tall clerestory. Tower with pyramidal roof over the crossing. A deliberately urban building: the chancel rises directly from the 86 street, with no windows and a buttress as central motif. It 'presents an exceedingly picturesque composition', says Eastlake. On the N side the church is partly hidden by a later three-bay porch and church buildings satisfyingly grouped around a small courtyard: SCHOOL, 1865, CLERGY HOUSE, 1873–4, MISSION HOUSE, 1893–8.

Fine, lofty interior with vaulted crossing, square chancel, and shallow transepts. Low lean-to aisles. The capitals of the stone piers are left undecorated. The W wall has a fine array of lancet windows in two tiers. Unsympathetically treated in the 1960s, when the red brick walls were whitened, and statues removed from the reredos. Mortuary chapel 1903–5 by Rev. *Ernest Geldart*. Black marble FONT and sturdy conical FONT COVER by *Brooks*. Ornate marble PULPIT added *c.* 1900. Splendid Gothic ORGAN CASE, 1874, S transept.

Former Congregational Tabernacle, Old Street. *See* Perambulation 1.

Niye Mosque, Kingsland Road. A cultural centre for the Turkish community. 1993–8 by *Networld Designs*. One of the largest buildings of its kind in London. Six storeys, faced in yellow brick. Formal front with a bowed centre. Tall minaret visible from afar. The double-height prayer hall is at first-floor level, marked by tall slim windows, with offices and classrooms above.

Wilson Street Chapel. Small, conventional late C19 Gothic (probably of the 1890s), red brick with stone dressings, plate tracery. Side entrances with crypt below.

## PUBLIC BUILDINGS

Borough Offices (former Town Hall), Old Street. Three main phases, reflecting the history of the borough. The E part dates from 1863–8, by *Caesar A. Long* for the Shoreditch Vestry, exceptionally grand for its date. Italian in a personal, not at all usual idiom. First floor with Corinthian columns, big keystones to the windows. The broken pediment was added after 1904. The more florid w extension of 1898–1902 by *W. G. Hunt* makes use of the same motifs but also sports an asymmetrical tower, an Ionic porch, and a big broken pediment with scrolled ends and reclining figures of Light and Power (cf. the Depot Buildings, below). Rear extension 1936–8. In the vestry hall, good original council chamber at the back. An imperial stair leads to the magnificent galleried first-floor public hall, an original feature, but reconstructed after a fire in 1904 by *A. G. Cross*, when it was given a new roof with plaster barrel vault and elaborate gilded decoration.

POLICE STATION and MAGISTRATES COURT, Old Street, opposite the Town Hall. 1906 by *J. D. Butler*. A good building of its date. A lively composition full of eclectic Baroque detail. Red brick above a granite base; stone-faced centre, ground floor and attic. The centre is recessed and has an open pediment. Busily blocked Venetian window on the first floor, set back above a shallow curved Ionic porch. The excessively elongated window brackets of the pediments are recognizable in Butler's other London police stations. Attic with porthole windows. Well-finished interior; a court on both ground and first floors, approached from a central waiting area. The Police Station included accommodation for thirty-seven constables.

Former CENTRAL LIBRARY, Pitfield Street (now used as orchestra rehearsal space). The best-preserved part of an ambitious civic group between Pitfield Street and Hoxton Market. 1895–7 by *H. T. Hare*. A Passmore Edwards building, of red brick and terracotta, in the fanciful semi-Loire, semi-Baroque style derived from Shaw's New Scotland Yard, with a bold striped corner turret. Interior restored after war damage, 1955–6 by *J. L. Sharratt*. Bust of Charles Bradlaugh, erected 1898. The adjoining baths by *Spalding & Cross*, with exteriors by *Hare*, have been demolished. For the LIBRARY in Hoxton Street *see* p. 528.

THE CIRCUS SPACE, Hoxton Market, occupies the former SHOREDITCH BOROUGH REFUSE DESTRUCTOR and GENERATING STATION, 1895–7, consultant engineer *E. Manville*. The façade in Fletton brick and terracotta, dated 1896, has the motto E PULVERE LUX ET VIS (Out of the dust, light and power). It refers to the use of a refuse destructor to raise steam for the municipal electricity station, the first successful works purpose-built to combine these two functions. The waste heat was used for the public baths. Sympathetically converted to a circus training school by *Philip Lancashire*, 1994, with a gymnasium in the old generating hall, and a training space in the former Combustion House, a large brick building in the yard to the E, its gable end with blind arches.

Former HAGGERSTON LIBRARY, Kingsland Road. House of *c.* 1880 adapted for a library in 1893 by *Richard J. Lovell*, extended by *Maurice B. Adams*. A fine tall palazzo, stone-fronted, with balustraded parapet, big cornice and pedimented entrance and first-floor windows. (Nice plasterwork inside; former reference library with painted decoration.)

HAGGERSTON BATHS, Whiston Road. 1903–4 by the baths specialist

*A. W. S. Cross*; a splendid example, built to impress. Red brick with centrepiece and dressings of stone, Baroque detail. The centre has a first-floor recessed loggia with Ionic columns; pediment with reclining figures of a man and a woman modelled by *Frederick Schenck*, carved by *Martyn & Co.* Domed cupola with a gilded ship weathervane. Originally with swimming bath, slipper baths and laundry. Main bath now subdivided.

GEFFRYE MUSEUM, Kingsland Road. One of the most pleasing almshouse groups in London, built for the Ironmongers in 1712–14, probably to designs of the builder *Robert Burford*, as a result of a bequest of 1704 by Sir Robert Geffrye. Converted by the LCC in 1912–13 to a museum of woodwork and furniture, to reflect the predominant local industry, a happy new use. Two-storeyed brick ranges on three sides of a spacious garden, low and comfortable-looking, just as almshouses should be. The chapel in the centre is

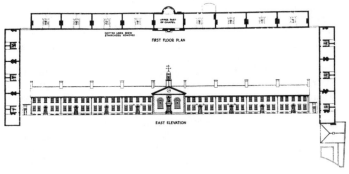

Geffrye Almshouses.
First-floor plan and east elevation

distinguished by taller arched windows, pediment and cupola. Above the doorway, a recess with the statue of Sir Robert Geffrye, 32 a replica of the original of 1723 by the *Nost* workshop, now at the company's C20 almshouses at Hook, Hampshire. The Victoria Room at the s end, built as a recreation room, is a tactful addition of 1896–7 by *Richard Roberts*. The almspeople had single rooms, grouped in fours around a staircase, each room with a small closet behind the stairs. From the front each group of four reads as a five-bay house. The original plan is preserved in No. 14. The rest were gutted in 1912–13 and 1925 to provide period rooms and exhibition space. Neat NE entrance hall by the *Conservation Practice*, 1991–4. Horseshoe-shaped SE wing for C20 displays, with glazed link to the old building, planned by *Branson Coates*, 1995, constructed in 1996–8 by *Sheppard Robson*.

The interior of the CHAPEL survives with its C18 fittings: three-decker PULPIT; decoratively lettered framed TEXTS; black and white marble floor. Shallow apse with delicate fan vault, a later C18 addition, possibly of *c.* 1791 by *Richard Jupp*, the company surveyor, who provided a communion table at this time. MONU-MENT to Sir Robert Geffrye †1703 and his wife †1676, made in

1704 by *Richard Saunders*, brought from St Dionis Backchurch in the City. Wall monument flanked by putti and crowned by an urn.

The GARDEN, divided from the road by (renewed) iron railings and gates, was grassed and planted with ninety lime trees in 1719, mostly replaced in the late C19 by planes. Small burial ground to the N. Nearby an early C18 NICHE of rubbed brickwork, from Bradmore House, Hammersmith. C20 herb garden to the E.

Former SHOREDITCH HEALTH CENTRE, Kingsland Road. 1920–2 by *Francis Danby Smith*. Built as a model mother-and-child clinic, a pioneering effort by the Borough of Shoreditch. Deliberately domestic seven-bay front of red brick in a handsome early C18 style reminiscent of the Geffrye Museum just down the road.

HAGGERSTON PARK. An extensive later C20 open space stretching S to Hackney Road, with a City Farm at the SE corner. Brick walls in the N part formed part of the Imperial Gasworks, established 1823, cleared away for the park in 1956.

ELECTRICITY SUBSTATION, Rivington Street and Garden Walk. *See* Perambulation 1.

CANALS. Along the REGENT'S CANAL from W to E. NEW NORTH ROAD has the first reinforced concrete tramway bridge in England, built in 1912 on the Hennebique system. At WHITMORE ROAD an original brick bridge of *c.* 1816–20. KINGSLAND BASIN of *c.* 1822–7 is still surrounded by late industrial buildings. On its E side the four-storey QUEBEC WHARF was a fodder warehouse over tramway stables, one of the very few warehouses remaining on London's canals. Another original bridge at HAGGERSTON ROAD. At QUEENSBRIDGE ROAD a handsome elliptical brick arch of *c.* 1840. BONNER HALL BRIDGE into Victoria Park has elaborate stone voussoirs. At the S end of the park is the junction with the HERTFORD UNION CANAL (Duckett's Cut), 1824–30 by *Francis Giles*, which joins the Regent's Canal to the Lee Navigation. Neat cast-iron beamed bridges.

RAILWAYS. THE NORTH LONDON RAILWAY extension from Dalston Junction to Broad Street, which cuts through on a viaduct, is of 1861–5 by *William Baker*. The RAILWAY BRIDGE over Great Eastern Street by the *MBW* under *Bazalgette* was shorn of its elaborate cast-iron decoration in the 1970s.

Former BISHOPSGATE GOODS STATION, Shoreditch High Street. Upon a brick viaduct. The Shoreditch passenger terminus of the Eastern Counties Railway, 1839–42, was rebuilt as a two-level goods station in 1877–82. Badly damaged by fire in 1964. Upper parts demolished, but a splendidly massive iron gate to the approach ramp remains, dated 1884.

*Educational Buildings*

Former CITY AND EAST LONDON COLLEGE, Pitfield Street. Built as the Haberdashers' Almshouses, 1825–7 by *D. R. Roper*, and very different from their predecessors, which had been built by *Robert Hooke* in 1690–5, and from the Geffrye Almshouses (*see* above). By the early C19 a big four-column Greek Doric portico seemed necessary to add status to the otherwise plain stock brick building. Flanking ranges of four bays; slightly projecting wings with tripartite windows. Extended with wings for National Schools in 1873; taken over by the LCC for use as Shoreditch Technical College, 1898. Residential use proposed, 1998.

SHOREDITCH COMMUNITY COLLEGE, Falkirk Street and Hoxton Street. By *Perkins Ogden Architects* and *Hampshire County Architects*. Phase One 1992–7, for 3,000 staff and students, an exceptionally ambitious and artistically interesting further education campus, made possible with the help of the Dalston City Partnership and lottery funding. Planned from 1989 on the site of a secondary school, and incorporating some Edwardian school buildings (adapted, alas rather clumsily, by *Hawkins Brown*). The new buildings form a dignified array around three sides of a spacious quadrangle: precise, reticent three-storey blocks faced with pale yellow brick, sensibly adaptable inside. In front runs a cloister of tall columns supporting a timber and cable structure for fabric canopies, an elegant, light-hearted touch. A corner entrance from Falkirk Street, a break in the w range, and the red brick Edwardian buildings to the s create pleasing visual variety, as does the unusual quantity of art work allied with good landscaping (by *Pearson Landscape Design*).

The surprise in the centre is the sunken Library and Resource Centre. To the N this is given light and space by a small amphitheatre stepping down, surrounded by wavy benches by *Bettina Furnee*, fancifully carved with a poem. To its s the centre looks out on a sunken garden designed by *Susanna Heron*, with brilliant blue curved wall as backdrop to two shallow pools, one with water flowing fast over granite sets, the other quieter, with a carved slate base. Big boulder at the upper level. Roof-lights appear as glazed garden pavilions. Within the basement foyer, two etched glass screens, and four windows to the adjoining Prayer Room, by *Alexander Beleschenko*. To the s of the main quadrangle, older buildings are grouped informally around a more secluded garden with 'Quarry', two massive Portland stone 'seat sculptures' by *Pat Kaufman*. In the building to the SE, adapted as a crèche, jolly ceramic mural of wild animals by *Dimitra Grivellis*. Especially happily integrated with the buildings is the memorable ironwork by *Matthew Fedden*, a mighty pair of gates and a series of smaller screens and gates which break up the brick walls along Hoxton Street (*see also* Perambulation 2), made up of strong simple curves and verticals. Behind one of the smaller gates, in a tiny courtyard, charming ceramic fountain with floating 'pebbles', by *Lotte Glob*. Planned for 1998 is the Art, Media and Design Centre, E of the main quadrangle, with Light Beacon by *Martin Richman*.

HAGGERSTON SCHOOL, Weymouth Terrace. A girls' secondary school by *Ernö Goldfinger*, 1962–7, his only secondary school for the LCC. Outstanding among schools of its period, and the best part of the almost total reconstruction of this area in the 1960s. Skilful and dignified composition in concrete and dark brick, whose good proportions and careful details repay examination. Concrete-framed, with strongly expressed horizontals of exposed pebbly aggregate. Main entrance from the w, through a low administration wing faced with blue engineering brick; the double-height hall on the N side has a glazed wall with tall black mullions and boxed-out doors, repeated for the internal wall between hall and entrance foyer. The hall has a pleasing variety of textures and patterns: timber cladding, an acoustic end wall of angled concrete bricks, and a coffered ceiling, which continues across both hall and foyer and above the first-floor offices to the s. These have, on the outside, an inset balcony and elegant spiral fire escape. A glazed link connects with the four-storey classroom range running N–S. On the w side cantilevered windows give greater depth to library and art room; on the E side the pattern of classroom windows is broken by recessed staircase glazing and projecting oriels near the N end, which light pairs of dining rooms. The roof has a concrete parapet on supports, acting like a cornice, lifting this block out of the purely utilitarian. (Goldfinger used it also at Trellick Tower in North Kensington.) Even the rooftop water tanks are arranged with care. Separate sports block to the E, with two gymnasia above a formerly open ground floor. Neat one-storey CARETAKER'S HOUSE to the N.

BOARD SCHOOLS. HOXTON HOUSE SCHOOLS, Hoxton Street. *See* Shoreditch Community College (above). LABURNUM STREET. With crowstepped dormers and an addition dated 1908. RANDALL CREMER PRIMARY, Ormsby Street. Very plain, with two hipped stair-turrets, one with a cupola, *c.* 1880.

## PERAMBULATIONS

### *1. South of Old Street*

A suburb of the City already in the C16, the centre of the wholesale furniture trade in the C19 and still one of the most evocative areas of C19 industrial buildings to be found in London.

SHOREDITCH HIGH STREET is a broad curving street leading N from the City. It was built up by the C16, but only scattered pre-Victorian houses survive among a now gap-toothed sequence of C19 commercial frontages. Starting from St Leonard at the N end, the E side begins with the little CLERK'S HOUSE, No. 118½, of 1735. Two storeys, gable to the road, four windows to the churchyard. Opposite, on the w side, Nos. 125–130, built *c.* 1878 as Edward Wells & Co.'s Commercial Ironworks, probably as showrooms. Surprisingly exotic: four bays, two giant arches of wrought-iron plates, flanked by two narrower ones. Lancet windows above, spiral terracotta corner shafts, mosaic decoration in Islamic style. On the E side, at the corner of Calvert Avenue, No. 112, a former London & South Western BANK, 1900, probably by *E. Gabriel*, Portland stone; then No. 110, a modest two-bay domestic survival.

The w side has small alleys opening off, relics of a long urban past. One such is FRENCH PLACE, which has at its corner Nos. 149–150, dated 1886; dormers with shaped gables. After some gaps, Nos. 181–182, former London & County Bank (now NatWest), a fine big four-storey palazzo, *c.* 1868, paired columns to first-floor windows and a heavy cornice. Nos. 187–189 are C18, partly refaced later. No. 190 is early C18, only two bays wide, but grandly flanked by giant pilasters, with segment-headed windows and dentilled cornice. Nos. 192–193, of 1886, was built for a tailor and outfitter, brick and terracotta, with a corner clock turret, and large plate-glass windows on both ground and first floor. No. 196, of five bays and four storeys, with segment-headed windows (said to have a date of 1693), the brickwork painted later. Further s the late C19 CROWN AND SHUTTLE, within a much altered and rebuilt urban terrace. No. 227 is recorded in rate books from 1703 but may be older behind.

w of the High Street lies a network of streets that grew up around the site of Haliwell (or Holywell) Priory. GREAT EASTERN STREET was cut through the area diagonally in 1872–6 by the MBW. This provided some challenging triangular corner sites: see for example, near the s end, the wedge-shaped No. 8, of *c*. 1882, with a narrow rounded end, floridly detailed; five storeys contained between three orders of pilasters. Further N, the OLD BLUE LAST, 1876, a grey brick and stucco pub, has a broad curved end spreading around the corner of Curtain Road. Facing it, Nos. 40–42, a handsome commercial building of the late 1870s, the first- and second-floor windows within large Gothic arches; splayed corner with elaborate Gothic porch, blue brick and terracotta decoration (partly, alas, painted over). Plainer four-storey factories with even lines of windows march N along Great Eastern Street. Exceptions are No. 73, 1881 by *Aston Webb*, more domestic-looking, formerly with crowstepped gable rising on the l. (unsympathetic new top floor), and No. 87, *c*. 1888, elaborately Gothic.

STREETS SW OF GREAT EASTERN STREET are still a rewarding area for authentic and varied late C19 industrial building, despite the advance N from Broadgate of flashy 1980s offices. Only highlights can be mentioned here. One can start at PHIPP STREET, with good plain surviving factories on both sides. At the corner, Nos. 6–8 Luke Street, a tactful newcomer (1995); clad in reused bricks, with angled recessed entrance. At LEONARD CIRCUS, Hitchcock's Reel, by *John Edwards*, 1996, a large painted 'reel' to commemorate a century of filmmaking. More factories in LUKE STREET, PAUL STREET, and LEONARD STREET, around the former St Michael's Church (q.v.), used at the time of writing as a centre for architectural salvage; its yard is spectacular. Nos. 65–83 Leonard Street are a terrace of furniture workshops of the 1870s; three storeys unified by the use of giant piers between the windows, 67 still with some prominent wall cranes. The domestic buildings in these streets have mostly gone. They included early examples of philanthropic housing (Langbourne Buildings, 1863) financed by Sir Sydney Waterlow (founder of the Improved Industrial Dwellings Company). Another block, between Paul Street, MARK STREET and Luke Street, survives in refurbished form as VICTORIA CHAMBERS; five storeys around a courtyard, originally with open stairwells. Waterlow's printing works were sited close by, in CLIFTON STREET and SCRUTTON STREET. The present buildings here are of *c*. 1900 onwards; brown glazed brick ground floor, large windows above. On the s side of Clifton Street, a bolder, more Baroque range, with lunette windows above a heavy cornice. Further s, CLIFTON HOUSE at the corner of Clifton Street and Worship Street, another printers (Williams Lea & Co.), built 1900; five storeys with handsome red brick arched windows. Further s, Paul Street becomes WILSON STREET. Here an increasing number of 1980s offices heralds the edge of the City. Domestic survivors among them: on the N side of CHRISTOPHER STREET,

Nos. 15–23, a tall late Georgian terrace with an unusual rhythm, widely spaced pairs of first-floor windows within blind arches. At the corner of SUN STREET, the FLYING HORSE, a C19 Italianate corner pub, next to another simpler late Georgian terrace.

Back now to WORSHIP STREET. At its junction with Clifton Street, HOLYWELL ROW is a small lane running NE. On its S side, a modest terrace, Nos. 10–27; partly of the early C19, partly rebuilt later as commercial buildings, but retaining the domestic scale and so giving an idea of what this area was like before the mid C19. Worship Street has a taller mixture. No. 60, premises of the *Mining Journal*, is a four-storey 1920s block remodelled in 1959 by *Tripe & Wakeham*; ground floor faced with granite sets, functional ribbon windows above. Near the E end, Nos. 91–101, a remarkably innovative and eclectic design of 1862–3 by *Philip Webb*, built for the philanthropist Colonel Gillum (for whom Webb later designed a house at East Barnet, q.v.). A domestic terrace with ground-floor shops and industrial basements. Five shallow shops with lean-to tiled roofs and thick glazing bars (restored to their original design in the 1990s). The shops are placed between buttresses, with a carriage arch at the W end. Above are two-light windows of Queen Anne shape but under Gothic arches (the same bold combination used by Webb elsewhere). The second floor has a simple band of small windows in groups of three. Dormers in the roof. Drinking fountain under a Gothic canopy.

STREETS NE OF GREAT EASTERN STREET. The most important route is CURTAIN ROAD, famous for its association with the Elizabethan Curtain Theatre (*see* above), but by the late C19 the hub of the furniture trade. On the r. side, Nos. 86–90, *c.* 1900 for Oakden & Sons, hardware factors, more glass than wall; likewise No. 96A. Further on, a few Georgian houses remain, then at the N end Nos. 134–146, 1890s, a warehouse built for the wholesale cabinet makers C. & R. Light, eight bays, five storeys, very impressive. RIVINGTON STREET, a winding back lane to Old Street, is more intimate, with some lower workshops. No. 54 was converted from a two-storey building as offices by and for *Charles Thomson*, 1989–90. Tall rendered front given formality by a row of small second-floor square windows below the cornice. CHARLOTTE ROAD cuts across, a canyon between variegated four-storey workshops. To the W, at the corner of Garden Walk, a former ELECTRICITY SUBSTATION for the LCC tramways, 1905–7, probably by *Vincent Harris* (cf. Upper Street, Islington, Perambulation 1a). The end wall to Rivington Street is a strikingly severe Baroque composition with a two-storey entrance arch and plain walls, relieved only by rusticated brick quoining. Rustication also on the longer front to Garden Walk. Across Great Eastern Street, filling the snub-ended wedge between Paul Street and Tabernacle Street, the FIREHOUSE, a restaurant in a former *LCC* Fire Station of 1895–6. A lively twin-turreted red brick château, six storeys with mansarded centre. Engine doors are still recognizable. A granite COLUMN marks the junction of the MBW's Great Eastern Street with OLD STREET. Between Rivington Street and Old Street, indifferent Neo-Georgian offices of the late 1980s incorporating the former Congregational Tabernacle, which faces CHAPEL PLACE off Old Street. Three-bay pedimented centre, stucco-trimmed, of *c.* 1840. Further E in Old Street, the former Town Hall and the Magistrates Court (*see* Public Buildings, above).

## 2. North of Old Street: Hoxton

Hoxton, an old hamlet, became a fashionable area in the late C17, when new squares of brick houses were laid out N of Old Street. During the C18, market gardens further N disappeared as development spread up Hoxton Street and, in the early C19, along New North Road. Only a few traces of this period remain. Industry and crowded working-class housing took over; the latter is now almost entirely replaced by C20 flats.

OLD STREET lost much of its character through widening of its W parts in 1872–7, but it narrows E of Coronet Street, and here, amidst tall commercial premises, there remain a few battered, much-altered buildings of C18 and early C19 domestic origin: Nos. 340–342 (S), with mansard roof, and Nos. 323 and 325–329 (N). To their N is HOXTON SQUARE, which was laid out shortly after 1683. The square itself (relandscaped in 1995) is still pleasantly spacious, with some of the buildings set back behind what were once front gardens. An impression of its original character can be gained from No. 32 on the E side, whose two-storey red brick frontage is a re-creation of a late C17 house. The N side is dominated by the C19 St Monica's R.C. Church and its attendant buildings (q.v.). By the mid C19 the residential character of the square had been replaced by furniture workshops. On the W side, No. 8, and No. 9 dated 1897, have workshop windows extending full width between the party walls. The quirky Gothic No. 10, with angular oriel, was built as a vicarage in the 1870s, probably by *R. W. Drew*, the architect of St Peter's, which stood at the NW corner. The newcomer near the S end is by *Maccreanor Lavington Architects*, 1997; gallery and cinema behind a bold grid of squares. In the lane to the SW, No. 56, C18, with later bowed shopfront.

From Hoxton Square W, CORONET STREET, a narrow cobbled lane with C19 workshops, leads into HOXTON MARKET, another square whose character was re-established by new buildings and conversions of the 1990s. On the E side, the former Christian Mission (Shaftesbury House), with a tall rear façade of 1913 added to an earlier building; well-detailed Neo-Georgian, the windows freely grouped. On the N side, THE CIRCUS SPACE is a former electricity generating station, part of a large complex of late C19 municipal buildings around Pitfield Street (*see* p. 520). The flattened W side was filled in 1995 by plain yellow brick student lodgings, ALEXANDER FLEMING HALLS. S side rebuilt 1997–8. In the square, a SCULPTURE, Juggling Figure, by *Simon Stringer*, 1994. Further W, CHARLES SQUARE, mostly post-war flats. The early character is represented by one good survival, No. 16, quite an ambitious house of *c.* 1725, five bays and three storeys, formerly with lower wings. Red brick, with the middle bay a little projected. Brick cornice above the first floor, stone keystones, doorway with fine carving.

PITFIELD STREET leads N with a few early C19 houses (Nos. 8–10, 17–21), and the HOP POLE pub, with green glazed ground floor and bold cornice lettering of *c.* 1900. Further N, past the Library and former Haberdashers' Almshouses, later City and East London College (qq.v.), No. 55, the former Varieties Picture Palace of 1914–15, with light-hearted classical detail, then the GEORGE AND VULTURE, with tall striped gable, *c.* 1900, at the corner of HABERDASHER STREET. This was rebuilt around the same time with artisan flats of an interesting design: red brick three-storeyed terraces enlivened by shallow bay windows and circular windows at the tops of the staircases. Unusually long back extensions with roof gardens to the upper flats. They keep in scale with the modest early C19 development of the HABERDASHERS' ESTATE around the former Almshouses. Terraces of *c.* 1823–30 remain in BUTTESLAND STREET and CHART STREET.

While the Haberdashers' Estate kept its residential character, the STURT ESTATE to its s and e was rebuilt with warehouses from the 1890s. The most interesting of these are by *Ernest Newton*, whose father was agent to the estate: Nos. 10 and 12 BACHES STREET, 1891, and the N side of CORSHAM STREET, where Nos. 18–24 of 1899 are an especially lively design. Stock brick is mixed with blue brick trim and stone keystones, arched windows alternate with segment-headed loading doors, with taller entrance bays at the ends. Nos. 25–33 are similar, built slightly later; they face another good group (not by Newton). In EAST ROAD the long five-storey warehouse on the w side (Nos. 49–69) is of 1901–8, by *Ernest Newton* with *Arthur Keen* (a fellow pupil from Norman Shaw's office), also carefully detailed, but in a more Neo-Georgian manner: channelled brick quoins; dentilled cornice. At the s end, SILBURY STREET, a cobbled passage, leads to VESTRY STREET, where Nos. 2–18 continue the Newton–Keen scheme. Vestry Street was cut through slums in the 1890s by Shoreditch Vestry. The improvements included the now demolished model dwellings nearby in Nile Street, of 1896–7 by *Rowland Plumbe*, some of the earliest local authority housing.

HOXTON STREET, running N from Old Street, is the centre of the former hamlet of Hoxton. It remains intimate, with a street market towards the N end, and a few remarkable C18 and C19 survivals. Domestic rebuilding of the 1970s onwards is indifferent but not out of scale. The principal contribution of the 1990s is the Shoreditch Community College (q.v.) on the e side, substantial but not unpleasantly dominant, its pale brick masses enlivened by decorative gates and successfully broken up by short wings. A PUBLIC LIBRARY facing the street, also with lively iron grille, is part of the same complex. All by *Hampshire County Architects* and *Perkins Ogden Architects*, 1992–7; ironwork by *Matthew Fedden*. Nos. 124–126 on the e side, hidden behind built-out shops, are good three-storey houses of *c.* 1725–30 (original fittings, especially well preserved in No. 126). HOXTON HALL (No. 130a) is hidden behind a former shop, but has pilasters and pediment to WILKS PLACE. Built in 1863 as a music hall, an early example of the type, with an additional storey and other alterations in 1867 as McDonalds Music Hall. Tall narrow hall with small stage and two tiers of balconies on three sides, supported on iron columns. Acquired in 1879 by a temperance group and in 1893 by the Quaker Bedford Institute. Community rooms added to the rear in 1910 by *Lovegrove*

*& Papworth.* Opposite, on the w side, Nos. 173 and 175, survivors from a group built after 1767; the last part of Hoxton Street to be built up. On the E side a public GARDEN of 1983 whose special feature is a cupola brought from the C19 Homerton Hospital (now demolished). Further N, No. 237, probably *c.* 1700, of five bays; windows with thick glazing bars and a canopied and bracketed doorcase concealed behind shops. Upper part rewindowed in the mid C18.

C20 slum clearance around Hoxton Street obliterated the dense poverty-stricken streets of the C19; only some of the institutional buildings and the big churches remain. On the E side, incorporated in 1990s housing, St Leonard's POOR RELIEF OFFICES, 1863, two storeys with central pediment; two further floors were added later. The grim workhouse buildings behind, later part of St Leonard's Hospital, were partly demolished in 1993. Among the council flats, the most noteworthy is the *LCC*'s largest enterprise in Shoreditch, the WHITMORE ESTATE between Hoxton Street and Kingsland Road. The original sixteen blocks of 1924–37 are arranged loosely and quite spaciously in three-sided courts opening off the side streets; decent Neo-Georgian detail, with steep tiled roofs. Post-war additions along Hoxton Street.

## 3. Haggerston

Haggerston was another hamlet. Today it is the area E of Kingsland Road straddling the Regent's Canal. As in Hoxton, the southern parts are mostly C20 and only a few older relics remain. The area N of the canal was built up in the first half of the C19, like the adjacent Hackney streets to the N (*see* Hackney, Perambulation 5).

The s end of KINGSLAND ROAD continues the character of Shoreditch High Street: mixed domestic and industrial, with some quite showy frontages of the late C19 to early C20. Note especially Nos. 41–49 (w side), Goddard & Gibbs's glass studios, three storeys; appropriately, all glass windows to the ground and first floors, divided by double-height fluted stucco pilasters. In Kingsland Road directly N of the Geffrye Museum (q.v.), a late C19 four-storey building, formerly stables for London Tramways horses. Much altered (but see the small windows at the back). Front originally with arcaded ground floor and cobbled ramps between the floors. Round the corner to the N, in PEARSON STREET, Nos. 2–16, a nice terrace of the second quarter of the C19; arched doorways with fluted quarter-columns and fanlights.

E of Geffrye Street, DUNLOE STREET leads to St Chad (q.v.). The big Brooks church once towered above Tudor villas of 1841 in Nichols Square, all swept away in comprehensive 1960s rebuilding by Shoreditch Borough Council. Low housing in a different form has been reintroduced by housing association groups of 1993 N of Dunloe Street; their yellow brick and deep eaves group nicely with the taller red brick gable of the church and the vicarage to the s. The landmarks of the 1960s rebuilding are two towers of FELLOWS COURT. Both have tapering piers and partly open ground floors in an effort to add some Corbusian panache. Hardly a success. The N one forms an overpowering w side to a bleak pedestrian shopping square at the N end of Weymouth Terrace. The bright spot here is the former LIBRARY AND COMMUNITY CENTRE, a colourful little building: orange mosaic-clad columns and blue and white tile panels above. Indifferent surrounding housing of three to six storeys, red brick, with pitched roofs added in the 1990s; more rewarding is *Goldfinger's* big Haggerston School E of Weymouth Terrace (q.v.). Further E, beyond Queensbridge Road, a scrappy area around the new HAGGERSTON PARK with a city farm. On its W side, the former St Augustine (q.v.), and in Dunloe Street, the MOTHER KATE HOMES of 1939 (Sisters of St Margaret), attached to the rebuilt St Saviour's Priory. Simple red brick vernacular, two storeys; E wing with blue brick ground floor; a small tower with sculpture of Crucifixion.

E of the park, GOLDSMITH'S ROW. On the E side and in GOLDSMITH'S SQUARE, two blocks of attractive working-class housing of 1894–5. Very early *LCC* work, built for some of the population cleared from Old Nichol, the slum area replaced by the Boundary Street Estate (Bethnal Green, Tower Hamlets: *see London 5: East*). The Housing Branch team included *C. C. Winmill*, who was possibly responsible for the design. An ingenious mixture of flats and houses, in two-storey blocks with mansards. Restrained polychromy: striped brick gable walls in red and yellow, purple-brown brick panels around the entrances. The poor interwar LCC blocks nearby are a sad comedown.

Finally the N side of HACKNEY ROAD, E–W. (The S side is in Bethnal Green, Tower Hamlets; *see London 5: East*.) Flanking the junction with Queensbridge Road, Nos. 237–241, plain four-storey early C19 terraces. Nos. 229–231 have little *Coade* stone heads to the arches over the first-floor windows. Further W the scene is scrappier in every sense. Next to a former burial ground, YE OLDE AXE, with tiled pub front, fruity swags and corner turrets. Stretching through to Kingsland Road, PERSEVERANCE WORKS, a cluster of C19 industrial buildings sensitively restored in the 1980s as offices and workshops.

### 4. *New North Road and the area to its west*

The NW corner of Shoreditch, like the adjacent parts of Islington, was built up in the earlier C19, but later rebuilding has left only pockets of interest. From the N end of Pitfield Street, NEW NORTH ROAD begins, with St John's Church (q.v.) on the E side, and a fragment of typical early C19 ribbon development on the W (Nos. 31–41). Nos. 27–29, 1903 by *S. N. Cranfield*, was built as Shoreditch Constitutional Club, rather grand, of red brick with terracotta trim. Opposite the church, ST LEONARD'S DWELLINGS, 1919–21 by the Shoreditch Borough Surveyor, *T. C. Hustler*.

Further N extensive clearance took place after the Second World War. Off the E side, in RUSHTON STREET, doctors' surgeries by *Penoyre & Prasad*, 1994–5. Further N, SHOREDITCH PARK, a post-war creation and still rather bleak, is overlooked by a tall Board school and by a gaunt and towering former POWER STATION in POOLE STREET. This was built for the Great Northern and City Railway, 1901, probably by *Sir Douglas Fox & Partners*. A steel frame clad in plain brickwork, formerly with a dominant chimney.

The station was intended to serve the Underground line between Finsbury Park and Moorgate, but it was closed in 1914 and converted to film studios in 1919. Early Hitchcock films produced by Gainsborough Pictures were among its productions.

The area w of New North Road was one of the borough's early post-Second-World-War redevelopment schemes; housing was planned together with school, community centre and library. The first block, LINALE HOUSE, was completed in 1949. Much of the area consists of the WENLOCK BARN ESTATE, with balcony-access flats up to seven storeys high, arranged in a loose grid plan which fails to give the area a distinctive identity. The later SHEPHERD MARKET ESTATE further w displays the 1970s shift to homelier low brown brick terraces. It extends as far as SHEPHERDESS WALK, where the tide turned, and the w side escaped the general clearance. Near the s end, an early C19 group: Nos. 1–5, and the William IV pub. Then Nos. 9–67, a long part-stuccoed two-storey terrace of the mid C19, preserved after a public enquiry in 1976. A taller early C19 terrace to the N (Nos. 87–131). In MICAWBER STREET, some more houses of this date, much repaired. Between Shepherdess Walk and Wenlock Road, WINDSOR HOUSE, 1926–7 by *E. E. Finch*, City Engineer, to house those displaced from the City by slum clearance in the Minories. Planned around a garden.

In the hinterland of the canal and its basins, industrial buildings take over. The best are along WHARF ROAD, between Wenlock Basin and City Road Basin. Nos. 44–48, early C20, were printing works; quite domestic-looking. Ground and first floor under brick arches; an internal courtyard. Opposite (on the Islington side of Wharf Road), PICKFORD WHARF and GRAND JUNCTION WHARF, with housing of *c.* 1990, arranged around two lozenge-shaped squares opening on to the City Basin. Interestingly varied heights, exploiting the views over the water. The groups build up to four-storey tower-like pavilions along Wharf Road, with asymmetrical balconies and cut-away corners on the side towards the basin.

# STOKE NEWINGTON

## INTRODUCTION

As Pevsner commented in 1951, Stoke Newington still does not seem entirely part of London. There lingers round the timber spire of the old church something of a village atmosphere, and the winding New River, with its two large reservoir ponds, and Clissold Park still maintain an illusion of parkland and open country. The population of the borough by 1951 was only 49,000; in 1820 it was 2,000. This is the time when Edgar Allan Poe lived at Stoke Newington, which he later described as 'a misty looking village of England' with 'gigantic and gnarled trees . . . deeply shadowed avenues . . . and a thousand shrubberies'. Shirley Hibberd, the nature writer, in 1864 still praises the nightingales and other wild birds of Stoke Newington, but adds that 'all around the builders are drawing a close cordon of bricks'. Population figures bear this out. The big jump was between 1870 and 1880 (1851: 6,100; 1861: 11,300; 1871: 17,500; 1881: 37,500; 1891: 47,800).

In the early C19 the village was chiefly a few large mansions and a row of houses along Stoke Newington Church Street, with some extension N and s on the High Street, and another small nucleus at Newington Green on the border with Islington. Defoe also, while he lived at Stoke Newington from 1709 to 1729, had his quarters at Church Street. The parish had a strong Nonconformist bias at this time. Isaac Watts lived here, wealthy Quaker families had houses in Stoke Newington, and the Newington Green Chapel was built as early as 1708.

The area between the Green and Church Street filled up from the 1830s, when Thomas Cubitt began to build stuccoed terraces and villas around Albion Road. The new church for this growing population in the s of the parish was *Butterfield*'s St Matthias, which became famous as one of London's principal centres of High Church ritual. It was built through the patronage of a Newington Green resident, Robert Brett (1808–74), later to be active in the Haggerston Church Scheme (*see* Shoreditch). A stately new mid-C19 church rose up too in the village centre beside the old church, while the N of the parish, developed with respectable middle-class housing from the 1860s, also received its quota of substantial churches of the later C19, now struggling to survive in changing social conditions.*

As with much of inner London, the status of Stoke Newington declined in the C20 as later suburbs spread into the countryside beyond. The larger houses nearly all disappeared. Church Street became the municipal centre and lost its select character; council housing encroached on the Victorian areas to the N, while the poorer and more crowded southern parts were drastically changed through a combination of slum clearance and war damage. But Stoke Newington has on the whole been fortunate: the Borough Council housing of between the wars was designed with care, the LCC's

---

* Demolished: St Faith, Londesborough Road, by *Burges*, 1872–3, and *Brooks*, 1881, destroyed in World War II; St John, Queen's Drive, by *F. Wallen*, 1869–78, demolished 1989–90.

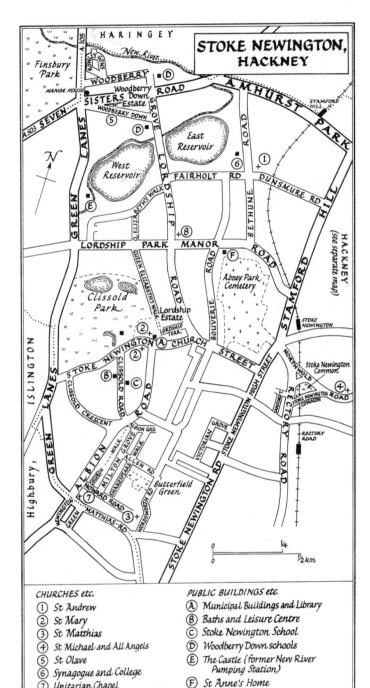

# STOKE NEWINGTON, HACKNEY

HARINGEY

Finsbury Park

MANOR HOUSE

New River

WOODBERRY

ROYAL GDNS.

A.105

SEVEN

A.503

SISTERS

Woodberry Down Estate

Woodberry Down

LANES

GREEN

WEST Reservoir

East Reservoir

AMHURST PARK

STAMFORD HILL

GROVE ROAD

LORDSHIP ROAD

FAIRHOLT RD

DUNSMURE RD

BETHUNE ROAD

STAMFORD HILL

HACKNEY (see separate map)

Q. ELIZABETH'S WALK

LORDSHIP PARK MANOR ROAD

Clissold Park

QUEEN ELIZABETH'S WALK

Lordship Estate

Lordship TERR.

STOKE NEWINGTON

ISLINGTON

Abney Park Cemetery

BOUVERIE ROAD

STOKE NEWINGTON

CHURCH STREET

STOKE NEWINGTON HIGH STREET

STOKE NEWINGTON

NORTHWOLD COMMON

Stoke Newington Common

STOKE NEWINGTON ROAD

CLISSOLD CRESCENT

STOKE NEWINGTON RD

CLISSOLD ROAD

ALBION ROAD

ALBION GRO.

MILTON GROVE

SHAKESPEARE WALK

ALLEN RD

CHURCH WALK

VICTORIAN GROVE

Butterfield Green

RECTORY ROAD

SANDFORD

RECTORY ROAD

Highbury, GREEN LANES

NEWINGTON GREEN

HOWARD ROAD

WORDSWORTH RD

MATTHIAS RD.

0       ¼
0                ½ km

CHURCHES etc.
1. St Andrew
2. St Mary
3. St Matthias
4. St Michael and All Angels
5. St Olave
6. Synagogue and College
7. Unitarian Chapel
8. United Reformed Church

PUBLIC BUILDINGS etc.
A. Municipal Buildings and Library
B. Baths and Leisure Centre
C. Stoke Newington School
D. Woodberry Down schools
E. The Castle (former New River Pumping Station)
F. St Anne's Home

Woodberry Down Estate of the 1940s is not without distinction, and there has been less wholescale post-war rebuilding here than in other parts of the present Borough of Hackney.

ARCHAEOLOGY. There was an important Paleolithic site at Stoke Newington, with flint working and possibly part of a woven shelter, but little later prehistoric evidence.

## RELIGIOUS BUILDINGS

### *1. Church of England*

ST ANDREW, Bethune Road. 1883–4 by *A. W. Blomfield*. Ragstone rubble, Dec; long nave with small transepts and spirelet. A tall, stately interior with stone quatrefoil piers, clerestory and plastered walls, unlike Blomfield's early brick churches. Notable for the coherent decorative scheme by *Heaton, Butler & Bayne*, which includes both STAINED GLASS, with standing figures (the S windows lost in the Second World War), and WALL PAINTING: in the nave, scenes from the life of Christ, pale and delicate beneath canopies, painted directly on to the walls, in the chancel a reredos with Crucifixion and evangelists, painted on canvas. W window by *Burlison & Grylls*, c. 1915–20, three pairs with saints. E window 1951 by *William Wilson*; stylized figures, hard colours not in harmony with the earlier decoration. Good iron SCREENS to chancel and baptistery, the latter made in 1921 in the SW corner. Alabaster FONT of 1884. Good *Willis* ORGAN.

ST MARY, Stoke Newington Church Street. The contrast between the Old Church on the edge of Clissold Park and the New Church across the road is impressive, one still the church of an English village, the other with the ambitions of a rising London suburb. The OLD CHURCH is a small homely building of brick, whose rendered W tower and wooden spire only just rise above the trees. The medieval church was rebuilt in 1563 – an unusual time for church building – by the Lord of the Manor, William Patten (date over the doorway), who added the W tower, S porch, S aisle and SE vestry. It was tactfully and economically repaired and enlarged in 1827–9 by *Sir Charles Barry*, who agreed to preserve its 'village-church like appearance'. The spire dates from 1829 (rebuilt c. 1930) The N side, rebuilt and extended in the C18 and C19, was reconstructed after war damage in 1940 without its outer N aisle, with a new NE vestry. The galleries were removed at this time. Inside, the C16 S aisle has low polygonal brick piers and four-centred chamfered brick arches. Odd blank recesses in the aisle S and W walls. Even odder is the way in which short cross-walls connect the older porch with the new outer S wall. This outer porch has a late C16 plaster vault. The windows of 1563 are still entirely in the Gothic tradition. Barry added the tracery spandrels in the clerestory. FURNISHINGS largely by Barry, including the good COMMUNION TABLE, RAILINGS, REREDOS (painted later) and PULPIT. Plain BOX PEWS, perhaps older, and reworked by Barry. STAINED GLASS. Post-war windows by *H. Vernon Spreadbury*, 1949. C16 fragments incorporated in the E window. MONUMENTS. John Dudley †1580. Standing wall monument with the usual kneeling figures facing each other. Joseph Hurlock

†1793 and wife. By *Thomas Banks*. Standing woman bent over a large urn, the detail very restrained.

The NEW CHURCH, also ST MARY, is by *Sir G. G. Scott*, 1854–8, on the site of the old rectory. The w tower with its spire, completed in 1890 by *J. Oldrid Scott*, makes a fine landmark, even if the big building is wholly insensitive to the pre-Victorian *genius loci*. Cruciform, of rubble stone, sizeable and competent. A Dec hall church with gabled aisles; tall arcades on columns with lushly naturalistic capitals. The chancel richer still, with angels around the arch soffits. Repaired by *N. F. Cachemaille-Day* after war damage; reopened 1957. REREDOS, *c.* 1908. Two large mosaic panels survive. Elaborately carved FONT by *R. Westmacott*; PULPIT in Italian Gothic style with busts in roundels and lozenges. STAINED GLASS all post-war: apse windows by *Francis Skeat*, 1957–8, traditional; N transept by *W. Carter Shapland*, 1960, striking panels in hard, bright colours. MONUMENTS. Several decorative early C20 wall monuments: David King Foster †1901, alabaster and mosaic; Harriet Sidney †1903, mosaic.

VICARAGE to the s, also by *G. G. Scott*. A robust gabled house on its own, with angular oriel above a Gothic door. Between it and the vestry room by *Oldrid Scott*, parish rooms planned 1995, by *Rebecca Cadie & Gordon Fleming*.

ST MATTHIAS, Matthias Road, facing Howard Road. Spearhead of the High Church campaign in Hackney and Stoke Newington, led by Robert Brett, a resident of Newington Green. By *William Butterfield*, 1849–53; one of his most remarkable designs. A towering w front with steep-pitched gable above low aisles and behind the gable the steep saddleback roof of a tall E tower over the chancel, a Butterfieldian innovation imported from Normandy. The central buttress dividing the large w window is derived from Dorchester Abbey, Oxon. The whole is of plain stock brick and harsh in all the details. The interior was unfortunately severely damaged in the Second World War and the notable Victorian fittings destroyed. The arcades remain, with richly moulded arches on quatrefoil piers; tall clerestory with traceried windows of three pointed lights. The post-war repairs, completed in 1954, introduced a plain timber roof in place of Butterfield's red brick and stone chancel vault, whitewashed walls, and a new w organ gallery. The sanctuary was closed off. The new fittings are dignified, although not in a Butterfieldian spirit. Post-war BAPTISTERY WALL PAINTING; bright STAINED GLASS in the E window by *A. F. Erridge*.

ST MICHAEL AND ALL ANGELS, Stoke Newington Common. 1883–5 by *J. E. K. Cutts*; his usual long red brick basilica with big slate roof. Small w porch in place of an intended w tower and spire. Brick arcades with plastered walls, plate tracery clerestory, large Dec E window. w end divided off by *Dennis Sexton*, 1972; plans for the E end under discussion at the time of writing. Good marble FONT and octagonal stone-traceried PULPIT of the 1880s. STAINED GLASS. By *Heaton, Butler & Bayne*: E window 1899, with outer lights of 1910. Nine N and one s aisle lancets, 1889; SE window †1884, naive Pre-Raphaelite style. VICARAGE to N, 1885.

ST OLAVE, Woodberry Down. 1893, a late work by *Ewan Christian*. Built from the proceeds of the sale of the City church of St Olave, Old Jewry (demolished *c.* 1891). Red brick inside and out, and agreeably spacious. An exceptionally broad nave, with flanking arches to the chancel arch, narrow passage aisles, and a nobly proportioned apse. Reordered 1994–5, with the nave cleared for multi-purpose use. Fine late C17 FONT, FONT COVER and PULPIT from the City church. The font is a small bowl decorated with cherubs' heads, on a polygonal stone baluster. Its pretty cover has eight volutes with cherubs' heads around a dove with an olive branch. The hexagonal pulpit, now without a base, has raised panels with foliage festoons. STAINED GLASS: much, and collectively quite impressive: apse window 1893 and 1897 by *Powell*, s transept E, 1897. Other windows 1903–17.

## 2. Roman Catholic and other places of worship

Apart from the Unitarian Chapel (*see* below), little remains from Stoke Newington's strong early Nonconformist tradition. The Friends Meeting House in Yoakley Road, 1828 by *William Alderson*, has been demolished, although the cemetery remains. The reconstruction of ABNEY CONGREGATIONAL CHURCH in Stoke Newington Church Street (1838, altered 1862, gutted in the Second World War) retained only parts of the walls. Surviving in other use is a mid-C19 former chapel, Bouverie Road, with pediment on four stuccoed pilasters, a late C19 chapel at the w end of Northwold Road, polygonal, Gothic, and another in Albion Grove, Gothic, converted to housing in 1993.

BAPTIST CHURCH, Wordsworth Road. 1894.

OUR LADY OF GOOD COUNSEL (R.C.), Bouverie Road. 1936 by *T. H. & T. G. B. Scott*. Plain red brick Romanesque, with low octagonal crossing tower. Plastered inside, but the crossing is of bare brick.

SYNAGOGUE and TALMUDICAL COLLEGE, No. 99 Bethune Road. 1967–8 by *Associated Design Partners* for the Union of Orthodox Hebrew Congregations, established in this area from 1926. A fortress-like block, of grey brick and concrete, with narrow upper windows and a taller four-storey wing at the back.

SYNAGOGUE, Lampard Grove. 1928 by *George Coles*. Brick, classical.

UNITARIAN CHAPEL, Newington Green. Built in 1708 by Edward Harrison, goldsmith, for a congregation established in 1682. Enlarged 1860. C19 cemented three-bay front with two large round-headed windows, Tuscan pilasters and a large pediment. Old views show that the original façade had a small pediment against a big hipped roof, with central oval window below. Apse of 1860, with pulpit. MONUMENTS to several notable Nonconformists: Dr Richard Price †1791; Anna Barbauld, Samuel Rogers and family.

UNITED REFORMED CHURCH (formerly Presbyterian), Manor Road. By *Peter F. Smith (Ferguson, Smith & Associates)*, 1969. Red brick, deliberately modest and practical (*see also* Perambulation 4). Cheerful blue-clad housing on the rest of the site of the previous church.

## 3. Cemetery

ABNEY PARK CEMETERY. Opened in 1840, one of the new hygienic metropolitan burial grounds, contemporary with Kensal

Green, Norwood and Brompton cemeteries, but, unlike them, non-denominational. George Collison, son of a Hackney Congregational minister, was a prime mover in its establishment. Buildings and landscaping are by *William Hosking*, Professor at King's College. The cemetery occupies the grounds of Abney House and Fleetwood House (*see* Perambulation 1), where Isaac Watts (†1748) had been a frequent visitor. The entrance from the s is through the fine wrought-iron gates of 1701 that originally belonged to Abney House, into Dr Watts Walk, a straight avenue leading to the chapel. The remarkable main entrance facing the High Street is in a different spirit: it has gates and lodges in the 52 Egyptian style, a thing which irritated Pugin no end. The hieroglyphics, which signify 'the gates of the Abode of the Mortal Part of Man' were provided by *Joseph Bonomi Jun*. From here, picturesque winding paths diverge to lead around the perimeter and towards the tall brick Gothic CHAPEL. It is on a Greek cross plan with a deep open s porch. Tracery rose windows and spire.

The planting of the cemetery, praised by Loudun as early as 1843, was conceived as an arboretum; trees and shrubs, supplied by the local nursery of George Loddiges, were all labelled. The Abney Park Cemetery Trust, founded after the cemetery company went bankrupt in 1972, preserves the N and W part of the grounds as a wild-life area: along the winding paths, tombs recede romantically into thickets of ivy. In the s part, where the monuments cluster more thickly, the undergrowth is kept at bay. Much-needed refurbishment of the buildings began with the lodges, by *Brady Mallalieu Architects*, 1992.

MONUMENTS. The most notable are in Dr Watts Walk. The one to Isaac Watts is by *E. H. Baily*, 1845. Among many others: bold Baroque sarcophagus on lion's paws erected *c.* 1854 to the son of *John Jay*, the cemetery's building contractor and mason, probably to his own design. – Samuel Robinson †1833, architect and surveyor. Gothic chest tomb, brought from the Retreat Almshouses, which he founded. – Nathaniel Rogers †1864, classical mausoleum, the only one in the cemetery. – Elizabeth Tollady †1855. White marble angel, well carved. – Agnes Forsyth †1864, with roundel carved by her father, the sculptor *James Forsyth*. – Henry Richards †1888, tall arcaded tomb-chest with portrait medallion. – On chapel lawn: John Spreat †1865, Gothic tower-like monument by *Waterhouse*, carved by *Farmer & Brindley*. NW of chapel lawn: Harriet Delph †1944, kneeling figure in Arts and Crafts tradition.

In the NE corner of the cemetery, 'Dr Watts' mound', formerly with a chestnut tree, traditionally his favourite retreat.

## PUBLIC BUILDINGS

MUNICIPAL BUILDINGS, Stoke Newington Church Street. 1935–7 by *Reginald Truelove*. Built as the Town Hall and Assembly Hall, on the site of an early C18 terrace which had replaced the Manor House. The council had previously occupied a vestry hall in Milton Grove. A spreading convex composition making use of a bend of the street; brick with much Portland stone, unaffected by the modern movement. Main entrance in a recessed centre, with two giant columns *in antis* and an awkward attic floor; assembly room to the E with four columns *in antis*. Inside, a grand imperial stair with iron and bronze balustrade leads to the first-floor council chamber. This has square panelled piers with gilded capitals. Its plaster dome survives above a crudely inserted suspended ceiling. Mayor's parlour and committee rooms along the front, with handsome panelled folding doors.

LIBRARY, Stoke Newington Church Street. 1892 by *Bridgman & Goss*, an early example of a borough library. Brick and stone, a gable at each end. Extended at the rear in 1904 to provide children's library and lecture hall. War Memorial entrance hall to the E added by *A. D. Porri*, 1923. This has a restrained 1920s-Baroque stone front, and a dignified stone-faced interior to the Memorial Hall, with good iron doors. Bust of Defoe (a local resident) by *Frank Ransome*, from a model by *Frampton*.

BRANCH LIBRARIES. BROWNSWOOD ROAD, 1960–2, decent single-storeyed building of stock brick. WOODBERRY DOWN, 1955 by *Gold & Aldridge*, extended *c.* 1961; part of the Woodberry Down Estate; *see* Perambulation 4.

LEISURE CENTRE, Clissold Road. By *Hodder Associates*, 1998. Steel framed, toplit, with glazed wings. It replaces baths by *Hobden & Porri*, 1930, which had an interesting arched concrete roof and a 1920s memorial hall.

STOKE NEWINGTON SCHOOL, Clissold Road. Forceful buildings of 1967–70 by *Stillman & Eastwick-Field* (*R. Smorczewski, D. McCoy, M. Plunkett*). Varied grouping of three-storey buildings around small courts; tough textured concrete surfaces and brick. The concrete is well detailed but overpowering. At the N end, a transparent boiler house, a cliché by this time but effective nonetheless.

WOODBERRY DOWN SCHOOLS, built by the *LCC* as part of the Woodberry Down Estate soon after the Second World War (*see* Perambulation 4, below). They reflect the idealism of the post-war years, before school building became a routine exercise. JUNIOR AND INFANTS, N end of Woodberry Grove, 1949–50. Quiet two-storey yellow brick group with pitched roofs, matching the Scandinavian mood of the neighbouring flats, looking out over the New River. Entrance court with sculpture. (Staircase mural in cement and plaster by *Augustus Lunn*.) SECONDARY SCHOOL, Woodberry Grove, S of Seven Sisters Road. Planned in 1949 as the first purpose-built London comprehensive; built 1950–5. Disused because of subsidence. Reticent four-storey classroom blocks, concrete-framed with brick infill, loosely ranged around a courtyard, enlivened by glazed stair-towers. The assembly hall has a latticed steel roof and a reinforced concrete gallery supported on a star beam resting on three columns (engineer *Frank Newby*). Several works of art acquired from the Festival of Britain (1951) were incorporated (since removed; painting by *Carel Weight*; wooden panels of ships by *Anthony Gilbert* and *H. J. E. Smith*; shell fountain by *C. W. Lewis*.)

BOARD SCHOOLS look very tall in relation to neighbouring two-storey Victorian housing. A good example in OLDFIELD ROAD, 1881–2, additions 1899, asymmetrical with prominent gables.

CLISSOLD PARK. Opened as a public park in 1889, rescued from building after the estate was sold. A flat area with plenty of trees, the lakes in the N part made from Hackney Brook. CLISSOLD HOUSE is near the S end, looking W across a stretch of the New River. It is named after Augustus Clissold, a C19 resident. This substantial Neoclassical villa, formerly Newington Park House, was built for Jonathan Hoare, a member of the well-known Quaker family, probably c. 1790, after he had acquired land in the area. The house appears on a print of 1793. Hoare was in financial difficulties by the late 1790s, and mortgaged the property in 1798.

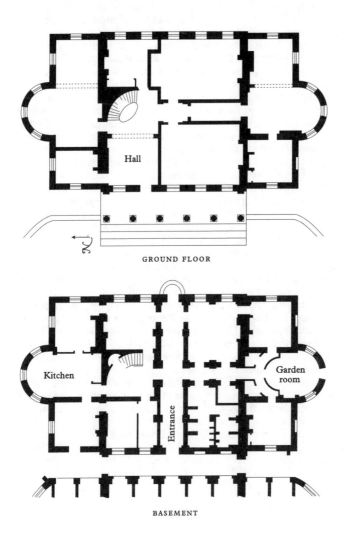

Clissold House. Plans

The C19 attribution of the house to his nephew Joseph Woods seems unlikely, as Woods was born only in 1776.

The five-bay centre is dominated by a severe one-storey colonnade of fluted Greek Doric columns, approached by a ramped forecourt which hides the basement and gives the house an elevated position. The rest is unassuming, but solidly built and elegantly finished: brick walls, moulded stone stringcourses, balustraded cornice hiding a flat roof, originally of copper. Lower one-bay wings, slightly set back, with a bow to N and S. Compact, slightly eccentric Neoclassical plan (partly altered when the house was converted to flats and café). The colonnade disguises the unusual asymmetry of the original entrance, formerly in the second bay from the l. Behind the entrance hall a toplit stair rises from the basement to the first floor against a semicircular wall. Four main reception rooms, those in the N and S wings each with a large bow. The basement has service rooms and stores, discreetly entered from beneath the colonnade, but also has a polite approach from the rear, where this floor is at ground level. From this entrance a groin-vaulted corridor provides access to the staircase. The kitchen and a former service stair were in the NW corner. Facing S, within the projecting bow, is a curious oval garden room, entered from outside; a curved corridor behind leads to corner rooms.

WATERWORKS, Green Lanes. Since 1946 the S termination of the NEW RIVER, which originally continued S to the New River Head in Finsbury (q.v.). E of Green Lanes are the two reservoirs built by *W. C. Mylne* in 1829–33, to the W were filter beds of 1856 (emptied *c.* 1990). Next to the W reservoir, THE CASTLE (converted to an indoor climbing centre in 1995). This is the PUMPING STATION of 1854–6, an amazing Scottish-baronial folly, designed for Mylne by *Robert Billings*, who exhibited drawings for it in 1856 at the Society of British Artists. The variety of motifs and outline is beyond belief. The chimney is a tall polygonal castle tower. In addition a big round angle tower for the standpipe, with a square top stage set diagonally, and at the opposite angle a stair-turret with a conical top. The keep itself is buttressed and has Gothic windows and a large monogram with Mylne's initials. The beam engines were removed in 1953; they were in a row inside, with flywheels tucked into the buttresses.

Contemporary ancillary building with crowstepped gable. PRIMARY FILTER HOUSE, 1936, Georgian-modern, the central hall entirely for show. GAS HOUSE, Lordship Road, earlier C19, four bays, one storey. N of the E reservoir, IVY HOUSE SLUICE, Newnton Close, across the New River. Mid-C19, small square building with manually operated sluice gate.

STOKE NEWINGTON STATION, Stamford Hill. 1974–5 by *E. J. Fletcher* of British Rail Eastern Region. Cheerful glass box, colourful inside.

## PERAMBULATIONS

*1. Stoke Newington Church Street*

The centre of the old village is still recalled by Church Street's informal character and scatter of older houses, although the big mansions which stood in their own grounds on the N side have all gone. The Manor House, which lay close to the church, on the site of the municipal buildings, disappeared already in the C18. A little further E stood the late C17 Abney House, built by Thomas Gunston in 1678, named after its early C18 owner Sir Thomas Abney, Lord Mayor, and demolished 1843, and Fleetwood House, of early C17 origin, demolished in 1872. Abney Park Cemetery (q.v.) occupies their grounds. Smaller C18 houses were built along the S side, and here examples of the changing style in terrace houses of the C18–C19 can still be spotted. Many retain good panelled rooms and staircases.

From E to W, first No. 11, early C18. Then Nos. 81–87, built 1733–5; exuberant eared doorcases with carved friezes. Nos. 89–93, of 1792–3, typical of the greater restraint of the 1790s; nice Doric porches to Nos. 89 and 91. Nos. 109–111 was built as a single house c. 1700; above the later shopfront is a projecting centre with rubbed brickwork. No. 129 is decent C19, with end pilasters and cornice. On the N side, at the corner with Lordship Road, the MAGPIE AND STUMP, early C20, with a forceful cranked gable, and original ground- and first-floor interiors. Behind is a stuccoed early C19 house with a N-facing bow, and the former parish lock-up. Then, set back from the S side of Church Street, recently restored, Nos. 135–137, of 1769. Two adjoining houses: the first has a five-bay N front with Doric porch; its neighbour faces the other way. Further on, opposite the library (*see* Public Buildings, above), Nos. 169–175, built by a local bricklayer, *Edward Newens*; No. 171 dated 1714, No. 173 much rebuilt but with original fittings inside. These two are each of three bays and three storeys; straight-headed windows, with the early C18 feature of a narrow blind window next to the central party wall. Gatepiers with urns. The outer houses were originally adjuncts, each with kitchen and coach-house. Nos. 179–183 of similar date, but much disguised by later alterations.

After the big C19 church and vicarage (q.v.), Nos. 207–223, a tall, urban stucco-trimmed quadrant of c. 1850–60, facing Clissold Park (rehabilitated in 1996 by *Pollard Thomas & Edwards*). Its counterpart to the W is MANTON HOUSE, also with a curved side, part of the LCC's CLISSOLD ESTATE, 1937 by *E. Armstrong*. Further W, some much-altered houses remain from a group built from 1721: No. 235, five bays, with Doric doorcase; Nos. 239 and 243, with remains of brick lacing.

### 2. South of Stoke Newington Church Street to Newington Green

This is an area of mid-C19 development between two old centres. Near the end of Church Street, CLISSOLD CRESCENT leads S, past ADEN TERRACE, a footpath by allotments which mark the former line of the New River continuing S from Clissold Park. No. 42 Clissold Crescent was *James Brooks*'s own house, 1861–2, probably his earliest work in London. A picturesque L-shaped Gothic house, reminiscent of Street's domestic work. Of red brick, unusual at this date. Stone porch with stumpy columns; steep slate and tiled roof, formerly with tall chimneys. All in feeling contrast to the conventional stucco-trimmed terrace round the corner in Burma Road. More stucco-trimmed houses further s. Beside them, No. 1a, the late C20 TURKISH ISLAMIC CULTURAL CENTRE, is cleverly fitted in behind a windowless brick wall, its glazed dome just visible. Entrance court with reused columns. The junction with ALBION ROAD is marked by the former ALBION pub, quite a stately detached Italianate building, ground floor remodelled 1890 by *W. G. Shoebridge*, converted to housing 1998. Albion Road was laid out after the land was sold for building in 1821. It forms the main road through an area developed by *Thomas Cubitt* 1823–39. The best of the remaining houses of this time are a little further s on the E side of Albion Road; three-storeyed stucco groups, with a lively rhythm of receding and projecting bays. N of the crossroads some single houses and groups remain, mostly on the E side: e.g. Nos. 156–162, and Nos. 174–178, a nice triplet. Larger mid-C19 Italianate pairs to the E along ALBION GROVE (Nos. 15–21, 25, 27, and Nos. 2–16, c. 1851–2).

The grander houses contrast with the humbler artisan neighbourhood to the SE, where a tight grid of small streets was laid out c. 1850. Among the survivals, MILTON GROVE has simple stuccoed terraces and a few larger houses: No. 66 with Ionic porch, Nos. 68–70 with tripartite windows of c. 1860, No. 110, detached ('The Cottage'). ALLEN ROAD is a mid-C19 shopping street; SHAKSPEARE WALK has a N end complete with plain terraces on both sides. To the s, C20 rebuilding: low council housing of the 1950s onwards, and BUTTERFIELD GREEN, an open space created around an old footpath to the N of *Butterfield*'s Church of St Matthias. Pretty former ELECTRICITY SUBSTATION, c. 1930, in WORDSWORTH ROAD.

w of Milton Grove, CHURCH WALK, another ancient footpath, leads to Newington Green; the N part, which led to the parish church, is now blocked by Stoke Newington School.

NEWINGTON GREEN is in Islington (*see* Islington 5, pp. 694–5), apart from the N side. The area was built up in the C17 and was then a smart place to live; the Unitarian Chapel (q.v.) on the N side is of late C17 origin. For the NE corner site and the area behind, *Rivington Street Studio*'s designs won a Peabody Trust competition in 1996 for housing and a health centre. Six-storey curved corner tower with a low range facing Victorian terraces along Albion Street. A fine gate and railings of c. 1715–20 from No. 42 Newington Green, demolished in the 1960s is to be incorporated. Further E, Nos. 35–38, two C18 houses hidden behind projecting shops, and the MILDMAY CLUB, thin Baroque of 1900 by *Alfred Allen*; overlarge segmental pedimented doorway, small cupola. (s of the green was the Mildmay memorial hospital and conference hall, now demolished.) It was one of several Christian missions based at Newington Green. In MATTHIAS ROAD to the E, Butterfield's church now towers over C20 council flats instead of low C19 terraces; plain five-storeyed blocks of the HEWLING ESTATE to the N by *Howes & Jackman*, for Stoke Newington, 1938; to the s the *LCC*'s MAYVILLE ESTATE, the interwar blocks with streamlined balconies contrasting with neat pale brick additions of the 1950s.

*3. Stoke Newington High Street and Stoke Newington Common*

STOKE NEWINGTON HIGH STREET forms a part of the long straight route of Ermine Street running due N from the City. At the narrow congested junction with Church Street it retains something of its pre-C19 character with Nos. 186–190 on the E side, perhaps C18 much altered. The outstanding buildings lie further N on the W side, Nos. 187, 189, and 191, a group of three excellent houses built between 1715 and 1728, each of five bays and three storeys. Later in institutional use, renovated in the 1980s, but only after they had stood empty and vandalized for twenty years and had lost most of their interior features. No. 187 (reconstructed behind the façade) is set back from the street behind big gateposts with urns. Probably built by Edward Lascelles, who built No. 189. This has straight-headed windows like its neighbour, but stands forward. The stucco quoins and porch were added in the C19, when it was used as a dispensary. No. 191, also set back behind gatepiers, has segment-headed windows. It was altered in the C19, when it was used first by the Infant Orphan Asylum and then as a female penitentiary. Opposite, THE JOLLY BUTCHERS, an 1850s pub with boldly bracketed ground floor.

Further N the portentous Egyptian entrance to Abney Park Cemetery (q.v.), with railings in complementary style added in 1993. It faces a Postmodern cornerpiece of the same date. N of this the street becomes STAMFORD HILL. On the W side, Nos. 1–25, set back, a decent large stucco-trimmed terrace of the mid C19, then Nos. 26–30, less regular, of similar date. Little worth pursuing N of Manor Road, except for Nos. 51–53, a once superior pair of *c.* 1800 with big bow windows, now, alas, the adjuncts of a service station and a bus depot. Further on, SAINSBURY'S, an extreme example of mangled classical detail, *c.* 1990. The BIRDCAGE pub opposite has a good early C20 interior.

Opposite the cemetery entrance, NORTHWOLD ROAD leads E towards Stoke Newington Common on the borders of Hackney. On the N side, WEST HACKNEY HOUSE, almshouses of 1888–9, brick and stone Tudor detail, recessed central loggia. RECTORY ROAD branches S through the remains of the common. SANFORD TERRACE on the W side is dated 1788; renovation began privately in 1967 (continued by the borough after a public inquiry in 1971 forbade demolition). Nos. 8–17 are three-storeyed, Nos. 18–21 two-storeyed and double-fronted, simple but well proportioned, with delicate fanlights of identical design. To the W, an area of rebuilding, *c.* 1980; minimally detailed terraces in brown brick, three storeys with flats above, intended but dismally failing to complement Sanford Terrace.

Back in the HIGH STREET S of Church Street there are only scattered items of interest. On the E side, Nos. 132–150, a C19 stucco-trimmed terrace. On the W side the ROCHESTER CASTLE, a tall pub with good ground floor of *c.* 1900, and further S VICTORIAN GROVE, with a few early C19 villas which must have faced open country when they were built. Nos. 9–11 have pretty curved bows and balconies, as at a seaside resort, and are indeed named 'Brighton Villas'. Nos. 13–19 are plainer. The VICTORIA, low and two-storeyed, is still on an early C19 scale. Then VICTORIAN

ROAD, which has on its s side, behind an arched screen, four robust mansion blocks. The wider spaces between the blocks are called CORONATION AVENUE and IMPERIAL AVENUE; the date must be *c.* 1901. Red brick with plain but decent Board-school-type detail, and slightly Arts and Crafts segmental hoods over the entrances (probably by *Joseph*, cf. Navarino Mansions, Dalston Lane: *see* Hackney Perambulation 7). On the N side, housing by *Pollard Thomas Edwards*, 1993–4.

STOKE NEWINGTON ROAD, the s continuation of the High Street, linking Stoke Newington and Dalston, has later C19 terraces, the best group attached to an elaborately stuccoed pub at the corner of Walford Road. No. 109 is older, *c.* 1800, three storeys, stuccoed, with central bow, lone survivor from a hamlet called the Palatine estate after an early C19 settlement of German Protestants. On the E side, the Somerford Estate (*see* Hackney, Perambulation 7). s of SOMERFORD GROVE a large former factory of 1929 by *Hobden & Porri*, now HALEVI COMMUNITY CENTRE, and a former Magistrates Court (*see* Hackney Public Buildings).

## 4. The north part of Stoke Newington

QUEEN ELIZABETH'S WALK, along the E side of Clissold Park, recalls a walk in the grounds which once extended N from the Manor House near the church. Facing the park, GREENAWAY CLOSE, low-rise flats, sensitively detailed in a traditional style. They form part of LORDSHIP ESTATE SOUTH, 1936 by *Howes & Jackman*, one of Stoke Newington's first big housing schemes. Behind are large blocks on a horseshoe plan. Here too the careful detail (private balconies and homely sash windows) is superior to much contemporary housing (cf. Hackney).

N of Clissold Park, the pumping station and reservoirs of the New River (q.v.) stood in open country until around 1860, when respectable villas and terraces began to be laid out. LORDSHIP PARK starts with ambitious houses at either end, their gaunt height relieved by some coloured brickwork, but has humbler two-storey terraces in between. In MANOR ROAD, the continuation of Lordship Park, ST ANNE'S HOME for the elderly, by *Edward Goldie*, for the Little Sisters of the Poor. Chapel and w wing, 1878–9; the rest 1893–6. Dauntingly large but decently detailed, red brick institutional classical, 2–21–2 bays, central pediment. Opposite and continuing along the E side of BETHUNE ROAD, an unusual development: ten blocks of three-storey self-contained middle-class flats in a generously leafy setting. Built from 1874 by *Matthew Allen* (a builder associated with Sydney Waterlow's Improved Industrial Dwellings Company). Eight of the blocks had ground-floor flats and two-storey houses above, with access to the gardens (originally laid out as a communal space with greenhouses and washhouses). Grey brick, with dressings in Allen's own patented artificial stone. Further N, LINCOLN COURT, three lumpy tower blocks of the late 1960s by *Howes, Jackman & Partners* overlooking the reservoirs of the New River. NE from here, AMHURST PARK, still with some big late Victorian villas. On the s side, in the back garden of No. 91, a single-storey laboratory by *Tom Kay Associates*,

1986. Cheerfully coloured and well detailed; steel, brick, glass and plastic, with curved roof.

Along SEVEN SISTERS ROAD replacement of the Victorian housing was planned from the 1930s. The site of the WOODBERRY DOWN ESTATE was acquired by the *LCC* in 1936, but the original scheme of 1938, delayed by the war, was rejected in favour of a revised layout devised in 1943 under *J. H. Forshaw* (co-author with Abercrombie of the *County of London Plan* of the same year). Building began in 1946; most of the housing was complete by 1952. This was the LCC's most progressive estate to be built immediately after the war, before housing was made the responsibility of the reformed architect's department under Sir Robert Matthew. In reaction against estates such as the pre-war White City, Hammersmith, it was planned together with schools and plenty of amenities. The 1943 plan adopted a *zeilenbau* lay-out, with tall blocks in parallel rows in progressive continental manner, to introduce plenty of light and air. The older type of five-storey LCC flats with their long brick balconies and recessed hipped roofs are easily recognizable, but there are also four eight-storey slabs, an experimental type with lifts, designed 1942–3 and built 1946–9, of concrete with 'Tyrolean' coloured render. Their projecting flat roofs give them a Swedish look. To the N and E are schools (qq.v.), a low shopping terrace along WOODBERRY GROVE, pale brick with monopitch roof, also looking a little Scandinavian, a Library (q.v.), and the JOHN SCOTT HEALTH CENTRE with Nursery School, 1948–52 by the *LCC* (*W. J. Durnford* and *A. E. Miller*), the first post-war London example of such a building. Beyond this, further flats, also in pale brick, like the shops, with enviable views over the New River reservoirs.

ROWLEY GARDENS, N of Seven Sisters Road, has more standard *LCC* mixed development in the Roehampton tradition: point blocks and terraces of 1958–62, in grounds by the New River surviving from an C18 mansion. The junction of Seven Sisters Road with GREEN LANES is marked by THE MANOR HOUSE, an ambitious crowstepped-gabled pub, 1931 by *A. W. Blomfield* for Watneys.

Finally some contrasts in infilling of the 1970s onwards. On the NE corner of LORDSHIP ROAD and Manor Road, a tightly planned L-shaped block of forceful flats clad in dark blue, buttressing the United Reformed Church (q.v.): 1967–75 by *Peter F. Smith*, intended as an exemplar for the redevelopment of over-large church sites. Housing of the 1990s prefers an eclectic historicism; SCHONFELD SQUARE by *Hunt Thompson*, 1993, for a Jewish Housing Association, has hefty cupola'd pavilions and terraces of yellow brick, arranged in a not quite symmetrical composition. Two curved blocks to the road; striped tiles below the eaves, entrances flanked by Romanesque columns, main square with central pediments. More Postmodern stripey brickwork in FAIRHOLT ROAD: bow-windowed terraces by *CGHP Architects*, 1995, in keeping with Victorian neighbours. BOUVERIE ROAD has a sequence of typical terraces of the 1860s–90s (earliest at the S end), interspersed with newcomers of the early 1990s: PEPPIE COURT and the more fanciful butterfly-plan MEROE COURT.

# HARINGEY

Haringey lies just to the N of the old boundary of the London County Council. The borough was created from the three Middlesex boroughs of Hornsey, Tottenham and Wood Green, becoming part of Greater London in 1965. The name is an old form of 'Hornsey' and confusingly also survives in use, as 'Harringay', for the area around Green Lanes near the centre of the modern borough. The population (1995) is *c.* 213,500.

# HORNSEY

## INTRODUCTION

Hornsey was a medieval parish to the w of Tottenham, extending over the easternmost hills of the Northern Heights up to Highgate. Until the mid C19 there was only a small village centre along the High Street, a hamlet at Crouch End to its sw, scattered farms and villas, and a few large houses, most of these on the fringes of Highgate. From the medieval church only the tower remains, and the big houses have also gone, replaced almost entirely by middle-class suburbs of the later C19 and early C20 with their attendant churches and civic buildings, and an agreeable quantity of open spaces and greenery. In 1894 Hornsey became an Urban District Council, in 1903 a borough. Expanding public transport allowed rapid commuting to the City. The Great Northern Railway opened a station at Hornsey in 1850; the railway line from Finsbury Park to Highgate via Crouch End was opened in 1867, with a branch to the newly opened Alexandra Palace added in 1873. Crouch End became the main shopping centre, transformed in the 1890s by showy new parades. At the same time builders began to develop the more remote Muswell Hill with superior houses and its own shopping centre; the area (part of it previously Clerkenwell Detached) was included in the new borough formed in 1903.

The local authority, run by the residents of those older mansions which survived into the early C20, took its suburban duties seriously, preserving woodland, creating parks, planting trees, providing libraries, and even building working-class housing on a small scale (Nightingale Lane and Highgate North Hill). Between the wars a progressively modern town hall was built, but the prestige of 'Healthy Hornsey' began to diminish, especially after the Second World War; its housing and amenities could not compete with the appeal of the new suburbs further out, accessible by Underground.

After 1965, the main energy of the new Borough of Haringey was directed towards the greater social challenges of Tottenham and to the creation of a major commercial centre at Wood Green (qq.v.). There were some new housing schemes (*see* the Introduction to Tottenham, below) and a few institutional buildings, but Hornsey escaped major change. The area remains a rich field for the study of suburban domestic architecture from 1870 to 1914 and onwards. A few older survivals of a cottagey nature remain at Fortis Green, beyond Muswell Hill (Perambulation 5). The largest historic centre was Highgate, which developed on the ancient boundary of the parishes of Hornsey and St Pancras, a division perpetuated by the modern boroughs of Haringey and Camden. The boundary runs along Highgate High Street. For ease of reference the centre of Highgate is described under St Pancras (*see* pp. 402–17).

ARCHAEOLOGY. Highgate Wood has produced a slight scatter of prehistoric finds, also Roman pottery kilns, and there are other indications of Roman settlement in this area.

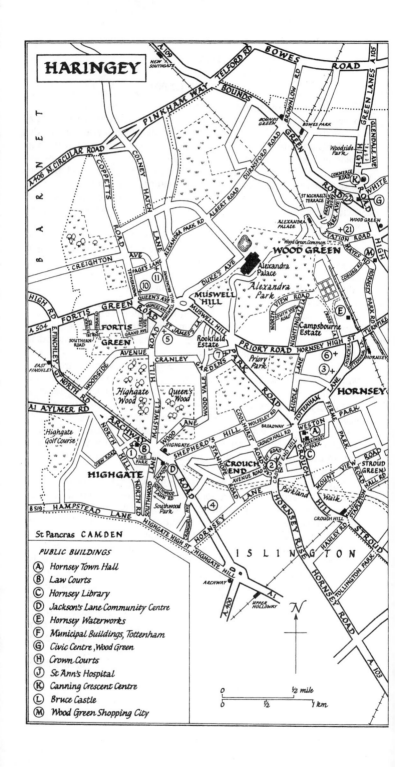

# HARINGEY

PUBLIC BUILDINGS

- (A) Hornsey Town Hall
- (B) Law Courts
- (C) Hornsey Library
- (D) Jackson's Lane Community Centre
- (E) Hornsey Waterworks
- (F) Municipal Buildings, Tottenham
- (G) Civic Centre, Wood Green
- (H) Crown Courts
- (J) St Ann's Hospital
- (K) Canning Crescent Centre
- (L) Bruce Castle
- (M) Wood Green Shopping City

0   ½ mile
0   ½   1 km

N

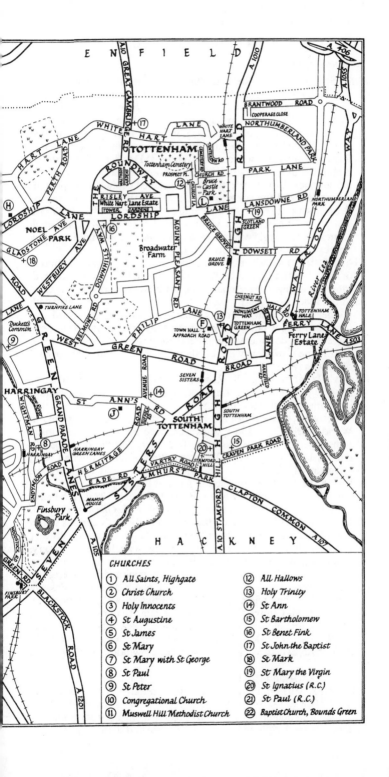

CHURCHES

| | | | |
|---|---|---|---|
| ① | All Saints, Highgate | ⑫ | All Hallows |
| ② | Christ Church | ⑬ | Holy Trinity |
| ③ | Holy Innocents | ⑭ | St Ann |
| ④ | St Augustine | ⑮ | St Bartholomew |
| ⑤ | St James | ⑯ | St Benet Fink |
| ⑥ | St Mary | ⑰ | St John the Baptist |
| ⑦ | St Mary with St George | ⑱ | St Mark |
| ⑧ | St Paul | ⑲ | St Mary the Virgin |
| ⑨ | St Peter | ⑳ | St Ignatius (R.C.) |
| ⑩ | Congregational Church | ㉑ | St Paul (R.C.) |
| ⑪ | Muswell Hill Methodist Church | ㉒ | Baptist Church, Bounds Green |

## RELIGIOUS BUILDINGS

*1. Church of England*

ALL SAINTS, Church Road, Highgate. Small stone cruciform church of 1864 by *A. W. Blomfield*; S aisle 1874, N aisle 1912 by *J. Stockdale*.

CHRIST CHURCH, Crouch End Hill. *A. W. Blomfield*'s first church in the area. Completed in stages: nave, chancel and N aisle 1861–2, S aisle 1867, tower and spire 1873, W porch 1881; N aisle enlarged in 1906 by *W. A. Pite*. Picturesquely sited on the slope of the hill. Ragstone outside, with some conventional Dec detail. The interior is of brick, and was progressively polychrome before it was whitened in the 1930s. Broad nave; the lush crocketed capitals were paid for by members of the congregation. S aisle with fancy plate tracery. Bronze WAR MEMORIAL with figure of St George by *L. F. Roslyn*. STAINED GLASS. Fine E window by *Lavers & Westlake*, small scenes, 1874. N aisle window by *Selwyn Image*, 1908; bold standing figures of Hope and Charity.

HOLY INNOCENTS, Tottenham Lane. Yet another *Blomfield* church, of 1877, this time with a brick exterior. Still in his early, less refined, more masculine style. An arresting pyramid-topped SE tower close to the road. Bold plate tracery; the tall chancel has an E wall with a wheel window over lancets. Nave with circular piers and two large dormers. W end partitioned off. STAINED GLASS. E window, three lancets commemorating Peter Robinson (of the department store), one N window with female figure against leafy background of Morris type.

HOLY TRINITY, Granville Road, Stroud Green. In a church hall of 1913 by *J. S. Alder*. The church of 1880 by *E. B. Ferrey* was demolished in 1960 after war damage.

ST ANDREW, Alexandra Park Road. 1903 by *J. S. Alder*; gutted in World War II; N, S and E walls were incorporated in the church remodelled by *R. S. Morris*, 1957. Red brick, conventional ingredients: a large incorrectly Dec W window; shallow pitched roof; clerestoried nave with stone octagonal piers and brick arches. VICARAGE by *Alder* opposite, in Curzon Road.

ST AUGUSTINE, Archway Road. By *J. D. Sedding*, 1884–7, the nave completed by *H. Wilson*, with a W end by *J. H. Gibbons*, 1914–15. Repaired by Gibbons after a fire in 1924. Gibbons's curious W end has a low central turret rising from a kind of W transept with very tall shouldered arches, and a W window with free Dec tracery. Sedding's unconventional interior has piers with dado panelling and no capitals, the low arches only slightly pointed. Tall clerestory with narrow windows framed by tall blank arcading. Passage aisles, the S one wider than the N, ending in a Lady Chapel by *Wilson*. High Church fittings: Baroque altar 1938 by *Adrian Scott*. Lady Chapel altar painting by *C. Whall*, 1895. STAINED GLASS by *Westlake* (N aisle). S aisle with two small windows by *M. E. Aldrich Rope*, c. 1930 and 1943. (Baptistery window by *Paul Quail*, 1965.)

VICARAGE and HALL by *J. S. Alder*, 1901 and 1905.

ST JAMES, Muswell Hill Road. The first church was a modest white brick affair of 1840–6 by *S. Angell*. It was replaced by an ambitious stone-faced building in *J. S. Alder*'s old-fashioned but accomplished Dec, planned 1898, built 1900–2, of a size and dignity appropriate to the burgeoning suburb. The NW tower with its tall spire of 1909–10 dominates the hill. Restored with a new roof by *Caröe & Partners* after war damage. ORGAN CASE by the same firm, 1955. STAINED GLASS. N chapel: two war memorial windows by *Morris & Co.*, 1919, each of two lights (one light and backgrounds post-Second World War). CHURCH HALL to the S, by *Caröe & Partners*, 1994–5.

ST LUKE, Mayfield Road. 1902–3 by *J. E. K. and J. P. Cutts*; w end completed 1903. A long, unexciting red brick church with Perp detail, converted to housing in the 1970s.

ST MARY, Hornsey High Street. In the old churchyard only the tower from the medieval parish church remains, of brick faced with local rubble stone. The tall belfry storey in the same materials was added by *George Smith* when he rebuilt the old church in 1832. The body of Smith's church was demolished in 1927. The tower has a NW corner turret and a Perp w window; above it are decayed carvings of angel busts with shields, which had arms of Bishops Savage and Warham (the Bishops of London were patrons), indicating a date of *c.*1500. Inside, blocked s arch to a former medieval s aisle; the respond capitals with sturdy shield-bearing angels. Tower ceiling of 1832, with Gothic leaf bosses naively carved in plaster. On the E face above the tower arch, traces of roof-lines indicate the low medieval church and Smith's taller replacement. This was superseded by a church by *Brooks* of 1889, built further E, also demolished. A few fittings are now in St Mary with St George, Cranley Gardens (*see* below). In the CHURCHYARD, railed tomb-chest to the poet Samuel Rogers †1855 and his brother and sister.

ST MARY WITH ST GEORGE, Cranley Gardens. 1959 by *Randall Morris*; built to replace St George, Priory Road (1906–7 by *J. S. Alder*, destroyed in World War II); in 1981 joined by the congregation from St Mary in Hornsey High Street (*see* above). Large windows of parabolic-arch shape. Ugly w front; light and spacious interior with passage aisles. FONT. Perp, octagonal, from the medieval church, via St George, Priory Road. Within the parish room of 1984 to the NE, the one important surviving MONUMENT from St Mary's, a remarkable large incised FLOOR SLAB to George p. 8 Rey †1599 and two wives, with one kneeling son. This monument of Midlands type has been convincingly attributed to *Jasper Hollemans*, the son of the Netherlandish sculptor Garrett Hollemans based at Burton-on-Trent. Rey was born in Staffordshire. A few small BRASSES (mounted on the wall). John Skevington *c.*1520, and two inscriptions (*c.*1420 and 1615, the latter a palimpsest).

ST PAUL, Wightman Road. By *Peter Jenkins* of *Inskip & Jenkins*, 1988–93, replacing a church of 1890–1 by *G. M. Silley* destroyed by fire in 1984. An exceptionally powerful building, small but uncompromisingly monumental; a traditional plan expressed with great originality through the use of simple geometric forms. An elemental rectangle, inspired by ancient Greece, is crowned by a 129 steeply pitched roof, which appears at each end as a forceful projecting triangular gable. Bold, apparently windowless red brick walls relieved by thin white bands. Broader stripes in the w wall frame a deeply recessed entrance between two triangular rooms. These ingeniously shield the large w windows of the body of the church, whose calm and lofty space is flooded with further light from splayed windows in the side walls and the glazed end gables. Austere white-painted brick walls and simple black furniture set off distinguished fittings by *Steven Cox*. Stone REREDOS depicting a Crucifixion above a map of the Mediterranean to show the journeys of St Paul; large ALTAR of porphyry on breccia supports, with effective contrast of polished and rough surfaces. Oval FONT, also of porphyry. Two SCULPTURES by *Danny Clahane*, St Paul and St Anthony. Vestries etc. are tucked below the E end. VICARAGE to the S, by the same firm.

ST PETER, Wightman Road. Now Greek Orthodox; *see* below.

### 2. Roman Catholic

OUR LADY OF MUSWELL, Colney Hatch Lane. 1938 by *T. H. B. Scott*. Plain Early Christian-Romanesque in brown brick; Byzantine-style capitals at the entrance.

ST AUGUSTINE, Mattison Road. 1963 by *Archard & Partners*; brick Gothic, adapted from a Primitive Methodist chapel of 1891.

ST PETER-IN-CHAINS, Womersley Road. By *A. J. C. Scoles*. S aisle 1896, nave and N aisle 1902.

### 3. Other places of worship

BAPTIST CHURCH, Stapleton Hall Road, Stroud Green. 1888 by *J. Wallis Chapman*. Red brick Gothic group of church with gable with two Dec windows (converted to housing) and school (now used by the church).

BAPTIST CHURCH, Duke's Avenue, Muswell Hill. 1900–1 by *G. & R. P. Baines*. Free Perp, with a cheerful little tower with a spike. Good interior with curved balcony.

CHOLMELEY EVANGELICAL CHURCH, Archway Road. 1989 by *Noel Isherwood Associates*. Entrance inset between classical columns, leading to a triangular foyer with church beyond.

CONGREGATIONAL CHURCH, Tetherdown, Muswell Hill. Reticent, nicely detailed Perp by *P. Morley Horder*, 1897–1900; roughcast with stone dressings. Handsome inside, with piers without capitals, broad barrel-vaulted roof, and galleried transepts. Vestries, lecture hall and parlour behind the E end. Institute opposite, in Jacobean style, 1928–9 by *Stanley Griffiths*.

FRIENDS MEETING HOUSE, Church Crescent. 1923–6 by *F. Rowntree*. Set on a slope, with the meeting room on the first floor above a classroom. In the vernacular tradition, with casement windows, steeply pitched tile roof, and heavy timber trusses visible inside. Tactful N extension with warden's house 1982–5 by *John Marsh*; S extension 1992, both continuing the original roofline.

HIGHGATE METHODIST CHURCH, Archway Road. *See* Public Buildings: Jackson's Lane Community Centre.

MORAVIAN CHURCH, Priory Road. 1907–8 by *W. D. Church & Son*. Perp, red brick with stone dressings, distinguished by an attractive octagonal corner turret with a spire.

MUSWELL HILL METHODIST CHURCH, Page's Lane. Part of a large complex on the North Bank Estate, given to the Methodists by Guy Chester in 1924. The church of 1984, by *Peter Knollt* and *Chris Lelliot* of *Daniel & Lelliot*, adjoins the original Victorian house (*see* Perambulation 5). A wide, light interior, with pitched boarded roof. E end with curved corners. Tall glazed side gable, incorporating STAINED GLASS from the previous Wesleyan Methodist church of 1899–1904 by *J. Gunton*, which stood on the E side of Colney Hatch Lane.

Former PARK CHAPEL, Crouch Hill. A crowded ragstone group with a flurry of gables near the foot of the hill. Its rapid expansion is evidence of the flourishing Congregational community of the later C19, especially under the Rev. Alfred Rowland, minister from 1876. The original building of 1854–5 faces down Haringey Park with a large Dec window and corner turret, progressively Gothic for mid-C19 Nonconformity. In 1861–2 this part became a transept, with a new nave to the s by *Lander & Bedells*, widened in 1876 and lengthened in 1886, to provide seating for 1,480. Corbin Hall to the N was added in 1893. Now in multiple use and altered inside.

Former PRESBYTERIAN CHURCH, Cromwell Avenue. 1887, stone; porch 1900 by *G. Lethbridge*. The Dec detail was preserved when it was converted to housing.

Former PRESBYTERIAN CHURCH, Muswell Hill Broadway. Like the nearby Baptist Church, by *G. & R. P. Baines*, 1903. A playful Art Nouveau composition, with blatant contrast of flint with hard red Ruabon brick dressings, a merry little spirelet on the NW tower, and a little turret on the crossing. Converted to a pub in 1996, retaining the general effect of the single square galleried space, with four stone piers supporting a steel trussed roof. HALL behind, 1898 by *Arthur O. Breeds*.

ST PETER (Greek Orthodox), Wightman Road. Formerly Church of England: a late work by *James Brooks & Son*, replacing an iron church of 1884. w end 1896–7, E end 1905. Red brick, with broad Perp w window flanked by octagonal corner turrets. Long nave with slim octagonal columns without capitals. Pointed barrel roof on laminated trusses, constructed in 1987 by *Clive Alexander & Partners*, after a fire. In the N chapel early C20 STAINED GLASS. The rest of the church with Greek Orthodox fittings, and extensive WALL PAINTINGS in traditional style, by *E. Foulides*, from 1987. VICARAGE by *Brooks* 1899–1900, his last; Georgian windows and big tiled gables.

UNITED REFORMED CHURCH (Whitefield Memorial), Alexandra Park Road. *See* Tottenham and Wood Green, below.

PUBLIC BUILDINGS

HORNSEY TOWN HALL (now Borough Offices), Crouch End Broadway. 1933–5 by the young New Zealand architect *R. H. Uren*, winner of a competition for a building on a new site, to replace older offices in Southwood Lane. The first English town hall demonstrably in the tradition of Dudok's modernist brick town hall at Hilversum. An asymmetrical L-shaped composition with a tower, set back from the street, its detail in obvious contrast to the late Victorian shopping centre. Plain walls faced with small hand-made brown bricks; elongated windows with pronounced keystones. The w front has on the l. a triple entrance to the public hall; on the r., below the tower, the entrance to the council offices, distinguished by decorative ironwork, and a band of stone carving by *A. J. Ayres*. The council chamber is upstairs in a projecting wing to the s. Well finished inside in a reticently modern style, with much use of high-quality materials. A handsome imperial stair with decorative metal balustrade leads to a toplit landing. Original panelling, floor surfaces, light fittings, furnishings and textiles throughout.

The modern town hall as symbol of enlightened local government was flanked by the agents of modern comfort: on the l. are the ELECTRICITY SHOWROOMS and offices, built for the borough, a straightforward brick range adapted by *Uren* from a former telephone exchange in 1938. On the r. is the former Hornsey Gas Company showrooms (now BARCLAYS BANK) by *Dawe & Carter*, 1936–7. This has below its upper windows a fine series of low-relief stone panels by *A. J. Ayres* illustrating the gas industry. Also by *Ayres* is a brick relief figure on the Electricity building.

LAW COURTS, Archway Road and Bishop's Road. 1955 by the MCC architect *C. G. Stillman*, area architect *D. R. Duncan*. Portland stone front broken by a glazed area with doors.

POLICE STATIONS. HORNSEY, Tottenham Lane, 1915 (future uncertain); MUSWELL HILL, No. 115 Fortis Green Road, 1900. Both by *J. D. Butler*.

HORNSEY LIBRARY, Haringey Park, Crouch End. 1965 by *Ley & Jarvis*. Light and airy, with galleried interior and a spacious foyer with open stair overlooking a small courtyard. Large glazed staircase window with engraved map of Hornsey by *F. J. Mitchell*. In front of the blank w exterior wall, a pool with bronze sculpture by *T. E. Huxley-Jones*.

LIBRARIES. HIGHGATE, Shepherd's Hill. 1901–2 by *W. H. Hyde*, half-timbered and domestic-looking, at the end of a terrace. STROUD GREEN, Quernmore Road. 1901, with nicely detailed red brickwork in the Queen Anne tradition, the ground floor similar to Highgate, so perhaps also by *Hyde*. MUSWELL HILL, Queen's Avenue. 1931 by *W. H. Adams*, Borough Architect. Formal Classical revival, with pilasters and pediment, and windows with diagonal glazing. Elaborate stair to the children's library on the first floor, which has original panelling and murals of local events, painted by members of the *Hornsey School of Art* in 1937–8.

SWIMMING POOL, Park Road. Open-air pool 1929; indoor pools *c.* 1974 by *Leonard Vincent, Raymond Gorbing & Partners*. Dark red ribbed cladding and tinted glazing.

TUC NATIONAL EDUCATION CENTRE, Crouch End Hill. This occupies the site of the Hornsey School of Art, founded in existing houses in 1882. In 1931 the school was given a demure classical centre by the *MCC*, and this was retained as the centrepiece of the extensions for the TUC by *Bertram Dinnage* of Haringey Architect's Department, 1980–3. Their restrained brick exteriors harmonize well with the older building.

JACKSON'S LANE COMMUNITY CENTRE, Archway Road and Jackson's Lane. Built as Highgate Methodist Church by *W. H. Boney & Cartwright*, 1905. Brick with stone dressings. High above

Archway Road; a prominent gable with a rhythm of wide and narrow lancets, flanked by turrets. To the N, former Sunday School with hall, behind a street front with elegant shallow bay windows with swept roofs. Interior radically transformed in stages from *c.* 1980. New entrance foyer between church and hall by *DEGW*; the church has an inserted floor; hall converted to a theatre by *Tim Ronalds Architects*, 1989, with lower walls lined in red brick.

HORNSEY CENTRAL HOSPITAL, Park Road. Built as Hornsey Cottage Hospital by the new borough, 1907–10 by *George Lethbridge*. Originally a modest three-bay building with central gable and two lower wings. Entrance hall and war memorial wing added 1921; nurses' home 1930; children's wing 1938.

ST LUKE'S HOSPITAL, Woodside Avenue. Three large Victorian villas adapted in 1928–30; pleasant Neo-Georgian centre. Much enlarged since.

HEALTH CENTRE, Middle Lane. *See* Perambulation 2.

HIGHGATE ARCHWAY. *See* Perambulation 3.

NEW RIVER. The C17 water supply from Hertfordshire to London (*see* Enfield, Hackney, Islington) ran through the E part of Hornsey. The 1,100-yd WOOD GREEN TUNNEL, completed 1859, a brick barrel 12 ft wide, constructed by cut and cover, cuts off a long former detour. To its S, remains of the former HORNSEY WATERWORKS, between Alexandra Park and Hornsey High Street. Constructed 1859, when the New River was realigned. The only surviving building of this date is the small SLUICE HOUSE across the river, originally flanked by two cottages. Built with two sluice gates (one remains). To the N, FILTER BEDS and RESERVOIRS (four filter beds of 1859, four of 1879). Nearby, in CROSS LANE, the CAMPSBOURNE WELL PUMPING STATION, 1887, small and chapel-like, with ornate red and yellow brickwork and attached boiler house. It supplemented the New River by pumping from the chalk, by a well 213 ft deep (now capped). To its S, MOSELLE COTTAGE, in similar style. Near Hornsey High Street, large, handsome Italianate ENGINE HOUSE, proposed for conversion to restaurant, 1998. Red brick with round-headed windows, 1903, with W extension for diesel engines 1935–7. Steam engines were replaced by electric pumps in 1964–6. By the main gates, LODGE and ENGINEER'S HOUSE, 1870s, in *cottage-orné* style, but much altered.

RAILWAYS. The PARKLAND WALK, opened in 1978, runs along two miles of the branch line (opened 1867, closed 1954), which climbs in a gradient of 1 in 65 or 70 along the embankment and through cuttings from Finsbury Park to East Finchley. There were stations at Stroud Green (1881), Crouch End and Highgate (both 1867). A twin tunnel remains S of the former Highgate Station. As part of abortive plans of 1935 to unite the line with the Underground, Highgate Station was rebuilt in 1939 in a minimal modernist idiom for electrification. A branch to Alexandra Palace (*see* Tottenham and Wood Green, p. 580), opened in 1873, carried by a viaduct over the S slope of Muswell Hill, is also now a path for much of its way.

UNDERGROUND. HIGHGATE, on the Northern Line from Archway to East Finchley, planned 1935, opened 1941. Deep below Archway Road, with ticket hall below ground. Intended as

an interchange with the overground line (*see* above). Elaborate
building plans were curtailed by the war: a single up escalator was
added in 1957 by *Adams Holden & Pearson*.

FINSBURY PARK. *See* Perambulation 4 p. 564.

PRIORY PARK. *See* Perambulation 1 p. 558.


*Educational buildings*

ST MICHAEL'S PRIMARY SCHOOL, North Hill, Highgate. *See* St
Pancras, p. 358.

BOARD SCHOOLS. The earliest survivor is HIGHGATE, North Hill.
1877–8 by *Chatfeild Clarke & Sons*. On a village scale, but much
altered: extended 1882, 1893–4 (corridors and assembly hall,
extra classrooms). By the same firm the taller CAMPSBOURNE,
Campsbourne Road, 1897. Yellow brick with sparing brick dressings; shaped gables. In the built-up area where space was tight,
the London School Board three-decker type was adopted:
NORTH HARRINGAY, Frobisher Road, by *Charles Bell*, 1893, is
tall and rather gaunt. STROUD GREEN, Woodstock Road, by
*Arnold Mitchell & Alfred Butler*, 1894–7, is more appealing, with
71      lively details in the Arts and Crafts spirit which inspired Mitchell's
domestic buildings: lunette windows on the top floor, bold rainwater heads. Low woodwork and cookery building in the same
style. SOUTH HARRINGAY, Mattison Road, a large cluster of
buildings, also by *Mitchell & Butler*, 1902–5, develops the style
further into a confident Free Baroque, with a variety of playful
little bell cupolas and steep dentilled gables enriched with egg-
and-dart. Junior School of two storeys, with a nice variety of window
shapes, above ground-floor openings emphasized by big stone
keystones. One-storey Infants' School, a swimming pool, and a
two-storey block to the E built as a Higher Elementary School
(later Hornsey County School).

ROKESLY, Rokesly Avenue. Low MCC buildings of 1934 (Infants)
and 1952–3 (Junior). The latter, by *C. G. Stillman*, makes ingenious
use of a sloping site. A circular hall with shallow concrete dome at
the upper level on the road side, is surrounded by a fan of classrooms at two levels, looking out over the grounds.

SECONDARY SCHOOLS. All in post-war buildings. The earlier parts
of FORTISMERE, Creighton Avenue, 1952–5 by *Richard Sheppard
& Partners*, and of HIGHGATE WOOD, Montenotte Road, 1956–7
by *Edward D. Mills & Partners*, were for Secondary Modern
schools, and reflect the new post-war trend for light and airy
interiors, modern materials and informal planning. Fortismere
(formerly Tollington School), is planned on a tight site: central
range with toplit corridor to its first-floor classrooms, and hall,
gymnasium and craftroom loosely grouped around it. Pleasantly
spacious double-height entrance foyer; patterned tiles near the
door. The original part of Highgate Wood is L-shaped: four-storey
curtain-walled classroom block at r. angles to hall and gymnasium. Both have extensive later additions. The two comprehensives of the 1970s, HORNSEY SCHOOL FOR GIRLS, Inderwick
Road, 1971 by *Haringey Architect's Department*, and ST DAVID
AND ST KATHARINE, Hillfield Avenue, by *Laurence King &
Partners* completed 1976, demonstrate the return to red brick,

the former with exposed concrete floorbands, in the idiom of the time.

HIGHGATE SCHOOL. *See* Camden: St Pancras, p. 357.


PERAMBULATIONS

*1. Hornsey High Street to the foot of Muswell Hill*

Chiefly a story of late Victorian and Edwardian suburban development, but with some older reminiscences around the High Street,
the centre of the former village, lying on low land between Muswell
Hill and the E end of the Northern Heights.

HORNSEY HIGH STREET is distinguished by a green island with
trees near the old churchyard to the S, and an open aspect to the
N due to the waterworks (*see* Public Buildings, p. 555), with
Alexandra Park beyond. A few buildings recall the rural village:
the medieval church tower (q.v.), and two houses on the N side:
No. 71, of three bays, stuccoed, early C19, and No. 69, a taller C18
house of three storeys, five windows wide, with later stucco, but
with its original brown brick visible at the side to Cross Lane. On
the other side of the lane is the GREAT NORTHERN RAILWAY
pub of 1897, by *Shoebridge & Rising*, festively Jacobean, with tall
shaped gable, and original fittings inside (interior alterations 1962
by *Roderick Gradidge*). The Music Room (originally separate,
beyond the Saloon) has elaborately decorated roof-lights. CROSS
LANE leads N past the remnants of the New River Company's C19
waterworks. The New River crossed and recrossed the High
Street before it was straightened in the C19 to run beside the railway line. Further W, the former Hornsey National Hall of 1888 by
*John Farrer*, a flat front with much red terracotta. Beyond were
large houses in their grounds. They began to disappear in the
1860s after they were sold up for building after the arrival of the
railway. BIRKBECK ROAD, S of the High Street, recalls the Birkbeck
Freehold Land Company, which developed the Grove House
Estate after 1866. Further S were more streets of the same date,
mostly rebuilt by Haringey with low-rise housing in 1967–76.

N of the High Street is the CAMPSBOURNE ESTATE, the result of
the borough's clearance of a grid of small and mean terraces built
by the British Land Company from 1867. Begun to a master plan
of 1950 (Borough Engineer *J. H. Melville Richards*) but modified
in execution. The original scheme includes Chasewater, Tivendale
and Goodwin Court, low flats of 1952; and, interrupting the old line
of Campsbourne Road, BOYTON CLOSE, 1957, which has more
imaginatively grouped short terraces of three and four storeys, some
set back to avoid monotony. Further N, WAT TYLER HOUSE, a
Corbusian seven-storey slab of maisonettes on stilts, planned 1963–4.

This area at the foot of Alexandra Park has a long history of
council activity. The Borough of Hornsey's very first council
housing is tucked away in NORTH VIEW and SOUTH VIEW
ROADS off Nightingale Lane. This was an early example of houses
built under Part III of the Housing Act of 1890, to provide
low-rent accommodation on the fringe of a fast-growing largely
middle-class suburb; 108 two- and three-bedroom cottages in red

brick terraces were built in 1896 by the Borough Engineer, *E. J. Lovegrove* (formerly Borough Surveyor to Richmond, where he had been responsible for a similar scheme). In NIGHTINGALE LANE 140 were added in 1904, this time with scullery with fitted bath and a hot-water system. RECTORY ROAD, with plain houses in a garden suburb tradition, followed in 1927.

PRIORY PARK to the s of Hornsey High Street and Priory Road was another early municipal enterprise, created as the built-up area threatened to expand: the land was bought in 1887, the park opened in 1894 and was enlarged in 1926. Granite FOUNTAIN of 1880, formerly in the churchyard of St Paul's Cathedral, moved here in 1909. DRINKING FOUNTAIN of 1879 from Crouch End Broadway. The High Street is continued by PRIORY ROAD, a broad tree-lined avenue which takes its name from The Priory, a Regency Gothic mansion of 1822–3 by *W. F. Pocock*, home in the later C19 of Henry Reader Williams (*see* Perambulation 2); it survived to the N until *c.* 1902. *John Farrer* (commemorated by FARRER ROAD), much involved with building throughout Hornsey, was responsible for developing the Priory Estate in the 1890s; Priory Road and the streets off it, with their relaxed terraces of gabled houses with decorative pargetting and timberwork, are quintessential Hornsey housing of those years.

Facing the junction at the foot of Muswell Hill is a little group of the earlier C19: Nos. 5–7 and No. 9 MUSWELL HILL, a pair and a single villa of plain stock brick with low pitched roofs and projecting eaves. Of the same period although altered, the VICTORIA STAKES, renamed to recall the former race track opposite at Alexandra Park. The ROOKFIELD ESTATE, immediately to the W, was laid out from *c.* 1901 by the builder *W. J. Collins* (active at the same time in Muswell Hill; *see* Perambulation 5). ETHELDENE AVENUE is conventionally straight, although the small, narrow-fronted houses are detailed in the Shaw tradition, with casements and some tile hanging. The more inventive later parts are due to the builder's two architect sons. *Herbert Collins* was responsible for the W side of ROOKFIELD AVENUE, built up 1906–11, with a series of asymmetrically gabled houses of Baillie Scott derivation climbing up the hill; *William Collins*, who established the Rookfield Garden Village Company in 1912, built CRANMORE WAY and ROOKFIELD CLOSE, completed 1915, after the demolition of the Collins family home, Rookfield House, on part of the site. Both are attractive essays in the precise domestic vernacular of Hampstead Garden Suburb: Cranmore Way has short terraces behind low privet hedges; white casements in canted bays, brick and rendered walls and tiled roofs (although these are still broken by party-walls, as demanded by building regulations, a requirement set aside at Hampstead Garden Suburb). Rookfield Close is a little more formal: three brick ranges laid out around the old garden and trees remaining from the early C19 property, with front doors set back within arched entrances.

On the E slope of MUSWELL HILL, hidden in trees, and with its own entrance lodge, GROVE LODGE, 1854, plain and stuccoed, converted for housing in 1995–6, when much of the rear was demolished. In ST JAMES'S LANE to the W, a mixture of small cottages, built after Muswell Hill Common was enclosed in 1816.

## 2. Crouch End

Crouch End lies sw of Hornsey village in a hollow between the sharp ridge of the Hog's Back to the s and Muswell Hill to the n. The c19 transformation of the crossroads hamlet from a cluster of cottages and a few large houses into a smart suburban shopping centre was encouraged by the opening in 1867 of the railway line (now closed) from Finsbury Park, with a station on Crouch End Hill. The boom years were the 1890s, when the large houses disappeared; the building of Hornsey Town Hall in 1933 set the seal on Crouch End as the official centre of the borough. Decline set in after 1965, when the town hall was demoted to municipal offices and trade was enticed to Wood Green Shopping City, but from the 1980s numerous specialist shops and eating places gave the area a new burst of life.

From the foot of Crouch Hill there is a vista up CROUCH END HILL, past the rotund corner turret of the KING'S HEAD, 1892, towards the spire of Christ Church (q.v.) in its leafy setting. Opposite is a big TELECOM building of 1953 by *F. W. Holder* (its w side curved to allow for a bypass that was never built) and the TUC National Education Centre (q.v.). The main shopping area, CROUCH END BROADWAY, developed slowly. On the e side, No. 6, DUNN'S, a baker's with the date 1850 below a wheatsheaf on the cornice above plain stock brick upper walls. Then a break, with the Town Hall complex set back (q.v.), and, further n, at the corner of Weston Park, a former BANK of c. 1888, slightly Jacobean with mullioned windows and shaped and striped gables. The Broadway finishes with a flourish: a jolly CLOCK TOWER of 1895 by *F. G. Knight.* 5 Free Classical, in an eclectic mixture of materials: granite base, striped terracotta and brick, topped by a cream terracotta cupola. It was put up as a testimonial to Henry Reader Williams (†1897), the energetic chairman of Hornsey Local Board, and bears his bronze portrait relief by *Alfred Gilbert.* TOPSFIELD PARADE forms a contemporary backdrop to the Clock Tower, a tall, exuberantly ornate shopping terrace in brick and stone with fancy gables, curving along Park Road to the l. and Tottenham Lane to the r. It was built on the estate of Henry Weston Elder, replacing Topsfield Hall, a Georgian mansion sold in 1892. The developers were Edmondsons of Highbury, who built identical shopping parades in Muswell Hill soon afterwards (*see* Perambulation 5). On the opposite side of Tottenham Lane the plainer BROADWAY PARADE was developed at the same time by Edmondsons' rival, *John Cathles Hill* of Highgate. It ends with the QUEEN'S HOTEL, 76 1898–1902, one of suburban London's outstanding grand pubs of the turn of the century (Hill's other masterpiece was the Salisbury, Green Lanes: *see* Tottenham, Wood Green, p. 595). Its special feature is the delicate floral Art Nouveau glass by *Cakebread Robey,* set in broad arched windows. Corner cupola above a recessed entrance with good ironwork; well-preserved interiors with original mahogany fittings dividing up the separate bars grouped around a central servery. The pub complemented the now vanished Queen's Opera House (opened in 1897 and destroyed in the Second World War), which stood behind the parades opposite.

ELDER AVENUE, together with Weston Park, on part of the Elder Estate, was built up by *John Farrer* from 1889. It continues behind the site of Topsfield Hall to MIDDLE LANE, an old route running N from Crouch End towards Turnpike Lane. The triangle between Middle Lane, New Road and Park Road has modest two-storey villas and cottages, a development of 1850–4 by *Joshua Alexander* and *William Bradshaw*. The best remaining group is Nos. 9–35 Middle Lane, unusually stylish for their size, semi-detached, with stuccoed ground floor and upper pilasters. To their N, CROUCH END HEALTH CENTRE, in plain pale brick with monopitch roofs, with a contrast provided by the inset timber balconies of the adjoining flats running back along New Road. By *Haringey Architect's Department* (*Bertram Dinnage*), 1984. The Health Centre neatly follows the angled building line of CLEMENCE COURT, pale brick post-war flats by *Hornsey Borough Council*, 1947. Further on, among Victorian housing, MARGARET HILL HOUSE by *Marden & Knight*, 1993, flats for Hornsey Housing Trust, with a sturdy corner turret of brick banded in stone. By LYNTON ROAD one reaches THE GROVE, chunky low red brick housing for the elderly, by *HKPA* for Haringey, 1970–4 (cf. their work in South Tottenham), nicely grouped around a lawn. Opposite, the corner of PARK ROAD and WOLSELEY ROAD is marked by the battlemented turret and half-timbered gable of a former school woodwork building, an addition of 1893 by *H. Chatfeild Clarke* to Hornsey's first Board school (the school itself was replaced by an awkward crescent of tightly packed houses in 1994). The neighbouring building to its N in Park Road, with diapered brick gables and two sedate bay windows, was built as a temperance coffee house. Further N, more patchy suburban expansion interspersed with Hornsey council housing: KELLAND HOUSE, 1937, has three ranges in a domestic style around a garden. Further on, RAMSEY COURT, 1952 (*B. Bancroft*); bomb-damage replacement of above-average quality, in the lighter style introduced in the 1950s. Four storeys, nicely set back from the road; generous balconies back and front, entrances flanked by decorative random stone panels.

*Streets around Crouch End, clockwise from the south-east*

During the later C19 middle-class housing, with grander houses on the slopes to the w, replaced scattered country villas and mansions. Nothing spectacular, but considerable variety.

Close to the Broadway is HARINGEY PARK, the first suburban street in Crouch End, laid out in 1845. It retains a few substantial stuccoed houses with Italianate detail. On the E side of CROUCH HILL a couple of low, somewhat altered villas of the 1820s, Nos. 118 and 120, reminders of a type common here before suburbia took hold. Further s, streets of the 1880s–90s; on the E, CECILE PARK, by *John Farrer*. Other parts of Crouch Hill, together with the streets to the w, are probably by the local builder *W.J. Collins*. Their style derives from the 'artistic' houses of Norman Shaw. No. 113 CROUCH HILL, perhaps built as a show house for the estate, is particularly elaborate, with decorative terracotta panels and tall chimney stacks. Other houses in the same style along

CHRISTCHURCH ROAD and WAVERLEY ROAD, leading towards the focus of Christ Church on Crouch End Hill, and in HASLEMERE ROAD, which curves around the site of Oakfield House (demolished in the 1930s). Good-quality details (typical of Collins): timber porches, front doors with stained glass, roofs with decorative cresting.

Around Christ Church on the other side of Crouch End Hill, CRESCENT ROAD was laid out by 1871, with large spiky Gothic houses, steeply gabled, of stock brick with coloured bands and a little carved decoration. Nine of the original houses remain scattered along the curve of Crescent Road amidst unsympathetic intrusions; fragments of a tenth, No.1 AVENUE ROAD, are ingeniously incorporated in a garden in front of flats for the elderly, a competition-winning design by *Marden & Knight* for Haringey, 1977–8.

Crouch End Hill runs uphill to the former station site. Beyond this, HORNSEY LANE continues to Highgate, an old route along the Islington border, once with 'first-class villas all the way to Crouch End Station' (Clarke, 1881). A few remain, but most have given way to an assortment of new arrivals demonstrating the eclecticism of the later C20. COLWICK CLOSE, by *David West* of *Mcmillan West Architects*, 1976, tucked away behind two Victorian houses, is an ingeniously sited retreat: small brown brick houses informally grouped, given character by some monopitch roofs. Among the tall blocks GARTON HOUSE is a crisply detailed nine-storey tower for single people, by *Colquhoun & Miller* for Haringey, completed 1980; faced in yellow brick, spandrels of glass blocks. RIDGEWAY GARDENS, 1988 by *Douglas Paskin Associates*, is an exclusive gated precinct dominated by two formal six-storey towers in banded brick with oversailing roofs on columns in the Postmodern manner. Yet more diversity around the corner in STANHOPE ROAD: Nos. 2–6, three blocks of busy Neo-Regency flats, 1959–61 by *Walter Grant* for Ideal Homesteads, face WYCHWOOD END, a neatly detailed close of modernist boxes, 1975 by *Duncan Medhurst*. Opposite is the stagey MAYBURY MEWS of 1988 by *Peter Newson Associates*, a steeply gabled red brick block attached incongruously to a half-timbered house of 1892, with a yellow brick range behind glimpsed through a clumsy archway.

The original houses of this area date from the 1890s. In STANHOPE ROAD most are tall and substantial, with timber attic balconies under projecting gables adding a little frivolity. Some more of the same period remain in SHEPHERD'S HILL, running E–W up to Highgate (*see also* Perambulation 3), and in COOLHURST ROAD, where No. 33 is a good Edwardian individualist, half-timbered and roughcast. From Coolhurst Road, Crouch End can be reached by CROUCH HALL ROAD, the main axis of a grid of streets laid out by the Imperial Investment Company on the Crouch Hall estate from 1882. In CLIFTON ROAD No. 42, with a monopitch roof and double-height entrance, is by *John Jenkins*, 1990, for himself.

*3. Around Archway Road, from Highgate Underground Station to Hornsey Lane*

Archway Road, an uncomfortably busy route taking the A1 into the City, was created in 1812 as a bypass around Highgate, in place of an unsuccessful tunnel, to avoid the steep climb of the Great North Road up Highgate Hill. It attracted an early straggle of ribbon development, but took off as a shopping street only in the later C19, serving the suburbs which developed after the opening of the branch line from Finsbury Park in 1867. As usual, the superior housing was built on the higher slopes, with artisan terraces tucked into the lower area between the main road and the railway line.

First N to the junction with MUSWELL HILL ROAD, past the WOODMAN pub, an inn of 1828 rebuilt in 1905 in solid roughcast Arts and Crafts style (note the porch roof brackets). Before the Enclosure Act of 1813 this area was Highgate Common. The woodland W of Muswell Hill Road (formerly Gravel Pit Wood) survives as HIGHGATE WOOD, 70 acres given to the Corporation of London in 1886 by the Ecclesiastical Commissioners. LODGE of 1886 in Muswell Hill Road; polished granite DRINKING FOUN- TAIN near the centre. To the SE, the quiet retreat of WOOD LANE; on the N side, the tall C19 garden walls of Southwood Hall (the house itself was replaced by dull flats in 1931), opposite some nicely individual early C19 houses on a modest scale: first a pair, Nos. 2–4; then No. 10, behind elegant railings and with a porch with fluted columns, and No. 12. No. 28 is a more elaborate *cottage orné*, with a Tudor-arched niche with a bust, a sharply pointed gable on either side, and angular stacks; Nos. 32–34 are a neat pair with shallow hipped roof and projecting eaves. On the N side, a few larger mid-C19 houses, but further development stopped in 1886, when Hornsey Local Board acquired the slopes beyond (known as Churchyard Bottom Wood), opened as QUEEN'S WOOD in 1898. The dense growth of oak and hornbeam still gives a surprisingly wild impression. Pretty half-timbered KEEPER'S LODGE of 1899. The successful fight to save the ancient wood- land of Highgate Wood and Queen's Wood was significant in pre- serving the leafy character of suburban Hornsey.

Back now to Archway Road. Further W on the N side a few humble box-like cottages, remnants of early C19 ribbon development, which were reprieved after prolonged road-widening threats and were given some new neighbours in 1995. Muswell Hill Road is continued s of Archway Road by SOUTHWOOD LANE, an old route leading uphill to Highgate. Until the mid C20 this was an area of large mansions in their own grounds; it remains pleasantly leafy. To the E was SOUTHWOOD HOUSE, replaced in 1958–62 by a triangle of low terraces by *Andrews, Emmerson & Sherlock*, enclosing a com- munal garden with trees surviving from the former grounds. Houses of pinkish brick with a broken rhythm of monopitch roofs. No. 123 on the W side, formerly a pair of tiny cottages, is early C18; steep tiled roof behind a parapet, an early weatherboarded and pantiled extension at the side, later additions behind. Beside it THE PARK, with detached villas of 1877, winding around the grounds of Park House, now occupied by Hillcrest, *T. P. Bennett*'s blocks of flats of 1946–9 for Hornsey (*see* Camden: St Pancras, Highgate). To the W, replacing two older houses, SOUTHWOOD PARK, two bold brutalist blocks by *Douglas Stephen & Partners*, 1963–5, of six and eight storeys, red brick with emphatic concrete floorbands. Cleverly sited, their bulk reduced by a slight curve, broken by stair towers in the romantic manner of Louis Kahn. On the garden side they are made less forbidding by large inset balconies. For Southwood Lane further w *see* Camden: St Pancras Perambulation 5a.

This route now turns back E towards Archway Road down JACKSON'S LANE, where an endearing narrow roadway leads past BANK POINT, a charming small stuccoed Georgian house wedged in the fork, with a two-storey porch and steep mansard roof, and HILLSIDE, also C18, with an upper bay window overlooking the passage from the S. On the N side of Jackson's Lane, part of the Southwood House development (*see* above), ringing the changes with a more urban three-storey terrace of timber and shuttered concrete, nicely proportioned.

The next lap, which follows Archway Road downhill, is chiefly late C19 suburban. First a detour E up SHEPHERD'S HILL. The N side starts with the Library (q.v.); then Nos. 3–25, a string of tall detached houses of the 1900s, occupying the top of the ridge, much altered but still with a picturesque assortment of shaped, roughcast and tile-hung gables. Opposite, the former GARDEN VIEW HOTEL, converted to flats in 1996–7, a broad red brick frontage with a variety of quirky bay windows. Its neighbours, Nos. 14–16, of 1882, were the first houses to be built in Shepherd's Hill.

On the w side of ARCHWAY ROAD substantial houses of slightly earlier date lie hidden behind trees. No. 225, with a big Ionic porch, is followed by a nearly complete sequence, Nos. 203–223, long neglected but repaired in the 1990s after road widening was abandoned. They have much notched brickwork, and look *c.* 1870. The E side is built up tightly with later C19 shops. Particularly characterful are a tall range of *c.* 1881, Nos. 164–198, and also the WINCHESTER HALL HOTEL, a pub with good corner entrance and ironwork at the corner of Northwood Road. All have topfloor balconies inset under big Gothic arches, with half-timbering within the arch and mullioned windows to the floor below. The group ends with the craggy profile of St Augustine's Church (q.v.). Opposite, steps lead up to WINCHESTER ROAD and CROMWELL AVENUE, an area of solid, respectable middle-class housing, with the distinguishing feature of basket-arched windows. Built by the Imperial Property Investment Company after the demolition of Winchester Hall, a late C17 mansion. Off Winchester Road, TILE KILN LANE, a path flanked by a little group of studio flats by *Peter Beavan*, 1978, tucked into the land above the Archway Road cutting. A crisp mixture of white concrete-block walls, projecting windows and slate roofs. The path emerges in HORNSEY LANE by a covered reservoir and small, neat New River Company ENGINE HOUSE of *c.* 1859, which pumped to the higher parts of Highgate and Hampstead. Stock brick with stucco pediment. HIGHGATE ARCHWAY carries Hornsey Lane over the cutting, with spectacular views S towards the City. The present bridge (*see also* p. 669) is of 1897–1900 by *Alexander Binnie*. It has elaborate cast-iron decorative spandrels and railings. The dolphin lamp stands are copies of the Embankment design by *Vulliamy*. The bridge replaced the first archway, which was an aqueduct-like structure designed by *Nash* in 1812.

At the w end of Hornsey Lane, a few worthwhile houses on the s side. No. 20 looks pre-c18 in origin, although given a *cottage-orné* treatment in the c19. Roughcast exterior with a projecting two-storey porch with mullioned window, flanked by two irregular gables, each with a tiny top casement window and a canted oriel below. Nos. 8–10 and Nos. 2–4 are c18, turning their irregular backs to the road to look s over London. Nos. 8 and 9 have upper Venetian windows with lunettes above.

## 4. Stroud Green and Harringay

STROUD GREEN ROAD, on the boundary between Hornsey and Islington, developed indifferently as a late c19 shopping street after the expansion of Finsbury Park Station at its southern end. The streets on the Islington side (*see* Islington, pp. 705–6) were laid out from the mid c19; the area to the e grew up later, a grid of streets with three-storey stock-brick-and-stucco-trimmed terraces of the later 1860s–1870s, interspersed now with patches of four-storey council flats on bomb sites, the borough's first post-war efforts. The very first flats, WALL COURT, Stroud Green Road, completed 1947, are in a solid brick style with rounded balconies in the progressive manner of the 30s; the blocks of the 50s are a little lighter, with Festival-style trimmings. The only pre-Victorian building is part of STAPLETON HALL, an unpromising-looking group at the beginning of Stapleton Hall Road. The two-storeyed e range with irregularly spaced windows, now cased in brick and stuccoed, is in origin a timber-framed building of three bays, probably early c17, with chamfered ceiling beams and a roof of four bays reconstructed from old timbers. In the early c19 it was modernized as a separate house with a new stuccoed front and porch. The parts to the s were demolished *c.* 1890 for Ferme Park Road. Converted to flats with new n and w ranges, 1989.

The houses along STAPLETON HALL ROAD (laid out 1876) and FERME PARK ROAD (1880), which branches n to run up over the hill, are happily eclectic, their details ranging from Gothic and Tudor to classical-French-château and terracotta trim. MOUNT VIEW ROAD along the ridge has stunning views s across a covered reservoir, and good houses of the 1890s further e. In QUERNMORE ROAD a group of shops and library (q.v.) by Harringay Station on the main line, where there is a footbridge to Wightman Road and Harringay.

HARRINGAY, the area e of the main railway line and w of Green Lanes, falls awkwardly between Hornsey and Wood Green. Its only notable buildings are the churches and schools (qq.v.) built to serve the 'ladder' of streets n of Finsbury Park, laid out unimaginatively by the British Land Company in 1880–1 over the site of Harringay House and its grounds. The New River used to loop picturesquely around the house; it now runs straight towards Finsbury Park.

FINSBURY PARK occupies a triangular area of 115 acres on the borders of Haringey, Islington and Hackney, on rising ground earlier occupied by Hornsey Wood. It was opened in 1869, laid out by *Alexander McKenzie* for the Metropolitan Board of Works, at the same time as Southwark Park, the Board's first enterprises of this kind. First proposals were for Albert Park, a grand open space for North London to complement the earlier Office of Works effort at Victoria Park, but the fields were overtaken by the builders and the park ended up smaller, and some distance from Finsbury, for whose inhabitants it had originally been intended. The original buildings have gone, but the main features of the Victorian lay-out remain: a perimeter drive, some good trees, 'American Gardens' with rhododendrons in the NW part, and a central boating lake with island. The NEW RIVER flows through the NE corner.

*5. Muswell Hill and Fortis Green: a circular tour starting at the top of Muswell Hill*

Muswell Hill forms a high plateau NW of Hornsey, looking out over the valleys of the Thames and the Lee, a once remote spot which derived its name from a holy well on land belonging to the medieval nunnery of St Mary Clerkenwell (the area remained a detached part of Clerkenwell parish until it became part of Hornsey in 1900). It was more accessible after the opening of a station on the branch line from Finsbury Park to Alexandra Palace (1873), but until the 1890s the prime sites were filled by a few large houses in spacious grounds, with only a scatter of Victorian villas among cottages further N. Then from 1896, as the big estates were released for building, the suburban centre suddenly took shape. Muswell Hill remains a remarkably coherent and stylish turn-of-the-century middle-class suburb, complete with shopping parades in flamboyant developers' Baroque, churches and chapels, and curving residential streets in the decorative 'Queen Anne' tradition established by Norman Shaw.

Near the top of MUSWELL HILL, close to the site of the former station, overlooking London, is the GREEN MAN, an old inn much rebuilt and enlarged. The low Swiss chalet opposite, dated 1900, began life as an Express Dairy. To their N four other roads with more urban buildings converge on a roundabout. The two old routes are MUSWELL HILL ROAD and COLNEY HATCH LANE, which bounded the Limes estate: here the shopping parades of MUSWELL HILL BROADWAY were built by *Edmondsons* in 1897, with a new residential road, QUEEN'S AVENUE, laid out between them. The Broadway is identical in design to the same firm's parades in Crouch End (*see* Perambulation 2); above each shop two storeys of pedimented windows and a central attic window in a shaped gable. Originally the buildings were of red brick with Bath stone dressings; the busy stone detail is now overemphasized by white paint. DUKE'S AVENUE, to the E, starts with shops, their upper floors to a different design, with much play with canted windows; then, opposite the Baptist Church on the s side (q.v.), comes a series of houses displaying lavishly pargetted gables and sgraffitoed eaves. Looking W along the BROADWAY the view is enlivened by the little spike of the former Presbyterian Church and by the taller and more serious spire of St James at the far end (qq.v.). One shop worth noting, MARTYNS (No. 135), a traditional grocery complete with fittings. The s side is less coherent: LLOYDS BANK by *Edward Maufe*, of 1927, is demure Neo-Georgian; further on is a pair of Victorian villas with Gothic upper windows, embedded in Marks

& Spencers. Opposite St James, FORTIS GREEN ROAD runs N. St James's Parade, 1900, on the E side, is a more informal and arty design, with large arched shop windows, and canted bays above with pargetting. This is the cultural end of Muswell Hill, once with an 'Athenaeum', a public hall provided by *Edmondsons*, but replaced in the 1960s by an unsympathetic lump of flats with Sainsbury's below. On the opposite corner is the ODEON, 1935–6, the fifth in this cinema chain to be built by *George Coles*, and his best work. An austere exterior faced in cream and black faience, linked to a shopping parade curving around the corner. The interior, although converted to three cinemas in 1974, retains its accomplished streamlined decoration, the curved surfaces of foyer and auditorium accentuated simply by subtle recessed lighting and by clever use of horizontal and vertical lines.

The residential areas of Muswell Hill can be sampled on either side of Fortis Green Road. To the E the curving streets are part of *Edmondsons*' development. First PRINCE'S AVENUE, laid out *c.* 1900 on the line of the drive to Fortis House, of which a stuccoed fragment (No. 38) may be a survival. Houses with pretty details: pargetting, small-paned upper sashes and playful timber balconies. QUEEN'S AVENUE has similar detail on a grander scale, somewhat eroded by hotel conversion and multi-occupation. The western houses are distinguished by bold semicircular canopies to the front doors; those E of KING'S AVENUE (laid out 1896) have elaborate two-storey balconies.

W of Fortis Green Road were the estates of The Firs and Fortismere. These were developed from 1900 by *W. J. Collins*, who had already been active in Crouch End (*see* Perambulation 2). BIRCHWOOD MANSIONS, Fortis Green Road, dates from 1907. Here the young *Collins* sons, *Herbert* and *William*, must have been at work (*see also* Rookfield Estate, Perambulation 1). The flats are in an inventive and eclectic Arts and Crafts style, in the romantic idiom of the entrances to Hampstead Garden Suburb. A long gabled range of four storeys, in brick and render, broken by recessed entrances below low brick arches and a half-timbered centre clasped between tall chimneystacks. Perky green-painted casement windows project as little triangular or rectangular oriels. Behind, in FIRS AVENUE, a picturesque group of former coach house and stabling around a courtyard. Firs Avenue and BIRCHWOOD AVENUE lead into the hubristically named GRAND AVENUE, from which other streets lead N to Fortis Green. They all have two-storey terraces with cleverly varied detail: compact houses no longer with the traditional London terrace house plan; central entrances but asymmetrical bays; minimal back extensions. The variety of surfaces echoes those found elsewhere in Muswell Hill, used here with greater discretion.

Back in Fortis Green Road, ST JAMES CHURCH HALL, by *Grey Wornum*, 1925, pinkish bricks in stretcher bond, with upstanding shaped gables in a mannered Scandinavian style, elegantly done. FORTIS COURT, Neo-Georgian flats of the same date, at the corner of FORTIS GREEN; other interwar flats opposite. Then on the S side of Fortis Green, FAIRPORT, a large steeply gabled, tile-hung block, followed by THE GABLES, another *Collins* enterprise of 1907. Similar in composition to Birchwood Mansions but enlivened with some panels of red and yellow chequerwork, and with delightful art nouveau iron railings to the top floor. Opposite, the Neo-Georgian flats with demure Regency balconies are by *William Collins*: TWYFORD COURT, 1933, and LONG RIDGES, 1930. They flank TWYFORD AVENUE, laid out 1935. It has pleasant low tile-hung houses with hipped gables in garden suburb style, with neatly integrated porches and garages.

Further w miscellaneous small cottages remain from the pre-suburban hamlet of FORTIS GREEN. On the N side, opposite the Police Station, COLERAINE COTTAGES, a rendered group with low-pitched roofs and central chimneystacks of the early C19; down an alley, Nos. 4–7 Fortis Green Cottages, a surprising survival of a back-to-back group; by Denmark Terrace, another alley, with WOODSIDE COTTAGES. CLISSOLD CLOSE is by *Lee & Miles*, 1978, for Haringey, one- and two-storey brown brick houses with projecting upper balconies and inset entrances, fitted in tightly around the edges of a narrow site. On the s side, FIELD COTTAGES, only one bay wide, then a few larger early-to-mid-C19 classical villas, nicely individual: Nos. 95–97, three storeys, with a pair of Doric porches; Nos. 91–93, lower, of grey brick with projecting eaves and recessed planes; Nos. 87–99 with a shared central gable, and Nos. 83–85 with some Gothick glazing. Of the same time, ALBION COTTAGE and LODGE, a pair on the N side. s of Fortis Green the HARWELL PARK ESTATE was laid out with WESTERN, EASTERN and SOUTHERN ROADS by the National Freehold Land Society from 1852, but built up only slowly. Early houses here are simple and elegant semi-detached villas at the s end of Eastern Road (Nos. 2–12) and a few more in Southern Road.

Finally a few pre-Edwardian outliers to the N. Among various Victoriana in TETHERDOWN, the continuation of Fortis Green Road, Nos. 58–60, a tall gabled Gothic pair. At the corner of PAGE'S LANE a cluster of mid-C19 cottages: No. 1, part of a group in COPPETTS ROAD, and a terrace to its E, Nos. 3–11, with Victoria Terrace behind. Page's Lane, an old road, winds past a C19 villa incorporated in a school, then WHITEHALL LODGE, flats of 1938, tall, white and austere, and NORTH BANK, a C19 house still with large grounds, now part of a group of Methodist buildings. Two steep gables, a w garden front with decorative bay. To the E, the church (q.v.) and an L-shaped stable group. 1980s sheltered housing in the grounds. Beyond is CHESTER HOUSE, Methodist Youth Headquarters and Youth Hostel, by *Charles Pike*, 1959–60, an excellent composition in pale brick, extending round the corner into COLNEY HATCH LANE. Here just a few early Victorian detached houses remain: Nos. 3–7, set back from the road, Nos. 5 and 7 with decorative bargeboards.

# TOTTENHAM AND WOOD GREEN

## INTRODUCTION

Tottenham High Road is part of the Roman Ermine Street, running straight N from Stamford Hill along a ridge to the W of the Lea Valley. Already in the early C18 Defoe records that it was continuously built up. The N part of the High Road still has a sprinkling of decent Georgian houses; to its W lies All Hallows, the former village church, and the manor house, Bruce Castle, forming a rural oasis N of Lordship Lane. The angular line of Bruce Grove, running SE, follows an avenue of Bruce Castle Park which appears on Roque's map. Otherwise there are few remains of before the C19. The old lanes connecting the High Road with Green Lanes and Wood Green High Road to the W are now busy roads – White Hart Lane, Lordship Lane, West Green Road, Philip Lane, St Ann's Road. They once linked scattered hamlets which had developed in forest clearings. Numerous surviving greens and commons and, just occasionally, a few older houses hint at these old settlements. Tottenham Green, West Green, Duckett's Common and Bounds Green are still recognizable. Even at Wood Green, beyond the brash late C20 commercial centre running along the High Road, greens remain to the N and two areas of common land to the W.

Robinson's C19 *History of Tottenham* records numerous C18 and older mansions in their own grounds. Some, such as Grove House at Tottenham Green, survived until the C20 in use as schools, but now only Bruce Castle remains. In 1831–3 the creation of Seven Sisters Road as a continuation of Camden Road provided a link to the West End, and middle-class villas began to spring up in South Tottenham, only to be swamped by the later C19 boom in working-class housing. This followed the introduction of workmen's fares in 1872 on the Enfield to Liverpool Street line of the Great Eastern Railway. The effect on Tottenham is shown by the population figures: 1861: 13,240; 1871: 22,869; 1881: 44,456; 1891: 97,174. Growth continued until 1931, when the figure for Tottenham stood at 157,752, and for Wood Green, 54,181. Wood Green, with few workmen's trains, and conscious of its aspiring middle-class status, was a separate local authority from 1888, until it became, with Tottenham and Hornsey, a part of Haringey in 1965.

The efforts to cater for the expanding population of the 1880s–1930s were reflected in a spate of churches – the Bishop of Bedford started five new missions in the 1880s – while the local authorities' efforts are still evident from the schools and parks of those years, which bring some distinction and diversity to the many indifferent flat streets of speculative two-storey terraces. Among these, two more coherent developments stand out: the pioneering planned estate of working-class terraces built at Noel Park in the 1880s, and the LCC's early C20 cottage estate at White Hart Lane. By then industries had for long been providing some local employment. Already in 1837 Robinson records steam factories in existence on the High Road, where crape and 'caoutchouc' (india-rubber) were manufactured in buildings formerly used for silk and lacemaking. Other works developed close to the New River and the main railway line to

the W, and, more extensively, along the Lee to the E. But by the late
C20 the industrial character of Tottenham was much diminished,
with old factory sites empty or, as at Tottenham Hale, replaced by
retail sheds and housing.

From the mid C20 the whole of Tottenham was affected by an
energetic housing programme, begun by the Borough of Tottenham
and continued after 1965 by Haringey. Under the Borough Architect
*C. E. Jacob* (formerly Hampstead Borough Architect), the new
borough embarked on a programme of rapid building, which produced
the unloved system-built linked slabs of Broadwater Farm Estate
and three large medium-rise blocks of identical design (two at
Tottenham: Kent, Northumberland Park; Tewkesbury, Lansdowne
Road; and one at Hornsey: Chettle Court). At the same time plans
were made to transform the nondescript Wood Green High Road into
a multi-level 'shopping city' and commercial centre, a process which
continued, with some changes of plan, into the 1980s. Despite its
central position it has not succeeded in providing a convincing focus
for the different parts of Haringey, which remain stubbornly distinct.
In the 1970s, under the Borough Architect *Alan Weitzel*, radical urban
restructuring was abandoned in favour of smaller and friendlier low-
rise housing schemes, mostly on small sites, scattered throughout
the borough. Some are by the Borough Architect's Department,
others by outside architects, which created some interesting variety.
The pattern was continued by housing associations in the 1980s–
90s. From *c.* 1984 the Borough Architect's Department was run as a
management co-operative. Later Borough Architects: *John Murray*
(1992–4), *Jacquie Quinn* (1994–6), *Greg Gordon* (1996– ).

## RELIGIOUS BUILDINGS

### 1. Church of England

ALL HALLOWS, Church Lane. The medieval church is memorable
for its contrasting building materials, each characteristic of its
date. Sturdy C14 W tower of four stages, with diagonal buttresses,
the lower parts of rubble stone, including patches of gravelly local
ferricrete and pebbles. The top has meagre C18 brickwork and
battlements. Late C15 S aisle faced with Kentish rag with tall
square-headed windows and a rood loft turret. Broad two-storey S
porch of *c.* 1500, with diaper brickwork and much-restored stone
dressings. The stack to an upper fireplace is corbelled out at the
side (the upper floor was used as a schoolroom; benches remain).
N aisle rebuilt 1816 in stock brick. At the E end there was until
1855 a circular mausoleum-cum-vestry built by Lord Coleraine in
1696. The present E end, 1875–7 by *William Butterfield*, which
attracted controversy at the time, is a picturesque but hard-edged
composition of low transepts and E vestries, in red brick with
some diapering. Butterfield worshipped here and is buried in the
cemetery to the N.

INTERIOR. Before Butterfield's additions, seven continuous
bays extended through both nave and chancel without a chancel
arch; a rood stair turret marks the former division. Arches on six
low octagonal piers with moulded capitals. These and the similar
tower arch are C14; the kingpost roof of the S aisle is late C15, but

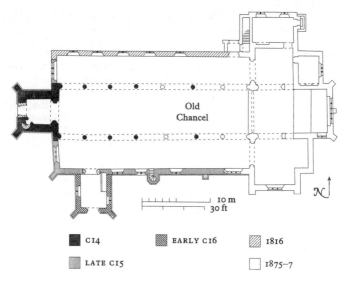

Old
Chancel

10 m
30 ft

| ■ C14 | ▨ EARLY C16 | ▱ 1816 |
| ▥ LATE C15 | | ☐ 1875–7 |

All Hallows. Plan

it is the C19 which dominates. Butterfield removed the N gallery
(added in 1821 by *William Beer*) and altered the proportions by
adding a clerestory and steep, intricately painted barrel roof. The
nave walls were redecorated in 1964–7. The C19 CHANCEL and its
FURNISHINGS retain their characteristic patterned Butterfield
surfaces: reredos and wall arcading with coloured tiles, brick walls
above broken up by stencilled stone bands. Elaborate tile floor and
painted timber vault. Stained glass of the E window, S transept and
first S aisle window by *Alexander Gibbs*, who often worked for
Butterfield; with the even tones and much use of red and pink with
which the architect liked to complement his colourful wall surfaces.
Also by *Butterfield* are the FONT with two layers of polished marble
columns, set in front of a tiled W nave wall, and the PULPIT, with
open arcading, of grey Derbyshire marble and alabaster.
    Other furnishings: COMMUNION TABLE. C17, small and deli-
cate, with arcading above the stretcher. ROOD FIGURES (N aisle).
Large carved figures by *Harry Hems*, brought from his Exeter
studio in 1942. STAINED GLASS, N aisle W. A rarity: French late
C16, presented in 1807; formerly in the E window. Three lights
with three large seated evangelists, brilliantly coloured, within
Renaissance canopies, three small seated prophets below. BRASSES.
1599 (inscription); Elizabeth Burrough †1616, two figures, *c*. 20 ins,
with children beneath; Margaret Irby †1640, engraved plate. MONU-
MENTS. Richard Canteler and wife, and Sir Fernando Heyborne
and wife (née Canteler), †1602, 1623, 1618, 1615. The two couples
kneel opposite each other in profile, each in front of a coffered
niche, and with a prayer desk between. The three short piers of
the niches are hidden by three obelisks (a less usual motif);
inscriptions below on the base. Sir John Melton †1640 and wife.
The couple kneel in the same way, flanking Corinthian columns,

broken segmental pediment; a conservative work for its date, as appears clearly by comparison with the monument to Mary Barkham †1644 and her husband, Sir Robert Barkham, signed by *Edward Marshall*. Of black and white marble, in contrast to the earlier painted monuments. Here stiffness is replaced by courtly ease and dignity. Frontal demi-figures; below, along the base, small kneeling figures in relief of eight children with two babies lying in front of them; the decoration also with the fuller and rounder forms of the Inigo Jones period. Very advanced in style. Large churchyard; some good C18 tombstones with decorative tops; many chests in bad condition; tapered Neo-Grecian stele to the Reeve family.

CHRIST CHURCH, Waldeck Road, West Green. 1982 by *Riley & Glanfield*, a replacement for a church of 1886–8 by *Hodson & Whitehead*.

HOLY TRINITY, Tottenham Green. 1828–30 by *James Savage*. Typical plain Commissioners' church; of white brick, with aisles, the nave and chancel slightly projecting to W and E, plain little turrets on the corners of aisles, and formerly on the nave as well; one had a bell. All rather thin and bare, with no excesses of feeling. Interior with slim Perp piers, tie-beams with tracery above. W gallery with Perp panelling. STAINED GLASS. One of c. 1830, two of the 1850s with medallions.

To the E, Sunday and Infants' SCHOOL, dated 1847; once pretty, with lozenge glazing and patterned slates.

ST ANN, St Ann's Road, South Tottenham. 1861 by *T. T. Bury*, a pupil of Pugin. Restored 1955. Part of a group with schools (q.v.) and model cottages (*see* Perambulation 3), paid for by Fowler Newsam, a resident of Stamford Hill, and built when the area was still semi-rural. Kentish rag, serious and substantial; Dec; with apse and SW tower with broached spire. Four-bay nave arcades on quatrefoil piers, taller transept arches. Much carving: musical angel corbels, naturalistic foliage on the capitals, and even on the soffit of the N chapel arch. ORGAN from Crosby Hall. Plentiful STAINED GLASS (apse and W by *Wailes*). MONUMENT. Rev. Frederick Rice †1927. Alabaster tablet with bronze relief portrait.

ST BARTHOLOMEW, Craven Park Road. 1904 by *W. D. Caröe*. A low, homely building of red brick alongside the road, with shingled spirelet over the crossing. Full of the inventive free Perp detail and careful craftsmanship typical of Caröe. W bellcote with overhanging gable, above a stair turret rising against the W window, flanked by steeply roofed porches. Interior of brick and stone, subtly mixed; a seven-bay nave with banded piers, dying mouldings, clerestory windows with varied cuspy tracery, and a handsome moulded arch-braced roof. Under the raised chancel, ingeniously lit by internal windows, a vaulted crypt with brick ribs on slim columns. Late C17 FONT, a marble bowl on four consoles, carved FONT COVER and octagonal PULPIT, probably of c. 1679, in the manner of *Gibbons*, from the City church of St Bartholomew Exchange via St Bartholomew, Moor Lane (demolished 1902). Good STALLS by *Caröe*. Attractive brick VICARAGE, with tile banding, tile-hung mansard and gables, and tall chimneys.

ST BENET FINK, Walpole Road. Like St Bartholomew, an Edwardian building funded from City church money, but totally different in character. 1911–12 by *J. S. Alder*, one of his least altered and most effective buildings. The exterior unusually quirky for this traditionalist architect, of red brick with stone dressings, enlivened by corner entrances to the low narthex, the N one topped by a bell-turret. Large Dec windows, the end bays of the nave treated transeptally. The tall, stately interior comes as a surprise; seven-bay nave with clustered stone piers, plastered walls and boarded barrel roof, very pure and light, with simple grisaille glass only. Good original stalls and pews. s of the chancel ample space for the ORGAN in a fine concave mahogany ORGAN CASE, 1784 by *Samuel Green*, from the City church of St Peter le Poer.

Contemporary VICARAGE by *Alder*, red brick, rendered gables, grouping well with the church.

ST CUTHBERT, Wolves Lane, Chitts Hill. 1906–7 by *J. S. Alder*. Three nave bays of the intended five were built. W wall 1930, with W window following Alder's design. Red brick with stone dressings. Light and airy interior.

ST GABRIEL, Bounds Green Road and Durnsford Road. 1936, built as a church hall. The church of 1905 by *E. B. Carter* demolished.

ST JOHN THE BAPTIST, Great Cambridge Road. 1939 by *Seely & Paget*. Funded from the sale of the Westminster church of St John, Great Marlborough Street. Red brick and concrete, in this firm's curiously eclectic mixture of traditional and modern. Red brick nave with pantiled roof, flanked by flat-roofed vestry and Lady Chapel. Above the W entrance, copper semi-dome on attenuated columns, sheltering a large statue of St John the Baptist. Side walls with copper cladding between the clerestory windows, and big buttresses. These support concrete parabolic transverse arches, which, together with narrow passage aisles, give the interior unexpected drama. Seely & Paget also used this construction at St Faith, Lee-on-Solent, Hampshire, 1933, and again (with interlocking arches) at St George, Stevenage, after the war. Across the second bay a flying gallery for the organ. Original pair of simple PULPITS; FONT in railed enclosure. CHURCH HALL to the E; rendered walls and big pantiled roofs.

ST MARK, Noel Park. 1889 by *Rowland Plumbe*, funded by the Shropshire Mission. The site was bought by Richard Foster (*see* Hackney: Shoreditch). A centrepiece of the Noel Park Estate (Perambulation 4). A tower was planned but not built. Similar to Plumbe's St Margaret, Streatham, also on an Artisans' estate. A big solid building of red brick outside and in, with grouped lancets; three at the E end, five at the W. Plain but consistent interior, the five-bay nave and transepts enlivened simply by hoodmoulds and stepped arches. Lofty roof with tie-beams and arched principals. Stone PULPIT with carved figures, including Bishop How with a model of the church. E end embellished by REREDOS and panelling in alabaster and mosaic, added gradually *c.* 1890–1914, likewise the STAINED GLASS in N chapel and aisles, with standing figures all of similar design. E window with more colourful Crucifixion and scenes from the life of Christ. CHURCH HALL to the S, 1884, with small turret. From the SE its roofs compose effectively with the taller tiled roofs of the church. The VICARAGE of 1903 by *J. S. Alder* completes the group.

ST MARY THE VIRGIN, Lansdowne Road. 1885–7 by *J. E. K.*

*Cutts*; a mission church founded by Marlborough College. The usual Cutts type; red brick, stone dressings, apsed E end, long nave with lancet clerestory. Low vaulted w baptistery; w bell-turret, and another bellcote to the NE morning chapel. Inside, as a result of the wealthy patrons, more ambitious than average. Apse and clerestory windows are set below quirky cusped rere-arches; the stone nave columns have scalloped capitals. Alabaster REREDOS by *Hems*, alabaster and marble FONT. Square oak PULPIT from Marlborough College. STAINED GLASS in apse and chapel. WALL PAINTINGS in chancel and w end are contemporary with the church. The quattrocento-style nave arcade spandrel paintings of the Life of Christ were completed in the 1890s. Paintings were favoured because they were more visible than stained glass to the working-class evening congregations. MONUMENT by *Hems* to the first vicar, E.F.N. Smith, †1908, alabaster effigy on a chest tomb.

St MICHAEL, High Road and Bounds Green Road. Wood Green's first Victorian church. A composite creation; a dignified stone-faced crossroads landmark, although the detail is disappointing. 1844 by *G. G. Scott & W.B. Moffatt*; reconstructed 1865 by *H. Curzon*; SE tower 1874, with spire of 1887.

St PAUL, Park Lane. By *Biscoe & Stanton*, 1971–7, replacing a church of 1859 by *W. Mumford*.

St PHILIP, Philip Lane. 1906 by the *Cutts*; chancel 1911. Their usual long brick clerestoried nave; inside, stone arcades and plastered walls. N aisle divided off. In the s chapel STAINED GLASS by *Morris & Co.*: Nativity, 1921, spread over four lights against a green landscape; three pairs of saints against vivid blue hangings, 1926, 1933, 1936.

St SAVIOUR, Alexandra Park Road. 1903–9 by *J. S. Alder*; demolished 1994. Alder's WAR MEMORIAL cross of 1919 remains.


*2. Roman Catholic*

St FRANCIS DE SALES, Tottenham High Road. 1895 by *Sinnott, Sinnott & Powell*. Entrance and baptistery 1946. Sanctuary 1966 by *Archard & Partners*.

St IGNATIUS, Tottenham High Road. A vast cruciform building whose twin w towers dominate South Tottenham and Stamford Hill. An early work by *Benedict Williamson*, in an earnest, dour Transitional Gothic of Spanish inspiration. Begun in 1902, to replace a temporary church founded by the Jesuits in 1892. Sanctuary and E chapels completed in 1906, w part 1911. Side walls of dark brick with flying buttresses and window surrounds of rough stone. Complex w front of Belgian brick: between the towers a triple entrance; giant arch and dwarf gallery above; two slim buttresses rising through all. Very broad but rather bleak nave, with barrel vault and transverse arches. Plastered walls; the plain arcade arches have small Romanesque capitals. Sumptuous HIGH ALTAR and REREDOS of marble, 1906, in a setting of ceramic and gilded MOSAICS covering both chancel and E chapels completed by 1923. STAINED GLASS by *Paul Woodroffe*: richly coloured lancets at the E end; s aisle window of 1915. The Jesuits also had a school here, which moved to Enfield in 1968.

St John Vianney, West Green Road. 1959 by *Archard & Partners*.
Mottled brick, with shallow pitched roof and low sw tower.

St Paul, Station Road, Wood Green. 1969–70 by *John Rochford &
Partners*. Better inside than out. To the road a low foyer, with
small round-arched windows in concrete panels. The windows
house STAINED GLASS from a former church; the best are the
earliest panels, †1882, SS Augustine and Gregory, by *George
Farmiloe & Sons*. Low SE morning chapel, with glazed wall to the
main church, which is hexagonal, with diagrid roof and hidden
clerestory lighting to the sanctuary. Huge w window with dramatic
pictorial STAINED GLASS by *Carmel Cauchi*, 1982, on the theme
of the Pilgrim Church. N and s windows, SS Peter and Paul and
Queen of Heaven, 1970 by *Moira Forsyth*. Stations of the Cross
and sanctuary statue by *M. Clark*.

*3. Other places of worship*

Baptist Church, Braemar Avenue. 1907 by *G. Baines & Son*.
Hard and spiky Art Nouveau, with striking colour contrasts of red
terracotta and white flint set in black mortar. Busy angular Perp
tracery; NW tower with battlements, gargoyles and corner turret.
Delightful intimate interior, unaltered; arcades with tapered timber
piers and traceried arches; curved benches, semicircular communion rail with simple Art Nouveau ironwork, tall E pulpit. Windows
enlivened by patterns of coloured glass.

Baptist Chapel, No. 697 Tottenham High Road. 1825 by
*J. Clark*; the main benefactor was Joseph Fletcher of Bruce Grove.
A handsome classical building of grey brick; projecting centre with
a Venetian window under an arch, above a porch with four Doric
columns. Nicely handled flank walls with windows under blind
arches. Galleries added 1836, enlarged 1876.

Christ Apostolic Church, High Road, South Tottenham.
Red brick front with a pair of castellated turrets; built as a Salvation
Army citadel, 1891–5.

Former Congregational Chapel, Lordship Lane. 1864 by
*Lander & Bedells*. Pilastered front with Venetian arch framing a
circular window within the pediment.

Friends Meeting House, Tottenham High Road. 1962 by *H. M.
Lidbetter*. Modest meeting room with rooftop forecourt over a shop.

Lutheran Church, Antill Road, South Tottenham. 1901, chancel
1935. Small red brick Gothic front squeezed between terraces.
Built for a group of German bakers.

Mosque (Sheik Nazim al-Haqqani Deighai), St Ann's
Road. In the buildings of a former Servite convent. A long yellow
brick front of 1876 with three gables and mullioned windows. A
flèche at the back marks the former chapel, added 1880–3. Rear
wing of 1906. The chapel is now the Prayer Room, a plain space
with paired lancets and two transverse arches on slim quatrefoil piers.

St Barnabas (Greek Orthodox), Finsbury Road. Built as a Baptist
Church in 1876. Brick, with SE turret.

St James-at-Bowes United Reformed Church, High
Road, Wood Green. 1901–9, brick and terracotta, free Perp.
(Original fittings, including hexagonal carved pulpit.)

St Mark Methodist Church, No. 461 Tottenham High Road.

A grey Art Deco tower of 1937 forms the centrepiece of a shopping parade. The church behind, originally of 1867, was reconstructed in 1963.

St Mary's Cathedral (Kimisis Panayias; Greek Orthodox from 1970), Trinity Road. Built as Trinity Methodist Church, 1871, to the Rev. *J. N. Johnson*'s own design. Brick, with eccentric Gothic detail: angular lancets, an elongated Dec w window, thin nw gabled tower and spire, with colonnettes set below the corner pinnacles. Much rebuilt after a fire in 1986.

United Reformed Church (Whitefield Memorial), Alexandra Park Road. 1907, for Congregationalists, by *Mummery & Fleming-Williams*. Planned as part of a larger complex which was not built. Cruciform, with a spike over the crossing, and big w window of rather thin intersecting tracery. Entrances below stone segmental arches with heavy straps.

Woodberry Down Baptist Church, Seven Sisters Road and Vartry Road. 1882–3 by *Paull & Bonella*. Large and sturdy, of red brick, with circular turrets clasping the w end, two large gables on each side, and grouped lancet windows. Formerly with a flèche. The main church, raised up on a basement, was subdivided in 1991 to create a well-lit first-floor church at the former gallery level, below the original timber vaulting. The room below preserves the gallery front as a cornice.

## 4. Cemetery

Tottenham Cemetery, Prospect Place. Opened 1858. A large area stretching n from All Hallows Church to White Hart Lane, extended to e and sw in 1881–7, and to the n after 1913. Two Kentish rag chapels of 1856–7 by *George Pritchett*, linked by a vaulted carriage arch with bellcote above; Dec detail. Near the churchyard a group of low cross-capped tomb-chests designed by *William Butterfield* (†1900) for himself and his sister's family. In the w extension, connected by a tunnel and opened 1883, War Memorial, 1919, *Sir Reginald Blomfield*'s design of Portland stone cross with bronze sword.

## PUBLIC BUILDINGS

Municipal Buildings. A pleasant Edwardian group in brick and stone on the w side of the Tottenham Green, built on the sites of older houses. Former Tottenham Town Hall by *A. S. Tayler & R. Jemmett*, 1905. Baroque, with columns, alternating pediments, and a hipped roof and cupola. Imperial staircase to a large front room, formerly the Council Chamber, with a barrel ceiling with festive plasterwork. By the same firm the Fire Station to the l., and the Public Baths to the r. (of which only the frontage remains), both with emphatic stone detail. n of the Baths the group is continued by the former County School of 1913 by *H. G. Crothall* (*see* below).

Civic Centre, Wood Green High Road. By *Sir John Brown, A. E. Henson & Partners*, 1955–8. Built on the site of the Fishmongers' and Poulterers' Almshouses. Intended as a focus for Wood Green, but now rather isolated on the N fringe of the later commercial centre. Plans were made in 1938 and ambitiously revised for the new site after the war, but only the first phase was completed. A long unassuming range to the road; the l. part, largely glazed, contains the Council Chamber on the first floor, approached by an airy double-height foyer with free-standing stair. The projecting rear wing on stilts was to have formed the S range of a courtyard with public hall and library to W and N.

MUNICIPAL OFFICES, No. 639 Tottenham High Road, at the corner of Lordship Lane. Built as the offices of Tottenham and Edmonton Gas Company (established 1847). 1901 by *John Sherwell Corder* of Ipswich, with extension of 1914 in the same style. Exuberant Free Jacobean: gabled red brick with terracotta ornament: a bulgy turret corbelled out at the corner.

CROWN COURTS, Lordship Lane. A huge Gothic pile of 1865, by *Edwin Pearce* and *Stephen Barton Wilson & Son*, built as the Royal Masonic Institute for Boys. The school moved to Bushey in the 1890s, and the building later became Gas Board Headquarters. A typically monumental Victorian institution: three storeys faced with white Suffolk brick with stone dressings, a central gable with a large Dec window above a canted bay; corner towers with steep iron-crested mansards. The frontage is now crushed by the angular roofs piled up behind, the result of remodelling in 1992 by the *Property Services Agency* to provide ten courtrooms. The new parts pay awkward homage to the Gothic design by including narrow windows with pointed heads.

POLICE STATIONS. No. 347 WOOD GREEN HIGH ROAD. 1907 by *J. D. Butler*, with his typical elongated door consoles. TOTTENHAM HIGH ROAD, E side. 1913, large, also by *J. Dixon Butler*, but Neo-Georgian.

LIBRARY, Wood Green High Road. By *Bertram Dinnage* of the *Borough Architect's Department*, 1975–8, part of the central redevelopment of Wood Green. Effectively set back from the road on the site of a former railway line, but now, alas, cluttered by later building. A dignified composition, distinguished by the use of pale buff ceramic facing tiles instead of the deep red brick of the surrounding buildings. Four stepped-back floors with a one-storey reading room in a cleverly angled projection. Double-height main library with children's library in gallery.

TOTTENHAM GREEN CENTRE, Philip Lane. L-shaped 1980s group with Sports Centre and MARCUS GARVEY LIBRARY, entered from a common foyer. Undistinguished Postmodern cladding in red and yellow brick.

BATHS, Western Road, Wood Green Common. 1911 by *Harold Burgess*. Converted to function suite, 1998. A shallow curved gable, slightly Art Nouveau in feeling (as were the fittings). Lower foyer decorated with volutes above the cornice.

ST ANN'S HOSPITAL, St Ann's Road. Founded as the North East London Fever Hospital in 1892. Much rebuilt and extended since, all low-rise. At the W end, GERIATRIC UNIT by *Kit Allsopp Architects*, c. 1989, neat one-storeyed blocks with shallow pitched roofs. Four wards in parallel pairs linked by common rooms, with spine-route meandering confusingly through. Friendly and informal interiors.

Former HOSPITALS in Tottenham High Road. *See* Perambulation 2.

Canning Crescent Centre, Wood Green High Road and Canning Crescent. By *MacCormac Jamieson Prichard*, 1994. A pioneering combination of mental health centre linked to a small acute day hospital. Of stock brick, domestic in character, with a striking series of chimney-like projections rising from cross-walls. They are ventilation flues operated by solar warmth. Light, non-institutional interior, with corridors broken up by wider spaces. The ground-floor rooms of different sizes, with shallow vaults of *in-situ* concrete, and the roof-lit upper corridors suggest that Soane provided some inspiration (cf. MacCormac's building at St John's College, Oxford).

Tottenham Hotspur Football Ground. The club was founded in 1880. E stand upgraded with new roof etc. by *W. R. L. Jenkins* in the 1990s. S stand redeveloped 1995, N stand 1998, both by *Igal Yawetz*.

Markfield Road Pumping Station. A former sewage works. Within a plain stock brick house, a very fine beam engine of 1883–6 by *Wood Bros.* of Sowerby Bridge. The beam stands on a splendid cast-iron platform, or 'entablature', on eight fluted columns, a free interpretation of the Doric order. The adjoining building was converted to a children's play centre by *Neil Thomson & Associates*, c. 1986. The former sludge settlement tanks of the 1850s, a model of their time, were converted to a playground.

Ferry Lane Pumping Station, by the River Lee. 1894 by *W. B. Bryan*, East London Waterworks Company. Pink brick with gabled hipped roof.

Stations on the Piccadilly Line Extension of 1932–3. These belong to the group by *Charles Holden* in the new and at the time quite revolutionary style which was then adopted for so many other Underground stations. Wood Green, on a corner site in the High Road, is the least successful, because not free-standing. Bounds Green, with its windows in the diagonals of the ticket iii hall block, and its recessed tower, is an interesting variant on the type used at Oakwood, Sudbury Town and Northfields. Fine original bronze uplighter in the centre of the ticket hall. The building incorporates a row of shops along the main road. Turnpike Lane makes use of its corner site for a pretty group with restaurant on a curved first floor and again a recessed tower. Good details; restored 1996.

Tottenham Hale Station. The overground station was remodelled as a junction for the line to Stansted Airport by *Alsop Lyall & Stormer*, 1989–92. Trim glazed walls with outré space-age elliptical tunnel-shaped waiting room; silvered walls, porthole windows. A colourful mural band above, by *Bruce McLean*. Remodelled Underground station with aluminium and steel canopies linking it to both the main line station and the bus station, planned by *John Lyall Architects*, 1993, begun 1995. The forecourt has three installations by the architects with *Bruce McLean*; Tower of Time, Bridge of Signs, Path of the People, 1998.

*Educational buildings*

The colleges and schools of Tottenham and Wood Green have undergone so many changes of name and function that classification is not easy. The selection which follows is grouped roughly by date of building.

VICTORIAN SCHOOLS. A few modest, once attractive pre-Education Act survivals. HIGH CROSS INFANTS' SCHOOL, Tottenham Green, close to Holy Trinity, 1847. Once pretty, with patterned lozenge glazing. Opposite St Ann's Church, in Avenue Road: one building remains from the 'HERMITAGE' schools established by the benefactors of the church (q.v.): the 'Junior and mixed school' of 1863, with steep gable, restored 1996. The GREEN SCHOOL, Somerset Road. Much altered. The Victorian teacher's house and Gothic school entrance preserved among C20 additions.

HIGH CROSS SCHOOL, Drapers Road, off High Road, converted to housing, 1998. A large earnestly Gothic institution in stock brick and stone, of 1860–2, built as Drapers College, by the company's architect, *Herbert Williams*. Originally flanked by a row of almshouses on each side. 1–7–1 bays, the ends gabled. Gables also to the Gothic first-floor windows projecting up into the steep patterned slate roof. Rear extensions of 1887–90 by *Charles Reilly (Sen.)* (partly demolished), made after the building became Tottenham High School for Girls. FELVUS HALL on Tottenham High Road is a neat, slightly Jacobean addition, with mullioned windows; 1926 by *H. G. Crothall* of the MCC. Grounds to the w built up for a housing association, by *West Faulkner Associates*, 1991.

BOARD SCHOOLS. Tottenham School Board was set up in 1879 and made plans for ten new schools to cater for the rapidly expanding population; its work was continued by Tottenham Education Committee after 1903. The early buildings are large and plain, given character by bold massing of roofs, gables and cupolas, and compactly planned, often with halls surrounded by classrooms on four sides (a type of plan generally avoided by the London School Board). From the late 1890s more ornament appears, and more variety of height, with separate lower buildings for infants and for manual instruction. *G. E. T. Laurence* was responsible for some of the most attractive examples.

The former SCHOOL BOARD OFFICES (now EDUCATION CENTRE) in Philip Lane, by *Albert E. Pridmore*, 1899, display the Board's confidence at this time: proud and showy, with splendidly gross terracotta detail; porch with hood on curly modillions and blocked columns; oriel windows. Panelled board room on the first floor.

Space permits only brief reference to individual schools. The first were COLERAINE PARK, Glendish Road, 1881 (altered 1907), and STAMFORD HILL, Berkeley Road, 1882–3 by *Edward Ellis & Son*. WEST GREEN, West Green Road. 1886; a formal, slightly cramped design: end gables and giant pilasters; enlarged 1909. DOWNHILLS, Philip Lane. A large site; Infants' School of 1893, two-storeyed with shaped end gables, the central dormers with brick stripes, as if half-timbered. Former Senior School buildings of 1913. EARLSMEAD, Broad Lane. 1897. Shaped gables, wings with arched windows, rather thin red brick detailing. WOODLANDS PARK, St Ann's Road. 1897–9 by *G. E. T. Laurence*, more lively: an attractive low Infants' School with Venetian windows and tripartite dormers. PARKHURST ROAD. 1907; one and two storeys, with enjoyable slightly Baroque decorative details; segmental arched windows in the gables with classical tops, lettering in curly plaques. RISLEY AVENUE, 1913, again by *Laurence*, reflects the cottage character of the neighbouring White Hart Lane Estate by the use of roughcast above brick; a long two-storey gabled range for both juniors and infants.

WOOD GREEN BOARD SCHOOLS. NOEL PARK, Gladstone Avenue, 1889, in the centre of the Artisans' estate (*see* Perambulation 4). A plain three-decker; a little pargetting brightens the N side. BOUNDS GREEN, Bounds Green Road. 1894–5 by *Charles Wall*. The usual low infants' and two-storey junior buildings, the latter with stone finials to the gables as its special feature. ALEXANDRA, Western Road. One-storey Infants' School, 1897–9, two-storey Junior, 1905. Another group by *Laurence*; pretty shaped gables with terracotta copings, and dates in curly cartouches.

SECONDARY SCHOOLS. Senior schools supplemented Board schools from the end of the C19. Early examples follow the Board school pattern, but the cheerful and confident English Baroque of the three early C20 schools built by the MCC makes much more of a show.

NIGHTINGALE, Bounds Green Road. Built as Tottenham Higher Grade Schools; later Trinity County Grammar School. 1899 by *Mitchell & Butler*, but less interesting than their Hornsey schools (q.v.). Hall range with a row of arches linking the dormers; hefty five-storey towers with hipped roofs.

Former TOTTENHAM GRAMMAR SCHOOL, Somerset Road. 1908–10 by *H. G. Crothall* of the MCC. Very large and grand, with big dentilled gables and a Baroque entrance at the side. Converted to workshops in 1984.*

ST THOMAS MORE, Glendale Avenue. Built as Wood Green County School. 1912 by *Crothall*. The main front is an excellent 72 example of the florid free Baroque of its time. Red brick with plentiful use of stone; entrances in the re-entrant towers, which turn octagonal and are capped with copper domes.

Former TOTTENHAM COUNTY SCHOOL, Town Hall Approach. 1913 by *Crothall*. The first co-educational school of its kind in Middlesex. A formal, rather busy classical façade, with a seven-bay centre with Ionic order; hipped roof with cupola.

TOTTENHAM TECHNICAL COLLEGE, now COLLEGE OF NORTH-EAST LONDON, Tottenham Green, founded 1892, was given a new principal building in 1936–9, in the austere classical style used in the interwar years by the *MCC* to dignify further education. Brick with sparing stone dressings, above a stone basement; fifteen bays, with recessed entrance under a pediment. Extensions of 1955 and 1972.

EARLHAM SCHOOLS, Glendale Avenue. 1939. In the plain brick modernist idiom initiated by the MCC in the mid 1930s.

COMPREHENSIVE SCHOOLS. Haringey adopted the comprehensive system in 1967, mostly entailing additions to and renaming of older schools. The new buildings are disappointing. NORTHUMBERLAND

---

* This building replaced one of 1840 for the school founded before 1600. The school moved in 1938 to new buildings in White Hart Lane, since demolished.

PARK SCHOOL, Paxton Road, completed 1971, is uninspiringly routine; ranges of breeze blocks and shuttered concrete on three sides of a courtyard. The community sports facilities added in 1974 are even less attractive externally. The LANGHAM SCHOOL, Langham Road, has extensive buildings of the 1970s.

POST-WAR PRIMARY and NURSERY SCHOOLS. ST ANN'S CHURCH OF ENGLAND, St Ann's Road. 1961 by *Rolls & Hall*. Two storeys, spacious foyer, main hall with shallow barrel vault. WELBOURNE, Stainby Road. Neat nursery school block near the road, by *S. & M. Craig*, *c.* 1977. ROWLAND HILL NURSERY SCHOOL, White Hart Lane. By *Michael Tilley* of *Building Design Services, Haringey Council*, 1991. A delightful polygonal building with green timber cladding and a shallow pitched roof in two steps. Inset entrance; on the playground side partly open.

MIDDLESEX UNIVERSITY, Bounds Green Road. A phased conversion of a warehouse for Middlesex Polytechnic by *Rock Townsend*, 1977–81. A trendy high-tech factory image created by recladding in profiled sheet steel, with much colourful pipework exposed in an open-plan interior.

MIDDLESEX UNIVERSITY, Tottenham Campus, White Hart Lane. Established here 1994–5. Teaching and administrative offices in much altered Board school buildings. Student housing in striped brick with pantiled roofs, on the site of the 1930s Tottenham Grammar School, from which the railings remain.

## ALEXANDRA PALACE AND PARK

The grand concept of a People's Palace on the high ground w of Wood Green was born in 1858. The designer *Owen Jones* and the engineer *Sir Charles Fox*, who had both been associated with the Crystal Palace re-erected on Sydenham Hill in 1852–4, proposed a N London counterpart in the form of a vast glass structure with a series of towers. It was to have two long naves, one devoted to Industry and Commerce, the other to the Arts and Sciences, and, to educate the masses, a lecture theatre for 10,000 above a railway station. No money was found, and the project foundered until the Great Northern Palace Company was established in 1860, with plans not only to build the palace but to lay out a park and promote a railway from Finsbury Park to provide access. The park was ready in 1863; the building took shape in 1865–6, and the railway (*see* Hornsey: Public Buildings, p. 555) was completed in 1873, the year the palace was opened. It had a long nave divided by three transepts, built not of glass, but in a hefty Italianate style, constructed from materials salvaged from the much criticized South Kensington Exhibition building of 1862 by the contractors of that building, John Kelk and Lucas Brothers. The design was by Kelk's associate architects *Alfred Meeson* and *John Johnson*. Sixteen days after it opened it burnt down, but it was rebuilt by *Johnson* and reopened in 1875.

Alexandra Palace belongs to the worldwide craze for large exhibition buildings which followed the success of the Crystal Palace, but in its proposed functions it differed from the big international exhibition halls. Owen Jones had envisaged for it a more precise and

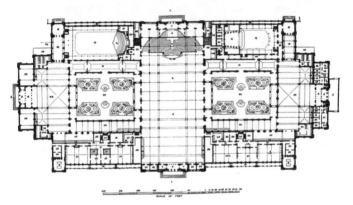

Alexandra Palace. Elevation and plan, 1874

a more permanent local and educational role, and this aspect was developed in the rebuilding of 1873–5 which provided theatre, concert hall and a Great Hall to seat 12,000, with a huge organ by *Henry Willis*, the largest in the country.

Despite a wide range of activities and entertainments the palace was not a financial success. Control passed through a series of struggling private companies until public ownership was established by Act of Parliament in 1901, supported by a consortium of local authorities. The N part of the park was sold for building, and in 1934 the SE part of the palace was leased to the BBC, attracted by the height of the site; by means of a mast on the heightened SE tower the first regular public television broadcasts took place in 1936.

Palace and park passed to the GLC in 1966, and to the Borough of Haringey in 1980. In the same year a major fire gutted nearly half the building, including the Great Hall. The first two phases of a remodelling programme, completed by 1990 by the *Alexandra Palace Development Team* under *Peter Smith*, included the Great

Hall and parts of the w wing; a new ice rink in the e wing followed. The rest awaits funding and remains under debate at the time of writing.

The existing building is essentially the reconstruction by *Johnson*, opened in 1875. He reused much of the shell, but the plan was altered to provide a central great hall between e and w ranges around courtyards, with concert room and theatre on the n side. Tall corner towers housing water tanks were added as a fire precaution. The long spreading bulk of the palace makes it one of the most prominent landmarks of n London. The s gable of the central hall is flanked by ranges with arcades on two levels, originally with refreshment rooms behind; the w range is derelict, the e one altered, its openings blocked for BBC studios. The corner towers are now asymmetrical; the SE one was heightened by the BBC and the others have lost their tall mansard roofs. Gables appear also over the entrances on the shorter e and w sides. The n and s gables of the Great Hall survived both fires. They clearly derive their form from Francis Fowke's South Kensington building of 1862, but their bold decoration, with patterns of red and yellow brick, reflects the growing interest in ornament and surface detail led by the Kensington museums in the 1860s; Fowke's 1862 building had been criticized for its plainness. In the s gable, within a deep arch on Corinthian columns, a Victorian circular window with new STAINED GLASS by *Maria Claffety*, a geometric pattern of solar reflective glass and coloured antique glass.

The GREAT HALL is an ingenious mixture of old and new. The remodelling after 1980 omitted the arcades of iron columns; marbled columns were added to the side walls to support the girders of a new roof, whose suspended fabric ceiling echoes the shape of the former glass barrel roof. The glazed roof is slung from two big external steel lattice girders, which make their own contribution to the skyline. The engineer was *Pell Frischmann*. The 1980s interiors in the w wing are decorated in an eclectic Neoclassical Grand Manner. The domed PALM COURT, built as a conservatory and undamaged by the fire, was reglazed and its iron columns sumptuously repainted. To the n, the LONDESBOROUGH ROOM, entirely new, has a green marble fireplace with figure of Solomon above, and large murals by *Cinelli*. Below the Great Hall the PALACE SUITE was created, with murals by *Christopher R. Bouller*, 1988. Other murals in the s corridor flanking the new WEST HALL made from the former courtyard. Disappointingly, neither this hall nor the ICE RINK created in the former e courtyard is architecturally distinguished. The C19 NW concert hall, later a skating rink, has gone, replaced by a works yard. In the NE wing the derelict THEATRE remains; an awkwardly long rectangular room with raked floor and balcony (an upper balcony has been removed) and thin Neoclassical plasterwork. Beneath the proscenium stage, original wooden machinery for scene changing (five sets of levers and pulleys), a rare survival.

Externally the tall gaunt n side has been little altered; the adjacent site of the railway, with its little booking hall (now a community centre), is still evident.

The PARK has unrivalled panoramic views S. It was laid out by *Alexander McKenzie* with formal beds close to the S terrace. The winding paths between clumps of planting on the steep slopes below remain, but the chief Victorian attractions have gone, including a banqueting hall (1864), racecourse and grandstand (1868) at the foot of the southern slope. To the W the park incorporates THE GROVE, the grounds of a house demolished in the 1870s. Some oaks and yews remain from the celebrated C18 landscaping carried out when it was the summer residence of Topham Beauclerk, a friend of Dr Johnson (whose name has been given to the early C20 lime avenue). N of the palace is a boating lake, originally part of a string of lakes, lost when the land was sold for building. The park originally included the former farmland to the N, which was laid out with an avenue aligned on the now disused N entrance. This part was sold for building after 1901.

## BRUCE CASTLE

Since 1906 a museum and archives department. The Tottenham manor house stands close to the church, in its own grounds N of Lordship Lane. Its name derives from its medieval ownership by Robert Bruce. It was acquired by Sir William Compton in 1514. The attractive E-plan S front is a composite creation, a late C17 and C18 remodelling of a house which probably goes back partly to

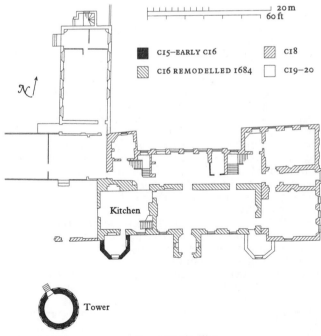

Bruce Castle. Plan

Compton's time – see the early brickwork of the lower part of the
24 polygonal bay at the E end – and partly to a later C16 rebuilding. The
s front may have formed part of a courtyard house of which the rest
has disappeared.

The main impression of the s front now is of the remodelling of 1684,
when Henry Hare, second Lord Coleraine, brought the house up
to date after his marriage to the Dowager Duchess of Somerset.
The central porch was given lively stone quoins, two orders of
pilasters, and a balustraded top, and surmounted by a tower and
little cupola. The polygonal end bays were heightened. Additions
were also made to the N and E, possibly after 1708, when Henry,
Lord Coleraine, succeeded his grandfather. An extra range of
rooms was added to the N, with a N front with heavy pediment
with the Coleraine arms over the centre five bays, and windows
within arches on the ground floor, probably originally intended as
an open loggia. The E wing was remodelled again after 1764 by
James Townsend, who married a daughter of Lord Coleraine.
The E front became an entrance front and was given the appearance of a plain Georgian house, eight bays and three storeys, with
a slightly off-centre doorway, which is explained by the plan of the
older building; the blind window to the l. of the door masks the
original back wall. The Georgian transformation was completed
by the replacement of the late C16 gabled attics of the s front (of
which evidence remains in the roof) by a top floor and parapet.
A w wing was demolished in 1813. The present three-storey NW
extension dates largely from c. 1870, when the house was in use as
a school.

The INTERIOR has been much altered, and now consists of a
series of exhibition spaces, with some C18 panelling here and
there. The arrangement of the late C17 house is known from a
plan of 1684. The hall was in the main range, then still only one
room deep, flanked by services to the w, great parlour and 'back
hall' to the E. On the first floor the main bedchamber was over the
kitchen, the dining room over the hall, a lady's chamber over the
porch. The C18 additions provided extra reception rooms; the sale
catalogue of 1789 lists, on the ground floor, hall, saloon, drawing
room, eating room and breakfast parlour, and library and billiard
room on the first floor. The w stair, on a dogleg plan, with open
string with carved tread ends and turned newels, looks early C18,
but its cramped position suggests it may have been moved. The
more spacious E stair, arranged around a well, and convincingly
sited NE of the hall, however, has details which look later and may
be a C20 reconstruction.

TOWER to the SW. A great puzzle. Circular, of red brick, 21 ft in
diameter and decorated with blank pointed arches; a fine military-
looking object, probably of early C16 date and of no known
purpose. Its origins were already obscure by c. 1700, when Lord
Coleraine wrote that 'in respect of its great antiquity more than
conveniency, I keep the old brick tower in good repair, although I
am not able to discover the founder thereof.'

The PARK was opened to the public in 1892, Tottenham's first public
park. BOWLING GREEN PAVILION, c. 1971 by *Andrews, Downie
& Kelly*. Neat and attractive, with interlocking monopitch roofs

and boarded walls. Alas, burnt 1998. The green is on the site of the kitchen garden, whose C17 brick wall remains on the S side.

## PERAMBULATIONS

*1. North Tottenham: a circular tour starting at All Hallows Church in Church Lane*

The parish church and the neighbouring manor house and park of Bruce Castle, together with the wide expanse of the cemetery stretching N from the churchyard, give this corner of Tottenham an unexpectedly rural feel. To the E is the old route of the High Road, still with considerable remains of a respectable C18 past; the land on either side of it was built up from the C19, and much rebuilt in the C20; its housing now ranges from cottage almshouse to C20 mega-structure.

The tour starts with one of the best of Tottenham's houses, THE PRIORY, Church Lane, from 1906 the vicarage. The house is set back behind an excellent C18 iron gate with curly overthrow, brought from No. 776 Tottenham High Road, used as the vicarage from 1870. The gate has been attributed to the smith *George Buncker*. A good early Georgian E front of five bays with rubbed red brick dressings, Doric doorcase with segmental pediment, and eaves cornice. But the steep roof and irregular chimneys indicate an older house remodelled, and repairs *c.* 1990 revealed remains of timber-framing behind the brick front. A N wing projects to the E, a S wing, with shallow early C19 bow, to the W.

The interior retains C17 work from the time of Joseph Fenton, a City barber-surgeon. A lavish plaster ceiling remains in the 18 ground-floor room to the r. The front part has the all-over surface decoration characteristic of the period. Fenton's rebus and the date 1620 appear in a strapwork surround in the centre of a pattern of broad, curving enriched ribs and floral sprays. The back of the room must be a later enlargement; it has a simpler ceiling with plain patterns and small centrepieces, one of them a Rococo cartouche. The fireplace on the wall adjoining the entrance passage has very fine, undercut carving of *c.* 1730–40. Of the same period are the details of the small SE room and the handsome staircase, with twisted balusters and carved tread ends, which rises around a well in a stairhall at the back to a landing with an Ionic arcade. First-floor rooms with C18 panelling, but the centre one on the N side has earlier panelling; small unpainted panels, a C17 corner overmantel with upright ovals, and a plaster roundel on the ceiling with the date 1621.

STREETS N OF THE PARK still have an early C19 village scale. In PROSPECT PLACE five pairs of tiny box-like cottages face the cemetery, the centre one with simple pediment and the date 1822. Along CHURCH ROAD a low parapeted terrace. In CEMETERY ROAD a slightly later terrace on the W side, and the cemetery gates at the end dated 1858. In BEAUFOY ROAD Sir William Staines Almshouses: simple gabled two-storey houses on three sides of a secluded garden. Founded in St Giles Cripplegate; rebuilt here in 1868. Opposite and in GRETTON ROAD and TENTERDEN ROAD is some of the most attractive of the low-rise housing built by *Haringey Architect's Department* in the 1970s (*A. Maestranzi*); completed 1971. Friendly groups of unfussy white-boarded two-storey terraces, respecting the character of the neighbourhood. Staggered frontages step down to another group of three-storey flats. Beyond is a small neat COMMUNITY CENTRE in Miesian mode, one-storeyed with exposed stanchions, by *Colquhoun & Miller*.

The E end of WHITE HART LANE has the scruffy character common around stations. On the S side a gaunt RAILWAY TAVERN, with terracotta corner gable dated 1895; opposite, one good house: Nos. 32–34, THE GRANGE, restored in 1985, early C18; five bays, two storeys and parapet, with rubbed brick window surrounds and an off-centre Doric doorcase; early C19 wings with blind arches, the r. one much altered. On the S side, No. 7, a neat stuccoed villa of *c.* 1840.

TOTTENHAM HIGH ROAD has at its N end a scattering of substantial Georgian houses, from the time when the village, like Stoke Newington further S, was a haven for prosperous London merchants. After long neglect, repairs from 1982 onwards have gradually restored some of their dignity. The best are on the E side, set back a little; the characteristic type is of three tall storeys above a basement. Directly opposite White Hart Lane is the largest group: Nos. 790–802. No. 790, Dial House, is the exception, standing close to the road, and possibly an addition to an older building. Largely reconstructed in 1982; the front survives, of five bays with central doorway and coved eaves cornice. It may date from 1691 (the date on the sundial). No. 792 is C18. Then Nos. 794–782, Northumberland Terrace, built in 1750–2 by Robert Plimpton, timber merchant, on the site of the Black House, a late medieval mansion sold off by its C18 owner, the Duke of Northumberland. The forecourt walls to No. 796, Percy House, with curly volutes and grand rusticated gatepiers, could be late C17 survivals from the older mansion. Good red brick dressings and cornice; parapet above. The houses are of irregular size; Nos. 794 and 796 are of five bays, the others narrower. Further N, Nos. 808–810 are a fine tall semi-detached early C18 pair with unusually elaborate detail in a Baroque spirit: seven bays in all, with blind centre window and narrower end ones; triple keystones to segmental window heads, brick aprons below. (Original interiors to No. 810.) Nos. 816–820, much altered by shops, retain a big Ionic doorcase to No. 818. No. 822 is early C19, with first-floor windows below arches.

On the W side of the High Road, starting at the N end close to the Edmonton boundary, Nos. 867–869, a very urban group, close to the roadway, like most of the houses on this side. Plain early C18; each of five bays, originally part of a group of four. Porch with carved brackets to No. 867. Nos. 859–863 were formerly a single three-bay house with extra carriage bay on the r.; early C18 with early C19 doorcases and sashes. The two-storey terrace, Nos. 847–851, may be early C18 but has been drastically altered. Nos. 819–821, three storeys, are also early C18, with later ashlar-lined rendering.

NORTHUMBERLAND PARK, to the E of the High Road on the land behind the site of the Black House (*see* above), started as an ambitious speculation of middle-class villas. They were laid out from the 1850s along a broad avenue sweeping E towards the station of the same name, but were mostly replaced by the sprawling NORTHUMBERLAND ESTATE, slab blocks and lower terraces begun by the Borough of Tottenham in the late 1950s and continued into the 1970s. Along PARK LANE, which became the service road to the S, to the E of the grounds of Tottenham Hotspur (q.v.), is a stuccoed row of shops dated 1866, a surprising survival. Near the High Road off BRANTWOOD ROAD, a contrast in C20 housing types: Haringey's last tower block, STELLAR HOUSE, completed 1971, and COOPERAGE CLOSE, low-rise groups built for Haringey by *Colin St J. Wilson & Partners*, 1973–5: a crisp cottagey group in dark brick with timber porches, and nicely scaled three-storey flats with balconies to a grassed courtyard. A common room at one end.

The HIGH ROAD S of White Hart Lane has only patches of interest. On the E side the former Tottenham and Edmonton Dispensary, Edwardian, with a stone ground floor enriched by an Ionic doorcase, and a few plain early C19 houses; on the w, Moselle House, with an early C19 side porch added when Church Road was laid out. Nos. 695–697 are a grander early C19 pair built in 1829 for Joseph Fletcher. Their porches have fluted Greek Doric columns which echo those of the dignified Baptist Chapel nearby (q.v.), which Fletcher helped to build. Opposite, No. 676 remains from the former Bull Brewery; one-storeyed, stock brick with stuccoed parapet to the road, and a clock above. Further S, other much altered C18 houses: No. 668, five bays with straight-headed brick window heads; Nos. 664–666, a refronting with rainwater head of 1817; and No. 662, whose lower proportions suggest an early C18 date.

At the junction with Lansdowne Road the classical corner turret of the white-walled CWS stores of 1930 looks across to the eclectic Gothic of the late Victorian RED LION on the S corner and the exuberant Edwardian Jacobean of the former Tottenham Gas Company offices (now Municipal Offices, q.v.). A short diversion w along LORDSHIP LANE can take in BRUCE TERRACE, three tall linked pairs of charming semi-detached villas with delicate iron verandas, dated 1826. MILLICENT FAWCETT COURT opposite, completed 1971, belongs to Haringey's phase of medium-rise pedestrian-segregated housing: two long three- and four-storey ranges in pale brick, plain but neatly detailed, stepping down on the w side, with a grass court in between.

Back in the High Road, on the E side, Nos. 614–620; the shaped brick gables above scruffy later shops are remnants of the former Blue School, a girls' charity school built 1833 by *Samuel Angell*, enlarged 1876. It lies on the edge of SCOTLAND GREEN, where some small C19 cottages remain on the S side.

Towards Bruce Grove Station the predominant mood of the High Road is shabby late Victorian. A few highlights on the w side. Nos. 583–585, set back from the road, are a fine three-storey C18 pair, with giant red brick pilasters, each of four bays, with entrances in side annexes (and an additional inserted doorcase to No. 583). No. 581, Charlton House, is a smaller cottage, C18 with Doric doorcase. In the adjoining alleyway, a surprisingly rustic relic behind No. 579, a two-storeyed, timber-framed, weatherboarded outbuilding with pantiled roof, perhaps C18. Further on, another alley leads to MORRISON YARD, with a late C19 brewhouse from the former Tottenham Brewery (No. 551b). No. 549, Barclays Bank, is a plain red brick palazzo, three storeys with balustraded parapet. On the E side all that need be noted is Nos. 530–536, a once good early C19 terrace disguised by shops in front, and, near Factory Lane, a strange commercial building with bands of purple glazed tiles. What is its date?

BRUCE GROVE, leading NW towards Bruce Castle, was built up along one of the avenues of Bruce Castle Park after the estate was sold up in 1789. On the W side, first a short early C19 terrace, then Nos. 5–16, five large early C19 pairs: each house of two or three bays and three storeys over basements. Once very handsome but now with sadly cluttered forecourts and extensions. Some good fanlights remain (Nos. 6, 8, 13, 14). Nos. 13–16 are the least spoilt. Opposite, next to the former Bruce Grove cinema, public conveniences with lavish railings. Further N, on the E side, the DRAPERS' ALMSHOUSES, a combination of three City foundations moved out to the countryside. 1868–9 by the company's architect, *Herbert Williams*. Spaciously laid out on three sides of a garden, with a central chapel with plate tracery window and angled flèche. Two-storey cottages in minimal Gothic, with red and black brick window arches, gabled dormers and pretty pairs of wooden porches. Bruce Grove leads to LORDSHIP LANE; opposite Bruce Castle, THE ELMHIRST, a decorative pub of 1903 with pargetting and corner turret.

Finally, to the W along LORDSHIP LANE, where the farm land which still survived until the beginning of the C20 was taken over for planned working-class housing. First a PEABODY ESTATE of 1907, then the much larger WHITE HART LANE ESTATE. This was one of the *LCC*'s first four cottage estates on the fringe of built-up London. The land was bought in 1901; initial plans were to house 33,000. The earliest part to be built (1903–13) lies just N of Lordship Lane: a grid of streets between TOWER GARDENS and RISLEY AVENUE with rows of two-storey terraced cottages made picturesque by a variety of slate-hung and tile-hung gables, hipped roofs and bay windows. The public garden S of Risley Avenue and the more generous private gardens in part of this first area were made possible by a donation by Sir Samuel Montagu; however, the houses were slow to let and less popular than those on the slightly cheaper Noel Park Estate at Wood Green (*see* Perambulation 4). The LCC response in 1912 was to plan for some houses with higher rents, in imitation of the greater social range of Hampstead Garden Suburb. Many extensions after the First World War: around WALTHEOF GARDENS to the N, a formal Neo-Georgian lay-out, 1921–3; TOPHAM SQUARE, flats off Risley Avenue, 1924; along LORDSHIP LANE, quiet terraces of cottage flats in pale render with modest Georgian features, 1925–6; around FLEXMERE ROAD to the NE, informally laid out cottages, 1926–7 (thinly detailed because of reduced funds). This last area is separated from the rest by THE ROUNDWAY, built in the 1920s as part of the bypass to the A10. N of the Roundway off Fryatt Road, LARKSPUR CLOSE, a delightfully secluded enclave of old people's housing, fitted on to a long, thin site. By *Lee, Quine & Miles*,

1973–6. All one-storeyed; stepped and undulating terraces with dark boarding on either side of an informal route. A larger block of sheltered housing with curved window at the entrance.

BROADWATER FARM, s of Lordship Lane off Mount Pleasant Road, was *Haringey Borough Architect's Department*'s most ambitious housing project in the first years of the new borough, planned 1966, completed in 1971; a system-built estate of plain slab blocks linked by walkways, planned for 1,063 households. The centre-piece is TANGMERE, a coarsely detailed concrete megastructure; U-shaped, with crude stepped-back angled balconies to the out-side, and an upper-level shopping street looking inward; five storeys of flats above. Later cosmetic decoration, removal of some of the walkways and other alterations have done only a little to dispel the bleakness and artificiality of the original concept, fenced off from the adjacent park and isolated from the more neighbourly surrounding streets.

LORDSHIP LANE RECREATION GROUND, a public park opened in 1932, has a pioneering model traffic area for training children in road safety, devised by *G. E. Harris* in 1938.

## 2. *From Tottenham Hale Station via Tottenham Green and the High Road to Seven Sisters Station*

Tottenham Hale began as a hamlet by the River Lee, but nothing old remains except the canal. There was a paper mill near the Lee in the late C18, but in the 1890s there were still nursery gardens, and it was only in the early C20 that the area became overwhelmingly industrial. The late C20 saw another transformation, nearly all the older factories replaced by nondescript sheds, and a new road cut through from Tottenham Green to Tottenham Hale Station (q.v.), whose importance grew after it became a junction of the Victoria Line with the line to Stansted Airport.

Much of the present domestic building is piecemeal rebuilding of the 1950s onwards. First, E of the railway, off Jarrow Road, the FERRY LANE ESTATE of the 1970s, a rare appearance of *GLC* work in this area. Pleasantly laid-out low-rise housing on former industrial land: two-storey terraces and three-storey flats in slightly stolid vernacular-revival; upper floors slate-hung. Then by numerous pedestrian crossings to HALE GARDENS, w of the Hale, which the new traffic routes have left pleasantly quiet. This was the site of an early post-war showpiece of mixed development by *Tottenham Borough Council*. The centrepiece is WARREN COURT, 1956, a Y-shaped nine-storey tower, clad in pale brick; end balconies to the s wing; short access balconies in a projecting frame on the N side. Not too large to overwhelm the surrounding crescent and shopping terrace of the same date. A low pub nearby (the City Arms) and a low later C19 terrace to the SW remain from the cluster of small streets (in existence by 1864) which were swept away by the post-war redevelopment. A subway beneath Monument Way leads N to the CHESNUT ESTATE. The s part is Haringey low-rise of the 1970s. The same type of pleasant white-boarded terraces as at Tenterden Road (see Perambulation 1) and the same type of small one-storeyed Community Centre by *Colquhoun & Miller*, but the lay-out is unimaginative, and badly in need of landscaping to pull it all together. The N part, completed in 1971 and separated by a much busier road until Monument Way was made, consists of a long brown brick ribbon of four-storey maisonettes by *Bertram Dinnage* of *Haringey Architect's Department*, with his characteristically austere but well-detailed lines of simple windows.

At the w end of CHESNUT ROAD, near the High Road, two quite grand Italianate houses of the C19 survive; the s one (Polo Club) of three bays with dentilled cornice, the N one (No. 1) more elaborate: a Doric frieze above bay windows and another frieze with medallions below bracketed eaves. Directly opposite in the HIGH ROAD is the former TOTTENHAM PALACE THEATRE, 1908, by *Oswald Cane Wylson* of *Wylson & Long*, the last and only survival of their chain for the United Variety Syndicate. Converted to a cinema in 1926 and for bingo in 1969. A stately Neo-Baroque front with striped quoins, segmental pediments to the wings, and a recessed centre with stone balcony in front of Ionic pilasters. Entrance lobby with three little domes, generous foyer, and a lavishly plastered and gilded auditorium, complete with its circle and upper gallery. Gilded female statues flank the proscenium arch. The original colours were described as cream and gold, salmon pink and turquoise blue, with crimson draperies and carpets. The raked stalls have gone, replaced by bingo tables.

The HIGH ROAD between here and Bruce Grove has little to single out: a group of much altered low C18 or C19 houses with some mansard roofs (Nos. 429–441), a plain but dignified taller C19 terrace (Nos. 479–491) and THE SHIP, whose predecessor was frequented by Izaak Walton; now elaborately Italianate, with ship reliefs on its projecting bay. (For the High Road further N, *see* Perambulation 1.)

To the s there is more of historical interest, though it is painful to see how the townscape has been split apart by the new road system. The High Road widens as it climbs towards the slightly higher ground which marks TOTTENHAM GREEN. On the w side first THE ZONE, built in 1909 as Canadian Royal Skating Rink, later a cinema and dance hall; a classical front on a curve, but exceedingly utilitarian behind, masking a view of the former High Cross School (q.v.), once the centre of a group with almshouses, now with new housing behind of the 1980s. s of this, behind a dismally neglected forecourt, a pair of C18 three-bay, three-storey houses (British Legion), much rebuilt after a fire. LIBRARY COURT, which follows, is more encouraging, a conversion of Tottenham's Edwardian library to flats, retaining the cheerful and informal frontage of 1896 by *Edmeston & Gabriel* (based on their library at Kilburn, Willesden). Lively striped quoins, corbelled-out balconies and pargetted gables. Across the road a small angular SCULPTURE: Embracing Forms, by *Vanessa Pomeroy*, 1983. The E side of the road has former school buildings (q.v.) built for the now defunct Tottenham Grammar School, on this site from the C16. A glimpse E down the disruptive Monument Way can take in another C18 house, now standing forlornly alone by Stainby Road; three bays, three storeys, with pedimented Doric doorcase.

TOTTENHAM HIGH CROSS, polygonal with a conical top, stands on a traffic island. A persistent survival. The thin Gothic details date from an 1809 stucco recladding of a brick structure of the early C17. This replaced a wooden wayside cross, recorded here in 1409. Beyond the cross is the Green proper, with the potentially attractive group of the low stuccoed SWAN inn, a small C19 Gothic school building and Holy Trinity Church (qq.v.). In front is HIGH CROSS PUMP, a well sunk in 1791 by the Lord of the Manor, Thomas Smith, after he had enclosed a previous well on common land in front of his house to the W of the Green. The well-head with tiled conical roof dates from a rebuilding in 1876 by *P. P. Marshall*, the parish surveyor. Only a little remains of the domestic buildings that once surrounded the green. Edwardian public buildings (qq.v.) now run along TOWN HALL APPROACH on the W side, where detached C18 houses formerly stood. The S side still has a decent early C19 pair, with ground-floor windows below blind arches, and the E side another pair, late C18, with a one-storey bowed addition to the N, which later belonged to the former hospital next door.

The former HOSPITAL is a quiet four-storey Neo-Georgian range of 1881, of brick with stone dressings; it was converted to flats by *Hunt Thompson Associates* from 1992. Its domestic character is explained by its origins: it was founded in 1868 as a Deaconesses' Institute, established at Avenue House by Dr M. Laseron for the training of voluntary Christian workers as nurses, modelled on the German Institute at Kaiserswerth. It became Tottenham Hospital in 1899, and was renamed the Prince of Wales Hospital in 1907. The later hospital buildings behind were replaced in the 1990s by *Hunt Thompson*'s low housing: traditional streets of two- and three-storey groups, with a few taller accents; red and yellow brick echoes the materials of the older building. They make an interesting comparison with the area immediately to the N of twenty years earlier, the SALTRAM CLOSE ESTATE, by *David Stern*, 1971–5. This combines the 60s traditions of traffic segregation and stark, precise forms, with the then growing concern to provide more homely low-rise housing. The crisp white brick terraces with split-pitched roofs are cleverly planned to lead gently from two-storey houses in COLSTERWORTH ROAD up to terraces along an upper deck over garaging.

Back to the High Road. At the end of the Green the TOTTENHAM WAR MEMORIAL, 1923, with a stone pillar bearing a slim bronze angel of peace by *L. F. Roslyn*. Then, on the W side, the College of North-East London (q.v.) and the former JEWISH HOSPITAL (No. 295), by *H. H. & Marcus Collins*, 1897–1901; S wing 1913. An amply proportioned Free Jacobean composition in red brick, with shaped and stepped gables, on a half-H plan. Two-storey bowed windows to the taller central block. On the E side, at the corner of Broad Lane, a former BANK of 1902, Free Classical; angled gable with pepperpot turrets. The green space with trees at the start of Broad Lane perpetuates the memory of a group of seven elm trees planted by seven sisters, the source of the name of SEVEN SISTERS ROAD, laid out from Camden Town to Tottenham in 1830–3.

### 3. South Tottenham: a circular tour starting at Seven Sisters Station

In the early C19, South Tottenham, like Stamford Hill to its S, had a sprinkling of large houses in their own grounds, homes of city merchants who established themselves on the country fringes. In 1861 St Ann's Church was built (q.v.), and a few middle-class villas appeared in the neighbouring streets of Avenue Road, South Grove and North Grove, laid out in 1857. Then the railway came in 1872, and with the introduction of workmen's fares the whole area was rapidly but haphazardly developed with small streets of two-storey terraces. This modest pattern has largely survived. Although some streets were swept away for grandiose post-war schemes, from the 1970s the area became a testing ground for Haringey's new low-rise housing policies. This perambulation takes in an assortment of the C20 interventions in the experimental variety of styles that replaced the heavier manner of the 60s.

Starting from Seven Sisters Station, in SEVEN SISTERS ROAD one's eye is caught first by a three-storey terrace with brown boarding and white projecting upper windows, typical of the light, picturesque approach of the 1990s. Behind is Haringey's extensive STONEBRIDGE ESTATE of c. 1974 (*Charles Grant*). Plain brown brick terraces, but tempered by a winding road preserved from the former lay-out, with carefully detailed garden walls and landscaping. (A similar development, also by *Charles Grant*, in PLEVNA CRESCENT, further S.)

To the NW of Seven Sisters Road the borough undertook extensive rebuilding. Nos. 545–583, two curiously detailed terraces on a curve, are of c. 1974 by *Haringey*, small houses with walls partly boarded, with a restless pattern of windows and blind recesses. Such detail was quite a novelty in public housing at the time. Behind, around KERSWELL CLOSE, two- and three-storey clusters in a pleasant series of informal courts, by *HKPA* for Haringey, 1971–81, the upper maisonettes reached by balconies and walkways. Sturdily detailed, red brick, painted concrete lintels and rather heavy pantiled roofs. N of this, a yellow brick cluster by *John Melvin & Partners*, 1974, a conscious contrast to KENT HOUSE, Haringey's tall block of the late 1960s to its N. The S side of ST ANN'S ROAD and SUFFOLK ROAD is different again: by *A. Maestranzi* of *Haringey Architect's Department*, completed 1971, narrow alleys of austere white brick terraces with monopitch roofs, Mediterranean-hill-village in inspiration, but lacking the quality detail needed to convince.

On the N side of St Ann's Road a few mid-C19 villas remain: Nos. 178–184. A few more of similar date are scattered along AVENUE ROAD N of the church. Here also is a little row of MODEL COTTAGES of 1858, built, like the adjacent schools, by Fowler Newsam, benefactor of St Ann's Church (qq.v.). Steep roofs with gables; gabled porches with Tudor doorways with portraits in relief (restored 1989). W of NORTH GROVE another mid-1970s development is fitted discreetly into the surrounding grid of roads: PENRITH ROAD and APPLEBY CLOSE, by *Douglas Stephen & Partners*. Plain buildings in dull brick, but cleverly planned around an attractive landscaped square. Two sides have houses over ground-floor flats, the other two have houses over garages with ingeniously raised private gardens.

WEST GREEN ROAD further N, winding E–W, is an old route linking the High Road and Green Lanes, mostly C20 now, and archi-

tecturally indifferent apart from No. 432, the Red House, a striking old people's home by *Colquhoun & Miller*, 1976. Orange brick.
An unusual lay-out on a triangular site, with a splayed wing (to
allow for a road which was not built). In the angle a common
room with bold convex eaves profile. To the N, SUMMERHILL
ROAD, laid out with cottages in 1857, and DORSET ROAD, with
WARBERRIES, a house with reliefs from a stonemason's yard. The
hamlet of West Green lay at the junction with Philip Lane, still
marked by the Blackboy pub. On the site of a C19 station on the S
side, picturesquely tucked into a slope, GRESLEY CLOSE, by *Dry
Halasz Dixon*, brown brick with jutting top balconies, somewhat
in the manner of Darbourne and Darke. This is one of a number
of small infill groups of the mid 1970s along a redundant railway
line between Seven Sisters and Turnpike Lane. By the same firm,
BRUNEL CLOSE further E, *c.* 1976. Near Seven Sisters Station,
BRUNSWICK ROAD and LOMOND CLOSE, two- and three-storey
white boarded terraces by Haringey, pleasantly straightforward, in
the manner of Tenterden Road (*see* Perambulation 1). The 1970s
move to provide low-cost housing acceptable to the occupiers
culminated in PELHAM COURT, N of West Green Road, where
the simple low-rise houses by *Bertram Dinnage* of *Haringey
Architect's Department*, 1976–9, incorporate plans and details
requested by the tenants' co-operative (e.g. a kitchen at the back
of the house). Further S BRAEMAR ROAD has a group which
shows the 1980s taste for fussier historicist detail: elaborate
balconies and gabled porches.

OUTLIERS. A diversion S down Seven Sisters Road can take in the
WOODBERRY DOWN TAVERN, late C19, coarsely picturesque in
a Norman-French manner, with prominent timberwork to its
large gables.

E from this, N of Vartry Road, DALEVIEW ROAD, with low-rise
housing by *Colin St John Wilson & Partners*, 1974–5. Further E,
at the end of Craven Park Road, GROVELANDS, an early and
attractive example of the borough's switch to low-rise: 1970–1 by
*Janina Chodakowska* of *Haringey Architect's Department*. Trim
rows of two-storey white-boarded terraces (with vertical not horizontal boarding like the later ones, and with flat roofs), and a
three-storey range of flats with balconies overlooking the River
Lee, nicely detailed.

## 4. Wood Green

Wood Green, once a hamlet within the parish of Tottenham, developed
after the opening of the station on the Great Northern line in 1859.
In 1881 Clarke's *Suburban Homes* called it 'almost an independent
colony'. It became a separate local authority in 1888 and, especially
in the new NW suburbs, maintained a middle-class respectability as
Tottenham became increasingly working-class. Radical change came
in the 1970s, when the area round the High Road was rebuilt as the
chief commercial centre of the new Borough of Haringey .

### South from Wood Green Station

The scene around the Underground station on the HIGH ROAD
is unhappily disparate: large and brash office buildings of the

1970s–80s confront a tiny Victorian shop and a couple of Edwardian pubs and Neo-Georgian banks, relics of a once uneventful suburban centre. To the s, opposite a scruffy market and open space awaiting redevelopment, a SAFEWAYS of the 1990s, with an unbelievably crude columned entrance. Further s, the huge former GAUMONT CINEMA of 1934 by *W. E. Trent & E. F. Tully*. Art Deco details to the foyers and the ovoid auditorium. Further s again, a jagged pile in deep red brick closes in on the High Street. This is WOOD GREEN SHOPPING CITY, a multi-level complex planned by *Sheppard Robson & Partners* (project architect *Richard Young*) from 1969. It was intended as a central focus for Haringey's three newly merged boroughs. The original plan, like many urban redevelopments of the 1960s, included elaborate pedestrian segregation, with diversion of the main road to the e, and a complex network of upper walkways. This was simplified in execution to a broad bridge with shops linking a short stretch of upper-level shopping on each side of the existing High Road, which remains a traffic route. Above the shops are multi-storey car parks and flats; the flats on the e, PAGE HIGH, by *Dry Halasz Dixon*, completed 1975, are arranged around a nicely secluded 'street in the air'. The larger shopping area to the w includes covered malls and a market hall (opened 1979), and a later covered shopping arcade wrapping around the side of the library, but the back of this part, as so often in such schemes, is messy and incoherent. Ramps for the abandoned flyover end in midair. The Library (q.v.) is the best individual contribution, standing out by its use of yellow ceramic tiles, but the open site in front has been compromised by indifferent additions.

NOEL PARK, e of the High Road, is grazed by the Shopping City, but was spared worse damage by the abandonment of the proposed road. This 100-acre estate of low-rent houses was created by the Artisans, Labourers and General Dwellings Company, which bought the land in 1881. It was laid out by *Rowland Plumbe* from 1883, and was largely complete by 1907. The n part was the first to be built; the streets s of Gladstone Avenue followed from the later 1890s.

As in the Artisans' two earlier estates, Shaftesbury Park, Battersea, and Queens Park, Paddington, the improved housing consists not of large blocks of tenements but of small houses. The streets are still straight, stock brick is still used extensively and long terraces exclusively. To that extent there is no influence yet from Norman Shaw's work of the 1870s at Bedford Park. But some streets have tree planting, and along GLADSTONE AVENUE the picturesque cluster of hall and vicarage by St Mark's and the tall school add two accents. The terraces are varied by their porches, and also have taller or projecting corner houses or occasional taller gables, sometimes with terracotta ornament. The row immediately n of the school (cottage flats, with two front doors under an arch) has gables patterned with green bricks. Along the High Road is a taller block with shops.

THE SANDLINGS, sw of Noel Park, off Glynne Road, is a medium-rise housing development of the early 1970s by *Haringey Architect's Department (Joyce Atkins)*, built on railway sidings. Completed 1975. Extensive but not oppressive: four-storey ranges over garages, with stepped-back balconies overlooking a pleasantly informal sequence of grassed courts. Faced in yellow brick with pebbly concrete lintels.

Around the junction of the HIGH ROAD and TURNPIKE LANE little of note, except for the Underground station (q.v.) and the long strip of DUCKETT'S COMMON. N of Turnpike Lane, in BURGHLEY ROAD, a former pumping station of 1897 with small decorative shaped gable, ingeniously converted in 1983 by *Marden & Knight* to a parents' and children's club; cart-shed converted to playroom opening on to a secluded open area. Finally, S down GREEN LANES, to the area known as HARRINGAY, where small cosmopolitan food shops occupy the long Victorian parades. At the corner of St Ann's Road, the SALISBURY HOTEL, built in 1898–9 by *J. C. Hill* (the firm which also built the Queen's Hotel, Crouch End; *see* Hornsey, Perambulation 2). One of the best examples in London of a bold and brash late Victorian pub on a grand scale: a broad curved corner, striped cupolas on fat polished granite columns, shaped gables and central tower with openwork iron crown. Fittings to match; excellent joinery and glass, and more exceptional Art Nouveau cut-glass mirrors, attributed to *Cakebread Robey.*

*West from Wood Green Station*

STATION ROAD leads past large 1970s offices to WOOD GREEN COMMON, a pleasant oasis, with the New River to the S and modest Victorian suburban housing round about. To the N, ST MICHAEL'S TERRACE, with a mixture of sheltered and other types of housing, *c.* 1983–7 by Haringey (*David Hayhow*). A friendly two-storey group in a variety of materials; pale brick with grey stripes and much timber boarding. Picturesque exterior stair, projecting porches. It occupies the site of the Palace Gates Station, and is the last and most attractive of the various low-rise housing groups built along the redundant branch line from Seven Sisters (*see also* Perambulation 3). Nearby in DORSET ROAD and BRIDGE ROAD, reticent cottages of *c.* 1900, in pale unembellished brick. At the corner of Buckingham Road, THE STARTING GATE, built in 1875 as The Palace Café; by the 1890s, a public house, the Alexandra Palace Hotel. Refitted 1899 by *Richard Dickenson.* Good pub interior with iron columns and engraved glass.

The skyline at the S side of the common has the shaped gables of the Board School and former Baths in Western Road (qq.v.). The area beyond developed from the 1860s after the opening of the Wood Green (now Alexandra Palace) Station in 1859. At the corner with MAYES ROAD, GRANTA HOUSE by *Dixon Del Pozzo DHP,* 1983–5; with bands of brickwork below low eaves sweeping elegantly around the curve. It replaces part of Barratts sweet factory (on this site 1880–1980), whose splendidly bombastic offices remain as No. 109, CAMBRIDGE HOUSE. This was industry at its most confident: a Baroque palace of red brick with generous stone dressings, four storeys and attics. A giant Roman Doric order rises above the ground floor; over the central archway the motto 'Labor et Probitas' in terracotta is crowned by an open pediment and clock turret (clock dated 1897). Between Mayes Road and the main railway line is a miscellaneous industrial area, where regeneration was encouraged by Haringey from the 1970s. As part of this, off COBURG ROAD, a group of six small flexibly planned industrial units around a courtyard, neatly mirror-glazed, by *Terry Farrell Partnership*, 1978–9.

### North-west from Wood Green Station to Bounds Green

At the N end of the High Road one has a glimpse of Wood Green as it was before the late C20 took over. The Victorian St Michael (q.v.), the area's first parish church, marks the junction with BOUNDS GREEN ROAD. To its s a line of low, pale brick villas of the early C19, still looking quite rural, faces a long strip of green with a tall OBELISK with drinking fountain, 1879, in memory of Mrs Smithies of Earlham Grove, founder of the Band of Mercy. The HIGH ROAD to the N also widens, with the Civic Centre (q.v.) on the W, built on the site of the Fishmongers' and Poulterers' Almshouses; the decent stucco-trimmed corner pub was formerly the FISHMONGERS ARMS. Opposite is a war memorial; on the E side a row of stuccoed Victorian villas faces another green. Further N, some newcomers of the 1990s add character: three-storey flats with a line of canted bays along the road, at the corner of King Street, then the Health Centre at Canning Crescent (q.v.) with its lively roof-line.

WOODSIDE HOUSE (Haringey Social Services), standing proudly on a rise within WOODSIDE PARK, E of the High Road, is an Italianate house of three storeys and five bays, 1864–6. Fomerly Earlham Grove Lodge. Converted to council offices in 1893 and enlarged in 1913 as Wood Green Town Hall, with a one-storey extension to the s containing council chamber and police court. The original stairs were replaced in iron at the same time. To the NW, near the road, a charming rustic LODGE, octagonal, with alternate faces inset, and a central chimney. Deep eaves, and eyebrow dormers within the patterned slate roof. Was it thatched originally? It was built *c.* 1822 for John Overend, the Quaker banker, and led to Chitts Hill House (built probably *c.* 1805, demolished 1896). The grounds, through which the New River ran until 1852, were admired by Keane in his *Beauties of Middlesex*.

COMMERCE ROAD, W of the High Road, first built up in the 1860s with middle-class villas, became a centre of post-war housing activity (as so often, a showpiece built within sight of the town hall). Good examples of the usual sequence of types: first LCC-type mixed development planned from 1959 under *A. J. Rebbeck*, Wood Green Borough Engineer: two seven-storey and two fifteen-storey brick-faced point blocks and a neat low terrace with shops. Plans for further high-rise were abandoned in favour of Haringey's traffic-segregated contribution of *c.* 1975, MORANT PLACE by *Ivor Smith & Cailey Hutton*: two long parallel ranges; they contain garaging below stepped-back flats of three and four storeys, approached by exterior stairs, overlooking a rather bleak plaza. To the W, around FINSBURY ROAD, unostentatious low-rise terraces of the 1970s. PALMERSTON ROAD continues N, its broad green strip marking an underground stretch of the New River made in 1852 to cut off the loop towards Tottenham. Off to the E, REDRUTH CLOSE, an example of picturesque small-scale infill of the 1970s: ingenious tightly knit houses with coloured brickwork, by *Dixon Haryett*, *c.* 1979.

The growth of the area further w followed the opening of Bowes Park Station in 1880. The Victorian shopping centre in MYDDLETON ROAD, leading to the station, still has some original shopfronts. To its s, in TRURO ROAD, large Victorian villas remain. In NIGHTINGALE ROAD, behind attractive Art Nouveau railings, ST LEONARD'S ALMSHOUSES, 1904 by *A. W. S. Cross*, a rebuilding of two foundations from Hackney Road and Old Street, Shoreditch. Back now to BOUNDS GREEN ROAD, which leads NW towards Southgate through a seamless growth of Edwardian and interwar housing, encouraged first by electric tramways and then by the arrival of the Piccadilly Line station (q.v.) in 1932. Opposite the station, in DURNSFORD ROAD, a row of cottage-style houses built for Wood Green UDC in 1921 by *T. H. Mawson* and *R. Dam*; attractively simple, with rendered walls, although compromised by rewindowing. Tucked away to the w near SCOUT PARK (opened 1928), BADEN COURT, an imaginative little 1970s group by *Dry Haryett Dixon*, of breeze blocks with timber cladding, around a tiny landscaped court with a fountain. Further s a large area of open land is preserved as Muswell Hill Golf Course (1893) and Albert Road Recreation Ground (1928), with the former Wood Green Lido (1934, now a garden centre). This was part of the Alexandra Park company land (*see* Alexandra Palace), and before that belonged to Tottenham Wood Farm. The early C19 portico of the farmhouse is preserved in the grounds of the primary school in RHODES AVENUE.

# ISLINGTON

The present borough, formed in 1965, is named from the larger of its two constituent Metropolitan Boroughs. The smaller one, Finsbury, on the fringe of the City, united several areas already largely built up by the later C17. Islington proper was in origin a medieval parish extending N for three miles from its main settlement around the High Street. Its development as a densely built-up suburb took place chiefly from *c.* 1790 to *c.* 1890. Since then the population of modern Islington has fallen dramatically: 174,500 in 1995, only little more than that of Finsbury alone in the mid C19.

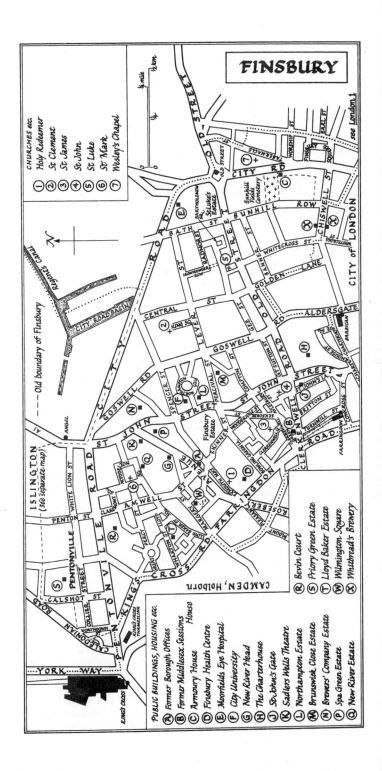

# FINSBURY

CHURCHES etc.
① Holy Redeemer
② St Clement
③ St James
④ St John
⑤ St Luke
⑥ St Mark
⑦ Wesley's Chapel

PUBLIC BUILDINGS, HOUSING etc.
Ⓐ Former Borough Offices
Ⓑ Former Middlesex Sessions House
Ⓒ Armoury House
Ⓓ Finsbury Health Centre
Ⓔ Moorfields Eye Hospital
Ⓕ City University
Ⓖ New River Head
Ⓗ The Charterhouse
Ⓘ St John's Gate
Ⓙ Sadler's Wells Theatre
Ⓚ Northampton Estate
Ⓛ Brunswick Close Estate
Ⓜ Brewers' Company Estate
Ⓝ Spa Green Estate
Ⓞ New River Estate
Ⓡ Bevin Court
Ⓢ Priory Green Estate
Ⓣ Lloyd Baker Estate
Ⓦ Wilmington Square
Ⓧ Whitbread's Brewery

see London 1

CITY of LONDON

ISLINGTON
(see separate map)

CAMDEN, HOLBORN

——— Old boundary of Finsbury

# FINSBURY

## INTRODUCTION

Finsbury, on the northern fringe of the City, was the second smallest of the LCC boroughs formed in 1901. It was composed of the Clerkenwell parishes of St James and St John, whose churches were successors to the C12 foundations of St Mary's Nunnery and the Priory of St John, and of St Luke Old Street further E, a parish carved out of St Giles Cripplegate in 1733.

The medieval and Tudor ages are more alive here than in most other inner London boroughs. The area was then bounded on the w by the valley of the Fleet River, winding along what is now King's Cross Road and Farringdon Road. On the higher ground were springs, which early on were appropriated for the City's water supply. One of them, the Clerk's Well which gave its name to Clerkenwell, is still visible off Farringdon Road. Further E, N of Cripplegate and Moorgate, was Moorfields, an area which Fitzstephen described in the C12 as a 'great fen or moor' on which skating on bones was a popular entertainment in the winter. The rest of Finsbury in Fitzstephen's time was 'fields for pasture and a delightful meadowland interspersed with flowing streams'. A causeway through Moorfields was built in 1415, and as the fields were much used for archery a special area was set aside for the sport in 1498. Moorfields long remained open land, but early in the C17 it was made into a public promenade by planting rows of trees flanking straight walks. To R. Johnson in 1607 Moorfields was 'a garden to the city . . . for citizens to walk and take the air and for merchants' maids to dry clothes in'.

By the end of the Tudor age much had changed in the built-up area of Clerkenwell. After the dissolution of the monasteries part of the nunnery site became Newcastle House, a mansion of the Duke of Newcastle, which survived until the 1790s. The Charterhouse, the third monastic foundation in the area, founded in the C14, had passed first to Sir Edward North, then to the Duke of Norfolk, and finally in 1611 to Sir Thomas Sutton, who converted it into a refuge for old men and a school for boys. In the C16–C17 the neighbourhood was of high social standing. Katherine Parr and the Venetian and French ambassadors had residences close to the Charterhouse, and Stow speaks of 'many fair houses for gentlemen' near the former Priory of St John. N of this area, which appears lightly built over on Agas's map of 1560, was open country, made uniquely interesting to Londoners of the time of James I by Sir Hugh Myddelton's adventurous and public-spirited creation of the New River to provide water for London. It came from Amwell, near Ware in Hertfordshire, over 39 miles away, to the site which later became the headquarters of the Metropolitan Water Board.

Like the suburban areas of Shoreditch and Southwark, Finsbury attracted activities proscribed within the City. There were theatres, among them the Fortune in Golden Lane, built for Philip Henslowe and Edward Alleyn. In the C17 and C18 the area became a great rallying point of Nonconformity, still recalled by the Bunhill Fields Burial Ground and Wesley's Chapel in City Road. Wesley had first preached in the remains of the brass foundry at Moorfields (abandoned after an explosion in 1717) – a reminder of early industrial activity. Breweries and distilleries appeared from the C18, a foretaste of the industrial growth of the next century; the pre-eminent survival is Whitbread's establishment in Chiswell Street. The open land also attracted institutional buildings. Robert Hooke's Bethlehem Hospital for the insane was built along the southern edge of Moorfields in 1675–6, and Finsbury received two of the many C18 hospitals attracted to the fringes of London: St Luke's Old Street, established in 1751 and the Lying-In Hospital of 1771, in City Road. All these have gone, as have the prisons which were a feature of Clerkenwell from the C17 to C19 (the exception being the basement levels of the 1840s House of Detention preserved beneath Kingsway College).

Meanwhile the northern parts assumed a different character, owing to the discovery of chalybeate springs late in the C17. The waters were first visited for medicinal reasons – an early example was the Cold Bath, of c. 1697, near the present Rosebery Avenue, around which Coldbath Square developed in the C18. Soon the new spas became places of amusement, with tea-gardens, grottoes and the like. The best known was Sadler's Wells, where the Music House of 1683 was the precursor of the present theatre. E of Sadler's Wells was the Islington Spa or Spa Fields or the New Tunbridge Wells; Bagnigge Wells lay between King's Cross Road and Gray's Inn Road.

Until the C19 much of the southern parts of Finsbury remained essentially a residential suburb. Its growth was encouraged by the arrival of refugees from the City after the plague of 1665 and the fire of 1666, and developers began to lay out new streets, as in Holborn further w. 416 houses were recorded in the parish of Clerkenwell in 1661, over 1,500 in 1724. In the early C18 it was still a smart address, as can be seen from some fine surviving houses in Charterhouse Square. The early C18 houses remaining in Britton Street, within the old precinct of St John's Priory, were built by a lawyer, Simon Michell, who also restored the chancel of the priory church as a new parish church. Further E was a denser suburban area, for which St Luke's Church was provided c. 1730. Ogilby and Morgan's map of 1676 shows the area between Golden Lane and Bunhill Row already fully built up, with houses beginning to spread N of Old Street.

Development further afield was encouraged by the New Road begun in 1756, a bypass designed to take traffic to the City from the West End, avoiding the old crowded streets. The Finsbury parts were complete by c. 1770, and in 1773 Henry Penton began to develop his estate, which lay just to the N of this line on the borders with Islington, calling it Pentonville. His spacious grid of streets and a few of his houses remain. At the same time Finsbury Square was laid out, on the edge of the City, by the City Surveyor *George Dance*, but this never quite achieved its intended status, and the handsome terraces have long given way to commercial buildings. By the end of the C18 the fringe of the City was no longer a fashionable address, and the steady growth in the earlier C19 was less ambitious socially. The population of Clerkenwell was already 23,000 in 1801; it grew to 31,000 in 1811 and 48,000 in 1831. For the whole of Finsbury at this time it was 102,000, rising to a peak of 173,000 in 1861.

The varied character of the surviving early C19 parts of Finsbury reflects the piecemeal land-ownership of the area, so different from the great estates of the West End. Much remains from this time, despite later encroachment. On the lands of the Northampton Estate there are the fragments of Northampton Square, laid out in 1805 to the E of St John Street, and Wilmington Square further W, of the 1820s. Just N of Clerkenwell Green is the tight little enclave of the Sekforde Estate, complete with chapel, built in the 1830s, further N are the more extensive developments of the New River Company of the 1820s onwards: Claremont Square, Myddelton Square and 55 neighbouring streets, and the delightful Lloyd Baker Estate of the 1830s–40s, on the land rising to the E of King's Cross.

By the mid C19 the whole area was built up, and overcrowding in the southern parts was widespread, particularly in the narrow courts and closes hidden behind the more respectable streets. In 1851 Clerkenwell had 7,549 houses, with an average of eight persons per house. Small-scale industries developed, particularly watch- and clockmaking, well established already in the C18. At first they were carried out in domestic buildings, adding to the congestion, but then 66 increasingly in the later C19 in purpose-built workshops and factories. These (although now empty or in other uses) still dominate Cowcross Street and St John Street and the new C19 roads which sliced through some of the worst slums: Farringdon Road laid out over the line of the Fleet River, and Clerkenwell Road, built up c. 1870.

To house some of the displaced population, working-class flats were built, the first (now demolished) in 1865 by the Corporation of London in Farringdon Road, others by philanthropic organizations, and from 1899 by the LCC. By 1901 there were 31 groups of 'model dwellings' in Finsbury, the largest of them the Peabody Estate in Whitecross Street, S of Old Street. But much overcrowding remained, and the pattern of slum clearance and rebuilding was continued energetically between the wars by the Borough of Finsbury. Five-storey walk-up flats of the 1920s in *E. C. P. Monson*'s conventional Neo-Georgian were followed by more radical plans for urban renewal drawn up by the architects of *Tecton*, led by the émigré *Berthold* 110 *Lubetkin* and continued by *C. L. Franck*. The Finsbury Health Centre (completed in 1938) was the enlightened herald, but the war put an end to the borough's ambitious Finsbury Plan, which proposed comprehensive redevelopment of the whole area around Rosebery Avenue. Instead, the flats built after 1945 were on scattered sites: 117 Spa Green, Bevin Court in Holford Square, and Priory Green in 118 Pentonville, all planned by Tecton before the firm split up; others followed on a larger scale around Skinner Street and King Square. By 1967, 7,000 people had been rehoused in the post-war rebuilding programme. These parts of Finsbury express a C20 urbanity more reminiscent of a continental city than any other part of London.

This C20 rebuilding paid little heed to the traditional pattern of London streets and squares, of narrow courts and closes reflecting the historic growth of the area. The clash around Northampton Square is particularly harsh. Reaction in favour of a more conservation-minded approach came after Finsbury became a part of the new Borough of Islington in 1965. Renovation of surviving domestic terraces was followed in the 1970s by growing appreciation of industrial buildings. Their future became doubtful as manufacturing activity declined, but their fabric proved amenable for conversion to small workshops, offices, studios and restaurants and (in the 1990s) to apartments. A new, smart, commercial Clerkenwell began to emerge. The intimacy of Clerkenwell contrasts with the less happy amorphous areas E of Goswell Road and with the clash on the City fringe around Chiswell Street between older remnants and monster offices of the 1980s.

## RELIGIOUS BUILDINGS

### 1. Church of England

HOLY REDEEMER, Exmouth Market. On the site of Spa Fields Chapel. 1887–8 by *J. D. Sedding*, completed by *H. Wilson*, 1892–5. Not in their exuberant free Gothic mood, but a powerful Italian 89 Renaissance design, exceptional among London's Victorian Anglican churches. The brick exterior hides a steel-framed construction. Tall front with round-arched doorway, boldly lettered frieze, and striped brick above with a circular window. Big deep-eaved pediment. On the r. the projecting SW campanile and clergy house (1906), on the l. a church hall (1916), all added by *Wilson*. They make bold use of tiles for stringcourses and arches. Inside, four groin vaults on an unbroken entablature, resting on giant Corinthian columns. Capitals carved by *F. W. Pomeroy*. Sedding planned frescoes, but these were not carried out. Behind the nave arcades, narrow aisles, and narrow, inorganically placed transepts. Marble High Altar under a massive domed baldacchino, on the pattern of Santo Spirito, Florence. Behind it, Wilson's E Lady Chapel, with altarpiece in pedimented Ionic frame. Large stone FONT, 1909, and other furnishings by *Wilson*. ORGAN from the Chapel Royal, Windsor, installed 1889.

ST CLEMENT, King Square. Built as St Barnabas, by *T. Hardwick*, completed 1826. Four-column giant Ionic portico without pediment. The needle-thin obelisk spire was intended to refer to the mother church of St Luke. Originally with a plain galleried interior. After Second World War damage reconstructed by *Norman Haines*, reopened 1954. Grand, spare spaces of nave, aisles and sanctuary divided by four cruciform piers with giant Corinthian columns; flat ceilings. Altar below a classical baldacchino. Nice hexagonal PULPIT, C18, from St Marylebone Chapel.

ST JAMES, Clerkenwell Close. 1788–92, by *James Carr*, a local architect and builder, on the site of the choir of the medieval nunnery (*see* Perambulation 1). An attractive landmark, giving an C18 flavour to Clerkenwell Green. A stock-brick box with a stone W tower topped by balustrade and vases. Open polygonal stage above, and an obelisk-like spire on a concave base (a variant on St Martin-in-the-Fields and St Giles). The steeple was rebuilt to the old design in 1849 by *W. P. Griffith*. S side with classical Tuscan Doric doorways in first and last bays, E side with large Venetian window (the centre originally blind), and a pediment; solid and competent rather than inspired. The interior has a curved W end, an unusual and successful feature, underlined by the gallery, also curved round on the W side. It is reached by two elegant staircases in rooms l. and r. of the tower. Early C19 upper galleries were added for charity children (reduced to a W gallery in 1940). Flat ceiling with restrained plaster decoration. Restored and reseated by *Blomfield*, 1883–4, but many Georgian furnishings remain. – FONT, carved rosewood, *c.* 1820. – Classical REREDOS with C19 texts. – C18 COMMUNION TABLE with bowed front. – C18 wrought-iron COMMUNION RAILS. – Also C18 the CHURCH-WARDENS' PEWS at the W end; and BOX PEWS in the gallery. Handsome mahogany ORGAN CASE by *G. P. England*, 1792, with feathery palm leaves. – ROYAL ARMS of *Coade* stone (George III). Over the nave W door, early C18 STATUE of St James, from a poor-box. – STAINED GLASS E window: Ascension by *Alexander Gibbs*, 1863, large figures in glaring colours. – BRASS. John Bell, Bishop of Worcester, †1556, relaid 1884 (lower part of figure lost). – MONUMENTS. (S aisle) Elizabeth Countess of Exeter †1653, armorial. – (N tower stairs) Elizabeth Partridge †1702, cartouche with bust and putti; of high quality. – (S of the tower) Henry Penton †1714, wall monument with gracefully ornamented obelisk. – Gilbert Burnet, Bishop of Salisbury, †1715, plain pedimented tablet with books and scrolls, by *R. Hartshorne*, an assistant of Stanton, also a large black marble floor slab below the altar. – Thomas Crosse †1712. Standing wall monument with two busts. – Beneath the tower, two CHARITY BOARDS, a BELL RINGERS' BOARD (Westminster Youths, 1800) and, more exceptionally, a monument to victims of Fenian riots, 1867. – Good VESTRY FURNISHINGS.

ST JAMES, Pentonville Road. Demolished. *See* Perambulation 5.

ST JOHN, St John's Square. *See* St John's Priory, below.

ST LUKE, Old Street. The parish was formed in 1733 from that of St Giles Cripplegate, and the church was funded by the Fifty New Churches Act. Built 1727–33 to designs by two of the Act's surveyors, *John James* and *Nicholas Hawksmoor*. Redundant by 1960, unroofed by the Church Commissioners, and left derelict after no buyers emerged. Consolidated as a ruin in 1994. The organ case and font went to St Giles Cripplegate, reredos and altar rails to the NW chapel at St Andrew Holborn (*see London 1: The City of London*). Conversion for the London Symphony Orchestra by *Levitt Bernstein Associates* began 1999. The body of the church is of stone all round, and so of unusual dignity, with a fine Venetian window in the E wall, and the remarkable W tower. This has as its spire a fluted obelisk, a concept of robust origi-nality (cf. Hawksmoor's St George, Bloomsbury), although one which did not find favour with classical purists. The W tower rises soundly and sturdily from the ground and the aisle roofs form a fragmentary pediment a little behind its front, thus avoid-ing the awkwardness of the St-Martin-in-the-Fields tower-on-pediment composition. The W entrance in the tower is flanked by staircase wings with N and S doorways. An oculus over each entrance. Domed vestibule beneath the tower. Flanking lobbies, each with an elegantly cantilevered stone stair in a curved end. The interior had tall unfluted Ionic columns, a shallow vault to the nave and transverse vaults to the aisles with galleries on three sides. Fine churchyard RAILINGS of 1852, and some good CHEST TOMBS.

ST LUKE'S CHURCH CENTRE, Roscoe Street. 1977 by *Biscoe & Stanton*. A replacement for the C18 St Luke's. No architectural pretensions.

ST MARK, Myddelton Square. 1826–8 by *W. Chadwell Mylne*, Surveyor to the New River Company. Stock brick, the usual Gothic box of the period, but with an exceptionally solid W tower adorned with a pinnacle-flanked portal of quite substantial richness. Some of the stone came from Wanstead House. The interior originally galleried on three sides. Reordered 1873 by *W. Slater* to create a chancel; reseated 1879. Bare interior (bombed in the war). STAINED GLASS. E window by *A. E. Buss* of *Goddard & Gibbs*, 1962; Ascension and local scenes.

ST SILAS, Penton Street. Begun 1860 by *S. S. Teulon*, completed 1863 by *E. P. Loftus Brock* to a simpler design. Chancel by *W. White*, 1884. Ragstone with some perverse use of brick. Gables over a clerestory with plate tracery. Plain interior with passage aisles and timber roof starting low down. Incomplete SW turret.

## 2. Roman Catholic

ST PETER AND ST PAUL, Amwell Street. Built 1835 by *John Blyth* for members of the Countess of Huntingdon's Connexion; R.C. from 1847. Sober Italianate front with central Venetian window, interior with galleries on thin iron columns, with ornate Gothic iron railings. Post-war STAINED GLASS of saints.

## 3. Other places of worship

ANGEL BAPTIST CHURCH, Chadwell Street, 1824, contemporary with adjacent houses on the New River estate. Stucco front with central pediment and Ionic porch. Built for Calvinistic Methodists.

ISLINGTON CLAREMONT UNITED REFORMED CHURCH, White Lion Street. Built as the Claremont Institute, 1906–10 by *Alfred Conder*. Three storeys, modestly decorated with striped pilasters and pierced parapet. A rear adjunct to the former Claremont Chapel of 1818–19 in Pentonville Road (Perambulation 5, p. 637).

KING'S CROSS WELSH TABERNACLE (Congregational), Pentonville Road. 1853–4 by *Henry Hodge*; porch, entrance lobby and vestries by *Alfred Conder*, 1904. Ragstone Gothic with slim Dec windows. Lofty, well-preserved interior: pitch-pine gallery of 1857, original fittings, hammerbeam roof with bold pierced spandrels. Dormer windows of 1904.

Former LEYSIAN MISSION, now IMPERIAL HALL, City Road. 1901–6 by *J. J. Bradshaw* of *Bradshaw & Gass*; the third home of the mission founded by the Methodist Leys school, Cambridge, in 1886. Intended for a mixture of secular and religious activities and so with a deliberately commercial-looking front to its offices and accommodation: tall, exceedingly sumptuous, with plenty of terracotta, a central dome and scrolly Arts and Crafts ornament. Great Hall behind, originally seating 1,750, rebuilt in 1953–5 by *W. H. Gunton* after war damage. The original staircase remains, with stained glass by *W. J. Pearce*. The Mission was amalgamated with Wesley's Chapel (*see* below) in 1989, and the building was remodelled as flats by *Planning Design Development* in 1994.

SOCIETY OF FRIENDS MEMORIAL BUILDING, Banner Street. *See* Perambulation 6, p. 643

VERNON BAPTIST CHAPEL, King's Cross Road. Three-bay brick front of 1843–4, minimal debased Perp detail. The Minister, the Rev. *Owen Clarke* (secretary of the British and Foreign Temperance Society), may have been his own designer, together with a local builder. Galleries added 1848; E extensions and small transepts 1869–70; interior remodelled 1937.

WESLEY'S CHAPEL, City Road. 'The Mother Church of World Methodism'. John Wesley established his London headquarters at the Foundery, Moorfields, in 1739. By the 1770s the movement had outgrown the small converted building, and Wesley laid the foundation stone of the new chapel himself, at the age of seventy-four, in 1777. The cost was met by subscription. Large broad oblong of stock brick, with two storeys of round-headed windows in five bays, a pediment over the centre three. Shallow stone apse. Greek Doric porch of 1815. Stone dressings, and probably the outer wings, by *Elijah Hoole*, 1891 and 1899. The interior has galleries on three sides, enlarged *c.* 1800 by curved corners, and an elaborate geometric ceiling with putti heads. The later enrichments give the room a C19 flavour: reseating by *W. W. Pocock* in 1862–4, who also created the vestibules; further work by *Charles Bell* after a fire in 1879; major restoration in the 1890s by *Elijah Hoole*, when the timber gallery columns were replaced by columns of jasper and the ceiling was raised to allow for tiered gallery seating. Some of the original Tuscan columns (made from ships' masts given by George III) are preserved in the vestibule. Original FITTINGS include the COMMUNION TABLE, RAILS and especially handsome mahogany PULPIT (the top tier of a three-decker, lowered in 1864). STAINED GLASS. Much, mostly late C19 pictorial, but three more dynamic designs by *Frank O. Salisbury* (S, second from E, 1930, and two flanking the W door, 1932, 1934). N gallery E, St John, by *H. Holiday*, 1900; gallery N, the Wesleys by *James Powell & Sons*, 1924. Many minor MONUMENTS, several of the early C19 ones by *Manning*, e.g. Joseph Butterworth †1826, with woman kneeling by a cross, and Lancelot Haslope †1838, woman reading a Bible beneath a palm tree; both delicately carved. In the 1880s portrait busts were popular: among them W. M. Punshon †1881 and Gervase Smith †1882, by *E. Onslow Ford*, twin busts beneath a pair of marble Gothic canopies; W. F. Moulton †1898 has a bespectacled bust in an odd classical aedicule, by *J. Adams-Acton*. F. J. Jobson †1881, also by *Adams-Acton*, is in profile, in a niche. To the S the FOUNDERY CHAPEL, rebuilt in 1899, toplit like a billiard room, with Wesley's own chamber ORGAN, and seating from the original foundry building. Small graveyard to the E, with plain chest tombs and a taller one with pyramid top and urn to Wesley †1791.

Forecourt with C18 iron gates, a bronze STATUE of Wesley, 1891 by *Adams-Acton*, and obelisk to Susannah Wesley, 1870 by *Albert Dunkley*.

The chapel was planned together with flanking houses along City Road. The one to the N was replaced by the MANSE of 1898. Three storeys, S porch with Doric columns *in antis*. Between it and the chapel, the LEYSIAN CENTRE, in the Benson Building of 1880, refurbished 1993 by *Watson Partners*, with meeting rooms and offices. To the S, WESLEY'S HOUSE, No. 47 City Road, occupied by Wesley himself and restored as a museum in 1897–8. Four storeys, brick with stucco and *Coade* stone dressings. Simple but elegant C18 joinery inside; fireplaces flanked by glazed fitted cupboards. On the first floor Wesley's bedroom in the back room, with his prayer closet opening off. Landing STAINED GLASS by *Osborne & Philips*, 1947.

Former WHITEFIELD TABERNACLE, Leonard Street. Now used by the Central Foundation School for Boys. By *C. G. Searle & Son*, 1868. Built to replace Whitefield's famous C18 Congregational Tabernacle at Moorfields. Ragstone Gothic, a huge and rather coarse Dec window in the gable over the triple entrance. Adjoining Sunday School with smaller gable. Inserted floors.

WOODBRIDGE CHAPEL (Clerkenwell and Islington Medical Mission), Hayward's Place off Sekforde Street. Built 1832–3 for Independent Calvinists. Simple brick exterior, the front with four round-arched upper windows, in keeping with the contemporary housing of the Sekforde Estate (*see* Perambulation 1, p. 625). Galleried interior, reconstructed in the C19, now floored.

## 4. Cemetery

BUNHILL FIELDS CEMETERY, City Road. The most celebrated Nonconformist burial ground in England, in use from the later C17 to 1854. Crowded with monuments, mostly minor, but many of them worth a glance. Near the centre, the Bunyan Memorial of 1862, by *Papworth*, a stone obelisk erected to Daniel Defoe in 1870 and a simple shaped headstone to William Blake †1827, and his wife. Gates and railings to City Road 1869, with big granite piers.

## PUBLIC BUILDINGS

Former BOROUGH OFFICES, Rosebery Avenue. On a triangular island site. Built as Clerkenwell Vestry Hall. 1895 by *C. Evans Vaughan*, rear extension of 1899. Nice irregular red brick and stone building in a free Flemish Renaissance, with a lantern and a fanciful glass and iron street canopy. The blunt-ended rear is more Baroque; broken segmental pediment with female figures, and carved frieze above the first floor. Grand first-floor public hall with apsidal end; coffered ceiling in fibrous plaster with elaborate Art Nouveau detail; winged figures hold sprays of light bulbs. Council chamber converted 1975 to mental health day centre. Further alterations 1985.

Former MIDDLESEX SESSIONS HOUSE, Clerkenwell Green. London Masonic Centre since *c.* 1980. Built 1779–82 by *Thomas Rogers*, Surveyor to the County of Middlesex, who was accused of cribbing designs by *John Carter*, the antiquarian. Much altered by *F. H. Pownall*, 1859–60. Palladian E front with centre pediment on engaged Ionic columns; decorative reliefs in medallions and panels by *Nollekens*. Pownall faced the originally plain brick sides in Roman cement with stone dressings, but his more elaborate plans for the W front (exposed by the opening of Farringdon Road) were not fully carried out. He also added an attic storey and altered the interior. The fine square central hall with circular coffered dome is original, but its cantilevered gallery, central staircase and lantern to the dome are by Pownall. Originally there were windows between the pendentives, and the stairs led in a curving double flight to the front Court Room. The Court Room retains its coffered ceiling. s extension of after 1876.

SHOREDITCH COUNTY COURT, Leonard Street. Built for the City and Guilds of London Technical College, 1881–3 by *E. N. Clifton*. Three storeys, ground- and first-floor windows arched. Porch with columns *in antis* and pediment carved with scientific books.

CLERKENWELL MAGISTRATES COURT, King's Cross Road and Great Percy Street. 1906 by *J. D. Butler*, a fine design, with his typical oversize keystones and a recessed centre with semicircular pediment.

TRAFFIC WARDEN CENTRE, King's Cross Road. A former POLICE STATION. 1869–70 by *T. C. Sorby*; five storeys, Italianate with big cornice. Bold stuccoed entrance with royal arms. Low cell block to the r.

POLICE BUILDINGS and PUBLIC CARRIAGE OFFICE, Penton Street. 1964–6 by *J. Innes Elliott*. With the pre-cast concrete panels with splayed reveals that were popular in the 1960s.

CLERKENWELL HOUSE OF DETENTION. *See* Kingsway College, below.

ST JOHN'S GATE MUSEUM. *See* St John's Priory, p. 623.

ARMOURY HOUSE, City Road and Bunhill Row. The Honourable Artillery Company was given a royal charter in 1537. Its oldest building is C18, approached through gates by *George Dance*, 1793, and faces s to a parade ground. Designs by *Thomas* (?) *Stibbs* were approved in 1729. Built 1734–6. Yellow brick with stone quoins. Palladian composition of five bays with slightly projecting three-bay centre with Doric portico, and tall arched first-floor windows with keystones. The parapet has five exploding cannon balls instead of the usual vases. A flagstaff rises from a central turret. Lower wings of five bays added *c.* 1828, with third storey of 1894. Inside, the central entrance hall was remodelled in the 1930s with a barrel vault, and iron gates of *c.* 1740. Behind, a broad dog-leg stair with closed string and column-and-urn balusters leads to the Long Room along the front. This has panelling of 1919, but C18 pedimented doorcases and chimneypieces of *c.* 1800. Above them the company arms (E) and royal arms (W), 1736. On the N side, small musicians' gallery, late C18 (added by Richard Pepys). To the NW the Court Room with mid-C18 decoration: panelling with a broad frieze with monochrome trompe-l'œil trophies painted by *Francis Holman* in 1758–9. Excellent chimneypiece with carved panel with trophies; above is a medallion of George II in a Rococo frame. Behind the President's chair a rather Batty Langley ogee canopy on trefoil columns. *Coade* stone royal arms above. At the rear on the ground floor, an austere mid-C19 drill hall with simple iron-trussed roof. On the City Road frontage, BARRACKS of 1857 by *J. J. Jennings*, demonstrably alluding to a heroic national past: a heavily rock-faced castellated fortress front with angle turrets and a broad gatehouse, refurbished 1994. Wilfully exclamatory angled link to the older buildings, faced in striped stone and granite, punched by openings of arbitrary shape. By *Arnold & Boston*, 1993–4.

FIRE STATION, No. 44 Rosebery Avenue. 1911–13 by *H. F. T. Cooper* of the LCC Fire Brigade Branch. Large, quite plain eighteen-window front, but with nice Arts and Crafts details and railings.

POST OFFICE SORTING OFFICE, Mount Pleasant. 1934 by *A. R. Myers* of the Office of Works. Vast. Built on the site of the Middlesex House of Correction of 1794. Refurbishment and extensions by *Watkins Gray International*, 1996.

LIBRARY, St John Street. By *C. L. Franck*, 1965–8. Planned together with the Finsbury Estate (*see* Perambulation 4). The two-storey curving front respects the line of the street, emerging from beneath a tower block. Precast units in black and white, with large glazed entrance to a broad foyer; on the l. a public hall, on the r. children's library and the main library behind, the latter given character by a generous N window and suspended barrel ceiling. Intended as a central library for Finsbury before it became part of Islington, replacing the library in Skinner Street of 1890 by *Karslake & Mortimer*.

MARX MEMORIAL LIBRARY, No. 37a Clerkenwell Green. Built 1738 by *James Steer* as a Welsh Charity School. Much altered in the C19; the front elevation was restored to a semblance of its simple pedimented C18 appearance in 1969. Used for radical meetings from 1872, when it became the headquarters of the London Patriotic Society, and by the socialist Twentieth Century Press from 1892 to 1922. Lenin had an office here in 1902–3. In the first-floor library, large forceful 1930s MURAL (exceptionally, in fresco) by *Jack Hastings*, pupil of Diego Rivera, depicting 'The Worker of the Future upsetting the Economic Chaos of the Present', including portraits of Marx, Lenin etc. Probably the most explicitly revolutionary public painting in England of its time.

PUBLIC BATHS and WASHHOUSES, Ironmonger Row. 1931 by the baths experts *A. W. S. & K. M. B. Cross*. Swimming pool added 1938. Stone-faced, in Roman revival style; two-storey front with patterned glazing to the upper windows, cornice, pantiled roof. Interior refurbished *c.* 1988.

FINSBURY LEISURE CENTRE, Ironmonger Row. 1972–5 by *Derek Lovejoy*. Large red brick windowless sports hall, NW of the Baths; part of the improved amenities for the St Luke's area (*see* Perambulation 7).

FINSBURY HEALTH CENTRE, Pine Street. 1935–8 by *Lubetkin* and 110 *Tecton*, their first public commission. One of the key buildings to demonstrate the relevance of the Modern Movement to progressive local authorities. This was the first achievement of the 'Finsbury Plan', the borough's brave effort, inspired by Alderman Harold Riley and Dr Katial, Chairman of the Public Health Committee, to create better living conditions for its overcrowded residents. H-shaped plan, two-storeyed with part-basement floor, with central entrance set in a gently curving projecting wall of glass blocks, between splayed wings. Borough arms over the entrance. The formality is tempered by a roof terrace to the centre, the name above in typical 1935–40 lettering. Light facing materials: the walls are faced with cream tiles, which on the wings frame curtain walling with teak frames, glazed spandrel panels and metal windows. The floating effect of the 'flashgap', a recessed plinth between walls and ground, is typical of Lubetkin. The light and airy entrance hall, given character by its curved glass wall, was originally enlivened by *Gordon Cullen*'s health education murals on the rear walls, and by a large map of London in the centre. Some original furniture

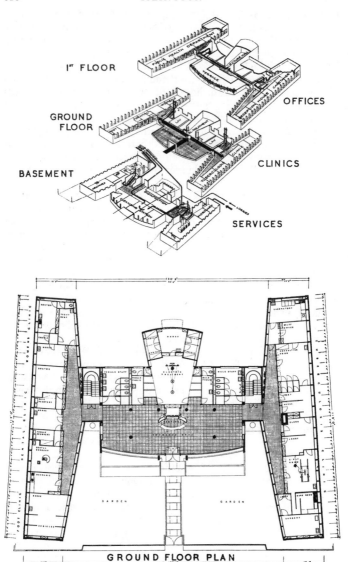

Finsbury Health Centre.
Axonometric and ground-floor plan

and light fittings remain. The lecture theatre behind has splayed walls, a curved back and a curved concrete roof. Consulting and treatment rooms, divided by non load-bearing partitions, are in the wings, where the splayed walls give extra space and light to the access corridors. Exemplary repairs by *Avanti Architects*, 1994–5, restored part of the exterior to its original appearance (asphalt reroofing, new tiles on the left-hand entrance wing, new thermolux glass panels, and the restoration of the original lively colour scheme of blue and terracotta to the painted concrete).

MOORFIELDS EYE HOSPITAL, City Road. An amalgamation of three C19 ophthalmic hospitals founded on different sites in 1804, 1816 and 1834. Main building of 1897–9 by *Keith Young & Bedell*; restrained classical front of red brick above rusticated stonework, a long spread-out composition of 2–3–1–3–2 bays. The end pavilions have shell niches to the attics. King George V Extension, 1933–5, by *Alec Smithers*, tall symmetrical front to Cayton Street, its steel frame faced in buff faience, upper storeys set forward. Above the entrance a small stone sculpture, Christ healing the Blind Man, by *Eric Gill*. Extended and replanned inside, with new outpatients' facilities, by *Watkins Gray International* (Phase 1) and *The Devereux Partnership* (Phase 2), 1979–88, when the branch in High Holborn was closed. Three of the delightful nursery rhyme tile pictures made for the Eye Hospital in High Holborn (now demolished) were transferred here (others went to the Hospital for Sick Children, Great Ormond Street). (CHAPEL with STAINED GLASS (slab and concrete) by *R. E. Rutherford*, 1971.)

INSTITUTE OF OPHTHALMOLOGY, Bath Street. 1989–92 by *GMW Partnership*. Dignified brick four-storey street range, articulated by bays projecting above a recessed ground floor and a tall off-centre entrance with gable. Taller upper parts set back, under a long pitched roof.

Former ST MARK'S HOSPITAL. *See* Perambulation 7.

SADLERS WELLS THEATRE, Rosebery Avenue. Rebuilt as a major dance theatre through Lottery funding. 1997–8 by *RHWL*; exterior by *Nicholas Hare Associates*. The wedge-shaped site is enclosed by tall, plain brick walls. At the s end a big glazed foyer with giant video screen. Auditorium seating 1,500; special attention to disabled access. Sadlers Wells can trace its history back to the theatre that in 1765 replaced a Music House built by Thomas Sadler. It stood by the chalybeate spring which had drawn visitors to Spa Fields from 1683. A well survives beneath the present building, which replaces a small theatre rebuilt in 1930 by *F. G. M. Chancellor* of *Frank Matcham & Co.*

NEW RIVER HEAD. Sir Hugh Myddelton's New River was completed in 1613. Its route from Amwell in Hertfordshire terminated p. 31 with a reservoir on the high ground above Clerkenwell, later known as Spa Fields. The former ponds are still open spaces in the heart of Finsbury, the Upper Pond in Claremont Square made in 1709 (now a covered reservoir), and the inner and outer round ponds of C17 origin (now dry) between Rosebery Avenue and Amwell Street. In the latter area some early buildings remain. Circular brick base of a WINDPUMP, *c.* 1708, now with conical roof (for pumping water to the Upper Pond). The tall ENGINE HOUSE is in origin the one in which a steam pumping engine was installed by *Smeaton* in 1767; enlarged by *Robert Myle* for *Boulton & Watt* engines *c.* 1790. The tapering square chimney of 1818, added by *W. C. Mylne*, was demolished in 1954. Two C19 boiler houses. In the area of the former inner pond a C14 CONDUIT was rather confusingly re-erected in 1927. It served originally as an extension to the White Conduit which supplied the Greyfriars (later Christ's Hospital).

The C20 buildings of the METROPOLITAN WATER BOARD facing Rosebery Avenue were converted to flats in 1997–8. HEADQUARTERS OFFICES are by *H. Austen Hall*, 1914–20; Neo-Georgian, with formal entrance to Hardwick Street and angled wings, not improved by the added top storey. Interior with circulation areas on an impressive scale, leading to the OAK ROOM, the board room of *c.* 1696–7, reinstalled from the previous offices on the site. It has sumptuous plasterwork and carved panelling, some of the best of its date in London. Ceiling oval with painted medallion of William III with allegorical figures, by *Henry Cooke*, within lushly modelled wreath and borders; charming small plaster panels with rural scenes. The fireplace is flanked in the grandest manner with two big Corinthian half-columns; the high-relief watery and fishy subjects flanking the royal arms on the overmantel are carved with all the exquisite realism of the *Gibbons* tradition, and must surely be by him. Carvings over doors and windows as well. LABORATORY BUILDING by *John Murray Easton* of *Easton & Robertson*, 1938, built on a curve, with continuous first-floor windows. At the SE end a semicircular glazed projection for a staircase, especially handsome inside, with a blue ceiling with incised figure of Aquarius by *F. P. Morton*, and original light fittings. One of the most pleasing structures of its date in London.

FARRINGDON STATION, Cowcross Street. The original terminus of the Metropolitan Railway, the world's first underground railway, as enlarged in 1866–8. Two iron and glass roofs over four platforms; brick buttressed retaining walls, paired columns down the centre. To the street, a low white faience-tiled classical front of 1922 by *C. W. Clark*.

*Educational buildings*

CITY UNIVERSITY, Northampton Square. So named from 1966. The historic nucleus is the NORTHAMPTON INSTITUTE, built as part of the late C19 improvements to the Northampton Estate (*see* Perambulation 4). It fills an awkward triangular site between St John Street and Northampton Square with public hall, offices, workshops and swimming bath. *E. W. Mountford* won the competition in 1893; the building was completed in 1898. Red brick with lavish stone dressings. An exceedingly successful example of the neo-French C16 style of the moment with its fresh and playful enrichments. At the NW corner, for example, a picturesque composition in three dimensions: a pert little turret with its cupola, a big bold curved gable higher up, and a lantern tower as a final flourish. The main front is asymmetrical but with a central tower. Doorway with lively figure-frieze by *Paul Montford* below the Baroque curved-up broken pediment. Windows partly French C16, partly Queen Anne. Many alterations: internal courtyard built over at basement level by 1901; five-storey extensions into it, 1909. After war damage the great hall on the St John Street front was rebuilt within existing walls, the gym to its E replaced by a five-storey block (1952–8), and the swimming pool at the Northampton Square corner was reroofed.

The main campus buildings by *Sheppard Robson & Partners*, 1971–9, adjoin the Institute to the NE, cutting brutally across the N corner of the square and the site of Charles Street. Tough exposed concrete and dark brick, as used in their earlier university buildings (Churchill College, Cambridge; Brunel University, Hillingdon), but here there are no alleviating open courts or greenery, and the heavy masses do little to lift the spirit. Circulation at first-floor level. The buildings include library, students' union, refectories, lecture theatres and laboratories etc. The Centenary Building was converted from High Voltage Laboratory to lecture theatres in 1993–4.

w of St John Street, CONNAUGHT BUILDINGS, with lecture theatres, offices etc., in a converted industrial building. In Owen's Row, the Optics Department occupies buildings of 1963, formerly part of Dame Alice Owen Girls' School. STUDENTS' RESIDENCES are scattered around the neighbourhood: in Bunhill Row, Northampton Hall, a twenty-storey tower by the *GLC Architect's Department* (*H. Bennett*), 1962–4; in Bastwick Street, Finsbury and Heyworth Halls, by *Sheppard Robson & Partners*, 1971, and Peartree Court, by *Geoffrey Reid & Associates*, 1991; in Graham Street, by the City Road Canal Basin, Walter Sickert Hall, by *Clark Renner Architects*, completed by *Holmes Bosley Associates*, begun 1992. In Goswell Road is the SADDLERS SPORTS CENTRE, by *Sheppard Robson & Partners*, begun 1973. Like the nearby halls in Bastwick Street, faced in brown brick, with some close-set black mullions. Tough but decent, nicely finished, and less dour than the firm's main campus buildings.

ST BARTHOLOMEW'S MEDICAL COLLEGE, Rutland Place, off Charterhouse Square. *See* Charterhouse, p. 620.

KINGSWAY COLLEGE, CLERKENWELL CENTRE, Sans Walk. This occupies the former Hugh Myddelton School of 1893, an excellent example of *T. J. Bailey's* tall and massive three-decker Board schools, on an H-plan, with plentiful yellow terracotta decoration. (Well-preserved interiors. The lower halls each have a vaulted aisle, with classrooms off; the top hall has a mansard roof on iron trusses.) Separate cookery and laundry building. Annexe of 1902, built as a Special Girls' School. The surprise is that the school stands on the site of the Clerkenwell House of Detention of 1845–7 by *William Moseley*, whose basement survives beneath. It had prison cells radiating from a central hall with cast-iron columns (cf. Pentonville: Islington, Public Buildings). The former female corridor is accessible; roofs of shallow brick arches; warders' hall and clerk's office with granite columns. SCHOOL KEEPER'S HOUSE, three storeys, brick and stucco; formerly the prison governor's house. The boundary wall incorporates part of the prison wall.

CENTRAL FOUNDATION SCHOOL FOR BOYS, Cowper Street. Founded 1866. Plain C19 buildings of stock brick; the centre of three storeys and eleven bays with Doric porch at the l. end; to the E a lower seven-bay range with arched top-floor windows, to the w a three-bay science extension of 1894. Extensions by *Ley, Colbeck & Partners*, 1966.

DAME ALICE OWEN SCHOOLS, Owen's Row. Gateposts of 1788 in Goswell Road remain from the school founded in 1613 by Dame Alice Owen. Boys' and girls' schools moved to Dugdale Hill Lane, Potters Bar, Herts, in 1973, taking with them the statue of Dame Alice by *George Frampton*, 1897, marble, bronze and alabaster; and nine figures rescued in 1751 from her tomb in St Mary, Islington. C20 buildings used by the City University (q.v.).

CLERKENWELL PAROCHIAL SCHOOL, Amwell Street. 1828–30 by *W. C. Mylne* and *John Blyth*. Eleven bays in minimal Gothic; two storeys. SUNDAY SCHOOLS, St James's Walk. *See* p. 627.

ST PETER AND ST PAUL R.C. SCHOOL, Compton Street. 1881, remodelled 1968–71 by *Farrington, Dennys & Fisher*.

BOARD SCHOOLS. Among the earliest: No. 10 BOWLING GREEN LANE, 1873–5, by *Robson*, picturesquely asymmetrical. Another in Eagle Court, St John's Lane, 1874, extended 1894. Plain, two U-shaped blocks, tall chimneys and gables. WHITE LION STREET, 1874; additions with steeply roofed pavilions, 1900.

ELIZABETH GARRET ANDERSON, Penton Street. Compact secondary school by *Architects' Co-Partnership*, 1962; house rooms around a central hall.

POST-WAR PRIMARY SCHOOLS. Several were built together with neighbouring housing in areas cleared after the war. The most interesting are the HUGH MYDDELTON SCHOOLS, Myddelton Street, angled across an incoherent cleared area between Spa Fields and Finsbury Estates. Attractive sturdy buildings, of brown brick with bold timber fascia, a departure from standard types. By *Julian Sofaer* for ILEA, 1966–70. The design makes much use of golden section proportions. The Infants' School has one-storey ranges formally arranged around a courtyard; the two-storey Junior School is linked to it, and also has a small courtyard. Separate Nursery School N of Lloyd's Row, similarly detailed. MOORFIELDS, Bunhill Fields, is a more usual *ILEA* type: three unassuming low single-storey linked blocks, built on the 'rationalized traditional' system, using standardized components. *c.* 1965–70; likewise MORELAND, Moreland Street, 1971.

ST LUKE'S CHURCH OF ENGLAND PRIMARY SCHOOL, Radnor Street, in the redeveloped area N of Old Street. By *Sheppard Robson and Partners*, completed 1974. Low buildings with an intimate entrance courtyard in which are displayed INSCRIPTION STONES from the old school buildings in Old Street (*see* Perambulation 7, p. 644). In the entrance hall, figures of Charity Boy and Girl from the original building of 1780 in Golden Lane.


## THE CHARTERHOUSE
### Charterhouse Square

The Charterhouse is infinitely the most important monument of Finsbury, and indeed one of the most important of all London. It was damaged during the Second World War and extensively repaired and reconstructed by *Seely & Paget*, 1950–9, but nevertheless still conveys a vivid impression of the type of large rambling C16 mansion that once existed all round London. Its complicated story was elucidated by excavations during the post-war reconstruction work and is still being unravelled by more recent research by the Survey of London, to which this account is much indebted.

The first period, from which only fragments remain, is that of the Charterhouse proper, the Carthusian Priory founded in 1370 by Sir

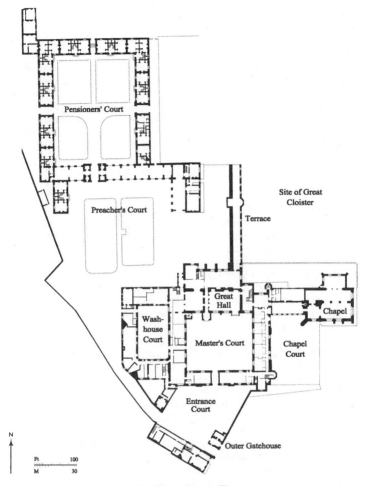

The Charterhouse. Plan

Walter de Manny on a site which he had acquired earlier and intended for plague burials. A chapel was built in 1349, but the intended college of priests was never established. The priory buildings were begun in 1371 under *Henry Yevele*, but not completed until *c.* 1414. The next phase is that of Sir Edward (later Lord) North, who bought the site in 1545 and died in 1564, followed by Thomas Howard, fourth Duke of Norfolk (†1572). The church was demolished and a mansion house created to the SW of the Great Cloister. Then in the early C17 these buildings were converted for the foundation of Thomas Sutton (†1611) for eighty pensioners and forty boys. The change typifies the C17 departure of the aristocracy from the City and its fringes. In the C19 there were extensions for the pensioners to the NW. The Carthusian Great Cloister became the Green of the school, and then of the Merchant Taylors' School, which took over the premises in

1872, when Charterhouse School moved to Godalming. This part became the Medical College of St Bartholomew's Hospital in 1933, and was much rebuilt after war damage.

The original Carthusian establishment consisted of a Prior and twenty-four brothers (twice the usual number). The general arrangement of the buildings is known from excavations and from early plans and surveys. The monks, as was customary in Carthusian houses, had separate minute houses with gardens around the Great Cloister, which was extremely large, 300 by 340 ft. The chapel lay to the s, the refectory to the w. The original prior's cell was at the sw corner. s of the refectory was the Little Cloister, which was enlarged and entirely rebuilt as the core of North's courtyard house in the mid C16 and became the Master's Court in the C17. To the w were the guesthouse and lay brothers' quarters, which partly survive in their early C16 form as Washhouse Court.

The precinct is entered from the s through the OUTER GATEHOUSE at the end of a wall of flint chequers. Early C15 archway with contemporary oak doors. The parts above belong with the adjoining red brick house to the l., built for the Charterhouse physician in 1716. Above the archway two lion brackets, possibly late C16, from Norfolk's time. Tucked into the r. side is the stuccoed Gothic PORTER'S LODGE of the 1840s. Straight ahead is the INNER GATE, an early C16 stone arch (reconstructed), and a CONDUIT HOUSE (a post-war interpretation from old drawings). The conduit house formed part of the C15 waterworks system. The celebrated plan of the medieval water supply is preserved in the Charterhouse.

The entrance to the MASTER'S COURT, the centre of the C16 MANSION, is to the r., at an odd angle. Consequently one does not at once notice that the buildings form a symmetrical composition as one approaches from the outer court. Their present appearance, however, owes much to *Seely & Paget*. The broad s front is of Kentish rag, with gables alternating with (restored) prominent chimneys. The windows are straight-headed under hoodmoulds, mullioned, and with each light arched. Centred archway with depressed arch and panelled soffit, in a square surround and much reconstructed. The battlements added c. 1830 by *Edward Blore* were removed after the war, when the attic floor was added. The later brick and stucco facings which formerly covered the walls on the courtyard sides were also removed, so that the effect is now more uniformly Tudor than before.

The GREAT HALL opposite does not lie on axis with the gateway. The hall has a porch at the w end, refaced with big rusticated quoins in the C17. The roof, parapet and surround to the sundial were rebuilt after the war. The rest is essentially C16 and largely of North's time, its inconsistencies perhaps resulting from the reuse of available material, as often happened with early post-Dissolution conversions. At the e end is a square straight-headed oriel window with arched lights and two transoms. Between oriel and porch, a central buttress, and two windows with four-centred arches and five lights with one transom, ending in ogee heads and Perp tracery; perhaps reused from elsewhere? Four straight-headed windows above, each of three lights, not aligned with the lower windows, and perhaps later additions. Just above the plinth, a row of large

p.
12

quatrefoils, very worn, presumably reused old material. The walls, otherwise of rubble, were rendered before the war. At the NW corner of Master's Court is a brick staircase tower, probably added by Norfolk. It has a window of three lights and two transoms, the lower part opened up after the war. The door E of the hall was also added by *Seely & Paget*. The E range, built in the C16 across the site of the monastic church, became the Master's House in the C17, and was gutted in the war. It was rebuilt (without its E wing) together with the matching s range, whose interior was also extensively reconstructed. The W range is the only one with some original stone dressings, of convincingly worn Reigate stone. On the paving of Master's Court is the outline of the smaller medieval Little Cloister, discovered in post-war excavations.

WASHCOURT COURT to the W was built as part of the monastic outbuildings and lay brothers' quarters in the early C16 and adapted as the service court of the Tudor mansion. The walls facing the courtyard are a picturesque mixture, partly of stone and partly of brick with a diaper pattern. The outer walls are of brick, with chimneystacks corbelled out at first-floor level. On the W range the initials I H in brick for John Houghton, Prior 1531–5, and a low blocked arch.

PREACHER'S and PENSIONERS' COURTS to the N were added as spacious new quarters for the Pensioners, begun in 1826–9 by *R. W. Pilkington* and completed by *Blore* in the 1830s, in a plain Tudor style. Apart from short three-storey stretches to N and S, Preacher's Court was destroyed after war damage; plans for a new SW building by *Michael Hopkins & Partners* were made in 1994.

Between the two courts a two-storey range with ground-floor arches (now blocked). Pensioners' Court, with nice iron lamp, is complete, although it has lost its battlements. Doorways (originally open) to apartments off common stairs, as in colleges or inns of court. In the N range a doorway with skulls in the spandrels leads to the former burial ground, now a garden.

To the N of the C16 mansion is Norfolk's long upper TERRACE (dated 1571), which led to his tennis court, later converted for the school and since rebuilt. The terrace is carried on a brick vaulted corridor which is on the site of the W walk of the CLOISTER of the Great Court. On the W side, square-headed brick recesses revealing medieval stonework.

INTERIORS: GREAT HALL. A composite creation of the C16, C17 and C20. The C16 oriel window has on the inside carved spandrels and panelled soffit and jambs. C16–C17 heraldic GLASS with arms of Somerset and Sutton. The large SCREEN of 1571 dates from Norfolk's time. Much repaired after war damage. Arched openings separated by Corinthian columns, gallery above with caryatids. 17 Along the N wall, an early C17 gallery added for Sutton's foundation, with arcades between tapering pilasters, elaborately decorated with heads and strapwork. Big stone fireplace of 1614, made by *Edmund Kinsman*, with Sutton's arms and strapwork. Cannons and gunpowder kegs commemorate Sutton's office of Master of 16 the Ordnance of the North. The hall was gutted in the war. The hammerbeam roof, originally open but ceiled later, was reconstructed by *Seely & Paget*. The spandrels with quatrefoils and pendants are largely original. The central ceiling was remade to a new design after the war, following the curved profile of the arched principals, and omitting the decorative wooden ribs which had been added by Blore. The longitudinal beams resting on the hammerbeams were reconstructed nearer the walls. In the SCREENS PASSAGE, three doorways to the service rooms, under one stringcourse, the centre one square-headed, the outer ones four-centred, with Renaissance detail in the spandrels.

The N range adjacent to the hall was also built in the 1540s, as tree-ring dating has shown. This rare early example of a double-pile plan is perhaps explained by the existing structures on the monastic site. The ground-floor room has wooden columns down its centre (perhaps added in the later C16) to support the Great Chamber above. Another early C17 stone chimneypiece with Sutton's arms and bold strapwork, similar to the hall fireplace, and a doorcase in the same style leading to the cloister. Beyond this door there may have been a staircase of the 1640s (removed when a grander stair was made E of the hall; *see* below). In the brick vaulted passage below the terrace, on the site of the Great Cloister W range, remains of the entrances to the cells of 1371. The foundation stone was laid by William Walworth, Lord Mayor. The SW corner cell is the best-preserved. The archway is two-centred, with a wave moulding, in a square surround with shields in the spandrels. Beside the door is a food hatch.

The Great Chamber is now approached by a STAIRCASE at the E end of the hall; a plain reconstruction by *Seely & Paget* of a differently arranged and richly carved staircase with open balustrades, the original one probably built by Norfolk, with Sutton's crest added later. On the landing, three stone doorcases, the smallest added to provide access to the early C17 hall gallery, cutting into an older brick archway (an internal window?). The northernmost archway leads to the GREAT CHAMBER, now a single long room, but formerly divided into chamber and ante-room. The decoration dates from Norfolk's time. Plaster ceiling (a *Seely & Paget* reconstruction, apart from the NW oriel), with intersecting ribs and Norfolk's arms. The W window is by *Blore*, reusing old glass. The unusual painted wooden and plaster chimneypiece is also later C16: Emblems of the Evangelists and twelve Apostles in medallions on columns, scenes of the Annunciation and the Last Supper, all in strapwork surrounds, more delicate than the early C17 work. The central panel was repainted in 1626 (signed on the back by *Rowland Bucket*, a leading decorative painter of the time).

The C16 mansion had apartments in the other ranges around the courtyard, and a long gallery, later subdivided, in the S range. In the ground-floor room E of the staircase, a plaster overmantel of *c.* 1620–30, of outstanding quality, brought down from a first-floor room in the Master's range. Large, elegantly Mannerist figures of Faith, Hope and Charity, based loosely on an engraving by Hieronymous Wierix.

CHAPEL COURT, CLOISTER and TOWER. These lie to the E of the Master's Court. CHAPEL COURT is on the site of the original Carthusian chapel, demolished in 1545–7. Excavations of 1947 showed that the C14 chapel was a plain rectangle to which N, S and W additions were made in the C15 and early C16. The founder's tomb was discovered in front of the high altar. In CHAPEL CLOISTER to the N, a fragment of the C14 TOMB CANOPY with miniature ribs, still with its original paint, also part of a STATUE of St Catherine, of high quality. Also in the cloister, two C17 stone figures of Moses and Aaron, possibly from a Laudian reredos. CHEST of c. 1600. Chapel Cloister dates from 1613–14 and is part of the alterations carried out for Sutton's foundation by *Francis Carter*. He had previously worked at Trinity College, Cambridge, and from 1614 was chief clerk of the King's Works under Inigo Jones. His work illustrates the latest Netherlandish Mannerist detail then fashionable, more sophisticated than Elizabethan work but still some way from Jones's purer classicism. The cloister has arches, originally open, with a kind of intermittent banded rustication. The contemporary doorway to the Chapel Tower is embellished with straps and imitation rings and pendants. The CHAPEL TOWER stands above the vestibule to the former Chapter House and contained the Monks' Treasury on the upper floor. Its N face was cut back in 1842. On the W side a much reconstructed stair-turret. On the ground floor the vestibule has a tierceron vault springing from angel corbels, bosses with symbols of the Passion, and the date 1512. The first floor has C14 two-light windows with cusped ogee heads, and a rib vault. The odd opening in the S wall was a squint from the Treasury into the monastic church. The upper part of the tower was added in 1613, its elaborate timber cupola of one square and one polygonal stage remarkable at this date.

The present CHAPEL was converted in the early C17 from the medieval Chapter House, an early C14 structure with windows of c. 1500. In the E wall an aumbry remains behind the panelling. Carter added a N aisle in 1612–14; its arcade has Tuscan columns with arches slightly decorated in a strapwork taste. The plaster ceiling is by *Blore*. The outer N aisle is of 1824, with screen and gallery above remade for the school in 1841. Excellent early C17 furnishings: fine small COMMUNION TABLE with thirteen pillars. – PULPIT by *T. Herring* and *E. Mayes*, with carving by *F. Blunt*, 1613. – ORGAN GALLERY, W end of N aisle, early C17; tapered piers decorated with musical instruments and firearms, two of the gallery panels with perspective views; Sutton's arms and the cherubs' heads look like later C17 additions. – SEATING by *Blore*, reusing C17 pew ends, with new Master's pew and stalls on the S side. PAINTING. The Visitation by *L. Giordano*. STAINED GLASS. E window, 1844, a dark pictorial Crucifixion by *Charles Clutterbuck*. Vestibule window by *W. Wailes*, 1853.

MONUMENTS. Thomas Sutton †1611, by *Nicholas Stone Sen.* and *Nicholas Johnson*, with *Edmund Kinsman*, completed 1615. The price paid was £360. A large and sumptuous affair, but confused in its composition. The monument starts quite reasonably with the recumbent alabaster figure of Sutton on a tomb-chest and Corinthian columns supporting the superstructure. The inscription tablet against the back wall between the columns is flanked by two bearded figures in armour (alluding to Sutton's career) keeping guard silently and holding the tablet. On it, a skull and the allegorical figures of Vanitas (blowing bubbles) and Father Time. In the superstructure, a long relief with the Brethren of the Charterhouse attending chapel. Sutton's arms above, standing figures of nine more allegories, with putti (originally on the outside). Much ribbon-work ornament of the type favoured by the Southwark school. The quality of *Stone*'s figures is high, the style clearly Mannerist, and the incongruity of the composition belongs to the style. Original RAILINGS by *William Shawe*. – John Law †1614, Sutton's executor, small tablet by *Stone*, with bust in oval niche and two allegorical figures in elegant, mannered attitudes. Vanity above (again as in the Sutton Monument) in the guise of a boy blowing bubbles. – Francis Beaumont †1624, small wall monument with kneeling figure flanked by shelves with books and instruments. Among lesser C18 tablets: Andreas Tooke, C18 cartouche with cherubs' heads; Henry Levett †1725, with classical surround; Thomas Walker †1728, with Ionic pilasters in coloured marble, with books below. John Christopher Pepusch, organist, †1752, erected 1767, with a lyre. – Dr Matthew Raine †1811, by *Flaxman*, with two flanking figures, nothing special. – Lord Ellenborough †1818, by *Chantrey*, with a large seated figure.

ST BARTHOLOMEW'S AND THE ROYAL LONDON SCHOOL OF MEDICINE AND DENTISTRY now occupies the site of the GREAT CLOISTER. The approach is from Charterhouse Square. The vast size of the cloister, larger than the present green, can be appreciated from the survival in the E boundary wall of the doorway to one of the monastic cells. The College took over the buildings of the Merchant Taylors' School, which had succeeded the Charterhouse School. From these there remain by the entrance in Rutland Place the former Headmaster's House, now DEAN'S HOUSE, ornate Franco-Flemish of 1894 by *W. Hilton Nash*, with oriel, canted bays, and carved foliage friezes with Merchant Taylor motifs. Opposite is the former LODGE, 1873–4 by *E.* (or possibly *E.B.*) *I'Anson*, French Gothic, with a circular stair-turret. The rest were damaged in the Second World War, and replaced by loosely grouped buildings for the Medical College. The first of these was COLLEGE HALL on the E side, by *Easton & Robertson*, 1949–52, a seven-storey hall of residence, carefully proportioned, with a light zigzag of balconies to the top floor. SCIENCE BUILDING at the NW corner, by the same firm, 1952–63, has a fine spacious entrance hall with corner staircase with sinuous landing balustrade, rising through four floors, remarkably generous for its date. Extended to the S by *Michael Squire Associates*, 1995. On the N side of the green, WOLFSON INSTITUTE OF PREVENTIVE MEDICINE, by *Sheppard Robson & Partners*, 1992, dark brick, with small glass spike over the first-floor library. Behind to the NE, the former school GYMNASIUM, with a row of red brick arched windows, dated 1884.

## ST JOHN'S PRIORY

The Knights Hospitallers' Priory of St John, a wealthy establishment which became head of the Order in England, was founded *c*. 1144 by Jordan Briset or Bricett, a Suffolk landowner who held property in Clerkenwell. Its precinct, covering about six acres, was bounded by

Turnmill Street, Cowcross Street, St John Street and Clerkenwell Green. Within this, an inner precinct was entered by the gatehouse in St John's Lane, leading to the church in the present St John's Square (the two brutally separated since the 1870s by Clerkenwell Road). Gateway and church are the chief survivals, but scattered evidence of medieval foundations has been found beneath buildings in and around the square (*see* Perambulation 1). The Museum in the gatehouse preserves many carved fragments, especially from the ornate late C12 chancel, and from large oriel windows of the late C15 or early C16. In the early C16, prominent members of the Priory staff had houses in the outer precinct; from one of these may come

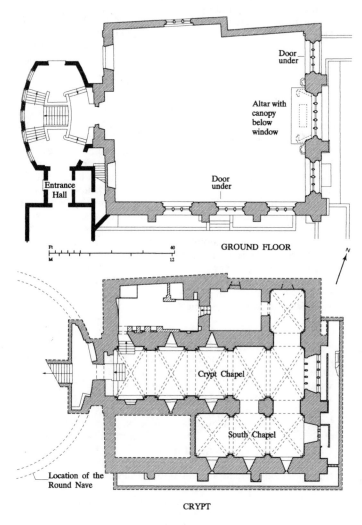

St John's Priory. Plan of church and crypt

early C16 terracotta fragments, possibly of continental origin, found in excavations in Albion Place in 1990–4.

St John. The exterior gives little sign that the crypt is one of London's major C12 treasures. It lies below a choir which was rebuilt in 1721–3 as a plain Georgian parish church, reusing parts of the medieval outer walls. After gutting in the Second World War the church was restored and extended in 1955–8 by *Seely & Paget*, and one sees first their one-storey Neo-Georgian elliptical narthex enclosing a new entrance for the crypt, and an early C18 w wall visible above, of red brick with stone pilasters. The w part of the medieval church has disappeared; it consisted in the C12 of a circular nave, inspired by the church of the Holy Sepulchre at Jerusalem, as was the practice of both this Order and the Templars. This was replaced by a more conventional aisled rectangle before 1381, when the church was sacked during the Peasants' Revolt. Both replacement nave and a massive NW tower added *c.* 1500 were destroyed by Protector Somerset after the Dissolution, to provide building material for Somerset House, leaving only the choir standing.

Inside the narthex, a C20 double stair, intended for processions, descends to the crypt. On each side is visible the start of the curved C12 wall of the round nave, with bases of two C12 internal pilasters. The CRYPT is of two dates. The unaisled mid-C12 w part has three bays with simple rib vaults and plain transverse arches, and a fourth w bay where only springers to the vault survive. The ribs appear to have had applied plaster enrichment with chevron, originally painted red. The late C12 enlargement (probably complete at the consecration of 1185) added two E bays, which extend transeptally for one bay on the N side and two on the S. These parts have the more elaborate mouldings of the late C12: triple-shafted responds, ribs with triple rolls, the centre one keeled, and transverse arches with pronounced angle rolls. W of the N transept is a vaulted chamber, from which the early C12 exterior wall is visible: ashlar-faced with pilasters with chamfered bases. The crypt was restored and refitted by *J. O. Scott* in 1900–1 and 1904–7 (s chapel).

FONT. Octagonal on a renewed quatrefoiled base. From the Preceptory at Hogshaw, Bucks. – ALTAR FRONTAL, embroidered with figures in ovals, Italian C16, brought from Florence. – STAINED GLASS, early C20, by *Nicholson*. – MONUMENTS. Sir William Weston, Prior of St John, †1540, emaciated corpse wrapped in a shroud and placed on a flat rush mat; a fragment of a larger tomb whose Gothic canopy is known from drawings. – Knight of St John, assumed to be Juan Ruiz de Vergara, proctor of the Langue of Castile in the Order of St John, originally in Valladolid Cathedral. Given in 1914. Alabaster, last quarter of C16. Recumbent effigy with sleeping son or page. Of a quality unsurpassed in London or England. Convincingly attributed to the Castilian sculptor *Esteban Jordan*. The pedestal was designed by *C. M. O. Scott*, 1916.

The post-war church has a frugal whitewashed aisleless interior. At the E end, responds of former aisles: late C12, with keeled shafts, four major, eight minor, important evidence of Transitional Gothic forms in London. Perp E, N and S windows. Two E corbels high up relate to the former C18 gallery. REREDOS. Two big carved consoles and a panel with cherubs' heads; they come from the early C18 W doorway. In the Museum, two fine painted wings from a late C15 Flemish altarpiece, formerly in the Priory church.

The area s of the church was laid out as a memorial garden after the war, approached from the w through a Tuscan archway below a caretaker's flat. On the s side of the church, blocked openings are visible between stone buttresses (restored in 1907–8). On the w one, some decoration, perhaps from the time of the early C16 Docwra Chapel which stood s of the church. To the E a C20 cloister arcade. In its centre a Crucifixion by *Cecil Thomas*, 1957, with flat terminal panels in an Eric Gill tradition.

ST JOHN'S GATE. The gatehouse to the inner precinct, built in 1504 by Prior Thomas Docwra, had a chequered career after the Dissolution; in the C18 it was offices and printing works for the *Gentleman's Magazine*, in the C19 the Old Jerusalem Tavern. In 1874 it became Headquarters and Museum of the revived Most Venerable Order of St John. Restored in 1846 by *W. P. Griffith*, in 1873–4 by *R. Norman Shaw*, and then from 1885–6 by *J. O. Scott*, who was involved in a ten-year programme of restoration, adaptation and building, including new offices to the SE (1901–3), and a new Chapter House (1901–4). The GATEHOUSE has an archway with room above, flanked by four-storey blocks. These have a main room on each floor with garderobe projection to the s and a square stair-turret to the N. The dressings are of Kentish rag, much restored, with inner walls of brick; those within the archway have some brick diapering. Archway with star-shaped tierceron vault, main window above of three lights, battlements of 1846 with additions of 1892–3. Stair-turrets with small Perp doorways, the w one reset to allow for the raised ground level. *Scott's* SE additions of 1901–3 are in matching Perp, with a broad doorway (planned for ambulances). The interiors are largely in Scott's Neo-Tudor, with plenty of panelling. His Chapter Hall has a big Perp fireplace, windows with heraldic glass, and a grand timber ceiling with central lantern rising above coving supported by well-carved stone angel corbels. On the same level is the Council Chamber in the room above the archway. This has a fireplace of *c.* 1700, panelling of 1900, and more heraldic glass (1911 by *Powells*). Roof with lantern of 1885–6 inserted above early C16 trusses with coarse openwork panelling. In the E wing a late C17 closed-string staircase with bulbous balusters; pretty plaster motifs on the soffit, added in the 1860s. On the second floor a fine late C16 stone fireplace, from the nearby Baptist's Head, formerly the town house of Sir Thomas Forster. Tapering pilasters, lintel carved with fruit, deer and other animals. The w wing stair-turret has its original timber newel stair. It leads to *Shaw's* library, with big Tudor fireplace dated 1874.

## PERAMBULATIONS

*1. Clerkenwell Green and the area around the monastic precincts*

The intricate street pattern of Clerkenwell was conditioned by three medieval religious foundations established just outside the City: the Knights Hospitallers' Priory of St John and St Mary's Nunnery, both founded in the C12, and the C14 Charterhouse. The Nunnery was N of Clerkenwell Green; St John's Priory lay a little to the SE, around St John's Square; the Charterhouse was further E. The Charterhouse was transformed into school and almshouses, and still forms a recognizable precinct N of Charterhouse Square. The other two monastic precincts became favoured places for superior mansions in the C16–C17, but as the social status of the area declined these gave way to smaller houses; along the narrow lanes that developed within the precincts C18 survivals now jostle with industrial premises and model dwellings, a characterful mixture consciously preserved from the mid 1970s by refurbishment and generally tactful infilling.

CLERKENWELL GREEN, in spite of a few trees, is now wholly urban and commercial, yet keeps some C18 reminiscences. The N side has as its main focus the simple stuccoed and pedimented front of No. 37a, built as a Welsh Charity School in 1738 by *James Steer*, now the Marx Memorial Library; the W side is dominated by the former Middlesex Sessions House of 1779–82 (for both, *see* Public Buildings, above). The S side is a mixture. It starts with Nos. 18–19, KLAMATH HOUSE, 1990 by *Huckle, Tweddle Partnership*; a sleek stone front with modish features: angled balcony, centre window stepping out in width, stair-tower to the r. with playful small window shapes. No. 16 has a good early C19 shopfront with Ionic columns, re-erected in 1978 when Nos. 15–17 were rebuilt with facsimile C18 fronts. Nos. 12–14a are characteristic warehouses of 1878 (builder *T. E. G. Channing*), with plenty of jolly terracotta and curved shaped gables enclosing large Gothic arches. On the N side, No. 29, a former public house of *c.* 1860, with narrow arched triplet windows on the top floor below bracketed eaves; No. 31, mannered classical of 1911, a narrow stone frontage with long thin windows. Then a development of 1984–6, designed to convey the small-scale C18–C19 variety that once existed here: flats and workshops with brick and rendered fronts and a variety of curved and angled bays. The site extends to Clerkenwell Close, with residents' car-parking hidden in the centre.

*Clerkenwell Close and St Mary's Nunnery*

CLERKENWELL CLOSE starts with the Crown Tavern, stucco-trimmed, *c.* 1860, then Nos. 54 and 56, early C19. The Close leads to St James's Church (q.v.), then winds to the W around the former site of St Mary's Nunnery, founded by Jordan Briset *c.* 1144. The C18 church is on the site of the medieval choir; the churchyard occupies the nave; part of St James's Gardens to the N covers the area of the cloister. The precinct is still clearly reflected in the topography, although the only medieval remains visible are the footings of the S cloister walk, with remains of C13 vaulting responds along the line of the nave of the church. W and N cloister ranges were transformed after the Dissolution into Newcastle House, a mansion occupied in the C17 by William Cavendish, Duke of Newcastle. This was demolished *c.* 1793 and replaced by terraced houses from which Nos. 47–48 survive N of the gardens. Converted to flats in 1991 by *Hunt Thompson*, with new flats behind, No. 1 Newcastle Row, which has a lively blue striped-brick ground floor and projecting eaves in sympathy with nearby buildings. Nos.

42–46 (of 1989) were intended as replicas of clockmakers' cottages demolished in 1974. Unconvincing detail.* The W side of the Close is shut in by Nos. 14–18, a tactful but bland mixture of C19 offices and warehouses refurbished and rebuilt in 1985–9. To the NW, PEAR TREE COURT, a large area of Peabody housing, built in 1883 to house over four hundred people displaced by clearance of the overcrowded small courts hidden behind the more select houses. A surviving C18 house is just visible at the back of THE HORSESHOE, a modest C19 pub built out in front.

CLERKENWELL WORKSHOPS, further N, Nos. 27–30, four- and five-storey warehouses converted to small workshops in 1975, were some of the first to challenge the post-war policy of replacement of Clerkenwell industry by housing. This sturdy and colourful brick range was built in 1895–7 for the London School Board by their works department, under *T. J. Bailey*, as the Board's central stores. 'Furniture', 'Stationery' and 'Needlework' appear in little cartouches over the entrances. Blue brick ground floor with segmental windows; three upper storeys with red brick pilasters. Opposite is the one jarring note in this area, THE OBSERVATORY, at the corner of Newcastle Row; flashy offices with a parade of mirror glass and crude Neo-Deco detail, 1987–8 by *Peter Tiggs Partnership*.

To the E of Clerkenwell Close more of the old network of narrow passages remains. By SANS WALK (with sheltered housing by *Levitt Bernstein*, 1995–6), one can reach a surprisingly complete early C19 enclave, the SEKFORDE (or WOODBRIDGE) ESTATE. It belonged to the Sekford Charity, used also to endow almshouses at Woodbridge, Suffolk, and was laid out from 1827 by *C. R. Cockerell*, surveyor to the charity, and his assistant *James Noble*. Most of the building took place in the 1830s–40s. Two new streets, Woodbridge Street and Sekforde Street, replaced a warren of small buildings that had grown up within the outer precinct of the nunnery.

First ST JAMES'S WALK, leading S off Sans Walk, with houses of *c*. 1827, and the PAROCHIAL SUNDAY SCHOOLS of 1828 by *William Lovell*, top floor added by *W. P. Griffith*, 1858. At the S end of WOODBRIDGE STREET, the former Woodbridge Chapel of 1833 (q.v.); at the junction with SEKFORDE STREET, the Sekforde Arms, with curved end, and WOODBRIDGE HOUSE, turning its back, with a five-bay front to the W, later used as the Finsbury Dispensary. Near the N end of Sekforde Street the FINSBURY SAVINGS BANK, of 1840 by *Alfred Bartholomew*, a festive stuccoed front in the spirit of Barry's Pall Mall Italian Renaissance clubs. Simple but nicely detailed three-storeyed terrace houses in between, some rebuilt in facsimile by *Pollard Thomas & Edwards* after Islington had acquired the run-down estate in 1975. On the E side is the contemporary rear of Nicholson's Distillery in St John Street (*see* Perambulation 2). At the N end of Woodbridge Street, round the corner in SKINNER STREET, an isolated C18 group, Nos. 35–45; straight-headed windows of rubbed brick, but much altered.

*Around St John's Priory*

AYLESBURY STREET marks the N boundary of the PRECINCT OF ST JOHN'S PRIORY (*see* above), which covered the whole area to

---

* The rear of No. 51, late C18, has a genuine workshop window in the middle floor.

its S, bounded by St John's Street, Cowcross Street and Turnmill Street. The street owes its name to a post-Dissolution mansion which belonged to the Earls of Aylesbury but had become tenements by the early C18. It is now dominated by the vast former premises of E. Pollard & Co., shopfitter and joiner, 1912–26 (*see also* Perambulation 2). To the S, JERUSALEM PASSAGE is on the site of a postern gate of the priory, demolished in 1780. Along the passage, a row of houses of mixed dates: No. 8 late C18, Nos. 9–10 *c.* 1830, No. 11 early C18, No. 12 mid C18. ST JOHN'S SQUARE, with the church (q.v.) on its E side, evolved from the inner courtyard of the priory; the S part of the court was regrettably lost to Clerkenwell Road, which now cuts it off from the medieval gatehouse in St John's Lane. The priory buildings, used by the Office of Revels in the C16, began to be replaced by individual houses from *c.* 1630. By the mid C19 these housed numerous specialized craftsmen, especially jewellers, watchmakers and printers. The N side of the square still has a pleasing C18 appearance, although only façades remain of Nos. 49–50, C18, and Nos. 51–52, 1806–7. Behind, all was rebuilt *c.* 1990. No. 48, also late C18, and No. 47, early C18 refaced in the C19, stand on late C16 brick vaulted cellars with a four-centred arch, probably remains of post-Dissolution buildings constructed within earlier outer walls which may have belonged to the priory bell tower demolished in 1550. S of the church, No. 2 ALBEMARLE WAY, with C18 interior behind a C19 front. The buildings in the S part of the square belong with the creation of Clerkenwell Road in 1879. On the N side of that road No. 84, a later C19 'flat iron' block, is topped off with attic workshop windows. At the SE corner, PENNYBANK CHAMBERS, 1879–80 by *Henman & Harrison*, towering model dwellings sparsely decorated with bands of tiles bearing the name of the National Penny Bank (founded 1875, modelled on the Yorkshire Penny Bank, where amounts as small as one penny could be deposited). Converted to craft workshops. Further W, in Clerkenwell Road at the corner of Britton Street, former BOARD OF GUARDIANS' OFFICES, built for Holborn Union. 1885–6 by *H. Saxon Snell & Sons*, a symmetrical classical block in blue and orange brick.

ST JOHN'S LANE is straddled by ST JOHN'S GATE (*see* St John's Priory, above). Adjoining on its NE side, No. 27 St John's Square, with a front of 1876 by *R. Norman Shaw* for Sir Edward Lechmere. Red brick, five storeys, with two levels of dormers. Linked to the priory by an addition of 1903.

BRITTON STREET, approached by narrow lanes and passages W of St John's Lane, has the best-surviving C18 houses in this area. It was laid out in 1719 as Red Lion Street, by a lawyer, Simon Michell, who was also responsible for rebuilding St John's Church. From that time several red brick houses on the E side, Nos. 54 and 59 with carved door brackets. No. 55, refronted in the early C19, has a good shopfront. Some clockmakers' attic workshop windows here (Nos. 28, 30–32, 54 and 56). Other C18 houses on the W side, partly rebuilt (Nos. 27–32). Adjacent to these is the monumental façade from BOOTH'S GIN DISTILLERY, 1903 by *E. W. Mountford*, re-erected rather meaninglessly here in 1975 as a condition of the demolition of the original building in Turnmill Street. The granite ground-floor arches are original, the brick upper floors facsimile reconstruction, incorporating *F. W. Pomeroy*'s attic frieze of carved panels showing gin-making processes. An archway leads through to a late C20 courtyard: behind the frontage are plain council flats and private offices, built by *YRM*, who took over the redevelopment of the site, building their own offices across the small yard at the back in 1973–6. These are in their impeccable sleek and anonymous style of the time: a red steel frame with glazed bands, two storeys above recessed ground floor, overlooking St John's Gardens (formerly Benjamin Street Burial Ground) on a lower level to the S. At the SE corner of Britton Street is a piece of whimsy, a private house with top-floor studio, by *CZWG*, 1987 for Janet Street-Porter. Successfully eye-catching, but the motifs fail to coalesce: the quiet buff and brown brick walls are overpowered by strident lozenge windows with large lattice panes and a forceful purple pantiled roof.

## 2. Cowcross Street and St John Street: Industrial Clerkenwell

Live cattle were driven down St John Street and across Cowcross Street to Smithfield until 1855. By then the area was an insanitary muddle of overcrowded C18 and early C19 housing interspersed with breweries, a distillery, and small-scale specialist industries, particularly metal manufacturing. Then the Metropolitan Railway arrived (opened in 1863), new roads (Farringdon Road, Clerkenwell Road) were sliced through, and much rebuilding followed, so that the dominant impression in these streets is of the sturdy warehouses and industrial buildings that transformed the area from the 1860s.

Starting in COWCROSS STREET from Farringdon Station (q.v.), rebuilt on its present site in 1922, the mood of this narrow street is at once established by Nos. 32–35 on the N side, curving round from Turnmill Street, a tall Italianate frontage of four storeys with big cornice, containing THE CASTLE pub, 1865 by *H. Dawson*. Warehouses and industrial buildings of the later C19 follow. Refurbishment of some as offices began in 1979. Conversions to apartments followed in the later 1990s. Along the N side, Nos. 29–31, 1864 by *Charles Hambridge* (*see* Highbury New Park, Islington Perambulation 4), are also Italianate, enlivened by polychrome brick window-heads to first and third floors. Nos. 26–27, 1879 by *Thomas Milbourn*, have even richer detail, with mosaic and brick patterned tympana. Nos. 20–24 and the area behind were cleared in 1985 for a grossly ambitious office scheme, reduced when built in 1997–8 to offices in front with flats at the back. No. 18 is by *J. H. Bethel*, 1886; Nos. 14–16 of similar date; Nos. 9–13, tall Venetian Gothic, 1878. By Peter's Lane a few low C18 terrace houses remain, converted to a hotel in 1997. Then No. 1, a tall C19 front with Gothic arches, four storeys and attics. On the S side at this end, leading round towards Smithfield, a good Italianate group of grey brick, 1870 by *Lewis Isaacs*, with THE HOPE, a pub remodelled c. 1900; a fine curved Art Nouveau front with engraved glass, good tiles inside.

CHARTERHOUSE STREET. The W part, which since 1994 forms the boundary with the City and is described in *London 1: The City of London*, was largely created by the Corporation of London in

1869–75 to provide a northern service street alongside their new Smithfield Market. In the narrower E end leading towards Charterhouse Square, two pubs: No. 103, the demure SMITHFIELD TAVERN, 'rebuilt 1871 by *J. H. Schraeder*', according to a small plaque, with basket-arched windows; and the much more exuberant No. 115, THE FOX AND ANCHOR, with a splendid Art Nouveau front by *W. J. Neatby* in cream and pale green Doulton faience, dated 1898; pictorial curved gable, tiles in the entrance as well, and a good interior. Between the two, Nos. 109–113, a sensitive Neo-Wren façade in a Dutch manner, built for the Charterhouse Cold Storage Company by *A. H. Mackmurdo*, 1900. Big stone and brick ground-floor arches; giant pilasters above with wreathed Ionic caps; thin windows in between. Remodelled as offices in 1988–9, with ground floor set back behind the original frontage. Behind No. 117, a plain warehouse, is a VESTRY ROOM for St Sepulchre's parish by *Lewis Isaacs* (Surveyor to Holborn District Board of Works), 1874. No. 119 is late C18; Nos. 121–123, 1907, built together with the hotel in Charterhouse Square and used as stock rooms by commercial travellers.

CHARTERHOUSE SQUARE was a respectable address in the early C18, given status by the Charterhouse to its N (q.v.). The square was planted with two avenues of trees in 1722, and ironwork of 1792 remains from its main entrances, but only a few houses remind one of the domestic past. Coming from Charterhouse Street, the first is No. 22 on the N side, of 1786–8, with *Coade* stone mask keystones and voussoirs (first-floor ceiling with roundels painted by the artist *Thomas Stowers*, a former resident). Nos. 18–21 were built as the CHARTERHOUSE HOTEL, 1902 by *E. B. I'Anson*. Then the entrance to the Charterhouse, with a handsome brick house of 1716 adjoining the Lodge. Along the N side a good group of C18 to early C19 houses: No. 14, Nos. 12–13 and No. 12a, early C19 with nice doorway with fanlight, and a two-storey bow to the square. At the NE corner the entrance to St Bartholomew's Medical School (*see* Charterhouse, above), which took over part of the Charterhouse site. On the E side Nos. 6–9, FLORIN COURT, service flats by *Guy Morgan*, 1936, ten storeys yet not oppressive; an undulating symmetrical front with recessed centre, poised between modernism and Art Deco. Then the earliest remaining houses, Nos. 4–5, a pair of *c.* 1700 (although probably refronted in the C19): they have adjoining entrances with later doorcases, and a total of six bays, with a narrow blind bay on the l. The S side of Charterhouse Square, with warehouses of the 1870s built in the wake of the Metropolitan Railway, is now in the City of London.

*St John Street from south to north*

ST JOHN STREET was an ancient thoroughfare leading N from Smithfield and the City between the precincts of St John's Priory and the Charterhouse. The W side starts at the corner with Cowcross Street with No. 1, plain apart from some polychrome brick and a panel with the address. The more flamboyant No. 3 was built as butcher's shop and offices by *W. Harris*, 1897. Tall Free Gothic gable facing Smithfield, and a skyline embellished by quirky chimneys and flourishes.

On the E side, first a more sober BARCLAYS BANK (built for

London Joint Bank), dated 1871, by *Lewis Isaacs*, a proud stone-faced palazzo, four storeys, elaborately detailed, with bowed corner oriel. The next buildings to note are all on the E side: Nos. 18–20, a late C19 warehouse with hoist between two big Gothic arches, and an oculus in the gable above. No. 22 is a tiny two-bay C18 house; No. 24, with C19 Italianate front of three bays, was ingeniously converted in 1986 by *D. Y. Davies Associates*: the ground floor was partly opened up, exposing the iron structural columns; a passage leads through to glazed showrooms in a bridge over the yard behind, linked to No. 24a, a backland warehouse. After No. 26, early C19, Nos. 34–36, George Farmiloe & Sons, lead and glass manufacturers, 1868 by *Isaacs*, an especially striking Victorian frontage; eclectic Italianate with busy stucco dressings. Four storeys, with ornate cornice and decoration over the round-headed first-floor windows. The plainer C19 buildings which follow make an effective foil: Nos. 40 and 42, brick, four storeys; Nos. 44–46, stucco, with row of six arched first-floor windows. After a C20 intrusion and an early C19 survivor (No. 72, with first-floor windows under arches), the next group of interest is Nos. 78–80. No. 78 is a fine Gothic warehouse of 1886, five storeys, with three storeys of loading bays contained within a Gothic arch with traceried top lights. Probably built for John Lawson & Co., brassfounders. Now linked to the C18 No. 80 (good first-floor ceiling), with a new entrance reached down a passage. A few four-storey houses follow: Nos. 82–84, earlier C18 altered, Nos. 86–88, early C19, with passage through to Hat and Mitre Court. No. 90 is dated 1926; tall and narrow, with windows grouped in a frame.

St John Street, W side from N to S. The area behind (to the S of Eagle Court), cleared for building in the 1980s boom, remains empty at the time of writing. Highlights along St John Street are No. 57, the White Bear, dated 1899, with terracotta panels and curved gable; Nos. 69–73, a late C18 group with a good early C19 Ionic pilastered shopfront to No. 69; and No. 99, elaborate Free Classical with curved gable, one of a group of narrow frontages in the stretch leading up to Clerkenwell Road. This was laid out in the 1870s; contemporary with it are the SE and NE corner blocks, with moderate Italianate trimmings.

To the N of Clerkenwell Road are a few domestic survivals: on the E side No. 122, early C19 with nice shopfront. Then a glimpse E down the narrow Great Sutton Street, lined with late C19 factories and warehouses; No. 30a was built as a dairy by *George Waymouth*: dairy scenes on ceramic lozenges. The next landmark on the E side is the former Cannon Brewery, on this site from the mid C18; much rebuilt in 1893 by *Bradford & Sons*, damaged in the Second World War and closed in the 1960s. First Nos. 148–154, a four-window office range in red brick and terracotta, then the larger Nos. 156–162, with rusticated brick ground floor with an archway; splendid Rococo-inspired metalwork on the timber gates. Terracotta panels between the two upper floors. Behind, a wedge-shaped counting house and office, 1876, restrained classical, but with whimsical Moorish doorcase. Further E is the vast fermenting house and offices, Tuscan-pilastered, backing on to Berry Street.

On the W side, Mallory Buildings, Nos. 115–121, replaced slum courts around the edge of St John's Square, 1906. Tall *LCC* flats over shops, five storeys and attics in austere grey and yellow brick, but with pretty ironwork and a picturesque roof-line with cranked dentilled gables and tall chimneys. A glimpse of the E end of St John's Church is flanked to the N by Nos. 145–157, tall ungainly 1970s offices: four tinted-curtain-walled floors over two recessed ones. Of the same height, but better balanced, Nos. 158–173, faience-faced, in simplified classical of the 1920s. These were showroom and factory for Pollards (see Perambulation 1), 1926 by *Malcolm Matts*. Then after Nos. 181–185, a little C18 group, a long sequence which formed NICHOLSON'S DISTILLERY (closed *c.* 1970), mostly of *c.* 1873–5. At the S end, Nos. 187–191, four bays with giant pilasters above a granite-faced ground floor with a low archway through to HAYWARD'S PLACE, where a row of much restored cottages of 1834, later used by distillery workers, remains on the S side. Then a long, sober frontage of about ten bays and four storeys, brick above a channelled stone-faced ground floor, with Doric pilasters and stone entablature. The attic is treated as a series of pavilions with arched windows. A further stretch of three storeys has an attic above a big cornice. No. 201 is the distillery buildings of 1828, by *John Blyth*, according to Pink's *Clerkenwell*. Austere and grand, three storeys of small windows between giant brick pilasters. A clumsy pastiche Georgian terrace of *c.* 1980 replaces Myerson's Ironworks (a surprisingly monumental Neoclassical building, a sad loss). This leads up to Sekforde Street (*see* Perambulation 1). Further N on the E side, No. 236 (Walmsley Building, City University), another stately industrial building of the late 1860s, by *Rowland Plumbe*: four storeys, grey brick, with tall windows, cornice, and segmental pediment to the centre bay. On a corner, No. 238, formerly the GEORGE AND DRAGON (see the carved panel), 1889 by the pub architect *H. J. Newton*. After the interruption of the C20 Finsbury Estate on the W side (*see* Perambulation 4) and the Northampton Institute and City University buildings on the E (*see* Public Buildings), St John Street changes character and is fringed on both sides by uneventful stretches of early C19 terraces as it continues N towards Islington. Breaking the skyline is No. 418, the OLD RED LION, 1898–1900 by *Eedle & Myers*. Terracotta panels and elaborate brick decoration.

Less interesting industrial building in GOSWELL ROAD, the parallel street to the E. The grandest lie E of Northampton Square. Nos. 137–157 stretches from Percival Street to Sebastian Street; a bold six-storey composition in red brick, which looks *c.* 1910. Around the Goswell Road–Clerkenwell Road junction, several extensively glazed commercial buildings of the 1870s, with much external cast-iron work, especially Nos. 2–7 and 8–11 Charterhouse Buildings, and Nos. 1–5 and 70–72 Clerkenwell Road. (*See also* Perambulation 6.)

### 3. Farringdon Road and Rosebery Avenue

The new C19 streets W of Farringdon Station drastically changed the nature of the Fleet valley. Farringdon Road N of Clerkenwell Green was laid out in conjunction with the Metropolitan Railway, which opened in 1863; Clerkenwell Road dates from 1872–8, Rosebery Avenue from 1888–92. The clearances of those years permitted industrial building on a grander scale than elsewhere in Clerkenwell. The printing industry, encouraged by the proximity of Fleet Street, was especially prominent here. Many buildings remain from this period, although their use has changed. Among them is a scatter of trendy commercial buildings from the boom years of the 1980s, but evocative names and a few older relics survive to give some inkling of the earlier history of the area.

Starting from Farringdon Station, one can first trace the old route out of London up TURNMILL STREET, formerly dominated by Booth's Distillery (for the façade re-erected in Britton Street, *see* Perambulation 1). In FARRINGDON LANE, the continuation of this route N of Clerkenwell Road (formerly Ray Street, now the E side of Farringdon Road), beneath No. 16, is the CLERK'S WELL, a rectangular enclosure with some medieval ashlar walling repaired with brick. It was rediscovered in 1924, and identified as the well mentioned by Fitzstephen and Stow which gave its name to the area. It lay just outside the precinct wall of the nunnery (*see* Perambulation 1). Fitzstephen describes it as 'frequented by scholars and youth of the City when they go out for fresh air on summer evenings'. Further on are warehouses of the 1870s, the most notable the tall gabled No. 34, designed in 1875 by *Rowland* 66 *Plumbe* for John Greenwood, watch and clock manufacturer, with Gothic details, a prominent clock, and other appropriate decoration (hourglass, scythe etc.) above the upper windows. Further on, past the Peabody Estate (*see* Perambulation 1) and a plainer warehouse, also of 1875, to BOWLING GREEN LANE to the E (bowling greens are shown on Ogilby and Morgan's map of 1676). On its S side, Nos. 16–17, a handsome four-storeyed factory of 1877 built for William Notting, typefounder and printer. Buff brick with segment-headed windows; red brick and terracotta trimmings. To the N, a vast multi-storey car park of the 1980s along Farringdon Road, with bland arched frontage of red and yellow brick. Low housing of the same date behind (CATHERINE GRIFFITHS COURT), its folksy brick detailing a painful contrast to *Tecton*'s Health Centre (*see* Public Buildings).

At the corner of Farringdon Road and Exmouth Market, Nos. 88–104, another group by *Plumbe*, 1872–3, built as a speculation. Gothic arches to the top floor, lush capitals. It includes a pub (the PENNY BLACK) and No. 94, Quality Chop House, a rare survival of an early C20 working-class restaurant, much refurbished in the 1980s but with some original fittings.

The W side of FARRINGDON ROAD begins at the N end with Nos. 143–155, a good example of a decently proportioned late C19 commercial terrace. A balanced design with slightly narrower end houses. The others each have a ground-floor shop and three floors of four-light upper windows extending almost full width between party walls. Then No. 119 (on the site of Corporation Dwellings of 1866), built as a warehouse *c.* 1976, and converted as offices of the *Guardian* by *Elsom Pack & Roberts*. An uncouth intruder, whose six storeys of drab brown precast panels contrast tellingly with the subtler articulation of the C19 buildings. A good example of these is Nos. 113–117 and the adjoining premises in RAY STREET, 1864–5 and 1875–6 by *Arding & Bond*, for V. & J. Figgis, typefounders.

The main building is of five storeys, with a sixth above a cornice; the windows of the four middle floors are enclosed in two series of giant arches; the whole is tied together by continuous rusticated brick piers. Nos. 109–111, 1865 by *Henry Jarvis*, for William Dickes, chromolithographer, is a splendid Venetian Gothic palazzo. Red and black brick, with close-set Gothic arcades. Nos. 105–107 and Nos. 99–101 are both dated 1887, slightly Gothic, with some black diapering. In between, No. 103, 1865 by *John Butler* for J. & R. M. Wood, printing press maker. (Machine hall behind with cast-iron columns.) The large site at the N corner of Clerkenwell Road has flats by *Chassay Architects*, 1993–4, building up from four to seven storeys, constructed around a deep-plan concrete frame intended for offices (the change of use during construction a sign of the times). Brick and rendered frontages, with glazed set-back top floor. Nos. 91–93, *c.* 1930–5, stone-faced and quiet. Nos. 77–79, large warehouse of the 1880s with a little classical detail. No. 75, indifferent, with the usual polished granite uprights of *c.* 1990. Then a long sequence of smaller groups of workshops and warehouses of the 1880s. (For buildings further s, *see* Camden: Holborn Perambulation 1a.) Opposite, along the curving sliver of land between road and railway, a flat canyon-like office frontage of polished granite, *c.* 1993, stepping up to a high tower at the corner of Cowcross Street (No. 20, SMITH NEW COURT HOUSE). Not an asset to the townscape.

### West of Farringdon Road

A few narrow streets and lanes on the slopes of the Fleet valley survived the improvements of the 1870s. Off Ray Street in HERBAL HILL, No. 1, an early C19 house. At the corner of WARNER STREET, opposite huge warehouses, the small and cheerful COACH AND HORSES, busy Neo-Jacobean of 1900. It is on the site of Hockley-in-the-Hole Bear Garden. ROSEBERY AVENUE cuts across the area. It flies over Warner Street on a pretty VIADUCT dated 1890, by *Westwood Baillie & Co.*; cast iron on brick jack arches; pierced trefoil balustrades. Climbing uphill to the N, BAKER'S ROW and BAKER'S YARD, redeveloped by *Kinson Architects*, 1988; three-storey warehouses in pale brick; a blue corner column between each garage and doorway adds some character. Further W, on the Holborn border, HOLSWORTHY SQUARE, off Elm Street, six-storey tenements rehabilitated for the St Pancras Housing Association by *Peter Mishcon* in 1981–7. Ingeniously replanned, with old staircases replaced by lifts and the exterior enlivened by elegant stairs and balconies.

ROSEBERY AVENUE was built up in the 1890s, soon after its construction. The Finsbury section starts N of Warner Street. On each side, tall mansion flats of 1892, with crowstepped gables and decorative Renaissance friezes. Less frugal in appearance than Rosebery Square to the s (*see* Camden: Holborn p. 332), although they were intended as low-rental accommodation by their developer, James Hartnoll. On the E side, ROSEBERY COURT, 1989 by *Kinson Architects*, part of the Baker's Row site (*see* above), prestige offices; six storeys with some fancy Mackintosh-inspired Arts and Crafts detail. On the same side, next to the Fire Station (q.v.), No. 40, a three-storey brick house, sole remnant of COBHAM

ROW, an C18 street developed around an older cold bath (commemorated in the name COLDBATH SQUARE). N of Mount Pleasant and its sprawling Sorting Office (*see* Public Buildings), some good industrial buildings on the E side dated 1897: Nos. 58–66, striped brick, with two sets of hoist doors. Further on after the former Vestry Hall of the 1890s (*see* p. 607), a late C20 stretch built on New River Company land. The E side, by *John Gill Associates*, 1987–9, is feebly Postmodern, with brick triangular oriels; the W side (Nos. 133–159) is bold and sleek, with a tall glazed frontage and transparent curved stair-tower behind. It adjoins a refurbished 1920s warehouse (No. 161 and Nos. 1–5 HARDWICK STREET), given a neat new steel fire escape to provide a focus at the back. All by *Troughton McAslan*, 1989–91. The rest of Rosebery Avenue has on the W side the New River Head and Sadlers Wells (*see* p. 611) and on the E Spa Fields (*see* Perambulation 4).

## 4. Northern Clerkenwell, a circular tour

The parts of Clerkenwell to the N of the medieval precincts around Clerkenwell Green were developed from the early C19 by a number of different landowners; each estate has a recognizable character, not only as regards its original houses, but also in the way it has been treated since. Approaches range from extensive preservation (Lloyd Baker and New River estates) to virtually complete rebuilding, in some cases more than once (Northampton Estate). Areas are described here in roughly anti-clockwise order, starting and ending at the Library in St John Street. For location of the estates *see* map p. 599.

NORTHAMPTON ESTATE, E of St John Street. Developed in the early C19 on land around the Manor House belonging to the Earls of Northampton, which survived until 1869. The names of COMPTON STREET to the S and SPENCER STREET to the N recall the family ownership. A modest terrace remains on the S side of Compton Street, some houses only one bay wide. Watch-and clockmaking spread to this area from Clerkenwell, and during the C19 specialist small-scale industries proliferated. By the C20 the minor streets had become notoriously slummy; hence the extensive rebuilding. Around PERCIVAL STREET, the old pattern was swept away for the BRUNSWICK CLOSE ESTATE, 1956–8 by *Emberton, Franck & Tardrew*. Three bold fourteen-storey slabs, rising from leafy gardens, on a staggered plan to allow for maximum light levels. Exposed reinforced concrete construction, with small projecting fire escape staircases ornamenting the top four storeys. The westernmost block has shops facing St John Street, and originally had an open way through it, a Corbusian concept which recurs in the firm's other Finsbury estates. Further E, in CYRUS STREET, a group of *Monson*'s 1930s flats, and THE TRIANGLE; an overbearing brown brick cluster of maisonettes of the 1970s, by *Clifford Culpin & Partners*, for the GLC, with a monumental entrance under a high-level bridge. They replaced an earlier low-rent housing scheme, the Improved Industrial Dwellings Company's Compton Dwellings of 1872–6. Quite suddenly to the N one comes to the remains of NORTHAMPTON SQUARE, set lozenge-wise to Percival Street. It was laid out *c.* 1805. Only the SE and SW

sides still have houses, with some more to the E in SEBASTIAN
STREET and ASHBY STREET. Attractive details; ground- and
first-floor windows within recessed arches. Three storeys with
attics (note the workshop windows in the attics of Nos. 26 and
29). The N corner is crassly sliced off by buildings for the City
University, adjoining the former Northampton Institute on the E
(qq.v.). S of this, in WYCLIF STREET, the site of the Northampton
Manor House is filled by a solid Gothic vicarage of 1871. It
belonged to the adjacent St Peter's Church (Smithfield Martyrs
Memorial Church, by *E. L. Blackburne*, 1869–71), demolished
after war damage.

BREWERS' COMPANY ESTATE. Small streets between St John
Street and Goswell Road, built up from the C18. The land was left
to the Brewers by Dame Alice Owen in 1613, with provision for
boys' and girls' schools (*see* Public Buildings). The schools moved
away in 1973; renovation and tactful infilling began after Islington
acquired much of the housing in 1974. In RAWSTORNE STREET,
houses of *c.* 1789; on the S side working-class tenements of 1871–83,
probably by the Brewers' Company Surveyor, *E. B. Martineau*.
Four storeys, quite pretty brick Gothic fronts. The taller block of
*c.* 1900 at the NW corner with St John Street was refurbished for
single homeless people by *Hunt Thompson*, 1986–7, enlivened by a
new brick stair-tower. Tiny streets off to the N with a mixture of
humble late Georgian terraces and late C20 infilling. OWEN'S ROW
is a little classier, with Nos. 2–5, *c.* 1780; doorcases with open
pediments.

*Spa Fields to Pentonville Road*

SPA FIELDS, between St John Street and Rosebery Avenue. The
neighbourhood of the former C18 pleasure gardens was a slum
clearance area by the 1930s, and formed the core of the Finsbury

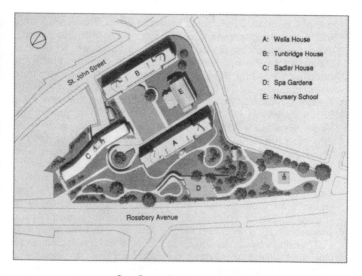

Spa Green Estate. Site layout

Plan, an ambitious scheme for borough-wide rebuilding, which was halted by the war. The original plan proposed a spine of eight-storey blocks ranged along Rosebery Avenue, with lower housing to E and W, complete with parks and amenities. First plans were made in 1937 by *Tecton*, then also busy with the Finsbury Health Centre (q.v.). Their revised and reduced scheme of 1946 for the SPA GREEN ESTATE was built in 1946–50. Three blocks of flats, 118 two of eight storeys, one of four. The lower one is on a curving plan, which does much to humanize the group and tie it in with its surroundings. Executive architects were *Lubetkin* and *Skinner*, the structural engineer (as at Tecton's Highpoint, Highgate; *see* Camden: St Pancras 5b, pp. 410–11) was *Ove Arup*. The flats were the most innovative public housing in England at the time, with many novelties, both structural (an early example of monolithic box-frame construction of *in-situ* concrete, the first Garchey refuse disposal system in London) and social (e.g. the ingenious aerofoil profile of the roof canopies on the tall blocks, designed to channel wind through the clothes-drying areas). The elevations too depart from the monotony of standard pre-war flats. The tall blocks, Wells House and Tunbridge House, are planned as a pair, with their bedrooms facing inward towards a landscaped area. The outer sides are deliberately livelier: plain brick-clad vertical panels containing the living-room windows are divided by a syncopated rhythm of inset balconies with grey ironwork against inner walls painted Indian red. Fanciful curved canopies to the central porches and the curved ramps on the inner sides are typically wayward Lubetkin touches. The four-storey Sadler House has a different version of rhythmic façade patterning, with alternating balconies contained within a tile-faced frame. Refurbishment in 1978–80 by *Peter Bell & Partners* included extensive retiling and restoration of much of the original colour scheme. Later decorative iron grilles; the lift extension to Sadler House was added in 1987.

In the public garden by Rosebery Avenue, WAR MEMORIAL, 1921 by *Thomas Rudge*, a bronze angel of Victory on a tall granite pedestal which bears a plaque showing 'Finsbury rifles attacking Gaza'; two other plaques have disappeared.

NEW RIVER ESTATE, W of Rosebery Avenue, S of Pentonville Road, close to the headquarters of the New River Company (*see* Public Buildings). Developed from the 1820s. The easternmost street is CHADWELL STREET, the SW boundary AMWELL STREET, both named from the Hertfordshire springs feeding the New River. Broad streets with agreeable terraces with stuccoed ground floors. Many doorways with fluted quarter-columns and pretty curving fanlight patterns characteristic of the earlier C19. Chadwell Street leads into MYDDELTON SQUARE, built 1824–7 by the Company Surveyor, *William Chadwell Mylne*. Pleasingly complete (N side rebuilt after war damage), with St Mark's Church (q.v.) in the centre. Further N, CLAREMONT SQUARE, 1821–8, built around the New River's Upper Pond of 1708, which became, less attractively, a raised covered reservoir in 1852. Tucked away to the E, CLAREMONT CLOSE, three-storey superior flats of 1935–6 in domestic revival style, built on former mews. AMWELL STREET, running downhill from Claremont Square, has terraces with small shops, many with good C19 shopfronts. No. 42, a dairy from 1914,

is notable for its tiled interior. From Amwell Street GREAT PERCY
STREET leads down to PERCY CIRCUS, 1841–3, a little circus of
stucco-trimmed houses, more Italianate than the earlier streets,
perched on a steep slope above King's Cross. Alas, it is no longer
complete, but is helped by some tactful replica fronts. They are
the back parts of the otherwise unappealingly bulky ROYAL SCOT
HOTEL, which occupies a triangular site behind KING'S CROSS
ROAD. By *Trehearne & Norman, Preston & Partners*, completed
1972. S of Great Percy Street, CUMBERLAND GARDENS with a
pair of 1840s semi-detached houses built to match a pair belonging to the Lloyd Baker Estate opposite (*see* below).

To the N, on the site of the bombed Holford Square of 1841–4,
the one major C20 addition: BEVIN COURT, 1952–5 by *Skinner,
Bailey & Lubetkin*, i.e. part of the Tecton firm after it had split up.
The first design, which preserved the form of the old square, was
rejected in favour of a cheaper solution of a seven- and eight-storey
Y-shaped block of 130 dwellings. The wings have the distinctive
Tecton surface patterning, achieved here through alternation of
windows, textures, and access-gallery uprights (private balconies were
too expensive); cf. Spa Green (above) and Hallfield, Paddington
117 (*London 3: North West*). The surprise is the stunning central staircase, one of the most exciting C20 spatial experiences in London.
Views out in different directions between the access points to each
wing. MURAL in the entrance by *Peter Yates*. HOLFORD HOUSE,
a four-storey block of maisonettes, is part of the same scheme.
The two-storey AMWELL HOUSE to the E of Bevin Court was
added by *Skinner, Bailey & Lubetkin* in 1956–8.

LLOYD BAKER ESTATE. Adjacent to the New River Estate, a
wedge-shape between Amwell Street and King's Cross Road.
Planned from 1818 but begun only in 1825, to designs chiefly by
*W. J. Booth*, son of the family estate surveyor. LLOYD STREET
and LLOYD SQUARE, 1833, are at the E end; WHARTON STREET
55 and LLOYD BAKER STREET run downhill from them towards
King's Cross Road. Especially attractive and complete. Mainly
semi-detached two-storeyed stock brick villas with emphatic Grecian
detail. The heavy shared pediments compose effectively in the
sloping views. In Lloyd Baker Street the houses also have their
windows framed by giant arches. Between the main streets is the
more routine three-storey GRANVILLE SQUARE, 1841–3. At the
top of Lloyd Baker Street, the YWCA, converted in 1962 from a
former convent, a House of Retreat for the Society of the Sisters
of Bethany, first established at No. 7 Lloyd Square in 1866. By
*Ernest Newton*, 1882–4, in robust Queen Anne-Board school style
rather than Gothic, the effect diminished since alteration of the
gables. Small cloister with balustraded corridor on two sides.
Chapel (now studio) rebuilt by Newton 1891–2; low N aisle and
high clerestory; free Dec detail. (Boarded barrel roof. Good Arts
and Crafts SCREENS; some STAINED GLASS.)

MARGERY STREET and WILMINGTON SQUARE, NE of Rosebery
Avenue. Another parcel which belonged to the Northampton
Estate, built up piecemeal 1819–31 by a builder, *John Wilson*. The
squalid courts which developed on the Northampton land
between Wilmington Square and the Lloyd Baker Estate were
cleared in the 1920s and replaced by Finsbury's most extensive

inter-war housing, between Lloyd Baker Street and MARGERY STREET. Five- and six-storey flats of 1930–4 by *E. C. P. Monson*. The conventional courtyard lay-out, with polite Neo-Georgian frontages but austere backs, should be contrasted with Tecton's work. More individual is CHARLES RONAN HOUSE of 1927–30, in MERLIN STREET, by *G. Mackenzie Trench*, architect to the Metropolitan Police. A rare early example of flats for married policemen. Five storeys, around a courtyard entered through large arches with tiled voussoirs. Drab courtyard elevations with the usual access balconies, but expressionist red brick exteriors with strong verticals ending in blocky chimneys; no period features at all. To the SW, WILMINGTON SQUARE, with complete 1820s terraces, the NW side of three storeys, the others of four. The longer NW and SE sides have their centres slightly emphasized by arched windows. Tactful rebuilding to the E of *c.* 1971: Nos. 38–39 at the corner with Atneave Street have flats behind replica fronts matching the square; in YARDLEY STREET old people's housing is hidden behind a Victorian frontage.

FINSBURY ESTATE, Skinner Street and St John Street. The last of Finsbury's major rebuilding schemes, completed only in 1968, after the borough had become part of Islington. By *C. L. Franck* of *Franck & Deeks* (successor to Emberton, Franck & Tardrew, *see* above). Four housing blocks, freely grouped to the N of a realigned sweep of Skinner Street; two blocks of four storeys, one of nine and one of twenty-five. The taller blocks have reinforced concrete frames, and are in shades of grey, with blue spandrel panels to the tallest. The different buildings interlock to a greater extent than in the firm's earlier work, a characteristic of the three-dimensional planning current in the 1960s. A covered car park is included, and also a Library (q.v.), crisply black and white, with a two-storey glazed front respecting the line of St John Street. There is a vista through the ground floor of the tower block beside it (cf. King Square, Perambulation 7), but the bulk of the car park compromises the view.

## 5. Pentonville to King's Cross

The NW corner of the old borough of Finsbury. Henry Penton's development of PENTONVILLE was begun in the 1770s. Until the early C19 it stood on its own, N of the part of the New Road now known as Pentonville Road. Penton's grid of streets remains, but was much rebuilt in the C20.

In PENTONVILLE ROAD, starting from the Angel, commercial buildings dominate the E end (*see* Islington Perambulation 1). W of this is a coherent early C19 domestic stretch: one complete terrace on the S side, Nos. 25–75, a dignified four-storey range of similar type to the streets of the New River Estate (*see* Perambulation 4). Opposite, Nos. 34–40 and 40–44, the last two with nice Gothic glazing to ground-floor arched windows. The CRAFTS COUNCIL next door (No. 44a), set back behind original railings, occupies the former Claremont Chapel, built for Independents in 1818–19, probably by *William Wallen*. It was funded by Thomas Wilson, benefactor to other Independent chapels. Well-proportioned

three-bay front with projecting centre with pediment and Ionic
porch with paired columns. Stuccoed *c.* 1860. The balustrading in
front, echoing C19 alterations, dates from the conversion for the
Crafts Council in 1991. Compactly planned with ground-floor
gallery and shop; café, library and offices upstairs. They have
patterned flooring by *Jennie Moncur* and curvaceous verdigris and
glass door furniture by *James Cox*.

In the streets to the N only a few original houses remain. PENTON
STREET has a few on the W side (Nos. 7 and 9). Opposite, some
much-altered terraces with shops. In WHITE LION STREET just
one good house, No. 57, four storeys, Doric porch with open
pediment; and the Claremont United Reformed Church (q.v.),
built as the Claremont Institute behind the older chapel in
Pentonville Road. In CHAPEL STREET further N, lesser houses,
overwhelmed by the street market. W of Penton Street, behind St
Silas (q.v.), WYNFORD ROAD ESTATE by *Westwood Piet Poole &
Smart* for the GLC, 1973–5.Three brown brick blocks linked by a
pedestrian deck over car-parking, squeezed onto a tiny site next to
a large secondary school (*see* p. 614).

Pentonville Road descends towards King's Cross, an incoherent
muddle of offices, warehouses, flats and garages. So one is grateful for the trim profile of No. 154a, GRIMALDI PARK HOUSE, by
*Allies & Morrison*, 1988–90, genteelly set within a little park
fringed with tombstones. It is a successor to St James's Church,
1787–8 by *Aaron Hurst*, made redundant and demolished in 1981.
A previous scheme (proposed by the Diocese as a concession to
those who had hoped to save the church) was for offices in the
form of a replica building. Allies & Morrison's solution is more
ingenious. The pretty pedimented and pilastered front is treated
as a quotation, separated by a small atrium from the brick-clad
offices behind, whose massing reflects the form of the church but
whose detail relates to its C20 function. Opposite, the skyline is
etched by stair- and lift-towers of a dramatic housing group in
WESTON RISE, a fortress-like cluster of eight-storey linked slabs
of maisonettes. By *HKPA* for the GLC, 1964–9. The folding plan
set on a slope is reminiscent of Parkhill, Sheffield, but this is a less
ambitious version, with access balconies rather than broad decks.
Transformed in the 1980s, when the aggressively brutalist concrete detail was disguised by painting, and enlivened at night by
clever lighting along the pierced concrete balconies. Further
downhill on the N side, No. 200, KINGS CROSS HOUSE
(National Westminster Bank); two overpowering curtain-walled
office blocks of identical design, 1975 and 1982, by *Chapman
Taylor & Partners*. Outside, a taut steel and cable SCULPTURE by
*William Pye*, 1974; inside, a TAPESTRY by *Robert Wallace*, 1975.
Behind them in KILLICK STREET, offices dressed in the Postmodern garb of the 1990s, with bowed fronts and jutting eaves.
On the W side, STUART MILL HOUSE, utilitarian indeed; six-
storey flats by *Joseph Emberton*, 1951. Long modernist concrete
balconies; none of Tecton's refinement.

PRIORY GREEN ESTATE, N of Killick Street, is the most ambitious
scheme among much public housing in this area, extending between
Collier Street and Wynford Road. First planned in 1937–9 as a
rebuilding of Busaco Street; replanned as part of Finsbury's grand

post-war housing programme, when the site was enlarged to E and N. The largest but least satisfactory of *Tecton's* Finsbury estates, completed by *Skinner, Bailey & Lubetkin*, 1947–57. Compromised by cost-cutting. Four blocks of four storeys, and to their E, six eight-storey blocks, formally arranged in two facing groups. N of these the U-shaped Wynford House and the three-storey Calshot House, added 1952–7. The circular building at the NW corner was designed as a laundry (with district boilerhouse beneath), the only amenity that survived drastic cuts. Dull access galleries instead of the intended stairs and lifts, also for economy. The private balcony sides are livelier, the lower blocks with typical Tecton chequer patterning. The tall blocks had open corner entrances, deliberately prominent, but now glazed in; their entrance halls originally had large murals by *Feliks Topolski*.

Down Collier Street one reaches the surprise of a complete early C19 terrace in NORTHDOWN STREET, Nos. 41–47, with grand Ionic pilastered and pedimented centrepiece and doorways with Doric columns. On the E side, POLLARD HOUSE, red and yellow brick, built as model dwellings by the East End Dwellings Company, 1895.

Around the road junctions at the foot of the hill the whole area has been mauled and blighted by successive transport schemes. Caledonian Road of 1826 was extended s by KING'S CROSS ROAD, created in 1910–12 over the line of the Metropolitan Railway of 1863. Then in the 1980s much was threatened by new rail proposals, as yet unrealized. A few good landmark buildings remain. Turning the corner from Pentonville Road to Caledonian Road is the terracotta-clad Nos. 272–276, 1900–1 by *Wylson & Long*, with a good pub interior. At the corner with King's Cross Road, Nos. 275–277, the former KING'S CROSS CINEMA, by *H. Courtney Constantine*, opened 1920. Grandiose classical; a corner dome, and paired Ionic columns to the upper floor.

*6. South of Old Street: the City fringe, a circular tour starting from Finsbury Square*

The street pattern and a few buildings still reflect the residential suburb of the C18, from which much survived up to the Second World War. The expansion of the commercial City is now everywhere apparent.

FINSBURY SQUARE, although now entirely commercial, was a late attempt at creating a West End residential atmosphere close to the City. Plans for the area were drawn up by the City Surveyor, *George Dance Sen.*, in 1751, but the details for Finsbury Square were settled only in 1777, when the W side was begun by *George Dance Jun.* The E side was built only from 1790. No original houses remain, although three on the W side survived until after the Second World War.* The original circular railed grass plot has gone, replaced, unforgivably, by a scruffy filling station and low restaurant. DRINKING FOUNTAIN at the SE corner by the marble masons *T. & W. Smith*, c. 1900. A frothily carved Portland stone affair with four arched aedicules and pyramidal top.

---

*They had an unusual rhythm, with giant stucco pilasters defining the single bay above each doorway, and pairs of windows in between, tied together by large segmental arches with garlands.

The N side has the most ostentatious of the C20 buildings, a group
built as ROYAL LONDON HOUSE (insurance headquarters). The
earliest part is at the corner of City Road, 1904–5 by *Belcher*, ornate
Baroque, with corner turret. Refurbished as TRITON COURT,
1980–5 by *Sheppard Robson*; a large new archway leads to a ten-
storey public atrium arranged on several levels, with water gardens
and much pale glossy marble. To the E, a harder, more angular
enlargement of 1929 by *Joass*, with an American-looking jagged
clock tower. 1950s addition beyond by *H. Bramhill*, the classical
tradition reduced to some ground-floor rustication. At the N end
of the E side, No. 27 is still fully in an Edwardian spirit, with giant
Ionic pilasters to the upper storeys. As for the rest, the 1950s and
1980s both contributed bland, mediocre stone-faced fronts of
seven to nine storeys. The only exception is the SW corner building, which ruthlessly displays its concrete structure.

In the streets to the E, on the fringe of Broadgate slick new
commercial buildings are interspersed with older survivals. No. 1
EARL STREET is by *Llewelyn-Davies & Weeks*, 1989–91, steel-
framed, with prefabricated cladding of grey granite and white
aluminium, built by fast-track methods. A tall late Georgian terrace
remains on the N side of CHRISTOPHER STREET, and a few other
isolated houses elsewhere. In the C19 this area became industrial,
like the neighbouring parts of Shoreditch (q.v.). Nos. 1–3 BONHILL
STREET is an impressive survivor from that time, surprisingly
grand; red and black engineering bricks, giant Ionic pilasters with
Portland stone capitals. Among the more eye-catching of the
brash newcomers, Nos. 28–30 WORSHIP STREET, with frontage
of 1980 by *Hulme Chadwick & Partners* with curved metal-clad
stair-tower and bowstring-braced glazing. Back to CITY ROAD
and the dignified Edwardian No. 1, LOWNDES HOUSE, with a
rusticated S front.

CHISWELL STREET, W of City Road. The S side E of Moor Lane
was transferred to the City in 1994. *George Dance Jun.* developed
terraces in this neighbourhood from *c.* 1776, but at the E end nothing of this time survives. Much was destroyed in the Second
World War, and the mid-1950s replacements have mostly been
rebuilt since. One later 1950s survival on the N side is No. 14,
LONGBOW HOUSE, by *Joseph*. A successfully varied stone-clad
composition; one-storey street range with free-standing columns,
seven-storey part set back, with windows in a big frame and small
decorative balconies enlivening the E side, and a lower W wing
with sculpture of an archer on its flank. The huge buildings
spawned by the booming City of the 1980s are much greedier for
space and have little respect for their context. The S end of
BUNHILL ROW has a crushingly mediocre group: a crude corner
block clad in grey marble and crimson trim, followed by
GAVRELLE HOUSE, 1990, a long front whose monotony is not
alleviated by its harsh contrasting panels of plain yellow and
moulded red brick. Opposite, the City has taken over, with a rash
of vast atrium buildings whose main sides face S to Ropemaker
Street (for more details *see London 1: The City of London*). No. 25
Ropemaker Street has a busy rhythm of horizontal sun screens,
and circular uprights projecting above the roof-line. MILTON
GATE, No. 1 Moor Lane, is more exceptional, both aesthetically

and functionally. By *Denys Lasdun, Peter Softley & Associates*, for Land Securities, 1987–91. A shimmering green glass cliff, its sheer glazing to Chiswell Street punctuated only by a pattern of small bolts, but breaking out into mysterious shallow projecting fins and bays higher up. The translucent quality is achieved by a double skin of glass, which has the practical purpose of housing hot air vents and cleaning balconies between the layers. Hipped roof, corner towers, and corner entrances marked by blue brick columns.

w of Milton Street we return to a more human scale. At the corner, the C19 ST PAUL'S TAVERN, tactfully extended in the C20 along the ground floors of three late C18 houses, each of three bays and three storeys. On the N side, No. 33, DIANA HOUSE, 1954–5 by *Hans Biel*, six storeys with aluminium-framed windows; cast stone STATUE of Diana in the forecourt by *Arthur Fleischmann*. No. 35, MICHAEL HOUSE, by *Architech*, 1989–90. After Whitbread's Brewery (*see* below), Nos. 42–46, a tall plain late C18 terrace, possibly by *Dance Jun.*, four storeys, arched doors with delicate fanlights.

## Whitbread's Brewery

The site straddles Chiswell Street. Breweries were not permitted within the City but grew up on its immediate fringes. Samuel Whitbread moved here in 1749, taking over a handsome dwelling house on the s side of the street for his own use (now the Partners' House) and an existing brewery, which he extended and rebuilt on an unprecedented scale. By the later C18 Whitbread's had become one of the sights of London, visited by the royal family in 1787, when there were 200 men and 80 horses. *John Smeaton* had designed the underground cistern for holding the beer; *John Rennie* supervised the introduction of steam power in 1785. What remains is only the historic core of the brewery; the late C19 buildings to N, s and E, developed after Whitbread's became a limited company in 1889, were demolished after the brewery ceased to operate in 1976. The earlier part, now company headquarters and conference centre, lies to the s, with an extension, converted to offices, around a narrow courtyard across the road to the N.

The PARTNERS' HOUSE is of red brick; it was in existence by 1716, altered and extended tactfully in 1756. Now of nine bays and four storeys, originally probably with a five-bay centre and stepped-back two-bay wings. A big coved cornice over all except the two l. bays. Central doorway with carved brackets and an iron overthrow with lamp. Ground-floor windows altered, but the three upper floors all with the very narrow blind recesses between the windows characteristic of *c.* 1700. Moulded floorbands, the lower one rising around the blind arched tympanum of the central first-floor window. The extension on the l. (E) side has a single large window on the first floor, for a reception room (now Board Room) created in 1756. Inside, a central passage leads to the stairs, back l. Lower flights with angular Chinese Chippendale balustrade, continued in the same mode by an extra half-flight to the Board Room, a fine room extending the whole depth of the house. Four symmetrically arranged doorcases with octagonal panels; fine Rococo fireplace with scrolled broken pediment and panel with musical instruments. The upper flights of the main stair still of *c.* 1700: closed string with spiral balusters. C18 fielded panelling in some other rooms, but the rest of the house much altered.

The stock brick BREWERY BUILDINGS cluster around a yard s of the Partners' House. The range E of the Partners' House dates from *c.* 1867; the carriageway through it is of 1891. Another entrance in Milton Street: a tall narrow archway of 1979 cut through a four-storey stable range rebuilt in the 1860s and 1880s. They had iron columns and brick vaults. The stables continue along the rear of the terrace with St Paul's Tavern, where a fragment of a ramp to the upper floors remains.

On the s side of the yard is the SUGAR ROOM of 1792, with two rows of arched windows. The low building housing the Speaker's Coach (drawn by Whitbread's horses from the 1840s) was added in 1986; the polygonal entrance lobby with tall brick arches was added in 1977–9 by *Wolff Olins*, in association with *Roderick Gradidge*, when the buildings were converted to a conference centre and the whole given a somewhat spurious 'heritage' flavour. A slate stair made from old fermenting vessels leads to the one survival from the early brewing buildings, the PORTER TUN ROOM, a storehouse where the beer barrels were kept to mature. Begun in 1774, now divided horizontally into two banqueting rooms. It is 160 ft (49 metres) long and has a 60-ft (18-metre) span. The important survival is the spectacular open timber kingpost roof of twelve bays. Brick vaults below.

On the N side of Chiswell Street there remains the brewery depot, where the beer was casked, brought here by pipes under the road. A long thin courtyard with gates to the road and buildings on three sides. These are of 1867, replacing buildings of 1771, as is recorded on the sundial at the end. W and N wings have continuous bands of windows. Converted in 1995 as student accommodation for the Guildhall School of Music, by *D. Y. Davies Associates*.

### Whitecross Street to Bunhill Road

WHITECROSS STREET runs N–S from the W end of Chiswell Street. On its E side the ungainly results of the redevelopment of *c.* 1980 which replaced Whitbread's later buildings, indifferent offices, then plain brown brick flats over a pedestrian shopping precinct and covered market. Further N are tall, close-set Peabody blocks of working-class flats of the 1880s, five and six storeys in the usual striped brick, evidence that this area was a major focus of slum clearance in the later C19. By the 1890s a new lay-out of regular side streets had replaced most of the crowded courts and alleys. On the s side, at the E end of DUFFERIN STREET, a more unusual group of the same period, DUFFERIN COURT, built as costermongers' dwellings, yellow and red brick, with barrow sheds on the courtyard side. In a few small lanes just to the N, miscellaneous industrial buildings give a faint flavour of the C19 scene. Further N and W much was rebuilt after war damage. The W side of Whitecross Street nevertheless still recalls the C18 character of the area, with a few older houses at the N end, and a vista of St Luke's Church beyond.

BANNER STREET has at its E end the *GLC*'s BANNER ESTATE of 1964–7: the best part is QUAKER COURT, quite pleasant four-storey maisonettes with a rhythm of boxed-out bays (with an intriguing variety of customized doors as recent counterpoint). An opening through to a garden made from part of a former Quaker Burial Ground. This was the burial place of George Fox †1691. At the NW corner, SOCIETY OF FRIENDS MEMORIAL BUILDING, 1881 by *W. W. Lee* (Bunhill Fields Meeting House, and offices of the Bedford Institute Association). One wing remains; the rest destroyed in the Second World War. Simple Queen Anne style, with red terracotta panel. The rest of the Banner Estate demonstrates the extremes required of mixed development on inner city sites where high-density housing was demanded: overlooking the garden, low old-people's housing to the W, and to the E, BRAITHWAITE HOUSE, a domineering twenty-one-storey slab of scissors-plan flats, on a bleak concrete plaza originally with garages below.

Finally the rest of BUNHILL ROW. On the W, Nos. 100–101, TURNBERRY HOUSE, 1990s Postmodern, not too large, three storeys and mansards, striped stonework with upper canted bays; the ARTILLERY ARMS, a modest C19 corner pub, and the ungainly slab-on-podium FINSBURY TOWER (reclad 1990). On the E side, first Bunhill Fields Cemetery (q.v.), then, backing on to the Artillery Company's grounds (*see* Armoury House), a neat early C19 terrace, Nos. 20–29, and a small warehouse with crane (No. 15).

## 7. Old Street and the area to its north

OLD STREET was the main W–E route through the parish of St Luke's, which developed as an C18 residential suburb on the fringe of the City. Only a few traces of this domestic period remain. Old Street became commercial and industrial in the C19, and the area to its N was extensively reconstructed after a combination of war damage and slum clearance.

The junction of Goswell Road, Clerkenwell Road and Old Street has tall, late C19 warehouses. At the NW corner the HAT AND FEATHERS, 1860 by *Hill & Paraire*, with ornate stuccoed front and a good bowed corner. The S side of OLD STREET starts with some late C19 buildings of quality. No. 2, 1872 for Thomas Mabe, colour merchant. Four storeys, with an elaborate unified elevation; giant pilasters linked by angular arches below a big cornice; paired windows with angular heads, patterned brickwork between floors. No. 12, dated 1876, a former pub, the OLD RODNEY'S HEAD, has a bust of Rodney under an arch, above an elaborate Venetian cornice and balustrade. Then the remarkable Nos. 20–24, 1880 by *Ford & Hesketh*, specialists in warehouse design. Built for Samuel Haskins, manufacturer of window blinds and rolling shutters. Seven bays, with six W bays added 1896–8. A five-storeyed frontage with bands of iron arcades framing the windows, as one might expect to find in Glasgow or New York rather than London. Attractively detailed with pierced decorative spandrels, the ground floor treated similarly but with doorways and broader arches for shopfronts.

Between Domingo Street and Honduras Street remains of a three-storey C18 domestic terrace. At the corner of Golden Lane, a stuccoed pub, formerly the Golden Hind, set back, with extension to Old Street in front of an older part. No. 78, BRAYFIELD HOUSE, 1989–92 by *Patrick Davies* of *Hanscomb Davies Ltd*. An elegantly transparent steel and glass front in a slot between drab neighbours. An angled curve on the l. White cladding, also to the rear which has a slight curve and some triangular windows to GARRETT STREET. This side is sandwiched between C19 industrial remnants: White Lion Court, with a crane, and a building with cast-iron windows. On the S side former STABLES for Whitbread's Brewery (*see* Perambulation 6), in use until 1992; three storeys with typical small windows, decorative plaque with the date 1897. Concrete jack-arched floors on iron columns, with horse ramps.

Back in Old Street big commercial façades dominate: the Postmodern Nos. 80–86 of 1989 has giant arches, but too flat to be effective; No. 88, *c.* 1900, busily decorated with terracotta, breaks up its six storeys by linking the middle ones in pairs, with a faster rhythm of windows to the top floor. No. 116 has an exuberant late C19 front with large central arched window, pilasters and decorative cornice. Opposite St Luke (q.v.), a few C18 domestic buildings (No. 90, and further on No. 118, No. 120). At the W corner of Whitecross Street, No. 142, CHURCHILL HOUSE, although rewindowed, is a stone-clad Edwardian building with very tall giant pilasters to ground and first floors. No. 148, Royal Mail, brown clad and brown glazed, demonstrates 1970s modernism at its dullest. Nos. 174–180, CLASSIC HOUSE, in 1930s style, is more fun, with its Art Deco and modernist touches: a recessed stair-tower and a framed black entrance on the r., a curved corner on the l., and upper floors with ribbon windows contrasting with the verticals of the stair-tower.

CITY CLOISTERS are the former ST LUKE'S PAROCHIAL SCHOOLS, now offices, 1870, with E wing of 1887 by *John Groom*. Tall and rather gaunt; main part with gables, top floor with Gothic arches (rebuilt after a fire in 1881). Niches for statues of Charity Boy and Girl from the previous building (now in St Luke's Church of England Primary School, q.v.).

The OLD STREET ROUNDABOUT, created as part of a street-widening scheme, was notorious for its dismal underpasses and aggressive concrete ventilators of the 1960–70s. The showy skeletal arches belong to a facelift of 1993–4 by *Hanscomb Davies Ltd*.

*North of Old Street*

The N side of OLD STREET, going W from the roundabout, is at first entirely later C20. The first, inhumanly scaled monster (Nos. 207–211) is a speculative 1970s tower, sleekly reclad for British Telecom offices in 1984. Then a shopping parade with flats above, part of ST LUKE'S ESTATE, on the site of St Luke's Hospital.* The estate extends on both sides of Bath Street whose name recalls Peerless Pool, a reservoir used in the C18 as a bathing pool. This is a total post-war remodelling of an area which had been

---

* The hospital was one of the two early London madhouses, founded in 1751, rebuilt by *George Dance Jun.* in 1782–4, with a restrained but harmonious front 493 ft long. Converted to the Bank of England Printing House, 1917–20. Demolished after war damage.

built up from the late C17 onwards. All that remains from its early development is the shell of St Luke's Church (q.v.) and a few houses to its W. The new housing is by the *GLC*, in two phases. E of Bath Street is the earlier part, completed 1969, on the mammoth scale still in vogue in the 1960s (cf. Pepys Estate, Deptford), and at the high density prescribed for innermost areas by the County of London plan. Behind the block with the shops, three linked ten-storey slabs with scissor-plan flats, and one separate taller twenty-storey tower. Yellow brick and concrete, the concrete in places quite sculpturally handled (see the open arches below the tower). New landscaping and gates etc. by *Pollard Thomas & Edwards*, 1988–9. W of Bath Street are more intimate L-shaped four-storey blocks in red brick of the 1970s, clustering around private and public spaces, clearly displaying the influence of Darbourne & Darke's Lillington Gardens, Westminster. The slightly cramped centre is BARTHOLOMEW SQUARE, a revival of an old name. To the W the plentiful open space around the shell of St Luke's Church is linked by a network of paths to amenities to the N: a pleasantly landscaped park, the Finsbury Leisure Centre and the older Public Baths in Ironmonger Row, and St Luke's School in Radnor Street (qq.v.).

To the N of Radnor Street the housing by Finsbury Borough Council is easily recognizable. 1959–60 by *Emberton, Franck & Tardrew*. Galway House and Grayson House are two formal seventeen-storey blocks, austere, brick-faced, with curved porches providing a little light relief. Like King Square (*see* below) constructed largely of prefabricated parts, without exterior scaffolding, an early example of this technique.

Back towards Old Street by HELMET ROW to the W of St Luke's Church, where No. 12 is the former C18 vicarage; five bays with late C19 bay window and side entrance. Nos. 1–3 are modest C18 survivals, as are Nos. 109–115 Old Street. Further W, narrow courts and yards behind the larger houses were replaced by PRIESTLEY (1964) and WENLAKE (1905), two *LCC* blocks, and by flats of between the wars.

Further W, a long range of plain post-war shops and offices along Old Street, built together with Finsbury's STAFFORD CRIPPS ESTATE to the N in GEE STREET, by *Emberton*, 1953–6. A high-density development (200 p.p.a.) achieved by three twelve-storey Y-shaped blocks, each with sixty flats, a similar plan to Bevin Court (*see* p. 636), but cheaper and without frills. The flats have balconies, but the landscaped foothills are little compensation for the bleak details and hopelessly cramped site.

CENTRAL STREET, which runs N from Old Street to City Road, has no coherent character. Further N, early rehousing efforts are now represented only by CHADWORTH BUILDINGS on the S side of LEVER STREET, LCC flats of 1906, probably by *J. G. Stephenson*. Spare Free Classical detail marred by reglazing. Four and five storeys around a courtyard entered by a big archway. Their tight plan contrasts with the large area further N rebuilt for Finsbury by *Emberton, Franck & Tardrew*, 1959–63. Five randomly grouped tower blocks of sixteen to nineteen storeys are sited where space became available. They are built largely of precast concrete units on a specially developed system (*F. Samuely & Partners*, engineers) and contain flats, not maisonettes, hence the insistent rhythm of long balconies on every floor. Balconies are of concrete precast panels, fluted to avoid staining. The tallest tower, TURNPIKE HOUSE (completed 1965 by *C. L. Franck*), forms the w side of the reconstructed KING SQUARE, between Central Street and Goswell Road, and is quite daringly opened up by a big arch at ground level. To the N are six-storey flats on columns, with private balconies facing the square. King Square was originally laid out in 1822–5, but from this time only the church on the E side remains (St Barnabas, now St Clement, q.v.), to the N of a new shopping precinct.

*City Road from west to east*

CITY ROAD, part of the C18 bypass around N London, divides the former boroughs of Finsbury and Islington. Opened 1761, but not built up until *c.* 1800. The w part retains a residential character, the E end, nearer the City, is commercial of *c.* 1900.

At the w end, near the Angel, there is a clear distinction between N and s sides. On the N side, Nos. 375–389 and 319–359, neat late Georgian terraces of *c.* 1810, part of the development of Duncan Terrace and Colebrooke Row (*see* Islington, below, pp. 677–8). On the s, Nos. 340–394, set back on the s side, early C19 with later stucco trimmings. Tall, close-set pedimented windows typical of the crowded details to be found *c.* 1860. No. 326 was formerly a detached mid-C19 villa of stock brick, three bays with two full-height bows, big cornice, and heavy doorcase with paired brackets. Restored as CITY AND GUILDS OF LONDON INSTITUTE, with a new link to the r. with archway and a further bay. To the l. another link to 'Cottage Place 1845', formerly a terrace of three houses. Behind is ANGEL GATE, a large precinct of brown brick offices, displaying the usual 1980s clichés of decorative red brick arches and hipped roofs. The former ST MARK'S HOSPITAL is of 1852–4 by *John Wallen*, heightened and extended to the s in 1895–6 by *Rowland Plumbe*. Domestic Classical five-bay front with stone rusticated ground floor, brick above. The first hospital for rectal diseases, an early example of a specialist hospital.

Further on the road crosses the CITY ROAD BASIN, where warehouses have been replaced by indifferent commercial buildings of the 1980s–90s; brown brick with some blue trimmings. After this, as the road approaches the City, the s side displays the undisciplined pomp of late Victorian and Edwardian commerce, still surprisingly undisturbed. Examples are Nos. 190–196, CITY HOUSE, *c.* 1895 by *King & Co.* a very large, ill-proportioned late C19 commercial range: elaborate Neo-Jacobean upper parts above giant arches. Converted to apartments 1997. Nos. 152–160, KEMP HOUSE, was built as a German YMCA (No. 160) and hotel (No. 158), 1908–10 by *George & W. Charles Waymouth*. Brick with stone dressings, Free Baroque with steep gable and elaborate Venetian window with an upper window tied in. Elongated scrolls and other fanciful Mannerist detail. GILRAY HOUSE, however, is interwar Art Deco, *c.* 1930–1 by *A. Scarlett*; four-storey front with giant polygonal columns to upper floors; steel windows in between. Then EMPIRE HOUSE, by *King & Co. c.* 1901, when it was the Alexandra Trust Dining Rooms; rather fussy Neo-French Renaissance, with three big floors with mullioned windows, all painted beige, which does not help. Nos. 124–130, Edwardian, five storeys and attics, has strong buttresses all the way up. In Baldwin Street behind, the OLD FOUNTAIN pub, an isolated modest Georgian survival.

## INTRODUCTION

The northern part of the modern borough consists of the parish of Islington, which became the Metropolitan Borough in 1899, stretching N to the foot of the Northern Heights from its main settlement at the S end. The broad High Street, with its green, and Upper Street, with the parish church, still reflect the pattern of the prosperous pre-Victorian village. It lay on an important medieval route from the City, which led N from Clerkenwell by St John Street to the High Street, and continued as Upper Street and Holloway Road up to Highgate. Until the late C18, in the countryside N of the village there was only a scatter of mansions and hamlets. The principal medieval houses belonged to religious institutions: Barnsbury to the Canons of St Paul's, Highbury to the Knights Hospitallers, Canonbury to the Canons of St Bartholomew. At the first two, only traces of moated sites survive amidst the later streets, but at Canonbury there are remains of a substantial courtyard house, partly dating from *c.* 1600 when it was a country retreat of the wealthy Sir John Spencer, Lord Mayor of London.

This is a good area to study the development of the suburban house. Islington and its hamlets attracted spasmodic development from the C17, appealing to Londoners looking for a rural home in convenient reach of the City. Newington Green, an old hamlet on the border with Stoke Newington, has an exceptional survival: a group 28 of the earliest remaining brick terrace houses in London, dating from the mid C17. From the C18 there are a few remains of the 1760s near Islington Green, and at Highbury Fields a bold and original isolated terrace of the 1770s, designed by *James Spiller.* During the C18 the banks of the New River to the E of the High Street proved a special attraction (*see* Colebrooke Row, Perambulation 1b), but systematic suburban expansion did not start until the end of the century. The handsome Highbury Terrace to the W of the Fields dates from the 1790s; at the same time, the Marquess of Northampton's estate around Canonbury House began to be laid out for building. W of Upper Street the Barnsbury Estate, which had been divided into a number of small landholdings, was developed piecemeal, chiefly from the 1820s–40s.

The shift in style from late Georgian elegance and restraint to mid-Victorian lushness and eclecticism can be illustrated in many places. A common early C19 type of terrace was four-storeyed, with arches framing ground- or first-floor windows, as at Compton Terrace, Upper Street, 1805, and Cloudesley Terrace, Liverpool Road, of the 1820s. More unusual are the all-stuccoed Annett's Crescent, Essex Road, of 1819–20, and, nearby, the eccentrically detailed terraces of the Scott Estate (pilasters with ammonite capitals). On the land behind the main roads, the conventional Georgian pattern of houses grouped around a square was sometimes adopted, although in a less ordered way than in Mayfair or Bloomsbury. Canonbury Square was the first, planned by 1805, followed by a delightfully haphazard 82 sequence of 'squares' of various shapes in Barnsbury, and by those of the Clothworkers' Estate S of Essex Road. The later terraces of the 1840s are generally recognizable by their more lavish use of stucco details, but, in the case of *Roumieu & Gough*'s startlingly austere Milner Square, were given proportions that departed radically 79 from Georgian tradition. Another theme is the contest between urban terrace and more rural villa. In the 1830s the ideal of the detached or semi-detached house affected parts of Barnsbury, e.g. the Neo-Tudor Lonsdale Square. It gained ground in the 1840s in Canonbury and at Highbury, which both sport ample stuccoed Italianate houses by *James Wagstaffe*, and reigned supreme in *Charles Hambridge*'s highly individual development of Highbury New Park, with its magnificent collection of grand, eclectic villas of the 1850s in a vaguely Lombard style. Tufnell Park had similar ambitions but they remained largely unachieved.

The line of the North London Railway, laid out in 1850, marks the edge of built-up Islington by the mid C19. By this time little remained of the pasture land which had been famous as the dairy of London, with its rustic pleasure resorts for Londoners at Highbury Barn and Copenhagen House. The land was divided up by new roads (Caledonian Road, Camden Road, both of the 1820s) and attracted typical fringe metropolitan services and industries. Pentonville Prison was built on Caledonian Road in 1840–2, and the Caledonian Market was laid out on Copenhagen Fields, 1850–5, in an effort to improve the insanitary collection of cowsheds and layers for cattle on their way to Smithfield. Closer to London noxious industries became concentrated in the sw around the Regent's Canal, and then along the railway line into King's Cross. In northern Islington, as public transport proliferated (first suburban stations 1852, first trams from Nag's Head, Holloway, from 1871), routine lower-class streets, no longer with any pretensions to fashion, rapidly filled up any empty areas until all was built over. By the C20 the borough had less public open space than any other within the LCC area. The population figures tell the story: 1811: 15,000; 1821: 22,000; 1831: 37,000; 1841: 56,000; 1851: 95,000; 1861: 155,000; 1871: 216,000; 1881: 283,000; 1891: 320,000. As the suburbs grew, shopping and commerce spread along the main routes of Upper Street and Holloway Road, both still predominantly C19 in character.

The Anglican churches built for the new suburbs, despite demolitions, also are still numerous, although several have found other uses. Only a few are architecturally outstanding.* The parish church of St Mary, with its enjoyable mid-C18 tower, was supplemented first by St Mary Magdalene, Lower Holloway (1814), then *Barry*'s churches of St John, St Paul, Holy Trinity and St Peter, all designed 82 in 1826 in a correct but dull Perp. In the 1830s *Inwood & Clifton* used a less accomplished Gothic for St Stephen, although their contemporary St James, Lower Holloway, is still Grecian. The *Rundbogenstil* popular from the 1840s is represented by *Scoles*'s St John of 1841–3, Islington's first R.C. church (another was *Roumieu*'s St Michael of 1863–4, demolished). By far the most rewarding of

---

*Demolished since World War II: All Saints, Caledonian Road, by *William Tress*, 1837–8; St Anne, Poole's Park, by *A. D. Gough*, 1871; St Matthew, City Road, by *Scott*, 1847–8 (an important early work destroyed in World War II); St Matthew, Essex Road, 1850, and St Philip, Arlington Square, 1855, by *A. D. Gough*; St Matthias, Caledonian Road, by *Barnett & Birch*, 1853 (originally Presbyterian); St Michael, Bingfield Street, by *Roumieu*, 1863–4.

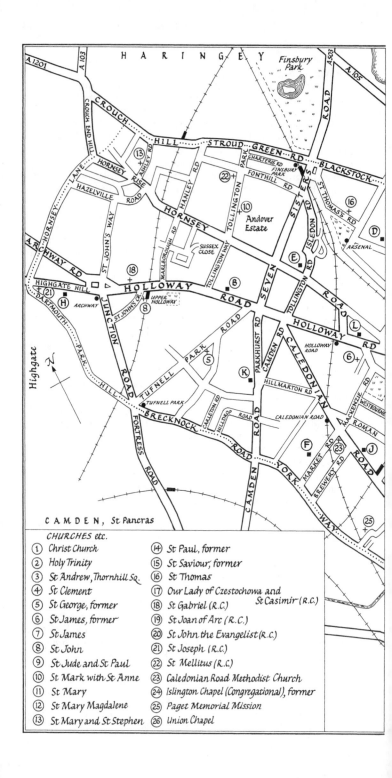

CHURCHES etc.
① Christ Church
② Holy Trinity
③ St Andrew, Thornhill Sq.
④ St Clement
⑤ St George, former
⑥ St James, former
⑦ St James
⑧ St John
⑨ St Jude and St Paul
⑩ St Mark with St Anne
⑪ St Mary
⑫ St Mary Magdalene
⑬ St Mary and St Stephen
⑭ St Paul, former
⑮ St Saviour, former
⑯ St Thomas
⑰ Our Lady of Czestochowa and St Casimir (R.C.)
⑱ St Gabriel (R.C.)
⑲ St Joan of Arc (R.C.)
⑳ St John the Evangelist (R.C.)
㉑ St Joseph (R.C.)
㉒ St Mellitus (R.C.)
㉓ Caledonian Road Methodist Church
㉔ Islington Chapel (Congregational), former
㉕ Paget Memorial Mission
㉖ Union Chapel

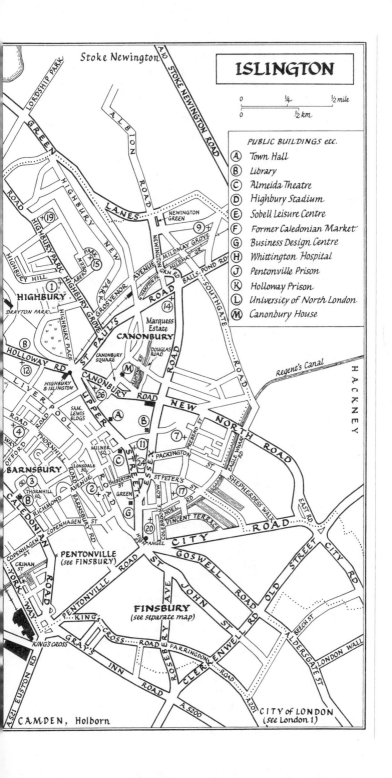

ISLINGTON

0        ¼        ½ mile
0              ½ km

PUBLIC BUILDINGS etc.

Ⓐ Town Hall
Ⓑ Library
Ⓒ Almeida Theatre
Ⓓ Highbury Stadium
Ⓔ Sobell Leisure Centre
Ⓕ Former Caledonian Market
Ⓖ Business Design Centre
Ⓗ Whittington Hospital
Ⓙ Pentonville Prison
Ⓚ Holloway Prison
Ⓛ University of North London
Ⓜ Canonbury House

Stoke Newington

STOKE NEWINGTON ROAD

ALBION ROAD

LORDSHIP PARK

GREEN LANES

HIGHBURY NEW PARK

HIGHBURY GROVE

HIGHBURY PARK

HIGHBURY HILL

HIGHBURY PLACE

NEWINGTON GREEN

NEWINGTON GRN.

MILDMAY GROVE

MILDMAY PK.

GROSVENOR AVE

ST. PAUL'S ROAD

BALLS POND RD

SOUTHGATE ROAD

DOUGLAS ROAD

CANONBURY ROAD

NEW NORTH ROAD

Regent's Canal

HACKNEY

HIGHBURY
Ⓐ①
DRAYTON PARK

PARK ⓧ⑮ ABER..

⑲
⑨

⑭

Marquess Estate
CANONBURY
CANONBURY SQUARE
Ⓜ
②⑥

HOLLOWAY RD
Ⓑ ⑫
⑧
LIVERPOOL ROAD
WAY
OFFORD RD
ⓧ④

HIGHBURY & ISLINGTON
SAM. LEWIS BLDGS
UPPER STREET

Ⓐ
Ⓑ
⑦ PREBEND ST.
PACKINGTON ST
EAGLE WHARF RD
SHEPHERDESS WALK

THORNHILL ROAD

BARNSBURY
Ⓚ③ THORNHILL SQ.
RICHMOND
COPENHAGEN ST
LONSDALE SQ.
MILNER SQ.
BARNSBURY RD
THEBERTON ST
ST PETER'S
ST. PETER'S
ST PETER'S GREEN
②
Ⓒ
Ⓖ
COLEBROOKE ROW
NOEL RD
VINCENT TERRACE
⑳ ⓧ ANGEL
⑪
②④
⑰

ESSEX ROAD

CALEDONIAN ROAD

COPENHAGEN ST
CRINAN ST
PENTONVILLE
(see FINSBURY)

CITY ROAD

GOSWELL ROAD

ST JOHN ST

OLD STREET

CITY RD

EAST RD

YORK WAY

KING'S CROSS

PENTONVILLE ROAD

KING'S CROSS ROAD

FINSBURY
(see separate map)

GRAY'S INN ROAD

ROSEBERY AVE

FARRINGDON ROAD

CLERKENWELL ROAD

BEECH ST

ALDERSGATE ST

LONDON WALL

A.201
A.501 EUSTON ROAD
A.5200

CAMDEN, Holborn

CITY of LONDON
(see London 1)

mid-Victorian churches is *William White*'s St Saviour, Aberdeen Park (1865–6), with its unusual central octagonal tower and its rich internal polychromy. *Scott*'s St Clement (1863–5) was a good runner-up but has been converted to flats. *A. D. Gough*'s numerous churches (of which only three survive) are a local peculiarity, characterized by rather wild rock-facing and asymmetrically placed thin spires. The *Ecclesiologist* disapproved of Gough. Also roguish and of the 1860s is *George Truefitt*'s St George's, Tufnell Park, its odd central plan prefigured by *Thomas Allom*'s Christ Church, Highbury Grove, of 1847–8. The more sober brick lancet style, which after the 1870s replaced the standard ragstone-and-Dec-tracery formula, is best represented by St Peter, Dartmouth Park (1879–80), by *C. L. Luck*. Most dramatic among R.C. churches is the Passionists' distinctly Italian St Joseph by *Albert Vicars*, 1887–9.

From the late C17 Islington was a popular refuge for Noncon-formists, and the best of their surviving buildings are more innova-tive than the Anglican churches. The Congregationalists erected three centralized Gothic buildings: Harecourt of 1855, Highbury Quadrant of 1880–2 (both mostly replaced) and, most splendid, the
95 well-preserved Union Chapel of 1876–8 by *James Cubitt*. Their other chapels are also notable, ranging from the classical New Court
94 Church (now St Mellitus, R.C.) by *C. G. Searle*, 1870–1, to Islington Chapel, one of the first in a domestic Queen Anne idiom (*H. J. Paull*, 1887–8). The majority of the churches and major chapels were intended for middle-class residents; the working classes were served by missions, most of which have gone. The Paget Memorial Mission, in the grimmest industrial area off York Way, must always have been an oddity, both for its façade by *Beresford Pite*, 1910–11, and for its curious fittings. Few later C20 churches need mention: the body of the parish church rebuilt by *Seely & Paget*, 1954–6, and two R.C. churches: St Joan of Arc, 1960–2 by *Walters & Kerr Bate*, and *Gerard Goalen*'s more radically modernist St Gabriel, 1966–8. The best of the many conversions and adaptations is Christ Church, Highbury Grove, by *Maurice Taylor*.

Among other buildings for the community by far the most notable are the distinctively individual Edwardian libraries: two by *Hare*, one
102 each by *Macartney* and *Pite*. Two interesting larger structures serving a wider catchment are the colossal iron-and-glass Royal Agricultural Hall of the 1860s (given a future as the Business Design Centre) and the Arsenal stadium at Highbury, whose East Stand is a uniquely lavish monument to 1930s football.

From the later C19 the middle classes began to move out of Islington to newer suburbs. The need to tackle overcrowding in the poorer areas was recognized already in the 1860s; the large Peabody Square s of Essex Road is a tough survivor from improvements of this time. Beyond the now cherished areas of the older squares and terraces (regenerated by gentrification from the 1950s onwards in Canonbury, and from the 1960s in Barnsbury), large tracts of public housing were put up, as well as many small estates, the result of widespread clearance before and after the Second World War. By 1951 the population had dropped to 236,000.

Landmarks from the early years of the century are the LCC's big Caledonian Estate off Caledonian Road and the progressively deco-rative blocks of the Samuel Lewis Trust in Liverpool Road. The borough's own housing programme took off from 1919, when *E. C. P. Monson* was appointed architect (though never directly employed by the council). His firm (later joined by his brother Harry and son John) designed 6,000 dwellings for the Metropolitan Borough (90 per cent of the council's housing) up to 1960. Inside, plans of flats varied little, but outside a number of popular guises were adopted: at first versions of Neo-Georgian (the modestly scaled showpiece flats of the 1920s around the new Town Hall), later on a more streamlined modern idiom. Much is downright dull; Aubert Park, Highbury, stands out as the most ambitious of the immediate post-1945 schemes, its ponderous monumentality a striking contrast to the light, Scandinavian-inspired blocks built by the LCC at Highbury Quadrant at the same time. In the 1960s, like other boroughs, Islington embarked on system-building, witnessed by towers still scattered over the borough, and by the lumpy, unsatisfactory, medium-rise Packington Square. A change came after *Alfred Head* became architect to the enlarged borough created in 1965, and commissioned more imaginative low- and medium-rise schemes from a variety of architects. The first, *Darbourne & Darke*'s intricate Marquess Estate of 1966–76, was still dauntingly large, but from the early 1970s, partly as a result of opposition to major demolition schemes, many small and ingenious high-density infill schemes were carried out, both for the borough and for housing associations (for example by *Andrews Sherlock & Partners* at Popham Street, by *Pring, White & Partners* in Barnsbury), often together with the creation of small parks and the rehabilitation of older housing. During the 1980s, a cosier village idiom, with quirky detail and pitched roofs, was cultivated by the Borough Architect's Department under *Chris Purslow* for both housing and neighbourhood centres, frequently at odds with the classically based styles of most of Islington's houses. This gave way to some more restrained and dignified designs in the 1990s (for example the streets off Isledon Road, by *Hunt Thompson*).

The Angel is Islington's only blatantly late C20 commercial quarter. It was greedily rebuilt in the 1980s after years of planning blight following proposals first for a motorway (in the GLC Development Plan of 1966–9), then for more modest road widening in the 1970s. Some more distinguished transformations and new building also began in the 1980s in the industrial area around the Battlebridge basin near King's Cross, initially for offices, but with housing playing a greater role in the 1990s.

ARCHAEOLOGY. A slight scatter of finds, mainly Paleolithic, relate to concentrations in the W end and the Stoke Newington area.


RELIGIOUS BUILDINGS

*1. Church of England*

Former ALL SAINTS, Tytherton Road, Tufnell Park. 1884–5 by *J. E. K. Cutts*. Redundant in 1994 and converted to flats. Long dull Perp red brick exterior that goes with the neighbouring red brick and terracotta terraces. Bellcote; polygonal E end. Restored after war damage by *A. Llewellyn Smith*, 1953. The interior was spacious, with arcade arches of very red brick.

CHRIST CHURCH, Highbury Grove. 1847–8 by *T. Allom*. Pinched ragstone Dec Gothic, with a fussy spire on the w (liturgically n) side. Remarkable for the original treatment of the awkward corner site with a big octagonal crossing at the hub of four short arms. Nave extended by three bays in 1872 by *Williams & Crouch*; this part divided off by *Maurice Taylor* in 1989 to form a two-storey community centre, a sympathetic scheme that includes some discreet new furnishing. Round the crossing an arcade of moulded arches, taller in the main directions. Polygonal apse with Dec blind arcading. Good Dec foliage capitals throughout. Arch-braced roof, the trusses especially decorative over the crossing. Original FONT and PULPIT. STAINED GLASS. Apse 1954 and transepts 1955 by *Francis Spear*. Vicarage to match to the s, post-1869.

EMMANUEL CHURCH, Hornsey Road, Upper Holloway. From the church of 1884 by *F.R. Farrow & E. Swinfen Harris* only the s aisle remains, red brick, lancet style, ingeniously incorporated in a new church, completed 1988, by *Keith Harrison & Associates*.

HOLY TRINITY (now Celestial Church of Christ), Cloudesley Square. 1826–9 by *Charles Barry*, the third of his Islington churches. In the middle of the square, designed like a miniature edition of King's College Chapel, a rectangle with corner pinnacles; no tower. The piers even slimmer than in St Paul and St John (*see* below), the same small clerestory; galleries removed 1900. The distinguishing feature inside is a tall four-centred arch separating a small vaulted chancel room; a crocketed three-decker pulpit originally stood in front of it. *Ewan Christian* refurnished the two e bays of the nave as a chancel in 1901. The ORGAN CASE is all that remains of the 1820s furnishings: Tudor-Gothic, perhaps by *Barry*. It originally stood in the w gallery. STAINED GLASS. Large e window by *Willement*, 1828, with a small kneeling figure of Richard Cloudesley (who gave the field which became the site of the church to the parish in 1517); royal arms below.

ST ANDREW, Thornhill Square. 1852–4 by *Francis B. Newman & John Johnson*; like a medieval village church transposed into this classical suburban lay-out. Kentish rag, Middle Pointed. Chancel, broad transepts (originally galleried) and aisled nave. sw tower and broach spire. Economical detail on the less important n side. Interior spoilt in the 1960s by ugly partitioning and the removal of the prominent Caen stone pulpit and pews. STAINED GLASS. e window 1873, highly coloured and pictorial.

ST ANDREW, Whitehall Park, Upper Holloway. On a difficult sloping site at the edge of the Victorian suburb. 1894–5 by *Frederick Hammond*, his only church. Mediocre exterior, red brick, lancet style. w end divided off for a hall, 1972. (c18 PULPIT, hexagonal with an inlaid panel. STAINED GLASS. In transept windows, two c16 figures of St James and St Simon from Ram's Chapel, Homerton, of 1729, demolished 1935).

ST AUGUSTINE, Highbury New Park. Provided by the suburb's developer, Henry Rydon (*see* Perambulation 4). 1869–70 by *Habershon & Brock*. Large and crude, of stock brick with a little blue and red brick. Unfinished sw tower. Broad five-bay nave and broad arcade arches with E.E. details; round clerestory windows and spare open roof trusses above. w end divided off c. 1970.

Former ST CLEMENT, Darcy Close, off Bride Street, Lower Holloway. 1863–5 by *Sir G.G. Scott*. Intended to be less Evangelical than other local churches, and hence rather ambitious for its modest neighbourhood. T. E. W. Cubitt paid for the church. E.E. in stock brick with three red brick portals. The front tall and steep with buttresses and bellcote, the nave pitch quite excessive to emphasize the craggy outline. Far less conventional and well bred than most of Scott's work. E end with three E lancets and a vesica. In 1976 the N aisle was unroofed to make a courtyard garden.

ST DAVID, Westbourne Road, Lower Holloway. 1935–6 by *T. F. Ford*, incorporating the arcades of *E. L. Blackburne*'s church of 1866–9 (burned down). Small, plain Perp, with lean-to porch.

ST GEORGE, Crayford Road. 1972–5 by *Clive Alexander*, the replacement for *Truefitt*'s St George's of 1865–8 in Tufnell Park Road (*see* below). A forceful red brick cube anchored on splayed plinths, with a flat lead-faced roof projecting on N, S and W. Interior with exposed brick, flat ceiling on thin steel piers, and restrained lighting: obscured clerestory glass, clear glass in the narrow slits below. In the front a large wooden cross and free-standing bell-frame.

Former ST GEORGE, Tufnell Park Road. 1865–8 by *Truefitt*, surveyor to the Tufnell Park Estate, for seceders from the Anglican church, known as the Free Church of England. Converted 1973–6 into a theatre (with some makeshift additions). The church is uninteresting in detail and materials (Kentish rag with bands of yellow brick) but uncommonly original and successful in plan and grouping, ingeniously fitted on to a sharp angled site (cf. Allom's Christ Church, Highbury). Its form follows the temporary circular timber church Truefitt put up in 1858.

Circular on the outside but with an octagonal core, arcaded internally and with a clerestory. E and W arms. The E one is a prelude to the sanctuary apse making a long stilted chancel; rectangular vestry beyond (encased by theatre buildings). Circular pepperpot (a closet) added 1883. The W arm has two-storey lobbies and flanking porches. Connected to it by a timber porte-cochère, now closed, and a long passage is the Rhenish tower, added 1875, originally with a tiled cap. The arcade has especially broad Gothic arches and cast-iron columns, faced in terracotta in 1883. Timber ceiling. Apron stage in the chancel, some windows blocked.

Former ST JAMES (now School of Audio-Engineering), Chillingworth Road, Lower Holloway. One of *Inwood & Clifton*'s few churches, 1837–8, extended in 1839 by *Hambley* of Holloway (E end) and in 1850 (SW tower). Altered after World War II bombing; converted 1980–2, when concrete-framed flats and studios were built within the shell by *Pollard Thomas Edwards Associates*. Originally of stock brick with stone dressings, now masked with a coat of black. To the street the S side of the nave: it originally had four Ionic pilasters, after the Erechtheum, and a spreading pediment; the hungry SW tower had a circular colonnaded top tier crowned by a wheat ear and grape ornament. The 1980s external alterations are more courageous than successful. In place of the central pilasters, two giant columns *in antis* front a scooped-out portico. Two ungainly extra storeys have vitreous panel cladding, deeply set end windows, and extensions between the rear buttresses.

ST JAMES, Prebend Street. 1873–5 by *F. W. Porter*, architect to the Clothworkers' Company. It stands in the middle of their estate and is the successor to their early C16 Lambe's Chapel, Monkswell Street, City of London, demolished 1872. Kentish rag, C13 detail, with a small, square tower and broach spire attached to the sanctuary. Inside, over the door, a half-figure of William Lambe, clothworker, dated 1612. STAINED GLASS. N chapel, four Flemish roundels, from Lambe's Chapel. Good E window by *Lavers & Barraud*.

ST JOHN, Holloway Road. Built with Commissioners' funds 1826–8 as Upper Holloway Parish Church. By *Charles Barry*, very similar to his other Islington churches. Uninspired Perp; in no other way – except perhaps correctness of detail – superior to the common run of Commissioners' churches. Yellow brick, the N (ritual W) front with a tower. Perp two-light windows separated by twin buttresses. Five-light E window, small clerestory. Inside, thin moulded piers carrying four-centred arches. Wooden galleries; box pews. E end remodelled to form a chancel (cf. Holy Trinity), with choir stalls, screen, organ case by *F. Hammond*, executed by *Jones & Willis*, 1901. Though pulpit, font and stalls were replaced in the later C19, the rest still has an atmosphere of early C19 austerity. STAINED GLASS. E window 1858, rich ornamental work. MONUMENTS. Ann Sykes †1835 and her daughter, Martha Venn, †1840, each with a standing allegorical figure (Faith and Charity). The decoration gracefully Grecian, unusually attractive for *Sievier*, their maker.

To the W the former NATIONAL SCHOOLS with gabled Tudor front.

ST JUDE AND ST PAUL, Mildmay Grove, Newington. 1855 by *A. D. Gough*. Cruciform, late Gothic, with a thin crocketed spire over the porch (restored 1911). Chancel, aisles and clerestory added in the same style by *Edwin Clare*, 1871. Choir vestry 1906. Interior remodelled c. 1965: N gallery and aisle arcades, with stiff-leaf capitals, partitioned off; not too disastrous as the focus is now on nave, chancel, broad high transepts and bold crossing, which have fine roofs with semicircular braces above the collar beams. Also by *Gough*, 1855, the tall former vicarage (W), the three cottages facing King Henry's Walk, and the school, making a good rag-stone group with the church.

ST LUKE, Hillmarton Road, Tufnell Park. 1859–60 by *Charles Lee*, builder *George Myers*. Dec in Kentish rag. Entrance through richly decorated porch in the NW tower; broach spire. Aisles, chancel and transepts: the N transept, destroyed in World War II, was rebuilt 1961 by *A. Llewellyn Smith*. This and the aisles have been partitioned off, but nave and chancel and the furnishings are intact. STAINED GLASS. E window 1960 by *Francis Spear*.

ST MARK WITH ST ANNE, Tollington Park, Hornsey. 1853–4 by *A. D. Gough*, the first of his Islington churches with emphatic ragstone exteriors and skinny Gothic details, which so irritated the ecclesiologists. 'Low church' plan, cruciform with small spirelet above a broad crossing, and a slim SW tower and spire. Arcades with thin marble columns, alternately circular and octagonal. Queenpost roof, more complex at the crossing. Aisles rebuilt by *F. R. Farrow* in 1884, when transept galleries were removed. The W two bays now divided off. Hefty carved stone PULPIT by *H. Hems*. STAINED GLASS. S transept by *Ward & Hughes*. E window,

1904, and early C20 aisle windows, by *A. L. Moore*. Matching HALL in Moray Grove.

ST MARY AND ST STEPHEN, Ashley Road, Hornsey Rise. By *A. D. Gough*, 1860–1 (cf. St Mark, St Jude). Ragstone, Dec tracery. Thin SW tower and spire 1868. Extended in 1883–4 by N, S and W porches (W replaced 1895), transept aisles, and W gallery. Busy interior with polished columns (replacements of 1883) and much carving. Corbels at alternating heights to the shafts between the small clerestory windows. Some PANELLING brought from *Teulon*'s St Paul, Avenue Road, Hampstead (1858–64, demolished 1958–9). Good traceried PULPIT. STAINED GLASS. Excellent E window of *c.* 1861 by *Lavers & Barraud* and W window by *Lavers, Barraud & Westlake, c.* 1870, a Tree of Jesse. S transept aisle, Dorcas window in Aesthetic style. HALL attached to N, 1878.

ST MARY, Upper Street. The medieval parish church of Islington was replaced in 1751–4 by a church by *Launcelot Dowbiggin*, 'citizen and joyner of London', built by *Samuel Steemson*. Dowbiggin's somewhat rustic floridity has resulted in a steeple of characteristic outline and robust detail. The tower and steeple are all that remain of his church. The rest was destroyed by World War II bombs. On the three-staged square tower of stock brick with broad quoins stand four corner vases and a polygonal balustrade surrounding a circular stage with narrowly placed alternatingly rusticated colonnettes. On this an obelisk spire of weird shape, with crockets and circular piercings, on a weird bulgy foot with giant gadrooning. The broad porch is of 1903 by *A. W. Blomfield & Sons*. The rebuilding of 1954–6 is by *Seely & Paget*, a neutral brick box with tall rectangular windows; not pastiche. Fine light interior with unexpected black marble, neo-Egyptian columns flanking the sanctuary and framing raised stone platforms for pulpit and lectern, backed by engraved glass screens. Woodwork neo-C18: organ gallery on Tuscan columns which carried the galleries of the C18 church. – Original C18 FONT of veined marble. – PAINTINGS by *Brian Thomas, c.* 1956, traditional with excellent figures; panels with the Eight Attributes of Christ in a reredos (E wall) and Christ the Judge (W wall). – FLOORING, W end. Christian Symbols in lino by *Charles Carter*, 1991. – Two C16 BRASSES survived the bombing: Robert Fowler and wife, 1540; Henry Savill and wife †1546, small standing figures.

Tucked away to the N, ST MARY'S NEIGHBOURHOOD CENTRE by *Keith Harrison & Associates*, 1976–7. Low concrete-block wings flank a small garden. Foundation stones by *Ralph Beyer*, with Christian symbols.

ST MARY MAGDALENE, Holloway Road, Lower Holloway. 1812–14 by *W. Wickings* (Surveyor to the County of Middlesex). Built as the chapel of ease to St Mary. Large, to cater for the huge increase in population in the area since the mid C18, and set in the spacious former burial ground: it became a parish church in 1894. A tall, gaunt six-bay box with three tiers of small windows, the lowest to the crypt. At the E end a lower one-bay frontispiece with N and S Tuscan stone porches (originally open) into vestibules flanking an E tower with a vestry in its base. The tower is square and not high, Ionic-pilastered and ending in a stone balustrade with urns (originally of *Coade* stone, replaced in 1910). W façade blank but for recessed brick arches, a Tuscan w porch, and aisle and gallery windows of 1894. Galleries on Tuscan columns on three sides, originally horseshoe-shaped but converted to a rectangular plan when the furnishings were altered in 1894–5 by *C. E. Child.* Most of the 1894 work was undone in 1983, when the choir stalls and pews were removed and the galleries partly underbuilt for meeting rooms. Gently coved ceiling. Pilastered reredos in a quasi-Venetian arrangement, enclosing tablets of the Law etc. and a PAINTING, 'Noli me tangere' by Mr *Tibbets,* a churchwarden in 1814. – Fine mahogany early C19 PULPIT with an altered ironwork stair balustrade, now at the w end. – FONT. Marble, neo-Renaissance, 1899. – Brass ALTAR RAILS, PAVING etc., presumably 1890s. – ORGAN. 1814 by *George Pike England,* with a handsome mahogany case; altered by *Willis,* 1867, and *N. P. Mander,* 1947. – WAR MEMORIAL (1914–18), s wall. From Offord Road Drill Hall (demolished), with a delicate bronze relief. – STAINED GLASS. N window by *Heaton Butler & Bayne,* post-1856. (Vestry in the base of the tower, with original fittings.)

Former ST PAUL (under conversion for a Steiner school 1997), Essex Road. 1826–8 by *Barry.* The Commissioners rejected a design by *Basevi,* and told Barry to reproduce his design for St John (q.v.). The exteriors in particular are similar to the point of confusion. The arcade, clerestory and ceiling also largely tally. The only change which was deliberately made is that St Paul has an e tower to mark the corner of Essex Road, with a vaulted tower hall inside which appears above the blind arcaded screen that forms the reredos at the back of the shallow chancel recess. VESTRY HALL, c. 1830, also Perp, extended N by one bay c. 1870. King-post roof.

ST PETER, Dartmouth Park Hill, Upper Holloway. 1879–80 by *C. L. Luck.* 'A rather good town church of the same plan as Luck's two churches in the Isle of Wight' (B. F. L. Clarke). Red brick, w end with corbelled-out central gable and corner buttresses instead of a tower. Plate tracery; no division between nave and chancel. Light interior, red and yellow brick patterning, narrow aisles with quadrant buttressing. STAINED GLASS of good quality; N and aisle e by *Lavers & Westlake,* others by *Clayton & Bell.*

Former ST PETER, St Peter's Street. 1834–5 by *Barry,* a plain minimum-Gothic box with corner pinnacles (costing £3,407) but crazily embellished by *Roumieu & Gough* in 1842–4. They added the spindly NW spire with flying buttresses, the thin papery E.E. w porch, transepts, and a short sanctuary and vestry. Converted into flats c. 1990.

Former ST SAVIOUR (since 1990 Florence Trust artists' studios), Aberdeen Park, Highbury. 1865–6 by *William White* for Rev. R. W. Morrice, an Anglo-Catholic. Made famous by Betjeman's poem. It remained an Anglo-Catholic stronghold within evangelical Islington. One of White's most interesting churches, with his characteristic polychrome brickwork. It is a competent and not unpleasing mixed Gothic design, with transepts and central tower which turns by buttresses and broaches into an octagonal lantern with iron flèche. Quite different in spirit from the surviving Italianate houses of Aberdeen Park (*see* Perambulation 4).

The interior has a sanctuary brick-vaulted at its end and a

crossing of a delicacy that contrasts with the bold two-and-a-half-bay nave arcades. They have moulded brick arches of odd profile on square brick piers with polychrome brickwork above; also over the chancel arch with a big Latin cross. The rich FURNISHINGS date from 1869. REREDOS. Stone triptych with mosaic Crucifixion by *Sir Henry Layard*, discoverer of Nineveh; two outer panels 1914. The sanctuary DECORATION of *c.* 1895 was designed by *White*, executed by *Henry Davies* (an assistant of Gambier Parry at Ely and Gloucester), who painted thinly over the brick with stencilled flowers, lozenges etc. STAINED GLASS. E window by *Lavers & Barraud*, designed by *Westlake*, 1865. Three windows by *Lavers & Barraud*.

ST SAVIOUR, Hanley Road, Upper Holloway. By *J. E. K. and J. P. Cutts*, nave and aisles 1887–8, chancel and vestries 1890, W porches 1900; tower never built. The usual Cutts red brick clerestoried basilica, fitted in closely between houses, hence the blind E wall. Inside, brick arcades; E wall with stone tracery filled with paintings of 1910.

ST STEPHEN, Canonbury Road. 1837–9 by *Inwood & Clifton*. Yellow brick with crude E.E. motifs and a starved octagonal E tower, of stone with spire and flying buttresses (detail was lost in war damage). Crazily pierced bell-openings. The nave was lengthened in 1850 and side windows altered by *A. D. Gough*, who added two porches (since removed). Reconstructed after war damage by *A. Llewellyn Smith* and *A. W. Waters*, 1957–8; the interior turned E to W with new vestries (E) and chapel (W) behind the altar wall, jazzed up by a neo-Baroque WALL PAINTING (Martyrdom of St Stephen) by *Brian Thomas*. Opposite, a STAINED GLASS window, by *Carl J. Edwards*, above the late C19 reredos which is the only trace of the original church left inside. HALLS and VICARAGE. 1968–74 by *Maurice Taylor*; quite a bold group behind the church.

ST THOMAS, St Thomas's Road. 1888–9 by *Ewan Christian*; additions 1901 and 1904, by *Edward Street*. Red brick inside and outside. Lancets. No accents except the flèche. Apsidal baptistery and narthex, entered at each end. Nave and chancel under one roof. Spacious three-bay nave with wide moulded brick arches on Purbeck columns; timber barrel vaults to both nave and aisles. The chancel (with its brickwork painted) is screened by a low wall and iron SCREEN by *Wippells*, 1920; a similar one to the apsidal-ended S aisle. Chancel ROOD by *Burnes & Oates*, 1922. Original FONT and cover. STAINED GLASS. E window by *C. E. Kempe*; six lights in the S chapel and five in the baptistery by *Clayton & Bell*. To the S, VICARAGE, Dec HALL and VESTRY 1901.

*2. Roman Catholic*

BLESSED SACRAMENT, Copenhagen Street. 1916 by *Robert L. Curtis*, red brick in a domestic-looking Free Style with large Romanesque doorways. Additions include the sanctuary by *T. G. Birchall Scott*, 1957–9, and a presbytery with monopitch roofs. Alterations in progress, 1998.

OUR LADY AND ST JOSEPH, Balls Pond Road. 1962–4 by *W. C. Mangan*. Yellow brick and stone. Westwork with three arched entrances and a central tower. Matching halls etc. Very plain inside: nave roof with shallow arched ribs.

OUR LADY OF CZESTOCHOWA AND ST CASIMIR, Devonia
Road. The former New Church College, until 1930 the
Swedenborgians' national seminary and school. Begun in 1852
by *Edward Welch*. The N wing, chapel and s wing 1865–79
by *Finch Hill & Paraire*. Simple Gothic Kentish rag chapel front
between three-storey ashlar-faced wings with mullioned windows;
symmetrical and hardly bigger than the adjacent houses. Inside,
the chapel is tall, narrow and very sweet. It still has its traceried
REREDOS of Caen stone by *Alexander Payne*, though without its
Swedenborgian centrepiece. On the altar a triptych (Last Supper)
painted by *Adam Bunsch*, 1939–45. The side chapel was originally
a s wing schoolroom. Pretty Gothic woodwork frames a row of
pointed s windows (into a first-floor room) and fronts the w gallery
and its twin organ cases. Miniature stone N gallery. STATIONS
OF THE CROSS, bronze, by *J.Z. Henelt*, 1945. STAINED GLASS.
An expressive series in tertiary colours by *Bunsch* (executed by
*Lowndes & Drury*) portraying the Polish struggle for sovereignty,
1939–45. E window and clerestory by *Stanley G. Higgins*, 1952–3,
abstract.

SACRED HEART OF JESUS, Eden Grove, Lower Holloway. 1869–70
by *F.H. Pownall*. E.E., stock brick with some blue brick and stone
dressings. A subtle composition of several different elements
(nave, tower, presbytery) clearly expressed, with a school detached
to the N. The nave is tall, long and dimly lit. Red brick walls with
precise black banding outlining the clerestory and arcades (with
stiff-leaf capitals by *Farmer & Brindley*). Hammerbeam roof.
Sanctuary remodelled 1960–1 by *Archard & Partners*. STAINED
GLASS. Some C19 and some post-1945 by *T. Grew*.

ST GABRIEL, Holloway Road. By *Gerard Goalen*, 1966–8. Facing
the noisy main road, only a plain side wall of dark brick, with
rounded ends and a pair of tiny projecting apsed chapels. The plan
is a rectangle with curved corners, with a shallow projection for
the altar on one of the long sides, and one for porch and baptistery
opposite. The interior is elegantly and unfussily handled. Its pale
brick and exposed concrete have been plastered and painted, but
there is still a telling contrast between the light porch, with windows
of concrete and obscure glass, and the calm, dim interior. It is lit
only by a clerestory above the level of the concrete grid ceiling, which
is supported like a canopy on slender piers round its perimeter.
Elegant polished concrete furnishings, incised lettering and SCULP-
TURE by *Willi Soukop* in bronzed fibreglass give the altar platform
a subdued drama.

ST JOAN OF ARC, Highbury Park. 1960–4 by *Walters & Kerr Bate*.
One of Islington's best post-war churches. Traditional but with
reduced Gothic forms in narrow orange-yellow bricks and stone.
The tower is the most effective stroke, tall, slender, and sharply
buttressed, with a pyramidal cap. Beyond the narthex, parabolic
arches span the nave, effectively lit from the clerestory over similar
low arches between nave and passage aisles. The sanctuary is defined
by two splayed walls, like the wings of an altarpiece. – STATUES.
St Joan (N aisle) by *Arthur Fleischmann*, 1962, perspex. – Virgin
and Child (N chapel) by *Ferdinand Stuflesser*, 1962. – RELIEFS in
baptistery, 1966. – STAINED GLASS. Symbols of the Passion etc.,
well drawn.

St John the Evangelist, Duncan Terrace. 1841–3 by *J. J. Scoles*. A large self-assured Neo-Romanesque façade almost flush with the terrace but with prominent twin towers, the N one taller, completed 1877 by *F. W. Tasker*. They were intended to be symmetrical and more elaborate. Spires copper-covered post-1945. The interior is rather in the style of the Basilica of San Clemente, Rome – roomy but somewhat bleak and barn-like. Pugin hated the design, mostly for not looking like a 'parochial' church, a true successor to St Mary's. He called it 'the most original combination of modern deformity that has been executed for some time past'. In return, Scoles's design was vigorously defended by Joseph Hansom in the *Builder*, 1843.

Nave with four chapels on each side (two N ones filled with confessionals) and a clerestory of narrowly set arched windows. The opening into the chapels also arched, with green marble responds. The chancel arch has two orders. The chapels have no windows at all, neither does the apse, where arched recesses contain bronze statues. Waterleaf capitals and much billet moulding. Blind arcading round chancel and Lady Chapel. Hammerbeam roof, a remodelling by *Tasker*, *c.* 1901, of the tie-beam one. One tie-beam truss left in the narthex. Crypt excavated 1977–8 for a youth centre by *Joan Davis*. – Original marble ALTARS supplemented by a handsome NAVE ALTAR of 1973 inlaid with Christian symbols. – FRESCOES by *Edward Armitage*, in St Francis Chapel and in the baptistery (and formerly in the apse). – STATUES. St Joseph by *Mayer & Co.* of Munich, from St Mary, Horseferry Road (S chapel); Virgin of Mercy *c.* 1964 (vestibule). – ORGAN. Reconstructed in 1963–4 by *Walkers*; bold modern case (W gallery).

St Joseph, Highgate Hill. The church of the Passionists' mother house in England, very large and a prominent landmark perched on the hillside at the meeting of two major roads. Designed by *Albert Vicars*, 1887–9, to replace *E. W. Pugin*'s church of 1859–62. Italian Romanesque (the church was built to celebrate Pope Leo XIII's Jubilee), with a dome on a tall octagonal drum. Extravagant W front with a crude wheel window and doorways within one deep arch; NW corner tower with tall domed bell-stage. Barrel-vaulted Italianate nave, more richly Renaissance at the E end. Low passage aisles with capitals extravagantly carved with Symbols of the Passion etc.; a staggered arrangement of side chapels because of the fall of the site. The dome is over the sanctuary; its lantern sheds dramatic light on an elaborate BALDACCHINO by *Sharp & Ryan* of Dublin, 1904.

Lady Chapel ALTAR by *Porter* of Fulham, 1897. – ALTAR in St Michael's Chapel, installed 1901 (shown at the Paris Exhibition 1900). RELIQUARY designed by *Cardinal Wiseman*. – Much PAINTED DECORATION. Nave ceiling (Te Deum) and arcade spandrels (Mysteries of the Rosary) by *N. H. J. Westlake* etc.; St Michael's Chapel, 1901; sanctuary walls by *C. Langlin*. – Crucifixion PAINTING (entrance to baptistery). Attributed to Lord *Leighton*. – CARVING by *R. L. Railton* of Cheltenham.

The church's exterior was 'freely treated to harmonize' with the clergy house (St Joseph's Retreat), S of the church, which was added to Pugin's church in 1874–5 by *F. W. Tasker*. Modelled on a rustic Italian villa, unusually for its date. It wraps round the

E end of the church. Of white brick with Doulton dressings and deep-eaved Italianate pantile roofs with small towers. Remarkably large arched windows in deep recesses on the ground floor. E wing slightly later, apsidal and used as the fathers' choir. Similar w wing. Low addition by *Alex Watson*, 1960.

ST JOSEPH AND ST PADARN, Salterton Road. 1873 by *J. & J. Belcher*. Built as St Padarn's Welsh Church. Yellow brick, E.E.

94  ST MELLITUS, Tollington Park. Built as New Court Congregational Church. 1870–1 by *C. G. Searle*. Grandly Corinthian with a large portico. The same giant order was used to frame the pulpit (replaced with an altar). Handsome horseshoe gallery with elaborate cast-iron front and columns. Later Art Nouveau electroliers.


### 3. *Other places of worship*

ARCHWAY CENTRAL METHODIST CHURCH, Archway Close. 1933–4 by *G. E. & K. G. Withers*. The last Methodist Central Hall to be built in London. On a prominent site and distinguishable from an average steel-framed commercial building only by a gable and cross on the w side. It has a huge cinema-style auditorium: J. Arthur Rank was a major contributor to the cost. Additional chapel made under the gallery *c.* 1970. Also halls, offices and classrooms on three floors.

Former CAMDEN ROAD BAPTIST CHAPEL, corner of Hilldrop Road. 1853–4 by *C. G. Searle*. Perp of the usual early C19 type, on the model of collegiate chapels. Hefty octagonal stair-towers, originally with spires. Kentish rag. Converted to a hostel, 1989–90; the former HALL of 1858 (Dec, probably by *Searle*) is now the church.

CALEDONIAN ROAD METHODIST CHURCH, corner of Market Road. 1870 by *T. & W. Stone* for the Primitive Methodists. A handsome palazzo in buff brick with voussoirs boldly striped in red and neat friezes of red brick Greek crosses. Almost square (four by five bays and two storeys plus basement) with a single-storey vestibule. Cast-iron windows. Simple interior with a coved and beamed ceiling, gallery with cast-iron-panelled front all round (partitioning below it *c.* 1972).

Former CAMDEN ROAD NEW CHURCH (now subdivided for Islington Arts Factory), Tufnell Park. 1873 by *Edward C. Gosling* for the Swedenborgians. Unexceptional Dec in Kentish rag. SW tower, aisles, apsidal sanctuary. Brick lecture hall etc. extended 1908 by *Ernest Trobridge*, himself a Swedenborgian.

CENTRAL METHODIST CHURCH, Palmer Place, Lower Holloway. 1962–3 by *Mauger, Gavin & Associates*. Church and halls in a long wedge between Palmer Place and Liverpool Road, with a patterned brick end wall.

ELIM PENTECOSTAL, Regina Road, Upper Holloway. 1961 by *John Diamond*. Prominent star-shaped roof. Built to succeed New Court Congregational Church (*see* St Mellitus R.C. Church, above).

HARECOURT CONGREGATIONAL CHURCH, St Paul's Road. By the *Habershons*, 1855. Burnt out in 1982, but its interesting central plan (octagonal, with three short arms in the main axes) is recalled by an octagonal reception and ancillary wing in the plain replacement by *Hodson Rivers*, 1991.

HIGHBURY PARK PRESBYTERIAN CHURCH, Grosvenor Avenue. 1863 by *E. Habershon*. Only the façade remains, of a neo-Hawksmoor type, with a low portico. The SW tower Italian but with a spire.

HIGHBURY QUADRANT CONGREGATIONAL CHURCH, Highbury Quadrant. 1954 by *Hastie, Winch & Kelly*. Portal-framed with STAINED GLASS by *Clifford Rankin*. It replaced *John Sulman*'s huge Gothic, centralized church of 1880–2 (cf. Harecourt Church, Union Chapel). The stubby neo-Norman W tower has chamfered corners to echo the octagonal schoolroom at the E end which, with other ancillary rooms, survives from Sulman's church; the schoolroom was galleried but is now two-storey.

HOLLOWAY ROAD SEVENTH DAY ADVENTIST CHURCH, Holloway Road. 1927–8 by *Samuel A. S. Yeo*. The Adventists' first permanent meeting place and national conference centre. Stripped classical façade.

HOLLOWAY WELSH CHAPEL, Sussex Way. 1873 by *Williams & Son*. Unremarkable Gothic brick exterior but well preserved inside, with a three-sided gallery of 1884 by *F. Boreham*.

Former ISLINGTON CHAPEL (Congregational), Upper Street. 1887–8 by *H. J. Paull* of *Bonella & Paull*, his last work. A remarkably handsome red brick front of Norman Shaw style, the first chapel in this style, according to the *Building News*. It has a large pedimented oriel window high in the gable and cupola above. Below it, four small arched windows and two big ones to the basement schoolroom. Either side two pilastered porches. To the side street, a row of gables above segment-headed windows. Decoratively patterned glazing bars and delicate cut brickwork. Handsome ironwork by the *St Pancras Iron Co*. Galleried interior divided up as studios and offices.

LEESON HALL. *See* Perambulation 7.

Former PAGET MEMORIAL MISSION, Nos. 18–26 Randell's Road. A simple red brick 1880s terrace with red and yellow brick banding and unexpected lunette windows back and front at Nos. 22–24. These light the mission hall, boldly carved out by *Beresford Pite* in 1910–11 for Rev. Sholto Douglas (later Lord Blythswood) in memory of his wife, Violet Paget, who had held a bible class in this tenement in 1887–9: the room she used is l. of the mission hall (Leader's Room). Missionaries' flats above. Drill hall on the ground floor of Nos. 18–20.

The mission hall is startlingly lavish. Big Jacobethan roof trusses and late C17-style minister's platform, with a pediment bearing Blythswood's arms. Arcaded panelling with cartouches inscribed VP, probably designed by *Travers*, pupil of Pite; stencilled violets on the cornices. The continental and pagan-looking woodwork was brought from the music room of Lord Blythswood's home, Douglas Support, near Coatbridge (Lanarks). On the pulpit, torchères representing Virtue and Vice, probably late C17 or early C18. Three elaborate fireplaces: SE with three figures above the pediment (the centre one Christ, after Thorwaldsen), SW with an overmantel portrait of Violet Paget; N with reused Jacobean carving. Organ on a gallery with Baroque twisted columns. Another C17 Baroque fireplace in the Leader's Room.

PROVIDENCE BAPTIST CHAPEL, Highbury Place. 1887 by *C. J. Bentley*. Simple brick front with North Italian Gothic stripes.

Barn-like interior with hammerbeam roof enlivened by a slightly later cast-iron-fronted gallery and raised pulpit. For the chapel's predecessor off Upper Street, *see* Perambulation 1a.

TOLLINGTON PARK BAPTIST CHURCH, Tollington Park. 1908 by *E. Douglas Hoyland*. Simple Perp box of hollow terracotta blocks. Porches demolished when the HALL of 1972 by *K. C. White & Partners* was added. Hammerbeam roof.

UNION CHAPEL (Congregational), Compton Terrace. 1876–7 by *James Cubitt* (tower completed 1889), replacing a modest chapel of 1806 built together with Compton Terrace (*see* Perambulation 3). The external show (and what a blustering High Victorian effect) is the big red brick tower crowned by an odd spirelet, breaking with the Georgian restraint of Compton Terrace. The style throughout is C13 French Gothic, but the central plan, an octagon with four short arms, was inspired by Santa Fosca, Torcello. James Cubitt was the author of *Church Designs for Congregations*, 1870, which emphasized the importance of congregations being able to see and hear easily. The central plan was favoured by several of the grander Congregational churches in the C19 (see, e.g., the earlier Harecourt Church, above, and Waterhouse's Congregational Church at Hampstead).

95        The interior is outstanding, both spatially and in the lavishness of its materials, red brick and stone decorated with marble and tile; the chapel served a smart congregation. Seating for 1,650 on two levels all round, including the tower in the w arm; all seats give an excellent view of the pulpit. The central octagon is defined by full-height Gothic arches which carry a timber roof with central ventilator. The galleries rest on broad segmental arches (NE, NW, SE, SW), with three-bay arcades across the wider transepts. Linking frieze of inlaid quatrefoils running along the gallery fronts. The quatrefoil motif appears also on the delicately carved stone and marble PULPIT. This and other carving is by *Thomas Earp*. Behind, a fine metalwork screen conceals the unaltered ORGAN by *Henry Willis*. Art Nouveau lights, the C19 GASOLIERS turned upside down and adapted. STAINED GLASS. Rose window in the E wall with musical angels. By *Frederick Drake* of Exeter. Fine quality. Six lancets in s wall by *Lavers & Westlake*, 1893; scenes of preaching and ministry commemorating Dr Henry Allon †1892, minister of the chapel when it was built.

Entered from Compton Avenue behind, the HALL and SUNDAY SCHOOL, unremarkable externally but well preserved inside. The school has wooden partitions within its gallery to divide individual classes. Library bay with rolling shutter to the bookshelves. Tortuous approach from the chapel, to be improved as part of a scheme to convert the whole building to multi-purpose use.

UNITARIAN CHAPEL, Newington Green. *See* Hackney, Stoke Newington.

### 4. Cemetery

JEWISH CEMETERY, Kingsbury Road. Founded 1788, in use until 1886. A secluded spot behind high walls. Headstones and chest tombs in crowded profusion; Goldsmid and Mocatta are among the eminent names.

## PUBLIC BUILDINGS

TOWN HALL, Upper Street. Designed by *E. C. P. Monson*, together
with Tyndale Mansions to the N. Built in 1922–3 (the wings of
committee rooms, offices etc. entered from Richmond Grove)
and 1925–6 (the council chamber, set back with a formal entrance
on Upper Street, and the housing). The town hall is not grand but
smallish, asymmetrical, and mixed in style, though all steel-framed
and Portland stone-faced with cast-iron panels. The first part is
restrained English Baroque, with an engaged temple front on Upper
Street marking the public hall. The later part is more Neoclassical.
The same mixture inside, with late C17 style predominant. Lavish
marble imperial stair to the octagonal council chamber; handsome
Graeco-Roman domed committee room corridor with pedimented
doorcases.

NEIGHBOURHOOD CENTRES (Borough Council offices). Twenty-
four local centres to house decentralized day-to-day services were
planned in 1982, following the lead of Walsall (Staffs). By *c.* 1985
thirteen had been built or converted from existing buildings by
*Chris Purslow*, Borough Architect. The new ones, e.g. BOLEYN
ROAD (the prototype), DRAYTON PARK, ROSEDALE (Lowther
Road), HANLEY ROAD and CALSHOT STREET, look cheap but
approachable with red brick, pantiled roofs and Mackintosh-style
gridded windows. Part-polygonal, mostly open-plan offices, with a
central clerestory-lit gallery useful for discreet surveillance and,
under it, tiny interview rooms and a waiting area that opens into a
garden segment.

POLICE STATION, HIGHBURY VALE, No. 211 Blackstock Road,
1903 by *John Dixon Butler*. Attractive domestic front in brick and
stone, with canted bay windows.

UPPER STREET FIRE STATION. By the Fire Brigade's in-house
architect *Peter J. Smith*, 1993. It follows a line of C19 terraces in
red and yellow brick. Jazzed up with a row of triangular oriels and
ship's rail balconies. Tower with oriels at the top.

NORTHERN DISTRICT POST OFFICE, No. 116 Upper Street. Of
1906 by the *Office of Works*. Edwardian Baroque, red brick with
quite lavish stone sculpture, including two caryatids supporting the
central pediment.

LIBRARIES. Described in chronological order, starting with an outstanding Edwardian group, which includes some of the best libraries
in London.

CENTRAL, Holloway Road. 1905–7 by *Henry T. Hare*, pre-
eminent designer of public libraries (cf. Shoreditch). Small, but still
in his early exuberant Mannerist style. The stone front has
Michelangelesque aedicules with thick strapwork linked to masks
and swags above. Statues of Spenser and Bacon flank the doorway. Striped red brick wing behind. Behind that an unexceptional
1970s addition with a new main entrance. The front block mostly
gutted but the rear wing has original decoration in the reading
room, and above that in the reference library, with big Mannerist
consoles supporting the barrel-vaulted ceiling. The first purpose-
built open-access library.

NORTH, Manor Gardens. 1905–6 by *Henry T. Hare*. Sweet, late
C17 style with a hipped roof, dormers and cupola. Richly detailed

with striped brick and stone, festoons between the upper windows and cartouches in the end pediments. Asymmetrical wing (r.) with a vaulted porch. The back is apsidal: on both floors Roman Doric colonnades, semicircular in plan. The original arrangement was lecture room above children's library (front) and reading room above the lending library (back): now open-plan.

WEST, Bridgeman Road. 1905–7 by *Beresford Pite,* a clever replacement for two terraced houses at the corner of Thornhill Square, restrained in style and modelling, self-confident in its narrow stripes of red and yellow brick. The regular bays continue the rhythm of the square; the entrance is tucked round the corner. The style is stripped classical with Roman and archaic Greek elements, such as the fret and acanthus motifs and the first-floor capitals based on the Temple of Epicurus at Bassae: the idiosyncratic mixture is paralleled in Lethaby's work. Also some Art Nouveau features, especially the railings and lantern. Despite 1950s alterations, a good interior, planned according to the progressive librarianship of James Duff Brown. Impressive entrance hall and staircase, intact children's lending library (unusual at that date) and many original furnishings.

ESSEX ROAD. 1916 by *Mervyn Macartney,* a good architect of the Norman Shaw school, rarely seen. Red brick with rubbed brick trim. Five-bay front, the entrance distinguished by stonework and a heavy scrolly pediment; single-storey reading room behind linked by an oval lobby, which has a flying staircase to a first-floor library with Doric columns and a shallow dome. Handsome late C17-style panelling in the main room.

Post-war libraries are much more modest, mostly built on the edges of new areas of housing, e.g.:

ARTHUR SIMPSON, Hanley Road, Upper Holloway, 1960, with green slate-panelled façade.

JOHN BARNES, Camden Road, *c.* 1974 by *Andrews, Sherlock & Partners* with *A. Head,* Borough Architect. The ground floor (with junior library) is tucked behind an embankment, with the entrance for adults at the jettied first-floor level. Nicely composed; the oriels by the main door are balanced by projecting brick carrels on the floor below. Inside, exposed steel trusses and toplit reading room.

MILDMAY, Mildmay Park. 1954; reclad *c.* 1990 by *Chris Purslow,* Borough Architect, in white tiles and dazzling primary colours. Cheap and cheerful. Glazed lean-to reading room added along the back, overlooking a play area.

ALMEIDA THEATRE, Almeida Street. Designed as the Literary and Scientific Institute, 1837–8 by *Roumieu & Gough,* architects of the nearby Milner Square (*see* Perambulation 2b). Used as a music-hall, as a Salvation Army citadel from 1890, and altered as a warehouse in 1956. Converted back to a theatre in 1982 by *Burrell Foley Architects.* Grecian, plain and blocky, with a suggestion of a portico *in antis* on the upper floor; no pediment, no ornament. The auditorium dates from the 1890s, when the original lecture hall was reversed in direction. Five-sided N gallery on cast-iron columns.

HIGHBURY STADIUM (Arsenal F.C.), Avenell Road. The club began in Woolwich in 1886 (hence the name), moving to Highbury in 1913, when the ground was laid out by *Archibald Leitch.* It was developed with the West and East Stands in the 1930s, when Herbert Chapman was manager. Chapman (†1934) recognized the entertainment value of football, and the stands were then the most lavish pieces of football architecture ever built. Huge and symmetrical, of brick, steel and concrete; Art Deco detailing. The WEST STAND, 1931–2 by *Claude Waterlow Ferrier*, built with seats for 4,000 and standing room for 1,700, had three flats and a restaurant as well. The even grander EAST STAND, 1936 by Ferrier's partner, *William Binnie*, is of five storeys, with seating for 8,000 in two tiers (seats for 5,500 in front added in 1969) and more bars and restaurants. Art Deco features continue inside; the marble hall has a bust of Herbert Chapman by *Epstein*, 1936, and a stylish staircase leading to a panelled board room. On the s side undistinguished boxes and club facilities, 1969 by *A. D. Consultants*. NORTH STAND 1992–3 by *Lobb Partnership*, project architect *Sean V. Jones*, more in sympathy with the 1930s stands, although domineering to the neighbouring streets. A massive brick and curtain-walled street front with curved ends, echoing the Art Deco styling, as does the glazing at the end of the seats. High-tech structure with cantilevered upper tier, seating 12,830.

SOBELL LEISURE CENTRE, Tollington Road. 1973 by *W. D. Laming* of *R. Seifert & Partners*. Of ribbed concrete, the ribs angled to form a sunburst around the broad glazed entrance arch. On a curved plan but with dull rectangular sports spaces and ice rink inside.

ARCHWAY ROAD LEISURE CENTRE. 1990s. Cheerfully brash stripey stonework, enclosing an informal pool.

HORNSEY ROAD BATHS. 1892–5 by *A. Hessell Tiltman*. Queen-Anne style with a tall red brick range with swimming pools and slipper baths screening a yard with a lower washhouse wing. Good cut brick, carved stone and lettering across the main oriel. On the s elevation, a diving lady in neon, probably the only survivor of a series of illuminated signs put on London swimming pools and lidos in the 1930s. Building restored after bombing and E wing built 1964.

Former CALEDONIAN MARKET. The Metropolitan Cattle Market was transferred here from Smithfield in 1852. The site, formerly Copenhagen Fields, then still on the fringe of built-up London, lies off Caledonian Road, between Market Road and North Road. Lay-out and buildings were by *J. B. Bunning*, architect to the City Corporation, 1850–5. The cattle market closed in 1939, the meat market in 1963, and much of the site is now occupied by council housing (*see* Perambulation 6). Principal survivor is the magnificent, once central CLOCK TOWER N of Market Road, 1850–5. Italianate in rusticated Portland stone, with swooping Baroque buttresses pierced by arches at the foot and a more conventional Quattrocento top. It originally had a low, twelve-sided, mostly timber structure (the telegraph and twelve banking offices) round its base. Also surviving are the sturdy cast-iron railings with debased Grecian posts (by *J. Bell*) along Market Road and Shearling Way, and four tall Italianate pubs with eyecatching chimneys. The BUTCHER'S ARMS is at the corner of York Way and Brewery Road. The WHITE HORSE (SE, now Gin Palace), the LAMB (NE) and the LION (NW) stood at the corners of the market (the Black Bull, at the SW corner, has gone). The first still has a cast-iron balcony on brackets: four storeys with bold stone cornices over the arched first-floor windows, segmental pediments over the ones above. Some original fittings inside. There were also Italianate administrative buildings, two large hostels for drovers on the N side (converted to flats by Islington in 1920), and iron sheds and stalls for 12,900 cattle, sheep and pigs. One lantern-roofed shed remains in warehouse use at Nos. 16–24 Brewery Road.

BUSINESS DESIGN CENTRE. Built as the ROYAL AGRICULTURAL HALL in 1861 by *Frederick Peck* of Maidstone. Converted into an American-inspired trade and exhibition centre in 1983–5 by *Renton Howard Wood Levin Partnership* with *John Melvin & Partners* (restoration work) and *Pietro Cavanna* (structural engineer) after having been used by the Post Office from 1943 to 1970 and then lying empty for another eleven years. Saved initially by statutory listing in 1972 and, practically, by a local businessman, Sam Morris, in 1981.

The enormous complex stretches from Liverpool Road to Upper Street and covers nearly five acres. The 1980s entrance (a crude but transitory range of Crystal Palace-inspired bays) is from the commercial Upper Street, but the main front was originally to Liverpool Road (then used by drovers), with a giant entrance arch and short angle towers with French pavilion roofs. The chief interest is still the interior, with its magnificent hall (384 by 217 ft), with ironwork by *Andrew Handyside & Co.* of Derby. It has an excellently proportioned curved wrought-iron roof of 123-ft span without tie-beams but braced along each diaphragm arch and by deep longitudinal girders acting as purlins. The covering is now poly-carbonate sheeting instead of glass, and profiled metal where it was timber and slate. The end walls lack their glazing bars (to be renewed in due course). Around the sides, galleries on two rows of columns (the outer ones function as drainpipes) and, beyond those, separately roofed aisles. The galleries were originally narrower but were widened in 1867 and in the 1920s, reusing the pierced iron balustrades. The details, as at Paddington Station ten years earlier, do not follow any period style. A mezzanine floor and partitioning for individual showrooms has been inserted, but this stands clear of the structure.

The immediate popularity of the hall, which was built by the Smithfield Club and used for meetings and entertainments as well as the annual Smithfield shows, led to additions on the Upper Street side, but except for the New Hall of 1930 (now the service bay) these were demolished for the forecourt and concealed multi-storey car park. On top of the car park, a large hotel by *Simon Powell Architects*, with a stylish entrance façade by *Rick Mather* (1994). Towards Barford Street on the site of the Gilbey Hall of 1895, THE GALLERIA, also by *Powell*, which externally apes the terraced houses opposite.

*Transport*

REGENT'S (GRAND UNION) CANAL. The stretch that runs through Islington from York Way to City Road belongs to the last section to be completed. It opened in 1820. MAIDEN LANE BRIDGE, over the canal in York Way, dates from 1850. Cast-iron girders and balustrade E of York Way, BATTLEBRIDGE BASIN, *see* Perambulation 6. E of it the ISLINGTON TUNNEL, Muriel Street to Vincent Terrace. By *James Morgan* (Company Engineer). 970 yards long, elliptical brick portals with sunburst rustication. Further E the CITY ROAD BASIN (*see* Perambulation 1C), which superseded Paddington as the main goods distribution point for London.

RAILWAYS. GREAT NORTHERN RAILWAY, 1846–50 by *Sir William Cubitt*, cuts diagonally through the borough with a tunnel under Copenhagen Fields. A diversionary route of 1872–4 passes beneath Highbury Hill to join the North London Railway. FINSBURY PARK STATION became a major interchange point, with platform buildings of 1874. NORTH LONDON RAILWAY: enacted in 1846 as the East and West India Docks and Birmingham Junction Railway; the name was changed in 1853. It carried goods to Blackwall, and from 1850, commuters to Fenchurch Street. A shorter route to Broad Street was opened in 1865. HIGHBURY AND ISLINGTON STATION at Highbury Corner had a grand station building and hotel of 1872 by *Horne*, destroyed in the Second World War. The Great Northern and City Underground line opened here in 1904; the Victoria line in 1968.

UNDERGROUND STATIONS. CALEDONIAN ROAD and HOLLOWAY ROAD. 1906 by *Leslie W. Green*. Well-preserved examples of former Great Northern, Piccadilly and Brompton Railway Company stations; frontages with rows of large arches; ox-blood faience outside, cream- and brown-tiled inside with handsome lettering. There is a similar disused station in York Way. TUFNELL PARK, 1907, on the Northern Line is of similar design. ANGEL. Now within the rebuilt SE corner of Islington High Street (*see* Perambulation 1). In the ticket hall, SCULPTURE, Angel, by *Kevin Boys*, 1996, figure of twisted metal bands.

THE ARCHWAY carries Hornsey Lane over the Archway Road. The present one (with splayed stone piers and richly moulded steel and cast-iron arch) is of 1897–1900 by *Sir Alexander Binnie*. The original one (demolished 1901), by *John Nash*, 1812, was built when the road was cut through to avoid the steeper Highgate Hill when travelling N (*see also* p. 563).

*Hospitals and Health Centres*

Former ROYAL FREE (originally LONDON FEVER) HOSPITAL. *See* Perambulation 2b.

Former ROYAL NORTHERN HOSPITAL, Holloway Road. Founded in 1856 as the Great Northern on a site near King's Cross; moved here in 1888; called the Royal Northern from 1921. On Holloway Road, a gabled Franco-Flemish red brick and terracotta block by *Keith Young & Henry Hall*, 1884–8. Extensions included a circular ward block of 1895. Demolition of rear areas in progress 1997.

WHITTINGTON HOSPITAL, Highgate Hill. An agglomeration of four separate hospitals, on sites divided by Highgate Hill and Dartmouth Park Road, united in 1944 by the LCC.

The F BLOCK, in the middle of the central site on the W side of Highgate Hill, was built as the Smallpox and Vaccination Hospital in 1848–50 by *Samuel Daukes* in his Italianate style (cf. his Middlesex Lunatic Asylum at Friern Barnet). Long front in stock brick with stone dressings: five-bay centre, seven-bay flanking ranges and three-bay wings pedimented to the sides. Distinctly early Victorian arched windows with moulded surrounds. In the centre, handsome lettering; above, an attic storey that originally had an open loggia and cupola. Later Roman Doric portico. In 1900 (after a replacement smallpox hospital was built in South Mimms, 1896) it became the administration block of the new St Mary's (Islington) Parish Workhouse Infirmary, remains of which stand to its s as ST MARY'S WING. Of 1900 by *William Smith*. Pairs of wings in red and yellow brick project to N and S, joined by open cast-iron galleries, with big canted bays of timber and cast iron at the ends. The NW part was replaced by the GREAT NORTHERN BUILDING of the 1990s, a ward block in yellow brick with windows in green slate bands. On the E edge of the site, ACCIDENT AND EMERGENCY WING, with expressed concrete frame; further N, the WATERLOW UNIT, red brick with slit windows to the road, 1980s, and, behind, an interwar MATERNITY WING in ungainly Neo-Georgian.

The HIGHGATE WING, on the W side of Dartmouth Park Road (now an administration block), was built for St Pancras (it is still in Camden) as one of the first metropolitan infirmaries on a site away from its workhouse. 1868–70 by *John Giles & Biven*. A totally plain building but with a logical pavilion plan (men's wards W of the central offices, women's wards E of it), which was praised by Florence Nightingale.

ARCHWAY WING, E side of Highgate Hill. For the Holborn and Finsbury Union in 1877 by *Henry Saxon Snell & Sons*. One of the most striking workhouse infirmaries (cf. Snell's St Charles Hospital, Kensington: *London 3: North West*) and a landmark at this muddled junction. It is a large hospital on a narrow site, hence the towering brick wings made bolder by tall water towers and windows rising into high dormers; alas, most of the brash plate tracery has gone. Pavilion plan; in the middle section the wards have an unusual lay-out with beds along hollow, ventilated partitions at r. angles to the windows. To the N a big block, now MIDDLESEX UNIVERSITY HEALTH CAMPUS, with the upper storeys cantilevered over the lower one. Yellow brick and concrete.

MANOR GARDENS HEALTH AND COMMUNITY CENTRE. *See* Upper Holloway, Perambulation 8, p. 703.

*Prisons*

PENTONVILLE PRISON, Caledonian Road. 1840–2 by *Col. Joshua Jebb*, first Surveyor General of Prisons, in association with *William Crawford* and *Whitworth Russell*. Pentonville was only the second national prison to be designed and built by the Home Department (the first was Millbank, 1812–16). Jebb used it as the model for all English prisons until it was superseded in the 1870s by the pattern of Wormwood Scrubs. It combined the main influences of the previous sixty years: Bentham's Panopticon plan of 1791, the salubrious planning and construction of William Blackburn's late C18 provincial gaols, the reforming solitude of de Haviland's Cherry Hill

Pentonville Prison, interior and plan, 1843,
showing the radiating wings, and circular and oval exercise yards

Penitentiary, Philadelphia, and the reforming silence of Auburn Penitentiary, N.Y. (both begun 1821). What was new was the 'depersonalized, mechanized, centralized and integrated' enforcement of these ideas (Robin Evans).

Main E–W range with the entrance at the W end and the chapel over governor's and commissioners' offices E of it. Four wings (N, NE, SE and S), originally of three storeys, radiate from the E end. In each wing, cells (originally 520 in all) down each side of a toplit galleried hall, all overlooked via bay windows that projected from the offices into the central space. Iron balconies and stairs so as not to impede the view. The cells were self-contained (solitary confinement was the method of reform) and had their own sanitation and ventilation through a system of hot-air flues. Extended by 220 cells in 1867. Vaulted roof removed and storey added 1871–90; windows altered 1910–14 and doubled in size c. 1985–1991. Further refurbishments c. 1995.

The main range is large, but it is Italianate, not castellated, and not as demonstratively forbidding as many other prisons. It originally had a clock tower over the E end. The entrance gateway must have originally looked more impressive and more like a porte-cochère, with tall arches open on all three sides. Flanking pilasters and engaged columns with diamond-faced blocking. The entrance, the flanking houses, the main block and the six lodges round the perimeter wall are all stuccoed; the wings are brick.

HOLLOWAY PRISON, Parkhurst Road. The original prison was demolished from 1970. It was designed as the City House of Correction by the City architect *Bunning*, 1849–51, and became a women's prison only in 1903. It had two front wings and four wings with 436 separate cells and large workrooms radiating from a tall central tower. The gatehouse and lodges and entrance block, copied from Caesar's Tower, Warwick Castle, looked thoroughly medieval. Its replacement (1970–7 by *Robert Matthew, Johnson-Marshall & Partners*) has unkind fortified red brick walls to the perimeter buildings, but, within this, the informal grouping of the red brick blocks round landscaped courts resembles a hall of residence rather than a prison. Equally low-key entrance. Classrooms, workshops and community buildings fulfil the Home Office focus (from 1968) on remedial custody for women, up to 500 here. To the S, anaemic Neo-Georgian prison officers' flats of the 1970s.

*Educational buildings*
Only a sample of schools can be mentioned here.

UNIVERSITY OF NORTH LONDON, Holloway Road. Created in 1993 from the Polytechnic of North London, which had its origins in the Northern Polytechnic Institute (founded 1896).

On Holloway Road, the TOWER BUILDING (opened 1966), replacing the main building of 1896–7 by *Charles Bell*. A logical design, strongly expressed. Bold horizontals at each floor level and equally forceful vertical emphasis on the service core and plant room. Eleven storeys cantilevered over two recessed ones; long low wing with concrete relief by *William Mitchell*. Disappointing interior. Next to it a former extension to the original building: weak classical red brick façade, 1902 by *A. W. Cooksey*. To the N, at the corner of Hornsey Road, the GLASS BUILDING, a learning centre, 1994 by *Geoffrey Kidd Associates*. Clichéd mirror-clad block. Further s, Nos. 6–40 Holloway Road, SCHOOL OF ARCHITECTURE AND INTERIOR DESIGN, new and converted buildings by *Brady & Mallalieu*, completed 1996. LADBROOKE HOUSE, Nos. 58–60 Highbury Grove, 1934–6, was built for the electrical valve firm of A. C. Cossor. A typical stripped classical brick factory-and-office block of its date. Many other teaching and residential buildings in the neighbourhood have been adapted from speculatively built commercial buildings.

SCHOOLS OF BEFORE 1870. Among church schools: ST JOHN'S, behind St John's Church, Holloway Road: 'gratuitously designed' by *Barry*, 1830–1; extended 1858, 1867. ST PETER, Devonia Road, stuccoed Tudor school and schoolhouse with bold chimney, an early work of *Roumieu & Gough*, 1837. ST JAMES, George's Road, 1854, Italianate (*see* Perambulation 7). ST JOHN'S, Conewood Road, a rebuilt National School of 1864. Stock brick with striped polychrome heads to the windows.

BOARD SCHOOLS by the London School Board. Early examples: ST WILLIAM OF YORK, Gifford Street. N side 1876–7 (extended *c*. 1890 with superimposed halls; s wing added 1915–16). BLESSED SACRAMENT (originally BUCKINGHAM STREET), Treaty Street. 1886–7. Asymmetrical, with an ogee-capped tower balanced by a gabled bay and big chimney. Among the best of numerous classic Board schools of the 1890s by *T. J. Bailey* are THORNHILL SCHOOL, Thornhill Road, 1894–5; HUNGERFORD SCHOOL, Hungerford Road, 1895–6, symmetrical with grand curved and balconied turrets. With an Infants' School of 1968–70 by the *GLC* (job architect *Barry Wilson*). Wedge-shaped teaching areas radiate from the main hall. MONTEM SCHOOL, Hornsey Road, 1897, boldly Baroque, remodelled inside 1968–71; low extension across the road with nice U-shaped railings. HORNSEY ROAD SIXTH FORM CENTRE (formerly Hornsey Road Upper School), 1897, is dramatically adapted to the site, with a Vanbrughian centrepiece canted towards Hornsey Road and flanked by ornate ogee-capped staircase towers at the angles with the bent-back wings. BARNSBURY PARK, Laycock Street (Finsbury pupil-teachers' centre), 1901, has Queen Anne windows arranged like Gothic ones between sketchy buttresses in the gable ends.

INTERWAR SCHOOLS. HIGHBURY HILL, 1928, stripped classical, brick with a hipped roof. Extension in Stirling and Gowan's red brick and glass style of the 1960s. HANOVER, Noel Road, 1932, a most unusual building. Squeezed in between canal and street and so with a rooftop playground carried upon giant piers in front of the street façade. End pavilions combine Arts and Crafts composition with Art Deco trim.

POST-WAR PRIMARY SCHOOLS. ASHMOUNT, Hornsey Lane. 1957–8 by *H. T Cadbury Brown*, with the Hills steel frame and glazing system then in vogue. The bold gesture to Hornsey Lane was the Junior School's wall of frosted green glass, but alas the pure, glacial effect has been destroyed by the many replacement panels of blue plywood and clear glass inserted 1991. On the boundary wall a Picasso-esque bronze cockerel by *John Willatts*. More conventional, the Infants' School just down the hill. VITTORIA, Half

Moon Crescent, an experimental design by the ILEA in conjunction with the DES, with reference to the 1966 Plowden Report's encouragement of a more domestic and informal approach. Pairs of classrooms, each with its own dining area, arranged round courtyards, all grouped round a multi-purpose hall. Split levels because of the sloping site. Monopitch roofs. DRAYTON PARK, Holloway Road. 1930s school with a good 1960s extension. Strongly expressed concrete floor beams and, between them, stock brick panels and timber windows in an asymmetrical arrangement. Bold oriel over the entrance canopy and in the end wall, with its split-pitched roof.

POST-WAR SECONDARY SCHOOLS. ISLINGTON GREEN, Rheidol Terrace. Compact six-storey block of c. 1965 by ILEA, contemporary with the rebuilding of the Packington Estate (*see* Perambulation 1c). Strong horizontal floor bands and twin Brutalist concrete service cores threaded through next to the entrance. Lower block in brick and board-marked concrete. HIGHBURY GROVE, Highbury Grove, 1967, by *James Cubitt*. Tough concrete exterior, more expansively planned, on the site of Victorian villas.


PERAMBULATIONS

*1. Islington town*

*1a. High Street, Upper Street, Cross Street, south part of Essex Road*

This tour starts with C20 rebuilding at the Angel; the rest is still recognizable as an old town centre overtaken first by extensive C18 domestic rebuilding and then by C19 and C20 commercial development for the expanding suburb.

Starting at the ANGEL, the chief landmark on the NW corner of this busy junction is the former ANGEL HOTEL of jolly commercial vulgarity, with a cupola and much terracotta in *Eedle & Myers's* Flemish manner (1899). Gutted by the GLC in 1980–1 and now a bank and offices. It was built on the site of the series of inns, in existence from the C16, which gave the crossroads its name. A little further N, a stuccoed campanile-style tower soars above the shops, all that remains of *H. Courtney Constantine's* ANGEL PICTURE THEATRE of 1913 (closed 1972); the main entrance was in White Lion Street.

The crossroads, after a road-widening scheme of the late 1970s, is dominated by huge office blocks. On the NE corner the brash ANGEL SQUARE, a greedy piece of Postmodernism by *Rock Townsend*, 1987–91, all drawn to a much bigger scale than its earlier neighbours. Four blocks with a busy variety of façades claiming local inspiration, and an Italianate campanile set at an angle, linked by bold polychrome stripes of brick and precast stone. At the centre, Angel Square itself, just a gloomy wedge-shaped light-well with ugly unresolved parts where the parts meet at high level. No joy for the public, apart from an incongruous bronze OBELISK to Thomas Paine †1809 (who is said to have written parts of the *Rights of Man* at the Angel) with relief portrait, 1991 by *Kevin Jordan*; provided by the developers. The self-conscious 'townscaping' of Angel Square was a reaction against the corporate monotony of *GMW*'s REGENT'S COURT (*c.* 1981–6) next on the E, also American in flavour but predating Postmodernism. Stock brick front with strong repetitive grid with triplets of rectangular windows and an open ground floor that looks well in the raking view; less successful the way this grid is peeled back at the entrance as if to reveal red and grey glass-clad innards. Generous colonnaded courtyard with façades angled back to reveal an exhilarating amount of light and sky.

ISLINGTON HIGH STREET widens into a spacious open wedge of the type found in old market towns, with a part of the space filled up by an island of buildings and the small alleys between them. On the W side the pavement is raised, and here and N of the Green the street is called Upper Street. It has a scatter of Georgian houses visible above later shops, interspersed with Victorian Franco-Flemish commercial frontages and later rebuilding, a mixture which continues along Upper Street to Highbury Corner and beyond up Holloway Road. From the W side of the High Street, Liverpool Road branches off, in origin the 'back street' of the old town (*see* Perambulation 2b).

On the E side the HIGH STREET has a dignified late C18 group, No. 80 with doorway on Tuscan columns, and Nos. 84–94, a terrace with open pedimented doorcase and some pretty fanlights. In between, the YORK public house, an Italianate rebuilding of 1872. The island is occupied by THE MALL, a former Electric Tramway Transformer Station by *Vincent Harris* for the LCC, 1905–6. Blind brick walls with rusticated Baroque entrance aedicules, inspired by Dance's Newgate Gaol (demolished 1902). Subdivided as a shopping arcade in 1979. Facing its N end, PHELPS COTTAGE, 1838, a small stucco villa typical of its date.

Behind these a pleasantly intricate mesh of small streets, much smartened up by the antique trade in the 1970s. To the E, CHARLTON PLACE, modest but complete on both sides, with a curving S side named Charlton Crescent, 1791–2, developed by *James Taylor*, the R.C. architect who designed houses in Duncan Terrace and probably City Road (*see* below). Plain two-bay houses, arched doorways without ornament, except for No. 15 on the N side, of three bays with *Coade* stone trim. To the N, CAMDEN PASSAGE continues the line of the High Street with small C18 houses, now over shops. No. 47–53 is a newcomer of the 1970s, facing Islington Green. Ground-floor shop windows in curved concrete surrounds. Camden Passage opens out before CAMDEN WALK, built in 1760 by Thomas Rosoman, manager of Sadlers Wells, and the CAMDEN HEAD, a pub of 1899 with much handsome engraved glass inside, refurbished appropriately by *Roderick Gradidge*. COLINSDALE leads off on the E. This discreet yellow brick Islington housing (*Borough Architect's Department*, 1965–9) lines well-landscaped pathways stepping down to Colebrooke Row (*see* Perambulation 1b).

ISLINGTON GREEN, at the N end of the High Street, was railed in 1781 and planted 1865. It has a dull statue of Sir Hugh Myddelton (creator of the New River for London's water supply; *see* Finsbury, Public Buildings) by the successful *John Thomas*, 1861–2. On the E side a tall, quite handsome late C19 WAREHOUSE (Nos. 30–34), refurbished as an antique bazaar by *O'Neilly Associates*, 1979, with a big mansard and mirror-glass canopy. Then ROSOMAN'S BUILDINGS (1758–69), remains of a three-storey terrace (Nos. 19–22), and a separate house (Nos. 23–24), another development by Thomas Rosoman. The N side was built up by 1817. Nos. 10–12, WATERSTONE'S shop of 1994–5, with Neo-Victorian iron canopy, occupies the site in front of the famous COLLINS MUSIC HALL. This was opened in 1862 at the back of the Landsdowne Tavern. The music hall, later used as a timber store, was destroyed by fire in 1958. Proposals for developing the site as an arts centre were under discussion in 1997.

On the W side of the Green, past the Dutch-gabled Nos. 71–73 of 1902, a few houses look C18 behind later commercial excrescences. One of these (No. 75) is the former ELECTRIC CINEMA, converted in 1908–9 from a shop projecting in front; it still has its small dome and (originally torch-bearing) figure. Close by a slightly larger competitor, the former Picture Theatre of 1911 (now THE SCREEN ON THE GREEN), refitted successfully by *Fletcher Priest*, 1981.

UPPER STREET continues from the Green NNE towards the parish church (q.v.). The triangle between them and Cross Street was already filled with houses by 1735, but Upper Street is now largely C19. On the W side the bright red brick Nos. 90–92 was a FIRE STATION by *William Wimble* for the London Salvage Corps, 1884–5; just to the N in Providence Place are the firemen's flats and the former PROVIDENCE CHAPEL of *c.* 1832, a simple pedimented box with altered round-arched windows. Next to the Post Office (q.v.), the KING'S HEAD, with a lavish late C19 front. The E side, rebuilt after road widening in 1888, has plain red brick terraces, the lively Islington Chapel (q.v.) and, next to the parish church, the Franco-Flemish former dispensary and soup kitchen (Nos. 303–304), founded 1821, rebuilt 1886.

On the W side, at the corner of Almeida Street, Nos. 140–143, late C19, by *Herbert Huntly-Gordon*, who had a special interest in the use of terracotta. Here the material (probably by Doulton & Co.) is bright orange, with ornate François I decoration. At the end of the tiny TERRETS PLACE, No. 3, an C18 sliver, well preserved inside. Front of 1720 with original door and shop-window under a dentilled moulding. Back of 1750 with richly carved Rococo chimneypiece on the first floor; central staircase. No. 149 Upper Street has an early C18 front above a C20 shop. The ROYAL MAIL, dated 1879, has a narrow front with mullioned windows and pediment over a delicate timber pub front with bowed centre; original fittings and engraved glass inside. Opposite the Town Hall, the SUTTON ESTATE, red and yellow brick, three-storey blocks of 1926 with Arts and Crafts details. Further blocks to the rear by *Neylan & Ungless*, 1985–90. Some way N, another early C18 front at Nos. 194–195, and, at the corner of Islington Park Street, the HOPE AND ANCHOR, *c.* 1880, a lavish stuccoed front with arched windows. This is opposite the S end of Compton Terrace, the start of Canonbury (*see* Perambulation 3). This tour now returns S to Cross Street, just N of the parish church.

CROSS STREET, linking Upper Street and Essex Road, has a good group of C18 houses: on the S side, Nos. 11–23, a terrace with open-pedimented Doric doorcases, and No. 25, an individual house with Tuscan doorcase. Nos. 33–35 of the 1770s have pretty Neoclassical doorcases with delicate guilloche on pilasters inspired by Adam's Adelphi Terrace of 1760–72. On the N side, an Ionic doorcase (No. 22) and a pretty fanlight (No. 28).

ESSEX ROAD (the former Lower Street, running NE from the Green) boasts as its most spectacular building the former CARLTON CINEMA. This lies N of Cross Street: a multicoloured Egyptian 116 front with two recessed columns, 1930 by *George Coles*. Interior in lavish Empire style. Further S, only a few very altered pre-C19 buildings remain. Nos. 79–85 were transformed in 1991–4 by *Pollard Thomas & Edwards* after fire damage in 1990. They were given a late C17 appearance, suggested by surviving quoins and interiors. These four houses were built in the late C17 as two joined pairs, with dog-leg staircases (some twisted balusters) side by side at the centre back of each pair. These were among the first speculative rows to take the place of individual mansions in this area, and may themselves have incorporated older fabric. Now part of a housing scheme (DRAPER PLACE) that stretches S along Essex Road and w to St Mary's Churchyard on Upper Street. Opposite, on the E side, No. 70 has an unsophisticated panelled interior of pre-1746, now quite rare: closed-string staircase from ground floor to attic. To the S the QUEENS HEAD, rebuilt in 1829 but incorporating a ceiling and fireplace of *c.* 1600 from an older inn on the site. The fireplace has a stone lintel carved with robust scenes of Diana and Actaeon, with terms on either side, and a wooden overmantel. Nearer the Green, Nos. 4–8, also minor C18.

### 1b. South-east: High Street to City Road

Georgian residential development, the Regent's Canal, and some C20 infilling.

COLEBROOKE ROW, SE of the High Street, built up piecemeal during the C18, is a good place to study the development of C18 terraces.* It starts opposite Islington Green and runs parallel to the High Street down to City Road. The attraction was the view of the New River, which ran in front until culverted in 1861. The oldest houses are near the N end, an irregular group of the early C18, consisting of Nos. 54–59. Nos. 56–57 (built in 1720) are the least altered, cottages each of three bays, flush window frames, heavy door canopies on carved brackets. Round a bend in the street to the N, Nos. 60–65, a plain group of 1767–74. Then, proceeding S, an excellent sequence of the later C18 (Nos. 41–53 and 34–36), three-storey terrace houses (some heightened) begun in 1768. Straight-headed windows with rubbed brick heads, and good open-pedimented Doric doorcases (cf. Cross Street above). No. 43 is a facsimile replacement.

DUNCAN TERRACE lay along the other side of the New River, whose site is now landscaped. The more varied mixture is instructive for minor changes of style from the later C18 to the mid C19. Starting from the N end, No. 64 (Charles Lamb's cottage), two-storeyed,

---

*Dates given here owe much to the research of Frank Kelsall and Mary Cosh; see M. Cosh, *The Squares of Islington, Part 2*, 1993.

with later stuccoed front, may date from the 1760s. Nos. 50–58, 'New Terrace', is dated 1791 on the pedimented centre. It has doorways with a little *Coade* stone ornament. No. 51 has two full-height bows on the return to Charlton Place (*see* Perambulation 1a); No. 49 opposite, with delicate Doric doorcase, belongs to a short terrace of 1793 (Nos. 46–49), with rusticated stuccoed ground floor to the end houses and individual bowed balconies. The next section is later, of the 1840s; two terraces flanking St John's R.C. Church. They have pronounced cornices, with arched windows above, a heavier, continuous first-floor balcony, and a rusticated stucco ground floor. The grander one is to the S: Nos. 22–32, doorcases with Greek Doric columns. Then older houses as one approaches City Road: Nos. 16–21 of 1829 (by *James Griffiths*, surveyor) have typical early C19 motifs: first-floor windows recessed in arches, anthemion balconies and delicate incised doorcases. Nos. 11–14 are a little older. Nos. 2–10, 1798–1803, have two arched ground-floor windows; straight-headed windows above. Similar terraces along the adjacent part of the CITY ROAD (Nos. 375–389), probably by *James Taylor*, who lived here, and was involved in the development of the area in the 1790s. The S end of Colebrooke Row has a less complete progression. Nos. 1–5, *c.* 1800; Nos. 13–19, 1837; Nos. 20–28, 1841 etc., interrupted by the different rhythm of WIDFORD HOUSE, late 1960s GLC flats.

ELIA STREET, E of Colebrooke Row, has ingeniously compact but cramped terraces by *Islington Architect's Department*, 1969–72. A dour street frontage with flats over a garage; lower houses immediately behind approached from the mews; in between are tiny upper back yards. NELSON TERRACE, nicely placed across the end of the street, a uniform terrace of *c.* 1802 with reeded doorcases. Behind it, in NELSON PLACE, more housing of *c.* 1970, attractively grouped around a triangular site. In other streets to the N, stucco-trimmed terraces of the 1840s and 50s: VINCENT TERRACE, facing the Regent's Canal, and NOEL ROAD, which has the special feature of castellated back extensions overlooking the canal.

The REGENT'S CANAL emerges at Colebrooke Row from the 970-yd Islington Tunnel (*see* Public Buildings) and soon after opens out S of Noel Road into the CITY ROAD BASIN, completed 1820. This area retains an industrial flavour, although the basin was commercially disused by the 1980s, when factories (which replaced earlier wharves) were mostly replaced by new housing and open space (for the E side, *see* Hackney: Shoreditch Perambulation 4). Between the wharf* and GRAHAM STREET, Diespeker & Co.'s terrazzo factory of *c.* 1908. A tall chimney remains beside the three-storey block converted by *Pollard Thomas & Edwards* in 1994 for their own offices. To the SW, between HAVERSTOCK STREET and City Garden Row, FALCON COURT, housing of 1970 by *P. S. Boyle*, an early example of infill following a traditional urban pattern: flat-roofed stock brick houses, using Modern Movement vocabulary.

Noel Road is continued along the canal by BALDWIN TERRACE, which has the NARROW BOAT pub and a warehouse very simply

---

* At No. 38 Graham Street, a surviving early C19 wharf cottage.

made into offices for themselves by *Edward Cullinan Architects*, *c.* 1991. In this area a scrappier mixture of humble terraces and council flats. In St Peter's Street, Cluse Court, *Monson*'s 1950s council housing with two ten-storey blocks of maisonettes, as mannered as 1950s furniture. Further N, around St Peter (q.v.) was the Hattersfield estate, initially laid out by *T. Cubitt* in the 1830s. A good terrace in Devonia Road, opposite the church (now flats) and the stuccoed Tudor former school and school-house (q.v.). The houses W of the church in Grantbridge Street (1855) show the disintegration of the simple Georgian style in the mid C19; they have busy fronts with stucco surrounds to the windows treated as vertical features.

On the E side of St Peter's Street, Nos. 7–21, handsome two-storey linked villas, 1848, with giant pilasters, instead of the usual terrace. Good studded doors and fancy railings. They were developed by James and Thomas Ward and possibly designed by *Samuel Angell*, Surveyor to the Clothworkers' Company (*see* below).

## 1c. South and east of Essex Road

Chiefly the attractive remains of the Clothworkers' and the Scott estates, both built up from the earlier C19, interspersed with varied types of urban renewal from the 1860s onwards.

In 1846 *Samuel Angell*, Surveyor to the Clothworkers, began to develop his company's property E of St Peter's Street, together with the Ecclesiastical Commissioners. The last part, the Packington Estate, was built up by 1861. Its unexceptional stucco-trimmed character is evident from the three-storey terraces surviving at the N end of Packington Street. Twelve acres further S were bought by Islington in 1963 and were rebuilt in 1967–9 to provide housing for *c.* 1,600 people. The controversial scheme was the newly enlarged borough's most ambitious industrialized building scheme (by *H. Moncrieff* of *Cooperative Planning Ltd*, using a Wates system). The new Packington Square is surrounded by unappealing five- and six-storey blocks with dark gritty panels, originally linked end-to-end by deck access, built partly below road level to minimize their impact on the surrounding terraces. Refurbished by *David Ford Associates* and *Islington Council Architect's Department* in 1989–94 with colourful but crude additions. Project-ing canopies and bridges span the sunken gardens: hipped-roofed service towers take the place of linking decks. In the centre, at road level, an eccentric brick community office with a curved front. To the E, S of Prebend Street, virtually unspoilt parts of the Clothworkers' Estate remain: surprisingly wide streets lined with quiet, uniform stucco-trimmed terraces of only two storeys. Taller terraces in Union Square of *c.* 1853 (E side only) and around the larger Arlington Square, *c.* 1846–50.

Prebend Street is named from a medieval estate of the Dean and Chapter of St Paul's Cathedral. On the N side, St James (q.v.), on the site of a C16 chapel. Close by, in Bishop Street, the Clothworkers Almshouses, 1855, gabled Tudor, attrac-tively asymmetrical. Opposite, Isledon House, 1949, by *Campbell Jones & Son*, built by the London Parochial Charities.

Unusual for its date in both provision and lay-out. Three blocks around a triangle, including both family flats and sheltered flats for the elderly, with a garden in the centre. Two ranges are four-storeyed with access balconies; the third, to Prebend Street, is a single-storey homely domestic row. All brick-faced with pantiled roofs, neatly detailed. The matron's house and communal rooms build up in a cluster of hipped roofs at the w corner.

POPHAM STREET, around the corner to the N, has borough housing by *Andrews, Sherlock & Partners*, planned 1968, built 1970–4, an ingenious example of the experiments with low-rise high-density development made at this time as an alternative to high building. 205 dwellings at 135 p.p.a. (70 per cent of them family houses with gardens), i.e. a remarkably high density for nothing over three storeys. Terraces at r. angles to the road, in closely set pairs, separated only by a passageway, which is spanned by bridges containing the kitchens of the flats above. Secluded back gardens are shut off from the street by brick walls. The passages emerge in DIBDEN STREET.

The PEABODY ESTATE, between Dibden Street and Greenman Street, is the only remnant of the C19 working-class housing that was built in this neighbourhood. PEABODY SQUARE, 1865 by *H.A. Darbishire*, is the first of that austere, vaguely Italianate type in striped grey brick which became standard for future Peabody estates. The average rent was 3s. 11d. for two rooms, i.e. intended for the skilled artisan. The square is typical of the more generous lay-out of the very early estates. Four-storeyed blocks with a fifth storey for drying rooms (note the smaller windows). There were also two-storey flatted workshops. 1880s additions along Dibden Street have five storeys of flats.

Round about is extensive but disjointed rebuilding of the 1950s onwards. Blocks of the later 1970s with decks over garaging, upper flats similar to the Popham Street lay-out but without their intimacy. One isolated survival: TIBBERTON SQUARE. Two terraces (converted to flats by *Andrews, Sherlock & Partners*, 1979) face each other across a garden. Built 1823–8 by the hat manufacturer Thomas Wontner in the grounds of his villa, which was demolished for the Greenman Street Public Baths in 1894 (replaced by housing in the 1970s). Along NEW NORTH ROAD a few more early C19 terrace houses on the NE side, with infilling of *c.* 1980.

New North Road runs N to ESSEX ROAD, where the most prominent building on the E side is No. 292, the preserved façade of a floorcloth manufactory built in 1812; balustrade and central pediment, giant Ionic pilasters to the upper floors. Later used as a beer bottling factory; converted to borough housing offices 1972. Next to it, ANNETT'S CRESCENT of 1819 by *William Burnell Hué*, an attractive sweep of stucco; first-floor windows within broad segment-headed arches. For Nos. 384–400 Essex Road, *see* Canonbury, Perambulation 3, p. 690.

The SCOTT ESTATE was developed from *c.* 1800, a grid of streets around the two roads which flank Annett's Crescent. Much bitty post-war rebuilding here, but some good survivals, restored after Islington acquired the whole estate *c.* 1973. In ROTHERFIELD STREET Nos. 61–83 have giant Ionic pilasters to the original houses. Further s the grander, three-storey Nos. 22–28, of *c.* 1826.

Here the giant fluted Ionic pilasters, more exceptionally, have Ammonite capitals, an invented order based on the shell, first employed by George Dance in 1788 for his Shakespeare Gallery, Pall Mall, but better known from its use by Amon Henry Wilds in Brighton (cf. also Old Kent Road and New Cross Road, Southwark, where this motif was used c. 1829). In SHEPPERTON ROAD linked pairs of villas, those towards the s end with shared pediments, nicely restored. On this sw fringe Islington infill of the 1970s provides some deliberate essays at contrasts; see e.g. along SHERBORNE STREET, staggered frontages with decisive projecting eaves and corner windows (*Borough Architect's Department*, 1979–80), and in ALMORAH ROAD, on a triangular church site, a mannered group with two tall monopitch-roofed wings linked by a low community centre. HALLIFORD STREET returns towards Essex Road, with plain, stucco-trimmed terraces of the 1840s, with Ionic and Tuscan porches.

## 2. Barnsbury

Barnsbury takes its name from a medieval manor belonging to the Canons of St Paul's, whose moated grange lay on the site of Barnsbury Square. The estate was split up in 1822, and the streets, squares and crescents w of Upper Street were nearly all laid out from the 1820s to the 1840s on small parcels of land; as a result there are many delightful variations in planning and style. It is a good place to study the shift of taste from terrace to villa. Despite some demolition since 1945, the area survives remarkably complete, enhanced by some sensitive restoration and new building. This route (which takes in only the most important features) meanders from s to n in roughly chronological order through the streets w of Liverpool Road, returns n–s down Liverpool Road, and then traverses the area between Liverpool Road and Upper Street.

### 2a. West of Liverpool Road

The tour starts at the s end of LIVERPOOL ROAD, opposite the former Royal Agricultural Hall (*see* Public Buildings: Business Design Centre) and near the exuberant Edwardian GEORGE pub.

The Stonefield or CLOUDESLEY ESTATE, planned from 1812, starts with CLOUDESLEY PLACE. The block on the se corner was largely rebuilt by the GLC in 1966–7; further on, the unadorned CLOUDESLEY MANSIONS was built by *Dove Brothers* in 1903–4 and 1907 (architect *Horace Porter*), screening their builders' yard. Much of the rest of the estate still has remarkably consistent terraces of c. 1818–26, with tall windows within a blind arcade on the first floor and arched doorways with fluted quarter columns. Minor variations in the spacing of the windows make the houses look more or less individual. The chief variation now (and a great delight, though much is not original) is the ironwork, which ranges from Greek to Gothic to Chinese fret. CLOUDESLEY SQUARE, laid out c. 1825, has Barry's Holy Trinity Church in the middle (q.v.). The square, Stonefield Street and the e end of RICHMOND AVENUE (Nos. 100–114) have the usual terraces, the special feature of the square being its canted corners; flanking the E exit, two detached villas. The terrace on the r. side of STONEFIELD STREET has houses clearly divided into pairs by recessed bays. CLOUDESLEY STREET to the S has lower villas linked by entrance wings, the last part of the estate to be built up. The attempt at keeping the continuity of terraces while avoiding monotony is a recurrent feature in the area. On the W side the former parish school, stucco Gothic, 1830 by *G. Legg*, enlarged 1840. W from here much clearance; some terraces remain at the S end of BARNSBURY ROAD, e.g. Claremont Row, 1818, and in COPENHAGEN STREET. On the N side of Copenhagen Street, terraces of one-, two- and three-storey houses by *Neylan & Ungless*, 1984, mediating between the busy street and the park to the N.

RICHMOND AVENUE, N of the park, has a cluster of good shopfronts, e.g. No. 94, near Cloudesley Road. Nearby, No. 185 Barnsbury Road faces Richmond Avenue with two tall bows poised on disturbingly insubstantial cast-iron columns: delicate doorcase between. Further W, Richmond Crescent, with villas of 1852.

The THORNHILL ESTATE was laid out by the estate surveyor, *Joseph Kay*, employed from 1810 to 1849. His Neoclassical taste can also be seen in his earlier work for the Foundling estate (*see* Camden, Holborn). The first part to be developed was Nos. 76–86 RICHMOND AVENUE (1829), with giant Ionic pilasters on the end houses and doorways with Greek Doric columns. The rest of this well-preserved estate is mostly of the 1840s; it was entirely built up by 1852. Nos. 46–72 (*c.* 1841) is a very long row of villas in threes (Nos. 62–72), then twos and ones (Nos. 46–60); they break into astonishing Graeco-Egyptian ground-floor detail, with sphinxes and obelisks flanking the entrances and odd round-topped, truncated pilasters dividing house from house (a motif repeated at the otherwise plain Nos. 44–47). Other linked villas of the 1840s in HEMINGFORD ROAD. Several pairs have pediments (E thin and stuccoed, W more Italianate with bracketed windows); some have hipped roofs. The HUNTINGDON ARMS and adjoining house have eccentric coupled pilasters linked into arches, with a taste of Milner Square (*see* Perambulation 2b); they stand at the corner of Bridgeman Road. This leads W into THORNHILL SQUARE (begun 1847) and THORNHILL CRESCENT (1846–52), a large elliptical composition, the kind of hippodrome arrangement often seen in contemporary plans but seldom carried out. It is impressively complete, curving round the contemporary St Andrew's Church (q.v.). Here, as in Hemingford Road, the detail is going Italianate (pediments over the windows, brackets under the eaves, rosette ornament). Back to the E, RIPPLEVALE GROVE climbs uphill with a variety of pretty two-storey cottages of 1839–41, some linked in pairs and terraces from the beginning, some detached and linked together later; most have delicate classical detail. A little further S, plainer villas (Malvern Terrace, 1836) also open on to Thornhill Road.

LONSDALE SQUARE, the Drapers' Company Estate built 1838–45, lies E of Thornhill Road. The agreement with the estate surveyor *Richard Carpenter*, who died in 1839, for pairs of classical houses was not carried out. It seems that it was his son, that excellent church architect *R. C. Carpenter*, who was responsible for the change to grey brick Tudor (cf. De Beauvoir Square, Hackney Perambulation 6). Each house has an asymmetrical, no longer entirely flat front, a sharp gable and squarish windows with hood-moulds and timber mullions. The houses at each end of the square are slightly different, but the total effect is uniform: indeed the projecting gabled bays are so rigidly repeated that the corners could only be turned by scooping them out for three entrances, the centre one to a wedge-shaped corner house. The sw corner remained just a façade until *Arup Associates* built behind it in the late 1960s: panels of windows between stepped brick piers. Tucked into the mews behind the se corner, a neat single-storey house (No. 1a) with a glazed front.

Opposite the N exit of the square is the elegant DRAPERS' ARMS, the very attenuated arched bays framing its windows. This stuc-coed frontispiece of *c.* 1839 stands in the middle of the N side of BARNSBURY STREET (*c.* 1830–41). The terrace was rescued by the Barnsbury Housing Association, and converted with new blocks of flats, in yellow brick with concrete lintels, added behind the w end by *Pring, White & Partners*, 1969–71, a pioneering attempt to fit well-detailed, high-density housing comfortably into an older area (cf. Popham Street off Essex Road, Perambulation 1c). The spine route, GISSING WALK, is a narrow alley, a little claustro-phobic perhaps, but with the compensation of elegantly finished open stairways leading from it to the raised courtyard gardens serving the upper flats. The housing turns on to Liverpool Road, where there are appropriately taller blocks. LONSDALE PLACE, s of Barnsbury Street, is a smaller group by the same firm, with a pleasant pedestrian walk at the back.

Further N, severe but complete terraces of the 1820s in BROOKSBY STREET and BEWDLEY STREET. These lead w to the irregular and badly mauled BARNSBURY SQUARE, the centre of the BISHOP ESTATE, of *c.* 1834 onwards. The square has stuccoed villas and, in the middle of the w side, a larger house, No. 15, MOUNTFORT HOUSE (really a disguised pair, built for the square's developer), on the moated site of the Barnsbury Manor farmhouse. Five bays, upper windows with shell decoration, big eaves brackets. Off the NW and SW corners of the square is the pretty peculiarity of two closes. The N one, MOUNTFORT CRESCENT, has pairs of semi-detached, bow-fronted stuccoed villas (1837–47). The s close has the Italianate MOUNTFORT TERRACE. On each side, a villa with double bows to the closes and a three-bay front to the square. Two villas on the N side have wreaths in the tympana of their broad windows, a feature typical of the 1830s.

THORNHILL ROAD leads N from Barnsbury Square. At the N end, THORNHILL HOUSE (1902) for the East End Dwellings Company, with huge circular porch hoods. Plainer houses just to the w in BELITHA VILLAS (1845, perhaps by *James Wagstaffe*), with examples, rare in Islington, of Italianate porches (cf. Arundel Square, Perambulation 7). OFFORD ROAD, with plain terraces, marks the boundary of this perambulation. (For similar streets N of the railway, *see* Perambulation 7.) At the e end of Offord Road, LEGION CLOSE, one of *Islington Architect's Department's* neat pieces of infilling; flats and houses with distinctive drum staircases (1970–5). For Liverpool Road, *see* Perambulation 2b.

*2b. Between Liverpool Road and Upper Street*

LIVERPOOL ROAD began as the back lane to Upper Street. It was
built up between 1820 and 1840. The w side has superior houses,
part of the development of Barnsbury; the e side was always more
miscellaneous and has been much rebuilt.

The route continues from the end of 2a above, proceeding s from
  the railway line. The main landmark on the e side is the SAMUEL
  LEWIS BUILDINGS of 1909–10, one of the first eight schemes for
  this housing trust, all by *C. S. Joseph & Smithem* (*see also* Hackney
  Perambulation 8). Five rows of flats with trees between. Mansard
  roofs, ogee-roofed towers and details of red brick and stone as in
  contemporary expensive Kensington flats, the best illustration in
  Islington of the tremendous improvement in standards of planning and humane appearance that became apparent in the best
  working-class housing around 1900.
    Then on the e side new housing which turns its back on the
  road, by *Islington Architect's Department*, 1977–80 (on the site of
  Park Place 1790; the sign remains). Nos. 202–266, MANCHESTER
  TERRACE, are modest stucco terraces, built from 1827 by *T. Cubitt*,
  some of them (Nos. 230–254 etc.) only one bay wide. Segment-
  headed windows on the first floor. Between Manchester Terrace
  and COLLEGE CROSS, another *Cubitt* development of *c.* 1827 to
  the e, and 1970s infilling incorporating a replica of a Victorian
  Turkish Bath.
  The w side of Liverpool Road has a series of classier blocks with the
  familiar pattern of round-headed ground-floor windows and first-
  floor windows recessed in arches: Nos. 331–345, 315–329, 295–307
  (Park Terrace, 1822). Between Barnsbury Road and Lofting
  Road, *Pring, White & Partners'* ingeniously intricate houses and
  flats for the Barnsbury Housing Association (*see* Perambulation
  2a), and a former REGISTRY OFFICE of 1872, with a quirky
  corner turret, converted to housing in 1994. After No. 291, an
  indifferent stretch until one reaches the long dignified terraces on
  raised pavements: Nos. 143–199 (CLOUDESLEY TERRACE, built
  *c.* 1825 to flank the entrance to Cloudesley Square); Nos. 111–141
  and Nos. 95–105, of *c.* 1821–4; and opposite, TRINIDAD PLACE
  (Nos. 84–124) of 1829–34, part of the Milner Gibson Estate (*see*
  below).
  OLD ROYAL FREE SQUARE on the e side is housing converted in
  1987–92 from the former London Fever (later Royal Free) Hospital
  of 1848–52 by *Charles Fowler & David Moccatta* – a model of useful after-life for redundant hospitals. Fowler's centrepiece is late
  classical, a Palladian composition of three blocks with low
  pilastered links to connect them, and two gate lodges. *Pollard
  Thomas & Edwards* (w part) and *Levitt Bernstein Associates* (e part)
  have linked this centre to two well-matched blocks of flats in
  highly finished red brick, and behind have enclosed a large
  Islington-style square with less formal red and yellow brick blocks.
  The central play area is screened by metal fences with well-drawn
  animal silhouettes, designed by the residents with *Jane Ackroyd*. e
  of the square two- and three-storey houses and a day centre
  (incorporating the hospital watertower), all more freely treated.

The MILNER GIBSON ESTATE e of Liverpool Road was laid out from 1823 by *Francis Edwards*, who designed the earliest houses. In THEBERTON STREET (1829–36), giant pilasters mark the corner blocks. N of it, the estate's two squares, more like wide streets with central gardens. First GIBSON SQUARE (1836–9), similar to Theberton Street, but with coarser detail. The E and W sides are unusual in Islington, complete compositions with applied temple fronts at the ends. In the central garden, a ventilation shaft for the Victoria Line disguised as an exquisite classical pavilion, designed by *Raymond Erith* in 1963, built 1968–9.

Beyond lies MILNER SQUARE, by *Roumieu & Gough*, 1839–44. The design has provoked extreme responses. The first edition of this book: 'Disintegration of the classical conventions shows itself sometimes naked, in sheer harshness and negation of harmonious proportions. A standard case is Milner Square ... The intention is to introduce as many tightly set unbroken uprights as could possibly be squeezed in.' Sir John Summerson, in *Georgian London*: 'It is possible to visit Milner Square many times and still not be absolutely certain that you have seen it anywhere but in an unhappy dream.' The square lost its projecting porches in the 1930s (their design appears in No. 2, a reconstruction at the N end) and also some of its decorative ironwork. It had become as dingy and barrack-like as the grimmest of C19 tenements by the time it was acquired by Islington Council in 1973 and converted and restored by *J. Godfrey-Gilbert & Partners*, 1973–7. Clean yellow brick and painted 79 stucco now make the terraces look less forbidding, and the eccentric and forceful play of extreme verticality and strong horizontals can be better appreciated. The ground floor is unexceptional: each house has a door and single, broad window. But on the upper floors the identity of the individual house is lost; first- and second-floor windows are separated by insistent giant pilasters in plain brick, broad and unadorned, standing proud of a stucco band between the two floors. Above is a massive continuous stucco cornice crowned by a ribbon of blind and windowed arches at attic level. The square closes in at each end in two steps, the outer angles of each block seamlessly curved to avoid unhappy junctions.

At the N end, the challenge of fitting a new building into this mid-C19 setting has been met successfully by *Pring, White & Partners'* replacement of the Richford ironworks (the former Barnsbury Chapel), at the corner of Barnsbury Street. The new building, 1974–6, has flats and maisonettes over garages. It echoes the general massing of the building it replaced (although it is slightly taller), the vertical emphasis of its long windows and the insistent repetition of the arches in the attic harmonizing with Milner Square while avoiding any obvious period allusions. The same is not true of WATERLOO GARDENS (1984–7 by *Christopher Libby*), which has taken the place of the Islington Proprietary School of 1830 on the opposite corner. A pretty Tudor plaque from the school has been incorporated into a sub-classical design whose broad bays and emphatic horizontals conflict with all its neighbours.

From the s side of Milner Square a passage leads to ALMEIDA STREET, where the Almeida Theatre (*see* Public Buildings) was built in 1837–8 by *Roumieu & Gough* as the neighbourhood's Literary and Scientific Institute. To the N NAPIER TERRACE,

Islington Borough infill with maisonettes by *Helen Stafford* (project architect) and a little sunken garden of 1971–5, walled by a long relief SCULPTURE by *Musgrave Watson*, originally from the Hall of Commerce of 1842 in Threadneedle Street (demolished 1922) and later at University College, an imaginative piece of rescue work. At the N end WATERLOO TERRACE; plain early C19 houses on the N side with good margin-light glazing, leading to Upper Street.

### 3. Canonbury

Canonbury owes its name to the estate of St Bartholomew's Hospital, which passed in 1570 to John Spencer, later Lord Mayor of London, †1610, and through his daughter to the Comptons, Earls of Northampton, with whom it remained until 1954. The remains of the Spencers' Canonbury House is the one precious relic of the time when Islington was open country and wealthy men built their houses here in spacious grounds. Building plans for the estate began in earnest around 1805 and the area was built up by the 1850s.

### East of Upper Street

Starting at Highbury Corner, COMPTON TERRACE, a long, respectable terrace, four-storey at the N end, three-storey at the S and pleasantly set back from Upper Street, was planned in 1805 by *Henry Leroux*, who intended a row of linked villas flanking a small Union Chapel (replaced by its overpowering successor, q.v., in 1876–7). He built only two pairs before he went bankrupt in 1809: the rest was continued in 1819 by *Henry Flower* (builder) and *Samuel Kell* (carpenter) but not completed until *c.* 1830. Leroux's houses are Nos. 17–20. Arches frame ground-floor windows (rather than those at the first floor, as is more common, cf. Liverpool Road, Perambulation 2b). Doorways with the quarter-round columns favoured at this time, and a good sequence of original doors. Towards the S end, a couple of big additional porticoes and a pretty cast-iron one.

Round the corner off Canonbury Lane, COMPTON AVENUE, the mews to Compton Terrace, were redeveloped at the S end with a terrace of late 1980s town houses by *Chris Libby*, set back behind a screen of gates and theatrical Neo-Graeco-Egyptian gateways. The pair of taller houses facing Canonbury Lane imitates the local mid-C19 Italianate villa style. Along CANONBURY LANE itself, on the S side, Nos. 1–11, built 1765–8 by *Thomas Bird*. They stand behind long gardens, less formal than subsequent developments in the area, stuccoed and with pretty pedimented doorcases.

CANONBURY SQUARE is a long rectangle, another of *Leroux*'s schemes. It was first mentioned in 1805, but little was completed before 1809. The E and S sides were built by *Richard Laycock c.* 1821–30. By that time the square had been carved in half by the line of the New North Road and Canonbury Road, laid out after 1812. The terraces are all different, and some have been rebuilt or reconstructed since 1945, but the square still gives a complete impression. The SW terrace of *c.* 1823–9, on a raised bank, is a 'palace' composition, whose slightly projecting centre and ends are emphasized by a stuccoed ground floor. The two centre houses share a Greek Doric portico; the end houses once had them also. In between, Greek Doric doorcases and first-floor windows within arches. Clockwise from here, the w end of the square has a single villa, No. 48. Then *Leroux*'s NW terrace, the first to be built, with unusually elongated first-floor windows within arches, still with the simplicity of *c.* 1800. Across Canonbury Road, No. 39, NORTHAMPTON LODGE, a brick villa with low curved wings, and a bow at the back. It was there by 1811 and is perhaps also by *Leroux*. Converted for the Estorick Collection of Modern Italian Art, 1988. *Laycock*'s SE and adjoining E terrace (1826–30) are plainer. Just to the N, off Canonbury Road, COLEBECK MEWS by *Dry, Halasz, Dixon Partnership*, 1977. Groups of simple two- to three-storey pitched-roofed terraces, brick with segment-headed windows, picturesquely set around a garden and stepped back along footpaths.

CANONBURY PLACE leads NE from Canonbury Square. For Canonbury Tower on the s side, *see* below. Opposite the tower is a delicate terrace by *Raymond Erith*, 1963–4 (Nos. 22–26) and 1968–70 (Nos. 27–30), displaying his typically eclectic use of Georgian detail: partly stuccoed, with flush-framed windows and hipped, pantiled roofs. At the w end an Ionic portico brought from King's College Hospital, Denmark Hill. COMPTON ROAD to the N is lined on the w side by busily stucco-trimmed mid-C19 terraces with big Greek porches. E of Canonbury Place a circuit can be made of CANONBURY PARK NORTH and SOUTH. Here development was begun in 1837 by *Charles Hamor Hill* and took the form of villas in a more spacious setting. First impressions, though, are of an outer-suburbia, because of the large number of small post-war houses and blocks of flats, for example those at the w end near Grange Grove, by *L. de Soissons Partnership*, planned in 1946–7. This was part of an ambitious rebuilding programme by the Northampton Estate which was not continued, but which attracted the middle classes back to the by then run-down neighbourhood. E of Alwyne Square, Canonbury Park North has large unspoilt paired villas of the 1840s. Canonbury Park South is more varied, with smaller houses on the s side; Nos. 50–52 have stuccoed pilasters, No. 44, MYDDELTON COTTAGE, of 1850–2, is rustic Italian in yellow and red brick, Nos. 40–42 are given a formal Italianate air by a shared triple-arched loggia-cum-porch and heavy eaves cornice. Now back to the s corner of Canonbury Place.

### Canonbury House

CANONBURY TOWER stands here, a very happy if accidental group. It formed the NW corner of Canonbury House, a manor house on a courtyard plan which until the Dissolution belonged to the Priors of St Bartholomew. The house was occupied from 1570 to 1610 by the wealthy merchant Sir John Spencer, Lord Mayor of London, who made improvements in the 1590s.

The brick tower is of uncertain date, perhaps mid C16, of four stages, with a parapet dating from the restoration of the tower by *C. E. Dance* in 1907–8 as a social centre for the Northampton Estate. Attached to it are short gabled wings, on the E side early C17 brick, with two later upper bay windows, to the S the steeply gabled stump of a tall timber-framed W range that once extended further to join the S range. The rest of the W range and the original S range (with a walled garden to the S) were replaced by houses in the later C18, but much of the gabled E RANGE survives as Nos. 6–9 CANONBURY PLACE. This was rendered and otherwise externally much altered in the late C18 and early C19, but its irregular E frontage still has stretches of possibly C16 brick and a variety of casement and cross windows. The courtyard is presumed to have been open on the N side; the position of the service rooms is unclear: were they at the N end of the E wing, or in another court further E?

INTERIORS. The remaining interior decoration from Spencer's time is of high quality. The good rooms are S of the tower and at the S end of the E range (presumably the lost S wing facing the garden also housed important rooms). The tower is filled by a newel stair (as is clear from the placing of the windows), which winds round a timber-framed core divided into cupboards: top balustrade 1907, of earlier timber. Painted inscription round the top floor, relating to monarchs up to Charles I. Opening off the staircase on the first and second floors, two elaborately panelled late C16 rooms in the W wing. In the E range, No. 7 at the S end has most C16 evidence, including an early C16 doorway (put here in the 1950s but recorded as in this range in 1907–8). The 'tun' or barrel in the spandrels is the rebus of William Bolton (Prior of St Bartholomew's 1509–32). In a first-floor room a fine plaster ceiling dated 1599: crisp strapwork, Roman emperors in the centre-piece. On the ground floor the remains of a late C16 chimney-piece; the architrave matches one at Compton Wynyates, where there is a chimneypiece with the Spencer arms supposedly moved from Canonbury. In Nos. 8–9 a ceiling with patterned circles, quatrefoils and pendants. Above it, another including emblems and heroes, dated 1599. Another smaller one partly destroyed.

Nos. 1–5 Canonbury Place, built by *John Dawes*, 1767–71, stand on the site of the S range. They are very irregular and look as if they may incorporate older work, but the details inside and out are C18 and early C19. Gibbs rustication round the doorways of Nos. 2–4. No. 5, of four bays, has an especially elaborate doorway, and a canted bay-window at the back. From the S No. 1 resembles a separate villa, with a three-bay side elevation with giant Ionic pilasters. On the site of the W range, facing W and detached, is CANONBURY HOUSE of c. 1795, of five bays and two storeys with a doorway with thin Ionic columns and ground-floor windows within blind arches on broad pilasters; stone balustrade and C19 or early C20 dormers. Original staircase, doors etc. In the garden by the tower, the community hall (now THEATRE) built in 1907, its roof modelled on that of Herne Church, Kent.

ALWYNE VILLAS and ALWYNE PLACE lead S to ALWYNE ROAD. They run roughly around the site of the old gardens of Canonbury House, as can be seen by the survival of two polygonal brick summerhouses. One, at the S end of Alwyne Villas (No. 4a), has a date 1526 and a late C19 upper floor: reset in the W wall, a late medieval cusped stone panel with Prior Bolton's rebus. The other, stuccoed, stands beside No. 7 Alwyne Road. Alwyne Villas starts on the W side with modest and irregular terraces developed *c.* 1824 by *Richard Laycock* at the same time as Canonbury Square. The rest of this area was built up only in the mid C19 with paired villas and terraces in leafy gardens (building agreement with *James Wagstaffe* of Highbury, 1847). Especially grand Italianate examples along Alwyne Road, where the gardens back on to the New River. The later ones in Alwyne Place have lush naturalistic foliage decoration to doorcases and window guards. One older house on the E side, No. 16, three bays, early C18.

Willow Bridge Road crosses over an old line of the New River; a simulated stretch has been created here as part of the delightful NEW RIVER PARK, a miniature linear park opened in 1954. On the S side, circular WATCHHOUSE and railings of the 1820s, when the New River was realigned. Overlooking the river, CANONBURY GROVE, with irregular terraces of two and three storeys, *c.* 1825, again by *Richard Laycock*. The towering Nos. 13–20 has flat bows at each end. By the WILLOW BRIDGE, *c.* 1850, the MARQUESS public house, with bold pilastered façades, 1848, part of Wagstaffe's development.

In DOUGLAS ROAD, slotted into a 20-ft gap between the Marquess pub and a plain terrace, is No. 40, a glass sliver of a house by *Future Systems* (*Jan Kaplicky, Amanda Levete*), 1993–4. Not a glass box on a spacious suburban site, like the Hopkins' in Hampstead (*see* Camden: Hampstead Perambulation 1b) but a glass version of the urban three-storey houses that surround it. The back is a slope of plate glass, frameless like Foster's Faber building (Ipswich), on which Kaplicky worked. It forms a triangular envelope with the front wall, which is predominantly of glass bricks, like Chareau's Maison de Verre, Paris, of 1932. Inside, the envelope is interrupted only by metal staircases to three living and bedroom decks and by the free-standing service core.

*North-east Canonbury, including the Marquess Estate*

Now an abrupt change. The MARQUESS ESTATE takes up almost the whole of the E corner of Canonbury, E of the New River between St Paul's Road and Essex Road. It is chiefly the work of *Darbourne & Darke* from 1966 to 1976, for Islington Borough Council, but enfolds some older council flats. It was Islington's first big estate following the creation of the larger boroughs under the GLC, and marked the council's turn away from high-rise housing but not from large-scale and very high-density development, which proved a nightmare to manage.

As in the later parts of the same architects' earlier Lillington Gardens, Westminster, most of the housing consists of terrace houses with their own small gardens rather than flats, but these are piled up into irregular ziggurats over garaging, with a complicated system of terraces and steps which, though picturesque, retain many of the disadvantages of conventional deck-access schemes. One-storeyed old people's flats are ingeniously sited above the houses, approached by lifts. They have their own front doors opening on to upper-level open-air streets. The materials are friendly brick and slate-hanging as at Lillington Gardens, though here the brick is a gloomier brown. Restructuring of the over-complex plan was begun in 1979 by *Shepheard Epstein Hunter*, with the aim of breaking the estate down into smaller, self-contained neighbourhoods by blocking off many of the walkways. Further remodelling planned 1998, by *PRP*.

The lay-out is informal to the point of confusion. From DOUGLAS ROAD on the NW border one wanders between and beneath the blocks along irregular, landscaped footpaths and roads, which open out into patches of greenery incorporating older trees. The largest open space lies along MARQUESS ROAD, near *Monson*'s older blocks of flats of the 1950s. W of this, near Essex Road, RED HOUSE SQUARE, the first neighbourhood to be remodelled, completed in 1995. Along ESSEX ROAD the Borough Architect, *Chris Purslow*, was responsible for the incongruous curved but cheap metal cladding converting car-parking below the Essex Road deck into industrial and office space.

Just S along Essex Road, more refurbishment by *Shepheard Epstein Hunter* at SICKERT COURT, a good example of the borough's careful improvement of housing stock since 1977. On the opposite side further N, MERCERS' HOUSE, Nos. 384–400. A bold group of twenty-eight sheltered flats and doctors' surgery by *John Melvin & Partners*, 1988 on, for the Mercers' Company Housing Association. The inspiration is the Edwardian Free Style mansion block. Three entrances between big projecting piers, chequered in brick and stone, which rise into dramatic stacks of flues flanking attic-level lunettes; rooftop towers with deep eaves house lift motor rooms.

The Marquess Estate was at first intended to continue by a bridge over ST PAUL'S ROAD. After some debate the *Borough Architect's Department* filled the gap on the N side of the road in 1969–73 with Nos. 62–82, a terrace with a façade replicating its early C19 neighbours (not a common solution at the time). Beyond, in NORTHAMPTON PARK, among early C19 detached villas, a little more of *Darbourne & Darke*: three-storey terraces with sunken ground floors. Further E, ST PAUL'S PLACE, with terraces of 1837; others to the W in St Paul's Road of *c*. 1845: No. 4 is a pretty Tudor villa of 1833–4 with bargeboarded gable.


## 4. Highbury

Development began in the 1770s after John Dawes, who had previously built in Canonbury Place (*see* Perambulation 3, p. 687), bought a large amount of land at Highbury. He built a new house (Highbury House, 1778–81) on the site of a manor house of the Knights Hospitallers which had been destroyed in the Peasants' Revolt of 1381. Its site lay N of the present Leigh Road, just W of Highbury Grove, which formed the approach from Islington. Building began around Highbury Fields in the 1770s, but progress was slow, and for at least fifty years only a handful of urban terraces stood alone among pasture land. Streets of large villas followed from 1840–60, then a mass of terraced housing (1860–90), after the opening of commuter lines from Highbury Corner in 1850. Attempts to preserve some open space came to nothing. In 1851 plans were drawn up by *Pennethorne* for a huge Albert Park, a northern counterpart to Victoria Park in the East End. The proposal was shortlived; the ambitious development of Highbury New Park covered what was to have been its S part, and the only result was Finsbury Park, much further N (*see*

Haringey). Towards Holloway Road minor late Victorian streets grew up around Drayton Park, interspersed with factories and railway yards. In 1885 the Metropolitan Board of Works responded to the desperate need for open space in the s of the area by buying Highbury Fields and laying them out with walks.

### East of Highbury Fields and Highbury Grove

The perambulation starts from the s end of Highbury Fields. At the entrance a BOER WAR MEMORIAL with bronze Victory by *Sir Bertram Mackennal*, 1905. On the Fields, the late C18 picture of open country and isolated terraces can still seize the imagination. HIGHBURY PLACE, the first development (1774–7), runs along the E side of the Fields. The builder was *John Spiller*, the architect probably his son *James Spiller* (friend of Soane and designer of St John, Hackney). The s end (Nos. 1–24) was built first: now much altered and so it is difficult to discern the original arrangement of pairs of villas linked by coachhouses and two flanking terraces. One pair of villas has gone, Calabria Road (part of the 1880s development behind Highbury Place) breaks in before Nos. 13–15, and the coachhouses have mostly been raised. The elevations are very plain, with round-headed doorways in two orders. It is in the second part (Nos. 25–39) that Spiller's originality comes out. The door pediments are handled in quite an unusual way, reduced to a thin, floating moulding on corbels. Marking the centre (No. 32), a Greek portico. Spiller lived at No. 39, a slightly separate house, balancing No. 25, with more conventional pilastered doorcase ground-floor windows within arches. At No. 40, an early C19 Neo-Grecian stucco ground-floor front, with a later house (1979) behind.

HIGHBURY TERRACE on the opposite side of the Fields was built further N to preserve the earlier terrace's open aspect. The original part (1789–94) is a long composition in three blocks, with lower links, echoing the Paragon, Blackheath (*see London 2: South*). Centre of eleven houses, N block with bold name and date. All have tall first-floor windows set in arches, starting at floor level in the latest fashion, and with individual curved balconies. Plain doorways with handsome fanlights. The links all vary slightly. At the s end, a pair of villas (Nos. 1–2) with *Coade* stone masks over the doorways, bows at the back. No. 12 has a curious portico with Roman Ionic columns and a key-pattern frieze in wrought iron. At the N end, a fourth terrace (Nos. 17–22) of 1817, with the end houses of a different build.

Covenants restricted building opposite Highbury Place until 1840. HIGHBURY CRESCENT was developed in 1844–50 by *James Wagstaffe* and *James Goodbody* with pairs of grand Italianate villas, generously spaced. (Wagstaffe seems to have played a role in introducing the semi-detached Italianate villa to this part of London; cf. Belitha Villas, Perambulation 2a, and Alwyne Road, Canonbury, Perambulation 3.) The central pairs, flanking Fieldway Crescent, are marked with stocky towers. Some have gone, the N ones replaced in 1937 by surprisingly sympathetic flats (CRESCENT MANSIONS), some of the s ones by later offices, e.g. HIGHBURY HOUSE, tall with insistent verticals of yellow brick.

Church Path leads from the top of Highbury Place NE to Christ Church (q.v.) and the small cast-iron CLOCK TOWER of 1897 at the junction of Highbury Hill and HIGHBURY GROVE. E of Highbury Grove, No. 56a, a brick garage with a corrugated iron roof that started life *c.* 1900 as the purpose-built balloon-making workshop of the Spencer Bros, aeronautical pioneers.

STREETS TO THE W, laid out in the 1840s, have some handsome Italianate villas and terraces, consistently three-storey and with rows of round-arched windows that echo Georgian houses elsewhere in Islington. Facing the clock tower at the corner of HIGHBURY HILL, the substantial Nos. 1–5 imitate a single Italianate villa with tall bows at either end. Good detached and paired villas follow; also, on the S side, Highbury Hill School (*see* Public Buildings), which in 1928 replaced Highbury Hill, a mansion of *c.* 1790 by *Daniel Asher Alexander*. LEIGH ROAD, to the N (reached from Highbury Grove), follows the line of the rectangular moat that enclosed the medieval manor house. The house which the developer John Dawes built on the site in 1778–81 was demolished in 1939 for a group of flats, ETON LODGE; the remaining service wing disappeared in 1997. Round the corner, BELFIORE LODGE, a large messy Italianate house of the 1840s in its own grounds. Then Islington council housing of the late 1970s by *Dixon Harvett Partnership*, discreetly stepping down between Highbury Grove and Hamilton Park West, incorporating a well-integrated children's home and older blocks. Lay-out and style are reminiscent of the Marquess Estate (*see* Canonbury, Perambulation 3, pp. 689–90), but the development is smaller, the houses and flats simpler and less mannered. They look on to well-treed gardens. On the other side of HAMILTON PARK WEST, pairs of two-storey three-bay villas with big Roman Doric or Ionic porticoes, 1841 onwards. They continue along the S side of AUBERT PARK.

AUBERT COURT, on the N side of Aubert Park, makes a magnificent display of the supreme confidence of post-war council housing; 1946–53 by *E. C. P. Monson* for Islington. A crisp and rational design. Linked brick blocks of seven to nine storeys are staggered down the hill, each block punctuated to the road by vertical accents of tall central stair-towers. On the W side, facing the garden, the horizontals are stressed by stringcourses and curved cantilevered balconies at the angles. The generous garden site is the legacy of the grand Neo-Grecian Highbury College for Dissenters, of 1825–6 by *John Davies*, which stood here. N of Aubert Park is Highbury Stadium, the Arsenal football ground (q.v.).

Back E along Aubert Park, past Nos. 1–3, a double villa masquerading as one, to HIGHBURY PARK, the N continuation of Highbury Grove. From here the road descends, later as Blackstock Road, towards Finsbury Park. On the E side a showy red brick shopping parade of the 1890s, and St Joan of Arc (*see* Churches); on the W side, NATIONAL CHILDREN'S HOME Headquarters, established here in 1925 in an earlier C19 building, Loxford House, refaced and extended by *Alan Brace*. Front with pedimented centre and pilasters. Some way further N in BLACKSTOCK ROAD, council flats by *John Melvin & Partners*, 1979. They look like linked deep-eaved villas, but have strong brick piers (after Kahn or perhaps Soane) and vertically linked windows between them. Odd recessed clerestory light high up over the entrance.

Returning S, PARK TERRACE on the W side of HIGHBURY PARK (S

of Aubert Park), 1829–36, raised above the road to command a (lost) prospect. Heavy late Regency with Greek details: a strong cornice; doorways with inset Doric columns, honeysuckle friezes and basket arches; palmette and fret on heavy, splayed-out balconies. Nos. 55 and 24 have porticoes. Opposite, a plain pair of villas (Nos. 54–56), the only ones left of five pairs built by *Thomas Cubitt*: they look like three-storey terrace houses. Two pairs have been lost to large council housing schemes by *E. C. P. Monson*. The northern one is THE CHESTNUTS, designed *c.* 1939, completed 1945, since refurbished; three formal blocks of flats open to a court to Highbury Grange. Opposite is Addington Mansions (now TAVERNER ESTATE), one of Islington's first groups of council flats (1922 by *Monson*), in a simple version of the Queen Anne style that had been used for earlier LCC flats; arranged round two squares. Further s the austere late C19 HIGHBURY BARN pub (No. 26) perpetuates the memory of popular C18 tea gardens that became a notorious pleasure resort in the C19. Further s down Highbury Grove is the turning to Aberdeen Park (*see* below).

Finally, back along St Paul's Road. In CORSICA STREET to the N, CIRCLE 33 HOUSING TRUST HEADQUARTERS, designed by *Jestico & Whiles*, executive architects *Pollard Thomas & Edwards*, 1993–4, three storeys, brick-faced, with rows of pierced squares as ornament; set-back glazed top floor.

### Aberdeen Park and Highbury New Park

ABERDEEN PARK, e of Highbury Grove, is a generously laid-out loop of 1853 with the splendid St Saviour (q.v.) at its centre. The N side had tennis courts, inappropriately filled in the 1930s with small houses of the bypass variegated type. Huge, gaunt, Italianate double villas survive on s and e sides; Nos. 26–32, with towers, likewise Nos. 56–62. Opposite the church, purpose-built flats of 1907. Nos. 42–44 and 50–52 have been sympathetically fitted into a small medium-rise housing scheme by *Darbourne & Darke*, 1979–81 (project architects *Peter M. Olley* and *Martin Cornelius*). Small houses and flats are piled up (cf. Marquess Road, Perambulation 3), like wings to the villas, with pathways that lead over the platform formed by the ground-floor garages and down to a spacious open green bordered with the low curved terraces of Seaforth Crescent, which lie behind the houses of Highbury New Park.

HIGHBURY NEW PARK, a 100–acre suburb, was planned in 1851 by Henry Rydon to attract City businessmen and their families, and built from 1853 as a long, broad tree-lined sweep lined by detached and paired villas, leading to St Augustine's Church (q.v.). In its grandeur and social aims it is comparable to, e.g., the slightly earlier Clapham Park in South London, but here styles and materials are mixed with all the exuberant originality of the mid-Victorian period, although the houses are more or less standard in plan. There has been much rebuilding at either end, but the central area is well preserved, reprieved from decline from the 1970s.

The wide and leafy road starts near the s end of Highbury Grove. The tone is set by a row of wealthy Italianate pairs on the s side, set back beyond stuccoed balustraded garden walls (now much depleted). The street continues e as GROSVENOR AVENUE, with No. 114 on the N side, a handsome detached villa with Venetian

windows flanking an Ionic porch (other houses replaced by flats).
Highbury New Park bends N, and, after Highbury Grove School,
early villas of 1853–6 remain on the w side. They include No. 23,
Rydon's own house, partially stuccoed with paired windows, and
No. 31, stuccoed with wreaths and swags in the pediment. Nos.
41–43 are eccentrically eclectic, with Grecian stuccoed ground
floor and polychrome brick above (likewise Nos. 53–55). The
detached houses Nos. 45 and 51 (1856) are completely stuccoed,
with Greek ornament, but Nos. 47 and 49 are in Lombardic style,
the brick inlaid with *Minton* encaustic tiles, and heavy corbelled-
out triple-windowed oriels. Rydon's architect and surveyor *Charles
Hambridge* certainly designed these and probably many of the
others. Off the E side BERESFORD TERRACE has a lower terrace,
Nos. 2–7, with pretty pierced tympana to the first-floor windows;
the same motif appears on some of the houses on the E side of
Highbury Park. Here Nos. 72 and 74 have Venetian loggias at
first floor. Nos. 82–90 are more Lombardic. Further N, Gothic
details are more prevalent, see Nos. 65 and 67 on the w side, but
towards St Augustine's the standard of invention declines, and
later houses further N, though still large, are less remarkable. Nos.
93–107, distinguished by rusticated ends, is among the best groups.
The estate was completed by various builders from the mid 1870s;
opposite the church are modest streets with terraces instead of the
crescent at first planned.

A path by St Augustine's leads E to PETHERTON ROAD, attractively
   wide to accommodate the course of the New River, culverted in
   1946. Smaller houses by a local builder, *J. G. Bishop*, were built
   here on the E part of Rydon's estate from 1868 to 1872, together
   with plain terraces in the roads up to Newington Green, completed
   *c.* 1876–80 by another builder, *Isaac Edmundson*.

HIGHBURY QUADRANT ESTATE, at the N end of Highbury New
   Park, has early post-war housing by the *LCC*, 1954. Swedish-
   modern flats in pale yellow brick are pleasantly scattered amidst
   lawns and trees. All of five storeys, a mixture of neatly detailed
   T-shaped and rectangular blocks. A short row of red brick shops
   with pitched roofs; other low red brick terraces around the edge.
   SCULPTURE: The Neighbours by *Siegfried Charoux*, 1957–9, of
   cemented iron. Unobtrusively sited but resonant with post-war
   idealism.


*5. Newington Green*

There was a small medieval settlement at Newington Green, on the
border of Islington and Stoke Newington, connected to the City by
what is now Essex Road. It attracted some affluent residents in the
C16 and early C17, and from the mid C17 a substantial number of
new houses were built, some speculatively, some replacing larger
houses. The green had become an urban square by 1742, when it
was given railings, and by the early C19 its surroundings were densely
built up. Further s houses spread along Balls Pond Road and, by
1837, w along St Paul's Road, but the Mildmay Estate SE of the
green remained open land until 1850, when the North London
Railway cut across it. Development followed, completed by 1865,
partly replaced by council flats between the wars and after 1945.

NEWINGTON GREEN has few survivors of before the C19, but on the W side is London's oldest surviving brick terrace (Nos. 52–55), dated 1658. It gives a good idea of speculative building in London before the Great Fire. There are not many houses of the mid C17 left anywhere in London, even in so fragmentary a state as these. The ground floors were altered by shops added c. 1880–2. Above, eight bays are divided into four two-bay houses by giant pilasters, the newly fashionable façade treatment introduced in Great Queen Street, Covent Garden, c. 1637. First-floor windows are set in arched panels with sunk square panels within the heads. Each house has a gable, with one rebuilt as a straight-topped attic storey. The plans are examples of an arrangement which preceded the standard type of C18 terrace house. The stairs are between the chimneystacks of front and back rooms, and the entrance lobby to each of the two inner houses is approached by a central passage (now between shops).The end houses probably also had side entrances before adjoining buildings went up. Between each pair of houses a tiny light-well to light the staircases. These are of the closed string type, with square newels and bulbous balusters. A little original panelling in the upper rooms. The back has segmental-arched windows.

Further N, the overpowering ALLIANCE CLUB has an Edwardian Baroque screen of gate arch with an open colonnade above spanning between severe blocks of flats. The red brick late Victorian NEWINGTON GREEN MANSIONS turns the corner into Green Lanes with a spirelet. The N side of the green with the Unitarian Chapel is within Stoke Newington (*see* Hackney: Stoke Newington Perambulation 2). On the E side Nos. 31–32, a plain early C19 pair; and on the S, the site of Mildmay House, unexceptional council flats of 1964–5.

The Mildmay Estate, built up 1850–65, lies SE of the green. MILDMAY PARK still has some of its large stucco-trimmed double villas with side porches. Crossing it, the surprising MILDMAY GROVE, laid out in 1850, where long terraces mirror each other across the deep crevasse of the North London Railway. At its E end, in ST JUDE'S STREET, some rehabilitation of the 1980s, ending in a varied two- and three-storey group of sheltered housing.

Mildmay Park leads to the BALLS POND ROAD, which has several plain terraces of pre-1817. Best is BRUNSWICK TERRACE of 1812 on the S side, with a pedimented pair of houses in the centre with Tuscan porches and the familiar arched ground-floor windows. Opposite, the ASYLUM OF THE METROPOLITAN BENEFIT SOCIETY, founded 1829, is the only survivor of several groups of early Victorian almshouses on the N side of the road. It lines three sides of a large forecourt. Two-storey stock brick Tudor N block by *S. H. Ridley*, 1836: central chapel (now hall) with a broad oriel and ogee-topped pinnacles, rebuilt 1931. W wing and E wing c. 1865–6. Further W, No. 198 (formerly ST PAUL'S MANSIONS), of 1891, has the beehive trademark of the builders *Studds & Sons*.

ST PAUL'S ROAD continues W on to Northampton land (*see* Canonbury, Perambulation 3, p. 690). No. 102 (Priory Cottage) at the corner of Newington Green Road dates from 1842.

### 6. Between Caledonian Road and York Way

An industrial area which developed between two main routes. The long, straight Caledonian Road was laid out in 1826 to link the New Road with Holloway Road. It took its name from one of its first buildings, the Royal Caledonian Asylum of 1827–8 by *George Tappen*, for the children of poor exiled Scots. Its Greek revival frontage stood on the site of the present Caledonian estate. York Way, fomerly Maiden Lane, an ancient route between the parishes of Islington and St Pancras, remains the division between the modern boroughs.

### Battlebridge and the south end of Caledonian Road

Battlebridge, once a hamlet by a bridge over the Fleet River, gave its name to the basin of the Regent's Canal, built E of York Road (then Maiden Lane) in 1820. The area developed with a mixture of canal-side industry and small streets of terraced houses opening off the Caledonian Road. Another settlement grew up from 1793 further w, around Maiden Lane. By 1830 this had become an enclave of noxious industries, and the industrial character of the area was intensified by the opening of King's Cross Station in 1852 and the development of the vast railway lands and goods yard to its N (*see* Camden: St Pancras). Regeneration of these declining industrial areas was encouraged from the 1980s. The King's Cross lands still (in 1998) await redevelopment, but the Battlebridge area was boosted as an early showpiece; the basin is now surrounded by some imaginatively converted warehouses, interspersed with new housing.

BALFE STREET, running N towards the canal from the s end of Caledonian Road, displays a characteristic mid-C19 combination of domestic and industrial building: Nos. 5–33 are a superior three-storey terrace with both ground- and first-floor openings within round-headed arches; near the centre, a works entrance dated 1846. To the N, around the canal and the BATTLEBRIDGE BASIN, a mixture of taller warehouses of the early C20 and low-key late C20 housing.

PORTERS SOUTH, No. 4 Crinan Street. The first, influential conversion in this area, of Porter's bottling works of 1906 onwards, which stretches all the way down the w side of the basin along CRINAN STREET. The two s blocks were recast in 1988 by *Fitch Benoy* for their architecture and design company, and later sold to Macmillan Publishing. The four-storey brick shells were retained; little was altered externally, and a tall, refined atrium was slotted into the wedge-shaped area in between the two blocks, with sleek frameless glazing towards the basin. The atrium is enlivened by the bold red curve of a stair-tower, and overlooked by meeting rooms at different levels. The open-plan N block was given new floor levels, an extra top floor, and lit by a light-well cut through the centre. This and the atrium are spanned by slender steel bridges that recall Ron Herron's contemporary infilling at the Imagination building in Store Street (*see* Camden: Holborn, Perambulation 6a). In PORTERS NORTH (No. 8), *DEGW* have more pragmatically fitted their well-planned offices into the existing fabric (*c.* 1989).

NEW WHARF ROAD along the E side of the basin has a mixture of new build and converted warehouses. A scheme for offices was devised by *David Marks & Julia Barfield* for the developers London Building, but the development that took place from 1993 was for housing, by various architects. No. 5, Gatti's Wharf, is a conversion. No. 10, MARINA ONE, is faced with pale yellow brick, with elegant curved end to the water; by *Munkenbeck & Marshall*, 1996. Next to it, the LONDON CANAL MUSEUM, formerly an ice warehouse of Carlo Gatti, popularizer of ice cream, with two deep wells of *c.* 1860 for the storage of Norwegian block ice. No. 14, MARINA TWO, similar to Marina One, by the same firm, 1998. Opposite, No. 20, a late 1940s factory, concrete with long lines of windows. Further N, a converted 1920s factory and new-build flats and offices in ICE WHARF and the PAVILION, 1994–7 by *Chassay Wright Architects*.

To the E, off ALL SAINTS STREET, crisp, pale brick housing for the Peabody Trust by *Avanti Architects* (job architect *Justin de Syllas*), private in LAVINA GROVE, for rent in KILLICK STREET. On the E side a HEALTH CENTRE (not part of the housing scheme), with, in its reception area, a TILE PICTURE of *c.* 1900 by *W. B. Simpson*: Playing Bowls in Copenhagen Fields in the reign of George III, rescued from the former Star and Garter pub, No. 80 Caledonian Road, and conserved by the *Jackfield Conservation Studio*, 1996.

REGENT'S WHARF, on the N side of All Saints Street, is a mixture of a boldly reconstructed C19 grain-milling complex and new offices in warehouse style, picturesquely grouped around a yard between the street and the canal. By *Rock Townsend*, 1991. Less domineering and more elegant than their contemporary work at the Angel (*see* Perambulation 1a). The new build consists of simple rectangular yellow brick blocks with attics and curious blind or part-blind oriels of copper sheeting. The older cattle-food mill and grain silo (*c.* 1890) have been partially opened up by glazed areas. An undulating timber-clad staircase wall and a block in striped red and yellow brick provide additional texture within the yard; along the street a lively red brick 1890s office block with Baroque doorway is also included. To the E a narrow building reproducing the form of a granary of *c.* 1860.

BRIDGE WHARF incorporates No. 152 and the detached No. 154 CALEDONIAN ROAD, both early C19 houses, and runs along the canal. A subtle design by *Chassay Wright Architects*, 1988, with flats above a podium for light industry. Mews-like entrances to the street; well-organized façade to the canal.

Returning S down Caledonian Road are good stretches of unspoilt terraces on the E side: Nos. 138–146, a short, symmetrically composed group which looks towards the THORNHILL pub, of the 1880s with good lettering on glazed tiles, then Nos. 106–136. On the W side the plain Nos. 75–87, with plaques on No. 77 (1845, 1855) to mark the boundary with Clerkenwell parish. Off the E side KEYSTONE CRESCENT, built *c.* 1845 across the parish boundary (see the markers), a minute late example of Neoclassical planning. Two-storey and basement houses on both sides. Near the scruffy S end of Caledonian Road, No. 7 is an exception, refronted in Queen Anne style, with cut brick, terracotta and tile-hanging, by *Romaine-Walker & Tanner*, 1885, with a former varnish factory of 'fireproof' buildings around a yard behind. For Pentonville Road *see* Finsbury, Perambulation 5.

*Caledonian Road north of Copenhagen Street and York Way*

Copenhagen Fields, with the C17 Copenhagen House, was a popular rural resort until the early C19. The eastern part of the Fields was bought in 1826 by Thomas Cubitt for clay extraction, and in 1839 became the site of Pentonville Prison; around it artisan housing grew up. From the mid C19 the unbuilt-up land behind the fringe of houses along Caledonian Road attracted large concerns serving the metropolis: the prison was followed by cattle market, breweries, and miscellaneous industry. The North London Railway cut across the area in 1850. N of this, Pentonville Prison remains a dominant feature, but much of the rest has been replaced since the Second World War by a maze of interlocking estates of public housing.

On CALEDONIAN ROAD mid-C19 terraces on the E side, e.g. Nos. 216–246, Italianate and set back from the road; some have rosettes above the windows like those in Thornhill Square to the NE (*see* Perambulation 2a). Beyond, three pairs of early C19 paired villas (Nos. 248–258), followed by a simple mid-C19 terrace and pub (Nos. 260–270). To the W, much low-rise housing of the 1970s onwards. Around DELHI STREET, towards the w end of Copenhagen Street, an estate by *Eric Lyons Cunningham Metcalfe*, 1973–8, humanely laid out with a high proportion of private gardens. To the NW, on the site of St Michael (1863–4 by *Roumieu*, demolished 1986) in what remains of BINGFIELD STREET, ten more houses by the same architects but in Surrey cottage style, 1984–6. NW in RANDELL'S ROAD, a red brick terrace of the 1880s (Nos. 18–26) that houses the former Paget Memorial Mission (*see* Churches) and CRUMBLES CASTLE, a fantasy play fort (built with stone from St Michael's?). N of these, less hospitable deck-access and ten-storey blocks of the 1960s and 70s.

CALEDONIAN ESTATE (No. 408 on), on the E side of Caledonian Road N of the prison, is a major scheme from the second phase of LCC housing, 1900–7, occupying the large site of the Royal Caledonian Asylum. Probably designed by *J. G. Stephenson* of the *LCC Housing Branch*. Five blocks, two parallel to the street with a bold entrance arch, the rest round a large court closed at the corners by brick arches. The access to the flats from iron balconies is typical of this phase. Serious five-storey blocks in red brick and some glazed terracotta, enlivened with Arts and Crafts details, e.g. the parapet curving up over the octagonal end bays and the pointed relieving arches over the windows filled with herringbone brick, as favoured at the same time by Holden at the Belgrave Hospital (*see London 2: South*, Lambeth). Playful but vandal-proof steel gates throughout by *Hutchinson & Partners*, 1988.

Further N, opposite Caledonian Road Underground Station (q.v.), the former MAYFAIR CINEMA (now the Cally Bingo Club), a late example of the streamlined cinema, 1937 by *F.E. Tasker*. Cement-rendered over faience tiles, faintly Egyptian columns, original plasterwork inside.

On the w side, No. 455 is a former ice depot of Carlo Gatti (*see also* Battlebridge Basin above, p. 697), eclectic Italianate. Further on, opposite Roman Road, MALLETT, PORTER & DOWD LTD, waste-cloth merchants and manufacturers, 1874, make a show on the w side of the road; name and date inscribed on a flat nine-bay composition in grey brick with bold debased classical details. Coachway at each end.

STREETS TO THE W of Caledonian Road have a mixture of post-war public housing, office conversions of industrial premises and late C20 commercial buildings. In BLUNDELL STREET opposite Pentonville Prison, No. 6, the offices of QUARTO publishers, occupy part of the site of Crosse & Blackwell's vinegar brewery, whose main entrance was in Brewery Road to the N. Converted *c.* 1990 by *Stewart Moss* of *Bennett Moss Construction* from a C19 Italianate stable block, with an atrium created in the mews yard.

In NORTH ROAD, N of Caledonian Road Underground Station, No. 39a, a narrow tile-hung Domestic Revival house, possibly by *Ernest George & Vaughan*, 1865, who designed workshops and stables here. The former coachbuilding premises of the LONDON GENERAL OMNIBUS COMPANY, built in 1900, stretch w in a plain red and yellow brick line; converted in 1990 by United Workspace into designers' studios, restaurants etc. MARKET ESTATE beyond replaced the N sheds of the Caledonian Market, demolished in 1965 (*see also* pp. 667–8). The MARKET CLOCK TOWER of 1850–5 survives in a huge, bleak square, flanked by Islington council housing (*Farber & Bartholomew, c.* 1967). Long deck-access blocks of red brick are linked by bridges to three eight-storey towers round two landscaped courtyards. Refurbished 1987 by *Shepheard Epstein Hunter*, who disconnected the towers and gave them big porches. Lower housing of the 1970s to the E. To its s, other vestiges of the market (q.v.).

YORK WAY, the old boundary between Islington and St Pancras, winds its way between derelict railway land and warehouses awaiting transformation through the arrival of the Channel Tunnel Rail link (*see* Camden: St Pancras). On the E side, at the corner of VALE ROYAL, once the centre of slaughterhouses and obnoxious trades, a colourful trailblazer: headquarters for the builders MARK FITZPATRICK, by *Chassay Architects*, 1988–91. Extravagantly Postmodern in the Michael Graves manner, with overlapping layers of rich and varied materials, ranging from polished green granite to terracotta render, and a glazed corner tower. Oriels on both façades of the Vale Royal wing. YORK CENTRAL is the former British Legion Poppy Factory, an interwar building transformed into neo-modern movement 'lofts' by *Harper Mackay*, 1995–6. The former YORK ROAD STATION (closed 1932) is still clearly recognizable as one of *Leslie Green*'s tiled stations of *c.* 1906 for the Great Northern, Piccadilly and Brompton Line.

Further s, near King's Cross, a mixture of Italianate industrial buildings of the later C19, also St Pancras Ironworks, 1866, around a courtyard, with frontage heightened in the 1890s.

## 7. Lower Holloway: the Holloway Road area south of Ring Cross

Suburban development in this area began in the late 1760s, with Paradise Row at the N end of Liverpool Road, from which one house remains. Holloway Road, the 'hollow way' recorded in 1307, was a medieval route leading N from Islington towards Highgate Hill. As the A1, it is still one of London's busiest main roads. By *c.* 1810 it was built up as far as Ring Cross, an early settlement at the junction of Holloway Road, Liverpool Road and Hornsey Road. Between Holloway Road and Liverpool Road a pleasant domestic enclave of the earlier C19 developed near St Mary Magdalene in its large churchyard. Mid- and later C19 housing further w and n has been extensively replaced by post-war council housing .

Starting from Highbury and Islington Station, the indifferent s end of HOLLOWAY ROAD has a scatter of decayed minor C19 ribbon development engulfed in later commercial development. On the E side, the former Underground station, dated 1904, and 1990s buildings for the University of North London (*see* p. 672).

EARLY to MID-C19 STREETS w of Holloway Road share the resi-dential character of Barnsbury further sw (*see* Perambulation 2a). FURLONG ROAD, laid out in 1839, and neighbouring streets have stuccoed terraces and paired villas. Rusticated ground floors with arched windows are common themes, but the details are subtly varied. Near the E end, ALBION LODGE, 1844, detached, with openwork parapet. Attached to Nos. 18–20, like an adapted base-ment storey, is the LEESON HALL (1886 by *T. S. Archer*), built for the Sandemanian Church. At the w end, some much tougher stock-brick infill by *L. R. Isaacson* (Nos. 23–27), typical of the early 1970s. LIVERPOOL ROAD has on its E side an attractive stretch of similar two- or three-storey terraces and pairs of villas of the 1830s and 40s, extending n to the large leafy churchyard beyond. On the w side, more urban terraces. To the w in ELLINGTON STREET, houses range from Nos. 14–28, 1839–40, two storeys, of brick with arched ground-floor windows and doors still in the Georgian tradition, to the grand, all-stuccoed composition of Arundel Terrace, Nos. 17–61, 1850, with giant pilasters and elaborate balconies. This backs on to ARUNDEL SQUARE, the last Victorian square to be built in Islington, developed piecemeal from 1850 on Pocock's Fields. E side 1852, n side 1855–60. n side with large Kensington-style porches (cf. Belitha Villas, Barnsbury, Perambulation 2a), and cramped vertical stucco panels, Victorian Italianate in its latest and busiest phase. The North London Railway cut through the square in 1850, and the s side was never completed. On the w side, the E end of the former St Clement's Church (q.v.).

Back now to LIVERPOOL ROAD. On the w side near the n end a short run of mid- to late C18 and early C19 houses, most of them raised above the present level of the road. They are the remnants of a development that began *c.* 1766 with *J. Pocock*'s Paradise Row (Paradise Passage echoes its name). No. 503 is the only early survivor. They stood isolated here for many years. Some of the houses have classical doorcases with Rococo decoration; see Nos. 513, 517, 519, 520 (with Roman Doric columns).

POST-WAR REDEVELOPMENTS w of Holloway Road can be explored around MACKENZIE ROAD. They reflect changing approaches to planning over three decades. The earliest, the *LCC*'s PAPWORTH GARDENS, completed *c.* 1958, has flats picturesquely disposed in a spacious lay-out: two five-storey point blocks and three- and four-storey ranges, all in yellow brick, with private balconies and neat 1950s details. Further w, the *GLC*'s RINGCROSS ESTATE, 1969, denser and more urban, with brick and concrete deck-access blocks enclosing a succession of four large courts, four storeys, with an eight-storey tower at one end. Though reasonable in size and detail and pleasantly landscaped, it suffers, like most schemes of this type, from cavernous underground garages and off-putting dead areas.

Along Mackenzie Road and s of it, a major redevelopment area by Islington: the WESTBOURNE ESTATE of 1976–9 by *Eric Lyons & Partners*, demonstrating the move back to conventional streets and terraced houses. Orange brick single-aspect terraces along Mackenzie Road and at r. angles to WESTBOURNE ROAD, with long continuous sweeps of monopitch roof diving down steeply to walled back gardens; at each end, a strip of dormer window where a flat has been inserted into the terrace. Vulcan Way has a mews arrangement, long walkways linking houses over gloomy garages; the small ADAM'S PLACE to the N, 1979, is an intimate version of multi-level housing.

In the C19 streets N of Mackenzie Road, a few Victorian and later remnants. Between GEORGE'S ROAD and EDEN GROVE, a large *LCC* estate of between the wars, now private. The core is Westbrook House, completed by 1936. Formal Neo-Georgian front; the back, to Eden Grove, has access balconies within giant arcades. Nearby, RINGCROSS SCHOOL, of the same period, two storeys, with pretty iron balconies. On the s side of George's Road, backing into the former St James's Church (q.v.), the former church SCHOOLS, 1854, a tall, gaunt Italianate composition of eleven bays with arcaded ground floor and central pedimental gable. At the N end of Eden Grove, the R.C. Sacred Heart Church (q.v.), next to Islington's first generating works, the former ELECTRIC LIGHTING STATION of 1893–6, glazed red brick with progressive details and moulded lettering. At r. angles a later screen wall with a Secessionist oriel. Further E, the former NOTRE DAME OF SION school, founded in the 1870s, twelve bays in severest Gothic with single, paired and triple-arched windows outlined in blue brick and a row of gabled dormers enlivened with corbelling. Across the back a two-storey cast-iron structure with access balcony; C19 NE wing and NE extension 1928.

## 8. Upper Holloway

Development in the upper part of the Holloway Road, N of the Hornsey Road junction, and in the countryside around it was sporadic until the later C19, with scattered groups of villas and terraces interrupted by large undeveloped pockets of land. E of Holloway Road villas went up along Hornsey Road, an old route, and to its E along the newly laid out Tollington Park and Hanley Road. To the W were brickfields, cemeteries and the House of Correction (Holloway Gaol). The spaciously laid out suburb of Tufnell Park, N of Camden Road, was planned from the 1840s but developed only from 1865. By the mid C19 Holloway Road had become a major shopping street, and by 1900 it was a flourishing centre with theatre and department stores. By then terraces had covered the green-field sites and gardens of earlier villas right up to the slopes of the Northern Heights, where both Holborn and Islington had found cheap land to build their workhouses and workhouse infirmaries (now the

Whittington Hospital). In the C20 many of the overcrowded C19 streets were replaced by public housing, at first in the form of big interwar blocks of flats, then by large new estates in the 1960s and 1970s.

*Holloway Road north of Holloway Road Station and streets off*

HOLLOWAY ROAD N of the viaduct of the North London Railway starts on the E side with tall red brick shopping parades of the 1890s in simple Franco-Flemish style: Nos. 262–268 with voluted central gable, Nos. 284–308 with a natty central turret. Then THE CORONET, a former cinema, now a pub, with trim faience-clad Art Deco front. Among larger C19 traders was the former JONES BROS (Nos. 350–356), a department store founded in 1867 and extended in the 1890s. The exuberant 1890s part survives, with a conical tower and clock over its big arched entrance, tall canted bays within multi-storey arches and rich stone details. WAITROSE replaced the earlier part *c.* 1990, copying some of the Edwardian tricks in a half-hearted way, but failing to convince because of its squat supermarket proportions. After the 1990s NAGS HEAD SHOPPING ARCADE, the OLD KING'S HEAD, a jolly mid-C19 pub in a very mixed commercial bag. Nos. 408–412, with emphatically pedimented C19 fronts, then a few smaller scale early C20 buildings: Nos. 416–418, MARKS & SPENCER, has chequered stonework enlivening its 1930s stripped-classical house-style. At the S corner of Seven Sisters Road, the former NAGS HEAD pub (now O'Neill's), stucco-trimmed Italianate. On the opposite corner, BATHURST MANSIONS (Nos. 459–462), dated 1891, with excellent François I decoration, originally one of two distinctive buildings that marked the entrance to Seven Sisters Road. (The other was BEALE'S RESTAURANT, a tall, rather Continental-looking specimen of the Gothic Revival by *F. Wallen*, 1889.)

On the W SIDE of Holloway Road interwar LCC flats predominate S of Camden Road. N of Camden Road the modest HALF MOON pub of *c.* 1860, with good Victorian interior, the Holloway Road Seventh Day Adventist Church (q.v.), and No. 383, MARLBOROUGH HOUSE, a big 1960s intruder, a classic combination of multi-storey office slab over a lower podium, now City and Islington College. It replaced *Matcham*'s Marlborough Theatre of 1903.

The ODEON on the W side vies with the Victorian display opposite. One of North London's most lavish cinemas, 1937–8, designed for Bernstein Theatres by *C. Howard Crane* (American architect of the Earl's Court exhibition centre) but built for Gaumont-British by *W. E. Trent*. Impressive classical cream faience exterior with an angled corner block crowned by a tall set-back attic. Giant fluted columns to the windows of the grand three-storey foyer, also classical inside. Originally with a mezzanine café (boxed in for a screen in 1973), which opened on to the raised terrace overlooking Holloway Road. After this Holloway Road assumes a more domestic, early Victorian scale, with Nos. 429–441, a terrace with cast-iron balconies to, unusually, pairs of windows. Nos. 443–445 is the former Holloway Hall, now NATIONAL YOUTH THEATRE, a C19 brick palazzo with a row of arched windows and decorated terracotta tympana, by *George Truefitt*, surveyor to the Tufnell

Park Estate (*see* below). On the E side ALBEMARLE MANSIONS, another curious late C19 palazzo front in Venetian manner (Nos. 544–554), with heavily moulded brick arches; it screens flats and shops, see the windows juggled to fit the staircases. More to see down MANOR GARDENS, where two pairs of plain classical villas (Nos. 6–9) form the wings of the MANOR GARDENS HEALTH AND COMMUNITY CENTRE, built in sympathetic style as the North Islington Infant Welfare Centre in 1927–8. On the S side, a library (q.v.) and, overpowering all, the vast former Money Order Office by *F. A. Llewellyn*, of *c.* 1932, converted into flats 1995–7 as the BEAUX-ARTS BUILDING. The style is in fact an angular version of Edwardian Baroque, on a harsh and scarcely comprehensible scale. Busy front with much dressed stone; rendered W elevation with parapets scooped up to tall ventilator shafts. Calmer N extension, with brick channelling, and a hint of Lutyens. To E and S utilitarian exposed steel framing with brick infill.

Beyond the former Royal Northern Hospital (q.v.), Holloway Road narrows as it climbs towards Highgate, past Victorian domestic terraces on the E side to Whittington Park, one of Islington's new open spaces of the 1970s, and St John's Church (q.v.). Further on, the traffic inferno of the Archway gyratory system, planned 1962.* The roads circle an island with the Archway Central Methodist Church (q.v.) and the large ARCHWAY TAVERN, rebuilt in 1886 by Watney's architect *J. G. Ensor* at the terminus of the tramway line. Stucco-trimmed with French mansard and clock. Looming over these is the sleek, dark seventeen-storey ARCHWAY HOUSE, the last part of the 1960s redevelopment that stretches W parallel with Junction Road; the rest has two curtain-walled twelve-storey slab blocks poised above a podium of shops with an upper-level pedestrian deck. In JUNCTION ROAD itself, the ROYAL LONDON FRIENDLY SOCIETY of 1903 by *Holman & Goodrham*, with a pretty asymmetrical Baroque front. Further S, by Tufnell Park Station (q.v.) at the angle of Junction Road and Dartmouth Park Hill, the Baroque corner tower of the expensively stone-trimmed BOSTON ARMS (1899 by *Thorpe & Furniss*) makes a good Edwardian *point-de-vue*.

## Tufnell Park

The secluded, residential Tufnell Park is bounded by Camden, Brecknock and Tufnell Park Roads. Plans to develop it with varied, superior residences were made *c.* 1840 by *John Shaw Jun.*, who had laid out part of the Eton Estate at Chalk Farm (*see* p. 241) from the 1830s. Shaw's scheme foundered, presumably at the death of the owner, Henry Tufnell, in 1845. Almost all that was achieved was the laying out of the pleasantly winding Carleton Road. Eventually more modest, higher-density development was carried out from the 1860s, largely under *George Truefitt*, surveyor to the estate 1865–90. He is supposed to have designed many of the villas, although the one or two that can certainly be identified lie to the S, just outside Tufnell Park proper, and predate his surveyorship. He also designed Holloway Hall in Holloway Road (*see* p. 702).

* A casualty of this in 1967 was the huge ensemble of WHITTINGTON ALMSHOUSES, 1822 by *George Smith*, Surveyor to the Mercers' Company. Organ and statue of Richard Whittington by *Joseph Carew* moved to new almshouses at Felbridge (Surrey).

CAMDEN ROAD, part of the route from Camden Town to Tottenham, begun in the 1820s, was built up along the Islington section from the 1850s with very large paired houses. On the SE side, especially elaborate, Nos. 350–352, gabled and rendered, with strapwork over the windows. To the SW, outside the Tufnell Park boundary, two *Truefitt* houses, the slightly roguish Nos. 1 and 8 MIDDLETON GROVE, *c.* 1859 (he lived at No. 1 before moving to the now demolished Fernbank in Carleton Road *c.* 1869). In between, three pairs of simpler semi-detached houses by *Charles Gray*. Opposite, ROWSTOCK GARDENS, neat mixed development *c.* 1960, low terraces and two point blocks set lozenge-wise to the road.

BRECKNOCK ROAD starts on the E side with the large HILLDROP ESTATE, built by the *LCC* from the 1930s onwards. Most of the original Tufnell Park houses here were replaced by the traditional type of walk-up four-storey flats (here, unusually, in pale brick). A good Italianate group remains in HILLDROP ROAD opposite Holloway School. In the spaciously laid out CARLETON ROAD, some of *Truefitt*'s more eccentric houses remain: most notable are Nos. 21 and 23, with crowstepped gables and Gothic details. ANSON ROAD, more densely built up, has large, varied examples, detached and semi-detached in both Gothic (e.g. Nos. 24, 26, 40, 44, 48) and Queen Anne styles (Nos. 32–4, 36–8). Some of the Gothic ones resemble *Truefitt*'s Villa Careno, a design illustrated in the *Building News* in 1866, and others his own house in Middleton Grove (*see* above). In all of these there is an inventive variety in the asymmetrical combination of features and levels.

Truefitt's St George's Church and its successor (qq.v.) stand at the E end of Carleton Road where it joins TUFNELL PARK ROAD, the main E–W artery from Holloway Road to Tufnell Park Underground Station. Near the E end, pairs of early Victorian villas (Nos. 9–21), still Georgian in style and linked to form a terrace. Later terraces are taller and plainly Italianate. On the N fringe, e.g. in TYTHERTON ROAD, modest gabled houses of red brick with terracotta ornament, dated 1889, opposite the former All Saints Church (q.v.).

### 9. North Islington

#### From Hornsey Road north to Tollington Park

Hornsey Road branches NE from Holloway Road. It was an old lane used as an alternative route to the N, avoiding the steep Highgate Hill, until a shorter bypass was provided by Archway Road, cut through in 1813. Development around the S end took off after Seven Sisters Road, the E continuation of Camden Road, was laid out in 1832. A few little roadside villas of *c.* 1830–40, used as garages etc., survived up to *c.* 1970. By *c.* 1850 its southern end was fringed with stucco-trimmed terraces, with a network of small side streets. Patchy Victorian survivals are now interspersed with an instructive variety of post-World War II housing types and some new open spaces.

Along HORNSEY ROAD, beyond the railway bridges, a mid-C19 part-stuccoed terrace and pub remain on the W side and, at No. 147, the former vicarage of Emmanuel Church (q.v.), quirkily

Italianate in the manner of *Roumieu & Gough*; streets of similar date behind. On the E is Islington's HARVIST ESTATE, 1967–70, with unappealing system-built nineteen-storey towers, reclad in 1996–7, rearing up close to the railway line behind lower terraces. To the SE, off ISLEDON ROAD, a large development for several housing associations by *Benjamin Derbyshire* of *Hunt Thompson*, 1991–4, fills former industrial space beside the railway. PARKSIDE CRESCENT looks down on the refurbished Isledon Road Gardens; to the S STEVE BIKO ROAD and RIXON STREET converge on a small circus in Beaux-Arts fashion. The tall, flat-fronted three-storey terraces of two-storey houses with flats above and in the corner pavilions are equally urban in character, and display the inventive eclecticism characteristic of this firm. Neoclassical allusions but also picturesque variety introduced by monopitch roofs and cut-away corners.

The former ASTORIA CINEMA at the junction of Isledon Road and Seven Sisters Road (later the Rainbow Theatre; currently used by Pentecostal Christians) was built for Paramount in 1930. At the time, one of the largest cinemas in the world. *Edward A. Stone* designed the faience exterior, the plain foil to an escapist 'atmospheric interior' by *Somerford & Barr*. Moorish foyer with fountain and arcaded tea balcony, crush hall like a Spanish courtyard and an auditorium recalling an Andalucian village at night.

Returning W along SEVEN SISTERS ROAD, mid-C19 streets remain to the S; e.g. MEDINA ROAD has typical stucco terraces, also a genteel Neo-Georgian EMPLOYMENT EXCHANGE ('Employers' over Gibbsian central door). Smaller streets to the N (including the notorious 'Campbell Bunk'*), built up cheaply after 1850, were slums by the early C20. They were swept away in a mammoth post-war rebuilding programme. The strikingly massed ANDOVER ESTATE (by the *GLC*, from 1972) was a late phase of this redevelopment. It builds up from two-storey terraces and four-storey deck-access maisonettes, to a towering group of ten-storey ziggurats on giant pilotis. Angular forms somewhat softened by universal use of brindled russet brick, brown pantiles and blue balcony planters. E of the Andover Estate, two groups of earlier Islington Borough Council flats: duller system-built 1960s maisonettes around DURHAM ROAD and Lennox Road, and 1950s flats further E, off BIGGERSTAFFE ROAD, with two later brick-faced eighteen-storey cluster blocks.

FONTHILL ROAD forms the E boundary of this redevelopment, still largely mid C19 and surprisingly broad, its S end dominated from the 1960s by ebullient rag-trade shops and factories. On the E side and behind in CLIFTON TERRACE, the ATHELSTANE ROAD ESTATE, homely two- and three-storey houses in brown brick by *Darbourne & Darke*, informally grouped. This was the start of an ambitious mid-1970s low-rise rebuilding scheme by Islington (cf. the earlier Marquess Estate, Canonbury, by the same firm; *see* Perambulation 3), but it was transformed into piecemeal infilling as comprehensive redevelopment fell out of favour. More of the same in CHARTERIS ROAD, and to the W of this (reached via a passage N of Moray Road), in EVERLEIGH STREET, where there

---

* See Jerry White, *The Worst Street in North London*, 1986.

is a play space and nicely detailed DAY NURSERY with a big slated roof. The plain yellow and red brick terraces of CHARTERIS ROAD benefited from the shift to rehabilitation. Its N end is a tiny street of very modest stucco-trimmed villas: Nos. 52–70 on the E side with shared pediments, Nos. 63–67 on the W side faintly Tudor, all c. 1840. It leads N to Tollington Park.

TOLLINGTON PARK (named from the manor of Tollington, which covered much of North Islington) was laid out, between the old routes of Hornsey Road and Stroud Green Road, as a superior residential development. Planned c. 1840, but built up slowly and irregularly and much eroded since. The survivals display the range of classical variants current in the mid C19. On the N side No. 89, sole remainder from a group of big austerely treated three-bay villas. On the S side Nos. 96–108, low single and paired villas, of an unusual design, but horribly maltreated. No. 104, the least altered, has the quirky narrow triple windows that appear in the work of Roumieu & Gough. Further W a more conventional stuccoed group on the N, Nos. 39–51; opposite are some more floridly ornate pairs, Nos. 66–72, and the tall, plainer late classical Nos. 62–64, next to St Mark (q.v.). In TOLLINGTON PLACE off to the N, one survival (No. 2) still in a stuccoed late Regency style.

### North of Tollington Park

HORNSEY ROAD narrows at the junction with Tollington Park. On the E side THE PLOUGH, with stuccoed arch to the former PLOUGH STABLES, then modest mid-C19 terraces with shops. The W side was rebuilt with dull Islington maisonettes in the late 1970s, crowding close to the road. It is worth penetrating these to explore further W via BAVARIA ROAD (where the Italianate REPLICA HOUSE was the Congregational Mission Halls by *Lander & Bedells*, 1883). The main landmark is SUSSEX CLOSE, S of Bavaria Road, an eight-storey crescent in red brick, with lower blocks enclosing a garden: an ambitious post-war Islington scheme of 1950 by *Monson*, spaciously laid out, in startling contrast to the tight streets of low stuccoed houses which then existed all around. Running W, CORNWALLIS SQUARE, of c. 1990, represents the return to semi-classical formality. Three-storey terrace houses with odd proportions and eclectic detail. Less formal groups around the square are blended in with C19 survivals. MARLBOROUGH ROAD leads back to Hornsey Road. On the S side the converted BELGRAVIA WORKSHOPS (Nos. 157–163) and an adjoining C19 factory (No. 165) are reminders that until the 1970s this was an area full of small industrial concerns. The factory backs on to Nos. 427–429 Hornsey Road, once a decent pair of mid-C19 villas. A few others opposite (Nos. 464 and 466, with narrow triple windows, cf. Tollington Park).

This area of Hornsey Road was a small hamlet already in the early C19. It expanded E with large stately houses along HANLEY ROAD, which looked out over fields until the later C19. An irregular group set back from the road, now rather battered and altered. Two stuccoed pairs, Nos. 9–15, then taller groups of three, three-storeyed above high basements, Nos. 17–45. No. 49 is a big Postmodern rebuild with large bow, part balcony, part window Then one of Islington's local council offices of the 1980s (*see* Public Buildings) and, by St Saviour (q.v.), HANLEY GARDENS, a cheerful housing association group of 1986–91 by *Anthony Richardson & Partners* (a Care in the Community project), well done in a friendly 1980s domestic idiom. Facing the road a day centre, made inviting by a big rendered bow and a first floor projecting like a conservatory. The embracing wings have interesting cut-away corner entrances to shared houses. Off ORMOND ROAD to the N, slotted into LAMBTON ROAD, a pocket of housing by *Avanti Architects* for the Guinness Trust; 1994–5, a crisp design in orange brick with contrasting porch projections. A combination of family maisonettes and flats for the disabled, with gardens and upper terraces. Further E, at the corner of Hanley Road and CROUCH HILL, FRIERN MANOR DAIRY, a remarkable arty frontage of the 1890s. Rubbed brick Queen Anne detail with quirky roof-line. Seven large sgraffito panels instructively depict old- and new-style milk production and delivery. Converted to a restaurant 1997.

Crouch Hill, on the border with Haringey, climbs the Northern Heights, the ridge of land continuing E from Hampstead and Highgate. The slopes once were scattered with select early C19 villas, but much was rebuilt between the wars and later with Islington council housing (cf. Hackney's colonization of Upper Clapton). Off Ashley Road, in HIGHCROFT ROAD (which still has one jolly Gothic villa of 1879) and HILLRISE ROAD, whimsical low terraces of *c.* 1983–6 by *Chris Purslow* (Borough Architect). They form a deliberate contrast to what they replaced, *Monson*'s austere Blythe Mansions, Viennese-type courtyard flats of the 1930s, a progressive but unpopular effort among Islington's pre-war housing. The new housing has plenty of cheerful polychrome brickwork inspired by the C19 surroundings, and is arranged in a huddled lay-out around a string of tiny mixer-courts in the manner of Ralph Erskine. Where Hillrise Road joins Hornsey Rise, the vocabulary is simpler, the planning more ingenious. Sheltered flats with good views from first-floor conservatories, and family houses with gated entrance courts and rooftop terraces.

Hillrise Road debouches in Hornsey Rise. On the W side, in CROMARTIE ROAD, a group of energy-efficient houses by *ECD Partnership*, 1987, shielded by a garden from the busy HORNSEY RISE, which climbs steeply to the forbidding tall stock brick slabs of the NEW ORLEANS ESTATE (*GLC*, 1972–4) at the corner of HORNSEY LANE. Here also earlier flats of the interwar Neo-Georgian type crowd along the S side of Hornsey Lane – a borough boundary, where, as so often, anything goes. A few substantial Victorian houses remain among them. (For the N side *see* p. 561.) The slopes stretching S from Hornsey Lane towards Archway Road are covered by terraces of the 1890s onwards, intermixed with dull ranks of four-storey council housing, partly pre-war, partly 1970s. They are leavened by ELTHORNE PARK and SUNNYSIDE GARDENS, nicely landscaped parks of the 1970s near Hornsey Rise, and by a cluster of amenity buildings, including Islington council offices, in BEAUMONT RISE.

# SOURCES AND
# FURTHER READING

The documentary information in this book is derived from a mixture of printed sources, planning records, local history collections and archives of individual boroughs, and in some cases, details kindly made available from those researching particular subjects or areas (*see* also acknowledgements, p. xviii). The following notes can provide only a selection from the vast range of material that exists.

## 1. General History and Topography

The most recent London bibliography is *The Bibliography of Printed Works of London History to 1939* (1994), edited by Heather Creaton. Comprehensive libraries with London material are those at Guildhall in the City of London, and at the London Metropolitan Archives, 40 Northampton Road, Islington, which incorporates the collections of the former Middlesex Record Office and the London County Council records and library. Roy Porter's excellent *London, a Social History* (1994), has a guide to further reading covering recent research on social background. *Public Housing* by Alan Cox (1993), a London archives guide, covers a useful range of sources, of wider relevance than its title suggests. An invaluable one-volume general reference book is *The Encyclopedia of London*, edited by B. Weinreb and C. Hibbert (2nd ed. 1992); a good one-volume guide is Ann Saunders, *Art and Architecture of London* (1984).

On the Prehistoric and Roman periods the most useful recent books are N. Merriman, *Prehistoric London* (1991); R. Merrifield, *The Archaeology of London* (London, 1975); D. Collins et al., *The Archaeology of the London Area: Current Knowledge and Problems* (Special Paper No. 1, London and Middlesex Archaeological Society) (London, 1976); *Time on our Side? A Survey of Archaeological Needs in Greater London* (Department of the Environment, Greater London Council, and Museum of London) (London, 1976); Gustav Milne, *Roman London* (English Heritage, 1985); Dominic Perring, *Roman London* (1991). R. Merrifield's last book on London was *London, City of the Romans* (1983). *The Archaeology of Surrey to 1540*, ed. J. Bird and D.G. Bird (Surrey Archaeological Society, 1987), covers the sw boroughs, with reference also to material beyond the Greater London boundary. Recent discoveries are reported in *London Archaeologist*, published quarterly, and in the annual reports of the Museum of London Archaeology Service (MoLAS). The county journal is the *Transactions of the London and Middlesex Archaeological Society*. There are major collections of London archaeological material in the British Museum and the Museum of London. There is also a book of essays, *Interpreting Roman London* (1996), ed. Joanna Bird, Mark Hassall and Harvey Sheldon.

The most comprehensive general histories available for most of the areas in this book are those provided in recent volumes of the *Victoria County History of Middlesex*. They are noted below under the relevant boroughs. For the areas outside the former LCC there is the still invaluable survey by Michael Robbins, *Middlesex* (1953), which has an excellent bibliography, and the same author's compilation on churches in *Transactions of the London and Middlesex Archaeological Society* 18 (1955). Older county books are D. Lysons, *Parishes of Middlesex* (1800), the *Little Guide* by J.B. Firth (1906), and M.S. Briggs, *Middlesex Old and New* (1934). *Memorials of Old Middlesex*, ed. J. Tavernor-Perry (1909), is especially useful for its chapters on churches and their furnishings (by Charles Cox and Aymer Vallance). On the same subject, J.H. Sperling's *Church Walks in Middlesex* (1849, revised 1853) is a valuable account by a critical ecclesiologist of buildings on the eve of Victorian restoration.

From the c18 onwards topographical surveys and guides appeared which provide a mixture of historical notes and contemporary descriptions about the neighbourhood of London. An early example was John Strype's edition of Stow's *Survey of London* (1720), which added details about the parishes around the edge of built-up London. The source used by many later guides was Daniel Lysons' invaluable *Environs of London* (1795, revised 1811). James Elmes, *London in the Nineteenth Century* (1829), and John Tallis, *London Street Views* (1838–47), both available in facsimile, have useful illustrations which include the inner London areas in this volume. Among later historical surveys are William Howitt, *The Northern Heights of London*, 1869, and Edward Walford, *Old and New London*, 1872–8. James Thorne's *Handbook to the Environs of London* (1876, reprinted 1970) is an especially comprehensive gazetteer to the area within twenty miles of London. His elegiac comments on the retreating countryside swallowed by the *Suburban Homes of London* contrasts with W. Clarke's amusingly enthusiastic eulogy of these in his book of that name (1881). The flavour of Middlesex at the turn of the century is given by such books as C.G. Harper's *Rural Nooks round London* (1907).

Topographical illustrations up to 1850 are listed in the admirable survey by Bernard Adams, *London Illustrated, 1604–1851* (1983), while the maps that chart the expansion and development of London have been usefully catalogued by J. Howgego, *Printed Maps of London c. 1553–1850* (2nd ed., 1978), and R. Hyde, *Printed Maps of Victorian London* 1851–1910 (1975). Two introductory histories based on maps are: Philippa Glanville, *London in Maps*, 1972, Felix Barker and Peter Jackson, *The History of London in Maps*, 1990. Helpful tools are the Godfrey editions of early Ordnance Survey maps. To bring such maps vividly to life one should look at the contemporary social investigations: Mayhew's *London Labour and the London Poor* (1851); Charles Booth's *Life and Labour of the People of London* (1889, reprinted by the London Topographical Society 1984), and *The New Survey of London Life and Labour* (1934).

Books dealing with the history of London during particular periods, relevant to the area within this volume, include vol. 1 of *Middlesex* VCH (1969), which covers medieval religious foundations, N.G. Brett-James, *The Growth of Stuart London* (1935), George Rudé, *Hanoverian London* (1971), Francis Sheppard, *London*

*1808–1870, the Infernal Wen* (1971), Priscilla Metcalf, *Victorian London* (1972), F.M.L. Thompson, *The Rise of Suburbia* (1982), and Alan A. Jackson, *Semi-Detached London, Suburban Development, Life and Transport, 1900–1939* (1979, 2nd ed. 1991). On the administrative background a basic reference book is K. Young and P. Garside, *Metropolitan London, Politics and Urban Change 1837–1981* (1982). Urban history, pioneered by H.J. Dyos in *Victorian Suburb, A Study of the Growth of Camberwell* (1961), is now a discipline in its own right, relevant alike to social, economic and architectural historians; recent research is published in the periodicals *Urban History* and the *London Journal*.

For after the Second World War the essential background books are the planning documents: Forshaw and Abercrombie's clear and attractively illustrated *County of London Plan* (1943) and Abercrombie's complementary *Greater London Plan* (1944), which describe London as it was then, and the proposals for post-war reconstruction and decentralization. These formed the basis for the official *County Development Plan* of 1951. *The London Plan, First Review* (1960) summarized the uneven progress made in the first few years. After the formation of the GLC in 1965 came the *Greater London Development Plan* (2 vols.: *Statement* and *Report of Studies* 1969) and numerous documents which emanated from the lengthy inquiry that followed. Later social and economic trends are considered briefly in *Changing London*, edited by Hugh Clout (1978).

## 2. Architectural History

A list of publications with more architectural detail starts with the Royal Commission on Historical Monuments, whose volumes on *West London* (1925), *East London* (1930) and *Middlesex* (1937), have descriptions of buildings up to 1714. For parts of the old LCC area these can be supplemented by the more detailed parish volumes of the *Survey of London*, (although the earlier ones generally ignore developments of the C19 onwards), and for all boroughs by the brief descriptions in the official *Lists of Buildings of Special Architectural and Historic Interest*. For five of the six boroughs in this volume these were issued as typescript 'greenbacks' in 1972–4, the list for Barnet dates from 1983. All have been supplemented since by numerous additions, which include buildings up to the 1960s; new, much expanded *Lists* for Camden and Islington are imminent at time of writing.

Research on individual periods and topics has multiplied fast in the last forty years, particularly on C19 and C20 subjects; only a sample of relevant works can be indicated here. The main landmarks of architectural history, in which the London area is so rich, are of course included in the general works, John Summerson's *Architecture in Britain 1530–1840* (revised 1991), *Victorian Architecture* by R. Dixon and S. Muthesius (1978), and *Edwardian Architecture* by A. Service (1977). Essential tools are H.M. Colvin's *Biographical Dictionary of British Architects 1600–1840* (1978, 3rd ed. 1996); *RIBA Directory of British Architects 1834–1900* (1993), A. Stuart Gray's *Edwardian Architecture, a Biographical Dictionary* (1985), excellently illustrated with London subjects; *Catalogues* of the Drawings Collection of the RIBA and *The History of the King's Works*, ed. H.M. Colvin, vols.

I–VI (1973–82). Nikolaus Pevsner's *A History of Building Types* (1976) provides an international perspective. The *Illustrated London News*, *The Builder*, *Building News* (later *Architect and Building News*), and *London* (later the *Municipal Journal*) have invaluable contemporary accounts of C19 buildings; for the C20 should be added the *Architectural Review*, the *Architects' Journal*, *RIBA Journal*, *Official Architecture and Planning*, and the *London Architect*. Individual articles in current architectural periodicals can found through the RIBA British Architectural Library database. For older buildings the publications of the London Topographical Society have much of interest. The *London Journal* and *Country Life* also include some articles on London architecture. To keep up to date with current research, *Architectural History*, and the publications of the Georgian Group, the Victorian Society and the Twentieth Century Society should be consulted. General books and articles on architectural history relevant for this and other *Buildings of England* volumes are listed in *The Buildings of England Further Reading, A Select Bibliography*, compiled by T. Blackshaw, B. Cherry and E. Williamson (1990, revised ed. 2000).

Mention of individual books should start with two on which *The Buildings of England* London volumes have leant heavily: John Summerson's lucid account of *Georgian London*, which first appeared in 1945 (latest revised edition 1988), and B.F.L. Clarke's *Parish Churches of London* (1966), which covers all Anglican churches in the old LCC area. More recent studies which focus on London buildings and monuments of the capital relevant to this volume include the following (in roughly chronological order of subject): 'Good and Proper Materials, The Fabric of London since the Great Fire', *London Topographical Society* 40, ed. A. Saunders (1989); A.F. Kelsall, 'The London House Plan in the later C17', *Post Medieval Archaeology* 8 (1974); M.H. Port (ed.) 'The Commissions for Building Fifty New Churches', *London Record Society* (1986); D. Cruickshank and N. Burton, *Life in the Georgian City* (1990); D. Cruickshank and P. Wyld, *London, The Art of Georgian Building* (1975); Andrew Byrne, *London's Georgian Houses* (1986), Alison Kelly, *Mrs Coade's Stone* (1990); essays by Andrew Saint and J. Mordaunt Crook, in *London, World City, 1800–1840* (1992, the catalogue of an exhibition held in Essen) edited by Celina Fox; Michael Port, *600 New Churches, 1818–1856* (1961); Donald J. Olsen, *The Growth of Victorian London*, (1976), is interesting on contemporary reactions to C19 expansion. Among much that has been published on C19 building activity are three influential essays by John Summerson, reprinted in his collection *The Unromantic Castle* (1990): 'Sir John Soane and the Furniture of Death', 'The London Building World of the 1860s', and 'The London Suburban Villa, 1850–1880'. Other milestones in appreciation of C19 subjects are *Victorian Pubs* (1975) and *Sweetness and Light, the Queen Anne movement 1860–1900* (1977) both by Mark Girouard; Martin Harrison, *Victorian Stained Glass* (1980); and Stefan Muthesius, *The English Terraced House* (1982).

On public housing, the best introduction is the guide by Alan Cox, mentioned above, p. 708. Working-class housing was the subject of one of Nikolaus Pevsner's pioneering studies, first published in 1943 (reprinted in his *Studies in Art, Architecture and Design*, vol. 2, 1968), and is examined in greater depth by J.N. Tarn: *see* his *Five per Cent Philanthropy* (1973), and The Peabody Donation Fund (*Victorian Studies*, 1966); also A.S. Wohl, *The Eternal Slum: Housing and Social Policy in Victorian London* (1977). The early role of the LCC is admirably dealt with by S. Beattie in *A Revolution in London Housing, L.C.C. Housing Architects and their Work, 1893–1914* (1980) and the next phase of public housing by Mark Swenarton in *Homes Fit for Heroes* (1981). The story of the county council's housing efforts is carried on more summarily up to 1975 by the GLC's *Home Sweet Home* (1976), and by contemporary records: the LCC's *Housing* (1928), *Housing 1928–30* (1931), *Housing 1945–9* (1949). *G.L.C. Architecture 1965–70* and later *G.L.C. Architect's Reviews* also cover other types of buildings. On private housing: M. Horsey, 'London Speculative Housing of the 1930s, Official Control and Popular Taste', *Lon. J.* 11(1985).

On schools, D. Gregory-Jones, 'The London Board Schools, E.R. Robson', in A. Service (ed.), *Edwardian Architecture and its Origins* (1975); *The Schools of the London School Board and the L.C.C. Education Department* (typescript, English Heritage) and for later ones as well, R. Ringshall et al., *The Urban School* (The Greater London Council, 1983), also A. Jackson in *London Topographical Record* 25 (1995). On schools generally: M. Seaborne, *The English School* vol. 1, 1370–1870 (1971); vol. 2 (with R. Lowe), 1870–1970 (1977). For the second half of the c20, A. Saint, *Towards a Social Architecture, the Role of School Building in Post-War England*, 1987. On public works in Middlesex there is much less available; the Minutes of the MCC are useful; a general account is C.W. Radcliffe, *Middlesex, the Jubilee of the County Council, 1889–1939* (1939).

Other studies on diverse subjects which have been useful include Hugh Meller's thorough gazetteer, *London Cemeteries* (1994), and on the same subject, Chris Brooks, *Mortal Remains* (1989); J. Glassman, 'London Synagogues in the late c19, design in context', *London Journal* 13 (1987–8); on libraries, A.W.G Ball, *The Public Libraries of Greater London* (1977), also Roger Bowdler and Steven Brindle, *A Survey of Pre-war Libraries in London* (English Heritage, typescript, 1992). On theatres of 1900–14 *Curtains!!!* (published by John Offord, Eastbourne, 1982), and on cinemas David Atwell, *Cathedrals of the Movies* (1980), and Richard Gray, *Cinemas in Britain* (1996), all with gazetteers.

Among monographs on architects and builders, especially relevant for this volume are Dorothy Stroud, *George Dance* (1971), J. Summerson, *John Nash* (1980), Hermione Hobhouse, *Thomas Cubitt* (1971), Geoffrey Tyack, *Sir James Pennethorne* (1992), Paul Thompson, *William Butterfield* (1971), Andrew Saint, *Richard Norman Shaw* (1976), A.P. Quiney, *John Loughborough Pearson* (1979), Jennifer Freeman, *W.D. Caröe* (1990), and John Allan, *Berthold Lubetkin* (1992). The London Ph.D. by Roger Dixon, *Life and Work of James Brooks* (1976), is also gratefully acknowledged. A useful general work is A. Service, *The Architects of London* (1979).

On sculpture, standard reference works are R. Gunnis, *Dictionary of British Sculpture 1660–1851* (1953, rev. 1968), Margaret Whinney, *Sculpture in Britain 1530–1830*, Pelican History of Art (1964, revised by John Physick, 1988), Benedict Read, *Victorian Sculpture* (1982), Susan Beattie, *The New Sculpture* (1983). For recent research *see* the journal *Church Monuments*, also Adam White, 'Westminster Abbey in the Early Seventeenth Century, A Powerhouse of Ideas', *Church Monuments IV* (1989), and the same author's London Ph.D. on church monuments. For C20 art: Margaret Garlake, 'The LCC as art patron 1948–65', *London Journal* 18 (1993).

On industrial archaeology the pioneer study was Ashdown, Bussell and Carter's *Industrial Monuments of Greater London* (1969). *London's Industrial Heritage* by A. Wilson (1967) discusses selected items in greater detail. For general coverage of individual aspects *see East Midlands* and *Eastern England* volumes in the *Canals of the British Isles* series, M. Denney, *London's Waterways* (1977), and Herbert Spencer *London's Canal* (1976) on the Regent's Canal, also B. Rudden, *The New River* (1985); R. Sisley, *The London Water Supply* (1899), H. W. Dickinson, *Water Supply of Greater London* (1954), and publications of the former Metropolitan Water Board (1953, 1961, etc.); S. Everard, *History of the Gas, Light and Coke Company* (1949), and the North Thames Gas Board's *Historical Index of Gas Works* (1957); Farries and Masons's *Industries of London since 1861* (1962) gives a geographical background to manufacturing. Much technical information can be found in the *Minutes of Proceedings of the Institution of Civil Engineers* and other contemporary publications; recent fieldwork is published by the Greater London Industrial Archaeology Society. Railway history, so significant for the development of outer London, is covered by T. C. Barker and Michael Robbins, *A History of London Transport*, 2 vols. (1963, 1974); H. P. White, *A Regional History of the Railways of Great Britain*, vol. 3, *Greater London* (2nd ed., 1971); Alan A. Jackson, *London's Termini* (2nd ed. 1986); H. V. Borley, *Chronology of London Railways* (1982). On King's Cross railway lands *see* Stephen P. Duckworth and Barry V. Jones, *Kings Cross Development Site, an Inventory of Architectural and Industrial Features* (English Heritage report), 1988. David Lawrence's *Underground Architecture* (1994) is an excellently illustrated survey.

For much of the C20 an adequate synthesis is lacking. Useful historical introductions are Gavin Weightman and Steve Humphries, *The Making of Modern London 1914–1939* (1984), and Steve Humphries and John Taylor, *The Making of Modern London 1945–1985* (1986). Lionel Esher's *A Broken Wave, the Rebuilding of England 1940–1980* (1981) has a chapter on London. *Tower Block* by Miles Glendinning and Stefan Muthesius, 1994, includes valuable detail on London's post-war public housing. On industrial building, private houses and churches *see* the Twentieth Century Society, *Twentieth Century Architecture* 1 (1996), 2 (1997), 3 (1998). Miranda H. Newton, *Architects' London Houses* (1992) discusses a selection of architects' own houses. Among brief guide books, one is retrospective (*Battle of Styles: A Guide to Selected Buildings in the London Region of the 1914–1939 Period*, RIBA London region, 1975), others record buildings of their time: Hugh Casson, *New Sights of London* (London Transport, 1938); S. Lambert (ed.) *New Architecture of London*, 1963; Ian Nairn, *Modern Buildings in London* (London Transport, 1964); Charles McKean and Tom Jestico, *Guide to Modern Buildings in London 1965–75* (RIBA, 1976), Samantha Hardingham, *London, A Guide to Recent Architecture* (1993 and later editions).

Finally in this section a few London anthologies can be mentioned: G. Stamp and C. Amery, *Victorian Buildings of London 1837–1887: An*

*Illustrated Guide* (1980), A. Service, *London 1900* (1979), and G. Stamp (ed.), *London 1900* (Architectural Design, 48, nos. 5–6, 1978). David Dean, *The Thirties: Recalling the Architectural Scene* (1983), is relevant for many London buildings. *Exploring England's Heritage, London*, 1991, by Elain Harwood and Andrew Saint, has an interesting selection with comments on different building types. Finally, personal responses to London that have stood the test of time can be recommended: S. E. Rasmussen's *London: The Unique City* (first published in 1934, revised in 1948) and *Nairn's London* by Ian Nairn (1966, revised 1988).

*3. Individual areas*

The following brief notes can only include a selection from what is available, with an emphasis on recent work. Many flourishing local societies have produced their own publications over the last thirty years, so that borough local history collections contain in addition to their archives, ever increasing published material on particular areas and, to a lesser extent, on individual buildings. The older borough guides with brief historical accounts and mention of the principal recent buildings remain useful. From the 1980s nostalgia for the past has been fed by a spate of books of old photographs, often knowledgeably annotated by local experts, which provide introductory visual histories, but usually little about the later c20 architectural scene. Two prolific series are Alan Sutton's *Britain in Old Photographs*, and the *Past* volumes published by Historical Publications. For existing older buildings more detail may be found in the official *Lists* (*see* above, p. 710); for some buildings English Heritage, the Royal Commission on Historical Monuments or local planning departments may hold historical evaluations and records made in advance of adaptation and repair (not always easy to track down). On recent architecture the most useful sources are architectural periodicals (*see* above, p. 711), architects' firms, and development control records of borough planning departments.

BARNET. The borough is covered by VCH *Middlesex* vol. IV (1975) (Edgware); vol. V (1979) (Hendon, Monken Hadley); vol. VI ( Friern Barnet, Finchley). Introductory books include two by Stewart Gillies and Pamela Taylor, *Finchley and Friern Barnet* (1992), *Hendon, Child's Hill, Golders Green and Mill Hill* (1993); also *The Barnets and Hadley* (*Britain in Old Photographs*) (1996); P. Reboul and J. Heathfield, *London Borough of Barnet Past and Present* (1997). Barnet Libraries have published a folder of material on Church Farm House, Hendon (1980). On Hampstead Garden Suburb: C. W. Ikin, *Hampstead Garden Suburb, Dreams and Realities* (1990); Mervyn Miller and A. Stuart Gray, *Hampstead Garden Suburb* (1992), which includes useful biographies of architects.

CAMDEN. The Camden History Society's publications include the *Camden History Review*, published from 1973, and a series of (mainly historical) *Streets* guides on Hampstead (1972, rev. 1984), Belsize (1991), West Camden (1984), Bloomsbury and Fitzrovia (1997). Introductory books include *Hampstead Past* by Christopher Wade (1989); *Highgate Past* (1989), *Camden Town and Primrose Hill Past* (1991), *Kentish Town Past* (1997) all by John Richardson; Christina

Gee, *Hampstead and Highgate in old photographs, 1870–1918* (1974); *Hampstead to Primrose Hill (Britain in Old Photographs)* by Malcolm J. Holmes.

Hampstead is covered in VCH *Middlesex* vol. XI (1992). F.M.L. Thompson's *Hampstead, Building a Borough* (1974) is an exemplary history based on original documents. J. Summerson's 'An Early Victorian Suburb', *London Topographical Record* 27 (1995), on Chalcots, Chalk Farm, and Alastair Service's *Victorian and Edwardian Hampstead* (1989) are excellent architectural accounts. *Belsize Park, a Living Suburb*, ed. L. Cohn (n.d.) for Belsize Park Conservation Area includes contributions on C19 and C20 buildings and their occupants. On individual buildings: Neil Burton, *St Stephen Rosslyn Hill*, GLC Historic Buildings Paper No. 1 (n.d.); *Rosslyn Hill Chapel* (1974); Alan Farmer, *Hampstead Heath*, 1984.

Holborn is partly covered by two *Survey of London* volumes: vol. 3, *St Giles-in-the Fields, part 1* (1912) dealing with Lincoln's Inn Fields; vol. 4, *St Giles-in-the-Fields, part 2* (1914), which includes the church of St Giles and its neighbourhood. D.J. Olsen *Town Planning in London, the Eighteenth and Nineteenth Centuries* (1982) has much on Holborn and St Pancras. General histories are John Lehmann, *Holborn* (1970), Gladys Scott Thomson, *The Russells in Bloomsbury (1669–1771)* (1940), Caroline M. Barron, *The Parish of St Andrew Holborn* (1979), and Nick Bailey, *Fitzrovia* (1981).

On individual sites particularly useful are: Andrew Byrne, *Bedford Square, an architectural study* (1990); Anthony Blee Consultancy, *Victoria House, Bloomsbury Square* (1997); Marjorie Caygill, *The story of the British Museum* (1992); J. Mordaunt Crook, *The British Museum* (1972); C. Cunningham, *Prudential Buildings, Holborn Bars* (n.d.); E.J. Davis, 'The University Site', *London Topographical Record* 17 (1936); Adrian Forty on Mary Ward House in *Architects' Journal* no. 2 August 1989; N. Harte and J. North, *The World of University College London 1828–1978* (1978); Penelope Hunting on Hatton Garden in *London Topographical Record* 25 (1985); Hugh Meller, *St George's Bloomsbury, an illustrated guide to the church* (1975); Philip Norman, 'Queen Square, Bloomsbury and its Neighbourhood', *London Topographical Record* 10 (1916); *Seven Dials and Covent Garden, the Environmental Handbook* (Seven Dials Monuments Trust, 1997). Richard Stone, *Gray's Inn, a short history* (1997); J. Summerson, 'The Old Hall of Lincoln's Inn', *Trans. Anc. Monuments Soc.*, 1984.

St Pancras. For the s part *see also* Holborn. Four *Survey of London* volumes have details on buildings and estate development up to the early C19: vol. 17, *The Village of Highgate* (1936); vol. 19: *Old St Pancras and Kentish Town* (1938); vol. 21: *Tottenham Court Road and neighbourhood* (1949); vol. 24, *King's Cross neighbourhood* (1952). Charles E. Lee, *St Pancras Church and Parish*, 1955, is a thorough history. *Change at King's Cross*, edited by Michael Hunter and Robert Thorne (1990), deals with the complex C19 and C20 history of the area around this main terminus. Gillian Tyndale's *The Fields Beneath* (1977) is a history of Kentish Town, John Richardson's *Highgate* (1983) is a well-illustrated general history with an appendix listing houses and their residents.

On individual sites: two important houses are well served by recent studies: Peter Barber et al. *Lauderdale Revealed*, 1993, Julius

Bryant, *Kenwood*, 1990. On Cromwell House there is an older *Survey of London* monograph (1926). On c20 developments, S. Pepper, Ossulston Street; early LCC experiments in high-rise housing, *Lon. Journal* 7 (1981).

ENFIELD. Both Enfield and Edmonton are covered in VCH *Middlesex* vol. v (1979). The standard c19 histories by William Robinson on Edmonton (1819) and Enfield (1823) are still of interest. *Enfield's Architectural Heritage* (Enfield Preservation Society, 1977), is a well-illustrated anthology, Graham Dalling's *Southgate and Edmonton Past* (1996) a useful recent introduction, David Pam, *A History of Enfield*, 3 vols., (1990–4), has much local detail. The Enfield Archaeological Society's *Industrial Archaeology in Enfield* (1971) is a comprehensive local survey. On individual buildings: Ian K. Jones and Ivy M. Drayton, *The Royal Palaces of Enfield* (Enfield Archaeological Society, 1984); Geoffrey Gillam, *Forty Hall*, 1997; T. Putnam and D. Weinstein, *A Short History of the Royal Small Arms Factory, Enfield*, Middlesex University, 1992; on Broomfield House studies by Steven Brindle and Richard Lea (English Heritage, 1994).

HACKNEY. VCH *Middlesex* vol. VIII (1988) covers Stoke Newington, vol. X (1995) the old parish of Hackney. The main c19 histories are again by William Robinson, *History and Antiquities of the Parish of Hackney* (1843), and *The History and Antiquities of the Parish of Stoke Newington*. Annotated collections of photographs include several by the borough archivist David Mander: *The London Borough of Hackney in old photographs* (1989 and 1991), and *Hackney, Homerton & Dalston; prints and engravings 1720–1948* (1996), Isobel Watson's *Gentlemen in the Building Line* (1989) is a detailed study of the development of South Hackney. The Hackney Society's many excellent publications began with *From Tower to Tower Block* (1979) and Michael Hunter's admirable *Victorian Villas of Hackney* (1981). *Hackney History* is published by the Friends of Hackney Archives, (vol. I, 1995).

Shoreditch: *Survey of London* vol. 8, *The Parish of St Leonard Shoreditch* (1922), deals with the development of the area up to the c18. More recent history is covered by the Hackney Society's survey: *South Shoreditch, Historic and Industrial Buildings* (1986), Christopher Miele, *Hoxton* (Hackney Society, 1993), and David Mander, *More Light More Power, an illustrated history of Shoreditch* (1996).

On individual subjects: T. F. Bumpus, *An Historical London Church, St Matthias Stoke Newington* (1913), Neil Burton, *The Geffrye Almshouses* (1979), David Mander, *St John-at-Hackney* (1993), Elizabeth McKellar, *The German Hospital at Hackney* (1991), Charles Poulsen, *Victoria Park*, (1976), Paul Joyce, *A Guide to Abney Park Cemetery* (1984). *Survey of London* monographs of 1904 and 1960 provide a record of the demolished Brooke House, Hackney. Other buildings are discussed in Elizabeth Robinson, *Lost Hackney* (1989).

HARINGEY. For Highgate *see also* Camden, St Pancras. VCH *Middlesex* vol. VI (1980) covers Hornsey, including Highgate. Much has been published by the Hornsey Historical Society; in addition to articles in its *Bulletin* (1973 onwards) and short guided walks in different areas. Useful general surveys include K. Gay, *From Forest to*

*Suburb* (1988), Jack Whitelaw, *The Growth of Muswell Hill* (1995), A. Aris et al., *Lost Houses of Haringey,* (1986), Joan Schwitzer (ed.) *People and Places* (1996), Joan Schwitzer and Ken Gay, *Highgate and Muswell Hill* (Archive Photograph series, 1995). R. Williams, *Herbert Collins 1885–1875* (1985) includes Collins' work at Muswell Hill.

Tottenham (including Wood Green) has a c19 history by William Robinson (1818, revised 1840) and is covered by VCH *Middlesex* vol. v (1979). On individual sites: J.M.M. Dalby, *Tottenham Parish Church and Parish* (1971), Ken Gay, *Palace on the Hill, Alexandra Palace and Park* (1992), R. Thorne, 'The White Hart Lane Estate. An LCC venture in suburban development', *Lon. Journal* 12 (1985)

ISLINGTON. The standard c19 works are J. Nelson, *History, Topography and Antiquities of the Parish of Islington* (1811), E.W. Brayley, *A Series of Views in Islington and Pentonville* (1819), and S. Lewis, *History and Topography of the Parish of St Mary Islington* (1842). More recent short surveys are by Pieter Zwart, *Islington, a history and a guide* (1973), Charles Harris, *Islington* (1974); comprehensive coverage of the parish of Islington is in VCH *Middlesex* vol. VIII (1988). *Islington Chapels* by Philip Temple (Survey of London, RCHME, 1992), is a pioneeringly comprehensive architectural survey with detailed gazetteer.

Well-researched studies on particular areas are two excellent books by Mary Cosh on *The Squares of Islington*, (1990, 1993), and Tanis Hinchcliffe, 'Highbury New Park, A Nineteenth Century Middle Class Suburb', *Lon. Journal*, 7 (1981). Good short accounts published by the Islington Archaeology and History Society are *Clerkenwell* (1980), *The New River* (1982), and *Barnsbury* (1981), all by Mary Cosh, and *History of Highbury* by Keith Sugden (1984).

On individual buildings early antiquarian studies are J.N. Nichols, *History and Antiquities of Canonbury,* 1790, and J. Nelson, *Canonbury House* (1811). Chris Draper, *Islington Cinemas and Film Studios* (n.d.) has a useful gazetteer. *The Hospital on the Hill* (1985) is a history by the Friends of Whittington Hospital. On c20 Finsbury *see* John Allan, *Berthold Lubetkin* (1992). The parish of Clerkenwell will be the subject of two forthcoming *Survey of London* volumes, one of them devoted to the Charterhouse. D. Knowles and W.F. Grimes, *Charterhouse* (1954) discusses the building in the light of the post-war excavations. On excavations at St John's Priory, *see* Kevin Wooldridge in *Lon. and Middlesex Archaeol. Transactions* 39 (1987). The Vergara monument at St John's Priory is discussed by Marjorie Trusted in *Varia* (Universidad de Valladolid, 1987).

# GLOSSARY

Numbers and letters refer to the illustrations (by John Sambrook) on pp. 728–35.

ABACUS: flat slab forming the top of a capital (3a).

ACANTHUS: classical formalized leaf ornament (4b).

ACCUMULATOR TOWER: see Hydraulic power.

ACHIEVEMENT: a complete display of armorial bearings.

ACROTERION: plinth for a statue or ornament on the apex or ends of a pediment; more usually, both the plinth and what stands on it (4a).

AEDICULE (*lit.* little building): architectural surround, consisting usually of two columns or pilasters supporting a pediment.

AGGREGATE: see Concrete.

AISLE: subsidiary space alongside the body of a building, separated from it by columns, piers, or posts.

AMBULATORY (*lit.* walkway): aisle around the sanctuary (q.v.).

ANGLE ROLL: roll moulding in the angle between two planes (1a).

ANSE DE PANIER: see Arch.

ANTAE: simplified pilasters (4a), usually applied to the ends of the enclosing walls of a portico *in antis* (q.v.).

ANTEFIXAE: ornaments projecting at regular intervals above a Greek cornice, originally to conceal the ends of roof tiles (4a).

ANTHEMION: classical ornament like a honeysuckle flower (4b).

APRON: raised panel below a window or wall monument or tablet.

APSE: semicircular or polygonal end of an apartment, especially of a chancel or chapel. In classical architecture sometimes called an *exedra*.

ARABESQUE: non-figurative surface decoration consisting of flowing lines, foliage scrolls etc., based on geometrical patterns. Cf. Grotesque.

ARCADE: series of arches supported by piers or columns. *Blind arcade* or *arcading*: the same applied to the wall surface. *Wall arcade*: in medieval churches, a blind arcade forming a dado below windows. Also a covered shopping street.

ARCH: Shapes *see* 5c. *Basket arch* or *anse de panier* (basket handle): three-centred and depressed, or with a flat centre. *Nodding*: ogee arch curving forward from the wall face. *Parabolic*: shaped like a chain suspended from two level points, but inverted. Special purposes. *Chancel*: dividing chancel from nave or crossing. *Crossing*: spanning piers at a crossing (q.v.). *Relieving or discharging*: incorporated in a wall to relieve superimposed weight (5c). *Skew*: spanning responds not diametrically opposed. *Strainer*: inserted in an opening to resist inward pressure. *Transverse*: spanning a main axis (e.g. of a vaulted space). *See also* Jack arch, Triumphal arch.

ARCHITRAVE: formalized lintel, the lowest member of the classical entablature (3a). Also the moulded frame of a door or window (often borrowing the profile of a classical architrave). For *lugged* and *shouldered* architraves *see* 4b.

ARCUATED: dependent structurally on the arch principle. Cf. Trabeated.

ARK: chest or cupboard housing the

tables of Jewish law in a synagogue.

ARRIS: sharp edge where two surfaces meet at an angle (3a).

ASHLAR: masonry of large blocks wrought to even faces and square edges (6d).

ASTRAGAL: classical moulding of semicircular section (3f).

ASTYLAR: with no columns or similar vertical features.

ATLANTES: see Caryatids.

ATRIUM (plural: atria): inner court of a Roman or C20 house; in a multi-storey building, a toplit covered court rising through all storeys. Also an open court in front of a church.

ATTACHED COLUMN: see Engaged column.

ATTIC: small top storey within a roof. Also the storey above the main entablature of a classical façade.

AUMBRY: recess or cupboard to hold sacred vessels for the Mass.

BAILEY: see Motte-and-bailey.

BALANCE BEAM: see Canals.

BALDACCHINO: free-standing canopy, originally fabric, over an altar. Cf. Ciborium.

BALLFLOWER: globular flower of three petals enclosing a ball (1a). Typical of the Decorated style.

BALUSTER: pillar or pedestal of bellied form. *Balusters*: vertical supports of this or any other form, for a handrail or coping, the whole being called a *balustrade* (6c). *Blind balustrade*: the same applied to the wall surface.

BARBICAN: outwork defending the entrance to a castle.

BARGEBOARDS (corruption of 'vergeboards'): boards, often carved or fretted, fixed beneath the eaves of a gable to cover and protect the rafters.

BAROQUE: style originating in Rome *c*.1600 and current in England *c*.1680–1720, characterized by dramatic massing and silhouette and the use of the giant order.

BARROW: burial mound.

BARTIZAN: corbelled turret, square or round, frequently at an angle.

BASCULE: hinged part of a lifting (or bascule) bridge.

BASE: moulded foot of a column or pilaster. For *Attic* base *see* 3b.

BASEMENT: lowest, subordinate storey; hence the lowest part of a classical elevation, below the piano nobile (q.v.).

BASILICA: a Roman public hall; hence an aisled building with a clerestory.

BASTION: one of a series of defensive semicircular or polygonal projections from the main wall of a fortress or city.

BATTER: intentional inward inclination of a wall face.

BATTLEMENT: defensive parapet, composed of *merlons* (solid) and *crenels* (embrasures) through which archers could shoot; sometimes called *crenellation*. Also used decoratively.

BAY: division of an elevation or interior space as defined by regular vertical features such as arches, columns, windows etc.

BAY LEAF: classical ornament of overlapping bay leaves (3f).

BAY WINDOW: window of one or more storeys projecting from the face of a building. *Canted*: with a straight front and angled sides. *Bow window*: curved. *Oriel*: rests on corbels or brackets and starts above ground level; also the bay window at the dais end of a medieval great hall.

BEAD-AND-REEL: see Enrichments.

BEAKHEAD: Norman ornament with a row of beaked bird or beast heads usually biting into a roll moulding (1a).

BELFRY: chamber or stage in a tower where bells are hung.

BELL CAPITAL: see 1b.

BELLCOTE: small gabled or roofed housing for the bell(s).

BERM: level area separating a ditch from a bank on a hill-fort or barrow.

BILLET: Norman ornament of small half-cyclindrical or rectangular blocks (1a).

BLIND: see Arcade, Baluster, Portico.

BLOCK CAPITAL: see 1a.

BLOCKED: columns, etc. interrupted by regular projecting blocks (*blocking*), as on a Gibbs surround (4b).

BLOCKING COURSE: course of stones, or equivalent, on top of a cornice and crowning the wall.

BOLECTION MOULDING: covering the joint between two different planes (6b).

BOND: the pattern of long sides (*stretchers*) and short ends (*headers*) produced on the face of a wall by laying bricks in a particular way (6e).

BOSS: knob or projection, e.g. at the intersection of ribs in a vault (2c).

BOW WINDOW: *see* Bay window.

BOX FRAME: timber-framed construction in which vertical and horizontal wall members support the roof (7). Also concrete construction where the loads are taken on cross walls; also called *cross-wall construction*.

BRACE: subsidiary member of a structural frame, curved or straight. *Bracing* is often arranged decoratively e.g. quatrefoil, herringbone (7). *See also* Roofs.

BRATTISHING: ornamental crest, usually formed of leaves, Tudor flowers or miniature battlements.

BRESSUMER (*lit.* breast-beam): big horizontal beam supporting the wall above, especially in a jettied building (7).

BRICK: *see* Bond, Cogging, Engineering, Gauged, Tumbling.

BRIDGE: *Bowstring*: with arches rising above the roadway which is suspended from them. *Clapper*: one long stone forms the roadway. *Roving*: *see* Canal. *Suspension*: roadway suspended from cables or chains slung between towers or pylons. *Stay-suspension* or *stay-cantilever*: supported by diagonal stays from towers or pylons. *See also* Bascule.

BRISES-SOLEIL: projecting fins or canopies which deflect direct sunlight from windows.

BROACH: *see* Spire and 1c.

BUCRANIUM: ox skull used decoratively in classical friezes.

BULLSEYE WINDOW: small oval window, set horizontally (cf. Oculus). Also called *oeil de boeuf*.

BUTTRESS: vertical member projecting from a wall to stabilize it or to resist the lateral thrust of an arch, roof, or vault (1c, 2c). A *flying buttress* transmits the thrust to a heavy abutment by means of an arch or half-arch (1c).

CABLE OR ROPE MOULDING: originally Norman, like twisted strands of a rope.

CAMES: *see* Quarries.

CAMPANILE: free-standing bell tower.

CANALS: *Flash lock*: removable weir or similar device through which boats pass on a flush of water. Predecessor of the *pound lock*: chamber with gates at each end allowing boats to float from one level to another. *Tidal gates*: single pair of lock gates allowing vessels to pass when the tide makes a level. *Balance beam*: beam projecting horizontally for opening and closing lock gates. *Roving bridge*: carrying a towing path from one bank to the other.

CANTILEVER: horizontal projection (e.g. step, canopy) supported by a downward force behind the fulcrum.

CAPITAL: head or crowning feature of a column or pilaster; for classical types *see* 3; for medieval types *see* 1b.

CARREL: compartment designed for individual work or study.

CARTOUCHE: classical tablet with ornate frame (4b).

CARYATIDS: female figures supporting an entablature; their male counterparts are *Atlantes* (*lit.* Atlas figures).

CASEMATE: vaulted chamber, with embrasures for defence, within a castle wall or projecting from it.

CASEMENT: side-hinged window.

CASTELLATED: with battlements (q.v.).

CAST IRON: hard and brittle, cast in a mould to the required shape. *Wrought iron* is ductile, strong in tension, forged into decorative patterns or forged and rolled into e.g. bars, joists, boiler plates; *mild steel* is its modern equivalent, similar but stronger.

CATSLIDE: *See* 8a.

CAVETTO: concave classical mould-ing of quarter-round section (3f).

CELURE OR CEILURE: enriched area of roof above rood or altar.

CEMENT: *see* Concrete.

CENOTAPH (*lit.* empty tomb): funer-ary monument which is not a burying place.

CENTRING: wooden support for the building of an arch or vault, removed after completion.

CHAMFER (*lit.* corner-break): sur-face formed by cutting off a square edge or corner. For types of cham-fers and *chamfer stops see* 6a. *See also* Double chamfer.

CHANCEL: part of the E end of a church set apart for the use of the officiating clergy.

CHANTRY CHAPEL: often attached to or within a church, endowed for the celebration of Masses prin-cipally for the soul of the founder.

CHEVET (*lit.* head): French term for chancel with ambulatory and radi-ating chapels.

CHEVRON: V-shape used in series or double series (later) on a Norman moulding (1a). Also (especially when on a single plane) called *zigzag*.

CHOIR: the part of a cathedral, mon-astic or collegiate church where services are sung.

CIBORIUM: a fixed canopy over an altar, usually vaulted and sup-ported on four columns; cf. Bal-dacchino. Also a canopied shrine for the reserved sacrament.

CINQUEFOIL: *see* Foil.

CIST: stone-lined or slab-built grave.

CLADDING: external covering or skin applied to a structure, especially a framed one.

CLERESTORY: uppermost storey of the nave of a church, pierced by windows. Also high-level windows in secular buildings.

CLOSER: a brick cut to complete a bond (6e).

CLUSTER BLOCK: *see* Multi-storey.

COADE STONE: ceramic artificial stone made in Lambeth 1769–c.1840 by Eleanor Coade (†1821) and her associates.

COB: walling material of clay mixed with straw. Also called *pisé*.

COFFERING: arrangement of sun-ken panels (coffers), square or polygonal, decorating a ceiling, vault, or arch.

COGGING: a decorative course of bricks laid diagonally (6e). Cf. Dentilation.

COLLAR: *see* Roofs and 7.

COLLEGIATE CHURCH: endowed for the support of a college of priests.

COLONNADE: range of columns supporting an entablature. Cf. Arcade.

COLONNETTE: small medieval column or shaft.

COLOSSAL ORDER: *see* Giant order.

COLUMBARIUM: shelved, niched structure to house multiple burials.

COLUMN: a classical, upright struc-tural member of round section with a shaft, a capital, and usually a base (3a, 4a).

COLUMN FIGURE: carved figure attached to a medieval column or shaft, usually flanking a doorway.

COMMUNION TABLE: unconsec-rated table used in Protestant churches for the celebration of Holy Communion.

COMPOSITE: *see* Orders.

COMPOUND PIER: grouped shafts (q.v.), or a solid core surrounded by shafts.

CONCRETE: composition of *cement* (calcined lime and clay), *aggregate* (small stones or rock chippings), sand and water. It can be poured into *formwork* or *shuttering* (temporary frame of timber or metal) on site (*in-situ* concrete), or *pre-cast* as components before construction. *Reinforced*: incor-porating steel rods to take the tensile force. *Pre-stressed*: with ten-sioned steel rods. Finishes include the impression of boards left by formwork (*board-marked* or *shut-tered*), and texturing with steel brushes (*brushed*) or hammers (*hammer-dressed*). *See also* Shell.

CONSOLE: bracket of curved outline (4b).

COPING: protective course of masonry or brickwork capping a wall (6d).

CORBEL: projecting block supporting something above. *Corbel course*: continuous course of projecting stones or bricks fulfilling the same function. *Corbel table*: series of corbels to carry a parapet or a wall-plate or wall-post (7). *Corbelling*: brick or masonry courses built out beyond one another to support a chimney-stack, window, etc.

CORINTHIAN: *see* Orders and 3d.

CORNICE: flat-topped ledge with moulded underside, projecting along the top of a building or feature, especially as the highest member of the classical entablature (3a). Also the decorative moulding in the angle between wall and ceiling.

CORPS-DE-LOGIS: the main building(s) as distinct from the wings or pavilions.

COTTAGE ORNÉ: an artfully rustic small house associated with the Picturesque movement.

COUNTERCHANGING: of joists on a ceiling divided by beams into compartments, when placed in opposite directions in alternate squares.

COUR D'HONNEUR: formal entrance court before a house in the French manner, usually with flanking wings and a screen wall or gates.

COURSE: continuous layer of stones, etc. in a wall (6e).

COVE: a broad concave moulding, e.g. to mask the eaves of a roof. *Coved ceiling*: with a pronounced cove joining the walls to a flat central panel smaller than the whole area of the ceiling.

CRADLE ROOF: *see* Wagon roof.

CREDENCE: a shelf within or beside a piscina (q.v.), or a table for the sacramental elements and vessels.

CRENELLATION: parapet with crenels (*see* Battlement).

CRINKLE-CRANKLE WALL: garden wall undulating in a series of serpentine curves.

CROCKETS: leafy hooks. *Crocketing* decorates the edges of Gothic features, such as pinnacles, canopies, etc. *Crocket capital*: *see* 1b.

CROSSING: central space at the junction of the nave, chancel, and transepts. *Crossing tower*: above a crossing.

CROSS-WINDOW: with one mullion and one transom (qq.v.).

CROWN-POST: *see* Roofs and 7.

CROWSTEPS: squared stones set like steps, e.g. on a gable (8a).

CRUCKS (*lit.* crooked): pairs of inclined timbers (*blades*), usually curved, set at bay-lengths; they support the roof timbers and, in timber buildings, also support the walls (8b). *Base*: blades rise from ground level to a tie- or collar-beam which supports the roof timbers. *Full*: blades rise from ground level to the apex of the roof, serving as the main members of a roof truss. *Jointed*: blades formed from more than one timber; the lower member may act as a wall-post; it is usually elbowed at wall-plate level and jointed just above. *Middle*: blades rise from halfway up the walls to a tie- or collar-beam. *Raised*: blades rise from halfway up the walls to the apex. *Upper*: blades supported on a tie-beam and rising to the apex.

CRYPT: underground or half-underground area, usually below the E end of a church. *Ring crypt*: corridor crypt surrounding the apse of an early medieval church, often associated with chambers for relics. Cf. Undercroft.

CUPOLA (*lit.* dome): especially a small dome on a circular or polygonal base crowning a larger dome, roof, or turret.

CURSUS: a long avenue defined by two parallel earthen banks with ditches outside.

CURTAIN WALL: a connecting wall between the towers of a castle. Also a non-load-bearing external wall applied to a C20 framed structure.

CUSP: *see* Tracery and 2b.

CYCLOPEAN MASONRY: large irregular polygonal stones, smooth and finely jointed.

CYMA RECTA and CYMA REVERSA: classical mouldings with double curves (3f). Cf. Ogee.

DADO: the finishing (often with panelling) of the lower part of a wall in a classical interior; in origin a formalized continuous pedestal. *Dado rail*: the moulding along the top of the dado.

DAGGER: *see* Tracery and 2b.

DEC (DECORATED): English Gothic architecture *c.* 1290 to *c.* 1350. The name is derived from the type of window tracery (q.v.) used during the period.

DEMI- or HALF-COLUMNS: engaged columns (q.v.) half of whose circumference projects from the wall.

DENTIL: small square block used in series in classical cornices (3c). *Dentilation* is produced by the projection of alternating headers along cornices or stringcourses.

DIAPER: repetitive surface decoration of lozenges or squares flat or in relief. Achieved in brickwork with bricks of two colours.

DIOCLETIAN OR THERMAL WINDOW: semicircular with two mullions, as used in the Baths of Diocletian, Rome (4b).

DISTYLE: having two columns (4a).

DOGTOOTH: E.E. ornament, consisting of a series of small pyramids formed by four stylized canine teeth meeting at a point (1a).

DORIC: *see* Orders and 3a, 3b.

DORMER: window projecting from the slope of a roof (8a).

DOUBLE CHAMFER: a chamfer applied to each of two recessed arches (1a).

DOUBLE PILE: *see* Pile.

DRAGON BEAM: *see* Jetty.

DRESSINGS: the stone or brickwork worked to a finished face about an angle, opening, or other feature.

DRIPSTONE: moulded stone projecting from a wall to protect the lower parts from water. Cf. Hoodmould, Weathering.

DRUM: circular or polygonal stage supporting a dome or cupola. Also one of the stones forming the shaft of a column (3a).

DUTCH or FLEMISH GABLE: *see* 8a.

EASTER SEPULCHRE: tomb-chest used for Easter ceremonial, within or against the N wall of a chancel.

EAVES: overhanging edge of a roof; hence *eaves cornice* in this position.

ECHINUS: ovolo moulding (q.v.) below the abacus of a Greek Doric capital (3a).

EDGE RAIL: *see* Railways.

E.E. (EARLY ENGLISH): English Gothic architecture *c.* 1190–1250.

EGG-AND-DART: *see* Enrichments and 3f.

ELEVATION: any face of a building or side of a room. In a drawing, the same or any part of it, represented in two dimensions.

EMBATTLED: with battlements.

EMBRASURE: small splayed opening in a wall or battlement (q.v.).

ENCAUSTIC TILES: earthenware tiles fired with a pattern and glaze.

EN DELIT: stone cut against the bed.

ENFILADE: reception rooms in a formal series, usually with all doorways on axis.

ENGAGED or ATTACHED COLUMN: one that partly merges into a wall or pier.

ENGINEERING BRICKS: dense bricks, originally used mostly for railway viaducts etc.

ENRICHMENTS: the carved decoration of certain classical mouldings, e.g. the ovolo (qq.v.) with *egg-and-dart*, the cyma reversa with *waterleaf*, the astragal with *bead-and-reel* (3f).

ENTABLATURE: in classical architecture, collective name for the three horizontal members (architrave, frieze, and cornice) carried by a wall or a column (3a).

ENTASIS: very slight convex deviation from a straight line, used to prevent an optical illusion of concavity.

EPITAPH: inscription on a tomb.

EXEDRA: *see* Apse.

EXTRADOS: outer curved face of an arch or vault.

EYECATCHER: decorative building terminating a vista.

FASCIA: plain horizontal band, e.g. in an architrave (3c, 3d) or on a shop front.

FENESTRATION: the arrangement of windows in a façade.

FERETORY: site of the chief shrine of a church, behind the high altar.

FESTOON: ornamental garland, suspended from both ends. Cf. Swag.

FIBREGLASS, or glass-reinforced polyester (GRP): synthetic resin reinforced with glass fibre. GRC: glass-reinforced concrete.

FIELD: see Panelling and 6b.

FILLET: a narrow flat band running down a medieval shaft or along a roll moulding (1a). It separates larger curved mouldings in classical cornices, fluting or bases (3c).

FLAMBOYANT: the latest phase of French Gothic architecture, with flowing tracery.

FLASH LOCK: see Canals.

FLÈCHE or SPIRELET (*lit.* arrow): slender spire on the centre of a roof.

FLEURON: medieval carved flower or leaf, often rectilinear (1a).

FLUSHWORK: knapped flint used with dressed stone to form patterns.

FLUTING: series of concave grooves (flutes), their common edges sharp (arris) or blunt (fillet) (3).

FOIL (*lit.* leaf): lobe formed by the cusping of a circular or other shape in tracery (2b). *Trefoil* (three), *quatrefoil* (four), *cinquefoil* (five), and *multifoil* express the number of lobes in a shape.

FOLIATE: decorated with leaves.

FORMWORK: see Concrete.

FRAMED BUILDING: where the structure is carried by a framework – e.g. of steel, reinforced concrete, timber – instead of by load-bearing walls.

FREESTONE: stone that is cut, or can be cut, in all directions.

FRESCO: *al fresco*: painting on wet plaster. *Fresco secco*: painting on dry plaster.

FRIEZE: the middle member of the classical entablature, sometimes ornamented (3a). *Pulvinated frieze* (*lit.* cushioned): of bold convex profile (3c). Also a horizontal band of ornament.

FRONTISPIECE: in C16 and C17 buildings the central feature of doorway and windows above linked in one composition.

GABLE: For types *see* 8a. *Gablet*: small gable. *Pedimental gable*: treated like a pediment.

GADROONING: classical ribbed ornament like inverted fluting that flows into a lobed edge.

GALILEE: chapel or vestibule usually at the W end of a church enclosing the main portal(s).

GALLERY: a long room or passage; an upper storey above the aisle of a church, looking through arches to the nave; a balcony or mezzanine overlooking the main interior space of a building; or an external walkway.

GALLETING: small stones set in a mortar course.

GAMBREL ROOF: see 8a.

GARDEROBE: medieval privy.

GARGOYLE: projecting water spout often carved into human or animal shape.

GAUGED or RUBBED BRICKWORK: soft brick sawn roughly, then rubbed to a precise (gauged) surface. Mostly used for door or window openings (5c).

GAZEBO (jocular Latin, 'I shall gaze'): ornamental lookout tower or raised summer house.

GEOMETRIC: English Gothic architecture c. 1250–1310. *See also* Tracery. For another meaning, *see* Stairs.

GIANT or COLOSSAL ORDER: classical order (q.v.) whose height is that of two or more storeys of the building to which it is applied.

GIBBS SURROUND: C18 treatment of an opening (4b), seen particularly in the work of James Gibbs (1682–1754).

GIRDER: a large beam. *Box*: of hollow-box section. *Bowed*: with its top rising in a curve. *Plate*: of I-section, made from iron or steel plates. *Lattice*: with braced framework.

GLAZING BARS: wooden or sometimes metal bars separating and supporting window panes.

GRAFFITI: *see* Sgraffito.

GRANGE: farm owned and run by a religious order.

GRC: *see* Fibreglass.

GRISAILLE: monochrome painting on walls or glass.

GROIN: sharp edge at the meeting of two cells of a cross-vault; *see* Vault and 2c.

GROTESQUE (*lit.* grotto-esque): wall decoration adopted from Roman examples in the Renaissance. Its foliage scrolls incorporate figurative elements. Cf. Arabesque.

GROTTO: artificial cavern.

GRP: *see* Fibreglass.

GUILLOCHE: classical ornament of interlaced bands (4b).

GUNLOOP: opening for a firearm.

GUTTAE: stylized drops (3b).

HALF-TIMBERING: archaic term for timber-framing (q.v.). Sometimes used for non-structural decorative timberwork.

HALL CHURCH: medieval church with nave and aisles of approximately equal height.

HAMMERBEAM: *see* Roofs and 7.

HAMPER: in C20 architecture, a visually distinct topmost storey or storeys.

HEADER: *see* Bond and 6e.

HEADSTOP: stop (q.v.) carved with a head (5b).

HELM ROOF: *see* IC.

HENGE: ritual earthwork.

HERM (*lit.* the god Hermes): male head or bust on a pedestal.

HERRINGBONE WORK: *see* 7ii. Cf. Pitched masonry.

HEXASTYLE: *see* Portico.

HILL-FORT: Iron Age earthwork enclosed by a ditch and bank system.

HIPPED ROOF: *see* 8a.

HOODMOULD: projecting moulding above an arch or lintel to throw off water (2b, 5b). When horizontal often called a *label*. For label stop *see* Stop.

HUSK GARLAND: festoon of stylized nutshells (4b).

HYDRAULIC POWER: use of water under high pressure to work machinery. *Accumulator tower*: houses a hydraulic accumulator which accommodates fluctuations in the flow through hydraulic mains.

HYPOCAUST (*lit.* underburning): Roman underfloor heating system.

IMPOST: horizontal moulding at the springing of an arch (5c).

IMPOST BLOCK: block between abacus and capital (1b).

IN ANTIS: *see* Antae, Portico and 4a.

INDENT: shape chiselled out of a stone to receive a brass.

INDUSTRIALIZED or SYSTEM BUILDING: system of manufactured units assembled on site.

INGLENOOK (*lit.* fire-corner): recess for a hearth with provision for seating.

INTERCOLUMNATION: interval between columns.

INTERLACE: decoration in relief simulating woven or entwined stems or bands.

INTRADOS: *see* Soffit.

IONIC: *see* Orders and 3c.

JACK ARCH: shallow segmental vault springing from beams, used for fireproof floors, bridge decks, etc.

JAMB (*lit.* leg): one of the vertical sides of an opening.

JETTY: in a timber-framed building, the projection of an upper storey beyond the storey below, made by the beams and joists of the lower storey oversailing the wall; on their outer ends is placed the sill of the walling for the storey above (7). Buildings can be jettied on several sides, in which case a *dragon beam* is set diagonally at the corner to carry the joists to either side.

JOGGLE: the joining of two stones to prevent them slipping by a notch in one and a projection in the other.

KEEL MOULDING: moulding used from the late C12, in section like the keel of a ship (1a).

KEEP: principal tower of a castle.

KENTISH CUSP: *see* Tracery and 2b.

KEY PATTERN: *see* 4b.

KEYSTONE: central stone in an arch or vault (4b, 5c).

KINGPOST: *see* Roofs and 7.

KNEELER: horizontal projecting stone at the base of each side of a gable to support the inclined coping stones (8a).

LABEL: *see* Hoodmould and 5b.

LABEL STOP: *see* Stop and 5b.

LACED BRICKWORK: vertical strips of brickwork, often in a contrasting colour, linking openings on different floors.

LACING COURSE: horizontal reinforcement in timber or brick to walls of flint, cobble, etc.

LADY CHAPEL: dedicated to the Virgin Mary (Our Lady).

LANCET: slender single-light, pointed-arched window (2a).

LANTERN: circular or polygonal windowed turret crowning a roof or a dome. Also the windowed stage of a crossing tower lighting the church interior.

LANTERN CROSS: churchyard cross with lantern-shaped top.

LAVATORIUM: in a religious house, a washing place adjacent to the refectory.

LEAN-TO: *see* Roofs.

LESENE (*lit.* a mean thing): pilaster without base or capital. Also called *pilaster strip*.

LIERNE: *see* Vault and 2c.

LIGHT: compartment of a window defined by the mullions.

LINENFOLD: Tudor panelling carved with simulations of folded linen. *See also* Parchemin.

LINTEL: horizontal beam or stone bridging an opening.

LOGGIA: gallery, usually arcaded or colonnaded; sometimes freestanding.

LONG-AND-SHORT WORK: quoins consisting of stones placed with the long side alternately upright and horizontal, especially in Saxon building.

LONGHOUSE: house and byre in the same range with internal access between them.

LOUVRE: roof opening, often protected by a raised timber structure, to allow the smoke from a central hearth to escape.

LOWSIDE WINDOW: set lower than the others in a chancel side wall, usually towards its w end.

LUCAM: projecting housing for hoist pulley on upper storey of warehouses, mills, etc., for raising goods to loading doors.

LUCARNE (*lit.* dormer): small gabled opening in a roof or spire.

LUGGED ARCHITRAVE: *see* 4b.

LUNETTE: semicircular window or blind panel.

LYCHGATE (*lit.* corpse-gate): roofed gateway entrance to a churchyard for the reception of a coffin.

LYNCHET: long terraced strip of soil on the downward side of prehistoric and medieval fields, accumulated because of continual ploughing along the contours.

MACHICOLATIONS (*lit.* mashing devices): series of openings between the corbels that support a projecting parapet through which missiles can be dropped. Used decoratively in post-medieval buildings.

MANOMETER or STANDPIPE TOWER: containing a column of water to regulate pressure in water mains.

MANSARD: *see* 8a.

MATHEMATICAL TILES: facing tiles with the appearance of brick, most often applied to timber-framed walls.

MAUSOLEUM: monumental building or chamber usually intended for the burial of members of one family.

MEGALITHIC TOMB: massive stone-built Neolithic burial chamber covered by an earth or stone mound.

MERLON: *see* Battlement.

METOPES: spaces between the triglyphs in a Doric frieze (3b).

MEZZANINE: low storey between two higher ones.

MILD STEEL: *see* Cast iron.

MISERICORD (*lit.* mercy): shelf on a carved bracket placed on the underside of a hinged choir stall seat to support an occupant when standing.

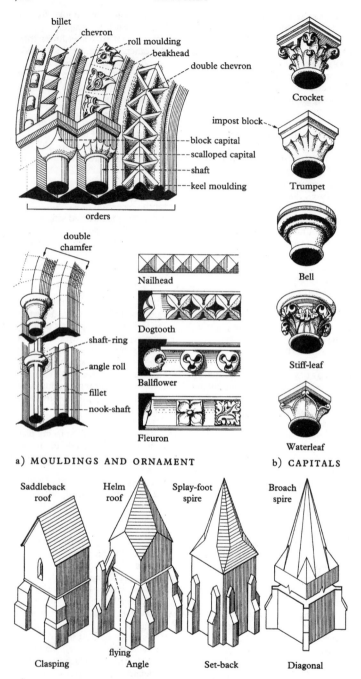

a) MOULDINGS AND ORNAMENT          b) CAPITALS

c) BUTTRESSES, ROOFS AND SPIRES

FIGURE I: MEDIEVAL

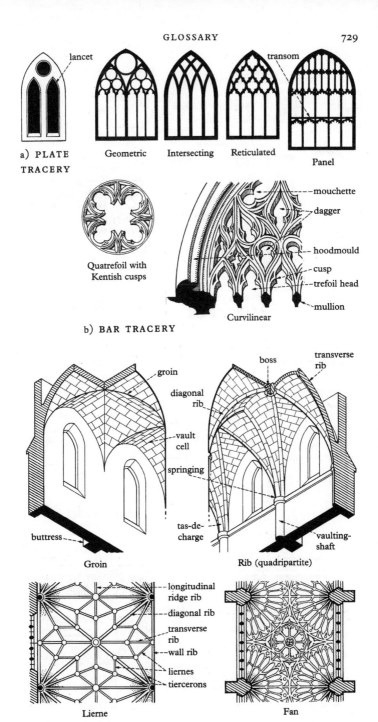

a) PLATE TRACERY — lancet

Geometric   Intersecting   Reticulated — transom   Panel

b) BAR TRACERY

Quatrefoil with Kentish cusps

Curvilinear — mouchette, dagger, hoodmould, cusp, trefoil head, mullion

c) VAULTS

Groin — groin, diagonal rib, vault cell, buttress

Rib (quadripartite) — boss, transverse rib, springing, tas-de-charge, vaulting-shaft

Lierne — longitudinal ridge rib, diagonal rib, transverse rib, wall rib, liernes, tiercerons

Fan

FIGURE 2: MEDIEVAL

# ORDERS

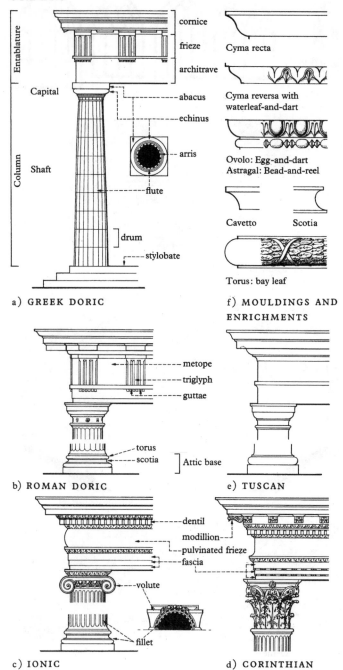

a) GREEK DORIC

f) MOULDINGS AND
ENRICHMENTS

b) ROMAN DORIC

e) TUSCAN

c) IONIC

d) CORINTHIAN

FIGURE 3: CLASSICAL

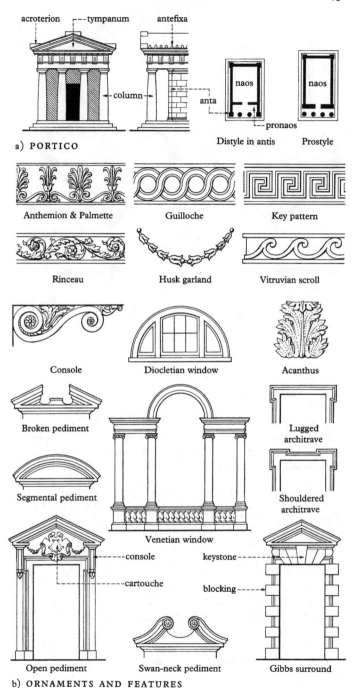

a) PORTICO

acroterion · tympanum · antefixa · column · anta · pronaos · naos · naos

Distyle in antis · Prostyle

Anthemion & Palmette · Guilloche · Key pattern

Rinceau · Husk garland · Vitruvian scroll

Console · Diocletian window · Acanthus

Broken pediment · Lugged architrave

Segmental pediment · Shouldered architrave

Venetian window

console · cartouche · keystone · blocking

Open pediment · Swan-neck pediment · Gibbs surround

b) ORNAMENTS AND FEATURES

FIGURE 4: CLASSICAL

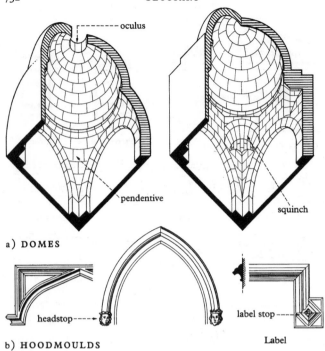

a) DOMES

b) HOODMOULDS

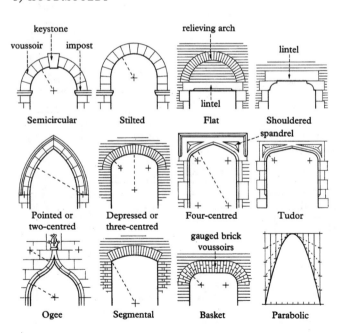

c) ARCHES

FIGURE 5: CONSTRUCTION

GLOSSARY 733

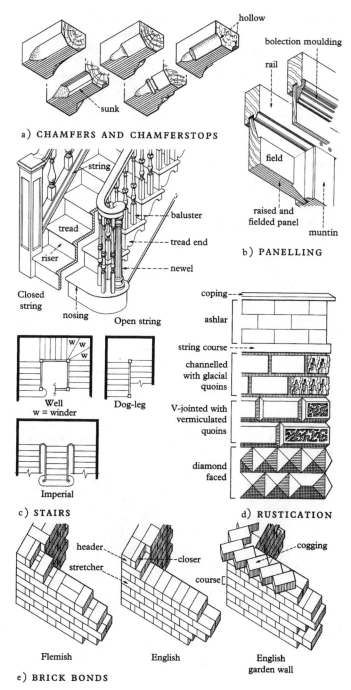

a) CHAMFERS AND CHAMFERSTOPS

b) PANELLING

c) STAIRS

d) RUSTICATION

e) BRICK BONDS

FIGURE 6: CONSTRUCTION

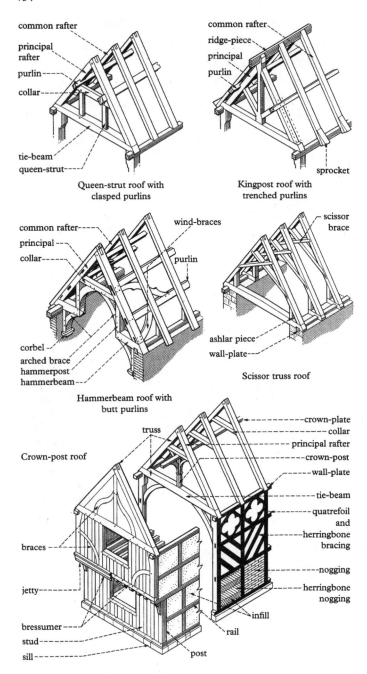

common rafter
principal rafter
purlin
collar
tie-beam
queen-strut

Queen-strut roof with
clasped purlins

common rafter
ridge-piece
principal
purlin
sprocket

Kingpost roof with
trenched purlins

common rafter
principal
collar
wind-braces
purlin
corbel
arched brace
hammerpost
hammerbeam

Hammerbeam roof with
butt purlins

scissor brace
ashlar piece
wall-plate

Scissor truss roof

Crown-post roof

truss
crown-plate
collar
principal rafter
crown-post
wall-plate
tie-beam
quatrefoil and herringbone bracing
nogging
herringbone nogging
braces
jetty
bressumer
stud
sill
post
rail
infill

Box frame:  i) Close studding     ii) Square panel

FIGURE 7: ROOFS AND TIMBER-FRAMING

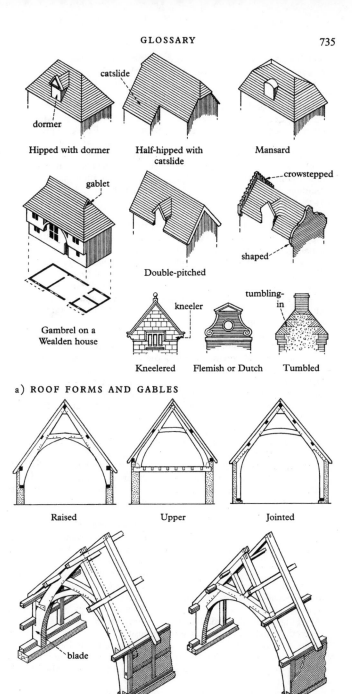

a) ROOF FORMS AND GABLES

b) CRUCK FRAMES

FIGURE 8: ROOFS AND TIMBER-FRAMING

MIXER-COURTS: forecourts to groups of houses shared by vehicles and pedestrians.

MODILLIONS: small consoles (q.v.) along the underside of a Corinthian or Composite cornice (3d). Often used along an eaves cornice.

MODULE: a predetermined standard size for co-ordinating the dimensions of components of a building.

MOTTE-AND-BAILEY: post-Roman and Norman defence consisting of an earthen mound (motte) topped by a wooden tower within a bailey, an enclosure defended by a ditch and palisade, and also, sometimes, by an internal bank.

MOUCHETTE: see Tracery and 2b.

MOULDING: shaped ornamental strip of continuous section; see e.g. Cavetto, Cyma, Ovolo, Roll.

MULLION: vertical member between window lights (2b).

MULTI-STOREY: five or more storeys. Multi-storey flats may form a *cluster block*, with individual blocks of flats grouped round a service core; a *point block*: with flats fanning out from a service core; or a *slab block*, with flats approached by corridors or galleries from service cores at intervals or towers at the ends (plan also used for offices, hotels etc.). *Tower block* is a generic term for any very high multi-storey building.

MUNTIN: see Panelling and 6b.

NAILHEAD: E.E. ornament consisting of small pyramids regularly repeated (1a).

NARTHEX: enclosed vestibule or covered porch at the main entrance to a church.

NAVE: the body of a church w of the crossing or chancel often flanked by aisles (q.v.).

NEWEL: central or corner post of a staircase (6c). Newel stair: see Stairs.

NIGHT STAIR: stair by which religious entered the transept of their church from their dormitory to celebrate night services.

NOGGING: see Timber-framing (7).

NOOK-SHAFT: shaft set in the angle of a wall or opening (1a).

NORMAN: see Romanesque.

NOSING: projection of the tread of a step (6c).

NUTMEG: medieval ornament with a chain of tiny triangles placed obliquely.

OCULUS: circular opening.

OEIL DE BOEUF: see Bullseye window.

OGEE: double curve, bending first one way and then the other, as in an *ogee* or *ogival arch* (5c). Cf. Cyma recta and Cyma reversa.

OPUS SECTILE: decorative mosaic-like facing.

OPUS SIGNINUM: composition flooring of Roman origin.

ORATORY: a private chapel in a church or a house. Also a church of the Oratorian Order.

ORDER: one of a series of recessed arches and jambs forming a splayed medieval opening, e.g. a doorway or arcade arch (1a).

ORDERS: the formalized versions of the post-and-lintel system in classical architecture. The main orders are *Doric, Ionic,* and *Corinthian.* They are Greek in origin but occur in Roman versions. Tuscan is a simple version of Roman Doric. Though each order has its own conventions (3), there are many minor variations. The *Composite* capital combines Ionic volutes with Corinthian foliage. *Superimposed orders*: orders on successive levels, usually in the upward sequence of Tuscan, Doric, Ionic, Corinthian, Composite.

ORIEL: see Bay window.

OVERDOOR: painting or relief above an internal door. Also called a *sopraporta.*

OVERTHROW: decorative fixed arch between two gatepiers or above a wrought-iron gate.

OVOLO: wide convex moulding (3f).

PALIMPSEST: of a brass: where a metal plate has been reused by turning over the engraving on the back; of a wall-painting: where one overlaps and partly obscures an earlier one.

PALLADIAN: following the examples and principles of Andrea Palladio (1508–80).

PALMETTE: classical ornament like a palm shoot (4b).

PANELLING: wooden lining to interior walls, made up of vertical members (*muntins*) and horizontals (*rails*) framing panels: also called *wainscot*. *Raised and fielded*: with the central area of the panel (*field*) raised up (6b).

PANTILE: roof tile of S section.

PARAPET: wall for protection at any sudden drop, e.g. at the wall-head of a castle where it protects the *parapet walk* or wall-walk. Also used to conceal a roof.

PARCLOSE: *see* Screen.

PARGETTING (*lit.* plastering): exterior plaster decoration, either in relief or incised.

PARLOUR: in a religious house, a room where the religious could talk to visitors; in a medieval house, the semi-private living room below the solar (q.v.).

PARTERRE: level space in a garden laid out with low, formal beds.

PATERA (*lit.* plate): round or oval ornament in shallow relief.

PAVILION: ornamental building for occasional use; or projecting subdivision of a larger building, often at an angle or terminating a wing.

PEBBLEDASHING: *see* Rendering.

PEDESTAL: a tall block carrying a classical order, statue, vase, etc.

PEDIMENT: a formalized gable derived from that of a classical temple; also used over doors, windows, etc. For variations *see* 4b.

PENDENTIVE: spandrel between adjacent arches, supporting a drum, dome or vault and consequently formed as part of a hemisphere (5a).

PENTHOUSE: subsidiary structure with a lean-to roof. Also a separately roofed structure on top of a C20 multi-storey block.

PERIPTERAL: *see* Peristyle.

PERISTYLE: a colonnade all round the exterior of a classical building, as in a temple which is then said to be *peripteral*.

PERP (PERPENDICULAR): English Gothic architecture c. 1335–50 to c. 1530. The name is derived from the upright tracery panels then used (*see* Tracery and 2a).

PERRON: external stair to a doorway, usually of double-curved plan.

PEW: loosely, seating for the laity outside the chancel; strictly, an enclosed seat. *Box pew*: with equal high sides and a door.

PIANO NOBILE: principal floor of a classical building above a ground floor or basement and with a lesser storey overhead.

PIAZZA: formal urban open space surrounded by buildings.

PIER: large masonry or brick support, often for an arch. *See also* Compound pier.

PILASTER: flat representation of a classical column in shallow relief. *Pilaster strip*: *see* Lesene.

PILE: row of rooms. *Double pile*: two rows thick.

PILLAR: free-standing upright member of any section, not conforming to one of the orders (q.v.).

PILLAR PISCINA: *see* Piscina.

PILOTIS: C20 French term for pillars or stilts that support a building above an open ground floor.

PISCINA: basin for washing Mass vessels, provided with a drain; set in or against the wall to the S of an altar or free-standing (*pillar piscina*).

PISÉ: *see* Cob.

PITCHED MASONRY: laid on the diagonal, often alternately with opposing courses (*pitched and counterpitched* or *herringbone*).

PLATBAND: flat horizontal moulding between storeys. Cf. stringcourse.

PLATE RAIL: *see* Railways.

PLATEWAY: *see* Railways.

PLINTH: projecting courses at the

foot of a wall or column, generally chamfered or moulded at the top.

PODIUM: a continuous raised platform supporting a building; or a large block of two or three storeys beneath a multi-storey block of smaller area.

POINT BLOCK: *see* Multi-storey.

POINTING: exposed mortar jointing of masonry or brickwork. Types include *flush*, *recessed* and *tuck* (with a narrow channel filled with finer, whiter mortar).

POPPYHEAD: carved ornament of leaves and flowers as a finial for a bench end or stall.

PORTAL FRAME: C20 frame comprising two uprights rigidly connected to a beam or pair of rafters.

PORTCULLIS: gate constructed to rise and fall in vertical grooves at the entry to a castle.

PORTICO: a porch with the roof and frequently a pediment supported by a row of columns (4a). A portico *in antis* has columns on the same plane as the front of the building. A *prostyle* porch has columns standing free. Porticoes are described by the number of front columns, e.g. tetrastyle (four), hexastyle (six). The space within the temple is the *naos*, that within the portico the *pronaos*. *Blind portico*: the front features of a portico applied to a wall.

PORTICUS (plural: porticūs): subsidiary cell opening from the main body of a pre-Conquest church.

POST: upright support in a structure (7).

POSTERN: small gateway at the back of a building or to the side of a larger entrance door or gate.

POUND LOCK: *see* Canals.

PRESBYTERY: the part of a church lying E of the choir where the main altar is placed; or a priest's residence.

PRINCIPAL: *see* Roofs and 7.

PRONAOS: *see* Portico and 4a.

PROSTYLE: *see* Portico and 4a.

PULPIT: raised and enclosed platform for the preaching of sermons. *Three-decker*: with reading desk below and clerk's desk below that.

*Two-decker*: as above, minus the clerk's desk.

PULPITUM: stone screen in a major church dividing choir from nave.

PULVINATED: *see* Frieze and 3c.

PURLIN: *see* Roofs and 7.

PUTHOLES or PUTLOG HOLES: in the wall to receive putlogs, the horizontal timbers which support scaffolding boards; sometimes not filled after construction is complete.

PUTTO (plural: putti): small naked boy.

QUARRIES: square (or diamond) panes of glass supported by lead strips (*cames*); square floor-slabs or tiles.

QUATREFOIL: *see* Foil and 2b.

QUEEN-STRUT: *see* Roofs and 7.

QUIRK: sharp groove to one side of a convex medieval moulding.

QUOINS: dressed stones at the angles of a building (6d).

RADBURN SYSTEM: vehicle and pedestrian segregation in residential developments, based on that used at Radburn, New Jersey, U.S.A., by Wright and Stein, 1928–30.

RADIATING CHAPELS: projecting radially from an ambulatory or an apse (*see* Chevet).

RAFTER: *see* Roofs and 7.

RAGGLE: groove cut in masonry, especially to receive the edge of a roof-covering.

RAGULY: ragged (in heraldry). Also applied to funerary sculpture, e.g. *cross raguly*: with a notched outline.

RAIL: *see* Panelling and 6b; also 7.

RAILWAYS: *Edge rail*: on which flanged wheels can run. *Plate rail*: L-section rail for plain unflanged wheels. *Plateway*: early railway using plate rails.

RAISED AND FIELDED: *see* Panelling and 6b.

RAKE: slope or pitch.

RAMPART: defensive outer wall of stone or earth. *Rampart walk*: path along the inner face.

REBATE: rectangular section cut out of a masonry edge to receive a shutter, door, window, etc.

REBUS: a heraldic pun, e.g. a fiery cock for Cockburn.

REEDING: series of convex mouldings, the reverse of fluting (q.v.). Cf. Gadrooning.

RENDERING: the covering of outside walls with a uniform surface or skin for protection from the weather. *Lime-washing*: thin layer of lime plaster. *Pebble-dashing*: where aggregate is thrown at the wet plastered wall for a textured effect. *Roughcast*: plaster mixed with a coarse aggregate such as gravel. *Stucco*: fine lime plaster worked to a smooth surface. *Cement rendering*: a cheaper substitute for stucco, usually with a grainy texture.

REPOUSSÉ: relief designs in metalwork, formed by beating it from the back.

REREDORTER (*lit.* behind the dormitory): latrines in a medieval religious house.

REREDOS: painted and/or sculptured screen behind and above an altar. Cf. Retable.

RESPOND: half-pier or half-column bonded into a wall and carrying one end of an arch. It usually terminates an arcade.

RETABLE: painted or carved panel standing on or at the back of an altar, usually attached to it.

RETROCHOIR: in a major church, the area between the high altar and E chapel.

REVEAL: the plane of a jamb, between the wall and the frame of a door or window.

RIB-VAULT: *see* Vault and 2c.

RINCEAU: classical ornament of leafy scrolls (4b).

RISER: vertical face of a step (6c).

ROACH: a rough-textured form of Portland stone, with small cavities and fossil shells.

ROCK-FACED: masonry cleft to produce a rugged appearance.

ROCOCO: style current *c.* 1720 and *c.* 1760, characterized by a serpentine line and playful, scrolled decoration.

ROLL MOULDING: medieval moulding of part-circular section (1a).

ROMANESQUE: style current in the C11 and C12. In England often called Norman. *See also* Saxo-Norman.

ROOD: crucifix flanked by the Virgin and St John, usually over the entry into the chancel, on a beam (*rood beam*) or painted on the wall. The *rood screen* below often had a walkway (*rood loft*) along the top, reached by a *rood stair* in the side wall.

ROOFS: Shape. For the main external shapes (hipped, mansard etc.) *see* 8a. *Helm* and *Saddleback*: *see* 1c. *Lean-to*: single sloping roof built against a vertical wall; lean-to is also applied to the part of the building beneath.
Construction. *See* 7.
*Single-framed* roof: with no main trusses. The rafters may be fixed to the wall-plate or ridge, or longitudinal timber may be absent altogether.
*Double-framed* roof: with longitudinal members, such as purlins, and usually divided into bays by principals and principal rafters.
Other types are named after their main structural components, e.g. *hammerbeam, crown-post* (*see* Elements below and 7).
Elements. *See* 7.
*Ashlar piece*: a short vertical timber connecting inner wall-plate or timber pad to a rafter.
*Braces*: subsidiary timbers set diagonally to strengthen the frame. *Arched braces*: curved pair forming an arch, connecting wall or post below with tie- or collar-beam above. *Passing braces*: long straight braces passing across other members of the truss. *Scissor braces*: pair crossing diagonally between pairs of rafters or principals. *Wind-braces*: short, usually curved braces connecting side purlins with principals; sometimes decorated with cusping.
*Collar* or *collar-beam*: horizontal transverse timber connecting a pair of rafter or cruck blades (q.v.), set between apex and the wall-plate.
*Crown-post*: a vertical timber set centrally on a tie-beam and supporting a collar purlin braced to it longitudinally. In an open truss

lateral braces may rise to the collar-beam; in a closed truss they may descend to the tie-beam.

*Hammerbeams*: horizontal brackets projecting at wall-plate level like an interrupted tie-beam; the inner ends carry *hammerposts*, vertical timbers which support a purlin and are braced to a collar-beam above.

*Kingpost*: vertical timber set centrally on a tie- or collar-beam, rising to the apex of the roof to support a ridge-piece (cf. Strut).

*Plate*: longitudinal timber set square to the ground. *Wall-plate*: plate along the top of a wall which receives the ends of the rafters; cf. Purlin.

*Principals*: pair of inclined lateral timbers of a truss. Usually they support side purlins and mark the main bay divisions.

*Purlin*: horizontal longitudinal timber. *Collar purlin* or *crown plate*: central timber which carries collar-beams and is supported by crown-posts. *Side purlins*: pairs of timbers placed some way up the slope of the roof, which carry common rafters. *Butt* or *tenoned purlins* are tenoned into either side of the principals. *Through purlins* pass through or past the principal; they include *clasped purlins*, which rest on queenposts or are carried in the angle between principals and collar, and *trenched purlins* trenched into the backs of principals.

*Queen-strut*: paired vertical, or near-vertical, timbers placed symmetrically on a tie-beam to support side purlins.

*Rafters*: inclined lateral timbers supporting the roof covering. *Common rafters*: regularly spaced uniform rafters placed along the length of a roof or between principals. *Principal rafters*: rafters which also act as principals.

*Ridge, ridge-piece*: horizontal longitudinal timber at the apex supporting the ends of the rafters.

*Sprocket*: short timber placed on the back and at the foot of a rafter to form projecting eaves.

*Strut*: vertical or oblique timber between two members of a truss,

not directly supporting longitudinal timbers.

*Tie-beam*: main horizontal transverse timber which carries the feet of the principals at wall level.

*Truss*: rigid framework of timbers at bay intervals, carrying the longitudinal roof timbers which support the common rafters.

*Closed truss*: with the spaces between the timbers filled, to form an internal partition.

*See also* Cruck, Wagon roof.

ROPE MOULDING: *see* Cable moulding.

ROSE WINDOW: circular window with tracery radiating from the centre. Cf. Wheel window.

ROTUNDA: building or room circular in plan.

ROUGHCAST: *see* Rendering.

ROVING BRIDGE: *see* Canals.

RUBBED BRICKWORK: *see* Gauged brickwork.

RUBBLE: masonry whose stones are wholly or partly in a rough state. *Coursed*: coursed stones with rough faces. *Random*: uncoursed stones in a random pattern. *Snecked*: with courses broken by smaller stones (snecks).

RUSTICATION: *see* 6d. Exaggerated treatment of masonry to give an effect of strength. The joints are usually recessed by V-section chamfering or square-section channelling (*channelled rustication*). *Banded rustication* has only the horizontal joints emphasized. The faces may be flat, but can be *diamond-faced*, like shallow pyramids, *vermiculated*, with a stylized texture like worm-casts, and *glacial* (frost-work), like icicles or stalactites.

SACRISTY: room in a church for sacred vessels and vestments.

SADDLEBACK ROOF: *see* IC.

SALTIRE CROSS: with diagonal limbs.

SANCTUARY: area around the main altar of a church. Cf. Presbytery.

SANGHA: residence of Buddhist monks or nuns.

SARCOPHAGUS: coffin of stone or other durable material.

SAXO-NORMAN: transitional Romanesque style combining Anglo-Saxon and Norman features, current c. 1060–1100.

SCAGLIOLA: composition imitating marble.

SCALLOPED CAPITAL: see 1a.

SCOTIA: a hollow classical moulding, especially between tori (q.v.) on a column base (3b, 3f).

SCREEN: in a medieval church, usually at the entry to the chancel; see Rood (screen) and Pulpitum. A *parclose screen* separates a chapel from the rest of the church.

SCREENS or SCREENS PASSAGE: screened-off entrance passage between great hall and service rooms.

SECTION: two-dimensional representation of a building, moulding, etc., revealed by cutting across it.

SEDILIA (singular: sedile): seats for the priests (usually three) on the S side of the chancel.

SET-OFF: see Weathering.

SETTS: squared stones, usually of granite, used for paving or flooring.

SGRAFFITO: decoration scratched, often in plaster, to reveal a pattern in another colour beneath. *Graffiti*: scratched drawing or writing.

SHAFT: vertical member of round or polygonal section (1a, 3a). *Shaft-ring*: at the junction of shafts set *en delit* (q.v.) or attached to a pier or wall (1a).

SHEILA-NA-GIG: female fertility figure, usually with legs apart.

SHELL: thin, self-supporting roofing membrane of timber or concrete.

SHOULDERED ARCHITRAVE: see 4b.

SHUTTERING: see Concrete.

SILL: horizontal member at the bottom of a window or door frame; or at the base of a timber-framed wall into which posts and studs are tenoned (7).

SLAB BLOCK: see Multi-storey.

SLATE-HANGING: covering of overlapping slates on a wall. *Tile-hanging* is similar.

SLYPE: covered way or passage leading E from the cloisters between transept and chapter house.

SNECKED: see Rubble.

SOFFIT (*lit.* ceiling): underside of an arch (also called *intrados*), lintel, etc. *Soffit roll*: medieval roll moulding on a soffit.

SOLAR: private upper chamber in a medieval house, accessible from the high end of the great hall.

SOPRAPORTA: see Overdoor.

SOUNDING-BOARD: see Tester.

SPANDRELS: roughly triangular spaces between an arch and its containing rectangle, or between adjacent arches (5c). Also non-structural panels under the windows in a curtain-walled building.

SPERE: a fixed structure screening the lower end of the great hall from the screens passage. *Spere-truss*: roof truss incorporated in the spere.

SPIRE: tall pyramidal or conical feature crowning a tower or turret. *Broach*: starting from a square base, then carried into an octagonal section by means of triangular faces; and *splayed-foot*: variation of the broach form, found principally in the south-east, in which the four cardinal faces are splayed out near their base, to cover the corners, while oblique (or intermediate) faces taper away to a point (1c). *Needle spire*: thin spire rising from the centre of a tower roof, well inside the parapet: when of timber and lead often called a *spike*.

SPIRELET: see Flèche.

SPLAY: of an opening when it is wider on one face of a wall than the other.

SPRING or SPRINGING: level at which an arch or vault rises from its supports. *Springers*: the first stones of an arch or vaulting rib above the spring (2c).

SQUINCH: arch or series of arches thrown across an interior angle of a square or rectangular structure to support a circular or polygonal superstructure, especially a dome or spire (5a).

SQUINT: an aperture in a wall or through a pier usually to allow a view of an altar.

STAIRS: see 6c. *Dog-leg stair*: parallel flights rising alternately in opposite directions, without an open well. *Flying stair*: cantilevered from the walls of a stairwell, without newels; sometimes called a *Geometric* stair when the inner edge describes a curve. *Newel stair*: ascending round a central supporting newel (q.v.); called a *spiral stair* or *vice* when in a circular shaft, a *winder* when in a rectangular compartment. (Winder also applies to the steps on the turn). *Well stair*: with flights round a square open well framed by newel posts. *See also* Perron.

STALL: fixed seat in the choir or chancel for the clergy or choir (cf. Pew). Usually with arm rests, and often framed together.

STANCHION: upright structural member, of iron, steel or reinforced concrete.

STANDPIPE TOWER: *see* Manometer.

STEAM ENGINES: *Atmospheric*: worked by the vacuum created when low-pressure steam is condensed in the cylinder, as developed by Thomas Newcomen. *Beam engine*: with a large pivoted beam moved in an oscillating fashion by the piston. It may drive a flywheel or be *non-rotative*. *Watt* and *Cornish*: single-cylinder; *compound*: two cylinders; *triple expansion*: three cylinders.

STEEPLE: tower together with a spire, lantern, or belfry.

STIFF-LEAF: type of E.E. foliage decoration. *Stiff-leaf capital see* 1b.

STOP: plain or decorated terminal to mouldings or chamfers, or at the end of hoodmoulds and labels (*label stop*), or string courses (5b, 6a); *see also* headstop.

STOUP: vessel for holy water, usually near a door.

STRAINER: *see* Arch.

STRAPWORK: late C16 and C17 decoration, like interlaced leather straps.

STRETCHER: *see* Bond and 6e.

STRING: *see* 6c. Sloping member holding the ends of the treads and risers of a staircase. *Closed string*: a broad string covering the ends of the treads and risers. *Open string*: cut into the shape of the treads and risers.

STRINGCOURSE: horizontal course or moulding projecting from the surface of a wall (6d).

STUCCO: *see* Rendering.

STUDS: subsidiary vertical timbers of a timber-framed wall or partition (7).

STUPA: Buddhist shrine, circular in plan.

STYLOBATE: top of the solid platform on which a colonnade stands (3a).

SUSPENSION BRIDGE: *see* Bridge.

SWAG: like a festoon (q.v.), but representing cloth.

SYSTEM BUILDING: *see* Industrialized building.

TABERNACLE: canopied structure to contain the reserved sacrament or a relic; or architectural frame for an image or statue.

TABLE TOMB: memorial slab raised on free-standing legs.

TAS-DE-CHARGE: the lower courses of a vault or arch which are laid horizontally (2c).

TERM: pedestal or pilaster tapering downward, usually with the upper part of a human figure growing out of it.

TERRACOTTA: moulded and fired clay ornament or cladding.

TESSELLATED PAVEMENT: mosaic flooring, particularly Roman, made of *tesserae*, i.e. cubes of glass, stone, or brick.

TESTER: flat canopy over a tomb or pulpit, where it is also called a *sounding-board*.

TESTER TOMB: tomb-chest with effigies beneath a tester, either free-standing (tester with four or more columns), or attached to a wall (*half-tester*) with columns on one side only.

TETRASTYLE: *see* Portico.

THERMAL WINDOW: *see* Diocletian window.

THREE-DECKER PULPIT: *see* Pulpit.

TIDAL GATES: *see* Canals.

TIE-BEAM: *see* Roofs and 7.

TIERCERON: *see* Vault and 2c.

TILE-HANGING: *see* Slate-hanging.

TIMBER-FRAMING: *see* 7. Method of construction where the structural frame is built of interlocking timbers. The spaces are filled with non-structural material, e.g. *infill* of wattle and daub, lath and plaster, brickwork (known as *nogging*), etc. and may be covered by plaster, weatherboarding (q.v.), or tiles.

TOMB-CHEST: chest-shaped tomb, usually of stone. Cf. Table tomb, Tester tomb.

TORUS (plural: tori): large convex moulding usually used on a column base (3b, 3f).

TOUCH: soft black marble quarried near Tournai.

TOURELLE: turret corbelled out from the wall.

TOWER BLOCK: *see* Multi-storey.

TRABEATED: depends structurally on the use of the post and lintel. Cf. Arcuated.

TRACERY: openwork pattern of masonry or timber in the upper part of an opening. *Blind tracery* is tracery applied to a solid wall.
*Plate tracery*, introduced *c.* 1200, is the earliest form, in which shapes are cut through solid masonry (2a).
*Bar tracery* was introduced into England *c.* 1250. The pattern is formed by intersecting moulded ribwork continued from the mullions. It was especially elaborate during the Decorated period (q.v.). Tracery shapes can include circles, *daggers* (elongated ogee-ended lozenges), *mouchettes* (like daggers but with curved sides) and upright rectangular *panels*. They often have *cusps*, projecting points defining lobes or *foils* (q.v.) within the main shape: *Kentish* or *split-cusps* are forked (2b).
Types of bar tracery (*see* 2b) include *geometric(al)*: *c.* 1250––1310, chiefly circles, often foiled; *Y-tracery*: *c.* 1300, with mullions branching into a Y-shape; *intersecting*: *c.* 1300, formed by interlocking mullions; *reticulated*: early C14, net-like pattern of ogee-ended lozenges; *curvilinear*: C14, with uninterrupted flowing curves; *panel*: Perp, with straight-sided panels, often cusped at the top and bottom.

TRANSEPT: transverse portion of a church.

TRANSITIONAL: generally used for the phase between Romanesque and Early English (*c.* 1175–*c.* 1200).

TRANSOM: horizontal member separating window lights (2b).

TREAD: horizontal part of a step. The *tread end* may be carved on a staircase (6c).

TREFOIL: *see* Foil.

TRIFORIUM: middle storey of a church treated as an arcaded wall passage or blind arcade, its height corresponding to that of the aisle roof.

TRIGLYPHS (*lit.* three-grooved tablets): stylized beam-ends in the Doric frieze, with metopes between (3b).

TRIUMPHAL ARCH: influential type of Imperial Roman monument.

TROPHY: sculptured or painted group of arms or armour.

TRUMEAU: central stone mullion supporting the tympanum of a wide doorway. *Trumeau figure*: carved figure attached to it (cf. Column figure).

TRUMPET CAPITAL: *see* 1b.

TRUSS: braced framework, spanning between supports. See also Roofs and 7.

TUMBLING or TUMBLING-IN: courses of brickwork laid at right-angles to a slope, e.g. of a gable, forming triangles by tapering into horizontal courses (8a).

TUSCAN: *see* Orders and 3e.

TWO-DECKER PULPIT: *see* Pulpit.

TYMPANUM: the surface between a lintel and the arch above it or within a pediment (4a).

UNDERCROFT: usually describes the vaulted room(s), beneath the main room(s) of a medieval house. Cf. Crypt.

VAULT: arched stone roof (sometimes imitated in timber or plaster). For types see 2c.
*Tunnel* or *barrel vault*: continuous semicircular or pointed arch, often of rubble masonry.

*Groin-vault*: tunnel vaults intersecting at right angles. *Groins* are the curved lines of the intersections.

*Rib-vault*: masonry framework of intersecting arches (ribs) supporting *vault cells*, used in Gothic architecture. *Wall rib* or *wall arch*: between wall and vault cell. *Transverse rib*: spans between two walls to divide a vault into bays. *Quadripartite* rib-vault: each bay has two pairs of diagonal ribs dividing the vault into four triangular cells. *Sexpartite* rib-vault: most often used over paired bays, has an extra pair of ribs springing from between the bays. More elaborate vaults may include *ridge ribs* along the crown of a vault or bisecting the bays; *tiercerons*: extra decorative ribs springing from the corners of a bay; and *liernes*: short decorative ribs in the crown of a vault, not linked to any springing point. A *stellar* or *star* vault has liernes in star formation.

*Fan-vault*: form of barrel vault used in the Perp period, made up of halved concave masonry cones decorated with blind tracery.

VAULTING SHAFT: shaft leading up to the spring or springing (q.v.) of a vault (2c).

VENETIAN or SERLIAN WINDOW: derived from Serlio (4b). The motif is used for other openings.

VERMICULATION: see Rustication and 6d.

VESICA: oval with pointed ends.

VICE: see Stair.

VILLA: originally a Roman country house or farm. The term was revived in England in the C18 under the influence of Palladio and used especially for smaller, compact country houses. In the later C19 it was debased to describe any suburban house.

VITRIFIED: bricks or tiles fired to a darkened glassy surface.

VITRUVIAN SCROLL: classical running ornament of curly waves (4b).

VOLUTES: spiral scrolls. They occur on Ionic capitals (3c). *Angle volute*: pair of volutes, turned outwards to meet at the corner of a capital.

VOUSSOIRS: wedge-shaped stones forming an arch (5c).

WAGON ROOF: with the appearance of the inside of a wagon tilt; often ceiled. Also called *cradle roof*.

WAINSCOT: see Panelling.

WALL MONUMENT: attached to the wall and often standing on the floor. *Wall tablets* are smaller with the inscription as the major element.

WALL-PLATE: see Roofs and 7.

WALL-WALK: see Parapet.

WARMING ROOM: room in a religious house where a fire burned for comfort.

WATERHOLDING BASE: early Gothic base with upper and lower mouldings separated by a deep hollow.

WATERLEAF: see Enrichments and 3f.

WATERLEAF CAPITAL: Late Romanesque and Transitional type of capital (1b).

WATER WHEELS: described by the way water is fed on to the wheel. *Breastshot*: mid-height, falling and passing beneath. *Overshot*: over the top. *Pitchback*: on the top but falling backwards. *Undershot*: turned by the momentum of the water passing beneath. In a *water turbine*, water is fed under pressure through a vaned wheel within a casing.

WEALDEN HOUSE: type of medieval timber-framed house with a central open hall flanked by bays of two storeys, roofed in line; the end bays are jettied to the front, but the eaves are continuous (8a).

WEATHERBOARDING: wall cladding of overlapping horizontal boards.

WEATHERING or SET-OFF: inclined, projecting surface to keep water away from the wall below.

WEEPERS: figures in niches along the sides of some medieval tombs. Also called mourners.

WHEEL WINDOW: circular, with radiating shafts like spokes. Cf. Rose window.

WROUGHT IRON: see Cast iron.

# INDEX OF ARTISTS

Entries for partnerships and group practices are listed after entries for a single surname. Minor differences in titles are disregarded.

Vicars, Albert 62, 652, 661
Vieira, Francesco, the Younger 259
Vigars, Allan F. 325
Vigers 284
Vinall, C. G. 115
Vincent (Leonard), Raymond
  Gorbing & Partners 554
Voelcker, John 111
Voysey, Charles Francis Annesley 38,
  199, 227, 232, 237, 241, 268
Vulliamy, George xiv, 61, 261, 319,
  563
Vulliamy, Lewis 58, 254n., 327, 347
Wade, Charles 147, 151
Wade, Robin 290, 294
Wadmore, J. F. 200
Wagstaffe, James 649, 683, 689, 691
Wailes, W. 184, 344, 571, 619
Wakelam, H. T. xv, 439
Wakley, Horace M. 310
Wales, George 503
Walford, W. J. 281
Walker, A. G. 327
Walker (John) & Co. 294
Walkers 661
Wall, Charles 579
Wallace, Robert 638
Wallace, W. 439
Wallen, F. 532n., 702
Wallen, John 646
Wallen, William 58, 637
Wallis, Gilbert & Partners 99, 189,
  329
Walters, A. G. 485; pl. 91
Walters, F. A. 254, 260
Walters, Sir Roger xiv
Walters & Kerr Bate 79, 652, 660
Ward, W. H. 148
Ward & Hughes 64, 191, 205, 435,
  656
Wardell, W. 62, 207, 484
Ware, Isaac 308
Ware, Samuel 29, 165
Waring & Gillow 364, 384
Warner, Ivor 135
Warre, E. L. 425
Warren, Gerald 154
Warwick, Septimus 70, 376
Waterhouse, Alfred 30, 43, 49, 62,
  199, 207, 264, 302–3, 304, 537; pls.
  63, 74
Waterhouse, Michael 265
Waterhouse, Paul 264–5; pl. 74
Waterlow, Sir Sydney 381
Waters, A. W. 659
Watkins, Jesse 214
Watkins Gray International 609, 611
Watkins Gray Woodgate International
  214
Watney, Dendy 308
Watson, Alex 662

Watson, M. L. 272
Watson, Musgrave 686
Watson, P. J. 359
Watson, T. H. 53, 112, 160
Watson Hart 150
Watson Partners 606
Watts, George Frederick 288
Waymouth, George 322, 629
Waymouth, George & W. Charles 646
Waymouth, W. Charles 170, 185, 187
Webb, Sir Aston 525
Webb, Christopher 159, 424, 480,
  484
Webb, David 396
Webb, E. Doran 424
Webb, Philip 37, 38, 49, 115, 199, 231,
  307, 455, 515, 526; pl. 68
Weedon, H. 244
Weekes, Henry 269
Weight, Carel 538
Weisner, Ekkehard 261
Weitzel, Alan 569
Welch, Edward 660
Welch, Herbert A. 137, 144, 148, 151,
  160, 162, 186
Welch, Cachemaille-Day & Lander
  154, 165
Welch & Hollis 43, 137, 150, 151
Welch & Lander 70, 159
Wells, Derek 355
West, David 561
West Faulkner Associates 578
Westlake 204, 351, 550, 659
Westlake, N. H. J. 344, 438, 661
Westlake, Philip 351
Westmacott, R. jun. 535
Westmacott, Sir Richard 202, 272,
  288, 291, 322, 326; pls. 41, 61
Westminster Marble Company 110
Westwood Baillie & Co. 632
Westwood & Emberton 69, 309
Westwood, Piet, Poole & Smart 306,
  638
Whall, Christopher 256, 283, 550
Wharmby (Philip) Architects 379
Wheeler, E. P. xiv, 263, 490
Whellock, R. P. 323
Whistler, Rex 273, 472
Whitburn, Henry A. 334
White, Henry 355
White, William 60, 605, 652, 658–9
White (K. C.) & Partners 163, 664
White (Sir Bruce), Wolfe Barry &
  Partners 162
Whitefriars Studios 207, 350
Whitfield & Thomas 201
Whitfield Partners 317
Wickings, William 57, 657
Wigg, George 284
Wigg, James 286
Wigg, Joseph 284

# INDEX OF STREETS, BUILDINGS
## AND LOCALITIES

Principal references are in **bold** type. References in *italic* are to buildings which no longer stand, and to defunct streets or street names. Reference in roman type within an italic entry are to remaining parts or furnishings of a vanished building.

Building types indexed together include: Baptist Chapels and Churches; Baths and Swimming Pools; Board Schools; Borough Offices; Cemeteries etc.; Cinemas; Community Centres; Congregational Chapels and Churches; Courts; Drill Halls; Fire Stations; Friends Meeting Houses; Health Centres, Clinics, Day Centres and Doctors' Practices; Hospitals and Asylums; Libraries; Manor Houses; Methodist Chapels and Churches; Police Stations; Post Offices; Presbyterian Churches; Reservoirs; Sports and Leisure Centres; Stations; Synagogues; Town Halls, Vestry Halls, Municipal Offices and Civic Centres; United Reformed Churches; Waterworks and Pumping Stations; Workhouses.

Buildings whose use has changed may be indexed under both present and former names. Broadways, High Roads and High Streets are indexed together. Streets mentioned in the gazetteer which bear the name of, and fall within, an indexed area (e.g. Canonbury) are not indexed separately.

The following abbreviations are used for boroughs:

Bowling Green Lane School (Is) 51, 614

Boyton Close (Hy) 557

Bracton House (Ca) 86, 303

Bradbury Street (Hc) 508

Braemar Road (Hy) 593

Braewood (Bn) 154

Braithwaite House (Is) 643

Bramley House (En) 449

Brampton Grove (Bn) 164

Branch Hill (Ca) 76, 230–1, 234, 342

Brantwood Road (Hy) 587

Brayfield House (Is) 644

Brecknock Road (Ca, Is) 704

Brecon House (En) 447

Brent Cross Flyover (Bn) 99, 162

Brent Cross Shopping Centre (Bn) 111

Brent House (Hc) 502

*Brent Lodge (Bn) 128*

Brent Reservoir (Bn) *see* Reservoirs

Brent Street (Bn) 166

Brent Terrace (Bn) 113

Brenthouse Road (Hc) 502

Brett Manor (Hc) 497

Brettenham School (En) 426–7

Brewers' Company Estate:
  Clerkenwell (Is) 634; St Pancras (Ca) 380

Brewery Road (Is) 668

Briardale Gardens (Ca) 233

Bridge Road (Hy) 595

Bridgeman Road (Is) 682

Brim Hill (Bn) 154

Brimsdown (En) 453

Brimsdown School (En) 442

Britannia House (Ca) 69, 317

British Legion Poppy Factory (Is) 699

British Library (Ca) 84, 86, 100, 372–5; pl. 121

British Medical Association (Ca) 265–6

British Museum (Ca) 17, 46, 82, 84, 100, 288–96; pls. 58, 61, 106; store (Ca) 306

British Newspaper Library, Colindale (Bn) 160–1

British Railways Board (Ca) *see* Euston House

British Telecom (Is) 644

British Telecom Tower (Ca) 80, 100, 262

British Theosophical Society (Ca) 265–6

Britton Street (former Red Lion Street) (Is) 20, 45, 85, 102, 626–7

Broad Walk (En) 469

Broadlands Road (Hy) 412

Broadside (Ca) 222

Broadwater Farm Estate (Hy) 75, 589

Broadway Market (Hc) 505

Broadway Parade (Hy) 559

Broadways: Cricklewood (Bn) 112–13; Crouch End (Hy) 559; Mill Hill (Bn) 174, 183; Muswell Hill (Hy) 565

Brocket (Bn) 111

Brockley Hill (Bn) *110*

Broke Road (Hc) *515n.*

Bromwich House (Ca) 414

Brondesbury Christian Centre (Ca) 207

*Brooke House: Hackney (Hc) 11, 489, 499; Holborn (Sir Fulke Greville's House) (Ca) 14–15, 249–52, 302*

Brooke's Court (Ca) 301

Brookfield Estate (Ca) 402

Brooklands Rise (Bn) 153

Brooklands School (Bn) 148

Brooklyn (En) 433

Brooksby Street (Is) 683

Brooksby's Walk (Hc) 501

Broomfield (En) 10, 23, 454, 461–2

Broomfield School (En) 459

Brownlow Road (Hc) 81–2, 506

Bruce Castle (Hy) 11, 57, 583–5; pl. 24

Bruce Grove (road) (Hy) 588

Bruce Terrace (Hy) 587

Bruges Place (Ca) 390

Brunel Close (Hy) 593

Brunner Close (Bn) 153

Brunswick Centre (Ca) 76, 328–9; pl. 7

Brunswick Close Estate (Is) 633

Brunswick Park (Bn) 115

Brunswick Road (Hy) 593

Brunswick Square (Ca) 32, 328

Brunswick Terrace (Is) 695

Buckingham Street School (Is) 673

Buckland Crescent (Ca) 240

Building Centre (Ca) 334

Bull, The (Hy) 411

Bull Brewery (Hy) 587

Bull and Gate (Ca) 394–5

Bulls Cross (En) 434, 450

Bullsmoor School (En) 442

Bunhill Fields (Is) 600, 607, 614
  *see also* Cemeteries

Bunhill Row (Is) 640, 643

Bunker's Dip (Bn) 154

Bunkers Hill (Bn) 152

Burgh House (Ca) 215

Burghley Road: Kentish Town (Ca) 401; Wood Green (Hy) 595

Burleigh Gardens (En) 466

Burleigh House (Ca) 233

Burnt Oak (Bn) 161, *162*, 168–9

Burroughs, The (Bn) 164

Burroughs House (Bn) 164

Burton Street (Ca) 330

Burton's (Montague): High Barnet (Bn) 172; Tottenham Court Road (Ca) 333

Kilburn Priory Estate (Ca) **246**
*Kilburn Priory (nunnery) (Ca)* 4, 6, **204**, *245*
Killick Street (Is) **638, 697**
Kiln Place (Ca) 74, **398**
King Alfred School (Bn) **136**
King Edward Hall (Bn) **129**
King Square (Is) **637**
King and Tinker (En) **449**
King William IV (Bn) **185**
King's Avenue (Hy) **566**
King's College, Kidderpore Avenue (Ca) **211–12**
King's Cross (area) (Ca, Is) 76, 83, *91*, 101, **378–81**
King's Cross Goods Yard (Ca) 97, **366–7**
Kings Cross House (Is) 86, **638**
King's Cross Road (Ca, Is) **636, 639**
King's Gardens (Ca) **246**
King's Head: Crouch End (Hy) **559**; Enfield (En) **445**; Upper Street (Is) **676**; Winchmore Hill (En) **469**
Kingsgate Estate (Hc) **508**
Kingsgate House (Ca) **327**
Kingsgate School (Ca) **213**
Kingsland (Bn) **181**
Kingsland (Hc) **484**
Kingsland Basin (Hc) 95, **508, 522**
Kingsland Crescent (Hc) **506**
Kingsland Passage (Hc) **508**
Kingsland Road (Hc) 16, **506, 529**
Kingsland School (Hc) **490**
Kingsley Close (Bn) **154**
Kingsley Place (Hy) **408**
Kingsley Way (Bn) **154**
Kingsmead Estate (Hc) **501**
Kingstown Street (Ca) **387**
Kingsway (Ca) 43, **314–15**
Kingsway College: (Is) 601, **613**, (Ca) 78, **263**
*Kingsway Hall (Ca) 320*
Kingsway Tram Tunnel (Ca) 98, **262–3**
Kingswell Shopping Centre (Ca) **220**
Klamath House (Is) **624**
Klippan House (Ca) **225**
Knights Lane (En) *425n.*
Kodak House (Ca) 43, **315**
La Sagesse Convent School (Bn) **137**
Laburnum Street School (Hc) **524**
Ladbrooke House (Is) **673**
Lady Hollis's School for Girls (Hc) **490**
Lady Margaret Methodist Church (Ca) *see* Our Lady Help of Christians
Lady Margaret Road (Ca) **401**
Lady Russell's Well (Bn) **182**
Lady Somerset Road (Ca) **401**
Lakis Close (Ca) **223**
Lamb, The (Is) **667**
Lamb Lane (Hc) **505**

Lamble Street (Ca) **398**
Lamb's Conduit Street (Ca) **312–13**
Lambton Road (Is) **707**
Land Registry (Ca) **307**
Lane House (Bn) **111**
*Langbourne Buildings (Hc) 525*
Langham School (Hy) **580**
Langhedge Road (En) **432**
*Langton Lodge (Bn) 164*
Langtry Way (Ca) **248**
Lansdowne Club (Hc) **496**
Lansdowne Drive (Hc) **505**
Lansdowne Terrace (Ca) **333**
Larkspur Close (Hy) **588–9**
Latymer School (En) 68, **427**
Lauderdale House (Ca) 11, 402, **405–7**
Laura Place (Hc) **497**
Laurel Farm (Bn) **189**
Laurier Road (Ca) **402**
Lauriston Road (Hc) 484, **503–4**
Lavender Road School (En) **442**
Lavers & Barraud works (Ca) 83, **319**
Lavina Grove (Is) **697**
Law Courts *see* Courts
Lawn Road (Ca) **243**
Lawrence Campe Almshouses (Bn) 25, 108, **132**; pl. 23
Lawrence Farm House (Bn) **183**
Lawrence Street (Bn) 179, **181**
Lawson & Co. (Is) **629**
Lea View (Hc) 85, **499**
Leather Lane (Ca) **300–1**
Leathersellers' Almshouses (Bn) 25, **173**
*Leatherville (Bn) 166*
Lee Navigation 95, (En) **426, 440–1**
Leeson Hall (Is) **700**
Legion Close (Is) **683**
Leigh Road (Is) **692**
Leigh Street (Ca) **330**
Leighton Crescent (Ca) **401**
Leighton Grove (Ca) **401**
Leighton Road (Ca) **394, 401**
Leisure Centres: *see* Sports Centres
Lennox House (Hc) 66, **502**
Leonard Circus (Hc) **525**
Leonard Street (Hc, Is) **525**; pl. 67
Lever Street (Is) **636**
Leverton Place (Ca) **394**
Leverton Street (Ca) **394**
Levita House (Ca) **380–1**
Lewis's bookshop (Ca) **273**
Leysian Centre (Is) **606**
Leysian Mission (Is) **605**
Libraries 53–4, 68, 80, 86
Bn 68, 80, 84, **117, 122–3, 132, 136,** 160, 161, 170, 179; Ca 53, 54, 80, 86, **210–11**, 262, 355; En 53, 54, 68, 80, **425–6**, 428, 430, 431, 440, 457–8; Hc 53, 54, **487**, 479n., *487*,

# COMPLETE LIST OF TITLES
## 2001

Volumes in the new, larger hardback format are marked (NF). Corrected reprints are not listed.

Bedfordshire and the County of Huntingdon and Peterborough *1st ed. 1968 Nikolaus Pevsner*

Berkshire *1st ed. 1966 Nikolaus Pevsner*

Buckinghamshire *1st ed. 1960 Nikolaus Pevsner, 2nd ed. 1994 revised Elizabeth Williamson* (NF)

Cambridgeshire *1st ed. 1954, 2nd ed. 1970, Nikolaus Pevsner*

Cheshire *1st ed. 1971 Nikolaus Pevsner and Edward Hubbard*

Cornwall *1st ed. 1951 Nikolaus Pevsner, 2nd ed. 1970 revised Enid Radcliffe*

Cumberland and Westmorland *1st ed. 1967 Nikolaus Pevsner*

Derbyshire *1st ed. 1953 Nikolaus Pevsner, 2nd ed. 1978 revised Elizabeth Williamson*

Devon *1st ed. in 2 vols. 1952 Nikolaus Pevsner, 2nd ed. 1989 revised Bridget Cherry* (NF)

Dorset *1st ed. 1972 John Newman and Nikolaus Pevsner*

Durham, County *1st ed. 1953 Nikolaus Pevsner, 2nd ed. 1983 revised Elizabeth Williamson*

Essex *1st ed. 1954 Nikolaus Pevsner, 2nd ed. 1965 revised Enid Radcliffe*

Gloucestershire 1: The Cotswolds *1st ed. 1970, 2nd ed. 1979, David Verey, 3rd ed. 1999 revised Alan Brooks* (NF)

Gloucestershire 2: The Vale and the Forest of Dean *1st ed. 1970, 2nd ed. 1976, David Verey, revision in progress*

Hampshire and the Isle of Wight *1st ed. 1967 Nikolaus Pevsner and David Lloyd (being revised and reissued as two volumes)*

Herefordshire *1st ed. 1963 Nikolaus Pevsner*

Hertfordshire *1st ed. 1953 Nikolaus Pevsner, 2nd ed. 1977 revised Bridget Cherry*

Kent, North East and East *1st ed. 1969, 2nd ed. 1976, 3rd ed. 1983, John Newman*

Kent, West, and the Weald *1st ed. 1969, 2nd ed. 1976, John Newman*

Lancashire, North *1st ed. 1969 Nikolaus Pevsner*

Lancashire, South *1st ed. 1969 Nikolaus Pevsner*

Leicestershire and Rutland *1st ed. 1960 Nikolaus Pevsner, 2nd ed. 1984 revised Elizabeth Williamson* (NF)

Lincolnshire *1st ed. 1964 Nikolaus Pevsner and John Harris, 2nd ed. 1989 revised Nicholas Antram* (NF)

London 1: The City of London *1st ed. 1997 Simon Bradley and Nikolaus Pevsner* (NF)

London 2: South *1st ed. 1983 Bridget Cherry and Nikolaus Pevsner* (NF)

London 3: North West *1st ed. 1991 Bridget Cherry and Nikolaus Pevsner* (NF)

London 4: North *1st ed. 1998 Bridget Cherry and Nikolaus Pevsner* (NF)

London 5: East and Docklands *1st ed. in progress*

London 6: Westminster *1st ed. in progress*

London 1: The Cities of London and Westminster *1st ed. 1957, 2nd ed. 1962, Nikolaus Pevsner, 3rd ed. 1973 revised Bridget Cherry, being revised and reissued as vols. 1 and 6 above*

London 2: Except the Cities of London and Westminster *1st ed. 1952 Nikolaus Pevsner, being revised and reissued as vols. 2–5 above*

Middlesex *1st ed. 1951 Nikolaus Pevsner, revised and reissued as vols. 3 and 4 above*

Norfolk 1: Norwich and North-East *1st ed. 1962 Nikolaus Pevsner, 2nd ed. 1997 revised Bill Wilson* (NF)

Norfolk 2: North-West and South *1st ed. 1962 Nikolaus Pevsner, 2nd ed. 1999 revised Bill Wilson* (NF)

Northamptonshire *1st ed. 1961 Nikolaus Pevsner, 2nd ed. 1973 revised Bridget Cherry*

Northumberland *1st ed. 1957 Nikolaus Pevsner with Ian A. Richmond, 2nd ed. 1992 revised John Grundy, Grace McCombie, Peter Ryder and Humphrey Welfare* (NF)

Nottinghamshire *1st ed. 1951 Nikolaus Pevsner, 2nd ed. 1979 revised Elizabeth Williamson*

Oxfordshire *1st ed. 1974 Jennifer Sherwood and Nikolaus Pevsner*

Shropshire *1st ed. 1958 Nikolaus Pevsner*

Somerset, North, and Bristol *1st ed. 1958 Nikolaus Pevsner*

Somerset, South and West *1st ed. 1958 Nikolaus Pevsner*

Staffordshire *1st ed. 1974 Nikolaus Pevsner*

Suffolk *1st ed. 1961 Nikolaus Pevsner, 2nd ed. 1974 revised Enid Radcliffe*

Surrey *1st ed. 1962 Ian Nairn and Nikolaus Pevsner, 2nd ed. 1971 revised Bridget Cherry*

Sussex *1st ed. 1965 Ian Nairn and Nikolaus Pevsner*

Warwickshire *1st ed. 1966 Nikolaus Pevsner and Alexandra Wedgwood*

Wiltshire *1st ed. 1963 Nikolaus Pevsner, 2nd ed. 1975 revised Bridget Cherry*

Worcestershire *1st ed. 1968 Nikolaus Pevsner*

Yorkshire: The North Riding *1st ed. 1966 Nikolaus Pevsner*

Yorkshire: The West Riding *1st ed. 1959 Nikolaus Pevsner, 2nd ed. 1967 revised Enid Radcliffe (being revised and reissued as two volumes)*

Yorkshire: York and the East Riding *1st ed. 1972 Nikolaus Pevsner, 2nd ed. 1995 revised David Neave* (NF)

SPECIAL PAPERBACK PUBLICATIONS

London: Docklands *1st ed. 1998, Elizabeth Williamson and Nikolaus Pevsner*

London: The City Churches *1st ed. 1998, Simon Bradley and Nikolaus Pevsner*

Manchester *1st ed. 2001, Clare Hartwell*

Looking at Buildings: the East Riding *1st ed. 1995 (with English Heritage), Hazel Moffat and David Neave*

Rahn